MW00974476

LET'S GO

■ THE RESOURCE FOR THE INDEPENDENT TRAVELER

"The guides are aimed not only at young budget travelers but at the indepedent traveler; a sort of streetwise cookbook for traveling alone."

—*The New York Times*

"Unbeatable; good sight-seeing advice; up-to-date info on restaurants, hotels, and inns; a commitment to money-saving travel; and a wry style that brightens nearly every page."

—*The Washington Post*

"Lighthearted and sophisticated, informative and fun to read. [Let's Go] helps the novice traveler navigate like a knowledgeable old hand."

—*Atlanta Journal-Constitution*

"A world-wise traveling companion—always ready with friendly advice and helpful hints, all sprinkled with a bit of wit."

—*The Philadelphia Inquirer*

■ THE BEST TRAVEL BARGAINS IN YOUR PRICE RANGE

"All the dirt, dirt cheap."

—*People*

"Anything you need to know about budget traveling is detailed in this book."

—*The Chicago Sun-Times*

"Let's Go follows the creed that you don't have to toss your life's savings to the wind to travel—unless you want to."

—*The Salt Lake Tribune*

■ REAL ADVICE FOR REAL EXPERIENCES

"The writers seem to have experienced every rooster-packed bus and lunar-surfaced mattress about which they write."

—*The New York Times*

"A guide should tell you what to expect from a destination. Here Let's Go shines."

—*The Chicago Tribune*

LET'S GO PUBLICATIONS

TRAVEL GUIDES

Alaska & the Pacific Northwest 2003
Australia 2003
Austria & Switzerland 2003
Britain & Ireland 2003
California 2003
Central America 8th edition
Chile 1st edition **NEW TITLE**
China 4th edition
Costa Rica 1st edition **NEW TITLE**
Eastern Europe 2003
Egypt 2nd edition
Europe 2003
France 2003
Germany 2003
Greece 2003
Hawaii 2003 **NEW TITLE**
India & Nepal 7th edition
Ireland 2003
Israel 4th edition
Italy 2003
Mexico 19th edition
Middle East 4th edition
New Zealand 6th edition
Peru, Ecuador & Bolivia 3rd edition
South Africa 5th edition
Southeast Asia 8th edition
Southwest USA 2003
Spain & Portugal 2003
Thailand 1st edition **NEW TITLE**
Turkey 5th edition
USA 2003
Western Europe 2003

CITY GUIDES

Amsterdam 2003
Barcelona 2003
Boston 2003
London 2003
New York City 2003
Paris 2003
Rome 2003
San Francisco 2003
Washington, D.C. 2003

MAP GUIDES

Amsterdam
Berlin
Boston
Chicago
Dublin
Florence
Hong Kong
London
Los Angeles
Madrid
New Orleans
New York City
Paris
Prague
Rome
San Francisco
Seattle
Sydney
Venice
Washington, D.C.

SPAIN & PORTUGAL
INCLUDING MOROCCO
2003

Andrew M. Torres Editor
Lucy B. Ebersold Associate Editor
Irin Carmon Associate Editor

Researcher-Writers
Sebastián Andrés Brown
Nate Gray
Josh Ludmir
Karen L. McCarthy
Paul Rubio
Marie C. Scott
Mosi Secret

Angela Mi Young Hur Managing Editor
Damian Williams Map Editor
Caleb S. Epps Typesetter

Macmillan

HELPING LET'S GO If you want to share your discoveries, suggestions, or corrections, please drop us a line. We read every piece of correspondence, whether a postcard, a 10-page email, or a coconut. Please note that mail received after May 2003 may be too late for the 2004 book, but will be kept for future editions. **Address mail to:**

Let's Go: Spain & Portugal
67 Mount Auburn Street
Cambridge, MA 02138
USA

Visit Let's Go at **http://www.letsgo.com,** or send email to:

feedback@letsgo.com
Subject: "Let's Go: Spain & Portugal"

In addition to the invaluable travel advice our readers share with us, many are kind enough to offer their services as researchers or editors. Unfortunately, our charter enables us to employ only currently enrolled Harvard students.

Published in Great Britain 2003 by Macmillan, an imprint of Pan Macmillan Ltd.
20 New Wharf Road, London N1 9RR
Basingstoke and Oxford
Associated companies throughout the world
www.panmacmillan.com

Maps by David Lindroth copyright © 2003 by St. Martin's Press.

Published in the United States of America by St. Martin's Press.

Let's Go: Spain & Portugal Copyright © 2003 by Let's Go, Inc. All rights reserved. Printed in the United States of America. No part of this book may be used or reproduced in any manner whatsoever without written permission except in the case of brief quotations embodied in critical articles or reviews. Let's Go is available for purchase in bulk by institutions and authorized resellers. For information, address St. Martin's Press, 175 Fifth Avenue, New York, NY 10010, USA.

ISBN: 1-4050-0080 5
First edition
10 9 8 7 6 5 4 3 2 1

Let's Go: Spain & Portugal is written by Let's Go Publications, 67 Mount Auburn Street, Cambridge, MA 02138, USA.

Let's Go® and the LG logo are trademarks of Let's Go, Inc.
Printed in the USA on recycled paper with soy ink.

ADVERTISING DISCLAIMER All advertisements appearing in Let's Go publications are sold by an independent agency not affiliated with the editorial production of the guides. Advertisers are never given preferential treatment, and the guides are researched, written, and published independent of advertising. Advertisements do not imply endorsement of products or services by Let's Go, and Let's Go does not vouch for the accuracy of information provided in advertisements.

If you are interested in purchasing advertising space in a Let's Go publication, contact: Let's Go Advertising Sales, 67 Mount Auburn St., Cambridge, MA 02138, USA.

HOW TO USE THIS BOOK

ORGANIZATION. Coverage of **Spain** spirals out counter-clockwise from Madrid, ending in the Canary Islands. Coverage of **Portugal** starts in Lisbon and then runs south-to-north. Coverage of **Morocco** runs roughly north to south. The black tabs on the side of the book should help you navigate your way through.

PRICE RANGES AND RANKINGS. Our researchers list establishments in order of value from best to worst. Our absolute favorites are denoted by the coveted Let's Go thumbs-up (☒). Since the best value does not always mean the cheapest price, we also give the price range for each listing according to the following system.

SPAIN AND PORTUGAL	❶	❷	❸	❹	❺
ACCOMMODATIONS	under €15	€15-25	€25-35	€35-50	over €50
FOOD	under €6	€6-10	€10-15	€15-25	over €25
MOROCCO	❶	❷	❸	❹	❺
ACCOMMODATIONS	under 60dh	60-100dh	100-150dh	150-200dh	over 200dh
FOOD	under 40dh	40-60dh	60-80dh	80-110dh	over 110dh

PHONE CODES AND TELEPHONE NUMBERS. Area codes for each city appear opposite the name of the city next to the ☎ icon and are always listed as part of local numbers. Phone numbers in text are also preceded by the ☎ icon.

WHEN TO USE IT

TWO MONTHS BEFORE. The first chapter, **Discover Spain, Portugal, and Morocco,** contains highlights of the region, including **Suggested Itineraries** (see p. 5) that might help you plan your trip. The **Essentials** (see p. 8) section contains practical information on planning a budget, renewing a passport, booking tickets, etc., and has other useful tips for traveling in Spain, Portugal, and Morocco.

ONE MONTH BEFORE. Take care of insurance, and write down a list of emergency numbers and hotlines. Make a list of packing essentials (see **Packing,** p. 24) and shop for anything you are missing. Read through the coverage and make sure you understand the logistics of your itinerary (catching trains, buses, ferries, etc.). Make any reservations necessary.

2 WEEKS BEFORE. Leave an itinerary and a photocopy of important documents with someone at home. Take some time to peruse the **Life and Times** sections for Spain (p. 62), Portugal (p. 577), and Morocco (p. 711), which have information on history, culture, recent events, and more.

ON THE ROAD. The **Appendix** contains a glossary, a phrase book, a distance chart, a climate chart, and other sundry bits of info to help you on your way. Now, arm yourself with a travel journal and hit the road.

A NOTE TO OUR READERS The information for this book was gathered by *Let's Go* researchers from May through August of 2002. Each listing is based on one researcher's opinion, formed during his or her visit at a particular time. Those traveling at other times may have different experiences since prices, dates, hours, and conditions are always subject to change. You are urged to check the facts presented in this book beforehand to avoid inconvenience and surprises.

LET'S GO
INTRODUCING THE NEW letsgo.com
READY TO GO?
BROWSE all our guides for free
ORDER plane tickets and railpasses
DOWNLOAD city guides for your Palm
EXCHANGE travel tips on our forums
CALIFORNIA
CENTRAL AMERICA
CHINA
EASTERN EUROPE
EUROPE
FRANCE
GERMANY
and 34 more titles
Fare Finder
From: New York
To: Reykjavik
Depart: 5/17/03
Return: 7/06/03
Budget Travel
Women Travelers
Recent News
Gay and Lesbian
Destinations
www.letsgo.com

CONTENTS

RESEARCHER-WRITERS

Sebastián Andrés Brown *Extremadura, Cantabria, Asturias, Galicia*

Native Chilean Sebastián has backpacked through the Atacama Desert, rafted in the river Pucòn, and hiked in the Antillanca volcano. But Seba brought more than his thirst for the wild; this budding economist has helped build more than 100 homes for the underprivileged in southern Chile, and tutored prison inmates in Boston. He attacked his route—especially the daytrips—with cheerful zeal, showering us with hilarious commentary along the way.

Nate Gray *La Rioja, Navarra, Pyrenees, País Vasco, Andorra*

Nate achieved international fame when the Associated Press and newspapers around the world ran front-page photos of his scuffle with a bull at the legendary *San Fermines* in Pamplona. Unruffled by danger and unspoiled by his celebrity status, he spun his researching feats into eloquent, edifying copy. An Eagle Scout, wordsmith, and rower, Nate has roamed Tanzania, Colombia, the Cayman Islands, and Belize, in addition to his frequent jaunts to Spain.

Josh Ludmir *Murcia, Valencia, Balearic Islands*

Josh was born to work for *Let's Go*. Not only is he fluent in Spanish, he also speaks French, Italian, and Hebrew, and has wandered all over Western Europe, South America, and North Africa. Gleaning adventures at every interval, he graced Spanish soap opera soirées and Mallorcan yacht extravaganzas, hitched rides on olive trucks, zipped around Benidorm on the back of a BMW motorcycle, and still had time to research social injustice and pen romantic musings.

Karen L. McCarthy *Andalucìa and the Algarve*

Fiery and energetic Karen has taught elementary school in Guatemala, studied wildlife ecology in East Africa, and worked with survivors of domestic violence in the US. A veteran traveler in Central America and Europe, she displayed an enthusiastic, unrelenting attention to detail. Always conscious of the dangers and difficulties for women traveling alone, Karen translated her experiences with overly friendly Spanish men into useful, compassionate copy.

Paul Rubio *Madrid and the Canary Islands*

Researching powerhouse Paul took a break from mitigating human-tiger conflicts in Malaysia and harvesting crops with Kikuyu women in Kenya to revel in Madrid's hottest nightlife for *Let's Go*. This Cuban-American environmental economist and developing-world specialist managed to engineer a staggering overhaul of the Canary Islands coverage, setting absurdly high goals for his research and exceeding them every time.

Marie C. Scott *Portugal*

A veteran of *Let's Go: Central America 2002*, Marie previously lobbied for human rights in Ecuador, worked for the National Legislative Assembly of Panama, and taught inner-city youth in Boston. Having already broken bread in Thailand, Cuba, and Russia, Marie's sojourn in Portugal added port, pastries, and pork to her travel menu. Her studies in Romance languages, literature, and religion smoothed the journey through Portugal's cathedrals and castles.

Mosi Secret *Morocco*

Mosi ventured into the medinas and deserts of Morocco, serene and intrepid. This religion scholar completed his thesis work on women's experience in Islam, for which he moved to Egypt. Morocco offered Mosi a seemingly unending obstacle course of hustler-dodging, *hammam* heat, and beleaguered donkeys. Still, he emerged unblinking, utilizing insider expertise, doggedly reworking his copy, and delivering side-splitting features.

Anna Elizabeth Byrne *Editor, Let's Go: Barcelona 2003*

Colleen Gargan *Researcher-Writer, Let's Go: Barcelona 2003*

Rei Onishi *Researcher-Writer, Let's Go: Barcelona 2003*

Adam Weiss *Researcher-Writer, Let's Go: Barcelona 2003*

CONTRIBUTING WRITER

Sarah Kenney was editor of *Let's Go: Barcelona 2002.* She lived in Barcelona for a year, where she learned to speak Spanish and Catalan. She is currently editing for a Spanish-language publishing company in Boston and teaching English for a non-profit organization. She is an avid fan of Floquet de Neu.

ASTURIAS & CANTABRIA
pp. 498- 524
Oviedo
ASTURIAS
Santander
CANTABRIA
Santiago de Compostela
GALICIA
pp. 525-547
León
Burgos
Viana do Castelo
Bragança
Valladolid
DOURO AND MINHO
pp. 687-704
TRÁS-OS-MONTES
pp. 705-710
CASTILLA Y LEÓN
pp. 158-196
Porto
Salamanca
Aveiro
THE THREE BEIRAS
pp. 674-686
MADRID
pp. 86-143
Coimbra
PORTUGAL
Madrid
RIBATEJO &
ESTREMADURA
pp. 654-673
Castelo Branco
Toledo
LISBON
pp. 593-627
Lisbon
Setúbal
EXTREMADURA
pp. 197-210
Mérida
Badajoz
CASTILLA
LA MANCHA
pp. 144-157
ALENTEJO
pp. 645-653
Évora
Beja
Córdoba
Sevilla
ANDALUCÍA
pp. 211-308
Lagos
Faro
ALGARVE
pp. 630-631
Granada
Málaga
ATLANTIC
OCEAN
Gibraltar
Algeciras
Canary Islands
pp. 548-576
Tangier
MOROCCO
pp. 711-792
TO
RABAT

Spain, Portugal, and Morocco:
Chapters
FRANCE
ANDORRA
pp. 435-438
NAVARRA
Pamplona
LA RIOJA
&
NAVARRA
pp. 459-475
CATALUÑA
pp. 407-434
Girona
Zaragoza
BARCELONA
pp. 365-406
ARAGÓN
pp. 439-458
SPAIN
Teruel
TO
MENORCA
Cuenca
Mallorca
Palma
Valencia
VALENCIA
BALEARIC ISLANDS
pp. 336-364
Ibiza
Eivissa/Ibiza
Formentera
Menorca
Ciudadela
Mahón
Alicante
Murcia
VALENCIA AND MURCIA
pp. 309-335
MURCIA
MEDITERRANEAN SEA
ALGERIA
0
50 miles
0
75 kilometers

Bay of Biscay
Ortigueira
El Ferrol
La Coruña
Betanzos
Ribadeo
Mondoñedo
Gijón
Oviedo
Ribadesella
Llanes
Santander
Bilbao
Corcubión
Santiago de Compostela
Lugo
Reinosa
Miranda de Ebro
Pontevedra
Ponferrada
León
Orense
Montforte
Astorga
Burgos
Vigo
Túy
La Guardia
Valença do Minho
Benavente
Palencia
Bragança
Medina de Rioseco
Venta de Baños
Aranda de Duero
Viana do Castelo
Braga
Guimarães
Tordesillas
Valladolid
Zamora
Porto
Vila Real
Medina del Campo
PORTUGAL
Salamanca
Segovia
Ovar
Viseu
Aveiro
Fuentas de Onoro
Cercedilla
Guarda
Ciudad Rodrigo
Béjar
Avila
Pampilhosa
El Escorial
Madrid
La Alberca
Figueira da Foz
Coimbra
Alcalá de Henares
Plasencia
Talavera de la Reina
Leiria
Batalha
Castelo Branco
Toledo
Aranjuez
Nazaré
Fátima
Tomar
Alcobaça
Peniche
Entroncamento
Valencia de Alcantara
Cáceres
Guadalupe
Óbidos
Marvão
Trujillo
Torre das Vargens
Portalegre
Mafra
Santarém
SPAIN
Ciudad Real
Sintra
Lisboa
Estremoz
Elvas
Mérida
Badajoz
Almagro
Puertollano
Setúbal
Casa Branca
Évora
Olivenza
Zafra
Jerez de los Caballeros
Service
High Speed Rail
Beja
Córdoba
Baeza
Espeluy
Funcheira
Jaén
Mértola
Ecija
Silves
Vila Real de Santo António
Huelva
Sevilla
Moreda
Vila do Bispo
Portimão
La Roda
Lagos
Ayamonte
Utrera
Antequera
Granada
Sagres
Albufeira
Faro
Olhão
Tavira
Osuna
Golfo de Cádiz
Bobadilla
Loulé
Arcos de la Frontera
Málaga
Nerja
Ronda
Jerez de la Frontera
Marbella
Torremolinos
Cádiz
Fuengirola
ATLANTIC OCEAN
Gibraltar
Tarifa
Algeciras
TO CANARY ISLANDS
Strait of Gibraltar
Ceuta
Tangier
N
0
50 miles
0
75 km
Al Hoceimo
MOROCCO

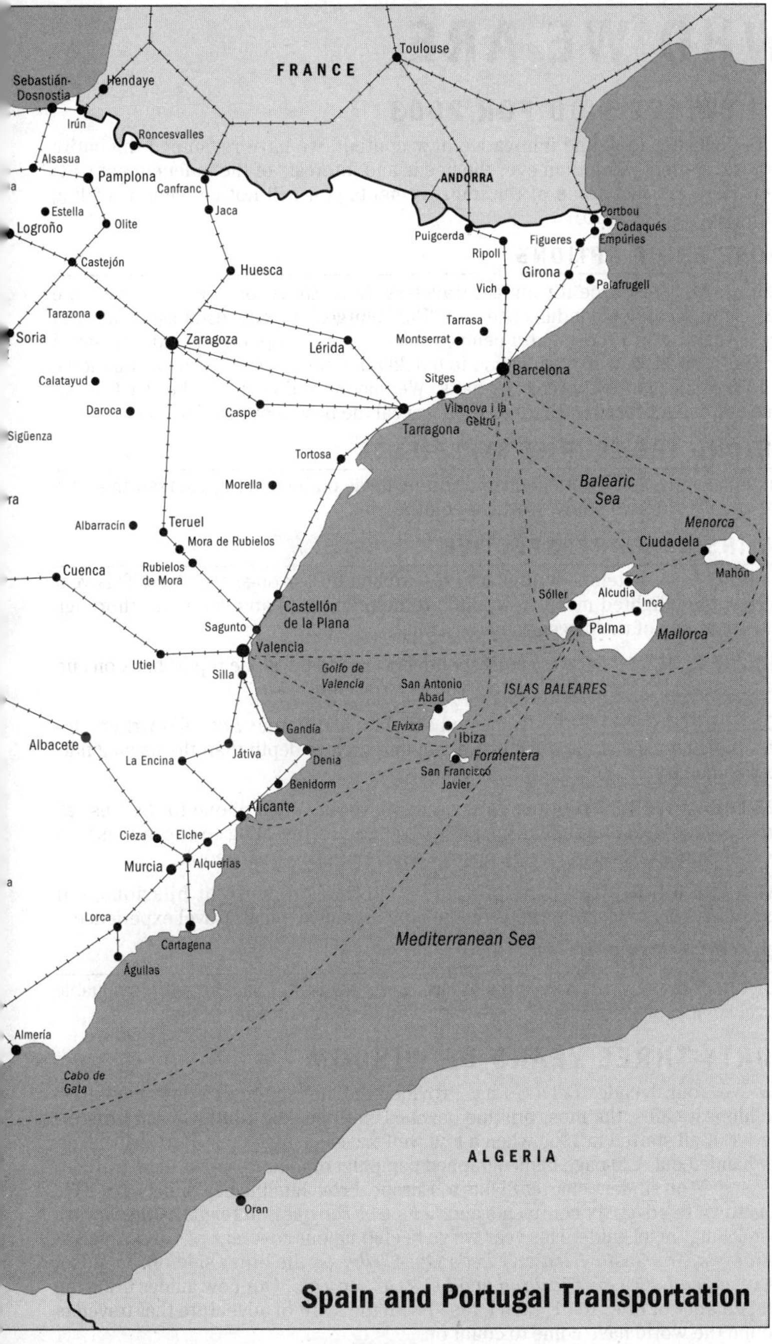

Spain and Portugal Transportation

WHO WE ARE

A NEW LET'S GO FOR 2003

With a sleeker look and innovative new content, we have revamped the entire series to reflect more than ever the needs and interests of the independent traveler. Here are just some of the improvements you will notice when traveling with the new *Let's Go*.

MORE PRICE OPTIONS

Still the best resource for budget travelers, *Let's Go* recognizes that everyone needs the occassional indulgence. Our "Big Splurges" indicate establishments that are actually worth those extra pennies (pulas, pesos, or pounds), and price-level symbols (❶ ❷ ❸ ❹ ❺) allow you to quickly determine whether an accommodation or restaurant will break the bank. We may have diversified, but we'll never lose our budget focus—"Hidden Deals" reveal the best-kept travel secrets.

BEYOND THE TOURIST EXPERIENCE

Our Alternatives to Tourism chapter offers ideas on immersing yourself in a new community through study, work, or volunteering.

AN INSIDER'S PERSPECTIVE

As always, every item is written and researched by our on-site writers. This year we have highlighted more viewpoints to help you gain an even more thorough understanding of the places you are visiting.

IN RECENT NEWS. *Let's Go* correspondents around the globe report back on current regional issues that may affect you as a traveler.

CONTRIBUTING WRITERS. Respected scholars and former *Let's Go* writers discuss topics on society and culture, going into greater depth than the usual guidebook summary.

THE LOCAL STORY. From the Parisian monk toting a cell phone to the Russian *babushka* confronting capitalism, *Let's Go* shares its revealing conversations with local personalities—a unique glimpse of what matters to real people.

FROM THE ROAD. Always helpful and sometimes downright hilarious, our researchers share useful insights on the typical (and atypical) travel experience.

SLIMMER SIZE

Don't be fooled by our new, smaller size. *Let's Go* is still packed with invaluable travel advice, but now it's easier to carry with a more compact design.

FORTY-THREE YEARS OF WISDOM

For over four decades *Let's Go* has provided the most up-to-date information on the hippest cafes, the most pristine beaches, and the best routes from border to border. It all started in 1960 when a few well-traveled students at Harvard University handed out a 20-page mimeographed pamphlet of their tips on budget travel to passengers on student charter flights to Europe. From humble beginnings, *Let's Go* has grown to cover six continents and *Let's Go: Europe* still reigns as the world's best-selling travel guide. This year we've beefed up our coverage of Latin America with *Let's Go: Costa Rica* and *Let's Go: Chile;* on the other side of the globe, we've added *Let's Go: Thailand* and *Let's Go: Hawaii.* Our new guides bring the total number of titles to 61, each infused with the spirit of adventure that travelers around the world have come to count on.

ACKNOWLEDGMENTS

TEAM SPAM THANKS: Our fabulous and attractive researchers, for their wonderful work and even better stories—we love you all; The Mangela, for unwaivering guidance and unpredictable affectations; our mapper Damian; and Team FRA for endless amusement. Just remember: it's not culturally insensitive if it's true. D&S forever.

ANDY THANKS: Most of all, I'd like to thank...myself, but also Lucy for El Salvador, second choices, and an uncertain future; Irin for Feminist Death Threat, topless hiking, and technological prowess; Anna for mimes, free spirits, and smoking for France—I see what you've done there; and Cody for everything—we'll always have Rio.

LUCY THANKS: Torres, for late-night cell phone calls, good hires, and sangría—we'll always have *mañana;* Irin, my partner in crime, for your free spirit and lewdness; Cody for the joint birthday party; Gretchen and Kathleen for sanity, trivia nights, and cut-up tshirts; Lowell's 11 for an ever-full inbox; Mom and Dad for roots and wings; Gagi for unconditional love and support. Can't you see the sunshine, can't you just feel the moonshine.

IRIN THANKS: Andy, head-flailing confusion and all. Lucy, fellow girl gone wild—I don't care what anyone says, you are funny. Angela for the movie club and Montreal. Everyman for RW phone calls, Annalise for movie nights and NY, Sarah for SATC breaks. Cogy, who knows what I'm talking about, and the Moldy Peaches cover band. My family for everything.

DAMIAN THANKS: Andy, Lucy, and Irin for their amazing work; my Mapland compadres; my mother, father, and sister for their unconditional love and support.

Editor
Andrew M. Torres
Associate Editors
Lucy B. Ebersold, Irin Carmon
Managing Editor
Angela Mi Young Hur
Map Editor
Damian Williams

LET'S GO

Publishing Director
Matthew Gibson
Editor-in-Chief
Brian R. Walsh
Production Manager
C. Winslow Clayton
Cartography Manager
Julie Stephens
Design Manager
Amy Cain
Editorial Managers
Christopher Blazejewski, Abigail Burger, D. Cody Dydek, Harriett Green, Angela Mi Young Hur, Marla Kaplan, Celeste Ng
Financial Manager
Noah Askin
Marketing & Publicity Managers
Michelle Bowman, Adam M. Grant
New Media Managers
Jesse Tov, Kevin Yip
Online Manager
Amélie Cherlin
Personnel Managers
Alex Leichtman, Owen Robinson
Production Associates
Caleb Epps, David Muehlke
Network Administrators
Steven Aponte, Eduardo Montoya
Design Associate
Juice Fong
Financial Assistant
Suzanne Siu
Office Coordinators
Alex Ewing, Adam Kline, Efrat Kussell
Director of Advertising Sales
Erik Patton
Senior Advertising Associates
Patrick Donovan, Barbara Eghan, Fernanda Winthrop
Advertising Artwork Editor
Leif Holtzman
Cover Photo Research
Laura Wyss
President
Bradley J. Olson
General Manager
Robert B. Rombauer
Assistant General Manager
Anne E. Chisholm

Meet the neighbors.

From the peaks of the Himalayas to the wilds of Bolivia and everywhere in between, FRONTLINE/World takes you on a journey of discovery to meet the people you won't see on the six o'clock news.

FRONTLINE

WORLD

stories from a small planet

A new documentary series airing on PBS

For broadcast schedule information, visit **www.pbs.org/frontlineworld**

A coproduction of WGBH Boston and KQED San Francisco

WGBH KQED

Major funding for FRONTLINE/World is provided by PBS and the Corporation for Public Broadcasting

Additional funding is provided by ABB, Ltd.

ABB

DISCOVER SPAIN, PORTUGAL, AND MOROCCO

SPAIN

Spain is colorful and playful, cultured and refined. It is a country offering equally generous portions of art, architecture, beaches, and nightlife. The people have a joyful, social lifestyle that they are eager to share, and the wildly diverse regions assure something for everyone. Art lovers flock to northeastern Spain to see trend-setting Barcelona, the rugged coastline that inspired Dalí, and Bilbao's shining Guggenheim museum. Adventure-seekers trek through the dizzying Pyrenees and the Picos de Europa, while architectural enthusiasts explore the Baroque cathedrals of Galicia, Antoni Gaudí's Modernista conjurings in Cataluña, and the Arab intricacies of Andalucía. Flamenco, bullfighting, and *tapas*, Spain's most familiar cultural expressions, also hail from Andalucía, while Madrid, Barcelona, and Ibiza do enough insane, all-night partying to make up for every early-to-bed grandmother the world over. Spain is the perfect destination for first-time travelers, for seasoned adventurers, for families with children, or for college students in search of fast, easy fun. Once you're in Spain, you'll wonder why you never came before.

PORTUGAL

Sandwiched between Spain and the Atlantic Ocean, Portugal is often unjustly overshadowed by its Western European neighbors. Most people know it only as the inventor of sugary-sweet port wine and the former home of intrepid, globe-trotting explorers. Travelers who come to Portugal today will discover one of Europe's newest hotspots. Lisbon, the capital and largest city, has the country's most impressive imperial monuments, while the southern Algarve boasts spectacular beaches and wild nightlife, drawing backpackers in droves. Northern Coimbra crackles with the energy of a university town, and Porto surpasses even Lisbon in sophisticated elegance. Portugal's small inland towns retain a timeless feel, with medieval castles overlooking rushing rivers and peaceful town squares. Portugal's wild northern hinterlands, where some villages have not changed in nearly a millennium, are perhaps the country's most unique region; the land in Trás-Os-Montes is among the most pristine in all of Europe.

MOROCCO

Morocco is an experience that goes beyond the common expectations of hustlers, drugs, snake charmers, and magic carpets. It is, above all, a land of beautiful extremes, characterized by both the snow-capped peaks of the Atlas mountains and the hot sun on Saharan dunes, by Europeanized coastal cities and isolated desert towns, by the sheer insanity of Marrakesh's Djema'a al-Fna and the peaceful seclusion of Essaouira's beaches. European travelers come to Morocco lured by exotic fantasies, "expat" legends, and Casablanca romance, but in place of some Hollywood set they find themselves face to face with the real Morocco, filled with bustling medinas, towering mosques, and crumbling *kasbahs*.

COUNTRY FACTS

SPAIN	PORTUGAL	MOROCCO
Population: 40,037,995	**Population:** 10,066,253	**Population:** 30,645,305
Size: 499,542 sq. km	**Size:** 91,951 sq. km	**Size:** 446,550 sq. km
Capital: Madrid	**Capital:** Lisbon	**Capital:** Rabat
Currency: euros (€)	**Currency:** euros (€)	**Currency:** dirham (dh)

...AND FIGURES

Pork consumed annually per capita in Spain: 67kg (147 lb.)

Mint tea consumed annually per capita in Morocco: 413.8 gallons

Ratio of yearly tourists to actual residents of Spain: 9 to 8

Amount of cork produced by Portugal annually: Enough to keep the entire population afloat—with each person wearing a 40lb. backpack.

Hours slept per capita each night in Madrid: 4.2

WHEN TO GO

Summer is **high season** (*temporada alta*) for coastal and interior regions in Spain, Portugal, and Morocco; winter is high season for ski resorts and the Canary Islands. In many parts of Spain and Portugal, high season extends back to **Semana Santa** (Holy Week; April 13-19 in 2003) and includes festival days. Tourism on the Iberian Peninsula reaches its height in August; the coastal regions overflow while inland cities empty out, leaving closed offices, restaurants, and lodgings.

Traveling in the **off-season** (*temporada baja*) has many advantages, most noticeably the lighter crowds and lower prices. Many hostels cut their prices by 30% or more, and reservations are seldom necessary. While major cities and university towns may burst with vitality during these months, many smaller seaside spots are left ghost towns, and tourist offices and sights cut their hours nearly everywhere. During **Ramadan** in Morocco (Oct. 27-Nov. 26 in 2003), there is little activity outside the sacred realm. For a temperature table, see **Climate,** p. 793. For a chart of **festivals** in Spain, see p. 85, in Portugal p. 592, and in Morocco p. 725.

WHAT TO DO

There are as many ways to see Spain, Portugal, and Morocco as there are places to go. One could search out every Baroque chapel, spend weeks trekking on some of Europe's best trails, or hop from city to city indulging cosmopolitan fantasies.

IT'S IN THE BLOOD

Spain, Portugal, and Morocco are *alive.* Two millennia of invaders have washed over these countries, resulting in a vibrant and eclectic culture filled with custom, religion, history, and an irrepressible energy. You can see it in Madrid's famous nightlife (p. 126), in the happy chaos of Fez's outdoor medina (p. 744), in the sidewalk cafes of Lisbon (p. 593), and above all in Spain's spectacular festivals. During **Carnaval** in Cádiz (p. 252), **Las Fallas** in Valencia (p. 310), the **Feria de Abril** in Sevilla (p. 231), and the infamous **San Fermines** in Pamplona (p. 469), there is no denying Spaniards' overwhelming cultural exuberance.

Still, like all passions, it's not entirely manic. Iberia's poignant expressions of heartbreak are often as blood-quickening as its celebrations. The ritually tragic emotions of flamenco and *fado* bring tears to the eyes of even the most macho of bullfighters, who in turn create their own tragedies of life and death on the bullring sand. Actual tragedy on a national scale scarred Spain during a good part of this century—Picasso's powerfully symbolic **Guernica** (p. 123) and the propagandistic **Valley of the Fallen** (p. 139) give travelers a taste of the pain of Fascism. All of this emotional heritage demands a break now and then. There is ample opportunity for peace and quiet here as well: the thin-aired reverence of **Montserrat** (p. 402), the calm of a rowboat in **Retiro** (p. 118), or the surreal peace of **Park Güell** (p. 384).

ARCHITECTURE

From traditionally conservative to unconventionally decadent, the buildings and monuments of Iberia form a collage of architectural styles. The remains of ancient civilizations are everywhere—from the Celtiberian tower of **O Castro de Baroña** (p. 533) to Roman ruins like the aqueduct in **Segovia** and Augusta Emerita in **Mérida** (p. 204). Hundreds of years of Moorish rule left breathtaking monuments all over Iberia, including Granada's spectacular **Alhambra** (p. 293), Córdoba's **Mezquita** (p. 235), and Sintra's **Castelo dos Mouros** (p. 621). The Catholic church has spent immense sums of money to build some of the world's most ornate religious complexes, ranging from the pastiche of the **Convento de Cristo** (p. 670) to the imposing **El Escorial** (p. 138), from which the Inquisition was conducted. Spain's magnificent cathedrals can be Gothic, Plateresque, or just plain bizarre, as with Gaudí's magnificent, still-unfinished **Sagrada Familia** in Barcelona (p. 387), a brilliant climax of the Modernista style. Modern additions to Iberia's rich architectural landscape include Lisbon's expansive **Park of Nations** (p. 608), Bilbao's shining **Guggenheim Museum** (p. 486), and Valencia's huge **Ciudad de las Artes y las Ciencias** (p. 315).

THE OUTDOORS

Iberia's best-kept secrets are its sprawling national parks and soaring, snowy mountain ranges. **Andorra,** in the heart of the Pyrenees, has easily accessible glacial valleys, rolling forests, and wild meadows (p. 436). In northern Spain, the **Parque Nacional de Ordesa** (p. 455) offers well-kept trails along jagged rock faces, rushing rivers, and thundering waterfalls, and the **Parc Nacional d'Agüestortes** (p. 334) hides 50 ice-cold mountain lakes in its 24,700 acres of rugged peaks and valleys. The **Picos de Europa** (p. 509) offer some of Europe's best mountaineering. Northern Portugal's **Parque Natural de Montesinho** (p. 705) is probably the most isolated, untouched land in all of Europe. Farther south, greenery-starved *madrileños* hike through the **Sierra de Guadarrama** (p. 140), and nature-lovers are drawn to Andalucía's huge **Parque Nacional Coto de Doñana** (p. 249), which protects nearly 60,000 acres of land for threatened wildlife. **Las Alpujarras** (p. 300), the southern slopes of the Sierra Nevada, are perfect for hiking among Spain's famous *pueblos blancos* (white towns), while trails in **Mallorca** (p. 338) and the **Canary Islands** (p. 548) juxtapose mountain peaks with ocean horizons. In Morocco, ambitious explorers trek to the top of the **Djebal Toubkal,** North Africa's highest peak (p. 782), or travel to the desert dunes near **Erfoud** (p. 791) and **M'Hamid** (p. 787).

BEACHES

It would be a shame to spend your *entire* time in Spain, Portugal, and Morocco beach-hopping, but if you were to insist, the options are virtually endless. Marc Chagall deemed the red-cliffed shores of **Tossa de Mar** (p. 411) "Blue Paradise."

San Sebastián's (p. 477) calm, voluptuous Playa de la Concha attracts young travelers from around the world, while **Santander** caters to an elite, refined clientele. The beaches of **Galicia** (p. 525) curve around kilometers of crystal-green, misty inlets. On the **Balearic** and **Canary Islands,** bronzed, glistening bodies crowd the chic beaches, and southern Spain's infamous **Costa del Sol** (p. 264) brings tourists to its scorched Mediterranean bays by the plane-load. The eastern **Costa Blanca** (p. 325) mixes small-town charm with ocean expanses, and the looming cliffs and turquoise waters of Portugal's southern **Algarve** adorn hundreds of postcards. In Morocco, beach-lovers flock to the ex-pirate cove **Essaouira** (p. 768).

NIGHTLIFE

Nightlife in Spain, Portugal, and Morocco can be relaxing—sipping a cold beer in a local bar or people-watching in the town square. But who really wants that? Just setting foot outdoors is likely to lead to events of unabashed hedonism unlike anything you've ever experienced. With countless bars and clubs and an incredible, intoxicating energy, **Madrid** (p. 86) has earned international renown as one of the greatest party cities in the world. **Barcelona**'s (p. 365) wild, edgy nightlife reflects the city's outrageous sense of style. Residents of **Sevilla** (p. 213) pack discos floating on the Río Guadalquivir to drink and dance the night away, and only on **Ibiza** (p. 356), the jetset's favorite party island, will you find the world's largest club filled with 10,000 decadent partiers. Student-packed **Salamanca** (p. 169) is a crazed, international game of "find-your-fling," and **Lagos,** Portugal (p. 628), has more bars and backpackers per square meter than any town in the world.

LET'S GO PICKS

BEST PLACE TO STUPIDLY ENDANGER YOUR LIFE: Pamplona (S), during the infamous "Running of the Bulls" (p. 463).

BEST UNFINISHED BUILDING: La Sagrada Familia, Gaudí's masterpiece in Barcelona (S). 120 years under construction, and counting (p. 387).

BEST PLACE FOR A SCANDALOUS AFFAIR: Mallorca (S), where Frédéric Chopin and George Sand spent a winter of passion and discontent (p. 338).

BEST PLACE TO HANDLE YOUR MONKEY OR CHARM YOUR SNAKE: Djema'a al-Fna, Marrakesh's (M) bizarre bazaar (p. 776).

BEST PLACE TO SEE A BURNING BUSH: Parque Nacional de Timanfaya, in the Canary Islands (S), where volcanic fires burn just below ground (p. 570).

BEST 5AM FOOD: Arroz de la calle ❶, Madrid's (S) cheap post-club fare (p. 107).

BEST MESSY FESTIVAL: La Tomatina, in tiny Buñol (S), where for two hours every August, the entire town has a massive, juicy tomato war.

BEST PLACE TO SPOON A STRANGER: Refugio L'Atalaya, in the Parque Nacional de Ordesa (S), where tight quarters make for fast friends (p. 455).

BEST RELIGIOUS MONUMENT MADE OF DEAD PEOPLE: 5000 unwitting skeletons went into the making of Évora's (P) macabre **Capella de Ossos** (Chapel of Bones) (p. 649).

BEST SINFULLY DELICIOUS DESSERTS: The heavenly **pastries** made by the cloistered nuns of Sevilla's (S) Convento de Santa Inés (p. 226).

BEST PLACE FOR SOME FUN FROM DOWN UNDER: Lagos (P), playground of too many tanned Kiwi and Aussie 20-somethings to count (p. 628).

SUGGESTED ITINERARIES

SPAIN, PORTUGAL, AND MOROCCO (6 WEEKS) Start the party off in **Madrid** (4 days, 4 nights, p. 86), with daytrips to the reserved palace of **El Escorial** (p. 138) and the medieval streets of **Toledo** (p. 146). Visit the ancient center of **Salamanca** (2 days, p. 169) before traversing north to the musical city of **Santiago de Compostela** (1 day, p. 458). Hop the border into **Portugal,** heading up to the unpretentious **Porto** (2 days, p. 687). Continue down to the vibrant university town of **Coimbra** (1 day, p. 674). Immerse yourself in the sights, sounds, and cafes of **Lisbon** (2 days, 3 nights, p. 593) with a daytrip to the town of **Sintra** (1 day, p. 621). To the south lie the beaches and cliffs of the Algarve; stop in **Lagos** (2 days, p. 628) to dance the night away. Catch your shut-eye on the 7hr. bus from Lagos to **Sevilla** (2 days, p. 213) and prepare for a romantic stroll along the Guadalquivir River. Delve deeper into Iberia's Arab roots and take a ferry from **Algeciras** to **Tangier, Morocco,** escaping immediately to the beaches of **Asilah** (1 day, p. 754). Move inland to the imperial cities of **Fez** (2 days, p. 744) and **Marrakesh** (2 days, p. 771) with their enchanting medinas. Stop by the coastal capital **Rabat** (1 day), and then swing back through Algeciras and Sevilla to **Córdoba, Spain** (2 days, p. 235), with its gargantuan Mezquita, and **Granada** (2 days, p. 287), home to the world-famous Alhambra. Enjoy the beaches and vibrant nightlife in **Alicante** (2 days, p. 286). Hop over to **Ibiza** (1 day, p. 490) in the Balearic Islands for decadence, discos, and debauchery. Head back to the mainland and up the Mediterranean Coast to **Valencia** (1 day, p. 310), where the food—*paella* and oranges—rivals the new planetarium as Valencia's top attraction.

BEST OF SPAIN, PORTUGAL, AND MOROCCO

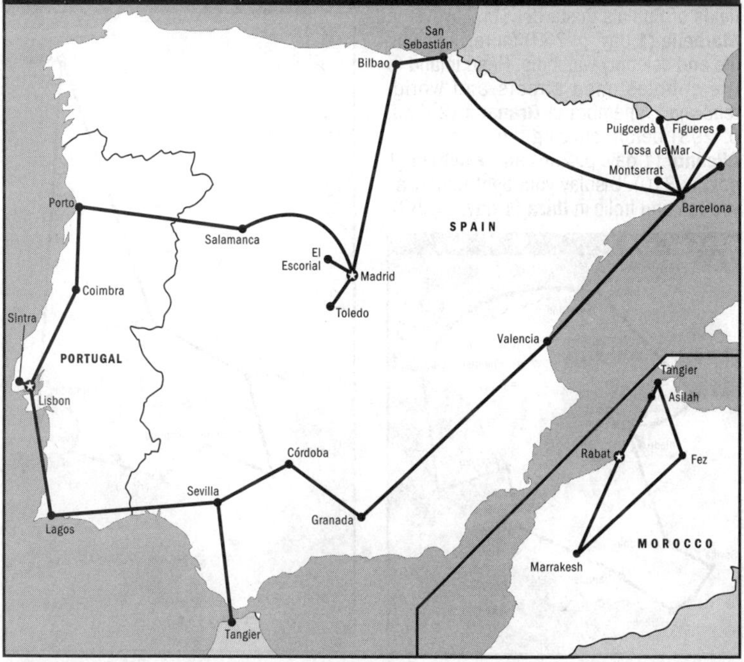

Onwards to **Barcelona** (4 days, p. 365), one of Europe's most vibrant cities full of Modernista architecture and fierce nightlife. During the summer, sun on the beaches in **Tossa de Mar** (1 day, p. 411), or visit the monastery in **Montserrat** (1 day, p. 402). In the winter, a better bet is skiing in **Puigcerdà** (1 day, p. 426). Visit Spain's second most popular museum, the Theatre-Museu Dalí in **Figueres** (1 day, p. 422) before heading on to **San Sebastián** (2 days, p. 477) and **Bilbao** (1 day, p. 486), home to the Guggenheim Museum. Enjoy the beaches and boardwalks of **Santander** (1 day, p. 444) for some relaxation on your final stop.

THE BEST OF SPAIN (3 WEEKS)

Begin *la marcha* in **Madrid** (4 days, 4 nights, p. 86), with daytrips to **El Escorial** (p. 138) and **Toledo** (p. 146). Then speed down to **Córdoba** (2 days, p. 235), and on to **Sevilla** (2 days, p. 213). Board the bus to the peaceful *pueblo blanco* of **Arcos de la Frontera** (1 day, p. 250). Next, make your way south to the tanning fields of Spain's Costa del Sol. Layover in **Marbella** (1 day, p. 269) for raging nightlife and celebrity-watching. Head inland to the cobblestoned streets and world-renowned Alhambra in **Granada** (2 days, p. 293) before cruising the coast up to **Alicante** (1 day, p. 286) and **Valencia** (1 day, p. 310). Display your tight tummy as you tan and frolic in **Ibiza** (1 day, p. 356).

BEST OF SPAIN

Venture north to Spain's coastal jewel, **Barcelona** (2 days, p. 365), a pleasure for art and nightlife lovers alike. Worthwhile daytrips in Cataluña abound: partake of **Tossa de Mar**'s beaches (1 day, p. 411), admire breathtaking mountain views from **Montserrat** (1 day, p. 402), or say Hello Dalí in **Figueres** (1 day, p. 421). Grab a bus to the beaches and *tapas* of **San Sebastián** (2 days, p. 477). Next, it's on to **Bilbao** (1 day, p. 486), home of the incredible Guggenheim museum, before a final stop in the charming university town of **Salamanca** (1 day, p. 138).

THE BEST OF ANDALUCÍA (2 WEEKS)

Whisk away from Madrid on the high-speed AVE train to **Córdoba** (2 days, p. 235) to tour the Mezquita mosque-turned-cathedral. Hop back on the AVE to **Sevilla** (3 days, p. 213) to inspect the three towers dedicated to gold, silver, and God. A quick trip down to Costa del Luz yields the soft-sanded stretches of **Cádiz's** beaches (2 days, p. 252).

BEST OF ANDALUCÍA

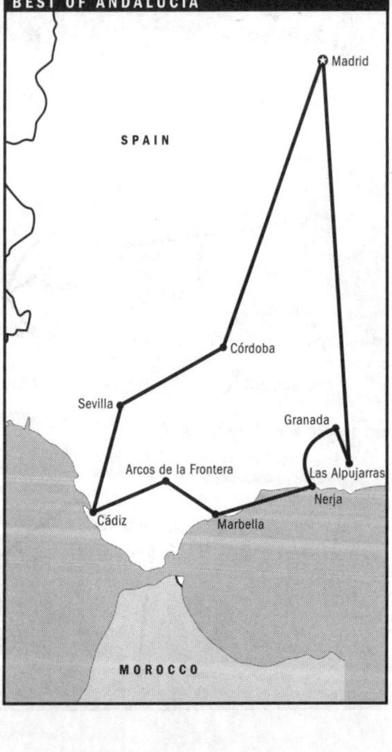

Move into the heart of Andalucía and the classic *pueblo blanco* **Arcos de la Frontera** (1 day, p. 250). Marvel at the *gorge*-ous sights in **Ronda** (1 day, p. 255) before partying in the Costa del Sol resort town of **Marbella** (2 days, p. 269). Continue inland to **Granada** (2 days, p. 287), where the Alhambra and Albaicín are sights for sore eyes. Mountain air awaits hiking from town to town in **Las Alpujarras** (1 day, p. 300). Ride the rails back to Madrid.

THE BEST OF PORTUGAL (2 WEEKS)

Begin in the busy capital **Lisbon** (3-4 days, p. 593) and daytrip to fairy tale **Sintra** (1 day, p. 593). Head down to the infamous beach-and-bar town **Lagos** (2-3 days, p. 628) and spend an afternoon in **Sagres,** once considered the end of the world. Check out the creepy bone chapel in **Évora** (1 day, p. 645) and the mysterious convent in **Tomar** (1 day, p. 670). Slam shut those dusty books in the university town of **Coimbra** (2-3 days, p. 674) and take in the youthful fun. Finish in **Porto** (2 days, p. 687), home of fine artwork and sweet port wine.

BEST OF PORTUGAL

THE BEST OF MOROCCO (2 WEEKS)

From Spain, hop on a ferry from Spanish **Algeciras** to **Tangier.** Once on land, move directly to **Asilah** (1 day, p. 754). Decamp to the enchanting stoned medina of **Chefchaoun** (1 day, p. 735) for sweet-smelling relaxation. Experience the dazzling imperial cities of **Fez** (2 days, p. 744), **Meknes** (2 days, p. 737), and **Marrakesh** (2 days, p. 771). Mounted on a camel, probe deeper into the deserts south of **Ouarzazate** (1 day, p. 784). Back track through Marrakesh to beaches of **Essaouira** (2 days, p. 768) before heading up the coast to the capital **Rabat** (1 day, p. 757) on your way back to Tangier.

BEST OF MOROCCO

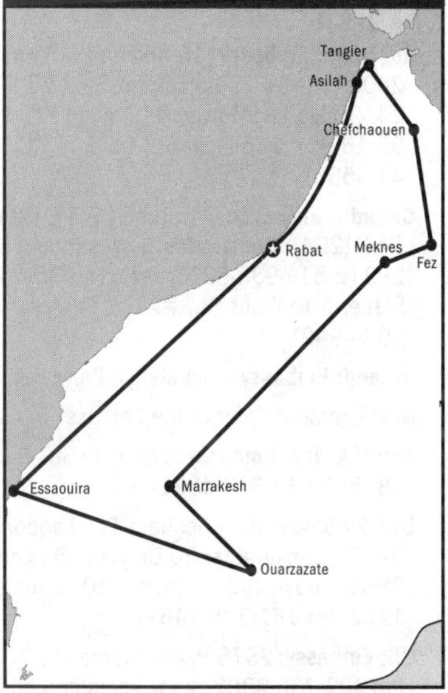

ESSENTIALS

FACTS FOR THE TRAVELER

ENTRANCE REQUIREMENTS

Passport (p. 10). Required for all citizens of Australia, Canada, Ireland, New Zealand, South Africa, the UK, and the US.

Visa (p. 12). Required in addition to a passport for South Africans going to Spain, Portugal, and Morocco.

Work Permit (p. 12). Required for all foreigners planning to work in Spain, Portugal, and Morocco.

International Driving Permit (p. 47). Recommended for those planning to drive in Spain, Portugal, and Morocco.

EMBASSIES AND CONSULATES

CONSULAR SERVICES ABROAD

The following listings are for Spanish, Portuguese, and Moroccan embassies and consulates in Australia, Canada, Ireland, New Zealand, South Africa, the UK, and the US. For listings of these embassies and consulates in Spain, Portugal, and Morocco, consult the country-specific **Essentials** sections (p. 85, p. 588, and p. 720).

SPANISH

Australia: Embassy: 15 Arkana St., **Yarralumla,** ACT 2600; P.O. Box 9076, Deakin, ACT 2600 (☎2 62 73 35 55; fax 2 62 73 39 18; www.embaspain.com). **Consulates:** Level 24, St. Martin's Tower, 31 Market St., **Sydney,** NSW 2000 (☎2 92 61 24 33; fax 2 92 83 16 95); 146 Elgin St., Carlton, VIC 3052 (**Melbourne**) (☎3 93 47 19 66; fax 3 93 47 3580).

Canada: Embassy: 74 Stanley Ave., **Ottawa,** ON K1M 1P4 (☎613-747-2252; fax 613-744-1224). **Consulates:** 1 Westmount Sq., #1456, Ave. Wood, **Montreal,** Quebec H3Z 2P9 (☎514-935-5235; fax 514-935-4655; www.docuweb.ca/spainincanada); Simcoe Place, 200 Front St., #2401 **Toronto,** Ontario M5V 3K2 (☎416-977-1661; fax 416-593-4949).

Ireland: Embassy: 17a Merlyn Park, Ballsbridge, **Dublin** 4 (☎1 269 1640).

New Zealand: Refer to the Embassy in Australia.

South Africa: Embassy: 169 Pine St., Arcadia, P.O. Box 1633, **Pretoria** 0083 (☎12 344 3875; fax 12 343 4891).

UK: Embassy: 39 Chesham Pl., **London** SW1X 8SB (☎207 235 5555; fax 207 235 9905). **Consulates:** 20 Draycott Pl., **London** SW3 2RZ (☎207 589 8989; fax 207 581 7888); #1A, Brook House, 70, Spring Gardens, **Manchester** M2 2BQ (☎161 236 1262; fax 161 228 7467).

US: Embassy: 2375 Pennsylvania Ave. NW, **Washington, D.C.** 20037 (☎202-738-2330; fax 202-738-2302; www.spainemb.org). **Consulates:** 150 E. 58th St., 30th fl., **New York,** NY 10155 (☎212-355-4080; fax 212-644-3751); **others** in Boston, Chicago, Houston, Los Angeles, Miami, New Orleans, San Juan (PR), and San Francisco.

PORTUGUESE

Australia: Embassy: 23 Culgoa Circuit, **O'Malley,** ACT 2606; P.O. Box 9092, Deakin, ACT 2600 (☎62 90 17 33; fax 62 90 19 57). **Consulate:** Level 9 #30, Clarence St., P.O. Box 3309, **Sydney,** NSW 2000 (☎92 62 59 91; fax 92 62 59 91; www.consulportugal-sydney.com).

Canada: Embassy: 645 Island Park Dr., **Ottawa,** ON K1Y OB8 (☎613-729-0883; fax 613-729-4236). **Consulates:** 438 University Ave., #1400, **Toronto,** ON M5G 2K8 (☎416-217-0966; fax 416-217-0973; www.cgportugaltoronto.com); 904-700 W. Pender St., #904, **Vancouver,** BC V6C 1G8 (☎604-688-6514; fax 604-685-7042).

Ireland: Embassy: Knocksinna House, Knocksinna Road, Foxrock, **Dublin** 18 (☎3531 289 4416; fax: 3531 289 2849).

New Zealand: Embassy: Refer to the Embassy in Australia. **Consulates:** 33 Garfield St., Parnell, P.O. Box 305, **Auckland** (☎9 309 1454; fax 9 308 9061); 21 Marion St., **Wellington** (☎4 382 7655; fax 4 382 6659).

South Africa: Embassy: 599 Leyds St., Muckleneuk, **Pretoria,** 0002; P.O. Box 27102, Sunnyside, 0132 (☎12 341 2340; fax 12 341 3975). **Consulates:** Barcley Sq., 296 Walker St., Sunnyside, **Pretoria,** 0002 (☎12 341 5522; fax 12 341 5690); Portuguese House, 1st fl., Ernest Oppenheimer Ave., 2198, Bruma, **Johannesburg;** P.O. Box 5092 (☎11 293 8206; fax 11 333 9009); Main Tower, Standard Bank Centre, Hertzog Boulevard, Hereengracht, **Capetown,** 8001; P.O. Box 3433, 8000; 320 W. St., 16th fl., P.O. Box 315, **Durban** (☎31 305 7511; fax 31 304 6063).

UK: Embassy: 11 Belgrave Sq., **London** SW1X 8PP (☎0171 581 8722; fax 20 7235 5331; fax 20 7245 1287). **Consulate:** Silver City House, 2nd-3rd fl., 62 Brompton Rd., **London** SW3 1BJ (☎0171 581 8722; fax 0171 581 3085).

US: Embassy: 2125 Kalorama Rd. NW, **Washington, D.C.** 20008 (☎202-328-8610; fax 202-462-3726 or 202-518-3694). **Consulates:** 630 5th Ave., 8th fl., #801, **New York,** NY 10111 (☎212-246-4580; fax 212-459-0190); **others** in Boston, Chicago, Coral Gables (FL), Houston, Honolulu, Los Angeles, Newark, New Bedford (MA), New Orleans, Philadelphia, Providence, San Francisco, Río Piedras (PR), and Waterbury (CT).

MOROCCAN

Australia: Embassy: 11 West St., #2, **North Sydney,** NSW 2060 (☎2 99 57 67 17; fax 2 99 23 10 53).

Canada: Embassy: 38 Range Rd., **Ottawa,** ON K1N 8J4 (☎613-236-7391 or 613-236-7392; fax 613-236-6164; www.ambassade-maroc.ottawa.on.ca). **Consulate:** 1010 Sherbrooke West St., #1510, **Montreal,** QU H3A 2R7 (☎514-288-8750; fax 514-288-4859; www.consulatdumaroc.ca).

Ireland: Embassy: 53 Ragland Rd., **Dublin** 4 (☎353 1 660 9449; fax 353 1 660 9468).

South Africa: Embassy: 799 Schoeman St., **Pretoria** (☎12 343 0230; fax 12 343 0613).

UK: Embassy: 49 Queens Gate Gardens, **London** SW7 5NE (☎20 7581 5001; fax 20 7225 3862).

US: Embassy: 1601 21st St. NW, **Washington, D.C.** 20009 (☎202-462-7979; fax 202-265-0161). **Consulates:** 10 East 40th. St., 23rd fl., **New York,** NY 10016 (☎212-758-2625; fax 212-779-7441); 1821 Jefferson Place NW, **Washington, D.C.** 20036 (☎202-462-7979; fax 202-452-0106).

TOURIST OFFICES

SPANISH

Spain's official tourist board operates an extensive website at www.tourspain.es. It also has offices in Canada, the UK, and the US.

Canada: Tourist Office of Spain, 2 Bloor St. West, Suite 3402, **Toronto,** ON M4W 3E2 (☎416-961-3131; fax 416-961-1992).

UK: Spanish National Tourist Office, 22-23 Manchester Square, **London** W1U 3PX (☎171 486 8077; fax 171 486 8034).

US: Tourist Office of Spain, 666 5th Ave., 35th fl., **New York,** NY 10103 (☎212-265-8822; fax 212-265-8864). Additional offices in **Chicago,** IL (☎312-642-1992), **Beverly Hills,** CA (☎323-658-7188), and **Miami,** FL (☎305-358-1992).

PORTUGUESE

The official Portuguese tourism website is located at www.portugal-insite.pt. There are also offices in Canada, the UK, and the US.

Canada: Portuguese Trade and Tourism Commission, 60 Bloor St. West, #1005, **Toronto,** ON M4W 3B8 (☎416-921-7376; fax 416-921-1353).

UK: Portuguese Trade and Tourism Office, 22-25A Sackville Street, 2nd-4th fl., **London** W1X 3LY (☎20 7474 1441; fax 20 7494 1508).

US: Portuguese National Tourist Office, 590 5th Ave., 4th fl., **New York,** NY 10036 (☎212-354-4403; fax 212-764-6137). Additional office in Washington D.C. (☎202-331-8222).

MOROCCAN

The official website for tourism in Morocco is www.tourism-in-morocco.com. There are also tourist offices located in Australia, Canada, and the US.

Australia: Moroccan National Tourist Office, 2/11 West St. North, **Sydney** NSW 2060 (☎2 9922 4999; fax 2 9923 1053).

Canada: Moroccan National Tourist Office, Place Montreal Trust, #2450, 1800, Ave. McGill, **Montreal** QC H3A 3J6 (☎514-842-8111; fax 514-842-5316).

US: Moroccan National Tourist Office, 20 East 46th St., #1201, **New York,** NY 10017 (☎212-557-2520; fax 212-949-8148). Additional office in **Lake Buena Vista,** FL (☎407-827-5337).

DOCUMENTS AND FORMALITIES

PASSPORTS

REQUIREMENTS. Citizens of Australia, Canada, Ireland, New Zealand, South Africa, the UK, and US need valid passports to enter Spain, Portugal, and Morocco and to re-enter their own countries. For citizens of some countries, neither Spain, Portugal, nor Morocco allows entrance if the passport expires in under six months. Returning home with an expired passport is illegal; fines may result.

NEW PASSPORTS. Citizens of Australia, Canada, Ireland, New Zealand, the UK, and the US can apply for a passport at any post office, passport office, or court of law. Citizens of South Africa can apply for a passport at any Home Affairs Office. Any new passport or renewal applications must be filed well in advance of the departure date. Most passport offices offer rush services for a very steep fee.

ONE EUROPE. The idea of European unity has come a long way since 1958, when the European Economic Community (EEC) was created in order to promote solidarity and cooperation. Since then, the EEC has become the European Union (EU), with political, legal, and economic institutions spanning 15 member states: Austria, Belgium, Denmark, Finland, France, Germany, Greece, Ireland, Italy, Luxembourg, the Netherlands, Portugal, Spain, Sweden, and the UK.

What does this have to do with the average non-EU tourist? In 1999, the EU established **freedom of movement** across 15 European countries—the entire EU minus Ireland and the UK, but plus Iceland and Norway. This means that border controls between participating countries have been abolished, and visa policies harmonized. While you're still required to carry a passport (or government-issued ID card for EU citizens) when crossing an internal border, once you've been admitted into one country, you're free to travel to all participating states. Britain and Ireland have also formed a **common travel area,** abolishing passport controls between the UK and Ireland. This means that the only times you'll see a border guard within the EU are traveling between the British Isles and the Continent. For more important consequences of the EU for travelers, see **The Euro** (p. 15) and **European Customs** (p. 11) and **Customs in the EU** (p. 13).

PASSPORT MAINTENANCE. Photocopy the page of your passport with your photo, as well as your visas, traveler's check serial numbers, and any other important documents. Carry one set of copies in a safe place, apart from the originals, and leave another set at home. Consulates also recommend that you carry an expired passport or an official copy of your birth certificate in a part of your baggage, separate from other documents.

If you lose your passport, immediately notify the local police and the nearest embassy or consulate of your home government. To expedite its replacement, you will need to know all information previously recorded and show ID and proof of citizenship. In some cases, a replacement may take weeks to process, and it may be valid only for a limited time. Any visas stamped in your old passport will be irretrievably lost. In an emergency, ask for immediate temporary traveling papers that will permit you to re-enter your home country.

VISAS

As of August 2003, citizens of South Africa need a visa in addition to a valid passport for entrance to Spain, Portugal, or Morocco; citizens of Australia, Canada, Ireland, New Zealand, the UK, and the US do not need visas to enter Spain, Portugal, or Morocco for less than three months. Visas vary in cost based on the length of stay and can only be obtained with extensive documentation on your planned activity in the country. Applications are available at the nearest consulate or embassy for the country to which you are traveling. In some cases they can also be filed in the foreign country, but generally speaking, visa applications must be filed in your home country. US citizens can take advantage of the **Center for International Business and Travel** (**CIBT;** ☎800-929-2428; www.cibt.com), which secures visas for travel to almost all countries for a variable service charge.

Double-check on entrance requirements at the nearest embassy or consulate of Spain, Portugal, or Morocco for up-to-date info before departure. US citizens can also consult www.pueblo.gsa.gov/cic_text/travel/foreign/foreignentryreqs.html.

IDENTIFICATION

When you travel, always carry two or more forms of identification on your person, including at least one photo ID; a passport combined with a driver's license or birth certificate is usually adequate. Many establishments, especially banks, may require several IDs in order to cash traveler's checks. Never carry all your forms of ID together; split them up in case of theft or loss.

TEACHER, STUDENT & YOUTH IDENTIFICATION. The **International Student Identity Card (ISIC)** provides discounts on sights, accommodations, food, and transport; access to 24hr. emergency helpline (in North America call ☎877-370-ISIC; elsewhere call US collect ☎+1 715-345-0505; www.isic.org); and insurance benefits for US cardholders (see **Insurance,** p. 24). The ISIC is preferable to an institution-specific card (such as a university ID) because it is more likely to be recognized and honored abroad. Applicants must be degree-seeking students of a secondary or post-secondary school and must be of at least 12 years of age. Because of the proliferation of fake ISICs, some services (particularly airlines) require additional proof of student identity, such as a school ID or a letter attesting to your student status, signed by your registrar and stamped with your school seal.

The **International Teacher Identity Card (ITIC)** offers teachers the same insurance coverage with similar but limited discounts. For non-student travelers 25 years old or under, the **International Youth Travel Card (IYTC)** offers many of ISIC's benefits.

Each of these identity cards costs US$22 or equivalent. ISIC and ITIC cards are valid for roughly one and a half academic years; IYTC cards are valid for one year from the date of issue. Many student travel agencies (see p. 34) issue the cards, including STA Travel in Australia and New Zealand; Travel CUTS in Canada; usit in the Republic of Ireland and Northern Ireland; SASTS in South Africa; Campus Travel and STA Travel in the UK; and Council Travel and STA Travel in the US. For a listing of issuing agencies, or for more information, contact the **International Student Travel Confederation (ISTC),** Herengracht 479, 1017 BS Amsterdam, Netherlands (☎31 20 421 28 00; fax 31 20 421 28 10; www.istc.org).

CUSTOMS IN THE EU. As well as freedom of movement of people within the EU (see p. 11), travelers in EU member countries (Austria, Belgium, Denmark, Finland, France, Germany, Greece, Ireland, Italy, Luxembourg, the Netherlands, Portugal, Spain, Sweden, and the UK) can also take advantage of the freedom of movement of goods. This means that there are no customs controls at internal EU borders (i.e., you can take the blue customs channel at the airport), and travelers are free to transport whatever legal substances they like as long as it is for their own personal (non-commercial) use—up to 800 cigarettes, 10L of spirits, 90L of wine (60L of sparkling wine), and 110L of beer. You should also be aware that duty-free was abolished on June 30, 1999, for travel between EU member states; however, travelers between the EU and the rest of the world still get a duty-free allowance when passing through customs.

CUSTOMS

Upon entering Spain, Portugal, or Morocco, you must declare certain items from abroad and pay a duty on the value of those articles that exceeds the allowance established by the country's customs service. Goods and gifts purchased at **duty-free** shops abroad are not exempt from duty or sales tax at your point of return and thus must be declared as well; "duty-free" merely means that you need not pay a tax in the country of purchase. Upon returning home, you must similarly declare all articles acquired abroad and pay a duty on the value of articles in excess of your home country's allowance. In order to expedite your return, make a list of any valuables brought from home and register them with customs before traveling abroad. Also be sure to keep receipts for all goods acquired abroad. Spain and Morocco have value-added taxes which can be redeemed upon leaving the country. See the **Essentials** sections for **Spain** (p. 80) and **Morocco** (p. 720) for more info.

▼ ▼ ▼ ▼ ▼ ▼ ▼ ▼ ▼ ▼ ▼ ▼ ▼ ▼ ▼ ▼ ▼ ▼ ▼ ▼

Learn Spanish & Portuguese

In Spain: Barcelona, Madrid, Granada, Sevilla, Marbella, Salamanca, San Sebastian
Also Portugal, Central & South America, the Caribbean

- ▼ Learn Spanish the RIGHT way FAST
- ▼ For all ages and all levels
- ▼ Most programs start weekly
- ▼ Private tutor or small groups
- ▼ 3-8 hours/day
- ▼ Academic credit available
- ▼ Pre-departure assistance
- ▼ Travel insurance
- ▼ Easy to book online
- ▼ All major credit cards accepted

▼ ▼ ▼ *¡Now Featuring!* ▼ ▼ ▼
University Semester Abroad Programs
Volunteer and Internship Placements

AmeriSpan programs can also be found at STA Travel offices around the world

For for free information:
USA & Canada: **1-800-879-6640**
Worldwide 215-751-1100
Fax: 215-751-1986
Email: info@amerispan.com
Web: **www.amerispan.com**

AmeriSpan Unlimited
THE BRIDGE BETWEEN CULTURES

FURTHER RESOURCES

Australia: Australian Customs National Information Line (☎1300 363 263, within Australia; from elsewhere call 2 6275 6666; www.customs.gov.au).

Canada: Canadian Customs, 2265 St. Laurent Blvd., Ottawa, ON K1G 4K3 (☎800-461-9999 (24hr.), within Canada; from elsewhere call ☎204-983-3500; www.revcan.ca).

Ireland: Customs Information Office, Irish Life Centre, Lower Abbey St., Dublin 1 (☎1 878 8811; fax 1 878 0836; ceadmin@revenue.ie; www.revenue.ie).

New Zealand: New Zealand Customhouse, 17-21 Whitmore St., Box 2218, Wellington (☎4 473 6099; fax 4 473 7370; www.customs.govt.nz).

South Africa: Commissioner for Customs and Excise, Private Bag X47, Pretoria 0001 (☎12 422 4000; fax 12 422 5186; http://www.sars.gov.za).

UK: Her Majesty's Customs and Excise, Passenger Enquiry Team, Wayfarer House, Great South West Road, Feltham, Middlesex TW14 8NP (☎0845 010 9000; www.hmce.gov.uk).

US: US Customs Service, 1330 Pennsylvania Ave. NW, Washington, D.C. 20229 (☎202-354-1000; fax 202-354-1010; www.customs.gov).

MONEY

CURRENCY AND EXCHANGE

The currency chart below is based on August 2003 exchange rates between European Union euros (EUR€) and Australian dollars (AUS$), Canadian dollars (CDN$), Moroccan dirham (DH), New Zealand dollars (NZ$), South African Rand (SAR), British pounds (UK£), and US dollars (US$). Check the converter on financial websites such as www.bloomberg.com and www.xe.com for current rates.

CURRENCY		
	1 AUS$ = 0.554 EUR = 5.808 DH	1 EUR = 10.449 DH = 1.804 AUS$
	1 CDN$ = 0.651 EUR = 6.822 DH	1 EUR = 10.449 DH = 1.536 CDN$
	1 NZ$ = 0.477 EUR = 4.996 DH	1 EUR = 10.449 DH = 2.096 NZ$
	1 ZAR = 0.097 EUR = 1.011 DH	1 EUR = 10.449 DH = 10.357 ZAR
	1 US$ = 1.0244 EUR = 10.731 DH	1 EUR = 10.449 DH = 0.976 US$
	1 UK£ = 1.564 EUR = 16.379 DH	1 EUR = 10.449 DH = 0.639 UK£

As a general rule, it's cheaper to convert money in Spain, Portugal, or Morocco than at home. However, you should bring enough foreign currency to last for the first 24 to 72 hours of a trip to avoid being penniless should you arrive after bank hours or on a holiday. Travelers from the US can get foreign currency from the comfort of home: **International Currency Express** (☎888-278-6628) delivers foreign currency or traveler's checks second-day (US$12) at competitive exchange rates.

When changing money, go only to bureaus with at most a 5% margin between their buy and sell prices. You lose money with every transaction, so **convert large sums** (unless the currency is depreciating rapidly), **but no more than you'll need.**

If you use traveler's checks or bills, carry some in small denominations (the equivalent of US$50 or less) for times when you are forced to exchange money at disadvantageous rates, but bring a range of denominations since charges may be levied per check cashed. Store your money in a variety of forms; ideally, you will always be carrying some cash, some traveler's checks, and an ATM and/or credit card. All travelers should also consider carrying some US dollars (about US$50 worth), which are often preferred by local tellers. Throwing around dollars for preferential treatment may be offensive, especially in Morocco, and it can attract thieves. It may also mark you as a foreigner and invite locals to jack up prices.

THE EURO. The official currency of 12 members of the European Union—Austria, Belgium, Finland, France, Germany, Greece, Ireland, Italy, Luxembourg, the Netherlands, Portugal, and Spain—is now the euro. All transactions are performed in euros and previous currencies are no longer in use.

TRAVELER'S CHECKS

Traveler's checks are one of the safest and least troublesome means of carrying funds. **American Express** and **Visa** are the most widely recognized. Many banks and agencies sell them for a small commission. Issuers provide refunds if the checks are lost or stolen, and many provide additional services, such as toll-free refund hotlines abroad, emergency message services, and stolen credit card assistance.

While traveling, keep check receipts and a record of which checks you've cashed separate from the checks themselves. Also leave a list of check numbers with someone at home. Never countersign checks until you're ready to cash them, and always bring your passport (or a copy) with you to cash them. If your checks are lost or stolen, immediately contact a refund center to be reimbursed; they may require a police report verifying the loss or theft. Ask about toll-free refund hotlines and the location of refund centers (there are more in Spain than in Portugal or Morocco) when purchasing checks, and always carry emergency cash.

American Express: Call ☎800 251 902 in Australia; in New Zealand ☎0800 441 068; in the UK ☎0800 521 313; in the US and Canada ☎800-221-7282. Elsewhere call US collect ☎801-964-6665; www.aexp.com. From Spain call toll-free ☎900 99 44 26; from Portugal toll-free ☎800 84 40 80; and from Morocco ☎441 273 35 71 00. Traveler's checks are available at no commission at AmEx offices, 2.5% at banks, and commission-free at AAA offices (see p. 47). *Cheques for Two* can be signed by either of 2 people traveling together.

Citicorp: In the US and Canada call ☎800-645-6556; from Spain call ☎900 97 44 30; from Portugal call ☎800 84 41 40; and from Morocco and anywhere else call US collect ☎813-623-1709. Traveler's checks available at 1-2% commission. Call 24hr.

Thomas Cook MasterCard: In the US and Canada call ☎800-223-7373; in the UK call ☎800 62 21 01; elsewhere call UK collect ☎1733 31 89 50. Checks available 2% commission. There are no Thomas Cook offices in Spain; banks accept their checks but charge commission. In Portugal, Marcus & Harting will cash checks commission-free in Faro, Lisbon, and the Algarve. In Morocco, Credit de Maroc will cash commission-free.

Visa: In the US call ☎800-227-6811; in the UK call ☎800 89 50 78; elsewhere call UK collect ☎20 7937 8091. Call for the location of their nearest office.

CREDIT CARDS

Credit cards often offer superior exchange rates—up to 5% better than the retail rate used by banks and other exchange bureaus. Credit cards may also offer services such as insurance or emergency help and are sometimes required to reserve hotel rooms or rental cars. **MasterCard** and **Visa** are the most welcomed; **American Express** cards work at some ATMs and at AmEx offices and major airports.

Credit cards are also useful for **cash advances,** which allow you to instantly withdraw euros or dirham from associated banks and ATMs throughout the country in which you are traveling. However, transaction fees for all credit card advances (up to US$10 per advance, plus 2-3% extra on foreign transactions after conversion) tend to make credit cards a more costly way of withdrawing cash than ATMs or traveler's checks. In an emergency, however, the transaction fee may prove worth the cost. To be eligible for an advance, you'll need to get a **Personal Identification Number (PIN)** from your credit card company (see **Cash (ATM) Cards,** below).

PIN NUMBERS & ATMS. To use a cash or credit card to withdraw money from a cash machine (ATM) in Europe, you must have a four-digit **Personal Identification Number (PIN).** If your PIN is longer than four digits, ask your bank whether you can just use the first four, or whether you'll need a new one. **Credit cards** don't usually come with PINs, so if you intend to hit up ATMs in Europe with a credit card, call your credit card company before leaving to request one. People with alphabetic, rather than numerical, PINs may also be thrown off by the lack of letters on European cash machines. The following handy list gives the corresponding numbers to use: 1=QZ; 2=ABC; 3=DEF; 4=GHI; 5=JKL; 6=MNO; 7=PRS; 8=TUV; and 9=WXY. Note that if you mistakenly punch the wrong code into the machine three times, it will swallow your card for good.

CASH (ATM) AND DEBIT CARDS

Cash cards—popularly called ATM cards—are widespread in Spain, Portugal, and Morocco. Depending on the system that your home bank uses, you can most likely access your personal bank account from abroad. ATMs get the same wholesale exchange rate as credit cards, but there is often a limit on the amount of money you can withdraw per day (around US$500), and unfortunately computer networks sometimes fail. There is also typically a surcharge of US$1-5 per withdrawal. Be sure to memorize your PIN code in numeric form since machines elsewhere often don't have letters on their keys. Also, if your PIN is longer than four digits, ask your bank whether you need a new number.

Debit cards can be used wherever its associated credit card company (usually Mastercard or Visa) is accepted, but the money is withdrawn directly from the holder's checking account. Debit cards often also function as ATM cards and can be used to withdraw cash from associated banks and ATMs.

The two major international money networks are **Cirrus** (US ☎800-424-7787; www.mastercard.com) and **Visa/PLUS** (US ☎800-843-7587; www.visa.com). Most ATMs charge a transaction fee that is paid to the bank that owns the ATM.

Visa TravelMoney is a prepaid, PIN-protected card that gives your 24-hour access to your funds in local currency at more than 700,000 Visa ATMs worldwide, including locations throughout Spain, Portugal, and Morocco. TravelMoney is safer than carrying cash and provides funds at favorable exchange rates. For local customer assistance or to activate a card in Spain, call ☎900 95 11 25, and in Portugal call ☎800 81 14 26. There is no number for local customer assistance in Morocco, but to activate a card call collect ☎410 581-9091.

GETTING MONEY FROM HOME

If you run out of money while traveling, the easiest and cheapest solution is to have someone back home make a deposit to your credit card or cash (ATM) card. Failing that, consider one of the following options.

WIRING MONEY. It is possible to arrange a **bank money transfer,** which means asking a bank back home to wire money to a bank in Spain, Portugal, or Morocco. This is the cheapest way to transfer cash, but it's also the slowest, usually taking several days. Note that some banks may only release your funds in local currency, potentially sticking you with a poor exchange rate; inquire about this in advance. Money transfer services like **Western Union** are faster and more convenient than bank transfers—but also much pricier. Western Union has many locations worldwide. To find one, visit www.westernunion.com, or call in the US ☎800-325-6000, in Canada ☎800-235-0000, in the UK ☎0800 83 38 33, in Australia ☎800 501 500, in New Zealand ☎800 27 0000, in South Africa ☎0860 100031, in Spain ☎902 11 41 89, in Portugal ☎800 20 68 68, and in Morocco ☎07 26 15 59. Money transfer services are also available at **American Express** and **Thomas Cook** offices.

US STATE DEPARTMENT (US CITIZENS ONLY). In dire emergencies only, the US State Department will forward money within hours to the nearest consular office, which will then disburse it according to instructions for a US$15 fee. If you wish to use this service, you must contact the Overseas Citizens Service division of the US State Department (☎202-647-5225; nights, Sundays, and holidays ☎202-647-4000).

COSTS

The cost of your trip will vary considerably, depending on where you go, how you travel, and where you stay. The most significant expenses will probably be your round-trip **airfare** to Spain, Portugal, or Morocco, and a **railpass** or **bus pass**. Before you go, spend some time calculating a reasonable per-day **budget** that will meet your needs.

STAYING ON A BUDGET. To give you a general idea, a bare-bones day (camping or staying in cheap hostels or pensions, buying food at grocery stores and markets) in Spain would cost about US$35 (€36), in Portugal about US$25 (€26), and in Morocco about US$18; a slightly more comfortable day (sleeping in nicer hostels and the occasional budget hotel, eating one or two meals a day at a restaurant, going out at night) would run US$55 (€56) in Spain, US$45 (€46) in Portugal, and US$35 in Morocco; and for a luxurious day, the sky's the limit. Also, don't forget to factor in emergency reserve funds (at least US$200) when planning how much money you'll need.

TIPS FOR SAVING MONEY. Search out opportunities for free entertainment, split accommodation and food costs with other trustworthy travelers, and buy food in supermarkets rather than eating out. Bring a **sleepsack** (see p. 25) to save on sheet charges in hostels, and do your **laundry** in the sink (unless you're explicitly prohibited from doing so). With that said, don't go overboard with your budget obsession. Though staying within your budget is important, don't do so at the expense of your health or a great travel experience.

Discover A New World Today!

Learn Spanish in Spain, Mexico, Central and South America ...

- Classes starting throughout the year
- Small group and private instruction
- Accommodations with host families
- Cultural Activities
- Excursions
- Academic Credit
- Airport Pickup
- Flight Info
- Country Info
- Plus Much More!

Spanish Abroad, Inc.
www.spanishabroad.com
1-888-722-7623
World wide: 602-778-6791 • Fax: 602-840-1545
5112 N. 40th St., #103 • Phoenix, AZ 85018 • USA

PRICE RANGES. Price ranges, marked by the numbered icons below, are included in food and accommodation listings. They are based on the lowest cost for one person during high season, excluding festivals.

SPAIN AND PORTUGAL	❶	❷	❸	❹	❺
ACCOMMODATIONS	under €15	€15-25	€25-35	€35-50	over €50
FOOD	under €6	€6-10	€10-15	€15-25	over €25
MOROCCO	❶	❷	❸	❹	❺
ACCOMMODATIONS	under 60dh	60-100dh	100-150dh	150-200dh	over 200dh
FOOD	under 40dh	40-60dh	60-80dh	80-110dh	over 110dh

ESSENTIALS

TIPPING, BARGAINING, AND TAXES

See the individual **Essentials** sections for **Spain** (see p. 70), **Portugal** (see p. 584), and **Morocco** (see p. 722) for specifics on tipping, bargaining, and taxes in each country.

SAFETY AND SECURITY

PERSONAL SAFETY

The following section is intended as a general guide; refer to the **Essentials** sections of **Spain** (p. 67), **Portugal** (p. 539), and **Morocco** (p. 662) for more detailed info.

EXPLORING. To avoid unwanted attention, try to blend in as much as possible. Respecting local customs (in many cases, dressing more conservatively) may placate would-be hecklers. Familiarize yourself with your surroundings before setting out, and carry yourself with confidence; if you must check a map on the street, duck into a shop. If you are traveling alone, be sure someone at home knows your itinerary, and **never admit that you're traveling alone.** When walking at night, stick to busy, well-lit streets; avoid dark alleyways. If you feel uncomfortable, leave as quickly as you can, but don't allow fear of the unknown to turn you into a hermit.

SELF DEFENSE. A good self-defense course will give you concrete ways to react to unwanted advances. **Impact, Prepare, and Model Mugging** can refer you to local self-defense courses in the US (☎800-345-5425). Visit www.impactsafety.org for a list of nearby chapters. Workshops start at US$50; full courses run US$350-500.

DRIVING. If you are using a **car,** learn local driving signals and wear a seatbelt. Children under 40 lbs. should ride only in a specially-designed carseat, available for a small fee from most car rental agencies. Study route maps before you drive, and if you plan on spending a lot of time on the road, you may want to bring spare parts. If your car breaks down, wait for the police to assist you. For long drives in desolate areas, invest in a cellular phone and a roadside assistance program (see p. 47). Be sure to park your vehicle in a garage or well-traveled area, and use a steering wheel locking device in larger cities. **Sleeping in your car** is one of the most dangerous (and often illegal) ways to get your rest.

TERRORISM. While Spain, Portugal, and Morocco are relatively stable countries, there are some terrorist activities that travelers should take note of. In Spain, the militant Basque separatist group ETA has carried out attacks on government officials and tourist destinations. Though the attacks are ongoing, the threat to travelers is relatively small. See p. 18 for more information. There are no particular terrorist threats in Portugal or Morocco, though the potential for transnational terrorism is relatively high in Morocco. Travelers should be aware of current levels of tension in the region and exercise appropriate caution.

TRAVEL ADVISORIES. The following government offices provide travel information and advisories by telephone, by fax, or via the web:

Australian Department of Foreign Affairs and Trade: ☎1300 555135; faxback service 02 6261 1299; www.dfat.gov.au.

Canadian Department of Foreign Affairs and International Trade (DFAIT): In Canada and the US call ☎800-267-6788, elsewhere call ☎+1 613-944-6788; www.dfait-maeci.gc.ca. Call for their free booklet, *Bon Voyage...But.*

New Zealand Ministry of Foreign Affairs: ☎04 494 8500; fax 494 8506; www.mft.govt.nz/trav.html.

United Kingdom Foreign and Commonwealth Office: ☎020 7008 0232; fax 7008 0155; www.fco.gov.uk.

US Department of State: ☎202-647-5225, faxback service 202-647-3000; travel.state.gov. For *A Safe Trip Abroad,* call ☎202-512-1800.

FINANCIAL SECURITY

PROTECTING YOUR VALUABLES. Spain and parts of Portugal are heavily touristed; along with that comes a thriving pickpocket trade. Morocco is notorious for the prevalence of theft, even in hostel rooms and other "secure" places. To minimize the financial risk associated with traveling: first, **bring as little with you as possible.** Second, buy a few combination **padlocks** to secure your belongings either in your pack or in a hostel or train station locker. Third, **carry as little cash as possible.** Keep your traveler's checks and ATM/credit cards in a **money belt** along with your passport and ID cards. Fourth, **keep a small cash reserve separate from your primary stash.** This should be about US$50 sewn into or stored in the depths of your pack, along with your traveler's check numbers and copies of important documents.

CON ARTISTS & PICKPOCKETS. In large cities **con artists** often work in groups, and children are among the most effective. Beware of certain classics: sob stories that require money, rolls of bills "found" on the street, mustard spilled onto your shoulder to distract you while they snatch your bag. **Don't ever let your passport and bags out of your sight.** Beware of **pickpockets** in crowds, especially on public transportation. Be alert in telephone booths: if you must say your calling card number, do so very quietly; if you punch it in, make sure no one can look over your shoulder.

ACCOMMODATIONS & TRANSPORTATION. Never leave your belongings unattended; crime occurs in even the most demure-looking hostel or hotel. Bring your own **padlock** for hostel lockers, and don't ever store valuables in any locker.

Be particularly careful on **buses** and **trains;** horror stories abound about determined thieves who wait for travelers to fall asleep. Carry your backpack in front of you where you can see it. When traveling with others, sleep in alternate shifts. When alone, use good judgement in selecting a train compartment: never stay in an empty one, and use a lock to secure your pack to the luggage rack. Try to sleep on top bunks with your luggage stored above you (if not in bed with you), and keep important documents and other valuables on your person. If traveling by **car,** don't leave valuables (such as radios or luggage) in it while you are away.

DRUGS AND ALCOHOL

Recreational drugs are illegal in Spain, Portugal, and Morocco. Possession of small amounts of marijuana sometimes goes unpunished in Spain and Portugal, but any attempt to buy or sell will definitely land you in jail or with a heavy fine. Morocco is infamous as a supplier of hashish to the Iberian Peninsula; don't be surprised if you are stopped and searched on your way into Spain. The Moroccan government enforces drug laws more strictly than most, and foreigners with drugs have regularly been arrested and severely punished.

HEALTH

Common sense is the simplest prescription for good health while you travel. Drink lots of fluids to prevent dehydration, and wear sturdy shoes and clean socks.

BEFORE YOU GO

In your **passport,** write the names of any people you wish to be contacted in case of an emergency, and list any allergies or medical conditions. Matching a prescription to a foreign equivalent is not always easy, safe, or possible, so carry up-to-date, legible prescriptions or a statement from your doctor stating the medication's trade name, manufacturer, chemical name, and dosage. While traveling, be sure to keep all medication with you in your carry-on luggage. For tips on packing a basic **first-aid kit** and other health essentials, see p. 25.

IMMUNIZATIONS AND PRECAUTIONS. Travelers over two-years-old should be sure that their following vaccines are up to date: MMR (for measles, mumps, and rubella); DTaP or Td (for diptheria, tetanus, and pertussis); OPV (for polio); HbCV (for haemophilus influenza B); and HBV (for Hepatitis B), although HBV is really only recommended for stays nearing six months. Adults traveling to Morocco on trips longer than four weeks should consider getting a Hepatitis A (or immune globulin) and typhoid vaccine four to six weeks before leaving. See the **Essentials** section for Morocco (p. 539) for more specific information on staying healthy during a stay in North Africa. For recommendations on immunizations and prophylaxis, consult the CDC (see below) in the US or the equivalent in your home country, and be sure to check with a doctor for guidance.

USEFUL ORGANIZATIONS AND PUBLICATIONS. The US **Centers for Disease Control and Prevention** (**CDC;** ☎877-FYI-TRIP; fax 888-232-3299; www.cdc.gov/travel) maintains an international traveler's hotline, an international fax information service, and a comprehensive travel website. The CDC's booklet *Health Information for International Travel*, an annual rundown of disease, immunization, and general health advice, is free online or US$25 via the Public Health Foundation (☎877-252-1200). For quick information on health and other travel warnings, call the **Overseas Citizens Services** (☎202-647-5225; after-hours 202-647-4000), or contact an embassy or consulate abroad. US citizens can send a self-addressed, stamped envelope to the Overseas Citizens Services, Bureau of Consular Affairs, #4811, US Department of State, Washington, D.C. 20520. For info on medical evacuation services and travel insurance firms, see the US government's website at http://travel.state.gov/medical.html or the **British Foreign and Commonwealth Office** (www.fco.gov.uk). For detailed info on travel health, including a country-by-country overview of diseases, try the **International Travel Health Guide,** Stuart Rose, MD (US$19.95; www.travmed.com). For general health info, contact the **American Red Cross** (☎800-564-1234).

MEDICAL ASSISTANCE ON THE ROAD. The following section offers general advice about medical help while traveling; see the **Essentials** sections for **Spain** (p. 82), **Portugal** (p. 590), and **Morocco** (p. 722) for more detailed info on each country.

If you are concerned about obtaining medical care while traveling, you may wish to employ special support services. *MedPass* from **GlobalCare, Inc.,** 6875 Shiloh Rd. East, Alpharetta, GA, 30005-8372, USA (☎800-860-1111; fax 678-341-1800; www.globalems.com), provides 24hr. international medical assistance and evacuation resources. The **International Association for Medical Assistance to Travelers** (**IAMAT;** US ☎716-754-4883, Canada ☎416-652-0137; www.iamat.org) has free membership, lists English-speaking doctors worldwide, and offers detailed info on immunization requirements and sanitation. If your regular **insurance** policy does not cover travel abroad, you may wish to purchase additional coverage (see p. 24).

Those with medical conditions (diabetes, allergies to antibiotics, epilepsy, heart conditions, etc.) can obtain a **Medic Alert** membership (first yr. US$35, annually thereafter US$20), which includes a stainless steel ID tag and a 24hr. collect-call number. Contact the Medic Alert Foundation, 2323 Colorado Ave, Turlock, CA 95382, USA (☎888-633-4298; outside US ☎209-668-3333; www.medicalert.org).

ONCE ABROAD

ENVIRONMENTAL HAZARDS

Neither Spain, Portugal, nor Morocco has a very extreme climate; the biggest environmental threat for most travelers is the sun. Stay aware of how much time you're spending lying on Spanish beaches or sweating in Moroccan sand dunes.

Heat exhaustion and dehydration: Heat exhaustion, characterized by dehydration and salt deficiency, can lead to fatigue, headaches, and wooziness. Avoid it by drinking plenty of fluids, eating salty foods (e.g. crackers), and avoiding dehydrating beverages (e.g. alcohol, coffee, tea, and caffeinated soda). Continuous heat stress can eventually lead to heatstroke, characterized by a rising temperature, severe headache, and cessation of sweating. Victims should be cooled off with wet towels and taken to a doctor.

Sunburn: Bring sunscreen with you (it's often more expensive and hard to find when traveling), and apply it liberally and often to avoid burns and risk of skin cancer. If you do get burned, drink more fluids than usual and apply Calamine or an aloe-based lotion.

High altitude: Allow your body a couple of days to adjust to less oxygen before exerting yourself. Note that alcohol is more potent and UV rays are stronger at high elevations.

INSECT-BORNE DISEASES

Be aware of insects while hiking and camping, especially in wet or forested areas. **Mosquitoes** are most active from dusk to dawn. Wear long pants and long sleeves, tuck your pants into your socks, and buy a mosquito net. Use insect repellents, such as DEET, and soak or spray your gear with permethrin (licensed in the US for use on clothing). Consider natural repellents that make you unattractive to insects, like vitamin B-12 or garlic pills. To stop the itch after being bitten, try Calamine lotion or topical cortisones (like Cortaid), or take a bath with a half-cup of baking soda or oatmeal. **Ticks,** responsible for Lyme and other disease, can be particularly dangerous in forested regions (in parts of northern Spain, for instance). Pause periodically while walking to brush off ticks using a fine-toothed comb on your neck and scalp. Do not try to remove ticks by burning them or coating them with nail polish remover or petroleum jelly.

Malaria: Extremely limited risk, only in some rural parts of Morocco. Transmitted by *Anopheles* mosquitoes that bite at night. The incubation period varies from 6-8 days to several months. Early symptoms include fever, chills, aches, and fatigue, followed by high fever and sweating, sometimes with vomiting and diarrhea. See a doctor for any flu-like sickness that occurs after travel in a risk area. Left untreated, malaria can cause anemia, kidney failure, coma, and death. To reduce the risk of contracting malaria, use mosquito repellent, particularly in the evenings and when visiting forested areas, and take oral prophylactics, like **mefloquine** (sold under the name Lariam) or **doxycycline** (ask your doctor for a prescription).

Tick-borne encephalitis: A slight risk in the few forested areas of Spain and Portugal. A viral infection of the central nervous system transmitted during the summer by tick bites (primarily in wooded areas) or unpasteurized dairy products. While a vaccine is available in Europe, the immunization schedule is impractical, and the risk of contracting the disease is relatively low, especially if precautions are taken against tick bites.

Lyme disease: Also a slight risk in forested areas of Spain and Portugal. A bacterial infection carried by ticks and marked by a circular bull's-eye rash of 2 in. or more. Later symptoms include fever, headache, fatigue, and aches and pains. Antibiotics are effective if administered early. Left untreated, Lyme can cause problems in joints, the heart, and the nervous system. If you find a tick attached to your skin, grasp the head with tweezers as close to your skin as possible and apply slow, steady traction. Removing a tick within 24hr. greatly reduces the risk of infection.

FOOD- AND WATER-BORNE DISEASES

Prevention is the best cure: be sure that everything you eat is cooked properly and that the water you drink is clean. Peel your fruits and veggies and avoid tap water (including ice cubes and anything washed in tap water, like salad). Watch out for food from markets or street vendors that may have been cooked in unhygienic conditions. Other culprits are raw shellfish, unpasteurized milk, and sauces containing raw eggs. Buy bottled water, or purify your own water by bringing it to a rolling boil or treating it with **iodine tablets.**

Traveler's diarrhea: Results from drinking untreated water or eating uncooked foods; a temporary (and fairly common) reaction to the bacteria in new food ingredients. Symptoms include nausea, bloating, urgency, and malaise. Try quick-energy, non-sugary foods with protein and carbohydrates to keep your strength up. Over-the-counter anti-diarrheals (e.g. Immodium) may counteract the problems, but can complicate serious infections. The most dangerous side effect is dehydration; drink 8 oz. of water with ½ tsp. of sugar or honey and a pinch of salt, try uncaffeinated soft drinks, or munch on salted crackers. If you develop a fever or your symptoms don't go away after 4-5 days, consult a doctor promptly. Consult a doctor for treatment of diarrhea in children.

Dysentery: Results from a serious intestinal infection caused by certain bacteria. The most common type is bacillary dysentery, also called shigellosis. Symptoms include bloody diarrhea (sometimes mixed with mucus), fever, and abdominal pain and tenderness. Bacillary dysentery generally only lasts a week, but it is highly contagious. Amoebic dysentery, which develops more slowly, is a more serious disease and may cause long-term damage if left untreated. Seek medical help immediately for both. A stool test can determine which kind you have. Dysentery can be treated with the drugs norfloxacin or ciprofloxacin (commonly known as Cipro). If you are traveling in Morocco (especially rural regions), consider obtaining a prescription before you leave home.

Hepatitis A: A viral infection of the liver acquired primarily through contaminated water. Symptoms include fatigue, fever, loss of appetite, nausea, dark urine, jaundice, vomiting, aches and pains, and light stools. The risk is highest in rural areas and the countryside, especially in Morocco, but it is also present in urban areas. Ask your doctor about the vaccine (Havrix or Vaqta) or an injection of immune globulin (IG).

Parasites: Microbes, tapeworms, etc. that hide in unsafe water and food. **Giardiasis,** for example, is acquired by drinking untreated water from streams or lakes all over the world, including Spain, Portugal, and Morocco. Symptoms include swollen glands or lymph nodes, fever, rashes or itchiness, digestive problems, eye problems, and anemia. Boil water, wear shoes, avoid bugs, and eat only thoroughly cooked food.

Typhoid fever: Caused by the salmonella bacteria; common in villages and rural areas in Morocco. While mostly transmitted through contaminated food and water, it may also be acquired by direct contact with another person. Symptoms include fever, headaches, fatigue, loss of appetite, constipation, and a rash on the abdomen or chest. Antibiotics can treat typhoid, but a vaccination (70-90% effective) is usually recommended.

OTHER INFECTIOUS DISEASES

Rabies: Really only a risk for those who may be exposed to wild or domestic animals during their travel. Transmitted through the saliva of infected animals; fatal if untreated. By the time thirst and muscle spasms appear, the disease is in its terminal stage. If you are bitten, wash the wound and seek immediate medical care. A rabies vaccine, which consists of 3 shots given over a 21-day period, is only semi-effective.

Hepatitis B: A viral infection of the liver transmitted via bodily fluids or needle-sharing. Symptoms may not surface until years after infection. Vaccinations are recommended for health-care workers, sexually-active travelers, and anyone planning to seek medical treatment abroad. The 3-shot vaccination series must begin 6 months before traveling.

Hepatitis C: Like Hep B, but the mode of transmission differs. IV drug users, those with occupational exposure to blood, hemodialysis patients, and recipients of blood transfusions are at the highest risk, but the disease can also be spread through sexual contact or sharing items like razors and toothbrushes that may have traces of blood on them.

AIDS, HIV, STDS

For detailed information on **Acquired Immune Deficiency Syndrome (AIDS)** in Spain, Portugal, and Morocco, call the **US Centers for Disease Control's** 24hr. hotline at ☎800-342-2437, or the **Joint United Nations Programme on HIV/AIDS (UNAIDS),** 20 av. Appia 20, CH-1211 Geneva 27, Switzerland (☎41 22 791 36 66, fax 41 22 791 41 87; www.unaids.org). Spain, Portugal, and Morocco may deny long-term residence to those who test HIV-positive, but they generally do not deny tourist, student and work visa applications on the basis of HIV status, even when medical tests are required. Contact the nearest consulate.

Sexually transmitted diseases (STDs) such as gonorrhea, chlamydia, genital warts, syphilis, and herpes are easier to catch than HIV and can be just as deadly. **Hepatitis B** and **C** are also serious STDs (see **Other Infectious Diseases,** above). **Condoms** may protect you from some STDs, but oral or even tactile contact can lead to transmission. Warning signs include swelling, sores, bumps, or blisters on sex organs, the rectum, or the mouth; burning and pain during urination and bowel movements; itching around sex organs; swelling or redness of the throat; and flu-like symptoms. If these symptoms develop, see a doctor immediately.

WOMEN'S HEALTH

Women traveling in unsanitary conditions are vulnerable to **urinary tract** and **bladder infections,** common and very uncomfortable bacterial conditions that cause a burning sensation and painful (sometimes frequent) urination. To try to avoid these infections, drink plenty of vitamin-C-rich juice and clean water, and urinate frequently, especially right after intercourse. Untreated, these infections can lead to kidney infections, sterility, and even death. If symptoms persist, see a doctor.

Vaginal yeast infections may flare up in hot and humid climates. Wearing loosely fitting trousers or a skirt and cotton underwear will help, as will over-the-counter remedies like Monistat or Gynelotrimin. Bring supplies from home if you are prone to infection, as it may be embarrassing, if not difficult, to explain your predicament to a foreign druggist. Since **tampons, pads,** and reliable **contraceptive devices** are sometimes hard to find when traveling, consider bringing supplies with you.

Abortions are illegal in Spain, Portugal, and Morocco, except to save the life of the woman, but women considering an **abortion** while traveling can contact the **International Planned Parenthood Federation (IPPF),** Regent's College, Inner Circle, Regent's Park, London NW1 4NS (☎020 7487 7900; fax 7487 7950; www.ippf.org), for guidance. In the US and Canada, the National Abortion Federation Hotline, (US ☎800-772-9100, Canada ☎800-424-2280; M-F 9am-10pm) provides referrals.

INSURANCE

Travel insurance generally covers four basic areas: medical or health problems, property loss, trip cancellation or interruption, and emergency evacuation. Prices generally run about US$50 per week for full coverage; trip cancellation or interruption may be purchased separately for about US$5.50 per US$100 of coverage.

Medical insurance (especially university policies) often covers costs incurred abroad; check with your provider. **US Medicare** does not cover foreign travel. **Canadians** are protected by their home province's health insurance plan for up to 90 days after leaving the country; check with the provincial Ministry of Health or Health Plan Headquarters for details. **Homeowners' insurance** often covers theft during travel and loss of travel documents (passport, plane ticket, etc.) up to US$500.

ISIC and **ITIC** (see p. 12) provide basic insurance benefits, including US$100 per day of in-hospital sickness for up to 60 days, US$3000 of accident-related medical reimbursement, and US$25,000 for emergency medical transport. Cardholders have access to a toll-free 24hr. helpline for medical, legal, and financial emergencies overseas (US and Canada ☎877-370-4742, elsewhere call US collect ☎+1 715-345-0505). **American Express** (US ☎800-528-4800) grants most cardholders automatic car rental insurance (collision and theft, but not liability) and travel accident coverage of US$100,000 on ticket purchases made with the card.

Council and **STA** (see p. 34) offer a range of plans to supplement your basic travel coverage. Other private insurance providers in the US and Canada include: **Access America** (☎800-284-8300; www.accessamerica.com); **Berkely Group/Carefree Travel Insurance** (☎800-323-3149; www.berkely.com); **Globalcare Travel Insurance** (☎800-821-2488; www.globalcare-cocco.com); and **Travel Assistance International** (☎800-821-2828; www.travelassistance.com). Providers in the **UK** include **Columbus Direct** (☎020 7375 0011; www.columbusdirect.net). In **Australia,** try **AFTA** (☎02 9375 4955).

PACKING

Pack lightly: lay out only what you absolutely need, then take half the clothes and twice the money. If you plan to do a lot of hiking, also see **Outdoors,** p. 28.

LUGGAGE. If you plan to cover most of your itinerary by foot, a sturdy **frame backpack** is unbeatable. (For the basics on buying a pack, see p. 29.) Toting a **suitcase** or **trunk** is fine if you plan to stay in one or two cities and explore from there, but a very bad idea if you're going to be moving around a lot. In addition to your main piece of luggage, a **daypack** (a small backpack or courier bag) is a must.

CLOTHING. No matter when you're traveling, it's a good idea to bring a warm jacket or wool sweater, a rain jacket (Gore-Tex® is both waterproof and breathable), sturdy shoes or hiking boots, and thick socks. Flip-flops or waterproof sandals are crucial for hostel showers. You may also want a nicer outfit than your jeans and t-shirt. Bringing light clothing is a wise idea since temperatures soar.

SLEEPSACK. Some hostels require that you either provide your own linen or rent sheets from them. Save cash by making your own sleepsack: fold a full-size sheet in half the long way, then sew it closed along the long side and one short side.

CONVERTERS AND ADAPTERS. In Spain and Portugal, electricity is 220 volts AC; most of Morocco runs on 220V as well, though some smaller towns still have 110V outlets. **Americans** and **Canadians** should buy an **adapter** (which changes the shape of the plug) and a **converter** (which changes the voltage; about US$20). **New Zealanders** and **South Africans** (who both use 220V at home), as well as **Australians** (who use 240/250V), won't need a converter, but will need a set of adapters. For more info on converters and adapters, check http://kropla.com/electric.htm.

TOILETRIES. Toothbrushes, towels, cold-water soap, deodorant, razors, tampons, and condoms are often available, but may be difficult to find, so bring extras along. **Contact lenses** may be expensive and hard to come by, so bring enough extra pairs and solution for your entire trip. Also bring your glasses and a copy of your prescription in case you need emergency replacements.

FIRST-AID KIT. For a basic first-aid kit, pack bandages, aspirin or other painkillers, antibiotic cream, a thermometer, a Swiss Army knife, tweezers, moleskin, decongestant, motion-sickness remedy, diarrhea or upset-stomach medication (Pepto Bismol or Immodium), an antihistamine (like Benadryl), sunscreen, insect repellent, and burn ointment.

FILM. Film and developing in Spain, Portugal, and Morocco can get expensive, so consider bringing along enough film for your entire trip and developing it at home. Despite disclaimers, airport security X-rays *can* fog film, so buy a lead-lined pouch at a camera store or ask security to hand inspect it. Always pack it in your carry-on luggage, since higher-intensity X-rays are used on checked luggage.

OTHER USEFUL ITEMS. For safety purposes, you should bring a **money belt** and small **padlock.** Quick repairs of torn garments can be done on the road with a needle and thread; also consider bringing electrical tape for patching tears. Doing your **laundry** by hand (where it is allowed) is both cheaper and more convenient than doing it at a laundromat. **Other things** you might forget: an umbrella; sealable **plastic bags** (for damp or dirty clothes, soap, food, shampoo, and other spillables); an **alarm clock;** safety pins; rubber bands; a flashlight; earplugs; and a small **calculator.**

ACCOMMODATIONS

For more specific information on accommodations, see the **Essentials** sections for **Spain** (p. 83), **Portugal** (p. 590), and **Morocco** (p. 724).

HOTELS, HOSTALES, AND PENSIONES

Hotel and **hostal** singles in Spain cost US$20-30 per night, doubles US$35-40. In Portugal rates run US$20-30. You'll typically share a hall bathroom; a private bathroom will cost extra. Smaller **pensiones** are often cheaper than hotels. If you make reservations in writing, indicate your night of arrival and the number of nights you plan to stay. The hotel will send you a confirmation and may request payment for the first night. Not all hotels take reservations, and few accept checks in foreign currency. Enclosing two International Reply Coupons will ensure a prompt reply (each US$1.05; available at any post office).

YOUTH HOSTELS

Youth hostels are generally dorm-style accommodations, often in single-sex large rooms with bunk beds, although some hostels do offer private rooms for families and couples. They sometimes have kitchens and utensils for your use, bike or moped rentals, storage areas, and laundry facilities. There can be drawbacks: some hostels close during certain daytime "lockout" hours, have a curfew, don't accept reservations, and impose a maximum stay, or, less frequently, require that you do chores. In Spain, a bed in a hostel will average around US$12-18 a night, while a night in a Portuguese hostel will be around US$10-15 a night.

HOSTELLING INTERNATIONAL

Joining the youth hostel association in your own country automatically grants you membership privileges in **Hostelling International (HI),** a federation of national hosteling associations that offer accommodations at significantly cheaper prices than private lodgings. HI hostels are scattered throughout Spain, Portugal, and Morocco and many accept reservations via the **International Booking Network** (www.hostelbooking.com, US ☎202-783-6161). To research hostelling in Spain and Portugal, check out HI's umbrella organization's web page (www.iyhf.org) or these other comprehensive websites: www.hostels.com and www.hostelplanet.com. All prices listed below are valid for **one-year memberships** unless otherwise noted.

Australian Youth Hostels Association (AYHA), 422 Kent St., Sydney NSW 2000 (☎2 9261 1111; fax 2 9261 1969; www.yha.org.au). AUS$49, under 18 AUS$14.50.

Hostelling International-Canada (HI-C), 400-205 Catherine St., Ottawa, ON K2P 1C3 (☎800-663-5777 or 613 237-7884; fax 613 237-7868; www.hihostels.ca). CDN$25, under 18 CDN$12.

An Óige (Irish Youth Hostel Association), 61 Mountjoy St., Dublin 7 (☎01 830 4555; fax 01 830 5808; www.irelandyha.org). €15, under 18 €7.50.

Youth Hostels Association of New Zealand (YHANZ), P.O. Box 436, 173 Cashel St., Christchurch 1 (☎3 379 9970; fax 3 365 4476; www.yha.org.nz). NZ$40, ages 15-17 NZ$12, under 15 free.

Hostels Association of South Africa, 3rd fl. 73 St. George's House, P.O. Box 4402, Cape Town 8000 (☎21 424 2511; fax 21 424 4119; www.hisa.org.za). ZAR55, under 18 ZAR30, lifetime ZAR250.

Scottish Youth Hostels Association (SYHA), 7 Glebe Crescent, Stirling FK8 2JA (☎1786 89 14 00; fax 1786 89 13 33; www.syha.org.uk). UK£6, under 18 UK£2.50.

Youth Hostels Association (England and Wales) Ltd., Trevelyan House, Dimple Rd., Matlock, Devonshire DE4 3YH, UK (☎1629 59 26 00; fax 1629 59 27 02; www.yha.org.uk). UK£13, under 18 UK£6.50, families UK£26.

Hostelling International Northern Ireland (HINI), 22-32 Donegall Rd., Belfast BT12 5JN, Northern Ireland (☎1232 32 47 33; fax 1232 43 96 99; www.hini.org.uk). UK£7, under 18 UK£3.

Hostelling International-American Youth Hostels (HI-AYH), 733 15th St. NW, #840, Washington, D.C. 20005 (☎202-783-6161 ext. 136; fax 202-783-6171; www.hiayh.org). US$25, under 18 free.

UNIVERSITY DORMS

Many **colleges and universities** open their residence halls to travelers when school is not in session; some do so even during term-time. Getting a room may take a few phone calls and require advance planning, but the low room rates are worth it.

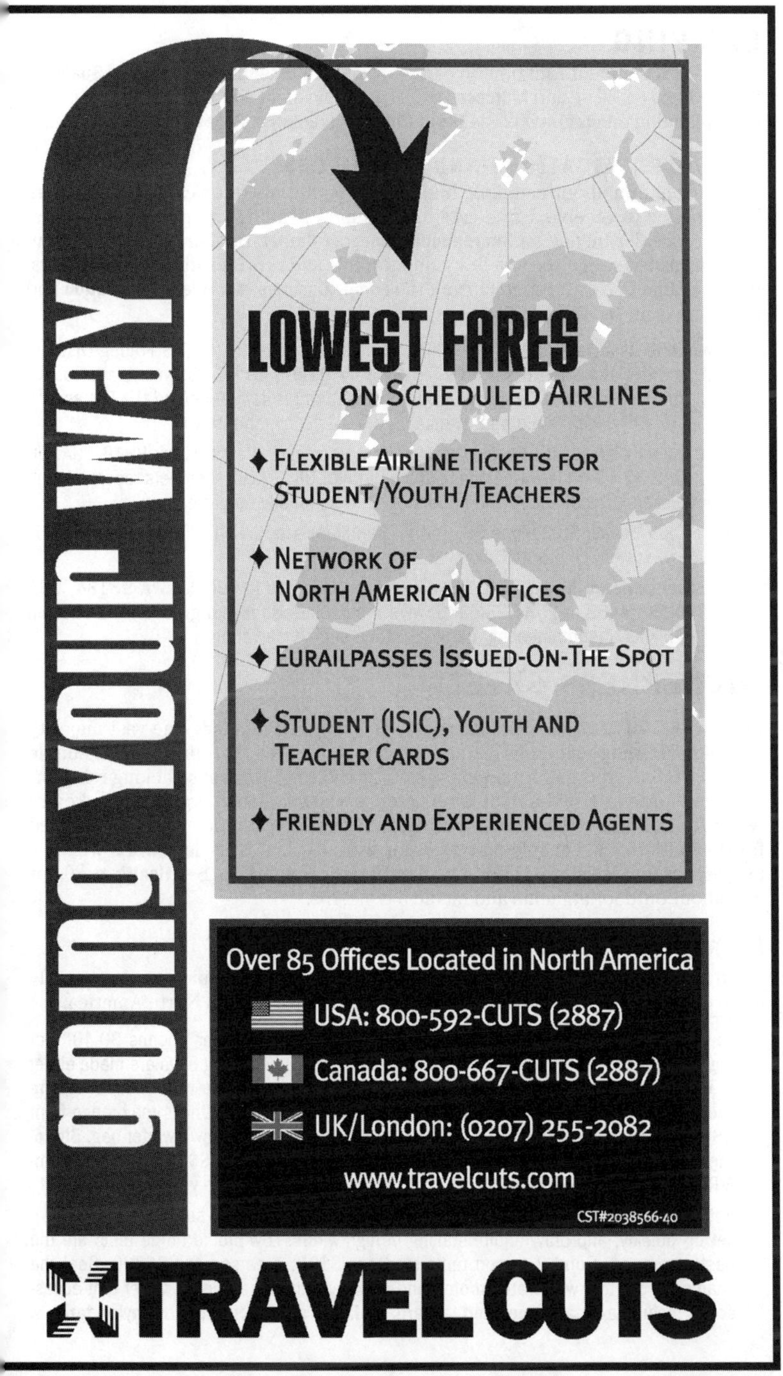
going your way
LOWEST FARES
ON SCHEDULED AIRLINES
✦ FLEXIBLE AIRLINE TICKETS FOR STUDENT/YOUTH/TEACHERS
✦ NETWORK OF NORTH AMERICAN OFFICES
✦ EURAILPASSES ISSUED-ON-THE SPOT
✦ STUDENT (ISIC), YOUTH AND TEACHER CARDS
✦ FRIENDLY AND EXPERIENCED AGENTS
Over 85 Offices Located in North America
USA: 800-592-CUTS (2887)
Canada: 800-667-CUTS (2887)
UK/London: (0207) 255-2082
www.travelcuts.com
CST#2038566-40
TRAVEL CUTS

CAMPING

For more specific information on camping, see the **Essentials** sections of **Spain** (p. 84), **Portugal** (p. 591), and **Morocco** (p. 724). An excellent general resource for travelers planning on camping is the **Great Outdoor Recreation Pages** (www.gorp.com).

USEFUL PUBLICATIONS AND RESOURCES

For information about camping, hiking, and biking, write or call the publishers listed below to receive a free catalog. Campers heading to Spain and Portugal should consider buying an **International Camping Carnet.** Similar to a hostel membership card, it's required at a few campgrounds and provides discounts at others. It is available in North America from the **Family Campers and RVers Association** and in the UK from **The Caravan Club** (see below).

Automobile Association, A.A. Publishing. Orders and enquiries to TBS Frating Distribution Centre, Colchester, Essex, CO7 7DW, UK (☎01206 25 56 78; www.theaa.co.uk). Publishes *Caravan and Camping: Europe* (UK£9) and *Britain & Ireland* (UK£8) as well as Big Road Atlases for Europe, France, Spain, Germany, and Italy.

The Caravan Club, East Grinstead House, East Grinstead, West Sussex, RH19 1UA, UK (☎01342 32 69 44; www.caravanclub.co.uk). For UK£27.50, members receive equipment discounts, a directory and handbook, and a monthly magazine.

Sierra Club Books, 85 Second St., 2nd fl., San Francisco, CA 94105, USA (☎415-977-5500; www.sierraclub.org/books).

The Mountaineers Books, 1001 SW Klickitat Way, #201, Seattle, WA 98134, USA (☎800-553-4453 or 206-223-6303; www.mountaineersbooks.org). Over 400 titles on hiking, biking, mountaineering, natural history, and conservation.

WILDERNESS SAFETY

THE GREAT OUTDOORS. Stay warm, stay dry, and stay hydrated—the vast majority of life-threatening wilderness situations can be avoided by following this simple advice. Prepare yourself for an emergency, however, by always packing raingear, a hat and mittens, a first-aid kit, a reflector, a whistle, high-energy food, and extra water for any hike. Dress in wool or warm layers of synthetic materials designed for the outdoors; never rely on cotton for warmth, as it is useless when wet. See **Suggestions for Hikers,** p. 511, for useful information on hiking. See **Health,** p. 20, for info about outdoor ailments and medical concerns.

CAMPING AND HIKING EQUIPMENT

Good camping equipment is both sturdy and light. Camping equipment is generally more expensive in Australia, New Zealand, and the UK than in North America.

Sleeping Bag: Most sleeping bags are rated by season ("summer" means 30-40°F at night; "four-season" or "winter" often means below 0°F). Sleeping bags are made either of **down** (warmer and lighter, but more expensive, and miserable when wet) or of **synthetic** material (heavier, more durable, and warmer when wet). Prices may range from US$80-210 for a summer synthetic to US$250-300 for a good down winter bag. **Sleeping bag pads** include foam pads (US$10-20), air mattresses (US$15-50), and Therm-A-Rest self-inflating pads (US$45-80). Bring a **stuff sack** to store your bag.

Tent: The best tents are free-standing (with their own frames and suspension systems), set up quickly, and only require staking in high winds. Low-profile dome tents are the best all-around. Good 2-person tents start at US$90, 4-person at US$300. Seal the seams of your tent with waterproofer, and make sure it has a rain fly. Other tent accessories include a **battery-operated lantern,** a **plastic groundcloth,** and a **nylon tarp.**

Backpack: Internal-frame packs mold better to your back, keep a lower center of gravity, and flex adequately to allow you to hike difficult trails. **External-frame packs** are more comfortable for long hikes over even terrain, as they keep weight higher and distribute it more evenly. Make sure your pack has a strong, padded hip-belt to transfer weight to your legs. Any serious backpacking requires a pack of at least 4000 in^3 (16,000cc), plus 500 in^3 for sleeping bags in internal-frame packs. Sturdy backpacks cost anywhere from US$125-420—this is one area in which it doesn't pay to economize. Either buy a **waterproof backpack cover,** or store all of your belongings in plastic bags.

Boots: Be sure to wear hiking boots with good **ankle support.** They should fit snugly and comfortably over 1-2 pairs of wool socks and thin liner socks. Break in boots over several weeks first in order to spare yourself from painful and debilitating blisters.

Other Necessities: Synthetic layers, like those made of polypropylene, and a **pile jacket** will keep you warm even when wet. A **"space blanket"** will help you retain your body heat and doubles as a groundcloth (US$5-15). Plastic **water bottles** are virtually shatter- and leak-proof. Bring **water-purification tablets** for when you can't boil water. Although most campgrounds provide campfire sites, you may want to bring a small **metal grate** or **grill** of your own. For those places that forbid fires or the gathering of firewood (this includes virtually every organized campground in Europe), you'll need a **camp stove** (the classic Coleman starts at US$40) and a propane-filled **fuel bottle** to operate it. Also don't forget a **first-aid kit, pocketknife, insect repellent, calamine lotion,** and **waterproof matches** or a **lighter.**

...AND WHERE TO BUY IT

Mail-order/online companies offer lower prices than many retail stores, but a visit to a local camping or outdoors store will give you a good sense of the look and weight of certain items. Popular outdoor gear companies include: **Campmor** (US ☎888-226-7667; elsewhere ☎+1 201-825-8300; www.campmor.com), **Discount Camping** (☎08 8262 3399; www.discountcamping.com.au), **Eastern Mountain Sports (EMS)** (☎888-463-6367 or 603-924-7231; www.shopems.com), **Mountain Designs** (☎07 3252 8894; www.mountaindesign.com.au), **Recreational Equipment, Inc. (REI)** (☎800-426-4840 or 253-891-2500; www.rei.com), and **YHA Adventure Shop** (☎020 7836 8541).

ORGANIZED ADVENTURE TRIPS

Organized adventure tours offer another way of exploring the wild. Activities include hiking, biking, skiing, canoeing, kayaking, rafting, climbing, photo safaris, and archaeological digs. Tourism bureaus can often suggest parks, trails, and outfitters; other good sources for info are stores and organizations that specialize in camping and outdoor equipment like REI and EMS (see above).

Specialty Travel Index, 305 San Anselmo Ave. #313, San Anselmo, CA 94960, USA (☎800-442-4922 or 415-459-4900; fax 415-459-9474; www.specialtytravel.com).

KEEPING IN TOUCH

BY MAIL

See the **Essentials** sections for **Spain** (p. 84), **Portugal** (p. 591), and **Morocco** (p. 724) for more detailed information about mailing from abroad.

SENDING MAIL HOME FROM ABROAD

Airmail is the best way to send mail home from Spain, Portugal, and Morocco. **Aerogrammes,** printed sheets that fold into envelopes and travel via airmail, are available at post offices. Write "par avion" on the front. Most post offices will charge exorbitant fees or simply refuse to send aerogrammes with enclosures. **Surface mail** is by far the cheapest and slowest way to send mail. It takes one to three months to cross the Atlantic and two to four to cross the Pacific—good for items you won't need to see for a while, such as souvenirs or other articles you've acquired along the way that are weighing down your pack.

SENDING MAIL ABROAD FROM HOME

Sending airmail to Spain from the US requires between four and seven days. To Portugal, allow seven to 10 days. Airmail to Morocco usually requires around two weeks, but it could either go more quickly or much more slowly. Mailing from European locations to any of these countries is a few days faster; from Australia, New Zealand, or South Africa, a couple of days slower. Mail sent to smaller towns will take longer. Envelopes should be marked "air mail" or "par avion." There are several ways to arrange pick-up of letters sent to you while you are abroad.

Mail can be sent internationally through **Lista de Correos** in Spain, **Posta Restante** in Portugal, or **Poste Restante** in Morocco. The mail will go to a special desk in the central post office, unless you specify a post office by street address or postal code. As a rule, it is best to use the largest post office in the area, and mail may be sent there regardless of what is written on the envelope. It is usually safer and quicker to send mail express or registered. When picking up your mail, bring a form of photo ID, preferably a passport. There is generally no surcharge; if there is a charge, it should not exceed the cost of postage. If the clerks insist there is nothing for you, have them check under your first name as well. Mark the envelope "HOLD" and address it with the last name capitalized and underlined, as follows:

Spain: TORRES, Andrew; Lista de Correos; City Name; Postal Code; SPAIN; PAR AVION.

Portugal: EBERSOLD, Lucy; Posta Restante; Post Office Street Address; City Name; Postal Code; PORTUGAL; PAR AVION.

Morocco: Moroccan post offices often misplace or automatically return held mail. If you want to try, mail should be addressed as follows: CARMON, Irin; Poste Restante; Post Office Address; City Name; MOROCCO; PAR AVION.

AMERICAN EXPRESS. AmEx's travel offices throughout Iberia will act as a mail service for cardholders if you contact them in advance. Under this free **Client Letter Service,** they will hold mail for up to 30 days and forward upon request. Address the letter in the same way shown above. Some offices will offer these services to non-cardholders (especially those who have purchased AmEx Travelers Cheques), but you must call ahead to make sure. *Let's Go* lists AmEx office locations for most large cities. AmEx also has a free complete list (☎800-528-4800).

OTHER OPTIONS. If regular airmail is too slow, **Federal Express** (US ☎800-247-4747, Spain ☎900 10 08 71, Portugal ☎800 24 41 44, Morocco ☎212 254 21 33; www.fedex.com) can get a letter from New York to Madrid in one day for a whopping US$300 or in two days for a slightly more reasonable US$40; rates among non-US locations are similarly expensive (London to Madrid, for example, costs upwards of US$35). For a cheaper alternative, try **DHL** (US ☎800-225-5345, Spain 902 12 24 24, Portugal 218 10 00 99, Morocco 212 297 20 20), which can get a document from New York to Madrid in one to two days for US$39. By **US Global Express Mail,** a letter from New York would arrive within four days and would cost US$17.

LENGUAVIVA
sevilla
CURSOS DE ESPAÑOL
SPANISH COURSES
SPANISCHKURSE
ESPAÑOL COMO LENGUA EXTRANJERA
Academia LENGUAVIVA
Viriato 24 (Plaza de San Martín)
41003 Sevilla, Spain
Fax: +34 - 954 905 123
ESPAÑOL
COMO LENGUA EXTRANJERA
www.lenguaviva.es info@lenguaviva.es
Infórmate en el teléfono 954 915 639
INTENSIVE COURSE
460 Euros
INTENSIVKURS
Horario de clase: 9.30 - 11.00 y 11:30 - 13.00 horas
4 semanas, 20 lecciones semanales

BY TELEPHONE

For more country-specific information about telephones abroad, see the **Essentials** sections of **Spain** (p. 62), **Portugal** (p. 577), or **Morocco** (p. 711). Most useful communication information (including **international access codes, calling card numbers, country codes, operator** and **directory assistance,** and **emergency numbers**) is also listed on the inside back cover of this book.

PLACING INTERNATIONAL CALLS. To call Spain, Portugal, or Morocco from home or to place an international call from abroad, dial:

1. The **international dialing prefix.** To dial out of **Australia,** dial 0011; **Canada** or the **US,** 011; the **Republic of Ireland, New Zealand, Morocco, Portugal, Spain,** or the **UK,** 00; **South Africa,** 09.
2. The **country code** of the country you want to call. To call **Australia,** dial 61; **Canada** or the **US,** 1; **Morocco,** 212; **Portugal,** 351; the **Republic of Ireland,** 353; **New Zealand,** 64; **South Africa,** 27; **Spain,** 34; the **UK,** 44.
3. The **local number,** including the **city** or **area code.** *Let's Go* lists city and area codes as part of local numbers. Phone codes for cities and towns in Spain, Portugal, and Morocco are also listed opposite the city or town name, alongside the ☎ icon. If the first digit is a zero (e.g., 09 for Tangier), omit it when calling from abroad (e.g., dial 011 212 9 from Canada to reach Tangier).

CALLING HOME FROM SPAIN, PORTUGAL, OR MOROCCO

Wherever possible, use a **calling card** for international phone calls, as the long-distance rates for national phone services are often exorbitant. You can usually make direct international calls from pay phones, but if you aren't using a calling card you may need to drop your coins as quickly your words. Where available, prepaid phone cards and occasionally major credit cards can be used for direct international calls, but they are still less cost-efficient. Look for pay phones in public areas, as private pay phones are often more expensive. Although incredibly convenient, in-room hotel calls invariably include an arbitrary and sky-high surcharge.

The expensive alternative to dialing direct is using an international operator to place a **collect call.** An English-speaking operator can be reached by dialing the appropriate service provider; they will usually place a collect call even if you don't have one of their phone cards.

CALLING WITHIN SPAIN, PORTUGAL, AND MOROCCO

The simplest way to call within the country is to use a pay phone. **Prepaid phone cards** (available at tobacco stores and newspaper kiosks), which carry a certain amount of phone time depending on the card's denomination, usually save time and money in the long run—in fact, some phones only accept cards. The computerized phone will tell you how much time, in units, you have left on your card. Another kind of prepaid telephone card comes with a Personal Identification Number (PIN) and a toll-free access number. Instead of inserting the card into the phone, you call the access number. These cards can be used to make international as well as domestic calls. Phone rates tend to be highest in the morning, lower in the evening, and lowest on Sunday and late at night.

CALLING CARDS

Setting up a calling card account is probably your best and cheapest bet for making calls from overseas. **MCI WorldPhone** also provides access to MCI's Traveler's Assist, which gives legal and medical advice, exchange rate information, and translation services. Other phone companies provide similar services to travelers.

To obtain a calling card from your national telecommunications service before you leave home, contact the appropriate company below.

Australia: Telstra Australia **Telstra Direct** (☎ 13 22 00).

Canada: Bell Canada **Canada Direct** (☎ 800-668-6878).

Ireland: Telecom Éireann **Ireland Direct** (☎ 800 40 00 00).

New Zealand: Telecom New Zealand (☎ 0800 00 00 00).

South Africa: Telkom South Africa (☎ 10 219).

UK: British Telecom **BT Direct** (☎ 800 34 51 44).

US: AT&T (☎ 800-361-4470), **Sprint** (☎ 800-877-4646), or **MCI** (☎ 800-444-3333).

Let's Go has recently partnered with **ekit.com** to provide a calling card that offers a number of services, including email and voice messaging. Before purchasing any calling card, always be sure to compare rates with other cards, and to make sure it serves your needs (a local phonecard is generally better for local calls, for instance). For more information, visit **www.letsgo.ekit.com.**

TIME DIFFERENCES

Spain is 1 hour ahead of **Greenwhich Mean Time (GMT)** and 6 hours ahead of US EST. **Portugal** and **Morocco** are on GMT and 5 hours ahead of EST. Thus, when it is noon in New York, it is 5pm in Portugal and Morocco and 6pm in Spain. Spain and Portugal, together with the rest of Europe, switch to Daylight Savings Time about one week before the US does; they switch back at the same time. Morocco does not switch, and so is 4 hours ahead of US EST and 2 hours behind Spain in summer.

EMAIL AND INTERNET

Email is quite easy to access in Spain and Portugal, but less so in Morocco. Though in some places it's possible to forge a remote link with your home server, this is a much slower (and thus more expensive) option than taking advantage of free **web-based email accounts** (e.g. www.hotmail.com and www.yahoo.com). **Internet cafes** and the occasional free Internet terminal at a public library or university are listed in the **Orientation and Practical Information** sections of major cities.

GETTING THERE

For country-specific information on traveling, travel organizations, and travel discounts within Spain, Portugal, and Morocco, see the **Transportation** sections for **Spain** (p. 79), **Portugal** (p. 588), and **Morocco** (p. 720).

BY PLANE

When it comes to airfare, a little effort can save you a bundle. If your plans are flexible enough to deal with the restrictions, courier fares are the cheapest. Tickets bought from consolidators and standby seating are also good deals, but last-minute specials, airfare wars, and charter flights often beat these fares. The key is to hunt around, to be flexible, and to ask persistently about discounts. Students, seniors, and those under 26 should never pay full price for a ticket.

AIRFARES

Airfares to Spain, Portugal, and Morocco peak between mid-June and early September; holidays are also expensive. The cheapest times to travel are December and January. Midweek (M-Th morning) round-trip flights run US$40-50 cheaper than weekend flights, but they are generally more crowded and less likely to permit frequent-flier upgrades. Traveling with an "open return" ticket can be pricier than fixing a return date when buying the ticket. Round-trip flights are by far the cheapest; "open-jaw" (arriving in and departing from different cities, e.g. New York-Madrid and Paris-New York) tickets tend to be pricier. Patching one-way flights together is an expensive way to travel. Flights between capitals or regional hubs—Madrid, Barcelona, Lisbon, Rabat, and Casablanca—tend to be cheaper.

If Spain, Portugal or Morocco is only one stop on a more extensive globe-hop, consider a **round-the-world** (RTW) ticket. Tickets usually include at least five stops and are valid for about a year; prices range US$1200-5000. Try **Northwest Airlines/KLM** (US ☎800-447-4747; www.nwa.com), **British Airways** (US ☎800-828-7797; www.britishairways.com), or **Star Alliance,** a consortium of 22 airlines including United Airlines (US ☎800-241-6522; www.star-alliance.com).

Fares for roundtrip flights to Madrid from the US or Canadian east coast cost US$500-750 in high season (mid-June to early Sept.), US$400-600 in the off season; from the US or Canadian west coast US$800-1100/US$550-800; from the UK, UK£175-250/UK£130-225; from Australia, AUS$2000-2500/AUS$1700-2100.

BUDGET AND STUDENT TRAVEL AGENCIES

While travel agents specializing in flights to Spain, Portugal, and Morocco can make your life easy and help you save, they may not spend the time to find you the lowest fare—they get paid on commission. Students and under-26ers holding **ISIC** or **IYTC cards** (see p. 12) qualify for big discounts from student travel agencies.

Council Travel (www.counciltravel.com). Countless US offices, including branches in Atlanta, Boston, Chicago, L.A., New York, San Francisco, Seattle, and Washington, D.C. Check website or call ☎800-2-COUNCIL (800-226-8624) for the nearest office. Also an office at 28A Poland St. (Oxford Circus), **London,** W1V 3DB (☎0207 437 77 67).

CTS Travel (www.ctstravelusa.com). Offices across Italy, in Paris, London, and now in New York. Call toll free ☎877-287-6665. In UK, 44 Goodge St., London W1T 2AD (☎0207 636 0031; fax 0207 637 5328).

STA Travel, 7890 S. Hardy Dr., #110, Tempe AZ 85284 (24hr. reservations and info ☎800-777-0112; fax 480-592-0876; www.sta-travel.com). A student and youth travel organization with over 150 offices worldwide (check their website for a listing of all their offices), including US offices in Boston, Chicago, L.A., New York, San Francisco, Seattle, and Washington, D.C. Ticket booking, travel insurance, railpasses, and more. In the UK, walk-in office 11 Goodge St., **London** W1T 2PF or call ☎0870-160-6070. In New Zealand, 10 High St., **Auckland** (☎09 309 0458). In Australia, 366 Lygon St., **Melbourne** Vic 3053 (☎03 9349 4344).

Travel CUTS (Canadian Universities Travel Services Limited), 187 College St., **Toronto,** ON M5T 1P7 (☎416-979-2406; fax 416-979-8167; www.travelcuts.com). 60 offices across Canada. In the UK, 295-A Regent St., **London** W1R 7YA (☎0207-255-1944).

usitWorld (www.usitworld.com). Over 50 usit campus branches in the UK (www.usitcampus.co.uk), including **London** (☎0870 240 1010), **Manchester** (☎0161 273 1880), and **Edinburgh** (☎0131 668 2221). Nearly 20 usit now offices in **Ireland,** including **Dublin** (☎01 602 16 00; www.usitnow.ie) and **Belfast** (☎028 90 327 111; www.usitnow.com). Affiliated offices are also in both **Spain** and **Portugal,** including Plaza Callao, 3, Madrid (☎902 25 25 75), Ronda Universitat, 16, Barcelona (☎93 412 01 04), and Rua Camilo Castelo Branco, 20, Lisbon (☎21 316 60 00). Offices also in Athens, Auckland, Brussels, Frankfurt, Johannesburg, Luxembourg, Paris, Sofia, and Warsaw.

20,160 minutes floating (in the sun).
5 minutes to book online (Boston to Fiji).

StudentUniverse.com

Real Travel Deals

Wasteels, Skoubogade 6, 1158 Copenhagen K., (☎3314-4633; fax 7630-0865; www.wasteels.dk/uk). A huge chain with 165 locations in Europe. Sells Wasteels BIJ tickets discounted 30-45% off regular fare, 2nd-class international point-to-point train tickets with unlimited stopovers for those under 26 (sold only in Europe). Locations in Iberia and Morocco are: Plaça Catalunya, **Barcelona** (☎933 01 18 81); Blasco de Garay, 13, **Madrid** (☎915 43 12 03); Rua dos Caminhos de Ferro, 90, **Lisbon** (☎218 86 97 93); 25 rue Leon l'Africain, **Casablanca** (☎02 314 060); 45 Bd. Mohamed V, **Meknes** (☎05 523 062), place de la Marche Verte, **Tangier** (☎09 938 185).

FLIGHT PLANNING ON THE INTERNET. Many airline sites offer special last-minute deals on the Web. For Spain, check Iberia (www.iberia.com), Spanair (www.spanair.com), and Air Europa (www.aireuropa.com); for Portugal, try TAP (www.tap-airportugal.pt); for Morocco, Royal Air Moroc (www.royalairmoroc.com). Other sites compile the deals for you—try www.bestfares.com, www.onetravel.com, and www.travelzoo.com. StudentUniverse (www.studentuniverse.com) and STA (www.sta-travel.com) sell student tickets and railpasses, while Orbitz (www.orbitz.com), Expedia (www.expedia.com), and Travelocity (www.travelocity.com) offer full travel services. Priceline (www.priceline.com) allows you to specify a price and obligates you to buy any ticket that meets or beats it; be prepared for antisocial hours and odd routes. Skyauction (www.skyauction.com) allows you to bid on tickets.

COMMERCIAL AIRLINES

The commercial airlines' lowest published fare is the **APEX** (Advance Purchase Excursion) fare, which provides confirmed reservations and allows "open-jaw" tickets. Generally, reservations must be made 7 to 21 days ahead of departure, with 7- to 14-day minimum-stay and up to 90-day maximum-stay restrictions. These fares carry hefty cancellation and change penalties (fees rise in summer). Book peak-season APEX fares early; by May you will have a hard time getting your desired departure date. Use **Orbitz** (www.orbitz.com), **Expedia** (www.expedia.com), or **Travelocity** (www.travelocity.com) to get an idea of the lowest published fares, then use the resources outlined here to try beat those fares.

TRAVELING FROM NORTH AMERICA

Standard commercial carriers like American (☎800-433-7300; www.aa.com) and United (☎800-241-6522; www.ual.com) will probably offer the most convenient flights, but they may not be the cheapest, unless you manage to grab a special promotion or airfare war ticket. You might find flying one of the following airlines a better deal, if any of their limited departure points is convenient for you.

Icelandair: ☎800-223-5500; www.icelandair.com. Stopovers in Iceland for no extra cost on most transatlantic flights.

Finnair: ☎800-950-5000; www.us.finnair.com. Cheap round-trips from San Francisco, New York, and Toronto to Madrid, Malaga and Lisbon; connections throughout Europe.

TRAVELING FROM THE UK & IRELAND

Because of the myriad carriers flying from the British Isles to the continent, we only include discount airlines or those with cheap specials here. The **Air Travel Advisory Bureau** in London (☎020 7636 5000; www.atab.co.uk) provides referrals to travel agencies and consolidators that offer discounted airfares out of the UK.

Aer Lingus: Ireland ☎01 886 88 88; www.aerlingus.ie. Return tickets from Dublin, Cork, Galway, Kerry, and Shannon to Madrid (€130-310).

12 minutes to defrost (medium heat).
5 minutes to book online (LA to Rome).

StudentUniverse.com Real Travel Deals

British Midland Airways: UK ☎0870 607 05 55; www.britishmidland.com. Departures from throughout the UK. London to Madrid and Barcelona (UK£90-110).

buzz: UK ☎0870 240 70 70; www.buzzaway.com. A subsidiary of KLM. From London to Jerez, Murcia, and Girona (UK£50-80). Tickets cannot be changed or refunded.

easyJet: UK ☎0870 600 00 00; www.easyjet.com. London to Barcelona, Madrid, Málaga, Palma, and Mallorca (UK£47-136). Online tickets.

Go-Fly Limited: UK ☎0845 605 43 21, elsewhere call UK +44 1279 66 63 88; www.go-fly.com. A subsidiary of British Airways. From London to seven locations in Spain and Portugal, including Barcelona and Faro (return UK£53-180).

TRAVELING FROM AUSTRALIA & NEW ZEALAND

Qantas Air: Australia ☎13 13 13; New Zealand ☎0800 808 767; www.qantas.com.au. Flights from Australia and New Zealand to London for around AUS$2400.

Singapore Air: Australia ☎13 10 11; New Zealand ☎0800 808 909; www.singaporeair.com. Flies from Auckland, Sydney, Melbourne, and Perth to Madrid.

Thai Airways: Australia ☎1300 65 19 60; New Zealand ☎09 377 38 86; www.thaiair.com. Auckland, Sydney, and Melbourne to Amsterdam, Frankfurt, and London.

TRAVELING FROM SOUTH AFRICA

Air France: ☎011 880 80 40; www.airfrance.com. Johannesburg to Paris; connections throughout Europe.

British Airways: ☎0860 011 747; www.british-airways.com/regional/sa. Cape Town and Johannesburg to the UK and the rest of Europe from SAR3400.

Lufthansa: ☎011 484 47 11; www.lufthansa.co.za. From Cape Town, Durban, and Johannesburg to Germany and elsewhere.

Virgin Atlantic: ☎011 340 34 00; www.virgin-atlantic.co.za. Flies to London from both Cape Town and Johannesburg.

AIR COURIER FLIGHTS

Those who travel light should consider courier flights. Couriers help transport cargo on international flights by using their checked luggage space for freight. Generally, couriers must travel with carry-ons only and must deal with complex flight restrictions. Most flights are round-trip, with short fixed-length stays (usually one week) and a limit of a one ticket per issue. Most of these flights also operate only out of major gateway cities, mostly in North America. Courier flights to Spain are common; those to Portugal or Morocco are scarcer. Generally, you must be over 21 (in some cases 18). In summer, the popular destinations usually require an advance reservation of about two weeks (you can usually book up to 2 months ahead). Super-discounted fares are common for "last-minute" flights (3-14 days ahead).

TRAVELING FROM NORTH AMERICA

Round-trip courier fares from the US to Spain run about US$200-500. Most flights leave from New York, Los Angeles, San Francisco, or Miami in the US; and from Montreal, Toronto, or Vancouver in Canada. The four organizations below provide members with lists of opportunities and courier brokers worldwide for an annual fee (typically US$50-60). Alternatively, you can contact a courier broker directly; most charge registration fees, but a few don't. Prices quoted below are round-trip.

Air Courier Association, 15000 W. 6th Ave. #203, Golden, CO 80401 (☎800-282-1202; www.aircourier.org). 10 departure cities throughout the US and Canada to Madrid (high-season US$150-360). 1yr. US$64.

90 minutes, wash & dry (one sock missing).
5 minutes to book online (Detroit to Mom's).
Save money & time on student and faculty travel at StudentUniverse.com
StudentUniverse.com
Real Travel Deals

International Association of Air Travel Couriers (IAATC), 220 South Dixie Highway #3, P.O. Box 1349, Lake Worth, FL 33460 (☎561-582-8320; www.courier.org). From North American cities to Western European cities, including Madrid. 1yr. US$45-50.

Global Courier Travel, P.O. Box 3051, Nederland, CO 80466 (www.globalcourier-travel.com). Searchable online database. 6 departure points in the US and Canada to Madrid. 1yr. US$40, 2 people US$55.

NOW Voyager, 74 Varick St. #307, New York, NY 10013 (☎212-431-1616; fax 219-1753; www.nowvoyagertravel.com). To Madrid (US$499-699). Usually 1 week max. stay. 1yr. US$50. Non-courier discount fares also available.

FROM THE UK AND IRELAND

Although the courier industry is most developed from North America, there are limited courier flights in other areas. The minimum age for couriers from the **UK** is usually 18. **Brave New World Enterprises,** P.O. Box 22212, London SE5 8WB (www.nry.co.uk/bnw) publishes a directory of all the companies offering courier flights in the UK (UK£10, in electronic form UK£8). **Global Courier Travel** (see above) also offer flights from London and Dublin to continental Europe. **British Airways Travel Shop** (☎0870 606 11 33; www.british-airways.com/travelqa/booking/) arranges flights from London to destinations in continental Europe (specials as low as UK£60; no registration fee).

STANDBY FLIGHTS

Traveling standby requires considerable flexibility in arrival and departure dates and cities. Companies dealing in standby flights sell vouchers rather than tickets, along with the promise to get to your destination (or near your destination) within a certain window of time (typically 1-5 days). Call before your specific window to hear flight options and the probability that you will be able to board each flight. You can then decide which flights you want to try to make, show up to the airport at the appropriate time, present your voucher, and board if space is available. You may receive a monetary refund only if every available flight within your date range is full; if you opt not to take an available flight, you can only get credit toward future travel. Read standby flight agreements carefully; tricky fine print can leave you in a lurch. To check on a company's service record in the US, call the **Better Business Bureau** (☎212-533-6200). It is difficult to receive refunds, and clients' vouchers will not be honored if an airline fails to receive payment on time.

TICKET CONSOLIDATORS

Ticket consolidators, or **"bucket shops,"** buy unsold tickets in bulk from commercial airlines and sell them at discounted rates. Look for consolidators in the Sunday travel section of any major newspaper (such as the *New York Times*), where many bucket shops place tiny ads. Call quickly, as availability is extremely limited. Not all bucket shops are reliable, so insist on a receipt that gives full details of restrictions, refunds, and tickets, and pay by credit card (in spite of the 2-5% fee) so you can stop payment if you never receive your tickets. For more info, see www.travel-library.com/air-travel/consolidators.html.

TRAVELING FROM THE US & CANADA

Travel Avenue (☎800-333-3335; www.travelavenue.com) searches for best available published fares and then uses several consolidators to attempt to beat that fare. **NOW Voyager,** 74 Varick St., #307, New York, NY 10013 (☎212-431-1616; fax 212-219-1793; www.nowvoyagertravel.com) arranges discount flights, mostly from New York, to Barcelona, London, Madrid, Milan, Paris, and Rome. Other consolidators are **Interworld** (☎305-443-4929; fax 305-443-0351); **Pennsylvania Travel**

(☎800-331-0947); **Rebel** (☎800-227-3235; www.rebeltours.com); **Cheap Tickets** (☎800-377-1000; www.cheaptickets.com); and **Travac** (☎800-872-8800; fax 212-714-9063; www.travac.com). Yet more consolidators on the web include the **Internet Travel Network** (www.itn.com); **Travel Information Services** (www.tiss.com); **TravelHUB** (www.travelhub.com); and **The Travel Site** (www.thetravelsite.com). Keep in mind that these are just suggestions for starting your research; *Let's Go* does not endorse any of these agencies. As always, be cautious before you hand over your credit card number.

TRAVELING FROM THE UK, AUSTRALIA, & NEW ZEALAND

In London, the **Air Travel Advisory Bureau** (☎0207-636-5000; www.atab.co.uk) can provide names of reliable consolidators and discount flight specialists. From Australia and New Zealand, look for consolidator ads in the travel section of the *Sydney Morning Herald* and other papers.

CHARTER FLIGHTS

Charters are flights a tour operator contracts with an airline to fly extra loads of passengers during peak season. Charter flights fly less frequently than major airlines, make refunds particularly difficult, and are almost always fully booked. Schedules and itineraries may also change or be cancelled at the last moment (as late as 48hr. before the trip, and without a full refund), and check-in, boarding, and baggage claim are often much slower. However, they can also be cheaper.

Discount clubs and **fare brokers** offer members savings on last-minute charter and tour deals. Study contracts closely; you don't want to end up with an unwanted overnight layover. **Travelers Advantage,** Trumbull, CT, USA (☎203-365-2000; www.travelersadvantage.com; US$60 annual fee includes discounts and cheap flight directories) specializes in European travel and tour packages.

BY TRAIN

Rail travel is common and convenient throughout the European continent, though not in Morocco. Connections are made through France into Spain and Portugal.

SHOULD YOU BUY A RAILPASS? Railpasses were conceived to allow travelers to hop on trains wherever and whenever they wanted through Europe. In practice, it's not so simple. You still must stand in line to validate your pass, pay for supplements, and fork over cash for seat and reservations. More importantly, railpasses don't always pay off. If you are planning to spend extensive time on trains, hopping between big cities, a railpass would probably be worth it. But in many cases, especially if you are under 26, point-to-point tickets may prove a cheaper option.

> **!** **JUST SAY NO.** If you are planning on traveling in just Spain and Portugal, do not buy a Eurailpass. Train travel in these countries is less expensive than the rest of Europe, where passes can save you from paying for expensive train fares. A Eurailpass only makes sense for those planning on traveling in other European countries as well.

EURAILPASS. Eurail (www.eurail.com.) is valid in Austria, Belgium, Denmark, Finland, France, Germany, Greece, Hungary, Italy, Luxembourg, The Netherlands, Norway, Portugal, the Republic of Ireland, Spain, Sweden, and Switzerland. It is not valid in the UK. Standard **Eurailpasses,** valid for a consecutive given number of days, are most suitable for those planning on spending extensive time on trains every few days. **Flexipasses,** valid for any 10 or 15 (not necessarily consecutive) days in a two-month period, are more cost-effective for those traveling longer distances less frequently. **Saverpasses** provide first-class travel for travelers in groups of two to five (prices are per person). **Youthpasses** and **Youth Flexipasses** provide second-class perks for those under 26. Starting in January 2003, Eurail will offer the **Selectpass,** which allows travel in your choice of 3, 4, or 5 adjoining countries for any 5, 6, 8, 10, or 15 days in a two-month period. This replaces the **Europass.**

EURAILPASSES	15 DAYS	21 DAYS	1 MONTH	2 MONTHS	3 MONTHS
Eurailpass	US$588	US$762	US$946	US$1338	US$1654
Eurailpass Saver	US$498	US$648	US$804	US$1138	US$1408
Eurailpass Youth	US$414	US$534	US$664	US$938	US$1160

FLEXIPASS	10 DAYS IN 2 MONTHS	15 DAYS IN 2 MONTHS
Flexipass	US$694	US$914
Flexipass Saver	US$592	US$778
Flexipass Youth	US$488	US$642

SELECTPASSES	5 DAYS	6 DAYS	8 DAYS	10 DAYS	15 DAYS
Selectpass: 3-country	US$356	US$394	US$470	US$542	N/A
4-country	US$398	US$436	US$512	US$584	N/A
5-country	US$438	US$476	US$552	US$624	US$794
Saver: 3-country	US$304	US$336	US$400	US$460	N/A
4-country	US$340	US$372	US$436	US$496	N/A
5-country	US$374	US$406	US$470	US$560	US$674
Youth: 3-country	US$249	US$276	US$329	US$379	N/A
4-country	US$279	US$306	US$359	US$409	N/A
5-country	US$307	US$334	US$387	US$437	US$556

Passholders receive a timetable for major routes and a map with details on possible ferry, steamer, bus, car rental, hotel, and Eurostar discounts. Passholders often also receive reduced fares or free passage on many bus and boat lines.

SHOPPING AROUND FOR A EURAIL PASS. Eurailpasses are designed by the EU itself, and are purchasable only by non-Europeans almost exclusively from non-European distributors. These passes must be sold at uniform prices determined by the EU. However, some travel agents tack on a US$10 handling fee, and others offer certain bonuses with purchase, so shop around. Also, keep in mind that pass prices usually go up each year, so if you're planning to travel early in the year, you can save cash by purchasing before January 1 (you have three months from the purchase date to validate your pass in Europe).

It is best to buy your Eurailpass before leaving; only a few places in major European cities sell them, and at a marked-up price. You can get a replacement for a lost pass only if you have purchased insurance on it under the Pass Protection Plan (US$10). Eurailpasses are available through travel agents, student travel agencies like STA and Council (see p. 34), and **Rail Europe,** 44 South Broadway, White Plains, NY 10601 (US ☎877-456-RAIL, Canada ☎800-361-RAIL; www.raileurope.com) or **DER Travel Services,** 9501 W. Devon Ave. #301, Rosemont, IL 60018 (US ☎888-337-7350; fax 800-282-7474; www.dertravel.com).

INTERRAIL PASS. If you have lived for at least six months in one of the European countries where InterRail Passes are valid, they prove an economical option. There are eight InterRail **zones,** one of which includes Spain, Portugal, and Morocco. The **Under 26 InterRail Card** allows either 14 days or one month of unlimited travel within one, two, three, or all eight zones; the cost is determined by the number of zones the pass covers (UK£159-259). If you buy a ticket including the zone in which you claim residence, you must still pay 50% fare for tickets inside your own country. Passholders receive **discounts** on rail travel, Eurostar journeys, and most ferries to Ireland, Scandinavia, and the rest of Europe. Most exclude **supplements** for high-speed trains. For info and ticket sales in Europe contact **Student Travel Center,** 24 Rupert St., 1st fl., London W1V 7FN (☎20 74 37 81 01; fax 20 77 34 38 36; www.student-travel-centre.com). Tickets are also available from travel agents or major train stations throughout Europe.

BY BUS

Though European trains and railpasses are extremely popular, buses are another viable option for travel to Iberia.

Busabout, 258 Vauxhall Bridge Rd., London SW1V 1BS (UK ☎207 950 1661; fax 207 950 1662; www.busabout.com), is a hop-on hop-off network linking 70 cities and towns in Europe including London, Paris, Madrid, Barcelona, and Lisbon. Consecutive-day Passes and Flexi-passes available. Consecutive-day standard/student passes range from US$269/239 for 2 weeks to US$1069/959 for a season pass. Flexi-pass standard/student passes range from US$259/229 for 6 days out of 1 month to US$839/759 for 25 days out of 4 months.

Contiki Holidays (888-CONTIKI; www.contiki.com) offers a variety of European vacation packages designed for 18- to 35-year-olds. For an average cost of $60 per day, tours include accommodations, transportation, guided sightseeing and some meals.

Eurolines, 52 Grosvenor Gardens, **London** SW1W 0AU (UK ☎1582 404 511; www.eurolines.co.uk or www.eurolines.com). Largest operator of Europe-wide services with offices in **Madrid** (Estación Sur de Autobuses, C. Méndez Álvaro, 83, ☎915 063 360; fax 915 063 365) and **Barcelona** (Ronda Universitat, 5, ☎933 425 180; fax 933 185 997).

BY BOAT FROM THE UK

Brittany Ferries: UK ☎0870 901 24 00; www.brittany-ferries.com. **Plymouth** to **Santander, Spain** (24-30hr., 1-2 per week, UK£80-145).

P&O European Ferries: UK ☎08702 42 49 99; www.poportsmouth.com. **Portsmouth** to **Bilbao, Spain** (35hr., 2 per week, UK£186).

GETTING AROUND

BY TRAIN

Trains in Spain and Portugal are generally comfortable, convenient, and reasonably swift. Second-class travel is pleasant, and compartments (seating 2-6) are great places to meet fellow travelers. Trains, however, are not always safe; for safety tips, see next page. For long trips make sure you are in the correct car, as trains sometimes split at crossroads. Towns listed in parentheses require a train switch at the town listed immediately before the parenthesis.

You can either buy a **railpass,** which allows you unlimited travel within a particular region for a given period of time, or rely on buying individual **point-to-point** tickets as you go. Many countries give students or youths (usually defined as anyone under 26) direct discounts on regular domestic rail tickets, and many also sell a student or youth card that provides 20-50% off all fares for up to a year.

BritRail
LETS GO READERS
EURAIL
Buy a Rail Pass
and get ALL this FREE...
Eurotrip Discount Coupons
Save at European shops, restaurants, museums and more.
One FREE night at The Pink Palace
Includes breakfast and dinner at the world famous youth resort in Corfu, Greece.
FREE Eurail timetable, guide & map
with every order.
Passes issued on the spot
Same day shipping! RUSH ORDERS are our specialty.
Expert Advice and Service
For over 20 years we have helped thousands of people travel Europe by rail. From Eurail to Britrail, we'll help you pick the perfect pass for your trip.
AND
Easy online ordering
Hundreds of passes to choose from
No handling fees
ORDER ONLINE and SAVE
www.LETSRAIL.com
1-866-RAIL-PASS
(1-866-724-5727)
GUARANTEED BEST PRICES
WINNER of the Eurail Award
Visit these helpful sites when planning your trip
EUROTRIP.com and RAILSAVER.com

RESERVATIONS. While seat reservations are required only for selected trains (usually on major lines), you are not guaranteed a seat without advance booking. Reservations are available on major trains up to two months in advance, and Europeans often reserve far ahead of time; you should strongly consider reserving during peak holiday and tourist seasons (at the very latest a few hours ahead). It will be necessary to purchase a **supplement** (US$10-50) or special fare for high speed or quality trains such as Spain's AVE.

OVERNIGHT TRAINS. Night trains have their advantages—you won't waste valuable daylight hours traveling, and you will be able to forego the hassle and considerable expense of securing a night's accommodation. However, night travel has its drawbacks as well: discomfort and sleepless nights are the most obvious. **Sleeping accommodations** on trains differ from country to country, but typically you can either sleep upright in your seat (for free) or pay for a separate space. **Couchettes** (berths) typically have four to six seats per compartment (about US$20 per person); **sleepers** (beds) in private sleeping cars offer more privacy and comfort, but are considerably more expensive (US$40-150). If you are using a railpass valid only for a restricted number of days, inspect train schedules to maximize the use of your pass: an overnight train or boat journey uses up only one of your travel days if it departs after 7pm (you need only write in the next day's date on your pass).

DISCOUNTED TICKETS

For travelers under 26, **BIJ** tickets (Billets Internationals de Jeunesse; a.k.a. **Wasteels, Eurotrain,** and **Route 26**) are a great alternative to railpasses. Available for international trips within Europe as well as most ferry services, they knock 20-40% off regular second-class fares. Tickets are good for 60 days after purchase and allow a number of stopovers along the normal direct route of the train journey. Issued for a specific international route between two points, they must be used in the direction and order of the designated route and must be bought in Europe. The equivalent for those over 26, **BIGT** tickets provide a 20-30% discount on 1st- and 2nd-class international tickets for business travelers, temporary residents of Europe, and their families. Both types of tickets are available from European travel agents, at Wasteels or Eurotrain offices (usually in or near train stations), or directly at the ticket counter in some nations. For more info, contact **Wasteels,** Plaça de Cataluña, **Barcelona** (☎933 01 18 81); Blasco de Garay, 13, **Madrid** (☎915 43 12 03); Rua dos Caminhos de Ferro, 90, **Lisbon** (☎21 886 97 93).

BY BUS

Though trains are quite popular in the rest of Europe, buses are often a better option in Spain, Portugal, and Morocco. In Spain, the bus and train systems are on par; in Portugal, bus networks are more extensive, more efficient, and often more comfortable. In Morocco, buses are the easiest way to get around, even though some may run infrequently. See the **Essentials** sections of **Spain** (p. 80), **Portugal** (p. 589), and **Morocco** (p. 721) for country-specific details on bus travel.

BY CAR

Cars offer speed, freedom, access to countryside, and an escape from the town-to-town mentality of trains. Unfortunately, they also insulate you from the *esprit de corps* of rail traveling, and driving in major cities can be hair-raising. Although a single traveler won't save by renting a car, a group of four usually will. If you can't decide between train and car travel, you may benefit from a combination of the two; Rail Europe and other railpass vendors offer rail-and-drive packages.

Before setting off, know the laws of the countries in which you'll be driving. The **Association for Safe International Road Travel (ASIRT)** can provide more specific information about road conditions in Spain, Portugal and Morocco. It is located at 5413 West Cedar Lane #103C, Bethesda, MD 20814 (☎301-983-5252; fax 301-983-3663; www.asirt.org). Western Europeans use unleaded gas almost exclusively.

RENTING

You can rent a car from a US-based firm with European offices, from a European-based company with local representatives, or from a tour operator which will arrange a rental for you at its own rates. Multinationals offer greater flexibility, but tour operators often strike better deals. Most available cars will have standard transmission—cars with automatic transmission are difficult to find and much more expensive. Reserve well before leaving for the region and pay in advance if possible. It is always significantly less expensive to reserve a car from the US than from Spain, Portugal, or Morocco. Ask your airline about special fly-and-drive packages; you may get up to a week of free or discounted rental. The minimum age in Spain and Portugal is usually 25 with the larger agencies (Hertz, Avis) and 21 at smaller, local businesses. Minimum age in Morocco is almost always 21. At most agencies, all you need to rent is a US license and proof that you've had it for a year, although in Spain, you may need an international driver's license (see below).

RENTAL AGENCIES. You can generally make reservations before you leave by calling major international offices in your home country. However, occasionally the price and availability information they give doesn't jive with what the local offices in your country will tell you. Try checking with both numbers to make sure you get the best price and accurate information. Local desk numbers are included in town listings; for home-country numbers, call your toll-free directory. Rental agencies in Spain, Portugal, and Morocco include:

Alamo (☎800-GO-ALAMO; www.alamo.com). Alamo has 85 offices in Spain and 13 in Portugal, including the airports of Barcelona, Lisbon, Madrid, and Sevilla. Frequent flyer deals available when flying on most major US airlines.

Auto Europe (US ☎888-223-5555; UK 0800 89 9893; www.autoeurope.com). Offers car rentals in Spain, Portugal and Morocco, as well flight and hotel bookings. Also rents cell phones to US citizens traveling in Europe.

Budget (☎800-527-0700; www.budget.com). Rentals in Spain, Portugal, and Morocco.

Hertz (US ☎800-654-3001; UK 08708 448844; Australia 61 3 9698 2555; www.hertz.com). Rentals in Spain, Portugal, and Morocco.

Europcar (US ☎800-227-3876; Canada 877 940 6900; UK 0870 607 5000; www.europcar.com; www.europcar.co.uk). Rentals in Spain, Portugal, and Morocco. Europcar is one of the few services that will rent to those ages 21-24 in most locations.

Europe by Car (☎800-223-1516; www.europebycar.com). Student discounts.

COSTS & INSURANCE. Rental car prices start at around US$20 per day from national companies. Expect to pay more for larger cars and for 4WD, less for minis or at local agencies. Cars with **automatic transmission** are considerably more expensive than those with standard transmission (stick shift), and in some places, automatic is hard to find in the first place. It is virtually impossible, no matter where you are, to find an automatic 4WD. National chains often allow one-way rentals, picking up in one city and dropping off in another. There is usually a minimum hire period and sometimes an extra drop-off charge of a few hundred dollars.

Be sure to ask questions before leaving the agency, including the number of kilometers included with the rental cost, the cost of returning a car without a full tank of gas, and the type of insurance included with the rental fee. Most credit cards

There's only one way to max out your travel experience and make the most of your time on the road: The International Student Identity Card.

Packed with travel discounts, benefits and services, this card will keep your travel days and your wallet full. Get it before you hit it!

Visit ISICUS.com to get the full story on the benefits of carrying the ISIC.

ISIC

Call or visit STA Travel online to find the nearest issuing office and purchase your card today:

www.statravel.com (800) 777-0112

90 minutes, wash & dry (one sock missing
5 minutes to book online (Detroit to Mom'

StudentUniverse.com

Real Travel Dea

cover standard insurance, though you should double-check with your credit card company. If you rent, lease, or borrow a car, you will need a **green card,** or **International Insurance Certificate,** to certify that you have liability insurance and that it applies abroad. Green cards can be obtained at car rental agencies, car dealers (for those leasing cars), some travel agents, and some border crossings. Rental agencies may require you to purchase theft insurance in countries that they consider to be high-risk. If you have a collision abroad, the accident will show up on your domestic records if you report it to your insurance company.

ON THE ROAD. Speed limits in Spain and Portugal are 60kph on main roads, 90kph on larger roads, and 120kph on highways. Police are often on the lookout for speeding tourists, and if you're caught you will face an on-the-spot fine. Petrol (gasoline) prices vary, but average about €0.85 per liter. Road conditions are fairly good throughout Spain and Portugal, with the most difficult conditions in the Pyrenees, although driving in Morocco can be difficult as well. For specific information on driving conditions, potential hazards, and car assistance see the country essentials sections for Spain (p. 81), Portugal (p. 589), and Morocco (p. 722).

DRIVING PRECAUTIONS. When traveling in the summer or in the desert, bring substantial amounts of water (a suggested 5 liters of **water** per person per day) for drinking and for the radiator. For long drives to unpopulated areas, register with police before beginning the trek, and again upon arrival at the destination. Check with the local automobile club for details. When traveling for long distances, make sure tires are in good repair and have enough air, and get good maps. A **compass** and a **car manual** can also be very useful. You should always carry a **spare tire** and **jack, jumper cables, extra oil, flares, a torch (flashlight),** and **heavy blankets** (in case your car breaks down at night or in the winter). If you don't know how to **change a tire,** learn before heading out, especially if you are planning on traveling in deserted areas; blowouts on dirt roads are exceedingly common. If you do have a breakdown, **stay with your car;** if you wander off, there's less likelihood trackers will find you.

DRIVING PERMITS & CAR INSURANCE

INTERNATIONAL DRIVING PERMIT (IDP). If you plan to drive a car while in the region, you should have an International Driving Permit (IDP), though Spain, Portugal, and Morocco allow travelers to drive with a valid American, Canadian, or EU member license. It may be a good idea to get an IDP, in case you're in a situation (e.g. an accident or stranded in a small town) where the police do not know English; information on the IDP is printed in 10 languages, including Spanish, French, Portuguese, and Arabic. Your IDP, valid for one year, must be issued in your own country before you depart. When you are on the road, you will always be asked to present your regular license in addition to your IDP. An application for an IDP usually needs to include one or two photos, a current local license, an additional form of identification proving that you are over 18, and a fee. To apply, contact the national or local branch of your home country's Automobile Association.

Australia: Royal Automobile Club (RAC) or National Royal Motorist Association (NRMA) if in NSW or the ACT (☎08 9421 4444; www.rac.com.au/travel). Permits AUS$15.

Canada: Contact any Canadian Automobile Association (CAA) branch office or write to: CAA, 1145 Hunt Club Rd., #200, Ottawa, Ontario, K1V 0Y3. (☎613-247-0117; www.caa.ca/CAAInternet/travelservices/internationaldocumentation/idptravel.htm). Permits CDN$10.

Ireland: Contact nearest Automobile Association (AA) office or write to The Irish Automobile Association, 23 Suffolk St., Rockhill, Blackrock, Co. Dublin (☎01 617 9988; www.aaireland.ie).

New Zealand: Contact your local Automobile Association (AA) or their main office at 99 Albert St., Auckland (☎9 377 4660; www.nzaa.co.nz). Permits NZ$10.

South Africa: Contact the Travel Services Department of the Automobile Association of South Africa at P.O. Box 7118, Johannesburg 2000 (☎011 403 5320; fax 011 403 5438; www.aasa.co.za). Permits SAR28.50.

UK: Visit your local AA Shop, contact the AA Headquarters (☎0870 600 0371; www.theaa.com), or write to: The Automobile Association, International Documents, Fanum House, Erskine, Renfrewshire PA8 6BW. Permits UK£4.

US: Visit any American Automobile Association (AAA) office or write to: AAA Florida, Travel Related Services, 1000 AAA Drive, Box 28, Heathrow, FL 32746 (☎407-444-4240; fax 407-444-4247; www.aaa.com). Permits US$10.

BY BICYCLE

Today, biking is one of the key elements of the classic budget Eurovoyage. With the proliferation of mountain bikes, you can do some serious natural sightseeing. If you are nervous about striking out on your own, **Blue Marble Travel** (in Canada ☎519-624 4760; in Paris ☎01 42 21 14 77; in US ☎973-326-8939; www.bluemarble.org) offers bike tours designed for adults aged 20 to 50.

Many airlines will count your bike as your second piece of luggage, and a few charge extra. The additional fee runs about US$60-110 each way. Airlines sell bike boxes at the airport (US$10), although it is easier and cheaper to get one from a local bike store. Most ferries let you take your bike for free or for a nominal fee. You can always ship your bike on trains, though the cost varies.

Riding a bike with a frame pack strapped on it or your back is about as safe as pedaling blindfolded over a sheet of ice; panniers are essential. The first thing to buy, however, is a suitable **bike helmet** (US$25-50). U-shaped **Citadel** or **Kryptonite locks** are expensive (starting at US$30), but the companies insure their locks against theft of your bike for one to two years. For mail order equipment, **Bike Nashbar,** 4111 Simon Rd., Youngstown, OH 44512 (☎800-627-4227; www.nashbar.com), beats all competitors' offers and ships anywhere in the US or Canada.

Renting a bike beats bringing your own if your touring will be confined to one or two regions. *Let's Go* lists bike rental shops for most larger cities and towns. Some youth hostels rent bicycles for low prices. Some train stations rent bikes and often allow you to drop them off elsewhere.

BY MOPED AND MOTORCYCLE

Motorized bikes don't use much gas, can be put on trains and ferries, and are a good compromise between the high cost of car travel and the limited range of bicycles. In Spain, they are an extremely popular method of transportation for locals, and they can be a fun alternative for tourist daytrips. However, they're uncomfortable for long distances, dangerous in the rain, and unpredictable on rough roads and gravel. Always wear a helmet, and never ride with a backpack. If you've never been on a moped, the windy roads of the Pyrenees and the congested streets of Madrid are not the place to start.

Before renting, ask if the quoted price includes tax and insurance, or you may be hit with an unexpected additional fee. Avoid handing your passport over as a deposit; if you have an accident or mechanical failure you may not get it back until you cover all repairs. Pay ahead of time instead.

INSTITUTO HEMINGWAY

the best choice to learn Spanish in Spain

At INSTITUTO HEMINGWAY you will find:

Spanish courses
Spanish courses throughout the year along with accomodations and cultural activties.

Internships
Wide range of possibilities for US and Canadian university students to carry out their practicum in businesses located in Spain. Accomodations included. Very good prices!!

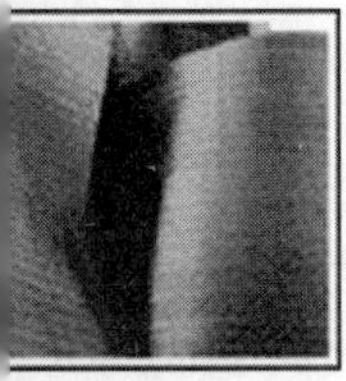

Au-pairs
Learn Spanish and its culture while working as an Au-pair.

Volunteer work
Live a different experience, learn Spanish and its culture, while collaborating with environmental and social service projects.

We have the widest range of offerings on the market to learn a language in its home country. Learn Spanish in Spain.

BY THUMB

No one should hitch without careful consideration of the risks involved. Hitching means entrusting your life to a random person who happens to stop beside you on the road and risking theft, assault, sexual harassment, and unsafe driving. In spite of this, there are gains to hitching. Favorable hitching experiences allow you to meet local people and get where you're going, especially in areas where public transportation is sparse or unreliable. For instance, hitching in southern Spain, particularly in Andalucía, and northern Portugal is easier than hitching in Murcia and allows you to mingle with the locals. The choice, however, remains yours.

Where one stands is vital. Experienced hitchers pick a spot outside of built-up areas, where drivers can stop, return to the road without causing an accident, and have time to look over potential passengers as they approach. Hitching (or even standing) on super-highways is usually illegal: one may only thumb at rest stops or at the entrance ramps to highways. Finally, success will depend on what one looks like. Successful hitchers travel light and stack their belongings in a compact but visible cluster. Most Europeans signal with an open hand, rather than a thumb; many write their destination on a sign in large, bold letters and draw a smiley-face under it. Drivers prefer hitchers who are neat and wholesome.

Safety issues are always imperative, even for those who are not hitching alone. Safety-minded hitchers avoid getting in the back of a two-door car and never let go of their backpacks. They will not get into a car that they can't get out of again in a hurry. If they ever feel threatened, they insist on being let off, regardless of where they are. Acting as if they are going to open the car door or vomit on the upholstery will usually get a driver to stop. Hitchhiking at night can be particularly dangerous; experienced hitchers stand in well-lit places. Expect drivers to be leery of nocturnal thumbers (or open-handers)

.

HITCHHIKERS BEWARE. *Let's Go* strongly urges you to seriously consider the risks before you choose to hitch. We do not recommend hitching as a safe means of transportation, and none of the information presented here is intended to do so. Women traveling alone should never hitch.

SPECIFIC CONCERNS

WOMEN TRAVELERS

Women exploring on their own inevitably face some additional safety concerns, but it's easy to be adventurous without taking undue risks. If you are concerned, consider staying in hostels which offer single rooms that lock from the inside or in religious organizations with rooms for women only. Communal showers in some hostels are safer than others; check them before settling in. Stick to centrally located accommodations and avoid solitary late-night treks or metro rides.

When traveling, always carry extra money for a phone call, bus, or taxi. **Hitching** is never safe for lone women, or even for two women traveling together. Choose train compartments occupied by other women or couples; ask the conductor to put together a women-only compartment if he or she doesn't offer to do so first. Look as if you know where you're going (even when you don't) and approach older women or couples for directions if you're lost or feel uncomfortable.

Generally, the less you look like a tourist, the better off you'll be. Dress conservatively, especially in rural areas. Wearing a conspicuous **wedding band** may help prevent unwanted overtures. Some travelers report that carrying pictures of a "husband" or "children" is extremely useful to help document marriage status. Even a mention of a husband waiting back at the hotel may be enough in some places to discount your potentially vulnerable, unattached appearance.

Your best answer to verbal harassment is no answer at all; feigning deafness, sitting motionless, and staring straight ahead will do a world of good. In extreme cases, the persistent can sometimes be dissuaded by a firm, loud, and very public "Go away!" in the appropriate language. In Morocco, however, it is more advisable to simply ignore advances, as local women do; rebuffs, or any kind of reaction, are often construed as playing hard to get. Don't hesitate to seek out a police officer or passerby if you are being harassed. Memorize emergency numbers in places you visit, and consider carrying a whistle or airhorn on your keychain. A self-defense course will not only prepare you for a potential attack, but will also raise your level of awareness and confidence (see **Self Defense,** p. 18). Refer to the **Essentials** section for **Morocco** (p.539) for more information on traveling there.

TRAVELING ALONE

There are many benefits to traveling alone, including independence and greater interaction with locals. However, a solo traveler is a more vulnerable target of harassment and street theft. Try not to stand out as a lone tourist, look confident, and be careful in deserted or crowded areas. If questioned, never admit that you are traveling alone. Maintain regular contact with someone at home who knows your itinerary. For more tips, pick up *Traveling Solo* by Eleanor Berman (Globe Pequot Press, US$17) or subscribe to **Connecting: Solo Travel Network,** 689 Park Rd., Unit 6, Gibsons, BC V0N 1V7, Canada (☎604-886-9099; www.cstn.org; membership US$35). **Travel Companion Exchange,** P.O. Box 833, Amityville, NY 11701, USA (☎631-454-0880, or in the US ☎800-392-1256; www.whytravelalone.com; US$48), will link solo travelers with companions with similar travel habits and interests.

OLDER TRAVELERS

Senior citizens are eligible for a wide range of discounts on transportation, museums, movies, theaters, concerts, restaurants, and accommodations. The books *No Problem! Worldwise Tips for Mature Adventurers*, by Janice Kenyon (Orca Book Publishers; US$16) and *Unbelievably Good Deals and Great Adventures That You Absolutely Can't Get Unless You're Over 50*, by Joan Rattner Heilman (NTC/Contemporary Publishing; US$13) are both excellent resources. For more information, contact one of the following organizations:

ElderTreks, 597 Markham St., Toronto, ON M6G 2L7 (☎800-741-7956; www.eldertreks.com). Adventure travel programs for the 50+ traveler in Morocco.

Elderhostel, 11 Ave. de Lafayette, Boston, MA 02111 (☎877-426-8056; www.elderhostel.org). Organizes 1-4 week "educational adventures" in Spain, Portugal, and Morocco on varied subjects for those 55+.

The Mature Traveler, P.O. Box 15791, Sacramento, CA 95852 (☎800-460-6676). Deals, discounts, and travel packages for the 50+ traveler. Subscription $30.

Walking the World, P.O. Box 1186, Fort Collins, CO 80522 (☎800-340-9255; www.walkingtheworld.com), organizes trips for 50+ travelers to a variety of destinations, including Spain and Portugal.

BISEXUAL, GAY, AND LESBIAN TRAVELERS

Attitudes toward homosexuality in Spain, Portugal, and Morocco vary by region. Gay and lesbian travelers may feel out of place in the smaller, rural areas of Spain and Portugal, given the countries' strong Catholic religious heritage, but overt homophobia is rare. The larger cities, especially Madrid, Barcelona, and Lisbon have well-developed gay men's scenes, and the lesbian scene is growing rapidly. In Spain, Sitges and Ibiza are internationally renowned as gay party destinations, and Madrid has one of the most lively gay scenes in Europe, including the epic parties of *Orgullo Gay* in June. Most Spanish newsstands carry the *Guía Gay Visado*, a publication dedicated to gay bars, discos, and contacts in Spain. (See **Gay and Lesbian Services,** p. 99, for more information.) The website www.guiagay.com has similar information. The Portuguese website www.portugalgay.pt also similar offers listings in Portuguese and English. There is no gay community in Morocco. Lesbianism is almost unheard of and unrecognized; male homosexuality is illegal under Islamic and civil law.

Listed below are contact organizations that offer materials addressing some specific concerns. **Out and About** (www.outandabout.com) offers a comprehensive site addressing gay travel concerns and publishes a monthly newsletter for gay and lesbian travelers.

International Gay and Lesbian Travel Association, 4331 N. Federal Hwy., #304, Fort Lauderdale, FL 33308, USA (☎800-448-8550; fax 954-776-3303; www.iglta.com). An organization of over 1350 companies serving gay and lesbian travelers worldwide. The website offers good links to Spanish and Portuguese gay websites.

International Lesbian and Gay Association (ILGA), 81 rue Marché-au-Charbon, B-1000 Brussels, Belgium (☎+32 2 502 2471; www.ilga.org). Provides political information, such as homosexuality laws of individual countries.

FURTHER READING: BISEXUAL, GAY, & LESBIAN.

Spartacus International Gay Guide 2002-03. Bruno Gmunder Verlag (US$33).

Damron Men's Travel Guide, Damron Women's Travel Guide, Damron Road Atlas, and Damron Accommodations. Damron Travel Guides (US$16-23). For more info, call ☎800-462-6654 or visit www.damron.com.

Ferrari Guides' Gay Travel A to Z, Ferrari Guides' Men's Travel in Your Pocket, and *Ferrari Guides' Inn Places*. Ferrari Publications (US$16-20).

TRAVELERS WITH DISABILITIES

Wheelchair accessibility varies widely in Iberia but is generally inferior to that in the US. Access in Morocco is minimal. In Spain and Portugal, handicapped access is common in modern and big city museums.

Those with disabilities should inform airlines and hotels of their disabilities when making reservations. Call ahead to restaurants, museums, and other facilities to find out about the existence of ramps, the widths of doors, etc. **Guide dog owners** should inquire as to the quarantine policies of each destination. At the very least, they will need to provide a certificate of immunization against rabies.

Rail is probably the most convenient form of travel for disabled travelers in Europe: many larger stations have ramps, and some trains have wheelchair lifts, special seating areas, and specially equipped toilets. Spain and Portugal's rail systems, however, have limited resources for wheelchair accessibility, especially in smaller stations. For those who wish to rent cars, some major **car rental** agencies (Hertz, Avis, and National) offer hand-controlled vehicles.

USEFUL ORGANIZATIONS

Mobility International USA (MIUSA), P.O. Box 10767, Eugene, OR 97440 (☎541-343-1284, voice and TDD; www.miusa.org). Sells *A World of Options: A Guide to International Educational Exchange, Community Service, and Travel for Persons with Disabilities* (US$35).

Moss Rehab Hospital Travel Information Service, MossRehab Hospital, 1200 West Tabor Rd., Philadelphia, PA 19141, USA (☎215-456-9900 or 800-CALL-MOSS; www.mossresourcenet.org). An information resource center on travel-related concerns for those with disabilities.

Society for Accesible Travel & Hospitality (SATH), 347 Fifth Ave., #610, New York, NY 10016 (☎212-447-7284; www.sath.org). An advocacy group that publishes free online travel information and the travel magazine *OPEN WORLD* (US$18, free for members). Annual membership US$45, students and seniors US$30.

Directions Unlimited, 123 Green Ln., Bedford Hills, NY 10507 (☎800-533-5343). Books individual and group vacations for the physically disabled; not an info service.

MINORITY TRAVELERS

Because of demographic homogeneity, Spanish people experience little interaction with other races. The infrequent incidents of racism are rarely violent or threatening, just a little awkward. They occur out of naiveté, ignorance, or curiosity rather than insensitivity. Portugal, with its rich ethnic composition, is actively anti-racist, and minority travelers have little to fear. Morocco encompasses a diverse cultural and racial spectrum; visitors are defined more by their foreign ways than by their skin color.

TRAVELERS WITH CHILDREN

Family vacations often require that you slow your pace, and always require that you plan ahead. When deciding where to stay, remember the special needs of young children; if you pick a hostel or a small hotel, call ahead and make sure it's child-friendly. If you rent a car, make sure the rental company provides a car seat for younger children. **Be sure that your child carries some sort of ID** in case of an emergency or in case he or she gets lost.

Museums, tourist attractions, accommodations, and restaurants often offer discounts for children. Children under two generally fly for 10% of the adult airfare on international flights (this does not necessarily include a seat). International fares are usually discounted 25% for children ages two to 11. Finding a private place for **breast feeding** is often a problem while traveling, so plan accordingly.

TAKING THE KIDS ALONG

The following books provide valuable information on how to prepare for a taking a trip with your kids:

Backpacking with Babies and Small Children, Goldie Silverman. Wilderness Press.

Take Your Kids to Europe, Cynthia W. Harriman. Cardogan Books.

How to take Great Trips with Your Kids, Sanford and Jane Portnoy. Harvard Common Press.

Have Kid, Will Travel: 101 Survival Strategies for Vacationing With Babies and Young Children, Claire and Lucille Tristram. Andrews McMeel Publishing.

Trouble Free Travel with Children, Vicki Lansky. Book Peddlers.

DIETARY CONCERNS

Spain and Portugal can be difficult places to visit as a strict vegetarian; in Spain meat or fish is featured in the majority of popular dishes. Most restaurants serve salads, however, and there are also many egg-, rice- and bean-based dishes that can be requested without meat. Be careful, though, as some servers may interpret a "vegetarian" order to mean "with tuna instead of ham." Eating as a vegetarian in Morocco is easier, as bean-based stews and couscous dishes are widespread. The **North American Vegetarian Society,** P.O. Box 72, Dolgeville, NY 13329 (☎518-568-7970; www.navs-online.org), publishes info about vegetarian travel, including *Transformative Adventures, a Guide to Vacations and Retreats* (US$12). For more info, visit your local bookstore, health food store, or library, and consult *The Vegetarian Traveler: Where to Stay if You're Vegetarian, Vegan, Environmentally Sensitive,* by Jed and Susan Civic (Larson Publications; US$16).

Keeping **kosher** is difficult in Spain, Portugal, and Morocco. If you are strict in your observance, you may have to prepare your own food. Travelers who keep kosher should contact synagogues in larger cities for information on kosher restaurants. Good resources include the website www.shamash.org/kosher and the *Jewish Travel Guide,* by Michael Zaidner (Vallentine Mitchell; US$17).

ESSENTIALS

OTHER RESOURCES

Let's Go tries to cover all aspects of budget travel, but we can't put *everything* in our guides. Listed below are books and websites that can serve as jumping off points for your own research.

USEFUL PUBLICATIONS

The Broadsheet, monthly magazine aimed at English speakers in Spain. Features current cultural and social events, as well as news. Commercially oriented. Web edition at www.spainalive.com.

Contemporary Spain: A Handbook, Christopher Ross. Broad and informative discussion of Spanish politics, culture, society, and travel (US$20/£13).

Culture Shock! Morocco, Orin Hargraves. An extremely helpful guide to the salient cultural characteristics of Morocco, the differences between this culture and ours, and how to manage those differences (US$14/£10).

Culture Shock! Spain, Marie Louise Graff. With a comprehensive coverage of Spain's history, beliefs, festivals, and working conditions, this book navigates the visitor through local customs, bureaucracy, and eating and entertaining habits (US$14/£10).

Focus Magazine (www.focusmm.com), monthly online magazine about the Mediterranean world. Includes information on Morocco.

A Traveller's History of Spain, Juan Lalaguna. Helpful for those seeking more background historical and cultural background information about Spain (US$15).

Worst Case Survival Handbook: Travel, Joshua Piven and David Borgenicht. Finally someone has filled the void: 2 experts offer advice on such things as how to stop a runaway camel or navigate a minefield (US$15).

THE WORLD WIDE WEB

Almost every aspect of budget travel is accessible via the Web. Within 10min. at the keyboard, you can make a reservation at a hostel in Spain, Portugal, or Morocco, get advice on travel hotspots from other travelers who have just returned, or find out how much a train from Madrid to Barcelona costs. Listed here are some budget travel sites to start off your surfing; other relevant websites are listed throughout the book.

THE ART OF BUDGET TRAVEL

How to See the World: www.artoftravel.com. A compendium of great travel tips, from cheap flights to self defense to interacting with local culture.

Rec. Travel Library: www.travel-library.com. A fantastic set of links for general information and personal travelogues.

Backpacker's Ultimate Guide: www.bugeurope.com. Tips on packing, transportation, and where to go. Also tons of country-specific travel information.

TravelPage: www.travelpage.com. Links to official tourist office sites through Europe.

COUNTRY-SPECIFIC INFORMATION

All About Spain: www.red2000.com/spain/index.html. Has an excellent photo tour of Spain, traveler's yellow pages, and information on major regions and cities.

Arab Net: www.arab.net/morocco/morocco_contents.html. Good historical, cultural, and tourist information on Morocco, including a list of links.

CIA World Factbook: www.odci.gov/cia/publications/factbook/index.html. Statistics on Spanish, Portuguese, and Moroccan geography, government, economy, and people.

CyberSpain: www.cyberspain.com. Has a wide variety of tourist and cultural info as well as links to other good sites inside and outside of Spain.

Geographia: www.geographia.com. Highlights, culture, and people of Morocco.

MadridMan: www.madridman.com. A site devoted entirely to the city of Madrid, with tons of useful info for visitors as well as history, culture, and current events sections.

Morocco Today: www.morocco-today.com. A comprehensive source of information on Moroccan current events, government, and society.

MyTravelGuide: www.mytravelguide.com. Country overviews, with everything from history to transportation to live web-cam coverage.

PlanetRider: www.planetrider.com. A subjective list of links to the "best" websites covering the culture and tourist attractions of Spain, Portugal, and Morocco.

Portugal-info: www.portugal-info.net. An excellent source for all types of information, from photos to wine descriptions to Portuguese personals.

Sí, Spain: www.sispain.org. Run by the Spanish Ministry of Foreign affairs, this site offers cultural and historical info, tourist info, and another great set of links.

SpainAlive: www.spainalive.com. From bars and concerts, to beaches and soccer, covers nightlife and recreation info for Spain's major tourism cities.

Spain Tourism: www.tourspain.es. The **official** Spanish tourism site. Offers national and city-specific info, an information request service, helpful links on all aspects of travel, cultural and practical info including stats on national parks and museums, and links to the biggest Spanish newspapers. In French, English, Spanish, and German.

Tourism in Morocco: www.tourism-in-Morocco.com. Helpful information on all aspects of traveling to and within Morocco, plus city-specific info.

AND OUR PERSONAL FAVORITE...

WWW.LETSGO.COM Our newly designed website now features the full online content of all of our guides. In addition, trial versions of all nine City Guides are available for download on Palm OS™ PDAs. Our website also contains our newsletter, links for photos and streaming video, online ordering of our titles, info about our books, and a travel forum buzzing with stories and tips.

ALTERNATIVES TO TOURISM

When it comes to natural beauty, vibrant spirit, and rich history, it doesn't get much better than Spain, Portugal, and Morocco. Not surprisingly, these countries grace many a traveler's itinerary, but often only briefly. Unfortunately, the rapid pace of such a tour can cause you to miss the more subtle and nuanced aspects of these multifaceted countries. If you crave a more in-depth travel experience, you may want to consider some alternatives to conventional tourism. Studying, working, or volunteering are some options that can help you understand and appreciate life in Spain, Portugal, or Morocco in ways that a mere tourist might not. This chapter outlines some of the different opportunities available for individuals who want something other than the typical budget traveler experience.

VISA INFORMATION

Spain: In Spain and Portugal, a visa is required for all travelers staying more than 90 days. A **student visa** is required for anyone planning on studying for 90 days or more. Student visas are valid for 90 days from the entry date. After that, a **student residency card** is required, which is valid for as long as the student is enrolled. To obtain a student visa, travelers must submit the following to their local Spanish consulate: a passport valid for at least six months, verification of enrollment from school or university, medical certificate, and proof of financial resources. The cost is US$45-60 depending on country of residence. A **residency visa** is required to work in Spain in addition to a **work permit.** To obtain a residency visa, travelers must submit a passport, certificate of good conduct, medical certificate, and a valid job offer. Cost is $45.

Portugal: To obtain a student visa, travelers must submit the same materials as for Spain plus a certificate of good conduct from the police. A **work visa** is required, which can be obtained with a work permit or work contract. All materials must be translated into Portuguese before being submitted to the consulate. The cost for each is US$24-48 depending on country of residence.

Morocco: All travelers must obtain a residency card from the local police headquarters once in Morocco if staying for longer than 90 days. A student visa is not required, nor is a work permit.

For an extensive listing of "off-the-beaten-track" and specialty travel opportunities, try the Specialty Travel Index, 305 San Anselmo Ave., #313, San Anselmo, CA 94960, USA (☎800-442-4922; fax 415-459-4974; www.spectrav.com).

STUDYING ABROAD

Spain is one of the most popular destinations in the world for study-abroad students. To find out more, contact US university programs and youth organizations that send students to Spanish universities and language centers. Many programs cluster around Madrid and Sevilla. While **Portugal** is not as common a destination for study abroad, most universities in Portugal open their gates to foreign students. Study abroad is rare in **Morocco,** though there are some programs available.

Studying in **Spain**, **Portugal,** or **Morocco** requires a good deal of regulatory paperwork. Students planning to stay longer than three months must obtain a visa from their national consulate (see p. 8). Those students studying only for the summer (i.e., for less than three months) need only a passport. Individual universities and programs have their own requirements, most of which involve a basic knowledge of the local language and a minimum grade point average.

Those relatively fluent in Spanish, Portuguese, French, or Arabic may find it cheaper to enroll directly in a university abroad, although getting college credit may be more difficult. Some American schools still require students to pay them for credits obtained elsewhere. Most university-level study-abroad programs are meant as language and culture enrichment opportunities, and therefore are conducted in the language of the country. Still, many programs offer classes in English as well as beginner- and lower-level language courses. A good resource for finding programs that cater to your particular interests is **www.studyabroad.com,** which has links to various semester abroad programs based on a variety of criteria, including desired location and focus of study. When contacting individual programs, ask for the names of recent participants to get their evaluation of the program. The following is a list of organizations that can help place students in university programs abroad, or have their own branch in Spain, Portugal, or Morocco.

AMERICAN PROGRAMS

Academic Programs International (API), 107 E. Hopkins, San Marcos, TX, 78666 (☎800-844-8124; www.academicintl.com). Programs available in Barcelona, Cádiz, Granada, Madrid, Salamanca, and Sevilla. Classes include international business, Spanish literature, and Spanish studies among others.

American Institute for Foreign Study, College Division, River Plaza, 9 West Broad St., Stamford, CT 06902 (☎800-727-2437, ext. 5163; www.aifsabroad.com). Organizes programs for high school and college study in universities in Spain.

Arcadia University for Education Abroad, 450 S. Easton Rd., Glenside, PA 19038 (☎866-927-2234; www.arcadia.edu/cea). Operates programs in Toledo.

Central College Abroad, Office of International Education, 812 University, Pella, IA 50219 (☎800-831-3629 or 641-628-5284; www.central.edu/abroad). Offers internships, summer-, semester-, and year-long programs in Granada.

School for International Training, College Semester Abroad, Admissions, Kipling Rd., P.O. Box 676, Brattleboro, VT 05302 (☎800-336-1616 or 802-257-7751; www.sit.edu). Semester- and year-long programs in Spain and Morocco. Also runs the **Experiment in International Living** (☎800-345-2929; fax 802-258-3428; www.usexperiment.org), 3- to 5-week summer programs that offer high-school students homestays, community service, ecological adventure, and language training in Spain.

Council on International Educational Exchange (CIEE), 633 3rd Ave., 20th floor, New York, NY 10017-6706 (☎800-407-8839; www.ciee.org). Sponsors study abroad and volunteer programs in Spain.

International Association for the Exchange of Students for Technical Experience (IAESTE), 10400 Little Patuxent Pkwy. Suite 250, Columbia, MD 21044-3519 (☎410-997-2200; www.aipt.org). 8- to 12-week programs in Spain and Portugal for college students who have completed 2yr. of technical study.

Institute of Spanish Studies, 17303 Southwest 80st Place, Miami, FL 33157 (☎888-454-6777; www.spanish-studies.com). Located in Valencia. Offers a range of courses in history, Spanish language, and literature. Students live with host families.

PROGRAMS IN SPAIN, PORTUGAL, AND MOROCCO

Universities in major cities like Madrid, Lisbon, and Rabat generally have options available for foreign students who wish to study abroad, but many other universities in smaller cities like Salamanca, Granada, and Coimbra have active study abroad programs and host thousands of foreign students every year. Check with the individual school for specific requirements and procedures for enrolling.

Universidad Complutense de Madrid, Vicerrectorado de Relaciones Internacionales, Isaac Peral s/n, 28040 Madrid, España (☎913 94 69 20; fax 913 94 69 24; www.ucm.es). Largest university in Spain. Hosts 3500 foreign students annually. Opportunities for study in a variety of fields with or without a specific study abroad program.

Universidade de Lisboa, Rectorate Al. da Universidade, Cidade Universitária, 1649-004 Lisbon, Portugal (☎217 96 76 24; fax: 217 93 36 24; www.ul.pt). Allows direct enrollment of foreign students in most of its divisions.

Al Akhawayn University, Office of Admissions, Al Akhawayn University, P.O. Box 104, Ifrane 53000, Morocco (☎+212 55 56 77 77; www.alakhawayn.ma) Welcomes direct enrollment by foreign students. Offers programs with an emphasis on Moroccan culture.

LANGUAGE SCHOOLS

Unlike American universities, language schools are frequently independently-run international or local organizations or divisions of foreign universities that rarely offer college credit. Language schools are a good alternative to university study if you desire a deeper focus on the language or a slightly less-rigorous courseload. These programs are good for high school students that might not feel comfortable with older students in a university program.

Arabic Language Institute in Fez, B.P. 2136, Ville Nouvelle, Fez 30000 (☎+212 562-4850). Specializes in Modern Standard Arabic and Colloquial Moroccan Arabic.

Don Quijote, Plaza San Marcos 7, 37002 Salamanca, Spain (☎923 26 88 60; www.donquijote.org). Offers Spanish language courses for all levels in Barcelona, Granada, Madrid, Málaga, Salamanca, Sevilla, and Valencia.

CIAL Centro de Linguas, Av. de República, 41-8° Esq., 1050-187 Lisbon, Portugal (☎217 940 448; www.cial.pt). Portuguese language courses for all levels. Locations in Lisbon, Porto, and Faro.

Eurocentres, 101 N. Union St. Suite 300, Alexandria, VA 22314, USA (☎703-684-1494; www.eurocentres.com), or in Europe, Head Office, Seestr. 247, CH-8038 Zurich, Switzerland (☎+41 1 485 50 40; fax 481 61 24). Spanish language programs for beginning to advanced students in Barcelona, Madrid, Salamanca, and Málaga.

WORKING ABROAD

When it comes to working abroad, there are two main schools of thought. Some travelers want long-term jobs that allow them to get to know another part of the world in depth while others seek out short-term jobs to finance their travel. This section discusses both short-term and long-term opportunities for working in Spain, Portugal, and Morocco. Make sure you understand the requirements for **visas** and **work permits** for working in these countries, as they are often complicated. See the box on p. 56 for more information on visas.

Travelers from within the European Union can work in any EU member country, but those from outside the EU need a work permit. All foreign workers in Morocco are required to have a permit. Obtaining a work permit in Spain and Portugal is a complicated process.

EU citizens, if they intend to stay for more than three months, must apply for a **residence card** (*tarjeta de residencia*) within 30 days of arrival. Application can be made at a regional police headquarters or a Foreigner's Registration Office. You will need a contract of employment, four photos, and a passport. Non-EU citizens must first obtain a residence visa prior to from the Spanish embassy in their country of residence, which requires the same materials as a residence card plus a copy of the employment contract, a medical certificate, and a certificate of good behavior from the police. Portugal's regulations are similar, although both EU and non-EU citizens can obtain a work permit with a residence visa. Friends in Spain or Portugal can often help expedite work permits or arrange work-for-accommodations swaps. Work permits are not required in Morocco.

LONG-TERM WORK

If you're planning on spending a substantial amount of time (more than three months) working in Spain, Portugal, or Morocco, search for a job well in advance. International placement agencies are often the easiest way to find employment abroad, especially for teaching English. **Internships,** usually for college students, are a good way to segue into working abroad, although they are often unpaid or poorly paid. Be wary of advertisements or companies that offer to get you a job abroad for a fee—the same listings are often available online or in newspapers.

In **Spain,** the national employment service (*Oficinas de Empleo*) has a monopoly on the job-finding market; begin your search here. Many seasoned travelers, however, go straight to a particular town's Yellow Pages (*Las Paginas Amarillas*) or even go door-to-door in the town in which they are staying. In **Portugal,** the English-language weekly newspaper *Anglo-Portuguese News* carries job listings. In **Morocco,** contact your national consulate for a list of schools with openings. Below are additional resources for finding jobs in Spain, Portugal, and Morocco.

Escape Artist (www.escapeartist.com/jobs/overseas1). Provides information on living abroad, including job listings for Spain, Portugal, and Morocco.

Go Jobsite (www.gojobsite.com). Lists jobs for European countries, including Spain.

Trabajos (www.trabajos.com). Provides job listings for all regions of Spain.

TEACHING ENGLISH

Teaching English is one of the most popular jobs in Spain and Portugal for those craving a more long-term experience. For non-EU citizens, teaching English is likely one of the few options available that avoid the long and bureaucratic process of obtaining a work permit through a sponsoring company. Teaching jobs abroad are rarely well-paid, though some elite private American schools pay somewhat competitive salaries. Volunteering as a teacher in lieu of getting paid is also a popular option, and even in those cases, teachers often get some sort of daily stipend to help with living expenses. In most cases, you must have at least a bachelor's degree to be a full-fledged teacher, though college undergraduates can often get summer teaching or tutoring positions. Finding a job teaching English in Spain is relatively easy. Positions tend to be fewer in Portugal and Morocco.

Many schools require teachers to have a Teaching English as a Foreign Language (TEFL) certificate. Those without the TEFL certificate can likely still find work, certified teachers often find higher paying jobs. Many schools provide an intensive course in TEFL prior to placement. Native English speakers working in private schools are most often hired for English-immersion classrooms. Those volunteering or teaching in public schools are more likely to be working in both English and the local language. Placement agencies or university fellowship programs are the best resources for finding teaching jobs in

Spain, Portugal, and Morocco. The alternative is to make contacts directly with schools or just to try your luck once you get there. If you are going to try the latter, the best time of the year is several weeks before the start of the school year. The following organizations are extremely helpful in placing teachers in Spain, Portugal, and Morocco.

International Schools Services (ISS), 15 Roszel Rd., P.O. Box 5910, Princeton, NJ 08543-5910, USA (☎609-452-0990; fax 609-452-2690; www.iss.edu). Hires teachers for more than 200 overseas schools including Spain and Morocco; candidates should have experience teaching or with international affairs, 2yr. commitment expected.

Office of Overseas Schools, US Department of State, Room H328, SA-1, Washington, DC 20522-0132, USA (☎202-261-8200; fax 202-261-8224; www.state.gov/m/a/os). Keeps a comprehensive list of schools abroad, including Spain, Portugal, and Morocco, and agencies that arrange placement for Americans to teach abroad.

AU PAIR WORK

Au-pairs are typically women, aged 18-27, who work as live-in nannies, caring for children and doing light housework in foreign countries in exchange for room, board, and a small spending allowance or stipend. Most former au-pairs speak favorably of their experience and of how it allowed them to get to know a foreign country without the high cost of traveling. Drawbacks, however, often include long hours and mediocre pay (€55-60 weekly). Ultimately, much of the au pair experience depends on the family you're placed with. The agencies below are good starting points for looking for employment as an au pair.

Accord Cultural Exchange, 750 La Playa, San Francisco, CA 94121, USA (☎415-386-6203; www.cognitext.com/accord).

Au Pair Homestay, World Learning, Inc., 1015 15th St. NW, Suite 750, Washington, DC 20005, USA (☎800-287-2477; fax 202-408-5397).

Au Pair in Europe, P.O. Box 68056, Blakely Postal Outlet, Hamilton, Ontario, Canada L8M 3M7 (☎905-545-6305; fax 905-544-4121; www.princeent.com/aupair).

Childcare International, Ltd., Trafalgar House, Grenville Pl., London NW7 3SA (☎+44 020 8906 3116; fax 8906-3461; www.childint.co.uk).

InterExchange, 161 Sixth Ave., New York, NY 10013, USA (☎212-924-0446; fax 924-0575; www.interexchange.org).

SHORT-TERM WORK

Traveling for long periods of time can get expensive. Those with unlimited time but not unlimited money often work odd jobs for a few weeks at a time to finance another month or two of travel. Because the process for obtaining a work permit is often long, complicated, bureaucratic, and requires a prior job contract, few travelers seeking short-term work have one. For non-EU citizens, working without a permit is illegal is Spain and Portugal, but many establishments hire travelers illegally, particularly in highly seasonal resort areas. These jobs often include bartending, waiting tables, or promoting bars and clubs. Another popular option is to work several hours a day at a hostel in exchange for free or discounted room and/or board. Most often, these short-term jobs are found by word of mouth, or simply by talking to the owner of a hostel, restaurant, or bar. Many places, especially because of the high turnover in the tourism industry, are always eager for help, even if only temporary. *Let's Go* does not recommend working illegally.

VOLUNTEERING

Volunteering is another option for those wishing for an alternative travel experience. Volunteer jobs are readily available in many parts of Spain, Portugal, and Morocco, and many provide room and board in exchange for labor. Most volunteers go through a parent organization that takes care of logistical details and frequently provides a group environment and support system. Unfortunately many of these services charge you a fee to participate in the program and to do work. These fees can be surprisingly hefty (although they frequently cover airfare and living expenses). However, you can sometimes avoid high application fees by contacting the individual workcamps directly.

Earthwatch, 3 Clocktower Pl. Suite 100, Box 75, Maynard, MA 01754, USA (☎800-776-0188 or 978-461-0081; www.earthwatch.org). Arranges 1- to 3-week programs in Spain to promote conservation of natural resources. Fees vary based on program location and duration, costs average $1700 plus airfare.

Elderhostel, Inc., 11 Avenue de Lafayette, Boston, MA 92111-1746, USA (☎877-426-8056; fax 877-426-2166; www.elderhostel.org). Sends volunteers age 55 and over around the world to work in construction, research, teaching, and many other projects. Costs average $100 per day plus airfare.

Habitat for Humanity International, 121 Habitat St., Americus, GA 31709, USA (☎229-924-6935 x2551; www.habitat.org). Volunteers build houses in over 83 countries, including Portugal, for anywhere from 2 weeks to 3 years. Short-term program costs range from US$1200-4000.

Peace Corps, Office of Volunteer Recruitment and Selection, 1111 20th St. NW, Washington, D.C. 20526, USA (☎800-424-8580; www.peacecorps.gov). Opportunities in 70 developing nations, including Morocco.

Service Civil International Voluntary Service (SCI-IVS), 3213 W. Wheeler St., Seattle, WA 98199, USA (☎/fax 206-350-6585; www.sci-ivs.org). Arranges placement in work camps in Spain, Portugal, and Morocco for those 18+. Registration fee US$65-125.

Volunteers for Peace, 1034 Tiffany Rd., Belmont., VT 05730, USA (☎802-259-2759; www.vfp.org). Arranges placement in work camps in Spain, Portugal, and Morocco. Membership required for registration. Annual *International Workcamp Directory* US$20. Programs average US$200-500 for 2-3 weeks.

FOR FURTHER READING ON ALTERNATIVES TO TOURISM

Alternatives to the Peace Corps: A Directory of Third World and U.S. Volunteer Opportunities, by Joan Powell. Food First Books, 2000.

How to Get a Job in Europe, by Sanborn and Matherly. Surrey Books, 1999.

How to Live Your Dream of Volunteering Oversees, by Collins, DeZerega, and Heckscher. Penguin Books, 2002.

International Directory of Voluntary Work, by Whetter and Pybus. Peterson's Guides and Vacation Work, 2000.

International Jobs, by Kocher and Segal. Perseus Books, 1999.

Overseas Summer Jobs 2002, by Collier and Woodworth. Peterson's Guides and Vacation Work, 2002.

Teaching English Abroad, Griffin and Pybus. Vacation-Work.

Work Abroad: The Complete Guide to Finding a Job Overseas, by Hubbs, Griffith, and Nolting. Transitions Abroad Publishing, 2000.

Work Your Way Around the World, by Susan Griffith. Worldview Publishing Services, 2001.

SPAIN

EUROS (€)		
	US $1 = €1.02	€1 = US $0.98
	CDN $1 = €0.65	€1 = CDN $1.54
	UK £1 = €1.56	€1 = UK £0.64
	AUS $1 = €0.56	€1 = AUS $1.79
	NZ $1 = €0.48	€1 = NZ $2.09
	ZAR 1 = €0.09	€1 = ZAR 3.73
	MOR 1DH = €0.09	€1 = MOR 10.50DH

Country Code: 34. **International dialing prefix:** 00.

SPAIN

LIFE AND TIMES

Imagine a parched central plateau surrounded by lush rolling hills, craggy snow-covered peaks, and glistening white sand beaches, a land where tradition and modern life collide with spectacular results, one whose glorious past is overshadowed only by its people's passion for living. This is Spain. Though travelers are drawn here by visions of flamenco and bullfighting, these are but one side of the country's personality. Spain's rich history spans more than a millenium of foreign invaders, artistic and literary geniuses, architectural masterpieces, and religious conflicts. Civilizations came and went, empires rose and fell, but with each new influence, Spain retained a portion as its own. The result is a country with an intoxicating amalgam of cultures, an incredible array of artistic and architectural treasures, and a definite flair for the celebratory. Modern Spain is a collection of autonomous regions, each with its own character, and often with its own language. Speaking of Spain as a whole is difficult, but there is a certain indefinable yet irrepressible spirit that binds the country together. Travelers who come here find breathtaking landscapes and priceless cultural riches along with some of the world's best nightlife and wildest festivals. Easily accessible and relatively inexpensive, Spain mesmerizes visitors with its vibrant energy and unforgettable soul.

OFFICIAL NAME: Kingdom of Spain.

GOVERNMENT: Parliamentary monarchy.

CAPITAL: Madrid.

POPULATION: 40,037,995.

LAND AREA: 499,542 sq. km.

GEOGRAPHY: Large, dry plateau surrounded by rugged hills, with the Pyrenees in the north.

CLIMATE: Temperate.

MAJOR CITIES: Barcelona, Córdoba, Granada, Madrid, Sevilla, Valencia.

LANGUAGES: Castilian Spanish (official), Catalan, Galician, Basque.

RELIGIONS: Roman Catholic (99%).

AVERAGE INCOME PER CAPITA: US$18,000.

MAJOR EXPORTS: Textiles and apparel, wine, metals, chemicals, automobiles.

HISTORY

With a history that spans over 50 constitutions, an endless array of amorphous kingdoms controlled by indigenous Iberians, Celts, Romans, Visigoths, Arabs, and French, and an empire that spread to the Americas, Spain can only be described as a *mestizo* (mixed) culture.

Spain has been colonized by a succession of civilizations who have left behind their cultural mark—**Basque** (considered indigenous), **Tartesian, Iberian, Celtic, Greek, Phoenician,** and **Carthaginian**—before the **Romans** dropped in with a vengeance in the 3rd century BC. In close to seven centuries, the Romans drastically altered the face and character of Spain, introducing Rome's language, architecture, roads, irrigation techniques, and use of grapes, olives, and wheat. A slew of Germanic tribes, including Swabians and Vandals, swept over Iberia in the early 5th century, but the **Visigoths,** newly converted Christians, emerged above the rest. The Visigoths established their court at Barcelona in 415 and effectively ruled Spain for the next three hundred years.

THE MOORISH OCCUPATION (711-1492). Following Muslim unification, a small force of Arabs, Berbers, and Syrians invaded Spain in 711. Practically welcomed by the divided Visigoths, the Moors encountered little resistance, and the peninsula soon fell under the dominion of the caliphate of Damascus. The Moors set up their Iberian capital in **Córdoba** (see p. 235). During **Abderramán III**'s rule in the 10th century, some considered Spain the wealthiest and most cultivated country in the world. Abderramán's successor, **Al Mansur,** snuffed out all opposition within his extravagant court and undertook a series of military campaigns that climaxed with the destruction of **Santiago de Compostela** (see p. 526), a Christian holy city, in 997.

THE CATHOLIC MONARCHS (1469-1516). It took almost 750 years, if you count the 718 victory of the Asturian Don Pelayo over a Muslim army in Covadonga as the start of *la Reconquista* or Reconquest of Spain, for the Christian kingdoms to "retake" Spain from the Moors. In 1469, the marriage of **Fernando de Aragón** and **Isabel de Castilla** joined Iberia's two mightiest Christian kingdoms. By 1492, the power couple had captured Granada (the last Moorish stronghold) and shuttled off Columbus to explore the New World. Jews and Muslims were forced to convert to Christianity or face expulsion. The Catholic Monarchs introduced the **Inquisition** in 1478, executing and then burning heretics, principally Jews (even those who had converted earlier). In approximately 50 years of rule, the Catholic Monarchs heightened Spain's position not only as the prime European exponent of Catholicism but also as a world economic, political, and cultural power—made even more enduring by lucrative conquests in the Americas.

THE HABSBURG DYNASTY (1516-1713). The daughter of Fernando and Isabel, **Juana la Loca** (the Mad), married **Felipe el Hermoso** (the Fair) of the powerful Habsburg dynasty. When *Señor Hermoso* passed away after a game of *jai alai* (an apparently lethal lacrosse/racquetball combination) *La Loca* refused to believe that he had died and dragged his corpse through the streets screaming. Juana and Felipe secured their genetic legacy with the birth of the half-Habsburg **Carlos I** (Charles V, ruled 1516-1556), who reigned as the last Roman Emperor.

After Carlos I died, his son **Felipe II** (1556-1598) was left holding Pandora's box: a handful of rebellious territories in the Protestant Netherlands. He decided to annex Portugal after its ailing King Henry died in 1580. One year later, the Dutch declared their independence from Spain, and Felipe began warring with the Protestants, spurring an embroilment with England. The war with the British ground to a halt when Sir Francis Drake undid Spain's **Invincible Armada** in 1588. Much of his European empire sapped, Felipe retreated to his grim, newly built palace, El Escorial, and remained there through the last decade of his reign.

Ortigueira
Ribadeo
La Coruña
Camariñas
Cabo de Finisterre
GALICIA
Santiago de Compostela
Oviedo
ASTURIAS
Santillana del Mar
Llanes
Santander
Picos de Europa
CANTABRIA
Potes
Bilba
León
Astorga
Carrion de los Condes
Pontevedra
Orense
Vigo
Túy
La Guardia
Miño
Santo Domingo
Burgos
CASTILLA Y LEON
Palencia
Valladolid
El Burgo de Osma
Duero
Zamora
Medina del Campo
Arévalo
Salamanca
Segovia
Ciudad Rodrigo
Alba de Tormes
Ávila
Guadalajara
El Escorial
Alcalá de Henares
Madrid
MADRID
Béjar
PORTUGAL
Toledo
Aranjuez
Tajo
Guadalupe
Cáceres
Trujillo
Consuegra
CASTILLA-LA MANCHA
EXTREMADURA
Guadiana
Mérida
Ciudad Real
Badajoz
Almagro
Zafra
Ubeda
Baeza
Cazorla
Aracena
Córdoba
Jaén
Guadalquivir
ANDALUCIA
Ecija
Huelva
Sevilla
Carmona
Guadix
Granada
Osuna
Golfo de Cádiz
Antequera
Sanlúcar de Barrameda
Chipiona
Arcos de la Frontera
Ronda
Nerja
Málaga
Almuñécar
ATLANTIC OCEAN
Jerez de la Frontera
Cádiz
Marbella
Vejer de la Frontera
Algeciras
La Línea
Gibraltar
Tarifa
Strait of Gibraltar
Ceuta
MOROCCO
Spain

SPAIN

Golfo de Vizcaya
FRANCE
San Sabastián
Hondarribia
Irún
Guernica
Roncesvalles
NAVARRA
Ansó
ANDORRA
Pamplona
Vitoria
Estella
Sangüesa
Tafalla
Olite
Torla
Pq. Na. de Ordesa
Jaca
Castillo de Loarre
Vielha
Puigcerdà
Seu d'Urgell
Núria
Ripoll
Portbou
Figueras
Empúries
Logroño
Ainsa
RIOJA
Tudela
Huesca
CATALUÑA
Girona
Palafrugell
Tossa de Mar
Soria
Tarazona
Ebro
ARAGON
Montserrat
Zaragoza
Lérida
Calatayud
Cariñera
Vilanova i la Geltrú
Barcelona
Sitges
Daroca
Tarragona
Sigüenza
Tajo
Balearic Sea
Morella
TO MENORCA
Albarracín
Teruel
Mora de Rubielos
Alcúdia
Cuenca
Palma
Sagunto
Golfo de Valencia
Mallorca
Valencia
VALENCIA
BALEARIC ISLANDS
Úcar
Cullera
San Antonio
Gandía
Eivissa
Játiva
Dénia
Ibiza
Albacete
S. Francisco
Formentera
Calpe
Menorca
Alicante
Ciutadella
Mahón
Elche
Murcia
MURCIA
Manga del Mar Menor
Lorca
Mediterranean Sea
Águilas
Mojácar
Almería
Cabo de Gata
ALGERIA
N
LG
0
50 mi
0
75 km

SPAIN

Felipe III (1598-1621) allowed his favorite adviser, the Duque de Lerma, to pull the governmental strings. In 1609, Felipe III and the Duke expelled nearly 300,000 of Spain's remaining Moors. **Felipe IV** (1621-1665) painstakingly held the country together through his long, tumultuous reign. Emulating his great-grandfather Carlos I, Felipe IV discerningly patronized the arts (painter Diego Velázquez and playwrights Lope de Vega and Calderón de la Barca graced his court) and architecture (the Buen Retiro in Madrid) and donned extravagant black garb. Then the **Thirty Years' War** (1618-1648) broke out over Europe, and defending Catholicism drained Spain's resources. It ended with the marriage of Felipe IV's daughter, María Teresa, and Louis XIV of France. Felipe's successor **Carlos II** (1665-1700), known as the "*hechizado*" (bewitched), was the product of generations of inbreeding: he was known to fly into fits of rage and epileptic seizures. From then on, little went right: Carlos II died, leaving no heirs because of his "problem," Spain fell into a depression, and cultural bankruptcy ensued. Rulers from all over Europe battled for the Spanish crown; the War of Spanish Succession had begun.

BOURBONS, CONSTITUTIONS, AND LIBERALS (1713-1930). The 1713 Peace of Utrecht ended the Spanish Succession ordeal and seated **Felipe V** (1713-1746), a Bourbon grandson of **Louis XIV,** on the Spanish throne. The king built ostentatious palaces to mimic Versailles in France and cultivated a flamboyant, debaucherous court. Still, Felipe competently administered the Empire, at last beginning to regain control of Spanish-American trade lost to northern Europeans. **Carlos III** (1759-1788) was probably Madrid's finest "mayor," founding academies and beautifying the capital. Spain's global standing recovered enough for it to team with France to help the American colonies gain independence from Britain, aid that was symbolized by Captain Gálvez's victories in the American South.

As part of his world domination trip, **Napoleon** then invaded Spain (1808-1814). The French occupation ended, ironically enough, when the Protestant Brits beat up the Corsican's troops at Waterloo (1814). This victory led to the restoration of arch-reactionary **Fernando VII** (1814-1833), who sought to revoke the progressive *Constitución de Cádiz* of 1812. Galvanized by Fernando's ineptitude and inspired by liberal ideas in the new constitution, most of Spain's Latin American empire soon threw off the colonial yoke. Domestically, parliamentary liberalism was restored in 1833 upon Fernando VII's death and survived the conservative challenge of the **Carlist Wars** (1833-1840); it would dominate Spanish politics until 1837, when the monarchy was so weakened that a **Spanish republic** was proclaimed. Despite the political anarchy that ensued until **Primo de Rivera's** mild dictatorship in the 1920s, rapid industrialization and prosperity marked the last two decades of 19th-century Spain. It was during this period that the wealth produced by Catalunya's industrial-inspired *Renaixença* (Renaissance) financed Barcelona's **Modernista** movement in architecture and design. But Spain's defeat to the US in the 1898 **Spanish-American War** cost the Spanish the Philippines, Puerto Rico, Cuba, and any dreams left of Latin American wealth.

THE ROAD TO NATIONAL TRAGEDY (1931-1975). In April 1931, **King Alfonso XIII** (1902-1931), disgraced by his support for Rivera's dictatorship, shamefully fled Spain, thus giving rise to the **Second Republic** (1931-1936). Republican Liberals and Socialists established safeguards for farmers and industrial workers, granted women's suffrage, assured religious tolerance, and chipped away at traditional military dominance. National euphoria, however, faded fast. The 1933 elections split the Republican-Socialist coalition, increasing the power of right wing and Catholic parties in the parliamentary *Cortes*. Military dissatisfaction led to a heightened profile of the **Fascist *Falange*** (founded by Rivera's son José), which further polarized national politics. By 1936, radicals, anarchists, Socialists, and Republicans had formed a loose, federated alliance to win the next elections, though the victory was short-lived. Once **Generalísimo Francisco Franco** snatched control of the Spanish army, militarist uprisings ensued, and the nation plunged into war. The three-year **Spanish Civil War** (1936-1939) ignited worldwide ideological passions. Germany and Italy dropped troops, supplies, and munitions into Franco's lap, while the US and liberal European states were slow to aid the Republicans. The Soviet Union, somewhat indirectly, called for a **Popular Front** of Communists, Socialists, and other leftist sympathizers to battle Franco's fascism. But soon after, the West abandoned the coalition, and aid from the Soviet Union waned as Stalin began to see the benefits of an alliance with Hitler. All told, bombings, executions, combat, starvation, and disease took nearly 600,000 lives, and in 1939, Franco's forces marched into Madrid and ended the war.

FRANCO AND THE NATIONAL TRAGEDY (1939-1975). As scientists, artists, and intellectuals emigrated or were assassinated en masse, the first decades of Franco's dictatorship were characterized by worker dissatisfaction, student unrest, regional discontent, and international isolation. Groups like the Basque ETA, resisted the dictatorship throughout Franco's reign, often via terrorist acts. In his old age, Franco tried to smooth international relations by joining NATO and encouraging tourism, but the **national tragedy** (as it was later called) did not officially end until Franco's death in 1975. King Juan Carlos I (1975-), grandson of Alfonso XIII and nominally a Franco protégé, carefully set out to undo Franco's damage. In 1978, under centrist premier Adolfo Suárez, Spain adopted a new constitution and restored the parliamentary government and regional autonomy.

TRANSITION TO DEMOCRACY (1975-2000). The post-Franco years have been marked by progressive social change. Divorce was finally legalized in 1981 and women now vote more and comprise over 50% of universities' ranks. After serving five years, Prime Minister Adolfo Suárez resigned in 1981, leaving the country vulnerable for an attempted coup d'etat on February 23, when a group of rebels took over Congress in an effort to impose a military-backed government. King Juan Carlos used his personal influence to convince the rebels to stand down, and order was restored. Charismatic **Felipe González** led the PSOE (Spanish Socialist Worker's Party) to victory in the 1982 elections. González opened the Spanish economy and championed consensus policies, overseeing Spain's integration into the European Community (EC; now the EU) in 1986. Despite unpopular economic stands, González was reelected in 1986 and continued a program of massive public investment. The years 1986 to 1990 were outstanding for Spain's economy, as the nation enjoyed an average growth rate of 3.8% a year. By the end of 1993, however, recession had set in. Revelations of large-scale corruption led to a resounding Socialist defeat at the hands of the *Partido Popular* in the 1994 European parliamentary elections. **José María Aznar** led the PP to power after González's support eroded and has managed to maintain a coalition with the support of the Catalán and Canary Islands regional parties. The PSOE achieved the worst results in 20 years in the 2000 elections; the PP won an absolute majority, restoring Aznar.

CURRENT EVENTS

Basque separatists in northwestern Spain have pressed on in their effort to establish an autonomous state. The movement's militant wing, Euskadi Ta Askatasuna (Basque Homeland and Freedom), is known for its terrorist activities; over 800 people have been killed since 1968, though the car bombings that are their favored line of attack commonly target politicians rather than civilians. In June 2002, authorities seized 288 pounds of dynamite near Valencia, charging that the ETA was planning to strike tourist spots along the Mediterranean coast. That same month, controversy ensued when the Spanish parliament moved towards banning Batasuna, a pro-independence Basque political party that Prime Minister Aznar said was allied with the ETA. Finally, during an EU summit in Sevilla, the ETA planted several car bombs in vacation resort towns along the Costa del Sol and in two cities in northern Spain, injuring several people but resulting in no fatalities.

For the past three hundred years, Spain has fought an uphill battle to regain control of Gibraltar, a strategic 6km territory in the south currently under British rule. Despite considerable resistance from the Gibraltarians, who are overwhelmingly loyal to the crown, Britain's desire to improve relations with Spain has paved the way for some concessions. In November 2001, Spain and Britain vowed to resolve the Gibraltar issue by summer 2002, with proposals such as joint Anglo-Spanish sovereignty and Gibraltarian self-government on the table. But Gibraltarians continue to delay agreements, registering their disapproval through massive pro-British marches and media campaigns against Spanish rule.

LANGUAGE

Spain's four regional languages and their various dialects differ far more than just cosmetically, although some spelling variations are merely superficial. **Castilian** (*castellano*), spoken almost everywhere, is Spain's official language. **Catalán** (*català*) is spoken in all of Cataluña. It has given rise through permutations to **Valencian** (*valencià*), the regional tongue of Valencia in the east, and **Mallorquín,** the principal dialect of the Balearic Islands. The once-Celtic northwest corner of Iberia gabs in **Galician** (*gallego*), which is closely related to Portuguese. Although more prevalent in the countryside than cities, Galician is now spreading among the young, as is **Basque** (*euskera*), spoken in País Vasco and northern Navarra.

SPAIN

City and provincial names in this text are usually listed in Castilian first, followed by the regional language in parentheses, where appropriate. Information within cities (i.e. street or plaza names) is listed in the regional language. For a **phrasebook, glossary,** and **pronunciation guide,** see p. 793.

RELIGION

CATHOLICISM. The Roman Catholic Church has played an important part in everyday life ever since the Christians ousted the Moors and Spain became unified under the Catholic Kings. Though Protestant churches are now treated more equally, the Catholic Church permeates Spanish life today. Treat shrines, sanctuaries, churches and cathedrals with respect, as most Spaniards are deeply religious and expect you to behave properly in their sacred places of worship.

CULTURE

FOOD AND DRINK

Spanish food's taste often ranks above appearance, preparation is rarely complicated, and many of the best meals are served not in expensive restaurants but in private homes or streetside bars. All of this has begun to change as Spanish food becomes increasingly sophisticated and cosmopolitan, but fresh local ingredients are still an integral part of the cuisine, varying according to each region's climate, geography, and history.

LOCAL FARE

Andalucian cuisine is the oldest in Spain—it was through Sevilla that New World products like corn, peppers, tomatoes, and potatoes first entered Europe. Andalucians have since mastered the art of *gazpacho*, a cool, tomato-based soup perfectly suited to the hot southern climate. The area is also known for its *pescadito frito* (fried fish), *rabo de toro* (bull's tail), egg yolk desserts, sherry wines, and tasty *tapas*. Spain's best cured ham, *jamón ibérico*, comes from the town of Jabugo, where black-footed pigs gain special flavor from daily oak acorn feasts.

Sheep share space with more of these prized pigs in nearby **Extremadura,** where a pastoral lifestyle has lent itself to hearty stews (*cocidos*), cheeses, and unique breadcrumb-based meals (*migas*). This type of dry-land "shepherd's cuisine" dominates central Spain. **Castilla-La Mancha** is famous for its sheep's milk *queso manchego*, the most widely eaten cheese in Spain, and lamb and roasted game are essential parts of menus here and in **Castilla y Léon.** *Escabeche*, an Arab tradition of sautéing with lemon or vinegar, has become a Castilian specialty, as has *tortilla española* (potato omelette) and *menestra de verduras*, a succulent vegetable mix. **Madrid** rivals Andalucia with its *tapas* offerings and is also renowned for the heavy *cocido madrileño*, a mix of meats with cabbage, carrots, and potatoes.

Further north, **Galicia** surpasses every other region with its 800 miles of coastline; most Galician shellfish dishes are prepared to emphasize freshness. Octopus, spider crab, and mussels are popular here, as is *empanada gallega*, the Galician pastry filled with everything from pork to chicken to fish. In **Asturias,** dried beans rule the kitchen; *fabada asturiana*, a bean and sausage stew, is the best-known hearty dish for regaining strength after a long work day. Apples, cider, and cow's milk are also especially good here. **Cantabrian** sardines, tuna, and anchovies are among the best in Spain. Food in the **País Vasco** rivals that of Catalunya in national prominence. Popular dishes include *bacalao* (salted codfish), *angulas* (baby eels), and squid *en su tinta* (in its own ink). It was also in Basque country that Spain's first gastronomic society was founded on January 1, 1900; these all-male cooking groups have grown over the past century and now number over 1,000.

In **Catalunya,** the Roman trilogy of olives, vineyards, and wheat dominates, and seafood, grilling, and unique sauces are key elements of many meals. **Aragonese** cuisine reflects the huge size of the region, ranging from cured hams to egg dishes to candied fruits. **Navarra** boasts the best red peppers in Spain, as well as the famous Roncal cheese; cooked game, sausages, and caldron stews are popular here. **La Rioja** is known for its pork, vegetables and above all *vino* (wine). **Valencia,** on the East Coast, has been the home of *paella* and oranges ever since Arab short-grain rice and American oranges were introduced to the area. Less than 200 years old, *paella* has evolved from a simple vegetable-rice dish to an increasingly elaborate mix of seafood, vegetables, poultry, and meats.

MEALS AND DINING HOURS

Discover the leisurely pace of the Spanish lifestyle through its dining hours. Spaniards start their day with a continental breakfast of coffee or thick, liquid chocolate combined with *bollos* (rolls) and *churros* (lightly fried fritters). Mid-morning they often have another cafe with a *tapa* to tide them over to the main meal of the day, *la comida*, eaten around 2 or 3pm. *La comida* consists of several courses: an appetizer of soup or salad; a main course of meat, fish, or a twist like *paella*; and a dessert of fruit, cheese, or sweets. Supper at home, *la cena*, tends to be light, usually a sandwich or tortilla consumed around 8pm. Eating out starts anywhere between 9pm and midnight. Going out for *tapas* is an integral part of the Spanish lifestyle; groups of friends will often spend several hours moving from bar to bar.

EATING OUT

While some restaurants are open from 8am to 1 or 2am, most serve meals from 1 or 2 to 4pm only and in the evening from 8pm until midnight. Some hints: eating at the bar is cheaper than at tables, and the check won't be brought to your table unless you request it. (*"La cuenta, por favor."*) Service in Spain is notoriously slow and at times frustrating. Many *bar-restaurantes* (and some *hostales*) have cozy *comedores* (dining rooms) on the premises. Diners will repeatedly come across three options. **Platos combinados** (combination platters) include a main course and side dishes on a single plate, plus bread and sometimes a drink. The **menú del día**—two or three dishes, bread, wine/beer/mineral water, and dessert—is Spaniards' common choice for the *comida*, a good deal at roughly €5-9. Those dining **á la carte** choose from individual entrees. Large *tapas*, often comparable in size to entrees, are called *raciones*.

DRINKY DRINKS

Cultivate your palate with the fine potpourri of Spanish wine. When in doubt among your choices, the *vino de la casa* (house wine) is an economical, often delectable choice. Also good are *vino tinto* (red wine), *vino blanco* (white wine), or *rosado* (rosé). For a taste, get a *chato* (small glass). Mild, fragrant reds are Spain's best vintages, but the crops of fine wines are vast. La Mancha's **Valdepeñas** are light, dry reds and whites, consumed without long aging. Catalunya's whites and **cavas** (champagnes) and Aragón's Cariñena wines pack bold punches. **Sidra** (alcoholic cider) from Asturias and País Vasco, and **sangría** (a red-wine punch with sliced peaches and oranges, seltzer, sugar, and a dash of brandy) are delicious alcoholic options. A popular light drink is *tinto de verano*, a cool mix of red wine and carbonated mineral water. **Jerez (sherry),** Spain's most famous wine, hails from Jerez de la Frontera in Andalucía. Try the dry *fino* and *amontillado* as aperitifs, or finish off a rich supper with the sweet dulce. The manzanilla produced in Sanlúcar has a salty aftertaste, ascribed to the region's salt-filled soil.

Wash down your *tapas* with a *caña de cerveza*, a normal-sized draft-beer. A *tubo* is a little bigger than a *caña*, and small beers go by different names—*corto* in Castilla, *zurito* in Basque. Pros refer to **mixed drinks** as *copas*. Beer and Schweppes is a **clara.** A **calimocho,** popular with young crowds, mixes Coca-Cola and red wine. Older drinkers prefer **sol y sombra** (brandy and anise). Spain whips up numerous non-alcoholic quenchers as well, notably **horchata de chufa** (made by pressing almonds and ice together) and the flavored crushed-ice **granizados.** *Café solo* means black coffee; add a touch of milk for a *nube*; a little more and it's a *café cortado*; half milk, half coffee and you have *café con leche*.

CUSTOMS & ETIQUETTE

Although Spaniards are known for being proud, they are generally polite, courteous, and kind to foreigners. Attempts at "correct behavior" will not go unnoticed; you'll be treated with cooperative friendliness if you make the extra effort.

TABOOS. As is to be expected, Spaniards take offense to critical comments about their country, their leaders, and their customs. Foreigners should be careful when approaching Spanish women; overly *macho* fathers, husbands, or boyfriends can be unusually sensitive and aggressive. Though dress in Spain is obviously more casual in the hot summer months than in winter, strapless tops on women and collarless t-shirts on men are generally unacceptable. Be cautious of shorts and flip-flops; they may be seen as disrespectful in some public establishments.

PUBLIC BEHAVIOR. Strongly individualistic, Spaniards are formally polite in mannerisms and social behavior. To blend in, it's a good idea to be as formal as possible upon a first meeting. Introduce yourself in detail, giving more than just your *nombre* (name). You'll be welcomed openly and made to feel at home if you mention who you are, where you're from, and what you are doing in Spain. Be sure to address Spaniards as *Señor* (Mr.), *Señora* (Mrs.), or *Señorita* (Ms.), and don't be surprised if you get kissed on both cheeks instead of receiving a handshake. Also, don't yawn or stretch in public; this is considered disrespectful, and your actions could garner some glares and grimaces from Spaniards.

TABLE MANNERS. Having a meal, whether at home or at a restaurant, is one of the most popular forms of socializing in Spain. The key to acceptance at a Spanish *mesa* is not imitating *how* Spaniards eat, but rather eating *when* they do. You'll encounter odd looks if you demand an evening meal at six o'clock. If you'd like to pick up a few Spanish table manners, be sure to eat with both your fork *and* your knife in hand at all times, and make sure both hands are visible during the meal.

THE ARTS

From the dark solemnity of El Greco's paintings to the playful exuberance of Gaudí's buildings, Spanish art and architecture ranges from the austere to the ostentatious. While the tradition has been shaped by foreign influences, Spain's dazzling architecture, paintings, and literature are distinctly Spanish.

ARCHITECTURE

Spanish architecture is as impressive and varied as the civilizations that have ruled the Iberian peninsula. Remnants of Spain's glorious past dot the landscape, hinting at the wealth and power that once flowed over the land. Bold postmodern projects promise to maintain Spain's proud architectural tradition for years to come.

ANCIENT AND EARLY MODERN. Scattered **Roman ruins** testify to six centuries of colonization. Highlights include some of the finest Roman ruins in existence: the aqueduct in Segovia, the theater in Mérida, and the town of Tarragona. Other vestiges of Spain's Roman past lie at the ruined towns of Itálica (near Sevilla), Sagunto (near Valencia), and Empúries (near Palafrugell).

After the invasion of 711, the **Moors** constructed mosques and palaces throughout southern Spain. Because the Qur'an forbade human and animal representation, Moorish architects thought of other ways to adorn their buildings, lavishing them with stylized geometric designs, red-and-white horseshoe arches, and ornate tiles. They combined intricate and elegant decorative work with courtyards, pools, and fountains to create buildings designed to delight the senses. The spectacular 14th-century **Alhambra** in Granada, said to be one of the most beautiful buildings in the world, and the **Mezquita** in Córdoba epitomize the Moorish style. Long periods of peaceful coexistence of Islam and Christianity created two architectural movements unique to Spain—**Mozarabic** and **Mudéjar.** Christians living under Muslim rule adopted Moorish design elements to create the distinctive Mozarabic style. The more prevalent and striking Mudéjar architecture was created by Moors living under Christian rule in the years between the Christian resurgence (11th century) and the Reconquista (1492). Sevilla's Alcázar is an exquisite example of Mudéjar.

The **Spanish Gothic** style brought experimentation with pointed arches, flying buttresses, slender walls, airy spaces, and stained-glass windows. The first Gothic cathedral in Spain was Burgos (begun 1221). Along with those in Toledo and León, the cathedral of Burgos is one of the finest examples of the Spanish Gothic style. The largest Gothic cathedral in world is in Sevilla.

THE RENAISSANCE. New World riches inspired the **Plateresque** ("in the manner of a silversmith") style, a flashy extreme of Gothic that transformed wealthier parts of Spain. Intricate stonework and extravagant use of gold and silver splashed 15th- and 16th-century buildings, most notably in Salamanca, where the university practically drips with ornamentation. In the late 16th century, Italian Renaissance innovations in perspective and symmetry arrived in Spain to sober up the Plateresque style. El Escorial (1563-1584), Felipe II's immense palace cum monastery, was designed by one of Spain's most prominent architects, Juan de Herrera.

BAROQUE. Opulence seized center stage in 17th- and 18th-century **Baroque** Spain. The Churriguera brothers pioneered a new style—called **Churrigueresque**—which reflected the wealth and ostentation of the era. Wildly elaborate ornamentation with extensive sculptural detail gave buildings of this period a rich exuberance.

MODERN AND POSTMODERN. In the late 19th and early 20th centuries, Catalunya's **Modernistas** burst on the scene in Barcelona, led by the eccentric genius of Antoni Gaudí, Lluís Domènech i Montaner, and Josep Puig y Cadafalch. Modernista structures defied any and all previous standards with their voluptuous curves and unusual textures. The new style was inspired in part by Mudéjar but far more so by organic forms and unbridled imagination. **La Sagrada Família** and **La Casa Milà,** both by Gaudí, stand as the most famous examples of Catalan Modernisme.

In the mid-20th century, Josep Lluís Sert helped introduce European Modernism to Spain with his stark concrete buildings. Spain's outstanding architectural tradition continues today with current stars like Ricardo Bofill, Rafael Moneo, and Santiago Calatrava, who has become the most recent sensation with his elegant steel-and-crystal buildings in Valencia and unmistakable bridges in Sevilla, Mérida, and Bilbao. Spain has also acquired more than a few landmarks from foreign architects including the stunning Guggenheim Museum in Bilbao by American Frank Gehry.

PAINTING

Over its long history, Spanish painting has seen a series of luminaries separated by several lulls. Flemish, French, and Italian influences have often predominated, but such heavy hitters as El Greco, Diego Velázquez, Francisco Goya, and Pablo Picasso have forged a dazzling, distinctive, and hugely influential body of work.

EARLY AND RENAISSANCE. In the 11th and 12th centuries, fresco painters and manuscript illuminators adorned churches and their libraries along the Camino de Santiago and in León and Toledo. **Pedro Berruguete's** (1450-1504) use of traditional gold backgrounds in his religious paintings exemplifies the Italian-influenced style of early Renaissance works. Not until after Spain's imperial ascendance in the 16th century did painting reach its **Golden Age** (roughly 1492-1650). Felipe II imported foreign art and artists in order to jump-start native production and embellish his palace, El Escorial. Although he supposedly came to Spain seeking a royal commission, Cretan-born Doménikos Theotokópoulos, known as **El Greco** (1541-1614), was rejected by Felipe II for his intensely personal style. Confounding his contemporaries, El Greco (or The Greek) has received newfound appreciation in the 20th century for his haunting, elongated figures and dramatic use of light and color.

Felipe IV's foremost court painter, **Diego Velázquez** (1599-1660), is generally considered one of the world's greatest artists. Whether depicting Felipe IV's family or lowly court jesters and dwarves, Velázquez painted with naturalistic precision; working slowly and meticulously, he captured light with a virtually photographic quality. Nearly half of this Sevillian-born artist's works reside in the Prado, notably his famous *Las Meninas* (1656; see **Museo del Prado,** p. 121). Other noteworthy Golden Age painters include **José de Ribera** (1591-1652), **Francisco de Zurbarán** (1598-1664), and **Bartolomé Estebán Murillo** (1618-1682).

FROM MODERN TO AVANT-GARDE. During the era of Spain's waning power, **Francisco de Goya** (1746-1828) ushered European painting into the modern age. Hailing from provincial Aragón, Goya rose to the position of official court painter under the degenerate Carlos IV. Not bothering with flattery, Goya's depictions of the royal family come closer to caricature, as can attest Queen María Luisa's haughty, cruel jawline in Goya's famous *The Family of Charles IV* (1800). His series of etchings *The Disasters of War* (1810-1814), which includes the landmark *El dos de mayo* and *El tres de mayo*, records the horrific Napoleonic invasion of 1808. Deaf and despondent in his later years, Goya painted more nightmarish and wildly fantastic visions, inspiring expressionist and surrealist artists of the next century. The Prado museum has a room full of his chilling Black Paintings (1820-1823).

It is hard to imagine an artist who has had as profound an effect upon 20th-century painting as Andalucian-born **Pablo Picasso** (1881-1973). A child prodigy, Picasso headed for Barcelona, then a hothouse for Modernist architecture and political activism. Bouncing between Barcelona and Paris, Picasso in 1900 inaugurated his Blue Period, characterized by somber depictions of society's outcasts. His permanent move to Paris in 1904 initiated his Rose Period as he probed into the engrossing lives of clowns and acrobats. With his French colleague Georges Braque, he founded **Cubism,** a method of painting objects simultaneously from multiple perspectives. His 1937 mural *Guernica* portrays the bombing of that Basque city by Nazi planes in cahoots with Fascist forces during the Spanish Civil War (see **The Tragedy of Guernica,** p. 493). A protest against violence and fascism, *Guernica* now resides in the Centro de Arte Reina Sofía in Madrid (see p. 391).

Catalan painter and sculptor **Juan Miró** (1893-1983) created simplistic, almost child-like shapes in bright, primary colors. His haphazard, undefined squiggles rebelled against the authoritarian society of the post-Civil War years. By contrast, fellow Catalan **Salvador Dalí** (1904-1989) scandalized society and leftist intellectuals in France and Spain by supporting the Fascists. Dalí's name is synonymous with **Surrealism.** A self-congratulatory fellow, Dalí founded the Teatro-Museo Dalí in Figueres, the second-most visited museum in Spain after the Prado.

Since Franco's death in 1975, a new generation of artists has thrived. With new museums in Madrid, Barcelona, Valencia, Sevilla, and Bilbao, Spanish painters and sculptors once again have a national forum for their work. Catalan **Antonio Tapiès** constructs unorthodox collages and is a founding member of the self-proclaimed "Abstract Generation," while **Antonio López García** creates hyperrealist paintings.

LITERATURE

Spain's rich literary tradition blossomed in the late Middle Ages (1000-1500). The 12th-century *Cantar de Mío Cid* (Song of My Cid), Spain's most important epic poem, chronicles national hero El Cid's life and military triumphs, from his exile from Castilla to his return to grace in the king's court. Fernando de Rojas's *La Celestina* (1499), a tragicomedy most noted for its strong, witch-like female character that helps two star-crossed lovers was made into a film with Penélope Cruz in 1996. *La Celestina* helped pave the way for picaresque novels like *Lazarillo de Tormes* (1554) and *Guzmán de Alfarache* (1599), rags-to-riches stories about mischievous boys (*pícaros*) with mostly good hearts. This literary form surfaced during Spain's **Golden Age,** which spanned the 16th and 17th centuries. Poetry thrived in this era; some consider the sonnets and romances of **Garcilaso de la Vega** the most perfect ever written in Castilian. Along with his friend **Joan Boscán,** Garcilaso introduced the "Italian" (or Petrarchan) sonnet to Iberia. The Golden Age also bred outstanding dramas, including works from **Calderón de la Barca** and **Lope de Vega,** who collectively wrote over 2,300 plays. Both espoused the Neoplatonic view of love, claiming it changes one's life dramatically and eternally.

Miguel de Cervantes's two-part *Don Quijote de la Mancha* (1605-1615)—often considered the world's first novel—is the most famous work of Spanish literature. Cervantes relates the hilarious parable of the hapless Don and his servant Sancho Panza, who think themselves bold caballeros (knights) out to save the world.

The 18th century brought a period of economic and political decline accompanied by a belated Enlightenment movement; one of the movement's most important figures was **José Cadalso,** author of the *Cartas Marruecas* (1789). The 19th century inspired contrasting variety, including the biting journalistic prose of **Mariano José de Larra, José Zorrilla's** romantic poem *Don Juan Tenorio* (1844), a reworking of Tirso de Molina's *El burlador de Sevilla,* **Benito Pérez Galdos's** prolific realism, and the naturalistic novels of **Leopoldo Alas ("Clarín").** Essayist **Miguel de Unamuno** (whose novel *El árbol de la ciencia* is still the most sold-out book in Spain) and cultural critic **José Ortega y Gasset** led the **Generación del 1898,** along with prose writers **Pio Baroja, Ramón María del Valle Incán,** and poets **Antonio Machado** and **Juan Ramón Jimenez;** reacting to Spain's defeat in the Spanish-American War (1898), these nationalistic authors argued, through essays and novels, that each individual must spiritually and ideologically attain internal peace before society can do the same. Unamuno and Ortega y Gasset single-handedly influenced the **Generación del 1927,** a group of experimental lyric poets who wrote Surrealist and avant-garde poetry. This group included **Jorge Guillén, Federico García Lorca** (assassinated at the start of the Civil War), **Rafael Alberti,** and **Luis Cernuda.**

In the 20th century, the Nobel Committee honored playwright and essayist **Jacinto Benavente y Martínez** (1922), poet **Vicente Aleixandre** (1977), and novelist **Camilo José Cela** (1989). Female writers, like **Mercè Rodoreda** and **Carmen Martín Gaite,** have likewise earned critical acclaim. As Spanish artists are again migrating to Madrid, just as they did in the early part of the century, an avant-garde spirit—known as *La Movida*—has been reborn in the capital. **Ana Rossetti** and **Juana Castro** led a new generation of erotic poets into the 80s, representing the first time in the panorama of Spanish literature that women have taken a place at the forefront.

MUSIC

Flamenco, one of the cultural aspects for which Spain is most famous, is a combination of *cante jondo* (melodramatic song), guitar, and dancing. It originated among Andalucian gypsies and has continued as an extremely popular tradition that today hypnotizes audiences all over the world. While it is possible to buy all manner of flamenco recordings, nothing compares to seeing a live performance. **Andrès Segovia** (1893-1987) was instrumental in investing the guitar with the same renown as the violin and the cello.

Pablo Casals (1876-1973), Spanish cellist, conductor, composer, pianist, and humanitarian, was one of the most influential musicians of the 20th century. To promote world peace, Casals composed the oratorio *The Manger* (1960), which he conducted throughout the world. Barcelona-born **José Carreras** and **Plácido Domingo,** of "three Tenors" fame, are recognized as two of the world's finest opera singers. While American rock is coveted by youth throughout Spain, there is considerable national pride in Spanish rock, which is plentiful and widespread. **Mecano** enthralls audiences around the world, and disco-goers dance all night long to pulsing **bakalao** (comparable to American house). Barcelona band **El Último de la Fila** and big-forum **Héroes del Silencio** are well worth a listen. **Ella Baila Sola** tops the best-selling charts, and other popular groups and soloists are **Presuntos Implicados, Los Rodríguez,** and **Manolo Tena.** And we can't forget **Julio Iglesias,** beloved the world over, and of course, his handsome offspring **Enrique Iglesias.**

PEDRO ALMODÓVAR

The Artistic Link Between Traditional and Modern Spain

There are few places in today's world where the ancient and the modern, the traditional and the unorthodox, and the dignified and the outrageous are intertwined so beautifully as in Spain. Where but Spain do Internet cafes in large cities still shut down for the traditional *siesta*? Where but Spain will the *matador*, that relic of a bygone era, speak to his sweetheart via cell phone before stepping out into the bull ring? Where but Spain do even the busiest of corporate professionals take time out of their hectic daily schedules to ritually engage in *la tertulia* (small talk) over coffee?

Yet Spain was not always such an exemplary amalgam of old and new. For 36 years (1939-1975), under the oppressive dictatorship of General Francisco Franco, Spain seemed to be cut off both from the cultural traditions of its past—Franco had many of the prominent cultural figures of the previous century assassinated, exiled, or censored—as well as the progressive trends of post-modernist Europe.

Pedro Almodóvar was born in Calzada de Calatrava, La Mancha in 1951, during that period of Franco's oppression. After an uninspiring primary school education, Almodóvar moved to Madrid at the tender age of 16 to pursue his passion: filmmaking. The weight of Franco's heavy rule could be felt everywhere in Madrid, but for a liberal adolescent like Almodóvar, the city was a cultural nexus of modernism and freedom. After working various odd jobs that introduced him to the country's emerging middle class, Almodóvar finally saved enough money to buy a cheap camera. Since Franco had closed the city's film schools and imposed harsh censorship on the film industry, Almodóvar learned on his own by going underground, producing a series of graphic flicks that first earned him a reputation as an outrageous and innovative film-maker. Almodóvar gradually gained notoriety in the avant-garde circles of Spanish society; by Franco's death in 1975, he was a leading pop culture figure at the head of *la movida*, the massive liberal movement which formed in response to the previous three decades of oppression.

It was in this period of flux, as Spain searched for its cultural identity in a rapidly changing world, that Almodóvar found the material that would characterize most of his films. Indeed, one of his first big box-office hits, *Law of Desire* (1986), which featured Antonio Banderas as an obsessive homosexual man, horrified the Spanish church with its defiance of traditional Spanish machismo and mores in favor of a more risqué and idiosyncratic portrayal of Spanish society in the early 1980s. *Matador* (1986), was harshly attacked by critics for satirizing bullfighting in the modern era. The turning point in Almodóvar's career came in 1988, when his hit film *Women On The Verge Of A Nervous Breakdown* was nominated for an Oscar for Best Foreign Film. He had succeeded in popularizing his vision of the paradoxical nature of Spanish society for the rest of the world. His characters—drug-dealing nuns, transvestites, and neurotic housewives—became symbols of modern Spain, ironically combining the traditional with the outrageous.

In 2000, Almodóvar's *All About My Mother* won the Oscar for Best Foreign Film. The director's irreverent style has inspired a new generation of Spanish artists, writers, and film makers to push the limits of their imaginations beyond established creative norms. Despite his flair for the unorthodox, Almodóvar remains staunchly Spanish, constantly turning down numerous offers to direct big-budget Hollywood films. Almodóvar is an illustration of the paradox he portrays in his films—that of modern Spain, rising into its promising future while firmly tied to, but also critical of, its past.

Josh Ludmir is a History and Romance Languages & Literature scholar at Harvard University. Josh is a Spanish language tutor and a Researcher-Writer for Let's Go Spain, Portugal, and Morocco 2003.

FILM

One of the greatest influences on Spanish film was not a filmmaker, but a politician: Franco's regime of censorship (1939-1975) defined Spanish film both during and after his rule. Spain's first film, *Ría en un Café* (directed by Fructuos Gelabert), dates to 1897, and director **Segundo de Chomón** is recognized world-wide as a pioneer of early cinema. The Surrealist **Luis Buñuel,** close friends with **Salvador Dalí,** produced several early classics, most notably *Un Chien Andalou* (1929). Later, in exile from Francoist Spain, he produced a number of brilliantly sardonic films including *Belle du Jour* (1967). Meanwhile, in Spain itself, Franco's censorship stifled most creative tendencies and left the public with nothing to watch but cheap westerns and bland spy flicks. As government supervision slacked in the early 1970s, Spanish cinema showed signs of life, led by **Carlos Saura's** dark, subversive hits such as *El Jardín de las Delicias* (1970) and *Cría Cuervos* (1975).

In 1977, in the wake of Franco's death, domestic censorship laws were revoked, bringing artistic freedom along with financial hardship for Spanish filmmakers, who found their films shunned domestically in favor of newly permitted foreign films. Depictions of the exuberant excesses of a super-liberated Spain found increasing attention and respect elsewhere. **Pedro Almodóvar's** *La ley del deseo* (1986), featuring **Antonio Banderas** as a gay man, captures the risqué themes of transgression and sexuality most often treated by contemporary Spanish cinema. (See **Pedro Almodóvar,** p.75). Other directors to look for in Spain include **Bigas Luna,** director of the controversial *Jamón Jamón* (1992), **Fernando Trueba** whose *Belle Epoque* won the Oscar in 1993 for Best Foreign Film, **Alejandro Amenabar**, who has received international acclaim for his 1997 release *Abre los Ojos*, **José Luis Cerda** with his touching film *La Lengua de la Mariposas* (2000), and **Vicente Aranda**.

BULLFIGHTING

The national spectacle that is bullfighting dates, in its modern form, to the early 1700s. Bullfighting's growing popularity meant that Roman amphitheaters like those in Sevilla and Córdoba were restored, and bulls were bred to possess aggressive instincts. The techniques of the modern bullfighter (matador) were developed around 1914 by Juan Belmonte, considered one of the greatest matadors of all time (others include Joselito, Manolete, and Cristina, the first female matador).

A bullfight is divided into three principal stages: in the first, picadors (lancers on horseback) pierce the bull's neck muscles to lower his head for the kill; next, assistants on foot thrust *banderillas* (decorated darts) into his back to enliven the tiring animal for the final stage; finally, the matador has ten minutes to kill his opponent with a sword between the shoulder blades. He can be granted up to five extra minutes if necessary, but after that the bull is taken out alive, much to the matador's disgrace. On the other hand, if the matador has shown special skill and daring, the audience waves white handkerchiefs to implore the bullfight's president to reward him with the coveted ears (and, very rarely, the tail).

Although bullfighting has always had its critics—the Catholic Church in the 17th century felt that the risks made it equivalent to suicide—the late 20th century has seen an especially strong attack from animal rights activists and social workers who feel that its prospect of social mobility leads too many young men to premature deaths. Whatever its merits and faults, bullfighting is an essential element of the Spanish national consciousness. Ernest Hemingway's *The Sun Also Rises* (1926) and *Death in the Afternoon* (1932) reflect on the myths of bullfighting.

THE MEDIA

NEWSPAPERS AND MAGAZINES. *ABC*, tangibly conservative and pro-monarchist, is the oldest national daily paper. It jostles with the more liberal *El País* for Spain's largest readership. *El Mundo* is a younger left-wing daily renowned for its investigative reporting. Barcelona's *La Vanguardia* maintains a substantial Catalan audience, while *La Voz de Galicia* dominates the northwest. *Diario 16*, the more moderate counterpart to *El Mundo*, publishes the popular newsweekly *Cambio 16*, whose main competition is *Tiempo*. *Hola*, the original *revista del corazón* (magazine of the heart), caters to Spain's love affair with aristocratic titles, Julio Iglesias, and "beautiful" people. The nosier, less tasteful tabloid *Semana* has gossip galore and readers aplenty.

TELEVISION. Tune in to news at 3 and 8:30pm on most stations. Programming includes dubbed American movies, sports, melodramatic Latin American *telenovelas* (soaps), game shows, jazzed-up documentaries, and cheesy variety extravaganzas. If all else fails, try *fútbol* games or bullfights.

SPORTS: THE CUP OF LIFE, BABY

¡Viva España! The beat and the glory go on for Spanish sports. **Miguel Indurain,** a Basque hero and Spain's most decorated athlete is remembered fondly by his fans. Old favorites like **Aranxta Sánchez-Vicario** and **Conchita Martínez** and up-and-comers like **Carlos Moya** and **Alex Corretja** have made their names in tennis. Regional specialties spice the sports scene, including *cesta punta* (known internationally as *jai alai*) from Basque country, wind surfing along the southern coast, and skiing in the Sierra Nevadas and the Pyrenees. The most popular sport is, of course, *fútbol*, a uniting passion for Spaniards. The 2002 World Cup enraged Spain, an early favorite, when its team lost to South Korea under a contested referee.

SPAIN

RECOMMENDED READING

English-speaking scribes have penned several first-class Spanish travel narratives. Richard Ford's witty *Handbook for Travellers in Spain and Readers at Home* is a favorite. Most time-honored classics are region-specific, including Washington Irving's *Tales of the Alhambra* and Bloomsbury Circle-expat Gerald Brenan's *South from Granada*. Look for Lucia Graves's account of her life in Mallorca titled *A Woman Unknown: Voices from a Spanish Life* (September 2000).

FICTION, SPANISH AND FOREIGN. Start with the epic story of *Poema del Mío Cid*. Alternatively, if you like reading about how a Spanish hunk steals the virtue of all the ladies in one medieval Spanish town, enjoy Tirso de Molina's *El burlador de Sevilla*. Whet your palate with the über-classic *Don Quijote* by Miguel de Cervantes. Get the abridged version or you'll never finish it. Ever. For gorgeous early 20th century prose, read Nobel-Prize winner Benito Pérez Galdós. His tale of friendship, love, and betrayal in *El Abuelo*, which was made into a movie and nominated for Best Foreign Film in the 2000 Academy Awards, will charm you with its prose and make you weep for its characters' follies. To get a taste of Spain during Franco's regime, read Ana María Matute's wondrous account of growing up in *Primera Memoria*. Spain has also inspired a number of American and British authors. Ernest Hemingway immortalized bullfighting, machismo, and Spain itself in *The Sun Also Rises* and *For Whom the Bell Tolls*.

ART AND ARCHITECTURE. The definitive work on Spanish art history is Bradley Smith's *Spain: A History in Art*. For late 20th-century art, check out William Dyckes's *Contemporary Spanish Art*. If you want to splurge, go for Fred Licht's *Goya* (2001), a must-read for fans of the artist. Books on Pablo Picasso, Salvador Dalí, and Antonín Gaudí can be found with minimal fuss. The standard text on Spanish architecture is Bernard Bevan's *History of Spanish Architecture*. For the 1980s and 90s scoop, peruse Anatzu Zabalbeascoa's *The New Spanish Architecture*. If you really want to know your *arquitectura*, get your hands on *Spain: Contemporary Art and Architecture Handbook* by Sidra Stich.

HISTORY AND CULTURE. Written in 1968, James Michener's best-seller *Iberia* continues to captivate audiences with its thoroughness, insight, and style. *Barcelona*, by Robert Hughes, delves deep into the culture of Catalunya. George Orwell's *Homage to Catalonia*, a personal account of the Spanish Civil War, rivals *Iberia* and *Barcelona* in quality and fame. A handful of other historians and works stand out—Richard Fletcher's comprehensive *Moorish Spain*, J.H. Elliot's masterful *Imperial Spain 1469-1716*, Raymond Carr's *Spain 1808-1975*, and Stanley Payne's *The Franco Regime 1936-1975* on the modern era.

ESSENTIALS

This section is designed to help travelers get their bearings once in Spain. For info about general **travel preparations** (including passports, money, health, packing, and more), consult **Essentials** (p. 8). **Essentials** also has important information for those with specific concerns: **women travelers** (p. 50); **older travelers** (p. 51); **bisexual, gay, and lesbian travelers** (p. 52); **travelers with disabilities** (p. 52); **minority travelers** (p. 53); **travelers with children** (p. 53); and travelers with **dietary concerns** (p. 54). See **Alternatives to Tourism** for information on studying and working in Spain (p. 56).

ENTRANCE REQUIREMENTS

Passport. Required for all citizens of Australia, Canada, Ireland, New Zealand, South Africa, the UK, and US.

Visa. Required only for citizens of South Africa.

Work Permit (p. 58) Required for all foreigners planning to work in Spain.

Driving Permit (p. 45). Recommended for those planning to drive.

EMBASSIES AND CONSULATES

Embassies and consulates are often open Monday through Friday, punctuated by *siestas*. Many consulates are only open mornings. Call ahead for exact hours.

Australian Embassy: Pl. Descubridor Diego de Ordás, 3, **Madrid** 28003 (☎914 41 60 25; fax 914 41 93 00; www.embaustralia.es). **Consulates:** Gran Vía Carlos III, 98, 9th fl., **Barcelona** 08028 (☎933 30 94 96; fax 934 11 09 04); Federico Rubio, 14, **Sevilla** 41004 (☎954 22 09 71; fax 954 21 11 45).

British Embassy: C. Fernando el Santo, 16, **Madrid** 28010 (☎917 00 82 00; fax 917 00 82 72). **Consulate-General:** Edificio Torre de Barcelona, Av. Diagonal, 477, 13th fl., **Barcelona** 08036 (☎933 66 62 00; fax 933 66 62 21). **Consulates:** Marqués de la Ensenada, 16, 2nd fl., **Madrid** 28004 (☎913 08 52 01; fax 913 08 08 82); Alameda de Urquijo, 2, 8th fl., **Bilbao** 48008 (☎944 15 76 00; fax 944 16 76 32); Pl. Mayor, 3D, **Palma de Mallorca** 07002 (☎971 71 24 45; fax 971 71 75 20); Av. Isidoro Macabich, 45, 1st. fl., Apartado 307, **Ibiza** 07800 (☎971 30 18 18; fax 971 30 19 72); Pl. Calvo Sotelo, 1-2, **Alicante** 03001 (☎965 21 60 22; fax 965 14 05 28);

Po. Pereda, 27, **Santander** 39004 (☎942 22 00 00; fax 942 22 29 41); Edificio Eurocom, Bloque Sur, C. Mauricio Moro Pareto, 2 **Málaga** 29006 (☎952 35 23 00; fax 952 35 92 11); Edificio Cataluña, C. Luis Morote, 6, 3rd fl., **Las Palmas** 35007 (☎928 26 25 08; fax 928 26 77 74).

Canadian Embassy: C. Núñez de Balboa, 35, **Madrid** 28001 (☎914 233 250; fax 914 23 32 51; www.canada-es.org). **Consulates:** Elisenda de Pinos, 10 **Barcelona** 08034 (☎932 04 27 00; fax 932 04 27 01); Edificio Horizonte, Pl. Malagueta, 3-1 **Málaga** 29016 (☎952 223 346; fax 952 224 023).

Irish Embassy: Po. Castellana, 46, 4th fl., **Madrid,** 28046 (☎914 36 40 93; fax 914 35 16 77). **Consulate:** Gran Vía Carlos III, 94, **Barcelona** 08028 (☎345 1 90 21; fax 345 11 29 21).

New Zealand Embassy: Pl. Lealtad, 2, 3rd fl., **Madrid** 28014 (☎915 23 02 26; fax 915 23 01 71). **Consulate:** Travesera de Gracia, 64, 2nd fl., **Barcelona** 08006 (☎932 09 03 99; fax 932 02 08 90).

South African Embassy: Claudio Coello, 91, 6th fl., **Madrid** 28006 (☎914 36 37 80; fax 915 77 74 14). **Consulates:** Teodora Lamadrid, 7-11, **Barcelona** 08022 (☎/fax 934 18 05 38); Las Mercedes, 31, Las Arenas, **Vizcaya** 48930 (☎ fax 944 64 11 24); C. Alvareda, 54, 2nd fl. **Las Palmas de Gran Canaria** 35008 (☎928 26 54 52; fax 928 22 49 75).

US Embassy: C. Serrano, 75, **Madrid** 28006 (☎915 87 22 00; fax 915 87 23 03). **Consulate General:** Po. Reina Elisenda de Montcada, 23, **Barcelona** 08034 (☎932 80 22 27; fax 932 05 52 06). **Consulates:** Po. de las Delicias, 7, **Sevilla** 41012 (☎954 23 18 85; fax 954 23 20 40); Edificio ARCA, C. Los Martínez Escobar, 3, Oficina 7, **Las Palmas** 35007 (☎928 27 12 59; fax 928 22 58 63); Dr. Romagosa 1-2 J **Valencia** 46002 (☎ 963 51 69 73; fax 963 52 95 65); Cantón Grande, 6-8 E, **La Coruña** 15003 (☎981 21 32 33; fax 981 22 88 08); Av. Jaime III, 26, Entresuelo H-1, **Palma de Mallorca** 07012 (☎971 72 26 60; fax 971 71 87 55).

TRANSPORTATION

Transportation to and within Spain is generally efficient, comfortable, and reliable. The easiest, quickest method of entering Spain is by plane, although Barcelona is well-connected to the European rail system. Despite the romanticized view of European train travel, buses offer the most extensive coverage and are the best option for short trips. Spain's islands are accessible by plane and ferry. For more specific info on island travel, see **Balearic Islands** (p. 62) and **Canary Islands** (p. 550). For general info on traveling in Europe, see **Getting There,** p. 33.

BY PLANE

All major international airlines offer service to Madrid and Barcelona, most serve the Balearic and Canary Islands, and many serve Spain's smaller cities. **Iberia** (in US and Canada ☎800-772-4642; in UK ☎45 601 28 54; in Spain ☎902 40 05 00; in South Africa ☎11 884 92 55; in Ireland ☎1 407 30 17; www.iberia.com) serves all domestic locations and all major international cities. **Aviaco,** a subsidiary of Iberia, covers mostly domestic routes, with a few connections to London and Paris. Some fares purchased in the US require a 21-day minimum advance purchase. Iberia's two less-established domestic competitors often offer cheaper fares and are worth looking into. **Air Europa** (in US ☎888-238-7672 or 718-244-6016; in Spain ☎ 902 30 06 00; www.air-europa.com) flies out of New York City and most European cities to Madrid, Málaga, Tenerife, and Santiago de Compostela. Discounts available for youth and senior citizens. No service Wednesdays or Sundays during the summer. **SpanAir** (in US ☎888-545-5757; in Spain ☎902 13 14 15; fax 971 49 25 53; www.spanair.com) offers international and domestic flights.

SpanAir Spain Pass: Good for flying to any airport within Spain, including Ibiza, Mallorca and Menorca. No minimum stay; maximum stay 6 months. Reservations must be made before arriving in Spain. Valid for 1 year. Under 12 65% discount. 3 tickets US$150 (€158), 4 tickets US$200 (€211), 5 tickets US$250 (€265). Additional tickets US$50 (€53). **SpanAir Spain Pass B** is the same as Spain Pass A, but also includes Lanzarote, Gran Canaria, or Tenerife. 3 tickets US$265 (€280), 4 tickets US$325 (€343), 5 tickets US$385 (€407). Additional tickets US$60 (€63).

Iberiabono España: One-way coupons good for all mainland airports and the Canary and Balearic Islands. Reservations must be made before arriving in Spain, and you must purchase your international return ticket before starting your trip. Minimum purchase 3 coupons. Mainland and Balearics, 3 coupons €200, 4 coupons €259. Mainland and Canary Islands, 3 coupons €348, 4 coupons €402.

BY TRAIN

Spanish trains are clean, relatively punctual, and reasonably priced, but tend to bypass many small towns. Spain's national railway is **RENFE** (www.renfe.es). Avoid *transvía*, *semidirecto*, or *correo* trains—they are very slow.

AVE (Alta Velocidad Española): High-speed trains dart between Madrid and Sevilla, Ciudad Real, Puertollano, and Córdoba. AVE trains soar above others in comfort, price, and speed. The 10am and noon trains are cheapest; student discounts available.

Talgo 200: Sleek trains zip passengers in air-conditioned compartments from Madrid to Málaga, Cádiz/Huelva, or Algeciras. It's more comfortable, possibly faster, and twice as pricey as Cercanías-Regionales trains. Changing a Talgo 200 ticket carries a 20% fine.

Grandes Líneas: RENFE's business unit for long distance travel. A wide range of lines including Euromed, Alaris, Arco, Talgo, and Trenhotel meet every traveler's needs.

Intercity: Cheaper than Talgo, but fewer stops. A/C and comfy. 5 lines: Madrid-Valencia, Madrid-Zaragoza-Barcelona, Madrid-Alicante, Madrid-Zaragoza-Logroño-Pamplona, and Madrid-Murcia-Cartagena.

Estrella: A pretty slow night train that has *literas* (bunks).

Cercanías: Commuter trains from large cities to suburbs and towns, with frequent stops.

Regional: Like cercanías but older; multi-stop, cheap rides to small towns and cities.

There is absolutely no reason to buy a Eurail pass if you are planning on traveling just within Spain and Portugal. Trains are cheap, so a pass saves little money. For the most part buses are an easier and more efficient means of traveling around Spain. Visit www.raileurope.com for more specific information on the passes below.

Spain Flexipass offers 3 days of unlimited travel in a 2mo. period. 1st-class €211; 2nd-class €164. Each additional rail-day (up to 7) €37 for 1st-class, €32 for 2nd-class.

Iberic Railpass is good for 3 days of unlimited 1st-class travel in Spain and Portugal for €217. Each additional rail-day (up to 7) €48.

Spain Rail n' Drive Pass is good for 3 days of unlimited 1st-class train travel and 2 days of unlimited mileage in a rental car within a 2mo. period. Prices €252-343, depending on how many travelers and type of car. Up to 2 additional rail-days and extra car days are also available, and a 3rd and 4th person can join in the car using only a Flexipass.

BY BUS

Bus routes, far more comprehensive than the rail network, provide the only public transportation to many isolated areas and almost always cost less than trains. They are generally quite comfortable, though leg room may be limited. For those traveling primarily within one region, buses are the best method of transport.

Spain has numerous private companies; the lack of a centralized bus company may make itinerary planning an ordeal. Companies' routes rarely overlap; it's unlikely that more than one will serve your intended destination. We list below the major national companies, along with the phone number of the Madrid or Igualada office; you will likely use other companies for travel within a region.

ALSA (☎902 42 22 42; www.alsa.es). Serves Madrid, Galicia, Asturias, and Castilla y León. Also to Portugal, Morocco, France, Italy, and Poland.

Alosa (☎934 90 00 00; www.alosa.es). Operating primarily in Northeastern Spain, Alosa serves Barcelona, Huesca, Jaca, Lérida, and Pamplona.

Alsina-Graels (☎954 41 88 11). Primarily serves Southern Spain, including Granada, Jaén, Sevilla, and Córdoba.

Auto-Res/Cunisa, S.A. (☎902 02 09 99; www.auto-res.net). From Madrid to Castilla y León, Extremadura, Galicia, and Valencia.

Busabout (www.busabout.com, see p. 43). Serves: Barcelona, Bilbao, Granada, Madrid, Pamplona, Salamanca, San Sebastián, Sevilla, Tarifa, Toledo, Valencia, and Zaragoza.

Daibus (☎902 27 79 99). Serving Algeciras, Madrid, Málaga, and Marbella.

Enatcar (☎915 27 99 27). Spain's major national long-haul bus company.

Julia Tours (☎913 35 18 97; www.julia-tours.es). Runs throughout Iberia and Western Europe, and to Morocco.

Linebús (☎914 26 28 03). Runs to France, the UK, Netherlands, Italy, and Morocco.

Samar, S.A. (☎914 68 48 39). To Aragón, Toulouse (in France), Andorra, and Portugal.

BY CAR

For more info on renting and driving a car, see p. 45. Spain's highway system connects major cities by four-lane autopistas with plenty of service stations. **Speeders beware:** police can "photograph" the speed and license plate of your car, and issue a ticket without pulling you over. Purchase **gas** in super (97-octane), normal (92-octane), diesel, and unleaded. Prices are astronomical by North American standards: about (€1.40-1.50 per liter). **Renting** a car in Spain is considerably cheaper than in many other European countries. Try **Atesa** (☎902 10 01 01), Spain's largest national rental agency. The Spanish automobile association is **Real Automóbil Club de España (RACE),** C. José Abascal, 10, Madrid (☎915 94 74 75; fax 915 94 73 29).

BY THUMB

Hitchers report that Castilla and Andalucía are long, hot waits; hitchhiking out of Madrid is virtually impossible. The Mediterranean Coast and the islands are much more promising. Approaching people for rides at gas stations near highways and rest stops purportedly gets results. Let's Go does not recommend hitchhiking.

MONEY

Banking hours in Spain from June through September are generally Monday through Friday 9am to 2pm; from October to May, banks are also open Saturday 9am to 1pm. Some banks are also open in the afternoon. **Santander Central Hispano** often provides good exchange rates. For more info on money, see p. 14.

Tipping is not very common in Spain. In restaurants, all prices include service charge. Satisfied customers occasionally toss in some spare change—usually no more than 5%—but this is purely optional. Many people give train, airport, and hotel porters €1 per bag while taxi drivers sometimes get 5-10%. **Bargaining** is really only common at flea markets and with street vendors.

Spain has a 7% **Value Added Tax,** known as IVA, on all restaurant and accommodations. The prices listed in *Let's Go* include IVA unless otherwise mentioned. Retail goods bear a much higher 16% IVA, although listed prices are usually inclusive. Non-EU citizens who have stayed in the EU fewer than 180 days can claim back the tax paid on purchases at the airport. Ask the shop where you have made the purchase to supply you with a tax return form.

SAFETY AND SECURITY

MEDICAL EMERGENCY ☎112	LOCAL POLICE: ☎092. NATIONAL POLICE: ☎091. GUARDIA CIVIL: ☎061.

PERSONAL SAFETY. Spain has a low crime rate, but visitors can always fall victim to tourist-related crimes. Tourists should take particular care in Madrid, especially in El Centro, and in Barcelona around Las Ramblas. If visiting the Costa del Sol in a car, be aware of the fact that this area has seen increased car theft in recent years. If using a car in Spain you happen to experience car problems, be wary of people posing as "Good Samaritans." Drivers should be extremely careful about accepting help from anyone other than a uniformed Spanish police officer or *Guardia Civil* (Civil Guard.) Travelers who accept unofficial assistance should keep their valuables in sight and at hand. For those travelers using public transportation, it is essential to be on the lookout for potential muggings and pickpocketing. Scams such as squirting mustard on clothing and asking for street directions are often employed for such purposes. For more general safety tips, see p. 18.

TERRORISM. Basque terrorism concerns all travelers in Spain and is a highly controversial issue both domestically and internationally. ETA, or Euskadi Ta Askatasuna (meaning Basque Homeland and Freedom), is the militant wing of the Basque separatist movement. It was founded in 1959 to fight for Basque self-determination, concentrating on establishing the Basque region as its own independent country, distinct from Spain and France. ETA attacks have resulted in more than 800 deaths since 1968. In 1998, the Spanish government issued the Lizarra Declaración, which called for an open dialogue between all involved parties, and ETA publicly declared a truce eight days later. However, ETA ended the cease-fire after 14 months. It is blamed for 39 deaths since November 1999, and 26 car bombings since January 2001. ETA has historically aimed its attacks at the police, military, and other Spanish government targets, but in March 2001, ETA issued a communique announcing its intention to target Spanish tourist areas. Though several suspected ETA members have been arrested in recent months and the Spanish government has succeeded in preventing numerous attacks, the ETA has continued a relatively active terrorist campaign. In June 2002, the ETA carried out a series of bombings in resort towns along the Costa del Sol and in northern Spain during an EU summit in Sevilla. While there may be some risk to the traveler, the attacks are very targeted and are not considered random acts of terrorism.

HEALTH

There are no particular health risks associated with traveling in Spain. Be sure to be up to date on your vaccinations for tetanus-diphtheria, measles, and chickenpox. If traveling during flu season, which runs from November through April, add the flu shot to your case. For more general info on travel-related **health** concerns, see p. 20. The public health care system in Spain is very reliable; in an emergency, seek out the *urgencias* (emergency) section of the nearest hospital. For smaller concerns, it is probably best to go to a private clinic to avoid the frustration of long lines.

Expect to pay cash up front (though most travel insurance will pick up the tab later) and bring your passport and other forms of identification. A single visit to a clinic in Spain can cost anywhere from €70-180, depending upon the service. You can visit the following site for the most recent updates on travel-related health concerns in Spain: www.mdtravelhealth.com/destinations/europe/spain.html.

Farmacias in Spain are also very helpful. A duty system has been set up so that at least one farmacia is open at all times in each town; look for a lighted green cross. Spanish pharmacies are not the place to find your cheap summer flip-flops or greeting cards, but they sell contraceptives, common drugs and many prescription drugs; they can answer simple medical questions and help you find a doctor.

ACCOMMODATIONS

YOUTH HOSTELS

Red Española de Albergues Juveniles (REAJ), C. Galera, 1a, Sevilla 41001 (☎954 216 803; fax 954 211 849), the Spanish Hostelling International (HI) affiliate, runs 165 youth hostels year-round. Prices depend on location (typically some distance away from town center) and services offered, but are generally €9-15 for guests under 26 and higher for those 26 and over. Breakfast is usually included; lunch and dinner are occasionally offered at an additional charge. Hostels usually lockout around 11:30am and have curfews between midnight and 3am. As a rule, don't expect much privacy—rooms typically have four to 20 beds in them. To reserve a bed in high season (July-Aug. and during fiestas), call in advance. A national **Youth Hostel Card** is usually required (see **Hostels,** p. 26). HI cards are available from Spain's youth travel company, **TIVE.** Occasionally, guests can stay in a hostel without one and pay extra, or pay extra per night for six nights to become a member.

SPAIN

PENSIONES, HOSTALES, AND HOTELES

Spanish accommodations have many aliases, distinguished by the different grades of rooms. The cheapest and barest options are **casas de huéspedes** and **hospedajes.** While **pensiones** and **fondas** tend to be a bit nicer, all are essentially just boarding houses. Higher up the ladder, **hostales** generally have sinks in bedrooms and provide sheets and lockers, while **hostal-residencias** are similar to hotels in overall quality. The government rates *hostales* on a two-star system; even establishments receiving one star are typically quite comfortable. The system also fixes each *hostal's* prices, posted in the lounge or main entrance. *Hostal* owners invariably dip below the official rates, especially in the off season (Sept.-May).

The highest-priced accommodations are **hoteles,** which have a bathroom in each room but are usually on the pricey side for the budget traveler. The top-notch hotels are the handsome **Paradores Nacionales**—castles, palaces, convents, and historical buildings that have been converted into luxurious hotels and often are interesting sights in their own right. For a *parador*, €75 per night is a bargain. If you have trouble with rates or service, ask for the **libro de reclamaciones** (complaint book), which by law must be produced on demand. The argument will usually end immediately, since all complaints must be forwarded to the authorities within 48 hours. Report any problems to tourist offices who may help you resolve disputes.

ALTERNATIVE ACCOMMODATIONS

In less-touristed areas, **casas particulares** (private residences) may sometimes be the only option. **Casas rurales** (rural cottages) and **casas rústicas** (farmhouses), referred to as *agroturismo*, have overnight rates from €6-21. In the Pyrenees and Picos de Europa, there are several **refugios,** rustic mountain huts for hikers.

CAMPING

In Spain, **campgrounds** are generally the cheapest choice for two or more people. Most charge separate fees per person, per tent, and per car; others charge for a *parcela*—a small plot of land—plus per-person fees. Although it may seem like an inexpensive option, prices can get high for lone travelers and even for pairs. Campgrounds are categorized on a three-class system, with rating and prices based on amenity quality. Like hostels, they must post fees within view of the entrance. They must also provide sinks, showers, and toilets. Most tourist offices provide information on official areas, including the hefty *Guía de campings*.

KEEPING IN TOUCH

Some useful **communication information** (including international access codes, calling card numbers, country codes, operator and directory assistance, and emergency numbers) is listed on the **inside back cover.**

TELEPHONES. The central Spanish phone company is *Telefónica*. Phone booths are marked by signs that say *Teléfono público* or *Locutorio*; most bars have pay phones, though they are often only coin-operated. The best way to make local calls is with a phone card, issued in denominations of €6 and €12 and sold at tobacconists (*estancos* or *tabacos*, identifiable by brown signs with yellow lettering and tobacco leaf icons) and most post offices. Ask tobacconists for calling cards known as *Phonepass*: for €6 it gives you 62 minutes on the public phones for calls to the US. For an additional €6, get 150 minutes. International calls can be made using phone cards but are very expensive; the best way to call home is with an international calling card issued by your phone company. Numbers for obtaining calling cards from home are in the **Essentials** section (see p. 32).

FAX. Most Spanish post offices have fax services. Some photocopy shops and telephone offices (*Telefónica*) also offer fax service, but they tend to charge more than post offices, and faxes can only be sent, not received. Cybercafes are also becoming increasingly popular places to send faxes at cheap rates.

MAIL. Air mail (*por avión*) takes five to eight business days to reach the US or Canada; service is faster to the UK and Ireland and slower to Australia and New Zealand. Standard postage is €0.70 to North America. Surface mail (*por barco*), while considerably less expensive than air mail, can take over a month, and packages will take two to three months. Registered or express mail (*registrado* or *certificado*), is the most reliable way to send a letter or parcel home, and takes four to seven business days. Spain's overnight mail is not worth the added expense, since it isn't exactly "overnight." For better service, try private companies such as DHL, UPS, or the Spanish company SEUR; look under *mensajerías* in the yellow pages. Their reliability, however, comes at a high cost. Stamps are sold at post offices and tobacconists (*estancos* or *tabacos*). Mail letters and postcards from yellow mailboxes scattered through cities, or from the post office in small towns.

EMAIL. Email is easily accessible within Spain and much quicker and more reliable than the regular mail system. An increasing number of bars offer Internet access for a fee of €1.20-4.20. Cybercafes are listed in most towns and all cities. In small towns, if Internet access is not listed, check the library or the tourist office (where occasionally travelers may get access for a small fee). The website www.tangaworld.com lists nearly 200 cybercafes in Spain by location and name.

NATIONAL HOLIDAYS

The following table lists the national holidays for 2003.

DATE	HOLIDAYS
January 1	New Year's Day
January 6	Epiphany
March 1	Victory Day
March 19	Saint Joseph's Day
April 17	Maundy Thursday
April 18	Good Friday
April 20	Easter
May 1	May Day/*Fiesta del Trabajo* (Labor Day)
May 2	Autonomous Community Day
July 6-14	Feast of San Fermín (Pamplona)
July 25	Saint James Day
August 15	*La Asunción* (Feast of the Assumption)
October 12	*Fiesta Nacional de España* (National Day)
November 1	All Saints Day
November 9	Virgen de la Almudena
December 6	*Día de la Constitución* (Constitution Day)
December 8	*La Inmaculada Concepción* (Feast of the Immaculate Conception)
December 25	*Navidad* (Christmas)
December 31	New Year's Eve

MADRID

The relentless summer sun parches sidewalks and sidestreets, blazing across a city filled with tremendous history and life. The dry air casts a spell throughout Madrid, inducing a hedonistic fever that sets in at sunset. In this city of restless energy, the morning rush hour coincides with the move to after-hours clubs, and fervent activity seems to pause only for an afternoon siesta. *Madrileños* never stop enjoying life, leaving straight from work to the city's many plazas, *tapas* bars, and romantic parks, surviving on minimal sleep and living each day to its fullest. While tourists inundate the city, spending their days absorbing its Old World monuments, world-renowned museums, and raging nightlife, Madrid's population of 5 million roams the labyrinthine neighborhoods with a simple and energetic joy.

Madrid's history does not read like that of rival European capitals. Although the city witnessed the coronation of Fernando and Isabel, Madrid did not gain importance until Habsburg King Felipe II moved the court here in 1561. Despite being far from vital ports and rivers, it immediately became a seat of wealth, culture, and imperial glory, serving as the center of Spain's 16th- and 17th-century Golden Age of literature, art, and architecture. In the 18th century, Madrid witnessed a Neoclassical rebirth as King Carlos III embellished the city with wide, tree-lined boulevards and scores of imposing buildings. In the 19th century, however, Madrid was scarred by the Peninsular Wars against Napoleon, the bloody inspiration for some of Francisco de Goya's most famous canvases.

In 1939, Madrid was the last city save Valencia to fall in the Spanish Civil War. Though it was hostile to Franco's nationalism, the city was forced to serve as the center of his government. This time, its location—smack in the center of the country—was considered its greatest strength. Franco's death nearly 40 years later brought an explosion known as *La Movida* ("Shift" or "Movement"). After decades of totalitarian repression, Madrid burst out laughing and crying in a breathtaking, city-wide release of inhibition. A 200,000-strong student population took to the streets and stayed there—they haven't stopped moving yet.

Today Madrid continues to serve as Spain's political, intellectual, and cultural center. It is not as cosmopolitan as Barcelona nor as charming as Sevilla, but it is undeniably the *capital*—the wild, pulsing heart of Spain. Students, families, and artists flock here in pursuit of their dreams, and Madrid continues to grow as a city of opportunity. Even its very architecture, with modern skyscrapers and shining industrial spaces expanding from narrow alleys and ancient plazas, epitomizes the mix of galvanizing history and passion for the present that so defines Spain.

INTERCITY TRANSPORT

BY PLANE

All flights land at **Aeropuerto Internacional de Barajas** (☎902 35 35 70 or 913 05 83 43), 20min. or 13km northeast of Madrid. A branch of the **regional tourist office** in the international arrivals area has maps and info. (☎913 05 86 56. Open M-F 8am-8pm, Sa 9am-1pm.)

The **Barajas Metro line,** inaugurated in June 1999, connects the airport to all of Madrid (€0.95). The Metro is the preferred method of transportation from the airport for the budget traveler. From the airport arrivals area, follow signs to the Metro.

(Be prepared; this can be quite a walk.) Take Line 8 (pink) to Nuevos Ministerios and switch to Line 10 (blue, towards Aluche). At Plaza de España, change to Line 3 (yellow, toward Legazpi), and two stops later you'll find yourself at Sol, smack in the middle of Madrid's best accommodations and sights. **Aero City** provides 24hr. pickup and drop-off service. (☎915 71 96 96; www.aerocity.com. €14, €17 at night.) Another option is the green **Bus-Aeropuerto #89,** which leaves from the national and international terminals and runs to the city center. (☎914 06 88 20. Look for "EMT" signs just outside the airport doors. Every 12min. 4:45am-2am. €2.40.) The bus stops underground beneath the Jardines del Descubrimiento in **Plaza de Colón** (M: Colón). After surfacing in Pl. Colón, walk toward the neo-Gothic statue that overlooks the **Paseo de Recoletos.** The Colón Metro station is across the street. Fleets of **taxis** swarm the airport. Taxi fare to central Madrid should cost €15-18, including the €4 airport surcharge, depending on traffic and time of day.

AIRLINES

Over 65 airlines fly in and out of the Barajas International Airport. Below are the numbers for the most relevant airlines in Madrid.

Iberia: Santa Cruz de Marcenado, 2 (☎915 87 47 47 or 917 22 96 00). M: San Bernardo. Open M-F 9:30am-2pm, 4-7pm. 24hr. reservations and info (☎902 40 05 00).

Air Europa: (☎902 40 15 01; www.aireuropa.com).

Air France: Pl. España, 18, 5th fl. (☎901 11 22 66 or 913 05 43 41; www.airfrance.es). M: Pl. España. Open M-F 9am-5pm.

American Airlines: C. Orense, 4, 1st fl. (☎902 11 55 70). Open M-F 9am-5:30pm. Reservations (☎914 53 14 00). Open M-F 9am-6:30pm, Sa 9am-2pm.

British Airways: Santiago de Compostela, 100 (☎913 87 43 00). Open M-F 9am-5pm. Reservations (☎913 76 96 66) open M-F 9am-7pm.

Continental: C. Leganitos, 47, 9th fl. (☎915 59 27 10). M: Pl. España. Open M-F 9am-6pm. Reservations open M-F 9am-7pm.

Delta Airlines: C. Goya, 8, 4th fl. (☎915 77 06 50 or 915 77 18 72).

KLM: Gran Vía, 59 (☎915 40 15 39; reservations and information 913 05 43 47).

Lufthansa: Cardenal Marcelo Española, 2 (☎913 83 51 13; reservations 902 22 01 01), located outside city limits.

Portugalia: Leganitos, 47, 6th fl. (☎ 902 40 04 55).

SpanAir: Terminal Nacional, Aeropuerto de Madrid-Barajas (☎913 93 67 40).

TAP Air Portugal: Gran Vía, 58 (☎915 41 20 00 or 915 41 20 08).

USAirways: Alberto Aguillera, 38, 2nd fl. (☎914 44 47 00). Open M-F 9am-6pm.

BY TRAIN

Two *Largo Recorrido* (long distance) **RENFE** stations, **Madrid-Chamartín** and **Madrid-Atocha,** connect Madrid to surrounding areas and the rest of Europe. Both stations are easily accessible by Metro. (For Madrid-Atocha, avoid lost tourist syndrome and get off the Metro at Atocha-Renfe, not Atocha.) Call RENFE (☎913 28 90 20 or 902 24 02 02; www.renfe.es) for reservations and info. Buy your tickets at the stations or at the **RENFE Main Office,** C. Alcalá, 44, at Gran Vía. (M: Banco de España. Open M-F 9:30am-8pm.) Schedules for **Regionales, Cercanias, AVE** (☎915 34 05 05), and **Talgo** trains are available at the stations and online.

Madrid Overview
1/2 mile
1/2 kilometer
TO AEROPUERTO DE BARAJAS
M30
Av. San Luis
C. de Arturo Soria
AV. DE LA PAZ
Parque Breogán
PARQUE DE LAS AVENIDAS
Alfonso XIII
Av. Aster
F. Nuñez
Av. Ramón y Cajal
C. Pradillo
ALFONSO XIII
Clara del Rey
PROSPERIDAD
CARTAGENA
Av. de América
C. Cartagena
Marqués de Torroja
PIO XII
C. Alfonso XIII
C. Costa Rica
C. Colombia
CONCHA ESPINA
Parque de Berlin
Auditorio Nacional
Lopez de Hoyos
AV. DE AMERICA
C. Francisco
CHAMARTÍN
Av. Pío XII
Estación de Chamartín
COLOMBIA
C. Príncipe de Vergara
CRUZ DEL RAYO
D. PASTRANA
Po. de la Habana
C. Potosí
PL. REP. EL SALVADOR
Av. Dr. Arce
REP. ARGENTINA
C. Diego de León
C. Serrano
C. Mateo Inurria
C. Fray B. Sahagún
Av. Alberto Alcocer
Habana
Av. Concha Espina
C. de Joaquín Costa
C. María de Molina
Agustín Foxa
C. Felix Boix
Damián
C. Padre
Po. de la
C. de Vitruvio
CASTILLA
CUZCO
Po. la Castellana
PL. DE CASTILLA
PL. DE CUZCO
PL. DE LIMA
SANTIAGO BERNABEU
Po. la Castellana
PL. S. JUAN DE LA CRUZ
GREGORIO MARAÑON
Museo Lazaro Galdiano
GLORIETA DE EMILIO CASTELAR
VENTANILLA
Australia
NUEVOS MINISTERIOS
Nuevos Ministerios
Museo Sorolla
VALDEACEDERAS
C. de Orense
C. de Alonso Cano
ALONSO CANO
C. José Abascal
C. Cmndte. Zofita
C. de Ponzano
C. Infanta Mercedes
Av. del General Perón
C. Sinesio Delgado
C. Bravo Murillo
TETUÁN
ALVARADO
CUATRO CAMINOS
C. Raimundo Fernández Villaverde
C. de Ríos Rosas
RÍOS ROSAS
C. Santa Engracia
IGLESIA
C. Capitán Blanco Argibay
ESTRECHO
C. de Bravo Murillo
CANAL
C. de Ofelia Nieto
GUZMÁN EL BUENO
Victoria
C. Francisco de Sales
Parque Santander
Av. Filipinas
C. Cea Bermúdez
FRANCOS RODRÍGUEZ
Av. de Pablo Iglesias
C. Guzmán el Bueno
PEÑAGRANDE
C. de Francos Rodriguez
Juan Montalvo
Av. Reina
Av. del Valle
Po. S. Francisco
ISLAS FILIPINAS
Po. Juan XXIII
METROPOLITANO
C. de Isaac Peral
PL. DE CRISTO REY
C. Antonio Machado
ANTONIO MACHADO
Denesa de la Villa
CIUDAD UNIVERSITARIA
Museo de América
Av. Arco de la Victoria
CIUDAD UNIVERSITARIA
Av. la Complutense
Av. la Puerta de Hierro

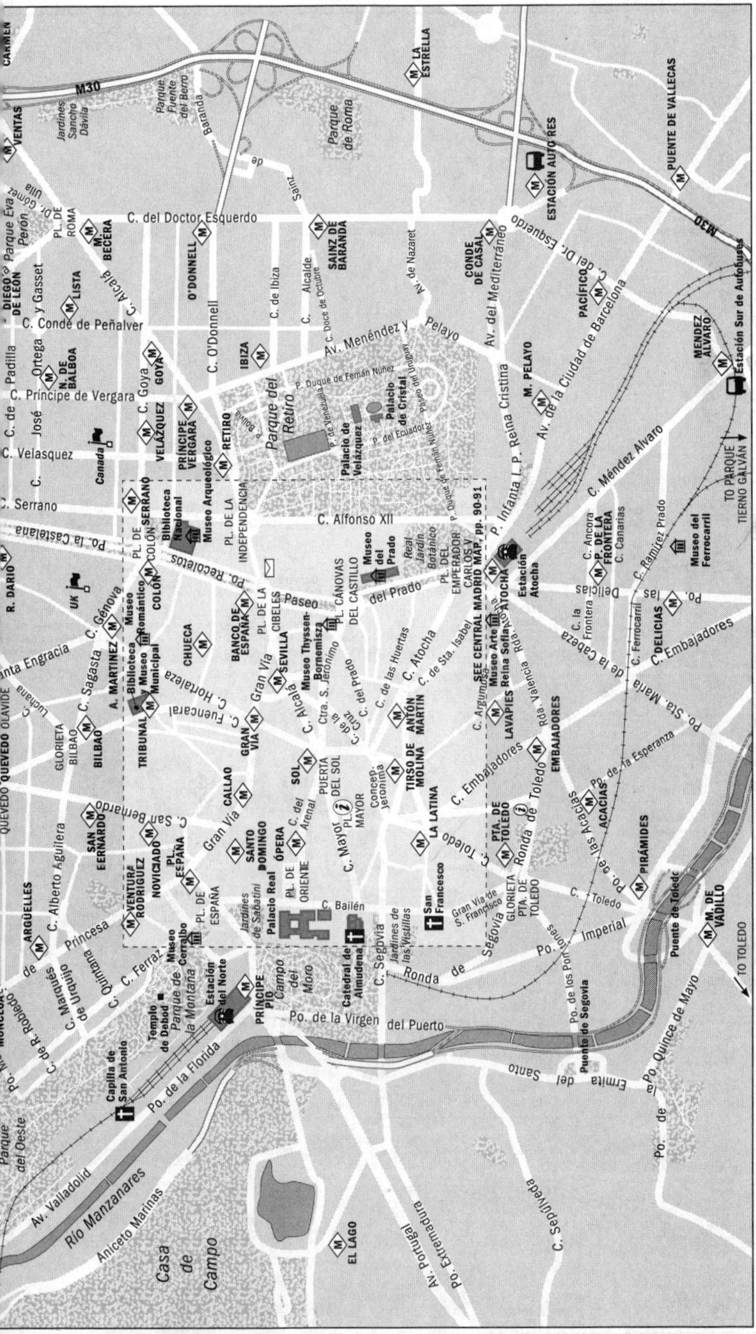
M30
VENTAS
Jardines Sancho Dávila
Parque Fuente del Berro
Baranda
Parque de Roma
LA ESTRELLA
ESTACIÓN AUTO RES
PUENTE DE VALLECAS
C. del Doctor Esquerdo
PL. DE ROMA
M. BECERA
DIEGO DE LEÓN
LISTA
C. Conde de Peñalver
O'DONNELL
C. O'Donnell
C. de Ibiza
SAINZ DE BARANDA
Av. de Nazaret
CONDE DE CASAL
Av. del Mediterráneo
C. del Dr. Esquerdo
PACÍFICO
Av. de la Ciudad de Barcelona
MENDEZ ALVARO
Estación Sur de Autobuses
N. DE BALBOA
GOYA
C. Goya
C. Príncipe de Vergara
IBIZA
Av. Menéndez y Pelayo
Parque del Retiro
Palacio de Velázquez
Palacio de Cristal
M. PELAYO
P. Infanta I. P. Reina Cristina
C. Méndez Alvaro
TO PARQUE TIERNO GALVÁN
C. Velasquez
Canada
VELÁZQUEZ
PRÍNCIPE VERGARA
RETIRO
PL. DE LA INDEPENDENCIA
Museo Arqueológico
Biblioteca Nacional
SERRANO
C. Serrano
C. Alfonso XII
Po. la Castellana
PL. DE COLÓN
COLÓN
Po. Recoletos
Museo del Prado
Real Jardín Botánico
PL. DEL EMPERADOR CARLOS V
SEE CENTRAL MADRID MAP, pp. 90-91
ATOCHA
Estación Atocha
C. Ancora
P. DE LA FRONTERA
C. Canarias
C. Ramírez Prado
Museo del Ferrocarril
R. DARIO
UK
C. Génova
Museo Romántico
PL. DE LA CIBELES
Paseo del Prado
PL. CÁNOVAS DEL CASTILLO
Po. las Delicias
DELICIAS
C. Embajadores
A. MARTÍNEZ
Biblioteca y Museo Municipal
CHUECA
BANCO DE ESPAÑA
SEVILLA
Museo Thyssen-Bornemisza
C. Atocha
C. de Sta. Isabel
Museo Arte Reina Sofía
C. la Frontera
C. Ferrocarril
Po. Sta. María de la Cabeza
C. Sagasta
C. Hortaleza
Gran Vía
C. Alcalá
C. de las Huertas
LAVAPIES
Rda. Valencia
QUEVEDO
OLAVIDE
GLORIETA BILBAO
BILBAO
TRIBUNAL
C. Fuencarral
GRAN VÍA
SOL
PUERTA DEL SOL
TIRSO DE MOLINA
ANTÓN MARTÍN
EMBAJADORES
Po. de la Esperanza
C. San Bernardo
SAN BERNARDO
NOVICIADO
CALLAO
PL. MAYOR
C. Mayor
LA LATINA
C. Toledo
PTA. DE TOLEDO
Ronda de Toledo
ACACIAS
Po. de las Acacias
PIRÁMIDES
C. Alberto Aguilera
VENTURA RODRÍGUEZ
PL. ESPAÑA
SANTO DOMINGO
ÓPERA
PL. DE ORIENTE
C. Bailén
San Francisco
Gran Vía de S. Francisco
GLORIETA PTA. DE TOLEDO
Po. Imperial
Puente de Toledo
M. DE VADILLO
TO TOLEDO
ARGÜELLES
C. Princesa
PL. DE ESPAÑA
Jardines de Sabatini
Palacio Real
Catedral de Almudena
Jardines de las Vistillas
C. Segovia
Ronda de Segovia
Po. de los Pontones
Puente de Segovia
C. Ferraz
Museo Cerralbo
Templo de Debod
Parque de la Montaña
Estación del Norte
PRÍNCIPE PÍO
Campo del Moro
Po. de la Virgen del Puerto
Ermita del Santo
Po. Quince de Mayo
MONCLOA
Po. de Rosales
C. Marqués de Urquijo
C. Quintana
Capilla de San Antonio
Po. de la Florida
Parque del Oeste
Av. Valladolid
Río Manzanares
Aniceto Marinas
Casa de Campo
EL LAGO
Av. Portugal
Po. Extremadura
C. Sepúlveda

MADRID

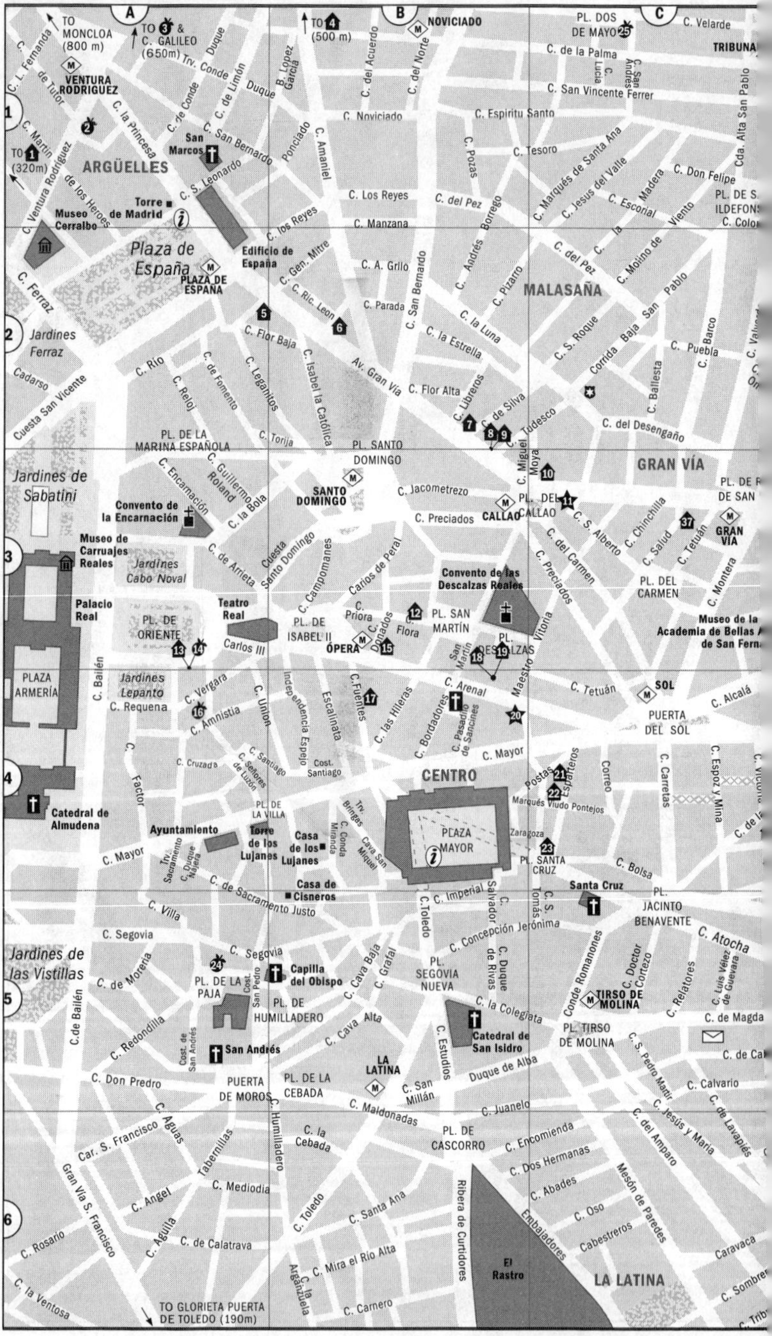

A
B
C
1
2
3
4
5
6
TO MONCLOA (800 m)
TO 3 & C. GALILEO (650m)
TO 4 (500 m)
TO 1 (320m)
NOVICIADO
PL. DOS DE MAYO
C. Velarde
TRIBUNAL
VENTURA RODRIGUEZ
ARGÜELLES
Museo Cerralbo
Torre de Madrid
San Marcos
Plaza de España
PLAZA DE ESPAÑA
Edificio de España
Jardines Ferraz
MALASAÑA
GRAN VÍA
PL. DE LA MARINA ESPAÑOLA
PL. SANTO DOMINGO
SANTO DOMINGO
CALLAO
Jardines de Sabatini
Convento de la Encarnación
Museo de Carruajes Reales
Jardines Cabo Noval
Convento de las Descalzas Reales
Palacio Real
PL. DE ORIENTE
Teatro Real
PL. DE ISABEL II
ÓPERA
PL. SAN MARTÍN
PL. DESCALZAS
PLAZA ARMERÍA
Jardines Lepanto
SOL
PUERTA DEL SOL
PL. DEL CARMEN
Museo de la Academia de Bellas Artes de San Fernando
CENTRO
PLAZA MAYOR
Catedral de Almudena
Ayuntamiento
Torre de los Lujanes
Casa de los Lujanes
Casa de Cisneros
PL. DE LA VILLA
PL. SANTA CRUZ
Santa Cruz
PL. JACINTO BENAVENTE
Jardines de las Vistillas
PL. DE LA PAJA
Capilla del Obispo
PL. DE HUMILLADERO
San Andrés
PL. SEGOVIA NUEVA
TIRSO DE MOLINA
PL. TIRSO DE MOLINA
Catedral de San Isidro
LA LATINA
PUERTA DE MOROS
PL. DE LA CEBADA
PL. DE CASCORRO
El Rastro
TO GLORIETA PUERTA DE TOLEDO (190m)
Gran Vía S. Francisco
Av. Gran Vía
C. Mayor
C. Arenal
C. Preciados
C. Atocha
C. de Bailén
C. Toledo
C. Segovia
Cuesta San Vicente
C. la Princesa
C. San Bernardo
C. Alcalá
Ribera de Curtidores
Embajadores

MADRID

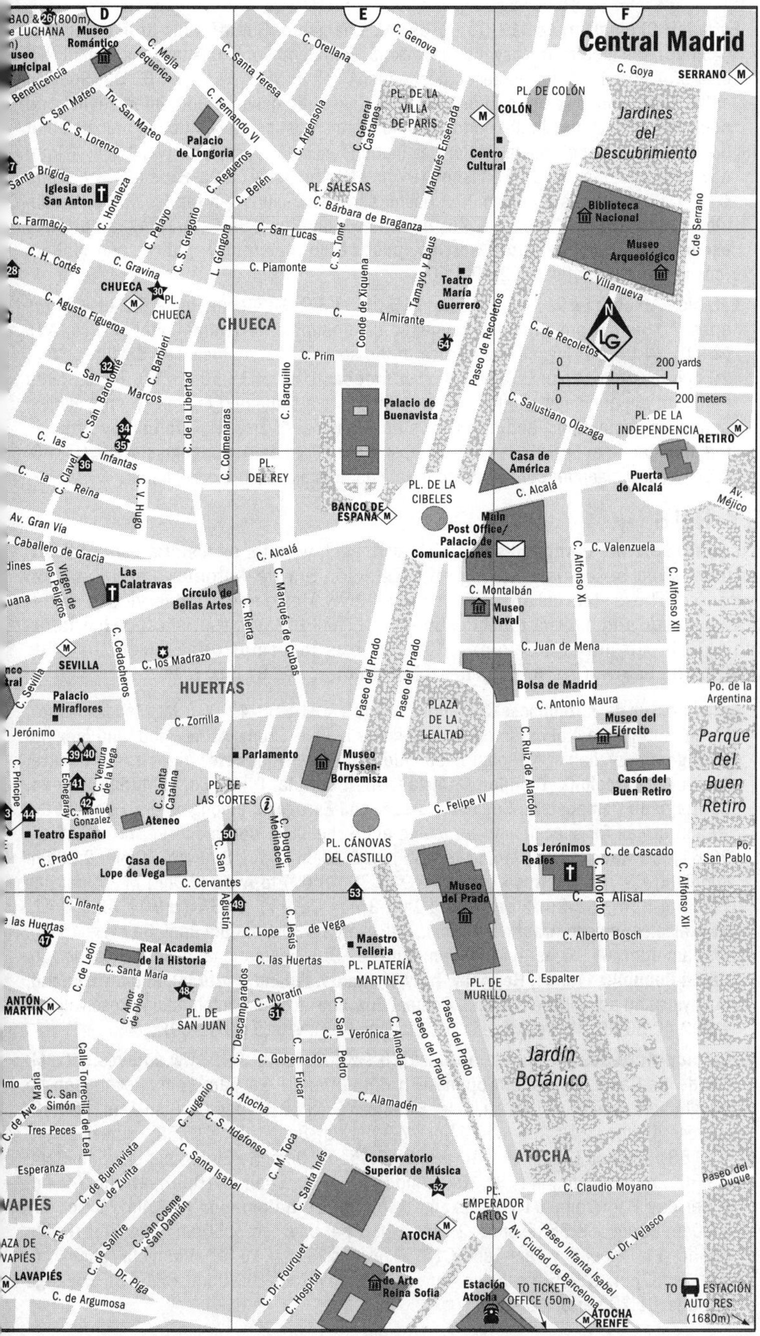
Central Madrid
D
E
F
Museo Romántico
Museo Municipal
C. Beneficencia
C. San Mateo
Trv. San Mateo
C. S. Lorenzo
C. Mejía Lequerica
C. Santa Teresa
C. Orellana
C. Genova
C. Goya
SERRANO
PL. DE COLÓN
COLÓN
PL. DE LA VILLA DE PARIS
C. Fernando VI
C. Argensola
C. General Castaños
Marqués Ensenada
Palacio de Longoria
Centro Cultural
Jardines del Descubrimiento
Santa Brígida
Iglesia de San Anton
C. Hortaleza
C. Regueros
C. Belén
PL. SALESAS
C. Bárbara de Braganza
Biblioteca Nacional
Museo Arqueológico
C.de Serrano
C. Farmacia
C. Pelayo
C. S. Gregorio
L. Góngora
C. San Lucas
C. S. Tomé
Tamayo y Baus
C. H. Cortés
C. Gravina
C. Piamonte
Teatro María Guerrero
C. Villanueva
CHUECA
PL. CHUECA
C. Agusto Figueroa
CHUECA
Conde de Xiquena
C. Almirante
Paseo de Recoletos
C. de Recoletos
C. Barbieri
C. Prim
C. San Bartolomé
C. Barquillo
0
200 yards
200 meters
Marcos
C. San
C. de la Libertad
C. Colmenaras
Palacio de Buenavista
C. Salustiano Olazaga
PL. DE LA INDEPENDENCIA
RETIRO
C. las Infantas
PL. DEL REY
Casa de América
Puerta de Alcalá
C. la Reina
C. Clavel
C. V. Hugo
PL. DE LA CIBELES
C. Alcalá
Av. Méjico
Av. Gran Vía
BANCO DE ESPAÑA
Main Post Office/ Palacio de Comunicaciones
C. Valenzuela
C. Caballero de Gracia
C. Alcalá
C. Alfonso XI
C. Alfonso XII
Virgen de los Peligros
Las Calatravas
Círculo de Bellas Artes
C. Marqués de Cubas
C. Montalbán
Museo Naval
C. Rlerta
C. Cedacheros
SEVILLA
C. los Madrazo
C. Juan de Mena
Paseo del Prado
Paseo del Prado
C. Sevilla
Palacio Miraflores
HUERTAS
Bolsa de Madrid
C. Antonio Maura
Po. de la Argentina
C. Zorrilla
PLAZA DE LA LEALTAD
Museo del Ejército
Parque del Buen Retiro
n Jerónimo
C. Ruiz de Alarcón
Parlamento
Museo Thyssen-Bornemisza
C. Príncipe
C. Ventura de la Vega
C. Echegaray
C. Santa Catalina
PL. DE LAS CORTES
Casón del Buen Retiro
C. Felipe IV
C. Manuel Gonzalez
Ateneo
C. Duque Medinaceli
Teatro Español
PL. CÁNOVAS DEL CASTILLO
Los Jerónimos Reales
C. de Cascado
Po. San Pablo
C. Prado
C. San Agustin
Casa de Lope de Vega
C. Cervantes
C. Moreto
Museo del Prado
C. Alisal
C. Alfonso XII
C. Infante
C. las Huertas
C. Jesús
C. Lope de Vega
Maestro Tellería
C. Alberto Bosch
C. de León
Real Academia de la Historia
C. las Huertas
PL. PLATERÍA MARTINEZ
C. Santa María
C. Espalter
PL. DE MURILLO
ANTÓN MARTÍN
C. Amor de Dios
PL. DE SAN JUAN
C. Descamparados
C. Moratín
C. San Pedro
C. Verónica
C. Almeda
Paseo del Prado
Paseo del Prado
Jardín Botánico
Calle Torrecilla del Leal
C. Gobernador
C. Fúcar
C. San Simón
C. de Ave María
C. Eugenio
C. Atocha
C. Alamadén
Tres Peces
C. S. Ildefonso
C. M. Toca
C. Santa Isabel
C. Santa Inés
Conservatorio Superior de Música
ATOCHA
Paseo del Duque
Esperanza
C. de Buenavista
C. de Zurita
C. Claudio Moyano
LAVAPIÉS
PL. EMPERADOR CARLOS V
C. Fé
C. de Salitre
C. San Cosme y San Damián
ATOCHA
Paseo Infanta Isabel
C. Dr. Velasco
PLAZA DE LAVAPIÉS
Av. Ciudad de Barcelona
LAVAPIÉS
Dr. Piga
C. Dr. Fourquet
C. Hospital
Centro de Arte Reina Sofía
Estación Atocha
TO TICKET OFFICE (50m)
ATOCHA RENFE
TO ESTACIÓN AUTO RES (1680m)
C. de Argumosa

Estación Chamartín: (☎913 00 69 69) M: Chamartín. Bus #5 runs to and from Sol (45min.); the stop is just beyond the lockers. For international destinations, call RENFE or ☎934 90 11 22; for domestic destinations call RENFE (☎902 24 02 02; Spanish only). Ticket windows open 8am-10:30pm. Chamartín services both international and domestic destinations in the northeast and south. Most *cercanías* (local) trains stop at both Chamartín and Atocha. Major destinations include: **Barcelona** (7-10½hr., 10 per day 7am-11:10pm, €40-42); **Lisbon** (9½hr., 10:45pm, €47.50); **Paris** (13½hr., 7pm, €117). Chamartín is a mini-mall of useful services, including a **tourist office** (Vestíbulo, Puerta 14, ☎913 15 99 76; open M-F 8am-8pm, Sa 9am-1pm), a **currency exchange, accommodations service, post office, car rental, police,** and **lockers** (*consignas automáticas;* €2.40-4.50).

Estación Atocha: (☎913 28 90 20 or 915 06 61 37). M: Atocha-Renfe. Ticket windows open 7:15am-10pm. Trains to domestic destinations; no international service. **AVE** (☎915 34 05 05) high-speed service to the south of Spain, including **Sevilla** (2½hr., 20 per day 7am-11pm, €52.50-60) via **Córdoba** (1¾hr., €38.50-45.50). The cast-iron atrium of the original station has been turned into a simulated rainforest. Art galleries, boutiques, restaurants, and cafes serve as additional diversions. **Information office** in the main terminal (☎902 24 02 02). Open 7am-10pm daily. **Luggage storage** (€2.40-4.50), follow signs for *consignas automáticas,* upstairs from the rainforest.

BY BUS

Numerous private companies serve Madrid, each with its own station set of destinations. Most buses pass through the Estación Sur de Autobuses and Estación Auto-Res. These stations are easily accessible by Metro and offer service to countless domestic and international destinations. The Pl. Mayor tourist office has information on the most relevant inter-city bus information. Search for your destination below. (For more general information, see **By Bus,** p. 80.)

Estación Sur de Autobuses: C. Méndez Álvaro (☎914 68 42 00). M: Méndez Álvaro; Metro stop inside station. Info booth open daily 7am-11pm. **ATMs,** food, and **luggage storage** are available. National destinations include: **Albacete, Algeciras, Alicante, Aranjuez, Barcelona, Benidorm, Cartagena, A Coruña, Gijón, Lugo, Murcia, Oviedo, Santiago de Compostela, Segovia, Toledo, and Zaragoza,** among others. Check at the station or call for specific info on routes and schedules. **Continental-Auto** (☎915 27 29 61) to **Toledo** (1½hr.; M-Sa every 30min. 6:30am-10pm, Su every 30min. 8:30am-midnight; €3.75). **Empresa Larrea** (☎915 30 48 00) to **Ávila** (2½hr.; M-F 8 per day 7:15am-8pm, Sa-Su 4 per day 10am-8pm; €5.91). **ALSA** (☎902 42 22 42; www.alsa.es) runs to **Aranjuez** (45min.; M-F every 15-30min. 6am-9pm, Sa every 45min. 7:30am-9pm, Su 10 per day 7:30am-9pm; €2.90). International destinations include: **Czech Republic, France, Germany, Italy, Romania, Poland, Portugal, and Switzerland,** but flying can actually be cheaper. Contact **Eurolines** for more information (Reservations: ☎902 40 50 40, Madrid office in bus station (#83): ☎915 06 33 60).

Estación Auto-Res: Pl. Conde de Casal, 6 (☎902 02 09 99; www.auto-res.net). M: Conde de Casal. Info booth open M-Th 6am-10pm, F-Sa 6am-1pm. Tickets can be bought here from 6am-1am daily. To: **Badajoz** (5¼hr., 9-10 per day 8am-1am, €20.58; express 4½hr., €24); **Càceres** (4¾hr., 7-9 per day 8am-1am, €15.58; express 3½hr., €16.58); **Cuenca** (3hr.; M-F 8-10 per day 6:45am-10pm, Sa-Su 5-6 per day 8am-8pm; €8.50. Express 2½hr.; M-F, Su 10am and 6:30pm, Sa 10am; €10.50); **Mérida** (4¼hr., 9 per day 8am-1am, €15.58. Express 4hr., €21); **Salamanca** (3-3¼hr., 7 per day 8:30am-10pm, €9.55; express 2½hr., 14-15 per day 7am-9:30pm, €14.17); **Trujillo** (3¼hr., 11-12 per day 8am-1am, €12.58; express 3hr., €16.58); **Valencia** (5hr., 4 per day 1am-2pm, €18.58; express 4hr., 10 per day 7am-10:30pm, €21.59). **Luggage storage** €1.20 per bag per day.

Central Madrid

ACCOMMODATIONS

Albergue Juvenil Santa Cruz de Marcenado (HI), **4**	B1
Hispa Domus, **32**	D2
Hostal A. Nebrija, **5**	A2
Hostal Abril, **29**	D2
Hostal Aguilar, **39**	D4
Hostal Alicante, **18**	B4
Hostal Armesto, **50**	D4
Hostal Cantábrico, **38**	D4
Hostal Chelo, **33**	D2
Hostal Esparteros, **22**	C4
Hostal Gonzalo, **49**	E5
Hostal Internacional, **41**	D4
Hostal Lauria, **8**	B2
Hostal Leones, **45**	C4
Hostal Lorenzo, **36**	D3
Hostal Madrid, **21**	C4
Hostal Margarita, **9**	B2
Hostal Medieval, **28**	D2
Hostal Palacios, **31**	C2
Hostal Portugal, **12**	B3
Hostal-Residencia Alibel, **10**	C3
Hostal-Residencia Carreras, **43**	D4
Hostal-Residencia Cruz-Sol, **23**	C4
Hostal-Residencia Domínguez, **27**	D1
Hostal-Residencia Lamalonga, **7**	B2
Hostal-Residencia Lido, **41**	D4
Hostal-Residencia Luz, **17**	B4
Hostal-Residencia Miño, **19**	B4
Hostal-Residencia Mondragón, **40**	D4
Hostal-Residencia Rios, **1**	A1
Hostal-Residencia Rober, **15**	B3
Hostal-Residencia Sud-Americana, **53**	E5
Hostal Ribadavia, **31**	C2
Hostal R. Rodríguez, **46**	C4
Hostal Santillan, **6**	B2
Hostal Triana, **37**	C3
Hostal Valencia, **13**	A3
Hotel Villar, **44**	D4
Hotel Mónaco, **34**	D2

FOOD THUMB-PICKS

Al-Jaima, **35**	D2
Ananias, **3**	A1
Arepas con Todo, **26**	D1
Café Gijón, **54**	E2
Café de Oriente, **14**	A3
Casa Alberto, **47**	D5
Cáscaras, **2**	A1
Champagneria Gala, **51**	E5
El Estragón Vegetariano, **24**	A5
La Granja Restaurante Vegetariano, **25**	C1
Inshala, **16**	A4
La Toscana, **42**	D4

NIGHTLIFE THUMB-PICKS

Acuarela, **30**	D2
El Café de Sheherezade, **48**	D5
Kapital, **52**	E6
Palacio Gaviria, **20**	B4
Pasapoga, **11**	C3

Estación Empresa Alacuber: (☎913 76 01 04), on Po. Moret. M: Moncloa. To: **El Pardo** (20min., every 15min. 6am-1:30am, €0.90).

Estación Empresa Continental Auto: Av. de América, 9 (☎917 45 63 00). M: Cartagena. To: **Alcalá de Henares** (40min.; M-Sa every 15min. 6:15am-10:45pm, Su every 30min. 7-9am and every 20min. 9am-11pm; €1.55) and **Guadalajara** (1hr., every hr. 7am-midnight, €3.46).

Estación Herranz: C. Princesa (☎918 96 90 28), in the Intercambio de Moncloa. M: Moncloa. To: **El Escorial** (50min., every 15min. 7am-9pm, €2.45) and **Valle de los Caídos** via El Escorial (20min.; departs El Escorial 3:15pm, returns 5:30pm; €6.20).

Estación La Sepulvedana: Po. de la Frontera, 16 (☎915 30 48 00). M: Príncipe Pío (via extension from M: Ópera). To: **Segovia** (1½hr., every 30min. 6:30am-10:15pm, €5.05) and **Ávila** (1½hr.; M-F 8 per day 6am-7pm, Sa-Su 3 per day 10am-7pm; €5.60).

ORIENTATION

The "Kilómetro 0" sign in front of the police station in **Puerta del Sol** marks the intersection of eight of Madrid's most celebrated streets, and the starting point of the country's major highways. To make Madrid's infinite plazas and serpentine streets more navigable, coverage of the city is broken down into five major neighborhoods: **Centro, Huertas, Malasaña and Chueca, Bilbao,** and **Argüelles,** all of which are within walking distance or a short taxi ride of one another.

MADRID

Most of Madrid's prominent sights, including the **Ópera** and **Plaza Mayor,** radiate from Sol in the Centro. Just west of Sol off C. Mayor, Plaza Mayor is the hub of activity for tourists and *madrileños* alike; the plaza houses both contemporary cafes and the churches and historical buildings of **Habsburg Madrid,** also known as **Madrid de los Asturias.** Farther west of Sol, by way of C. Arenal, lies the reigning monument of **Bourbon Madrid,** the Palacio Real. This section of Madrid, also known as **Ópera,** hosts fantastic gardens and churches.

To the southeast of Sol lies **Huertas,** once the literary district and now the center for exploring the city's three great museums (see **Museums,** p. 121) or the lush **Parque del Buen Retiro** (see p. 118). Bordered by C. Alcalá to the north, Po. Prado to the east, and C. Atocha to the south, the neighborhood is the home of traditional cafes, lively theaters, and intoxicating nightlife. Centered around **Plaza Santa Ana,** Huertas is crowded with some of the best budget accommodations in the city, as well as some of the best traditional *tapas* bars.

Also south of Sol and west of Huertas is the area around the Metro stop **La Latina,** which has less prestige and fewer tourists than the rest of Old Madrid. Small markets line winding lantern-lit streets, perfect for an evening of gourmet tradition. **El Rastro,** a gargantuan ancient flea market, is staged here every Sunday morning. Farther south lies **Lavapiés,** a working-class neighborhood.

North of Sol, the busy avenue **Gran Vía** is the commercial center of Madrid, littered with fast-food joints and a handful of skyscrapers. Linked to C. de Fuencarral, it acts as the southern border of **Malasaña** and **Chueca,** both full of trendy restaurants and shops. Beyond Gran Vía and east of Malasaña and Chueca lies modern Madrid. Running the length of Madrid from **Atocha** in the south to **Plaza de Castilla** in the north, **Paseo del Prado, Paseo de Recoletos,** and **Paseo de la Castellana** pass the Prado, the fountains at the **Plazas Cibeles** and **Colón,** and the elaborate skyscrapers beyond Pl. Colón, including the twin towers of the **Puerta de Europa.**

The area northwest of Sol holds the **Plaza de España** and the soaring **Torre de Madrid,** the pride of 1950s Spain. Still farther northwest of Sol lie **Argüelles** and **Bilbao,** energetic neighborhoods spilling over from **Moncloa.** Both are student districts, filled with cheap eateries and neon nightclubs.

Madrid is much safer than most major European cities, but Sol, Pl. España, Pl. Chueca, and Malasaña's Pl. Dos de Mayo are still intimidating late at night. As a general rule, avoid the parks and quiet residential streets after dark and always watch out for thieves and pickpockets in crowds.

READ THIS The **Guía del Ocio,** available behind the counter of any news kiosk, should be your first purchase in Madrid (€1). It has concert, theater, sports, cinema, and TV schedules, and lists exhibits, restaurants, bars, and clubs. Although it's in Spanish, alphabetical listings of clubs and restaurants are invaluable even to non-speakers. The *Guía* comes out on Thursday or Friday, so be sure that you're buying an up-to-date copy instead of last week's issue. For an English magazine with articles on new finds in and around the city, pick up **In Madrid,** distributed free at tourist offices and many restaurants. Live Music and Nightlife sections are basically an English-language translation of the *Guía*. **The Broadsheet,** free at bookstores, is a no-frills listing of English-language classifieds. The weekly **Segundamano,** on sale at kiosks, is essential for apartment or roommate seekers. Gay travelers will want to pick up the free magazine **Shanguide,** which lists activities and nightspots for every town in Spain, or buy **Zero** magazine at any kiosk (€3.60). **Minerva** keeps you up to date on the art scene.

LOCAL TRANSPORTATION

MAPS

The free *Plano de Madrid* (street map) and *Plano y Guía de Transportes* (public transportation map) are fantastic. Pick them up at the tourist office in the arrivals area of the airport terminal or from any other tourist office. Public transportation info can also be accessed by phone (☎012) or by web (www.ctm-madrid.es). **El Corte Inglés** (see p. 98) offers a one-page map of Madrid. For a comprehensive map with street index, pick up the *Almax* map (€4) at any newsstand.

METRO

Safe, speedy, and spotless, Madrid's Metro puts most major subway systems to shame. Trains run frequently; green timers above most platforms show increments of five minutes or less since the last train departed. The free *Plano del Metro* (available at any ticket booth) and the wall maps of surrounding neighborhoods are clear and helpful. Fare and schedule info is posted in every station.

Eleven lines, totaling more than 171km, connect Madrid's 158 stations, making the city incredibly easy to get around. Lines are distinguished by color and number. An individual Metro ticket costs €0.95, but frequent riders opt for the **bonotransporte** (ticket of 10 rides for either the Metro or bus system) at €5. Buy them at machines in any Metro stop, *estancos* (tobacco shops), or newsstands. Remember to hold on to your ticket until you leave the Metro—riding without one incurs outrageous fines. For more details, call **Metro info** (☎915 53 59 09) or ask at any ticket booth. For a comprehensive guide, visit www.metromadrid.es.

Trains run every day from 6am to 1:30am. Violent crime in the Metro stations is almost unheard of, and women usually feel safe traveling alone. Pickpockets tend to do their best work in crowded cars, though. If you feel uncomfortable, avoid empty cars and ride in sight of the conductor. At night, avoid the stations to the north, which tend to be less frequented. Metro stations Chueca, Gran Vía, La Latina, Plaza de España, Sol, and Tirso de Molina can be intimidating after midnight if alone. These areas are usually busy all through the night with bar- and club-hoppers, but many crimes are reported in the area. Use caution and common sense.

BUS

While the Metro makes the most sense for trips across Madrid, buses cover areas inaccessible by the Metro and are a great way to see the city. Like the Metro, the bus system is exceptionally organized. Most stops are clearly marked, but if you want extra guidance in finding routes and stops, try the handy *Plano de los Transportes*, free at the tourist office, or *Madrid en Autobús*, free at bus kiosks.

The fare is €0.95 for a single ride. Ten-ride *bonotransporte* passes are sold at newsstands and *estancos* for €5. Buses run from 6am to 11:30pm. From midnight until 3am, the night bus service, **Búho** (owl), travels from Pl. Cibeles (and other marked routes) to the outskirts every 20min.; from 3-6am, they run every hr. Night buses (N1-N20), the cheapest form of transportation for late-night revelers, are listed in a special section of the *Plano*. For more info, call **Empresa Municipal de Transportes.** (☎914 06 88 10. Spanish only. Open 6am-midnight.)

TAXI

Madrid is filled with taxis around the clock. On major streets, it's easy to catch a taxi in just a few minutes. If one does not appear when you need it, or if you want to summon one to your door, call **Radio Taxi** (☎914 47 51 80), **Radio-Taxi Independiente** (☎913 71 21 31), or **Teletaxi** (☎913 71 37 11). A green *"libre"* sign in the window or a lit green light indicates availability. Base fare is €1.35, plus €0.63-0.81 per kilometer from 6am-10pm and €0.81-0.91 from 10pm-6am. Common fare supplements include: airport (€4); bus and train stations (€2); luggage charge (€0.50 per bag). Fare from the city center to the airport is €15-18, depending on traffic.

Check that the driver starts the meter. If you have a complaint or think you've been overcharged, demand a *recibo oficial* (official receipt) and *hoja de reclamaciones* (complaint form), which the driver is required to supply. Take down the license number, route taken, and fare charged. Drop off the forms and information at the **Oficina Municipal del Taxi,** C. Vallehermoso, 1, 2nd fl. (☎915 88 96 32; fax 915 88 96 35) or **Ayuntamiento** (City Hall), Pl. Villa, 4 (☎914 47 07 15 or 914 47 07 14), to request a refund. To request **taxi service for the disabled,** call ☎915 47 85 00 or 915 47 86 00. Rates are same as other taxis. If you leave possessions in a taxi, visit or call the **Negociado de Objetos Perdidos,** Pl. Legazpi, 7. (☎915 88 43 46. Open M-F 9am-2pm.) Drivers are obligated to turn in items within 48 hours.

CAR RENTAL

There is no reason to rent a car in Madrid. If congested traffic and nightmarish parking don't drive you into hysterics, aggressive drivers and annoying mopeds will. Don't drive unless you're planning to zoom out of the city, and even then bus and train fares will be cheaper. Tobacco shops sell parking permits for designated street parking. If driving to destinations outside of Spain, a larger car rental chain is your best bet. The tourist office has a complete list of car rental companies.

Atesa, Reservations: ☎902 10 01 01; www.atesa.com. Offices: Gran Vía, 80, in Pl. Mostenses (☎915 42 50 15); airport (☎913 93 72 32).

Avis, Reservations: ☎902 13 55 31; www.avis.com. Offices: Estación de Atocha (☎915 30 01 68); Gran Vía, 60 (☎915 48 42 03); airport (☎913 93 72 22).

Budget, Reservations: ☎901 20 12 12; www.budget.com. Offices: Av. Aragon, 336 (☎913 74 94 50); airport (☎913 93 72 16).

Europcar, Reservations: ☎902 10 50 30; www.europcar.com. Offices: Estación de Atocha (☎915 30 01 94); airport (☎913 93 72 35).

Hertz, Reservations: (☎902 402 405 or 913 72 93 00; www.hertz.com). Offices: Gran Vía, 88, #18 (☎915 42 58 05); Estación de Atocha (☎914 68 13 18); Estación de Chamartín (☎917 33 04 00); airport (☎913 93 72 28).

MOPED RENTAL

Fortunately for pedestrians, Madrid is not scarred by the moped mayhem that has taken over other parts of Europe. Though mopeds are swift and convenient, Madrid's stellar public transportation system is more than sufficient for getting around. A lock and helmet are necessary if you decide to rent one.

Motocicletas Antonio Castro, C. Conde Duque, 13 (☎915 42 06 57). M: San Bernardo. Mopeds start at €27 per day or €117 per week, including unlimited mileage and insurance. €241 deposit required. Min. age 18. **International Driver's Permit** required for mopeds larger than 125cc. Open M-F 8am-1:30pm and 5-8pm, Sa 9-11am.

PRACTICAL INFORMATION

TOURIST AND FINANCIAL SERVICES

Tourist Offices: English is spoken at most tourist offices. Those planning trips outside the Comunidad de Madrid can visit region-specific offices within Madrid; ask the tourist offices below for their addresses. **Regional/Provincial Office of the Comunidad de Madrid,** main office: Duque de Medinacelia, 2 (☎914 29 49 51; info line 902 10 00 07; www.comadrid.es/turismo). M: Pl. de España. Brochures, transportation info, and maps for towns in the Comunidad. Extremely helpful; make this your first stop.

English spoken. **Municipal Tourist Office,** Pl. Mayor, 3 (☎913 66 54 77 or 913 58 816 36; fax 913 66 54 77). M: Sol. Hands out indispensable city and transportation maps and a complete guide to accommodations, as well as *In Madrid* and *Enjoy Madrid,* monthly activities and information guides. Open M-Sa 10am-8pm, Su 10am-3pm. **Secondary office** at Mercado Pta. de Toledo, Ronda de Toledo, 1, stand #3134 (☎913 64 18 75). M: Pta. de Toledo. In a gallery with large banners on a plaza across from the Metro station. Open M-F 9am-7pm, Sa 9:30am-1:30pm. **Other offices** at Estación Chamartín (see **By Train,** p. 87) and the airport (see **By Plane,** p. 87). Megastore **El Corte Inglés** has **free maps** and information (see p. 98).

General Info Line: ☎901 30 06 00. Run by the Ayuntamiento. They'll tell you anything about Madrid, from police locations to zoo hours. Ask for *inglés* and they will transfer you to an English-speaking operator.

Websites: www.comadrid.es/turismo; www.tourspain.es; www.cronicamadrid.com; www.guiadelocio.com; www.madridman.com; www.red2000.com/spain/madrid.

Tours: Tours can be pricey but informative. Read the fine print before signing on. Tourist office has details as well as offering their own **walking tours** of Habsburg Madrid every Saturday (Pl. Mayor office; 10am; €3.50). **Madrid Vision** (☎917 79 18 88 or 915 41 63 21) offers tours of the city on double decker buses. A great option for those with limited time. There are 3 routes (Madrid Historico, Moderno, and Monumental) each of which makes about 20 key stops around the city. Get off and on the bus as you please. Weekdays €9.62, weekends €10.82. **Juliá Tours,** Gran Vía, 68 (☎915 59 96 05). M: Pl. de España. Offers pricey tours of Andalucía, Portugal, and Morocco.

Budget Travel: Viajes TIVE, C. Fernando el Católico, 88 (☎915 43 74 12; fax 915 44 00 62). M: Moncloa. Walk straight down C. Arcipreste de Hita, and turn left on C. Fernando el Católico; it's on your left. A great resource for long-term visitors. ISIC €4.25, HI card €10.85. Organizes group excursions and language classes. Lodging and student residence info. English spoken. Open M-F 9am-2pm; Sa 9am-noon, information only. Arrive early to avoid lines. If you don't need tickets, try **Comunidad de Madrid,** Dirección General de Juventud, C. Gran Vía, 10 (☎917 20 11 82; www.comadrid.es/infojoven). M: Banco de España. It offers many of the same services as TIVE. Open M-F 9am-2pm and 5-8pm; in Aug. mornings only. **ASATEJ Group,** Fernardo el Católico, 60 (☎915 43 47 61; www.asatej.com). M: Arguelles. Backpackers sell student airfares, tours, car rental, bus passes, ISIC cards, and other travel needs. (Open M-F 10am-8pm, Sa 10:30am-1:30pm). **USIT,** Pl. Callao, 3 (☎902 25 25 75 or 915 24 70 40; www.usitworld.com) is part of a travel megaplex, arranging trips, car rentals, and documentation. Student friendly. **Viajes Barceló,** C. Princesa 3 (☎902 11 62 26; www.barceloviajes.com). M: Ventura Rodríguez or Pl. España, has student travel services. (Open 10am-7pm.)

Currency Exchange: Santander Central Hispano charges no commission on traveler's checks up to about €500. Also offers the best rates on AmEx traveler's checks. **Main branch,** Pl. Canalejas, 1 (☎915 58 11 11). M: Sol. Follow C. San Jerónimo to Pl. Canalejas. Open Apr.-Sept. M-F 8:30am-2:30pm, Sa 8:30am-1pm; Oct.-Mar. M-Th 8:30am-4:30pm, F 8:30am-2pm, Sa 8:30am-1pm. **Banks** usually charge 1-2% commission (minimum charge €3). Booths in Sol and Gran Vía, open as late as midnight and on weekends, have poor rates and are not a good deal for cashing traveler's checks. On the other hand, for small-denomination bills, they may be the best option. **ATMs** are everywhere in Madrid and can be operated in English. **Servi Red, Servi Caixa,** and **Telebanco** machines accept bank cards with one or more of the Cirrus, PLUS, EuroCard, or NYCE logos. See **Cash Cards,** p. 15.

American Express: Pl. Cortés, 2 (Traveler services: ☎913 22 54 40; currency exchange: ☎917 43 77 83). M: Sevilla. From the Metro stop, take a right on C. Alcalá, another right down C. Cedacero and a left on C. San Jerónimo; it's on the left. "Agencia de Viajes" is written in big letters on the windows. Offers **currency exchange** (no commission on cash or AmEx traveler's checks; small set fee for non-AmEx traveler's checks), will hold mail for 30 days, and can help send and receive wired money. In an emergency, will cash personal checks up to US$1000 for cardholders. Traveler services open M-F 9am-5:30pm, Sa 9am-noon; currency exchange M-F 9am-7:30pm, Sa 9am-2pm. 24hr. Express Cash machine outside. Also airport office (☎913 93 82 22). To report or cancel lost traveler's checks, call toll free ☎902 37 56 37. To report other problems, call ☎900 94 14 13 or 900 99 44 26.

Lost or stolen credit cards: American Express (☎915 72 03 03); VISA (☎900 97 44 45); MasterCard (☎915 19 21 00); any credit card (☎915 81 18 11)

LOCAL SERVICES

Luggage Storage: Barajas Airport. Follow the signs to *consigna*. 1 day €2.60, 2-15 days €3.25-4.55 per day, after day 15 €0.65-1.30 per day. **Estación Chamartín.** Self-serve, automatic lockers in the *consignas automáticas* area by the bus stop. Lockers €2.40-4.50 per day. Open daily 6:30am-10:15pm. **Estación Atocha.** Same services, prices, and hours. Follow signs to *consignas automáticas* above the rainforest area. **Estación Sur de Autobuses.** Bags €4.85. **Estación Auto-Res.** Bags €1.20.

El Corte Inglés: C. Preciados, 3 (☎913 79 80 00). M: Sol. **C. Goya, 76** (☎914 32 93 00). M: Goya. **C. Princesa, 56** (☎914 54 60 00). M: Argüelles. **C. Raimundo Fernández Villaverde, 79** (☎914 18 88 00). M: Nuevos Ministerios. Various other locations in Madrid and throughout Spain. *La mama grande* of department stores, the chain's official motto is: "A place to shop. A place to dream." No matter what you need, be it clothes, groceries, or train tickets, you can find it here. Currency exchange with no commission but mediocre rates. Open M-Sa 10am-9:30pm, Su 11am-9pm.

English-Language Periodicals: International edition dailies and weeklies available at kiosks everywhere, especially on the Gran Vía, Paseos del Prado, Recoletos, and Castellana, and around Pta. Sol. If you're dying for the *New York Times (*€2.70), try one of the **VIPS** restaurants (see **Red-Eye Establishments,** p. 107).

Language Service: Forocio, C. San Jerónimo, 18, 1st fl. (☎915 22 81 96 or 915 22 56 77; www.forocio.com). M: Sol. An organization dedicated to bringing foreigners and natives together to share languages and good times. Sponsors weekly international parties. Open M-F 10am-10pm.

Libraries: The municipal tourist office has a comprehensive list of *bibliotecas* around the city. These include **Bibliotecas Municipales Especializadas,** and numerous branches of the **Bibliotecas Publicas Municipales por Distritos** (22 locations), and **Bibliotecas Populares** (18 locations). Large branch at M: Puerta de Toledo with English-language periodicals. (☎913 66 54 07. Info line ☎914 45 98 45. Open M-F 8:30am-8:45pm, Sa 9am-1:45pm.) **Washington Irving Center** (☎915 87 22 00), in the American Embassy, C. Serrano, 75. M: Serrano or Colón. Anyone over 16 can check books out for 2 weeks by filling out a form. Allow 1 week for processing. (Open M-F 2-6pm.)

Religious Services: Our Lady of Mercy, C. Alfonso XIII, 165 (☎917 73 98 29 or 914 16 90 09), at Pl. Habana. Sunday Mass in English 11am, followed by coffee and doughnuts. **Immanuel Baptist Church,** C. Hernández de Tejada, 4 (☎914 07 43 47). English services Su 11am and 7pm. **Community Church of Madrid,** C. Bravo Murillo, 85. M: Cuatro Caminos. At the Colegio El Porvenir. Multi-denominational Protestant services in English Su 10am. **British Embassy Church of St. George,** C. Núñez de Balboa, 43 (☎915 76 51 09). M: Velázquez. Services Su 8:30, 10, and 11:15am. **Sinagoga Beth Yaacov,** C. Balmes, 3 (☎915 91 31 31), near Pl. Sorolla. M: Iglesia. Services F 8pm, Sa 9:15am. Kosher restaurant can be reserved. Passport sometimes required. Spanish only. **Centro Islámico,** C. Alonso Cano, 3 (☎914 48 05 54). M: Iglesia. Services and language classes. Open M-F 10:45am-2pm.

Women's Services: For general information on women's services in Spain or to report an incident, call **Instituto de la Mujer** (☎900 19 10 10). For literature concerning women's issues, try the **Librería de Mujeres,** C. San Cristóbal, 17 (☎/fax 915 21 70 43; www.unapalabraotra.org/libreriamujeres.html), near Pl. Mayor. M: Sol. From Sol, C. San Cristóbal is the 2nd left off C. Mayor. The shop's motto is *"Los libros no muerden, el feminismo tampoco."* (Books don't bite; neither does feminism.) Books and gifts, but more of a resource for Spanish speakers. Helpful with finding local support and discussion groups. Open M-F 10am-2pm and 5-8pm, Sa 10am-2pm.

Gay and Lesbian Services: Most establishments in Chueca carry a free guide to gay nightlife in Spain called **Shanguide.** If you can't find one right away, just ask someone in a store near the Pl. Chueca and they will tell you where to get one. This guide book offers detailed listings and maps of the many gay bars, clubs, cafes, restaurants, bookstores, shops, and associations in and around Madrid. Alternatively, you can purchase **Zero** magazine (€3.60) at any kiosk stand. The magazine includes a small pull-out guide to nightlife and gay activities. These listings are often more up to date than the **Spartacus International Gay Guide,** sold at almost any newsstand or bookstore in Madrid. Support groups and associations: **Colectivo de Gais y Lesbianas de Madrid (COGAM),** C. Fuencarral, 37 (☎/fax 915 23 00 70 or 915 22 45 17). M: Gran Vía. Provides a wide range of services and activities of interest to gays, lesbians, and bisexuals. English usually spoken. Free screenings of gay-interest movies, COGAM youth group (25 and under), and HIV-positive support group (☎915 22 45 17; M-F 6-10pm). Reception daily M-Sa 5:30-9pm. Free counseling M-Th 7-9pm. Library open daily 7-9pm. Once every 2 months, COGAM publishes **Entiendes...?,** a magazine in Spanish about gay issues that also lists activities and nightspots for every town in Spain. **Berkana Librería Gay y Lesbiana** (☎915 22 55 99; www.libreriaberkana.com) has guidebooks, contact information, and listings (see **Books,** p. 135). Most entertainment guides list gay and lesbian clubs. **GAY-INFORM,** a gay info line (☎915 23 00 70), provides information in Spanish (and sometimes French and English) about gay associations, leisure activities, and health issues. The same number has info on sports, workshops in French and English, dinners, and **Brujulai,** COGAM's weekend excursion group. Open daily 5-9pm.

Laundromat: Lavandería Ondablu, C. León, 3 (☎913 69 50 71). M: Antón Martín. **Lavandería,** C. Cervantes 1. M: Puerta del Sol or Banco de España. From Pl. Santa Ana follow C. Prado, turn right on C. León, then left on C. Cervantes. Wash €4, dry €1 for 9min. Open M-Sa 9am-8pm. **Lavandería Automática SIDEC,** C. Don Felipe, 4. M: Tribunal. Wash €4.50, detergent €0.20. Open M-F 10am-9pm.

EMERGENCY AND COMMUNICATIONS

Emergency: ☎112 (for all emergencies). ☎091 or 092 (national and local police).

Police: C. de los Madrazo, 9 (☎915 41 71 60). M: Sevilla. From C. Arenal a right onto C. Cedacneros and left onto C. los Madrazo. English forms available. To report crimes in the **Metro,** go to the office in the Sol station (☎915 21 09 11). Open daily 8am-11pm. **Guardia Civil** (☎062 or 915 34 02 00). **Protección Civil** (☎915 37 31 00).

Crisis Lines: Poison Control (24hr. ☎915 62 04 20). **Rape Hotline** (☎915 74 01 10). Open M-F 10am-2pm and 4-7pm (other times machine-recorded instructions).

Help Lines: AIDS Info Hotline (☎900 11 10 00). Open M-F 10am-10pm. **Detox** (☎900 16 15 15). English spoken. Open daily 9am-9pm. **Alcoholics Anonymous,** C. Juan Bravo, 40, 2nd fl. (English ☎913 09 19 47; Spanish ☎913 41 82 82). M: Núñez de Balboa. **English-Language Helpline** (☎915 59 13 93). Trained volunteers offer confidential help. €0.14 per min. Open daily 7-11pm.

Late-Night Pharmacy: Dial ☎098, the general Madrid info line, to find the nearest one. One located at **C. Mayor, 59** (☎915 48 00 14), near M: Sol. Listings of the nearest on-duty pharmacy are also posted in all pharmacy windows.

First Aid Stations: Scattered about the city, all open 24hr. C. Navas de Tolosa (☎915 21 00 25); General Ricardos, 14 (☎924 71 03 50); Av. del Paseo de Extremadura, 147 (☎914 64 76 32).

Hospitals: Prompt appointments are hard to obtain, but public hospitals don't require advance payment. Emergency rooms are the best option for immediate attention. US insurance is not accepted, but get a receipt, and your insurance may pick up the tab when you get home. General emergency exam runs €150. For non-emergency concerns, **Anglo-American Medical Unit,** Conde de Aranda, 1, 1st fl. (☎914 35 18 23), is quick and friendly. M: Serrano or Retiro. Doctors, dentists, and optometrists. Run partly by British and Americans. Regular personnel on duty 9am-8pm. Not an emergency clinic. Initial visit €54 for students, €60-90 for non-students. AmEx/MC/V. Embassies and consulates keep lists of English-speaking doctors in private practice. **Hospital Clínico San Carlos** (☎913 30 30 00), on Pl. Cristo Rey. M: Moncloa. Open 24hr.

Emergency Clinics: In a **medical emergency,** dial ☎061 or 112. **Hospital de Madrid,** Pl. Conde del Valle Suchil, 16 (☎914 47 66 00; www.hospitaldemadrid.com). **Equipo Quirúrgico Municipal No. 1,** C. Montesa, 22 (☎915 88 51 00). M: Manuel Becerra. **Hospital Ramón y Cajal** (☎913 36 80 00), Ctra. Colmenar Viejo. Bus #135 from Pl. Castilla. **Red Cross** (☎915 22 22 22, info 902 22 22 92).

Telephones: Information ☎1003. No English spoken. (For further information, see **Keeping in Touch,** p. 29.)

Internet Access: New Internet centers are surfacing everywhere. Listed below are 5 of possibly hundreds of Internet cafes spread across the city. The rates are generally consistent (roughly €0.80-1.50 per 30min., €1.30-2.50 per hr.).

Easy Everything, C. Montera, 10 (☎915 23 29 44; www.easyeverything.com). M: Sol. From the Puerta del Sol, look for C. Montera which goes towards Gran Vía. Open daily 24hr. with lots of computers, unbeatably fast connections, good music, a cafe, tons of travelers, and cheap rates. You are not obligated to use all of your purchased time at once, making quick email checks easy and cost-efficient. Rates fluctuate based on the number of computers in use.

Conéctate, C. Hilarión Eslava, 27 (☎915 44 54 65; www.conectate.es). M: Moncloa. A computer zone for students with over 300 flat-screens and some of the lowest rates in Madrid. Open 24hr. Also has stations in several VIPS restaurants (C. Serrano, Alcalá, Parque, Velázquez).

Yazzgo Internet, Puerta del Sol, 6; Gran Vía, 60; Gran Vía, 69; Gran Vía, 84; Estación Chamartín; Estación Méndez Alvaro. (☎915 22 11 20; www.yazzgo.com). Trendy work center with locations throughout Madrid. Open daily 8:30am-10:30pm, except Gran Vía, 69, open 8:30am-1am.

Oficina13, C. Mayor, 1, 4th fl., office 13. M: Sol. Take the elevator up and buzz the office. A nice new office; friendly service and U2 songs abound. Open daily 10am-11pm.

La Casa de Internet, C. Luchana, 20 (☎915 94 42 00). M: Bilbao. Open M-Sa noon-2am, Su 4pm-2am.

Post Office: Palacio de Comunicaciones, C. Alcalá, 51, on Pl. Cibeles (☎902 19 71 97). M: Banco de España. Enormous, ornate palace on the far side of the plaza from the Metro. Info (main vestibule) open M-Sa 8am-9:30pm. Windows open M-Sa 8:30am-9:30pm, Su 9am-2pm for stamp purchases. Receive **Lista de Correos** (Poste Restante) at windows 80-82; passport required. For **certified mail, telex,** and **fax** service, and the information booth, enter main door. Send packages at windows marked "Todos Los Productos" in main area behind info counter or through door N (enter from C. Montalbán). Postal Express is at door K (enter from Po. del Prado). **Postal Code:** 28080.

ACCOMMODATIONS

The demand for rooms in Madrid is always high and increases dramatically in summer. Though the city is filled with hostels, good quality at good prices can be hard to find. Prices range from €17 to €50 per person, depending on location, amenities, and season. Don't be deceived; higher prices do not necessarily translate into nicer accommodations. Reservations are strongly recommended at the top listings in the sections below. Try negotiating the price if you plan on staying awhile.

Because there are so many reasonably priced hostels *(hostales)* in Madrid, the listings here focus on them almost exclusively. Be aware that there are other accommodation options in Madrid, including hotels and *pensiones*. In Madrid, the difference between a one-star *hostal* and a *pensión* is often minimal. A room in a one- or two-star *hostal* has at least the basics: bed, closet space, desk with chair, sink and towel, window, light fixture, fake flowers, a lock on the door, and the occasional religious icon. Winter heating is standard; air-conditioning is not. Unless otherwise noted, communal bathrooms (toilet and shower) are the norm. Most places accept reservations, but none require them. Still, reservations are recommended in summer and on weekends year-round, especially in the Puerta del Sol area and at the first place *Let's Go* lists in each district. Hostels in Madrid are generally well-kept and comfortable; some are simply spectacular. Owners are usually accustomed to opening the doors, albeit groggily, at all hours or providing keys for guests, but ask before club-hopping into the wee hours; late-night lockouts or confrontations with irate owners are never fun. *Pensiones* are like boarding houses: they sometimes have curfews and often host guests staying for longer periods of time. Good deals can often be found outside central locations, and Madrid's stellar public transportation makes virtually any place central.

EL CENTRO: SOL, ÓPERA, AND PLAZA MAYOR

Puerta del Sol is the center of the city in the center of the country. All roads converge here (it's Spain's km 0) and most visitors ramble through at least once. Signs indicating *hostales* and *pensiones* stick out from flower-potted balconies and decaying facades on narrow, sloping streets. For better deals in quieter spots, stray several blocks from Sol. Don't be afraid to climb that extra flight of dusty stairs to find a good deal. The following listings fall in the area between the Sol and Ópera Metro stops. Price and location in the Centro are as good as they get, especially if you are planning to brave the legendary nightlife. Buses #3, 25, 39, and 500 serve Ópera; buses #3, 5 (from Atocha), 15, 20, 50, 51, 52, 53, and 150 serve Sol.

Hostal Paz, C. Flora, 4, 1st and 4th fl. (☎915 47 30 47). M: Ópera. Don't be deterred by the dark street, parallel to C. Arenal, off C. Donados or C. Hileras. Unbeatable hospitality from wonderful owners. Peaceful rooms with large windows, satellite TV, A/C, and spotless bathrooms. Reservations advised. Laundry €8. Singles €17; doubles €27-32; triples €40. Monthly rentals available but must be arranged far in advance. MC/V. ❷

Hostal-Residencia Luz, C. Fuentes, 10, 3rd fl. (☎915 42 07 59 or 915 59 74 18; fax 915 42 07 59), off C. Arenal. M: Ópera. 12 sunny, newly redecorated rooms exude comfort: hardwood floors, elegant furniture, beautiful curtains and bedspreads. Satellite TV, A/C, fax, and public phone. Laundry €6. Singles €15; doubles €27.50-33; triples €33-39. Discounts for longer stays. ❶

Hostal-Residencia Rober, C. Arenal, 26, 5th fl. (☎915 41 91 75). M: Ópera. Quiet *hostal* with brilliant balcony views down Arenal. Smoking strictly prohibited. All 14 pristine sound-proof rooms have their own tiny TVs and A/C. Singles with double bed and shower €25, with bath €33; doubles with bath €38; triples with bath €58. Good discounts for longer stays. ❸

Hostal Valencia, Pl. Oriente, 2, 3rd fl. (☎915 59 84 50). M: Ópera. Narrow glass elevator leads you to elegant rooms, each uniquely decorated, overlooking the gorgeous Plaza Oriente and the Palacio Real. All rooms have TV. Interior singles €42; interior doubles €60; double with view €68; master suite €78. ❹

Hostal Esparteros, C. Esparteros, 12, 4th fl. (☎/fax 915 21 09 03). M: Sol. Cheap, small, sparkling rooms with balcony or large windows (no fans or A/C). English-speaking owner ensures a terrific stay. Laundry €7. Singles €20; doubles €35; triples €42. 10% discount for longer stays. ❷

Hostal Cantábrico, C. de la Cruz, 5 (☎915 31 01 30 or 915 21 33 03), near Pl. Canalejas. M: Sol. Welcoming hallways and reception lead to spacious rooms all with complete bath, some with nice balcony views. Over 100 years in operation. Singles €31; doubles €46; triples €61. ❸

Hostal-Residencia Cruz-Sol, Pl. Santa Cruz, 6, 3rd fl. (☎915 32 71 97; info@hostalcruz-sol.com). M: Sol. Modern rooms with parquet floors, double-paned windows, safes, heat, phones, Internet jacks, A/C, and baths. Vending machines satiate late-night thirst. Laundry €11. Singles €36; doubles €48; triples €60; quads €72. AmEx/MC/V. ❹

Hostal Portugal, C. Flora, 4, 1st fl. (☎915 59 40 14). M: Opera. Mediocre rooms with TV and bath, but great location, especially if Hostal Paz is full and you don't want to schlep your luggage around anymore. Doubles €33; triples €45. ❷

Hostal-Residencia Miño, C. Arenal, 16, 2nd fl. (☎915 31 50 79 or 915 31 97 89). M: Ópera. Deer's head at the entrance. Several different rooms, some with hardwood floors and balconies. Singles €21-29; doubles €36-39; triples with bath €51. ❷

Hostal Madrid, C. Esparteros, 6, 2nd fl. (☎915 22 00 60; fax 915 32 35 10; www.hostal-madrid.com), off C. Mayor. M: Sol. Average hostel with TVs, telephones, safes, A/C, new bathrooms, and high prices. Reservations 4 days ahead advised. Singles €48-55; doubles €66; triple with balcony €84. AmEx/MC/V. ❹

Hostal Alicante, C. Arenal, 16, 2nd fl. on the left. (☎915 31 51 78). M: Ópera or Sol. Typical hostel fare with TV and heat. Singles €23; doubles €38, with bath €41; triples with bath €60. MC/V. ❷

HUERTAS

Although *madrileños* have never settled on a nickname for this neighborhood, the area between C. San Jerónimo and C. de las Huertas is generally referred to as Huertas. Once a seedy area and a Hemingway hangout, Huertas has shaped up to be a cultural hotbed of food and drink. Though quieter than El Centro, Malasaña, and Chueca, **Pl. Santa Ana, C. Príncipe,** and **C. Echegaray** offer some of the best bars in Madrid, and **C. Ventura de la Vega** some of the best restaurants. Sol, Pl. Mayor, *el triángulo del arte*, and the Atocha train station are all within walking distance. Sol-bound buses stop near accommodations on C. Príncipe, C. Núñez de Arce, and C. San Jerónimo; buses #14, 27, 37, and 45 run along Po. Prado. The Metro stops are Sol, Sevilla, and Antón Martín.

Hostal Gonzalo, C. Cervantes, 34, 3rd fl. (☎914 29 27 14; fax 914 20 20 07), off C. León. M: Antón Martín. A budget traveler's dream. The friendly staff welcomes you to this lively *hostal* with newly renovated rooms, pristine baths, firm beds, TVs, and fans in summer. Leather-plush lounge. Singles €35; doubles €43; triples €55. AmEx/MC/V. ❸

Hostal Internacional, C. Echegaray, 5, 2nd fl. (☎914 29 62 09). With extensive renovations completed in the summer of 2002, Internacional's rooms are new and crisp, all with TV. Also boasts a nice common room. Singles €30; doubles €36. ❸

Hostal-Residencia Lido, C. Echegaray, 5, 2nd fl. (☎914 29 62 07). M: Sol or Sevilla. Across the hall from Internacional, Lido also recently finished a makeover, showcasing new rooms with comfy beds, TV, and complete bath. Singles €18; doubles €30. ❷

Hostal Villar, C. Príncipe, 18, 1st-4th fl. (☎915 31 66 00; fax 915 21 50 73; www.arrakis.es/~h-villar). M: Sol or Sevilla. From the Sol Metro, walk down C. San Jerónimo and turn right on C. Príncipe. The 1970s stormed through this building, leaving behind 46 decidedly brown and unintentionally retro rooms with TV and phone, some with A/C. Big lounge for socializing. Singles €20, with bath €23; doubles €26.50, with bath €35; triples €37, with bath €49. AmEx/MC/V. ❷

Hostal Armesto, C. San Agustín, 6, 1st fl. (☎914 29 90 31), in front of Pl. Cortés. M: Antón Martín. This small hostel offers exceptional hospitality and a quiet night's sleep for the less boisterous. Some rooms have garden view, all have private baths, TVs, A/C. Older crowd. Singles €39; doubles €45; triples €53. AmEx/MC/V. ❹

Hostal-Residencia Carreras, C. Príncipe, 18, 3rd fl. (☎/fax 915 22 00 36), off C. San Jerónimo, between Pl. Santa Ana and Canalejas. M: Antón Martín, Sol, or Sevilla. Be sure to ask for a room with a balcony–they tend to be larger. Most rooms have been renovated recently. Small, central lounge. Singles €21, with bath €48; doubles €36, with bath €42-48; triples €54, with bath €60. AmEx/MC/V. ❷

Hostal Aguilar, C. San Jerónimo, 32, 2nd fl. (☎914 29 59 26 or 914 29 36 61; fax 914 29 26 61; www.hostalaguilar.com). M: Sol or Sevilla. More than 50 clean, expansive, and modern rooms with vast bathrooms, telephones, A/C, safe boxes, and TVs. Elegantly spare lounge with deep couches serves as a meeting ground for clubbers. Singles €30; doubles €42; triples €47; quads €69. MC/V. ❸

Hostal R. Rodríguez, C. Núñez de Arce, 9, 3rd fl. (☎915 22 44 31), off Pl. Santa Ana. M: Sol or Sevilla. Reception decor makes even the cheapest of travelers feel like royalty. Clean shared baths and spacious rooms. 24hr. reception. English spoken. Singles €25; doubles €42-47; triples €65. AmEx/MC/V. ❸

Hostal-Residencia Sud-Americana, Po. Prado, 12, 6th fl. (☎914 29 25 64), across from the Prado. M: Antón Martín or Atocha. Airy doubles facing the Prado with views of the Paseo. Great location, simple rooms. Singles €18; doubles €33; triples €52.50. ❷

Hostal Leones, C. Núñez de Arce, 14, 2nd fl. (☎915 31 08 89). Basic hostel with inviting staff and spotless bathrooms. Singles €17; doubles €29, with bath €33. ❷

Hostal-Residencia Mondragón, C. San Jerónimo, 32, 4th fl. (☎914 29 68 16). M: Sol. Cheap prices come at the expense of service. Site of Spain's first motion picture film in 1898 (see p. 76). Ask for a room off the gardenia-filled terrace overlooking the street. Hot water runs only in communal bathrooms. Singles €13; doubles €19; triples €27. ❶

GRAN VÍA

The neon lights of Broadway and the Champs-Élysées have met their match in Gran Vía. The massive avenue glows and pulsates with the sharp lights of sex shops, McDonald's, and five-star hotels in a 24-hour parade of flashing cars, swishing skirts, and stack-heeled shoes. *Hostal* signs scatter the horizon, but accommodations tend to be pricier and less comfortable than in other areas. Have your wits about you when returning late at night. El Centro and Huertas provide safer bargains. Buses #1, 2, 44, 46, 74, 75, 133, 146, 147, and 148 reach Pl. Callao; buses #1, 2, 3, 40, 46, 74, 146, and 149 service both Pl. España and Pl. Callao. The closest Metro stops are Gran Vía, Callao, Santo Domingo, and Banco de España.

Hostal A. Nebrija, Gran Vía, 67, 8th fl., elevator A (☎915 47 73 19). M: Pl. España. A grandson continues his grandparents' tradition with pleasant, spacious rooms offering magnificent views of the city. A very tidy building, and heavily furnished in classic style. All rooms have TVs and fans. Singles €26; doubles €36; triples €49. AmEx/MC/V. ❸

Hostal Margarita, Gran Vía, 50, 5th fl. (☎/fax 915 47 35 49). M: Callao. Warm and inviting family offers simple rooms with large windows, TV, and telephone, most with street views. Plush lounge and big kitchen. Laundry €10. Reservations recommended. Singles €25; doubles €36, with bath €38; triples with bath €48. MC/V. ❸

Hostal Triana, C. de la Salud, 13, 1st fl. (☎915 32 68 12; fax 915 22 97 29; www.hostaltriana.com). M: Callao or Gran Vía. From Gran Vía, turn onto C. Salud; the sign is quite visible. Catering to those seeking a little more comfort than the standard *hostal.* All rooms have TV, fans, and private baths. Reserve 2 weeks ahead. Singles €30; doubles €41, with A/C €46. ❸

Hostal Santillan, Gran Vía 64, 8th fl. (☎/fax 915 48 23 28). M: Pl. España. Take the glass elevator to the top floor. If the Beatles, little dwarfs, and familial portraits don't welcome you, the friendly management will. Simple rooms with showers and sinks. All have TV, fan, safe box, and phone. Singles €30; doubles €45; triples €55. MC/V. ❸

Hostal-Residencia Alibel, Gran Vía, 44, 8th fl. (☎915 21 00 51). M: Callao. Well-lit rooms with great views show off Alibel's recent face-lift. Doubles €35; triples €42. ❹

Hostal-Residencia Lamalonga, Gran Vía, 56, 2nd fl. (☎915 47 26 31 or 915 47 68 94). M: Santo Domingo. Rooms with views, A/C, full bath, and phone. Singles €36; doubles €48; triples €58. 10% discount for stays over 5 days. MC/V. ❹

Hostal Lauria, Gran Vía, 50, 4th fl. (☎/fax 915 41 91 82; www.geocities.com/hostal lauria). M: Callao. Sleeping quarters are well endowed with large beds, baths, phones, fans, and TVs. Lounge with couches, TV, and stereo. English spoken. Singles €33; doubles €42; triples €57. MC/V. ❸

MALASAÑA AND CHUECA

Split down the middle by C. Fuencarral, Malasaña and Chueca are two of Madrid's best hard-core party pits. Beyond outrageous nightlife and numerous drinking outlets, the area offers a wide range of excellent restaurants, great shopping, and charming plazas. Even though *hostales* and *pensiones* in Malasaña and Chueca are usually located on the upper floors of old, and sometimes dilapidated, buildings, accommodations tend to be a bit pricier here than in other areas of the city. Don't be deterred by the occasional sketchy street—Chueca is hip, fun, funky, and wild. It is the pleasuredome of Madrid's gay population, but offers something for everyone. Buses #3, 40, and 149 run along C. Fuencarral and Hortaleza. Metro stops Chueca, Gran Vía, and Tribunal service the area.

Hostal-Residencia Domínguez, C. Santa Brígida, 1, 1st fl. (☎/fax 915 32 15 47). M: Tribunal. Down C. Fuencarral toward Gran Vía, left on C. Santa Brígida, and up 1 flight. The doubles on the 3rd fl. are immaculate and brand new. Hospitable young owner is ready with tips on local nightlife. English spoken. Singles €21, with bath €30; doubles with bath and A/C €40. ❷

Hostal Chelo, C. Hortaleza, 17, 3rd fl. (☎915 32 70 33; www.chelo.com). M: Gran Vía. In addition to its great location, the biggest draw of this *hostal* is the helpful staff, educated on everything and anything about Madrid. Rooms are clean and spacious, with TV and complete bath. English spoken. Singles €30; doubles €36. ❸

Hostal Lorenzo, C. Clavel, 8 (☎915 21 30 57; fax 915 32 79 78). M: Gran Vía. From the Metro, walk down Gran Vía and make a left on C. Clavel. In the process of converting from a *hostal* to a hotel, Lorenzo has renovated 2 floors to produce elegant and affordable accommodations equipped with crisp, new furniture, modern baths, and soundproof windows. Older rooms on the 3rd fl. are cheaper. Reservations recommended. Singles €45; doubles €65-80. IVA not included. AmEx/MC/V. ❹

Hostal Palacios and **Hostal Ribadavia,** C. Fuencarral, 25, 1st-3rd fl. (☎915 31 10 58 or 915 31 48 47). M: Gran Vía. Both hotels are run by the same cheerful family. Palacio (1st and 2nd fl.) offers large, tiled rooms with elegant modern furniture. Older Ribadavia (3rd fl.) has comfortable rooms with TVs. Singles €20, with bath €27; doubles €28, with bath €35; triples €45, with bath €48; quads with bath €60. AmEx/MC/V. ❷

Hispa Domus, C. San Bartolomé, 4, 2nd fl. (☎915 23 81 27; www.hispadomus.com). M: Chueca or Gran Vía. Small hostel that caters to a mostly gay clientele. Gregarious staff and colorful rooms, complete with A/C, bath, and postmodern decor. English and Italian spoken. Reservations required. Singles €40; doubles €46-57. MC/V. ❹

Hostal Abril, C. Fuencarral, 39, 4th fl. (☎915 31 53 38). M: Tribunal or Gran Vía. Singles reminiscent of your college dorm. Rooms with balconies are surprisingly tranquil for the spicy location. Singles €17-18; doubles with bath €32; triples with bath €44. ❷

Hostal Medieval, C. Fuencarral, 46, 2nd fl. (☎915 22 25 49). M: Tribunal. Older rooms, central location, and hospitable owners. TV lounge honors Real Madrid. Singles €22; doubles €30, with bath €36; triples €44. ❷

Hotel Mónaco, C. Barbieri, 5 (☎915 52 46 30; fax 915 21 16 01). M: Chueca or Gran Vía. From Pl. de Chueca, follow C. Barbieri all the way. Once a brothel catering to Madrid's high society, this hotel still encourages naughtiness. Frescoes of Eve-like temptresses excite the imagination while hundreds of mirrors and *palacio*-sized beds fulfill the reality. Green-lit lounge and a lively bar/cafeteria area. Adventurous older crowd. Simple singles €48; doubles €66; triples €86; quads €105. AmEx/MC/V. ❹

ELSEWHERE

Budget lodgings are rare near the **Chamartín** train station, as is the case in most of the residential districts located away from the city center. There are a handful of hostels near the **Atocha** train station, the closest of which are down Po. Santa María de la Cabeza. Be aware that this neighborhood is not as safe as those that are more central. The tourist office in Pl. Mayor has a full list of lodgings.

Albergue Juvenil Santa Cruz de Marcenado (HI), C. Santa Cruz de Marcenado, 28 (☎915 47 45 32; fax 915 48 11 96). M: Argüelles. From the Metro, walk 1 block down C. Alberto Aguilera away from C. Princesa, turn right on C. Serrano Jóve, then left on C. Santa Cruz de Marcenado. Lounge is great for meeting people and late-night card playing. The 72 beds fill quickly, even in winter. English spoken. Rooms have cubbies, but use the lockers outside the rooms (€2 extra). Breakfast included. Sheets (but no towels) provided. 3-day max. stay. Quiet hours after midnight. Reception daily 9am-10pm. 1:30am curfew is strictly enforced. Reserve a space (by mail, fax, or in person) in advance, or arrive early and pray. Closed Christmas and New Year's. An HI card is required and can be purchased for €12. Dorms €8, over 26 €11.50. ❶

Hostal-Residencia Rios, C. Juan Álvarez Mendizábal, 44, 4th fl. (☎915 59 51 56). M: Ventura Rodríguez or Argüelles. Face the green shrubbery, walk 3 blocks left up C. Princesa to C. Rey Francisco, go 3 blocks to J. A. Mendizábal, and turn left again. Nothing fancy; just clean, cheap, comfortable rooms close to the park, some with A/C (€6). Singles €17; doubles with shower €32; triples €45. ❷

CAMPING

Tourist offices provide info about the 13 campsites within 50km of Madrid. Similar info can be found in the *Guía Oficial de Campings* (official camping guide), available at most bookstores or on reserve at the tourist offices. The *Mapa de Campings* shows the location of every official campsite in Spain. Also ask for the brochure *Hoteles, Campings, Apartamentos,* which lists hotels, campsites, and apartments in and around Madrid. For further camping info, contact the *Consejería de Educación de Juventud* (☎915 22 29 41).

Camping Alpha (☎916 95 80 69; fax 916 83 1659), on a tree-lined site 12.4km down the Ctra. de Andalucía in Getafe. M: Legazpi. From the Metro station take bus #447, which stops next to the Nissan dealership (10min., every 30min. until 10pm, €1.25). Ask driver to let you off at the pedestrian overpass for the campsite. Cross the bridge and walk 1.5km back toward Madrid along a busy highway; camping signs lead the way. Pool, showers, and laundry. €4 per person, €4.50 per tent, €4 per car. ❶

Camping Osuna (☎917 41 05 10; fax 913 20 63 65), on Av. Logroño. M: Canillejas. From the Metro, cross the pedestrian overpass, walk through the parking lot, and turn right along the freeway. Pass under 2 bridges (the 1st a freeway and the 2nd an arch) and look for campground signs on the right. Or grab the #101 bus from the Metro toward Barajas and ask for the campsite. Closer than Alpha, but not as nice. Showers, laundromat, supermarket, and bar (sandwiches €2.50, salads €1.85). Reception open daily 8:30am-10pm. €4.50 per person, per tent, and per car. €2.85 for electricity. ❶

FOOD

In Madrid, it's easy to eat without emptying your wallet. You can't walk a block without tripping over at least five *cafeterías*, where a sandwich, coffee, and dessert go for €3.60. Vegetarians should check out the *Guía del Ocio* (€1), which has a complete listing of Madrid's vegetarian havens under the section *Otras Cocinas*. Check out www.mundovegetariano.com. Even carnivores may appreciate a veggie meal, given Madrid's indulgence in fatty meats and fried preparation.

Expect to spend at least €7 for a full meal at a *restaurante*, one step up from the typical *cafetería*. Most restaurants offer a *menú del día*, which includes bread, one drink, and a choice from the day's selections for appetizers, main courses, and desserts. For €6.75-9, it's a fantastic way to fill up. Keep the following buzz words in mind for quicker, cheaper *madrileño* fare: *bocadillo* (a sandwich on a long, hard roll, €2-2.75); *sandwich* (a sandwich on sliced bread, ask for it *a la plancha* if you want it grilled, €2.25); *croissant* (with ham and cheese, €1.50); *ración* (a large *tapa*, served with bread €1.85-3.75); and *empanada* (a puff pastry with meat fillings, €1.25-1.85). See the **Glossary,** p. 794, for additional translations.

In general, *restaurantes* are open 1-4pm and 8pm-midnight or 1am; in the following listings, this is the case unless otherwise noted. More casual establishments such as *mesones*, *cafeterías*, *bares*, *cafés*, *terrazas*, and *tabernas* serve drinks and foodstuffs all day until midnight, though some are closed on Sundays.

FOOD SHOPPING

In general, groceries get cheaper the farther you get from the center. Specialty items may require a visit to a pricey store in the center, but for daily fare, slipping into any corner store will reward you with an inexpensive selection of standards at drastically lower prices than would be found in a major chain.

Groceries: %Dia and **Simago** are the cheapest city-wide supermarket chains, though their locations tend to be a bit far from the city center. To satisfy grocery needs near El Centro, try the numerous *alimentaciones* (food marts) on side streets that sell drinks, candy, ice cream, and some basics. The *supermercado* in the basement of **El Corte Inglés** (see p. 98) near Puerta del Sol is somewhat pricier but über-convenient. Other more upscale options are **Mantequerías Leonesas, Expreso,** and **Jumbo.**

Markets: Mercado de San Miguel, a covered market on Pl. San Miguel, off the northwest corner of Pl. Mayor, sells the finest seafood and produce in the city at high prices. A wide selection of tourists can be found on display between the *bacalao* and the tuna. Open M-F 9:30am-2:30pm and 5:15-8:15pm, Sa 9am-2:30pm. **Mercado de la Cebada,** at the intersection of C. Toledo and C. San Francisco, is larger and less expensive and caters to many more locals. Open M-Sa 8am-2pm and 5:30-8pm.

Pastry Shops: These are everywhere. The sublime **Horno La Santiagüesa,** C. Mayor, 73, sells everything from *roscones de reyes* (sweet bread for the Feast of the Epiphany) to *empanadas* and pastries doused in rich chocolate. Don't pass through without trying the *tarta de santiago* (almond sweet bread). Open M-Sa 8am-9pm, Su 8am-8pm. **Horno San Onofre,** C. San Onofre, 4 (☎915 32 90 60), off C. Fuencarral, serves sumptuous fruit tarts and *suspiros de modistilla* (seamstress's sighs), a *madrileño* specialty. Open M-Sa 9am-9pm, Su 9am-8pm.

Red-Eye Establishments: *Guía del Ocio* lists late-night eateries under *Cenar a última hora.* The chain **VIPS,** at Gran Vía, 43 (☎915 42 15 78; M: Callao); Serrano, 41 (M: Serrano); C. Princesa, 5 (M: Ventura Rodríguez); Fuencarral 101 (M: Tribunal); and other locations are a standard late-night option. An American-style diner with cushioned booths, average service, and overpriced burgers with cheese fries, VIPS also carries English books and magazines, records, and canned food. Open daily 9am-3am. **7-Eleven** stores are scattered in Ópera, Alonso Martínez (C. Mejía Lequerida), and Av. América. **Hot & Cool,** C. Gaztambide in Moncloa-Argüelles, serves fresh *bocadillos* until 3am on weekends. **Street vendors** sell cheap *bocadillos* and Chinese food to hungry clubbers until late. Open *cervecerías* aren't hard to find within a few blocks until 2am.

EL CENTRO: SOL, ÓPERA, AND PLAZA MAYOR

Flooded with tourists looking for "traditional" fare, this area abounds with mediocre food at high prices. However, sifting through the dirt can lead to some amazing restaurants at decent prices. Streets off M: Ópera teem with crowded cafes, markets, and restaurants. Side streets off Puerta del Sol offer cuisine from all over the world. Places with menus in several different languages tend to be tourist traps; avoid them like green *gambas*. Cruise to nearby Pl. Santa Ana for better deals. The surrounding streets, especially through the **Arco de los Cuchilleros** in the southwest corner of Pl. Mayor, house specialty shops and renowned *mesones.* Head here for garlicky *tapas* and pitchers of sangría in a festive, albeit touristy, atmosphere.

Inshala, C. Amnistia, 10 (☎915 48 26 32). M: Opera. Eclectic menu filled with delicious Spanish, Mexican, Japanese, Italian, and Moroccan dishes. Weekday lunch *menú* €7.25. Dinner €8-15. Occasional cover of €1.25. Reservations strongly recommended for both lunch and dinner. Open M-Th 1:30pm-2am, F-Sa 1:30pm-3am. ❸

Anatolia, C. de la Cruz, 10. M: Sol. One of the many Turkish restaurants in Madrid. Serves succulent *Doner Kebap* (chicken or lamb gyro sandwich). Probably the most delicious and least expensive lunch in Madrid. *Tavuk Kebap* with all the trimmings €3. Other Turkish specialties €2.70-4.50. Closed Su. ❶

Restaurante Casa Botín, C. de Cuchilleros, 17 (☎913 66 42 17 or 913 66 30 26), off of Pl. Mayor. The self-proclaimed oldest restaurant in the world (founded 1725), Casa Botín serves a variety of simple but filling Spanish dishes (€7-20). A favorite among tourists. Lunch served all week 1-4pm, dinner 8pm-midnight. ❸

Museo del Jamón, C. San Jerónimo, 6 (☎915 21 03 46). M: Sol. 5 other locations throughout the city, including C. Mayor, 7 (☎915 31 45 50). A vegetarian's nightmare and pork lover's dream. Dodge hooves and shanks at the metallic bar or head to the upstairs dining room (open at 1pm) for the chef's specialties (€3.75-7). Generous combo plates €4-6. Open M-Th 9am-12:30pm, F-Sa 9am-1am, Su 10am-12:30pm. ❶

El Cuchi, C. Cuchilleros, 3 (☎913 66 44 24). Just outside Pl. Mayor, and better and cheaper than the restaurants inside it. Delicious Mexican food in a festive setting. Entrees €5.40-17.50. Open M-Sa 1pm-1am, Su 1-midnight. AmEx/MC/V. ❸

Lhardy Restaurante, C. San Jerónimo, 8 (☎915 21 33 85), at C. Victoria. M: Sol. Get slicked-up and bring an overstuffed wallet for an expensive but delicious meal. This gorgeous 150-year-old restaurant is replete with original wallpaper and woodwork. The house specialty, *cocido* (chick pea stew; €25), has won deserved fame as a *madrileño* specialty. Open M-Sa 1-3:30pm and 8:30-11:30pm, Su 1-3:30pm. AmEx/MC/V. ❺

Matador Parilla, C. De La Cruz, 13 (☎915 22 35 95), off C. San Jerónimo. Cooks grill a variety of meats and vegetables a la carte (€8.50-14) or as part of a 7-course meal (€27-36). Open daily 1-4:30pm, Su-Th 8pm-midnight, F-Sa 8pm-1am. ❹

HUERTAS

A popular place among locals, Pl. Santa Ana is perfect for killing some time with a drink and snack. Straying slightly from its center, **Calles Echegaray, Ventura de la Vega,** and **Manuel Fernández González** offer the best food options; quality is high and prices low. As the evening grows and wine flows, these streets become the first stop of a night out in Madrid.

Champagneria Gala, C. Moratín, 22 (☎914 29 25 62; www.paellas-gala.com). M: Antón Martín. Down the hill on Moratín from C. Atocha. The *paella* buck stops here, with decor as colorful and varied as its specialty. *Menú* (€14) offers choice of *paella*, along with the usual salad, bread, wine, and dessert. Enjoy a romantic meal under the high, lit roof of the vine-covered interior garden. Reserve on weekends. Open daily 1:30-5pm and 9pm-12:30am. No credit cards accepted. ❸

Al Natural, C. Zorrilla, 11 (☎913 69 47 09). M: Sevilla. From the Metro stop, a left off of C. de Cedaceros, behind the Congress building. A unique offering of vegetarian Mediterranean dishes (€8-12) served in a lively, candle-lit atmosphere. Open daily 1-4pm, M-Sa 7pm-midnight. ❸

La Farfalla, C. Santa María, 17 (☎913 69 46 91). M: Antón Martín. 1 block from the Metro along C. Huertas; look for the butterfly above the entrance. La Farfalla's specialty is Argentine-style grilled meat, but don't miss their thin-crust pizzas (€5). Open for dinner Su-Th 9:30pm-3am, F-Sa 9:30pm-4am. AmEx/MC/V. ❷

Gula Gula, C. Infante 5 (☎914 20 29 19), off C. Echegaray near C. Huertas. M: Antón Martín. New location also at C. Gran Vía, 1 (☎915 22 87 64). You better work! Outrageous drag and cabaret shows complement the all-you-can-eat buffet (lunch €9; dinner €18.75, includes cold buffet plus an ordered hot dish). Reserve for weekend dinner 1 week ahead. Open daily 1-5pm and 9pm-3am. AmEx/MC/V. ❹

Pizzería Cervantes, C. Leon, 8 (☎914 20 12 98), off C. del Prado. Hands down one of the best cheap *menús* (€7; served M-F) in the area offering much more than pizza and including a selection of exquisite desserts. Most entrees €6. Open daily 1:30-4:30pm and 8:30-11:30pm. Closed Tu afternoon. Open F-Sa until 1am. AmEx/MC/V. ❷

Restaurante Integral Artemisa, C. Ventura de la Vega, 4 (☎914 29 50 92), off C. San Jerónimo. M: Sol. 2nd location in Pl. del Carmen, at Tres Cruces, 4 (☎915 21 87 21). Elegant veggie food served in a long, mellow dining area. Veggie *menú* €7.50. Open daily 1:30-4pm and 9pm-midnight. AmEx/MC/V. ❷

LAVAPIÉS, LA LATINA AND ATOCHA

The neighborhoods south of Sol, bounded by C. Atocha and C. Toledo, are generally residential and working class. No caviar or champagne here, but you'll find plenty of *menús* for around €6.50. Grab some chow in a funky outdoor eatery on **Calle Agurrosa,** or head up the hill toward Huertas for more tasty options.

El Estragón Vegetariano, Pl. de la Paja, 10 (☎913 65 89 82; www.menudeldia.com); on the far side of the plaza. M: La Latina. From the Metro, follow C. Duque de Alba, turn right through Pl. Puerta de Moros and keep the church to your right. Perhaps the best medium-priced restaurant—of any kind—in Madrid, with vegetarian food that could convince even the most die-hard carnivores to switch teams. Treat yourself to *crepes a la Museliño,* the house specialty, or try the delicious and creative *menú* (M-F €9; Sa-Su and evenings €18). Open daily 1:30-4:30pm and 8pm-1am. AmEx/MC/V. ❸

El Granero de Lavapiés, C. Argumosa, 10 (☎914 67 76 11), off the plaza. M: Lavapiés. For 16 years, frescoes and inventive specials have kept this hideaway packed with locals. Vegetarian *menú* M-Sa €8. Open daily 1-4pm, F-Sa 8:30-11pm. MC/V. ❷

GRAN VÍA

Tourist and locals alike battle their love/hate relationships for the Golden Arches, KFC, and Burger King under the shimmering lights of Gran Vía. Long lines at fast food joints demonstrate that convenience and time often outweigh fine dining. Fear not—there are still some culinary diamonds hidden in the fast-food rough.

La Finca de Susana, C. Arlaban, 4 (☎913 69 35 57). M: Sevilla. Probably the most popular lunch eatery in all of Madrid, where delicious fine dining comes at an extremely low price (*menú* €6.50). Be prepared to wait in line. Open daily 1-4pm, 8-11:30pm. ❷

Museo Chicote, C. Gran Vía, 12 (☎915 32 97 80). M: Gran Vía. Lose yourself in green leather booths amidst pictures of stars from Ava Gardner and John Wayne to Lola Flores and Luis Buñuel. Throw back a cocktail with Madrid's socialites after 11pm. Lunchtime *menú* €8.50. Open M-Sa 8am-12:30am. Lunch served 1-4pm. ❷

MALASAÑA AND CHUECA

Before the nighttime insanity begins, Malasaña and Chueca offer some of the best dining options in all of Madrid. The area showcases exceptional vegetarian, Middle Eastern, and Italian restaurants. Most eateries are small and intimate, with high quality and low prices.

La Granja Restaurante Vegetariano, C. San Andrés, 11 (☎915 32 87 93), off Pl. 2 de Mayo. M: Tribunal or Bilbao. Dimmed yellow lights glow above intricately-tiled walls in this Arabic-themed restaurant. Youthful crowd, friendly owner, and big portions. *Menú* €7.25. Open W-M 1:30-4:30pm and 9pm-midnight. Closed Su in summer. ❷

Al-Jaima, Cocina del Desierto, C. Barbieri, 1 (☎915 23 11 42). M: Gran Vía or Chueca. Lebanese, Moroccan, and Egyptian food in intimate North African setting. Specialties include the *pastela,* couscous, *shish kebabs,* and *tajine* (€4-8). Open daily 1:30-4pm and 9pm-midnight. Dinner reservations highly recommended, sometimes required. ❷

Pizzeria Vesuvio, C. Hortaleza, 4 (☎915 21 51 71). M: Gran Vía. Mix and match pasta and sauce or try the 30+ varieties of personal pizzas. Fresh, delicious food and fast service. Try the *pasta fresca.* Fight the crowd for a seat (counter seating only), or order to go. Meals €3.30-5. Open M-Sa 1-4pm and 8pm-midnight, F-Sa until 1am. ❶

Chez Pomme, C. Pelayo, 4 (☎915 32 16 46), off C. Augusto Figueroa. M: Chueca. Quiet, artsy spot that serves filling portions of French vegetarian cuisine. Try the *berenjenas al horno* (baked eggplant dish), one of the many tofu dishes, or a creative salad (€4.50-5.60). *Menú* €6. Open M-Sa 1:30-4pm and 8:30-11:30pm, F-Sa until midnight. ❶

Pizzaiolo, C. Hortaleza, 84 (☎913 19 29 64). M: Chueca. Authentic Italian pizza with incredibly fresh ingredients. Friendly staff wants to ensure your satisfaction. Open Tu-Su 12:30pm-midnight, F-Sa until 1am. ❷

Vegaviana, C. Pelayo, 35 (☎913 08 03 81). M: Chueca. Wholesome vegetarian cuisine. Very popular with locals and tourists. Lunch *menú* €7.25, meals €7-10. Open Tu-Sa 1:30-4pm and 9pm-midnight. ❷

La Sacristía, C. Infantas, 28 (☎915 22 09 45). M: Gran Vía or Chueca. Creative Spanish cuisine, including 60 types of *bacalao* (codfish). Dinner *menú* changes weekly (M-Th only, €16). Serves breakfast, lunch, and dinner. Open M-Sa 8am-2am. ❹

La Carreta, C. Barbieri, 10 (☎915 32 70 42 or 915 21 60 97), off C. las Infantas. M: Gran Vía or Chueca. Small, friendly spot specializing in Argentinian, Uruguayan, and Chilean meals. Beef specialties. Lunch *menú* €10. Entrees €8-15. Occasional tango performances on weekend evenings (call for schedule). Reservations recommended. Open W-M 1:30-5pm and 9pm-5am. ❸

La Gata Flora, C. San Vicente Ferrer, 33 (☎ 915 21 27 92 or 915 21 20 20), about a block from Pl. 2 de Mayo, and across the street at C. 2 de Mayo, 1. M: Noviciado or Tribunal. Pizza, pasta, drinks, and desserts in a festive setting. Pitcher of sangría €6.40. Open daily Su-Th 2-4pm and 8:30pm-midnight, F-Sa until 1am. ❷

El Tazumal, C. Madera, 36 (☎915 22 79 82). M: Tribunal. From the Metro, walk down Fuencarral and make a right onto C. Santa Barbara which becomes C. Don Felipe after the plaza, then turn left onto C. Madera. Tasty and unique cuisine from El Salvador. Entrees €1.75-7.85. Open W-M 1:30-4:30pm and 8pm-midnight. ❶

La Gastroteca de Stephane y Arturo, Pl. Chueca, 8 (☎915 32 25 64 or 915 22 88 04). M: Chueca. Appropriate attire required for this upscale French restaurant located in the heart of Chueca. A knock on the door may or may not let you in. Entrees €14.50-18. Open M-F 1-3:30pm and 9-11:30pm. ❹

BILBAO

The area north of Glorieta de Bilbao (M: Bilbao), in the "V" formed by C. Fuencarral and C. Luchana and including Pl. Olavide, is the ethnic food nexus of Madrid; it overflows with bars, clubs, cafes, and restaurants of all nationalities. **C. Hartzenbusch** and **C. Cisneros** present endless options for cheap *tapas* to the youthful crowd that swarms the area at night.

Arepas con Todo, C. Hartzenbusch, 19 (☎914 48 75 45), off C. Cardenal Cisneros, from C. Luchana. Hanging gourds and waitresses in festive dress fill this classic Colombian restaurant. A rotating *menú* (€10-12), plus 60 fixed dishes (€11-14.50). Only the live music repeats itself. For dinner, make reservations. Open daily 2pm-1am. MC/V. ❸

Collage, C. Olid, 6 (☎914 48 45 62), 3rd street on your right off C. Fuencarral. M: Bilbao. A group of Swedish chefs mix and match in style. Entrees €10-17. Open Su-M 1:30-4pm, Tu-Sa 1:30-4pm and 8:30pm-midnight. AmEx/MC/V. ❸

Tanger, C. Cardenal Cisneros, 11 (☎915 94 44 61). Middle-Eastern and Moroccan dishes (€6-7.25) are served in a mirrored dining room replete with low, backless seats and engraved, wooden tables. Midday *menú* €6.75. Open Tu-Su 12:30pm-2am. ❷

Bar Samara, C. Cardenal Cisneros, 13 (☎914 48 80 56). From M: Bilbao, walk up C. Luchana and take a quick left onto C. Cisneros. Bills itself as Egyptian. Middle Eastern staples. Kebabs and other entrees €10-13.25. Open M 8:30pm-midnight, Tu-Th 2-4pm and 8:30pm-midnight, F-Su 2-4pm and 8:30pm-1am. ❸

MADRID

ARGÜELLES

Argüelles is a middle-class neighborhood near the Ciudad Universitaria. It's geared toward locals rather than tourists and is therefore full of inexpensive markets, moderately priced restaurants, and informal neighborhood bars. Check out the quiet *terrazas* on C. Pintor Rosales, overlooking the park.

Cáscaras, C. Ventura Rodríguez, 7 (☎ 915 42 83 36), your 1st right off C. Princesa. M: Ventura Rodríguez. Sleek interior enhances the dining experience. Popular for *tapas, pinchos,* and ice-cold Mahou beer in the early afternoon and evening. Exotic vegetarian entrees €4.85-6. Open M-F 7am-1am, Sa-Su 10am-1am. AmEx/MC/V. ❷

Ananias, C. Galileo, 9 (☎914 48 68 01). M: Argüelles, a left off C. Alberto Aguilera. Swirling waiters serve Castilian dishes with a flourish. *Torero* paraphernalia covers the walls in the front room, while regulars enjoy the elegance of the back room. Entrees €9-15. Open Su-Tu, Th-F 1-4pm, 9-11:30pm, Sa 9-11:30pm. AmEx/MC/V. ❸

La Crêperie, Po. Pintor Rosales, 28 (☎915 48 23 58). M: Ventura Rodríguez. The cherub decorations are almost as sweet as the dessert crepes (€2.25-3.90). Eat the lunch and dinner crepes (€3.25-5) on the chic Po. Rosales *terraza*. Open Su-Th 1:30-4:15pm and 8pm-1am, F-Sa 1:30-4:15pm and 8pm-1:30am. ❶

TAPAS So finally you've found a hostel, only been lost twice, and are ready to experience the *madrileño* lifestyle. Clearly, it's time for some drinks and *tapas*. The only problem is, what are you going to order? To the untrained reader, *tapas* menus are often cryptic and undecipherable—if the bar has even bothered to print any. To make sure you don't end up eating the stewed parts of the oxen you rode in on, keep the following words in mind. Servings come in three sizes: *pincho* (normally eaten with toothpicks between sips of beer), *tapa* (small plate), or *ración* (sizable, meal portion). *Aceitunas* (olives), *albóndigas* (meatballs), *anchoas* (anchovies), *callos* (tripe), *chorizo* (sausage), *croquetas* (croquettes), *gambas* (shrimp), *jamón* (ham), *patatas bravas* (fried potatoes with spicy sauce), *pimientos* (peppers), *pulpo* (octopus), and *tortillla* (omelette) comprise any basic menu. More adventurous travelers should try *morcilla* (blood sausage) or *sesos* (cow's brains). Bartenders will often offer tastes of *tapas* with your drink and strike up a conversation in the spirit of Madrid's generosity and charm. To ensure full treatment and local respect, the house *cerveza* is always a good choice. Sangria, a mixture of wine and fruit juices, seems innocent but packs a kick—natives drink it by the jar and box in the sweltering summers.

La Vaca Argentina, Po. Pintor Rosales, 52 (☎915 59 66 05). M: Moncloa or Argüelles. Follow C. Marqués de Urquijo downhill, then take a left on Po. Rosales. 1 of 10 of its kind in Madrid, this restaurant is famous for its steak specialties (€7-27) and infamous for the cowhide wallpaper. Open daily 1-4:30pm and 9pm-12:30am. AmEx/MC/V. ❹

TAPAS

Not so long ago, bartenders in Andalucía used to cover *(tapar)* drinks with saucers to keep the flies out. Later, servers began putting little sandwiches on top of the saucers, and there you have it: *tapas*. Hopping from bar to bar gobbling *tapas* is an active alternative to a full sit-down meal and a fun way to sample food you might never even dream of trying. Most *tapas* bars (a.k.a. *tascas* or *tabernas*) are open noon to 4pm and 8pm to midnight or later. Some, like **Museo del Jamón** (see p. 107), double as restaurants, and many cluster around **Pl. Santa Ana** and **Pl. Mayor** (beware the tourist traps!). Authentic bars pack **C. Cuchilleros** and **C. de la Cruz.**

Casa Alberto, C. Huertas, 18 (☎914 29 93 56). M: Antón Martín. Patrons spill out into the night air to wait for a spot at the bar. Cervantes wrote the 2nd part of "El Quijote" here. The *tapas* are all original house recipes. Sample the *gambas al ajillo* (shrimp in garlic and hot peppers; €7.50) or the filled *canapés* (€1.75-2). Sit-down dinner is a bit pricey. Open Tu-Sa noon-5:30pm and 8pm-1:30am. AmEx/MC/V. ❷

La Toscana, C. Manuel Fernández González, 10-12 (☎914 29 60 31), at C. Ventura de la Vega. M: Sol or Sevilla. A local crowd hangs out over *tapas* of *mocillo asado* (€8). Despite the antique lettering and wrought iron, the range of dishes is anything but medieval. Spacious bar jam-packed on weekends. Open Tu-Sa 1-4pm and 8pm-midnight. ❷

Los Gabrieles, C. Echegaray, 17 (☎914 29 62 61), near Villa Madrid. The tiled mural at the back depicts famous artists—from Velázquez to Goya—as stumble-drunks. Serves *tapas* by afternoon and drinks by night. Flamenco night Tu. Open daily 1pm-late. ❶

Casa Amadeo, Pl. de Cascorro, 18 (☎913 65 94 39). M: La Latina. The jovial owner of 60 years supervises the making of house specialty *caracoles* (snails; *tapas* €4.25, big *ración* €9) and *chorizo* made with snails (€4.50). Other *raciones* €2-5.50. Open M-F 10:30am-4pm and 7-10:30pm, Su 7-11pm. ❶

La Trucha, C. Núñez de Arce, 6 (☎915 32 08 82). M: Sol. Impressive selection of seasonal veggies (€5-9) and daily specials. Don't skip the *rabo de toro* (stewed bull's tail; €9.50). Entrees €12-15. Open M-Sa 12:30-4pm, 7:30pm-midnight. AmEx/MC/V. ❸

Taberna del Alabarder, C. Felipe V, 6 (☎915 47 25 77 or 915 41 46 70), near Café Oriente in Pl. Oriente. M: Ópera. Overlooking the glorious Palacio Real, try the nationally-famous *patatas al pobre* (potatoes with garlic) or *tigres unidad* (fried muscles). *Tapas* €3.75-6.75. Open M-Sa 1-4pm and 7pm-midnight. AmEx/MC/V. ❶

La Princesita, C. Princesa, 80 (☎915 43 70 71). M: Argüelles. Students crowd in to enjoy *tapas* like *queso de cabrales* (goat cheese; €1). Open M-Sa 10am-11:30pm. ❶

Cafetería-Restaurante El Encinar del Bierzo, C. Toledo, 82 (☎913 66 23 89). M: La Latina. A neighborhood landmark. House specialties *conejo al ajillo* (rabbit with garlic; €12) and *gambas a la plancha* (grilled shrimp; €6.75). *Menú* €6.75, €8 on Su. Open daily 1-4:30pm and 9-11:30pm. MC/V. ❷

CAFES

Madrid's cafes offer ambiance as well as caffeine, allowing contemplative coffee drinkers to lose themselves in atmosphere, history, and image. Marvel at the scenery, be reflective, and linger for an hour or two in these historic cafes, an economical way to soak up a little of Madrid's culture and finally write those postcards you bought a few days ago. You won't be bothered with the check until you ask.

Café de Oriente, Pl. Oriente, 2 (☎915 47 15 64). M: Ópera. An old-fashioned cafe catering to a ritzy, older crowd. Spectacular view of the Palacio Real from the *terraza,* especially at night when floodlights illuminate the facade. Prices are cheaper inside. Specialty coffees (€1.80-5.55) live up to their price. Open daily 8:30am-1:30am.

Café Gijón, Po. Recoletos, 21 (☎915 21 54 25). M: Colón. Enjoy thought-provoking conversation and good coffee in this historic landmark. Recognized for its intellectual significance, Café Gijón makes the perfect stop during your walking tour of the Paseos. Coffees from €3.75. Open daily 9am-1:30am. AmEx/MC/V.

Café Comercial, Glorieta de Bilbao, 7 (☎915 21 56 55). M: Bilbao. Founded in 1887, Madrid's oldest cafe boasts high ceilings, cushioned chairs, and huge mirrors perfect for people-watching. Frequented by artists and Republican aviators alike, the first anti-Franco protests took place here. Coffee €1 at the bar, €1.55 at a table. Open M-Th 7:30am-1:30am, F-Sa 8am-2am, Su 10am-1am.

El Obrador del Cafe de Oriente, Carlos III, 3 (☎915 48 28 93). M: Ópera. On the side of the opera house, before the Pl. de Oriente. Classy shop in front filled with candies, pastries, and sweets leads to a small cafe in back with sophisticated wall decorations, pristine tables, and bottles of wine. Coffee starts at €1.20. Open daily 9am-midnight.

La Botilleria del Cafe de Oriente, Pl. Oriente, 4 (☎915 48 46 20). M: Ópera. Yet another gorgeous cafe situated at the entrance to the Plaza de Oriente with views of the gardens, the plaza, and the palace. Both a cafe and a restaurant, with a variety of coffees (€2.25) and teas (€2.40).

Eucalipto, C. Argumosa, 4. M: Lavapiés. Take a break from the normal coffee fare and head for refreshing *zumos tropicales* (fresh fruit drinks; €2.40-3.30). Spike up the night with a *daiquiri* (€3.75-4), or enjoy a fantastic fruit salad for 2 (€6). Lively sidewalk seating. Open daily M-Th 6pm-2am, F-Sa 6pm-3am, Su 2pm-midnight.

Cafe del Real, Pl. Isabel II, 2 (☎915 47 21 24). Hang out at the cafe upstairs, lined with tables surrounded by theatrical pictures on burgundy and gold walls, or go downstairs to the pizzeria for a quick bite. Coffee €1.20 at the bar, €1.80 at the table.

SIGHTS

Madrid, large as it may seem, is a walker's city. Its fantastic public transportation system should only be used for longer distances, or between the day's starting and ending points. Although the word *paseo* refers to a major avenue (such as *Paseo de la Castellana* or *Paseo del Prado*) it literally means "a stroll." Do just that from Sol to Cibeles and from the Plaza Mayor to the Palacio Real—sights will kindly introduce themselves. The city's art and architecture and its culture and atmosphere convince wide-eyed walkers that it was once the capital of the world's greatest empire. While Madrid is perfect for walking, it also offers some of the world's best places to relax. Whether soothing tired feet after perusing the *triángulo de arte* or seeking shelter from the summer's sweltering heat, there's nothing better than a shady sidewalk cafe or a romantic park.

For hardcore visitors with a checklist of destinations, the municipal tourist office's *Plano de Transportes* map, which marks monuments as well as bus and Metro lines, is indispensable. In the following pages, sights are arranged by neighborhood. Each section has a designated center from which all directions are given. If you are trying to design a walking tour of the entire city, it is best to begin in El Centro, the self-evident nucleus of Madrid. The neighborhoods naturally fall in geographical order from there; a good day of sightseeing might move from historic Madrid, to the cafes of Huertas, to the celebrated *paseos*, to a stroll through the Retiro. El Pardo falls last as a separate trip.

EL CENTRO

The area known as El Centro, spreading out from the Puerta del Sol ("Gate of the Sun"), is the gateway to the history and spirit of Madrid. Although several rulers carved the winding streets, the Habsburg and Bourbon families left the Centro's most celebrated monuments. As a result, the Centro is divided into two major sections: Madrid de los Habsburgs and Madrid de los Borbones. Most Habsburg directions are given from the Puerta del Sol and Bourbon directions from Ópera. The sights are easily accessible by Metro and by foot, and the neighborhood itself is quite easy to navigate. For convenience, the Metro stop closest to each sight is listed. All of El Centro can be conquered in a single day, but take more time to leisurely enjoy the sights and marvel at their beauty.

PUERTA DEL SOL

Kilómetro 0—the origin of six national highways fanning out to the rest of Spain—marks the country's physical center in the most chaotic of Madrid's numerous plazas, Puerta del Sol. Sol bustles day and night with the taxis, bars, street performers, and newsstands. A web of pedestrian-only tributaries originating at the Gran Vía leads a rush of consumers down a gallery of stores, funneling them into Sol.

It was not until the late 19th century that Sol became the true nucleus of Madrid. In the 16th century, an eastward-facing gate known as the Gateway to the Sun stood in Puerta del Sol. Today, government buildings dominate the plaza, where citizens and tourists alike converge upon *El oso y el madroño*, a bronze statue of a bear and a strawberry tree, now a symbol of Madrid. On New Year's Eve, citizens congregate in Sol to gobble up one grape per chime as the clock strikes midnight.

HABSBURG MADRID

"Old Madrid," the city's central neighborhood, is the most densely packed with both monuments and tourists. In the 16th century, the Habsburgs built **Plaza Mayor** and the **Catedral de San Isidro** from scratch. Many of Old Madrid's buildings, however, date from much earlier, some from as far back as the Moorish empire. When Felipe II moved the seat of Castilla from Toledo to Madrid (then only a town of 20,000) in 1561, he and his descendants commissioned the court architects (including Juan de Herrera, the architect of the austere El Escorial) to update many of Madrid's buildings to the latest styles. After only a century of development and expansion, Madrid more than doubled in population. Today, central Madrid, from the celebrated street of Alcalá to the iron verandas of Plaza Mayor, still reflects the power of the Habsburgs and the architecture of Juan de Herrera.

PLAZA MAYOR. In 1620, Pl. Mayor was completed for Felipe III; his statue, installed in 1847, graces the plaza's center. Though designed by Juan de Herrera, Pl. Mayor is much softer in style. Its elegant arcades, spindly towers, and pleasant verandas are defining elements of the "Madrid style," which inspired architects across the city and throughout the country. With lances of exaggerated length, 17th-century nobles on horseback spent Sunday afternoons chasing bulls in the plaza. The nobility had such a jolly time that eventually everyone joined in the fun. Citizens, on foot and armed with sticks, also began running after those pesky bulls. The tradition came to be known as a *corrida*, from the verb *correr* (to run).

Toward evening, Pl. Mayor awakens as *madrileños* resurface, tourists multiply, and cafe tables fill with lively patrons. Live performances of flamenco and music are a common treat. While the cafes are a nice spot for a drink, food is overpriced; save dinner for elsewhere. On Sunday mornings, the plaza holds a rare coin and stamp sale, marking the starting point of **El Rastro** (see p. 134). During the annual **Fiesta de San Isidro** (May 15-22, see p. 133), the plaza explodes with celebration. *(From Pta. Sol, walk down C. Mayor. The plaza is on the left. M: Sol.)*

CATEDRAL DE SAN ISIDRO. This cathedral, which commemorates San Isidro, protector of crops and patron saint of Madrid, has had a turbulent history. It was designed in the Jesuit Baroque style at the beginning of the 17th century; in 1769 San Isidro's remains were brought here. During the Civil War, rioting workers burned the exterior—only the primary nave and a few Baroque decorations remain from the original. San Isidro, which has since been restored, reigned as *the* cathedral of Madrid from the late 19th century until the Catedral de la Almudena (see p. 115) was consecrated in 1993. *(From the Pta. Sol, take C. Mayor to Pl. Mayor, cross the plaza, and exit onto C. Toledo. The cathedral is located at the intersection of C. Toledo and C. Sacramento. M: Latina. Open for Mass only at 9, 10, 11am, and noon daily.)*

PLAZA DE LA VILLA. When Felipe II made Madrid the capital of his empire in 1561, most of the town huddled between Pl. Mayor and the Palacio Real; Pl. Villa marks the heart of what was once Old Madrid. Though only a handful of medieval buildings remain, the plaza still features a stunning courtyard (surrounding the statue of Don Álvara de Bazón), beautiful tile-work, and eclectic architecture. The horseshoe-shaped door on C. Codo is one of the few examples of Gothic-Mudéjar left in Madrid, and the 15th-century Torre de los Lujanes (on the left when looking from C. Mayor) is the sole remnant of the once lavish residence of the Lujanes family. Across the plaza is the 17th-century Ayuntamiento (Casa de la Villa), designed in 1640 by Juan Gómez de Mora as both the mayor's home and the city jail. Inside is Goya's *Allegory of the City of Madrid* (1819). The neighboring Casa de Cisneros, a 16th-century Plateresque house, also served as a government building when Habsburg officials annexed it for the city's growing bureaucracy. *(From Pta. Sol, go down C. Mayor, past Pl. Mayor. The plaza is on the left. M: Sol.)*

ALONG RÍO MANZANARES. Past the **Puerta de Toledo,** the triumphal arch commissioned by Joseph Bonaparte to celebrate his brother Napoleon, the Río Manzanares, Madrid's notoriously puny river, snakes its way around the city. The broad Baroque **Puente de Toledo** makes up for the river's inadequacies. Sandstone carvings on both sides of the bridge depict San Isidro and his family. The **Puente de Segovia,** which fords the river along C. Segovia, was conceived by Juan de Herrera. Both bridges afford gorgeous views and are popular with young couples. *(To reach Puente de Toledo from Pta. Sol, go down C. Mayor, through the Pl. Mayor, and onto C. Toledo; follow Toledo to the bridge (about a 15min. walk). M: Puerta de Toledo. M: Ópera.)*

OTHER SIGHTS. As the legend goes, the **Iglesia de San Pedro** began as a Mudéjar mosque. A 17th-century overhaul, commissioned by Felipe IV, infused the original structure with Baroque intricacies. *(Facing the Palace, go left on C. Bailén and take a right* *on C. Segovia. The church will be on your right when you reach Cost. San Pedro and C. del Nuncio. San Pedro is open for Mass only, daily 9, 11am, 7pm. Free.)* Next to the Iglesia de San Pedro is the **Museo de San Isidro**, where the saint was said to have resided and home to the sarcophagus of San Isidro, the **Capilla de San Isidro.** *(From the San Pedro church, take C. Príncipe, take a left at Pl. de la Paja, and then another left onto San Andrés. M: La Latina. Open Tu-F 9:30am-8pm, Sa-Su 10am-2pm. Free.)*

BOURBON MADRID

Weakened by plagues and political losses, the Habsburg era in Spain ended with the death of Carlos II in 1700. Felipe V, the first of Spain's Bourbon monarchs, ascended the throne in 1714 after the 12-year War of Spanish Succession. Bankruptcy, industrial stagnation, and widespread moral disillusionment compelled Felipe V to embark on a crusade of urban renewal. His successors, Fernando VI and Carlos III, fervently pursued the same ends, with astounding results. Today, the lavish palaces, churches, and parks that remain are the most touristed in Madrid; a walk around them will require planning and patience.

PALACIO REAL. The impossibly luxurious Palacio Real lounges at the western tip of central Madrid, overlooking the Río Manzanares. Felipe V commissioned Giovanni Sachetti to replace the Alcázar, burned down in 1734, with a palace that would dwarf all others; he succeeded. When Sachetti died, Filippo Juvara took over the project, basing his new facade on Bernini's rejected designs for the Louvre. The shell took 26 years to build, and the decoration of its 2000 rooms with a vast collection of porcelain, tapestries, furniture, armor, and art dragged on for over a century. When Alfonso XIII abdicated in 1931, the Second Republic abandoned the costly construction. Today, the unfinished palace is only used by King Juan Carlos and Queen Sofía on special occasions. Although only a fragment is complete, the palace stands as one of Europe's most grandiose residences.

The palace's most impressive rooms are decorated in the *Rococo* style. The **Salón de Gasparini,** site of the king's ceremonial dressing before the court, houses Goya's portrait of Carlos IV and a Mengs ceiling fresco. The **Salón del Trono** (Throne Room) also contains a ceiling fresco, painted by Tiepolo, outlining the qualities of the quintessential ruler. The **Real Oficina de Farmacia** (Royal Pharmacy) features crystal and china receptacles used to hold royal medicines, and the **Biblioteca** shelves first editions of *Don Quijote.* Also open to the public is the **Real Armería** (Armory), which displays the finest armor of the age, that of Carlos V and Felipe II, as well as other medieval weapons and artillery. *(From Pl. Isabel II, head towards the Teatro Real; the palace will be behind it, past the Pl. de Oriente. M: Ópera. ☎914 54 88 00. M: Sol. Open Apr.-Sept. M-Sa 9am-6pm, Su 9am-3pm; Oct.-Mar. M-Sa 9:30am-5pm, Su 9am-2pm. €6, with tour €6.90; students €3, with tour €6.90. EU citizens free W. Arrive early to avoid lines and skip M, when it is one of the only sights open.)*

MADRID

CATHEDRAL DE LA ALMUDENA. Take a break from the cherub-filled frescoes of most cathedrals in Spain for refreshingly modern decor. Begun in 1879 and finished a century later, this cathedral is a stark contrast to the gilded Palacio Real. After a 30-year hibernation, the building received a controversial face-lift. The reasons are apparent, as the cathedral's frescoes and stained glass windows contain a discordant mix of traditional and abstract styles: gray stone walls clash with the ceiling panels of brilliant colors and sharp geometric shapes. *(The cathedral is to the left of the Palacio Real on C. Bailén. M: Ópera. Closed during Mass. Open M-Sa 1-7pm. Free.)*

PLAZA DE ORIENTE. A minor architectural miscalculation was responsible for this sculpture park. Most of the statues were designed for the palace roof, but because they were too heavy and the queen had a nightmare about the roof collapsing, they were instead placed in this shady plaza. An equestrian **statue** of Felipe IV, sculpted by Pietro Tacca, dominates the plaza; other structures include the **Teatro Real,** inaugurated by Isabel II. Treat yourself to a pricey coffee at the elegant *terrazas* that encompass the plaza. *(From Pl. Isabel II, walk past the Teatro Real; you will stumble across the Plaza de Oriente. M: Ópera.)*

OTHER SIGHTS. The **Jardines de Sabatini,** just to the right when facing the palace, is the romantic's park of choice. Wade in the fountain and lie amongst sculpted hedges. Be sure to catch the **sunset** from the walls above the garden. Below the Palace, the **Campo de Moro,** opened to the public just 13 years ago, is straight out of a fairy tale. *(Enter the Campo from the side opposite the Palace. Free.)* The **Parque de las Vistillas,** named for the tremendous *vistillas* (views) of Palacio Real, Nuestra Señora de la Almudena, and the surrounding countryside, provides a stunning photo-op. Be cautious, as it can be dangerous at night. *(Located near the Pl. Gabriel Miró. Facing the palace, turn left on C. Bailén, and then right on C. Don Pedro into the plaza.)*

HUERTAS

The area east of Sol is a wedge bounded by C. Alcalá to the north, C. Atocha to the south, and Po. del Prado to the east. Off C. San Jerónimo a myriad of streets slope downward, outward, and eastward toward various points along Po. del Prado and Pl. Cánovas de Castillo. **Plaza Santa Ana** and its *terrazas* are the center of this old literary neighborhood; all directions in this section start from there. Huertas's sights, from authors' houses to famous cafes, are reflections of its artistic past. Home to Cervantes, Góngora, Quevedo, Calderón, and Moratín at its heyday during the "Siglo de Oro" (see **Literature,** p. 73), Huertas enjoyed a fleeting return to literary prominence when Hemingway frequented the neighborhood in the 1920s.

CASA DE LOPE DE VEGA. Although Golden Age writers Lope de Vega and Miguel de Cervantes were bitter rivals, Vega's 17th-century house is ironically located on C. Cervantes. (More ironic still, Cervantes is buried on C. Lope de Vega.) A prolific playwright and poet, Lope de Vega spent the last 25 years of his life writing over two-thirds of his plays in this house. *(C. Cervantes, 11. With your back to Pl. Santa Ana, turn left on C. Prado, right on C. León, and left on C. Cervantes. ☎914 29 92 16. Open Tu-F 9:30am-2pm, Sa 10am-2pm. €1.50, students €0.90, Sa free.)*

CÍRCULO DE BELLAS ARTES. Designed by Antonio Palacios, this building encloses two stages and several studios for lectures and workshops run by prominent artists. The Círculo is the energetic hub of much of Madrid's art, sponsoring and organizing performances and shows around the city. Pick up their free monthly magazine, *Minerva*, at the entrance. Many facilities are for *socios* (members) only, but exhibition galleries are open to the public. *(C. Alcalá, 42. From Pl. Santa Ana, go up C. del Príncipe, cross C. San Jerónimo, and continue toward C. Alcalá. Turn right on C. Alcalá; the building is on the right. ☎913 60 54 00. Hours and admission vary with exhibitions.)*

OTHER SIGHTS. Juan de Villanueva's simple **Real Academia de la Historia** houses an old library, an example of Madrid-style architecture. *(At the C. León and C. Huertas intersection. From Pl. Santa Ana, take C. Príncipe; turn left on C. Huertas. Library open M-F 9am-1pm and 4-8pm.)* Also impressive are the facades of the **Palacio Miraflores** and the **Palacio del Marqués de Ugena** designed by the 18th-century architect Pedro de Ribera. *(Palacio Miraflores, C. San Jerónimo, 15. Palacio de Marqués de Ugena, Pl. Canalejas, 3.)*

GRAN VÍA

Urban planners paved the Gran Vía in 1910 to link C. Princesa with Pl. Cibeles, creating the cosmopolitan center of life in the city. After Madrid gained wealth as a neutral supplier during WWI, the city funneled much of its earnings into making Gran Vía one of the world's great thoroughfares. Today, movie theaters and fast-food joints line the most commercialized street in Madrid. Still, Gran Vía is a sight in itself—be sure to stroll (quickly) among the shops and skyscrapers.

Sol's shopping streets converge at Gran Vía's highest elevation in **Plaza de Callao** (M: Callao), C. Postigo San Martín splits off southward, where you'll find the famed **Monasterio de las Descalzas Reales** (see p. 125). Westward from Pl. Callao (left when facing the conspicuous sex shop), the Gran Vía makes its descent toward **Plaza de España** (M: Pl. España), where a statue commemorates Spain's most prized fictional duo: Cervantes's Don Quijote and Sancho Panza (riding horseback and muleback respectively). Next to Pl. España are two of Madrid's tallest skyscrapers, the **Telefónica building** (1929) and the **Edificio de España** (1953). Louis S. Weeks of the Chicago School designed the Telefónica building, the tallest concrete building in existence at the time (81m), and Franco's architect designed the Edificio de España. Tucked between the two skyscrapers on C. San Leonardo is the small **Iglesia de San Marcos,** a Neoclassical church composed of five intersecting ellipses—this Euclidean dream of a church doesn't have a straight line.

MALASAÑA AND CHUECA

Devoid of the numerous historic monuments and palaces that characterize most of Madrid, the labyrinthine streets of Malasaña and Chueca house countless undocumented "sights," from platform-shoe stores to spontaneous street performers. These streets are an ultra-modern, funkafied relief for travelers weary of crucifixes and brushstrokes. Chueca, in particular, remains the ideal area for people-watching and boutique shopping. By night, both of these districts bristle with Madrid's alternative scene. Overall, most of the scenery lies in the people, though the region between **Calle de Fuencarral** and **Calle de San Bernardo** contains some of Madrid's most avant-garde architecture and current art exhibitions.

IGLESIA DE LAS SALESAS REALES. Bourbon King Fernando VI commissioned this church in 1758 at the request of his wife, Doña Bárbara. The Baroque-Neoclassical domed church is clad in granite, with facade sculptures by Alfonso Vergaza and a dome painting by the brothers González Velázquez. The church's ostentatious facade and interior prompted critics to pun on the queen's name: "Barbaric queen, barbaric tastes, barbaric building, barbarous expense," they said, giving rise to the expression "*¡qué bárbaro!*" Today, the expression refers to absurdity, extravagance, or just plain craziness. *(C. Bárbara de Braganza, 1. M: Colón. From Pl. Colón, go down Po. Recoletos and make a right on C. Bárbara de Braganza; the church will be on your right. ☎913 19 48 11. Open daily 9am-1pm and 5-6pm. Free.)*

ARGÜELLES

The 19th century witnessed the growth of several neighborhoods around the core of the city, north and northwest of the Palacio Real. Today, the area known as Argüelles and the zone around **Calle San Bernardo** form a cluttered mixture of middle-class houses, student apartments, and bohemian hangouts, all brimming with cultural activity. Heavily bombarded during the Civil War, Argüelles inspired Chilean poet Pablo Neruda, then a resident, to write *España en el corazón.*

TEMPLO DE DEBOD. Built by Pharaoh Zakheramon in the 4th century BC, it's the only Egyptian temple in Spain. In appreciation of Spanish archaeologists who helped rescue the Abu Simbel temples from the floods of the Aswan dam, the Egyptian government shipped the temple stone by stone to Spain. The **Parque de la Montaña** is home to the temple and two of its three original gateways and provides a peaceful haven with beautiful views. At sunset, marvel at the landscape from the look-out points. *(M: Ventura Rodríguez. From the Metro, walk down C. Ventura Rodríguez to Parque de la Montaña; the temple is on the left. ☎917 65 10 08. Tu-F 9:45am-1:15pm and 4:15-5:45pm; Sa-Su 10am-1:45pm. W and Su free. Park free and always open.)*

ERMITA DE SAN ANTONIO DE LA FLORIDA. Although out of the way, the Ermita is worth the trouble. It contains Goya's pantheon—a frescoed dome arches above his buried corpse. Goya's skull, apparently stolen by a phrenologist, was missing when the corpse arrived from France. Every 12th of June, single *madrileñas* pay homage to the statue San Antonio's to beg his help in the husband-hunt. *(M: Príncipe Pío. From the Metro, go left on C. de Buen Altamirano, walk through the park, and turn left on Po. Florida; the Ermita is at the end of this street. ☎915 42 07 22. Open Tu-F 10am-2pm and 4-8pm, Sa-Su 10am-2pm. €1.80, student €0.90. W and Sa Free.)*

CASA DEL CAMPO. Take the **Teléferico** from Rosales into the city's largest park. Shaded by pines, oaks, and cypresses, large numbers of families, joggers, and walkers roam the grounds by day. Early morning reveals evidence of questionable nighttime activities; it's wise to stay away after dark. Inside the amusement park, **Parque de Atracciones,** relive your childhood on the roller coaster. One of Madrid's largest pools is in the corner of the park, next to M: Lago. *(Take bus #33 or M: Batán. Walk up the main street away from the lake and through the park. ☎915 26 80 31. Open Su-F noon-11pm, Sa noon-midnight. www.parquedeatracciones.es.)* The **Zoo/Aquarium** is 5min. away. *(☎915 12 37 80. Open daily 10:30am-sunset. €10, children under 8 €8.)*

OTHER SIGHTS. Parque del Oeste is a large, sloping park known for the **Rosaleda** (rose garden) at its bottom. A yearly competition determines which award-winning rose will be added to the permanent collection. *(M: Moncloa. From the Metro, take C. Princesa. Garden open daily 10am-8pm.)* A prime example of Fascist Neoclassicism, the arcaded **Cuartel General del Aire (Ejército del Aire)** commands the view on the other side of the Arco de la Victoria (by the Moncloa Metro station). The renovation of Felipe V's soldiers' barracks has produced one of Madrid's finest cultural centers, the **Centro Cultural Conde Duque,** which hosts travelling exhibitions. *(C. Conde Duque, 11. ☎915 88 58 34. M: Noviciado.)* The fabulous **Museo de América** (see p. 124) is a bit farther down the avenue, past the **Arco de Moncloa.** The **Faro de Moncloa** is a 92m high metal tower near the museum that offers views of the city. On a clear day, you can see El Escorial. *(Av. Arco de la Victoria, ☎902 15 19 12. Open daily 10am-1:45pm, 5-8:45pm. €1.50 to ascend the Faro de Moncloa.)*

RETIRO

With the construction of the 300-acre **Parque del Buen Retiro,** Felipe IV intended to transform the former hunting grounds into a personal retreat, *un buen retiro*. Today, the magnificent park and its accompanying gardens are filled with palm-readers, sunbathers, young couples, soccer players, reflective students, and aggressive drug pushers (just ignore them and they should leave you alone). The northeast corner of the park enchants with medieval monastic ruins and waterfalls. The park also houses the spectacular Palacio de Cristal and Estanque Grande. On weekends, the promenades fill with musicians, families, and young lovers; on summer nights (when only the north gate remains open), the lively bars and cafes scattered around the park become quite active. The park is easily accessible from the Retiro Metro stop. There are four entrances to Retiro: C. Alfonso XII, C. Alcalá, Pl. de la Independencia, and Av. Menéndez Pelayo. Avoid venturing alone after dark.

ESTANQUE GRANDE. Overlooked by Alfonso XII's mausoleum, rowers crowd the rectangular lake in the middle of the park, the Estanque Grande. The lake has been the social center of Retiro ever since aspiring caricaturists, fortune-tellers, sunflower-seed vendors, and drug pushers first parked their goods along its marble shores. The colonnaded monument is the perfect spot for late afternoon relaxation and people-watching. *(M: Retiro. With your back to the Metro stop, turn right on C. Alcalá and walk until you reach Pta. Alcalá/Pl. de la Independencia. Enter the park at Independencia which takes you to Av. Méjico, the gateway to the lake.)*

PALACIO DE VELÁZQUEZ. This Velázquez creation has billowing ceilings, marble floors, and ideal lighting. The Palacio de Velázquez exhibits works in conjunction with the Museo de Arte Reina Sofía (see p. 123). Exhibits change quite frequently. *(From the Estanque, walk straight to Pl. de Honduras and turn left on Po. Venezuela. The palace will shortly be on your right. Walk slightly downhill and around the building to get to the main entrance. ☎915 75 62 45. Closed Tu. Open Apr.- Sept. M-Sa 11am-8pm, Su 11am-6pm; Oct.-Mar. M-Sa 10am-6pm, Su 10am-4pm. Free.)*

PALACIO DE CRISTAL. Built by Ricardo Velázquez to exhibit Philippine flowers in 1887, this exquisite steel-and-glass structure hosts a variety of art shows and exhibits, with subjects ranging from Bugs Bunny to Spanish portraiture to vocal recognition of bird calls. *(From Palacio de Velázquez, continue straight out the main door until you reach the lake and the palace. ☎915 74 66 14. Always closed Tu. Open Apr.- Sept. M-Sa 11am-8pm, Su 11am-6pm; Oct.-Mar. M-Sa 10am-6pm, Su 10am-4pm. Free.)*

OTHER SIGHTS. Bullets from the 1921 assassination of prime minister Eduardo Dato permanently scarred the eastern face of **Puerta de Alcalá** (1778), outside Retiro's Puerta de la Independencia. To the south, the **Casón del Buen Retiro** faces the park (see p. 123); behind it sits the **Museo del Ejército** (see p. 126). The two buildings are remnants of Felipe IV's palace, which burned down in 1764.

EL PARDO

Built as a hunting lodge for Carlos I in 1547, El Pardo was enlarged by generations of Habsburgs and Bourbons. Though Spain's growing capital eventually engulfed El Pardo, it still stands as one of Spain's greatest country palaces. El Pardo gained attention in 1940 when Franco decided to make it his home; he resided here until his death in 1975. Although politics have changed, the palace is still the official reception site for distinguished foreign visitors. Renowned for its collection of **tapestries**—several of which were designed by Goya—the palace also holds a Velázquez painting and Ribera's *Techo de los hombres ilustres (Ceiling of the Illustrious Men).* You can also see the bedroom cabinet in which Franco kept Santa Teresa's silver-encrusted hand. Entrance to the palace's **capilla** and the nearby **Casita del Príncipe,** created by Juan de Villanueva of Museo del Prado fame, is free. *(Take bus #601 from the stop in front of the Ejército del Aire building above M: Moncloa (every 15min., €0.90). ☎913 76 03 29. Palace open Apr.-Sept. M-F 10:30am-6pm, Su 9:25am-1:40pm; Oct.-Mar. M-F 10:30am-5pm, Su 9:55am-1:40pm. Compulsory 45min. guided tour in Spanish. €4.80, students €1.50. W free for EU citizens.)*

THE PASEOS: A WALKING TOUR

Madrid's thoroughfare *paseos* connect the city through three fused segments, **Po. Prado, Po. Recoletos,** and **Po. Castellana,** running from Madrid-Atocha in the south to Madrid-Chamartín in the north. The *paseos* are a great starting point for walking tours, since most major sights branch out from the main avenue. Plants, gardens, and cafes separate traffic along the *paseos*. A walking tour could last several hours, an entire day, or even several days, depending on how much time you want to spend at the various sights and how far you stray from the main *paseo* path. You may be tempted to head to El Retiro after the Museo del Prado or venture to Puerta del Sol once you have reached Pl. Cibeles. Regardless of the path chosen, the *paseos* are a simple way to get your bearings and organize your daily itinerary.

The first *paseo*, Po. Prado, connects Atocha to Pl. Cibeles, passing the **Museo del Prado** (see p. 121), the **Thyssen-Bornemisza** (see p. 124), and the Ritz Hotel. Along Po. Recoletos, extending from Pl. Cibeles to Pl. Colón, the newest members of the *clase alta* (upper class) congregate at luxuriously shaded *terrazas*. Contemporary Madrid stretches farther north along Po. Castellana (lined with bank buildings from the 1970s and 80s) to Pl. Castilla's twin towers (Puerta de Europa).

PASEO DEL PRADO

Modeled after the Piazza Navona in Rome, Paseo del Prado is the center of Madrid's art district. Virtually every major museum is in the vicinity of this museum mile, known as the *triángulo de arte.* Directly across from Estación Atocha, the **Centro de Arte Reina Sofía** (see p. 123), home to Picasso's *Guernica,* presides over Pl. Emperador Carlos V. Its innovative glass elevators and outdoor sculptures hint at the impressive collection of modern art within.

Walking up Po. Prado, you'll pass the **Jardín Botánico** on the right. Opened during Carlos III's reign, the garden showcases over 30,000 species of plants, ranging from traditional roses to medicinal herbs. Just about anyone will appreciate the garden's vast collection of imported trees, bushes, and flowers. *(Pl. de Murillo, 2, next to the Museo del Prado. ☎914 20 30 17; www.ejb.scic.es. Open in summer daily 10am-8pm; in winter 10am-6pm; in spring and fall 10am-7pm. €1.50, students €0.75.)* Next to the Jardín Botánico is the world-renowned **Museo del Prado** (see p. 121) and behind it, on C. Ruiz de Alarcón, stands the **Iglesia de San Jerónimo,** Madrid's royal church. Built by Hieronymite monks and re-endowed by the Catholic Monarchs, the church has witnessed a few joyous milestones, including the coronation of Fernando and Isabel and the marriage of King Alfonso XIII. These days, only the highest of high-society weddings are held in the church. *(Open daily 8am-1:30pm and 5-8:30pm.)* Back on Po. Prado, to the north in Pl. Lealtad, stands the **Obelisco a los Mártires del 2 de Mayo,** filled with the ashes of those who died in the 1808 uprising against Napoleon. Its four statues represent Constancy, Virtue, Valor, and Patriotism, and the flame burns continuously in honor of the patriots. Behind the memorial sits the colonnaded Greco-Roman-style **Bolsa de Madrid** (Stock Exchange), designed by Repullés. Ventura Rodríguez's **Fuente de Neptuno,** in Pl. Cánovas de Castillo, is one of three aquatic masterpieces along the avenue.

The arts of the Po. Prado transform into the Po. Recoletos at the tulip-encircled **Plaza de Cibeles** (see **Sex in the Cibeles,** below). Madrid residents protected this emblem of their city (best viewed at dusk) during Franco's bomb raids by covering it with a pyramid of sandbags. From the plaza, the small **Museo Naval** is to the right. *(Entrance at Po. Prado, 5. ☎913 79 52 99; www.armada.mde.es. Open Tu-Su 10am-1:30pm. Closed in Aug. Free.)* In the southeast corner of the plaza, the spectacular neo-Baroque **Palacio de Comunicaciones** (see p. 100), designed by Antonio Palacios and Julián Otamendi of Otto Wagner's Vienna School in 1920. Looking to your right up C. Alcalá from the Palacio de Comunicaciones is Sabatini's **Puerta de Alcalá,** the 18th-century emblematic gateway and court symbol. On the northeastern corner of the plaza roundabout (behind black gates) is the former **Palacio de Linares,** a 19th-century townhouse built for Madrid nobility. Proven by a team of "scientists" to be inhabited by ghosts, it was transformed into the **Casa de América,** with a library and lecture halls for the study of Latin American culture and politics. It sponsors art exhibitions, tours of the palace, and guest lectures. *(Po. de Recoletos, 2. M: Banco de España. ☎915 95 48 00. Open F 10am-12:30pm, Sa-Su 10am-1:30pm.)*

PASEO DE RECOLETOS

Continuing north toward the brown **Torres de Colón** (Columbus Towers), you'll pass the **Biblioteca Nacional,** where the sleek **Museo del Libro** displays treasures from the monarchy's collection, including a first edition copy of *Don Quijote. (Entrance at #20. Open Tu-Sa 10am-9pm, Su 10am-2pm. Free.)* Behind the library lies the massive **Museo Arqueológico Nacional** (see p. 125). The museum entrance is on C. Serrano, an avenue lined with pricey boutiques in the posh **Barrio de Salamanca.** The museum and library huddle just beyond the modern **Plaza Colón** (M: Colón) and the adjoining **Jardines del Descubrimiento** (Gardens of Discovery). At one side loom huge clay boulders, inscribed with odd trivia about the New World, including

SEX IN THE CIBELES The Plaza de Cibeles, with its infamous marble fountain, has been Madrid's spiritual center since its construction in 1781. Depicting the fertility goddess's triumph over the emblematic Castilian lions, the fountain's image of Cybele has long captivated citizens. Legend has it that the fleet-footed Atlanta, one of Cybele's maids, would take as her lover only the man who could outrun her. No man was up to the challenge until one cunning suitor instructed his cohorts to scatter golden apples (as distractions) in Atlanta's path. The goddess Cybele, watching the prank, was overcome with rage at men's evil ways. After punishing the plotters by turning them into lions, she hitched them up to her own carriage. This assertion of power and sexuality charmed Madrid, resulting in the proverb *"más popular que Cibeles."*

Seneca's prediction of the New World's discovery, the names of the mariners on board the caravels, and passages from Columbus's diary. From a thundering fountain in the center of the plaza rises a neo-Gothic spire to Columbus. A huge inlaid map detailing Columbus's journey covers the wall behind the waterfall. Concerts, lectures, ballets, and plays are held in the **Centro Cultural de la Villa** (☎915 75 60 80), the underground municipal art center beneath the statue and waterfall.

PASEO DE LA CASTELLANA

Nineteenth- and early 20th-century aristocrats dislodged themselves from Old Madrid to settle along Po. de la Castellana. During the Civil War, Republican forces used the mansions as barracks. Most were torn down in the 1960s when banks and insurance companies commissioned new, innovative structures. Competition begat architectural excellence, offering the lowly pedestrian a rich man's spectacle of architecture and fashion. Some notables include: Rafael Moneo's **Bankinter,** #29, the first to integrate rather than demolish a townhouse; **Banco Urquijo,** known as "the coffeepot"; the Sevillian-tiled **Edificio ABC,** #34, the former office of the conservative, monarchical newspaper and now a shopping center; the pink **Edificio Bankunion,** #46; **Banca Catalana Occidente,** #50, which looks like an ice cube on a cracker; and the famous **Edificio La Caixa,** #61.

Just south of the American Embassy, between Pl. Colón and Glorieta de Emilio Castelar, is an **open-air sculpture museum** displaying works by Miró, González, and Chillida. Look up—works are also hanging from the bridge. Intimate, private museums, including the **Museo Lázaro Galdiano** (see p. 125), are just off Po. Castellana. At **Plaza de Lima** is the 110,000-seat **Estadio Santiago Bernabéu** (M: Lima), home to the beloved **Real Madrid,** winner of its 8th European Championship in 2000 and its 28th Spanish Championship in 2001. Farther north, the **Puerta de Europa,** with its two 27-story leaning towers connected by a tunnel, dominates Pl. Castilla (M: Pl. Castilla). They were designed by American John Bergee as a doorway to the city.

MUSEUMS

Madrid's great museums need no introduction. If you plan on visiting the big three, your best bet is the **Paseo del Arte** ticket (€7.66), which grants admission to the Museo del Prado, Centro de Arte Reina Sofía, and Museo Thyssen-Bornemisza. The pass is available at all three museums.

MUSEO DEL PRADO

Po. Prado at Pl. Cánovas del Castillo. M: Banco de España or Atocha. ☎/fax 913 30 28 00; museoprado.mcu.es. Open Tu-Sa 9am-7pm, Su 9am-2pm. €3, students €1.50. Sa after 2:30pm, Su, and holidays free.

The Prado is Spain's most prestigious museum, as well as one of Europe's finest centers for art from the 12th through 17th centuries. In 1785, architect **Juan de Villanueva** began construction of the Neoclassical building, following Carlos III's order for a museum of natural history and sciences. In 1819 Fernando VII transformed it into the royal painting archive; the museum's 7000 pieces are the result of hundreds of years of Bourbon art collecting. The walls are filled with Spanish and foreign masterpieces, including a comprehensive selection from the Flemish and Venetian schools. The museum is well-organized: each room is numbered and described in the museum's free guide. The sheer quantity of paintings means you'll have to be selective—walk past the rooms of imitation Rubens and Rococo cherubs and into the groves of the masters. The ground floor houses Spanish painting from the 12th through 16th centuries and 15th through 16th century Flemish, German, and Italian paintings. The first floor contains 17th-century works, and 18th-century paintings are located on the second floor. In addition to the free, indispensable floorplan you receive upon entry, the museum's guidebooks help you sift through the floors and offer extensive art history and criticism (€0.60-18).

DIEGO VELÁZQUEZ. The first floor houses Spanish, Flemish, French, Dutch, and Italian works from the 16th and 17th centuries. The most notable of these are an unparalleled collection of works by Diego Velázquez (1599-1660), court painter and interior decorator for Felipe IV (portraits of the foppish monarch abound). Because of their unforgiving realism and use of light, Velázquez's works resonate even in the 21st century. Several of his most famous paintings are here, including *Las hilanderas (The Tapestry Weavers)*, *Los borrachos (The Drunkards)*, and *La fragua de Vulcano (Vulcan's Forge)*. With *Las lanzas (The Spears* or *The Surrender of Breda)*, Velázquez began to experiment with spatial perspective, developing the technique to imply continuous movement. Smoke from a recent battle clears in the background as an anxious horse dominates the foreground. Velázquez's technique, called illusionism, climaxed in his magnum opus *Las meninas (The Maids of Honor)*, dubbed an "encounter" rather than a painting. The "snapshot quality" of the figures transformed painting in the 17th century.

FRANCISCO GOYA. In 1785, Francisco de Goya y Lucientes (1746-1828) became the court portraitist. Perhaps the most interesting aspect of his works is that he managed to depict the royal family so unflatteringly and satirically without being expelled from court. Some suggest that he manipulated light and shadow to focus the viewer's gaze on the figure of the queen (rather than the centrally located king) in *La familia de Carlos IV*—a discreet way of supporting popular contemporary opinion about the true power behind the monarchy. The stark *Dos de Mayo* and *Fusilamientos de Tres de Mayo*, which depict the terrors of the Revolution of 1808, may be Goya's most recognized works. Also notable is the expressionless woman in *La maja vestida* and *La maja desnuda*. Perhaps the most evocative pieces in the Goya collection are the *Pinturas Negras (Black Paintings)*. These paintings were aptly named for the darkness of both the colors and the subject matter—Goya painted them in the house where he lived at the end of his life, deaf and alone. *Saturno devorando a su hijo (Saturn Devouring His Son)* stands out among the *Pinturas Negras*, a reminder from an ailing artist that time eventually destroys its creations. Goya violently captures the moment when Saturn eats his children upon hearing a prophesy that one of them would overthrow him.

ITALIAN, FLEMISH, AND OTHER SPANISH ARTISTS. The ground floor of the Prado displays many of **El Greco's** (Doménikos Theotokópoulos, 1541-1614) religious paintings. *La Trinidad (The Trinity)* and *La adoración de los pastores (The Adoration of the Shepherds)* are characterized by El Greco's luminous colors, elongated figures, and mystical subjects. On the second floor are other works by

Spanish artists, including **Murillo's** *Familia con pájaro pequeño (Family with Small Bird),* **Ribera's** *El martirio de San Bartholomeo (Martyrdom of Saint Bartholomew),* and **Zurbarán's** *La inmaculada.*

The collection of **Italian** works is formidable, including **Titian's** portraits of Carlos I and Felipe II and **Raphael's** *El cardenal desconocido (The Unknown Cardinal).* **Tintoretto's** rendition of the homicidal seductress Judith and her hapless victim Holofernes, as well as his *Washing of the Feet* are here as well. Some minor **Botticellis** and a slew of his imitators are also on display. Among the works by **Rubens,** *The Adoration of the Magi* bests reflect his voluptuous style.

As a result of the Spanish Habsburgs' control of the Netherlands, the **Flemish** holdings are also top-notch. **Van Dyck's** *Marquesa de Legunes* is here, as well as works by **Albrecht Durer.** Especially harrowing is **Peter Breughel the Elder's** *The Triumph of Death,* in which death drives a carriage of skulls on a decaying horse. **Hieronymus Bosch's** moralistic *The Garden of Earthly Delights* is a favorite, with detailed depictions of hedonism and the destiny that awaits its practitioners.

CASÓN DEL BUEN RETIRO. Three minutes from the Prado Museum is the Casón del Buen Retiro, which, while closed for renovations, is still worth a peek. Once part of Felipe IV's Palacio del Buen Retiro, the Casón was destroyed in the Napoleonic wars. The rebuilt version normally houses the Prado's 19th- and 20th-century works, currently on loan to the Reina Sofía. *(C. Alfonso XXII, 28. ☎913 30 28 60. Closed for renovations until at least 2003.)*

MUSEO NACIONAL CENTRO DE ARTE REINA SOFÍA

C. Santa Isabel, 52, opposite Estación Atocha at the south end of Po. Prado. M: Atocha. ☎914 67 50 62 or 914 67 47 61; museoreinasofia.mcu.es. Open M and W-Sa 10am-9pm, Su 10am-2:30pm. €3.01, students €1.50. Sa after 2:30pm, Su and holidays free.

Since Juan Carlos I decreed this renovated hospital a national museum in 1988, the Reina Sofía's collection of **20th-century art** has grown steadily. Entrance through the soaring glass elevators adds to the mystique and character of the museum. The second and fourth floors are mazes of permanent exhibits charting the Spanish avant-garde and contemporary movements. Rooms dedicated to Juan Gris, Joan Miró, and Salvador Dalí display Spain's vital contributions to the Surrealist movement. Miró's works show a spare, colorful abstraction, while Dalí's paintings, including *Monumental Imperial a la mujer niña* and *El enigma sin fin,* portray the artist's Freudian nightmares and sexual fantasies.

Picasso's masterpiece **Guernica** is the highlight of the Reina Sofía's permanent collection. Now freed from its restrictive glass cover, it depicts the Basque town bombed by the Germans at Franco's request during the Spanish Civil War (see **The Tragedy of Guernica,** p. 493). Picasso denounced the bloodshed in a huge, colorless work of contorted, agonized figures. The screaming horse in the center represents war, and the twisted bull—an unmistakable national symbol—represents Spain. When asked by Nazi officials whether he was responsible for this work, Picasso answered, "No, you are." He gave the canvas to New York's Museum of Modern Art on the condition that they return it to Spain when democracy was restored. In 1981, five years after Franco's death, *Guernica* was delivered to Madrid's Casón del Buen Retiro. The subsequent move to the Reina Sofía sparked an international controversy—Picasso's other stipulation had been that the painting hang only in the Prado, to affirm his equivalent status with artists like Titian and Velázquez. Basques want the painting relocated to the Guggenheim in Bilbao, but Madrid officials declare it too delicate to move. Preliminary sketches and a myriad of other Picasso paintings surround *Guernica,* testimony to his breadth of talent. Two other Picasso works of note are *Woman in Blue* and *Painter with Model.*

MUSEO THYSSEN-BORNEMISZA

On the corner of Po. Prado and C. San Jerónimo. M: Banco de España. Bus #6, 14, 27, 37, or 45. ☎913 69 01 51; www.museothyssen.org. Open Tu-Su 10am-7pm. No admission after 6:30pm. €4.20, seniors and students with ISIC €2.40, under 12 free.

Unlike the Prado and the Reina Sofía, the Thyssen-Bornemisza covers a wide range of periods and media; exhibits range from 14th-century canvases to 20th-century sculptures. The museum is housed in the 18th-century **Palacio de Villahermosa** and contains the former collection of Baron Heinrich Thyssen-Bornemisza. The baron donated his collection in 1993, and today the museum is the world's most extensive private showcase. To view the collection in chronological order and observe an evolution of styles, begin on the top floor and work down.

The top floor is dedicated to the **Old Masters** collection, which includes such notables as Hans Holbein's austere *Portrait of Henry VIII* and El Greco's *Annunciation.* The organization of the Thyssen-Bornemisza provokes natural comparisons across centuries—note how the representation of the body evolves from Lucas Cranach's *The Nymph of the Spring* to Titian's *Saint Jerome in the Desert* to Anthony van Dyck's *Portrait of Jacques Le Roy.* In both variety and quality, the Thyssen-Bornemisza's **Baroque** collection, including pieces by Caravaggio, José de Ribera, and Claude Lorraine, overshadows that of the Prado.

The movement from the dark canvases of the top floor to the vibrant ones below reflects the revolutionary command of light and the arbitrary use of color that became popular in the 17th century. During this period, Dutch works, such as Frans Hals's *Family Group in a Landscape,* began to display a mastery of natural light. The **Impressionist** and **Post-Impressionist** collections explode with texture and color—look for works by Renoir, Manet, Degas, Monet, van Gogh, Cézanne, and Matisse. Though less well-known, the **Expressionist** artists are well-represented, with noteworthy works by Nolde, Marc, and Beckmann. The museum is also home to Europe's only collection of North American 19th-century painting.

The highlight of the tour is the museum's **20th-century** collection. The modern artists represented include Picasso, Léger, Mondrian, Miró, Kandinsky, Gorky, Pollack, Rothko, Dalí, Hopper, Chagall, Ernst, Klee, and O'Keefe, among others.

OTHER MUSEUMS

MUSEO DE AMÉRICA. This under-appreciated museum reopened after painstaking renovations; it is now a must-see. It documents the cultures of America's pre-Columbian civilizations and the legacy of Spanish conquest with detail and insight. Artifacts include solid gold Columbian ornaments and Mayan treasures. *(Av. Reyes Católicos, 6, next to the Faro de Moncloa. ☎915 49 26 41. M: Moncloa. Open Tu-Sa 10am-3pm, Su 10am-2:30pm. €3, students €1.50. Su free.)*

MUSEO DE LA REAL ACADEMIA DE BELLAS ARTES DE SAN FERNANDO. Following the example of Italy and France, Spain's Old Masters convinced Ferdinand VI to declare a royal academy in 1752 to train the country's most talented artists. The collection of Old Masters in this beautiful museum represents their legacy; it is surpassed only by the Prado. Goya's *La Tirana* and Velázquez's portrait of Felipe IV are masterpieces; the Raphael and Titian collections are also excellent. Other attractions include a room dedicated to Goya (a former academy director) and 17th-century canvases by Ribera, Murillo, Zurbarán, and Rubens. The top floor also has Picasso sketches. The **Calcografía Real** (Royal Print and Drawing Collection) houses Goya's studio and organizes temporary exhibitions. The front desk has comprehensive guides for all collections. *(C. Alcalá, 13. ☎915 22 08 64. M: Sol or Sevilla. Open Tu-F 9am-7pm, Sa-M 9am-2:30pm. €2.50, students €1.25. W free.)*

MUSEO LÁZARO GALDIANO. This small palace, once owned by 19th-century financier Lázaro Galdino, displays a private collection of Italian Renaissance bronzes and Celtic and Visigoth brasses. Paintings include Leonardo da Vinci's *The Savior* and Hieronymus Bosch's *Ecce Homo*, as well as works by the Spanish trifecta: El Greco, Velázquez, and Goya. *(C. Serrano, 122. Turn right off Po. Castellana onto C. María de Molina. ☎915 61 60 84. M: Rubén Darío or Nuñez de Balboa. Open Sept.-July Tu-Su 10am-2pm. €3. W free. Closed for renovations until at least late 2002; call ahead for re-opening information.)*

MUSEO SOROLLA. The former residence and studio of the Valencian painter displays his own priceless paintings and sculptures, accompanied by works of other painters of his time. Sorolla's charming house and garden are as captivating as his work, including *Trata de Blancas* and *Clotilde con traje de noche*. *(Po. General Martinez Campos, 37. ☎913 10 15 84. M: Iglesia or Rubén Darío. Open Tu-Sa 10am-3pm, Su 10am-2pm. €3, Su Free. Call ahead; closed for renovations at least until late 2002.)*

MONASTERIO DE LAS DESCALZAS REALES. In 1559 Juana of Austria, Felipe II's sister, converted the former royal palace into a convent; today it is home to 26 Franciscan nuns who watch over Juana's tomb. The **Salón de Tápices** contains 10 renowned tapestries based on cartoons by Rubens, as well as Santa Ursula's jewel-encrusted bones and *El viaje de Santa Úrsula y las once mil vírgenes (The Journey of Santa Úrsula and the Eleven Thousand Virgins)*. Claudio Coello's magnificent 17th-century frescoes line the staircase. Lines are long in the summer; arrive early. *(Pl. Descalzas, between Pl. Callao and Pta. de Sol. ☎915 59 74 04 or 915 47 53 50. M: Callao or Sol. Open Tu-Th and Sa 10:30am-12:45pm and 4-5:45pm, F 10:30am-12:45pm, Su 11am-3pm. €4, students €2.40. W free for EU citizens.)*

MUSEO ARQUEOLÓGICO NACIONAL. After countless moves, Madrid's display of the history of the Western world settled in this huge museum in 1895. Founded by a decree of Isabel II, the museum houses an astounding collection of items from Spain's past, including the country's most famous archaeological find, *Dama de Elche*, a 4th-century funerary urn, Felipe II's astrolabe, and a 16th-century porcelain clock belonging to Lady Baza. Outside stands a replica of the Altamira caves and their Paleolithic paintings. *(C. Serrano 13, behind the Biblioteca Nacional. ☎915 77 79 12; www.man.es. M: Serrano. Open Tu-Sa 9:30am-8:30pm, summer until 6:30pm; Su 9:30am-2:30pm, summer until 2pm. €3, students €1.50. Sa after 2:30pm and Su free.)*

THE INSIDER'S CITY

HUERTAS HOPPING

With endless options for Madrid's nightlife-lovers, the Huertas neighborhood is one of the city's best places to party. Countless bars and clubs surround the Plaza de Santa Ana and radiate out to smaller side streets. Drink up, have fun, and go wild!

1. Sip enormous, volcanic drinks in a Hawaiian paradise at **Mauna Loa** (☎914 29 70 62).
2. Throw back a cold *cerveza* overlooking Plaza Santa Ana at **Naturbrier** (☎914 29 39 18).
3. Request your favorite hip-hop and reggae hits from DJ Jay at **La Comedia** (☎915 21 51 64).
4. Enjoy a night with that special someone at the romantic **Viva Madrid** (☎914 29 36 40).
5. Clack your heels and clap your hands at **Cardamomo** for a night of flamenco fun (☎913 69 07 57).
6. Looking for live music? Catch a show at **La Boca del Lobo** (☎914 29 70 13).
7. Break out your dance grooves at the energetic **No Se Lo Digas a Nadie** (☎913 69 17 27).

THE RIGHT TO PARTY After 40 years of Franco-imposed repression, Madrid was a cultural explosion waiting to happen. Franco's death in 1975 served as a catalyst for change; not a day passed before every newspaper printed a pornographic photo on its front page. *El Destapeo* ("the uncorking" or "uncovering" that followed Franco's regime) and *La Movida* ("the Movement," which took place a few years later) exploded in Madrid, inspiring political diversity, apolitical revelry, and eccentricity of all kinds. Filmmaker Pedro Almodóvar became a reflection of the movement and its most famous member, creating farcical films about loony grandmothers, outgoing young women, unapologetic homosexuals, and troubled students. Gradually, *La Movida* became too much for the city. Artists and club-rats were forced to give up their favorite pastimes for practical jobs—no one could afford to keep up the careless and eccentric lifestyle that *La Movida* represented. Remnants of *La Movida* are still visible, however, in today's outrageous clubs, ambitious bars, and in the excitement of young *madrileños* planning to *ir de marcha* ("to party," literally "to go marching").

MONASTERIO DE LA ENCARNACIÓN. Designed by Juan de Herrera's disciple Juan de Gómez, the monastery is an oasis in the middle of Madrid's bustle, housing 1500+ relics of saints, including a vial of San Pantaleón's blood believed to liquify every year on July 27. According to the legend, if the blood does not liquify, disaster will strike Madrid. *(Pl. Encarnación, off C. Bailén just east of the Palacio Real. ☎915 42 00 59. M: Ópera. Open W and Sa 10:30am-12:45pm and 4-5:45pm, Su 11am-1:45pm. €2.55, students €1.35. W free for EU citizens.)*

MUSEO MUNICIPAL. An Isabelline facade leads to a collection of documents and artwork detailing the history of Madrid, including the first complete 16th-century map of the city. *(C. Fuencarral, 78. ☎915 88 86 72. M: Tribunal. Open Tu-F 9:30am-8pm, Sa-Su 10am-2pm. €1.80. W and Su free. Call ahead; closed for renovations during 2002.)*

MUSEO DEL EJÉRCITO. In this stately fragment of the Palacio del Buen Retiro stands a vast collection of over 27,000 military artifacts tracing the history of the Spanish military. Each room is dedicated to a different period or conquest; the most famous contains the *Tizona* sword of Cid Campeador and a fragment of the cross Columbus wore when he arrived in the New World. *(C. Méndez Núñez, 1, just north of Casón del Buen Retiro. ☎915 22 89 77. M: Retiro or Banco de España. Open Tu-Su 10am-2pm. €0.60, students €0.30, under 18, over 65 free. Sa free.)*

MUSEO CERRALBO. This unusual palatial museum displays an eclectic collection of furniture and ornamentation, including a Louis XVI-style French piano and El Greco's *The Ecstasy of Saint Francis* in the chapel. *(C. Ventura Rodríguez, 17. ☎915 47 36 46. M: Ventura Rodríguez or Plaza de España. Open Tu-Sa 9:30am-2:30pm, Su 10am-2pm. €2.40, students €1.20. W and Su free.)*

MUSEO ROMÁNTICO. Housed in a 19th-century mansion, this museum is a time capsule of the Romantic period's decorative arts. *(C. San Mateo, 13. ☎914 48 10 71; www.mcu.es/nmuseos/romantico. M: Alonso Martínez. Open Sept.-July Tu-Sa 9am-3pm, Su 10am-2pm. €2.40, students €1.20. Su free. Call ahead; closed for renovations until late 2002.)*

NIGHTLIFE

Madrid offers some of the greatest nightlife in the world. As the sun sets, the streets and plazas begin to exude a frenetic energy, an intoxicating mixture of excitement and alcohol. Partying in Madrid is a celebration of life, a true demonstration that *la vida es un carnaval.* Undeterred by occasional spells of bad weather, traffic jams on small streets, and shady characters that always seem to appear in Madrid's plazas, party-goers in Madrid have only one goal for the night: fun. Both gay and straight bar- and club-hoppers will be overwhelmed by the countless ways to spend a single evening. Proud of their nocturnal offerings—*madrileños* will tell you with a straight face that they were bored in Paris or New York—they insist that no one goes to bed until they've "killed the night" and, in some cases, a good part of the following morning.

An average night includes several neighborhoods and countless venues; half the party is the in-between. A typical evening might start in the *tapas* bars of Huertas, moving to a first-session disco in Malasaña, and then to the wild parties of Chueca. Some clubs don't even bother opening until 4 or 5am; the only (relatively) quiet nights of the week are Monday and Tuesday. For clubs and discos, life begins around 2am. Many discos have "afternoon" sessions for teens (7pm-midnight; cover €1.50-6), but the "night" sessions (lasting until dawn) are when people really let their hair down. The *entrada* (cover) often includes a drink and can be as high as €13; men may be charged up to €3 more than women, if women are charged at all. Venues often change their prices depending on the night, with Saturdays being the most expensive. Keep an eye out for *invitaciones* and *oferta* cards—in stores, restaurants, tourist publications, tourist offices, and in the streets—that offer discounts or free admission. For the most up-to-date info on what's going on, scan Madrid's entertainment guides (see **Read This,** p. 94).

EL CENTRO: SOL, ÓPERA, AND PLAZA MAYOR

In the middle of Madrid and at the heart of the action are the grandiose and spectacular clubs of El Centro. With multiple floors, swinging lights, cages, and disco-balls, they fulfill even the wildest clubber's expectations. The mainstream clubs found among these streets are often tourist hotspots; as a result, a night of fun here is the most expensive in the city. El Centro includes more territory than Madrid's other neighborhoods, so make a plan for your night and bring a map.

Palacio Gaviria, C. Arenal, 9 (☎915 26 60 69; www.palaciogaviria.com). M: Sol or Ópera. A red carpet leads to 2 ballrooms turned club spaces, complete with dancers and blazing light shows. Different theme every night. Cover varies; Su-Tu cover starts at €7, W-Th €9, F €12, Sa €15. Open M-Th 11pm-late, F-Sa 11:30pm-late, Su 9pm-late.

Suite, Virgen de los Peligros, 4 (☎915 21 40 31), off C. Alcalá. M: Sevilla. Classy restaurant, bar, and club boasts *tapas* by day and sleek drinks by night (€5-6). Upstairs dance floor rolls with house while the crowd downstairs at the bar and on the terrace makes its own music. Mixed crowd. Open daily 11am-6pm and 8pm-3:30am.

Joy Madrid, C. Arenal, 11. (☎913 66 37 33). M: Sol or Ópera. Next to the Palacio Gaviria, a well-dressed crowd parties the night away to disco, techno, and R&B on a 3-tiered dance floor. Cover €12. F-Sa €15. Open daily 11:30pm-5:30am.

El Barbu, C. Santiago, 3 (☎915 42 56 98). M: Sol or Ópera. Chill to lounge music in a brick 3-room interior. Open Tu-Sa 8pm-3am. Su transforms the bar to "8th," a rave-like setting with popular local DJs. Cover €8. Open 7pm-5:30am.

Kathmandú, C. Señores de Luzón, 3 (☎915 41 52 53), a right off C. Mayor from Puerta del Sol, after Pl. Mayor and facing the Ayuntamiento. M: Sol. Jammed with locals dancing to high-energy techno and acid jazz until the wee hours of the night and morning. Cover €4.80-6, includes 1 drink. Open Th 11pm-5am, F-Sa 11pm-6am.

Sweet Club Dance, C. Dr. Cortezo, 1 (☎918 69 40 38), off C. Colegiata, close to C. Atocha. M: Tirso de Molina. Steel doors covered in steel vines lead to an outrageous gay scene. Cages and disco-ball dance floor get packed after 3am. Cover €9 with flyer, €12 without. Cover includes 1 drink. Open F-Sa 1am-dawn.

HUERTAS

The heart of Huertas lies at **Plaza Santa Ana,** brimming with *terrazas*, bars, and live street music. Many bars convert to clubs as the night unfolds, spinning house and techno on intimate dance floors. With its variety of styles, Huertas is one of the best places to party. C. Príncipe is lined with smaller spots, but be sure to check out the larger *discotecas* on **C. Atocha.** Most locals begin their evenings here and emerge, slightly worn out, from El Centro and Chueca (see p. 130) in the morning.

DISCOTECAS

Kapital, C. Atocha, 125 (☎914 20 29 06), a block off Po. del Prado. M: Atocha. *Thumba la casa* (bring down the house) on 7 floors of *discoteca* insanity. From hip-hop to house, open *terrazas* to cinemas, lose yourself (and maybe your friends) in the madness. Dress to impress (the bouncer). Drinks €9. Cover €12, includes 1 drink. Open Th-Su midnight-6am and afternoon sessions Sa-Su (5:30-11pm). Gets going around 2am.

Sundance, Vieja Estación. M: Atocha. Celebrate the middle of the week in style in Madrid's old train station, now transformed into a outdoor *terraza* equipped with hot bartenders, mist sprays, and room for thousands of club-goers. Mixed crowd. Drinks €6. Cover €6, includes 1 drink. Open May- Sept. W only 9pm-4am.

No Se Lo Digas a Nadie, C. Ventura de la Vega, 7 (☎913 69 17 27), next to Pl. Santa Ana. M: Sevilla. Head through the garage doors onto the packed dance floor and throw in a quick dance along your bar crawl. Drinks €3-5. Open W-Sa until 3:30am.

Azúcar, Po. Reina Cristina, 7 (☎915 01 61 07). M: Atocha. Sweet, sweet salsa. No sneakers. Salsa classes daily 10-11pm. Su-Th cover €6, includes 1 drink; F-Sa €10, includes 1 drink. Open daily 11pm-5:30am.

Villa Rosa, Pl. Santa Ana, 15 (☎925 21 36 89). M: Sol or Sevilla. American pop meets Moorish architecture in this Alhambra-inspired disco, which sports 4 bars and a raised dance floor. Frescoed and tiled walls compete with flat-screen TVs for attention. Cover F-Sa €6. Drinks €6. Open M-Sa 11pm-5am.

BAR-MUSICALES

Cardamomo, C. Echegaray, 15 (☎913 69 07 57). M: Sevilla. Flamenco music spins all night. A local crowd dances flamenco occasionally, but come W nights to see professionals do it. Mondays bump with Brazilian and other exotic beats. Open 9pm-4am.

La Comedia, C. Príncipe, 16 (☎915 21 51 64). M: Sevilla. Americans feel at home in a crowd dancing to hip-hop, R&B, and reggae. Hit up DJ Jay with requests; he spins to please. Beer €3.60, drinks €6. Open daily 9pm-4am.

Café Jazz Populart, C. Huertas, 22 (☎914 29 84 07; www.populart.es). M: Sevilla or Antón Martín. This intimate, smoke-filled scene hosts local and foreign talent. Live jazz, blues, reggae, and flamenco. Shows Su-W 11pm, F-Sa 11pm and 12:30am. Open Su-Th 6pm-12:30am, F-Sa 6pm-3am.

Café Central, Pl. Angel, 10 (☎913 69 41 43), off Pl. Santa Ana. M: Antón Martín or Sol. Art Deco meets old-world cafe in one of Europe's top jazz venues. Mesmerized listeners recline in each others' arms. An older audience. Shows nightly. Beer €2. Cover €8-15. Open daily 1:30pm-1:30am, F and Sa until 3:30am.

La Boca del Lobo, C. Echegaray, 11 (☎914 29 70 13). M: Sevilla. Live shows of reggae, funk, blues, and rock bands hit this 2-story joint, drawing a varied crowd. Waterfall mirrors in the bathrooms may drench you. Cover €6. Open daily 11pm-dawn.

BARS

El Café de Sheherezade, C. Santa María, 18 (☎913 69 24 74), a block from C. Huertas. M: Antón Martín. Recline on opulent pillows while sipping exotic infusions in a bohemian atmosphere. Surrounded by Middle Eastern music and decor, groups cluster around *pipas* (€7-10) that filter sweet, incense-like smoke through whiskey or water. Late nights sometimes end with belly dancing. Open daily 7pm-5am.

MADRID

Trocha, C. Huertas, 55 (☎914 29 78 61). M: Antón Martín or Sol. Come here for Brazilian *capirinhas* (lime, ice, rum, and sugar drinks; €4.50). The delicious and potent drinks (ask for *flor de caña)* are served in a chill setting with jazz tunes and cushioned wicker couches. Open Su-Th 8pm-3am, F-Sa 8pm-4am.

Viva Madrid, C. Manuel Fernández González, 7 (☎914 29 36 40), off C. Echegaray. M: Sol or Sevilla. *"Lo mejor del mundo"* is the humble motto of this daytime cafe/nighttime foray. A local favorite for a romantic evening. Cocktails €7. Open daily 1pm-2am.

Mauna Loa, Pl. Santa Ana, 13 (☎914 29 70 62). M: Sevilla or Sol. Feels like Hawaii—birds fly freely between low chairs and the scantily clad dance to upbeat tunes. Sip on a *fuerte volcano* (€6-10) through an enormous straw at this crowded pre-party destination. Open Su-Th 6pm-2am, F-Sa 6pm-3am.

Naturbier, Pl. Santa Ana, 9 (☎914 29 39 18). M: Sol or Sevilla. Join the locals who pour in for the excellent locally-brewed *bier,* inspired by their motto "beer is important to human nutrition." Superior lager €1.80-4.20; it gets cheaper as you progress to the innermost of the 3 bars. Open daily 10am-2:30am.

GRAN VÍA

The deepest drum and bass pounds in the boisterous landmark clubs on the side streets of Gran Vía well into the early morning. Subtlety has never been a strong suit for this area, nor is it known for its safety; a mix of sketchy tourists and sketchier locals makes Gran Vía less than ideal for late-night wandering.

Pasapoga, Gran Vía, 37 (☎915 47 57 11 or 915 32 16 44), around the corner from Pl. Callao. M: Callao. Gay nightlife explodes here on weekends, especially on Saturdays. Strut down the ivory-banistered staircase and feel like the princess or *reina que tú eres*. Circular dance floor and spectacular chandelier. Pumping techno, pop, and house. Beautiful interior, beautiful people. Cover €15. F and Sa are gay nights. Midnight-late.

Cool, Isabela La Católica, 6 (☎915 48 20 22 or 915 42 34 39). M: Santo Domingo. Heavenly drag performances and the occasional underworldly goth party for a wild, mixed crowd. Mesmerizing video projections give this club the production-value of international venues, which fits with the mix of locals, Brits, and Americans yelling to be heard over the latest house. Special **Shangay Tea Dance** for primarily gay crowd on Sundays. Drinks €5-8. Cover varies, usually includes 1 drink. F-Sa midnight-late. Sunday opens at 9pm; free with flyer before 9:30pm.

IN RECENT NEWS

DEATH IN THE AFTERNOON

There is nothing in Spanish culture as ingrained and controversial as the bullfight. While the sport takes place in France, Spain, Portugal, and Latin America, it is the contested emblem of Spanish culture. Even in its early days, this spectacle of life versus death, of man against nature, faced considerable opposition. Pope Pius V forbade the bullfight in 1567, claiming that "exhibitions of tortured beasts or bulls are contrary to Christian duty and piety." Still, the rituals continued.

Today, bullfighting is under attack by animal rights activists across the world. They lobby politicians, stage massive protests, besiege the Vatican with postcards, and cite the negative psychological effects bullfighting has on children. They believe the bullfight is not a fight at all, but a spectacle devoid of competition. Their efforts have been met with some success. In 1992, 400 Spaniards protested the sport in Madrid; in 1993, an anti-bullfighting petition garnered over one million signatures, and recent polls show that younger generations are less captivated by the sport.

Still, as Europe unifies, the anti-bullfight movement has become a tense point of cultural resistance for much of southern Europe. Portuguese laws that ban the killing of the bull continue to be defied by southern cities, which have more in common culturally with their Spanish neighbors. Meanwhile, funds are being pumped into revitalizing and ensuring the permanence of the sport, and tourists arrive every day believing they haven't seen Spain unless they've witnessed a bullfight.

Soul Kitchen, Mesonero Romanos, 13 (☎915 32 15 24), off Gran Vía. M: Callao or Gran Vía. Get your freak on at the only real hip-hop club in town. Those in the know arrive around 3am to a packed dance floor. Open W-Sa 1pm-5am.

MALASAÑA AND CHUECA

Chueca and Malasaña come to life in the early evening, especially in **Pl. Chueca** and **Pl. 2 de Mayo.** By sunset, these plazas are social meccas—places to hang out, meet your friends, and get drunk. Bar-filled streets radiate from the plazas; though people eventually migrate away from the plazas, they still remain busy with activity well into *la madrugada.* The alcoholic circus known as Chueca nightlife guarantees entertainment from locals, tourists, and random, questionable characters who tend to pass out on plaza benches. Outside the plazas, most nightlife tends toward classy cafes, cruisy bars, and shady clubs. Though Chueca is largely gay, most of the establishments in the area are quite mixed. The area is ideal for bar-hopping until 2 or 3am, when it's time to hit the clubs near Sol, Centro, and Gran Vía.

Acuarela, C. Gravina, 10 (☎915 22 21 43), on the corner of Pl. Chueca. M: Chueca. A welcome alternative to the club scene. Buddhas and candles surround antique furniture, providing inspiration for good conversation and a nice buzz. Coffees and teas €3-4.25. Liquor €4. Open daily 3pm-3am.

Why Not?, C. San Bartolomé, 7. M: Chueca. Small downstairs bar packed almost every night of the week with a wild, mixed crowd. When in doubt at 1-3am, people flock to Why Not?. Open daily 10pm-4am. The same owners manage **Polana,** C. Barbieri, 8-10 (☎915 32 33 05), which gets going around 2:30am, blasting campy Spanish pop music for a mainly gay crowd. Open daily 11pm-late.

La Sastrería, Hortaleza, 74 (☎915 32 07 71), and **Mama Ines,** Hortaleza, 22 (www.mamaines.com). Chic cafes/bars with perfect diva lighting. Good desserts, light meals, and teas. Open Su-Th 10am-2am, F-Sa 11am-3am.

Star's Café, C. Marqués de Valdeiglesias, 5 (☎915 22 27 12). M: Chueca. A stylish cafe during the week complements a vivacious dance club downstairs on the weekends. Come well-dressed. Open M-Th 1pm-2am, F-Sa 1pm-4am.

Liquid, C. Barquillo, 8 (☎915 32 74 28). M: Chueca or Banco de España. Water bubbling through glass near the front door leads to a video bar that plays mainly English songs. Clientele is quite refined and mostly gay. Open Tu-Su 9pm-3am, F-Sa until 3:30am.

Vía Láctea, C. Velarde, 18 (☎914 66 75 81). M: Tribunal. Dive into the Brit underground scene every night from 8 to 9pm when soft drinks and beer on tap are €2 each. After midnight, a late 20s crowd gets groovy between the pink walls. The loudspeakers can be deafening. Th funk. Open daily 7:30pm-3am.

Café la Palma, C. La Palma, 62 (☎915 22 50 31). M: San Bernardo or Noviciado. Slip back into the comfy pillows of this decadent venue for live music and late-night whispering. Beer €2.10. Mixed drinks €5. Open daily 4pm-3:30am.

El Truco, C. Gravina, 10 (☎915 32 89 21). M: Chueca. Watch the smoky windows from Pl. Chueca to see shadows of people dancing inside. Bar features local artists' works and pop artists' hits. Lesbian-friendly. Open Su-Th 8pm-2am, F-Sa 9pm-4am. Same owners run **Escape,** a club down the street. Both strong enough for a man, but designed for a woman. Open F-Sa midnight-7am.

Bolero Terraza, Po. Castellana, 33 (☎915 54 91 51). M: Rubén Darío. Flashy smiles and pressed collars. *The* ultra-fashionable yuppie *terraza*. Outside seating centered around a bar. Drinks €7. Open daily 7:30pm-3am.

BILBAO

In the student-filled streets radiating from **Glorieta de Bilbao,** it's easy to find a cheap drink. Although discos are plentiful, revelers don't come here to dance; it's the *terrazas* that are packed late into the night with lively customers sipping icy Mahou on Pl. Olavide, C. Fuencarral, and C. Luchana.

Barnon, C. Santa Engracia, 17 (☎914 47 38 37). M: Alonso Martínez or Tribunal. Barnon actually bars many from its hip-hop scene if you're not as cool as the owner, Real Madrid's stud *fútbol* forward. Dress well. Tu is salsa night, free lessons 11pm-midnight. Drinks €10. Open daily 9pm-6am.

Clamores Jazz Club, C. Albuquerque, 14 (☎914 45 79 38), off C. Cardenal Cisneros. M: Bilbao. Swanky, neon setting and Madrid's more interesting jazz. The cover (€3-9) gets slipped into the bill if you're there for the jazz, starting around 10:30pm Tu-Su. Check posters outside and arrive early for a seat. Open Su-Th 6pm-3am, F-Sa 6pm-4am.

Big Bamboo, C. Barquillo, 42 (☎915 62 88 38). M: Alonso Martínez. Walk 3 blocks east of C. Pelayo on C. Gravina and turn left on C. Barquillo. Infiltrate the Rasta scene at this international club that grooves to smooth reggae. W and Th theater shows. Drinks €2.40-3. Open 10:30pm-6am, F-Sa 10:30pm-7am.

MONCLOA

High-schoolers dominate Moncloa's streets. Unless you're Lolita, or looking for one, the only reason to leave Madrid's better nighttime areas for Moncloa is **Los Bajos,** a concrete megaplex of diminutive bars serving incredibly **cheap drinks.** The bars tend to be slightly grimy, the dance floors small, and the crowd pre-pubescent, but at €1 each, the *chupitos* (shots) are hard to turn down. (Bars are usually only open F-Sa and close 1-2am. From M: Moncloa, cross C. Isaac Peral in front of Pl. Moncloa, passing under the gate onto C. Gatzambide, 35.)

ENTERTAINMENT

Anyone interested in the latest on live entertainment—from music to dance to theater—should stop by the **Círculo de Bellas Artes,** C. Alcala, 42 (☎913 60 54 00; fax 915 23 28 12), at M: Sevilla or Banco de España. The six-floored building not only houses performance venues and art exhibits but also serves as an organizing center for events throughout Madrid; it has virtually all current information on performances. Their monthly magazine, *Minerva*, is indispensable.

MUSIC

In summer, Madrid sponsors free concerts, ranging from classical and jazz to bolero and salsa, at Pl. Mayor, Lavapiés, Oriente, and Villa de París; check the *Guía del Ocio* for the current schedule. Many nightspots also have live music.

The **Auditorio Nacional,** C. Príncipe de Vergara, 146, home to the National Orchestra, features Madrid's best classical performances. (☎913 37 01 00. M: Cruz del Rayo. €5-25.) The **Fundación Juan March,** C. Castelló, 77, hosts a lecture series (Tu-W 7:30pm) and sponsors free weekend concerts. (☎914 35 42 40. M: Núñez de Balboa.) **Teatro Monumental,** C. Atocha, 65, is home to Madrid's Symphonic Orchestra. Reinforced concrete—a Spanish invention—was first used in its construction in the 1920s, so be prepared for unusual acoustics. (☎914 29 81 19. M: Antón Martín.) For opera and *zarzuela* (Spanish light opera), head for the ornate **Teatro de la Zarzuela,** C. Jovellanos, 4, modeled on Milan's La Scala. (☎915 24 54 00. M: Banco de España.) The city's principal performance venue is the prestigious **Teatro Real,** Pl. de Isabel II, featuring the city's best ballet and opera. (☎915 16 06 06. M: Ópera.) The grand 19th-century **Teatro de la Ópera** (☎915 59 35 51), in Pl. Ópera, is the city's principal venue for classical ballet. Most theaters shut down in July and August.

FLAMENCO

Flamenco in Madrid is tourist-oriented and expensive. A few nightlife spots are authentic (see **Cardamomo,** p. 128), but they are pricey. **Casa Patas,** C. Cañizares, 10, offers excellent quality for a bit less than usual. Summer courses are taught in flamenco dance and song. (☎913 69 04 96; www.casapatas.com. M: Antón Martín. Call for prices and reservations.) **Café de Chinitas,** C. Torija, 7, is as overstated as they come. Shows start at 10:30pm and midnight, but memories last forever—or at least they should, given the price. (☎915 47 15 02 or 915 59 51 35. M: Santo Domingo. Cover €24 and up.) At **Corral de la Morería,** C. Morería, 17, by the Viaducto on C. Bailén, shows start at 9:45pm and last until 2am. (☎913 65 84 46. M: Ópera or La Latina. Cover €24, includes 1 drink.) **Teatro Albéniz,** C. Paz, 11, hosts an annual *Certamen de Coreografía de Danza Española y Flamenco* that features original music and extraordinary flamenco. (☎915 21 99 98. M: Sol. Tickets €4.25-12.)

FILM

In summer, the city sponsors free movies and plays, all listed in the *Guía del Ocio* and the entertainment supplements of Friday's newspapers. In July, look out for the **Fescinal,** a film festival at the Parque de la Florida. Most cinemas show three films per day, at around 4:30, 7:30, and 10:30pm. Tickets cost €2.40-5.40. Some cinemas offer weekday-only matinée student discounts for €3.65. Wednesday (sometimes Monday instead) is *día del espectador*, when tickets cost around €3—show up early. Check the *versión original (V.O. subtitulada)* listings in the *Guía del Ocio* for English movies subtitled in Spanish. Three excellent movie theaters cluster near M: Ventura Rodríguez, between Pl. España and Argüelles. **Princesa,** C. Princesa, 3 (☎915 41 41 00), shows mainstream Spanish films and subtitled foreign films. The theater/bar **Alphaville,** C. Martín de los Héroes, 14 (☎915 59 38 36), behind Princesa and underneath the patio, shows current alternative and mainstream Spanish titles. **Renoir,** C. Raimundo Fernández Villaverde, 10 (☎915 41 41 00), shows highly acclaimed recent films, many foreign and subtitled. Check the *Guía del Ocio* for other cinema megaplexes in and around the city.

THEATER

Huertas, east of Sol, is Madrid's theater district. In July and August, Pl. Mayor, Lavapiés, and Villa de París frequently host plays as theaters move outdoors. For a complete list of theaters and shows, consult the *Guía del Ocio*. Seeing a play in Madrid is an entertaining way to participate in traditional culture and to practice your Spanish. Tickets to shows start around €24, but special deals for as low as €12 are not uncommon. Theater-goers should consult the magazines published by state-sponsored theaters, such as **Teatro Español,** C. Príncipe, 25, in Pl. Santa Ana (☎914 29 62 97. M: Sol), **Teatro de la Comedia,** C. Príncipe, 14 (☎915 21 49 31. M: Sevilla), and the superb **Teatro María Guerrero,** C. Tamayo y Baus, 4 (☎913 19 47 69; M: Colón). Tickets can be purchased at theater box offices or at ticket agencies. (**FNAC** ☎915 95 62 00. **Librería Crisol** ☎913 22 47 00. **TelEntrada** ☎902 210 12 12.)

FÚTBOL

Spaniards obsess over *fútbol* (soccer to Americans). The festivities start hours before matches as fans congregate in the streets, earphones and radio in one hand and *cerveza* in the other, listening to pregame commentary and discussing it with other die-hards. If either **Real Madrid** or **Atlético de Madrid** wins a match, count on streets clogged with honking cars. Every Sunday and some Saturdays between September and June, one of these two teams plays at home. Real Madrid plays at **Estadio Santiago Bernebéu,** Po. Castellana, 104. (☎914 57 11 12. M: Lima.) Atlético de Madrid plays at **Estadio Vicente Calderón,** C. Virgen del Puerto, 67. (☎913 66 47 07. M: Pirámides or Marqués de Vadillos.) Tickets cost €18-42 and sell out quickly.

RECREATIONAL SPORTS

For **bicycle rental,** try **Karacol Sport,** C. Tortosa, 8. (☎915 39 96 33. M: Atocha. Rental €12 per day with €3 deposit and passport. Open daily 10:30am-8pm, Th until 10pm, Sa until 2pm.) For **cycling info** and bicycle repair, cruise over to **Calmera Bicicletas,** C. Atocha, 98. (☎915 27 75 74; www.calmera.net. M: Anton Martín.)

Madrid's swimming pools provide the perfect solution to summertime heat and land-locked shortcomings. Gawkers be warned; most women go topless. (☎915 40 39 39 for pool information. Municipal tourist office offers a comprehensive list of the 25 pools in and around Madrid. All pools have same time-table and prices.) Swimmers splash in the outdoor pools at **Lago/Casa de Campo,** on Av. Angel. The Lago pools are yet another one of Madrid's social meccas, with several pools and sunbathing areas, including Madrid's equivalent of a "gay beach." Lots of kids, ice cream stands, and fun. Watch your valuables. (☎914 63 00 50. M: Lago. Open 10:30am-8pm. €3.20.) Other cooling relief includes-the pool at **Peñuelas,** on C. Arganda. (☎914 74 28 08. M: Acacias, Piramides, or Embajadores; or bus #18.)

Gallop over to the **Hipódromo de Madrid,** Ctra. de La Coruña, km 7800 (☎913 57 16 82), for **horse-racing.** Call the **Oficina de Información Deportiva** (☎914 63 55 63) for more information on outdoor recreation in Madrid. The tourist office's *Plano de las Instalaciones Deportivas Municipales* lists areas open to the public.

BULLFIGHTS

Bullfighters are either loved or loathed. So, too, are the bullfights themselves. Nevertheless, bullfights are a Spanish tradition, and locals joke that they are the only things in Spain ever to start on time. Hemingway-toting Americans and true fans of a contorted struggle between man and nature clog Pl. de Ventas for the heart-pounding, albeit gruesome events.

From May 15 to May 22 every year, the **Fiestas de San Isidro** provide a *corrida* (bullfight) every day with top *matadores* and the fiercest bulls. The festival is nationally televised; those without tickets crowd into bars. There are also bullfights every Sunday in summer from March to October, and less frequently throughout the rest of the year. Look for posters in bars and cafes for upcoming *corridas* (especially on C. Victoria, off C. San Jerónimo). **Plaza de las Ventas,** C. Alcalá, 237, east of central Madrid, is the biggest ring in Spain. (☎913 56 22 00. M: Ventas.) A seat runs €5-92, depending on location in the sun (*sol*) or shade (*sombra*); shade is more expensive. Tickets are available the Friday and Saturday before and the Sunday of the bullfight. **Plaza de Toros Palacio de Vista Alegre,** a new ring in town, hosts bullfights and cultural events. (☎914 22 07 80. M: Vista Alegre. Ticket window open M-F 10am-2pm and 5-8pm.) To watch amateurs, head to the **bullfighting school,** which has its own *corridas.* (☎914 70 19 90. M: Batán. Open Sa 7:30pm. Tickets €7, children €3.50.)

FESTIVALS

The city bursts with street fiestas, dancing, and processions during **Carnaval** in February, culminating on Ash Wednesday with the beginning of Lent and the burial of the Sardine in the Casa de Campo. In late April, the city bubbles with the renowned **International Theater Festival.** The Comunidad de Madrid celebrates its struggle against the French invasion of 1808 during the **Fiestas del 2 de Mayo** with bullfights and concerts. Starting May 15, the month-long **Fiestas de San Isidro** honor Madrid's patron saint with a pilgrimage to the saint's meadow, various concerts, parades, and Spain's best bullfights. At the end of June, Madrid goes mad with **Orgullo Gay** (Gay Pride). Outrageous floats filled with drag queens, muscle boys, and politically active lesbians shut down traffic between El Retiro and Puerta del Sol on the Saturday of pride weekend. The weekend is filled with free concerts in

MADRID

Pl. Chueca and Pl. Vázquez de Mella and bar crawls among the congested streets of Chueca. Throughout the summer, the city sponsors the **Veranos de la Villa,** an outstanding and varied set of cultural activities, including free classical music concerts, open-air movies, plays, art exhibits, an international film festival, opera, *zarzuela* (light Spanish opera), ballet, and sports. The **Festivales de Otoño** (Autumn Festivals), from September to November, also bring an impressive array of music, theater, and film. On November 1, **Todos los Santos** (All Saints' Day), an International Jazz Festival, brings great musicians to Madrid. On New Year's Eve, **El Fin del Año,** crowds gather around Puerta del Sol to countdown to the new year and eat 12 grapes (*uvas*), one by one, as the clock strikes midnight. The brochure *Las Fiestas de España,* available at tourist offices and bigger hotels, contains comprehensive information on Spain's festivals.

SHOPPING

For upscale shopping, sashay down swanky **C. Serrano** and **C. Velázquez** in the famous **Salamanca** district (near Pl. Colón), where fine boutiques and specialty stores line the streets. Stores like Gucci, Prada, and Calvin Klein provide fabulous shopping bags to showcase your purchases. Most major department stores can be found between Puerta del Sol and Callao, with smaller clothing stores scattered along Gran Vía. **El Cortes Inglés,** Spain's unavoidable, all-in-one store, sports over 10 locations throughout the city. Countless clothing boutiques in **Chueca** specialize in hot clubwear, tight jeans, and sexy day-wear. The **Mercado Fuencarral,** C. Fuencarral, 42, specializes in funky attire and tattoo/piercing parlors. Most stores in Madrid are open 10am-2pm and 5-8pm. Some stay open on Saturday afternoon and during *siesta.* By law, *grandes almacenes* (department stores) may open only the first Sunday of every month, a vestige of the country's Roman Catholic heritage. Many boutiques close in August, when almost everyone flees to the coast. Non-residents of the EU can shop tax-free at major stores, as long as they remember to ask for their VAT return form (☎600 43 54 82 for more info). **Inal** publishes a yearly *Guía Esencial para vivir en Madrid,* which includes descriptions of most stores.

MADRID

MALLS

Mallrats may go through a bit of withdrawal in Madrid, since smaller, scattered stores are the norm. **La Vaguada** (M: Barrio del Pilar; bus #132 from Moncloa), in the northern neighborhood of **Madrid-2,** is Madrid's first experiment in super-malls. It offers everything the homesick Anglophone could want: 350 shops, including The Body Shop, Burberry's, a food court with a trusty McDonald's, multi-cinemas, and a bowling alley (open daily 10am-10pm). **ABC,** C. Serrano, 61, in the old ABC Newspaper headquarters, has a modern complex of food courts and Spanish clothing chains from Zara to Mango. (M: Castellano, right next to Metro stop. Open M-Sa 10am-9:30pm, Su noon-8pm.) Madrid's outlet mall is **Las Rozas,** Juan Ramón Jiménez, a 20min. drive from the center, with up to 60% off favorite brands. (☎916 40 49 08; www.valueretail.com.) By far the poshest shopping mall is the **Galería del Prado,** Pl. Cortes, located beneath the Hotel Palace and across the Castellana from the Ritz. (M: Banco de España. Open M-Sa 10am-9pm.)

EL RASTRO (FLEA MARKET)

For hundreds of years, El Rastro has been a Sunday morning tradition in Madrid. The market begins in La Latina at Pl. Cascorro off C. Toledo and ends at the bottom of C. Ribera de Curtidores. Get lost in the insanity and the excitement as your senses become overwhelmed with sights, sounds, and smells from every direction.

Seek out that souvenir you've been dying for since your first day in Madrid and haggle for it until you're blue in the face. In El Rastro you can find anything, from pots to jeans to antique tools to pet birds. As crazy as the market seems, it is actually thematically organized. The main street is a labyrinth of cheap jewelry, incense, and sunglasses, branching out into side streets, each with its own concert of vendors and wares. Antique-sellers contribute their peculiar mustiness to C. del Prado. *Tapas* bars and small restaurants line the streets and provide an air-conditioned respite for market-weary bargain-hunters. The flea market is a pickpocket's paradise, so leave your camera in your room, bust out with the money belt, or turn that backpack into a frontpack. Police are everywhere if you have any problems. El Rastro is open Sundays and holidays from 9am to 2pm.

BOOKS

FNAC, C. Preciados, 28 (☎915 95 62 00; www.fnac.es). M: Callao. Best music and book selection. English books on 3rd fl. Open M-Sa 10am-9:30pm, Su noon-9:30pm.

Casa del Libro, Gran Vía, 29 (☎915 22 66 57; www.casadelibro.com). M: Callao. Madrid's largest and most comprehensive bookstore. Branch at Maestro Victoria.

Booksellers, C. José Abascal, 48 (☎914 42 79 59, 914 42 81 04, or 913 99 33 87). M: Gregorio Marañón. A vast array of books, videos, magazines, and children's literature in English. Open M-F 9:30am-2pm and 5-8pm, Sa 10am-2pm.

Librería de Mujeres, C. San Cristóbal, 17 (☎915 21 70 43), near Pl. Mayor. International bookstore. English spoken. (See **Women's Services,** p. 99.)

Berkana Librería Gay y Lesbiana, C. Horaleza, 64 (☎/fax 915 22 55 99). M: Chueca. Gay and lesbian bookstore with loads of contact info for foreigners and a free map of gay Madrid. Open M-F 10:30am-2pm and 5-8:30pm, Sa noon-2pm and 5-8:30pm.

Altair, C. Gaztambide, 31 (☎915 43 53 00). M: Moncloa or Argüelles. Comprehensive travel bookstore, with the world's best travel guides and others. Knowledgeable staff. Open M-Sa 10:30am-2:30pm and 4:30-8:30pm.

COMUNIDAD DE MADRID

The Comunidad de Madrid is an autonomous administrative region, smack in the middle of Spain, bordered by Castilla y Leon to the north and west and Castilla La Mancha to the south and east. Beyond Madrid proper, the Comunidad offers travelers a variety of daytrips to exquisite cultural landscapes and small town serenity.

ALCALÁ DE HENARES

Alcalá (pop. 165,000) draws intellectuals to continue the tradition of the city's distinguished offspring, including Miguel de Cervantes, and Golden Age authors Francisco de Quevedo and Lope de Vega. Alcalá's famous history and exceptional Renaissance architecture make the city well worth a peek.

TRANSPORTATION AND PRACTICAL INFORMATION. The **train station** is on Po. Estación (☎915 63 02 02). **Cercanías** trains run to **Madrid's Estación Atocha** (50min., every 10min. daily 6:06am-10:36pm, €2.01) and return (M-F 5:49am-11:58pm, Sa-Su 6:12am-11:58pm). The **Continental-Auto bus station,** Av. Guadalajara, 5 (☎918 88 16 22), runs between Alcalá and **Madrid** (45min., every 15min., €1.77). To reach the city center from the bus station, turn right on Av. Guadalajara and continue as it turns into C. Libreros. The **tourist office,** Callejón de Santa María, 1, at Pl. Cervantes, has a map, and a list of accommodations and restaurants. (☎918 89 26 94. Open June and Sept. daily 10am-2pm and 5-7:30pm;

July-Aug. Tu-Sa 10am-2pm and 5-7:30pm; Oct.-May 10am-2pm and 4-6:30pm.) **Santander Central Hispano,** C. Libreros, 19, has an **ATM.** Important phone numbers include **emergency** ☎112; **ambulance** ☎061; and **police** ☎918 81 92 63. **Alcal@.3,** on C. San Diego, 3, offers 15 speedy computers and friendly service. (☎918 83 40 24. €0.60 per 15min. Open July-Aug. M-F 10am-2pm and 3-10pm, Sa 10am-10pm, Su 4-10pm; Sept.-June also open Sa 10am-2pm and 3-10pm.) The **post office,** Pl. Cervantes, 5, is inside Banco Argentina. (☎912 19 71 97. Open M-F 8:30am-7pm, Sa 9:30am-1pm.) The **postal code** ranges from 28801 to 28807.

ACCOMMODATIONS AND FOOD. Some of the least expensive rooms are at **Hostal Jacinto ❷,** Po. Estación, 2, 2nd staircase, 1-D. Pleasant tiled rooms all have sinks, TVs, and heat during the winter. (☎/fax 918 89 14 32. Singles €18, with shower €19; doubles €34, with bath €37; triples €40.) Or try **Hostal El Torero ❷,** Av. de Madrid, 14, past Pl. de los Santos Niños. (☎918 89 03 73. Singles €19; doubles with bath €40.) For food, Alcalá's famed *almendras garrapiñadas* (honey- and sugar-coated almonds) beg to be sampled. For groceries, stop at the gigantic **Champión** on Vía Complutense, located just behind the bus station. Or, from the train station, take a left at the traffic circle. (☎918 89 36 37. Open June 15-Sept. 15 M-Sa 9am-10pm; rest of year M-Sa 9:15am-9:15pm. MC/V.) For fantastically cheap *menús*, turn left on C. Mayor from Pl. Cervantes, and check out the restaurants on the right side of the street. Try **El Gringo Viejo ❸,** on C. Ramón y Cajal, 8. Take C.

Mayor from Pl. Cervantes, then your first left onto C. Ramón y Cajal, and the entryway will be on your right. (☎918 78 89 01. Mexican entrees €5.30-17.30. Open M-Th 8:30am-midnight, F 8:30am-1am, Sa 10:30am-1am, Su 11am-midnight. MC/V.)

SIGHTS. Plaza de Cervantes, filled with cafes, rose bushes, and a statue of its namesake, bursts with color in the summertime. At the end of the plaza opposite C. Libreros lie the **Ruinas de Santa María,** the remains of a 16th-century church destroyed during the Spanish Civil War. In the surviving **Capilla del Oidor,** art exhibits surround the fountain where Cervantes was christened. (Open Oct.-May Tu-Su noon-2pm and 6-9pm; June-Sept. Tu-Su noon-2pm and 5-8pm. Free.) Just before Pl. Cervantes in Pl. San Diego, take a left off C. Libreros onto C. Bedel to see the **Colegio Mayor de San Ildefonso** (☎918 85 40 00). In the **Paraninfo,** where doctorates were once awarded, the king now presents the "Premio Cervantes," Spain's most prestigious literary award. The Paraninfo and **Capilla de San Ildefonso** both have spectacular Mudéjar ceilings made of crafted wood pieces held together by pressure. (By tour only. June-Sept. M-F 11:30am, 12:30, 1:30, 7pm; Sa-Su 11, 11:45am, 12:30, 1:15, 2, 5, 5:45, 6:30, 7:15, 8pm. Oct.-May M-F 11:30am, 12:30, 1:30, 4:30, 5:30pm; Sa-Su 11, 11:45am, 12:30, 1:15, 2, 4, 4:45, 5:30, 6:15, 7pm. €2.50.) The town's **Catedral Magistral,** at the end of C. Mayor in Pl. de los Santos Niños, is one of two in the world with this title (the other is in Lovaina, Belgium); to be so named, each priest must be a university professor. (Open M-Sa 9-11:30am and 6:30-8:30pm, Su 9am-12:45pm and 6:30-9pm. Free.) Down C. Mayor from Pl. Cervantes is the **Casa de Cervantes,** the reconstructed house where the author was born. Currently undergoing expansion, the house displays a variety of period furniture and editions of *Don Quijote* in languages Cervantes never knew. (☎918 89 96 54. Open Tu-Su 10am-2pm and 4-7pm. Free.) The **Convento de San Bernardo** hides a gorgeous 17th-century elliptical interior behind a simple facade. (Mandatory tour meets in the courtyard and begins June-Sept. M-F 1:45, 6:30pm; Sa-Su 12:30, 1:30, 5, 5:45, 6:30, 7:15, 8pm; Oct.-May M-F 1:45, 5:30pm; Sa-Su 12:30, 1:30, 4, 4:45, 5:30, 6:15, 7pm. €2.10.)

MADRID

SAN LORENZO DEL ESCORIAL ☎918

San Lorenzo's El Escorial—half monastery and half mausoleum—is the most popular daytrip from Madrid. Although Felipe II constructed El Escorial for himself and for God, the complex, with its magnificent library, palaces, and art, seems as if it were made for tourists. Don't go on Monday; the whole town is closed. Also, don't miss the nearby Valle de los Caídos (see p. 139). Visits are popular during the *Fiestas de San Lorenzo* (Aug. 10-20), when parades of giant figures line the streets and fireworks fill the sky, and on Romería a la Ermita de la Virgen de Gracia, the second Sunday in September, when folk dancing contests fill the forests.

TRANSPORTATION AND PRACTICAL INFORMATION. Autocares Herranz buses (☎918 96 90 28) travel from Madrid's **Moncloa Metro station** (50min.; every 15min. M-F 7am-11:30pm, Sa 9am-10:15pm, Su 9am-11pm; €2.75) to El Escorial and back (every 15min. M-F 6:15am-10:30pm, Sa 7:45am-9pm, Su 9am-10pm). El Escorial's **train station** (☎918 90 00 15; RENFE info 902 24 02 02), on Ctra. Estación, is 2km outside of town. Trains run to **Madrid-Atocha** and **Madrid-Chamartín** (1hr.; M-F every 30min., Sa-Su 1 every hr. 5:47am-10:15pm; round-trip €4.80).

With your back to the **bus station,** turn right down C. Juan de Toledo and continue until its end. Turn right at the corner onto Po. de José Antonio; the monastery will be on your left. The **tourist office** is to the right, underneath the walkway connecting the two buildings at C. Grimaldi. (☎/fax 918 90 53 13. Open M-Th 11am-6pm, F-Su 10am-7pm.) From the **train station,** take the shuttle to the bus station (M-F every 15-20min. 7:23am-10:38pm, Sa-Su every 20-60min. 9:44am-10:38pm; €0.90) or exit the train station, walk straight ahead, and follow the signs toward the monastery (25min. walk uphill). For a more peaceful walk, exit the train station and straight ahead enter the Casita del Príncipe main entrance. Start walking uphill and take the C. de los Tilos path, which leaves you by the monastery (25min.). In an **emergency** call ☎ 112 or the **police,** Pl. de la Constitución, 1 (☎ 918 90 52 23).

ACCOMMODATIONS AND FOOD. Because of its proximity to Madrid, El Escorial is usually done as a daytrip. However, for those wishing to stay, budget options include **Hostal Cristina ❸,** C. Calvario, 45, which has private baths, TVs and phones. (☎918 90 19 61; fax 918 90 12 04. July-Aug. doubles €43; rest of year €40. MC/V.) To reach **Residencia Juvenil El Escorial (HI) ❶,** C. Residencia, 14, from C. Rey, turn right on C. Tozas, left onto C. Claudio Coello, left again onto Po. Unamuno, then right onto C. Residencia. (☎918 90 59 24; fax 918 90 06 20. HI card required. Closed Sept. Laundry €2. Dorms €8, with dinner €10.75, with lunch and dinner €12.75; over 26 €10/€13/€16. IVA not included. MC/V.) **Restaurante El Trillo ❷,** C. Duque de Medinaceli, 11 (☎918 90 73 19), a straight shot uphill from the tourist office, serves a traditional *menú* indoors for €7.25, outside for €9. (Open 1:30-4:30pm and 8pm-midnight. MC/V.) Self-caterers head to **Mercado Público,** C. Rey, 7, just off of the central plaza (open M-Sa 9am-2pm and 6-9pm).

EL ESCORIAL

☎918 90 59 03 or 918 90 59 04. Complex open Apr.-Sept. Tu-Su 10am-6pm; Oct.-Mar. Tu-Su 10am-5pm. Last admission to palaces, pantheons, and museums 1hr. before closing. Complete visit takes 2hr. Spanish tours leave every 15min., ask at the desk for the next English tour. Monastery €6, students and seniors €3, guided tour €7. W free for EU citizens.

MADRID

THE MONASTERY. The **Monasterio de San Lorenzo del Escorial,** a gift from Felipe II to God, his people, and himself, was meant to commemorate his victory over the French at the battle of San Quintín in 1557 and includes a royal monastery and mausoleum. He commissioned Juan Bautista de Toledo to design the complex in 1561; when he died in 1567, Juan de Herrera inherited the job. Except for the Panteón Real and minor additions, the monastery was finished in just 21 years. According to tradition, Felipe oversaw much of the work from a chair-shaped rock, **Silla de Felipe II** (Felipe's Chair), 7km from the site.

Considering the resources that Felipe II commanded, the building is noteworthy for its symmetry, and simplicity; Felipe described it as "majesty without ostentation." Fulfilling the *desornamentado* style, the monastery is pieced together with granite hewn from the surrounding quarries. The entire structure is built around a gridiron pattern: four massive towers pin the corners, and a great dome surmounts the towers of the central basilica, giving the ensemble a pyramidal shape. At Felipe II's behest, steep slate roofs—the first of their kind in Spain—were introduced from Flanders. Slate spires lend grace to the grim structure, further mellowed by the glowing *piedra de Colmenar* stone.

GALLERIES AND LIVING QUARTERS. To avoid the worst of the crowds, enter El Escorial by the traditional gateway on the west side (C. Floridablanca), where you'll find a collection of Flemish tapestries and paintings. The collection exudes much of the same severity as the monastery, with dark paintings like El Greco's *Martirio de San Mauricio y la Legión* and Roger van der Weyden's glowing *Calvary.* The adjacent **Museo de Arquitectura and Pintura** has an exhibition comparing the construction of El Escorial to other related structures; there is also a display of wooden models of 16th-century machinery. Though masterpieces by Bosch, Dures, El Greco, Titian, Tintoretto, Zurbarán, Van Dyck, and others hang from the walls, most of the collection is now housed in Madrid's Museo del Prado.

The **Palacio Real,** lined with *azulejos* from Toledo, includes the **Salón del Trono** (Throne Room) and two dwellings: Felipe II's spartan 16th-century apartments and the more luxurious 18th-century rooms of Carlos III and Carlos IV. Pastoral images cover the **Puertas de Marguetería,** German doors made from 18 different species of wood. The **Sala de Batallas** (Battle Room) links the two parts of the palace with frescoes by Italian artists Grabelo and Castello. Castile and Spain's greatest victories—including Juan II's 1431 triumph over the Muslims at Higueruela, Felipe's II's successful expeditions in the Azores, and the Battle of San Quintín—are detailed on the walls and ceiling. Maps line the walls; the last one on the right portrays the world, as (mis)understood by the 16th-century Europeans. Downstairs, in the royal chambers, Felipe II's miniscule bed attests to his asceticism.

LIBRARY. The **biblioteca** (library) on the second floor holds numerous priceless books and manuscripts (though several fires have reduced the collection). Alfonso X's *Cantigas de Santa María*, the Book of Hours of the Catholic monarchs, Saint Teresa's manuscripts and diary, the gold-scrolled *Aureus Codex* (by German Emperor Conrad III, 1039), and an 11th-century *Commentary on the Apocalypse* by Beato de Liébana are just a sampling of the manuscripts. Frescos of history's most prized academic figures cover the ceiling.

BASILICA. The lower cloister leads to the basilica. Marble steps lead up to an altar adorned by two groups of sculptures. The figures on the left represent assorted relatives of Felipe II, including his parents Carlos I and Isabel, his daughter María, and his sisters María (Queen of Hungary) and Leonor (Queen of France). Those on the right depict Felipe II with his three wives and his son Carlos. The **Coro Alto** (High Choir) has a magnificent ceiling fresco of an angel-filled heaven. The **cloister** shines under Titian's fresco of the martyrdom of St. Lawrence.

PANTHEONS. The nearby **Panteón Real,** filled with tombs of past monarchs, glistens with intricate gold and marble designs completed in 1654. Felipe II ordered that its design allow for Mass to be conducted over his father's tomb. The connecting **Pudreria,** where bodies would dry before being buried, is thankfully out of commission. Two centuries later, the **Panteón de los Infantes** was built for the youngest of the royals and has space for over 50 babies. It is rumored that many of the royalty's illegitimate children, including a son of Charles V, lie within the crypts.

THE CASITAS. Commissioned by the Prince of Asturias, later to become Carlos IV, the **Casita del Príncipe** displays a collection of ornaments, including chandeliers, lamps, rugs, furniture, clocks, tapestries, china, and engraved oranges. Though the French roughed up the *casita* during the Napoleonic invasions, many rooms were later redecorated by Fernando VII in the then-popular Empire style. *(Approx. 1km from the monastery on the way to Madrid. Open Sa-Su 10am-1pm and 4-6:30pm. Visitors may only enter with a guided tour; every 30min., 10-person max. Call ahead for reservations ☎918 90 59 03. €3.50 per person; students and seniors €1.80.)* 3km toward Ávila, the simpler **Casita del Infante,** commissioned by Carlos's brother, Gabriel de Borbón, in the mid-16th century as a retreat, was meant to entertain guests with stunning views and musical performances. *(Open Semana Santa and July-Sept. Tu-Su 10am-7pm; €3.)*

NEAR EL ESCORIAL: EL VALLE DE LOS CAÍDOS

In a once-untouched valley 8km north of El Escorial, Franco forced prisoners to build the overpowering monument of Santa Cruz del Valle de los Caídos (Valley of the Fallen) as a memorial to those who gave their lives in the Civil War. Although ostensibly a monument to both sides, the massive granite cross (150m tall and 46m wide) implicitly honors only those who died "serving Dios and España," (i.e. the Fascist Nationalists); many of the Republican prisoners-of-war died under the grueling conditions of its construction. To climb to the base of the cross, use the stairs adjacent to the automatic lift or follow the paved road up to the trailhead just past the monastery on the right. Apocalyptic tapestries line the cave-like **basilica,** where lies the ghost of Fascist architecture, and death-angels carry swords and angry light fixtures. Behind the chapel walls lie a multitude (9 levels) of the dead. The high altar, located directly underneath the mammoth cross with its mammoth statues, is testimony to modern Spain's view of Franco—although Franco lies buried underneath, there is no mention of his tomb in tourist literature. El Valle de los Caídos is accessible only via El Escorial. (Mass M-Sa 11am; Su 11am, 12:30, 1, and 5:30pm. Entrance gate open Tu-Su 10am-6pm; Basilica open 10am-6:30pm. €5, seniors and students €2.50. W free for EU citizens. Funicular to the cross €2.50.) **Autocares Herranz** runs one bus to the monument. (☎918 90 41 25 or 918 96 90 28. 20min., leaves El Escorial from C. Juan de Toledo Tu-Su 3:15pm and returns 5:30pm, round-trip plus admission €6.30, funicular not included.)

SIERRA DE GUADARRAMA

The Sierra de Guadarrama is a pine-covered mountain range halfway between Madrid and Segovia. With *La Mujer Muerta* (The Dead Woman) to the west, the *Sierra de la Maliciosa* (Mountain of the Evil Woman) to the east, and the less-imaginatively-named *Siete Picos* (Seven Peaks) between the two, the Sierra draws both summer and winter visitors to hike and ski.

CERCEDILLA ☎918

A picturesque chalet town blessed with great weather, Cercedilla is the ideal base for venturing into the Sierras. In the summer, cooler temperatures and a relaxed pace lure sweltering city-dwellers; in the winter, skiers enjoy the nearby resorts. For those weary of Madrid's sights, Cercedilla has no monuments, churches, or museums. Instead, it offers great day hikes that provide an escape from the city.

MADRID

TRANSPORTATION AND PRACTICAL INFORMATION. Cercedilla makes an easy daytrip from Madrid. Camping is not allowed in the area, so pack for a day hike or reserve a hostel in advance for extended stays. The **train station** (☎918 52 00 57), at the base of the hill on C. Emilio Serrano, sends trains to: **El Escorial** via **Villalba** (1hr.; 20 per day Su-F 6:07am-11:35pm, Sa 6:37am-11:35pm; €1); **Los Cotos** (45min.; Su-F every hr. 9:35am-7:35pm, Sa every 2hr. 10:35am-6:35pm; €3.25); **Madrid-Atocha** or **Madrid-Chamartin** via **Villalba** (1½hr.; over 20 per day Su-F 6:07am-11:35pm, Sa 6:37am-11:35pm; €3.35); **Puerto de Navacerrada** (30min., on the way to Los Cotos, €3.25); **Segovia** (45min., 8-9 per day 7:20am-9:20pm, €2.40); **Villalba** (30min.; M-Sa 6:07am-10:35pm, Sa-Su 6:37am-10:35pm; €1). The **bus station,** Av. José Antonio, 2 (☎918 52 02 39), sends buses to **Madrid** (M-F 29 per day 6am-8:45pm, Sa 15-17 per day 6:20am-8:45pm, Su 17 per day 8:30am-9:30pm; €2.50).

Upon arrival in Cercedilla, first-timers should proceed to the **Consejería de Medio Ambiente** to pick up tourist information and great hiking maps, some even in English. This is the starting point for several hikes (see **Hiking,** below). To get there from the train or bus station, call a **taxi** (☎918 52 03 24, 650 26 30 43, or 619 22 62 72) or just wait for one, though this can take a while. The Consejería is roughly 3km from the train station on **Ctra. Las Dehesas,** km 2. By foot, go straight uphill and stay left at the fork (40min.). Services include: **emergency** (☎112), **police** (☎639 35 17 91), and the **Centro Médico** (☎918 52 30 31).

ACCOMMODATIONS AND FOOD. Many of the youth hostels in Cercedilla are booked during the summer by camp groups and other organizations. For most *albergues* and *hostales*, reservations should be made more than 15 days in advance.

The closest to the train station is **Hostal Longinos ❸**, right across the street from the station. Longinos has spacious rooms, all with private bath and a retro feel. (☎918 52 15 11 or 918 52 06 86. Singles €29; doubles €40.) For cheaper, more rustic accommodations, try **Villa Castora (HI) ❶**, about 1km up Ctra. Las Dehesas on the left. (☎918 52 03 34; fax 918 52 24 11. All rooms with private bath. Reception open daily 8am-10pm. Rooms and 3 meals €12.60, with 2 meals €10.60, only breakfast €7.80; over 26 €16.80/€14/€11.) **Hostal La Maya ❹**, C. Carrera del Señor, 2, has rooms with TVs, sofas, and modern private baths. (☎91 852 22 52. Doubles €40. MC/V.) **Camping** is strictly controlled throughout the Sierra de Guadarrama and is prohibited throughout the area surrounding Cercedilla. The Consejería can provide a list of Cercedilla's restaurant choices. For groceries, **Supermarket Gigante,** C. Doctor Cañados, 2, is in the town center off Av. Generalísimo. (☎918 52 23 19. Open M-Sa 9:30am-2pm and 5:30-9pm, Su 9:30am-2pm.) Convenience stores outside the bus and train stations sell all the essentials.

HIKING. The **Consejería de Medio Ambiente** functions as a **tourist office** and offers hiking information. (☎/fax 918 52 22 13. Open daily 9am-6pm. M-F English-speaking staff.) The Consejería provides detailed maps of six trails and day hikes through the surrounding Sierra region, ranging from the 14.3km (5-6hr.) **El GR-10** to the 4km (1½hr.) **Camino Puricelli.** Some of the hiking around Cercedilla begins up the **Carretera las Dehesas,** near the Consejería. Atop the *carretera*, the **Calzada Romana** (about 1.5km from the Consejería), offers hiking along a Roman road that once connected Madrid to Segovia (1½hr. trail).

PUERTO DE NAVACERRADA AND LOS COTOS

A year-round magnet for outdoorsy types, **Puerto de Navacerrada** offers **skiing** in the winter (late Dec.-early Apr.) and beautiful **hiking** in the summer. Backpackers in search of challenging hikes often take the popular **Camino Schmid,** a 7km trail which goes from Navacerrada to Pradera de los Corralillos; from there it is another 3km to the Consejería in Cercedilla. For hiking information, try **Deporte y Montaña,** 1.5km from the train station. (☎918 52 14 35. Open Sa-Su 10:30am-5pm in summer.) To head straight for the trails, exit the train station, turn left at the highway, and turn left again (off the road) at the large intersection marking the pass. The dirt path leads uphill to several trailpaths through the pine forests. A **train** leaves for Navacerrada from the Cercedilla station (30min.; Su-F every hr. 9:35am-7:35pm, Sa every 2hr. 10:35am-6:35pm; €3.25). For budget accommodations in Navacerrada, try the **Albergue Alvaro Iglesias** (☎918 52 38 87). **Los Cotos** is another popular winter resort, but it is difficult to find a place to stay there; accommodations are more plentiful in Navacerrada. For information, try the **Parque Nacional Peñalara** (☎915 22 87 43), a few kilometers from the train station. **Valdesqui** (☎918 52 33 02) is a ski resort in nearby **Rascafria,** a 2.5km hike from the Cotos station.

ARANJUEZ

History and natural beauty converge at the heart of green Aranjuez (pop. 43,000). Once a getaway for generations of Habsburg and Bourbon royalty, Aranjuez still maintains a pastoral elegance thanks to its dazzling gardens and palaces. UNESCO recently declared this small city, famed for its strawberries, asparagus, and aesthetic landscape, a "World Heritage Cultural Landscape." Aranjuez is an easy day trip from either Madrid or Toledo, but consider staying a bit longer during festivals at the end of May, during September, and during *Carnaval* (www.aranjuez.net).

TRANSPORTATION. Trains (RENFE info ☎902 24 00 42) go to: **Cuenca** (2hr.; 4-5 per day M-F 6:10am-8:14pm, Sa-Su 9:23am-8:14pm; €6.30); **Madrid** (45min.; *cercanías* to **Atocha** every 15-30min. M-F 5:30am-11:30pm, Sa-Su 6am-11:30pm; *regionales* to **Chamartín** 8-10 per day M-F 6:57am-9:27pm, Sa-Su 8:57am-9:27pm; €2.40); **Toledo** (30min.; 7-10 per day M-F 7:20am-9:12pm, Sa-Su 9:17am-9:12pm; €2.40). **ALSA** runs from the **bus station,** Av. Infantas, 16 (☎918 91 01 83), to: **Madrid's Estación Sur de Autobuses** (45min.; M-F every 15-30min. 6am-9pm, Sa every 45min. 7:30am-9pm, Su 10 per day 7:30am-9pm; €2.90). For **taxis,** try ☎918 91 11 39 or ☎669 81 53 00 between 10pm and 6am.

ORIENTATION AND PRACTICAL INFORMATION. To enter the city by foot, exit the train station parking lot, take a right, and then follow the signs toward El Palacio Real, which takes you to the left until you reach the palace. From the bus station, walk down C. Infantas toward the main fountain. Orienting yourself from the palace is fairly easy, and friendly locals can point you toward your destination or the tourist office. Alternatively, on the corner outside the palace, climb aboard the **Chiquitren de Aranjuez** (☎902 08 80 89 or 617 46 95 00) to catch all the major sights of Aranjuez in one day (€4, not including admission to the museums and sights; www.promotrain.com).

The **tourist office** is in Pl. San Antonio, 9. (☎918 91 04 27. Open Tu-Su 10am-7:30pm.) Local services include: **emergency** ☎112; **police,** C. Infantas, 36 (☎918 09 03 60); and a **pharmacy,** on the corner of C. Capitán Gómez and C. Real. (Open M-F 9:30am-1:15pm and 5-8:30pm, Sa 9:30am-1:15pm. MC/V.) For **Internet** access, head to **Arancyb,** up the street from the tourist office, through the plaza arches. From Ctra. Andalucía, take a left on C. Gobernador, 67. (☎918 91 28 62. €0.60 for 15min., €2.40 per hr. Open M-Sa 11am-3am, Su 4-11pm.) The **post office** is on C. Peña Redonda, 3, off C. Capitán Gómez. (☎918 91 11 32. Open M-F 8:30am-2:30pm, Sa 9:30am-1pm.) **Postal code:** 28300.

ACCOMMODATIONS AND FOOD. Aranjuez has a wide variety of choices for accommodations and food, especially for a city its size. **Hostal Infantas ❶**, Av. Infantas, 4-6, will be on your left when your back is to the bus station. All the rooms have sinks, TV, and phones, and doubles with shower or bath have A/C. (☎918 91 13 41; fax 918 91 66 43. Singles €13.50, with shower €21, with bath €23.50; doubles €23/€38/€40. MC/V.) The rooms at **Hostal Castilla ❸,** Ctra. Andalucía, 98, face a garden terrace and several have been recently renovated. All have TV, A/C, telephone, bath. (☎918 91 26 27; fax 918 91 61 33. Singles €33; doubles €40.) The same owners run **Hostal Rusinol ❷** on C. San Antonio with fewer amenities and cheaper prices. (☎918 91 01 55.) **Camping Soto del Castillo ❶,** across the Río Tajo and off the highway to the right, sits amid lush fields and offers a restaurant, supermarket, and a swimming pool. (☎918 91 13 95. €3.90 per person, €3.46-4.21 per tent, €3.31 per car. Open Apr.-Sept. MC/V.) For groceries or a quick meal, try the **Mercado de Abastos** on Ctra. Andalucía. With your back to the tourist office go left through the arch; the market is on your left. (Open M-F 9am-2pm and 6-9pm, Sa 9am-2pm.) Be sure to grab some delicious *fresas con nata* (strawberries and cream) from the vendors just over the small river bridge near the main fountain (in front of the palace gardens). For some savory asparagus specialties and typical Spanish entrees, head to **El Rana Verde ❸,** C. Reina, 1 (☎918 01 15 71) or **La Alegría de la Huerta ❸,** Ctra. de Madrid, 4 (☎918 91 29 38). Dinner runs €12-16.

SIGHTS. The stately **Palacio Real,** resplendent in white brick, was originally designed by Juan de Herrera, chief architect of El Escorial, under the direction of Felipe II. In subsequent years, Felipe V, Fernando VI, and Carlos III all had the palace enlarged and embellished to suit their own tastes. The Oriental **porcelain room,** with three-dimensional wallpaper and Rococo ceramic work, and the Mozarabic **smoking room,** which bears a striking resemblance to the Alhambra, are particularly remarkable. *(☎918 91 07 40. Open Apr.-Sept. Tu-Sa 10am-6:15pm; Oct.-Mar. Tu-Sa 10am-5:15pm. Compulsory 30min. tours in Spanish, English, or Italian leave about every 15min. €4.81, students €2.40. EU citizens free W.)* Just outside the palace begins a labyrinth of river walkways, freshly trimmed hedges, and mythological statues. The garden motif continues further down from the palace on C. de la Reina with the **Jardín del Príncipe,** built for the amusement of Carlos IV. *(Both open daily 10am-sunset. Free.)* A 30min. walk through the park leads to the **Casa del Labrador,** a mock cottage full of Neoclassical decorative arts. *(Located 3km down C. de la Reina from the Palacio Real. ☎918 91 03 05. Open daily 10am-sunset. €4.81, students and children under 16 €2.40.)*

The **Falúas Museum,** once home to the Tajo's sailing squad, stores royal gondolas. *(Open June-Aug. Tu-Su 10am-6:15pm; Sept.-May Tu-Su 10am-5:15pm. €3, students and under 16 €1.51. EU citizens free W.)* **Aranjuez, Una Gran Fiesta,** has exhibits that take you through the history of the *corrida*. *(Plaza de Toros. ☎918 92 16 43. Open Apr.-Sept. Tu-Su 11am-7:30pm, Oct.-Mar. 11am-5:30pm. €3; students, seniors, and under 16 €1.20.)*

CASTILLA LA MANCHA

Cervantes chose to set Don Quijote's adventures in La Mancha (*manxa* means parched earth in Arabic, and *mancha* means stain in Spanish) in an effort to evoke a cultural and material backwater. While Castilla La Mancha is one of Spain's least developed regions, this battered, windswept plateau possesses an austere beauty. Its tumultuous history, gloomy medieval fortresses, and brooding cliffs evoke both melancholy and reverence. Long ago, this region was at the epicenter of conflict between Christians and Muslims. When Christian forces arrived in Muslim Spain, La Mancha became the domain of the military orders Santiago, Calatrava, Montesa, and San Juan, which were modeled after such crusading institutions as the Knights Templar, a society of powerful warrior-monks. In the 14th and 15th centuries, the region saw fearsome struggles between the kingdoms of Castilla and Aragón. All this warring left La Mancha in a state of utter destruction.

The region is Spain's largest wine-producing area (*Valdepeñas* and *Manzanares* are popular table wines), and its abundant olive groves and hunting influence many local recipes. Stews, roast meats, and game are all *manchego* staples. *Gazpacho manchego* (a hearty stew of rabbit, lamb, chicken, and pork) and *queso manchego* (Castile's beloved cheese) are both indigenous specialties.

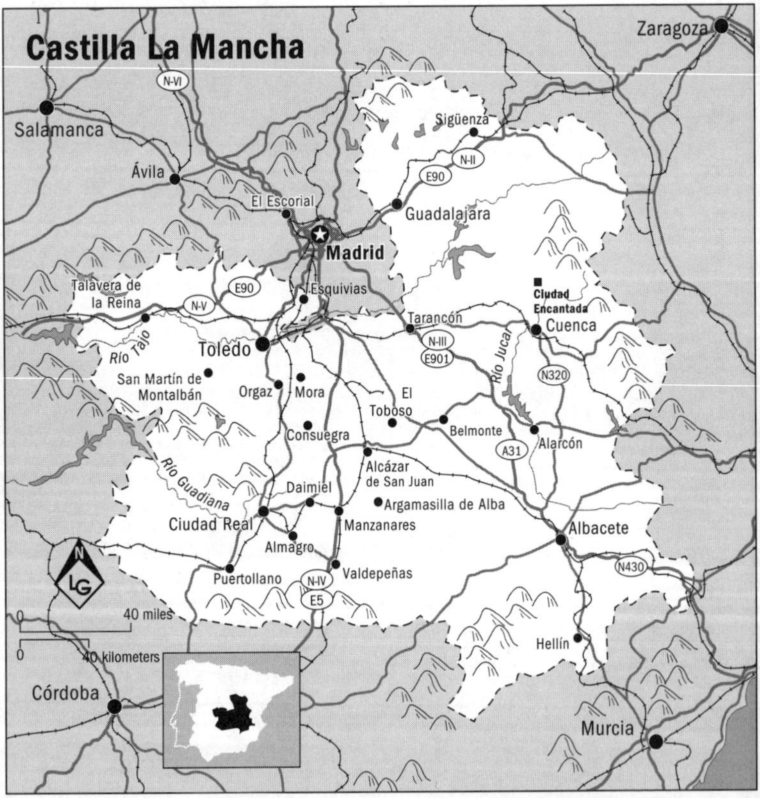

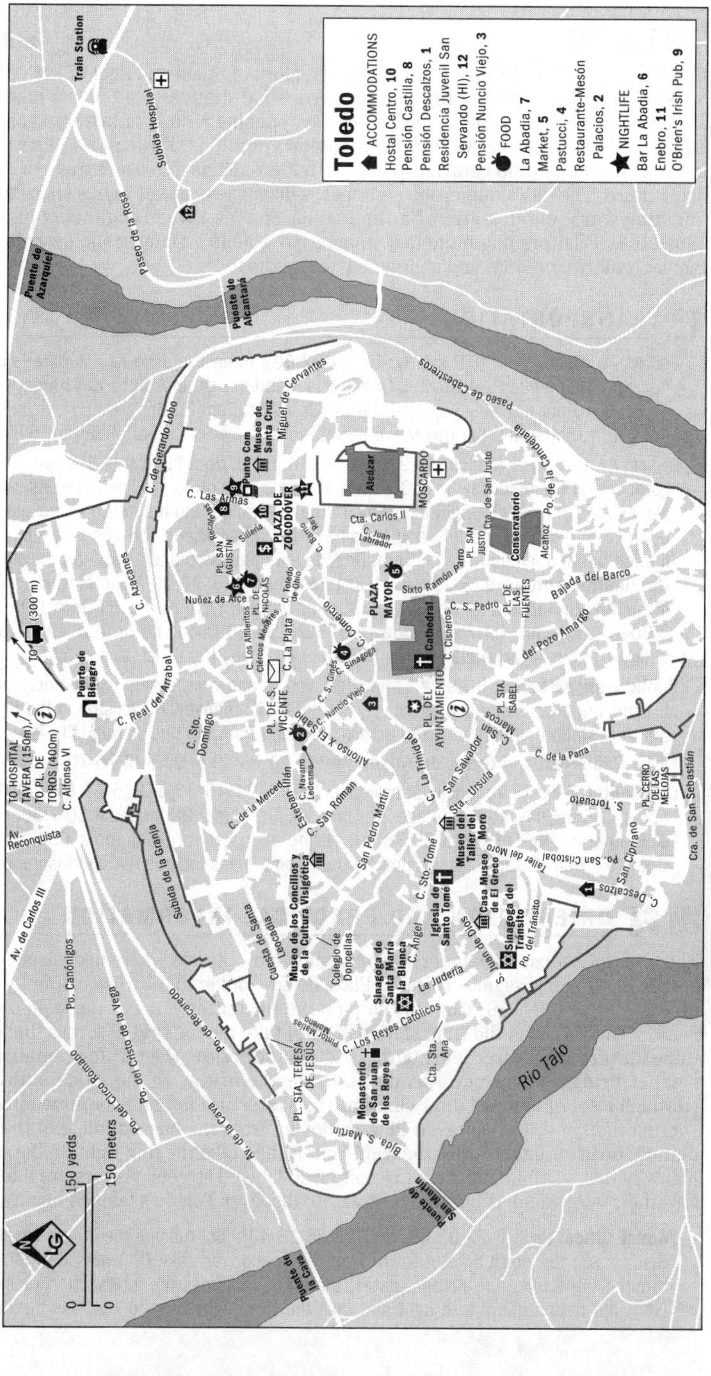

CASTILLA LA MANCHA

TOLEDO ☎925

For Cervantes, Toledo was a "rocky gravity, glory of Spain and light of her cities." Cossío called it "the most brilliant and evocative summary of Spain's history." Toledo holds a special mystique and charm, opening a page of history against a spectacular backdrop. Modern-day Toledo (pop. 66,000) may be marred by swarms of tourists and caravans of kitsch, but it remains a treasure trove of Spanish culture. The city's numerous churches, synagogues, and mosques share twisting alleyways, emblematic of a time when Spain's three religions coexisted peacefully. Visitors pay monetary homage to Toledo's Damascene swords and knives, colorful pottery, and almond-paste marzipan.

TRANSPORTATION

Trains: Po. Rosa, 2 (RENFE Info ☎902 24 02 02), in an exquisite neo-Mudéjar station just over the Puente de Azarquiel. One line to Madrid to either **Atocha** or **Chamartin** (1-1½hr.; 9-10 per day M-F 6:30am-8:58pm, Sa-Su 8:25am-8:58pm; €4.81), usually via Aranjuez (35min.; 8-9 per day M-F 6:30am-8:58pm, Sa-Su 8:25am-8:58pm; €2.41).

Buses: Av. Castilla-La Mancha (☎925 21 58 50), 5min. from **Puerta de Bisagra,** the city gate. From **Pl. Zocodóver,** take C. Armas and its extension to the Puerta de Bisagra; as you exit the old city turn right following Ronda de Granadal to the next traffic circle. Just before the bridge, take a left, and the station is straight ahead (15-20min. walk). Information booth open daily 7am-11pm. Despite multiple companies, destinations are few. **Continental-Auto** (☎925 22 36 41 in Toledo and 915 27 29 61 in Madrid) runs to **Madrid-Estación Sur** (1½hr.; every 30min. M-F 6am-10pm, Sa 6:30am-10pm, Su 8:30am-11:30pm; €3.75). **Alsina** (☎925 21 58 50 in Toledo or 963 49 72 30 in Valencia) goes to **Valencia** (5½hr.; M-F 3pm; €17, buy the ticket on the bus).

Public Transportation: Buses #5 and 6 get you to and from several city points, mainly the bus and train stations and the very central **Pl. Zocodóver.** Buses stop to the right of the train station, underneath and across the street from the bus station (€0.78).

Taxis: Radio Taxi and **Gruas de Toledo** (☎925 25 50 50 or 925 22 70 70.)

Car Rental: Avis, C. Venancio González, 9 (☎925 21 45 35 or 925 21 57 94). From about €60 per day. Minimum age 23. Open M-F 9:30am-2:30pm and 4:30-7:30pm, Sa 9:30am-2pm. **Hertz** (☎925 25 38 90), at the train station. From about €50 per day. Open M-F 9am-1:30pm, 4:30-7pm; Sa 9am-1pm. Prices include IVA and insurance.

ORIENTATION AND PRACTICAL INFORMATION

Toledo is an almost unconquerable maze of narrow streets where pedestrians and cars battle for sovereignty. To get to Plaza de Zocodóver in the town center by bus, take bus #5 or 6 (€0.78) from the stop on the right after you exit the train or bus station. On foot from the train station, *do not* take the big bridge across the Tajo. Instead, turn right after leaving the station and follow the left fork uphill to a smaller bridge, Puente de Alcántara. Cross the bridge to the stone staircase (through a set of arches); after climbing the stairs, turn left and continue upward, veering right at C. Cervantes to Pl. Zocodóver. From the bus station, exit the restaurant, head straight toward the traffic circle, and take the first right on the steep highway that surrounds the city. Despite well-labeled streets, visitors are likely to lose their way; wandering is the best way to discover Toledo's tangled beauty.

Tourist Office: (☎925 22 08 43; fax 925 25 26 48), just outside the Puerta Nueva de Bisagra, on the north side of town. From Pl. Zocodóver, take C. Armas downhill and through the Puertas de Bisagra gates; the office is across the intersection (10min.). From the train station, turn right and take the busy right-hand fork across the bridge

(Puente de Azarquiel), following the city walls until you reach the second traffic circle; the office is across the road, outside the walls. English-speaking staff offers handy maps. Open July-Sept. M-Sa 9am-7pm, Su 9am-3pm; Oct.-June M-F 9am-6pm, Sa 9am-7pm, Su 9am-3pm. **Second office** in Pl. Ayuntamiento (☎925 25 40 30), opposite the cathedral. English spoken. Open Tu-Su 10:30am-2:30pm and 4:30-7pm.

Currency Exchange: Santander Central Hispano, C. Comercio, 47 (☎925 22 98 00). No commission and a 24hr. **ATM.** Open Apr.-Sept. M-F 8:30am-2:30pm; Oct.-Mar. M-F 8:30am-2:30pm, Sa 8:30am-1pm.

Luggage Storage: At the **bus station** (€0.80-1.20). Open daily 7am-11pm. At the **train station** (€3). Open daily 7am-9:30pm.

Emergency: ☎112. **Police:** ☎092, where Av. Reconquista and Av. Carlos III meet.

Pharmacy: (☎925 22 17 68), Pl. Zocodóver. Posts list of various late-night pharmacies.

Hospital: Hospital Virgen de la Salud (☎925 26 92 00), Av. Barber.

Internet Access: Punto Com, C. Armas, 4, 2nd fl. (☎925 25 62 08), in Pl. Zocodóver, on the right as you begin to walk downhill. The cheapest, most convenient connection in town. €0.90 for 15min., €2.40 per hr. Open M-Sa 11:30am-10pm, Su 3:30-10pm.

Post Office: C. Plata, 1 (☎925 22 36 11; fax 21 57 64). Take C. Comercio from Pl. Zocodóver and turn right on C. Toledo de Ohio which turns into C. Plata. **Lista de Correos.** Open M-F 8:30am-8:30pm, Sa 9am-2pm. **Postal Code:** 45070.

ACCOMMODATIONS AND CAMPING

Toledo is chock-full of accommodations, but finding a bed during the summer can be a hassle, especially on weekends. Reservations are strongly recommended, especially during the summer. Last-minute planners, try the tourist office if you run into trouble. There are several camping grounds around Toledo. Out of town sites bring quiet and shade; those in town trade convenience for noise.

Residencia Juvenil San Servando (HI), Castillo San Servando (☎925 22 45 54). Cross the street from the train station, turn left, then immediately right up Callejón del Hospital. When the steps reach a road, turn right, then right again, following the signs to Hospital Provincial. The steep walk uphill past the hospital leads to the *hostal,* housed in a 14th-century castle. From the bus station, exit the restaurant, go toward the traffic circle, and continue straight uphill; cross the footbridge to the left and head up to the castle. Attractive, monumental building has 38 rooms, each with 2-4 bunk beds and private bath, some with views. Pool in summer. TV room. Free sheets. Reception open 7am-midnight. Dorms €8.50, with breakfast €10; over 26 €11/€13. Must have HI card. ❶

Hostal Centro, C. Nueva, 13 (☎925 25 70 91), on the northwest corner of Pl. Zocodóver. Centrally located for discovering the city. Clean, spacious rooms with TV, bath, A/C, phone. Friendly staff. Singles €30; doubles €42; triples €60. MC/V. ❸

Pensión Descalzos, C. Descalzos, 30 (☎925 22 28 88), down the steps off Po. del Tránsito, near the Sinagoga del Tránsito. Recently refurbished hostel with stunning views. Modern rooms with TV, A/C, full bath, and phone, some with balconies. Rooms #41 and 42 are favorites. Small pool/big jacuzzi in backyard. Breakfast €1.35-4.80. Apr.-Oct. singles €24; doubles €39-44. Oct.-Mar. €23/€34-39. IVA not included. MC/V. ❷

Pensión Castilla, C. Recoletos, 6 (☎925 25 63 18). Take C. Armas downhill from Pl. Zocodóver, then the first left up C. Recoletos (opposite the Caja Madrid bank); the hostel is up the stairs in the corner. Singles €15; doubles with bath €25. ❷

Pensión Nuncio Viejo, C. Nuncio Viejo, 19, 3rd fl. (☎925 22 81 78). 7 rooms close to the cathedral are cramped, but they're bright and clean. The motherly owner is a great cook. Breakfast €1.50. Meals €6.50. Single €17; doubles €28, with bath €32. ❷

Camping El Greco (☎925 22 00 90), 1.5km from town on Ctra. CM-4000, km0.7. Bus #7 (from Pl. Zocodóver) stops at the entrance. Shady, wooded site between the river and an olive grove. Restaurant, bar, and supermarket. Pool during the summer. Open year-round. €4 per person, €3.90 per tent, €3.90 per car. IVA not included. ❶

FOOD

Toledo grinds almonds into marzipan of every shape and size, from colorful fruity nuggets to half-moon cookies; *pastelería* windows beckon on every corner. Alternatively, grab fresh fruit and the basics at **Alimentación Pantoja,** C. Arrabal, 30, inside the Puerta de Bisagra and across from the tourist office. (Open June-Aug. M-Sa 9am-11pm, Su 9am-3pm; Sept.-May 9am-10pm/9am-3pm.) The **market** is in Pl. Mayor, behind the cathedral. (Open M-Sa 9am-8pm.)

La Abadía, Pl. San Nicolás, 3 (☎925 25 11 40). With your back to the McDonald's in Pl. Zocodóver, take C. Sillería (to the left of the pharmacy). Bear left when the road splits; when you reach a small plaza, Abadía is to your right. The dining room is a maze of cave-like underground rooms. The delicious lunch *menú* is a steal (€8.30). Open M-Th 8am-midnight, F 8am-1:30am, Sa noon-2:30am, Su noon-midnight. AmEx/MC/V. ❸

Pastucci, C. Sinagoga, 10 (☎925 21 48 66). From Pl. Zocodóver take C. Comercio; keep to the right through the underpass. Cheerful atmosphere. Pastas €5-6. Pizza €6. 10% discount with your *Let's Go* guide. Open daily 12:15pm-midnight. MC/V. ❶

Restaurante-Mesón Palacios, C. Alfonso X El Sabio, 3 (☎925 21 59 72), off C. Nuncio Viejo. Two daily *menús* loaded with meat, fish, and egg dishes. Toledo's famous partridge dish is an option on the more expensive *menú* (€6-10.22). Entrees €7.21-12. Open M-Sa 1-4pm and 7-11pm, Su noon-4pm. AmEx/MC/V. ❷

SIGHTS

Toledo's excellent museums, churches, synagogues, and mosques make the city impossible to see in one day. Within its fortified walls, attributed to 7th-century King Wamba, Toledo's attractions form a belt around its middle. An east-west tour, beginning in Pl. Zocodóver, is mostly downhill. Most sights are closed Mondays.

EL GRECO'S THREE MISTAKES Upon a visit to the sacristy of Toledo's cathedral, the eye is quickly drawn to the large El Greco painting at the end of the room. El Greco painted *El Espolio*—his first painting—specifically for the cathedral, although neither party had thought to negotiate costs before the completion of the work. The cathedral's clergy were unhappy with the painting due to three mistakes El Greco had inadvertently made. The first is an anachronism: the scene depicts the point in the Bible at which the Roman soldiers are about to remove Jesus's gown, but the soldier standing to his left is wearing distinctly 16th-century armor. El Greco's second mistake was painting three women in the bottom left corner; according to the New Testament, no women were present at that moment. The clergy's final complaint was that the artist painted ordinary men's heads above the head of Jesus; even in art, Christ is more holy than mere humans. The two parties went to court over the matter, eventually working out a compromise. In the end, El Greco won something more valuable than money—the court battle threw him into the spotlight, earning him a slew of new commissions and spreading his reputation.

CATHEDRAL. Built between 1226 and 1498, Toledo's cathedral boasts five naves, delicate stained glass, and unapologetic ostentation. Noteworthy pieces include the 14th-century Gothic *Virgen Blanca* by the entrance, El Greco's *El Espolio*, and Narciso Tomés's *Transparente*, a Spanish-Baroque whirlpool of architecture, sculpture, and painting. In the **Capilla Mayor,** the massive Gothic altarpiece stretches to the ceiling. The tomb of Cardinal Mendoza, founder of the Spanish Inquisition, lies to the left. Beneath the dome is the **Capilla Mozárabe,** the only place where the ancient Visigoth Mass (in Mozarabic) is still held. The **treasury** flaunts interesting ornamentations, including a replica of one of Columbus's ships and a 400-pound, 16th-century gold monstrosity lugged through the streets during the annual Corpus Christi procession. The **sacristy** is home to 18 El Grecos and two Van Dycks, along with the portrait of every archbishop of Toledo. The red hats hanging from the ceiling mark the cardinals' tombs. *(At Arco de Palacio, up C. Comercio from Pl. Zocodóver. ☎925 22 22 41. Cathedral open daily June-Aug. 10am-noon and 4-7pm; Sept.-July 10am-noon and 4-6pm. Cathedral is free, but it's worth the extra money to see the sacristy and the capillas, open June-Aug. M-Sa 10:30am-6:30pm, Su 2-6pm; Sept.-May M-Sa 10:30am-6pm, Su 2-6pm. €4.81. €2.70 for the audio guide available in English, French, and Italian. Tickets sold at the store opposite the entrance. Modest dress required.)*

ALCÁZAR. Toledo's most formidable landmark, the Alcázar served as a military stronghold for the Romans, Visigoths, Moors, and Spaniards. Much of the building was reduced to rubble during the Civil War, when Fascist troops used the Alcázar as their refuge. Don't miss the room detailing Colonel Moscardó's refusal to surrender the Alcázar, even at the cost of his son's life. Visit the dark, windowless basement refuge where over 500 civilians hid during the siege. The rooms above ground have been turned into a national military museum complete with armor, swords, guns, knives, and comparatively benign dried plants. *(Cuesta Carlos V, 2, a block down from Pl. Zocodóver. ☎925 22 16 73. Open Tu-Su 9:30am-2pm. €2. Free W.)*

EL GRECO. Greek painter Doménikos Theotokópoulos, commonly known as El Greco, spent most of his life in Toledo. Many of his works are displayed throughout town, but the majority of his masterpieces have been carted off to the Prado and other big-name museums. On the west side of town, the **Iglesia de Santo Tomé** houses his famous *El entierro del Conde de Orgaz (The Burial of Count Orgaz)*. The stark figure staring out from the back is El Greco himself, and the boy is his son, Jorge Manuel, who built Toledo's city hall. *(Pl. Conde. ☎925 25 60 98. Open daily Mar.-Oct.15 10am-6:45pm; Oct.16-Feb. 10am-5:45pm. €1.20; children under 18, students, and seniors €0.90.)* Downhill and to the left lies the **Casa Museo de El Greco,** containing 19 works, including a copy of the detailed *Vista y plano de Toledo (Landscape of Toledo)*. *(C. Samuel Levi, 2. ☎925 22 40 46. Open Tu-Sa 10am-2pm and 4-6pm, Su 10am-2pm. €1.20; students, under 18, and over 65 free. Sa-Su afternoons free.)* Outside handsome Puerta Nueva de Bisagra, 16th-century **Hospital Tavera** displays five El Grecos as well as several works by his mentor, Titian. *(Cardenal Tavera, 2. ☎925 22 04 51. Near the tourist office. Open daily 10:30am-1:30pm and 3:30-6pm. €3.)*

THE OLD JEWISH QUARTER. Samuel Ha Leví, diplomat and treasurer to Pedro el Cruel, built the **Sinagoga del Tránsito** (1366). Its simple exterior hides an ornate sanctuary with Mudéjar plasterwork and an *artesonado* (intricately designed wood) ceiling. The Hebrew-inscripted walls are mostly taken from the Psalter. Inside, the **Museo Sefardí** is packed with artifacts, including a Torah (parts of which are over 400 years old) and a beautiful set of Sephardic wedding costumes. *(C. Samuel Leví. ☎925 22 36 65. Closed for renovations in summer 2002; call ahead. Open Tu-Sa 10am-1:45pm and 4-5:45pm, Su 10am-2pm. €2.40, students and under 18 €1.20. Free Sa after 4pm and Su.)* **Sinagoga de Santa María la Blanca,** down the street to the right, was originally built to be a mosque, but was then purchased by Jews and used as the city's principal synagogue; in 1492, it was converted into a church. Now secular, its Moorish arches and tranquil garden make for a pleasant retreat. *(☎925 22 72 57. Open daily June-Aug. 10am-1:45pm and 3:30-6:45pm; Sept.-May 10am-1:45pm and 3:30-5:45pm. €1.20; students, children under 16, seniors €0.90.)*

MONASTERIO DE SAN JUAN DE LOS REYES. At the far western edge of the city stands the Franciscan Monasterio, commissioned by Isabel and Fernando to commemorate their victory over the Portuguese in the Battle of Toro (1476). The cloister, covered with the initials of the *Reyes Católicos*, melds Gothic and Mudéjar architecture. The Catholic monarchs planned to use the church as their burial place but changed their minds after the victory over Granada. *(☎925 22 38 02. Open daily Apr.-Sept. 10am-1:45pm and 3:30-6:45pm; Oct.-Mar. 10am-2pm and 3:30-6pm. €1.20.)*

OTHER SIGHTS. Toledo was the seat of Visigoth rule and culture for three centuries prior to the 711 Muslim invasion. The **Museo del Taller del Moro,** on C. Bulas near Iglesia de Santo Tomé, features outstanding woodwork, plasterwork, and tiles. *(Taller de Moro, 200. ☎925 22 45 00. Open Tu-Sa 10am-2pm and 4-6:30pm, Su 10am-2pm. €0.60.)* The exhibits at the **Museo de los Concilios y de la Cultura Visigótica** pale in comparison to their beautiful setting in a 13th-century Mudéjar church. *(C. San Clemente, 4. ☎925 22 78 72. Open Tu-Sa 10am-2pm and 4-6:30pm, Su 10am-2pm. €0.60, students €0.30.)* The impressive and untouristed **Museo de Santa Cruz** (1504) exhibits a handful of El Grecos in its eclectic art collection, which also includes the remains from archaeological digs throughout the province. *(C. Cervantes, 3, off Pl. Zocodóver. ☎925 22 10 36. Open Tu-Sa 10am-6:30pm, Su 10am-2pm. Usually free.)*

NIGHTLIFE

For nightlife, head through the arch and to the left from Pl. Zocodóver to **C. Santa Fé,** brimming with beer and local youth. **Trébol,** C. Sante Fe, 1, has excellent *tapas*, and their *bombas* (stuffed potato bombs; €2.25) are famous and deservedly so. (☎925 21 37 02. Open M-Sa 10am-3:30pm and 7pm-midnight, Su 1-3:30pm and 7pm-midnight.) **Enebro,** tucked away on small Pl. Santiago Balleros off C. Cervantes, lures in customers with free evening *tapas*. (☎925 22 21 11. Beer €1.20. No cover. Open daily 11am-4pm and 7pm-2:30am.) **C. Sillería** and **C. Alfileritos,** west of Pl. Zocodóver, are home to a few upscale bars and clubs, including **Bar La Abadía,** (☎925 25 11 40. See directions under Food.) **O'Brien's Irish Pub,** C. Armas, 12, fills with 20-somethings later in the evening. There is live music on Thursdays at 10:30pm. (☎925 21 26 65. Open Su-Th noon-2:30am, Sa-Su noon-4am. MC/V.)

DAYTRIP FROM TOLEDO

CONSUEGRA

Samar buses (☎925 22 39 15) depart for Consuegra from the Toledo bus station (1¼hr.; M-F 10 per day 9:15am-8:30pm, Sa 5 per day 9:15am-11pm, Su 3 per day 10:30am-11pm; €3.30). Buses return to Toledo from C. Castilla de la Mancha (1¼hr.; M-F 8 per day 6:45am-5:45pm, Sa 3 per day 7am-1:30pm, Su 3 per day 7am-6pm). In Toledo, buy tickets at the office; upon return, buy tickets from the driver.

Of all Manchegan villages, tiny Consuegra provides the most raw material for an evocation of Quijote's world. The village **castle,** called *Crestería Manchega* by locals, was a Roman, then Arab, then Castilian fortress. (Call for ever-changing hours.) **El Cid's** only son, Diego, died in the stable; you can visit a lavish monument in his honor near the Ayuntamiento. Though small, Consuegra is home to a palace, a Franciscan convent, and a Carmelite monastery. The **tourist office,** located on the same road as the castle, about halfway up on the left, will gladly provide more information. (☎925 47 57 31. Open June-Sept. M-F 9:30am-2pm and 4:30-7pm, Sa 10:30am-2pm and 4:30-7pm, Su 10:30am-2pm; in winter, afternoon hours 3:30-6pm.) Plan around bus departure times so you don't have to spend the night.

ALMAGRO ☎926

Situated in the heart of the Campo de Calatrava plain, the sleepy town of Almagro, with its narrow cobblestone streets and endless rows of whitewashed and half-timbered houses, evokes a vivid image of Spain as it was during the Renaissance. Despite its small size (pop. 8643), Almagro hosts an annual theater festival of international renown which attracts visitors during the first three weeks in July.

TRANSPORTATION. Find the **train station** at Po. Estación (☎926 86 02 76), outside the city center, at the end of the pedestrian street. To get from the station to the Pl. Mayor, walk down Po. Estación and turn left onto C. Rondo de Calatrava; turn right onto C. Madre de Dios (a sign points to Centro Urbano), which becomes C. Feria and leads to the plaza. To: **Aranjuez** (2hr., 2 per day, €8.41-9.62); **Ciudad Real** (15min., 5 per day 8:40am-9pm, €1.65-4.81); **Madrid** (2¾hr., 2:59 and 6:05pm, €11.27-12.77). Change at Ciudad Real for Córdoba, Sevilla, Granada, and Valencia. **Buses** (☎926 86 02 50) stop at a brick building at the far end of Ejido de Calatrava, left of the Hospedería Municipal de Almagro. **AISA** buses go to **Ciudad Real,** the connection point for most other cities (20min.; M-F 7 per day 8am-6:15pm, Sa 9:15am and 3pm; €1.35) and **Madrid** (2¼hr., M-F 5 per day 7am-6:45pm, €10.22).

ORIENTATION AND PRACTICAL INFORMATION. The center of Almagro is the long, arcaded Pl. Mayor. From the bus station, turn left on C. Madre de Dios and follow it straight to the plaza. The **tourist office,** Pl. Mayor, 1, is located on the first floor of the Ayuntamiento, directly underneath Pl. Mayor's clocktower. (☎926 86 07 17. Open Apr.-June and Sept. Tu-F 10am-2pm and 5-8pm, Sa 10am-2pm and 5-7pm, Su 11am-2pm; July-Aug. same hours except Tu-Sa 6-9pm; Oct.-Mar. same hours except Tu-F 4-7pm, Sa 10am-2pm and 4-6pm.) **Banks** and **ATMs** line C. Mayor de Carnicerías. Services include: **emergency** ☎926 86 00 33; **police,** C. Mercado, 1 (☎609 01 41 36), adjacent to the Pl. Mayor; the **Centro de Salud,** C. Mayor de Carnicerías, 11 (☎926 86 10 26); and the **post office,** C. Mayor de Carnicerías, 16. (☎926 86 00 52. Open M-F 8:30am-2:30pm, Sa 9:30am-1pm.) **Postal code:** 13270.

ACCOMMODATIONS AND FOOD. Hospedería de Almagro ❷, Ejido de Calátrava, s/n, resembles the austere decor of the monastery to which it is attached. The rooms are bright and spacious, and many overlook a pleasant courtyard. Clean baths, phones, and TVs provide for a comfortable stay. Reservations months ahead are needed for the theater festival. (☎926 88 20 87; fax 926 88 21 22. Aug.-June singles with bath €19.75; doubles with shower €27, with bath €33. July €22.50/€33/€39. MC/V.) To the right of the Hospedería de Almagro is the slightly more expensive **Hotel Don Diego ❸,** C. Bolaños, 1, which has brightly lit hallways and equally clean and comfortable rooms, all complete with bath, shower, TV, and phone. (☎926 86 12 87; fax 926 86 05 74. Aug.-June singles €31; doubles €43; triples €58. July €48.25/€66.50/€73.) Closer to the Pl. Mayor is **La Posada de Almagro ❹,** C. Gran Maestre, 5. From the tourist office, head towards the opposite end of the Pl. Mayor, passing the small park and **statue** of Diego de Almagro on your left. Make an immediate right on C. Gran Maestre, and the hotel will be on your left. Inside the large wooden gate is a beautiful courtyard with hanging vines and potted flowers. Rooms are charming and rustic, with colorfully tiled bathrooms.

(☎926 26 12 01; fax 926 24 12 01. Aug.-June singles €36; doubles €55; triples €67. July €48/€75/€90. All prices excluding 7% IVA tax.) Outdoor **restaurants** crowd on Pl. Mayor; they offer some of the best (and most expensive) food in town. Inside the **Hospedería de Almagro** is the cozy dining hall of **Restaurante Dos Toreadores ❷,** which has an extensive selection of seafood, meat, poultry, and vegetable entrees (€5-11). Especially good is the *pisto manchego*, a regional green pepper and tomato stew. (Open daily from July-Aug. 1:30-4pm and 9-11:30pm. Sept.-June same lunch hours, dinner 8:30-11pm.) Fresh fruits and veggies are sold at the outdoor **market.** From the Pl. Mayor, walk down C. Mayor de Carnicerías for one block, then turn left on Rastro de San Juan. (Open W 8am-3pm.)

SIGHTS AND ENTERTAINMENT. The center of Almagro, the **Plaza Mayor,** is also the city's cultural hub. Here you can find the **Corral de Comedias,** an open-air multilevel theater resembling Shakespeare's Globe. This theater is the only one left intact from the "Golden Age" of Spanish drama, and its stage was home to the works of such literary masters as Cervantes and Lope de Vega. (☎926 86 15 39. Open Apr.-June and Sept. Tu-F 10am-2pm and 5-8pm, Sa 11am-2pm and 5-8 pm, Su 11am-2pm and 4-6pm; July-Aug. Tu-Sa 10am-2pm and 6-9pm, Su 11am-2pm and 5-7pm; Oct.-Mar. same hours except Tu-F 4-7pm, Sa-Su 4-6pm. €1.80, children and groups of 15 or more €0.90.) Directly across the plaza from the *corral* and through a few arches, **Museo Nacional del Teatro** displays the history of Spanish drama. Ticket includes entrance to the museum's temporary exhibits on different aspects of Spanish theater such as costumes and stage design, which are housed in the Iglesia de San Agustín past the tourist information office on the corner of C. San Agustín and C. Feria. (☎/fax 926 88 22 44. Open Tu-F 10am-2pm and 4-6pm, Su 11am-2pm. €1.20, children under 18 and all on Sa afternoon and Su morning free.) The final stop on the theater tour is the **Teatro Municipal,** C. San Agustín, 20. Follow C. San Agustín out of Pl. Mayor and look for a crimson and white building on the right. Inside is a renovated theater and a small collection of elaborate costumes. (☎926 86 13 61. Open Apr.-June and Sept. Tu-F 10am-2pm and 5-8pm, Sa 11am-2pm and 5-8pm, Su 11am-2pm; July-Aug. same hours except Tu-F 6-9pm, Sa 10am-2pm and 6-9pm; Oct.-Mar. same hours except Tu-F 4-7pm, Sa 10am-2pm and 4-6pm.)

Every year, prestigious theater companies and players from around the world descend on the town for the **Festival Internacional de Teatro Clásico de Almagro** from the first Thursday to the last Sunday in July. Daily performances of Spanish and international classics take place in the Corral de Comedias, Teatro Hospital de San Juan de Dios, Teatro Municipal, Claustro de los Domínicos, Teatro Infantil, Teatro en la Calle, Patio de Fucares and Seminarios. The **box office** is in the Palacio de los Medrano, C. San Agustín, 7. (☎902 10 12 12; www.festivaldealmagro.com. Open May-June Th 11am-1:30pm; July daily 11:30am-2pm and 7:30-10:30pm. MC/V.) There are daily shows in July at 10:45pm at all venues except Teatro Infantil (8:30pm) and Teatro en la Calle (9pm); tickets are €11-16 (Tu half-price) and should be purchased in May before the festival begins as they tend to sell out very quickly. The festival also has an office in Madrid at C. Príncipe, 14 (☎915 21 07 20), and the 2003 program is listed online. From Sept.-June, there are classical theater performances nearly every weekend at the *corral.* (7, 7:30, or 9pm, depending on the date. Tickets, €9.50, can be purchased either at the *corral* itself, or by calling ☎926 88 24 58. Ask for the program there or at the tourist information office.)

CUENCA ☎969

Cuenca (pop. 50,000) owes its fame to its location. Perched atop a hill, the city is flanked by two rivers and the stunning rock formations they have created. These natural boundaries have served the city well; Muslims and then Christians settled in Cuenca because it was a nearly impenetrable fortress. Yet the city now strains against its boundaries with its modern commercial life spilling down the hill into New Cuenca. The enchanting old city still safeguards most of Cuenca's treasures, including the famed *casas colgadas* (hanging houses), dangling high above the Río Huécar, and the magnificent Catedral de Cuenca in the colorful Plaza Mayor.

TRANSPORTATION

Trains: C. Mariano Catalina, 10 (☎902 24 02 02). Trains to: **Aranjuez** (2hr., 5-6 per day 7:05am-6:55pm, €6.30); **Madrid** (2½-3hr., 5-6 per day 7:05am-6:55pm, €8.60); **Valencia** (3-4hr.; 3-4 per day M-F 7:45am-6:40pm, Sa-Su 11:19am-7pm; €9.50).

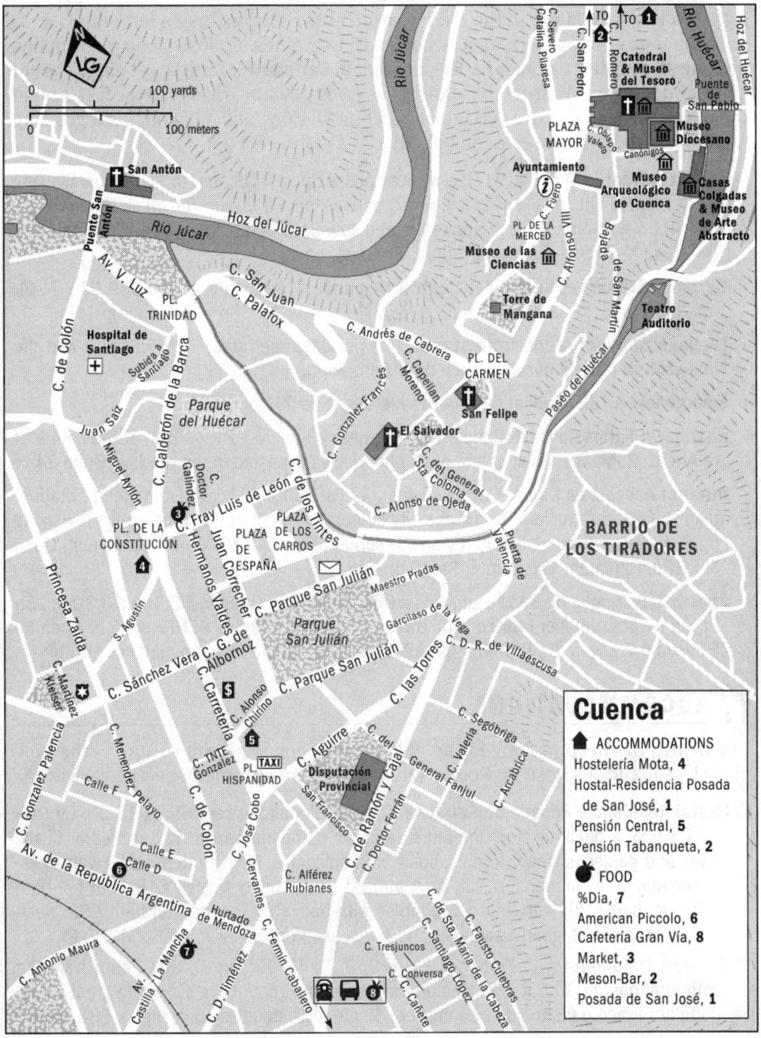

Buses: C. Fermín Caballero, 20 (☎969 22 70 87). Info open M-F 7am-10pm, Sa-Su 7am-9pm. **SIAL** (☎969 22 27 51) to: **Barcelona** (3½hr.; M-Sa 9:30am, July-Aug. extra bus Su at 2pm; €27). **AutoRes** (☎969 22 11 84) to: **Madrid** (2½hr.; 8-9 per day M-Sa 7:30am-8pm, Su 8am-10pm; €8.20-10.15). **AISA** to: **Toledo** (3hr.; M-F 6:30am and 4:30pm, Su 5:30pm; €9.75).

Taxis: Radio-Taxi (☎969 23 33 43). From the train station to Pl. Mayor €3.60.

ORIENTATION AND PRACTICAL INFORMATION

Upon exiting the train station, the back of the bus station (a large brick building) will be directly in front of you; head up the steps to C. Fermín Caballero and turn right. To reach **Pl. Mayor** in the old city from either station, take a left onto C. Fermín Caballero, following it as it becomes C. Cervantes, C. José Cobo, and finally, bearing slightly left through Pl. Hispanidad, **C. Carretería.** Large street signs should show you the way. Alternately, take #1 bus (every 20min., €0.50) to the last stop in the old city. From C. Carretería, turn right on C. Fray Luis de León; it's a grueling uphill walk to Pl. Mayor and the old city (20-25min.).

Tourist Office: (☎969 23 21 19; www.aytocuenca.org). Located in Pl. Mayor. Walking up C. Alfonso VIII, look to your left as it broadens into Pl. Mayor. The office is just before the archway. Some English spoken. Open July-Sept. M-Sa 9am-9pm, Su 9am-2pm; Oct.-June M-Sa 9am-2pm and 4-6pm, Su 9am-2pm.

Currency Exchange: Santander Central Hispano, C. Carretería, 23 (☎969 211 726). Apr.-Sept. M-F 8:30am-2:30pm; Oct.-Mar. M-F 8:30am-2:30pm, Sa 8:30am-1pm.

Luggage Storage: At the **train station** (€3 per day; open daily 7am-9:30pm) and the **bus station** (€1.80 per day; open daily 6am-9pm).

Emergency: ☎112. **Police:** C. Martínez Kleyser, 4 (☎091 or 092).

Pharmacy: Farmacia Castellanos, C. Cervantes, 20 (☎969 21 23 37), at the corner of C. Alferez Rubianes. A list of late-night pharmacies is posted in the window. Open 24hr.

Internet Access: La Repro, C. Jorge Torner, 39 (☎ 969 24 01 36). From the bus station, take C. Fermín Caballero toward the city center; turn right at the 1st stop light, walking up C. Julio Larrañaga 1 block. It's on the corner at the 1st left. €0.60 per 30min. Open M-F 10am-2pm and 5-8:30pm, Sa 10am-2pm.

Post Office: Parque de San Julián, 16 (☎969 22 90 16). Open M-F 8:30am-8:30pm, Sa 9:30am-2pm. Smaller **branch** with fewer services right next to **RENFE** station. Open M-F 8:30am-2:30pm, Sa 9:30am-2pm. **Postal Code:** for the large post office, 16004.

ACCOMMODATIONS

The dearth of cheap lodging in the old city may convince you to stay in the new city's less luxurious hostels. Rooms on the hill charge for their spectacular views.

Hostal-Residencia Posada de San José, C. Julián Romero, 4 (☎ 969 21 13 00; fax 969 23 03 65), a block up from the left side of the cathedral next to C. San Pedro. Cushy beds and gorgeous views. Rooms, some with balconies, have modern baths with sinks. Reservations recommended. July-Aug. and F-Sa year-round singles €18, with full bath €39; doubles €29, with bath €57; triples with bath €77; quads with bath €92. *Semana Santa* prices higher; weeknight and low season prices lower. AmEx/MC/V. ❷

Pensión Tabanqueta, C. Trabuco, 13 (☎969 21 12 90), up C. San Pedro from the cathedral past Pl. Trabuco. Rooms on the side of the gorge have sinks and great views. Popular terrace bar shouldn't be missed. Single €12; doubles €24; triples €36. ❶

Hostelería Mota, Pl. Constitución, 6, 1st fl. (☎969 22 55 67), at the end of C. Carretería. Marble floors, polished wooden walls, and A/C. Cheerful modern rooms have sinks and TVs. Singles occasionally available in winter. Doubles €27, with bath €37. ❷

Pensión Central, C. Alonso Chirino, 7, 2nd fl. (☎969 21 15 11), off C. Carretería. From the bus station, follow signs to Parque San Julián past Pl. Hispanidad. Clean, old-fashioned rooms with big windows, high ceilings and sinks. Be prepared to wait in line for the common bathroom. Breakfast €1.50. Lunch or dinner €6. July-Sept. singles €11; doubles €20; triples €25. Sept.-June prices €1.20 lower. ❶

FOOD

The area around Pl. Mayor is filled with mid- to high-priced restaurants, but a short walk along sidestreets near the plaza yields cheaper alternatives. Budget eateries line **C. Cervantes** and **C. República Argentina;** the cafes off **C. Fray Luis de León** are even cheaper. Area specialties *Resoli*, a liqueur of coffee, sugar, orange peel, and eau-de-vie, and *alajú*, a nougat of honey, almonds, and figs, are a heavenly match. The **market** is on C. Fray Luis de León, near Pl. Constitucíon (open M-Sa 8:30am-2pm). Grab **groceries** at **%Día,** Av. Castilla La Mancha and Av. República Argentina (open M-Th 9:30am-2pm and 5:30-8:30pm, F-Sa 9am-2:30pm and 5:30-9pm).

Meson-Bar Tabanqueta, C. Trabuco, 13 (☎ 969 21 12 90), beneath the pension of the same name. This little joint bustles with patrons enjoying views of the gorge over cheap food and drinks. Wide range of options including a *menú del dia* (€7.20) and sandwiches (€2.40-4.20). Open Tu-Su noon-2am. ❶

Posada de San José, C. Julián Romero, 4 (☎969 21 13 00). Outdoor wooden terrace offers spectacular views. Soak in the ambiance with a serving of *pisto* (stew made of tomatoes, peppers, and onions; €3.45). *Bocadillos* and omelettes €1.80-3.60. Lamb, tenderloin, and fried trout €5-9. Open Tu-Su 8-11am and 6-10:30pm. AmEx/MC/V. ❶

Cafetería Gran Vía, C. Fermín Caballero, 4 (☎969 23 62 26). Enjoy the elegant wooden interior or go outdoors for abundant seating and watch the street life of New Cuenca. The well-dressed waiters are quick and attentive. Combination plates of fish and pork €7-10. Open daily 7:30pm-1am MC/V. ❷

American Piccolo, Av. República Argentina, 14 (☎969 21 28 55). Ignore the cheesy sign and enjoy the photos and prints on the walls of this cheerful *trattoria*. Pizzas and pastas €5-8. Lunch *menú* €8. Open Th-Tu 1:30-4pm and 8pm-midnight. MC/V. ❷

SIGHTS

CASAS COLGADAS. Cuenca draws its fame from the gravity-defying *casas colgadas* that have dangled over the riverbanks for six centuries. These "hanging houses" are believed to have been the summer home of monarchs during the 14th century. Walk across the Puente de San Pablo at sunset for a spectacular view of the *casas* and the surrounding cliffs. Stroll along two trails that flank Hoz del Júcar and Hoz del Huécar (the steep river gorges on either side of the old city) for fantastic views of Cuenca. Maps are available from the municipal tourist office.

MUSEO DE ARTE ABSTRACTO ESPAÑOL. Inside one of the *casas*, the award-winning Museo de Arte Abstracto Español exhibits works by the odd yet internationally renowned "Abstract Generation" of Spanish painters. All pieces, most by Canogar, Tápies, Chillida, and Fernando Zóbel, were chosen by Zóbel himself. Don't miss the "White Room." Striking views of the gorge are an added plus. *(Pl. Ciudad de Ronda, follow signs from Pl. Mayor. ☎969 21 29 83. Open Tu-F and holidays 11am-2pm and 4-6pm, Sa 11am-2pm and 4-8pm, Su 11am-2:30pm. €3, students and seniors €1.50.)*

LIVING ON THE EDGE Very little is known about Cuenca's unique 14th-century *casas colgadas*. They were supposedly built to house kings; one is even named Casa del Rey. Casa de la Sirena, the only other remaining original hanging house, got its name from the siren-like screams emitted by a Cuenca *señorita* when she flung herself out of the window after her son was killed by her lover. Despite their striking appearance, the *casas* did not become famous until recently. Indeed, the *casas* were completely run down when the city of Cuenca decided to rehabilitate them early in this century, transforming them into magnificent museums. Now one of Central Spain's greatest tourist attractions, the houses draw thousands of visitors each year.

CATEDRAL DE CUENCA. Constructed under Alfonso VIII six years after he conquered Castile, the cathedral dominates Pl. Mayor. A perfect square, 25m on each side, it is the only Anglo-Norman Gothic cathedral in Spain. A Spanish Renaissance facade and tower were added in the 16th and 17th centuries, only to be torn down when deemed aesthetically inappropriate. A 1724 fire prevented a subsequent attempt to build a front, leaving the current exterior strangely reminiscent of a Hollywood set. Colorful stained-glass windows illuminate the entrance. Inside, the **Museo del Tesoro** houses late medieval psalters and gold jewelry. More impressive is the **Sala Capitular** with its delightful ceiling. *(Cathedral and museum open Aug.-Sept. Tu-Sa 8:45am-2pm and 4-6pm, Su 9am-2pm. Oct.-July same hours except Tu-Sa 4-7pm. Mass daily 9:20am, plus Su noon and 1pm. Cathedral free, museum €1.20.)*

OTHER SIGHTS. Down C. Obispo Valero, the **Museo Arqueológico de Cuenca** is a treasure trove of Roman mosaics, ceramics, coins, and Visigoth jewelry. *(☎969 21 30 69. Open June-Sept. Tu-Sa 10am-2pm and 5-7pm, Su 11am-2pm; Oct.-July Tu-Sa 10am-2pm and 4-7pm, Su 10am-2pm. €1.20, students €0.60. Sa afternoon and Su free.)* Perhaps the most beautiful of the museums along this street is the **Museo Diocesano,** whose exhibits include Juan de Borgoña's altarpiece from local Convento de San Pablo, colossal Flemish tapestries, splendid rugs, and two El Grecos—*Oración del huerto* and *Cristo con la cruz*. *(☎969 22 42 10. Open July-Sept. Tu-Sa 11am-2pm and 5-8pm, Su 11am-2pm; Oct.-June Tu-Sa 11am-2pm and 4-7pm, Su 11am-2pm. €1.80.)*

ENTERTAINMENT AND NIGHTLIFE

Cuenca rings with song during the **Festival of Religious Music,** a famous international celebration the week before *Semana Santa.*

Cuenca's nightlife scene extends into the wee hours of the morning. The older crowd stays near Pl. Mayor, while teens and 20-somethings flock to the newer city. Several bars with young, well-dressed crowds line C. Galíndez, off C. Fray Luis de León, a hot spot in the new city but a long, dark walk down the hill from Old Cuenca; a taxi will be about €3.60. **BarClays** (opens at 7pm), **Malibu** (opens at 11:30pm), **Rodeo** (open Tu, Th-Su and "sometimes" M and W, 11pm), and **Don Temístocles** (opens at 11pm) along C. Galíndez are virtually identical with fun-loving bartenders, darts, and a plethora of mixed drinks. Closing hours are generally between 2 and 4:30 am. For two floors of dance and drink, don't miss the **Big Red Bus** on C. Galíndez. Almost empty for the first hour, the spacious dance floors fill quickly as partiers from nearby bars suddenly and simultaneously feel the urge to groove to techno, pop, and hip-hop. (Beer €2; mixed drinks €4. 11:30pm-4am.)

For more nightlife options, take the winding street/staircase just off Pl. Mayor across from the cathedral toward the Río Júcar to find several small bars. Also, check out the bar under **Pensión Tabanqueta** on C. Trabuco (see above).

SIGÜENZA ☎949

The quintessential small Spanish town, Sigüenza (pop. 5000) is peaceful and lovely, but somewhat humdrum for any longer than a day. Its rosy stone buildings and red-roofed houses surround a storybook Gothic cathedral and castle, both of which deserve a peek. During the Civil War, the Republicans seized the cathedral while the Nationalists took the castle, providing the most action this small town has seen since. Sigüenza's medieval architecture has been painstakingly restored, and a walk through the streets—from the 12th-century medieval city to the 18th-century Baroque neighborhoods—make an enjoyable escape from Madrid.

TRANSPORTATION AND PRACTICAL INFORMATION. The **train station** (☎949 39 14 94) is at the end of Av. Alfonso VI. Trains run to: **Madrid-Chamartin** (1½-2hr., 6-7 per day 10:08am-9:18pm, €7.06-17); **Soria** (1½hr.; daily 9:45am, 5:20, 8:48pm; no 5:20pm train on F; €4.91); **Zaragoza** (2hr.; 4:05, 7:40, 11:35pm; €15-17). For a **taxi** call ☎949 39 14 11. **Luggage storage** is at the train station (€1.80 per locker). To get to the **tourist office,** follow Av. Alfonso VI to the first intersection after Parque de la Alameda (on the left). The office is just around the corner in the restored Ermita. (☎949 34 70 07. Open M-F 10am-2:30pm and 4-6:30pm, Sa 9:30am-3pm and 3:30-7pm, Su 9:30am-3:30pm. Closed M Oct.-Apr.) Across the intersection is **Santander Hispano Central,** Av. Calvo Siteco, 9, with a 24hr. **ATM.** (Open M-F 8:30am-2:30pm.) **Internet** is available at a coin-operated machine in **Don Rodrigo Pizzeria,** C. Cardenal Mendoza, 16, on the corner of C. Humilladero. (☎949 39 16 19. €1 per 15min. Open 8am-midnight.) Services include: **emergency** (☎949 30 00 19); **Red Cross,** Ctra. Madrid (☎949 39 13 33); and **police,** Ctra. de Atienzo (☎949 39 01 95). **Post office:** C. Villaviciosa, 10, off Pl. Hilario Yabén. (☎949 39 08 44. Open M-F 8:30am-2:30pm, Sa 9:30am-1pm.) **Postal code:** 19250.

ACCOMMODATIONS AND FOOD. Although you can "do" Sigüenza in a few hours, train schedules might have you spending the night. The slightly crumbling **Pensión Venancio ❶,** C. San Roque, 3, is old but charming. From the station, follow Av. Alfonso VI, turn left at the first intersection onto Av. Pio XII, then take the first right. (☎949 39 03 47. Singles €14; doubles €26; triples €32.) Small places to eat are everywhere. **Bar-Restaurante Sánchez ❷,** C. Humilladero, 11, has a cheap, delicious *menú* for €7.21. (☎949 39 05 45. Open daily 1:45-4pm and 9:45-11:30pm.)

SIGHTS. The tourist office offers guided city tours, including entrance to all parts of the cathedral, for €6. From the bottom of the hill, two buildings jut out from Sigüenza's low skyline: the cathedral and the fortified **castle,** a 12th-century castle-turned-*parador* (luxury hotel). Restored in the 1970s, the castle merits an uphill stroll through the cobblestone streets, even just for a peek into the luxuriously decorated *parador* and its marvelous view. To get to the **cathedral,** follow Av. Alfonso VI uphill (it changes to C. Humilladero), then take a left onto C. Cardenal Mendoza. Work on the cathedral began in the mid-12th century and continued until the 16th century; it combines Romanesque, Mudéjar, Plateresque, and Gothic styles. One of the structure's most renowned features is the 15th-century Tumba del Doncel, commissioned by Isabel in memory of a page who died fighting the Muslims in Granada. The sacristry's Renaissance ceiling boasts 304 stone portraits carved by Alanso de Covarrubias. The adjoining chapel houses El Greco's *Anunciación.* (☎619 36 27 15. Cathedral open daily 9am-1:30pm and 4:30-8pm. Free. Tours in Spanish, required for entry to sacristy and chapel. Tours year-round Tu-Sa 11am, noon, 12:45, 4:30, 5:30pm; June-Nov. 12 Su noon, 5:30pm; Nov. 13-May Su noon, 1, 5:30pm. €3.) Opposite the cathedral, the small **Museo de Arte Antiguo** (Museo Diocesano) houses medieval and early modern religious works, including a Ribera and a Zurbarán. (☎949 39 10 23. Open Tu-Su 11am-2pm and 4-7pm. €2.)

CASTILLA Y LEÓN

The aqueduct of Segovia, the Gothic cathedrals of Burgos and León, the Romanesque belfries along Camino de Santiago, the sandstone of Salamanca, and the city walls of Ávila: these images, ingrained in the collective memory of the Spanish consciousness, all belong to Castilla y León. Age-old traditions are preserved particularly vehemently here: in the public slaughter of pigs in Medina de Rioseco, in the fire bull at Coca, and in the *Cabezadas* (bowling) in León. Well before Castilla's famous 1469 confederation with Aragón, when Fernando of Aragón and Isabel of Castilla were united in world-shaking matrimony, it was clear that Castilla had its act together. During the High Middle Ages, the region emerged from obscurity to lead the Christian charge against Islam. Castilian nobles, sanguine from the spoils of combat, introduced the concept of a unified Spain (under Castilian command, of course), and *castillano* ("Spanish") became the dominant language throughout the nation. Castilla's comrade in arms, imperious León, though chagrined to be lumped with Castilla in a 1970s provincial reorganization, has much in common with its co-province.

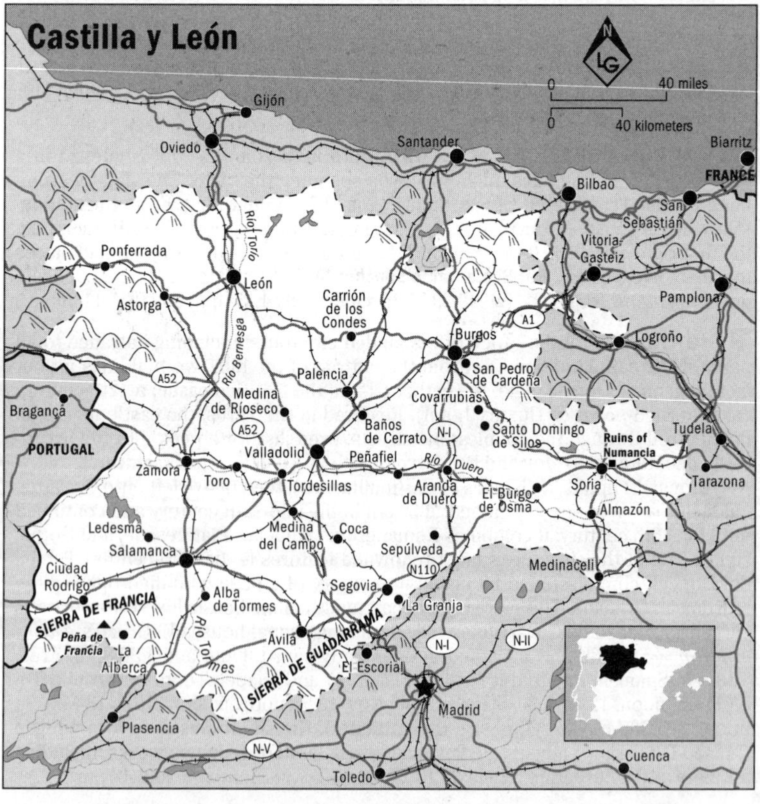

SEGOVIA ☎921

Segovia (pop. 56,000) is immersed in legend. The history that surrounds each monument in the "Stone Ship" that is Segovia—so named because of the prow-shaped profile of the city's Alcázar and its cathedral's mast-like tower—are told and retold. Legend has it that the devil constructed the famed aqueduct in one night in a failed effort to win the soul of a Segovian water-seller named Juanilla. Segovia's aqueduct may not have won Juanilla's soul, but it certainly draws its share of Spanish and international tourists. Twisted alleyways lead to streets lined with shopping stalls. However, such old-town charm comes at a price tag; food and accommodations are more expensive here than in Madrid. Finding the city an ideal place for language practice, international students flock to Segovia.

TRANSPORTATION

Trains: Po. Obispo Quesada, (☎921 42 07 74). To **Madrid** (2hr.; 7-9 per day, M-F 5:55am-8:55pm, Sa-Su 8:55am-8:55pm; €4.90) and **Villalba** (1hr., €3.21), the transfer for El Escorial, Ávila, León, and Salamanca.

Buses: Estacionamiento Municipal de Autobuses, Po. Ezequiel González, 12 (☎921 42 77 07), at the corner of Av. Fernández Ladreda. **La Sepulvedana** (☎921 42 77 07) to: **La Granja** (20min.; 9-12 per day M-Sa 7:40am-9:30pm, Su 10:30am-10:30pm; round-trip €1.38); **Madrid** (1½hr.; M-F every 30min. 6-11am and 8:30-11:30pm; €5.33). **Renfe-Iñigo** (☎921 44 12 52) to: **Ávila** (1hr.; M-F 10:30am, 2, 7:30pm; Sa 2pm; Su 7:45pm; €3.75). **Linecar** (☎921 42 77 06) to: **Salamanca** (3hr.; 4 per day M-F 8:50am-5:45pm; Sa 8:50am, 1:30, 5:45pm; Su 5:45pm; €8.25); **Valladolid** (2hr.; 6-13 per day M-Sa 6:45am-9pm, Su 9am-9pm; €5.80).

Public Transportation: Transportes Urbanos de Segovia, Pl. Mayor, 8 (☎921 46 03 29). Fare €0.65; 10-trip **Bono-Bus** pass €4, sold at the office.

Taxis: Radio Taxi (24hr. ☎921 44 50 00). Taxis pull up by the train and bus stations.

ORIENTATION AND PRACTICAL INFORMATION

Take any bus from the train station (€0.65) to **Pl. Mayor,** the city's historic center, or to **Pl. del Azogeojo,** just downhill from Pl. Mayor. The **Po. del Salón** bus (M-F every 30min. 7:45am-10:15pm) runs directly to the steps of **Puerta del Sol.** From the top of the stairs, turn right on C. Judería Vieja, and make the first left onto C. Isabel la Católica. The Pl. del Azoguejo bus (M-F every 30min. 7:30am-10pm, Sa-Su 7:45am-10:15pm) goes to the **aqueduct** and **municipal tourist office.** On foot from the **train station,** turn right, cross the street, and walk toward town along Po. Obispo Quesada, becoming Av. Conde de Sepúlveda, then Po. Ezequiel González, before coming to the bus station (20min.) From the **bus station** (15min.), cross main Po. Ezequiel González, and follow Av. Fernández Ladreda to Pl. del Azoguejo. Both Pl. Mayor (10min.) and the **Alcázar** (20min.) are uphill from Pl. de Azoguejo.

Tourist Office: Regional Office, Pl. Mayor, 10 (☎921 46 03 34; fax 921 46 03 30), in a corner opposite the cathedral. Indispensable map. Open June-Aug. Su-Th 9am-8pm, F-Sa 9am-9pm; Sept.-May M-F 9am-2pm and 5-7pm, Sa-Su 10am-2pm and 5-8pm. **Municipal Office,** Pl. Azoguejo, 1 (☎921 46 29 06; fax 921 46 04 92), at the stairs leading to the aqueduct. Open daily 10am-8pm.

Currency Exchange: Av. Fernández Ladreda is lined with **ATMs. Santander Central Hispano,** C. Fernández Ladreda, 17, just before the aqueduct. Open Apr.-Sept. M-F 8:30am-2pm, Oct.-Mar. M-F 8:30am-2pm, Sa 8:30am-1pm.

Luggage Storage: Lockers at the **train station** (€3). Open daily 6am-10pm.

Emergency: Municipal Police, C. Guadarrama, 26 (☎921 43 12 12).

Hospital: Policlínico, C. San Agustín, 13 (☎921 41 92 72).

Internet Access: Neociber, C. Santa Isabel, 10 (☎921 43 80 42). From Pl. Azoguejo, follow the aqueduct up C. Teodosio el Grande, then turn right on C. Santa Isabel. €0.50 per 15min. Open year-round M-Th 11am-2pm and 4:30-10:30pm, F 11am-2pm and 4:30-11:30pm; Sept.-May Sa 11am-2pm and 5pm-midnight, Su 5-10:30pm; June-Aug. Sa 6pm-midnight, Sun 6-10:30pm.

Post Office: Pl. Dr. Laguna, 5 (☎921 46 16 16), up C. Cronista Lecea from Pl. Mayor. Open M-F 8:30am-8:30pm, Sa 9:30am-2pm. **Postal Code:** 40001.

ACCOMMODATIONS AND CAMPING

Segovia's numerous sights and proximity to Madrid and La Granja make rooms scarce during the summer. Reservations are a must for any of the hotels, especially those in or around major plazas. The *pensiones* are significantly cheaper, but rooms tend to be on the less comfortable side of "basic."

Hotel Las Sirenas, C. Juan Bravo, 30 (☎921 46 26 63; fax 921 46 26 57), down C. Cervantes. Luxurious rooms with TV, shower, telephone, and A/C. Reservations encouraged. Singles €35-40, with bath €40-45; doubles with bath €50-60. AmEx/MC/V. ❶

Pensión Ferri, C. Escuderos, 10 (☎921 46 09 57), off Pl. Mayor. A fortifying experience: rustic but tidy rooms with stone walls, some with windows, overlooking a bountiful garden. Showers €2. Singles €12; doubles €18. ❶

Hostal Don Jaime, Ochoa Ondategui, 8 (☎921 44 47 87). From Pl. Azoguejo, follow the aqueduct down C. Teodosio and turn left. The hostel is around the bend and up the slope. Wood paneling and white walls in rooms with large mirrors. Breakfast €3. Singles €22, with bath €30; doubles €30, with bath €38; triples with bath €48. MC/V. ❷

Hostal Juan Bravo, C. Juan Bravo, 12, 2nd fl. (☎921 46 34 13). From Pl. Azoguejo, take C. Cervantes to Pl. Mayor; look just past Iglesia de San Martín on the left. Doubles €27-28, with bath €29-32; triples €36-38, with bath €39-43. MC/V. ❷

Residencia Juvenil Emperador Teodosio (HI), Av. Conde de Sepulveda, 4 (☎921 44 11 11 or 921 44 10 47). Look for bright red fire escape in front. From the train station, turn right down Po. Obispo Quesada, continuing as it becomes Av. Conde de Sepúlveda (10min.). From the bus station, turn right on Po. Ezequiel González, continuing as it becomes Av. Conde de Sepúlveda (10min.). Private baths. HI card required. Same-day reservations only. Max. 3-night stay. Lockout 2am. Breakfast €1. Open July 1-Aug. 31. Dorms €6.61, with full meals €13.82; over 26 €9.32/€18.63. ❶

Camping Acueducto, C. Borbón, 49/Ctra. Nacional 601, km 112 (☎/fax 921 42 50 00), 2km toward La Granja. Take the AutoBus Urbano (€0.65) from Pl. Azoguejo to Nueva Segovia. Restaurant, supermarket, hot showers, pool, and laundry. Open *Semana Santa*-Sept. Summer €4 per person, per tent, and per car; winter €3.75. ❶

FOOD

To avoid tourist traps, steer clear of Pl. Mayor, Pl. Azoguejo, and any menus posted on worn "medieval" parchment. *Sopa castellana* (soup with bread, eggs, and garlic), *cochinillo asado* (roast suckling pig), and lamb are all regional specialities. Segovia's many sights and steps are ideal for picnicking. **Produce stands** dot C. Juan Bravo and its neighbors, and a **market** comes to Pl. de la Reina Dona Juana every Th, 9am-2:30pm. Buy **groceries** at **%Día,** C. Gobernador Fernández Giménez, 3, off C. Fernández Ladreda (open M-Th 9:30am-8:30pm, F-Sa 9am-9pm).

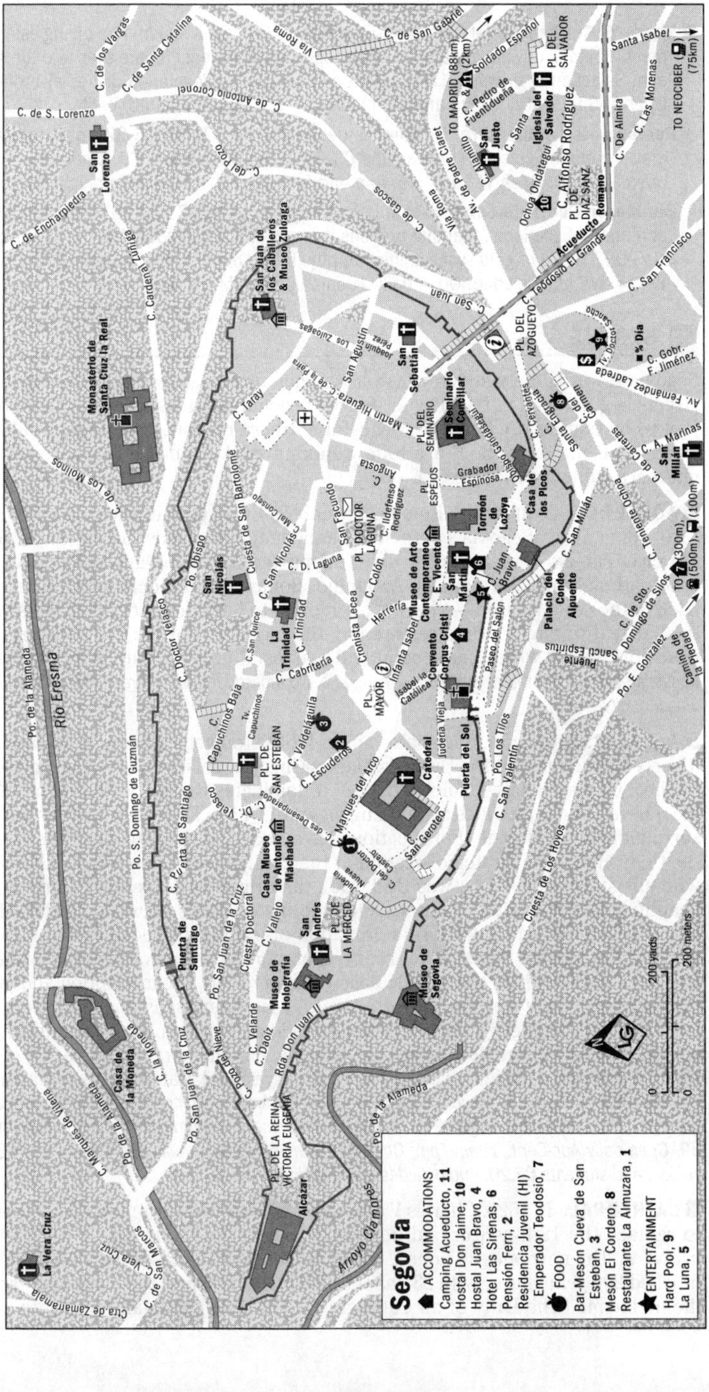
Segovia
ACCOMMODATIONS
Camping Acueducto, 11
Hostal Don Jaime, 10
Hostal Juan Bravo, 4
Hotel Las Sirenas, 6
Pensión Ferri, 2
Residencia Juvenil (HI) Emperador Teodosio, 7
FOOD
Bar-Mesón Cueva de San Esteban, 3
Mesón El Cordero, 8
Restaurante La Almuzara, 1
ENTERTAINMENT
Hard Pool, 9
La Luna, 5
Alcázar
Casa de la Moneda
La Vera Cruz
Monasterio de Santa Cruz la Real
San Lorenzo
San Juan de los Caballeros & Museo Zuloaga
San Sebastián
Seminario Conciliar
Casa de los Picos
Torreón de Lozoya
Palacio del Conde Alpuente
San Martín
Museo de Arte Contemporaneo E. Vicente
Convento Corpus Cristi
Catedral
Puerta del Sol
Puerta de Santiago
Museo de Segovia
Museo de Holografía
San Andrés
Casa Museo de Antonio Machado
La Trinidad
San Nicolás
San Millán
Iglesia del Salvador
San Justo
Acueducto Romano
PL. MAYOR
PL. DE SAN ESTEBAN
PL. DE LA MERCED
PL. DE LA REINA VICTORIA EUGENIA
PL. DEL AZOGUEYO
PL. DEL SEMINARIO
PL. DOCTOR LAGUNA
PL. DE DÍAZ SANZ
PL. DEL SALVADOR
Río Eresma
Arroyo Clamores
TO MADRID (88km) & 11 (2km)
TO NEOCIBER (75km)
TO 7 (300m), (500m), (100m)
200 yards
200 meters

Mesón El Cordero, C. del Carmen, 4-6 (☎921 46 33 45). A superb fine-dining establishment. Spreads of wine, meats, and other specials are a feast for the eyes and the stomach. Selection of *menús* €11-12. Meat entrees €9-15. Vegetarian dishes also offered. Open M-Sa 12:30-4:30pm and 8pm-midnight, Su 12:30-6pm. MC/V. ❸

Restaurante La Almuzara, C. Marqués del Arco, 3 (☎921 46 06 22), past the cathedral. Vegetarian cuisine. Large salads €3.60-9. Luncheon *menú* €9. Meat entrees also offered €6-10. Open W-Su 12:45-4pm and 8pm-midnight, Tu 8pm-midnight. MC/V. ❷

Bar-Meson Cueva de San Esteban, C. Vadelaguila, 15 (☎921 46 09 82), off Pl. Esteaban and C. Escuderos. Plentiful portions in a cavernous *comedor*. Ask the owner about his 2002 "nose of gold" wine-sniffing trophy. Lunch *menú* M-F €8, Sa-Su €10. Entrees €7-14. IVA not included. Open daily 10am-midnight. MC/V. ❸

SIGHTS

Segovia rewards the wanderer. Its picturesque museums, palaces, churches, and streets beg that you put aside your tourist brochure and just explore. Often overlooked by tourists are Segovia's peaceful northern regions, outside the walls and away from the Alcázar. For a long, relaxing walk, tour the monasteries and churches along the Río Eresma.

AQUEDUCT. Built by the Romans around 50 BC to pipe in water from the Río Frío, 18km away, Segovia's serpentine aqueduct commands the entrance to the old city. The two tiers of 163 arches, supported by 128 pillars, span 813m and reach a height of 29m near Pl. Azoguejo. Some 20,000 blocks of granite were used in the construction—without any mortar to hold them together. This spectacular feat of engineering, restored by the monarchy in the 15th century, can transport 30L of water per second and was used until the late 1940s. *(Aqueduct begins just above the tourist office in Pl. Azoguejo. No individual tours offered; consult the tourist office for city tours.)*

ALCÁZAR. From afar, Segovia's Alcázar looks strangely familiar; the rumor that it served as the model for Disney's Magic Kingdom palace may not seem so far-fetched. Of classic late-medieval design, it dominates the far northern end of the old quarter, and it provides astounding views of Queen Eugenia's gardens and the surrounding countryside. Fortifications have occupied this site since the time of the Celts, due to its strategic location at the confluence of two rivers. Alfonso X, who allegedly believed he was God, took the original 11th-century fortress and beautified it. Successive monarchs added to the Alcázar's grandeur, and the final touches were added for the 1474 coronation of Isabel I as Queen of Castilla. The walls of the **Sala de Reyes** (royal room) are adorned with wood- and gold-inlaid friezes of monarchs. In the **Sala de Solio** (throne room), the inscription above the throne reads: "*tanto monta, monta tanto*" (she mounts, as does he). Get your mind out of the gutter—it means that Fernando and Isabel had equal authority as sovereigns. The **Museo Real Colegio de Artilleria,** commemorates the period (1764-1862) in which the Alcázar was used as a artillery school. Canons, charts, and models abound. *(From the Pl. Mayor, follow C. Marqués del Arco, to your right when facing the cathedral entrance, and walk through Pl. de la Merced, following signs through the park. ☎921 46 07 59. Open daily Apr.-Sept. 10am-7pm; Oct.-Mar. 10am-6pm, Oct. weekends 10am-7pm. €3.10, seniors and students €2.20. Audio guides available in English €3.)*

CATHEDRAL. In 1525, Charles V commissioned the construction of a cathedral to replace the 12th-century edifice destroyed in the *Revuelta de las Comunidades*. The new one, he hoped, would tower over the Pl. Mayor. When it was finished 200 years later, with 23 chapels and a gilt treasury, the cathedral earned the nickname "The Lady of all Cathedrals." The **Sala Capitular,** hung with 17th-century tapestries, displays an ornate silver-and-gold chariot. Off the cloister is the **Capilla de Santa Catalina,** filled with incredible crucifixes, chalices, and candelabras. *(☎921 46 22 05. Cathedral open daily Apr.-Oct. 9am-6:30pm, Nov.-Mar. 9:30am-6pm; final entrance 30min. before closing. €2, under 14 and Su until 2:30pm free. Mass M-Sa 10, 11am; Su 11am, 12:30, 2pm.)*

MUSEUMS. The elegant **Museo de Arte Contemporáneo Esteban Vincente** holds a permanent collection of native Segovian Vincente's works and a prestigious exhibition of contemporary art. *(Pl. de las Bellas Artes, just above Pl. de San Martín, off C. de Cervantes. ☎921 46 20 10. Open Tu-Sa 11am-2pm and 4-7pm; Su and festivals 11am-2pm. €2.40, students and seniors €1.20. Th free.)* Ceramics fans shouldn't miss the **Museo Zuloaga,** Pl. Colmenares, a former church and palace that was the home and workshop of Daniel Zuloaga, an early 20th-century artist whose tile murals grace many walls in Madrid. It now holds his paintings, tiles, and ceramics. *(☎921 46 33 48. Open Tu-Sa 10am-2pm and 5-7pm, Su 10am-2pm. €1.20; students, seniors €0.60; Sa-Su free.)*

CASA-MUSEO DE ANTONIO MACHADO. Antonio Machado—literature professor, playwright, and, above all, author of love poems and melancholic verse—never made much money. The poet lived in this small *pensión*-turned-museum from 1919 to 1932, paying 3ptas per day in rent. A short, informative museum tour (in Spanish and English) details major influences in Machado's poetry, including the 1909 death of his first wife, and a later love affair with a married Segovian woman he called "Guiomar" in his writing. The poet's modest room has been left untouched, filled with original manuscripts and portraits (including a Picasso) on its walls. Of his room Machado once wrote (upside down) "*Blanca Hospedería, Celda de Viajero, ¡Con la Sombra Mi!*" (Modest and clean lodging, traveler's cell, alone with my shadow!). Though significantly more humble than the Alcázar, this museum holds its own among Segovia's treasures. *(C. Desamparados, 5. ☎921 46 03 77. From Pl. Mayor, take C. Marqués del Arco, and then right on C. Desamparados. Open W-Su 11am-2pm and 4:30-7:30pm. Spanish and English tours every 30min. €1.20, W free.)*

OUTSIDE THE WALLS. A walk away from the city past the meandering Eresma River offers a welcome change of pace. Be prepared, however, for a grueling uphill trek back to the city. Nearby is the **Iglesia de la Vera Cruz,** a mysterious 12-sided basilica built by the mystical Knights Templar in 1208. *(Follow C. Pozo de la Nieve, on the left with your back to the Alcázar, down the 2nd stone staircase to Po. San Juan de la Cruz. 20min. walk from the bottom. ☎921 43 14 75. Open Apr.-Sept. Tu-Su 10:30am-1:30pm and 3:30-7pm; Nov.-Mar. Tu-Su 10:30am-1:30pm and 3:30-6pm. €1.50.)*

LA MUJER MUERTA According to local folklore, the picturesque mountain silhouette south of Segovia known as **La Mujer Muerta** (The Dead Woman) commemorates a bloody but moving turn of events. *La mujer,* the wife of a chief, was widowed when her twin sons were but young boys. As only one of the two could inherit his father's rule, the mother grew fearful of impending fratricide once the children came of age. She offered her life to God as a sacrifice, hoping this act would save both her sons. Unfortunately, it settled nothing. On a summer's day years later, as the two young men prepared to fight each other for supremacy, it suddenly began to snow. By the time the storm dissipated, a snow-capped mountain had materialized upon the scene of the proposed battleground. As all soon acknowledged, it was the resting body of the twins' mother. *Segovianos* insist that two small clouds float closer to the mountain at dusk—the two sons kissing their mother goodnight.

FESTIVALS AND NIGHTLIFE

From June 24-29, Segovia holds a **fiesta** in honor of San Juan and San Pedro. During the festival there are free open-air concerts on Pl. Azoguejo, as well as dances and fireworks on June 29. **Zamarramala,** 3km northwest of Segovia, hosts the **Fiestas de Santa Agueda** on the weekend following February 5. Women parody men to commemorate a sneak attack on the Alcázar in which the townswomen distracted the castle guards with wine and song. Women take over the town's administration for a day, dress in period costumes, and parade through the streets.

Though the city isn't known for its sleepless nights, when it comes to nightlife, native Segovians go all out. Packed with bars and cafes, Pl. Mayor is the center of Segovian nightlife. The bars filling Pl. Azoguejo and C. Carmen, near the aqueduct, are frequented by the high school set. Club headquarters are C. Ruiz de Alda, off Pl. Azoguejo. You can count on a party every night of the week at **La Luna,** C. Pta. de la Luna, 8. From Pl. Mayor, head down C. Isabel la Católica onto C. Juan Bravo and take your second right. A young local and international crowd mixes it up in this popular discopub, downing cheap shots and Heineken. (☎921 46 26 51. Shots €1. Beer €1.35. Open daily 5pm-4am.) Pick up a cue at **Hard Pool,** C. Dr. Sancho, 4. Take a left at the end of Tr. de Dr. Sancho, off of Av. Fernández Ladreda, just before the bank. The downstairs dance floor has two side bars open on weekends. The club features funk, soul, and Latin jazz nights (Th-Sa 11pm-3am) and occasional rock concerts. (Pool €2.50 per game. Beer €1-1.30. Mixed drinks €3.50-4.50, 2-for-1 mixed drinks daily 11pm-midnight. Open July-Aug. Su-Th 8am-2am, F-Sa 8pm-4am, rest of the year Su-Th 6am-2am, F-Sa 6am-4am.)

DAYTRIP FROM SEGOVIA

LA GRANJA DE SAN ILDEFONSO

La Sepulvedana buses (☎921 42 77 07) run from Segovia to La Granja (20min.; 9-12 per day M-Sa 7:40am-9:30pm, Su 10:30am-10:30pm; return M-Sa 7:20am-9pm, Su 11am-10pm; €1.38 round-trip). From the bus stop, walk uphill through the ornate gates. Signs will lead to the palace and gardens.

A must-see for any visitor to Segovia, the royal palace of La Granja, 9km southeast of the city, is the most extravagant of Spain's four royal summer retreats (the others being El Pardo, El Escorial, and Aranjuez). Felipe V, the first Bourbon King of Spain and grandson of Louis XIV, detested the Habsburgs' austere El Escorial. Nostalgic for the Versailles, where he spent his childhood, he commissioned La Granja in the early 18th century, choosing the sight based on its hunting and gardening potential. A fire destroyed the living quarters in 1918, but the structure was rebuilt in 1932 to house one of the world's finest collections of Flemish tapestries. The highlight of the collection is the nine-tapestry series entitled *The Honours* by Pierre van Aelst; it was said to be an allegory of Emperor Charles's moral development. (☎921 47 00 19. Open daily Apr.-Sept. Tu-Su 10am-6pm; Oct.-Mar. Tu-Sa 10am-1:30pm and 3-5pm, Su 10am-2pm. Mandatory guided tours in Spanish depart every 15min. €4.81; students, under 16, and EU seniors €2.40; children under 5 free. EU citizens free W.) Surrounding the palace are **gardens** designed by Frenchman René Carlier. Carefully manicured hedges form labyrinthine pathways around impressive flowerbeds, but even they are no match for the decadent **Cascadas Nuevas,** an ensemble of illuminated fountains, pools, and pavilions that represents the continents and seasons. (Fountains usually run W-Th and Sa-Su at 5:30pm; consult with the tourist office. Gardens open Nov.-Feb. 10am-6pm, Mar. and Oct. 10am-6:30pm, Apr. 10am-7pm, May-June 16 and Sept. 10am-8pm, June 17-Aug. 10am-9pm. W, Sa, Su €3; students €1.50. M-Tu and Th-F free.)

ÁVILA ☎920

Long ago, "do not enter" was an appropriate message for what are now Ávila's (pop. 50,000) two main attractions: the isolated abode of Santa Teresa de Jesús, and an impressive set of restored 12th-century stone city walls. That message has changed over the years; with recent renovations of many monuments and massive efforts on the part of the city's tourist office, the city begs to be seen. Museums and monuments welcome outsiders to learn about Santa Teresa, depicting her divine visitations and ecstatic visions in exhaustive detail; the celebration of her day (Oct. 15) lasts a full week. The popular and plentiful *yemas de Ávila*, gooey pastry balls made with honey and egg, lure hungry visitors inside the city's walls, which are untouched by pollution, advertisements, or the blare of tourist traffic. Ávila is well worth at least a daytrip from Segovia or Madrid.

TRANSPORTATION

Trains: (☎902 24 02 02), on Av. José Antonio. Info open daily 7am-2pm, 3-8:30pm. To: **El Escorial** (1hr.; 9 per day M-F 5:30am-9:26pm, Sa 9:15am-8:12pm, Su 9:15am-8:15pm; €3); **Madrid** (1½-2hr.; 15-19 per day M-F 5:30am-9:50pm, Sa 8:20am-9:50pm, Su 8:56am-10:13pm; €6.81); **Salamanca** (1¾hr., 5-6 per day 6:40am-8:52pm, €6.81); **Valladolid** (1½hr.; 5-9 per day M-F and Su 9:53am-9:53pm, Sa 9:53am-8pm; €6.81); **Villalba,** for transfer to **Segovia** (1hr., 16 per day, €6.81).

Buses: Av. Madrid, 2 (☎920 22 01 54), at Av. Portugal on the northeast side of town. Schedules are posted in windows. To: **Madrid** (1½hr.; M-F 8 per day 6am-7pm, Sa-Su 4 per day 10am-7pm; €6.05); **Salamanca** (1½hr.; M-Sa 4 per day 9:15am-10pm; Su 6, 10pm; €4.50); **Segovia** (1hr.; M-F 9:30am, 12:45, 6:30pm; Sa 9am; Su 6:45pm; €3.75). **Luggage storage** at bus station. Large bags €0.70, small bags €0.30. Open 9am-7pm.

Taxis: Pl. Santa Teresa (☎920 21 19 59) and at the train station (☎920 35 35 45).

ORIENTATION AND PRACTICAL INFORMATION

The tangled city has two main squares: **Plaza de la Victoria** (or Pl. del Mercado Chico) inside the city walls, and **Plaza de Santa Teresa** just outside. The recently revamped Pl. Santa Teresa is the city's social center. Stick to labeled streets; unidentified alleys usually wind out of town. To get to Pl. Santa Teresa from the **train station,** go straight onto **Po. de la Estación** from the exit, turn right on Av. del Dieciocho, left on Av. Madrid, then left again onto C. Duque de Alba, which leads to the plaza. Alternatively, take bus #1 (€0.60) to Pl. Victoria from the stop 1 block from the station. From the **bus station,** cross the intersection in front, and follow the length of the park to C. Duque de Albe, which leads into Pl. Santa Teresa.

Tourist Office: Pl. Catedral, 4 (☎920 21 13 87; fax 25 37 17), opposite the cathedral. From Pl. Santa Teresa, pass through the gate and take your 2nd right onto C. Alemania. English-speaking staff. Open Su-Th 9am-8pm, F-Sa 9am-9pm.

Currency Exchange: Santander Hispano Central, P. José Tomé, 2 (☎920 21 11 50). Open Apr.-Sept. M-F 8:30am-2pm; Oct.-May M-F 8:30am-2pm, Sa 8:30am-1pm.

Emergency: ☎112.

Police, Av. Inmaculada, 11 (☎920 35 24 24).

Medical Services: Hospital Provincial, Jesús del Gran Poder, 42 (☎920 35 72 00). **Ambulance:** ☎920 22 22 22.

Internet Access: Arroba@25, C. Ferreol Hernández, 1. From Pl. de Italia, take a left onto C. F. Hernández. €0.60 per 15min.

Post Office: Pl. Catedral, 2 (☎920 35 31 06), to the left when facing the cathedral entrance. Open M-F 8:30am-8:30pm, Sa 9:30am-2pm. **Postal Code:** 05001.

ACCOMMODATIONS

Ávila's walls surround numerous comfortable, affordable accommodations. Those near the cathedral and Pl. Santa Teresa fill up in the summer, so call early.

Pensión Continental, Pl. Catedral, 6 (☎920 21 15 02; fax 920 21 15 63), next to the tourist office. TV lounge. All rooms with phones, some with TV. Singles €15.05; doubles €25.84, with bath €33.06; triples €39.07. IVA not included. AmEx/MC/V. ❷

Hostal Jardín, C. San Segundo, 38 (☎920 21 10 74). Older rooms with TV and phone. Breakfast €3. June-Oct. singles €21, with bath €28; doubles €27, with bath €38; triples €40.50, with bath €51. Nov.-July €18/€21/€24/€30/€36/€46. MC/V. ❷

Hostal Casa Felipe, Pl. Victoria, 12 (☎920 21 39 24), near the cathedral. Well-lit rooms with TVs and sinks. Private baths. Singles €19; doubles €32, with bath €38. MC/V. ❷

FOOD

Budget sandwich shops circle Pl. Victoria. The most affordable restaurant area is C. San Segundo, off Pl. Santa Teresa, while the plaza itself holds the more expensive fare. The city has won fame for its *ternera de Ávila* (veal), *mollejas* (sweetbread), and *yemas de Santa Teresa* or *yemas de Ávila.* Every Friday, the **mercado** in Pl. Victoria sells produce from 10am to 2pm. The **supermarket,** C. Juan José Martín, 6, stocks all the basics. From Pl. Teresa, turn left off C. Duque de Alba after the Monasterio de San José (open M-Sa 9:45am-2pm and 5-8pm).

La Taberna del Lagartijo, C. Martín Carramolino, 4 (☎920 22 88 25), just behind the Iglesia de San Juan in Pl. Victoria. An impressive collection of autographed bullfighter photos hang from the walls. *Menú* (M-Th 1-3:30pm and 8-10:30pm; €9). ❷

Restaurante La Posada de la Fruta, Pl. Pedro Davila, 8 (☎920 25 47 02). Airy terrace creates a serene dining experience. *Menú* €12. Sandwiches and a less expensive *menú* (up to €7.90) are offered inside the cafeteria. Open daily 1-4pm and 8:30-11:30pm. ❸

SIGHTS

THE CITY WALLS (LAS MURALLAS). Each summer, shutter-happy hordes attack Ávila's **city walls,** the first stop on the way into its inner city. Modern research has placed construction of the 2500 battlements, 88 towers, and six gates in the 12th century, though legend holds that they are the oldest in Spain, dating back to 1090. **Cimorro,** the most imposing of the towers, doubles as the cathedral's apse. On the inside, in the corner to the right of the cathedral, are all that remains of a former Alcázar, the mere outlines of two windows and two balconies. If you wish to walk along the 2½km of walls, start from the Puerta del Alcázar. *(Walk straight ahead with your back to Pl. Santa Teresa. Open Semana Santa-Oct. 15 daily 11am-8pm; rest of the year Tu-Su 10am-2pm and 4-6pm. €3.50, student groups and under 8 €2.)* The best view of the walls and of Ávila itself is from the **Cuatro Postes,** a four-pillared structure past the Río Adaja, 1½km along the highway to Salamanca. It was here that Santa Teresa was caught by her uncle as she and her brother tried to flee the Islamic south. *(From Pl. Santa Teresa, walk through the inner city and out the Puerta del Puente. Cross the bridge and follow the road to your right for about 1km. Total walk 25min.)*

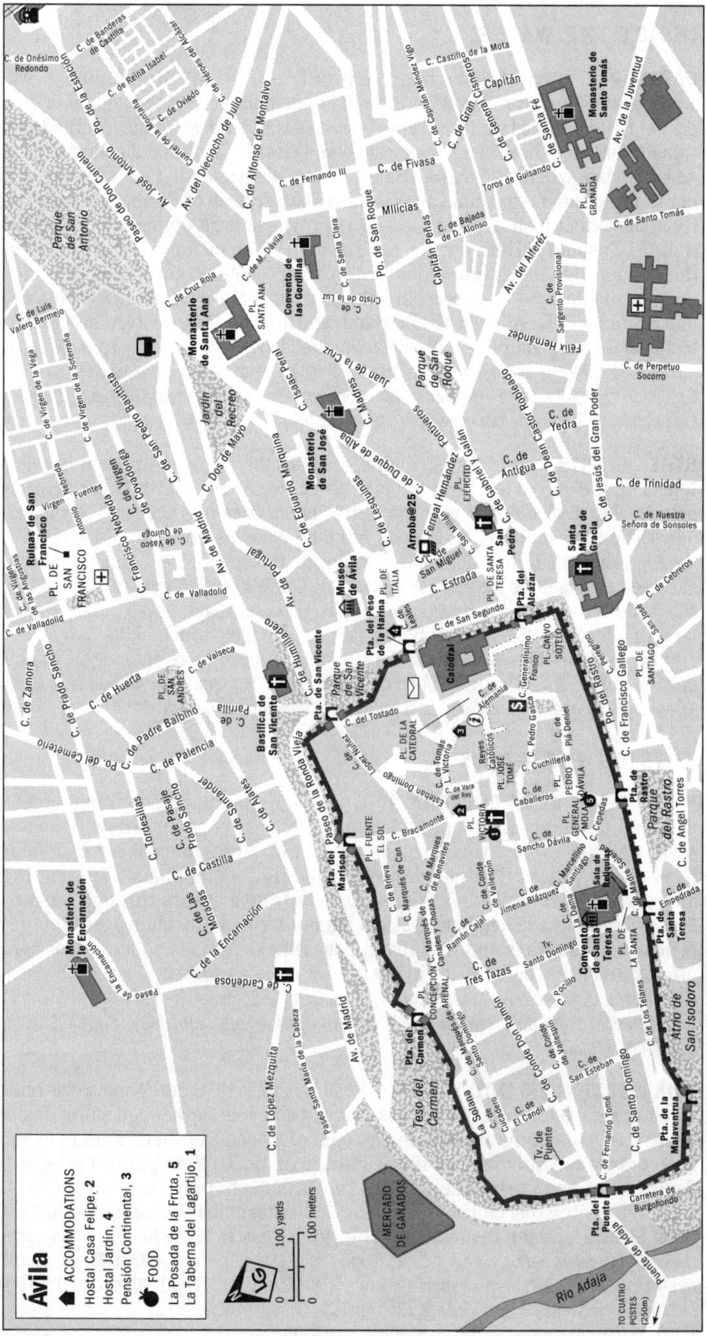

CASTILLA Y LEÓN

INSIDE THE WALLS

CATHEDRAL. Some believe that the profile of the cathedral looming over the watchtowers inspired Santa Teresa's famous metaphor of the soul as a diamond castle. Begun in the late 12th century, Avila's is the oldest Spanish cathedral in the transitional style between Romanesque and Gothic. Look for the **Altar de La Virgen de la Caridad,** where 12-year-old Santa Teresa prostrated herself after the death of her mother. Behind the main altar is the alabaster **tomb** of Cardinal Alonso de Madrigal, an Ávilan bishop and prolific writer whose dark complexion won him the title "El Tostado" (The Swarthy, or "Toasted"). The nickname spread, and during the Golden Age, it became popular to call an aspiring author *un tostado.* The **museum** displays an El Greco portrait, enormous *libros de canti* (hymnals) that make you feel like Alice in Wonderland, and Juan de Arfe's silver, six-leveled **Custodia del Corpus,** complete with swiveling bells. *(From Pl. Santa Teresa, walk through the Puerta, and take the 1st right onto C. Cruz Vieja, which leads to the cathedral. ☎920 21 16 41. Open daily June-Oct. M-Sa 10am-7pm, Su noon-7pm; Nov.-Apr. 10am-1:30pm and 3:30-5:30pm. Last entrance 30min. before closing. Museum €2.50.)*

OTHER SIGHTS. Santa Teresa's admirers built the 17th-century **Convento de Santa Teresa** on the site of her birth. *(From Pl. Santa Teresa, turn left onto C. San Segundo, right onto Po. Rastro, then right through Pta. Santa Teresa. Open daily 8:30am-1:30pm and 3:30-9pm.)* The **Sala de Reliquias,** a small building near the convent, holds some Santa Teresa relics, including her right ring finger, the sole of her sandal, and the cord she used to flagellate herself. *(Open daily Apr.-Oct. 9:30am-1:30pm and 3:30-7:30pm; Nov.-Mar. Tu-Su 10am-1:30pm and 3:30-5:30pm. Last entrance 30min. before closing. Free.)* For a larger collection of items that Santa Teresa may have touched, looked at, or lived among, visit the **Museo de Santa Teresa,** built into the convent's crypt around the corner left of its entrance. *(Open daily Apr.-Oct. 10am-2pm and 4-7pm; Nov.-Mar. Tu-Su 10am-1:30pm and 3:30-5:30pm. Last entrance 30min. before closing; €2.)*

OUTSIDE THE WALLS

MONASTERIO DE LA ENCARNACIÓN. Santa Maria must have found comfort in Christ; it definitely wasn't provided in her 30-year residence, now known as the Monasterio de la Encarnación. Among its interesting relics is a wooden log she used as her pillow. The mandatory guided tour visits Santa Teresa's tiny cell and the small rooms where nuns observed their guests through barred windows. Santa Teresa had her mystical encounter with the child Jesus on the **main staircase.** Upstairs from the cloister, a **museum** features a collection of personal effects given to the convent by wealthier nuns as bribes to procure entrance. *(Po. Encarnación. From Av. Madrid, turn right on C. de la Encarnatión and follow it to the monastery. Museum open daily June-Aug. 9:30am-1pm and 4-7pm; Sept.-May 9:30am-1:30pm and 3:30-6pm. €1.20.)*

MONASTERIO DE SANTO TOMÁS. The Monasterio de Santo Tomás was built as a summer refuge for Fernando and Isabel and as a seat of the Inquisition. Inside the church, in front of the *retablo,* is the tomb of Prince Don Juan, Fernando and Isabel's only son, who died in 1497 at the age of 19. To the right of the altar is the **Capilla de l Santo Cristo,** where Santa Teresa came to pray and confess. Also here are three contrasting cloisters: the Tuscan **Cloister of the Noviciate,** the Gothic **Cloister of Silence,** and the Renaissance-Transition **Cloister of the Kings.** *(Pl. Granada, 1. At the end of C. Jesús del Gran Poder. Church open daily 10am-1pm and 4-8pm. The museum is currently closed for 2-3yr. of renovation. Cloisters Nov.-Mar. Tu-Su 10am-1:30pm and 3:30-5:30pm. Last entrance 30min. before closing. Cloisters €1. Church free.)*

SALAMANCA ☎923

Almost 1100 hundred years after its colonization, Salamanca maintains a distinctly medieval feel. It is a place of sandstone arches, cobblestoned streets, and tall, graceful bell towers. Against this ancient backdrop, however, modern life carries on. During medieval times, La Universidad de Salamanca was grouped with those of Bologne, Paris, and Oxford as one of the "four leading lights of the world." Countless eminent Spanish intellectuals have graced its hallowed halls, including Fray Luis de León, San Juán de la Cruz, Antonio de Nebrija, Fernando de Rojas, and Miguel de Unamuno. The university's fame can be summed up in the Old Latin quote, "Quod deus non dat, nec Salamanca praestat." ("What God does not give, Salamanca doesn't either.") La Universidad de Salamanca continues to add energy, character, and prestige to the city today, attracting thousands of students from all over the world who enliven what locals claim to be Spain's best nightlife.

TRANSPORTATION

Trains: Po. de la Estación (☎ 923 12 02 02). Walk up C. Toro away from Plaza Mayor, take a right onto Av. de Mirat at the large intersection, then a left onto Po. de la Estación keeping the large park to your right. To: **Ávila** (1¾hr.; daily 7:45am, 3:45, 7:40pm, plus M-F 12:45pm; €5.30); **Hendaya** (7hr.; 2:20am, 10:30am; €26); **Lisbon** (6hr., 4:38am, €33); **Madrid** (2½hr., 4 per day 7:45am-7:40pm, €13); **Palencia** (2hr., 1:35pm, €7.80); **Valladolid** (2hr., 4 per day 2:20am-8:50pm, €5.30).

Buses: Av. Filiberto Villalobos, 71-85 (☎923 23 67 17). Walk down C. Prior away from Pl. Mayor to Pl. de las Agustinas. Go straight between the 2 churches into C. Ramón y Cajal, continue to Po. San Vicente. Cross this avenue, and C. Ramón y Cajal becomes C. Filiberto Villalobos. Go straight; the bus station will be on your left. Info window open M-F 8am-8:30pm, Sa 9am-2:30pm and 4:30-6:30pm, Su 10am-2pm and 4-7:30pm. To: **Ávila** (1½hr.; M-Sa 4 per day 6:30am-8:30pm, Su 3:30 and 8:30pm; €4.50); **Barcelona** (11hr.; daily 7:30am and noon, Su and F 4pm; €37.72); **Ciudad Rodrigo** (1hr.; M-F 12 per day 7am-9:30pm, Sa 6 per day 8:30am-6pm; €4.73); **León** (2½hr.; M-F 3 per day 11am-6:30pm, Sa 11am, Su 10pm; €10.60); **Madrid** (3hr.; M-Sa 15 per day 6am-9:30pm, Su 15 per day 8am-11pm; €9.55); **Segovia** (3hr.; M-F 7:30am, 1:30pm; Sa 7:30, 9:30am; Su 1:30, 8:45pm; €8.28); **Valladolid** (1½hr.; M-Sa 6 per day 8am-8pm, Su 4 per day 10:30am-10pm; €6.12); **Zamora** (1hr.; M-F 22 per day 6:40am-10:35pm, Sa 10 per day 7:45am-8:30pm; €3.54).

Taxis: Auto-Taxi (24hr. ☎923 25 00 09) and **Radio Taxi** (24hr. ☎923 25 00 00).

Car Rental: Avis, Po. Canalejas, 49 (☎923 26 97 53). Open M-F 9:30am-1:30pm and 4-7pm, Sa 9am-1:30pm. **Europcar,** Po. Canalejas, 123 (☎923 26 90 41). Open M-F 9am-1:30pm and 4:30-7:30pm, Sa 9am-1:30pm.

ORIENTATION AND PRACTICAL INFORMATION

Majestic **Plaza Mayor** is the social and geographic center of town. Most budget hostels lie south of the plaza around R. Mayor. The **Universidad** and most tourist sights lie south of Pl. Mayor, near **Plaza de Anaya.** From the **train station,** catch bus #1 (€0.60) to Gran Vía and ask to be let off at Pl. San Julián, which is a block from Pl. Mayor. To walk, with your back to the station, turn left down Po. Estación to Pl. España and walk down C. Azafranal (or C. Toro) to Pl. Mayor (20min.). From the **bus station,** either catch bus #4 to Gran Vía or walk down C. Filiberto Villalobos, cross busy Av. Alemania/Po. San Vicente, and go straight down C. Ramón y Cajal. Keep the park on your left; at the end (just after the Iglesia de la Purísima), head left and then right on C. Prior, which runs to Pl. Mayor.

Tourist Office: Municipal, Pl. Mayor, 14 (☎923 21 83 42). Large, helpful office. Open M-Sa 9am-2pm and 4:30-6:30pm, Su 10am-2pm and 4:30-6:30pm. **Provincial,** R. Mayor, 70 (☎923 26 81 71), at the Casa de las Conchas. Entrance on R. Mayor. Open M-F 9am-2pm and 5-7pm, Sa-Su 10am-2pm and 4-7pm. **Information booths** open occasionally July-Sept.

Currency Exchange: ATMs on C. Toro and R. Mayor. **Banesto:** C. Toro, 13 (☎902 30 70 30). Open Oct.-Mar. M-F 8:30am-2pm, Sa 8:30am-1pm.

Luggage Storage: At the train station, Po. de la Estación (€3) and bus station, Av. Filiberto Villalobos (€0.60 per item, 7am-7:45pm).

Emergency: ☎112. **Police:** ☎092 or 923 27 91 38.

Pharmacy: Farmacia Amador Felipe, C. Toro, 25 (☎923 21 41 24), at the corner of Brocense. Friendly service. English spoken. Open daily 9:30am-10pm.

Hospital: Hospital Clínico Universitario, Po. San Vicente, 108 (☎923 29 11 00).

Internet Access: Informática Abaco Bar, C. Zamora, 7 (☎923 26 15 89), near Pl. Mayor. €1.20 per hr. Open M-F 9:30am-2am, Sa-Su 11am-2am.

Post Office: Gran Vía, 25-29 (☎923 28 09 02). **Lista de Correos.** Open M-F 8:30am-8:30pm and Sa 9:30am-2pm. **Postal Code:** 37080.

ACCOMMODATIONS AND CAMPING

Thanks to floods of student visitors, reasonably priced *hostales* and *pensiones* pepper the streets of Salamanca (especially off Pl. Mayor and C. Meléndez). Try to make reservations a day or two in advance, especially during July and August, when Salamanca becomes overrun by hostel-hungry students and tourists.

Pensión Las Vegas, C. Meléndez, 13, 1st fl. (☎923 21 87 49). Accessible by R. Mayor and R. Antigua. TVs and friendly owners. Doubles €24; triples with bath €36. MC/V. ❶

Pensión Estefanía, C. Jesús, 3-5 (☎923 21 73 72), off Pl Mayor. Comfortable rooms and convenient location. Doubles with private shower €22; triples with shower €30. ❶

Pensión Lisboa, C. Meléndez, 1 (☎923 21 43 33). Everything in this place is pink—the stucco walls, the bedspreads, even the radiators. Rooms are small but clean, beds are comfortable, and some rooms have rooftop city views. Singles €12; doubles €24. ❶

Pensión Villanueva, C. San Justo, 8, 1st fl. (☎923 26 88 33). Exit Pl. Mayor via Pl. Poeta Iglesias, cross the street, and take the first left. Let Sra. Manuela share her local lore and gossip. Reservations only accepted for F-Su. Singles €12; doubles €24. Extra beds available at €12 per person. ❶

Hostal Emperatriz, R. Mayor, 18 (☎/fax 923 21 91 56). This hostel operates out of the 2-star hotel next door. To register, go to the hotel lobby. Spacious rooms include full bathroom and telephone. Try to get a room facing R. Mayor for a great view. Breakfast €2.10. Singles €24; doubles €33; triples €42. Prices don't include tax. MC/V. ❷ Next door, the pricier **Hotel Emperatriz** offers rooms with a medieval ambiance: wooden old-style beds and hand-carved drawers. Singles €36; doubles €51. MC/V. ❹

Hostal Anaya, C. Jesús, 18 (☎923 27 17 73). Steps away from the Pl. Mayor and most historical sights, Hostal Anaya offers clean rooms, heating, and friendly service that will make you feel at home. Singles €24; doubles €42; triples €54; quads €72. ❷

Camping: Regio on Ctra. Salamanca (☎923 13 88 88), 4km toward Madrid. Albertur buses leave from Gran Vía every 30min. near Pl. de San Julián. First-class sites with hot showers. Tennis courts and restaurants in a tourist complex next door. €2.70 per person, €5.11 per tent, and €2.70 per car. MC/V. ❶

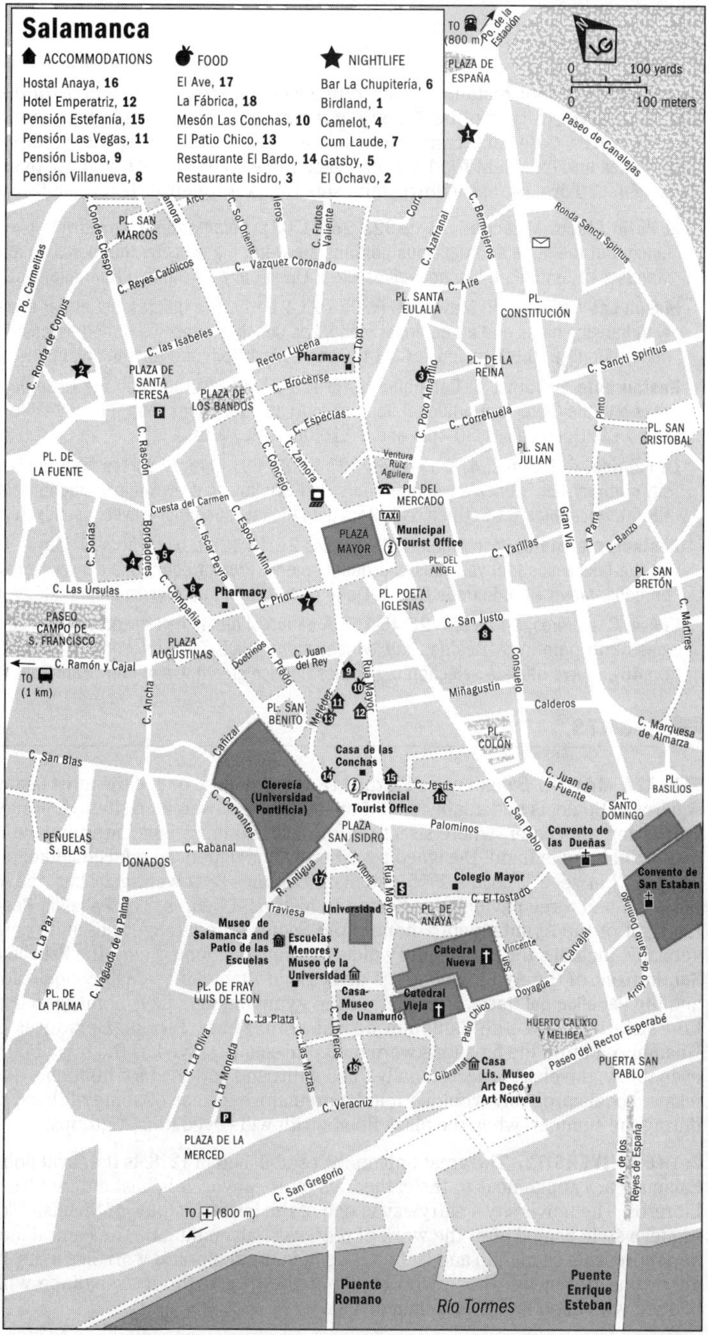
Salamanca
ACCOMMODATIONS
Hostal Anaya, 16
Hotel Emperatriz, 12
Pensión Estefanía, 15
Pensión Las Vegas, 11
Pensión Lisboa, 9
Pensión Villanueva, 8
FOOD
El Ave, 17
La Fábrica, 18
Mesón Las Conchas, 10
El Patio Chico, 13
Restaurante El Bardo, 14
Restaurante Isidro, 3
NIGHTLIFE
Bar La Chupitería, 6
Birdland, 1
Camelot, 4
Cum Laude, 7
Gatsby, 5
El Ochavo, 2
TO (800 m) Po. de la Estación
PLAZA DE ESPAÑA
0 100 yards
0 100 meters
Paseo de Canalejas
Ronda Sancti Spiritus
C. Bermejeros
C. Azafranal
PL. SAN MARCOS
Condes Crespo
C. Reyes Católicos
C. Sol Oriente
C. Frutos Valiente
C. Vazquez Coronado
Po. Carmelitas
C. Ronda de Corpus
C. Aire
PL. SANTA EULALIA
PL. CONSTITUCIÓN
C. las Isabeles
Rector Lucena
Pharmacy
C. Toro
C. Brocense
PLAZA DE SANTA TERESA
PLAZA DE LOS BANDOS
C. Pozo Amarillo
PL. DE LA REINA
C. Sancti Spiritus
C. Especias
C. Correhuela
C. Pinto
PL. SAN CRISTOBAL
PL. DE LA FUENTE
C. Rascón
C. Concejo
C. Zamora
Ventura Ruiz Aguilera
PL. SAN JULIAN
PL. DEL MERCADO
Cuesta del Carmen
C. Iscar Peyra
C. Espoz y Mina
TAXI
PLAZA MAYOR
Municipal Tourist Office
Gran Via
La Parra
C. Banzo
C. Sorias
Bordadores
PL. DEL ANGEL
C. Varillas
C. Las Úrsulas
C. Compañía
Pharmacy
C. Prior
PL. POETA IGLESIAS
PL. SAN BRETÓN
PASEO CAMPO DE S. FRANCISCO
PLAZA AUGUSTINAS
C. San Justo
C. Mártires
TO (1 km)
C. Ramón y Cajal
Doctrinos
C. Prado
C. Juan del Rey
Rua Mayor
Consuelo
Miñagustin
C. Ancha
PL. SAN BENITO
Meléndez
Calderos
C. Marquesa de Almarza
Cañizal
PL. COLÓN
C. San Blas
Casa de las Conchas
C. Juan de la Fuente
C. Jesús
Clerecía (Universidad Pontificia)
Provincial Tourist Office
PL. BASILIOS
PL. SANTO DOMINGO
C. Cervantes
C. San Pablo
PLAZA SAN ISIDRO
Palominos
Convento de las Dueñas
PEÑUELAS S. BLAS
C. Rabanal
DONADOS
Convento de San Estaban
R. Antigua
F. Vitoria
Rua Mayor
Colegio Mayor
C. El Tostado
Traviesa
Universidad
PL. DE ANAYA
Arroyo de Santo Domingo
C. La Paz
C. Vaguada de la Palma
Museo de Salamanca and Patio de las Escuelas
Escuelas Menores y Museo de la Universidad
Catedral Nueva
Vincente
San
C. Carvajal
PL. DE LA PALMA
PL. DE FRAY LUIS DE LEON
Casa-Museo de Unamuno
Catedral Vieja
Doyagüe
C. La Plata
Patio Chico
HUERTO CALIXTO Y MELIBEA
C. Libreros
C. Las Mazas
C. La Oliva
C. La Moneda
C. Gibraltar
Casa Lis. Museo Art Decó y Art Nouveau
Paseo del Rector Esperabé
PUERTA SAN PABLO
C. Veracruz
PLAZA DE LA MERCED
Av. de los Reyes de España
C. San Gregorio
TO (800 m)
Puente Romano
Río Tormes
Puente Enrique Esteban

FOOD

Salamanca is full of restaurants offering everything from *salamantinto* dishes like *chanfaina* (a type of beef stew) and *tostón asado* (roasted baby pork) to cheeseburgers. Cafes and restaurants surrounding Pl. Mayor provide great views of the plaza and excellent food; you can get a three course meal for a little over €8. **Champión,** C. Toro, 64, has a downstairs supermarket (open M-Sa 9:15am-9:15pm).

El Patio Chico, Meléndez, 13 (☎923 26 51 03). *Salamantinos* crowd this place at lunch, but the large and delicious portions are worth the wait. Try the *morcilla picante*. *Menús* €11, entrees €4-8, *bocadillos* €2-3. Open daily 1-4pm and 8pm-midnight. ❷

Mesón Las Conchas, R. Mayor, 16 (☎923 21 21 67). The quintessential *bar español*. With hanging hams and a traditional *menú*, Las Conchas offers great food at reasonable prices. *Menú* €10.50, *raciones* €6-14. Open daily 1-4pm and 8pm-midnight. MC/V. ❸

Restaurante El Bardo, C. Compañía, 8 (☎923 21 90 89), between the Casa de Conchas and the Clerecía. Traditional Spanish food and low prices keep the tiled tables full. *Menú* €9. Open daily 1:30-4pm and 9-11:30pm. MC/V. ❷

La Fábrica, C. Libreros, 47 and 49 (☎923 26 85 69). Directly across from the University's library, La Fábrica's wooden floors and 30s music draw mainly students. *Menú* €8.50, *bocadillos* €3-6. Open daily 9am until the last customer leaves, usually 2am. ❷

Restaurante Isidro, Pozo Amarillo, 19 (☎923 26 28 48), a block from Pl. Mayor. Don't let the fake roses fool you—this is a quality place. Prompt courteous service and large portions. *Menú* €10. Entrees €7-11. Open daily 1-4pm and 8pm-midnight. MC/V. ❷

El Ave, C. Libreros, 24 (☎923 26 45 11). A beautiful dining hall decorated with stained glass and paintings. Besides the typical *menús* (€8.70) and entreés (starting at €5.40), El Ave offers a selection of pastries and ice cream. Open daily 8am-2am. ❷

SIGHTS

PLAZA MAYOR. Salamanca's Plaza Mayor, considered one of the most beautiful squares in Spain, is undeniably one of the best people-watching sites. Hundreds of tables ring the center, where street performers and musicians entertain and couples stroll hand in hand. Designed by Alberto Churriguera (see **Architecture,** p. 71) and built between 1729 and 1755, the plaza contains 88 towering arches, the **Ayuntamiento,** and three pavilions dedicated to historical figures. The **Pabellón Real,** to the right of the Ayuntamiento, honors the Spanish monarchy (and, quite controversially, includes the 20th-century dictator Franco among them); the **Pabellón del Sur,** in front of the Ayuntamiento, is dedicated to famous Spanish conquistadors; and the **Pabellón del Oeste,** to the left of the Ayuntamiento, pays homage to important *salmantinos* like San Juan de Sahagún, Santa Teresa, Cervantes, and Unamuno. Before the pavilions were built, the square served as the town bullring; even today, the plaza is occasionally filled with sand and used for bullfights during feasts. Locals probably wouldn't mind a premature release of some of those bulls during the summer, when the plaza floods with wide-eyed tourist groups.

THE UNIVERSITY. The great university, established in 1218, is the focal point of Salamanca. Though next to the cathedrals on R. Mayor, it is best entered from C. Libreros. The university's entryway is one of the best examples of Spanish Plateresque, a style named after the work of *plateros* (silversmiths). The central medallion represents Fernando and Isabel. Hidden in the sculptural work lies a tiny frog; according to legend, those who can spot the frog without assistance will be blessed with good luck and even marriage.

UNDER PRESSURE Look closely at the walls of the University and Cathedral and you'll see faded red scrawlings on the sandstone; this is not graffiti. Eight hundred years ago, students of the University of Salamanca used to attend class in the Old Cathedral. They would come to the church the night before their final exam to pray for success; the rigorous oral test (in logic and rhetoric) was administered the next day in front of *La Capilla de Santa Bárbara,* now known as *La Capilla del Estudiante.* Those who were fortunate enough to pass left the Cathedral through the main entrance to shouts of congratulations from the throng of anxious *salmantinos* waiting outside. Later that evening, the town would host a bullfight in honor of the new graduates; the fresh blood of the bull was then mixed with a flour paste and used to paint the names of the new doctors on the University and Cathedral walls.

The old lecture halls inside are open to the public. Entering the cool stone foyer feels like stepping into another era; a cough echoes through the building and outdoor noise disappears. The 15th-century classroom **Aula Fray Luis de León** has been left in more or less its original state; students in medieval times considered the hard benches luxurious, as most students then sat on the floor. A plaque bears Unamuno's famous love poem to the students of Salamanca. The **Paraninfo** (auditorium) contains Baroque tapestries and a portrait of Carlos IV attributed to Goya. The 18th-century **chapel,** almost gaudy with red curtains on the walls, red velvet chairs, and a red altar, contains the burial sight of Fray Luis. The **Antigua Biblioteca** (one of Europe's oldest libraries), on the second floor, is the most spectacular room of all, located atop a magnificent Plateresque staircase.

The university entrance faces the **Patio de las Escuelas.** The statue here portrays Fray Luis de León, a university professor and one of the most respected literati of the Golden Age. A Hebrew scholar and classical Spanish stylist, Fray Luis was arrested by the Inquisition for translating Solomon's *Song of Songs* into Castilian and for preferring the Hebrew version of the Bible to the Latin one. After five years of imprisonment, he returned to the university and began his first lecture, *"Como decíamos ayer..."* ("As we were saying yesterday..."). The patio is surrounded by the **Escuelas Menores,** with a smaller version of the main entryway's Plateresque facade. Don't miss the **University Museum.** Walk through the hallway on the left corner of the patio; the museum is on your left. The reconstructed **Cielo de Salamanca,** the library's famous 15th-century fresco of the zodiac painted on the ceiling by the celebrated Fernando Gallego, is preserved here in all its splendor. Take a peek at the intricate strongbox with its many locks. *(From Pl. Mayor follow R. Mayor, veer right onto R. Antigua, then left onto C. Libreros; the university is on the left. University ☎ 923 29 44 00. Museum ☎ 923 29 12 25. Open M-F 9:30am-1:30pm and 4-7:30pm, Sa 9:30am-1:30pm and 4-7pm, Su 10am-1:30pm. University and museum €2.40, students and seniors €1.20.)*

CATEDRAL NUEVA. It took 220 years to build this striking Gothic Spanish building (1513-1733). While several architects decided to retain the original late Gothic style, they could not resist adding touches from later periods, most notably to its Baroque tower, one of the tallest in Spain. Inside, the cathedral is separated into many small chapels dedicated to various saints or important locals. These surround a center chapel and the enormous organ, whose pipes rise up toward the high ceiling. The cathedral was recently renovated, and the architects left their marks: look for the astronaut in the left side of the main door. *(From Pl. Mayor, walk down R. Mayor into Pl. Anaya; the Catedral Nueva is in front of you. Open Apr.-Sept. daily 9am-2pm and 4-8pm; Oct.-Mar. 9am-1pm and 4-6pm. Free.)*

CATEDRAL VIEJA. The smaller Catedral Vieja (1140) was built in the Romanesque style. Inside the cupola, apocalyptic angels separate the sinners from the saved. The oldest original part of the cathedral is the **Capilla de San Martín,** with brilliant frescoes dating from 1242. Look for the image of the Virgen de la Vega, Salamanca's patron saint. The **Capilla de Santa Bárbara,** or the Capilla del Título, was what students used to face as they took their final exams. Other points of interest include a document signed by El Cid Campeador and the crucifix he held at his death. The **museum** features a paneled ceiling by Fernando Gallego and houses the Mudéjar Salinas organ, one of the oldest in Europe. Be sure to check out the famed **Patio Chico,** behind the cathedral, where students congregate to chat and play music. It is ideal for getting a splendid view of both cathedrals. *(Enter through the Catedral Nueva. Museum ☎923 21 74 76. Cathedral open Apr.-Sept. daily 10am-1:30pm and 4-7:30pm. Cathedral, cloister, and museum €3, students €2.25, children €1.50.)*

CASA LIS MUSEO ART NOUVEAU Y ART DECO. Cross the threshold of this odd-looking building and enter the bizarre. Salamancan industrialist Miguel de Lis collaborated with modernist architect Joaquín Vargas to design the building, which now showcases Lis's eclectic art collection. Exhibits range from the elegant (fans signed by such noteworthies as Salvador Dalí) to the odd (porcelain dolls with two faces), to the racy (small sculptures of animals and people in compromising positions). *(C. Gibraltar, 14, behind the cathedrals. ☎923 12 14 25. Open Apr.-Oct.15 Tu-F 11am-2pm and 5-9pm, Sa-Su 11am-9pm; Oct. 16-Mar. 31 Tu-F 11am-2pm and 4-7pm, Sa-Su 11am-8pm. €2.10, students €1.50, children and Tu mornings free.)*

CONVENTO DE SAN ESTEBAN. While on a fundraising endeavor, Columbus spent time in one of Salamanca's most dramatic monasteries, the Convento de San Esteban, off of C. San Pablo and Palominos. When illuminated by the afternoon sun, the stoning of St. Stephen and the crucifixion of Christ come alive on its facade. The beautiful **Claustro de los Reyes** (Kings' Cloister), with its Gothic interior and Plateresque exterior, is visibly the product of two different eras. José Churriguera's central altarpiece (1693) is a masterpiece of Spanish Baroque. Also worth seeing is the **Panteón de los Teólogos,** home to the remains of the most decorated Dominican theologians of the University. *(☎923 21 50 00. Open Apr.-Sept. Tu-Su 9am-1pm and 4-8pm; Oct.-Mar. 9am-1pm and 4-6pm. €1.20, free W mornings.)*

CASA DE LAS CONCHAS. From Pl. Mayor, exit onto pedestrian R. Mayor (through the archway opposite the clock). Follow this street until you reach a plaza with a water fountain. Take a right and look up at the face of the building on your right. Yup, those are sandstone shells. The 15th-century Casa de las Conchas (House of Shells), with over 300 large scallop halves, is one of Salamanca's most famous landmarks. Pilgrims who journeyed to Santiago de Compostela (see p. 526) traditionally wore shells to commemorate their visit to the tomb of St. James. According to legend, the owner of the *casa* created this monument either to honor the renowned pilgrimage or to honor his wife, whose family shield was decorated with scallops. Legend has it that the Jesuits leveled every house in the area to build the college; the Casa de las Conchas was the only one that was not bought, despite the Jesuits' shady offer of one gold coin for every sandstone shell. The building now serves as a public library and houses the provincial tourist office. *(C. Compañía, 39. Library ☎923 26 93 17. Open M-F 9am-9pm, Sa-Su 9am-2pm and 4-7pm. Free.)*

LA CLERECÍA. Directly across from the Conchas is the Clerecía (Royal College of the Holy Spirit), the main building of La Pontíficia Universidad de Salamanca, a private educational institution unaffiliated with La Universidad de Salamanca. When Saint Ignatius of Loyola, founder of the Jesuits, arrived in Salamanca in the early 16th century, he was imprisoned for 20 days for heresy. Once the Jesuits were finally recognized by the Church, Loyola decided to claim recompense for

LA TUNA...MORE FRAT THAN FISH In Spain, it's not dolphins who are threatened by the "tuna industry." According to legend, it is young women who need to watch out, lest their hearts be captured unawares by a charming bard. *Las tunas* are university student music bands dating back to the reign of King Alfonso X the Wise, in 1215. Originally founded by students who needed to earn money for their studies, *tunas* have become a form of social competition in modern universities, as well as paid entertainment for private parties and high-class restaurants. To become a *tuna*, candidates *(pardillos)* must prove their wit and artistic ability in a series of tests, culminating with the consumption of a bowl of The Soup of Charity, a painfully fiery concoction mixed by veteran *tunas*. The chosen ones take an oath over a tambourine, the symbol of the *tuna*, and are given a *tuna* sash and nickname for life.

his mistreatment by creating an enormous church and college of the Jesuit Order. Founded in 1611 with the financial aid of Queen Margarita de Austria (Felipe III's wife), the college actually owes its name to King Carlos III, who expelled the Jesuits from Spain and made the institute property of the Real Clerecía in the 18th century. The building has a unique U-shaped groundplan, allowing visitors to peer over the Cloister of Studies into the lower gallery and courtyard. *(☎923 26 46 60. Open for Mass M-Sa 1:15 and 7pm, Su noon. Free.)*

MUSEO DE SALAMANCA. Across from the university in the Patio de Escuelas, the Museum of Salamanca occupies an astounding 15th-century building that was once home to Alvarez Albarca, physician to Fernando and Isabel. Along with the Casa de las Conchas, this structure is among Spain's most important examples of 15th-century architecture. The museum has an intriguing collection of painting and sculpture as well as some temporary archaeology and ethnology exhibits. Its most important canvases are Juan de Flandes's portrait of Saint Andrew and Luis de Morales's *Llanto por Cristo muerto*. *(Po. de Escuelas, 2. ☎923 21 22 35. Open Tu-Sa 8am-2pm and 4:30-8pm, Su 9:30am-2:30pm. €1.20, students free.)*

CASA MUSEO DE UNAMUNO. Miguel de Unamuno, Rector of the University at the beginning of this century, is revered as one of the founding figures of the Spanish literary movement known as the "Generation of '98." Unamuno passionately opposed dictatorship and encouraged his students to do so as well. His stand against General Primo de Rivera's 1923 *coup d'état* led to his dismissal from the rector's post; he was triumphantly reinstated some years later. Unamuno lived in this house during his years as rector and his original furniture has been preserved, along with many framed photos and letters. *(To the right of the university's main entrance. ☎923 29 44 00, ext. 1196. Open July-Sept. Tu-F 9:30am-1:30pm, Sa-Su 10am-1:30pm; Oct.-June Tu-F 9:30am-1:30pm and 4-6pm, Sa-Su 10am-2pm. Research room open M-F 9am-2pm. Mandatory tour in Spanish every 30min., €1.80. Ring bell if house appears closed.)*

PUENTE ROMANO. This 2000-year-old Roman bridge, spanning the scenic Río Tormes at the edge of the city, was once part of an ancient Roman road called the *Camino de la Plata* (Silver Way). The *Camino* ran from Mérida in Extremadura to Astorga and was heavily traveled during the Roman occupation of Spain. In medieval times, the *Camino de la Plata* was the route most Andalucian and Castilian Christians took to complete their pilgrimage to Santiago de Compostela. The bridge is guarded at its end by a headless granite bull called the **Toro Ibérico.** Though it dates back to pre-Roman times, the bull gained fame in the 16th century when it appeared in *Lazarillo de Tormes*, the prototype of the picaresque novel and a predecessor of *Don Quijote;* in one episode the novel's hero gets his head slammed into the bull's stone ear after he cheats his employer.

ENTERTAINMENT

Lugares, a free, slim pamphlet distributed at the tourist office and at some bars, lists everything from movies and special events to bus schedules. Posters at the **Colegio Mayor** (Palacio de Anaya, across from the Catedral Nueva) advertise university events, free films, and student theater. The city hosts many events and festivals during the summer. On June 12, in honor of San Juan de Sahagún, there is a **corrida de toros** charity event in **La Plaza de Toros** en Plaza Glorieta to the northeast of old city as well as parades and instant craft fairs throughout the city. September 8-21, Salamanca indulges in festivals and exhibitions, most honoring the bullfight that has made the region's *ganaderías*, or bull farms, the best in all Spain. This is also a fun place to be during *Semana Santa*, with local traditions like **Lunes de Aguas,** celebrated the Monday after Easter. This feast remembers the tradition of banishing local prostitutes across the river during the 40 days of Lent; they used to return triumphantly on *Lunes de Quasimodo*, when eager *salmantinos* would picnic along the bridge to await their arrival.

NIGHTLIFE

Salmantinos claim Salamanca to be the best place in Spain *para salir de marcha* (to party). It is said that there is one bar for every hundred people that live here; though this may sound exaggerated, it may well be true. *Chupiterías* (bars mostly selling shots), *bares*, and *discotecas* line nearly every street, and when some close at 4am, others are just opening. *La Marcha* starts in Pl. Mayor, where members of local college or graduate-school **tunas** (medieval-style student troubadour groups) finish their rounds. Dressed in traditional black capes, they strut around the plaza with guitars, mandolins, *bandurrías*, and tambourines, serenading women while students start drinking in the many bars and *mesones* in the area. Student nightlife spreads out to **Gran Vía, C. Bordadores,** and side streets. Spacious discos/bars, or *pafs*, blast music into the wee hours of the morning. **C. Prior** and **C. Rúa Mayor** are full of bars; locals gather in the charming *terrazas* on **Pl. de la Fuente,** off Av. Alemania. More intense partying occurs off **C. Varillas.**

Birdland, C. Azafranal, 57, facing Pl. España. Drink to modern funk jazz. Take a break from the club scene to enjoy a lower-decibel conversation. Beer €1.50-2.40. Mixed drinks €3-6. Open Su-Th 4pm-3am, F-Sa 4pm-4:30am; opens at 6:30pm in summer.

Bar El Ochavo, Pl. San Juan Bautista, 7. A typical *bar de copas* where Spaniards begin their nights of partying. Drink the famous *litros* of beer or sangría for €3, or just buy a bottle of wine, starting at €4, and talk until you feel like dancing.

Bar La Chupitería, Pl. Monterrey, at C. Prior and Bordadores. Unusually low prices have built La Chupitería's reputation among students as a premier pre-gaming establishment. Shots €0.90, *chupitos* (slightly larger than shots) €1.

Gatsby, C. Bordadores, 6 (☎923 21 72 74). Across the street from Camelot, this club draws American and Salamancan students from their rooms with its disco beat. Beer €1.80. Sangría €2.10. Mixed drinks €4.25. Specials nearly every night. Open Su-Th 10pm-4am, F-Sa 7pm-6:30am.

Cum Laude, C. Prior, 5. On this bar's dance floor, a replica of the Plaza Mayor, partying starts at 11pm and doesn't stop until 4:30am. Mixed drinks €4-7. No sneakers.

Camelot, C. Bordadores, 3. Holy ruins shake to the techno beat–this club was built in the remains of an old church. Mixed drinks start at €3.

DAYTRIPS FROM SALAMANCA

CIUDAD RODRIGO

Buses come from the Salamanca station, Av. Filiberto Villalobos, 71-85 (1hr.; M-F 13 per day 7am-9:30pm, Sa 6 per day 8:30am-6pm, Su 4 per day 11am-10pm; €4.57). Buy tickets from La Pilar, windows 23 and 24. Last bus leaves Ciudad Rodrigo at 7:30pm.

The hushed, labyrinthine streets and 18th-century ramparts of Ciudad Rodrigo, a sleepy town just 27km from Portugal, harbor myriad sandstone cathedrals, Roman ruins, and medieval masonry. Although the town was originally a Roman outpost, today it is known for its namesake, Conde Rodrigo González Girón, the count who brought the site back to life in 1100 after the destruction of the Moorish invasions. The **cathedral** is the town's masterpiece. Originally a Romanesque church commissioned by Fernando II of León, it was later modified in the 16th-century Gothic style. The **coro** (choir) was the masterpiece of Rodrigo Alemán, who worked on it from 1498 to 1504. Look for the sculptor's signature—a carving of his head hidden among the rest of the carvings. The two 16th-century organs star in a series of concerts every August. The cathedral's **claustro** (cloister) alone merits a trip to Ciudad Rodrigo. The columns are covered with figures doing everything from making love to playing peek-a-boo to flirting with cannibalism. The cathedral's **museum** is filled with unique pieces, including an ancient clavichord, the cathedral's "ballot box," richly embroidered robes and slippers worn by bishops and priors, and Velázquez's *Llanto de Adán y Eva por Ariel muerto*. (Cathedral open daily 10am-1pm and Su 4-7pm. Free. Cloister and museum open daily 10am-1pm and Su 4-7pm. €2. Tours in Spanish.) To reach the cathedral from the tourist office (see below for more info on the tourist office), turn left onto Pl. Amayuelas into town, and then take your first right onto Pl. de San Salvador. The cathedral is to your left.

Also of note is the 14th-century **Castillo de Enrique II de Trastámara,** built by Gonzalo Arias de Genizaro. Ciudad Rodrigo was once the site of a bloody face-off between Trastámara and Pedro I El Cruel; today the castle serves as a tranquil *parador*. The castle's surroundings afford a view of the Río Agueda and the **ancient Roman bridge** that spans it. An ancient **verraco** (pig), Ciudad Rodrigo's only other remnant of its ancient Roman settlers, stands guard in front of the castle.

The **bus station** (☎923 46 10 09) is on Campo de Toledo, 3-25. From the station entrance, take a left onto Campo de Toledo (with the station behind you) and then the second right onto Av. Yurramendi (uphill). Pass through the stone arch; the **tourist office,** Pl. Amayuelas, 5, is immediately on your left, across the street and before the cathedral. (☎923 46 05 61. Open M-F 9am-2pm and 5-7pm, Sa-Su 10am-2pm and 5-8pm. French also spoken.) Most **restaurants, bars, and cafes** in town cluster on Pl. Mayor and on the streets around it. If you are looking for traditional Spanish cuisine, try **Cafetería Arcos** 2, Pl. Mayor, 17 (☎923 46 06 64), where a three-course menu is €8.50. Also near Pl. Mayor is **Pizzaria Tussilago** 1, C. Julián Sánchez, 7 (☎923 48 22 26), that offers pizzas and other dishes starting at €5. To get to Pl. Mayor from the tourist office, continue straight on Pl. de Amayuelas into town, then turn left onto C. del Cardenal Pacheco just before Pl. de San Salvador and make a left again in C. Julián Sánchez; Pl. Mayor is at the end of this street.

ZAMORA

Zamora is most easily reached by buses, which are more frequent and travel to more cities than trains. Trains leave from Zamora's C. de Estación (24hr. ☎980 52 11 10) at the end of C. Alfonso Peña and go to: Madrid (3hr.; 3:50am, 2:23, 6:20pm; €21.08) and Valladolid (1½hr., 8:32am and 7:40pm, €6.30).

Alone atop a cliff over the Río Duero, Zamora (pop. 65,000) is a beguiling mix of modern and medieval: 11th-century churches rub shoulders with Mango and Zara,

15th-century palaces harbor Internet cafes and luxury hotels, tangled and narrow streets empty onto grand *avenidas*, and the magnificent 12th-century cathedral overlooks modern subdivisions and steel bridges in the distance. While locals enjoy the town's modern conveniences, it is Zamora's history as one of the most powerful cities in medieval Castile that constantly lures Spanish tourists. In nearly every plaza and street, monuments stand to Zamora's infamous figures, from Viriato, the fierce Roman warrior born in Zamora, and El Cid, the Spanish hero who played fugitive here, to Sancho II, who died here during his attempt to overthrow his sister Doña Urraca and claim the House of Castile as his own. Zamora is only a short bus ride from Salamanca, making it an easy—and worthwhile—daytrip.

Zamora's foremost monument is its Romanesque **cathedral,** built from the 12th to 15th centuries. Its Byzantine cupola is notable for its **Bishop's Door,** an entrance in the side of the dome that can only be reached by a vertigo-inducing flight of stairs. Inside, the cathedral's highlights are its intricately carved choir stalls (complete with seated apostles laughing and singing) and the main altar, an ornate marble and gold structure. Golden angels keep watch from a blue sky above. Inside the cloister, the **Museo de la Catedral** features the priceless 15th-century **Black Tapestries,** which tell the story of the Trojan War and Achilles's defeat. (☎980 53 06 44. Cathedral and museum open Tu-Su 10am-2pm and 5-8pm; Mass daily at 10am, also Sa 6pm and Su 1pm. Cathedral free; museum €1.80.) To reach the cathedral from Pl. Mayor, walk left (with your back to the Ayuntamiento) up C. Ramón Carrión, following it until its name changes to R. de Los Francos and R. de Los Notarios. After R. de Los Notarios curves to the left, it will bring you to Pl. de la Catedral. Behind the cathedral is the **Parque del Castillo,** a great spot for an afternoon picnic.

Twelve striking **Romanesque churches** remain within the walls of the old city, gleaming in the wake of recent restoration. Almost all these churches were built in the 11th and 12th centuries; their ornate altars, however, were usually added in the 15th and 16th centuries. Most visitors follow the **Romanesque Route,** a self-guided tour of all of the churches available from the tourist office. With their gray stone, dark interiors, and sculptures of Christ in the sepulcher, all twelve churches tend to blend together. There are, however, a few standouts. In Pl. Mayor, the **Iglesia San Juan** is notable for its luminescent, marble-veined windows. **La Magdalena,** straight up C. Ramón Carrión from Pl. Mayor, features an intricately carved south door; it also houses a Mary Magdalene icon, one of the most revered religious works of art in Zamora. Across the street from La Magdalena on C. Ramón Carrión is the **Convento del Transito,** a convent of Carmelite nuns who watch over *La Virgen del Transito*, the patron saint of Zamora; she is credited with miracles ranging from bringing rain during a drought to protecting El Cid.

Farther up C. Ramón Carrión on the left is **Iglesia San Ildefonso,** noted for its bright green-and-orange organ and its statues of *La Virgen Amor y Hermosa*, another important Zamoran saint. Finally, **Iglesia Santa María La Nueva** was the site of one of Zamora's most significant historical events, *El Motín de la Trucha;* in 1158 villagers set the church on fire (with Zamoran nobility inside) to protest a law giving noblemen priority over plebeians in buying trout. While it may sound silly, the event was one of the first in a series that led to the rise of the Spanish bourgeoisie. To get to the church from Pl. Mayor, walk up C. Sacramento and then turn right onto C. Barandales; the church is in Pl. Santa María la Nueva. (All open Tu-Sa 10am-1pm and 5-8pm. Free.) The **Museo de Semana Santa,** Pl. Santa María La Nueva, 9, is a rare find. Hooded mannequins stand guard over elaborately sculpted floats that depict the stations of the Vía Crucis. These mannequins were used during the *romerías*, processions honoring *Semana Santa*; Zamora has one of the most decorated Easter celebrations in all of Spain. To reach the museum from Pl. Mayor, take C. Sacramento and turn right on C. Barandales. (☎980 53 22 95. Open M-Sa 10am-2pm and 5-8pm, Su 10am-2pm. €2.70.) The train and bus stations are both a 15min. walk from Pl. Mayor. The **tourist office** is at C. Santa Clara, 20. (☎980 53 18 45; fax 980 53 38 13. Open M-Sa 9am-2pm and 5-7pm.) **Restaurant Casa Bernardo** 2, Plazuela de San Miguel, 2 (☎980 53 27 41), is in Plaza Mayor, the historical center of the city, and serves delicious food on a sunny terrace. Entrees €5-€7.80, *menú* €9. Open daily from 1-4pm and 5-10pm.

LEÓN ☎987

The residents of León (pop.300,000) are proud of their riverside oasis. From the tangled streets of the *barrio gótico* to the stunning cathedral, locals boast that their city is the best in Castille, if not in Spain. It's fitting that the city's unofficial mascot is the oh-so-proud lion—images of lions are everywhere and *leones*, the local moniker for natives of the area, literally means "lions" in Spanish. Strangely enough, the city's name has nothing to do with lions—it stems from *legio* (Latin for legion), a name that the Roman Legion gave the town in AD 68. During the Middle Ages, the city was an important stop on the pilgrim's route to Santiago de Compostela—and continues to be, as attested to by gold shells marking the *camino*'s path through the city center. León was an essential defense point against Moorish invaders during the *Reconquista*. Today the city is best known for its cathedral, whose spectacular blue stained-glass windows have earned León the nickname *La Ciudad Azul.* While history provides León with its local prominence, it is the city's serene parks and vibrant outdoor life that make it worth exploring.

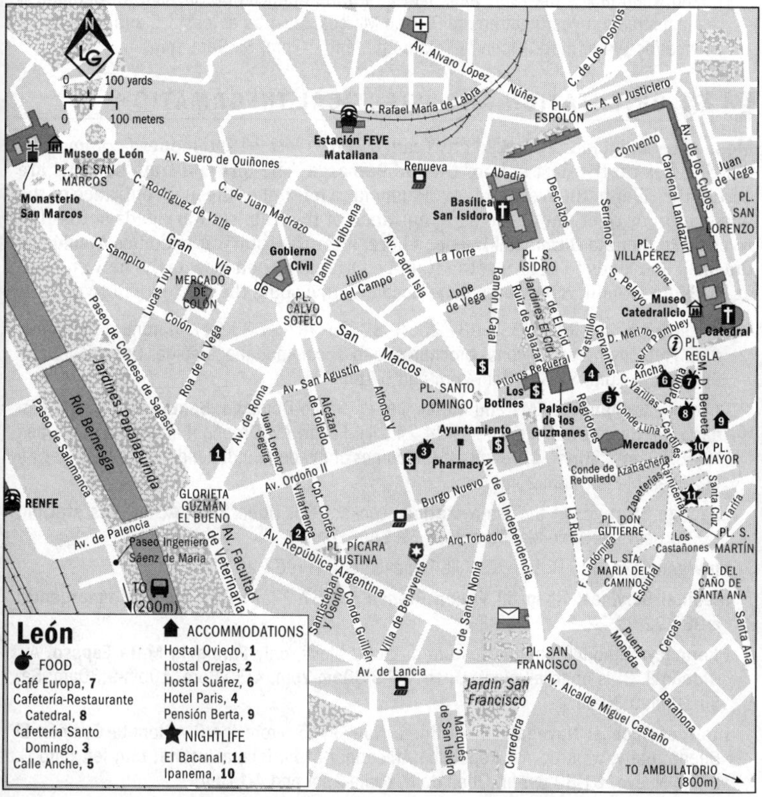

TRANSPORTATION

Trains: RENFE, Av. Astorga, 2 (☎902 24 02 02). With Pl. Guzmán el Bueno behind you, cross the river and continue on Av. Palencia as it curves to the right; the station is on your left. Open 24hr. Trains to: **Barcelona** (9½hr.; 12:25am, 9:47pm; €30); **Bilbao** (5½hr., 3:10pm, €24); **Burgos** (2-3hr.; 12:25am, 9:47pm; €14.50); **La Coruña** (7hr., express 4½hr.; 4:45am, 4:59pm; €25); **Madrid** (4½hr., M-Sa 7 per day 1:12am-6:12pm, €27.50); **Oviedo** (2½hr., 7 per day 4:45am-7:40pm, €5.85-14); **Palencia** (1½hr.; Su-F 13 per day 12:15am-9:47pm, Sa 12 per day 12:25am-9:47pm; €11.20); **Valladolid** (2½hr., M-Sa 10 per day 1:12am-8:35pm, €7.90-18). **FEVE,** Av. Padre Isla, 48 (☎987 22 59 19), north of Pl. Santo Domingo, sends trains to local destinations. Train and bus schedules are printed daily in *Diario de León* (€0.65).

Buses: Estación de Autobuses, Po. Ingeniero Sáenz de Miera (☎987 21 00 00). Info open M-Sa 7:30am-9pm. To: **Madrid** (4½hr.; M-F 12 per day 2:30am-10:30pm, Sa-Su 8 per day 2:30am-7:30pm; €16.10); **Santander** (5hr., F 4pm and Su 7:30pm, €16.23); **Valladolid** (2hr., 8 per day 2:30am-10:30pm, €7.02); **Zamora** (2½hr.; M-F 9 per day 8am-9:15pm, Sa 6 per day 8am-5pm, Su 4 per day 10:15am-7pm; €7.12).

Taxis: Radio Taxi (☎987 24 24 51 or 987 24 12 11). 24hr. service.

Car Rental: Hertz, C. Sampiro, 20 (☎987 23 19 99). From Pl. Glorieta Guzmán el Bueno when facing the river, walk right up Po. de Condesa de Sagasta; C. Sampiro is the last street on your right before Pl. San Marcos. Must be at least 25 and have had a license for 1yr. or more. Open M-F 9am-2pm and 4-7pm, Sa 9am-1pm.

ORIENTATION AND PRACTICAL INFORMATION

Most of León, including the old city (called *León Gótico*) and modern commercial district, lies on the east side of the **Río Bernesga.** The bus and train stations are across the river in the west end. Av. Palencia (a left out of the main entrance of the bus station or right out of the main entrance of the train station) leads across the river to **Pl. Glorieta Guzmán el Bueno,** where, after the rotary, it becomes **Avenida de Ordoño II** and leads to León's cathedral. Av. Ordoño II then bisects the new city and at Pl. Santo Domingo becomes **Calle Ancha,** which splits the old town in two.

Tourist Office: Pl. Regla, 3 (☎987 23 70 82; fax 987 27 33 91), in front of the cathedral. Free city maps, regional brochures, and accommodations guide. Open M-F 9am-2pm and 5-7pm, Sa-Su 10am-2pm and 5-7pm.

Currency Exchange: ATMs and **banks** line Pl. Santo Domingo. **Santander Central Hispano,** Pl. Santo Domingo (☎902 24 24 24). Follow Av. Ordoño II into the plaza. Open M-F 8:30am-2:30pm. **Citibank,** at the corner of Av. de la Independencia and C. Legión VII. Open M-F 8:30am-2pm.

Luggage Storage: At the **train station.** Lockers €3. Open 24hr. At the **bus station,** €0.60 per bag. Open M-F 9am-8pm, Sa 9am-2pm.

Emergency: ☎112. Police: C. Villa Benavente, 6 (☎987 20 73 12).

Medical Services: Hospital Virgen Blanca (☎987 23 74 00). **Medical emergency:** ☎987 22 22 22.

Pharmacy: Although pharmacies are on every block, only **Farmacia Mata Espeso,** Av. Ordoño II, 3, is open all night. Open M-F 9:30am-2pm, 4:30-8pm, 10pm-9:30am; Sa-Su 10pm-9:30am.

Internet Access: NavegaWeb, C. Burgo Nuevo, 15. From the Pl. Glorieta Guzmán El Bueno rotary, walk up Av. República Argentina; at Pl. Pícara Justina, turn left onto C. Burgo Nuevo. €1.80 per hr. Open daily 10am-2pm and 4-11pm.

Post Office: Jardín San Francisco (☎987 23 90 79; fax 987 87 60 78). From Pl. Santo Domingo, go down Av. Independencia; the post office is on the right just before Av. de Lancia. **Lista de Correos** (windows #12-13) and **fax** service available. Open M-F 8:30am-8:30pm, Sa 9:30am-2pm. **Postal Code:** 24004.

ACCOMMODATIONS

Budget beds are fairly easy to come by in León, thanks to the yearly influx of pilgrims on their way to Santiago, but *pensiones* do tend to fill during the June fiestas. Many accommodations cluster on **Av. de Roma, Av. Ordoño II,** and **Av. República Argentina,** which lead into the old town from Pl. Glorieta Guzmán el Bueno. The tourist office has a free brochure listing all accommodations in town.

Hostal Orejas, C. Villafranca, 6, 2nd fl. (☎987 25 29 09; janton@usarios.Retecal.es). Just down Av. República Argentina from Pl. Glorieta Guzmán el Bueno. Brand-new rooms, complete with bath, shower, and cable TV. Free Internet access. Singles Su-W €28, Th-Sa €39; doubles Su-W €34 and Th-Sa €47; triples €62; extra bed €10. V. ❸

Hostal Oviedo, Av. Roma, 26, 2nd fl. (☎987 22 22 36), off Pl. Glorieta Guzmán el Bueno. Street-side rooms have terraces. Shared bathrooms are kept impeccably clean. Singles €14; doubles €23; triples €36. ❶

Pensión Berta, Pl. Mayor, 8, 2nd fl. (☎987 25 70 39). From Pl. Santa Domingo, walk up C. Anche, and turn right on C. Mariano Domínguez Berrueta just before the cathedral. When you reach Pl. Mayor, turn left onto the 1st walkway; the pension is on your left. Although rooms are small and a little dim, Berta is centrally located in the *barrio hûmedo,* with all-night bars right at the doorstep. Singles €11; doubles €20. ❶

Hostal Suárez, C. Ancha, 7 (☎987 25 42 88). Prime location, seconds away from the cathedral. Rooms are spacious with high ceilings and soft beds. No heat. Open Apr.-Nov. Doubles €18; triples €22. ❷

Hotel Paris, C. Ancha, 18 (☎927 23 86 00, fax 927 27 15 72). All the facilities and services of a modern 3-star hotel in the midst of León's old neighborhood. Singles €44; doubles €63. AmEx/MC/V. ❹

FOOD

Inexpensive eateries fill the area near the cathedral and on the small streets off C. Ancha; also check Pl. San Martín, near Pl. Mayor. Meat-lovers will rejoice, as many variations of pork top the local menus. In June, León's 3500km of trout-fishable streams draw the **International Trout Festival.** Fresh produce as well as bread, cheese, and milk are available at the **Mercado Municipal del Conde,** Pl. Conde, off C. General Mola. From Pl. Santo Domingo, walk up C. Anche, and then turn right onto C. Regidores, which empties into the market. (Open M-Sa 9am-3:30pm.)

Cafetería-Restaurante Catedral, C. Mariano Domínguez Berrueta, 17 (☎987 21 59 18). From Pl. Santo Domingo, walk up C. Anche and turn right onto C. Mariano Domínguez Barreuta. Huge portions, garlic-laden trout, and homemade desserts. *Menú del día* €8. Open M, Th-Sa 10am-midnight; Tu, W, Su 10am-4pm. AmEx/MC/V. ❷

Café Europa, Pl. Regla, 9 (☎987 25 61 17). The spacious, sunny terrace offers great views of the cathedral that complement the delicious varieties of coffee and pastries. Offers breakfast (€3), coffee (€2), and tasty ice cream (€1). Open 9am-11pm. ❶

Cafetería Santo Domingo, C. Ordoño II, 3 (☎987 26 13 84). A family restaurant specializing in ice creams and pastries. 3-course *menús* for €9. Open daily 8am-midnight. ❷

Calle Ancha, C. Ancha, 11 (☎987 21 01 83). Between C. Regidores and C. Conde Luna, a 2min. walk from the cathedral. Bring a breath mint–*everything* comes with *ajo* (garlic) at this bright cafe. The *menú del día* (€6.61) includes a bottle of wine. Open daily noon-4pm and 9:15pm-midnight, F-Sa until 3:30am. MC/V. ❷

Restaurant Bodega Regia, C. Regidores, 9 (☎987 21 31 73). Part of the hotel of the same name, Bodega Regia specializes in *cocina leonesa* and has won several awards. Full *menú* with wine included costs €15. Open daily 1:30pm until late. AmEx/MC/V. ❸

SIGHTS

CATHEDRAL. The 13th-century Gothic cathedral, *La Pulchra Leonina*, is arguably the most beautiful cathedral in Spain. It is also one of Spain's best examples of Gothic architecture. The exceptional facade depicts smiling saints amidst bug-eyed monsters munching on the damned. But the real attractions are its stained-glass windows, which feature angelic saints and brilliant flowers, and the elaborate altar painting of the stations of the Vía Crucis. *(On Pl. Regla. ☎987 87 57 70. From Pl. Santo Domingo, walk straight up C. Anche. Cathedral open in summer daily 8:30am-2:30pm and 5-7pm; in winter daily 8:30am-1:30pm and 4-7pm. Free. Museum open in summer daily 9:30am-1:30pm and 4-6:30pm; in winter M-F 9:30am-1pm and 4-6pm, Sa 9:30am-1:30pm. Cathedral €3.50, Claustro €0.60.)*

BASÍLICA SAN ISIDORO. The Romanesque Basílica San Isidoro was dedicated in the 11th century to San Isidoro of Sevilla. After his death, his remains were brought from Muslim-dominated Andalucia to the Christian stronghold of León. The corpses of countless royals rest in the Panteón Real, where the ceilings are covered by vibrant 12th-century frescoes. The unusual Annunciation and Roman agricultural calendar are noteworthy. Admission to the pantheon includes entrance to the library, which houses a 10th-century handwritten Bible, and to the treasury, home of Doña Urraca's famous agate chalices. *(On Pl. San Isidoro. From Pl. Santo Domingo, walk up C. Ramón y Cajal; the basilica is up the flight of stairs on the right just before C. La Torre. Open M-Sa 9am-1:30pm and 4-6:30pm, Su only from 9am-1:30pm. €3.)*

OTHER SIGHTS. The **Museo de León** displays an extensive archaeological collection with pieces dating from the Paleolithic era; particularly stunning are the 4th-century Roman mosaics. *(Pl. San Marcos. From Pl. Santo Domingo, walk up Gran Vía de San Marcos to its end at Pl. San Marcos. ☎987 24 50 61. Open July-Sept. Tu-Sa 10am-2pm and 5-8pm, Su 10am-4pm; Oct.-Jun Tu-Sa 10am-2pm and 4-7pm, Su 10am-4pm. €1.20, free for students Sa-Su.)* **Los Botines** is one of the few buildings outside Cataluña designed by modernist architect Antoni Gaudí, the most famous member of the *Modernisme* movement in Spain. The relatively restrained structure contains hints of his later style in its turrets and windows (see **Barcelona,** p. 365). It now serves as bank offices and is not open to the public. *(From Pl. Santo Domingo, walk up C. Ancha toward the cathedral; Los Botines is immediately on your left in front of Pl. San Marcelo.)* Some of León's most enjoyable attractions are its myriad parks and promenades where locals spend their evenings picnicking and exchanging *besos.* Two of the most peaceful are the **Jardines El Cid,** directly behind Los Botines on Pilotos Tegueral between El Cid and Ruiz de Salazar, and the **Jardines Papalaguinda,** running along the river from Pl. San Marcos in the north to the Pl. de Toros in the south.

ENTERTAINMENT AND NIGHTLIFE

Festivals commemorating **San Juan** and **San Pedro** occur from June 21 to 30. Highlights include a *corrida de torros* (bullfight) and the feast days of San Juan on

June 23 and San Pedro on June 30. King Juan Carlos I and his wife Sofía sometimes attend the fiestas and the cathedral's **International Organ Festival** on October 5.

For nearby bars, discos, and techno music, head to the *barrio húmedo* (drinker's neighborhood) around **Plaza de San Martín** and **Plaza Mayor.** Walk up C. Ancha toward the cathedral and take a right on C. Varillas (which becomes Platerías Candiles). To reach P. San Martín, take a right where the street ends at C. Carnicerías; to reach Pl. Mayor, take a left onto C. Plegaria at the end of C. Platerías Candiles. All bars here are open until 2am daily and until 5-6am on Friday and Sunday. In Pl. San Martín, **El Bacanal,** C. Mulhacín, 5, attracts crowds to its Caravaggio-covered walls. (☎987 21 38 51.) Around Pl. Mayor, León's hippest partygoers flock to **Ipanema,** C. Plegarias, 8; the upstairs is a dim, bossa nova-infused cafe, while the downstairs dance floor sticks to standard Spanish beats. After 2am, the crowds weave to the many discos and bars of **C. Lancia** and **C. Conde de Guillén.**

DAYTRIP FROM LEÓN

ASTORGA

Astorga is most easily reached by ***bus*** *from León, Po. Ingeniero Saenz de Miera (45min.; M-F 16 per day 6:15am-9:30pm, Sa 7 per day 8:30am-8:30pm, Su 6 per day 8:30am-8:30pm; €3). RENFE runs* ***trains*** *to Astorga from León (45min.; M-Tu and Th-F 5 per day 2:04am-8:29pm, W 6 per day 2:04am-8:29pm, Sa 4 per day 2:04am-8:29pm, Su 3 per day 2:15am-8:29pm; €3), but the station is a 15min. walk uphill from the main sights.*

Astorga reached its maximum splendor in the 15th century as an important stop on both *La Ruta de la Plata*, the Roman silver route, and *El Camino Santiago*, the pilgrim's path to Santiago de Compostela that begins in the French Pyrenees. In the early 17th century it became one of the world's main chocolate-making centers; a few die-hards still produce bars of authentic *chocolate de Astorga.*

Today Astorga is perhaps most distinguished by the **Palacio Episcopal,** designed in the late 19th century by Antoni Gaudí. The palace's turrets, main entryway, and beveled stone exterior are most characteristic of Gaudí's style. Gaudí built the palace to replace the one which burned down in 1886, but no bishop has actually ever lived there. Now the fascinating palace houses the **Museo de los Caminos,** dedicated to the various paths toward Santiago de Compostela that converge in 2000-year-old Astorga. (☎987 61 88 82. Open M-Sa 10am-1:30pm and 4-7:30pm, Su 10am-1:30pm. €1.50.) The **cathedral,** directly to the left when facing Gaudí's palace, is definitely worth a quick visit. While it is not as well-preserved or as opulent as León's cathedral, its emptiness—there are no pews, chapel gates, or candle tables—affords a rare opportunity to experience the immensity of Gothic architecture. The cathedral's **museum** has 10 rooms filled with religious relics and the series of paintings depicting the temptations of St. Anthony—including several panels of his gruesome attack by demons—are well worth the small admission fee. (Cathedral and museum open daily 10am-2pm and 4-8pm. Cathedral free; museum €1.50, €2.40 for a joint ticket with the Museo de los Caminos.) Kids and the sweet-toothed should stop by the **Museo de Chocolate,** C. José María Goy, 5. From the Palacio Episcopal, walk up Los Sitios to Pl. Obispo Alcolea; veer to the right onto C. Lorenzo Segura and C. José María Goy is on the right. (Open Tu-Sa 10:30am-2pm and 4:30-8pm, Su 10:30am-2pm. €0.90.) Learn everything you ever wanted to know about chocolate. The museum sells chocolates by the dozen, but you can also purchase their sugary delights next door at the **Confitería la Mallorquina,** C. Lorenzo Segura, 7. (Open daily 10am-2pm and 4-7pm.) Visiting Astorga without buying a box of *milagritos* or *hojaldres* pastries just might classify as a sin.

The **bus station,** Av. las Murallas, 54 (☎987 61 93 51), faces the back of the Palacio Episcopal. From the station's main entrance, cross Av. las Murallas and the new-age Parque de "El Melgar"; the stairs in the city walls will lead you straight up to the cathedral and palace. To get to the town center from the RENFE **train station** (☎987 84 21 22), Pl. Estación, cross the parking lot in front of the station and follow C. Pedro de Castro until it crosses Puerta de Rey. A large building (Casa Granell) is on the right. Walk through the city wall onto C. Enfermas and turn right onto Los Sitios, which will bring you to the palace. With your back to the palace, the **tourist office,** Glorieta Eduardo de Castro, 5, is directly in front of you across the plaza. (☎987 61 82 22. Open Sa-M 9am-8:30pm, Tu-F 10am-2pm and 4-8:30pm.)

VALLADOLID ☎983

For nearly 300 years, Valladolid was the most important town in Castile; when Fernando and Isabel were married here in 1469, it stood at the forefront of Spanish politics, finance, and culture. Explorers Magellan and El Cano came to Valladolid to discuss their plans for voyages to circumnavigate the globe, newly discovered to be round. Miguel de Cervantes, creator of the romantic hero Don Quijote, lived here; in 1506, famous explorer Christopher Columbus died here. Close to a century later, shady dealings by minister Conde Duque de Lerma brought the city's glory days to an end. In return for a whopping bribe, Lerma took Valladolid (then capital of Castile) out of the running for capital of Spain. Today, the city has little to offer visitors beyond its sculpture museum and relics of a Renaissance past. It does, however, offer a glimpse of the unaffected Spanish urban life.

TRANSPORTATION

Flights: Villanubla Airport, León Highway (N-601), km13 (☎983 41 54 00). Daily flights to **Barcelona** and **Paris.** June-Oct. service to the **Balearic Islands.** Info open daily 8am-8pm. **Iberia** (☎983 56 01 62). Open daily 8am-8pm. Taxi to airport €11-12.

Trains: Estación del Norte, C. Recondo, s/n (☎902 24 02 02), at the end of Campo Grande. Info open daily 7am-8pm. Trains to: **Barcelona** (9¾-11hr.; Su-F 9:18am and 9:30pm, Sa 8:10pm; €35.50); **Bilbao** (4hr.; M, W, F 6:27pm; €18.50); **Burgos** (1¾-2½hr.; M-F 11 per day 7am-1:42am, Sa-Su 7 per day noon-11:45pm; €5.85); **León** (2-3hr.; M-Sa 8 per day 10:26am-1:42am, Su 7 per day 10:26am-5:25pm; €7.90); **Lisbon/Oporto** (7¾hr., 3:20am, €40); **Madrid** (3-3¾hr.; M-F 13 per day 4am-8:41pm, Sa 12 per day 4am-8:41pm, Su 11 per day 7am-9pm; €11.40-22); **Oviedo** (4-5½hr.; M-Sa 1:42, 10:26am, 5:25pm; Su 10:26am, 5:25pm; €25); **Paris** (11hr., 9:20pm, €83.50); **Salamanca** (1¾-2¾hr.; M-F 7 per day 7:15am-10:02pm, Sa 7 per day 9:45am-8:15pm, Su 6 per day 7:05am-10:02pm; €5.35-11.50); **Santander** (3-6hr.; M-F 7 per day 9:35am-1:42am, Sa 8 per day 7:15am-1:42am, Su 7 per day 7:15am-6:40pm; €11.40-24); **San Sebastián** (5hr.; 3:41, 11:47am, 12:25pm; €21.50-28); **Zamora** (2hr., 8:36am, €6.45-12).

Buses: Puente Colgante, 2 (☎983 23 63 08). Info open daily 8am-10pm. **La Regional** runs to Palencia and Zamora; **ALSA** serves all others. Info open M-Sa 6am-10pm, Su 8am-10pm. To: **Barcelona** (10hr.; 9:45am, 12:15, 9:45pm; €33.50-35); **Bilbao** (5hr.; M-Th and Sa 1:35, 5:30pm; F 1:35, 3:30, 5:30pm; Su 5:30, 7:15pm; €18.50-24); **Burgos** (1¾-2¾hr., Su-Th 5 per day 9:45am-9:45pm, €5.85); **León** (2hr.; M-F 9 per day 2:45am-12:45am, Sa 7 per day 2:45am-12:45am, Su 6 per day 2:45am-9:45pm; €7.90); **Madrid** (2¼hr.; M-Sa 18 per day 4:15am-12:30am, Su 19 per day 10:15am-10pm; €11.40); **Oviedo** (3¼-4¼hr., 4 per day 2:15am-7pm, €12.25); **Palencia** (45min.; M-F every hr. 7am-9pm, Sa 6 per day 8am-8:15pm, Su 3 per day 10am-10pm; €3); **Santander** (4hr.; M-Th and Sa 9:45am, 4:45pm; F and Su 4:45, 8pm;

€11.40); **Zamora** (1½hr.; M-F 7 per day 7am-6:30pm; Sa 5 per day 8am-5:30pm; Su 10:30am, 5, 10pm; €6.45).

Taxis: Agrupación de Taxistas de Valladolid 24hr. ☎983 20 77 55.

ORIENTATION AND PRACTICAL INFORMATION

The bus and train stations sit on the southern edge of town, beneath the Parque de Campo Grande. To get from the **bus station** to the **tourist office** (15min.), exit at the corner of Po. del Arco de Ladrillo and C. San José. (Do not exit onto the corner of Po. del Arco de Ladrillo and C. de Puente Colgante.) Turn left onto Po. del Arco de Ladrillo, and keep right onto C. Ladrillo at the rotary. Follow C. Ladrillo to Po. de Los Filipinos. At the edge of the Campo, take the pedestrian path through the park. When you reach Pl. de Zorrilla at the end of the park, C. Santiago—the street the tourist office is on—will be directly across the rotary. From the front entrance of the **train station** (10min.), take the sidewalk to your left onto C. Estación del Norte, following it to Pl. de Colón. Follow the rotary to the right; C. Acera de Recoletos will be the third street on your right, running alongside the park, and will take you directly to Pl. de Zorilla. C. Santiago is the second street to the right from this rotary (10min.). **Pl. Mayor** is straight up C. Santiago from the tourist office; the **cathedral** and **sculpture museum** are 10min. to the north.

Tourist Office: C. Santiago, 19 (☎983 34 40 13). Open daily 9am-2pm and 5-7pm.

Currency Exchange: Santander Central Hispano, C. Perú, 6 (☎902 24 24 24), on the corner of Av. Acera Recoletos. Open M-F 8:30am-2:30pm. **Citibank,** C. Miguel Iscar, 7, off Pl. Zorrilla. Open M-F 8am-2pm.

Luggage Storage: At the **train station** 24hr. (lockers €2.50). At the **bus station** (€0.60 per bag). Open M-Sa 8am-10pm.

Emergency: ☎091 or 092. **Local Police:** In the Ayuntamiento (☎983 42 61 07).

Medical Services: Ambulance/emergencies: ☎061. **Hospital Pío del Río Hortega,** Rondilla de Santa Teresa, s/n (☎983 42 04 00). **Red Cross** (☎983 22 22 22).

Pharmacy: Pharmacies line C. Santiago. **Lcda. López,** Po. Zorrilla, 85, is the only all-night pharmacy. Open Sa-Th 10pm-9:30am, F 10pm-10am.

Internet Access: Ciberc@fé Segafredo, Po. de Zorrilla, 46 (☎983 33 80 63). From Pl. de Zorrilla, walk down Po. de Zorrilla alongside park; cafe is on right before Av. García Morato. Exact change for machines. €0.60 per 15min. Open daily 8am-midnight.

Post Office: Pl. Rinconada, s/n (☎983 33 02 31). From Pl. Mayor, take C. Jesús to the left of the Ayuntamiento. **Faxes** and **Lista de Correos.** Open M-Sa 8:30am-8:30pm, Su 8:30am-2pm. **Postal Code:** 47001.

ACCOMMODATIONS

Cheap lodgings with winter heating are easy to come by. The streets off Av. Acera Recoletos near the train station are packed with *pensiones*, as are those near the cathedral and behind Pl. Mayor at Pl. Val.

Pensión Dani, C. Perú, 11, 1st fl. (☎983 30 02 49). Following the directions from the train station to the tourist office, turn right onto C. Perú before Pl. de Zorrilla. Has 4 comfortable rooms near Valladolid's beautiful park. Singles €10.60; doubles €19. ❶

Pensión Dos Rosas, C. Perú, 11, 2nd fl. (☎983 20 74 39). The rooms at Dos Rosas are just as spacious and well-kept as those at Dani. Not surprisingly, the prices are also identical. Portable heaters in winter. Singles €10.60; doubles €19. ❶

Hostal Residencia Val II, Pl. Val, 6, 1st fl. (☎983 37 57 52). From Pl. Mayor, turn left onto Pl. Corrillo, 2 streets to the right when facing the Ayuntamiento. Walk up C. Val, the 3rd street on the right in the plaza. TV common area and quiet lounge. Huge rooms with eclectic quilts open onto private terraces. Singles with sink €17, with toilet €24.04; doubles with sink €27.05, with toilet €33.06. ❷

Hotel Olid Meliá, Pl. San Miguel, 10 (☎983 35 72 00; fax 983 33 68 28). A huge 7-story building with conference rooms, bars, a nice restaurant, and comfortable, fully-equipped rooms. Singles €77.05; doubles €133. AmEx/MC/V. ❺

FOOD

Though bars and cafes abound, the search for a meal beyond *tapas* may leave visitors with an empty stomach. Search for eateries between Pl. Mayor and Pl. Val and explore the area near the cathedral for *tapas*. The **Mercado del Val,** in Pl. Val just off Pl. Mayor, has fresh foods. (Open M-Sa 6am-3pm.)

Cantina La Puñeta, C. Santa María, 19 (☎983 20 71 36). With a wooden bar, pastel-colored walls, and delicious burritos, La Puñeta is a great place for Tex-Mex fanatics. Salads €5-6, entrees €5-8. Open daily 1-5pm and 8pm-midnight. ❷

Casa San Pedro Regalad, Pl. Ochavo, 1 (☎983 34 45 06). From Pl. Mayor, walk up C. Lencería and turn left onto C. Lonja, which runs into Pl. Ochavo. Descend into the cavernous depths of this 16th-century *bodega* to enjoy elegant dining. *Menú* €7.25. Open daily 1:30-3:30pm and 8-11:30pm. AmEx/MC/V. ❷

Restaurante Chino Gran Muralla, C. Santa María, 1 (☎983 34 23 07), to the right off C. Santiago, north of Pl. Zorrilla. Neon dragons greet patrons at this Spanish pagoda. 4-course *menú del día* (€4.25). Open daily 11:30am-5pm and 7pm-12:30am. ❶

SIGHTS

CATHEDRAL METROPOLITANA. Although this Romanesque cathedral was partly designed by Juan de Herrera, creator of El Escorial (see p. 138), it is still an excellent example of Herrera's *desornamentado* style of plain masonry. Apparently, other architects felt the need to ornament the cathedral; ranks of gargoyles leer down at parishioners. The extensive **Museo Diocesano,** in the cathedral's Gothic addition, houses the remains of the original 11th- to 13th-century structure as well as Herrera's model of the basilica. *(C. Arribas, 1, in Pl. Universidad. From Pl. Mayor, walk up C. Ferrari. After 2 blocks, veer left onto Bajada de la Libertad. At Pl. Libertad, turn right; the cathedral is directly in front of you. ☎983 30 43 62. Cathedral and museum open Tu-Sa 10am-1:30pm and 4:30-7pm, Su 10am-2pm. Cathedral free. Museum €2.50.)*

CASA DE CERVANTES. The supposed home in which Cervantes penned his epic *El Quijote* from 1603-1606, the *casa* houses an amusing collection of old books and furniture; the medieval bed-warmer is its only unique highlight. *(☎983 33 88 10. C. Rastro. From Pl. de Zorrilla, walk up C. Miguel Iscar; C. Rastro will be 2 blocks up on your right. Open Tu-Sa 9:30am-3:30pm, Su 10am-3pm. €2.50, students with ID €1.25. Under 18 and over 65 free. Su free.)*

ENTERTAINMENT

Valladolid's cafes and bars are lively, though nothing to write home about. A student crowd fills the countless bars on **C. Paraíso,** just beyond the cathedral. From Pl. de la Universidad at the cathedral, turn left onto C. Duque de Lerma, then right onto C. Marqués del Duero; C. Paraíso will be on the right. For pubs, try **Pl. San Miguel** (from Pl. Mayor, walk up Pl. Corrillo, turn left onto C. Val, and after the plaza, continue straight onto C. Zapico; at Pl. Los Arces, turn left onto C. San Antonio de Padua, which brings you to Pl. San Miguel) and **C. Santa María,** off C. Santiago. Cafes on **C. Vincente Moliner** draw an older crowd; from Pl. Mayor, walk up C. Ferrari, and at Pl. Fuente Dorada, C. Vicente Moliner is on the left. The neighborhood around **Pl. Martí Monsó,** however, is the most central nightlife in Valladolid. In addition to its numerous all-night *tapas* bars such as **El Concho,** C. Correos, 2 (open daily 8:30pm-2:30am), and chic wine bars like **Vino Tinto,** C. Calixto Fernández de la Torre, 4 (open M-Sa 7pm-4am), this neighborhood also houses Valladolid's two best dance clubs. **TinTin,** C. Campañas, 12, is deservedly the most popular bar in Valladolid (open Tu-Sa 10pm-sunrise). From Pl. Mayor, walk up Calixto Fernández de la Torre (to the left when facing the Ayuntamiento), turn right onto Pl. Martí Monso, then right again onto C. Campanas. **Club 38,** C. Mayor, 30, is the other dance hotspot. (☎983 74 52 82. Open 7pm-late.)

With over 12 movie theaters, Valladolid has one of the highest cinema-to-citizen ratios in all Spain. Each movie theater features a different genre of film. **Cines Casablanca,** C. Platerias, 1 (☎983 33 89 14), features *film noir* classics, while the **Cines Coca,** Pl. Marti Monso, 10 (☎983 33 02 90), shows recent British and American films. (Tickets €6.75.) The **International Cinema Week** (Oct. 21-31) features indie European films. The week of September 21 marks the **Fiesta Mayor,** which features bullfights, carnivals, and parades.

BURGOS ☎947

Upon entering Burgos (pop. 346,000) one first sees its cathedral; the magnificent Gothic spires tower over even the remotest *calle* and plaza. While this architectural and religious landmark is the city's claim to fame, there is much more to the town than transepts and altars. From its duck-filled riverbanks to its elegant denizens sipping sangria in sidewalk cafes, Burgos emits an aura of vivacity, prosperity, and elegance. Perhaps modern Burgos's ease and confidence are due to its 500-year stint as Castile's capital. Every street seems to mark some historical legacy, from the return of Christopher Columbus from the New World to the conquests of El Cid Campeador, and nearly every plaza and *paseo* is graced with architectural marvels like the Puente de Santa María and the Monasterio de Las Huelgas. Perhaps the heroes and kings of yore just knew a good thing when they saw it; what with its debaucherous nightlife and delectable cuisine, Burgos is simply splendid.

TRANSPORTATION

Trains: Av. Conde Guadalhorce, s/n (☎947 20 35 60). 10min. walk or €3 taxi ride to the city center. Info open daily 7am-10pm. To: **Barcelona** (9-13¾hr., 4 per day 2:17am-11:40pm, €32); **Bilbao** (2½-4hr.; M-F 5 per day 3:17am-6:44pm, Sa 4 per day 3:17am-6:44pm, Su 3 per day 12:57-6:44pm; €14); **La Coruña** (6-9hr.; daily 2:38am, 12:13, 3:16pm; €30.50-38); **León** (2-3hr.; M-Sa 4 per day 2:38am-3:16pm, Su 3 per day 2:38am-3:16pm; €15-19); **Lisbon** (8-10hr., 1:32pm, €34.50); **Madrid** (3-5½hr.; M-F 10 per day 2:20am-11:07pm, Sa-Su 9 per day 2:20am-11:07pm; €22-28); **Palencia** (45min.; M-F 8 per day 2:38am-8:20pm, Sa-Su 6 per day 2:38am-8:20pm; €3.40-12); **Oviedo** (5hr.; M-Sa 6:48am, 3:16pm; €20.50); **San Sebastián** (3-3½hr., 8 per day 5:12am-6:44pm, €17.50); **Valladolid** (1-2hr., 12 per day 1:44am-11:07pm, €5.85-11.50).

Buses: C. Miranda, 4 (☎947 28 88 55). To: **Barcelona** (7½hr.; 5 per day noon-12:35am, €29.19); **Bilbao** (2-3hr., M-F 4 per day 8:30am-7pm, €9); **La Coruña/Santiago** (7hr., 10am, €33.18); **León** (3½hr., M-Sa 10:45am, €19.82); **Madrid** (2¾hr., M-F 12 per day 7:30am-3:45am, €12.80); **Oviedo** (4-5hr., 4 per day 4:45am-9:15pm,

€11); **Salamanca** (4hr., M-Sa 10:45am, €12.59); **San Sebastián** (4-5hr., 7 per day 7:15am-3:15am, €12.61); **Santander** (2¾hr., 4 per day 10:30am-3:15am, €8.85); **Valladolid/Zamora** (2hr., M-Sa 4 per day 5:15am-6:30pm, €6.50); **Vitoria-Gasteiz** (1¾hr., 9 per day 7:15am-3:15am, €6.03).

Taxis: Abutaxi (☎947 27 77 77) or **Radio Taxi** (☎947 48 10 10). 24hr. service. Taxis line up by Pl. de Santo Domingo de Guzmán, Pl. de Vega, and Pl. de Conde Jordana.

Car Rental: Hertz, C. Progreso, 5 (☎947 20 16 75, reservations ☎902 40 24 05). From the main entrance of the bus station, turn left onto C. Miranda, left again onto C. de Madrid, and left again onto C. Progreso. Min. age 25; credit card in driver's name required for deposit. Small cars with unlimited mileage €66 per day, longer rentals less. Open M-F 9am-1pm and 4-7pm, Sa 9am-1pm. AmEx/MC/V.

ORIENTATION AND PRACTICAL INFORMATION

The Río Arlanzón splits Burgos north-to-south. While the **train** and **bus stations** are on the south side, the **Santa Iglesia Cathedral** and most other sights of interest are located to the north. From the **train station** at Av. Conde de Guadalhorce, s/n, follow Av. Conde de Guadalhorce away from the station, then turn right onto C. La Merced before the river. At the second bridge, **Puente de Santa María,** turn left. Continuing through the gate will bring you to the cathedral, while turning right onto the **Po. del Expolón** leads to **Pl. Mayor** and **Pl. de la Libertad,** both on the left. From the main entrance of the **bus station,** C. Miranda, 4, turn left onto C. Miranda and right onto **C. Madrid** across the river and to the cathedral.

Tourist Office: Pl. Alonso Martínez, 7 (☎947 20 31 25; fax 947 27 65 29). Open M-F 9am-2pm and 5-7pm, Sa-Su and holidays 10am-2pm and 5-8pm.

Currency Exchange: Santander Central Hispano, Pl. de España, 6 (☎904 24 24 24). Open M-Th 8:30am-6:30pm, F 8am-3pm.

Emergency: ☎091 or 092. **Guardia Civil,** Av. Cantabria, 87-95 (☎062 or 947 22 22 63). **Police,** Av. Cantabria, s/n (☎947 28 88 39).

Pharmacy: Farmacia Natividad Combarro Rodríguez, C. San Juan, 25 (☎947 20 12 89). Open M-F 9:45am-2pm and 5-8pm, Sa 10:15am-2pm. All pharmacies post a list of late-night and Su pharmacies in their windows.

Medical Services: Ambulance ☎947 23 22 22. **Hospital General Yagüe,** Av. del Cid, 96 (☎947 28 18 00).

Internet Access: Café Cabaret Ciber-Café, C. La Puebla, 21 (☎947 20 27 22). €1.20 per 15min. Printing €0.10 per page. Open M-Th 4pm-2am, F 4pm-4am, Sa 5pm-4am, Su 5pm-2am.

Post Office: Pl. Conde de Castro, s/n (☎947 26 27 50, info ☎902 19 71 97; fax 947 26 57 11). From Pl. de la Libertad, cross the river on Puente de San Pablo; it will be directly on your right. **Lista de Correos** and **fax** services (€11 1st page, €3 each additional page). Open M-F 8:30am-8:30pm, Sa 9:30am-2pm. **Postal Code:** 09070.

ACCOMMODATIONS AND CAMPING

Inexpensive *pensiones* line the streets near **Pl. Alonso Martínez.** The C. San Juan area is also dotted with reasonably priced hostels. Otherwise, the tourist office distributes a complete list of Burgos's accommodations. Reservations are crucial on summer weekends, for the festivals in June and July, and in August.

Pensión Peña, C. La Puebla, 18, 2nd fl. (☎947 20 63 23). From the Puente de Santa María, turn right onto C. Vitoria, then left at Pl. del Cid. Cross Pl. de la Libertad to your right and turn left onto C. La Puebla. Doubles €18. ❶

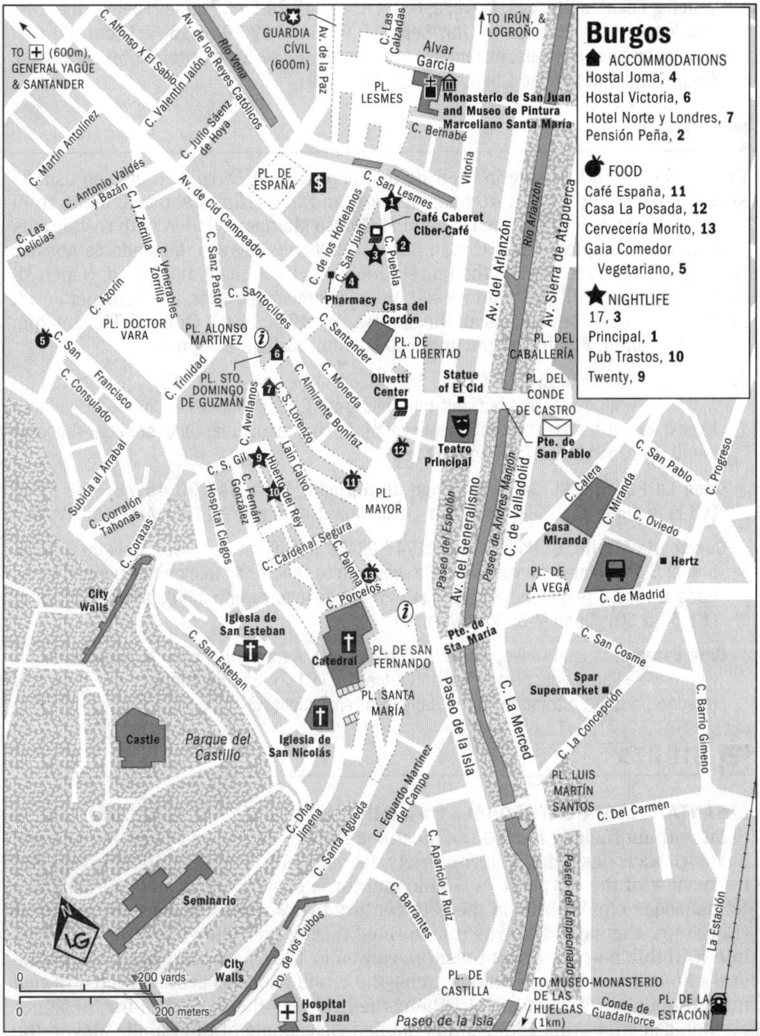

Hostal Joma, C. San Juan, 26, 2nd fl. (☎947 20 33 50). From Puente de Santa María, turn right onto C. Vitoria, and at Pl. del Cid, turn left onto C. Santander; C. San Juan is the 2nd left. Spotless rooms in a large, modern building. Singles €15; doubles €20. ❷

Hostal Victoria, C. San Juan, 3, 2nd fl. (☎/fax 947 20 15 42), down the street from Hostal Joma. Sunny rooms have big beds, desks, and sinks. Public phone and luggage storage. Singles €18; doubles €31. Extra bed €15. ❷

Hotel Norte y Londres, Pl. Alonso Martínez, 10 (☎947 26 41 25; fax 947 27 73 75). A few steps away from the tourist office towards the cathedral. Enormous rooms with bath, TV, and great views of the city. Singles €43; doubles €65. ❹

Camping Fuentes Blancas, Pl. Vega, 6, 1st fl. (☎947 20 54 57). The "Fuentes Blancas" bus leaves from Pl. España (July-Sept. 15 9:30am, 12:30, 4:15, 7:15pm; €0.50). Swimming pool, showers, restaurant, and currency exchange on site. €3.50 per person, €3 per tent and per car. Open Apr.-Sept. MC/V. ❶

FOOD

Burgos natives take pride in their delicious *queso de Burgos*, a cheese usually served with honey or in a *tarte* as dessert, and *morcilla*, a sausage made from tripe, blood, and rice. The area around **Pl. Alonso Martínez** is laden with restaurants serving these staples, while C. San Lorenzo is *tapas* heaven. **Mercado de Abastos (Sur),** on C. Miranda next to the bus station, sells fresh meat and bread. (Open M-Sa 7am-3pm, or until the vendors sell out.) **Supermercado Spar,** C. Concepción, 14, near the train station, carries all the staples. (☎947 26 00 07. Open M-Th 9am-2pm and 5:30-8:30pm, F 9am-2:30pm and 5:30-8:30pm, Sa 9am-2:30pm.)

Gaia Comedor Vegetariano, C. San Francisco, 31 (☎947 23 76 45). From Pl. Alonso Martínez, walk up C. Trinidad and turn right onto C. San Francisco. The earth goddess herself would be delighted by this vegetarian, counter-cultural luncheonette. 4-course *menú* €7. Open M-Sa 1:30-4pm. ❷

Casa La Posada, Pl. Santo Domingo de Guzmán, 18 (☎947 20 45 78). The *menú* (€11) features a rotating local dish. Open daily 1-4pm and 9-11pm. AmEx/MC/V. ❸

Cervecería Morito, C. Porcelos, 1 (☎947 21 73 21). From Pl. Mayor, walk up C. Sombrería; C. Porcelos is on your right. Be prepared to fight for a table on this popular *tapas* bar's terrace. The enormous salads (€4-6) are definitely worth a little scuffle. *Raciones* (€1.50-5.50). Open M-Sa 7pm-2am. ❶

Café España, C. Laín Calvo, 12 (☎947 20 53 37). A traditional cafe, founded in 1921, with a wide variety of cafes, teas, and infusions (€1-2). Its bright terrace is a great way to spend a quiet afternoon. Open daily 10am-midnight. ❶

SIGHTS

SANTA IGLESIA CATHEDRAL. Officially named a UNESCO World Heritage Sight and unofficially named the most beautiful cathedral in Spain, the **Catedral Santa Iglesia** is deserving of its notoriety. Its magnificent spires find their way into every view of the city, and its Gothic interior is equally remarkable. Originally a Romanesque church built in the 13th century by *Reconquista* hero Fernando III (El Santo), the cathedral was transformed during the following three centuries into a Gothic marvel. Devout visitors can enter the Chapel of Christ, the cathedral's holiest and most infamous arch—the crucified Jesus is constructed of real human body parts. Fortunately, the cathedral has other wonders for those not attending services: the 16th-century stained-glass dome of the Capilla Mayor; the eerily lifelike *papamoscas* (fly-catcher), a strange creature high up near the main door in the central aisle that tolls the hours by opening its mouth and gulping; and, under the transept, marked only by a small brick, the remains of El Cid and Doña Jimenez. The cathedral's museum displays a Visigoth Bible and El Cid's nuptial documents. *(☎947 20 47 12. Open M-Sa 9:30am-1pm and 4-7pm, Su 9:30-11:45am and 4-7pm. Cathedral free. Museum €3.60, students €2.40. Audioguide in English €0.50.)*

MUSEO-MONASTERIO DE LAS HUELGAS REALES. Built by King Alfonso VIII in 1188, the austere Museo-Monasterio de las Huelgas Reales is slightly out of the way, but certainly worth the trip. Once a summer palace for Castilian kings and later an elite convent for Cistercian nuns, today's monastery-as-museum allows

WINDOWS TO THE SOUL After a few Castilian towns, the region's cathedrals and churches often blend together, and unless you're an art history major or an aficionado of Catholic churches, all the terms–Romanesque and Gothic, apse and transept–mean little, and the buildings themselves even less. So here's a quick lesson in cathedral architecture. Every Catholic cathedral is built in the shape of the cross. The vertical arm of the cross is called the **nave;** the horizontal arm of the cross is the **transept.** Where the transept and nave meet is usually where the **altar** stands; below the altar in the nave are the **choir stalls.** The segment of the nave above the transept is the **apse,** usually the site of several **chapels,** or altars in honor of saints and apostles other than the patron of the cathedral. Underneath the main floor is the **sepulchre,** or **catacomb,** a burial place for royal and holy figures. The **cloister** is situated off the apse or the transept and is a square structure with a garden in the middle.

Romanesque, dating from the 11th to 13th centuries, is the older of the two styles. Based on Roman architecture, Romanesque relied on strict geometric shapes mathematically proven to support the weight of the building. The hallmarks of a Romanesque structure are perfectly round arches, walls of even thickness, and a scarcity of windows. Columns are all symmetrically placed, and vaults–the arched ceilings–are never more than half the width of the height they support. In other words, Romanesque churches are dark, blocky, and full of right angles and perfect circles.

Gothic architecture, named after the Visigoths as an insult, defied all rules of Romanesque geometry. With the invention of flying buttresses and ribbed vaults, Gothic architects made taller and brighter cathedrals. The walls of the cathedral were freed from supporting the entire weight of the building–a job now given over to the buttresses and the ribbings–and the result was more windows and a less visible structure. Gothic cathedrals are renowned for their enormous, elaborate stained glass windows. Thanks to rib vaulting, the cathedrals could also be taller than Romanesque churches, creating imposing new spires on local skylines. While in practice Gothic cathedrals may seem as dark and geometrically rigid as the Romanesque, they are in theory lighter, brighter, and taller, helping their parishioners to be just a little bit closer to God.

visitors a glimpse of the austerity and glory of medieval Castillian royalty. In fact, the monastery has been closely associated with Spanish royalty since the Middle Ages; the abbess of Las Huelgas has traditionally served as a personal advisor to the king. Burial wardrobes can be viewed in the **Museo de Telas** (Textile Museum). *(Take the "Barrio del Pilar" bus (€0.50) from Pl. España to the Museo stop. ☎947 20 56 87. Open Tu-Sa 10am-1:15pm and 3:45-5:45pm. €4.80, students and under 14 €2.40, under 5 and EU passport-holders free. W free. Obligatory tours in Spanish every 30min.)*

PARQUE DEL CASTILLO. Atop a hill high above the cathedral, the ruins of a medieval castle and a sprawling, tangled park preside over Burgos. Sections of the walls and building demolished by Napoleonic troops are still undergoing reconstruction. The bleached castle rocks offer astounding views of the red roofs of Burgos below and the surrounding countryside. *(From the front entrance of Iglesia San Esteban, climb the 200 steps directly across the street.)*

CASA MIRANDA. This sprawling 16th-century mansion houses four floors of provincial Burgalese art and archaeology. Included in the exhibits are the remains of Cluny, a piece of the front facade of the monastery at Santo Domingo de Silos, and the sepulchre of Don Juan de Padilla. While the provincial art tends toward the usual devotional images, the first floor archaeological collection is a fascinating collection of artifacts and bones. *(C. Miranda, 13. ☎947 26 58 75. Open Tu-F 10am-2pm and 4:30-7:30pm, Sa 10am-2pm and 5-8pm, Su 10am-2pm. €1.20; under 18, senior citizens, and students with ID free. Sa and Su free.)*

CASA DEL CORDÓN. The restored Casa del Cordón—named for the Franciscan Friar's belt that hangs from the doorway—was built by Castilian constables in the 15th century. On April 23, 1497, Columbus met with Fernando and Isabel here after his second trip to America, and here Felipe el Hermoso breathed his last ragged breath after an exhausting game of *jai alai*. Upon his death, his wife Juana dragged his corpse through the streets, earning her nickname, Juana la Loca (the Mad). *(C. Santander, on the other side of the statue of El Cid, on the right. Hours vary.)*

ENTERTAINMENT AND NIGHTLIFE

Like a typical Spanish town, Burgos's nightlife starts late into the night. By midnight C. Avellanos (across from Pl. Alonso Martínez) fills with night owls, migrating from C. Avellanos onto nearby C. Huerto del Rey. If you have to hit the sack early on a Saturday night, wake up Sunday to join the crowds still dancing at *discotecas* along C. San Juan, C. La Puebla, and in the disco complex on Pl. San Lesmes. Nightlife shifts into overdrive during the last week in June, when Burgos honors its patron saints with concerts, parades, fireworks, bullfights, and dances. The day after **Corpus Christi** (May 29th in 2003), citizens parade through town with the *Pendón de las Navas*, a banner captured from the Moors in 1212.

Twenty, Pl. Huerto del Rey, 20 (☎947 26 46 92). Easily the most popular and crowded stop on the Huerto del Rey clubhopping route. Techno predominates on the multi-level dance floor. Beer €2. Open M-Sa 7pm-5am, Su 7pm-midnight.

17, C. La Puebla, 17. Burgos's trendsetters enjoy evenings at this cavernous bar. Entertain yourself with the caveman-like drawings of "couples" on the bright orange walls. Open Tu-Sa from 4pm until the last person leaves.

Principal, C. La Puebla, 40, at the corner of C. San Juan and C. San Lesmes. Sleek limestone-and-glass bar attracts an older, low-key crowd. Open daily 5pm-3am.

Pub Trastos, Pl. Huerto del Rey, 7-9. Cheap liquor keeps backpackers dancing until dawn. Arrive after 1am. Beer €1.50. Open daily 7pm-5am, later on F and Sa.

DAYTRIP FROM BURGOS

SANTO DOMINGO DE SILOS

To get from Burgos to Santo Domingo de Silos (50km) by car, take N-234 toward Salas de los Infantes to Hortigüela. From there, C-110, which borders the Arlanza River, will pass the monastery of San Pedro de Arlanza before arriving at Covarrubias; it's only 17km farther. Arcoredillo runs a bus to Santo Domingo from Burgos, Miranda, 4 (1½hr.; departs Burgos M-F 5:30pm; departs Santo Domingo M-F 8:30am; €4.65).

Since 1993, the Benedictine monks of Santo Domingo de Silos (pop. 380) have sold 5 million recordings, including the Gregorian chant album that reached #1 on global charts. In the **Abadía de Santo Domingo de Silos,** listeners are transported back in time as black-cloaked monks chant along with the organ and the soothing echoes of their own voices. Sit in at morning song at high Mass at 9am (Su at noon), vespers at 7pm (Th in summer at 8pm), and compline at 9:40pm. Perhaps more interesting than the monastery are the **museum** and **cloister** next door, where highlights include an ancient pharmacy of 300-year-old chemicals, skulls, and preserved animal parts. (☎947 39 00 68. Museum and cloister open Tu-Sa 10am-1pm and 4:30-6pm, Su-M 4:30-6pm. €1.50.) Rooms are easy to find in this friendly (though pricey) little town—a good thing since visitors without cars are almost obligated to stay the night. **Hostal Cruces ❷,** Pl. Mayor, 20, offers clean, sunny rooms with baths. (☎947 39 00 64. Singles €21; doubles €33. V.) Near the bus station, **Hostal Santo Domingo ❷,** C. Santo

Domingo, 14-16, has well-kept, air-conditioned rooms with full baths, phones, and TVs. (☎947 39 00 53. Singles €22; doubles €33-48.)

SORIA ☎975

Ruins and remains are not the only reasons to visit burgeoning Soria (pop. 35,000). Though museums and surrounding archaeological sites are the city's biggest attractions, Soria also claims the edenic Parque Alameda, a lively city center, and, in its outskirts, the intriguing Monasterio de San Juan de Duero and the Ermita San Saturio. Though built as a fortress against Aragón, the city proper is idyllic and peaceful. Locals religiously observe their evening *paseo*, strolling and chatting with friends and neighbors before dinner.

TRANSPORTATION

Trains: Estación El Cañuelo (☎975 23 02 02), Ctra. de Madrid. Shuttle buses run from Pl. Mariano Granados to the station 20min. before each train departs (€0.45), and return with new arrivals. To: **Madrid** (3hr.; M-F 7:40am, 5:40pm; Sa 8:45am, 5:40pm; Su 8:45am, 5:25, 7:50pm; €11.44) via **Alcalá de Henares** (2¾hr., €9.66).

Buses: Av. Valladolid (☎975 22 51 60), at Av. Gaya Nuño. Info open M-Sa 7am-10:30pm, Su 9am-10:30pm. **Therpasa** (☎975 22 20 60) to: **Burgos** (2½hr.; 1-3 per day M-F 7am-6:30pm; Sa 7am, 2:15pm; Su 6pm; €8.35); **Zaragoza** (2¼hr.; 3-6 per day M-Sa 7:30am-8pm, Su noon-9pm; €7.75) via **Tarazona** (1hr., €3.90). **Linecar** (☎975 22 15 55) to: **Valladolid** (3hr.; 3 per day M-Sa 9:45am-6:45pm, Su 11:15am-6:45pm; €10.90). **Continental Auto** (☎975 22 44 01) to: **Logroño** (1½hr.; 4-7 per day M-Sa 11am-7:45pm, Su 11am-11:30pm; €5.27); **Madrid** (2½hr.; 6-9 per day M-Th and Sa 9:15am-8:45pm, F and Su 9:15am-11:45pm; €11.28); **Pamplona** (2hr.; 4-7 per day M-Th and Sa 10:45am-10:15pm, F and Su 10:45am-12:15am; €10.10).

Taxis: ☎975 21 30 34. Stands at Pl. Mariano Granados and bus station.

Car Rental: Europcar, C. Angel Terrel, 3-5 (☎975 22 05 05), off C. Sagunto. Min. age 21. €70 per day, €335 per week (plus IVA; insurance included). Open M-F 9:30am-1:30pm and 4:30-8pm, Sa 10:30am-1pm. AmEx/MC/V.

ORIENTATION AND PRACTICAL INFORMATION

The city center is about a 15min. walk from the **bus station.** From the traffic circle outside the station, **Av. Valladolid** runs downhill to the *centro ciudad.* Keep walking for five blocks, then bear right at the fork onto Po. Espolón, which borders the **Parque Alameda.** When the park ends, **Plaza Mariano Granados** will be directly in front of you. To reach the center from the **train station,** either take the shuttle or turn left onto **C. Madrid** and follow the signs to *centro ciudad.* Continue on C. Almazán as it bears left and becomes Av. Mariano Vicen, follow the road for six blocks, keep left at the fork onto C. Alfonso VIII until you reach Pl. Mariano Granados. From the side of the plaza opposite the park, C. Marqués de Vadillo leads to C. El Collado, the shopping street cutting through the old quarter to **Plaza Mayor.**

Tourist Office: Pl. Ramón y Cajal (☎/fax 975 21 20 52; www.sorianitelaimaginas.com; www.turismodesoria.com), on the side of Pl. M. Granados opposite the park. English-speaking staff present only on weekends. Open Su-Th 9am-8pm, F-Sa 9am-9pm.

Currency Exchange: Santander Central Hispano, C. Collado, 56 (☎975 22 02 25). Open Apr.-Sept. M-F 8:30am-2pm; Oct.-May M-F 8:30am-2pm, Sa 8:30am-1pm.

Luggage Storage: At the **bus station.** 1st day €0.60, €0.15 each additional day. Open M-Sa 7am-10:30pm and Su 9am-10:30pm.

Emergency: ☎112 or 062.

Municipal Police: C. O. Agustín, 1 (☎092 or 975 21 18 62).

Medical Services: Hospital General, Po. Santa Barbara (☎975 23 43 00).

Internet: Cyber Centro, Pasaje Tejera, 16 (☎/fax 975 23 90 85). Turn into the small tunnel between C. Las Casas and C. Caro on C. Tejera and walk halfway down. €2.40 per 30min.; €3.60 per hr. Open M-F 10:30am-2pm and 5-9pm, Sa 10:30am-3pm.

Post Office: Po. Espolón, 6 (☎ 975 23 35 70; fax 975 23 35 61), off Pl. Mariano Granados. Open M-F 8:30am-8:30pm, Sa 9:30am-2pm. **Postal Code:** 42070.

ACCOMMODATIONS AND CAMPING

Solar de Tejada, C. Claustrilla, 1 (☎/fax 975 23 00 54; perso.wanadoo.es/solardetejada), on the corner of C. Collado, off Pl. Mariano Granados. Look for a blue sign with a moon. Stained-glass lamps, glass floors, and a rocking horse delightfully decorate. June-Aug. singles €39; doubles €51; triples €60. Sept.-May €36/45/54. MC/V. ❹

Hostal Residencia Alvi, C. Alberca, 2 (☎975 22 81 12; fax 975 22 81 40), on the street just beyond the tourist office, away from the park. Convenient location in the *centro ciudad*. Comfortable rooms, sparingly decorated. Singles €26; doubles €46. ❸

Residencia Juvenil Juan Antonio Gaya Nuñoz (HI), Po. San Francisco (☎975 22 14 66). With your back to the tourist office, take C. Nicolás Rabal along the park from Pl. Mariano Granados. Take your 2nd left onto C. Luisa Marillac and look for half-yellow dorms ahead. Spacious dorm-style rooms with large bathrooms. Extremely convenient location and great price. Check-in before 8pm. Curfew at midnight. Open July 1-Sept. 15. Doubles have private bath. 3-night max. stay when full. HI members only. Breakfast €1. Dorms €6.51, over 26 €8.71. ❶

Pension Ersogo, C. Alberca, 4 (☎975 21 35 08), the 1st right on C. Alberca off Pl. Ramón y Cajal. Seven 4th fl. rooms with 2 squeaky clean common baths. Large single beds next to wide windows. Singles €13; doubles €20; triples €28. ❶

Casa Diocesana Pío XII, C. San Juan, 5 (☎975 21 21 76; fax 975 24 02 78). From Pl. Marciano Granados, go up C. El Collado and right on C. San Juan, just after Pl. San Blas y el Rosel; in the tall building set back from the street. Hide away in monasterial rooms. Public telephone and laundry. July-Aug. singles €10.73, with bath €19.23; doubles €19.73, with bath €28.83. Sept.-June €8.75/€15.93/€15.03/€23.44. MC/V. ❶

Camping Fuente la Teja (☎975 22 29 67), 2km from town on Ctra. Madrid (km 233). Swimming pool open July-Aug. €3 per person, €3.25 per car, €3.75 per tent (IVA not included). Open *Semana Santa*-Sept. MC/V. ❶

FOOD

Soria's specialties include *chorizo* and *migas* (fried bread crumbs). C. M. Vicente Tutor is peppered with bars and inexpensive restaurants. Buy fresh foods at the small **market** in Pl. Bernardo Robles on C. Estudios, left off C. Collado. (Open M-Sa 8:30am-2pm.) **SPAR supermarket** is at Av. Mariano Vicen, 10, four blocks from Pl. M. Granados toward the train station. (Open M-Sa 9am-2pm and 5:30-8:30pm. MC/V.)

La Parilla, C. Tejera, 20 (☎975 21 44 32). From Pl. Mariano Granados, take C. Ferial and continue 3 blocks up the hill to C. Tejera. Traditional dining in a friendly atmosphere. Popular *menú* available at every meal except Sa dinner (€8.35). Entrees €7-13. Open M-F and Su 1-4pm and 9-11pm, Sa 1-4pm and 9pm-midnight. MC/V. ❷

Café-Bar Don Quijote, Av. Mariano Vicen, 37 (☎975 22 30 07), on the way to the train station. Locals crowd this cafe-bar, exchanging daily tidbits between bites of *tapas*. Luncheon *menú* (€9) served M-Sa 1-4pm in a pleasant dining room. MC/V. ❷

Callado 58, C. Callado, 58 (☎975 24 00 53). Large meals; larger frozen desserts. Unique ice cream concoctions (€4.25-5.35), shakes (€3.50), and heaping banana splits (€4.25). Combo plates €8.25-12.45. Open daily 8am-11pm. ❸

SIGHTS

The great 20th-century poet Antonio Machado once likened the **Río Duero** to a drawn bow arching around Soria. To find the river from Pl. M. Granados, walk past the sign for Restaurant Nueva York and straight down C. Zapatería, which changes to C. Real. Follow this road to Pl. San Pedro, and the bridge lies ahead.

ERMITA DE SAN SATURIO. Soria's biggest draw is well worth the 1½km trek downstream. The 17th-century Ermita de San Saturio, built into the side of a cliff, is a heavenly retreat where light seeps into the caves through stained-glass windows. San Saturio himself keeps vigil over the upstairs chapel, whose every inch of wallspace is covered by *frescos*. To get to the hermitage by car, cross the bridge onto Ctra. De Ágreda, turning right with the road. On foot, take the shorter, cooler, and more scenic route through the lush **Soto Playa.** Turn right just before the main bridge and cross the red and green footbridge. Keeping the river to your left, walk along the small island, meandering across small footpaths and boardwalks until you see the hermitage. *(Open May-Sept. Tu-Su 10am-2pm and 5-7pm; Oct.-Apr. Tu-Su 10am-6:30pm. Free.)*

MONASTERIO SAN JUAN DE DUERO. The Monasterio San Juan de Duero sits quietly by the river amid cottonwoods and grass. The church, dating from the 12th century, is quite simple. Its graceful arches blend Romanesque and Islamic styles and are all that remain of the 13th-century cloister. Inside, an annex to the Museo Numantino displays medieval artifacts. *(Turn left after crossing the bridge. Museo Numantino ☎975 22 13 97 for info. Open June-Aug. Tu-Sa 10am-2pm and 5-9pm, Su 10am-2pm; Sept.-Oct. and Apr.-May Tu-Sa 10am-2pm and 4-7pm, Su 10am-2pm; Nov.-Mar. Tu-Sa 10am-2pm and 3:30-6pm, Su 10am-2pm. €0.60; under 18, over 65, and students free. Sa-Su free.)*

MUSEO NUMANTINO. The museum exhibits an impressive collection of Celto-Iberian and Roman artifacts excavated from nearby Numancia. *(Po. Espolón, 8. ☎975 22 13 97. Open June-Sept. Tu-Sa 10am-2pm and 5-10pm, Su 10am-2pm; Oct.-May Tu-Sa 10am-2pm and 4-7pm, Su 10am-2pm. €1.20; under 18, over 65, and students free. Sa-Su free.)*

ENTERTAINMENT AND NIGHTLIFE

In the first week of August, Soria hosts a festival of concerts and street theater, as well as other events throughout the summer. Pick up the free *Actividades Culturales* in the tourist office for specific dates. As the moon rises, revelers of all ages crowd **Pl. Ramón Benito Aceña** and the adjacent **Pl. San Clemente,** off C. Collado. Late-night disco-bars center around the intersection of **Rota de Calatañazer** and **C. Cardenal Frías,** near Pl. Toros. On weekends, youths convene in **Parque Alameda** with store-bought spirits. A selection of small clubs lie within the **C. Zapatería** vicinity, but seek out the midnight island paradise of chic **El Son,** C. Zapatería, 24. Facing the clock tower in Pl. Mayor, head left through the arch to C. Zapatería at the end of the street and take a right. Sip on a daiquiri (€3.10-3.30) amid tropical tunes, or hit the dance floor. Try the hot rum for €3.30. (☎975 22 29 30. Open 7pm-4am.) The intimate tables of **Bar Ogham,** C. Nicolás Rabal, 3, draw a young crowd. (☎975 22 57 71. Open daily noon-3am.) **Kavanagh's,** C. Campo, 14, offers a friendly setting with great deals on large quantities of alcohol. If you're tired of the traditional wine or beer, try a *calimocho* or the lemon- or orange-flavored *orgasmo* (€3 per liter). (☎975 22 47 01. Open M-Sa noon-midnight.)

DAYTRIP FROM SORIA

RUINS OF NUMANCIA

Getting to Numancia without a car proves a problem. The bus to Garray comes within 1km of the ruins (15min.; summer M-F 2 and 5:45pm, Sa 5:45pm; winter M-F 2pm, F and Sa also 6pm; €1), but the return buses only run in summer (summer M-F 8:50am and 2:20pm, Su and holidays 2:20pm; winter M-Sa no 2:20pm return). Ruins ☎975 22 1397. Open June-Aug. Tu-Sa 10am-2pm and 5-9pm, Su 10am-2pm; Sept.-Oct. and Apr.-May Tu-Sa 10am-2pm and 4-7pm, Su 10am-2pm; Nov.-Mar. Tu-Sa 10am-2pm and 3:30-6pm, Su 10am-2pm. €1; under 18, over 65, and students free. Sa-Su free.

Archaeology fans will enjoy the ruins of Numancia, a hilltop settlement 7km north of Soria that dates back more than over 4000 years. The Celto-Iberians settled here by the 3rd century BC and resisted Roman conquest. It took 10 years of the Numantian Wars and the direction of Scipio Africanus to dislodge them. Scipio encircled the town in a system of thick walls in order to starve its residents. After his victory, he kept 50 survivors as trophies, sold the rest into slavery, burned the city, and divided its lands among his allies. Numancia lived on as a metaphor for patriotic heroism in Golden Age and Neoclassical tragedies, and the ruins, though battered, are worth a visit.

EXTREMADURA

The aptly named Extremadura is a land of harsh beauty and cruel extremes. Arid plains bake under the intense summer sun, relieved only by scattered patches of sunflowers. Yet the traveler who braves the Extremaduran plains is rewarded with stunning ruins and peaceful towns. Compared to the hectic pace of nearby Madrid, life in Extremadura is unhurried and far less modern, as though the region's history still dominates its present character. Though these are the lands that hardened New World conquistadors like Hernán Cortés and Francisco Pizarro, Extremadura itself has remained unexplored by most Spaniards. Mérida's Roman ruins and the hushed ancient beauty of Trujillo and Cáceres are only beginning to draw their flocks of admirers looking for the traditional Spanish countryside. Beyond the region's rugged landscape, its hearty pastoral cuisine is especially appealing; local specialties include rabbit, partridge, lizard with green sauce, wild pigeon with herbs, and *migas* (fried bread) with hot chocolate. Thick *cocido* (chick pea stew) warms *extremeños* in winter, while the many varieties of *gazpacho* (including an unusual white variation) cool in summer.

CÁCERES ☎927

Founded by Romans in 34 BC, this thriving provincial capital (pop. 90,000) is the closest Extremadura comes to a big city. Named a World Heritage City in 1986, Cáceres's *barrio antiguo* offers plenty of architectural wonder. Between the 14th and 16th centuries, rival noble families vied for social and political control, each building a miniature palace to demonstrate their power and wealth. As a result, the old city is a wonderful maze of palaces, museums, and churches. Although Cáceres's newer areas are less interesting, the *Parque del Príncipe* and a healthy nightlife scene provide ample amusement for a short stay. From Cáceres it is possible to enter Portugal by bus or by train via Badajoz or Valencia de Alcántara.

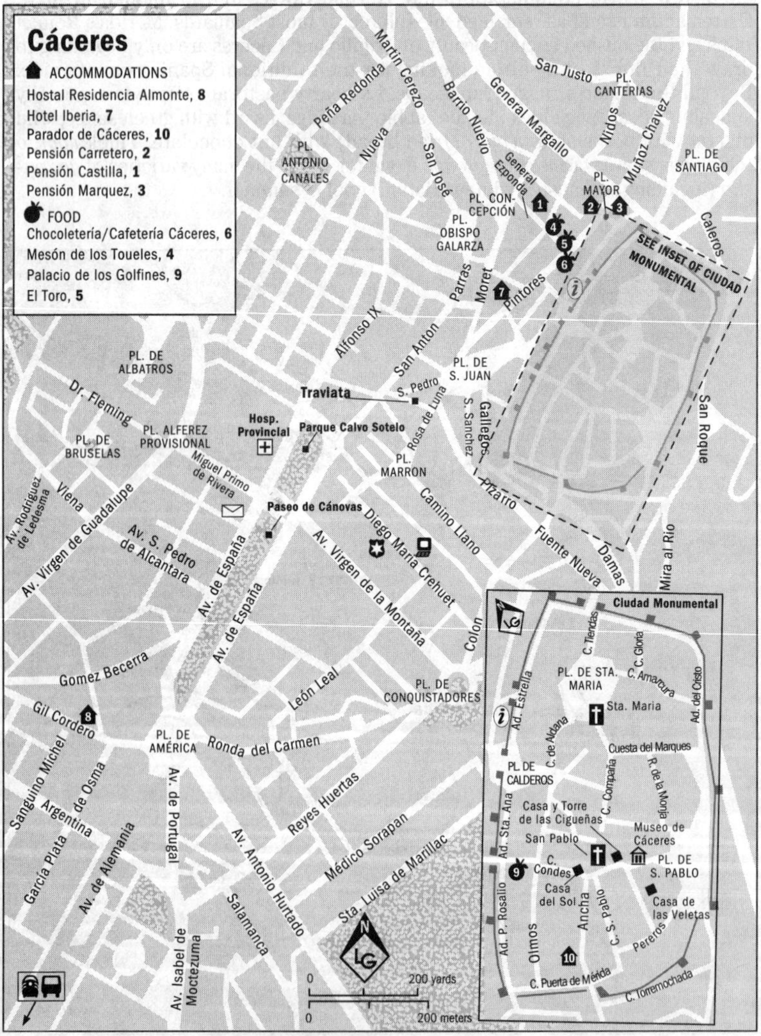

TRANSPORTATION

Trains: (☎902 24 02 02), on Av. Alemania, 3km from the old city across the highway from the bus station. Info window open daily 9am-9pm. Trains to: **Badajoz** (2hr.; noon, 1:44, 6:45pm; €6.60-13); **Lisbon** (6hr., 2:59am, €29); **Madrid** (4hr., 5-6 per day 4:01am-5:55pm, €15-29); **Mérida** (1hr., 5 per day 8:19am-6:45pm, €3.50-10.20); €6.60-13); **Sevilla** (4hr.; 8:19am, 2pm; €13).

Buses: (☎902 42 22 42), on Ctra. Sevilla, across from the train station. Info window open M-Th 7:30am-8:30pm, Sa 8:30am-9pm, Su 8:30am-11:30pm. Buses to: **Badajoz** (1½hr.; M-Sa 12:45, 6:45pm; Su 12:45, 9:15pm; €6.50); **Madrid** (4-5hr.; 6-7 per day M-Sa 1:45am-6pm, Su 1:45am-7pm; €15); **Mérida** (1hr.; M-F 8 per day 4:20am-9:30pm, Sa 4 per day 1-9:30pm, Su 9:30pm; €4.05); **Salamanca** (4hr.; 3-6 per day M-Sa 7am-6pm, Su 5-6:45; €10.55); **Sevilla** (4hr.; 4 per day M-F 4:10am-9:45pm, F-Su extra bus at 1pm, F and Su extra bus at 2:15 am; €13); **Trujillo** (45min.; 4-7 per day M-F 6am-6pm, Sa 6am-2pm, Su 8:15am-7pm; €2.55); **Valencia de Alcántara** (2½hr.; M-F 4 per day 12:15-6:30pm, Sa 2:30pm, Su 8pm; €6.60); **Valladolid** (5½hr.; daily at 1:25 and 5:15pm, extra bus on F and Su at 2:30am; €16).

Taxis: Stands at Pl. Mayor and bus and train stations. **Radio Taxi** (☎927 21 21 21).

Car Rental: Avis (☎689 84 90 18), in the bus station. On the right when you face the station from the outside. 1-day rental starting at €72. Minimum age 23. Open M-F 9:30am-1pm and 5-8pm (in winter 5-8pm only); Sa 9:30am-1pm.

ORIENTATION AND PRACTICAL INFORMATION

The **Ciudad Monumental** (a.k.a. *barrio antiguo*) and the commercial street **Av. de España** flank **Pl. Mayor** (a.k.a. Pl. General Mola). The plaza is 3km from the **bus** and **train stations,** which face each other across the rotary intersection of Av. Hispanidad and Av. Alemania. From the bus or train station, the best way to get to the center of town is via the #1 bus (€0.60); hop off at Pl. Obispo Galarza, next to the big blue and red "FLEX" sign. Facing the bus stop, start right and take your first left down the steps. At the first intersection, turn right, then left to continue downhill. When you reach the arches, Pl. Mayor will be to your left. Bus #2 stops on Av. Hispanidad, around the corner to the right as you emerge from the bus station, and runs to **Pl. de América,** hub of the new downtown area. From there, "Ciudad Monumental" signs point up the tree-lined Av. España (Po. Cánovas) toward Pl. Mayor.

Tourist Office: Pl. Mayor, 10 (☎927 62 50 47). English spoken. Open Oct.-June M-F 9am-2pm and 4-6pm, Sa-Su 9:45am-2pm; July-Sept. M-F 9am-2pm and 5-7:30pm, Sa-Su 9:45am-2pm. The **Patronato de Turismo** (☎927 25 55 97), C. Amargura, in the Palacio de Caravajal in the old city, provides quality maps of the monuments and hosts a modern art museum. From Pl. Mayor, pass under Arco de la Estrella (facing the tourist office, it is the first arch on your left) into the old city and continue straight until you face the Catedral in the Plaza de Santa Maria; it's opposite the left side. Open M-F 8am-9:30pm, Sa-Su 10am-2pm.

Currency Exchange: Banks line Av. España and the streets leading to Pl. Mayor.

Luggage Storage: At the train station (€3 per day) and bus station (€0.60 per day).

Emergency: ☎091. **Police: Municipal** (☎927 24 84 24), on C. Diego M. Crehuet.

Late-Night Pharmacy: Farmacia Castel, Pl. Mayor, 28A (☎927 24 50 87), **Farmacia Jiménez Rebolledo,** Pintores, 23 (☎927 24 55 18), and **Farmacia Acedo,** Pintores 31 (☎927 24 55 26), post the list of *farmacias de guardia* (24hr. pharmacies).

Hospital: Hospital Provincial (☎927 25 68 00), on Av. España, off Pl. Mayor.

THE BIG SPLURGE

J'ADORE LE PARADOR

Indulge your decadent side at the **Parador de Cáceres.** One of the many luxurious *paradores nacionales* scattered throughout Spain, the Parador de Cáceres gives its guests a taste of aristocratic Extremaduran life in the heart of the *ciudad monumental*. The hotel is situated in the beautiful 14th-century Palacio de Torrergaz, built by Diego García de Ulloa, a knight of the Order of Santiago and the Knight Commander of Alcuéscar, on the foundations of an earlier Moorish structure. The facade of the tower still bears the original coat of arms.

The Parador combines modern luxury with traditional Extremaduran culture. With a sunny interior courtyard, a manicured garden, and luxuriously appointed rooms, you may forget you are in Spain's harshest region. The restaurant specializes in regional cuisine, incorporating local game, fish, cheese, and desserts into the menu. Look for upscale versions of traditional specialties like venison with Casar cheese and roast kid with rosemary.

The hotel also offers excursions to historical and cultural sites in the region and can arrange activities ranging from golf to hot-air balloon rides.

C. Ancha, 6 (☎927 21 17 59). From the Arco de la Estrella, make a right onto Adarve la Estrella, then make a left onto C. Condes and follow it to C. Ancha; the hotel is on the right. Singles €84; doubles €105. MC/V. ❺

Internet Access: Ciberjust, C. Diego M. Crehuet, 7 (☎927 21 46 77). From Pl. Mayor take C. Pintores to Pl. San Juan and continue down C. Rosa de Luna to Pl. Marron; C. Diego M. Carhuet is the third left. €2 per hr. Open M-Sa 10am-2:30am, Su 4pm-2am.

Post Office: C. Miguel Primo de Rivera (☎927 62 66 81; fax 927 21 42 16), off Av. España on the left from Pl. de América. Open for stamps and Lista de Correos M-F 8:30am-8:30pm, Sa 9:30am-2pm. **Postal Code:** 10071.

ACCOMMODATIONS

Hostales are scattered throughout the new city and line Pl. Mayor in the old town. Prices rise during festivals, and advance reservations are recommended on summer weekends. Late-night arrivals, never fear—24hr. reception is the norm.

Pensión Carretero, Pl. Mayor, 22 (☎927 24 74 82; pens_carretero@yahoo.es). Some rooms have balconies onto Pl. Mayor. Spacious TV lounge. No winter heating. Singles €13; doubles €22; triples €30. MC/V. ❶

Hostal Residencia Almonte, C. Gil Cordero, 6 (☎927 24 09 25; fax 927 24 86 02). Heading away from Pl. Mayor on Av. España, C. Gil Cordero is right off Pl. de América. A/C €2.40 extra. A bit of a hike from the Plaza Mayor, it has a parking garage for 3 lucky cars (€3). Singles €21; doubles €32; triples €38; quads €44. MC/V. ❷

Pensión Castilla, Ríos Verdes, 3 (☎927 24 44 04). From Pl. Mayor, take C. General Ezponda, then take a right. Quiet rooms near the old city. Singles €15; doubles €30. ❷

Pension Márquez, Gabriel y Galán, 2 (☎927 24 49 60), off Pl. Mayor, opposite the town hall. The friendly owner makes Márquez feel like home. No winter heating. Doubles €20; triples €30. ❷

Hotel Iberia, C. Pintores 2 (☎927 24 76 34), right off Pl. Mayor, across from the Ayuntamiento. Excellent rooms with TV and private bathrooms for relatively low prices. Newly renovated in 2002. Breakfast €3.30. Singles €39; doubles €51; triples €57. MC/V. ❹

FOOD

Like every Pl. Mayor, the one in Cáceres is full of restaurants and cafes serving up *bocadillos, raciones,* and *menús.* Explore the side streets for less touristed local bars and pastry shops. For groceries, hit up the big **Hiper Tambo,** C. Alfonso IX, 25. From Pl. de América follow the left side of Av. de España to its extension. (☎927 21 17 71. Open M-Sa 9:30am-9pm.)

El Toro, C. General Ezponda, 2 (☎927 21 15 48). Serves yuppified Spanish cuisine in a terra cotta and marble setting. Entrees €6.60-15. *Menú* €9-12. Open Tu-Sa 11am-5pm and 8pm-1am. MC/V. ❸

Mesón de los Toneles, C. General Ezponda, 8 (☎927 21 61 70). Traditional *cocina extremeña* in a dim but folkloric setting. Don't leave without trying the delicious *migas extremeñas* (€5). Entrees €5-13. *Menú* €10. Open daily 11am-5pm and 7pm-2:30am. ❷

Chocolatería/Cafetería Cáceres, Plaza Mayor, 16 (☎927 24 97 63). A convenient restaurant with a spacious terrace and quick service. Serves breakfast (€5), lunch, and dinner. Entrees €6-12, *Menú* €7-9. ❷

Palacio de los Golfines, Adarve del Padre Rosalío, 2 (☎927 24 24 14). Situated in a gorgeous 15th-century palace in the old city, the Palacio has received numerous awards for its exquisite Spanish cuisine. Appetizers €3.50-10. Entrees €11-25, *Menú* €25. MC/V. ❹

SIGHTS AND ENTERTAINMENT

CIUDAD MONUMENTAL. Golden, stork-filled Old Cáceres is home to one of the most varied architectural ensembles in Europe. Roman, Arabic, Gothic, Renaissance, and even Incan influences (brought back by the conquistadors along with all that gold) can be detected throughout the old city. The main attraction is the neighborhood as a whole, since most buildings don't open their doors to tourists. The best way to experience the *barrio antiguo* is to suppress your internal compass and wander along the narrow, winding streets. Though the area is small, a tourist office map will come in handy. *(From Pl. Mayor, take the stairs from the left of the tourist office to the Arco de la Estrella, the entrance into the walled old city.)*

MUSEO DE CÁCERES. Inside the Casa de los Caballos, Museo de Cáceres is a must-see, housing a tiny but brilliant *Who's Who* of Spanish art. The museum features originals by El Greco, Picasso, Miró, and recent abstractionist stars, along with rotating exhibitions. Also called the Museo Arqueológico Provincial, the **Casa de las Veletas** (House of Weathervanes), connected to the Casa de los Caballos, displays Celtiberian stone animals, Roman and Visigothic tombstones, and an astonishing Muslim cistern. *(Across from the Casa y Torre de las Cigueñas. ☎927 24 72 34. Open Apr. 14-Sept. Tu-Sa 9am-2:30pm and 5-8:15pm, Su 10:15am-2:30pm; Oct.-Apr. 13 Tu-Sa 9am-2:30pm and 4-7:15pm. €1.20; students, seniors, EU citizens free. Su free for all.)*

CATEDRAL DE SANTA MARÍA. A statue of San Pedro de Alcántara, one of Extremadura's two patron saints, eyes the plaza from a corner pedestal of the Catedral de Santa María. His shiny boots are the result of years of good-luck toe-rubbing. Built between 1229 and 1547, the Romanesque and Gothic cathedral has a Renaissance ceiling and an impressive wood-carved altar.

CASA Y TORRE DE LAS CIGUEÑAS. Cáceres's aristocracy was a war-like lot. The city's monarchs removed all battlements and spires from local lords' houses to punish their violent quarreling. Due to his loyalty to the ruling family, Don Golfín's Casa y Torre de las Cigueñas (House and Tower of the Storks) was the lone estate allowed to keep its battlements. Storks still nest atop its spires each spring. *(From the Arco de la Estrella, take a right up the hill, a left onto Adarve de Santa Ana, another right, then a quick left onto C. Condes. Pass through Pl. de San Mateo to Pl. de Conde Canilleros; La Casa is on your left.)* Nearby **Convento de San Pablo** is late-Gothic eye candy for architecture addicts. The cloistered nuns sell delicious pastries through a peculiar door that prevents customers from seeing them. *(To the left of Casa y Torre de las Cigueñas.)*.

THE THINGS WE DO FOR LOVE Legend has it that the daughter of the Moorish King of Cáceres fell head over heels for the Christian conqueror Alfonso IX, then vying for control over Cáceres. Alfonso was badly disadvantaged, but his sweetheart gave him the keys to the walled city, enabling a successful surprise attack. Every April 22, the day before St. George's Day (the patron saint of the city), the legend is reenacted by citizens of Cáceres who break into groups of Christians and Moors and act out the battle, casting a dragon into fake flames at its finish.

OTHER SIGHTS. The 16th-century **Casa Del Sol** is the most famous of Cáceres's numerous mansions; its crest is the city's emblem. The **Casa de Toledo-Moctezuma** was built by the grandson of the Aztec princess Isabel Moctezuma to represent a unification of the old and new worlds. *(In Pl. de San Mateo, to the left as you enter the Arco de la Estrella.)* On October 26, 1936, in the **Palacio de los Golfines de Arriba,** yet another Golfín family palace, Francisco Franco was proclaimed head of the Spanish state and General of its armies. *(Sandwiched by C. Olmos and Adarve de Santa Ana.)*

ENTERTAINMENT. Weekend revelry starts in the **Pl. Mayor** and along **C. Pizarro,** lined with live-music bars. For live jazz music, poetry festivals, and tarot reading, head to **El Nido de las Cigueñas,** Cuesta de Aldana, 6 (☎927 21 58 36), in the old city. **Traviata,** Donoso Cortés, 10 (☎927 21 13 74), is a hip musical cafe blasting both techno and pop. Drinks start at €3, and there's no cover. Later on, the party migrates to **La Madrila,** a club-filled area near Pl. Albatros in the new city. From the Pl. Mayor, take Av. España, make a right onto Primo de Rivera, cross the intersection onto C. Dr. Fleming, then make another right into La Madrila.

DAYTRIP FROM CÁCERES

GUADALUPE

Transportation to and from Guadalupe can be somewhat tricky; most visitors arrive via tour bus or in their own cars. Empresa Mirat (☎927 23 48 63) sends buses from Cáceres to Guadalupe via Trujillo (2½hr., M-F 1:30 and 5:30pm, €7.50) and back (M-F 6:30 and 7:30am). Bus schedules quite regularly force an overnight stay in Guadalupe, but the pleasant calm can be a relief from bigger cities.

Two hours east of Trujillo and four hours southwest of Madrid, Guadalupe rests on a mountainside in the Sierra de Guadalupe. The **Real Monasterio de Santa María de Guadalupe,** with its eclectic history and decadent architecture, is a worthy daytrip, particularly for pilgrims and backpackers. The fairy-tale monastery has even been nicknamed "the Spanish Sistine Chapel." At the Battle of Salado in 1340, Alfonso XI, believed to have been aided by the Virgin Mary, defeated a much superior Muslim army. As a token of his gratitude, he commissioned the lavish Real Monasterio. Years later, it became customary to grant licenses for foreign expeditions on the premises; in fact, Columbus finalized his contract with Fernando and Isabel here. To pay homage to the city, he named one of the islands he discovered Guadalupe (now known as Turugueira). The most prominent object in the basilica is the **Icon of the Virgin,** carved of wood, blackened with age, and cloaked in robes of silver and gold. (Monastery open daily 9:30am-1pm and 3:30-6:30pm. €1.80.)

The **tourist office** in **Plaza Mayor** posts information on the door; follow signs from the bus station. (☎927 15 41 28. Open Tu-Su 10am-2pm and 5-7pm.) Travelers looking for food or beds should head to Pl. Mayor.

TRUJILLO ☎927

The gem of Extremadura, hill-top Trujillo (pop. 10,000) is an enchanting old-world town unspoiled by modern influences. Often called the "Cradle of Conquistadors," Trujillo furnished history with over 600 explorers of the New World, including Peru's conqueror Francisco Pizarro and the Amazon's first European explorer, Francisco de Orellana. Scattered with medieval palaces, Roman ruins, Arabic fortresses, and churches of every era, Trujillo is a hodgepodge of histories and cultures. Its most impressive monument is also its highest: the 10th-century Moorish castle commands a stunning panoramic view of the surrounding plains. Twentieth-century residents take pride in the well-preserved beauty of their churches, palace, and castle, adorning them with lovely gardens and flowering vines.

TRANSPORTATION. The **bus station** (☎927 32 18 22 or 927 32 06 61) is at the corner of C. de las Cruces and C. del M. de Albayada; look for the **AutoRes** sign. As most buses stop only en route to larger destinations, there are not always seats available—check ahead. Buses run to: **Badajoz** (2hr.; 9-10 per day M-Th, Sa 3:55am-11:50pm, F and Su 12:50-11:50pm; €7.55); **Cáceres** (45min.; 5-7 per day M-Th and Sa 11:15am-10:25pm, F and Su 11:15am-12:20am; €2.70); **Madrid** (2½hr.; 12-14 per day M-F 2:25am-6:15pm, Sa 6:40am-6:15pm, Su 8:55am-8:25pm; €13).

PRACTICAL INFORMATION. The English-speaking **tourist office** is in Plaza Mayor, on the left when facing Pizarro's statue. Info is posted in the windows when it's closed. (☎927 32 26 77. Open June-Sept. 9:30am-2pm and 4:30-7:30pm; Oct.-May 9:30am-2pm and 4-8pm.) Guided tours leave from Pl. Mayor at 11:30am and 5pm (€6.50). **Currency exchange** and an **ATM** are at **Santander Central Hispano,** Pl. Mayor, 25. (☎927 24 24 24. Open Oct.-Mar. M-F 8:30am-2:30pm and Sa 8:30am-1pm; Apr.-Sept. M-F 8:30am-2:30pm.) In a medical **emergency** call ☎112 or 927 32 20 16. The **police** are at C. Carnicería, 2 (☎927 32 01 08 or 608 70 65 17), just off Pl. Mayor. The **post office,** Po. Ruiz de Mendoza, 28, is on the way from the station to Pl. Mayor. (☎927 32 05 33. Open M-F 9am-2:30pm, Sa 9:30am-1pm.) **Postal code:** 10200.

ACCOMMODATIONS AND FOOD. Get medieval at **Hostal Trujillo ❷,** C. de Francisco Pizarro, 4-6. From the bus station, turn left on C. de las Cruces, right on C. de la Encarnación, then right again onto C. de Francisco Pizarro. The armor, lance, and shield-bedecked halls of this renovated 15th-century hospital lead to simple but comfortable rooms with full bath, A/C, and TV. (☎927 32 26 61; ☎/fax 927 32 22 74; www.orrakis.es/~hstruji/hostal.htm. Singles €21; doubles €39; triples €49.) The pleasant **Pensión Boni ❶,** C. Mingo de Ramos, 11, is off Pl. Mayor to the right of the church. Close to the plaza without the noise, Boni has airy patio rooms and a comfy TV lounge. (☎927 32 16 04. Singles €12; doubles €21, with bath €30; triples with full bath and A/C €39-42.) **Posada Dos Orillas ❺,** C. Cambreras, 6, offers top notch rooms in Trujillo's historic center. The decor of Dos Orillas' seven exclusive rooms are inspired by the seven cities in Latin America named Trujillo, giving this 16th-century building and its beautiful garden an eclectic feel. (☎927 65 90 79; posada@dosorillas.com. Doubles €93.50.) The best spot for a meal in Trujillo is a shaded table in the garden of **Meson Alberca ❸,** C. Victoria, 8. Enjoy a three-course *menú* (€15) with regional favorites in this tourist-free sanctum. (☎927 32 22 09. Open Su-Tu, Th-Sa 11am-5pm and 8:30pm-1am. AmEx/MC/V.) Sample the delicious *jamones ibéricos* and *pruebas de cerdo* (€6-10) in the more traditional **Mesón La Cadena ❷,** Pl. Mayor 8. (☎927 32 29 19. Open daily 1-4pm and 8:30-11pm.) Another dining option in the historic area is the **Cafe Bar Escudo ❶,** Pl. de Santiago, 2 (☎927 32 19 07). The friendly staff serves *bocadillos* (€3-6), *tapas* (€2), and entrees (€10) in the sunny terrace every day beginning at 10am.

SIGHTS. An afternoon stroll through Trujillo's *barrio* may be the best in Extremadura. Sights run €1.20-1.50 and are open daily June-Sept. 10am-2pm and 5-8:30pm, Oct.-May 9:30am-2pm and 4:30-7:30pm, except where otherwise indicated. A *bono* ticket (€4.20), available at the tourist office, allows entrance to the Casa-Museo de Pizarro, the Arab castle, and Iglesia de Santiago, and includes a guide book. The tourist office offers tours of the old city, including the Museo del Traje.

Trujillo's **main plaza** was the inspiration for the Plaza de Armas in Cuzco, Perú, constructed after Francisco Pizarro defeated the Incas. Palaces, arched corridors, and cafes surround the central fountain and the Estatua de Pizarro. The gift of an American admirer of Pizarro, the bronze statue was erected in 1929 and, like the plaza, has a twin in Lima, Perú. Festooned with stork nests, Iglesia de San Martín dominates the plaza's northeastern corner. The church has several historic tombs, but contrary to local lore, Francisco de Orellana does not rest here. (Opens 20min. before Mass. Mass M-Sa at 7:30pm, Su 1 and 7:30pm. Free.) Across the street, the seven chimneys of the **Palacio de los Duques de San Carlos** symbolize the religions conquered in the New World. (Open daily 9:30am-1pm and 4:30-6:30pm. €1.20.)

The Gothic **Iglesia de Santa María** is still farther up the hill. According to legend, the giant soldier Diego García de Paredes picked up the fountain (now located next to the rear door) at age 11 and carried it to his mother. After a fatal fall from a horse, the giant was buried here. Commonly known as the "Extremaduran Samson," the giant is referenced in chapter 32 of Cervantes's *Don Quijote*. The church's 25-panel Gothic altar-piece was painted by master Fernando Gallego in 1480. Climbing the tiny steps of the church tower is exhausting, but the view of Trujillo from the top is breathtaking. (Open May-Oct. 10am-2pm and 4:30-8pm, Nov.-Apr. 10am-2pm and 4-7pm. €1.20. Mass Su 11am.) To the left of the church is the restored **Museo de la Coria,** which explores the relationship between Extremadura and Latin America during *la Conquista* and the later independence of the new continent. (Open Sa-Su 11:30am-2pm. Free.) To the right of the church, inside a restored convent, is the **Museo del Traje,** exhibiting the spectacular evening gowns worn by royalty and famous actresses from the 17th century on. (Open 10am-2pm and 5-8:30pm. €1.50.) To get to the **Casa-Museo de Pizarro,** walk uphill on the stone road to the right of the Iglesia de Santa María. The bottom floor of the house is a reproduction of a 15th-century nobleman's living quarters, while the top floor is dedicated to the life and times of Francisco Pizarro. Crowning the hill are the ruins of a 10th-century **Arab castle.** Pacing the battlements and ramparts is like playing in your best Lego creation. Enjoy a view of unspoiled landscape, with Trujillo on one side and fields scattered with ancient battlements on the other.

MÉRIDA ☎924

For quality of Roman ruins per square foot, it doesn't get better than Mérida (pop. 60,000). In 26 BC, as a reward for services rendered to the Roman Empire, Augustus Caesar granted a heroic group of veteran legionnaires a new city in Lusitania, a province comprised of Portugal and part of Spain. The veterans chose a lovely spot surrounded by hills on the banks of the Río Guadiana to found their new home, which they named "Augusta Emerita." Not content to rest on their laurels and itching to gossip with fellow patricians in Sevilla and Salamanca, soldiers built the largest bridge in Lusitania, now the Puente Romano. The nostalgic crew adorned their "little Rome" with baths, aqueducts, a hippodrome, an arena, and a famous amphitheater. Modern Mérida complemented the Roman buildings with walkways, small plazas, and the world-class Museo Romano. In July and August, the spectacular *Festival de Teatro Clásico* presents some of Europe's finest classical and modern theater and dance, performed among the ruins.

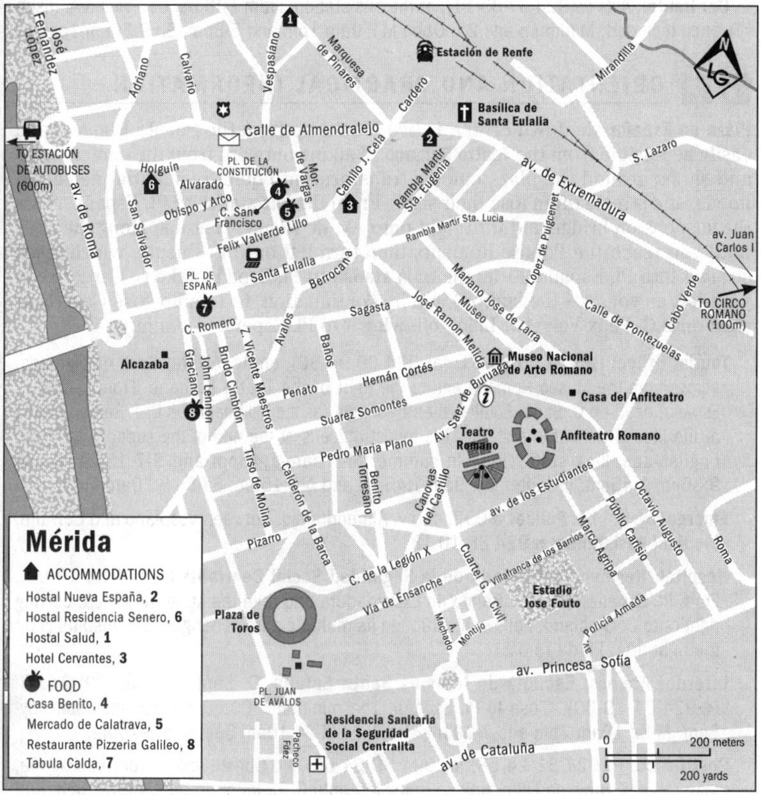

TRANSPORTATION

Trains: (RENFE info ☎902 24 02 02), C. Cardero. Info window open daily 7am-10pm. Trains to: **Badajoz** (1hr.; M-Sa 7:12am-10:16pm, Su 2:18-10:16pm; €2.50-9.60); **Cáceres** (1hr., 3-4 per day 9:06am-9pm, €3.16-10.22); **Lisbon** (transfer in Cáceres); **Madrid** (4hr.; M-F, Su 1:26 and 9pm, Sa 1:26pm; €18-26); **Sevilla** (4½hr., 9:25am, €10.20); **Zafra** (1hr., 9:25am, €3.16).

Buses: (☎924 37 14 04), Av. Libertad, in the Polígono Nueva Ciudad. Info booth open M-F 7am-11pm, Sa-Su 7am-1pm and 3:15-11pm. **LEDA** (☎924 37 14 03) sends buses to: **Badajoz** (1hr.; 4-9 per day M-F 8am-12:30am, Sa 8:45am-10:50pm, Su 11:40am-10:50pm; €3.65); **Cáceres** (1hr.; 2-4 per day M-Th 9:10am-9:15pm, F-Sa 9:10am-3:50pm, Su 5:50-8:30pm; €4); **Sevilla** (3hr.; 7-9 per day M-F 7am-8:30pm, Sa 7am-6pm, Su 9am-8:30pm; €9.75); **Zafra** (1¼hr.; M-Sa 11 per day 7am-9:50pm, Su 8:30 and 10:20pm; €3.60). **Alsa** (☎902 42 22 42) goes to: **Salamanca** (5hr.; 4-5 per day M-Sa 9:15am-1:30am, Su 9:15am-12:10am; €15); **Sevilla** (3hr., 6-8 per day 5:05am-10:45pm, €9.75). **AutoRes** (☎924 37 19 55) goes to **Madrid** (5½hr.; 7-8 per day M-F 8:45am-7:15pm, Sa 8:45am-4:45pm, Su 9:45am-7:15pm; €17-20).

Taxis: Teletaxi (24hr. ☎924 31 57 56).

Car Rental: Avis (☎924 37 33 11), at the bus station. From €48 per day plus IVA. Insurance included. Minimum age 23. Open M-F 9am-1pm and 5-8pm, Sa 9:30am-1pm.

ORIENTATION AND PRACTICAL INFORMATION

Plaza de España, the town center, is two blocks up from the Puente Romano and easily accessible from the **Teatro Romano.** Walking outward from the center, cafes and shops around the plaza quickly transform into quiet residential neighborhoods, and streets often lose their signs. From the **bus station** to Pl. España, cross the suspension bridge and turn right onto Av. de Roma. Continue along the river until you reach the Puente Romano, then turn left onto C. Puente, which leads straight into Pl. España. From the **train station** to Pl. España, take C. Cardero (on your left as you exit the station) and its continuation, C. Camilo José Cela; bear right onto C. Felix Valverde Lillo, following it to Pl. España (5-10min.).

Tourist Office: (☎924 00 97 31; fax 924 00 97 30), on Av. Álvarez Saez de Buruaga, across from the Museo Romano and to the right of the Teatro Romano. From central Pl. España, head up C. Santa Eulalia, then bear right (as the hill peaks) on C. J. Ramon Melida at the little circle with the statue. The tourist office is at the end of the street to the right. English-speaking staff. Open in summer M-F 9am-1:45pm and 5-7:15pm, Sa-Su 9:30am-1:45pm; in winter M-F 9am-1:45pm and 4-6:15pm, Sa-Su 9:30am-1:45pm.

Emergency: ☎112. **Police:** ☎092, on Av. Almendralejo, between Vespiano and Calvario. **Medical Assistance:** ☎924 38 10 18.

Hospital: Residencia Sanitaria de la Seguridad Social Centralita (☎924 38 10 00). From Pl. España, face the Banco de Extremadura and take the street to its left, curving right onto C. Graciano. Follow this through its multiple name changes; the hospital is on the right after Pl. de Toros.

Internet Access: Escuela de Idiomas Santa Eulalia, C. Santa Eulalia, 19, 2nd fl. (☎924 31 19 60). Close to Pl. España. 1hr. minimum. €0.60 per 30min. Open July-Sept. M-Sa 10am-2pm and 7-10pm; Oct.-June M-Sa 10am-3pm and 5-10pm.

Post Office: (☎924 31 24 58; fax 924 30 24 56), Pl. Constitución. From Pl. España, take C. Félix Valverde Lillo, make a quick left onto C. Trajano, go through the arch, and follow the road to the right; the post office is in the left corner. Open Sept. 16-July 14 M-F 8:30am-8:30pm, Sa 9:30am-1pm; July 15-Sept. 15 M-F 8:30am-2:30pm, Sa 9:30am-1pm. **Postal Code:** 06800.

ACCOMMODATIONS

Despite Mérida's crowds of visor-sporting tourists, it's not usually not a problem finding a reasonably priced room. Check the tourist office for complete listings.

Hostal-Residencia Senero, C. Holguín, 12 (☎924 31 72 07). From Pl. España, take the street to the left of Hotel Emperatriz to C. Holguín. Lively, charming owners make Mérida feel like home. A/C €4.20 extra. Apr.-Oct. and Dec. 22-31 singles €16, with bath €19; doubles with bath €31. Nov.-Dec. 21 and Jan.-Apr. €14/€18/€28. MC/V. ❷

Hostal Salud, C. Vespasiano, 41 (☎626 32 41 67; fax 924 31 22 59). From the train station, follow C. Cardero to the 1st intersection; take a sharp right onto C. Marquesa de Pinares. C. Vespasiano is the 3rd left. From the bus station, cross the bridge, head straight up Av. Almendralejo, and take the 3rd left onto C. Vespasiano. Large, nicely furnished rooms with TV and private bath. Singles €18; doubles €35. AmEx/MC/V. ❷

Hostal Nueva España, Av. Extremadura, 6 (☎924 31 33 56 or 31 32 11). Private baths. Apr.-Sept. singles €23; doubles €34; triples €44. Oct.-Mar. €20/€31/€40. MC/V. ❷

Hotel Cervantes, Camilo José Cela, 8 (☎924 31 49 01 or 31 13 42). Centrally located, modern building with comfortable facilities. Breakfast offered (€3.90). Singles €40; doubles €60. MC/V. ❹

FOOD

Plaza de España is filled with overpriced outdoor cafes. Buy fresh foods at the **market, Plaza Mercado de Calatrava,** on C. San Francisco. From Pl. España, take C. Félix Valverde Lillo; C. San Francisco is the second right. (Open M-Sa 8am-2pm.) Buy **groceries** at **El Arbol,** C. Félix Valverde Lillo, 8, 1½ blocks from Pl. España. (☎924 30 13 56. Open M-Sa 9:30am-2pm and 6-8:30pm. MC/V.)

Restaurante-Pizzeria Galileo, C. John Lennon, 28 (☎924 31 55 05). A glass-floored dining room reveals the Roman ruins below. 34 creative varieties of pizza, fresh salads, and pastas. Entrees €3.85-6. Open Th-Tu 1:30-4pm and 8pm-midnight. MC/V. ❶

Casa Benito, C. San Francisco, 3 (☎924 31 55 00). From Pl. España take C. Santa Eulalia for 2 blocks. The ivy-walled terrace is the perfect place for a beer. *Tapas* €0.60-3, *bocadillos* €2.10-6. Open M-Sa 9am-midnight. ❶

Tabula Calda, C. Romero y Leal, 11 (☎924 30 49 50; www.tabulacalda.com). Tables in an interior garden make Tabula the perfect setting for an intimate meal. Entrees start at €10 and 3-course *menús* at €15. Open daily 1-4:30pm and 8:30pm-midnight. ❷

SIGHTS

From the **Puente Romano** to the astrological mosaics, Mérida offers Spain's best view of Roman civilization in Iberia. A **combined ticket,** valid for all the listings below—except the Museo Nacional de Arte Romano—can be purchased at any of the sights. (€7.20, EU students €3.60. Valid for several days and includes a guide book to the ruins.) The ruins are all open June-Sept. daily 9:30am-1:45pm and 5-7:15pm; Oct.-May 9:30am-1:45pm and 4-6:15pm.

MUSEO NACIONAL DE ARTE ROMANO. Enormous, elegant galleries under brick arches house all the Roman memorabilia you could ask for: statues, dioramas, coins, and other relics. The **Cripta** displays parts of an ancient Augusta Emerita street found at the time of the museum's construction. *(Follow C. Santa Eulalia from Pl. España; at the traffic circle turn right on C. Juan Ramón Melida. ☎924 31 16 90. Open Oct.-May Tu-Sa 10am-2pm and 4-6pm, Su and holidays 10am-2pm; June-Sept. Tu-Sa 10am-2pm and 5-7pm, Su and holidays 10am-2pm. €2.40; EU students €1.20. Sa afternoon and Su free.)*

ANFITEATRO ROMANO AND TEATRO ROMANO. Inaugurated in 8 BC, the *anfiteatro* was used for contests between any combo of animals and men, so long as blood was shed. *(In the park across from the Museo Nacional. €5.10, covers Teatro as well.)* The spectacular *teatro* was a gift from Agrippa, a Roman administrator, in 16 BC. Its 6000 seats face a *scaenaefrons*, an incredible marble colonnade built upstage. Today the stage features performances of Teatro Clásico. *(Performances almost daily July-Aug. 10:45pm. Info ☎924 317 847; www.festivaldemerida.com. Tickets €9-36.)*

CASA DEL MITREO AND CASA DEL ANFITEATRO. These ruins of Roman homes showcase some of the world's finest Roman mosaics. Of special note is the Casa del Mitreo's **Mosaico Cosmólogico,** depicting the ancient Romans' conception of the world and forces of nature. *(From the entrance of the Teatro Romano, follow the right side of the ruins down Av. Alvarez Saenz de Buruaga and take a right onto Vía Ensarele. Casa del Anfiteatro is located between the Anfiteatro Romano and the Museo de Arte Romano. Each €2.55.)*

BULLBOARDS Staring glassy-eyed out the window of your preferred mode of transportation, you may notice rather unusual monuments along the highway: massive, black paper cut-outs of solitary bulls. Once upon a time (in the 1980s) these cut-outs were advertisements for Osborne Sherry. In the early 1990s, however, billboards were prohibited on national roads. A plan was drafted to take the bulls down, but Spaniards protested, as the lone bull towering along the roadside had become an important national symbol. After considerable clamoring and hoofing, the bulls were painted black and left to loom proudly against the horizon. The familiar shape now decorates t-shirts and pins in souvenir shops, but the real thing is still impressive. Keep your eyes peeled as you ride through the countryside.

OTHER RUINS. At the end of C. Rambla Mártir Santa Eulalia stand the **Museo, Basílica,** and **Iglesia de Santa Eulalia,** all commemorating the child martyr. In 1990, in the midst of repairs to the 6th-century church, layers of previous construction were uncovered to reveal the ruins of Roman houses dating from the 3rd to 1st centuries BC, a 4th-century necropolis, and a basilica dedicated to Santa Eulalia. *(From Pl. España, take C. Santa Eulalia to the traffic circle and bear left onto C. Rambla. Admission to the museum and basilica €2.55. Church open daily during services at 8:30am and 8pm. Free.)* Near the theater complex is the **Circo Romano,** or hippodrome. Diocles, the most famous Lusitanian racer, had his start here; he ended his career with a whopping 1462 victories. Once filled with spectators, the arena (capacity 30,000) is currently under excavation and is closed to the public—though the view from the outside is still worth the trip. Next to the Circo stand the remains of the **Acueducto de San Lázaro.** *(With your back to the Teatro Romano entrance, follow the road to the right, turn left on C. Cabo Verde, and take the pedestrian walkway underneath the train tracks.)* Built from materials discarded by the Visigoths, the **Alcazaba** was designed by the Moors to guard the Roman bridge. *(Down the banks of the Guadiana and near Pl. España. €2.55.*

BADAJOZ ☎924

Badajoz (pop. 120,000) is little more than a necessary stop en route to or from Portugal. Nonetheless, the contemporary art museum is worth a visit, and the Moorish ruins and 13th-century cathedral provide for an afternoon's distraction. The city has cleaned up much of the industrial pollution that once plagued it, making layovers more pleasant. While most people are just passing through, some have been here for a long time: archaelogical evidence suggests that humans first settled in Badajoz during the Lower Paleolithic period. Historical sights are not the only attraction in Badajoz; parties erupt in the evening in Pl. España and along the river. Jealous Portuguese revelers often cross the border to partake in the fun.

TRANSPORTATION

From Badajoz, buses to Portugal are faster and more convenient than trains.

Flights: Aeropuerto de Badajoz (☎902 21 04 00), Carretera Madrid-Lisboa, 10km east of the city. This small airport is forever closing or changing airline companies—be sure to ask the tourist office or a travel agency if flights are running. **AirEuropa** currently sends flights to **Madrid.** From Pl. España, a taxi to the airport is €15.

Trains: Av. Carolina Coronado (☎924 27 11 70). From the train station to Pl. Libertad, take bus #1 (€0.60). Info booth open daily 9am-10pm. Trains to: **Cáceres** (2½hr.; Su-F 8:10am and 2:40pm, Sa 8:10am; €5.35-16.50); **Madrid** (5hr.; Su-F 3 per day 8:10am-2:40pm, Sa 8:10am and 12:30pm; €21-30); **Mérida** (1½hr., 7 per day 6:40am-7:40pm, €2.60-10.50).

Buses: Central Station, C. José Rebollo López, 2 (☎924 25 86 61). Info booth open daily 7:45am-1am. Buses #3, 6a, 6b, and 9 run between the station and Pl. Libertad (€0.60). **Alsa** sends buses to: **Cáceres** (1½hr.; M 3 per day 8am-4:30pm, Tu-Sa 9:30am and 4:30pm, Su 4:30pm; €6.50-7.70) on its way to **Salamanca** (5hr., €17-19); **Lisbon** (3½hr., daily at 3:45am and 4pm, €15). **AutoRes** (☎924 23 85 15 or 902 02 09 99) to: **Lisbon** (2½hr.; daily 5pm and 2am, plus F 8:30pm; €12); **Madrid** (4hr.; 7-8 per day M-F and Su 8am-6:30pm, Sa 8am-4pm; €20-24); **Trujillo** (2hr.; 6 per day M-Th and Sa 8am-4pm, F 8am-6:30pm, Su 9am-6:30pm; €7.55). **Caballero** (☎924 25 57 56) to **Cáceres** (1½hr.; M-F 8:30am and 4pm, Sa 8:30am and 2pm, Su 6pm; €5.30). **Damas** to **Sevilla** (4½hr.; M-F 6:45am-8pm, Sa-Su 9am-8pm; €10.95). **LEDA** (☎924 23 34 78) goes to **Mérida** (1½hr.; M-F 8 per day 8am-9pm, Sa 6 per day 9:30am-9pm, Su 7:30 and 9:30pm; €3.65) and **Zafra** (1hr.; 6-8 per day M-F 6:45am-8:15pm, Sa 6:45am-6pm, Su 9am-8:15pm; €4.50).

Taxis: At bus and train stations and Pl. de España. **Radio-Taxi** (24hr. ☎924 24 31 01).

ORIENTATION AND PRACTICAL INFORMATION

Across the Río Guadiana from the **train station** and home to the municipal tourist office, **Plaza de España** is the heart of Badajoz. From the plaza, C. Juan de Ribera and C. Valdivia lead to Pl. Dragones Hernan Cortes; one block to the right is **Pl. Libertad** (5min.) and the regional tourist office. Between Pl. España and Pl. Libertad is the small park of **Po. San Francisco,** home to the **post office** and **supermarket.** From the **train station,** follow Av. Carolina Coronado straight to the Puente de Palmas, cross the bridge, then continue straight on C. Prim. Turn left onto C. Juan de Ribera at Pl. Minayo to get to Pl. España, or right to Pl. Libertad (35min.). The #1 bus runs from the train station to Pl. Libertad, stopping directly across from the regional tourist office. From the **bus station** entrance, turn left, take a quick right, and then turn left onto C. Damión Tellez Lafuente. Pass straight through Pl. Constitución and Pl. Dragones Hernan Cortes to Pl. España (20min.).

Tourist Office: Municipal Tourist Office, Pasaje San Juan (☎924 22 49 81). Facing the Ayuntamiento from Pl. España, take C. San Juan to its left; the tourist office is tucked into a small passageway on the right. English-speaking staff. Open M-F 10am-2pm and 5-7pm, Sa 10am-1:30pm. **Regional Tourist Office,** Pl. Libertad, 3 (☎924 22 27 63), across the street from the Consum supermarket. No English. Open M-F 9:30am-2pm and 4-6:30pm, Sa-Su 10am-2pm. For tips on nightlife, visit the helpful, friendly, and knowledgeable staff at the **Oficina de Información Juvenil,** Ronda de Pilar, 20 (☎924 22 44 49). Open M-F 9am-2pm and 5:30-7:30pm.

Luggage Storage: In the bus station (€0.60) and train station (€3).

Emergency: ☎092. **Police:** Av. Ramón y Cajal (☎091 or 924 21 00 72) off Pl. Libertad.

Hospital: Hospital Provincial, Pl. Minayo, 2 (☎924 20 90 00). From Pl. de España, walk down C. Juan de Riberato Pl. Minayo; it's on your left.

Internet Access: HD Zone, Antonio Moreno, 6A (☎924 24 86 16). Email, *bocadillos,* and *raciones* make a great combination. €1.50 per hr. Open daily from 8am until late.

Post Office: Po. San Francisco, 4 (☎924 22 25 48). **Lista de Correos.** M-F 8am-9pm, Sa 9am-2pm. **Postal Code:** 06001.

ACCOMMODATIONS

Hotels line the streets that originate in Pl. España. For **groceries,** head to **Consum,** next to the post office on Pl. San Francisco. (Open M-Sa 9am-9pm. MC/V.) Beyond Pl. España, cafes and eateries crowd **Po. San Francisco.**

Hostal Niza II, C. Arco-Agüero, 45 (☎924 22 38 81 or 924 22 31 73; hniza@coeba.es). From Pl. de España take C. San Blas downhill, then take your first right onto C. Arco-Agüero. Large rooms with A/C, TV, private bath. Owner is eager to provide maps, brochures, history. Singles €23; doubles €38; triples €47. ❷

Pension Pintor, C. Arco-Agüero, 26 (☎924 22 42 28). Close to the heart of the old city, and down the street from Hostal Niza II. You may need to ring the bell across the street at #33. One single with bath €20; doubles €23, with bath, TV, and A/C €35. ❷

Hotel Condedú, Muñoz Torrero, 27 (☎924 20 72 47; fax 924 20 72 84). Centrally located in Badajoz's commercial district, rooms are equipped with TV, bathroom, A/C, telephone, and those irresistible minibars. Singles €36.40; doubles €53.50. ❹

FOOD

Restaurante La Buena Pasta, C. Muñoz Torrero, 3 (☎924 22 03 64), one block off Pl. España, in a romantic setting. Pastas €3.90-6 and pizzas €6.60-8.40. Open W-M 1-4pm and 8:30pm-midnight. ❷

Restaurant La Traviata, Av. María Auxiliadora, 6 (☎924 24 48 95). From Pl. España go down Pedro de Valdivia, go right on Ronda del Pilar, left on Av. de Huelva which becomes Av. de Villanueva and then Av. María Auxiliadora (25min.). Great selection of wine, pasta, meat, and pizzas (€5-12). Open daily 1:30-5pm and 8:30pm-12:30am. ❸

Restaurant Simbo, C. J. María Alcaraz y Alenda, 33 (☎924 25 24 74). From Av. María Auxiliadora (above), take a right onto Av. S.Madroñero; its the 3rd street on the right. Large portions of delicious Cantonese food. Entrees €3. Open Su-Th 11:30am-2:30pm and 8pm-midnight, F-Sa 11:30am-2:30pm and 7:30pm-12:30am. ❶

SIGHTS AND ENTERTAINMENT

In 1995, Badajoz renovated its high-security prison to make way for the **Museo Extremeño e Iberoamericano de Arte Contemporáneo.** Five floors exhibit recent works from Spain, Portugal, and Latin America. The permanent collection includes controversial pieces, including Marta María Pérez Bravo's photo of a woman's breasts as a communion offering. From Pl. España, head down C. Juan Ribera, continuing as it turns into Av. Europa; the museum is on the left after Pl. Constitución. (☎924 26 03 84. Open Tu-Sa 10am-1:30pm and 5-8pm, Sun 10am-1:30pm. Free.) Badajoz's old quarter, including **Plaza de España** and **Po. San Francisco,** is rich with history. With one Renaissance, one Gothic, and one Plateresque window, the 13th-century **cathedral** (a converted mosque) in Pl. España is an artistic timeline. (Open 11am-1pm. Free.) The ruins of the **Alcazaba,** a Moorish citadel, stand at the top of the hill. (Ruins free. Archaelogical museum open Tu-Su 10am-3pm. Free.) Badajoz **nightlife** starts in the old quarter of the city where every street off of Pl. España has at least three different bars. **La Tetería,** Meléndez Valdéz, 14, offers 25 different kinds of tea in a relaxed setting with cushions on the floor. For a more sophisticated atmosphere, visit bar **Samaskarda,** Virgen de la Soledad, 3F. Comfortable couches and jazz music make it a great spot for intimate conversations. Later on, Badajoz draws partiers from as far as Portugal to **Pl. Santa Marta's** C. Francisco Lujan and C. Rafael Lucenqui. From Pl. España head downhill past Pl. Constitucion, and take the second right onto C. General Palafox, which becomes C. Francisco Lujan.

ANDALUCÍA

Andalucía is what most everyone comes to Spain to see, whether they know it or not. This area derives its spirit from an intoxicating amalgam of cultures. The ancient kingdom of Tartessus—the same Tarshish mentioned in the Bible for its fabulous troves of silver—grew wealthy off the Sierra Nevada's rich ore deposits. The Greeks and Phoenicians established colonies and traded up and down the coast, and the Romans later cultivated wheat, olive oil, and wine from the fertile soil watered by the Guadalquivir. In the 5th century AD, the Vandals flitted through the region on their way to North Africa leaving little more than a name—Vandalusia (House of the Vandals). The Moors provided a more enduring influence. Arriving in AD 711 and establishing a yet unbroken link to Africa and the Muslim world, they endowed the region with far more than the flamenco music and gypsy ballads proverbially associated with southern Spain.

Under Moorish rule, which lasted until 1492, Sevilla and Granada reached the pinnacle of Islamic arts, and Córdoba matured into the most culturally influential city in Islam. The Moors preserved, perfected, and blended Roman architectural techniques with their own, creating a style that became distinctively and uniquely Andalucian—patios, garden oases with fountains and fish ponds, and alternating red brick and white stone bands are its hallmarks. Two descendent peoples, the Mozarabs (Christians of Muslim Spain), and later the Mudéjares (Moors who remained in Spain after *la Reconquista)*, made further architectural impacts, the former with horseshoe arches and the latter with intricate wooden ceilings. The mingling of Roman and Moorish influences sparked the European Renaissance, merging Classical wisdom and science with that of the Arab world.

Andalucía has been the source of the many popular images of Spanish culture—bullfighting, flamenco, white-washed villages, sherry *bodegas*, sandy beaches, and the blazing sun. Beyond these obvious attractions lie Spain's most vivacious and warm-hearted residents. Despite (or perhaps because of) the poverty and high unemployment in their homeland, Andalucians have always maintained a passionate, unshakable dedication to living the good life. The *festivales*, *ferias*, and *carnavales* of Andalucía are world-famous for their extravagance.

SEVILLA ☎954

Sevilla (pop. 700,000) is arguably the most charming and romantic of Spain's great cities. Narrow, tangled streets unfold from the center leading to an awe-inspiring cathedral, the third largest in the world. Tourists and locals stroll among the horse-drawn carriages and chat over *tapas* in numerous outdoor cafes, while musicians perform in the many plazas. Contemporary Sevilla is the product of an ancient and impressive history. Once the site of a Roman acropolis founded by Julius Caesar, it later became the capital of the Moorish empire and a focal point of the Spanish Renaissance. Sevilla is now the guardian of traditional Andalucian culture; flamenco, *tapas*, and bullfighting are at their best here, and the city's many historical sites are stunning. Sevilla's *Semana Santa* and *Feria de Abril* are among the most lavish celebrations in all of Europe, and in the summer, crowds gather to drink and dance along the Guadalquivir River.

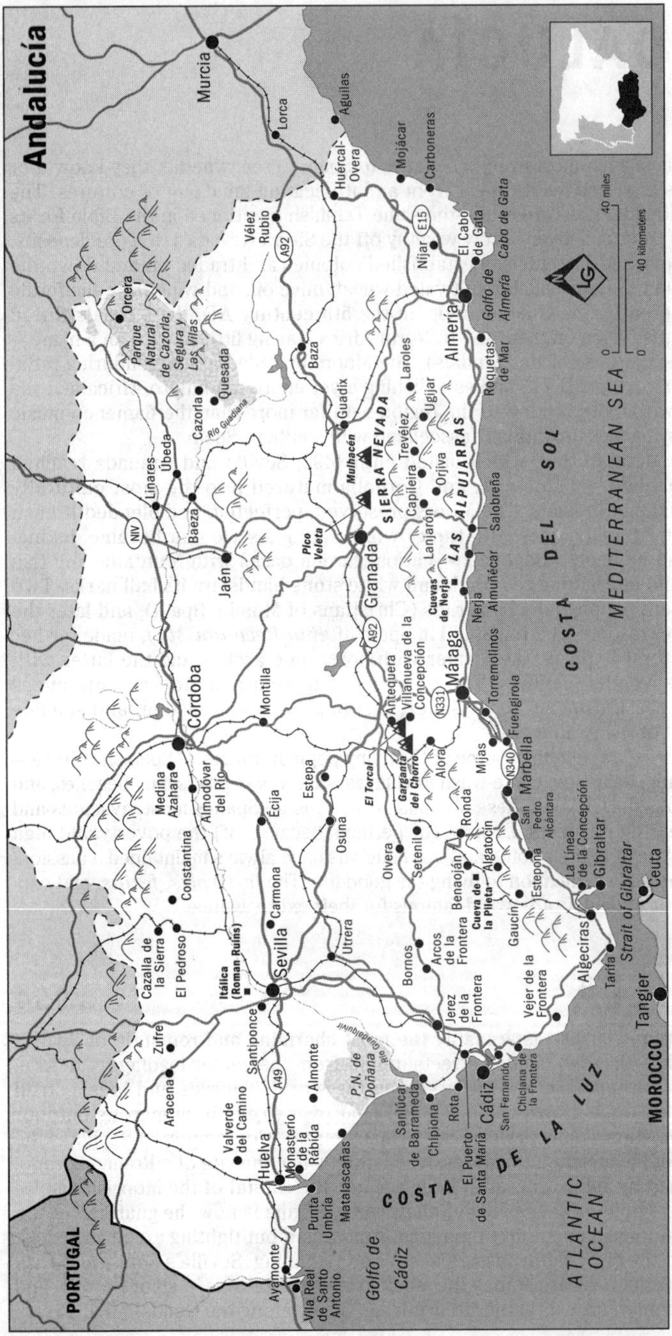
Andalucía
Murcia
Lorca
Aguilas
Huércal-Overa
Vélez Rubio
Mojácar
Carboneras
Níjar
E15
El Cabo de Gata
Cabo de Gata
Golfo de Almería
Almería
Roquetas de Mar
Laroles
Ugíjar
Trevélez
Órjiva
Capileira
Lanjarón
Salobreña
Almuñécar
Nerja
Cuevas de Nerja
LAS ALPUJARRAS
SIERRA NEVADA
Mulhacén
Pico Veleta
Granada
Guadix
Baza
Orcera
Parque Natural de Cazorla, Segura y Las Villas
Quesada
Cazorla
Río Guadiana
Úbeda
Linares
NIV
Baeza
Jaén
A92
Córdoba
Montilla
Antequera
Villanueva de la Concepción
Málaga
N331
Torremolinos
Fuengirola
Mijas
N340
Marbella
Álora
Garganta del Chorro
El Torcal
Estepa
Osuna
Écija
Almodóvar del Río
Medina Azahara
Constantina
Carmona
Sevilla
Itálica (Roman Ruins)
Cazalla de la Sierra
El Pedroso
Utrera
Olvera
Setenil
Ronda
Benaoján
Cueva de la Pileta
Algatocín
Estepona
Gaucín
San Pedro Alcántara
La Línea de la Concepción
Gibraltar
Ceuta
Strait of Gibraltar
Algeciras
Tarifa
Tangier
MOROCCO
Bornos
Arcos de la Frontera
Jerez de la Frontera
Vejer de la Frontera
Chiclana de la Frontera
San Fernando
Cádiz
El Puerto de Santa María
Rota
Chipiona
Sanlúcar de Barrameda
P.N. de Doñana
Río Guadalquivir
Almonte
Santiponce
A49
Zufre
Aracena
Valverde del Camino
Huelva
Monasterio de la Rábida
Punta Umbría
Matalascañas
Ayamonte
Vila Real de Santo Antonio
PORTUGAL
Golfo de Cádiz
COSTA DE LA LUZ
ATLANTIC OCEAN
COSTA DEL SOL
MEDITERRANEAN SEA
0
40 miles
0
40 kilometers
N
LG

INTERCITY TRANSPORTATION

BY PLANE

All flights arrive at **Aeropuerto San Pablo,** Ctra. Madrid (☎954 44 90 00), 12km out of town. A taxi ride from the town center costs about €13. **Los Amarillos** (☎954 98 91 84) runs a bus from outside the Hotel Alfonso XIII at the Pta. Jerez (M-F every 30-45min., Sa-Su every hr. 6:15am-11pm; €2.25). **Iberia,** C. Guaira, 8 (☎954 22 89 01; nationwide 902 40 05 00; open M-F 9am-1:30pm) books flights to **Barcelona** (55min., 6 per day) and **Madrid** (45min., 6 per day).

BY TRAIN

Sevilla is served by **Estación Santa Justa,** Av. Kansas City (☎954 41 41 11). Services include **luggage storage** and **ATM.** In town, the **RENFE** office, C. Zaragoza, 29, is near Pl. Nueva. (☎954 54 02 02. Open M-F 9am-1:15pm and 4-7pm.) International bookings must be made at this office.

AVE trains run to: **Córdoba** (45min., 18-20 per day 6:30am-9pm, €15-17) and **Madrid** (2½hr., 18-20 per day 6:30am-9pm, €62).

Talgo trains run to: **Almería** (5½hr., 3 per day 7am-5:40pm, €26.65); **Antequera** (2hr., 5 per day 7am-6pm, €10); **Barcelona** (12hr.; M-F 8:05, 9:43am, 8:20pm; €53); **Cáceres** (5½hr., 4:30pm, €18.60); **Cádiz** (2hr.; 7-12 per day M-F 6:35am-9:27pm, Sa-Su 9am-9:27pm; €8.05); **Córdoba** (1½hr., 6 per day 6:30am-9pm, €8.05); **Granada** (3hr., 5 per day 7am-5:40pm, €16.65); **Huelva** (1½hr., M-F 3 per day 8:50am-8:45pm, €6.61); **Jaén** (2hr., 6:46pm, €14.15); **Málaga** (2½hr., 4-7 per day 7:40am-€8.10pm, €13.35); **Valencia** (8½hr., 4 per day 8:11am-9:50pm, €35.50).

BY BUS

The bus station at **Prado de San Sebastián,** C. Manuel Vázquez Sagastizabal (☎954 41 71 11), serves most of Andalucía. Look carefully; this station is in a yellow building (next to the restaurant) and is not marked on the street. Sevilla has a second bus station at **Plaza de Armas** (☎954 90 80 40), primarily serving areas outside of Andalucía. Several bus lines are in the process of changing the station from which they depart. If in doubt, phone ahead or check with the tourist office.

PRADO DE SAN SEBASTIÁN

Transportes Alsina Graells (☎954 41 88 11). Open daily 6:30am-11pm. To: **Almería** (7hr., 3 per day 7am-midnight, €25.16); **Córdoba** (2hr., 10-12 per day 7:30am-9:30pm, €8.28); **Granada** (3hr., 10 per day 8am-11pm, €15.43); **Jaén** (4hr., 6 per day 7:30am-6pm, €14.75); **Málaga** (2½hr., 10-12 per day 7am-midnight, €12.59); **Murcia** (8hr., 3 per day 8am-11pm, €30.10).

Transportes Comes (☎954 41 68 58). Open M-Sa 6:30am-9:30pm, Su 7:15am-10:30pm. To: **Algeciras** (3½hr., 4 per day 9am-8pm, €13.75); **Cádiz** (1½hr., 11-13 per day 7am-10pm, €9); **Jerez de la Frontera** (2hr., 6 per day 8:30am-10pm, €5.62); **Tarifa** (3hr., 4 per day 9am-8pm, €13.54).

Los Amarillos (☎954 98 91 84). Open M-F 7:30am-2pm and 2:30-8pm, Sa-Su 7:30am-2pm and 2:30-8pm. To: **Arcos de la Frontera** (2hr.; 8am, 4:30pm; €5.89); **Marbella** (3hr.; 8am, 4, 8pm; €6.30); **Ronda** (2½hr., 3-5 per day 7am-5pm, €8.38); **Sanlúcar and Chipiona** (2hr., 10 per day 7am-9pm, €6.31).

PLAZA DE ARMAS

Enatcar-Bacoma (☎902 42 22 42). Open daily 9:30am-9pm. To **Valencia** (9-11hr.; 9:30am, 5:30pm; €40-47) and **Barcelona** (12-18hr.; 9:30am, 5:30pm; €61-73).

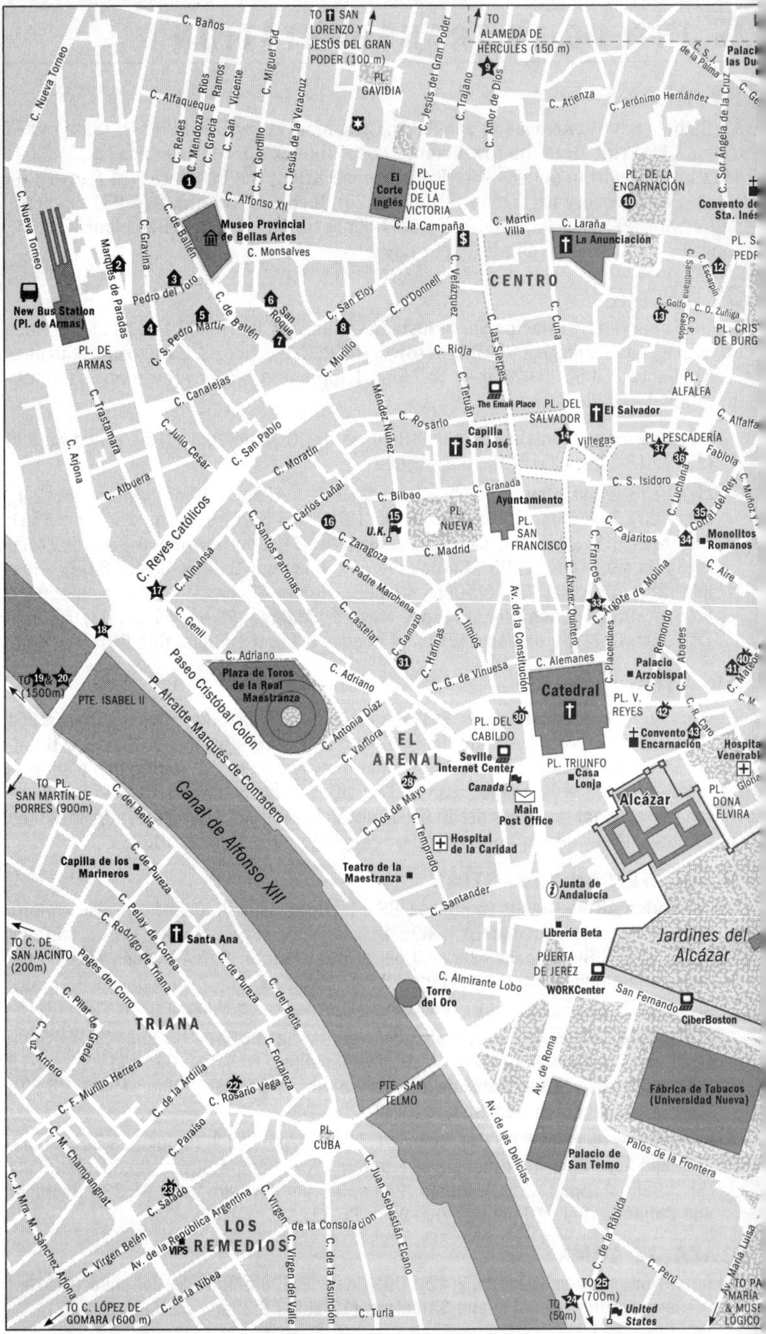

TO SAN LORENZO Y JESÚS DEL GRAN PODER (100 m)
TO ALAMEDA DE HÉRCULES (150 m)
C. Baños
C. Nueva Torneo
C. Alfaqueque
PL. GAVIDIA
C. Jesús del Gran Poder
C. Trajano
C. Amor de Dios
C. Atienza
C. Jerónimo Hernández
C. Sor Ángela de la Cruz
Palacio de las Dueñas
El Corte Inglés
PL. DUQUE DE LA VICTORIA
PL. DE LA ENCARNACIÓN
Convento de Sta. Inés
C. Alfonso XII
Museo Provincial de Bellas Artes
C. la Campaña
C. Martín Villa
C. Laraña
La Anunciación
C. Monsalves
CENTRO
New Bus Station (Pl. de Armas)
PL. DE ARMAS
C. Nueva Torneo
Marqués de Paradas
C. Gravina
Pedro del Toro
C. de Bailén
C. S. Pedro Mártir
San Roque
C. San Eloy
C. O'Donnell
C. Velázquez
C. Cuna
C. Murillo
C. Rioja
C. las Sierpes
C. Tetuán
C. Canalejas
C. Trastamara
C. Julio César
C. San Pablo
Méndez Núñez
C. Rosario
The Email Place
PL. DEL SALVADOR
El Salvador
Capilla San José
Villegas
PL. ALFALFA
PL. PESCADERÍA
Fabiola
C. Arjona
C. Albuera
C. Moratín
C. Reyes Católicos
C. Carlos Cañal
C. Bilbao
U.K.
PL. NUEVA
C. Granada
Ayuntamiento
PL. SAN FRANCISCO
C. S. Isidoro
C. Luchana
Conde del Rey
Monolitos Romanos
C. Almansa
C. Santos Patronas
C. Zaragoza
C. Madrid
C. Pajaritos
C. Padre Marchena
C. Francos
C. Álvarez Quintero
Av. de la Constitución
C. Argote de Molina
C. Aire
C. Genil
C. Castelar
C. Gamazo
C. Harinas
C. Jimios
C. Placentines
C. Remondo
C. Abades
TO 19 & 20 (1500m)
PTE. ISABEL II
P. Alcalde Marqués de Contadero
Paseo Cristóbal Colón
C. Adriano
Plaza de Toros de la Real Maestranza
C. Antonia Díaz
C. Vaflora
C. G. de Vinuesa
C. Alemanes
Catedral
Palacio Arzobispal
PL. V. REYES
Convento Encarnación
PL. DEL CABILDO
EL ARENAL
Seville Internet Center
Canada
Main Post Office
PL. TRIUNFO
Casa Lonja
Alcázar
PL. DONA ELVIRA
Hospital Venerables
TO PL. SAN MARTÍN DE PORRES (900m)
C. del Betis
Canal de Alfonso XIII
C. Dos de Mayo
C. Temprado
Hospital de la Caridad
Capilla de los Marineros
C. de Pureza
Teatro de la Maestranza
Junta de Andalucía
C. Santander
Librería Beta
Jardines del Alcázar
C. Pelay de Correa
C. Rodrigo de Triana
Santa Ana
TO C. DE SAN JACINTO (200m)
Pages del Corro
C. de Pureza
C. del Betis
PUERTA DE JEREZ
C. Almirante Lobo
Torre del Oro
WORKCenter
San Fernando
CiberBoston
C. Pilar de Gracia
TRIANA
C. Luz Arriero
C. F. Murillo Herrera
C. de la Ardilla
C. Rosario Vega
C. Fortaleza
PTE. SAN TELMO
Av. de Roma
Fábrica de Tabacos (Universidad Nueva)
C. M. Champagnat
C. Paraíso
PL. CUBA
Av. de las Delicias
Palacio de San Telmo
Palos de la Frontera
C. J. Mra. M. Sánchez Arjona
C. Salado
Av. de la República Argentina
C. Virgen de la Consolación
C. Juan Sebastián Elcano
C. de la Rábida
LOS REMEDIOS
VIPS
C. Virgen Belén
C. de la Nibea
C. Virgen del Valle
C. de la Asunción
C. Perú
Av. María Luisa
TO PL. MARÍA LUISA & MUSEO ARQUEOLÓGICO
TO C. LÓPEZ DE GOMARA (600 m)
C. Turia
TO 24 (50m)
TO 25 (700m)
United States

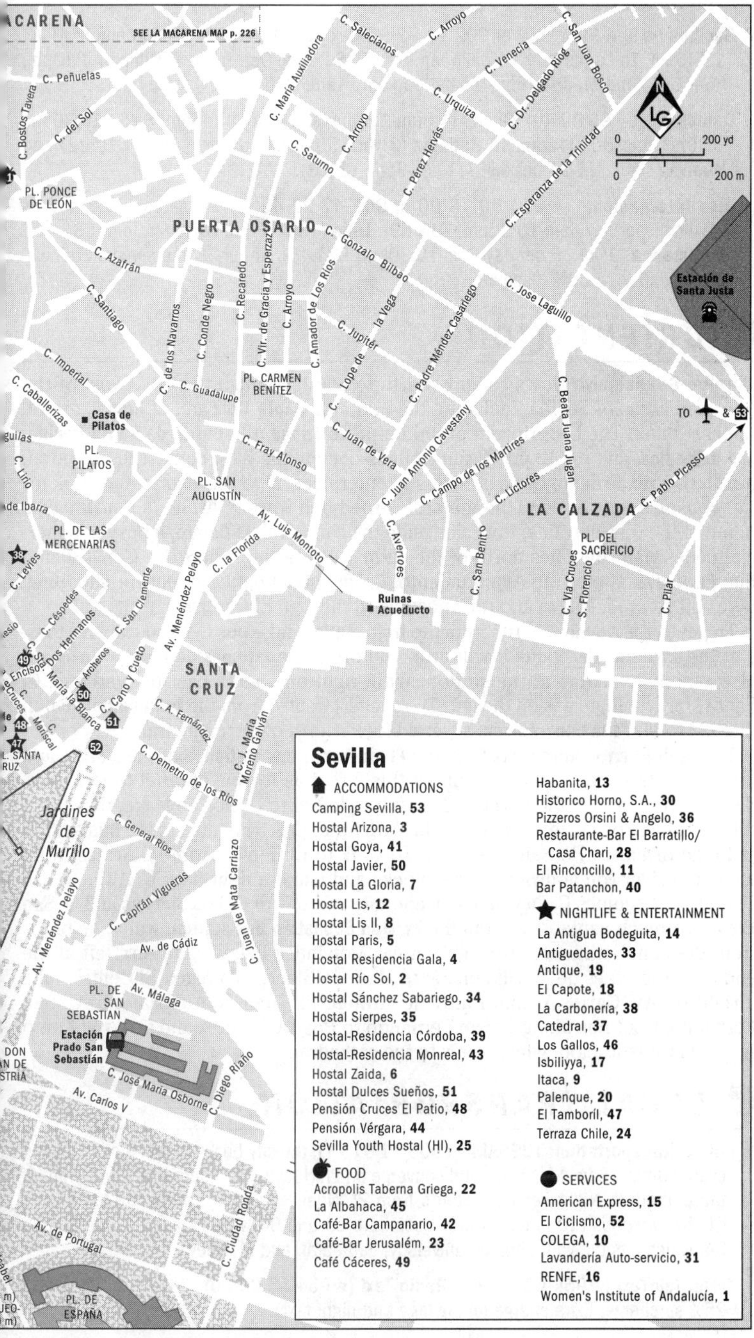

Sevilla

ACCOMMODATIONS

Camping Sevilla, **53**
Hostal Arizona, **3**
Hostal Goya, **41**
Hostal Javier, **50**
Hostal La Gloria, **7**
Hostal Lis, **12**
Hostal Lis II, **8**
Hostal Paris, **5**
Hostal Residencia Gala, **4**
Hostal Río Sol, **2**
Hostal Sánchez Sabariego, **34**
Hostal Sierpes, **35**
Hostal-Residencia Córdoba, **39**
Hostal-Residencia Monreal, **43**
Hostal Zaida, **6**
Hostal Dulces Sueños, **51**
Pensión Cruces El Patio, **48**
Pensión Vérgara, **44**
Sevilla Youth Hostal (HI), **25**

FOOD

Acropolis Taberna Griega, **22**
La Albahaca, **45**
Café-Bar Campanario, **42**
Café-Bar Jerusalém, **23**
Café Cáceres, **49**
Habanita, **13**
Historico Horno, S.A., **30**
Pizzeros Orsini & Angelo, **36**
Restaurante-Bar El Barratillo/ Casa Chari, **28**
El Rinconcillo, **11**
Bar Patanchon, **40**

NIGHTLIFE & ENTERTAINMENT

La Antigua Bodeguita, **14**
Antiguedades, **33**
Antique, **19**
El Capote, **18**
La Carbonería, **38**
Catedral, **37**
Los Gallos, **46**
Isbiliyya, **17**
Itaca, **9**
Palenque, **20**
El Tamboríl, **47**
Terraza Chile, **24**

SERVICES

American Express, **15**
El Ciclismo, **52**
COLEGA, **10**
Lavandería Auto-servicio, **31**
RENFE, **16**
Women's Institute of Andalucía, **1**

Socibus (☎954 90 11 60 or 902 22 92 92; fax 954 90 16 92). Open daily 8:30am-12:45am. To **Lagos** (6hr.; 1 daily Jan.-May Th-Su, June-Oct. Tu-Su 7:30am or 4:30pm; from €15) and **Madrid** (6hr., 11 per day 9am-1am, €16.89).

Damas (☎954 90 80 40). Open M-F 8am-1:30pm and 4:30-10:45pm, Sa-Su 10:30am-1:30pm and 8-10:45pm. To **Badajoz** (3½hr., 5 per day 6:45am-8pm, €10.22) and **Huelva** (1¼hr., 21-24 per day 7:30am-9pm, €5.53).

Alsa Internacional (☎954 90 78 00 or 902 42 22 42; www.alsa.es). To: **Cáceres** (4¼hr., 7 per day 6am-10:30pm, €13.69); **León** (13hr., 3 per day 6am-9pm, €34.40); **Salamanca** (9½hr., 5 per day 6am-10:30pm, €24.45). Under 26 and seniors 10% discount, under 12 50% discount.

ORIENTATION

The **Río Guadalquivir** flows roughly north to south through the city. Most of the touristed areas of Sevilla, including the **Barrio de Santa Cruz** and **El Arenal,** are on the east bank. The historic and proud **Barrio de Triana,** the **Barrio de Santa Cecilia, Los Remedios,** and the Expo '92 fairgrounds occupy the west bank. The cathedral, next to Barrio de Santa Cruz, is Sevilla's centerpiece. If you're disoriented, look for the conspicuous Giralda (the minaret-turned-bell tower). **Av. de la Constitución,** home of the tourist office, runs alongside the cathedral. **El Centro,** a busy commercial pedestrian zone, lies north of the cathedral, starting where Av. Constitución hits **Pl. Nueva,** site of the Ayuntamiento. **C. Tetuan,** a popular street for shopping, takes off from Pl. Nueva and runs northward through El Centro.

To get to Barrio Santa Cruz from the **train station,** take bus C-2 and transfer to C-3 at the Jardines del Valle; it will drop you off at the **Jardines de Murillo. Taxis** are also readily available at the station. Walk right one block past the gardens; C. Santa María la Blanca is on the left. To reach El Centro from the **train station,** catch bus #32 to **Pl. de la Encarnación,** several blocks north of the cathedral.

To reach Barrio Santa Cruz from the **Pl. de Armas bus station,** exit the station and cross the street to C. Arjona. Follow this street as it runs parallel to the river. Shortly after passing the Plaza de Toros, turn left onto C. Dos de Mayo; the end of this street will place you in front of the cathedral. Bus C4 connects the bus station at Pl. de Armas to Pr. San Sebastián. To walk to El Centro from Pl. Armas, walk along the river (on your left) three blocks and make a right onto C. Alfonso XII. This street becomes C. La Compaña, and intersects with C. Los Sierpes and C. San Elroy. To reach Santa Cruz from the **Pr. San Sebastián bus station,** walk one block from the main entrance, turn right on Av. Menéndez Pelayo, and turn left at the end of the Jardines de Murillo on Santa María la Blanca. To reach El Centro, take a right on Av. Carlos V, and follow it through Pl. Juan de Austria onto C. San Fernando. Continue along C. San Fernando to Puerta de Jerez and turn right onto Av. de la Constitución, which leads to the cathedral.

LOCAL TRANSPORTATION

Public Transportation: TUSSAM (☎900 71 01 71), the city bus network. Most lines run every 10min. (6am-11:15pm) and converge on Pl. Nueva, Pl. Encarnación, or in front of the cathedral. Night service departs from Pl. Nueva (every hr. midnight-2am). Fare €0.90, *bonobús* (10 rides) €4.50. Useful are C3 and C4, which circle the center, and 34, which hits the youth hostel, university, cathedral, and Pl. Nueva.

Taxis: TeleTaxi (☎954 62 22 22). **Radio Taxi** (☎954 58 00 00). Base rate €2.15, Su 25% surcharge. Extra charge for luggage and night taxis.

Car Rental: Hertz, at the airport (☎954 51 47 20) or train station (☎954 53 39 14). General information and reservations ☎902 40 24 05. Min. age 25. From €54 a day. Open daily 7am-11pm. AmEx/MC/V. **Triana Rent A Car,** C. Almirante Lobo, 7 (☎954 56 44 39 or 954 33 68 97). Minimum age 21, but they will negotiate. €54 per day, discounts for longer rentals.

Moped Rental: Alkimoto, C. Fernando Tirado, 5 (☎954 58 49 27), near the train station. €18 per day. Open M-F 9am-1:30pm and 5-8pm.

Bike Rental: El Ciclismo, Po. Catalina de Ribera, 2 (☎954 41 19 59), off Menéndez Pelayo, at the end of the Jardines de Murillo. €12 per weekday, €24 for the weekend. Open M-F 10am-1:30pm and 5-8pm.

PRACTICAL INFORMATION

TOURIST AND FINANCIAL SERVICES

Tourist Offices: Centro de Información de Sevilla, Av. Constitución, 21B (☎954 22 14 04; fax 954 22 97 53), 1 block from the cathedral. English spoken. Open M-F 9am-7pm, Sa 10am-2pm and 3-7pm, Su 10am-2pm. **Info booths** at the train station and Pl. Nueva carry maps and bus guides.

Currency Exchange: Santander Central Hispano, C. la Campaña, 19 (☎902 24 24 24). Open M-F 8:30am-2pm, Sa 8:30am-1pm. Money-changing shops are scattered around the cathedral and are useful when banks are closed; most are open daily until 8pm. While they claim to be "commission-free," the exchange rate will be better at a bank.

Banks and **ATMs:** All along Av. Constitución and near Pl. Nueva.

American Express: Pl. Nueva, 7 (☎954 21 16 17). Open M-F 9:30am-1:30pm and 4:30-7:30pm, Sa 10am-1pm.

LOCAL SERVICES

Luggage Storage: At Pr. San Sebastián bus station (€0.90 per bag per day; open 6:30am-10pm), Pl. Armas bus station (€3 per day), and the train station (€3 per day).

English Bookstore: Librería Beta, C. Constitución, 27 (☎954 56 07 03), past the tourist office on the corner near Pta. Jerez. Has a good selection of English language books and travel guides, including *Let's Go.* Open M-F 10am-2pm and 5:30-9pm, Sa 10am-2pm. MC/V. **Vértice,** C. San Fernando, 33 (☎954 21 16 54), near Pta. Jerez. Open M-W 9:30am-2pm and 6-8:30pm, Th-Sa 9am-3pm. Closed Sa in July.

VIPS: C. República Argentina, 25 (☎954 27 93 97), 3 blocks from Pl. Cuba, in Triana. International newspapers, liquor, non-perishable groceries, and an American-style restaurant. Open Su-Th 8am-1:30am, F 8am-3am, Sa 9am-3am. MC/V.

Women's Services: Women's Institute of Andalucía, C. Alfonso XII, 52 (24hr. toll free hotline ☎900 20 09 99; office ☎955 03 49 53; www.iam.juntadeandalucia.es). Info on feminist and lesbian organizations, plus legal and psychological services for rape victims. Employment listings for women. Open Oct.-May M-Th 8am-8pm, F 8am-3pm; June-Sept. M-F 8am-2:30pm.

Gay and Lesbian Services: COLEGA (Colectiva de Lesbianas y Gays de Andalucía), Pl. Encarnación, 23, 2nd fl. (☎954 50 13 77; fax 954 56 33 66; www.colegaweb.net). Look for the sign in the window; the door is not marked. Open M-F 10am-2pm.

Laundromat: Lavandería Auto-servicio, C. Castelar, 2 (☎954 21 05 35). From the cathedral, walk 2 blocks down C. Vinuesa and turn left. Wash and dry €6 per 5kilos. Open M-Sa 9:30am-1:30pm and 5-8:30pm.

EMERGENCY AND COMMUNICATIONS

Emergency: Medical: ☎061. **Police:** Po. Concordia (Local ☎092; national ☎091).

Late-Night Pharmacy: Check list posted at any pharmacy for those open 24hr.

Medical Assistance: Red Cross: (☎913 354 545). **Ambulatorio Esperanza Macarena** (☎954 42 01 05). **Hospital Universitario Virgen Macarena,** Av. Dr. Fedriani (☎954 24 81 81). English spoken.

Internet Access:

Sevilla Internet Center, C. Almirantazgo, 2, 2nd fl. (☎954 50 02 75), across from the cathedral. €3 per hr. Open M-F 9am-10pm, Sa-Su 10am-10pm.

CiberBoston, C. San Fernando, 23 (☎954 21 94 49). €3 per hr. Open M-F 9am-1am, Sa-Su noon-midnight.

The Email Place, C. Sierpes, 54 (☎954 21 85 92). €2.20 per hr. Open Oct.-May M-F 9am-11pm, Sa-Su noon-9pm; June-Sept. M-F 10am-10pm, Sa-Su noon-8pm.

WORKcenter, C. San Fernando, 1 (24hr. ☎902 11 50 11; www.workcenter.es), on the corner of C. San Fernando near Pta. de Jerez. An office center providing Internet (€2.40 per hr.), fax, photocopy, and other services. Sells office supplies and film. Open daily 24hr. MC/V.

Post Office: Av. Constitución, 32 (☎954 21 64 76), opposite the cathedral. **Lista de Correos** and **fax.** Open M-F 10am-8:30pm, Sa 9:30am-2pm. **Postal Code:** 41080.

ACCOMMODATIONS

During **Semana Santa** and **Feria de Abril,** rooms vanish and prices soar; it would be wise to make reservations many months ahead. The tourist office has lists of *casas particulares* that open for visitors on special occasions.

BARRIO DE SANTA CRUZ AND EL ARENAL

The narrow streets east of the cathedral around C. Santa María la Blanca are full of cheap hostels with virtually identical rooms. The neighborhood is overwhelmingly touristed, but its disorienting streets and shady plazas are all within a few minutes' walk of the cathedral, the Alcázar, and El Centro. Watch your bag on less crowded streets—*ladrones* on motorcycles are known to snatch them.

Pensión Vergara, C. Ximénez de Enciso, 11, 2nd fl. (☎954 21 56 68), at C. Mesón del Moro. Beautiful rooms of varying size with lace bedspreads, antique-style furniture, and a sitting room with book swap. All rooms have fans. Towels provided on request. Singles, doubles, triples, and quads available. €15-18 per person, depending on the room. ❷

Hostal Dulces-Sueños, Santa Maria la Blanca, 21 (☎954 41 93 83). Comfortable rooms, all with A/C, and 3rd fl. terrace with laundry lines. Singles €20; doubles €40, with bath €50; one triple with bath €60. MC/V. ❷

Hostal Sánchez Sabariego, C. Corral del Rey, 23 (☎954 21 44 70). Comfortable rooms with unique furnishings. A/C upstairs, fans in all other rooms. Singles €15-30; doubles with bath €30-60; triples with bath €40-90. ❷

Hostal Goya, C. Mateos Gago, 31 (☎954 21 11 70; fax 954 56 29 88), 3 blocks from the cathedral. Spacious and sparkling-clean rooms have A/C and showers. Rooms with bath are more luxurious. Doubles €51, with bath €57; triples €72/€80. MC/V. ❸

Hostal-Residencia Córdoba, C. Farnesio, 12 (☎954 22 74 98), off C. Fabiola. This *hostal,* run by a friendly and helpful family, offers immaculate and spacious air-conditioned rooms. A/C functions from 4pm-4am. 3am curfew. Singles €25, with shower €33; doubles €40, with shower €51. *Semana Santa* and *Feria* €33/€45/€50/€60. ❷

Hostal Javier, C. Archeros, 16 (☎954 41 23 25). Rooms with framed prints and floral-patterned bed sheets. Singles €21, with bath €30; doubles €33, with bath €39-42 depending on the room. MC/V. ❷

Hostal Sierpes, C. Corral del Rey, 22 (☎954 22 49 48; fax 954 21 21 07), on the continuation of C. Argote de Molina. All rooms with baths, many with A/C. Parking €10. Mar.-Oct., Dec. 5-8, Dec. 23-Jan. 7 singles €34; doubles €50; triples €66; quads €82. Holidays, festivals €56/€72/€95/€120. Nov.-Feb. €27/€37/€47/€57. MC/V. ❸

Hostal-Residencia Monreal, C. Rodrigo Caro, 8 (☎954 21 41 66). From the cathedral, walk up C. Mateos Gago and take the 1st right. Very basic rooms, some with verandas overlooking a nearby plaza. The downstairs cafe caters to backpackers. Singles €20; doubles €40, with bath €60. MC/V. ❷

Pensión Cruces El Patio, C. Cruces, 10 (☎954 22 96 33 or 954 22 60 41). Fans provided on request. Up to 6 people in a room. Laundry €9. Mar. 15-Oct. singles €30, with shower €36; doubles €60, with shower or bath €65. Nov.-Mar. 14 €21/€24/€39/€42. €12 per additional person. ❷

EL CENTRO

El Centro, a mess of narrow streets radiating from Pl. Encarnación, is a bustling shopping district during the day, but most streets are deserted at night.

Hostal Lis, C. Escarpín, 10 (☎954 21 30 88), on an alley near Pl. Encarnación. Nice-sized rooms with traditional Spanish tile. Owner is currently adding TV and A/C to all rooms. Free Internet service, laundry, full baths, and a rooftop terrace. All rooms have fans. Singles with shower €21; doubles with bath €42; triples with bath €63. MC/V. ❷

Hostal Lis II, C. Olavide, 5 (☎954 56 02 28), off San Eloy. Pleasant rooms all have fans. On-site Internet. May 16-Dec. singles €22.41; doubles €35.37, with bath €41.80; triples with shower €51.45, with bath €54.67; quad with shower €67.52. Jan.-Mar. 15 €3-5 less. Mar. 15-May 15 substantially higher. MC/V. ❷

Hotel Zaida, C. San Roque, 26 (☎954 21 36 12; fax 954 21 88 10). Hotel-sized lobby disguises simple rooms beyond. All rooms have bath, TV, and A/C. Mar. 16-Oct. singles €42; doubles €55. *Semana Santa* and *Feria de Abril* €51.05/€109.50. Nov.-Mar. 15 €35.50/€48.40. MC/V. ❹

Hostal La Gloria, C. San Eloy, 58, 2nd fl. (☎954 22 26 73), at the end of a lively shopping street. Faded white rooms. Singles €18; doubles €30, with bath €36; limited triples available. *Semana Santa* and *Feria* €36/€60/€76. ❷

NEAR ESTACIÓN PLAZA DE ARMAS

Most hostels are near the Pl. Armas bus station center on C. Gravina, parallel to C. Marqués de las Paradas and two blocks from the station. These are the most convenient for exploring El Centro and C. Betis on the west bank of the river.

Hostal Río Sol, C. Márquez de Parada, 25 (☎954 22 90 38), 1 block from Pl. de Armas bus station. Singles €15, with bath €18, with bath, TV, and fan €21; doubles with bath, TV, and A/C €42.10. MC/V. ❷

Hostal Paris, C. San Pedro Mártir, 14 (☎954 22 98 61 or 954 21 96 45; fax 954 21 96 45), off C. Gravina. Pricey but comfortable. All rooms have baths, A/C, phone, and TV. Mar.-Oct. singles €38.52; doubles €51.36; triples €72.90. Nov.-Feb. €32.10/€44.94/€62.90. AmEx/MC/V. ❸

Hostal Residencia Gala, C. Gravina, 52 (☎954 21 45 03). Clean rooms with framed prints and spacious bathrooms. Singles €25, with bath €30; doubles €50, with bath €60; limited triples available. All prices double during *Semana Santa* and *Feria.* ❸

Hostal Arizona, C. Pedro del Toro, 14 (☎954 21 60 42), off C. Gravina. Some rooms have balconies. Mar.-Oct. singles €30.05; doubles €48.10, with bath €54.10. Nov.-Apr. €15.05/€27.05/€33.10. ❸

ELSEWHERE AND CAMPING

Sevilla Youth Hostel (HI), C. Isaac Peral, 2 (☎954 61 31 50; fax 954 61 31 58; reservas@inturjoven.junta-andalucia.es). Take bus #34 across from the tourist office near the cathedral; the 5th stop is behind the hostel. Isolated and difficult to find. A cab from the cathedral should cost about €5. Doubles, triples, and quads available. A/C. Many private baths. Breakfast included. Dorms Mar.-Oct. €12.90, over 26 €17.25; Nov.-Feb. €10.90/€15.20. Non-members can pay an additional €3 a night for 6 nights to become members. ❶

Camping Sevilla, Ctra. Madrid-Cádiz, km 534 (☎954 51 43 79), near the airport. From Pr. San Sebastián, take bus #70 (stops 800m away at Parque Alcosa). Hot showers, supermarket, and pool. €3 per person, €3 per car, €2.50 per tent. ❶

Club de Campo, Av. Libertad, 13, Ctra. Sevilla-Dos Hermanas (☎954 72 02 50), 8km out of town. Los Amarillos buses leave from C. Infante Carlos de Borbón, at the back of Pr. San Sebastián, to Dos Hermanas (every 45min., €0.75). Lots of grass and a pool. €3.40 per person; €3 per child; €3.40 per car; €3.40 per tent. ❶

FOOD

Sevilla is a city of *tapas;* locals spend their evenings relaxing and socializing over plates of *pacoles* (snails), *cocido andaluz* (thick chick pea soup), *pisto* (tomato and eggplant hash), *espinacas con garbanzos* (spinach with chick peas), and fresh seafood. *Pescado frito,* lightly fried fish, is a *sevillano* specialty. For those on a stricter budget, there are markets such as **Mercado del Arenal,** near the bullring on C. Pastor y Leandro, between C. Almansa and C. Arenal, which has fresh meat and produce (open M-Sa 9am-2pm). For a supermarket, try **%Día,** C. San Juan de Ávila, near El Corte Inglés (open M-F 9:30am-2pm and 6:30-9pm, Sa 9am-1pm).

BARRIO DE SANTA CRUZ AND EL ARENAL

Restaurants near the cathedral cater almost exclusively to tourists. Beware the unexceptional, omnipresent *menús* featuring *gazpacho* and *paella* for €7. Food and prices improve in the backstreet establishments between the cathedral and the river in El Arenal and along side streets in the Barrio Santa Cruz.

Restaurante-Bar El Baratillo/Casa Chari, C. Pavía, 12 (☎954 22 96 51), on a tiny street off C. Dos de Mayo. A backpacker and local favorite; the hospitable owner will help you practice your Spanish. Ask at least 1hr. in advance for the tour-de-force: homemade *paella* (vegetarian options available) with a jar of wine, beer, or sangría (€18 for 2). *Menú* €4-9. Open M-F 10:30am-11pm, Sa noon-5pm; open later when busy. ❷

Histórico Horno, S.A., Av. de la Constitución, 16 (☎954 22 18 19), across from the Cathedral. Excellent pastries, cookies, and cakes will satisfy any sugar craving. Enjoy your delicacy at the bar or in the upstairs seating area with a *café con leche,* or have it *para llevar* (to go). Open daily 7:30am-11pm. MC/V. ❷

Café-Bar Campanario, C. Mateos Gago, 8 (☎954 56 41 89), ½ block from the cathedral, on the right. Mixes the best (and strongest) jugs of sangría around (half-liter €7.25, liter €9.65). *Tapas* €1.50-2, *raciones* €6-8.40. Open daily 11am-midnight. ❷

Café Cáceres, C. San José, 24. The closest thing to a buffet-style breakfast in Sevilla. Choose from a spread of cheeses, jams, and countless condiments, fresh squeezed orange juice, and numerous omelets. *Desayuno de la casa* (orange juice, coffee, ham, eggs, toast) €5. Open M-F 7:30am-8pm, Sa-Su 7:30am-midnight. ❶

Bar Patanchon, C. Mateos Gago, 13 (☎954 22 47 08), 1 block from the cathedral on the left. Outdoor seating and great service. Vegetarian options. Specialties include baked goat cheese (€6.61) and roasted red peppers stuffed with seafood (€10.22). *Raciones* €9-13.22 (*media-raciones* available). Open daily noon-2am. MC/V. ❸

La Albahaca, Pl. de Santa Cruz, 12 (☎954 22 07 14). Dine by candlelight *al fresco* or in one of the stately dining rooms. The elegant *menú* of 4 dishes (such as sea bass baked with hazelnut sauce) plus dessert will set you back €42. Appetizers €7-12, entrees €16-20. Open M 8pm-1am, Tu-Sa noon-4pm and 8pm-1am. AmEx/MC/V. ❺

EL CENTRO

This area belongs to professionals and shoppers by day and young people by night. Inexpensive *tapas* bars line the streets radiating from **Pl. Alfalfa.**

Pizzeros Orsini & Angelo, C. Luchana, 2 (☎954 21 61 64), 2 blocks from Pl. del Salvador. Crisp and filling pizza served straight from the oven. Romantic outdoor seating in front of a Baroque church. Pizzas €3.60-6.61, pasta €4.81-7.21, salads €3.61-5.11, and Italian desserts €2.40. Open daily 1-4pm and 8pm-1am. ❷

Habanita Bar Restaurant, C. Golfo, 3 (☎606 71 64 56; www.andalunet.com/habanita), on a tiny street off of C. Perez Galdos. Popular cafe serving Cuban fare, pastas, salads, and Caribbean drinks. Warm orange walls and Cuban jazz grace the indoor dining room, while outdoor seating provides cool breezes. Vegetarian and vegan options. Meals €4.80-9.95. Open daily 12:30-4:30pm. MC/V. ❷

El Rinconcillo, C. Gerona, 40 or C. Alhóndiga, 2 (☎954 22 31 83), behind Santa Catalina Church. Founded in 1670, this *bodega* attracts loyal patrons. Sip *cerveza* and savor *olivas* on top of discarded Tito Pepe barrels. *Tapas* €1.25-3.70, *raciones* €3.90-13.15. *Media-raciones* available. Open Th-Tu 1pm-2am. AmEx/MC/V. ❷

TRIANA AND BARRIO DE SANTA CECILIA

This old maritime neighborhood, on the far side of the river, was once a separate village. Avoid overpriced C. Betis and plunge down the less expensive side streets, where fresh seafood and *caracoles* abound. *Tapas* bars cluster around **Pl. San Martín** and along **C. San Jacinto.**

Acropolis Taberna Griega, C. Rosario Vega, 10 (☎954 28 46 85), 2 blocks from the Pl. Cuba. This small restaurant serves delicious Greek food. Many vegetarian options. Very popular with foreign students and locals. Call and reserve a table for the busy weekends. Entrees and appetizers €2.50-4. Open Aug.-June M 8:30-11:30pm, Tu-Sa 1:30-3:30pm and 8:30-11:30pm. July M-Sa 9pm-midnight. MC/V. ❶

Café-Bar Jerusalém, C. Salado, 6, at C. Virgen de las Huertas. Bar with an international crowd and creative *tapas*. Chicken, lamb, or pork and cheese *schwarmas* (€3-4.50) called a *bocadillo hebreo*—it's not kosher, but it sure is tasty. Open daily 8pm-3am. ❶

SIGHTS

While it is Sevilla's ambiance which lingers longest in travelers' memories, there are plenty of postcard-worthy monuments in Barrio de Santa Cruz.

THE CATHEDRAL. Legend has it that in 1401 the *reconquistadores* wished to demonstrate their religious fervor by constructing a church so great, they said, that "those who come after us will take us for madmen." With 44 individual chapels, the Cathedral of Sevilla is the third largest in the world, after St. Peter's Basilica in Rome and St. Paul's Cathedral in London, and the world's biggest Gothic edifice ever constructed. Not surprisingly, it took more than a century to build.

In 1401, the 12th-century Almohad mosque was destroyed to clear space for a massive cathedral. All that remains is the **Patio de Los Naranjos,** where the faithful would wash before prayer, the Puerta del Perdón entryway from C. Almanes, and the famed minaret **La Giralda,** built in 1198. The tower and its twins in Marrakesh and Rabat are the oldest and largest surviving Almohad minarets. There are 35 ramps inside leading to the tower's top. These once allowed the *muezzin* to climb up on his horse for the call to prayer; today they enable tourists to take pictures.

In the center of the cathedral, the **Capilla Real** (main chapel), built in Renaissance style, stands opposite **choirstalls** made of mahogany recycled from a 19th-century Austrian railway. The **retablo mayor** (altarpiece), one of the largest in the world, is a golden wall of intricately wrought saints and disciples. Nearby is the **Sepulcro de Cristóbal Colón** (Columbus's tomb). The black and gold coffin-bearers represent the eternally grateful monarchs of Castilla, León, Aragón, and Navarra. Considerable mystery surrounds the actual whereabouts of Columbus's remains, since he has four alleged resting places throughout the world. The Sepulcro was inaugurated in 1902, 396 years after Columbus died; chances are this tomb isn't it.

Farther on and to the right stands the cathedral's treasury, the **Sacristía Mayor,** which holds gilded panels of Alfonso X el Sabio, done by Juan de Arefe, as well as works by Ribera and Murillo, and a glittering Corpus Christi icon, **La Custodia Processional.** A small, disembodied head of John the Baptist eyes visitors who enter the gift shop. It overlooks keys presented to the city of Sevilla by Jewish leaders after King Fernando III ousted the Muslims in 1248. In the northwest corner of the cathedral lie the architecturally stunning **Sala de Las Columnas** and **Cabildo.** *(☎954 21 49 71. Open M-Sa 9:30am-4:30pm, Su 2:30-7pm. Tickets sold until 1hr. before closing. €6, seniors and students €1.50, under 12 free. Su free. Mass held in the Capilla Real M-F 8:30, 9, 10am; Sa 8:30, 10am, 8pm; Su 8:30, 10, 11am, noon, 1pm.)*

ALCÁZAR. Like the Alhambra in Granada, Sevilla's Alcázar has Moorish architecture and gardens that are nothing short of magnificent. Constructed by the Moors in the 7th century, the palace was embellished greatly during the 15th century and now serves as the residence of the King and Queen of Spain during their stays in Sevilla. Visitors enter through the **Patio de la Montería,** directly across from the intricate Almohad facade of the Moorish palace. Through the archway lies the Arabic residences, including the **Patio del Yeso** and the exquisitely carved **Patio de las Muñecas** (Patio of the Dolls), so named because of miniature faces carved into the bottom of one of the room's pillars. Of the Christian additions, the most notable is the **Patio de las Doncellas** (Patio of the Maids). Court life in the Alcázar revolved around this colonnaded quadrangle, which is encircled by archways adorned with glistening tilework. The golden-domed **Salón de los Embajadores** is allegedly the site where Fernando and Isabel welcomed Columbus back from America. Nearby, the **Corte de las Muñecas** contains the palace's private quarters, decorated with the building's most exquisite carvings. Peaceful **gardens** stretch from the residential quarters in all directions. *(Pl. Triunfo, 7. ☎954 50 23 23. Open Tu-Sa 9:30am-7pm, Su 9:30am-5pm. €5; students, disabled, over 65, and under 16 free. Tours of the upper palace living quarters every 30min. from 10am-1:30pm, €3. Worthwhile audioguides give anecdotes, historical info, and a clearly marked route through the complex; €3.)*

CASA LONJA. Between the cathedral and the Alcázar stands the 16th-century Casa Lonja, built by Felipe II as a *Casa de Contratación* (commercial exchange) for trade with the Americas. In 1785, Carlos III converted the building into the **Archivo General de las Indias.** Today it contains a collection of over 44,000 documents relating to the discovery and conquest of the New World. Among its books is Juan Bautista Muñoz's "definitive" history of the conquest, commissioned by Carlos III. Other highlights include Juan de la Costa's wildly inaccurate *Mapa Mundi*, letters from Columbus to Fernando and Isabel, and a 1590 letter from Cervantes (pre-*Don Quijote*) requesting employment in America. *(☎954 21 12 34. Exhibits open M-F 10am-1pm. Free. Full access to documents is limited to scholars.)*

LOYALTY REMEMBERED During the civil wars of the 1270s, King Alfonso X the Wise was betrayed by his own son Don Sancho, who wrestled from his father all of Castilla, León, Galicia, Extremadura, and Andalucía—with the sole exception, that is, of Sevilla, whose people remained loyal to the old king. Alfonso is recorded as having sighed in gratitude *"No m'a dejado"* ("She has not forsaken me"). To remind generations to come of the city's loyalty, the king added a new logo to the city shield which has since become the emblem and motto of Sevilla: a NO and DO with a double knot in between, similar to "NO&DO." *Nudo* in Spanish means "knot," and *madeja* means "skein." The rebus reads *No m'a dejado* perfectly and is a particularly clever word play which proud Sevillians have emblazoned all over the city, from the sides of buses to government buildings.

BARRIO DE SANTA CRUZ

The tourist office has a detailed map of the winding alleys, wrought-iron gates, and courtyards of the Barrio de Santa Cruz. King Fernando III forced Jews in flight from Toledo to live in this former ghetto. The fragrance of jasmine lingers at sunset and every street corner echoes with legend. On **Calle Susona,** the ceramic tile of a skull, resting above a door, evokes the tale of beautiful Susona, a Jewish girl who fell in love with a Christian knight. When Susona learned that her father and

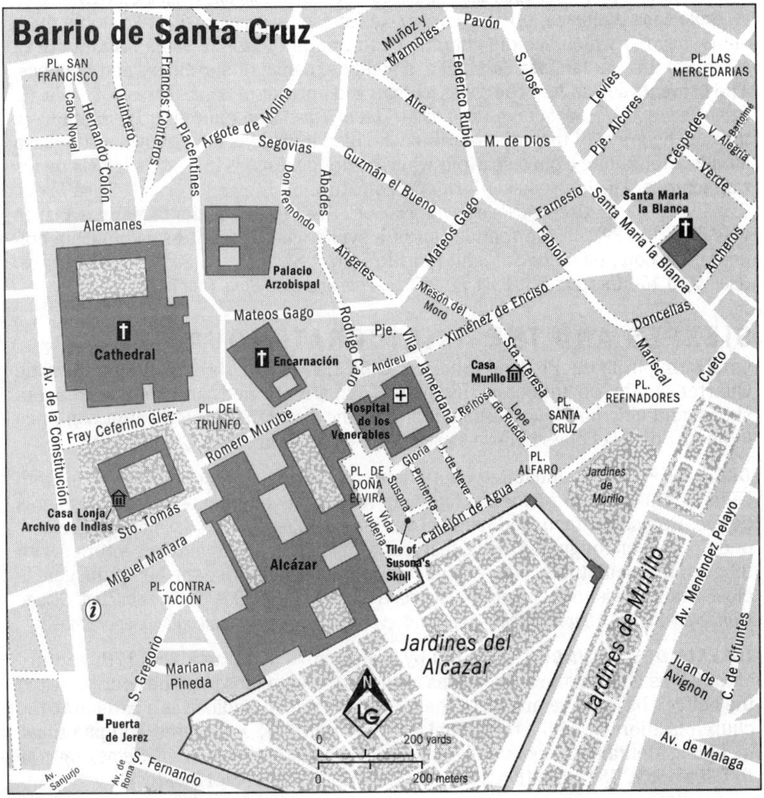

PILATE IN SEVILLA? When most people hear the name Pilate, they think biblical Jerusalem, not 17th-century Spain. At the time of the Inquisition, Pilate was not a name frequently chosen for children, let alone plazas and palazzos. By what heresy were Casa de Pilatos and the adjoining Plaza de Pilatos named? Local legend has it that the central courtyard of the palace was modeled after that of Pilate's villa in Jerusalem. Given the utter lack of resemblance between the two, this seems hardly plausible. Most likely, Casa de Pilatos—officially named the Palacio de San Andrés—received its epithet because of the role it played in annual Good Friday processions; each year worshippers would gather by a large wooden cross outside the palace to recreate Jesus's appearance before Pontius Pilate.

friends planned to kill several inquisitors, including her knight, she warned her lover. A bloody reprisal was unleashed on the Jewish ghetto, during which Susona's entire family was slaughtered. She requested that her skull be placed above the doorway in atonement for her betrayal, and the actual skull supposedly remained until the 18th century. C. Susona leads to **Plaza Doña Elvira,** where Sevillian Lope de Rueda's works, precursors to the dramas of Spain's Golden Age, were staged. A turn down C. Gloria leads to Pl. Venerables, site of the 17th-century **Hospital de los Venerables,** a hospital-church adorned with art from the Sevillian school. *(☎954 56 26 96. Open daily for guided visits 10am-2pm and 4-8pm. €3.61.)*

Calle Lope de Rueda, off C. Ximénez de Enciso, is graced with two noble mansions, beyond which lies the charming and fragrant **Plaza de Santa Cruz.** South of the plaza are the **Jardines de Murillo,** a shady expanse of shrubbery and benches. The **Convento de San José** cherishes a cloak and portrait of Santa Teresa of Ávila. *(C. Santa Teresa, off Pl. Santa Cruz. Open daily 9-11am. Free.)* The church in Pl. Santa Cruz houses the grave of the artist Murillo, who died in what is now known as the **Casa Murillo** after falling from a scaffold while painting frescoes in Cádiz's Iglesia de los Capuchinos. The house has information on Murillo's life and work. *(C. Santa Teresa, 8. ☎954 22 12 72. Open M-F 8am-3pm and 4-8pm. Free.)* **Iglesia de Santa María la Blanca** was built in 1391 on the foundation of a synagogue. It features red marble columns, Baroque plasterwork, and Murillo's *Last Supper*. *(C. Santa María la Blanca. Open M-Sa 10-11am and 6:30-8pm, Su 9:30am-2pm and 6:30-8pm. Free.)*

SIERPES AND THE ARISTOCRATIC QUARTER

Originating from the Pl. San Francisco, **Calle Sierpes** cuts through the Aristocratic Quarter. At the beginning of this pedestrian street lined with shoe stores, fan shops, and chic boutiques, a plaque marks the spot where the royal prison once loomed. Some scholars believe Cervantes began writing *Don Quijote* here.

CASA DE PILATOS. Inhabited continuously by Spanish aristocrats since the 15th century, this private residence has only recently been opened to the bourgeois public. Roman artifacts and tropical gardens coexist in Mudéjar patios. The second floor, open for guided visits, features rooms decorated over the centuries with oil portraits, sculptures, painted ceilings, and tapestries. Use the bell if the gate is closed during visiting hours. *(Pl. Pilatos. ☎954 22 52 98. Open daily 9am-7pm. Guided tours every 30min. 10am-5:30pm. €5 ground level only, €8 ground level and upper chambers.)*

IGLESIA DEL SALVADOR. Fronted by a Montañés sculpture, this 17th-century church was built on the foundations of the city's main mosque. The courtyard and the belfry's base are remnants of the old building. As grandiose as a cathedral, the church is adorned with exceptional Baroque *retablos*, sculptures, and paintings, including Montañés's *Jesús de la pasión*. *(Pl. Salvador, 1 block from C. Sierpes. Open M-Th 7:30am-9pm, F-Su 10am-1pm. Mass M-F 9:15am and 8:30pm, Su 11am-1pm.)*

OTHER SIGHTS. A few blocks southeast of Pl. Salvador stand the excavated ruins of an old **Roman temple.** The remaining columns rise 15m from below street level and offer a glimpse of the literal depth of Sevilla's history; river sediment that accumulated after the construction of the temple caused the ground level to rise. *(C. Mármoles.)* The **Ayuntamiento** has 16th-century Gothic and Renaissance interior halls, a richly decorated domed ceiling, and a Plateresque facade. It often displays art exhibitions; check with the tourist office for information. *(Pl. San Francisco. ☎954 59 01 01. Open Tu-Th 5:30-6:30pm. Call ahead to confirm hours.)* The **Iglesia de la Anunciación** features a pantheon honoring illustrious *sevillanos*, including poet Gustavo Adolfo Bécquer. *(Pl. Encarnación, enter on C. Laraña. Open daily 9am-1pm.)*

EL ARENAL, TRIANA, AND PASEO ALCALDE MARQUÉS DE CONTADERO

Immortalized by *Siglo de Oro* (Golden Age) writers Lope de Vega, Quevedo, and Cervantes, Triana was Sevilla's chaotic 16th- and 17th-century mariners' neighborhood. El Arenal was once a stretch of sand by the harbor on the opposite bank, exposed when the river was diverted to its present course. The inviting riverside esplanade Po. Marqués de Contadero stretches along the banks of the Guadalquivir from the base of the Torre del Oro. Bridge-heavy boat tours of Sevilla leave from in front of the tower (1hr., €4.20).

MUSEO PROVINCIAL DE BELLAS ARTES. Cobbled together from decommissioned convents in the mid-1800s, this museum contains Spain's finest collection of works by painters of the Sevilla school, most notably Murillo, Valdés Leal, and Zurbarán, as well as El Greco and Dutch master Jan Breughel. Spanning patios and chapels, the grounds are a work of art. *(Pl. Museo, 9, off C. Alfonso XII. ☎954 22 07 90. Open Tu 3-8pm, W-Sa 9am-8pm, Su 9am-2pm. €1.50, EU citizens free.)*

PLAZA DE TOROS DE LA REAL MAESTRANZA. A tiled boardwalk leads to Pl. Toros de la Real Maestranza, Spain's most beautiful, renowned bullring. Construction began in 1761 and took over 120 years to build. Home to one of the two great bullfighting schools (the other is in Ronda), the plaza fills to capacity (14,000) for the 13 *corridas* of the *Feria de Abril* as well as for weekly fights. Multilingual tour guides take visitors behind the ring to a chapel where *matadores* pray before fights and a medical emergency room used when their prayers go unanswered. *(☎954 22 45 77. Open on non-bullfight days 9:30am-2pm and 3-7pm, on bullfight days 9:30am-3pm. Tours in English and Spanish every 20min. €3. See* **bullfights,** p. 230, *for tickets.)*

HOSPITAL DE LA CARIDAD. A 17th-century complex of arcaded courtyards, this hospital was founded by Don Miguel de Marañe, believed to be the model for legendary Sevillian Don Juan. This notorious playboy converted to a life of piety and charity after allegedly stumbling out of an orgy into his own funeral cortège. Don Miguel's body rests inside the crypt of the **Iglesia de San Jorge,** part of the hospital. The church's walls display paintings and frescos by Valdés Leal and Murillo, who couldn't refrain from holding his nose when he saw Leal's morbid *Finis Gloria Mundi*, which depicts corpses of a peasant, a bishop, and a king beneath a rendition of Justice and the Seven Deadly Sins. *(C. Temprado. ☎954 22 32 32. Open M-Sa 9am-1:30pm and 3:30-7:30pm, Su 9am-1pm. €3.)*

TORRE DEL ORO. The 12-sided Torre del Oro (Gold Tower), built by the Almohads in 1200, overlooks the river from Po. Cristóbal Colón. Glistening golden tiles once covered the entire tower; today a tiny yellow dome is all that remains. Inside is the **Museo Náutico,** a storehouse of naval relics with illustrations of Sevilla as a bustling 17th-century port. *(☎954 22 24 19. Open Sept.-July Tu-F 10am-2pm, Sa-Su 11am-2pm. €1. Tu free.)* On the far bank of the river, the **Torre de la Plata** (Silver Tower) used to be connected to the Torre de Oro by underwater chains designed to protect the city from river-borne trespassers. With piracy no longer a concern, the Torre de la Plata has since been absorbed by a bank building, but one side is still visible near the corner of C. Santander and C. Temprado.

OTHER SIGHTS. The **Capilla de los Marineros** in Triana was constructed in the 18th century to worship the Esperanza de Triana, who, along with the Virgin Mary and the "Macarena," is one of the most adored figures of Sevilla. *(C. Pureza, 53.)* One block farther inland, midway between Puente de Isabel II and Puente de San Telmo, stands the **Iglesia de Santa Ana,** Sevilla's oldest church and the focal point of the exuberant July fiestas that take over the area in July. *(Open M and W 7:30-8:30pm.)* The terraced riverside promenade **Calle Betis** is an ideal spot from which to view Sevilla's skyline and sparkling nights.

LA MACARENA

La Macarena is the virgin of the city and namesake of an enchanting church and neighborhood northwest of El Centro.

CONVENTS. The founder of **Convento de Santa Inés,** as legend has it, was pursued so insistently by King Pedro the Cruel that she disfigured her face with boiling oil so he would leave her alone. Cooking liquids are used more positively today—the

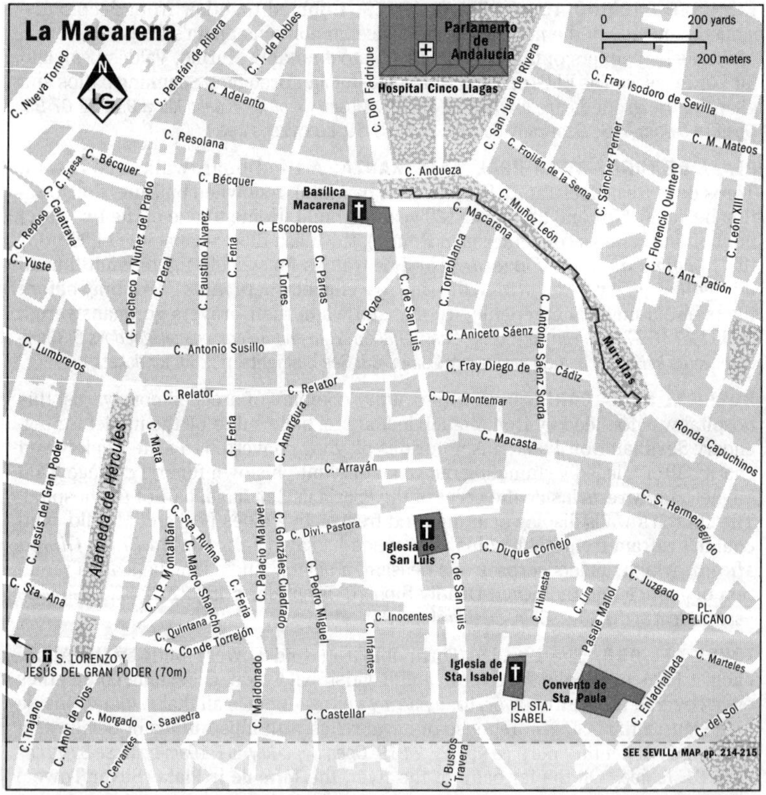

cloistered nuns sell puff pastries and coffee cakes through the courtyard's revolving window. *(C. María Coronel. Sweets sold M-Sa 9am-1pm and 4-7pm.)* **Convento de Santa Paula** includes a church with Gothic, Mudéjar, and Renaissance elements, a magnificent ceiling, and Montañés sculptures. *(Pl. Santa Paula. ☎954 53 63 30. Open Tu-Su 10:30am-12:30pm and 4:30-6:30pm.)* The **museum** has religious sculptures and paintings including Ribera's *St. Jerome.* Nuns peddle scrumptious homemade marmalades and angel-hair pastry. Knock if the door is closed. *(Pl. Santa Paula, 11. Open Tu-Su 10am-1pm, 4:30-6:30pm. Museum €2; marmalades €2.70 for 300g.)*

CHURCHES. A stretch of **murallas** (fortress walls) created in the 12th century runs between Pta. Macarena and Pta. Córdoba on the Ronda de Capuchinos road. Flanking the west end of the walls, the **Basilica Macarena** houses the venerated image of *La Virgen de la Macarena,* who is borne through the streets in the climax of the *Semana Santa* processions. A **treasury** glitters with the virgin's jewels and other finery. *(Pl. San Gil. ☎954 37 01 95. Basilica open daily 9:30am-1pm and 5-9pm. Free. Sunday Mass 10:30am, 12:30pm. Treasury open daily 9:30am-1pm and 5-8pm. €2.70.)* Opposite the belfry of the Iglesia de San Marcos rises **Iglesia de Santa Isabel,** featuring an altarpiece by Montañés. Nearby stands the exuberantly Baroque **Iglesia de San Luis,** crowned by octagonal glazed-tile domes. The site of the church was the endpoint of a 12-step prayer route based on the ascent to Golgotha. *(C. San Luis. ☎954 55 02 07. Open Tu-Th 9am-2pm, F-Sa 9am-2pm and 5-8pm.)* Toward the river is **Iglesia de San Lorenzo y Jesús del Gran Poder,** with Montañés's remarkably lifelike sculpture *El Cristo del gran poder.* Worshipers kiss Jesus's ankle. *(Pl. San Lorenzo. ☎954 38 45 58. Open Sa-Th 8am-1:45pm and 6-9pm, F 7:30am-10pm. Free.)*

OTHER SIGHTS. A large garden beyond the *murallas* and the basilica leads to the **Hospital de las Cinco Llagas,** a spectacular Renaissance building recently renovated to host the Andalucian parliament. Thursday mornings from 9am-2pm, a large flea market is held along C. La Feria, C. Maldonado, and C. Regina.

ELSEWHERE

PARQUE DE MARÍA LUISA. In 1929, Sevilla made elaborate plans for an Ibero-American world fair. Though plans were interrupted by the stock market crash, the lovely landscapes of the Parque de María Luisa remained, framed by Av. Borbolla and the river. The park offers innumerable courtyards, tiled benches, and tropical gardens. *(Park open daily 8am-10pm. Boat rides €4.25 for 1-3 people.)*

PLAZA DE ESPAÑA. On the northeast edge of Parque María Luisa, the twin spires of Plaza de España tower above the city skyline. Horse-drawn carriages clatter in front of the plaza and rowboats can be rented to navigate its narrow moat. Mosaics depicting every provincial capital in Spain line the crumbling colonnade. The balconies above offer a beautiful view of the surrounding gardens.

NIGHTLIFE

The tourist office distributes *El Giraldillo,* a free monthly magazine with complete listings on music, art exhibits, theater, dance, fairs, and film. Sevilla's reputation for partying is tried and true. A typical Sevillian sampling of *la marcha* (going out) begins with visits to several bars for *tapas* and *copas,* continues with dancing at *discotecas,* and culminates with an early morning breakfast of *churros con chocolate.* Most clubs don't get crowded until well after midnight; the real fun often starts after 3am. Popular bars can be found around C. Mateos Gago near the cathedral, C. Adriano by the bullring, and C. Betis across the river in Triana. Sevilla is also famous for its *botellón,* the (mostly student) tradition of getting drunk in massive crowds in plazas or at bars along the river to start the night. In the winter,

FROM THE ROAD

SANTA'S COMING TO TOWN

During the spectacular *Semana Santa,* Sevilla is transformed into a weeklong display of faith and penitence. The smell of orange blossoms mingles with candle wax and incense, and the sounds of chapel music, trumpets, and drums fill the air. Women don black clothing and lace shawls in mourning for Christ's crucifixion, while men in *confradías* (brotherhoods) parade through the streets, carrying elaborate floats.

The tradition dates back to Ferdinand III's recapture of Sevilla from the Moors in 1248. Developed in its present form in the 16th century as an accessible teaching of the lessons of Christ, *Semana Santa* is now the largest holy week festival in the world.

In the procession, *confradías* may carry two floats: one bearing a life-sized carving of Christ and another of Mary. (A typical float carried by 20-30 men can weigh 2 tons; it is considered a great honor to be among the carriers.) The ornate floats depict scenes from Christ's passion, death, and resurrection, and the *dolor* (pain) of Mary, signified by her crystal teardrops. The brothers wear the color of the patron saint of their church and may carry a book containing the rules and statutes of the brotherhood.

Fifty-seven brotherhoods and 60,000 brothers participate in the ceremonies, and more than a million spectators flock to Sevilla every year. Processions occur daily from Palm Sunday to Easter Sunday. Crowds are thick, especially along the *carrera official.* Newspapers and the tourist office provide maps and details.

the most popular places to *botellón* are in Pl. Alfalfa and Pl. del Salvador. In summer, the crowds sweep toward the river in hopes of a breeze, and even on "slow" nights, most *terrazas* stay open until 4am. New locations open every summer; check with the Centro de Información de Sevilla for the latest info.

BARRIO DE SANTA CRUZ

Terraza Chile, Po. de las Delicias, at Av. Uruguay and Av. Chile. Loud salsa and Spanish pop keep this small breezy dance club packed and pounding throughout the early morning hours. Young *sevillano* professionals mingle with Euro-chic American exchange students. Beer €2. Mixed drinks €4.50. Open in summer daily 9pm-6am.

La Carbonería, C. Levies, 18 (☎954 21 44 60), off C. Santa María La Blanca. Don't let the drab entrance hall deter you—beyond lies a popular bar with free live flamenco and an outdoor patio replete with banana trees, picnic tables, and guitar-strumming Romeos. Mostly a backpacker crowd. Flamenco nightly at midnight, and occasional theatrical performances earlier. Beer €2.50. Open M-Sa 8pm-3:30am, Su 8pm-2:30am.

Antigüedades, C. Argote de Molina, 40, 1 block up from the cathedral. This mellow bar with small tables plays jazzy soul for a mid-20s and up crowd. Creative redecorating every few months. Beer €1.29, mixed drink €4. Open daily 9pm-4am.

El Tamboril, Pl. Santa Cruz (☎954 56 15 90). See authentic *sevillanas* and *rumbas* in this intimate Santa Cruz hideaway. Somewhat older, local crowd. Midnight music and dancing. Sangría €15 per large jar, beer €3, mixed drinks €6. Open daily 10pm-dawn.

EL CENTRO AND TRIANA

Isbiliyya, Po. de Colon, 2 (☎954 21 04 60), across from Pte. Isabel II. Friendly mixed gay and lesbian bar with outdoor seating and a good dance floor. Plays percussion-filled dance music, and hosts drag performances on Th and Su (approx. 1:30am). Beer €2-2.50, mixed drinks €5. Open M-W 7pm-4am, Th-Su 7pm-5am.

El Capote, next to Pte. Isabel II, at C. Arjona and C. Reyes Católicos. A popular outdoor bar with live music performances in summer. Experience *botellón* as you head toward the river, past young *sevillanos* swigging *cuba libres.* Open daily in summer 11pm-3am.

La Antigua Bodeguita, Pl. del Salvador, 6 (☎954 56 18 33). The crowds can't be contained at any hour of the day in this bustling *bodega.* Beer €1, *tapas* €1.20-1.80. Open daily 12:30-4pm and 8pm-midnight.

Catedral, Cuesta del Rosario, 12 (☎630 61 55 02), 1 block from Pl. del Salvador. Underground disco with a metal, stone, and wood decor. No cover for women and those with coupons (available in stores, restaurants, and hostels). Older crowd. Cover for men €6, includes 1 drink or 2 beers. Open W-Sa midnight-6am. Sporadic summer hours.

Itaca, C. Amor de Dios, 31. Knock on the black unmarked door or ring the bell. Dark and slightly cavernous; plays house music until the early morn. Caters to a primarily gay male crowd. Open daily 10:30pm-5am.

CARTUJA '93

A bit of a jaunt from Sevilla center, the area across the Guadalquivir from Pte. de la Barqueta is still worth an evening foray during the summer. Forged from the idle remnants of Expo '92, the massive clubs located here form part of a surreal landscape of spaceship replicas, abandoned gondolas, pork vending stands, and empty rum bottles. (The A2 night bus runs at midnight, 1 and 2am from Pl. Nueva; ask to be let off near Pte. de la Barqueta. Cabs from Pl. Nueva should cost around €5.)

Palenque, Av. Blas Pascal, on the grounds of Cartuja '93. From Pte. de la Barqueta, follow C. Materatico Rey, turn left and walk toward the spaceship on the horizon. Once a stadium-sized auditorium, now the largest dance club in Sevilla. Multiple floors with a live DJ spinning salsa and Latin pop. Mainly *sevillano* university crowd. Mixed drinks €4.20, beer €2. Cover €6 for men, €4 for women. Open summer Th-Sa midnight-7am.

Antique, C. Materatico Rey Pastor. Cross Pte. de la Barqueta; it's on the left. Decorated entirely in white, with swirling spotlights and Ottoman pavilions doubling as bars in the yard and patio. Mixed age crowd. Plays mostly Spanish pop and house. Transforms during the winter into one of the city's most popular indoor dance clubs. No cover for women, cover for men €7. Open Th-Sa midnight-7am.

ENTERTAINMENT

THEATERS

Cine Avenida, C. Marqués de las Paradas, 15 (☎954 29 30 25) and **Cines Warner Lusomundo,** Co. Comercial, Pl. Legión (☎902 23 33 43) show American films dubbed in Spanish. **Corona Center,** Pagés del Corro y Paraíso, in the mall between C. Salado and C. Paraíso, screens subtitled films, often in English. (☎954 27 80 64. M-F movies €3, Sa-Su €3.50.) For more info, look under "Cinema" in *El Giraldillo.*

Sevilla is a haven for the performing arts. The venerable **Teatro Lope de Vega** (☎954 59 08 53), near Parque María Luisa, has long been the city's leading stage. Ask about scheduled events at the tourist office or check the bulletin board in the university lobby on C. San Fernando. If you can't see a show, at least stop by for a drink at **Casino,** the popular *terraza* outside. **Sala la Herrería** and **Sala la Imperdible** put on avant-garde productions in Pl. San Antonio de Padua. (Both ☎954 38 82 19.) **Teatro de la Maestranza,** on the river next to Pl. Toros, is a splendid concert hall accommodating both orchestral performances and opera. (☎954 22 33 44. Box office open M-F 10am-2pm and 6-9pm.) On spring and summer evenings, *barrio* fairs are often accompanied by free **open-air concerts** in Santa Cruz and Triana.

FLAMENCO

Flamenco, originally brought to Spain by the *gitanos* (Roma people), is at its best in Sevilla. Traditionally consisting of dance, guitar, and song, it expresses the passion and soul of the region. Rhythmic clapping, intricate finger work on the guitar, throaty wailing, and rapid foot-tapping form a mesmerizing backdrop for the swirling dancers. Flamenco can be seen in either a *tablao,* where skilled professional dancers perform, or in *tabernas,* bars where locals merrily dance *sevillanas* (folk flamenco). Both have merit, but for those on a budget the *tabernas* tend to be free. The tourist office provides a complete list of both *tablaos* and *tabernas.*

SEVILLANAS When in Sevilla, do as the *sevillanos* do. *Sevillanas* is the widely popular folk form of flamenco. While elegant flamenco dancers must study technique for years, just about anyone can perform *sevillanas.* In little bars in Sevilla, yuppie couples, chic young women, and toothless old men take the dance floor side-by-side when the guitar begins to play its song. A partnered dance, *sevillanas* consists of four segments that act out a courting ritual. The basic step is easy to pick up; ask sweetly for an impromptu lesson, and before long you'll be twisting your wrists like a native. During the *Feria de Abril* the whole city takes to the streets, stomping their feet, flipping their skirts, and holding their heads high as they turn and sashay. If you can't catch the dancing live, check out Carlos Saura's movie *Sevillanas*.

TABLAOS

Small and intimate **Los Gallos,** Pl. Santa Cruz, 11, is probably the best tourist show in Sevilla. Buy tickets in advance at hostels or stores in Barrio Santa Cruz and arrive early. (☎954 21 69 81. Shows nightly 9 and 11:30pm. Cover €27.05, includes 1 drink.) **El Arenal** is also a *tablao-restaurante*, so you can eat a meal while watching. (Shows nightly 9 and 11pm. Cover €29, includes 1 drink.) **El Patio Sevillano,** Po. de Colón, 11, offers nightly performances at 7:30 and 10pm. (☎954 21 41 20. €27, includes 1 drink). **El Palacio Andaluz,** Av. Auxiliadora, 18, has a mixed flamenco and classical dance show. (☎954 53 47 20. Shows nightly at 7:30 and 10pm. Cover includes 1 drink.) Though somewhat farther afield, **Las Brujas,** Gonzalo de Bilbao, 10, is certainly worth the trek. (☎954 41 36 51. Shows M-Sa 9 and 11:30pm. €22.84 cover includes 1 drink.)

TABERNAS

El Tamboril, Pl. de Santa Cruz, hosts a primarily Spanish mixed-age crowd. **La Carboneria,** C. Levies, 18 is a large club with a courtyard, popular with young backpackers. Three are located across the river in Triana: **El Simpecao,** Po. Nuestra Senora de la O, **Casa Anselma,** C. Pages del Corro, and **El Rejoneo,** C. Betis.

SHOPPING

Sevilla is a great place to find Andalucian crafts such as hand-embroidered silk and lace shawls, and traditional flamenco wear. C. Sierpes is in the center of the main shopping area. Its environs, including C. San Eloy, C. Velazquez and C. Francos, have a wide array of crafts, as well as modern clothing, shoe stores, and jewelry. A large **flea market** is held Th 9am-2pm, extending from C. Feria to C. Regina in the Macarena neighborhood.

FÚTBOL

Sevilla has two wildly popular pro teams within its city limits that play in the **Estadio Sámche Pizjuán** (☎954 53 53 53), east of Av. Menéndez Pelayo on Av. Eduardo Dato. Buy tickets at the stadium; price and availability depend on the quality of the match-up. Even if you can't make it, you'll know who's won by the colors worn by the crowds in the streets (Betis wears green and white, Sevilla white and red).

BULLFIGHTS

Sevilla's bullring is generally considered to be the most beautiful in Spain. The cheapest place to buy tickets is at the ring on Po. Marqués de Contadero. However, when there's a good *cartel* (line-up), the booths on C. Sierpes, C. Velázquez, and Pl. Toros might be the only source of advance tickets. Ticket prices, depending on the quality of both seat and matador, can run from €18 for a *grada de sol* (nosebleed seat in the sun) to €75 for a *barrera de sombra* (front-row seat in the shade). Buying a ticket from a scalper usually adds 20% to the ticket price. *Corridas de toros* (bullfights) or *novilladas* (apprentice bullfighters and younger bulls) are held: on the 13 days around the *Feria de Abril* and into May, every Sunday Apr.-June and Sept.-Oct., more often during Corpus Christi in June and early July, and during the *Feria de San Miguel* near the end of Sept. During July and August, *corridas* occur on occasional Thursdays. It's obvious when a top-notch matador is scheduled to fight; hours before the big event, the ring is surrounded by throngs of young female fans donned in their most seductive dresses and alluring lipstick in hopes of catching the eye of their hero. Some of the most popular Sevillian bullfighters include El Juli, Joselito, and Jose Tomás. (For current info and **ticket sales,** call ☎954 50 13 82. For more info on **Bullfighting,** see p. 76.)

FESTIVALS

Sevilla swells with tourists during its *fiestas*, and with good reason—they are insanely fun. If you're in Spain during any of the major festivals, head straight to Sevilla—you won't regret it (if you can remember it, that is).

SEMANA SANTA. Sevilla's world-famous *Semana Santa* lasts from Palm Sunday to Easter Sunday (Apr. 13-20 in 2003). In each neighborhood of the city, thousands of penitents in hooded cassocks guide *pasos* (stunning, extravagant floats), through the streets, illuminated by hundreds of candles. The climax is Good Friday, when the entire city turns out for the procession along the bridges and through the oldest neighborhoods. Book rooms well in advance, and expect to pay triple the usual price. The tourist office has a helpful booklet of advice on where to eat and sleep during the week's festivities.

FERIA DE ABRIL. Two or three weeks after *Semana Santa* (Apr. 29-May 4 in 2003) the city rewards itself for its Lenten piety with the *Feria de Abril.* Begun as part of a 19th-century revolt against foreign influence, the *Feria* has grow into a massive celebration of all that is Andalucian. Circuses, bullfights, and flamenco shows roar into the night in a showcase of local customs and camaraderie. A spectacular array of flowers and lanterns decorates over 1000 kiosks, tents, and pavilions, collectively called *casetas*. Each has the elements necessary for a rollicking time: small kitchen, bar, and dance floor. Locals stroll from one to the next, sharing drinks and food amid the lively music and dance. Most *casetas* are privately owned by families and businesses, and the only way to get invited is by making friends with the locals. There are a few large public *casetas* where you can find drink and dancing though. Either way, people-watching from the sidelines can be almost as exciting, as costumed girls dance *sevillanas* and men parade on horseback through the streets. *(The fairgrounds are on the southern end of Barrio Los Remedios.)*

ROMERÍA DEL ROCÍO. Folklore and religion unite in the *Romería del Rocío* which takes place 50 days after Easter on Pentecost and involves the veneration of the *Virgen del Rocío*. More than 70 brotherhoods of pilgrims from around the world make their way to the small town of Almonte, near Huelva, from all points in Spain. They arrive in flower-decorated carriages or on horses saddled in typical Andalucian style wearing traditional gypsy costumes. In the best Spanish fashion, the Romería is half penitence, half party. The solemnity of the days are broken with singing, dancing, and drinking around campfires from dusk until dawn.

DAYTRIPS FROM SEVILLA

OSUNA

Trains from Sevilla (1hr., 6 per day 7am-5:40pm, €6.26). Empresa Dipasa/Linesur (☎954 98 82 22) runs buses to and from Sevilla's Pr. de San Sebastián station (1½hr., 5-11 per day 7:30am-10pm, €5.48).

Julius Caesar founded Osuna (pop. 17,500), naming it after the *osos* (bears) that once lumbered about its hills. Most sites of interest are found on the hill which rises above town. The **Colegiata de Santa María de la Asunción,** C. Callejón de las Descalzas, was commissioned by the Dukes of Osuna in the Renaissance style and now houses the **Museo de Arte Sacro Panteón Ducal.** The Colegiata contains a spectacular array of paintings, including religious artifacts and five Riberas. (From Pl. Mayor, walk to the adjacent Pl. Duquesa Osuna and then uphill to Pl. Encarnación; knock to enter. ☎954 81 04 44. Open May-Sept. 10am-1:30pm and 4-7pm; Oct.-Apr. Tu-Su 10am-1:30pm and 3:30-6:30pm. €2.) On the right side of the church sits the university and **Convento de la Encarnación,** Pl. Encarnación, 2, a Baroque church founded by the Duke of Osuna in the 17th century and lavishly decorated in the 18th. A resident nun will show you room upon room of polychromed wooden sculptures, silver crucifixes, painted tiles, and handmade Christ-doll clothes. Make sure to knock and wait until the previous tour group finishes. (☎954 81 11 21. Open Tu-Su 10am-1:30pm and 3:30-6:30pm. €1.50.)

To reach Pl. Mayor from the **train station** (☎/fax 954 81 03 08; open 7am-8pm), walk up Av. Estación, curving right on C. Mancilla. At Pl. Salitre, turn left on C. Carmen and then right on C. Sevilla, which leads into the plaza. The **bus station** is on Av. Constitución. (Open M-F 6:50-9am, 10:15am-2:30pm, and 3:30-7:40pm; Sa 7:30-9am and 10:30am-2pm; Su 3:30-4:30pm and 7-7:40pm.) To get to Pl. Mayor from the bus station, walk downhill on C. Santa Ana past Pl. Santa Rita; continue on Av. Arjona until the plaza. The **tourist office** is in Pl. Mayor. (☎955 82 14 00. Open M-F 10am-1:30pm and 4-7pm, Sa 10am-2pm and 4-7pm, Su 10am-3pm.)

ITÁLICA

Take the Empresa Casal bus (☎954 41 06 58) toward Santiponce from the Pl. Armas bus station, platform 34. Tell the driver you're going to Itálica, and get off at the last stop (30min.; M-Sa every 30min. 6:30am-midnight, Su every hr., on the ½hr. 7:30am-midnight; €0.75). Pay on-board. The entrance to the ruins is located next to the gas station where the bus drops you. When returning to Sevilla, wait at the bus sign in front of the entrance to Itálica, the bus will turn around in the neighboring gas station.

Just 9km northwest of Sevilla and right outside the village of **Santiponce** (pop. 6200) lie the excavated ruins of Itálica, the first important Roman settlement in Iberia. The birthplace of emperors Trajan (AD 53) and Hadrian (AD 76), Itálica was founded in 206 BC as a settlement for soldiers wounded in the Battle of Illipa, and was later utilized as a strategic military outpost. During the 4th and 5th centuries AD, the city burgeoned into a cosmopolitan trading center, but by the early 500s, Sevilla had become the regional seat of power. Archaeological excavations began in the 18th century and continue today, although the oldest neighborhoods in Itálica are still buried under downtown Santiponce, and may never be recovered. The **Casa del Planetario** (The House of Planets) has intricate **mosaic floors** depicting the seven gods that represent planets, whose names are given to the days of the week. There are also reconstructed patios and a bakery depicting life as it was during the decline of the city. The **anfiteatro,** among Spain's largest, seats 25,000. It was once used to stage fights between gladiators and lions; today it hosts more mellow classical music performances in the summer. (☎955 99 73 76.

Open Apr.-Sept. Tu-Sa 8:30am-8:30pm, Su 9am-3pm; Oct.-Mar. Tu-Sa 9am-5:30pm, Su 10am-4pm. €1.50, EU citizens free.) For info on the annual **Festival Internacional de Itálica,** which brings dance, classical music, and theater to Itálica in July and August, check Sevilla's *El Giraldillo*. While the restaurant directly across the road from Itálica is less than inspiring, wonderful *hornos* populate the left side of the road back to Santiponce. Not for the vegetarian, these grills serve delicious meat-and-potato entrees best washed down with a jug of *tinto de verano*.

CARMONA

Buses to Carmona depart Sevilla from the Pr. de San Sebastián station, platform 25. (1hr.; M-F 25 per day 6:15am-8:30pm, Sa 10 per day 6:30am-8:30pm, Su 7 per day 8am-8:30pm; €2.10; pay on the bus.) In Carmona, buses return to Sevilla from the main square, along Av. Jorge Bonsor (23 per day 6:15am-9pm).

Thirty-three kilometers east of Sevilla, ancient Carmona (pop. 25,000) dominates a tall hill overlooking the countryside. Founded by the Carthaginians, it became an important trade city during Roman occupation in later centuries and a Moorish stronghold thereafter. Moorish palaces mingle with Renaissance mansions in a network of streets partially enclosed by fortified walls. The **Puerta de Sevilla,** a horseshoe-shaped passageway with both Roman and Arab architectural elements, and the Baroque **Puerta de Córdoba,** on the opposite end of town, once linked Carmona to the east and west. From the bus stop, walk from the back of the bus onto C. San Pedro. Cross the roundabout and walk through the Puerta de Sevilla, noting the **Iglesia de San Pedro,** whose Mudéjar tower is a scaled-down copy of Sevilla's Giralda. Enter the **Alcázar de la Puerta Sevilla** through the tourist office on your right. The Alcázar originally served as a Carthaginian fortification against Roman attack. During the reign of Augustus, the structure was expanded to its current size. (☎954 19 09 55. Open M-Sa 10am-6pm, Su 10am-2pm. €2; students, seniors, and children under 12 €1.) From the Alcázar, take C. Prim and then C. Martín to find Pl. Marqués de las Torres, where the late-Gothic **Iglesia de Santa María** was built over an old mosque. The splendid **Patio de los Naranjos** remains from Moorish days. An even older Visigothic liturgical calendar graces one of the columns. (☎954 14 13 30. M-Sa 9am-2pm and 5:30-7:30pm, Su 9am-2pm and 6-8:30pm. Free. Mass daily 8pm.) The **Alcázar del Rey Don Pedro,** an old Almohad fortress and now a ritzy hotel, guards the eastern edge of town. In the opposite direction from the bus stop, along C. Enmedio, lie the ruins of

THE BIG SPLURGE

A TOUCH OF CLASS

Looking for a little luxury in your next Cordoban dining experience? Head to El Churrasco, where you'll eat like a king. An elegant yet unpretentious break from budget fare, this restaurant ensures royal treatment with cloth napkins, a complimentary apertif, and attentive and friendly service.

Complementing El Churrasco's regal atmosphere are its delicious dishes. While prices are slightly higher than those at your average budget eatery, the *menú* is neither boring nor exorbitant. Enjoy multiple courses, then cleanse your palate with a selection from El Churrasco's decadent dessert menu. Enjoy the complete *menú* for €22, or go *a la carte* with starters (€4-15), eggs and vegetarian options (€4.50-14), fish dishes (€11-30), meat dishes (€11-38), and dessert (€4.25).

With no official dress code at El Churrasco, there's no need to break out your *finest* duds. However, you'll stand out if you arrive in a t-shirt and jeans; if you're clean and presentable, El Churrasco will welcome you and your empty stomach with open arms.

C. Almanzor Romero, 16 (☎957 29 08 19; fax 957 29 40 81; www.elchurrasco.com). From the top left side of the Mezquita follow C. Cardinal Herrero through C. Judería. Take a right onto C. Deanes and a quick left onto C. Romero; the restaurant is near the Pl. Card. Salazar, on the right. Delicious dishes. Open daily 1-4pm, 8:30-11:30pm. Closed in August. MC/V. ❺

the **Necrópolis Romana,** Av. de Jorge Bonsor, 9 (☎954 14 08 11). Highlights include the **Tumba de Servilia** and **Tumba del Elefante,** where depictions of Mother Nature and Eastern divinities are overshadowed by the presence of a giant stone elephant. The **Museo Arqueológico** has remains from over a thousand tombs unearthed at the necropolis. (Both open June-Aug. Tu-Sa 8:30am-2pm; Sept.-May Tu-Sa 9am-5pm. €1.50, EU citizens free.) The **tourist office,** on Arco de la Pta. de Sevilla, is located at the Pta. de Sevilla, down C. San Pedro from the bus stop. (☎954 19 09 55; fax 954 19 00 80. Open M-Sa 10am-6pm, Su 10am-3pm.) The **police** (☎954 14 00 08) are in Pl. San Fernando.

HUELVA ☎959

While many Spaniards vacation on the beaches of the Huelva province, the capital city offers little more than an industrial port; not much is appealing about Huelva (pop. 140,000) other than its proximity to the towns from which Columbus mustered men. That said, travelers heading to or from Portugal shouldn't shy away from an opportunity to spend the night in a place truly free of tourism.

TRANSPORTATION. RENFE **trains** on Av. de Italia (info: ☎902 24 02 02; station: ☎959 24 56 14) run to: **Córdoba** (2¼hr., 4:32pm, €16.32); **Madrid** (4¼hr., 4:32pm, €53.32); **Sevilla** (1½hr., 7:15am-7pm, €6.15). **Buses** depart from Av. Dr. Rubio (☎959 25 69 00) to: **Cádiz** (5hr., 9:30am, €14.88); **Faro, Portugal** (2½hr.; 9am, 6pm; €4.57); **Lagos, Portugal** (5hr.; 9am, 6pm; €9.98); **Lisbon, Portugal** (6½hr.; M, W, F 1:15pm; €24.80); **Madrid** (6hr., 4 per day 9:45am-11:15pm, €21.45); **Málaga** (3pm, €18.82); **Sevilla** (1hr., 9-20 per day 7am-9pm, €5.88).

ORIENTATION AND PRACTICAL INFORMATION. The central axis of the city is **Av. Martín Alonso Pinzón** (or Gran Vía). To reach it from the train station, go out the front door, cross the street, and go straight down the street in front of you, C. Alonso XII. From the bus station, exit across Av. Alemania. Take C. Gravina, turn left onto C. M. Núñez, then right onto C. Concepción. Follow C. Concepción for three blocks, then turn left. Av. Martín Alonso Pinzón is one block over. The **tourist office** is at Av. de Alemania, 12, across from the bus station and half a block to the right. (☎959 25 74 03 or 959 21 01 01. Open M-F 9am-7pm, Sa 10am-2pm.) The bus station has large lockers for **luggage storage** (€3 per day). **Police** are on Av. Tomás Domínguez de Ortiz, 2 (national ☎091; local ☎959 24 93 50). For **Internet access,** go to **Cybercafe Interpool,** C. Vázquez Limón, 9. (☎959 80 24 78. Open M-F 10am-2pm and 5pm-2am, Sa-Su 5pm-2am. €1 per 30min.) **Santander Central Hispano** is at C. Palacios, 10. (☎902 24 24 24. Open M-F 8:30am-2pm, Sa 8:30am-1pm.) The **post office** is at Av. Tomás Domínguez de Ortiz, 1 (☎959 24 91 84).

ACCOMMODATIONS AND FOOD. Most of the accommodations in Huelva cluster between the train station and Av. Martín Alonso Pinzón. A decent option is the somewhat out-of-the-way **Albergue Juvenil Huelva ❶,** on Av. Marchena Colombo, 14. (Take city bus #6 from the central bus station, €0.90. ☎959 25 37 93. Up to 4 people per room. Breakfast included. Some wheelchair-accessible rooms. July-Aug. €12.90 per person, over 26 €17.25. Sept.-June €10.90/€15.20. €3 extra per day for non-members. AmEx/MC/V.) **Mercado de Carmen,** the town's market, is at the intersection of C. Barcelona, C. Carmen, and C. Duque de la Victoria; it sells fresh fish and produce daily 8am-2pm. *Cafeterías* can be found in the center of town on the pedestrian streets, such as C. Concepción, C. Palacios, and C. Arq. Carasca. At night, locals gather at the bars near **Av. Pablo Rada.**

CÓRDOBA ☎957

Charming Córdoba (pop. 310,000), perched on the south bank of the Río Guadalquivir, was once the largest city in western Europe. Islamic architecture, abundant courtyards, and flowers dripping from balconies make this a captivating and romantic city. The narrow and winding streets of the old city fill daily with the unhurried pace of enchanted tourists and strolling locals. Nowhere else are the remnants of Spain's Islamic, Jewish, and Catholic heritages so visibly intermixed. For three centuries, Córdoba was the hub of the Moorish Empire, whose legacy is visible in the famed Mezquita and its dazzling *mihrab* (prayer niche). The Judería is one of Spain's oldest Jewish quarters, containing one of the few synagogues in the Iberian peninsula, and the 14th-century Palacio del Marqués de Viana anticipates Spain's Golden Age of the 16th-17th centuries. Springtime festivals, friendly locals, and a rich and diverse history make Córdoba an essential destination.

TRANSPORTATION

Trains: Pl. de las Tres Culturas, Av. América (☎957 40 02 02). To: **Algeciras** (AVE 4hr., 10:20am, €20.50; regular 5½hr., 5am and 10:15pm, €19-20.59); **Barcelona** (10-11hr., 3 per day 9:45am-10:20pm, €46-60); **Cádiz** (AVE 2¾hr., 12:15am and 6pm, €22; regular 3-4hr., 5 per day 6am-8pm, €15.11-22); **Madrid** (AVE 2hr., 18 per day 7:11am-9:42pm, €38-45); **Málaga** (AVE 2¼hr., 6 per day 9:09am-10:09pm, €12-13.50; regular 3hr., 10 per day 6:40am-10:10pm, €10-18); **Sevilla** (AVE 45min., 18 per day 8:40am-11:40pm, €14.50-17.50). For international tickets, contact **RENFE,** Ronda de los Tejares, 10 (☎957 49 02 02).

Buses: Estación de Autobuses, (☎957 40 40 40; fax 957 40 44 15), on Av. América across from the train station.

Alsina Graells Sur (☎957 27 81 00) covers most of Andalucía. To: **Algeciras** (5hr., 2 per day, €17.50); **Almería** (5hr., 8am, €18); **Antequera** (2½hr., 3 per day 9am-7pm, €6.50); **Cádiz** via Los Amarillos or Comes Sur (4-5hr.; 10am, 6pm; €17.28); **Granada** (3hr., 8-9 per day 8am-8:30pm, €10.01); **Málaga** (3-3½hr., 5 per day 8am-7pm, €10.12); **Sevilla** (2hr., 10-12 per day 5:30am-9:30pm, €8.29). **Bacoma** (☎957 45 65 14) goes to: Baeza, Ubeda, Valencia, and **Barcelona** (10hr., 6:25pm, €51). **Secorbus** (☎902 22 92 92) provides cheap service to **Madrid** (4½hr., 6 per day 1-8pm, €10.45), departing from Camino de los Sastres in front of Hotel Melía.

Transportes Ureña (☎957 40 45 58) runs to **Jaén** (2hr., 7 per day 7:30am-8pm, €5.95). Intra-provincial buses depart from Av. República and Po. Victoria: **Autocares Priego** (☎957 40 44 79), **Empresa Carrera** (☎957 40 44 14), and **Empresa Rafael Ramírez** (☎957 42 21 77) run buses to surrounding towns and camping sites.

Local Public Transportation: 12 bus lines (☎957 25 57 00) cover the city, running from the wee hours until 11pm. **Bus #3** makes a loop from the bus and train stations through Pl. Tendillas, along the river, and up C. Doctor Fleming. **Bus #10** runs from the train station to Barrio Brillante. Purchase tickets onboard for €0.80.

Taxis: Radio Taxi (☎957 76 44 44) has stands at most busy intersections throughout the city. Be sure that the meter is turned on before you start off. From the Judería to the bus and train stations €3-5; to Barrio Brillante €3.60-6.

Car Rental: Hertz (☎957 49 29 61; fax 957 40 20 60), in the train station. Car €61.39 per day for a small car, discounts for longer time periods. Minimum age 25. Open M-F 8:30am-9pm, Sa 9am-1pm and 3:30-7pm, Su 9am-1pm.

ORIENTATION AND PRACTICAL INFORMATION

Córdoba is split between two parts: the old city and the new. The modern and commercial northern half extends from the train station on Av. América down to **Plaza de las Tendillas,** the center of the city. The old section in the south is a medieval maze known as the **Judería** (Jewish quarter). This tangle of beautiful and disorienting streets extends from Pl. Tendillas to the banks of the Río Guadalquivir, winding past the **Mezquita** and **Alcázar.** The easiest way to reach the old city from the train station and the bus station is to take city bus #3 to **Plaza Campo Santo de los Mártires** (€0.80). Alternatively, the walk is about 20min. From the train station, with your back to the platforms, exit left, cross the parking plaza, and make a right onto Av. de los Mozárabes. When you reach the Roman columns, turn left and cross Gta. Sargentos Provisionales. Make a right on Po. de la Victoria and veer toward the left until you reach Puerto Almodóvar; you are now in the old city.

Tourist Offices: Oficina Municipal de Turismo y Congresos, Pl. Judá Leví (☎957 20 05 22; fax 957 20 02 77). Open M-F 8:30am-2:30pm. **Tourist Office of Andalucía,** C. Torrijos, 10 (☎957 47 12 35; fax 957 49 17 78), in the Junta de Andalucía, across from the Mezquita. From the train station, take bus #3 along the river until a stone arch appears on the right. Office is 1 block up C. Torrijos. General info on Andalucía. English-speaking staff with free map of the monument section. Open May-Sept. M-F 9:30am-8pm, Sa 10am-7pm, Su 10am-2pm; Oct.-Apr. M-F 9:30am-6pm, Su 10am-2pm.

Tours: Córdoba Vision, Av. Doctor Fleming, 10 (☎957 76 02 41; fax 957 20 03 68). From the old city bus stop at Pl. Campo Santo de Los Martires, walk about 100m up Av. Doctor Fleming; Córdoba Vision will be on the right. Offers 4 hour-long guided tours in English, French, and Spanish. Walking tour of Córdoba's monuments Tu-Su 10:30am, €25. Tour of Medina al-Zahra: winter Tu-F 4pm, Sa 10:30am and 4pm, Su and holidays 10:30am; summer Tu-F 6pm, Su and holidays 10:30am; €18.

Currency Exchange: CajaSur, Ronda de los Tejares, 18-24 (☎957 21 42 42; fax 957 47 51 29), across from the Corte Inglés. Charges 10% commission, €4.21 minimum. Open M-F 8:30am-2:30pm. **Banks** and **ATMs** are abundant in Córdoba; you will find many in the streets surrounding La Mezquita and around the Pl. Tendillas.

Luggage Storage: Coin-operated lockers at the train and bus stations open 24hr. (€2.40-4.50).

El Corte Inglés: Av. Ronda de los Tejares, 30 (☎957 47 02 67), on the corner of Av. Gran Capitán. Sells an excellent street map (€3.10). Open M-Sa 10am-10pm.

Laundry: Teleseco, Ronda de Isasa, 10 (☎957 48 33 56), 1 block from La Mezquita across from the river. Coin service or dry cleaning. Washers €4.80, dryers €3.

Emergency: ☎092. **Police:** Av. Doctor Fleming, 2 (☎957 59 45 80).

Late-Night Pharmacy: On a rotating basis. Refer to the list posted outside the pharmacy in Pl. Tendillas or the local newspaper.

Medical Assistance: Emergencies ☎061. **Red Cross Hospital,** Po. de la Victoria (emergency ☎957 22 22 22, main line 957 42 06 66). English spoken. Open M-F 9am-1:30pm, 4:30-5:30pm. **Ambulance:** ☎902 50 50 61 (urgent), ☎957 76 73 59.

Internet Access: e-Net, C. García Lovera, 10 (☎957 48 14 62). Leave Pl. Tendillas on C. Claudio Marcelo; C. García Lovera will be the second left. €1.20 per hr., €8 per 10 hr., and €15 per 20 hr. Computer printing, €0.15 per page, €0.30 in color. Faxing available €1 per page to send internationally. Open daily 9am-2pm and 5-10pm.

Post Office: C. Cruz Conde, 15 (☎957 47 97 96), 2 blocks up from Pl. Tendillas. **Lista de Correos.** Open M-F 8:30am-8:30pm, Sa-Su 9:30am-2pm. **Postal Code:** 14070.

ACCOMMODATIONS AND CAMPING

Hostels cluster between the **Mezquita** and **C. de San Fernando.** Córdoba is especially crowded during *Semana Santa* and from May-Sept.—you may have to call two to three months in advance for reservations. Prices are higher in summer.

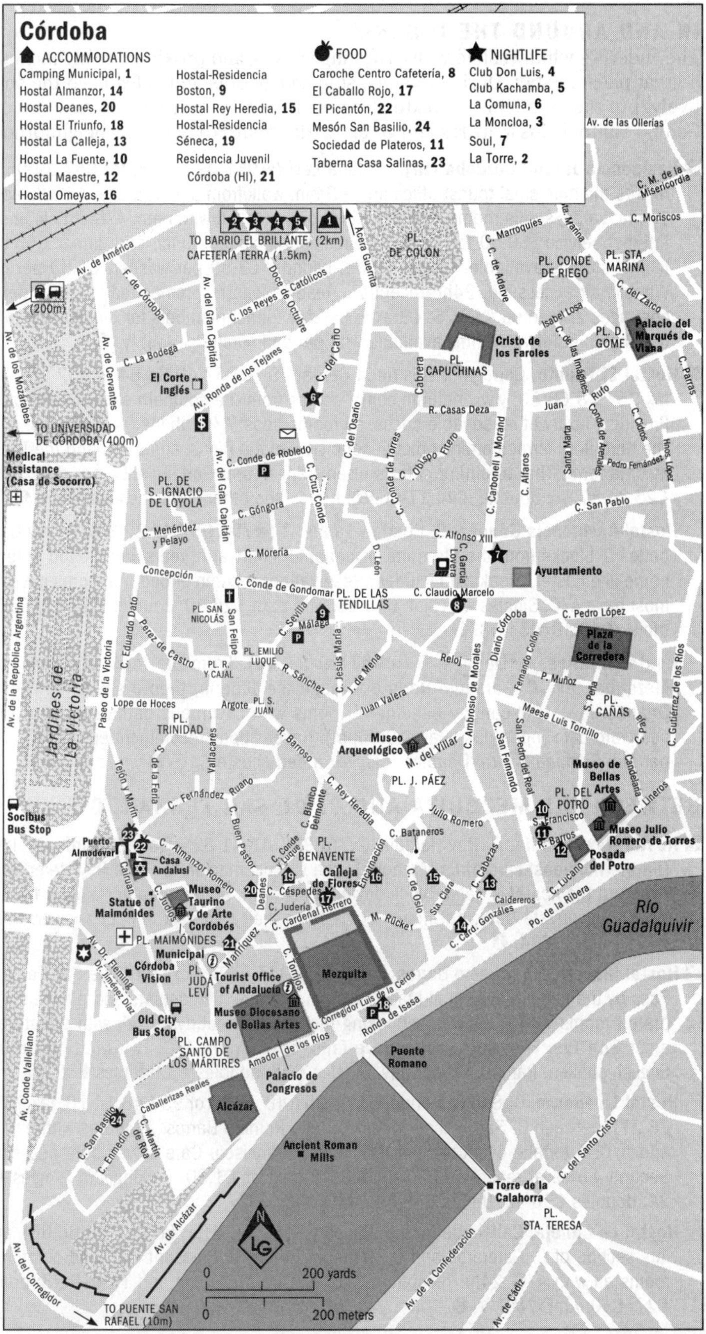
Córdoba
ACCOMMODATIONS
Camping Municipal, 1
Hostal Almanzor, 14
Hostal Deanes, 20
Hostal El Triunfo, 18
Hostal La Calleja, 13
Hostal La Fuente, 10
Hostal Maestre, 12
Hostal Omeyas, 16
Hostal-Residencia Boston, 9
Hostal Rey Heredia, 15
Hostal-Residencia Séneca, 19
Residencia Juvenil Córdoba (HI), 21
FOOD
Caroche Centro Cafetería, 8
El Caballo Rojo, 17
El Picantón, 22
Mesón San Basilio, 24
Sociedad de Plateros, 11
Taberna Casa Salinas, 23
NIGHTLIFE
Club Don Luis, 4
Club Kachamba, 5
La Comuna, 6
La Moncloa, 3
Soul, 7
La Torre, 2
TO BARRIO EL BRILLANTE, (2km)
CAFETERÍA TERRA (1.5km)
(200m)
Av. de América
F. de Córdoba
Av. del Gran Capitán
C. los Reyes Católicos
Doce de Octubre
Acera Guerrita
PL. DE COLÓN
C. Marroquíes
C. de Adarve
Sta. Marina
PL. CONDE DE RIEGO
PL. STA. MARINA
C. M. de la Misericordia
C. Moriscos
Av. de las Ollerías
C. del Zarco
Isabel Losa
PL. D. GOME
Palacio del Marqués de Viana
Cristo de los Faroles
PL. CAPUCHINAS
Cabrera
C. de las Imágenes
Rufo
C. Parras
C. La Bodega
Av. de Cervantes
Av. de los Mozárabes
El Corte Inglés
Av. Ronda de los Tejares
C. del Caño
C. del Osario
R. Casas Deza
Juan
Conde de Arenales
C. Cidros
Hnos. López
Pedro Fernández
Santa Marta
TO UNIVERSIDAD DE CÓRDOBA (400m)
Medical Assistance (Casa de Socorro)
C. Conde de Robledo
C. Cruz Conde
C. Conde de Torres
C. Obispo Fitero
C. Carbonell y Morand
C. Alfaros
PL. DE S. IGNACIO DE LOYOLA
C. Góngora
C. San Pablo
C. Menéndez y Pelayo
C. Morería
C. Alfonso XIII
D. León
C. García Lovera
Ayuntamiento
Concepción
C. Conde de Gondomar
PL. DE LAS TENDILLAS
C. Claudio Marcelo
Av. de la República Argentina
PL. SAN NICOLÁS
San Felipe
C. Sevilla
Málaga
Diario Córdoba
C. Pedro López
C. Eduardo Dato
Pérez de Castro
PL. EMILIO LUQUE
PL. R. Y CAJAL
R. Sánchez
C. Jesús María
J. de Mena
Reloj
Plaza de la Corredera
Fernando Colón
P. Muñoz
Jardines de La Victoria
Paseo de la Victoria
Lope de Hoces
Argote
PL. S. JUAN
Juan Valera
C. Ambrosio de Morales
S. Peña
PL. CAÑAS
Maese Luis Tornillo
C. Gutiérrez de los Ríos
PL. TRINIDAD
Vallacares
S. de la Feria
R. Barroso
Museo Arqueológico
M. del Villar
C. San Fernando
San Pedro del Real
C. Peña
Museo de Bellas Artes
Candelaria
PL. J. PÁEZ
Tejón y Marín
C. Fernández Ruano
C. Buen Pastor
C. Blanco Belmonte
C. Rey Heredia
Julio Romero
PL. DEL POTRO
S. Francisco
C. Lineros
Socibus Bus Stop
Puerto Almodóvar
C. Almanzor Romero
Casa Andalusí
C. Conde y Luque
PL. BENAVENTE
C. Bataneros
R. Barros
Museo Julio Romero de Torres
Posada del Potro
Cairuan
Statue of Maimónides
Museo Taurino y de Arte Cordobés
C. Judíos
Deanes
C. Céspedes
Calleja de Flores
Encarnación
C. de Osio
Sta. Clara
C. Cabezas
C. Lucano
Caldereros
Po. de la Ribera
Río Guadalquivir
C. Judería
C. Cardenal Herrero
M. Rücker
C. Card. Gonzáles
PL. MAIMÓNIDES
Municipal
Manríquez
C. Torrijos
Mezquita
Av. Dr. Fleming
Dr. Jiménez Díaz
Córdoba Vision
PL. JUDÁ LEVÍ
Tourist Office of Andalucía
C. Corregidor Luis de la Cerda
Ronda de Isasa
Museo Diocesano de Bellas Artes
Old City Bus Stop
PL. CAMPO SANTO DE LOS MÁRTIRES
Amador de los Ríos
Puente Romano
Palacio de Congresos
Av. Conde Vallellano
Caballerizas Reales
Alcázar
C. San Basilio
C. Enmedio
C. Martín de Roa
Ancient Roman Mills
C. del Santo Cristo
Torre de la Calahorra
PL. STA. TERESA
Av. de Alcázar
Av. del Corregidor
Av. de la Confederación
Av. de Cádiz
0
200 yards
0
200 meters
TO PUENTE SAN RAFAEL (10m)

IN AND AROUND THE JUDERÍA

The Judería's whitewashed walls, twisting streets, and proximity to sights make it a great place to stay. During the day, souvenir booths and cafes keep the streets lively, but the area feels desolate at night. Take bus #3 from the train station to Campo Santo de los Mártires and go up C. Manríques to reach the neighborhood.

Residencia Juvenil Córdoba (HI), Pl. Juda Leví (☎957 29 01 66; fax 957 29 05 00), next to the municipal tourist office and a 2min. walk from the Mezquita. A backpacker's utopia. Large, sterile rooms, either doubles or quads, all with bath. A/C. Public phones. Internet service (€0.50 for 12 min.). Breakfast included, lunch and dinner €4.70. No locked storage available. Towels €1.05. Laundry €2.50 per washer, €1.50 per dryer. Wheelchair accessible. 24hr. reception. Reservations recommended. €12.90 per person; ages 26 and up €17.25; €3 extra per day for nonmembers for 6-night stay to gain membership. Private rooms available with per-bed surcharge. MC/V. ❶

Hostal El Triunfo, Corregidor Luis de la Cerda, 79 (☎957 49 84 84 or 902 15 83 92; fax 957 48 68 50; www.htriunfo.com), across from the southern side of La Mezquita. Providing luxury at reasonable prices, all rooms boast A/C, phone, TV, bath, and a safe. The third floor terrace offers a picturesque view of the Río Guadalquivir and the Torre de la Calahorra. The adjoining cafe is open 8am-11pm. Parking €12 per day. Singles €25.24-37.86; doubles €44.17-56.80; triples and other capacities available. ❸

Hostal-Residencia Séneca, C. Conde y Luque, 7 (☎/fax 957 47 32 34). Follow C. Céspedes 2 blocks from the Mezquita. A beautiful courtyard greets you as you enter this home-like hostel. Breakfast included. Reservations recommended. All rooms have fans, most have A/C. Singles with sink €15-18, with bath €26-30; doubles €27-32/€35-39; triples €40-48/€54-58. ❷

Hostal Deanes, C. Deanes, 6 (☎957 29 37 44). From the top left corner of the Mezquita, take C. Cardenal Herrero through the Judería, then a sharp right onto C. Deanes. In a 16th-century building, 5 rooms with cavernous baths surround a busy courtyard cafe (open daily 9am-10:30pm). Reservations recommended during December and *Semana Santa*. Doubles €31, extra bed charge €10. ❷

BETWEEN THE MEZQUITA AND C. DE SAN FERNANDO

Hostal Rey Heredia, C. Rey Heredia, 26 (☎957 47 41 82). From C. Cardenal Herrero (on the northeast side of La Mezquita) take C. Encarnación to C. de Rey Heredia, turn right and the *hostal* is half a block down on the right. A great deal for budget travelers. No A/C or private bath, but many rooms have their own sink and/or shower. Singles €12; doubles €24. ❶

Hostal Maestre, C. Romero Barros, 4-5 (☎/fax 957 47 53 95), off C. de San Fernando. Pass by the neighboring Hotel Maestre and head here. Immaculate and pleasantly decorated rooms with windows overlooking the street or courtyard. All with private bath, most with TVs. First floor rooms have fans, other floors A/C. Two pretty courtyards. English spoken. Parking €6 per day. Singles €18; doubles €32; triples €38. ❷

Hostal La Fuente, C. San Fernando, 51 (☎957 48 78 27 or 957 48 14 78; fax 957 48 78 27), between C. San Francisco and C. Julio Romero Barros. All rooms with bath, TV, and A/C. A terrace overlooks the Iglesia San Francisco. Cafe serves beer and coffee. Security boxes at reception for valuables. Breakfast €1.80. Parking €6. Singles €20-24; doubles €36-40; triples €48-50. AmEx/MC/V. ❷

Hostal La Calleja, Calleja de Rufino Blanco y Sánchez, 6 (☎/fax 957 48 66 06), at the intersection of C. Calereros and C. Cardenal González. Pleasant staff and comfortable rooms all with A/C. 24hr. reception. Singles €17, with bath and TV €19.23; doubles €27/€30. AmEx/MC/V. ❷

Hostal Almanzor, C. Cardenal González, 10 (☎/fax 957 48 54 00), 3 blocks from the Mezquita at the end of C. Rey Heredía. All singles have king-sized beds. Spotless rooms with balcony-like windows, TVs, bath and A/C. Parking included. 24hr. reception. Singles €9-12; doubles €18-30. AmEx/MC/V. ❶

Hostal Los Omeyas, C. Encarnación, 17 (☎957 49 22 67 or 957 49 21 99; fax 957 49 16 59). From C. Cardenal Herrero (on the top right side of La Mezquita) you will find C. Encarnación; Los Omeyas is midway up on the right. Pleasant rooms all with A/C, TV, phone, and bath, surround a pleasant courtyard. Breakfast served (€3.50) 8-11am. Parking available €12 per day. Singles €32-38; doubles €50-62. ❹

OTHER AREAS

Hotel Residencia Boston, C. Málaga, 2 (☎957 47 41 76; fax 957 47 85 23), on the corner of Pl. Tendillas, near the new town. All rooms equipped with A/C, TV, phone, safe, and bath. Breakfast €3. Laundry service. Parking nearby. Singles €27-30; doubles €42-49; triples €51-55. AmEx/MC/V. ❸

Camping Municipal, Av. Brillante, 50 (☎957 40 38 36, fax 957 28 21 65). From the train station, turn left on Av. América, left on Av. Brillante, and walk uphill for 20min., or take bus #10 or 11 from Av. Cervantes, which stops across the street. Pool, currency exchange, supermarket, restaurant, free hot showers, laundry. Camping equipment for rent. Wheelchair accessible. IVA not included. One person and tent €8; two people and tent €11.60; two people, car, and tent €15.60; two people and camper €16.85. ❶

FOOD

The Mezquita area falls flat with many hyper-touristed restaurants, but a five-minute walk in any direction yields local specialties at reasonable prices. In the evenings, locals converge at the outdoor terrazas between C. Severo Ochoa and C. Dr. Jiménez Díaz for drinks and *tapas.* Cheap eateries cluster farther away from the Judería in **Barrio Cruz Conde,** and around **Av. Menéndez Pidal** and **Pl. Tendillas.** Regional specialties include *salmorejo* (a gazpacho-like cream soup topped with hard-boiled eggs and pieces of ham) and *rabo de toro* (bull's tail simmered in tomato sauce). **El Corte Inglés,** Av. Ronda de los Tejeres, 30 (open M-Sa 10am-10pm) contains a grocery store.

El Picantón, C. F. Ruano, 19, 1 block from the Puerta de Almodóvar. From the right corner of the Mezquita, walk up Romero and turn left; alternatively, follow C. Judíos to the end, turn right at Puerto Almodóvar, and continue until you see El Picantón on your right. No seats. Great for budget travelers; take ordinary *tapas*, pour on *salsa picante,* stick it in a roll, and voilà, you've got a cheap, hearty meal. *Bocadillos* €1-3, *tapas* €1-3, beer €1. Open daily 10am-3:30pm and 8pm-midnight. ❶

Taberna Casa Salinas, Puerto Almodóvar (☎957 29 08 46). A few blocks from the synagogue, up C. Judíos and to the right. Pepe Salinas has been running this place for over 35 years. Eschew the jam-packed bar and request a table on the romantic outdoor patio, or enjoy A/C in the mellow dining room. *Media raciones* €4.80-8.40. Open M-Sa 11:30am-4:30pm and 8:30pm-12:30am, Su 11:30am-4:30pm. Closed in Aug. ❷

Mesón San Basilio, C. San Basilio, 19 (☎957 29 70 07). From Campo Santo de los Mártires take Caballerizas Reales until the end, turn right onto C. Martín de Roa and then left onto C. San Basilio. 2 floors surrounding a breezy patio. *Menú* M-F €6, Sa-Su €9. *Raciones* €2.70. Entrees dishes €6-13.50. Open daily 1-4pm and 8pm-midnight. ❷

Sociedad de Plateros, C. San Francisco, 6 (☎957 47 00 42), between C. San Fernando and Pl. Potro. White-haired Spanish men play dominoes as tourists cool off in the shaded patio. A Córdoba mainstay since 1872. *Media raciones* and *raciones* €2.60-6.20. Bar open Tu-Su 8am-4:30pm and 8pm-midnight, restaurant 1-4pm and 8pm-midnight. Open June-Aug. M-Sa, Sept.-May Tu-Su. MC/V. ❶

Caroche Centro Cafetería, C. García Lovera, 7 (☎957 49 25 71). Don't let the address fool you. Caroche Centro sits on C. Claudio Marcelo *across* from C. García Lovera. From Pl. Tendillas, walk 1 block down C. Claudio Marcelo. The large-screen TV and blustery A/C combine with affordable food to make this a great refuge from the heat. *Menú* €6. Entrees €4-9. Open daily 7:30am-4am. ❷

El Caballo Rojo Restaurante, C. Cardinal Herrero, 28 (☎957 47 53 75). Walk up the alley-like corridor off C. Cardinal Herrero on the northeast side of La Mezquita. Advertises traditional favorites and "constant investigations in the cuisine of Mozarabs with their spices and virgin olive oil." Eat *tapas* in the bar (€2-15), or enjoy a fancier meal in the restaurant. Fish and vegetarian options. Open daily 9am-midnight. MC/V. ❸

SIGHTS

LA MEZQUITA

☎957 47 05 12. Open Apr.-June M-Sa 10am-7:30pm, Su and holidays 2-7:30pm; July-Oct. daily 10am-7pm; Nov.-Mar. daily 10am-6pm. €6.50, children under 10 free. Wheelchair accessible. Last ticket sold 30min. before closing. Opens M-Sa 8:30am for Mass starting at 9:30am; Su Mass 11am, noon, and 1pm.

Built in 784 on the site of a Visigothic Basilica, this architectural masterpiece is considered the most important Islamic monument in the Western world. Over the course of the next two centuries, the Mezquita was enlarged to cover an area the size of several city blocks with more than 850 columns, making it the largest mosque in the Islamic world at the time of its completion. Carved from granite and marble, the pillars are capped by the characteristic banded Mudéjar arches of different heights. Visitors enter through the **Patio de los Naranjos,** an arcaded courtyard featuring carefully spaced orange trees, palm trees, and fountains, where the dutiful would wash before prayer. The **Torre del Alminar** encloses remains of the minaret from where the *muezzin* would call for prayer.

The most elaborate additions, consisting of the dazzling **mihrab** (prayer niche) and the triple **maksourah** (caliph's niche), were created in the 10th century. The *mihrab*, which faces Mecca, formerly housed a gilt copy of the Qur'an; worn stones evince where pilgrims knelt in reverence. Estimated at close to 35 tons, the intricate gold, pink, and blue marble Byzantine mosaics shimmering across the arches of the *mihrab* were given by the Emperor Constantine VII to the caliphs.

At the far end of the Mezquita lies the **Capilla Villaviciosa,** where Caliphal vaulting appeared for the first time. Completed in 1371, it was the first Christian chapel to be built in the mosque, thus beginning the transition of the Mezquita to a place of Christian worship. In 1523, Bishop Alonso Manrique, an ally of Carlos V, proposed the construction of a cathedral in the center of the mosque. The town rallied violently against the idea, promising painful death to any worker who helped tear down the Mezquita. Nevertheless, a towering **crucero** (transept) and **coro** (choir stall) were eventually erected, incongruously planting a richly adorned Baroque cathedral amidst far more austere environs. The townspeople were less than pleased, and even Carlos V regretted the changes to the Mezquita, lamenting, "You have destroyed something unique to create something commonplace." What remains, though, is far from commonplace, for the juxtaposition of the two architectural styles and programs accentuates the individual qualities of each one.

IN AND AROUND THE JUDERÍA

A combined ticket for the Alcázar, Museo Taurino y de Arte Cordobés, and Museo Julio Romero is available at all three locations. €7.05, students €3.60.

ALCÁZAR. Along the river on the left side of the Mezquita lies the Alcázar. Built in 1328 during *la Reconquista*, the building was both a fortress and residence for Alfonso XI. Fernando and Isabel bade Columbus farewell here, and from 1490 to 1821, it served as a headquarters for the Inquisition. Its walls enclose a garden with terraced flower beds, ponds, palm trees, and fountains. The museum displays 1st-century Roman mosaics and a 3rd-century Roman marble sarcophagus. Don't miss the Arab bath turned Counter-Reformation interrogation chamber in the basement. *(☎957 42 01 51. Open May-June and Sept. Tu-Sa 10am-2pm and 5:30-7:30pm, Su and holidays 9:30am-2:30pm; Oct.-Apr. Tu-Sa 10am-2pm and 4:30-6:30pm, Su and holidays 9:30am-2:30pm; July-Aug. 8:30am-2:30pm. Closed M. €1.87, students €0.94.)*

SINAGOGA. Built in 1315, the Sinagoga is a hollow remnant of Córdoba's once vibrant Jewish community. Adorned with Mozarabic patterns and Hebrew inscriptions, the walls of the small temple have been restored to much of their original intricacy, although little else has been preserved. The only other synagogues to survive the 1492 expulsion of the Jews from Spain are in Toledo. *(C. Judíos, 20, just past the statue of Maimonides. ☎957 20 29 28. Open M-Sa 10am-2pm and 2:30-5:30pm, Su 10am-1:30pm. €0.50, free for EU citizens.)*

MUSEO TAURINO Y DE ARTE CORDOBÉS. The museum is dedicated to the history and lore of the bullfight with rooms containing uniforms, posters, and artifacts from decades of bullfighting in Spain. The main exhibit includes a replica of the tomb of Spain's most famous matador, the dashing Manolete, and the hide of the bull that killed him. *(Pl. Maimónides. ☎957 20 10 56. Open Sept.-June Tu-Sa 10am-2pm and 5:30-7:30pm, Su 9:30am-2:30pm; July-Aug. Tu-Sa 8:30am-2:30pm, Su 9:30am-2:30pm. Last entrance 15min. before closing. Sa-Th €2.91, students €1.48, seniors free. F free.)*

MUSEO DIOCESANO DE BELLAS ARTES. Once the home of Córdoba's bishops while the Inquisition raged within the Alcázar, this 17th-century ecclesiastical palace houses a modest collection of Renaissance and Baroque religious art. *(C. Torrijos, 12, across from the Mezquita in the Palacio de Congresos. ☎957 49 60 85. Open July-Aug. M-Sa 9:30am-3pm; Sept.-June M-F 9:30am-1:30pm and 2-6pm, Sa 9:30am-1:30pm. €1.20, under 12 free, free with admission to Mezquita.)*

OTHER SIGHTS. Townspeople take great pride in their traditional **patios,** many dating from Roman times. These open-air courtyards, tranquil havens of orange and lemon trees, flowers, and fountains, flourish in the old quarter. Among the streets of exceptional beauty are **Calleja del Indiano,** off C. Fernández Ruano at Pl. Angel Torres, and the aptly named **Calleja de Flores**, off C. Blanco Belmonte where lustrous geraniums in full bloom crowd along the white walls of the alley. In Pl. Tiberiades, rub the toes of the statue of **Maimonides** to gain the knowledge of this 12th-century Jewish philosopher and religious rationalist. The statue was used as the model for the face of the New Israeli Shekel. Further past the statue is **Casa Andalusi,** a house restored to its 12th-century state. The tranquil home features mosaic floors, fountains, old Arabic texts and coins, a replication of a paper factory, and an ancient well in the basement. *(C. Judios, 12, between the Sinagoga and the Puerta de Almodóvar. Open M-Sa 10:30am-8:30pm. €2.50.)*

OUTSIDE THE JUDERÍA

MUSEO JULIO ROMERO DE TORRES. Spice up your life with Romero's sensual portraits of Cordoban women, exhibited in the artist's former home. Only the Andalucian sun gets hotter. *(Pl. Potro, 5-10min. from the Mezquita. ☎957 49 19 09. Open May-Sept. Tu-Sa 10am-2pm and 5:30-7:30pm, Su and holidays 9:30am-2:30pm. Last entrance 30min. before closing. Sa-Th €2.95, students €1.48. F free. Combined tickets to Alcázar, Museo Taurino y de Arte Cordobés, and Museo Julio Romero Torres €7.05, students €3.60.)*

MUSEO DE BELLAS ARTES. Across the courtyard from the Museo Julio Romero de Torres, this museum now occupies a building that served as a hospital during the reign of Fernando and Isabel. Its small revolving collection displays Renaissance sketches and works by modern Cordoban artists. Don't miss the sculptures by Mateo Inurria and Juan de Mesa on the ground floor. *(Pl. Potro, 5-10 min. from the Mezquita. ☎957 47 33 45. Open Tu 3-10pm, W-Sa 9am-8pm, Su and holidays 9am-3pm. Enter 15min. before closing. €1.50, EU citizens free.)*

PALACIO DEL MARQUÉS DE VIANA. An elegant 14th-century mansion, the palace displays 12 Cordoban patios complete with sprawling gardens, majestic fountains, tapestries, furniture and porcelain. *(Pl. Don Gome, 2. A 20min. walk from the Mezquita. ☎957 49 67 41. Open June 16-Sept. M-Sa 9am-2pm; Oct. 1-May M-F 10am-1pm and 4-6pm, Sa 10am-1pm; closed June 1-16. Complete tour €6, garden and courtyards only €3.)*

OTHER SIGHTS. From the train station take a moment to see the **Zona Arquelogica de Cercadillas,** the ruins of a 3rd-century Roman palace that was discovered when they built the station. Viewable from the parking lot behind the train station with signs explaining the area; a free guided tour meets at the information stand in the station Sa and Su at 10am and noon. Near the Palacio del Marqués de Viana in Pl. Capuchinos (also known as Pl. Dolores) and next to the monastery is the **Cristo de los Faroles** (Christ of the Lanterns). This is one of the most famous religious icons in Spain and is the site of frequent all-night vigils. The eight lanterns that are lit at night symbolize the eight provinces of Andalucía. Facing the Museo de Bellas Artes and the Museo Julio Romero de Torres is the **Posada del Potro,** a 14th-century inn mentioned in *Don Quijote*. Remnants of 2nd-century Roman water wheels line the sides of the Guadalquivir River. Originally believed to be used by Romans as **mills,** they were later used to bring water to the Calipha's palace. The mills continued to function until Elizabeth "the Catholic" demanded they be shut down as they disturbed her sleep. Crossing the river from the Mezquita is the **Puente Romano,** a restored Roman bridge used by pedestrians. The bridge passes through a natural bird sanctuary on its way to the **Torre de la Calahorra,** a Muslim military tower which was built in 1369 to protect the Roman bridge. The tower now houses a museum that covers Córdoba's cultures during the Middle Ages. Open daily 10am-2pm, 4:30-8:30pm; €3.60, students €2.40, audio-tour €3.60.

ENTERTAINMENT

For the latest cultural events, pick up a free copy of the *Guía del Ocio* at the tourist office. Cheap flamenco isn't easy to come by in Córdoba. Tourists fill the **Tablao Cardenal,** C. Torrijos, 10, facing the Mezquita, where prize-winning dancers perform *flamenco puro*. Reserve seats at the Tablao or your hostel. (☎957 48 33 20. Shows M-Sa 10:30pm. €18, includes 1 drink.) Another option is **La Bulería,** C. Pedro López, 3, with nightly shows at 10:30pm. (☎957 48 38 39. €11, includes 1 drink).

NIGHTLIFE

Nightlife in Córdoba is focused around the city center and in the chic Barrio Brillante. During the cooler months of winter, nightlife tends to center in the neighborhood where the Universidad de Córdoba used to be, especially in pubs on C. Alderetes and C. Julio Pellicer, and near the Pl. de la Corredera. From there, the crowds move on to Av. Gran Capitán and C. Cruz Conde.

Soul, C. Alfonso XIII, 3 (☎957 49 15 80). A hip, relaxed bar where you can chat with your friends at cozy tables or mingle with locals, international students, and dreadlocked bartenders. Offering reggae, drum and bass, deep house, DJ and jazz music. Beer €1.20, mixed drinks €3.60. Open 9pm-3am, closed July and Aug. MC/V.

La Comuna, C. del Caño, 1 (☎610 71 55 63; www.lacomuna.es.fm). An upbeat crowd gathers for friendly service and alternative music. La Comuna is popular with exchange students. Beer €2, mixed drinks €4. Open noon-4am, closed July and Aug.

From the first weekend of June until the heat subsides, the cool **Barrio Brillante,** uphill from Av. América, is the place where most young *cordobéses* head at night. Throngs of well-dressed, young people walk the streets, hopping from one packed outdoor bar to another until reaching a dance club. Bus #10 goes to Brillante from the train station until about 11pm, but the bars do not wake up until around 1am (most stay open until 4am). A taxi should cost €3-6. If you're walking, head up Av. Brillante (45min. from the bottom of the old city), passing along the way **Pub BSO** at C. Llanos de Pretorio. Right around the corner is **Brujas Bar,** where every Tuesday and Thursday, witches can tell your fortune.

La Torre, C. Poeta Emilia Prados. An outdoor nightclub with a slightly younger crowd that plays a mix of well-known Latin music and Spanish pop. Beer €1.50, mixed drinks around €4. Open 11pm-4:30am. Across the street is **Cafetería Terra** where locals converge before hitting Brillante's bars and clubs.

La Moncloa, Av. Brillante (☎957 27 23 11), near McDonalds and Camping Municipal. Taking its name from Madrid's presidential palace, Moncloa draws a crowd of 20-somethings for Spanish and Latin dance music. Beer €2-2.50, mixed drinks €3-5.

Club Don Luis, Av. Brillante. Much like its neighbor La Moncloa, the party at Don Luis doesn't start until around 1am. Young crowd, cheap beer (€2). Open midnight-4am.

Club Kachamba, Av. Brillante. The friendly staff at Kachamba makes it another entertaining place to stop on a tour of Av. Brillante's popular nightclubs. With the same owners as Club Kachamba, **Cachao** and **La Toscana** offer late-night dancing starting at 3am. You'll need to take a cab to these hip *discotecas*, located at Corretera de Trasierra.

DAYTRIP FROM CÓRDOBA

MADINAT AL-ZAHRA

Madinat al-Zahra can be hard to reach. The 0-1 bus (☎957 25 57 00) leaves from Av. República Argentina in Córdoba for Cruce Madinat Al-Zahra, 3km from the site (10min. past every hr., €0.80) and from Puerta del Puente (every hr., €0.80). From the bus stop, it's a 45min. walk, mostly uphill. The return bus stops along the highway at the cross, on the opposite side of the street from the gas station. A taxi from Córdoba to the site costs about €24. Córdoba Visión also offers transportation and tours (see p. 236).

Legend has it that Abd al-Rahman III built the city of Madinat Al-Zahra for his favorite wife, Zahra. Since Zahra pined for the snow-capped peaks of her hometown in Granada, the thoughtful Abd al-Rahman planted white-blossoming almond groves to substitute for the snowcaps of the Sierra Nevada. Archaeologists, on the other hand, tend to believe that Madinat al-Zahra was built to demonstrate Abd al Rahman III's power as the new caliph in al-Andalus. If so, he must have been effective, for this 10th-century medina was considered one of the greatest palaces of its time before it was sacked by Berbers in 1010. The city was rapidly built out of the world's best materials; 10,000 people worked day and night to complete it within 50 years. It was constructed in three terraces (one for the nobility, another for servants, and a third for an enclosed garden and almond grove), and included roads, bridges and aqueducts. Today, Madinat al-Zahra rests in ruins, but with the help of some reconstructions one can still get a sense of its past. A complete tour of the ruins takes between 20-45min., depending on your level of interest. (☎957 32 91 30. Open May-mid Sept. Tu-Sa 10am-8:30pm, Su and holidays 10am-2pm; mid Sept-Apr. Tu-Su and holidays 10am-2pm; closed M all year. €1.50, EU citizens free.)

JEREZ DE LA FRONTERA ☎956

Jerez de la Frontera (pop. 200,000) is the cradle of three staples of Andalucian culture: flamenco, Carthusian horses, and, of course, *jerez* (sherry). It is the sheer quantity and quality of this third staple that draws in the tourists, most of whom are older, well-to-do Europeans. The city also makes a good departure point for the *ruta de los pueblos blancos*, but those not particularly interested in *bodega* tours or horse shows would be better off spending their time elsewhere.

TRANSPORTATION

Flights: Airport, Ctra. Jerez-Sevilla (☎956 15 00 00), 7km from town. Taxi to the airport €11. **Iberia** (☎956 18 43 94) has an office at the terminal. Flights operate regularly to and from **Madrid** and **Barcelona,** as well as other major European cities.

Trains: Pl. Estación (☎956 34 23 19), at the end of C. Medina after it becomes C. Cartuja. **RENFE,** C. Larga, 34 (☎902 24 02 02). To: **Barcelona** (12hr.; 8:36am, 9pm; €51.63-74); **Cádiz** (45min., every 30min. 6:45am-10:15pm, €2.41); **Madrid** (4½hr.; 8:36am, 5pm; €48.16-70.16); **Sevilla** (1¼hr., 12 per day 6:23am-9pm, €5.66).

Buses: C. Cartuja (☎956 34 52 07), at the corner of C. Madre de Dios, 2 blocks from the train station. **Transportes Generales Comes** (☎956 34 21 74). To: **Cádiz** (1hr., 19 per day 7am-11:15pm, €2.37); **Puerto Santa María** (30min., 5-7 per day 7am-8:30pm, €1.30); **Ronda** (2¾hr., 4 per day 7:45am-3:30pm, €8.33). **Los Amarillos** (☎956 32 93 47) goes to **Arcos de la Frontera** (30min., 8 per day 9am-8:15pm, €1.94) and **Córdoba** (4hr., 5pm, €12.74). **Linesur** (☎956 34 10 63) runs to: **Algeciras** (2hr., 7-9 per day 7am-9:45pm, €7.10); **Chipiona** (1hr., 11 per day 7am-10pm, €1.93); **Sanlúcar** (30min., every hr. 7am-10pm, €1.31); **Sevilla** (1½hr., 7-8 per day 8:30am-7:45pm, €4.81). **Secorbus** (☎902 22 92 92) goes to **Madrid** (7hr., 6 per day 8:50am-11:50pm, €19.57). **City Buses:** Each of the 12 lines runs every 15min., most passing through Pl. Arenal and by the bus station. Fare €0.70. **Info office** (☎956 34 34 46) in Pl. Arenal.

Car Rental: Niza, Ctra. N. IV Madrid-Cádiz, KM, 634 (☎956 30 28 60). Take Av. Alvaro Domecq to the highway NIV towards Sevilla. Starts at €57 per day. Min. age 21. Open daily 8:30am-8pm.

ORIENTATION AND PRACTICAL INFORMATION

The labyrinthine streets of Jerez are difficult to navigate without a map. Get one free from the tourist office at Pl. Arenal or buy one at any bookstore or newsstand (€2.60). To reach the town center from the **bus station,** with your back to the ticket counter exit left onto C. Cartuja, which becomes C. Medina, which leads into **Pl. Romero Martínez** (the city's commercial center). From here, walk left on C. Cerrón, which leads to C. Santa María and C. Lancería, heading into **Plaza del Arenal. C. Lancería** and **C. Larga** make up the main pedestrian thoroughfare in the center of the city. From the **train station,** exit to the right and take C. Cartuja to the bus station, then follow the directions above.

Tourist Office: Pl. Arenal (☎956 35 96 54). English-speaking staff has free maps and info on sherry production, *bodega* tours, and horse shows. Open June-Sept. M-F 9am-2:30pm and 4:30-6:30pm, Sa-Su 9:30am-3:30pm; Oct.-May M-F 8am-3pm and 4-7pm, Sa-Su 10am-2pm.

Currency Exchange: Santander Central Hispano, C. Larga, 11 (☎902 24 24 24). Open M-F 8:30am-1pm.

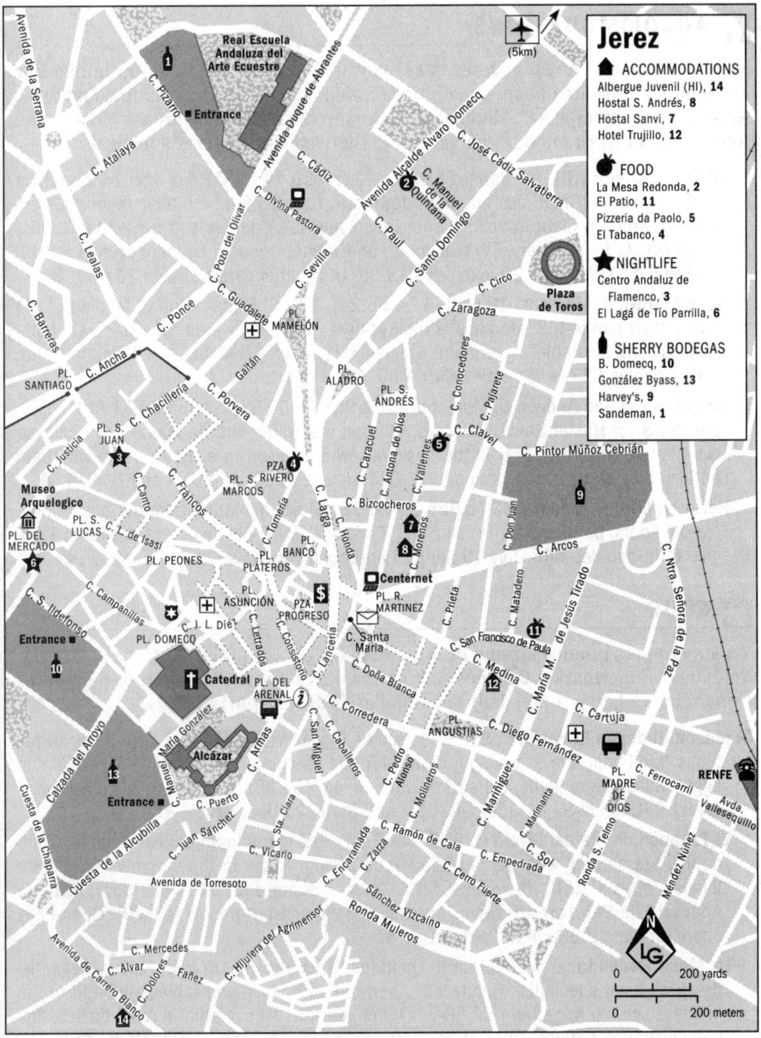

Emergency: ☎061. **Police:** ☎091 or 956 33 03 46.

Medical Assistance: Ambulatorio de la Seguridad Social, C. José Luis Díez (☎956 32 32 02).

Internet Access: Centernet, C. Arcos 3 (☎956 32 49 39). €1.80 per hr. Open daily 10:30am-2:30pm and 4:30-11pm.

Post Office: Main Office, C. Cerrón, 2 (☎956 34 22 95), off Pl. Romero Martínez. Open M-F 8:30am-8:30pm, Sa 9am-2pm. **Lista de Correos** open M-Sa 9am-2pm. **Postal Code:** 11480.

ACCOMMODATIONS

Finding a place to crash in Jerez is as easy as finding a cork to sniff, though few accommodations are cheap. Look along C. Medina, near the bus station, and on C. Arcos, which intersects C. Medina at Pl. Romero Martínez. The area is close to the fountains and *terrazas* of C. Larga. Prices increase during Jerez's festivals.

Albergue Juvenil (HI), Av. Carrero Blanco, 30 (☎956 14 39 01; fax 956 14 32 63), a 25min. walk or 10min. bus ride from downtown (bus L-8 from the bus station, bus L-1 from Pl. Arenal). Clean rooms, a pool (open July-Aug.), tennis and basketball courts, small soccer field, library, TV/VCR room, and rooftop terrace. Laundry service €1.80. Call ahead. Dorms €10.90, over 26 €15.20. HI member card €5, over 26 €11. ❶

Hostal Sanvi, C. Morenos, 10 (☎956 34 56 24). Take C. Fontana (off C. Medina), for 1 block, then turn left; C. Morenos is the 1st right. Newly renovated rooms. Private bathrooms. Fans available on request. Singles €21, during festivals and *Semana Santa* €30; doubles €27/€42; triples €45/€60. ❷

Hostal/Hotel San Andrés, C. Morenos, 12 (☎956 34 09 83; fax 956 34 31 96). Follow directions for Hostal Sanvi. Hallways adorned with vines and Andalucian tile enclose two plant-filled patios. Stay in the basic *hostal* or splurge on a "hotel" room with bath and TV. Singles €20, with bath and TV €24; doubles €24, with bath and TV €38. ❷

Hotel Trujillo, C. Medina, 38 (☎956 34 24 38). Down the street from the bus station. Marble floors, bath, phone, TV, and A/C. Parking €12.90 per day. Sept. 16-July 14 singles €25; doubles €48. July 15-Sept.14 and during festivals €50/€75. MC/V. ❹

FOOD

Tapas-hoppers bounce around Pl. Arenal, C. Larga, and in the old town around Pl. del Banco. Supermarket **Cobreros** sells the basics on the second floor of the Centro Comercial, C. Larga (open daily 9am-2pm and 5:30-9:30pm).

Mesón Bodegon El Patio, C. San Francisco de Paula, 7 (☎956 34 07 36). Savor sumptuous traditional fare in a dining room with brightly-colored oil paintings. Loaded with eggs, sausage and garlic, the sizzling *sopa de ajo* (€4.25) is a meal in itself. *Raciones* €4.81-9. Open M-Sa 11:30am-4:30pm and 8pm-12:30am. MC/V. ❷

El Tabanco, Pl. Rafael Rivero (☎956 33 40 24). *Tapas* bar in an unrivaled setting. Outdoor plaza seating with frequent flamenco performances in the summer. Filled with locals. *Tapas* €1.50. *Raciones* €5-11. Open 7:30pm until late. Next door, **Antigua Abaceria de San Lorenzo** serves an exquisite almond tart *postre* (€1.70). Open daily noon-3pm and 8:30pm-1:30am. MC/V. ❷

La Mesa Redonda, C. Manuel de la Quintana, 3 (☎956 34 00 69). Serves elegantly-prepared local specialties (many with sherry). Peach walls and tablecloths add to the intimate setting. Appetizers €4.50-7.50. Entrees €6-13.55. Fish and meat dishes; limited vegetarian options. Open M-Sa 1:30-4pm and 9-11:30pm. AmEx/MC/V. ❸

Pizzeria da Paolo, C. Clavel at C. Valientes. The best pizza in Jerez. Pizza €4.80-7.50, pasta €4.50-7.50, salads €2.50-4.85. Open Tu-Su 1:15-4:30pm and 8:45pm-12:30am. MC/V. ❶

SHERRY BODEGAS

People come to Jerez for the *jerez*. Multilingual tour guides distill the sherry-making process for you, then give you free samples. The best time to visit is early September during the harvest; the worst is August when many *bodegas* close down. *Bodegas* are plotted on any map, and the tourist office can help find the right one for you.

LIQUOR FOR LINGUISTS The Islamic prohibition against consumption of alcohol did not prevent Jerez's Moorish merchants from exporting wine to the infidel English in the 12th century. "Sherry," an anglicization of Shir-az, the Arabic name for Jerez, is a legacy of this early commerce. Today, only wines produced in Jerez, Sanlúcar de Barrameda, and El Puerto de Santa María are considered sherries. There is no vintage sherry; wines from various years are continuously mixed together in what is known as the *solera* process. Placing burnt distilled wine in old sherry casks results eventually in the creation of cognac. Unable to use the term for the same reason that wineries in other regions cannot call their products sherry, Jerez's merchants have settled with "brandy," another English bastardization, this time of the Dutch word "brandewyn," meaning "burnt wine." Impress your friends at dinner parties by knowing the trinity of major sherry types: **Fino:** A dry, light colored sherry served chilled and sipped with *tapas*. Most popular in Andalucía. Manzanilla, a type of fino from Sanlúcar de Barrameda, is slightly salty in taste. **Amontillado:** Somewhat sweeter and amber in color. Excellent with white meat and cheese. **Oloroso dulce:** A dessert wine, dark in color, with a raisin-like taste. Go ahead, be pretentious. You know you want to.

Group reservations for tours must be made at least one week in advance; reservations for individuals are usually unnecessary. Call ahead for exact times.

B. Domecq, C. San Idelfonso, 3 (☎956 15 15 00; www.domecq.es). Founded in 1730, Domecq is the oldest and largest *bodega* in town. Tours include an informative 15min. video followed by a stroll through some of the warehouses and gardens of the sprawling complex. With unlimited sampling from 3 sherries and 2 brandies, Domecq's tasting is by far the most generous in Jerez. Celebrity visitors have included Franco and Alexander Fleming. Tours every hr. M-F 10am-1pm, €5. Noon tours conducted in Spanish, English, and German. Reservations required. Group visits available on weekends. MC/V.

González Byass, C. Manuel María González, 12 (☎956 35 70 16; www.gonzalezbyass.es). The Disneyworld of *bodegas*: uncomfortably commercial and definitely overblown, but worth visiting at least once. Trolleys whisk visitors past the world's largest weathervane and a storage room designed by Gustave Eiffel (of Eiffel Tower fame). At the end of the tour, a trained mouse climbs a miniature ladder to sip a glass of *oloroso*. Celebrity visitors have included Margaret Thatcher and Orson Welles. Tours in English M-Sa 11:30am-5:30pm, Su 10am-1pm. €7, 2pm tour with light *tapas* €10. MC/V.

Sandeman, C. Pizarro, 10 (☎956 31 29 95; www.sandeman.com), next to the Royal Andalucian School of Equestrian Art. Although most associated with port, Sandeman is also a leading sherry producer. Their labels sport a stylish black-caped Don. Tours M, W, F 10:30am-2:30pm; Tu, Th 10:30am-3pm; Sa 11:30am-1:30pm. €4. MC/V.

Harvey's, C. Arcos, 54. (☎956 34 60 04; www.jerezharveys.es). Makers of Harvey's Cream, the best selling sherry in the world. Visit includes a video of the production process and a tour featuring peacocks, countless oak barrels, and a crocodile. Open M-F 9am-1pm, weekends and holidays 2-8pm. €3. Reservations required for groups. MC/V.

SIGHTS

ALCÁZAR. Seized by Christian knights under Alfonso X during *la Reconquista* of Jerez in 1255, the Alcázar has slowly changed over the centuries. During the 1300s, the Moorish governor's private mosque was transformed into a chapel to commemorate the intercession of the Virgin Mary on behalf of Christian raids into the Kingdom of Granada. Later, in the 17th century, the neighboring Arab baths became servants' quarters for the Palacio de Villavicencio, where the **Cámara Oscura** resides today.

Designed along a model by Leonardo Da Vinci, the Cámara Oscura uses reflective lenses to project panoramas of the city. *(☎956 31 97 98. Open May-Sept. 15 M-Sa 10am-8pm, Su from June 15-Sept. 15 10am-3pm; Sept. 16-Apr. daily 10am-6pm. Alcázar only €1.29, students €0.64; Alcázar and Cámara Oscura €3.25, students €2.57.)*

REAL ESCUELA ANDALUZA DE ARTE EQUESTRE. Jerez's love for wine is almost matched by its passion for horses. During the first or second week of May, the Real Escuela Andaluza de Arte Equestre (Royal Andalucian School of Equestrian Art) sponsors a **Feria del Caballo** (Horse Fair) with shows, carriage competitions, and races of Jerez-bred Carthusian horses. During the rest of the year, weekly shows feature a troupe of horses dancing in choreographed sequences. The training sessions are almost as impressive. *(Av. Dunque de Abrantes. ☎956 31 96 35; www.realescuela.org. Training sessions year-round. M, W, and F 10am-1pm. Up to €12. Shows year-round Th noon and March-Oct. Tu noon. €12-18, children and students 40% off. MC/V.)*

ENTERTAINMENT AND NIGHTLIFE

FLAMENCO. Rare footage of Spain's most highly regarded flamenco singers, dancers, and guitarists is available for viewing at the **Centro Andaluz de Flamenco,** in Palacio Pemartín, on Pl. San Juan. *(☎956 34 92 65; www.caf.cica.es. Open M-F 9am-2pm. Audio-visuals every hr. 9am-2pm. Free.)* Most *peñas* and *tablaos* (clubs and bars that host flamenco) hide in the old town and host special performances during July and August. Ask for details in the tourist office or look for posters along the main streets. For more frequent (and touristy) shows, make the trek to **El Lagá de Tío Parrilla,** Pl. Mercado. *(☎/fax 956 33 83 34. Shows M-Sa 10:30pm. Cover €12, includes 1 drink.)*

FESTIVALS. Autumn, in addition to being grape harvest season, is festival season, when Jerez showcases its best equine and flamenco traditions. In September, the **Fiesta de la Bulería** celebrates flamenco, as does the **Festival de Teatro, Música, y Baile.** These festivals are collectively known as the **Fiestas de Otoño,** occurring from early September until the end of October. The largest **horse parade** in the world, with races in Pl. Arenal, is the highlight of the final week. Check at the tourist office for details; schedules are available in September for the upcoming year.

NIGHTLIFE. Visitors to Jerez tend to be on the older side; *tapas* bars are more popular than dance clubs here, although plenty of people go out on weekends. For bars and *terrazas,* look around the triangle formed by **C. Santo Domingo, C. Salvatierra,** and **Av. Méjico.** Also of interest is Pl. Canterbury, a mini-mall of nightspots located on C. Paul at C. Santo Domingo. **Cancún,** C. Pajarete, 18, a huge, trendy *bar-musical* off C. Zaragoza (a block from Pl. Canterbury), features Caribbean themes, but the usual techno-pop blasts from the speakers. *(☎956 33 17 22. Couples, ladies, and "members" only. Free.)*

SANLÚCAR DE BARRAMEDA ☎956

Sanlúcar de Barrameda (pop. 62,000), at the mouth of the Río Guadalquivir, borders both the Parque Nacional Coto de Doñana (see **Fine Feathered Friends,** below) and some pristine beaches. Home to a handful of sherry *bodegas* and palaces, Sanlúcar is a cross between a Spanish *pueblo blanco* and a European seaside resort. Its industrial outskirts are a bit of an eyesore, but it boasts superbly fine sands, forming the seaside corner of the illustrious "sherry triangle," along with Jerez and El Puerto de Santa María.

FINE FEATHERED FRIENDS Bust out your binoculars—the 60,000 acre **Parque Nacional Coto de Doñana** on the Río Guadalquivir delta is home to flamingos, vultures, and thousands more of your feathered favorites, along with geese (and mongeese), wild boars, and lynx. Despite a huge mining spill on a tributary of the Guadalquivir River in April 1998 that threatened to be one of Spain's biggest ecological disasters, the park has done surprisingly well, and tourist visits have continued relatively unaffected. If ornithological delights don't entice you, the salt marshes, sand dunes, wooded areas, and beach might. Nature purists beware, though, lest you stumble upon the lair of the dreaded species *turgrupus touristicus*—the park borders the town of Matalascañas, with a concrete shopping center and hotel complex.

Access to most of the park is restricted, and back-country hiking and camping are prohibited. The western end of the park is accessible from Huelva and Matalascañas. Also, boat tours on **S.S. Real Fernando** depart from **Sanlúcar.** (☎956 36 38 13. 4hr.; June.-Sept. daily 10am and 5pm; Apr., May, and Oct. 10am and 4pm; Nov.-Mar. 10am; €14.50.) Call or visit the office in the old ice factory by the dock on Av. Bajo de Guía. Those more interested in sand than life on the wild side can take the launch across the bay (8am-8pm, €3) to one of the few non-touristed beaches in Spain. To get a taste of Doñana, stop by the **Visitor Center,** also in the ice factory. (☎956 38 16 35. Open June-Aug. daily 9am-8pm; Sept.-May 9am-2:30pm and 4-7pm.)

TRANSPORTATION. **Los Amarillos** (☎956 38 50 60), on Pl. Pradillo at the end of C. San Juan, runs **buses** to: **Cádiz** (1hr., 10 per day 6:15am-6:20pm, €2.55); **Chipiona** (30min., every hr. 6:15am-10:45pm, €0.70); **Sevilla** (2hr., 13 per day 6:45am-9:15pm, €6). **Linesur La Valenciana** (☎956 34 10 63) is 2 blocks toward the beach from Pl. Cabildo. Buses run to **Chipiona** (30min., every hr. 8am-9pm, €0.70) and **Jerez** (45min., every hr. 7:20am-10:20pm, €1.50). Buy tickets on the bus. For **taxis,** call ☎956 36 11 02 or 956 36 00 04.

PRACTICAL INFORMATION. The **tourist office** is on Calzada del Ejército, which runs perpendicular to the beach. English-speaking staff has info on the **Parque Nacional de Doñana.** (☎ 956 36 61 10; fax 956 36 61 32. Open June-Aug. M-F 9am-2pm and 6-8pm, Sa-Su 10am-2pm and 6-8:30pm; Sept.-May M-F 10am-2pm and 5-7pm, Sa 10am-1pm.) Services include: **emergency** ☎061; **Ambulatorio de la S.S.** on Calzada del Ejército (☎956 36 71 65); **police,** Av. Constitución (☎956 38 80 11); and the **post office,** C. Correos and Av. Cerro Falcón, toward the beach from the tourist office. (☎956 36 09 37. Open M-F 8:30am-2:30pm, Sa 9am-1pm.) **Postal code:** 11540.

ACCOMMODATIONS AND FOOD. Few true bargains exist in Sanlúcar; it may be worth it to inquire at doorway signs reading *"se alquilan habitaciones"* (rooms for rent). **Hostal La Blanca Paloma ❷,** Pl. San Roque, 15, keeps spacious, clean rooms, a few with balconies. (☎956 36 36 44. Mar.-Oct. singles €15; doubles €27. Nov.-Feb. €13/€21.) Sanlúcar is famous for its *langostinos* (king prawns). For a sit-down meal, head for the side streets off C. San Juan. *Terrazas* fill Pl. San Roque and Pl. Cabildo, its tree-lined neighbor. **Bar-Restaurante El Cura ❶,** C. Amargura, 2, between the two plazas, serves up divine *paella* (€3) and other entrees. (☎956 36 29 94. Open daily 1:30-4pm and 7:30pm-midnight.)

SIGHTS AND ENTERTAINMENT. Two impressive palaces compete with the enormous 14th-century **Iglesia de Nuestra Señora de la O,** Pl. Paz, for the attention of sun-struck tourists. (☎956 36 05 55. Open 30min. before and after Mass. Mass M-F 7:30pm; Su 9am, noon, 8pm. Free.) The **Palacio Medina Sidonia** is inhabited by the

Duque de Medina Sidonia. (☎956 36 01 61. Call to arrange group visits on Su or M. Free.) The 19th-century **Palacio Infantes de Orleans** now houses the Ayuntamiento. (☎956 38 80 00. Open for guided visits Th 11:15am. Free.) Several **bodegas** tower over Sanlúcar's small streets. Check at the tourist office for their schedules. (Tours M-Sa. €1.80-3.) For €4 per person, the tourist office organizes tours of the monuments and *bodegas*. Locals celebrate their sherry during the **Feria de la Manzanilla** (late May or early June). In August, **Carreras de Caballos** (horse races) thunder along the beach, and the **Festival de la Exaltación del Río Guadalquivir** brings poetry readings, a flamenco competition, dancing, and bullfights.

ARCOS DE LA FRONTERA ☎956

The Spanish novelist Azorín once described Arcos (pop. 33,000) by saying: "Imagine a long, narrow ridge, undulating; place on it little white houses, clustered among others more ancient; imagine that both sides of the mountain have been cut away, dropping downward sheer and straight; and at the foot of this wall a slow, silent river, its murky waters licking the yellowish stone, then going on its destructive course throughout the fields...and when you have imagined all this, you will have but a pale image of Arcos." The most popular of Spain's *pueblos blancos*, Arcos is a historic and romantic gem. Emanating like gossamer strings from the Plaza del Cabildo, the convoluted medieval streets lead visitors past geranium-lined balconies and tranquil farmers' markets lying unperturbed in the sun.

TRANSPORTATION

Buses: Station, C. Corregidores. **Transportes Generales Comes** (☎956 70 20 15). To: **Cádiz** (1½hr., 6 per day 7:20am-7:25pm, €4.45); **Costa del Sol** (3-4hr., 4pm, €9.21-12.36); **Ronda** (1¾hr., 3 per day 8:15am-2pm, €6). **Los Amarillos buses** (☎956 70 02 57) go to **Jerez** (30min.; M-F 8-18 per day 6:30am-8:15pm, Sa-Su 8am-6:30pm; €1.94) and **Sevilla** (2hr.; 7am, 5pm; €6.12).

Taxis: RadioTaxi (24hr. ☎956 70 13 55). Taxis cluster around C. Debajo del Corral.

ORIENTATION AND PRACTICAL INFORMATION

To reach the town center from the bus station, exit left, turn left, then continue uphill for two blocks on C. Josefa Moreno Seguro, taking a right on C. Muñoz Vásquez. From there it's a 20min. walk uphill. Continue straight until reaching Pl. de España, then veer left onto Debajo del Coral, which quickly changes into C. Corredera; the old quarter is 500m ahead. Mini-buses run every 30min. from the bus station to C. Corredera (€0.80). A taxi costs €4.

Tourist Office: Pl. Cabildo (☎956 70 22 64). Open Mar. 15-Oct. 15 M-Sa 10am-2pm and 4-8pm; Oct. 16-Mar. 14 M-Sa 10am-2pm and 3:30-7:30pm. Offers tours of the old city. (M 10:30am, 10:30pm; Sa 10:30am. €3, children free.) Also gives patio tours. (M-F noon, 6:30pm; Sa noon. €3.)

Bank: Santander Central Hispano, C. Corredera, 62 (☎902 24 24 24). Open M-F 8:30am-2pm, Sa 8:30am-1pm.

Emergency: ☎091. **Police:** C. Nueva (☎956 70 16 52).

Medical Emergency: ☎061 or 956 51 15 53. **Hospital: Centro de Salud,** C. Rafael Benat Rubio (☎956 70 0787), in the Barrio Bajo.

Pharmacy: Ldo. Ildefonso Guerrero Seijo, C. Corredera, 11 (☎956 70 02 13). Open Apr.-Sept. M-F 9:30am-1:30pm and 5-9pm; Oct.-Mar. M-F 9:30am-1:30pm and 4:30-8pm, Sa 9:30am-1:30pm.

Post Office: C. Murete, 24 (☎956 70 15 60), overlooking the cliffs and the river. Open M-F 8:30am-2:30pm, Sa 9:30am-1pm. **Postal Code:** 11630.

ACCOMMODATIONS

Arcos has only a few budget hostels; call ahead during *Semana Santa* and in the summer to be safe. As usual, the tourist office has a list of accommodations.

Hostal San Marcos, C. Marqués de Torresoto, 6 (☎956 70 07 21), past C. Dean Espinosa and Pl. Cabildo. Bright, modern rooms with large private baths. Restaurant below serves one of the cheapest *menús* in town (€6). Singles €25; doubles €36. MC/V. ❷

Pensión El Patio, C. Dean Espinosa, 4 (☎956 70 23 02), shaded by the buttresses of Iglesia de Sta. María. Entrepreneurial owner runs a hostel in addition to a restaurant and barbershop on the ground floor. Spotless rooms, all with TV and A/C. Singles €18, with bath €22; doubles €27, with bath €33. MC/V. ❷

Hotel El Convento, C. Maldonado, 2 (☎956 70 23 23; fax 956 79 41 28). Pleasant rooms set in a restored 17th-century convent. Shared terrace provides breathtaking views. All rooms have phone, TV, A/C, and bath. Parking in plaza €3 per day, in garage €4.81 per day. Closed Jan. 7-Jan. 22. Mar.-Oct. singles €52; doubles €65, with private terrace €78. Nov.-Feb. €33/€46/€58. AmEx/MC/V. ❷

FOOD

Restaurants huddle at the bottom end of C. Corredera, while *tapas* nirvana can be found uphill in the old quarter.

Bar Típico Alcaraván, C. Nueva, 1 (☎956 70 33 97), down from Pl. Cabildo. In a cave under a 900-year-old castle. The perfect place for a romantic *tête-à-tête. Tapas* €1.50-3, *raciones* €6-9. Open Tu-Su noon-4pm and 7:45pm-midnight. MC/V. ❷

Los Faraones, C. Debajo del Corral, 8 (☎956 70 06 12), downhill from C. Corredera. Arab cuisine and hearty Spanish staples prepared by a friendly Egyptian-Spanish couple. Extensive vegetarian *menú* €10. Open Tu-Su 9:30am-5pm and 8pm-midnight. ❷

Cafetería Albéniz, C. Muñoz Vázquez, 10 (☎956 70 14 99). Plenty of outdoor seating makes this cafe an extremely popular rest-stop. Coffee €0.90. Entrees €5.50-10. *Paella* €5.40-7.20. Vegetarian options. Open M-Sa noon-midnight. ❷

Restaurante El Convento, C. Marqués de Torresoto, 7 (☎956 70 41 28), across from Hostal San Marcos. Andalucian fare served in a 17th-century setting. Fish, meat, and game dishes. Appetizers €4-9, entrees €7-15. Open June-Sept. 1-4pm and 7:30-10:30pm, Oct.-May 1-4pm and 7-10pm. Closed the 1st or 2nd week of July. MC/V. ❸

SIGHTS AND ENTERTAINMENT

The most beautiful sights in Arcos are the winding white alleys, Roman ruins, and hanging flowers of the old quarter, combined with the view from **Plaza Cabildo.** The plaza earned the nickname *Balcón de Coño* because the view is so startling that people often exclaim *¡coño!* (expletive) in disbelief. In this square stands the **Iglesia de Santa María,** a mix of Baroque, Renaissance, and Gothic styles, built between the 15th and 18th centuries. Its most impressive attribute is the 14th-century mural painting. A symbol of the Inquisition—a circular design within which exorcisms were once performed—is still etched into the ground on the church's left side. (Open M-F 10am-1pm and 3:30-6:30pm, Sa 10am-2pm. €1.) The late-Gothic **Iglesia de San Pedro** was built on the site of an Arab fortress in the old quarter. A collection of religious paintings by Murillo, Zurbarán, and Ribera decorate the interior. (Open Sa

10am-1pm and 4-7pm, Su 10am-1:30pm. €1. Service 11:30am.) An artificial **lake** built in 1960 laps at Arcos's feet, its gentle waters inviting overheated travelers to take a dip; most choose to swim near Porto Alegre, a beach-like strip. Urban buses descend to this beach, **Mesón de la Molinera** (M-Sa 5 per day 9:15am-8:15pm, €0.80). The **Oficina de Deportes** (☎956 70 30 11) has information on water sports at the lake. **Festivals** in Arcos are highly spirited. A favorite is the **Toro de Aleluya,** held on the last Sunday of *Semana Santa.* Two bulls run rampant through the steep, cobbled streets as residents drink and dance flamenco.

CÁDIZ ☎956

Located on a peninsula, Cádiz (pop. 155,000) has a powerful ocean on one side and a placid bay on the other. Despite this, one can wander through the narrow streets of the old town, strolling from plaza to plaza between soaring cathedrals and outdoor cafes, without realizing the city is surrounded by water. Cádiz is both a thriving metropolis and a touristed beach town. Founded by the Phoenicians in 1100 BC, Cádiz is thought to be the oldest inhabited city in Europe. From the 16th to the 18th century, the Spanish colonial shipping industry transformed the port into one of the wealthiest in Europe. The city is renowned for its extravagant *Carnaval*, the only festival of its size and kind not suppressed by Franco's regime. Perhaps Spain's most dazzling party, *Carnaval* makes Cádiz an essential stop on February itineraries. During the rest of the year, Cádiz offers a little of everything to visitors—a thoroughly Spanish city trimmed by golden sand beaches.

TRANSPORTATION

Trains: RENFE, Pl. Sevilla (☎956 25 43 01), off Av. Puerto. A free shuttle bus runs between the 2 stations every 30min. To: **Córdoba** (3hr., 4 per day 8am-8:25pm, €25); **Jerez** (40min., 12 per day 5:55am-7:57pm, €3); **Madrid** (5hr.; 8am, 4:25pm; €61); **Sevilla** (2hr., 12 per day 5:55am-7:57pm, €8.10).

Buses: Transportes Generales Comes, Pl. Hispanidad, 1 (☎956 22 78 11). To: **Arcos de la Frontera** (1½hr., 4 per day 7am-6pm, €4.45); **Algeciras** (3hr., 10 per day 6:45am-8pm, €8.22); **Córdoba** (5hr.; 7am, 4pm; €17.28); **Granada** (6hr., 4 per day 9am-9pm, €24.43); **Jerez de la Frontera** (1hr., 7-12 per day 7am-4pm, €2.28); **La Línea** (3hr.; 1:30, 2:17pm; €9.72); **Málaga** (4hr., 6 per day 6:45am-8pm, €17.24); **Sevilla** (2hr., 11 per day 7am-10pm, €9); **Vejer de la Frontera** (1½hr., 7 per day 9am-10pm, €3.85). **Transportes Los Amarillos** (☎956 28 58 52) depart from beside the port in front of the park Paseo de Canalejas, off Pl. San Juan de Dios. Purchase tickets on the bus or at the office on nearby Av. Ramón de Carranza (open M-F 9:30am-1:30pm and 5-8:30pm, alternate Sa 10am-1pm). To: **Arcos de la Frontera** (1hr., 7 per day 12:30-7:15pm, €3.78); **Chipiona** (1½hr., 5-11 per day 7:15am-7:30pm, €3.13); **Sanlúcar** (1hr., 5-11 per day 7:15am-7:30pm, €2.55). **Secorbus** (☎902 22 92 92) has service to **Madrid** (8hr., 6 per day 8:10am-11:10pm, €18.48). Buses leave from next to Estadio Ramón de Carranza, just past Pl. Glorieta Ingeniero, in new Cádiz.

Ferry: El Vapor (☎956 87 02 70), departs from a dock next to the Comes station and runs to **Pto. de Sta. María** (45min., 4 per day 10am-6:30pm, €2).

Catamaran: (☎670 69 79 05). Leaves from Estación Marítima near Plaza de España for **Pto. de Sta. María** (25min., 5-8 per day 7:50am-9pm, €2.80).

Municipal Buses: (☎956 26 28 06). Pick up a map/schedule and *bonobus* (discount packet of 10 tickets for €6) at the kiosk across from the Comes bus station. Most lines run through Pl. España. Beach bums' favorite bus #1 (Cortadura) runs along the shore to new Cádiz (every 10min. 6:40am-1:10am, €0.80). Bus #7 runs the same route, leaving from **Playa de la Caleta.**

Taxis: ☎956 21 21 21.

ORIENTATION AND PRACTICAL INFORMATION

Cádiz's old town was built on the end of the peninsula, and the new town grew up behind it farther inland. The old town hosts most of the cheap hostels and historic sights (not to mention the bus and train stations), while the new town is home to high-rise hotels, numerous bars and restaurants, kilometers of lovely sand, and deep blue seas. To reach **Plaza San Juan de Dios** (the town center) from the **Comes bus station,** walk along Av. Puerto for about 5min., keeping the port on the left; the plaza lies to the right, just after a park. From the **Los Amarillos bus stop,** walk inland about 100m. From the **train station,** walk past the fountain, keeping the port on the right, for about two blocks; Pl. San Juan de Dios is the first plaza on the left. The tangled *casco viejo* is disorienting—a map is necessary. When you take the bus into new Cádiz (down the main avenue), hop off at the square with the McDonald's and the modern-looking Hotel Victoria. This square is **Glorieta Ingeniero.**

Tourist Office: Municipal, Pl. San Juan de Dios, 11 (☎/fax 956 24 10 01). Bright yellow "i" marks the spot. Useful free map. English spoken. Open M-F 9am-2pm and 5-8pm. On weekends, a kiosk opens in front of the main office (open Sa-Su and holidays 10am-1pm and 5-7:30pm). **Junta de Andalucía,** Av. Ramón de Carranza (☎956 25 86 46) Free map of Cádiz. Open M and Sa 9am-2pm, Tu-F 9am-7pm.

Currency Exchange: Santander Central Hispano, C. Columela, 13 (☎902 24 24 24). Open M-F 8:30am-2pm, Sa 8:30am-1pm.

Luggage Storage: Lockers at train station (€3), to the right on the way out to the platforms. Open daily 8am-11pm.

Emergency: ☎061. **Municipal police:** ☎091. In Campo del Sur in the new city.

Medical Assistance: Ambulatorio Vargas Ponce (☎062 or 956 28 38 55). **Hospital: Centro de Salud,** Av. Ana de Viya (☎956 24 21 00).

Internet Access: Enred@dos, C. Sacramento, 36 (☎956 80 81 81). Open M-Sa 11am-11pm. **Ciber La Sal,** C. Dr. Marañón, 14 (☎956 21 15 39). Enter on C. Felipe Abarzuza. Computers €2.40 per hr. Open M-Sa 9am-midnight. **Ahi.com,** C. Rosario, 15 (☎800 40 08 00). Open M-F 10am-3pm and 5-10:30pm, Sa 11am-2pm and 5-10:30pm, Su 11am-5pm. €1.80 per hr.

Post Office: (☎956 21 39 45), the red building in Pl. Flores, next to the market. Open M-F 8:30am-8:30pm, Sa 9:30am-2pm. **Postal Code:** 11070.

ACCOMMODATIONS

Most hostels huddle around the harbor, in Pl. San Juan de Dios, and just behind it on C. Marqués de Cádiz. Others are scattered throughout the old town. Singles and private bathrooms are scarce. Call months in advance to find a room during February's *Carnaval;* calling a few days ahead during the summer should be fine.

Quo Qádis, C. Diego Arias, 1 (☎/fax 956 22 19 39), 1 block from Pl. Falla. Clean rooms, roof terrace, TV room, laundry facilities, and a social atmosphere. Offers flamenco classes, planned excursions, and vegetarian dinners (€3.50). Breakfast included. Sheets €1.20. Lockout 11am-5pm for dorms. Dorms €6; singles €12.60; doubles €24; triples €36. 10% discount if you arrive by bike. ❶

Hostal Colón, C. Marqués de Cádiz, 6 (☎956 28 53 51), off Pl. San Juan de Dios. Spotless rooms with sinks, colorful tiles, and balconies. Has a terrace with a great view of the cathedral surrounded by hundreds of TV antennas. July-Sept. and *Semana Santa* 2 windowless singles €17; doubles €30; triples €42. Oct.-June €15/€24/€35. ❷

Hostal San Francisco, C. San Francisco, 12 (☎956 22 18 42), 2 blocks from Pl. España. Spacious rooms surround a Spanish patio with Japanese decor. Large communal baths. May-June singles €15.60; doubles €26, with bath and TV €34. July-Sept. €17/€28/€37.50. Oct.-Apr. €15/€25/€31.50. AmEx/MC/V. ❷

Camas Cuatro Naciones, C. Plocia, 3 (☎956 25 55 39), on a corner of Pl. San Juan de Dios. One of the cheapest places to stay in Cádiz. Rooms are small and pleasant, some with sunny terraces. June-Sept. singles €12; doubles €24. Oct.-May €10.20/€21. ❶

FOOD

Once you leave Pl. San Juan de Dios, finding eateries can be a trying experience. Opt for cafes and *heladerías* around Pl. Flores, near the post office and the municipal **market.** If you detest seafood, head to **Supermarket Champión,** next to the municipal market, off Pl. Flores (open M-Sa 9am-10pm).

Bar-Restaurante Pasaje Andaluz, Pl. San Juan de Dios, 9 (☎956 28 52 54). Sip *café con leche* (€1.05) and sit on the plaza where the Constitución de Cádiz was proclaimed in 1812. Great *menú* featuring *paella,* gazpacho, salad, chicken, pork, or fish, and dessert €7.85. Open daily 12:30-4:30pm and 8-11:30pm. ❷

Meson La Nueva Marina, C. Plocia, 3 (☎956 28 93 81). Outdoor seating, on the corner of Pl. San Juan de Dios. Fabulous food and desserts. Entrees €6-24 (most €8-11). Open daily noon-5pm and 8pm-1am (sometimes later). AmEx/MC/V. ❸

Arte Serrano Tapeo y Restaurante, Po. Marítimo, 2 (☎956 27 72 58). 1 block below Pl. Glorieta in the new town. Ocean views and excellent meats, seafood, salads, and cheeses. Entrees €7-15. Open daily 12:30-5pm and 8pm-1am. AmEx/MC/V. ❸

Mesón Churrasco, C. San Francisco, 3 (☎956 22 03 73), 1 block from Pl. San Francisco. Traditional *bodega* packed with locals and legs of ham. Opt for the hearty *menú* (offered M-Sa, €6). Open daily 9am-4:30pm and 7:30pm-midnight. ❷

SIGHTS

CATHEDRAL. This gold-domed 18th-century masterpiece is considered the last great cathedral built by colonial riches. Its treasury bulges with valuables—the *Custodia del Millón* is said to be set with a million precious stones. *(From Pl. San Juan de Dios, follow C. Pelota. ☎956 28 61 54. Museum open Tu-F 10am-12:45pm and 4:30-6:45pm, Sa 10am-12:45pm. €3, children €2. Cathedral open W, F 7-8pm, Su 11am-1pm. Free.)*

PASEO. Cádiz's seaside *paseo* runs around the old city and along the Atlantic; walking the path is a good way to get a feel for the layout of the city. Stupendous views of ships leaving the harbor recall Spain's golden age; at the end of the *paseo,* infinite rows of antennae rising from the rooftops recall the 1950s. Exotic trees, fanciful hedges, and a few chattering monkeys enliven the adjacent **Parque Genovés.** *(Paseo accessible via Pl. Argüelles or C. Fermín Salvochea, off Pl. España.)*

MUSEO DE CÁDIZ. Thanks to the fusion of a Fine Arts and Provincial Archaeological Museum, Murillo, Rubens, and Zurbarán live here in unholy union with Phoenician sarcophagi, ancient jewelry, blown glass, and pottery. *(Pl. Mina. ☎956 21 22 81. Open for guided tours Tu 9am-2:30pm; for public Tu 9:30am-8pm, W-Sa 9am-8pm, Su 9:30am-2:30pm. €1.50, EU citizens free.)*

ENTERTAINMENT AND NIGHTLIFE

Carnaval insanity is legendary. The gray of winter gives way to dazzling color as the city hosts one of the most raucous *carnavales* in the world (Feb. 27-Mar. 9 in 2003). Costumed dancers, street singers, ebullient residents, and spectators from the world over take to the streets in a week-long frenzy that makes New Orleans's Mardi Gras look like Thursday night bingo at the old folks' home.

Cádiz's nightlife migrates depending on the season; in winter the scene is situated primarily in the old city, while summer takes the party closer to the beach in the new city. For the cafe scene, try the area around **Pl. Mina** (especially lively on winter weekends). **C. de Manuel Rances,** nearby off C. Antonio López, lines up some of the hippest bars in the old city. **Pub La Luna,** C. Dr. Zurita, on the corner of C. General Luque, hosts a mixed gay and lesbian scene with Friday night drag queen performances at midnight. (Open year round Tu-Su 11pm-4am.) **Cafe Poniente,** Beato Diego de Cádiz, 18, has a similar crowd with drag queen performances Thursdays at midnight. (Open year-round daily 10:30pm-4am.) In the new city, C. General Muñoz Arenillas off Pl. Glorieta Ingeniero and the **Paseo Marítimo,** the main drag along Playa Victoria, have some of Cádiz's best bars. **Marimba,** on Po. Marítimo, has tables on the beach (open daily at midnight), while **Barabass,** on C. General Muñoz Arenillas, features sparkling lights, a dance floor, and pop music. (Open daily 4pm-6am.) Clubrats will prefer **Punto de San Felipe,** a strip of 10 bars and clubs reached by walking north along the sea from Pl. España, just beyond the Comes station (take a right before the tunnel); these spots don't get going until 4 or 5am. Look for signs on the boardwalk advertising theme parties.

BEACHES

As Cádiz was built on a peninsula, the exhaust-spewing ships on one coast don't pollute the pristine beaches on the other. **Playa de la Caleta** is most convenient beach to the old city. Better sand and more space can be found in the new city, serviced by bus #1, leaving from Pl. España (€0.80). The first beach beyond the rocks is the unremarkable **Playa de Santa María del Mar.** Next to it, **Playa de la Victoria** has earned the EU's *bandera azul* for cleanliness. Get off bus #1 at Pl. Glorieta Ingeniero in front of McDonald's. A more natural landscape, with fewer hotels, belongs to **Playa de Cortadura,** where the coveted *bandera azul* also flaps proudly. Take bus #1 until it almost reaches the highway, where the bus turns around. The boardwalk ends here, and sunbather density falls steadily the farther one walks.

VEJER DE LA FRONTERA ☎956

Glistening white above a sea of golden wheat, beautiful Vejer (pop. 13,000) is one of Andalucía's most enchanting *pueblos blancos.* Fourteenth-century homes line cobblestoned alleys, and gray-haired men discuss politics on street corners. The hike up to town is nothing short of painful, but pure relaxation and beautiful views await. A mere village, Vejer is a great place to unwind for a few days. For the more restless, it is best explored as a daytrip from Cádiz or a stop en route to Tarifa.

TRANSPORTATION. Getting to Vejer can be difficult. While some buses stop at the end of **Avenida de Los Remedios,** which leads uphill into La Plazuela (10min.), many just leave you by the highway at **La Barca de Vejer,** a small town at the base of the hill. Take one of the numerous taxis waiting by the bus stop (€5). The alternative, an arduous 20min. uphill climb, is extremely difficult with a backpack. If you do make the trek, climb the cobbled track to the left of the restaurant. When you reach the top, keep walking straight; all roads lead to quiet **Plaza de España,** not to be confused with La Plazuela, which is a tiny intersection (where Av. Los Remedios and C. Juan Bueno meet).

For **bus** info, visit either the tourist office or the mall shop on C. La Plazuela toward Av. Los Remedios, where tickets are sold (☎956 44 71 46). Short-distance buses run from Av. Los Remedios to **Cádiz** (1½hr., 9 per day 7:15am-8:30pm, €3.85). For other destinations, descend the hill (1km) to **La Barca de Vejer.** (Buses leave for La Barca de Vejer every 15min. 10:15am-8:15pm, €0.90.) Service to: **Málaga** (4hr.; 7:45am, 5pm; €13.31); **Algeciras** (2hr., 10 per day 7:50am-10:45pm, €4.57); **Sevilla** (3½hr., 8:30am, €10.43); **Tarifa** (1hr., 10 per day 7:50am-10:45pm, €3.07). For a **taxi,** call ☎956 45 04 08.

PRACTICAL INFORMATION. The staff at the **tourist office,** C. Marqués de Tamarón, 10, speaks English. (☎956 45 17 36; fax 956 45 16 20. Open June-Aug. M-F 8am-2pm, in Aug. Sa 10:30am-2pm; Sept.-May M-F 8am-3pm and 5-9:30pm.) Services include: **Santander Central Hispano,** C. Juan Bueno, 5 (☎ 902 24 24 24; open M-F 8:30am-2pm, Sa 8:30am-1pm); **Centro de Salud,** Av. Andalucía (☎956 44 76 25); **police** (☎956 45 04 00); and the **post office** at C. Juan Bueno, 22. (☎956 45 02 38. Open M-F 8:30am-2:30pm, Sa 9:30am-1pm.) **Postal code**: 11150.

ACCOMMODATIONS AND FOOD. The most affordable places to stay in Vejer are *casas particulares* (private houses). Two such *casas* are on C. San Filmo, up a stone staircase from Av. Los Remedios. The friendly Sra. Rosa Romero owns **Casa Los Cántaros ❶,** C. San Filmo, 14, a beautifully restored Andalucian home with a grape-vined patio. The spotless suites have sitting rooms, antique furniture, private bathrooms, and kitchen access. (☎956 44 75 92. Doubles June-Sept. €24. Oct.-May €18.) Next door, Sra. Luisa Doncel keeps tidy little rooms with common bathrooms in **C. San Filmo, 12 ❶.** If Doña Luisa is not at #12, try #16. (☎956 45 02 46. June-Sept. singles €12; doubles €21. Oct.-May €9/18.) A more luxurious option is the charming **Hotel La Casa Del Califa ❹,** Pl. de España, 16. All rooms have brick floors, A/C, TV, phone, and beautiful views. Breakfast included. (☎956 44 77 30; fax 956 45 16 25; www.vejer.com/califa. June-Sept. singles €44.47-51.09; doubles €55.29-59.50. Oct.-May €39.07-44.47/€44.47. AmEx/MC/V.) The cheapest eats are *tapas* or *raciones* at the bars around the Plazuela. Renowned for its *jamón ibérico*, family-run **Mesón Pepe Julián ❷,** C. Juan Relinque, 7, prepares the best *tapas* in town (€1-1.50) and serves reasonably priced entrees (€4.20-12) in a warmly lit dining room. (Open daily 11:30am-4pm and 7:30pm-midnight; Oct.-June closed W. MC/V.) At peaceful **Bar El Cura ❶,** Po. Cobijadas, 1, near the bottom of C. Juan Bueno, locals place bets on who can make the solemn owner laugh (or at least crack a smile). Enjoy the view while sipping *fino* (dry sherry) for a mere €0.50. (☎956 45 07 76. Open daily 7am-3pm and 5:30pm-late.)

SIGHTS. The best way to enjoy Vejer is by wandering along the labyrinthine streets and cliffside *paseos*, stopping occasionally for drinks or *tapas*. As for monuments, the **Castillo Moro,** down C. Ramón y Cajal from the church, offers the usual assortment of battlements and crenelated walls. (Open July-Aug. roughly M-Sa 11am-2pm and 6-9pm; Sept.-June M-Sa 10am-2pm. The gates open only when a Boy Scout troop is available to lead tours.) **Iglesia del Divino Salvador,** behind the tourist office, is a choice blend of Romanesque, Mudéjar, and Gothic styles (Mass daily 8:30pm). Ten kilometers from Vejer on the road to Los Caños lies **El Palmar,** 7km of fine white sand and clear waters easily accessible by car or bus (4 per day 11:45am-8:45pm, €0.80). Many beach-goers hitch rides at the bend of Av. Los Remedios or catch the Cádiz-bound bus to **Conil de la Frontera** and walk southeast along the beach for 3-4km. For information on the town and outdoor activities, consult **Discover Andalucía,** Av. Los Remedios, 45b, across from the bus stop. (☎956 44 75 75. Bikes from €12.50 per day. Surfboards from €6 per day. Open M-F 10:30am-2pm and 6-9pm, Sa 10:30am-2pm. AmEx/MC/V.)

NIGHTLIFE AND FESTIVALS. Vejer's old quarter hops at night. Leave another little piece of your heart at **Bar Janis Joplin,** on C. Marqués de Tamarón, 6. Sit on plush wicker chairs and keep an eye out for Bobby McGee. (Open nightly 9:30pm-late.) Several popular pubs lie downhill from the Plazuela on C. Sagasta and C. Santísimo. From July to August, everyone dances among the thatched huts at *discoteca* **La Carpa** in Parque de Los Remedios, behind the bus stop. Stupendous terrace views make **Café-Bar El Arriate,** C. Corredera, 55 (☎956 44 71 70 or 956 45 13 05), a good place for a *copa* anytime. Vejer throws brilliant *fiestas*. Soon after the **Corpus Christi** revelry in June comes the **Candelas de San Juan** (June 23), climaxing with the midnight release of the *toro de fuego* (bull of fire) at midnight. A local (obviously, one with a death wish) dressed in an iron bull costume charges the crowd as the firecrackers attached to his body fly off in all directions. The town demonstrates its creativity again during the delirious **Semana Santa** celebrations, when a *toro embolao* (sheathed bull) with wooden balls affixed to the tips of his horns is set loose through the narrow streets of Vejer on the Sunday of the Resurrection. The good-natured **Feria de Primavera** (2 weeks after *Semana Santa*) is a bit tamer, with people dancing *sevillanas* and downing cups of *fino* until sunrise.

TARIFA ☎956

When the wind picks up in Tarifa (pop. 15,000), the southernmost city in continental Europe, visitors can easily understand why it is known, even to locals, as the Hawaii of Spain. Shelter-seeking residents and tourists leave miles of white sandy beaches desolate but for the few, the proud—the windsurfers. You'll see more frame backpacks, stickered vans, Quicksilver attire, and Reefs than you could ever imagine. Still, there is more to Tarifa than just windsurfing—sandy beaches and an enchanting old city make for pleasant afternoon and evening walks.

TRANSPORTATION. Transportes Generales Comes buses roll in from C. Batalla del Salado, 19. (☎956 67 57 55. Open M-F 2:30-7pm, Sa-Su 3-8pm. When the office is closed, the bus schedule is posted on the window; buy your tickets from the driver.) **Buses** run to: **Algeciras** (30min., 7-12 per day 6:30am-8:15pm, €1.44); **Cádiz** (2¼hr., 7 per day 7:25am-8:55pm, €6.60); **Sevilla** (3hr., 4 per day 7:55am-5:10pm, €13.50). **Ferries** leave from the **FRS** at the port (☎956 68 18 30; www.frs.com) for **Tangier** (35min.; M-Th and Sa 9:30, 11:30am, 6:30pm; F 10am, noon, 7pm; Su 10am, 6pm; €22.50, children €11, small car €69.50, motorcycle €21.50). Prices and travel length for the return trip are the same, though the schedule is not. (M-Th, Sa 8:30am, 1:30, 5:30pm; F 9am, 1:30, 6pm; Su 1, 5pm. Times local to Morocco.)

ORIENTATION AND PRACTICAL INFORMATION. The small **bus station** is on C. Batalla del Salado. With your back to the station turn right and walk a short distance to the intersection with C. Andalucía. To reach the center of the old town, cross C. Andalucía and pass under the arch. To the left is C. Nuestra Señora de la Luz; follow this street to its end and you will be on C. Sancho IV el Bravo, the location of many cafes and restaurants. To reach the **tourist office,** turn right on C. Andalucía. The pedestrian thoroughfare Paseo de la Alameda will be about one block ahead on the left; the tourist office is in the center. The tourist office has good adventure sports information. (☎956 68 09 93 or 956 68 04 31. Open July 15-Aug. daily 10:30am-2pm and 6-8pm; Sept.-July 14 M-F 10am-2pm and 5-7pm.) Services include: **emergency** ☎091; **police,** Pl. Santa María (☎956 68 41 86); **Centro de Salud** ☎956 68 15 15. **Internet** access is available at **Planet,** C. Santísima Trinidad, 20 (€3 per hr.; open M-F 10:30am-2:30pm and 5:30-10pm, Sa 10:30am-2:30pm and 7-10pm), or **Ciber-Papelería Pandor@'s,** C. Sancho IV Bravo, 5 (€3 per hr.; open Sept.-May daily 10am-2pm and 5pm-midnight, June-Aug. 10am-1am). The **post office,** C. Coronel Moscardó, 9, is near Pl. San Maleo. (☎956 68 42 37. Open M-F 8:30am-2:30pm, Sa 9:30am-1pm.) **Postal code:** 11380.

ACCOMMODATIONS AND FOOD. Affordable rooms line main C. Batalla del Salado. Prices rise significantly in summer; those visiting in August should call ahead and arrive early. Comfortable **Hostal Villanueva ❷,** Av. Andalucía, 11, features a rooftop terrace with an ocean view. (☎956 68 41 49. All rooms with bath.

Singles €18; doubles €35-40.) The dining room downstairs serves its specialty *paella* for €7. (Open Tu-Su 1-4pm and 8-11pm.) Uphill, where Av. Andalucía becomes C. Amador de los Ríos, **Hostal El Asturian ❹** keeps clean, tiled rooms with full baths, some with ocean views. (☎956 68 06 19. July-Sept. and *Semana Santa* doubles €52-55; triples €82-115. Dec. 24-Jan. 6 and Mar. 1-22 €37-40/€61-85. Rest of the year €30-33/€48-66. MC/V.) Official **campgrounds** lie a few kilometers west on the beach (€4.20-5 per person); ask the bus driver to let you off.

Serving *bocadillos* (€3-4), entrees (€9-10), and specialty drinks to locals and backpackers, **Café-Bar Central ❷,** C. Sancho IV El Bravo, has one of the few wind-free *terrazas* in town. (☎956 68 05 90. Open daily 8am-3am.) Across the street, **Bagoeteria La Badeguita ❶,** C. Sancho IV Bravo, 5, serves sandwiches (€1.80-2.40) and tasty *tapas* (€0.75). For an excellent meal head to **Mandrágora ❷,** C. Independencia, 3. From C. Sancho IV el Bravo continue to the end, which becomes C. General Copons. C. Independencia is a tiny alley on the right. This small restaurant serves exquisite meat, seafood, and vegetarian options to the accompaniment of soft latin jazz. (Salads and appetizers €2-6. *Raciones* €8-12. Open daily 8pm-1am.)

SIGHTS AND ENTERTAINMENT. Next to the port and just outside the old town, stand the ruins of the **Castillo de Guzmán el Bueno.** In the 13th century, the Moors kidnapped Guzmán's son and threatened his life if Guzmán didn't relinquish the castle. Surprisingly, the father didn't surrender, even after his son's throat was slashed before his eyes. (Open daily 10am-2pm and 6-8pm. Oct.-Apr. 11am-2pm and 4-6pm. €1.80; free Su afternoon.) Those with something less historic in mind can head 200m south to **Playa Lances** for 5km of the finest white sand on the Atlantic coast. Bathers should be aware of the occasional high winds and a strong undertow. Adjacent to Playa Lances is **Playa Chica,** which is smaller but more sheltered from the winds. **Tarifa Spin Out Surfbase,** 9km up the road toward Cádiz (ask the bus driver on the Cádiz route to stop, or take a taxi for about €6), rents windsurfing boards and instructs all levels. (☎956 23 63 52. Rental €22.50 per hr., €47.50 for 4+hr.; instruction €49 for 2hr.) Many campgrounds and hotels along CN-340 between km70 and km80 provide instruction and gear for outdoor sports.

At night, sunburnt travelers mellow out in the old town's many bars, which range from jazz to psychedelic to Irish. Follow the crowds as they barhop along C. Nuestra Señora de la Luz and C. San Francisco. The *terrazas* on C. Sancho IV el Bravo fill at night with locals and windsurfers chatting over beer or coffee. **Moskio,** C. San Francisco, 11, has a dance floor and lots of young people milling about. **La Tribu,** on the corner of C. Nuestra Señora de la Luz and C. Sancho IV el Bravo, has neon lighting, small circular tables, techno, and TV. **Tanakas,** Pl. San Hiscio, is a large disco which gears up late night/early morning. In July and August, they move their party to the beach (buy tickets at Tanakas for €1.50).

ALGECIRAS ☎956

Franco dreamt of transforming Algeciras into a burgeoning southern metropolis that would eclipse Gibraltar as the commercial center of the southwestern Mediterranean and force the Royal Army out of Iberia. Innumerable concrete wharfs and slapdash highrises remain, but so do the British. Hidden beyond Algeciras's seedy port is a more serene, old neighborhood, worthy of visiting for those with a few hours to spare. For most travelers, however, this is a city to be seen in transit.

TRANSPORTATION

Trains: RENFE, Ctra. Cádiz (☎902 24 02 02), down C. Juan de la Cierva. To: **Granada** (4hr., 3 per day 7:40am-3:55pm, €15.11); **Ronda** (1½hr., 4 per day 7am-7:25pm, €6). Also to **Bobadilla** (€10), with connections to: **Córdoba** (5hr., 6 per day 7:40am-9:35pm, €15.82-21.22); **Madrid** (6hr., 5 per day 7:40am-9:35pm, €32.16-57); **Málaga** (3½hr.; noon, 3:55pm; €13.20); **Sevilla** (6hr., 4 per day 7:40am-3:55pm, €19).

Buses: Buses depart from the separate addresses as indicated.

Empresa Portillo, Av. Virgen del Carmen, 15 (☎956 65 43 04). To: **Córdoba** (6hr., 3-4 per day 8am-3:15pm, €18); **Granada** (5hr., 4 per day 10:30am-5pm, €16); **Málaga** (3hr., 8-9 per day 9:30am-10pm, €8.70); **Marbella** (1hr., 8-9 per day 9:30am-10pm, €4.85).

Transportes Generales Comes, C. San Bernardo, 1 (☎956 65 34 56), by Hotel Octavio. To: **Cádiz** (2½hr., 6 per day 7am-10:30pm, €8.25); **La Línea,** for **Gibraltar** (45min., every 30min. 7am-9:30pm, €1.50); **Madrid** (8hr., 4 per day 8:10am-9:45pm, €22.08); **Sevilla** (4hr., 4 per day 7:30am-4:45pm, €13.75); **Tarifa** (40min., 7-10 per day 7:05am-9pm, €1.44).

Empresa Bacoma, Av. Marina, 8 (☎956 66 50 67), left of Banco Zaragozano. To **Barcelona** (19hr., 5 per day 10am-10pm, €70.80).

Ferries: From the bus and train stations, follow C. San Bernardo to C. Juan de la Cierva, and turn left at its end; the port entrance will be on your right. Tickets are overpriced at the train station; book at a travel agency in town or at the port. Only Trasmediterránea (☎902 45 46 45), at the entrance of the port, offers Eurail discounts. *Embarcaciones rápidas (*fast ferries), depart for Ceuta, a Spanish enclave in North Africa; normal ferries leave for the Moroccan port of Tangier (see p. 728). Allow 30min. to clear customs and board, 90min. with a car. Summer ferries to **Ceuta** (35min.; depart every hr. 7am-10pm, return 6am-9pm Morrocan time; €21, under 12 €10.50; small car €70.70; motorcycle €19.60) and **Tangier** (2½hr.; depart every hr. 7am-10pm, return 6am-9pm Morrocan time; €22, with Eurail pass €18.64, under 12 €11.75; small car €71.90; motorcycle €22.20. Limited service in winter. MC/V.

ORIENTATION AND PRACTICAL INFORMATION

Lined with travel agencies, banks, and hotels, **Av. de la Marina** runs along the coast, eventually turning into Av. Virgen del Carmen north of the port. **C. Juan de la Cierva** runs perpendicular to the coast from the port, becoming **C. San Bernardo** as it nears the **train** and **bus stations.** The train station is directly across the street from the Comes Bus Station; the Portillo bus station is near the port. To reach the **tourist office** from the train station, follow C. San Bernardo along the abandoned tracks toward the port, past a parking lot on the left. From the **port,** take a left onto Av. Virgen del Carmen, then a quick right onto C. Juan de la Cierva; the office is on the left. All services necessary for transit to Morocco cluster about the port, accessible by a single gate and driveway. Be wary of imposters peddling ferry tickets.

Tourist Office: C. Juan de la Cierva (☎956 57 26 36; fax 956 57 04 75), in the tube-shaped, pink glass building. Provides maps (free for Algeciras, €0.60 for maps of other cities). Some English spoken. Open M-F 9am-2pm.

Currency Exchange: Santander Central Hispano, Av. Virgen del Carmen, 9-11. Open M-F 8:30am-2pm, Sa 8:30am-1pm. For a daytrip to Tangier, buying **dirham** may not be necessary; many places accept euros and you will not be able to convert your dirham back once you return. For longer trips, change money in Morocco.

Luggage Storage: At **Empresa Portillo bus terminal,** lockers €3 per day. Open daily 7:40am-9:50pm. At **RENFE,** €3 per day. Open daily 5:30am-10:30pm. At the **port,** lockers €3. Open daily 7am-9:30pm.

Camping Gear: Adventura Sport, Ventura Morón, 5 (☎956 66 92 34), off Pl. Alta. Open M-F 10am-1:30pm and 5-9pm, Sa 10am-2pm. MC/V.

Emergency: ☎061. **Police: Local,** C. Ruiz Zorilla, (☎956 66 01 55).

Medical Assistance: Ambulatorio Central, Pl. Menéndez Tolosa (☎956 66 19 56).

Internet Access: Locutorio Carnes y Telefono, C. Jose Santacana. Open daily 9am-3pm and 5:30pm-midnight. Computers will not take disks; Internet only. €3 per hr.

Post Office: Ruiz Zorilla, 42 (☎956 66 36 48). **Lista de Correos.** Open M-F 8:30am-2:30pm, Sa 9:30am-1pm. **Postal Code:** 11203.

ACCOMMODATIONS

Hostels line **C. José Santacana,** parallel to the seafront along Av. Marina and about a 10min. walk from the bus and train stations. From either station, follow C. San Bernardo, turning left before the bush-lined median; take a right onto Av. Segismundo Moret and then take the 3rd left, C. José Santacana. Ask for back rooms—local teenagers cruise the narrow streets on Vespas at ungodly hours.

Hostal Residencia Versailles, C. Moutero Rios, 12 (☎/fax 956 65 42 11), off C. Cayetano del Toro. If the Sun King had stayed here, he would have been close to the bus station. Clean, well-sized rooms, all with phones, TV, and bathrooms. Singles with shower €15; doubles with shower €27, with bath €30. ❷

Hostal Rif, C. Rafael de Muro, 11 (☎956 65 49 53). Follow C. José Santacana into the small market square, bear left around the large kiosk and continue up C. Rafael del Muro for 1 block. Upstairs in a restored 18th-century home with a palm-shaded patio. Backpackers share stories on the rooftop. Communal showers. Info available on forays into Morocco. Laundry €4.25. Singles €8; doubles €17; triples €24. ❶

Hotel Reina Christina, Po. de la Conferencia (☎956 60 26 22). Spend your days in Morocco and your nights in luxury at this 4-star hotel. The gardens have great views of the strait. All rooms have bath, safe, A/C, TV, and phone. The hotel also boasts a pool and a restaurant. Singles €55.86, doubles €78.25. AmEx/MC/V. ❺

FOOD

Outdoor cafes line C. Regino Martínez, Algeciras's main drag. Celebrate your return from Morocco with *pollo asado* (baked chicken) on Av. Virgen del Carmen, near the port, or C. Juan de la Cierva. The **supermarket** is on the corner of C. José Santacana and C. Maroto. (Open daily 9am-2pm and 5-8pm.) The outdoor **market** at Pl. Palma is one block from Av. Virgen del Carmen. (Open M-Sa 8:30am-2pm.)

Montes Restaurante, C. Juan Morrison, 22 (☎956 65 42 07). With white linens on the tables and liquor bottles on the wall, this air-conditioned restaurant offers fish, meat, and egg dishes. *Menú* €7.21. Open daily noon-5pm and 7pm-midnight. MC/V. ❷

La Alegría, C. José Santacana, 6. Huge portions of Moroccan favorites. No written menu; choose from chicken, lamb, and vegetarian entrees €5.40. Open daily 7am-1am. ❶

GIBRALTAR

Emerging from the morning mist, the Rock of Gibraltar's craggy face menaces those who pass by its shores. Ancient seafarers referred to the rock as one of the Pillars of Hercules, believing that it marked the end of the world. Today, it is known affectionately to locals as "Gib," and is home to more fish 'n' chips plates and pints of bitter per capita than anywhere else in the Mediterranean. Though Gibraltar is officially a self-governing British colony, Spain continues to campaign for sovereignty. When a 1969 vote showed that Gibraltar's populace favored its colonial ties to Britain (a near-tie: 12,138 to 44), Franco sealed off the border. After 16 years of isolation and a decade of negotiations, the border re-opened on February 4, 1985. Tourists and residents now cross with ease, but Gibraltar has a culture all its own, one that remains detached from Spain. While the peculiar mix of wild roaming primates (the only to be found in Europe) and curious enclave of not-quite-British-definitely-not-Spanish culture definitely make Gibraltar worth visiting, it is in many ways a tourist trap. Cross the border, spend a day exploring the Rock and stocking up on duty-fee liquor and tobacco, then scurry back to Spain.

TRANSPORTATION

Flights: Airport (☎730 26). **British Airways** (☎793 00) flies to **London** (2½hr., £138.50/€207) for those scared to set foot back in Spain.

Buses: From **La Línea,** on the Spanish border, to: **Algeciras** (40min., every 30min. 8:45am-10:15pm, €1.50); **Cádiz** (3hr., 4 per day 6:30am-8pm, €9.72); **Granada** (5-6hr.; 1, 2:15pm; €16.82); **Madrid** (7hr.; 12:10, 10:15pm; €2.47); **Málaga** (3¼hr., 4 per day 7:30am-4:45pm, €8.74); **Marbella** (1¾hr., 4 per day 7:15am-5:15pm, €5.01); **Sevilla** (6hr.; 7am, 3, 4:15pm; €17.25).

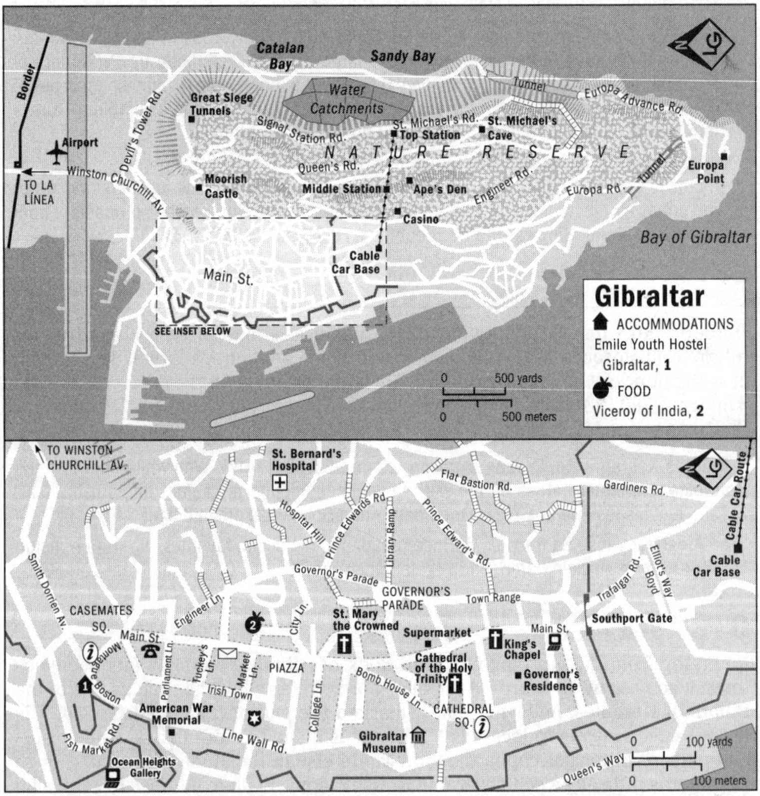

POUNDS OR EUROS. Although **euros** are accepted most everywhere (except in pay phones and public establishments), the **pound sterling (£)** is the preferred method of payment in Gibraltar. Merchants sometimes charge a higher price in euros than in the pound's exchange equivalent. Change is often given in English currency rather than euros. As of press date, **1£ = €1.58.**

Ferries: Turner & Co., 65/67 Irish Town (☎783 05; fax 720 06). To: **Tangier** (1¼hr.; F 6pm, return Sa 5:30pm Moroccan time; £18/€32, under 12 £9/€16.20).

Public Transport: Most bus lines run from one end of the Rock to the other. Buses #9 and 10 go between the border and the Rock for 45 pence or €0.70.

Taxis: ☎700 27.

ORIENTATION AND PRACTICAL INFORMATION

Buses from Spain terminate in the nearby town of **La Línea.** From the bus station, walk directly toward the Rock; the border is 5min. away. Once through Spanish customs and Gibraltar's passport control, catch bus #9 or 10 or walk across the airport tarmac (look both ways and hold hands) into town (20min.). Cars take longer to enter and exit Gibraltar; the queue often takes an hour or more. If walking, stay left on Av. Winston Churchill when the road forks with Corral Lane. Gibraltar's **Main Street,** a pedestrian-only commercial strip lined with most services, begins at the far end of a square, past the Burger King on the left.

Tourist Office: Duke of Kent House, Cathedral Sq. (☎450 00; tourism@gibraltar.gi), across from Gibraltar Museum. Open M-F 9am-5:30pm. **2nd office,** Watergate House, Casemates Sq. (☎749 82). Open M-F 9am-5:30pm, Sa-Su 10am-3pm.

Luggage Storage: Lockers at the bus station in La Línea (€3). Open daily 7am-10pm.

Bookstore: Gibraltar Bookshop, 300 Main St. (☎718 94). The best English bookstore on the Iberian Peninsula. Open M-F 10am-6:30pm, Sa 11:30am-2:30pm. AmEx/MC/V.

Emergency: ☎199. **Police:** 120 Irish Town St. (☎725 00).

Hospital: St. Bernard's Hospital on Hospital Hill (☎797 00).

Telephone Code: From Britain (00) 350. From the US (011) 350. From Spain 9567.

Internet Access: Café Cyberworld, Ocean Heights Gallery, Queensway Rd. (☎514 16; cyberworld@gibnynex.gi) £4.50/€8.50 per hr. Open daily noon-midnight. A cheaper option (with a slower connection) can be found at the **John McIntosh Hall Library,** 308 Main St., 2nd fl. 75 pence per 30min. Euros not accepted. Open M-F 9:30am-7:30pm.

Post Office: 104 Main St. (☎756 62). Possibly the world's easiest **Poste Restante** address: DYDEK, Cody. Poste Restante, Gibraltar (Main Post Office). Open June to mid-Sept. M-F 9am-2:15pm, Sa 10am-1pm. Mid-Sept. to May M-F 9am-4:30pm, Sa 10am-1pm. Euros not accepted.

ACCOMMODATIONS AND FOOD

Gibraltar is best done as a daytrip. The few accommodations in the area are often full, especially in the summer, and camping is illegal. At worst, you can crash across the border in **La Línea.** Back on the Rock, **Emile Youth Hostel Gibraltar ❷,** Montague Bastian, off Line Wall Rd., has bunkbeds in cheerfully-painted rooms with clean communal bathrooms. (☎511 06. Breakfast included. Lock-out 10:30am-4:30pm. Dorms £12/€19; singles £15/€24; doubles £27/€44.) Located near the base of the cable cars, **Queen's Hotel ❷,** 1 Boyd St., has rooms with terraces and TV. (☎740 00. English breakfast included. Singles £24, with bath £39.60; doubles

IN RECENT NEWS

WHEN IN *ROMA*...

Ever since *Gitanos* (gypsies, or *Roma*) arrived in Spain from India in the 15th century, they have faced discrimination, forced assimilation, and expulsion. Ironically, Spain owes this marginalized people such national art forms as flamenco.

The *Gitano* situation has improved only slightly since the 1978 constitution, which granted *Gitanos* equal rights. The situation is sensitive; the government hopes to integrate *Gitanos* into modern Spanish life without compromising cultural traditions.

About 600,000 *Gitanos* reside in Spain, nearly half of them in Andalucia. Most live in rural areas below the poverty line at a rate five times poorer than the rest of the population. School absenteeism is common, and the literacy rate is among the lowest in Spain. Unfortunately, slow transfer of funds for national reform programs and a lack of cooperation between officials have largely stymied government efforts to improve the situation.

In 1999, a new parliamentary commission was created to address the issue, and results have been promising. *Gitanos* are pursuing vocational educations, and programs fostering better relations between *Gitanos* and the Spanish have had success.

The recent influx of immigrants from North Africa has dually impacted the *Gitano*. Immigrants have tended to adopt Spanish ways and rise up the socioeconomic ladder more quickly than the *Roma,* who live in virtually self-imposed isolation. Still, the issue of discrimination against immigrants has once again shed light on the problems facing the Gitano.

£36, with bath £46-55, with bath and seaview £66. 20% student discount with cash payment, 15% with credit card. MC/V.) International restaurants are easy to find, but you may choke on the prices. A good choice is **The Viceroy of India ❸,** serving fabulous Indian food. (Entrees £3.75-4.75 for vegetarian dishes; meat and seafood £6.95-9.75. Open M-F noon-3pm and 7-11pm, Sa 7-11pm. MC/V.) As a back-up, there's the **Checkout** supermarket on Main St. next to Marks & Spencer. (Open M-F 8:30am-8pm, Sa 10am-6pm, Su 1am-3pm. Accepts both pounds and euros. MC/V.)

SIGHTS

THE ROCK OF GIBRALTAR

Top of the Rock Nature Reserve is accessible by car or cable car. Cable cars depart daily every 10min. 9:30am-5:15pm. It's possible to buy a ticket for only the cable car (£6/€9, children £4/€6), but if you plan on visiting any of sights highlighted below, it's better to buy a combined admittance ticket, including one-way cable car ride for £7/€10.64, children £5/€8.15. The walk down takes 2hr. Tickets sold until 5:15pm.

About halfway up the Rock is the infamous **Apes' Den,** where a colony of **Barbary apes** cavorts on the sides of rocks, the tops of taxis, and tourists' heads. These disturbingly tail-less apes have inhabited Gibraltar since the 18th century. When the ape population nearly went extinct in 1944, Churchill ordered reinforcements from North Africa; now they are proliferating at such at rate that population control has become an issue. At the northern tip of the Rock, facing Spain, are the **Great Siege Tunnels.** Originally used to fend off a combined Franco-Spanish siege at the end of the American Revolution, the tunnels were later expanded during WWII to span 33mi. underground. The eerie chambers of **St. Michael's Cave,** located ½km opposite the siege tunnels, were cut into the rock by thousands of years of water erosion. At the southern tip of Gibraltar, guarded by three machine guns and a lighthouse, **Europa Point** commands a view of the straits. Nearby the **Ibrahim-Al-Mosque,** Europe's largest, and the **Shrine of Our Lady of Europe** face each other in pluralistic harmony. (Take bus #3 or 1B from Line Wall Rd., just off Main St., all the way to the end. Departs every 15min., 45 pence/ €0.70.)

COSTA DEL SOL

The coast has sold its soul to the Devil, and now he's starting to collect. Artifice covers the once-natural charms as chic promenades and swanky hotels burgeon between small towns and the shoreline. The Costa del Sol officially extends from Tarifa in the southwest to Cabo de Gata, east of Almería; post-industrial Málaga lies smack in the middle. To the northeast, coastal hills dip straight into the ocean, where rocky beaches have helped to preserve some of the shore's natural beauty. To the southwest, waves seem to wash up onto more concrete than sand. That said, nothing can take away from the coast's major attraction: eight months of spring and four months of summer. News of Costa del Sol's fantastic weather has spread far and wide, and July and August bring swarms of pale-skinned Brits and thick-walleted German tourists. Make reservations days in advance to avoid having to sleep on the beach (not recommended for solo travelers and women). Alternatively, ask around for *casas particulares*. June is the best time to visit, when summer has already hit the beach but tourists haven't. Private bus lines offer connections along the coast itself—trains only go as far as Málaga and Fuengirola. Railpasses are not valid on the Costa del Sol, but train prices are reasonable.

MÁLAGA ☎952

Once celebrated by the likes of Hans Christian Andersen, Málaga (pop. 531,140) is the largest Andalucian city on the coast and the birthplace of Pablo Picasso. While Málaga's beaches are better known for bars than sand, the city has much to offer. You'll find locals strolling and meeting in sidewalk cafes for beer and *tapas*, exuberant nightlife, a dash of foreign exchange students, and all the requisite historical monuments—fortress, cathedral, and bullring. Because it is a critical transportation hub, many see Málaga en route to other coastal stops, but it is well worth a day or two in its own right. Neighboring Torremolinos (30min. by bus or train) attracts some package-tourists with its mediocre beaches and sketchy nightlife, but Málaga and nearby Fuengirola and Nerja (see p.273) are more worthwhile.

TRANSPORTATION

Flights: (☎952 04 88 04). From the airport, bus #19 (every 30min., €1.20) runs from the "City Bus" sign, stopping at the bus station and at the corner of C. Molina Lario and Postigo de los Abades behind the cathedral. RENFE trains connecting the city and the airport are cheaper (€0.81) and quicker (12min.). **Iberia,** C. Molina Larios, 13 (☎952 13 61 66; 24hr. reservations 902 40 05 00).

Trains: Estación de Málaga, Esplanada de la Estación (☎952 36 02 02). Take bus #3 at Po. Parque or #4 at Pl. Marina to the station. **RENFE** office, C. Strachan, 4 (☎902 24 02 02), off C. Molina Lario. To: **Barcelona** (13hr.; 7:05am, 9pm; €48.66); **Córdoba** (2hr., 6 per day 6:45am-9pm, €18.66); **Fuengirola** (30min., every 30min. 7:15am-10:30pm, €1.66); **Madrid** (5hr., 5 per day 8:40am-7:45pm, €44.32); **Sevilla** (3hr., 6 per day 7:45am-8:08pm, €13.36); **Torremolinos** (20min., every 30min. 5:45am-10:13pm, €1.11). Reservations on long-distance trains are highly recommended.

Buses: Po. Tilos (☎902 24 02 02; Alsa ☎902 42 22 42; Alsina Graells Sur ☎952 31 82 95; Casado ☎952 31 59 08; Daibus ☎952 31 52 47; Portillo ☎952 36 01 91), 1 block from the RENFE station along C. Roger de Flor. To: **Algeciras** (3hr., 16 per day 5am-9:45pm, €8.74-9.02); **Almería** (8 per day 7am-3am, €12.77); **Antequera** (1hr., 9-12 per day 7am-10pm, €3.61); **Cádiz** (5hr., 4 per day 6:45am-8pm, €17.24); **Córdoba** (3hr., 5 per day 9am-7pm, €10.11); **Fuengirola** (30min., every 30min., €1.95); **Granada** (2hr., 17 per day 7am-9pm, €7.76); **La Línea** (3hr., 4 per day 7am-5pm, €8.26); **Madrid** (7hr.; 4-7 per day M-Th and Sa 8:45am-1am, F and Su 2:15pm-12:30am; €17.33); **Marbella** (1½hr., approx. every hr. 7am-8pm, €4.20); **Murcia** (6hr., 5 per day 8:30am-midnight, €24); **Nerja** (1hr., approx. every hr. 7am-11pm, €3.05); **Ronda** (3hr., 4 per day 8:15am-4:30pm, €7.92); **Sevilla** (3hr., 11-12 per day 7am-3am, €12.59); **Torremolinos** (20min., every 15min. 6:15am-1am, €0.95).

Taxis: Radio-Taxi (☎952 32 00 00 or 952 33 33 33). A taxi from the town center to the waterfront costs €6 and to the airport €10.

ORIENTATION AND PRACTICAL INFORMATION

The bus and train stations lie a block away from each other along C. Roger de Flor; be aware of potential thieves in this area. To get to the town center from the **bus station** (20min.), exit right onto C. Perchel, walk straight through the big intersection with Av. Aurora, take a right on Av. Andalucía, and cross the Puente Tetuán. From here, **Alameda Principal** leads into **Plaza de la Marina.** Or take bus #4 or 21 along the same route (€0.81). From Pl. Marina, C. Molina Lario leads to the **cathedral** and the old town. C. Marqués de Larios connects Pl. Marina to **Plaza de la Constitución,** while Po. Parque leads past the **Alcazaba.** Seaside Po. Marítimo stretches toward the lively beachfront district **El Pedregalejo** (bus #11 or a 40min. walk). After dark, be wary of the neighborhoods of **Alameda de Colón, El Perchel** (toward the river from the train and bus stations), **Cruz del Molinillo** (near the market), **La Esperanza/Santo Domingo** (up the river from El Corte Inglés), and the beaches.

Tourist Offices: Municipal, Av. Cervantes, 1 (☎/fax 952 60 44 10), in a little house along Po. Parque. Also a kiosk near the post office on Av. Andalucía. Open M-F 8:15am-2pm and 4:30-7pm, Sa-Su 9:30am-1:30pm. **Junta de Andalucía,** Pasaje de Chinitas, 4 (☎952 21 34 45), off Pl. Constitución at the corner of C. Nicasio. Enter the alley through the arch, and take the 1st right. Open M-F 8:30am-8:30pm, Sa-Su 10am-2pm.

Currency Exchange: Banco Español de Crédito, Alameda Principal, 8 (☎952 21 15 41), at the intersection with Pta. Mar. Open M-F 8:30am-2pm.

Luggage Storage: Lockers at the **train station** (open daily 7am-10:45pm) and **bus station** (open daily 6:30am-11pm). Both €3 per day.

Foreign Language Bookstore: Rayuela Idiomas, Pl. de la Merced, 17 (☎952 22 48 10). A wide range of classic literature and contemporary novels. The best foreign bookstore within 100km. Open M-F 9:45am-1:30pm and 5-8:30pm, Sa 10am-2pm.

Emergency: ☎112. **Police:** ☎952 12 65 00.

Pharmacy: Farmacia Palouix García, C. Cortina del Vuelle, 5 (☎052 21 91 95). Open M-Sa 9:30am-1:30pm and 5-8:30pm.

Medical Services: ☎952 30 30 34 (urgent), ☎952 39 04 00 (non-urgent). **Medical Emergency:** ☎061.

El Corte Inglés: Av. Andalucía, 4-6 (☎952 07 65 00), across the street from the post office, over the Puente Tetuán. Department store with a supermarket downstairs; sells a street map of Málaga. Open M-Sa 10am-10pm. AmEx/MC/V.

Internet Access: Internet Meeting Point, Pl. de la Merced, 14. Has a pool table, video games, liquor, and coffee. Internet access €1 per hr. Open daily 10am-2am.

Post Office: Av. Andalucía, 1 (☎902 19 71 97), just over the Puente Tetuán. **Lista de Correos.** Open M-F 8:30am-8:30pm, Sa 9:30am-2pm. **Postal Code:** 29080.

ACCOMMODATIONS

Budget establishments can generally be found in the old town, between Pl. Marina and Pl. Constitución.

Hostal La Palma, C. Martínez, 7 (☎952 22 67 72), off C. Marqués de Larios. Spotless, with a great family atmosphere. Downstairs rooms have communal baths; upstairs doubles are brand new with A/C, mini-terraces, and private baths. Call ahead to make sure the owner is in. Singles €12-18; doubles €24-39; triples €27-42. ❷

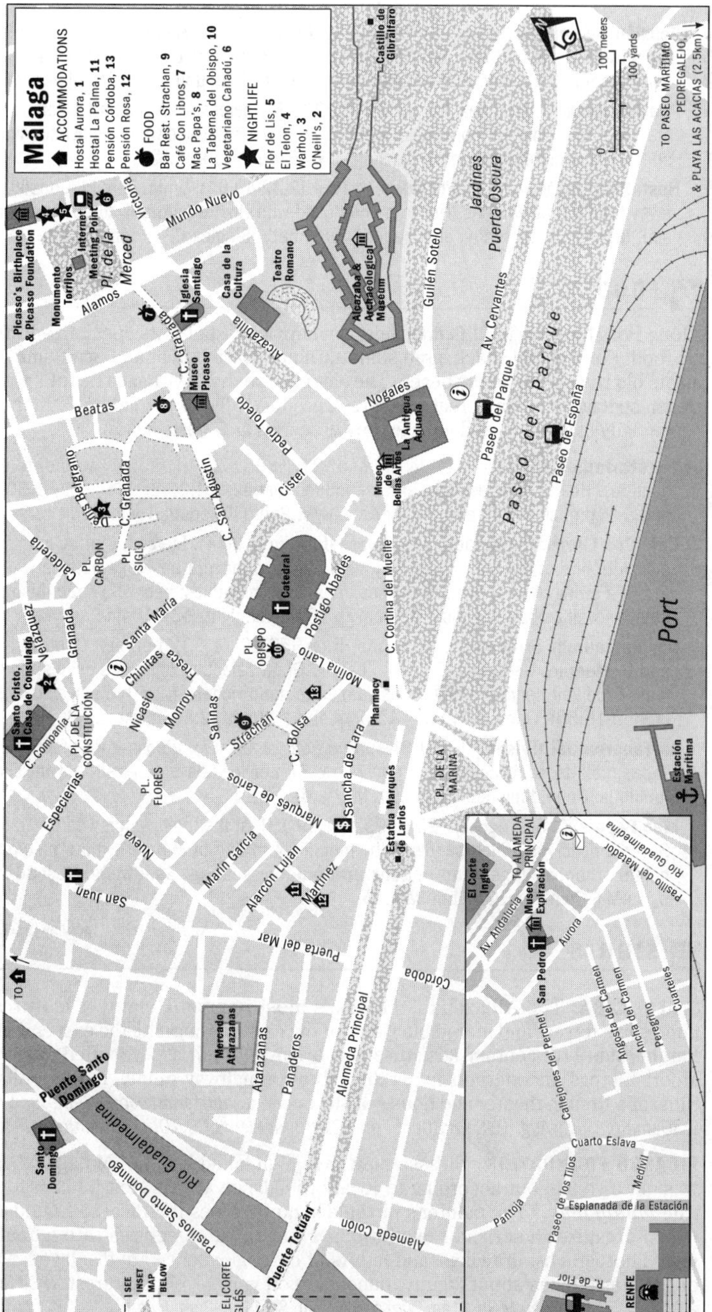
Málaga
ACCOMMODATIONS
Hostal Aurora, 1
Hostal La Palma, 11
Pensión Córdoba, 13
Pensión Rosa, 12
FOOD
Bar Rest. Strachan, 9
Café Con Libros, 7
Mac Papa's, 8
La Taberna del Obispo, 10
Vegetariano Cañadú, 6
NIGHTLIFE
Flor de Lis, 5
El Telon, 4
Warhol, 3
O'Neill's, 2
0 100 meters
0 100 yards
TO PASEO MARÍTIMO, PEDREGALEJO, & PLAYA LAS ACACIAS (2.5km)
Castillo de Gibralfaro
Jardines Puerta Oscura
Paseo del Parque
Paseo de España
Av. Cervantes
Guilén Sotelo
Alcazaba & Archaeological Museum
Teatro Romano
Casa de la Cultura
Alcazabilla
Mundo Nuevo
Victoria
Picasso's Birthplace & Picasso Foundation
Internet Meeting Point
Monumento Torrijos
Pl. de la Merced
Alamos
Iglesia Santiago
C. Granada
Museo Picasso
Beatas
Pedro Toledo
Nogales
La Antigua Aduana
Museo de Bellas Artes
Cister
C. San Agustín
Belgrano
Calderería
PL. CARBON
PL. SIGLO
Catedral
Postigo Abades
C. Cortina del Muelle
Santa María
Velázquez
Granada
Santo Cristo, Casa de Consulado
Chinitas
Fresca
Nicasio
Monroy
PL. OBISPO
Molina Lario
Pharmacy
Salinas
Strachan
C. Bolsa
Sancha de Lara
PL. DE LA MARINA
PL. DE LA CONSTITUCIÓN
C. Compañía
Especierías
PL. FLORES
Marqués de Larios
Estatua Marqués de Larios
Port
Estación Marítima
Nueva
Marín García
Alarcón Luján
Martínez
San Juan
Puerta del Mar
TO 1
Córdoba
Alameda Principal
Mercado Atarazanas
Atarazanas
Panaderos
Puente Santo Domingo
Santo Domingo
Río Guadalmedina
Pasillos Santo Domingo
Puente Tetuán
Alameda Colón
SEE INSET MAP BELOW
TO EL CORTE INGLÉS
El Corte Inglés
TO ALAMEDA PRINCIPAL
Av. Andalucía
Museo Expiración
San Pedro
Aurora
Pasillo del Matador
Río Guadalmedina
Callejones del Perchel
Angosta del Carmen
Ancha del Carmen
Peregrino
Cuarteles
Cuarto Eslava
Medívil
Paseo de los Tilos
Esplanada de la Estación
Pantoja
R. de Flor
RENFE

ANDALUCÍA

Pensiõn Córdoba, C. Bolsa, 11 (☎952 21 44 69), off C. Molina Lario. Decently-sized rooms with sinks and antique furniture surround a patio filled with clotheslines. Spotless common baths and a great location. Singles €15; doubles €25-28; triples €42. ❶

Pensión Rosa, C. Martínez, 10 (☎952 21 27 16), across from Hostal La Palma off C. Marqués de Larios. All rooms have a sink, and many have nice windows overlooking the street. Clean common bathrooms. Singles €25; doubles €35. ❸

Hostal Aurora, Muro de Puerta Nueva, 1 (☎952 22 40 04), 5min. from Pl. Constitución, away from the busy areas. Not to be confused with Hostal Aurora II, run by the owner's son. Rooms are cool, airy, and clean. Shared bath. Singles €24; doubles €39. ❷

FOOD

Along Po. Marítimo in **El Pedregalejo,** beachfront restaurants specialize in fresh seafood. For a cheap snack, grab some sardines roasted over an open flame (usually in old rowboats) on the beach. The eateries around C. Granada near Pl. Constitución specialize in land creatures. Fresh produce fills the **market** on C. Afaranzas (open daily 8am-2pm), and you can buy groceries at **El Corte Inglés.**

Vegetariano Cañadú, Pl. de la Merced, 21 (☎952 22 90 56; www.cuidate.com/canadu). Hearty meatless fare and smoothies. Entrees €4.20-6. Open daily 1:30-4pm and 8-11pm, closed Tu evening. AmEx/MC/V. Photo ID required with credit cards. ❶

Café Con Libros, C. Granada, 73, 1 block down from the Pl. Merced. Curl up in this cozy cafe with one of the many multi-language books, or have a beverage outside while sitting in a swing. A wide array of coffees, teas, and smoothies; beer and liquor also available, as well as baked goods. Open M-Th 10am-midnight, F-Sa 10am-2am. ❶

Bar Restaurant Strachan, C. Strachan, 5 (☎953 22 75 73), between C. Molina Lario and C. Marqués de Larios. Outdoor seating. Great selection of liquors, wines, and coffees. Excellent service, tasty *tapas*, baguette sandwiches (€2.70-3.50), and entrees (€3.50-15.50). Open daily noon-4:30pm and 7:30pm-12:30am. AmEx/MC/V. ❷

La Taberna del Obispo, Pl. del Obispo (☎952 21 93 67), across from the cathedral. *Tapas*, salads, sandwiches, and *paella* (€6-7). Service is a bit relaxed, but the food is fabulous. Open daily noon-midnight. MC/V. ❷

Mac Papa's, C. San Agustín, 23 (☎952 21 59 13), at the intersection with C. Granada. Savor a delicious grilled sandwich by moonlight in one of Málaga's more picturesque neighborhoods. Vegetarian options and outdoor seating. Sandwiches €1.80-2.70. Open M-F 6pm-1am, Sa 6pm-3am. ❶

SIGHTS

ALCAZABA. The Alcazaba is Málaga's most imposing sight; it features 10 impressive towers and incredible views of the harbor. Guarding the east end of Po. Parque, this 11th-century structure was originally built as a fortified palace for Moorish kings. Incongruously perched above a highway tunnel, it overlooks the ruins of a Roman theater and houses a Moroccan **art museum.** *(Open Sept.-June Tu-Su 9:30am-8pm, July-Aug. Tu-Sa 8:30am-7pm. €1.80, students €0.70, children under 7 free.)*

PICASSO FOUNDATION. Picasso may have high-tailed it out of Málaga when he was quite young, but according to local officials, he always "felt himself to be a true *malagueño.*" The painter's birthplace now houses the Picasso Foundation, which organizes a series of exhibitions, concerts, and lectures throughout the year. Photographs, drawings, and letters of correspondence are displayed; a tour of the house takes about 30min., depending on your level of interest. *(Pl. Merced. ☎952 21 50 05. Open M-Sa 11am-2pm and 5-8pm, Su 11am-2pm. Free.)*

CASTILLO DE GIBRALFARO. An Arab lighthouse was built in this Phoenician castle, which offers sweeping views of Málaga and the Mediterranean. Exploring the grounds alone can be dangerous though. *(Bus #35 to Castillo leaves every 20min. from the plaza below on Av. Cervantes, €1.80; otherwise it's an uphill hike. Open daily 9:30am-8pm.)*

CATHEDRAL. Málaga's breathtaking cathedral is a blend of Gothic, Renaissance, and Baroque styles. The cathedral's second tower, under construction from the 16th to 19th century, was never completed—hence the cathedral's nickname *La Manquita* (One-Armed Lady). Small museum upstairs displays religious art. The organs date from 1781. *(C. Molina Larios. ☎952 22 03 45. Open M-Sa 10am-6:45pm. €2.)*

MUSEO DE BELLAS ARTES. The local fine arts museum, in the Palacio de la Aduana, displays collections of Renaissance religious works and devotes a wing to Picasso. *(C. Alcazabilla, 2. Open Tu 3-8pm, W-F 9am-8pm, Sa-Su 9am-3pm. Free.)*

MUSEO PICASSO. Expected to be completed in October 2003, a new museum dedicated to the life and works of Pablo Picasso, Málaga's native son, will reside on C. San Agustín on the corner of C. Granada.

NIGHTLIFE

In summer, young *malagueños* crowd the boardwalk bars in the beachfront neighborhood of El Pedregalejo, a short distance east of Málaga. The **Nocturno 1 bus** takes over the Pedragalejo line nightly from 12:45 to 5:45am (every hr.); a taxi should cost €5-7. Once in El Pedregalejo, **La Tortuga** redefines "international relations," as Spanish-language students practice their lessons over mixed drinks and beer. Monday is particularly popular with exchange students. (Drinks €2.40-6. Open daily 10pm.) The other bars in El Pedragalejo, especially on C. Bolivia and a few blocks up from the beach, stay open a bit later. Stop by **Donde 41,** C. Bolivia, 97, for dance music with a Latin beat (drinks €2-3.50, open daily 11pm-6am), or mellow out among shrubbery, pillows, and a pool table next door at **Bolivia.** On weekends, crowds invade the bars and pubs closer to Málaga's center, particularly in the area between C. Comedias and C. Granada, near Pl. Constitución and Pl. Merced. Expatriates and Spaniards alike enjoy drafts at **O'Neill's,** C. Luis de Velázquez, 3, which has all the charisma of an Irish pub including dark wooden decor, pints of Guinness (€3.35), and bartenders imported from the Emerald Isle. (☎952 60 14 60. Open Su-Th noon-3am, F-Sa noon-4am.) More bars surround Pl. Merced like **Flor de Lis,** a primarily gay bar with great ambiance and live DJs spinning house (open 10pm-3am). Right next door is **El Telon,** which entertains a mixed crowd with hip-hop Latino dance music (open 9:30pm-3am). To seriously get your dance on, head to **Warhol,** C. Denis Belgrano, 8, where an international crowd pulsates to jazz-infused house music spun by excellent DJs (open 11pm-6am).

MARBELLA ☎952

Like your vacation spots shaken, not shtirred? Scottish smoothie Sean Connery and a host of other jet-setters choose Marbella (pop. 100,000) as their vacation home. With gorgeous beaches that stretch for kilometers and a decidedly more sophisticated atmosphere than much of the Costa del Sol, its no wonder that Marbella attracts the rich and famous. While now primarily a chic resort, Marbella has a long history as an important merchant town utilized by the Phoenicians, Greeks, Romans, and Arabs. Remnants of this history can be felt in the well-preserved architecture and streets of the *casco antiguo.* Today Marbella serves as an elegant beachside retreat for a wealthy international crowd. Although there are more yachts than hostels, it's still possible to visit on a budget.

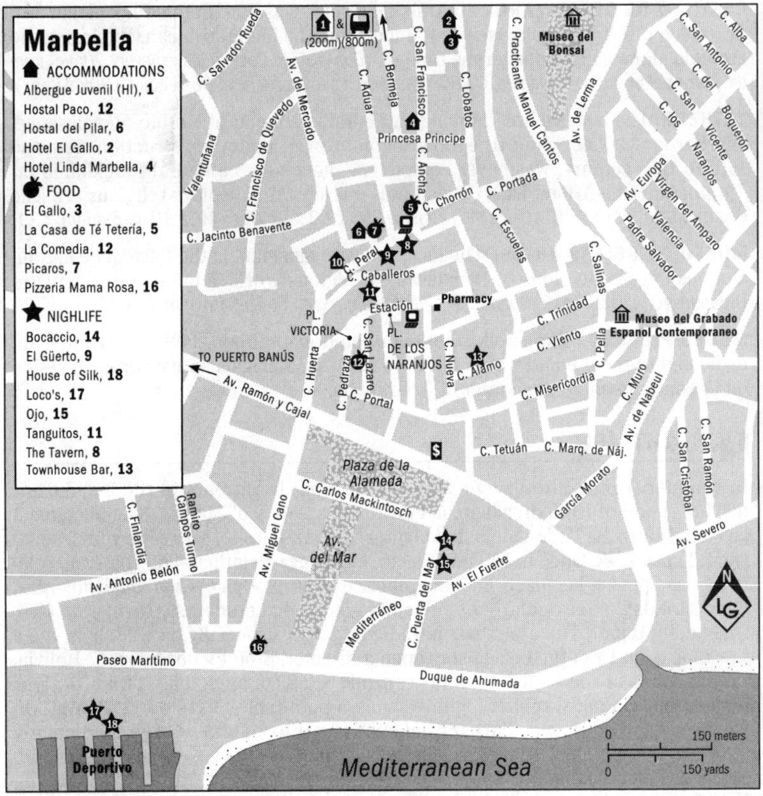

TRANSPORTATION

Buses: Av. Trapiche (☎952 76 44 00). To: **Algeciras** (1½hr., 7 per day 11am-8:30pm, €5.01); **Cádiz** (4hr., 6 per day 7:30am-8:45pm, €13.34); **Fuengirola** (1hr., approx. every 35min. 6:45am-10:30pm, €2.99); **Granada** (4hr., 8 per day 8:30am-6:55pm, €11.77); **Madrid** (7½hr., 10 per day 7:30am-midnight, €19.15); **Málaga** (1½hr., every 30min. 7am-2:30am, €4.18); **Ronda** (1½hr., 7 per day 9am-8:55pm, €4.13); **Sevilla** (4hr.; 9am and 4pm, F and Su also 8:30pm; €12.82).

Taxis: Taxi Sol, (☎952 82 35 35) serves Marbella center (€4) and Puerto Banús (€12).

Boats: To **Puerto Banús** from the port (30min.; every hr.; €5 1-way, €8 roundtrip).

ORIENTATION AND PRACTICAL INFORMATION

Marbella, 56km south of Málaga, can only be reached by bus. The **bus station** sits at the top of Av. Trapiche. To reach the city center, exit the train station, walk left, make the first right onto Av. Trapiche, and turn right at the end of the road onto C. Salvador. Continue downhill on Av. del Mercado and turn left on C. Castillejos, which leads to the perpendicular Av. Ramón y Cajal, the main street in the new town—this becomes Av. Ricardo Soriano on the way to the swanky harbor of **Puerto Banús.** C. Peral curves up from Av. Ramón y Cajal around the **casco antiguo.**

Tourist Office: Pl. Naranjos (☎952 82 35 50), in the *casco antiguo*. From C. Castillejos, pass through Pl. Victoria and follow C. Estación into Pl. Naranjos. **Second office,** C. Glorieta de la Fontanilla (☎952 77 14 42). English spoken. Both open June-Aug. M-F 9:30am-9pm, Sa 10am-2pm.

Currency Exchange: Santander Central Hispano, Av. Ramón y Cajal, 9 (☎902 24 24 24). Good exchange rates. Open M-F 8:30am-2pm, Sa 8:30am-1pm. **ATMs** abound, especially near the *casco antiguo.*

Luggage Storage: At the **bus station** (€3). Open daily 6:30am-11:30pm.

Emergency: ☎091. **Police:** Av. Juan de la Cierva (☎952 82 24 94).

Medical Emergency: ☎061. **Hospital: Comarcal,** CN-340, km187 (☎952 86 27 48).

Pharmacy: Farmacia Espejo, Pl. Naranjos, 4 (☎952 77 12 91). Open M-F 9:30am-2pm and 5:30-9:30pm. In the winter, M-F 9:30am-2pm and 4-8:30pm.

Internet Access: Neotel Locutorios, Pl. Puente de Ronda, 6 (☎655 54 73 11; fax 952 82 43 21). €3 per hr. Open daily 10am-2pm and 4pm-midnight. MC/V. **Marbell Telecom,** C. Estación (☎952 86 11 28), on the corner, near Pl. de los Naranjos. Offers photocopying, fax, and Internet (€3 per hr.). Open daily 10am-2pm and 5-11pm.

Post Office: C. Jacinto Benavente, 26 (☎952 77 28 98), uphill from C. Ricardo Soriano. Open M-F 8:30am-8:30pm, Sa 9:30am-1pm. **Postal Code:** 29600.

ACCOMMODATIONS AND CAMPING

If you are reservationless, especially from June to September, arrive early and pray for a miracle. The area around **Pl. Naranjos** is loaded with hostels.

Hostal del Pilar, C. Mesoncillo, 4 (☎952 82 99 36), off C. Peral. Run by an accommodating Scot, this 17th-century inn was originally run by monks as a home for traveling pilgrims. Now it's a haven for backpackers, with clean, comfortable rooms, shared bathrooms, and a pool table. Crackling fires warm the downstairs bar during winter. Hearty English breakfast €5. €15 per person, July-Aug. €20; roof mattresses €12. ❶

Albergue Juvenil (HI), Av. Trapiche, 2 (☎952 77 14 91; fax 952 86 32 27). Exit left from the bus station, turn right and follow Av. Trapiche for ½km. Like a proper hotel, only affordable. Facilities include a large pool, garden, TV room, pool table, and basketball court. Doubles and quads, many with private bathrooms. June to Sept. 15 €12.90 per person; over 26 €17.25. Apr.-June, Sept. 15-Oct. €10.60/€15.20. Nov.-Mar. €8.50/€11.50. €3 fee for non HI-members. MC/V. ❶

Hotel Linda Marbella, C. Ancha, 21 (☎/fax 952 85 71 71), located on a quiet street in the *casco antiguo*. Colorfully painted rooms all have bath, TV, phone, safe, and A/C. June 15-Sept. singles €50; doubles €80. Oct.-June 14 €30/€50. MC/V. ❹

Hostal Paco, C. Peral, 16 (☎952 77 12 00; fax 952 82 22 65). Large cheerful rooms all with bath. Phone and TV in lobby. July-Oct. 15 and *Semana Santa* singles €30; doubles €45. Oct. 16-June €27/€39. MC/V. ❸

Hotel El Gallo, C. Lobatas, 46 (☎952 82 79 89), next to Restaurante El Gallo in the *casco antiguo.* Brand new, clean, and comfortable rooms, all with bath, TV, and A/C. Doubles €45. MC/V. ❸

El Castillo, Pl. San Bernabé, 2 (☎952 77 17 39; fax 952 82 11 98), in the *casco antiguo*, a few blocks uphill from Pl. Naranjos. Sunny rooms with high ceilings, fans, and spacious baths. July-Sept. singles €24; doubles €39. Mar.-June and Oct. €22/€36. Nov.-Feb. €19/€29.50. MC/V. ❷

Camping Marbella Playa, (☎952 83 39 98), 2km east on N-340, on the Marbella-Fuengirola bus line (€1.20); ask the bus driver to stop at the campground. Open year-round. €4 per person, €7 per tent. ❶

FOOD

Terrazas filling Pl. Naranjos are not particularly budget-friendly—the multilingual menus spell tourist trap. Restaurants farther uphill are less picturesque but easier on the wallet. Locals retreat to Av. Nabeul for cheap eats while seaside **Av. Miguel Cano** and **Av. Pta. Mar** host more lively bars and cafes. The municipal **market** is on Av. Mercado, uphill from C. Peral (open M-Sa 8am-2pm). The **24hr. minimarket** at the corner of C. Pablo Casals and Av. Fontanilla is a beacon in the night.

El Gallo, C. Lobatas, 44 (☎952 82 79 98). A perennial favorite with backpackers, El Gallo serves up tasty meals for next to nothing. Ultra-cheap *tapas* (from €1). Hamburger with chips and salad €3.30. Open M-W and F-Su, 8am-midnight. MC/V. ❶

La Casa del Té Tetería, C. Ancha, 7 (☎639 16 79 18). Cozy candlelit rooms filled with cushions, paintings, and incense. Vegetarian sandwiches and crepes (€1.80-2.25), Indian yogurt drinks (€1.18), and an array of teas and coffees. Open W-M 5-11pm. ❶

Picaros, C. Aduar, 1 (☎952 82 86 50). Enjoy excellent cuisine in the beautiful courtyard, or stay cozy inside during winter. Great wine list and a wide range of dishes (€12-18.50). 3-course meal €30. Open Tu-Su 7:30-11:30pm. AmEx/MC/V. ❹

La Comedia, Pl. Victoria (☎/fax 952 77 64 78). Creative modern cuisine in a stylish atmosphere. Entrees €11.80-18.70. Some half-portions and vegetarian options available. Open Tu-Su 7pm-1am. AmEx/MC/V. ❸

Pizzería Mama Rosa, Po. Marítimo (☎952 82 00 11), at Av. Miguel Cano. Pizza and pasta served alongside a popular beachfront promenade. Pizza €5.26-8.11, pasta €5.71-9. Take-out available. Open daily noon-1am. MC/V. ❷

SIGHTS

Although most visitors come to Marbella for the 320 days of sunshine a year, no visit would be complete without a stroll through the **casco antiguo,** a maze of cobbled streets and white-washed facades trimmed with wild roses. The **Museo del Grabado Español Contemporáneo,** C. Hospital Bazán, in a restored hospital for the poor, is a treasure-trove of engravings by Miró, Picasso, Dalí, Goya, and contemporary artists. (☎952 82 50 35. Open M 10am-2pm, Tu-Sa 10am-2pm and 6-9pm; €2.50.) To the northeast is the **Parque Arroyo de la Represa,** site of the **Museo del Bonsai,** home to four rooms of bonsai trees, including a 500-year-old Chinese ficus. (☎952 86 29 26. Open daily 10am-1:30pm and 5-8pm. €3, under 12 €1.50.)

NIGHTLIFE

Nightlife in Marbella begins and ends late. The rowdiest corner of the *casco antiguo* is where C. Mesoncillo meets C. Peral. Loud music and cheery Spaniards spill from **El Güerto,** C. Peral, 9, while a mixed crowd of backpackers and locals enjoy the pub scene at **The Tavern,** C. Peral, 7. (Both open at 8:30pm; El Güerto opens only on weekends.) A mellower ambiance suffuses the **Townhouse Bar,** C. Alamo, tucked down an alley off C. Nueva, downhill from Pl. Naranjos. Ask for a shot of apple pie; it ain't mama's. (Open daily at 10pm.) **Tanguitos,** C. Buitrago off C. de los Caballeros, also hosts a mellow crowd with groups congregating on the couches near the fireplace or under the stars in the back courtyard. (Open daily at 11pm.) Many clubs and bars are located down by the port (at the bottom of Av. Miguel Cano), including the waterfront **House of Silk,** or the more grungy **Loco's;** both play dance hits. Between the beach and the *casco antiguo*, C. Puerta del Mar is home to several gay bars, including **Ojo,** C. Puerta del Mar, 9 (open daily at midnight), and the younger **Bocaccio,** C. Puerta del Mar, 17 (opens at 11pm).

While the *casco antiguo* gets crowded on weekends, the elite scene at **Puerto Banús** is hopping all week long. The bars and clubs lining the yacht port and C. Ribera are hard to miss. Buses run on the hour all night from Av. Ricardo Soriano (destination San Pedro, €0.90). Taxis from Marbella center (€8.40) stop near the port's popular celebrity-sighting hangout, **Sinatra Bar.** (Mixed drinks €4.20-8. Open daily 11pm.) Around 4am, the action shifts to the clubs. **Comedia,** (terrace-level, C. Ribera) draws in the dancing crowd with a glam ambiance and high energy music (open daily at midnight, €10 cover on weekends), and **Terra Blues,** (further down C. Ribera) provides a more eclectic mix of music and a less touristy scene.

BEACHES

City buses along Av. Richard Soriano (destination San Pedro or Hipercor, €0.90) bring you to chic and trendy **Puerto Banús** where beautifully clean beaches are buffered by imposing, white yachts and row upon row of boutiques and fancy restaurants. On exceptionally clear days, the Moroccan coast is barely visible. The port has been frequented by the likes of Sean Connery, King Fahd of Saudi Arabia (who built a palace modeled on the White House), Antonio Banderas, and even the late Princess Diana. Throngs of well-dressed Euro-chicks and chicos mill about the marina, in search of well-banked spouses. With 22km of **beach,** Marbella offers a variety of settings despite its ultra-chic facade. Beaches to the east of the port are popular with British backpackers; those to the west attract a more posh crowd. **Funny Beach,** popular with families, is a 10min. bus ride (take the bus to Fuengirola and ask the driver to stop, €1), or walk 2km east along the beach. You'll find a paradise of beach games, including jet-skiing and volleyball. Because of the mountains nearby, Marbella's winter temperatures tend to be 5-8°F warmer than Málaga's, and beach season lasts at least 10 months.

NERJA ☎952

Renowned for its beaches and caves, Nerja (pop. 15,000) offers all the comforts and clutter of a coastal resort town. Spectacular beaches are crowded with bikini-clad tourists and flip-flopped anglophones. At the **Balcón de Europa,** hordes gather to catch a glimpse of one of the Costa del Sol's most stunning ocean views.

PRACTICAL INFORMATION. The **bus station,** C. San Miguel, 3 (☎952 52 15 04), sends buses to: **Almería** (4hr., 6 per day 8am-7:50pm, €9.69); **Almuñécar** (30min., 9 per day 6:30am-8:30pm, €1.97); **Granada** (2¼hr.; 6:30am, 4:45, 7:15pm; €7.38); **Málaga** (1½hr., 17 per day 6:30am-9:45pm, €3.06); **Sevilla** (4hr., 2 per day 7:30am and 4:30pm, €15.38). For a good map of Nerja, head to the multilingual **tourist office,** Pta. del Mar, 2. From the bus ticket counter, cross the street (Av. de Pescia) and walk downhill on C. Pintada until the end; the tourist office is on the left beside the Balcón de Europa. (☎952 52 15 31; fax 952 52 62 87. Open June-Aug. M-F 10am-2pm and 5-8pm, Sa 10am-1pm; Sept.-May M-F 10am-2pm and 5-8pm, Sa 10am-1pm.) Services include: **pharmacy,** P. De San Cristóbal (☎958 63 06 98); **medical emergency** ☎112; **police** C. Virgen del Pilar, 1 (☎952 52 15 45); **Internet**, Med Web Cafe, Av. Castilla Perez, 21 (☎952 52 72 02), at the bottom of the Av. on the right, open daily 10am-midnight, with a helpful multi-lingual staff, printing, coffee, snacks, and smoothies; and the **post office,** C. Almirante Ferrándiz, 6 (☎952 52 17 49. Open M-F 8:30am-2:30pm, Sa 9am-1pm). **Postal code:** 29780.

ACCOMMODATIONS AND FOOD. It's worth breaking a sweat for **Hostal Estrella del Mar ❷,** C. Bellavista, 5. From the bus station, cross the street, but stay on Av. de Pescia past the traffic circle and take your fourth right on C. Andalucía.

Make another right on C. Asensio Cabanillas and then a left on C. Bellavista; the *hostal* is on your left. Spacious rooms with baths and terraces, many with ocean views. (☎952 52 04 61. Breakfast €2.55. Closed Nov.-Feb. July-Sept. 15 singles €18, doubles €25.25; Sept. 16-June €25.25/€33.05; €6 charge per extra person.) Otherwise, **Pensión Residencia Mena ❷,** C. El Barrio, 15, conveniently located off the Balcón de Europa, has comfortable, if bare, rooms. (☎952 52 05 41; fax 952 52 83 45. Oct.-Apr. singles €17; doubles €24. May-Sept. €19.50/€30; Aug., *Semana Santa*, and holidays €23/€36.50, €3.50 extra for a room with a view.) Overpriced restaurants near and along the Balcón de Europa tempt passersby with views. On Playa de Burriana, **Merendero Montemar** specializes in fresh fish and *paella* (€4.81). For those who are craving a British pub, **Big Al's,** Castilla Perez, 26, on the corner of C. Tutti Frutti, brings a taste of England to Spain with British television in the restaurant, a friendly staff, and outdoor dining. Al's is famous for their Sunday English roast (€6.95). At night, the most happening place in town is the unfortunately named **C. Tutti Frutti,** where young Brits congregate at lively local bars. A **supermarket** can be found on C. Antonio Ferandiz. (Open M-Sa 9:30am-9:30pm.)

SIGHTS. To get to the **Balcón de Europa,** a promenade overlooking the Playa de la Caletilla that was once part of a 9th-century castle, cross Av. de Pescia from the bus station and turn right on C. Pintada, which leads downhill to the *balcón*. The **Nerja caves** are the 3rd most visited monument in Spain. Approx. 3km outside of town, they are best reached by taxi or bus (15 per day, €0.70). Below the cliff are more **caves** worthy of exploration, best approached from the **Paseo de los Carabineros** (off the stairs to the right of the tourist office). The walkway winds along the rocky shore to the east, past **Playa de Calahonda, Playa Carabeo,** and to **Playa Burriana,** which earned an EU blue flag for cleanliness. Burriana is the most crowded beach with lots of tourists and restaurants. To reach the sprawling and less crowded **Playa de la Torrecilla** (also a blue flag beach) from the *balcón*, cut west through town to the Playa de la Torrecilla apartments and follow the shoreline (15min.). Closer and popular with locals, but more crowded, is **Playa del Salón,** accessible through an alley off the *balcón*, to the right of Restaurante Marisal.

ALMUÑÉCAR ☎958

In the 4th century BC, a booming fish-salting industry brought prosperity to this Phoenician port town known as **Sexi.** The Romans seized control a century later, constructing temples and a massive aqueduct. Though not quite as exciting as its Phoenician name suggests, Almuñécar entices visitors with expansive boardwalks and an alluring tropical environment.

PRACTICAL INFORMATION. The **bus station** (☎958 63 01 40) is at the corner of Av. Fenicia and Av. Juan Carlos I. Buses run to: **Nerja** (30min., 18 per day 7:15am-9:15pm, €1.97); **Málaga** (1½hr., 7 per day 7am-9:15pm, €5.03); **Granada** (1½hr., 7 per day 6:30am-8pm, €5.55); and **Madrid** (7hr., 8:15am, €15.77). The **tourist office** is in a mauve mansion at the bottom of Av. Europa. From the bus station, exit right and head downhill to the beach. Turn right and walk along the beach until you reach the lookout on the left and Hotel Casablanca. Turn onto C. Bikini, and follow to Av. Europa which begins on the right. (☎958 63 11 25. Open daily 10am-2pm and 5-8pm.) **Luggage storage** at lockers in the bus station. (€2. Open daily 6:30am-9:30pm.) Services include: **medical emergency** ☎061 or ☎112; **police** at the Ayuntamiento in Pl. Constitución (emergency ☎092 or non-emergency ☎958 63 94 30); and **medical care** (☎958 63 20 63).

THE FIFTH BOMB In the 1960s, as Spain was debating whether to join NATO, a USAF B-52 bomber carrying five hydrogen bombs blew up during an in-flight refueling mishap over the village of Palomares, 20km north of Mojácar. Locals looked on as US personnel in radiation suits combed the town in search of the bombs. Four were recovered and identified; the fifth supposedly emerged wrapped in a plastic tarp and without a serial number (Spanish Greenpeace still doubts that it was ever found). Much of Spain boycotted the area's produce (primarily tomatoes), and anti-NATO sentiment reached new heights. To downplay the accident, the US Ambassador and Franco's Minister of the Interior staged a seaside photo-op, swimming in the water before a dozen CIA agents. To top it off, the US built a health clinic in the town. Palomares has since prospered, with copious harvests of tomatoes, leeks, and melons, but some locals still blame defects and illnesses on the mysterious fifth bomb.

ACCOMMODATIONS AND FOOD. Several reasonably priced hostels lie on Av. Europa. From the bus station walk downhill to the beach, turn right and follow the beach until you see the lookout on the left. Av. Europa runs perpendicular to the beach off C. Bikini. Situated across from the tourist office, **Hotel Goya ❷,** Av. Europa, 31, has comfortable rooms with dark wood furniture, baths, and phones. (☎958 63 05 50 or 958 63 11 92; fax 958 63 11 92. July-Sept. and *Semana Santa* singles €25; doubles €44. Oct.-Mar. €17/€26. Apr.-June €17/€32; €12 to add an extra bed. AmEx/MC/V.) **Hostal Residencia Tropical ❸,** Av. Europa, 39, a half-block from the beach, has spotless, well-furnished rooms with private bath. (☎958 63 34 58. June 21-Aug. 1 and Aug. 18-Sept 14 singles €25; doubles €42; triples €48. Aug. 2-Aug. 17 €30/€45/€51. Sept. 15-30 and Apr. 20-June €20/€35/€41. MC/V.) Plenty of beach-front *terrazas* line Po. Puerta del Mar and Po. San Cristóbal, providing the place to savor the catch of the day. Locals frequent **Bar Avenida Lute y Jesús ❶,** Av. Europa, on the corner of C. Pablo Iglesias, which specializes in *fritura de pescado* (€3.90-6). (☎958 63 42 76. *Menú* €4.80-7.20. Open daily 8am-1:30am. AmEx/MC/V.) Further down the road is **Restaurante Pizzería Da Nicola ❷,** Av. de Europa, 28, with Italian favorites including pasta (€5.30-8.80) and pizza (€4.20-7.50), as well as fish and meat dishes (€9.80-14.50). Italian liquors available. (☎958 63 31 04. Open 8am-midnight, depending on the season. MC/V.)

SIGHTS AND BEACHES. Almuñécar's historical protagonists, the Phoenicians, Romans, and Moors, all fought over this subtropical paradise, and each left their distinct mark. The Moorish **Castillo de San Miguel** rests atop a massive hill at the front of Pl. Puerte del Mar. Bombarded by the British during the Napoleonic Wars, it was cleared of rubble and converted to a cemetery before finding its most recent incarnation as a museum. (Open Tu-Sa 10:30am-1:30pm and 5-7:30pm, Su 10:30am-2pm, closed M. €2.02, children €1.40.) The 1900-year-old, 8km long **aqueduct** watered the ancient Roman town; parts of it are still in use. It lies in many pieces along the Río Seco as you leave town, and is best reached via a hike along the river, or with a four-wheel drive vehicle. Almuñécar is also home to nearly 100 different species of birds, which nest in the **Parque Ornitológico Loro Sexi** beside El Castillo de San Miguel, 100m from the beach. (☎958 88 08 65. Open daily 11am-2pm and 5-7pm. €2, children under 12 €1.40.) Uphill from the tourist office, **Parque El Majuelo** has 400 varieties of imported plants and great views of the ruins of a Roman-Punic fishing factory. (Free.)

Located on the **Costa Tropical,** Almuñécar is known for its excellent beaches. Jutting into the sea, **Peñón del Santo,** a point of land crowned by a giant cross, separates the two main beaches. Both **Playa San Cristóbal** and **Playa del Mar** feature gray sands and stunning views of the surrounding sea cliffs. To reach either beach, follow Av. Europa to the sea; San Cristóbal is on the right, del Mar is on the left. Beyond Puerta del Mar lies the beautiful and less frequented **Playa de Velilla.** Buses to Málaga go through **La Herradura** (15min., 11 per day 7am-9:15pm, €0.80), a suburb/beach frequented by windsurfers and scuba divers. The largest **nude beach** on the Costa Tropical is **Playa Cantarriján,** accessible by car or taxi, en route to Nerja.

ALMERÍA

Exciting nightlife, flowery promenades, and an extensive coastline have turned the once-poor city of Almería into a choice spot for weekend getaways. The cranes, bulldozers, and other construction equipment that frame the city are a testimonial to its growing popularity. Despite the ugly urban sprawl of the city's outskirts, the beautiful plazas, streets, and port make the city center a desirable destination. A huge Moorish fortress, the Alcazaba, presides over the city, but the best parts of Almería are the kilometers of sand stretching along the sea toward Cabo de Gata, at the eastern edge of the Costa del Sol.

TRANSPORTATION. The **airport** (☎950 21 37 00), 9km out of town, has daily flights to Madrid and Barcelona. **Trains,** Pl. Estación (☎902 24 02 02), run to: **Barcelona** (14hr.; W,F, Sa 7:30am; €38.45); **Granada** (2hr., 4 per day 6am-6:10pm, €9.90-10.90); **Madrid** (7hr.; 7:15am, 3:45pm; €34.25-43.25); **Sevilla** (6hr., 3 per day 6am-2:40pm, €26.15); **Valencia** (8hr.; W, F, Sa 7:30am; €33). **Buses** (☎902 42 22 42) leave from Pl. Estación. **Alsa/Enatcar** goes to: **Barcelona** (14hr., 4 per day 9:30am-9:30pm, €44.70); **Mojácar** (1½hr., 6 per day 6:30am-8pm, €5.10); **Murcia** (3hr., 6 per day 6:30am-8pm, €13.20); **Valencia** (8hr., 4 per day 9:30am-9:30pm, €25.75). **Alsina Graells** sends buses to: **Córdoba** (6hr., 1 per day, €18.80); **Granada** (2hr., 12 per day 7am-8pm, €8.55); **Málaga** (3½hr., 10 per day 6:30am-11pm, €15.60); **Sevilla** (5½hr., 3 per day, €23.45). **Almeraya** goes to **Madrid** (8hr., 4 per day 9:30am-midnight, €18).

ORIENTATION AND PRACTICAL INFORMATION. The city revolves around **Puerta de Purchena,** a six-way intersection just down C. Tiendas from the old town. To reach Pta. Purchena from the **bus station** or the connected **train station** on Pl. Estación, walk straight out the front door and take a left onto Av. Estación after one block; turn right onto Av. Federico García Lorca, then left onto Rbla. Obispo Orbera. Po. Almería runs out of Pta. Purchena to the port—any services, including banks with **ATMs,** can be found on Po. Almería or just off it. The **tourist office,** is in Parque Nicolás Salmerón. Follow Po. Almería out of Pta. Purchena toward the port, and turn right onto Parque de Salmerón. (☎950 27 43 55. Open M-F 9am-7pm, Sa-Su 10am-2pm.) The commercial **port** of Almería lies directly in front of the Parque de Salmerón. Services include: **emergency** (☎112); **police,** C. Santos Zarate (☎92); **Hospital Torre Cardenas** (☎950 01 60 00). **Internet access** is available at **DC-9 Ciberclub,** C. Martínez Almagro, 8, several blocks behind the post office. Fax service and a coffee bar are also available. (☎950 25 71 96. Internet €2.10 per hr., faxes €1.50 each. Open M-Th 9am-10:30pm, F 9am-2am, Sa 10:30am-2am, Su 3:30-11pm.) **Post office,** Pl. Juan Cassinello, down Po. Almería. (☎950 24 02 31. Open M-F 8:30am-8:30pm, Sa 9:30am-2pm.) **Postal code:** 04080.

ACCOMMODATIONS. Rooms in Almería tend to be rather uninspiring—high prices are charged for average quality. The tourist office provides a list of accommodations, most of which surround Pta. Purchena. **Hostal Americano ❷,** Av. Estación, on the corner of C. Federico García Lorca, is one of the simpler hostels in town. (☎950 28 10 15. Singles €16.80-18, with bath €21-24.65; doubles €30.65-33, with bath €36-39.37.) Those seeking quiet rooms with private bath, TV, and A/C should check out **Hostal Residencia Nixar ❷**, C. Antonio Vico, 24, a few blocks up from Pl. del Carmen. (☎950 23 72 55. Sept.-May singles €20.35; doubles €33.60; triples €41. June-Aug. €23.80/€40.30/€48.15.) Less than a block down the street from Hostal Nixar is **Hotel La Perla ❹**, Pl. del Carmen, 7, which has recently-refurbished rooms with bath, TV, and A/C that are popular with an older crowd. (☎950 23 72 55. Singles €35-46.28; doubles €40-57.10.)

FOOD. Cafes line Po. Almería. Eat a traditional Andalucian meal on barrels of olive oil amidst photos of famous *matadores* at **Bodega Las Botas ❷**, C. Fructuoso Perez, 3, on a side-street off Po. Almería one block before Pta. Purchena. The *bodega* offers good cold cut platters (€5.45-9) and fresh fish entrees (€10-14). (☎950 26 22 72. Open daily noon-4pm and 8pm-2am.) If you're looking for a break from Spanish food, head to **Pizzeria-Ristorante Nello ❷**, Av. de la Estacion, 26, one block down from Hostal Americano towards the bus station, which serves excellent pizza (€7.25) and pasta (€7-8.50) in a traditional Italian setting. (☎950 26 77 39. Open daily noon-4pm and 8pm-midnight.) With ham chandeliers and over 70 types of *tapas* (all €0.60), **Casa Puga ❶**, C. Jovellanos, 7, in the old quarter, packs them in. (☎950 23 15 30. Open M-Sa 11am-4pm and 8pm-midnight.) The local supermarket is **Champíón,** Po. Almería. (☎950 23 28 00. Open M-Sa 9:15am-9:15pm.)

SIGHTS. Built in 995 by order of Abderramán III of Córdoba, the **Alcazaba,** a magnificent 14-acre Moorish fortress, spans two ridges overlooking the city and the sea. Time your visit so you can make the short trek up to the fortress for stunning views of the city at sunset. Also, visit the small museum containing Moorish artifacts recovered from archaeological digs in the area. *(From Pl. Carmen next to Pta. Purchena, follow C. Antonio Vico. ☎950 27 16 17. Open Tu-Sa 9am-8:30pm. Closed M. €1.50, free with EU passport.)* The **cathedral,** in the old town, resembles a fortress; its design was intended to prevent raids by Berber pirates. Though spartan and blockish on the outside, the inside is all Renaissance with a touch of Baroque on the altar. *(☎609 57 58 02. Open M-F 10am-4:30pm, Sa 10am-1pm, and during Mass. €1.80.)*

NIGHTLIFE. Pubs, bars, and discos fill the small streets behind the post office, where throngs of students and adults can be seen partaking in *la marcha* as early as 11pm. By far the most popular hot spot is the disco **Dolce Vita,** Po. Almería, where several cavernous dance floors, numerous bars, and pulsating music keeps the tight-bodied crowd going until nearly 6am. (M-F no cover, Sa cover €6, Su cover €5. Cover includes one drink. Mixed drinks €5, beer €2.50. Open nightly 11pm-6:30am.) Student-aged partiers start the night off at the bar **Babel,** C. San Pedro, 7, where the owner offers free dance lessons M and Tu from 10pm-1am. (Mixed drinks €4, beer €2. Open Su-Th 3pm-3am, F-Sa 3pm-4am.) The next stop for the younger crowd is **Enebro,** C. San Pedro, a lively pub that features loud Spanish pop. (Mixed drinks €4, beer €2.50. Open nightly until 4am.) **Chupitería Dalia,** C. Dalia, 3, serves up a variety of not-so-subtly-named shooters like *orgasmo de manga*. (☎950 26 25 84. Cocktail shots €7.20, shots €1.20, *copas* €3.60.) Those too old to giggle at a buttery nipple gather at the outdoor tables and by the bar at **The Irish Tavern,** C. Antonio González Eges, 4 (mixed drinks €4.20, beer €2-3; open daily 3pm-3am), then head over to dance at **Velvet,** C. Trajana at the corner of C. San Pedro (no cover; mixed drinks €3.50; open Th-Sa 11pm-4am). When the weekend partying is done, locals head to **Vertice Pub,** C. Eduardo Perez, 4, for beer (€2.10) and chill jazz music. (☎652 95 09 32. Open daily 10:30pm-4am.)

BEACHES. There is nothing unique or inspiring about Almería's beaches, but they serve their purpose when the weather gets unbearably hot in the city. From the port, walk past La Rambla Belén along Po. Marítimo. To your right you'll find

Playa Almadravillas, whose waters are often churned up by the traffic of private yachts motoring in and out of the nearby marina. Further down Po. Marítimo, well past the marina are **Playa Ciudad Luminosa** and **Playa del Zapillo,** which offer swimmers calmer waters flanked by numerous stone jetties. The beaches generally improve as you head north of the city towards the protected coast of **Cabo de Gata.**

DAYTRIP FROM ALMERÍA: CABO DE GATA

Alsina Graells (☎950 23 51 68) sends buses to San Miguel de Cabo de Gata (1hr.; M-F 6 per day 8am-9pm, Sa-Su 4 per day 8am-8pm; €1.65); Autocares Bernardo (☎950 25 04 22) runs to San José (45min.; M-F 1:15 and 6:30pm, Sa 2:15pm; returns M-F 7am, 3 and 9pm, Sa 7am; €2.50).

Thirty kilometers east of urban Almería lies pristine **Parque Natural de Cabo de Gata-Níjar,** a 60km stretch of protected coast and inland environs. The near-desolate peninsula juxtaposes tropical and barren climates; flamingos flock to the area's salt marshes, while a desert and mountains farther inland draw visitors for hiking. The park has served as a movie set for *The Good, the Bad, and the Ugly* and *Lawrence of Arabia*. Many come to Cabo de Gata to dive at **Mermaid's Reef** or windsurf off **Playa de San Miguel. Grupo J. 126** (☎950 38 02 99) and **Ocio y Mar** (☎608 05 64 77) provide info and tours of the park; contact them a day or two in advance for tours and equipment rental (prices based on availability). Long stretches of pleasant beaches await in the fishing town of **San Miguel de Cabo de Gata** (or simply **Cabo de Gata**). As Cabo de Gata has nary a budget lodging, it's best to head back to Almería for the night. Farther south, the little resort of **San José** boasts an even more pristine beach and serves as a base for exploring the park. Contact the **tourist office** (☎950 38 02 99) in San José for information on water sports, bike and car rentals, and maps for visiting the numerous **calas** (coves) along the coast on the outskirts of town, which offer the most secluded and untouched beaches.

MOJÁCAR

Mojácar is the kind of vacation spot one might expect to see on a postcard: a white-stoned, picture-perfect, hilltop village with 17km of smooth coastline and firecracker nightlife. Stunning sunsets find tourists and residents relaxing on the numerous outdoor terraces or strolling along the stone boardwalk by the beach. During the day, the village clears out as the tourists head downhill to the turquoise Mediterranean to escape the heat. The beachfront resorts fill up quickly in July and August when hordes of international visitors join the large contingent of German, British, and American expats who have made Mojácar their home—don't be surprised to hear more English than Spanish from visitors and residents alike.

TRANSPORTATION. The main bus stop (there is no station) is in front of the shopping plaza near the beach. **Alsa/Enatcar** buses (☎902 42 22 42) leave for **Almería** (1½hr.; M-Sa 7 per day, Su 2 per day 7:50am-11:10pm; €5.10); **Barcelona** (12hr., 2 per day, €39.65); **Madrid** (8hr., 1-2 per day, €26.10); **Murcia** (2½hr.; M-F 8 per day, Sa-Su 4-5 per day 7:05am-9:35pm; €8.10). For a **taxi** call ☎950 47 81 84, or wait at the stop in Pl. Nueva in town. The tourist office has a list of **car rental** agencies—with so many tourists around, there are a dozen or so to choose from. **Scooters** can be rented at **Star Moto,** Po. del Mediterraneo, 293. (☎950 61 51 56. €27 per day. Driver's license and €35 deposit required.)

ORIENTATION AND PRACTICAL INFORMATION. Mojácar is split into two parts: the beach, lined with pricey hotels, tourist-oriented restaurants, and the best nightlife spots which all lie along Po. del Mediterraneo, and the *pueblo*, where everyday life centers around Pl. Nueva. The town rests atop a hill and is connected to the beach by a winding road. Most buses stop both at the "official" stop in front of the shopping plaza by the beach, as well as at the lowest point of the village itself; since most budget lodging is in town, get off at the latter stop. The 30min. hike up the hill from the beach or the main bus stop to Pl. Nueva is not for the faint of heart, but yellow **Transportes Urbanos** buses run to and from town and the beachfront bus stop for your convenience. (2 per hr. 9:30am-1:30pm and 5pm-midnight, 1 per hr. 1:30-5pm; €0.60.) This same bus line also services the various beaches along the coast. From the main bus stop, take **Line A** to the golf course and northern residential areas along Po. del Mediterraneo towards the town of Garruchas. **Line B** services the southern beaches heading towards the town of Carboneras and most of the beach bars and clubs in that direction. Check the main bus stop or the tourist office for schedules. The main **tourist office** (☎/fax 950 61 50 25; open M-F 8am-3pm, Sa 10:30am-1:30pm), **police** (☎950 47 20 00), and **post office** (open M-F 8:30am-2:30pm, Sa 9:30am-1pm) are all in Pl. Nueva, although there is also another tourist office on Po. del Mediterraneo on the beach across the street from the large shopping center (same hours as the main office). **Postal code:** 04638.

ACCOMMODATIONS. Finding a bed at the last minute in Mojácar can be difficult, especially in high season (July and Aug.) when the city is taken over by partying tourists. Those wishing to stay on the beachfront have several options along Po. del Mediterraneo. **Hostal Flamenco ❸**, Po. Mediterraneo, s/n, 1 block past Star Moto rental coming from town, has simple and airy rooms with bath, TV, and A/C. All doubles have terraces overlooking the sea, and guests can use the swimming pool across the road for relief after a day in saltwater. (☎950 47 82 27. Sept.-May singles €24, with terrace €30; doubles €42. June-Aug. €30/€35/ €60.) The five elegant bedrooms at **Pensión Torreón ❷**, C. Jazmín, 4, are decorated with a resort aesthetic, which is appropriate since they open onto fantastic oceanfront views. From Pl. Nueva, follow C. Indalo and take the second right on C. Enmedio, then take a left downhill along C. Unión, and a right at the end of the hill onto C. Jazmín. (☎950 47 52 59. Call early to reserve a room. Doubles with shared bath €36.) The simple but pleasant accommodations at **Casa Justa ❶**, C. Morote, 7, give you the most for your money. From Pl. Nueva, take a right on C. Alcalde Jacino, a left on C. Estacion Nueva, a right on C. Esteve, a sharp right again and go down the hill to C. Morote; the hostel is on the left. (☎950 47 83 72. Singles €15, doubles €24-42.)

FOOD. You'll find more variety and better value in town than at the beach, although the fresh seafood restaurants with their feet in the sand are occasionally worth the splurge. **Pizzeria Pulcinella ❶**, C. Puntica, 5, three blocks from Pl. Nueva (follow the large green signs), caters to the tourist but still prepares some of the best Italian cuisine in town. (☎950 47 84 01. Pizzas €4.66-7.50, pasta €5.85. Open Tu-Su 8pm-midnight. MC/V.) If you wish to dine close to the beach, or are just too lazy to schlep uphill, try **Focus ❶**, Po. del Mediterraneo, 325, for lunch. Order from the short list of international favorites like club sandwiches (€3.90) and chef salads (€6) or from the daily *menú*. (☎950 47 25 85. Open M-Sa noon-6pm.) For dinner, head to **La Cantina ❷**, Po. del Mediterraneo, 2, in Tito's Beach complex, for quite possibly the most authentic tacos and quesadillas (€5-7) in southern Spain. Never mind the Dutch cook. (☎950 47 88 41. Open daily 7:30pm-midnight.)

ENTERTAINMENT AND BEACHES. Tourists come to Mojácar for the beaches. Buses run twice an hour between the town and beach and along the shore (see **practical information,** above). In town, buses leave from the stop below Pl. Nueva. From the beach, get on at a stop along Po. del Mediterraneo. There are many beaches to choose from, from the crowded **Playa del Cantal** and **Playa del Cueva del Lobo** to the more sedate **Playa Piedra Villazar. Playa de las Ventanicas** marks the start of a gorgeous palm-lined path that stretches several kilometers to the south. The best beaches are to the right at the bottom of the hill from town.

Mojácar pulses with nightlife. Tented *chiringuitos* (beach bars) sprawl out along the water by Po. del Mediterraneo and are the most popular places to begin (or end) a night. Go by car or scooter if you can; buses stop running at 11pm, taxis disappear at sundown, and walking the poorly lit highway is a dangerous alternative. Some of the best *chiringuitos* include **Tito's,** Po. del Mediterraneo, 2, on Playa de las Ventanicas, which serves excellent margaritas (€3.60-4.50) in a relaxed setting and holds open-air jazz festivals every summer; call for schedules. (☎629 48 25 69. Open daily 10am-8pm. Internet access from bar €0.60 per 30min.) **El Cid** and **El Patio,** both on Playa del Cantal, offer a similarly laid back atmosphere amidst palm trees and tiki torches. (Beer €2. Both open daily 10am-1:30am.) An upscale *chiringuito* is **Lua** on Playa de las Ventanicas, about a block from Tito's heading toward the main bus stop on Po. del Mediterraneo. (Beer €2.10. Open daily noon-4am.) Pre-game before the *discoteca* at the hip new cocktail lounge **Oasis,** right next door to Tito's. (Cocktails €5-6. Open daily 7pm-3am.) A popular *discoteca* is **Pachá,** Po. del Mediterraneo, where palm trees grace the bar. For a midnight dip to sober up before bed, the pool at **Master Disco,** on the highway between the beach and the town, is open until 5am. (☎950 46 81 33.) Back in town, expats run more laid-back watering holes. **Time and Place,** in Pl. Flores, serves soothing drinks to a sunburnt crowd. (☎950 47 25 38. Open W-M 7pm-1:30am.) Because Mojácar has more than 19 pubs and discos and over 11 beach bars, the "in" place seems to be changing constantly; pick up the free *Mojácar Viva* leaflet at the tourist office for more detailed info. In the second week of June, Mojácar goes haywire with the **Festival de Moros y Cristianos,** a week filled with beautiful costumes of both sides of *la Reconquista,* loud parades, and revelry. War and reconciliation are recreated as Christian troops surround the Moorish city, fire rockets, make speeches, and later join the night-long *fiesta* in peace.

RONDA ☎952

The picturesque "old town," with its narrow stone streets and plethora of sites, is separated from the new by a 100m gorge. From the bridge which spans it, one can look out across miles of rolling farms that spread out from the city's lofty perch. Ronda (pop. 38,000) was a pivotal commercial center in Roman times. Fortunes dwindled under Moorish rule after Al Mutadid ibn Abbad drowned the ruling lord in his bath and annexed the city for Sevilla. More recently, Ronda—the birthplace of modern bullfighting—has attracted such forlorn artists as Rainer Maria Rilke, who wrote his Spanish Elegies here, and Orson Welles, whose ashes are buried on a bull farm outside of town. Brimming with sights, Ronda makes an excellent base for exploring the *pueblos blancos*.

TRANSPORTATION

The **train** and **bus stations** are in the new city three blocks away from each other on Av. Andalucía. To reach the tourist office and the town center from the **train station,** turn right on Av. Andalucía and follow it through Pl. Merced past the **bus station** (it becomes C. San José) to its end.

Trains: Av. Alférez Provisional (☎902 24 02 02). **Ticket office,** C. Infantes, 20 (☎952 87 16 62). Open M-F 10am-2pm and 6-8:30pm. To: **Algeciras** (2hr., 4 per day 7:10am-8:28pm, €5.66); **Madrid** (4½hr.; 7:35am, 4:35pm; €52.32). Change at Bobadilla for: **Granada** (3hr., 3 per day 8:44am-5:58pm, €10.11); **Málaga** (2hr., 4 per day 7:50am-4:45pm, €8).

Buses: Pl. Concepción García Redondo, 2 (☎952 18 70 61 or 952 87 22 62), near Av. Andalucía. To: **Cádiz** (4hr., 4 per day 9:30am-5:30pm, €11.08); **Málaga** (2½hr.; 5 per weekday 6am-7:30pm, fewer on weekends; €8.09); **Marbella** (1½hr., 4 per day 6:30am-7:45pm, €4.73); **Sevilla** (2½hr.; M-F 5 per day 7am-7pm, Sa-Su 3-4 per day 7am-7pm; €8.69).

Taxis: (☎952 87 23 16 or 670 20 74 38). From the train station to Pl. España €3.80.

ORIENTATION AND PRACTICAL INFORMATION

The 18th-century **Puente Nuevo** connects Ronda's old and new sections. On the new side of the city, **Carrera Espinel** (the main street, including the pedestrian walkway known as **C. la Bola**) runs perpendicular to C. Virgen de la Paz. Cra. Espinel intersects C. Virgen de la Paz between the bullring and Pl. España.

Tourist Office: Po. Blas Infante (☎952 18 71 19; fax 952 18 71 47), across from the bullring in a sleek, black building. **Regional Tourist Office:** Pl. España, 1 (☎952 87 12 72). Open M-F 9am-7pm, Sa-Su 10am-2pm.

Currency Exchange: Santander Central Hispano, Ctra. Espinel, 17 (☎902 24 24 24), near C. Remedios.Open M-F 8:30am-2pm, Sa 8:30am-1pm.

Luggage Storage: At the **bus station** (€3 per day). Open daily 9am-8pm.

Emergency: ☎092. **Police:** Pl. Duquesa de Parcent, 3 (☎952 87 71 25).

Medical Emergency: ☎952 87 17 73. **Centro de Salud** (☎952 87 56 75), on the road to El Burgo.

Internet Access: Abolengo@Bocateria Internet, C. Niño, 6 (☎952 19 02 33), off Pl. Merced. €2 per hr. Open daily 10am-2am.

Post Office: C. Virgen de la Paz, 20 (☎952 87 25 57), across from Pl. Toros. **Lista de Correos.** Open M-F 8:30am-2:30pm, Sa 9:30am-1pm. **Postal Code:** 29400.

ACCOMMODATIONS

Most budget lodgings are concentrated in the new city near the bus station, along the streets perpendicular to Carrera Espinel—try C. Naranja and C. Lorenzo Borrego. Expect room shortages during the *Feria de Ronda* in September.

Hotel Goyesca, C. Infante, 39 (☎952 19 00 49; fax 952 19 06 57; www.andaluciahoteles.com). Beautiful apartment-like rooms with living room, washing machine, bath, and TV surround a fragrant courtyard. Breakfast included. Doubles €72. MC/V. ❹

Hostal González, C. San Vincente de Paul, 3 (☎952 87 14 45). Clean and sunny rooms. The best budget deal in town. Singles €10; doubles €16. ❶

Hostal Ronda Sol, C. Almendra, 11 (☎952 87 44 97). Spotless, pleasant rooms surround a leafy patio. Singles €10.30; doubles €17; triples €25. ❶

Hotel Morales, C. Sevilla, 51 (☎952 87 15 38; fax 952 18 70 02). With its myriad framed maps, the lobby is a cartographer's fantasy. New rooms, all with bath, some with TV. Singles €18-21; doubles €33-39. MC/V. ❷

FOOD

Restaurants and cafes abound in Ronda, although many are geared to tourists and tend to be overpriced. Stay away from Pl. España and check out some of the listings below. Rabbit and stewed bull's tail are local specialties.

A WHOLE LOT OF BULL Bullfighting *aficionados* charge over to Ronda's **Plaza de Toros,** Spain's oldest bullring (est. 1785) and cradle of the modern *corrida.* The **Museo Taurino** inside tells the story of local hero Pedro Romero, the first matador to brave the beasts *a pie* (on foot) and to use the red cape. (☎952 87 15 39. Open daily Nov.-Feb. 10am-6pm; Mar.-Apr. 15 10am-7pm; Apr. 16-Oct. 10am-8pm. €4.) Romero killed his first bull at age 17 in 1771, the start of a glorious career: "From 1781-1799, it can be said that I killed in each year 200 bulls, whose sum totals 5600 bulls, yet I am persuaded that there may have been more." Though no mathematician (if you're a nerd, do the math and see how he relied on hyperbole rather than reality), Romero knew his way around the ring. The museum displays heads of bulls legendary for their ferocity and bloodied matador shirts, including the shirt of Francisco Rivera ("Paquirri"), who was gored to death in 1984. Elaborate *trajes de luces,* the traditional costumes of the bullfighters, are kept behind glass cases. An exhibit on 20th-century bullfighting showcases photos of Orson Welles and Ernest Hemingway. In early September, the Plaza de Toros hosts *corridas goyescas* (bullfights in traditional costumes) as part of the **Feria de Ronda.** The town fills to capacity—book rooms months ahead.

Relax Bar and Restaurant, C. los Remedios, 27 (☎952 87 72 07; www.relaxcafebar.com). Red walls and candle-lit tables invite diners for exquisite vegetarian fare. *Tapas* €1, salads €4-5, and pastas €5.90. Vegan options. Happy Hour (Tu, Th, F 10-11pm) offers half-priced beer and wine. Open M-F 1-4pm and 8pm-midnight. ❶

Carmelitas Descalzas, Pasaje S. Juan de la Cruz, 1 (☎952 87 29 65), to the left of the church entrance. A divine pastry shop. Place your money on the round table, and a cloistered nun will fill your order. €1.50-2.50 for ¼kg of pastries. Open daily 10:15am-1:15pm and 4:45-6:45pm. ❶

Pizzería Ristorante Italiano Nonno Peppe, C. Nueva, 18 (☎952 87 28 50). Fabulous pizzas (€3.50-8) and pastas (€3.50-6) with many ingredients imported from Italy. Wide array of Italian desserts (€1.55-3.31). Open daily noon-4:30pm and 8pm-1am. ❶

Restaurante Hnos. Macías, C. Pedro Romero, 3 (☎952 87 42 38). Delicious cuisine elegantly served on a quaint pedestrian throroughfare. Exquisite pork entrees and rice desserts. Seafood and vegetable entrees (€5.50-12). Open daily 8am-1am. MC/V. ❷

SIGHTS

BRIDGES. Carved by the Río Guadalevír, Ronda's gorge falls 100m below the **Puente Nuevo,** across from Pl. España. Arrested highwaymen were once held in a prison cell beneath the bridge's center; during the Civil War, political prisoners were thrown from the top. Two other bridges span the gap and can be reached by walking on C. Santo Domingo past the Casa del Rey Moro: the innovative **Puente Viejo** was rebuilt in 1616 over an earlier Arab bridge, and the **Puente San Miguel** (or **Puente Árabe**) is a prime Andalucian hybrid of a Roman base and Arab arches.

CASA DEL REY MORO. A colonnaded walkway leads to the House of the Moorish King, which, despite its name and Moorish facade, dates from the 18th century. Sixty meters below the palace lies an Islamic well constructed during the 1300s. Four hundred Christian prisoners were once employed in the arduous task of drawing water; today visitors climb down passageways and stone steps to survey the ravine's depths. Don't miss the view of the countryside from the serene Forestier gardens, built in 1915 and located near the museum exit. *(Cuesta de Santo Domingo, 9. ☎952 18 72 00. Open daily summer 10am-8pm; winter 10am-7pm. €4, children €2.)*

IGLESIA DE SANTA MARÍA. Following the Christian reconquest of Ronda in 1485, this church was slowly assembled over the next two centuries. Part Gothic, part Renaissance, part Baroque, its incense-filled nave provides a view of the town's evolution. A small Moorish arch near the entrance and a verse from the Qur'an engraved behind the sacristy are the last vestiges of the mosque which once stood in its place. *(Off C. Marqués de Salvatierra. ☎952 87 22 46. Open daily summer 10am-8pm; winter 10am-6pm. €2, groups €1.50 per person.)*

PALACIO DE MONDRAGÓN. Originally inhabited by Don Fernando Valenzuela, a prominent minister under Carlos III, this 17th-century palace has since been transformed into a fascinating anthropological museum. Exhibits on ancient life in the area fill former sitting rooms and libraries. No doubt Don Fernando would not have approved of the Neolithic hut replicated in his bedroom. *(☎952 87 84 50. Open summer M-F 10am-7pm, Sa-Su 10am-3pm; winter M-F 10am-6pm, Sa-Su 10am-3pm. €2, students and groups €1 per person, under 14 and disabled free.)*

OTHER SIGHTS. Frequented by Hemingway and widely regarded as the world's most beautiful bullring, Ronda's **Plaza de Toros** was inaugurated in 1785, placing it among the oldest in Spain. *Corridas* take place in September; tours are available all year. *(Virgen de la Paz, 15. ☎952 87 15 39; fax 952 87 03 79. Open daily Nov.-Feb. 10am-6pm, Mar.-Apr. 15 10am-7pm, Apr. 16-Oct. 10am-8pm. €4.)* For something just as bloody, visit the **Museo del Bandolero,** C. Armiñán, 59, dedicated to presenting "pillage, theft, and rebellion, in Spain since Roman times." *(☎952 87 77 85. Open daily summer 10am-8:30pm, winter 10am-6pm. €2.70.)* The **Museo de Caza** displays mounted hunting trophies from four continents to the melodious strains of Spanish soft rock. With its mountains of taxidermy, it's definitely not a good place for vegetarians. *(C. Armiñán, 59. ☎952 87 78 62. Open daily 10:30am-7pm. €1.20.)*

NIGHTLIFE

At night, Rondans congregate in the pubs and *discotecas* along C. Jerez and the streets behind Pl. Socorro, including C. Pozo. Popular with young Spaniards is **Bar Antonio,** C. San José 4, which starts drawing a crowd between midnight and 1am. (Open M-Sa 7am-1:30am.) For a more tranquil evening, head to **Tetería Al-Zahra,** C. Tiendas, 19, where patrons drink yogurt smoothies and sip tea from all over the world. The Islamic decor, floor pillows, and soothing New Age tunes invite long stays. (☎952 87 16 98. Open W-M 4pm-midnight.)

DAYTRIP FROM RONDA

CUEVAS DE LA PILETA

By car, take highway C-339 north (Ctra. Sevilla from the new city). The turnoff to Benaoján and the caves is about 13km out, in front of an abandoned restaurant. Taxis will go round-trip from Ronda for €43. A cheaper alternative is the train, via the town of Benaoján. Trains run to Benaoján from Ronda (7:10, 9:47am, 2:34pm; return 9:01am, 1:21, 5:13, 7:51pm. €1.36). From the train station at Benaoján, it's a tough but scenic 1-1½hr. climb to the caves. The hike is mostly uphill and there is little shade; bring water. With your back to the train station, exit left and follow the road parallel to the tracks for 100m until the sign for Hotel Molino del Santo. Take a right and continue past the hotel until you see a sign on the left for the caves. Follow the wide path for 1km up to a dilapidated farm; on the right, just after the abandoned refrigerator, is a goat path leading up to the hill. There, near the summit, is a narrow highway; turn left and follow the road for 500m. A walkway from the train station to the caves is under construction. Caves open daily 10am-1pm and 4-6pm. Tours last 1hr. Groups up to 8 €6.50 per person; 9 or more €6.01 per person.

Twenty-two kilometers west of Ronda are the **Cuevas de la Pileta** (☎952 16 73 43 or 952 16 72 02), a dark expanse of stalactites and Paleolithic paintings, stretching for over a kilometer underground. More than 22,000 years ago local inhabitants took refuge in these caves, painting the walls with cryptic symbols and animal imagery. The highlights are the *Yegua preñada* (pregnant mare) and the beautifully preserved *Pez* (fish). The abstract depiction of human genitalia in the *sala finale* is somewhat more open to criticism. The chamber walls are darkened with soot and small human bones have been discovered in a number of locations; it's believed that the caves held special ceremonial significance during Neolithic times and were the scene of child sacrifices. Today, children are still welcome (€2.40-3), although to preserve the interior climate, only 25 people are admitted at a time. Guides lead gas-lantern tours in Spanish and English. Reservations are possible in the winter, but long queues line up in the summer. Wear comfortable shoes and dress warmly—even in the summer, the caves are 30°F colder than outside.

ANTEQUERA ☎952

Few sunsets rival those seen from atop Antequera's old Moorish fortress, with views extending over the town and into the mountains. The Romans gave Antequera (pop. 42,000) its name, but older civilizations preceded them. Their mark can be seen on the outskirts of town in the pre-Roman *dólmenes* (funerary chambers built from rock slabs), the oldest in Europe. The alluring Sierra de Torcal, a Mars-like wasteland of eroded rock, is another nearby attraction. Wise travelers kick back here for a few days of inland visual splendor among Antequera's rolling hills and rich history.

TRANSPORTATION

Trains: Av. Estación (☎902 24 02 02). To: **Algeciras** (4hr., 3 per day 8:23am-7:25pm, €10.11); **Granada** (2hr., 4 per day 8:30am-7:52pm, €5.76-6.26); **Ronda** (1½hr., 3 per day 8:15am-7pm, €4.81); **Sevilla** (2½hr., 5 per day 9:28am-1:53am, €10) via **Bobadilla.**

Buses: Po. García del Olmo (☎952 84 13 65), near the Parador Nacional. To: **Córdoba** (2¼hr.; 9:45am, 5:45pm; €7.22); **Granada** (2hr., 5 per day 6:30am-1am, €5.98); **Málaga** (45min., 9-12 per day 8:15am-10pm, €3.36); **Murcia** (5½hr., 9:45am, €20.10); **Sevilla** (2¼hr., 7 per day 4:10am-6:45pm, €9.58).

Taxis: Taxi Radio Antequera (☎952 84 55 30) services Antequera and will go to Sierra de Tocal. From the town center to either station costs €3.60, but the walk is not long.

ORIENTATION AND PRACTICAL INFORMATION

From the train station, it's a 10min. hike up a shadeless hill along Av. Estación to the town center. At the top, continue straight past the market, turn right on C. Encarnación, and go past the Museo Municipal to reach **Plaza San Sebastián,** the city center. Alternatively, from the bus station it is just under a 10min. walk down a shadeless hill. Exit the station and turn right on Ctra. del Albergue, then left onto C. Almeda de Andalucía which, keeping to the right, becomes C. Infante Don Fernando and leads to the tourist office and Pl. San Sebastián.

Tourist Office: Pl. San Sebastián, 7 (☎/fax 952 70 25 05). Open June-Sept. M-Sa 10am-2pm and 5-8pm, Su 10am-2pm; Oct.-May M-Sa 9:30am-1:30pm and 4-7pm, Su 10am-2pm.

Banks: Santander Central Hispano, C. Infante Fernando, 51 (☎902 24 24 24). Open M-F 8:30am-2pm, Sa 8:30am-1pm.

Laundry: Pressto, Merecillas, 7 (☎952 84 55 44).

Emergency: ☎112. **Medical Emergency:** ☎952 84 19 66. **Municipal Police:** on Av. Legión (☎952 70 81 04).

Pharmacy: on C. Encarnación, near C. Calzada. Open M-F 9:30am-1:30pm and 5-8:30pm, Sa 10am-1:30pm.

Hospital: Hospital Comarcál, C. Polígono Industrial, 67 (☎952 84 62 63).

Internet: Ant@kira.net, C. Barrero, 20 (☎952 84 29 53; fax 952 70 66 37; www.antakira.net), off C. Calzada. Internet access €1.80 per hr. Open M-Th 10:30am-2pm and 4:30pm-1am, F 10:30am-2pm and 4:30pm-2am, Sa 11am-2pm and 4:30pm-2am, Su 2:30pm-1am.

Post Office: C. Nájera (☎952 84 20 83). Open M-F 8am-2pm, Sa 9:30am-1pm. **Postal Code:** 29200.

ACCOMMODATIONS

Pensión Toril, C. Toril, 3-5 (☎/fax 952 84 31 84), off Pl. San Francisco. Grandfatherly owner lets bright, clean rooms with fans and TV. Locals gather on the patio to chat over dominoes. The restaurant downstairs has entrees for €3 and a filling *menú* accompanied by a bottle of wine for €5.40. Meals served daily 1-4pm and 8-9:30pm. Parking included. Singles €9.60, with bath €12; doubles €20, with bath €24. ❶

Pensión Madrona, C. Calzada, 25 (☎952 84 00 14), through Bar Madrona, across from the supermarket. Newly renovated, with A/C, TV, bath, and heating. Restaurant downstairs offers a tasty *menú* (€4-9). Singles €17.69; doubles €24.76. AmEx/MC/V. ❷

Hotel Antequera, C. Infante Don Fernando, 40 (☎/fax 952 84 30 90; www.hotelcastilladeantequera.com). Pleasant, sunny rooms with phone, TV, bath, and A/C. Singles €25; doubles €39. AmEx/MC/V. ❸

FOOD

For traditional cuisine, your best bet is to sample a *menú* at a *pensión* listed above. Other options exist for those weary of pork and seafood. Get fresh produce, fish, and meats at the **market,** in Pl. San Francisco (open M-Sa 8am-3pm). **Mercadona,** C. Calzada, 18, has all the basics. (Open M-Sa 9am-9pm. MC/V.)

La Espuela, C. San Agustín, 1 (☎952 70 30 31; fax 952 70 34 24), on a narrow street where C. San Agustín meets C. Infante Fernando. An elegant Italian restaurant serving pizza and pasta, as well as fish, meat, and bona fide veggie options (€8-16). *Menú* €13.50. Open daily noon-4pm and 7-11pm. MC/V. ❸

Manolo Bar, C. Calzada, 14 (☎952 84 10 15), downhill from the market. This dark, cavernous bar is filled with cowboy paraphernalia and good-humored patrons. Ultra-cheap *tapas* (€1). Open W-Th 5pm-1am, F-Sa 5pm-3am. ❶

El Angelote, Pl. Coso Viejo (☎952 70 34 65), off C. Encarnación in front of the Museo Municipal. Open daily noon-5pm and 7:30-11:30pm. MC/V. ❷

SIGHTS

LOS DÓLMENES. Antequera's three ancient caves are the oldest in Europe. Once burial chambers with storerooms for the riches of the dead, they were long ago looted but remain highly worthy of spelunking. Marvel at the 200-ton roof hauled five miles to the **Cueva de Menga** (2500 BC). Carved millennia ago, the four figures engraved on the chamber walls typify Mediterranean Stone Age art. **Cueva de Viera**

THE BIG SPLURGE

SLEEPING IN PARADISE

Location, location, location; **Hotel America,** settled in the heart of the elegantly beautiful Alhambra, offers Granada's most unique lodging experience. If you are willing to shell out a fair share of euros, you can tell friends back home that you spent the night within the walls of the Alhambra, just like Washington Irving.

Don't be discouraged by the name; Hotel America isn't a stars-and-stripes themed homage to the good ol' US of A. The hotel has charming, spacious, and cozy rooms which overlook the Generalife. Colorful woven bedspreads and curtains from *Las Alpujarras* add a bright, cheery touch. The hotel has a beautiful internal courtyard with a vine canopy where you can sit outside and dine by the light of hanging lanterns. Meals are home-cooked and reasonably priced. The sitting room is crowded with interesting old family heirlooms including china, pottery, photographs, rocking chairs, ornaments, and sofas.

Unfortunately, America isn't an undiscovered secret. The hotel's beauty is well-known, and guests must make reservations at least two months in advance.

Real de la Alhambra, 53 (☎958 22 74 71; fax 22 74 70). All room rates include breakfast. Singles €70.75; doubles €110. ❺

(2000 BC), uncovered in 1905, begins with a narrow passageway leading deep into the darkness of the earth. Somewhat farther afield, **Cueva de El Romel** (1800 BC) is still explored by visitors with gas lamps. Relive eighth-grade *Tom Sawyer* fantasies amidst the gentle sizzle of gas and the warmly illuminated domed ceilings of the interior. *(It is a 1km walk to reach the Cuevas de Menga and Viera; follow signs toward Granada from the town center (20min.), and watch for a small sign past the gas station. To reach Cueva de Romeral from the other caves, continue on the highway to Granada for another 3km. On the left side of the street, across from Hotel Restaurante Camas, a gravel road leads to a narrow path bordered by cyprus trees. Take this path across the tracks to reach the cave. Sometimes the guard falls asleep; if the gate is locked, give a shout. All 3 caves open Tu 9am-3:30pm, W-Sa 9am-6pm, Su 9:30am-2pm. Free.)*

OTHER SIGHTS. Back in town, all that remains of the **Alcazaba** are its two towers, the wall between them, and some well-trimmed hedges. The view of the city at dusk is magnificent. *(Open Tu-F 10:30am-2pm and 4:30-6:30pm, Sa 10:30am-2pm, Su 11:30am-2pm. Free.)* Next door, the towering **Colegiata de Santa María** was the first church in Andalucía to incorporate Renaissance style. *(Open Tu-F 10:30am-2pm and 4:30-7:30pm, Sa 10:30am-2pm, Su 11:30am-2pm. Free.)* The plaza in front of the church offers views across the city to the **Peña de los Enamorados** (Lovers' Rock), a small mountain which looks exactly like the Sphinx lying down, if you tilt your head sideways. Legend has it that a Christian man and his Moorish girlfriend, fearing separation by invading soldiers, leaped to their deaths from atop the rock. Downhill, the **Museo Municipal** exhibits avant-garde 1970s paintings by native son Cristóbal Toral alongside dozens of Roman artifacts, including the graceful **Efebo,** a rare bronze statue of a Roman page. *(☎952 70 40 21. Open Tu-F 10am-1:30pm and 4-6pm, Sa 10am-1:30pm, Su 11am-1:30pm. €2.)* The new **Museo Conventual de las Descalzas** is housed in the Convento de las Carmelitas Descalzas and exhibits 16th- and 17th-century paintings, sculptures, and bronze works. *(Open Tu-F 10am-2pm and 5-7pm, Sa 10am-12:30pm and 5-7pm, Su 10am-12:30pm. €2.10.)*

DAYTRIP FROM ANTEQUERA

SIERRA DE TORCAL

Two-thirds of the 13km to the Sierra de Torcal can be covered by bus. Ask the driver to let you off at the turnoff for El Torcal; from there it is a 5km walk. Casado ***buses*** *(☎952 84 19 57) leave from Antequera (M-F 1pm, €2); the return bus leaves from the turnoff (M-F 4:15pm). You can also* *take a **taxi** (have the tourist office call one for you, or the fare may be higher) to the refugio (round-trip €18), and the driver will wait for 1hr.*

A garden of wind-sculpted boulders, the Sierra de Torcal glows like the surface of a barren and distant planet. The central peak **El Torcal** (1369m) takes up most of the horizon, but the surrounding clumps of eroded rocks are even more extraordinary. Several trails circle the summit. The green arrow path (1½km) takes about 45min.; the red arrow path (4½km) takes over 2hr. All but the green path require a guided tour; call the **Centro de Información** for more details. (☎952 03 13 89. Open daily 10am-8pm.) Each path begins and ends at the *refugio* (lodge) at the mountain base. Try to catch the sunset and the spectacular mountain view from the striking **Mirador de las Ventanillas.**

GRANADA ☎958

When Moorish ruler Boabdil fled Granada, the last Muslim stronghold in Spain, his mother berated him for casting a longing look back at the Alhambra—the magnificent palace which crowns the highest point of the city—saying, "You do well to weep as a woman for what you could not defend as a man." Indeed, throughout history, Granada has aroused the passions of all those who have gazed upon her many splendors. To this day, visitors are still captivated by the charm, the mystery, and the indescribable sense of romance that emanates from the very stones of its ancient and winding streets. As the famous song begins, *"Granada, tierra soñada por mi..."*—Granada, land of which I have dreamed.

Conquered by invading Muslim armies in 711, Granada blossomed into one of Europe's wealthiest, most refined cities. As Christian armies turned back the tide of Moorish conquest in the 13th century, the city became the last Muslim outpost on the peninsula, surrounded by a unified Christian kingdom. Due to the relentless Christian onslaught and growing disputes and corruption within the ruling dynasty, Moorish domination over Granada began to wane by the end of the 15th century. Fernando and Isabel capitalized on the ensuing chaos, finally capturing Boabdil—the last Moorish ruler of Granada—and the Alhambra on the momentous night of January 1, 1492. Although the Christians torched all the mosques and the lower city, embers of Granada's Arab past still linger. The Albaícin, an enchanting maze of Moorish houses and twisting alleys, is Spain's best-preserved Arab quarter and the only part of the Muslim city to survive *la Reconquista* intact.

TRANSPORTATION

Flights: Airport (☎958 24 52 37), 17km west of the city. **Autocares J. Gonzales** (☎958 13 13 09) runs a bus from Gran Vía, in front of the cathedral, to the airport. (5 per day 8am-7pm, €3). A **taxi** to the airport costs €15. **Iberia** (☎902 40 05 00) flies to **Barcelona** (1¼hr., 2-3 per day) and **Madrid** (45min., 2-3 per day). Customer service representatives available by phone M-F 9am-1:45pm and 4-7pm.

Trains: RENFE Station Av. Andaluces (☎902 24 02 02). From Pl. Isabel la Católica, follow Gran Vía to the end, then bear left on Av. Constitución, or take bus #3, 4, 5, 6, 9, or 11 from Gran Vía to the stop marked Constitución 3. Turn left on Av. Andaluces; RENFE is at the end. To: **Algeciras** (5-7hr., 3 per day 7:15am-5:50pm, €16.29); **Almería** (3hr., 4 per day 10am-9:05pm, €10.86); **Antequera** (2hr., 3 per day 7:15am-5:50pm, €6.12); **Barcelona** (12-13hr.; daily 10:10pm, M, Th, Sa 8:30am; €38-46.16); **Madrid** (5-6hr., 7:55am and 4:40pm, €26-32.60); **Ronda** (3-4hr., 3 per day 7:15am-5:50pm, €10.80); **Sevilla** (4-5hr., 4 per day 8:18am-8:15pm, €16).

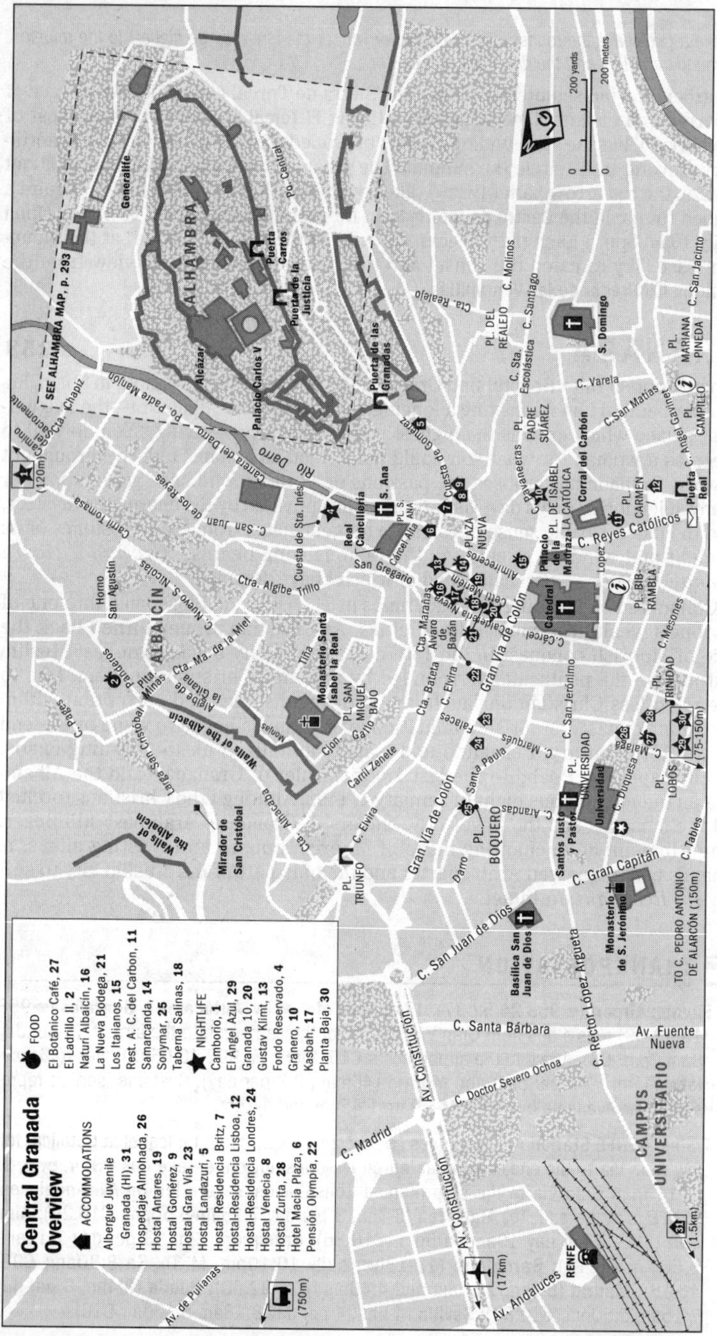
Central Granada Overview
ACCOMMODATIONS
Albergue Juvenile Granada (HI), 31
Hospedaje Almohada, 26
Hostal Antares, 19
Hostal Gomérez, 9
Hostal Gran Vía, 23
Hostal Landazuri, 5
Hostal Residencia Britz, 7
Hostal-Residencia Lisboa, 12
Hostal-Residencia Londres, 24
Hostal Venecia, 8
Hostal Zurita, 28
Hotel Macía Plaza, 6
Pensión Olympia, 22
FOOD
El Botánico Café, 27
El Ladrillo II, 2
Naturi Albaicín, 16
La Nueva Bodega, 21
Los Italianos, 15
Rest. A. C. del Carbon, 11
Samarcanda, 14
Sonymar, 25
Taberna Salinas, 18
NIGHTLIFE
Camborio, 1
El Ángel Azul, 29
Granada 10, 20
Gustav Klimt, 13
Fondo Reservado, 4
Granero, 10
Kasbah, 17
Planta Baja, 30
SEE ALHAMBRA MAP, p. 293
ALHAMBRA
Generalife
Alcázar
Palacio Carlos V
Puerta de la Justicia
Puerta Carros
Puerta de las Granadas
ALBAICÍN
Walls of the Albaicín
Mirador de San Cristóbal
Monasterio Santa Isabel la Real
Real Cancillería
S. Ana
PLAZA NUEVA
Catedral
Palacio de la Madraza
Corral del Carbón
S. Domingo
Santos Justo y Pastor
Universidad
Basílica San Juan de Dios
Monasterio de S. Jerónimo
CAMPUS UNIVERSITARIO
RENFE
Gran Vía de Colón
C. Reyes Católicos
Av. Constitución
C. San Juan de Dios
C. Gran Capitán
Río Darro
Carrera del Darro
PL. TRIUNFO
PL. BIB-RAMBLA
PL. DE ISABEL LA CATÓLICA
Puerta Real
TO C. PEDRO ANTONIO DE ALARCÓN (150m)
200 yards
200 meters

Buses: All major intercity bus routes originate from the **bus station** on the outskirts of Granada on Ctra. Madrid, near C. Arzobispo Pedro de Castro.

Alsina Graells (☎958 18 54 80) to: **Almería** (2¼hr., 12 per day 6:45am-9:30pm, €8.80); **Almuñecar** (1½hr., 11 per day 7:30am-8pm, €5.10); **Antequera** (2hr., 3-5 per day 3-7pm, €5.82); **Cádiz** (4hr., noon and 3:30pm, €23.55); **Córdoba** (3hr., 10 per day 7:30am-8pm, €10.01); **Jaén** (1½hr., 15 per day 7am-9:30pm, €5.82); **Málaga** (2hr., 16 per day 7am-9pm, €7.79); **Sevilla** (3hr., 9 per day 8am-3am, €15.46).

Bacoma (☎958 15 75 57). To: **Alicante** (6hr., 5 per day, €21.06); **Barcelona** (14hr., 3 per day, €49.80); **Valencia** (8hr., 4 per day, €30.87). All buses run 10:15am-1:45am.

Junta de Andalucía, the regional government, charters buses to **Veleta** from the Granada bus station. Call ahead (☎630 95 97 39) for reservations and information. (45 min.; 5-7 per day 9am-6:40pm; €3 one-way, €4.80 round-trip, 50% discount for seniors and children 4-9m, under 3 free.

La Línea runs to: **Algeciras** (5hr., 6 per day 9am-8pm, €16.23); the villages in **Las Alpujarras** (10:30am, noon, 5:15pm; €6-12); **Gibraltar** (4½hr., 8am and 3pm, €15.48); **Madrid** (5hr., 14 per day 7am-1:30am, €12.45).

Public Transportation: (☎958 81 37 11). Important buses include: "Bus Alhambra" #30 from Pl. Nueva to the Alhambra; #31 from Pl. Nueva to the Albaícin; #10 from the bus station to the youth hostel, C. de Ronda, C. Recogidas, and C. Acera de Darro; and #3 from the bus station to Av. Constitución, Gran Vía, and Pl. Isabel la Católica. Rides €0.85, bonobus (10 tickets) €5.02. Caja General de Ahorros de Granada, Pl. de Isabel la Catolica, 6, sells a "bono turístico" pass (€18.03) good for 1 week, which provides direct access to the Alhambra and several other sights throughout Granada without having to wait in line at the ticket counter. Also includes 10 free trips on any local bus lines to destinations within the city. (☎902 10 00 95. Open M-F 8:30am-2:15pm all year and November 1-March 30 also on Th 5:15-7:30pm.)

Taxis: Teletaxi, (24hr. ☎958 28 06 54), with service to Granada and environs.

Car Rental: Atasa, Pl. Cuchilleros, 1 (☎958 22 40 04). Cheapest car €276 per week with unlimited mileage and insurance. Prices rise with shorter rentals. Min. age 20, and must have had license for at least 1 year.

ORIENTATION AND PRACTICAL INFORMATION

Municipal **buses** cover practically the entire city, but the best way to explore is on foot. The geographic center of Granada is the small **Pl. de Isabel la Católica,** the intersection of the city's two main arteries, **C. de los Reyes Católicos** and **Gran Vía de Colón.** On Gran Vía, you'll find the **cathedral.** Two short blocks uphill on C. Reyes Católicos sits Pl. Nueva. Downhill, also along C. Reyes Católicos, lie Pl. Carmen, site of the **Ayuntamiento,** and Puerta Real, the six-way intersection of C. Reyes Católicos, C. Recogidos, C. Mesones, C. Acera de Darro, C. Angel Gavinet, and C. Acero del Casino. The **Alhambra** commands the steep hill up from Pl. Nueva.

Tourist Office: Oficina Provincial, Pl. Mariana Pineda, 10 (☎958 24 71 28; fax 958 22 89 16). From Pta. Real, turn right onto C. Angel Ganivet, then take a right 2 blocks later to reach the plaza. English spoken. Open M-F 9am-8pm, Sa 10am-7pm, and Su 10am-4pm. **Junta de Andalucía,** C. Mariana Pineda (☎958 22 10 22; fax 958 22 39 27; otgranada@andalucia.es). From Pta. Real, take C. Reyes Católicos to Pl. Carmen; C. Mariana Pineda is the 1st left. Hotel guide (€4.80) and brochures on hiking, hunting, and golf (€2.40). Open M-Sa 9am-7pm, Su 10am-2pm.

Currency Exchange: Santander Central Hispano, Gran Vía, 3 (☎958 21 73 00), off Pl. Isabel la Católica. Exchanges money and AmEx traveler's checks; no commission. Open May-Sept. M-F 9am-2pm; Oct.-Apr. M-Sa 9am-2pm.

American Express: C. Reyes Católicos, 31 (☎958 22 45 12), between Pl. Isabel la Católica and Pta. Real. Open M-F 9am-1:30pm and 2-9pm, Sa 10am-2pm and 3-7pm.

Gay and Lesbian Services: Juvenós, C. Lavadero de las Tablas, 15, organizes weekly activities for gay youth. **Información Homosexual Hotline** ☎958 20 06 02.

Luggage Storage: At the **train** and **bus stations** (€2.40). Open daily 4-9pm.

El Corte Inglés: C. Genil, 20 and 22 (☎958 22 32 40). Follow C. Acera del Casino from Pta. Real to C. Genil. Good map for €2.85. Open M-Sa 10am-10pm.

Foreign Language Bookstore: Metro, C. Gracia, 31 (☎958 26 15 65). Vast foreign language section. Open M-F 10am-9pm, Sa 10am-2pm.

Laundromat: C. La Paz, 19. From Pl. Trinidad, take C. Alhóndiga, turn right on C. La Paz, and walk 2 blocks. Wash €3; dry €0.90 per 15min. Open M-F 9:30am-2pm and 4:30-8:30pm, Sa 9am-2pm.

Emergency: ☎112. **Police:** C. Duquesa, 21 (☎958 24 81 00). English spoken.

Pharmacy: Farmacia Gran Vía, Gran Vía, 6 (☎958 22 29 90). Open M-F 9:30am-2pm and 5-8:30pm.

Medical Assistance: Clínica de San Cecilio, C. Dr. Oloriz, 16 (☎958 28 02 00 or 958 27 20 00), on the road to Jaén. **Ambulance:** ☎958 28 44 50.

Internet Access: Net (☎958 22 69 19) has 3 locations: C. Santa Escolástica, 13, up C. Pavaneras from Pl. Isabel la Católica; Pl. de los Girones, 3, 1 block away from first locale; C. Buensucesco, 22, 1 block from Pl. Trinidad. English spoken. €1.20 per hr. All open M-Sa 9am-1am, Su 3pm-1am.

Post Office: Pta. Real (☎958 22 48 35; fax 958 22 36 41), at Carrera del Darro and C. Angel Ganinet. **Lista de Correos** and **fax** service. Open M-F 8am-9pm, Sa 9:30am-2pm. Wires money M-F 8:30am-2:30pm. **Postal Code:** 18009.

ACCOMMODATIONS AND CAMPING

NEAR PLAZA NUEVA

Hostels line Cuesta de Gomérez, the street leading uphill to the Alhambra, to the right of Pl. Nueva. Crashing in this area is wise for those planning to spend serious time at the Alhambra complex, but these spots tend to fill up the quickest.

Hostal Venecia, Cuesta de Gomérez, 2, 3rd fl. (☎958 22 39 87). This cozy abode is one of the most appealing bargains in town, as owners Sergio and Maria del Carmen spoil their guests with attentive service and tea. Rooms near the street can be noisy. Singles €14; doubles €26; triples and quads €13 per person. ❶

Hostal Residencia Britz, Cuesta de Gomérez, 1 (☎/fax 958 22 36 52), on the corner of Pl. Nueva. Laundry €4. 24hr. reception. Singles €18; doubles €27.50, with bath €38. 6% discount off all room rates if you show reception your copy of *Let's Go.* MC/V. ❷

Hostal Landazuri, Cuesta de Gomérez, 24 (☎958 22 14 06). Plain hallways open into colorfully decorated rooms, all of which have their own motif. A rooftop terrace with potted flowers and an ivy covering provides guests with splendid views of the Alhambra and Sierra Nevada. Front door is locked after 1am every day. Singles €20, with bath €28; doubles €27/€36; suite €40. ❷

Hostal Gomérez, Cuesta de Gomérez, 10 (☎958 22 44 37). Spartan rooms with hall baths. Multilingual owner will assist guests planning longer stays. Laundry €6 per load. Singles €15; doubles €24; triples €30. ❷

Hotel Macia Plaza, Pl. Nueva, 4 (☎958 22 75 36; fax 958 22 75 33). A modern, comfortable hotel centrally located on the plaza. All rooms are carpeted, with marble baths, TV, phone, A/C. Singles €42; doubles €63; triples €84 (prices exclude 7% IVA tax). ❹

NEAR THE CATHEDRAL/UNIVERSITY

Hostels surround Pl. Trinidad, at the end of C. Mesones when coming from Pta. Real. Many *pensiones* around C. Mesones cater to students during the academic year but free up during the summer. The ones listed below are open year-round.

Hospedaje Almohada, C. Postigo de Zarate, 4 (☎958 20 74 46. If Mercedes, the proprietor, isn't in, call her cell phone at ☎627 47 25 53). From Pl. Trinidad, follow C. Duquesa to C. Málaga and take a right; it's the red door with the small sign on your right. A successful experiment in communal living: guests cook for themselves and often for each other, gathering at the end of the day to fraternize over Cruzcampo and olives in the cozy den. Laundry €5 per load. Dorms €11 per person; singles €13.50; doubles €24; triples €32.50. Discounts available for those staying longer than 1 week. ❶

Hostal Zurita, Pl. Trinidad, 7 (☎958 27 50 20). Bright rooms with floral sheets and sound-proof balcony doors. High quality beds, A/C, and 24hr. hot water. Singles €15; doubles €27, with bath €33; triples €39/€45. ❷

Hostal-Residencia Lisboa, Pl. Carmen, 29 (☎958 22 14 13 or 958 22 14 14; fax 958 22 14 87). Take C. Reyes Católicos from Pl. Isabel la Católica; Pl. Carmen is on the left. Singles €16, with bath €24; doubles €24/€35; triples €32/€47. MC/V. ❷

ALONG GRAN VÍA DE COLÓN

Hostels are sprinkled along Gran Vía. In all cases, rooms with balconies over the street are much noisier than those that open onto an inner patio.

Hostal Antares, C. Cetti Meriém, 10 (☎958 22 83 13), on the corner of C. Elvira, 1 block from the cathedral. Singles €18; doubles €30, with bath €36. ❷ Rooms with A/C and TVs available. July-Aug. doubles €45; triples €63. Sept.-May €36/€51. ❸

Hostal-Residencia Londres, Gran Vía, 29, 6th fl. (☎958 27 80 34), perched atop a fin-de-siecle edifice with multiple patios. One large bath for every 2 bedrooms. Singles €18; doubles €21; €9 for each additional person. ❷

Pensión Olympia, Alvaro de Bazán, 6 (☎958 27 82 38). From Pl. Isabel, walk 6 blocks down Gran Vía and turn right. A standard pensión with simple rooms. Singles €15; doubles €18, with shower €24, with bath €30. MC/V. ❶

Hostal Gran Vía, Gran Vía, 17 (☎958 27 92 12), about 4 blocks from Pl. Isabel la Católica. Singles with shower €18; doubles €21, with shower €24, with bath €30; triples with shower €36, with bath €42. ❷

ELSEWHERE

Albergue Juvenil Granada (HI), Ramón y Cajal, 2 (☎958 00 29 00 or 958 00 29 01; fax 958 00 29 08). From the bus station take #10; from the train station #11; ask the driver to stop at "El Estadio de la Juventud." Across the field on the left. Towels €1.50. 24hr. reception. Dorms €10-12, over 26 €14-16. Non-HI guests can join for an extra €3 per night for 6 nights.

CAMPING

Buses serve five campgrounds within 5km of Granada. Check the departure schedules at the tourist office, sit up front, and ask bus drivers to alert you to your stop.

Sierra Nevada, Av. Madrid, 107 (☎958 15 00 62; fax 958 15 09 54). Take bus #3 or 10. Shady trees, modern facilities, a large outdoor pool, and free hot showers. If you arrive when the town fair is here, stay elsewhere—you'll have clown nightmares. €3.78 per person, children under 10 €3.15. Open Mar.-Oct. ❶

María Eugenia, Ctra. Nacional, 342 (☎958 20 06 06; fax 958 20 94 10), at km 436 on the road to Málaga. Take the Santa Fé or Chauchina bus from the train station (every 30min.). €3 per person, children €2.40. Open year-round. ❶

FOOD

Granada offers a variety of ethnic restaurants to relieve those who have had a bit too much fish. North African cuisine can be found around the **Albaicín,** while more typical *menú* fare awaits in Pl. Nueva and Pl. Trinidad. The adventurous eat well in Granada—*tortilla sacromonte* (omelette with calf's brains, bull testicles, ham, shrimp, and veggies), *sesos a la romana* (batter-fried calf's brains), and *rabo de toro* (bull's tail) are common. Picnickers can gather fresh fruit and vegetables at the **market** on C. San Augustín. Get groceries at **Supermercado T. Mariscal,** C. Genil, next to El Corte Inglés (open M-F 9:30am-2pm and 5-9pm, Sa 9:30am-2pm).

NEAR PLAZA NUEVA

Plaza Nueva abounds with large, generic indoor/outdoor cafes located right on the square itself. Those seeking more authentic fare (and not the kind whose menus are translated into five different languages) would do better to look around the small side streets which lead from the plaza. The bars around Pl. Nueva, like most everywhere in Granada, offer *tapas* for **free** (with a drink).

Taberna Salinas, C. Elvira, 13 (☎958 22 14 11). Rustic tavern which serves generous portions. Share a *tabla salinas surtida* with friends (plate of cheeses, pâté, and cold cuts; €10.41), and choose from a wide selection of grilled meats and seafood for your main course (€9-11). Open daily 12:30pm-2am. ❸

La Nueva Bodega, C. Cetti Meriém, 9 (☎958 22 59 34), out of Pl. Nueva on a street off C. Elvira. Locals stake out the bar as tourists dine on hearty traditional cuisine. *Menús* €6-6.60. *Bocadillos* €1.65. Open daily noon-midnight. ❶

Restaurant Sonymar, Pl. Boquero, 6 (☎958 27 10 63). Relish in the nouveau Moorish decor of this secluded neighborhood eatery. *Menú* €5.10. Entrees €7.20-12.60. Open daily 1-4pm and 8-11:30pm. AmEx/V. ❷

THE ALBAICÍN

Wander the romantic, winding streets of the Albaicín and you'll discover a number of budget bars and restaurants on the slopes above Pl. Nueva. C. Caldereria Nueva, off C. Elvira leading from the plaza, is crammed with teahouses and cafes.

Naturi Albaicín, C. Caldereria Nueva, 10 (☎958 22 06 27). Excellent vegetarian restaurant with a serene Moroccan ambiance. Tasty options include *berenjenas rellenas* (stuffed eggplant), quiche, and *kefir* (a yogurt drink). No alcohol served. *Menús* €5.70-6.90. Open Sa-Th 1-4pm and 7-11pm, F 7-11pm. ❶

Samarcanda, C. Caldereria Vieja, 3 (☎958 21 00 04). Experience Lebanese cuisine at its finest. Excellent hummus (€6.25), couscous (€6-9), and shish kebab (€10) can be ordered a la carte, or for €38, ask for a *Mesa Libanesa* platter to share; it comes with a bottle of Lebanese wine. Open Th-Tu 1-5pm and 7:30pm-midnight. ❸

El Ladrillo II, C. Panaderos, 13 (☎958 29 26 51), off Cuesta del Chapiz near the Iglesia El Salvador, high on the Albaicín. Feast on seafood under the stars while listening to the romantic strains of *sevillanas*. *Menú* claims—with some credibility—to offer "the biggest portions in Spain." Entrees €6.60-12. Open daily 12:30pm-1:30am. MC/V. ❷

GRAN VÍA AND ELSEWHERE

Restaurante Asador Corrala del Carbón, Mariana Pineda, 8 (☎958 22 38 10). Savor traditional Andalucian grilled meat in an indoor re-creation of an old neighborhood courtyard in Granada. Entrees €8-17. Open daily 1-4pm and 8:30pm-midnight. ❸

Botánico Café, C. Málaga, 3 (☎958 27 15 98), 2 blocks from Pl. Trinidad. Manhattan minimalism meets Spanish modernity at this student hangout where a fusion of cultural food traditions brings new life to Spanish favorites. Entrees €4.80-9. Open M-Th 10am-3am, Su noon-1am. ❷

Los Italianos, Gran Vía de Colón, 4 (☎958 22 40 34). Popular gelato parlor with 26 heavenly flavors draws nightly crowds from the discos in the area after the parties have ended. 2 scoops €1, ice cream sundaes €1.20-2.40. Open daily 9am-3am. ❶

SIGHTS

THE ALHAMBRA

To reach the Alhambra, take C. Cuesta de Gomérez off Pl. Nueva, and be prepared to pant (20min.; no unauthorized cars 9am-9pm), or take the quick Alhambra-Neptuno microbus from Pl. Nueva (every 5min., €0.78). ☎958 22 15 03. Open Apr.-Sept. daily 8:30am-8pm; Oct.-Mar. M-Sa 9am-5:45pm. Nighttime visits June-Sept. Tu, Th, Sa 10-11:30pm; Oct.-May Sa 8-10pm. All visits €7, free for the handicapped and children under 8. Limited to 7700 visitors per day June-Sept., 6300 Oct.-May, so get there early. Enter the Palace of the Nasrids (Alcázar) during the time specified on your ticket, but stay as long as desired. It is possible to reserve tickets a few days in advance at banks for a €0.75 charge; this is recommended especially July-Aug. and Semana Santa. Reservations ☎902 22 44 60. Audioguides available, narrated by "Washington Irving" in Spanish, English, French, German, and Italian (€3).

From the streets of Granada, the Alhambra, meaning "the red one" in Arabic, appears simple, blocky, faded—a child's toy castle planted in the foothills of the Sierra Nevada. Up close, however, you will discover an elaborate and detailed

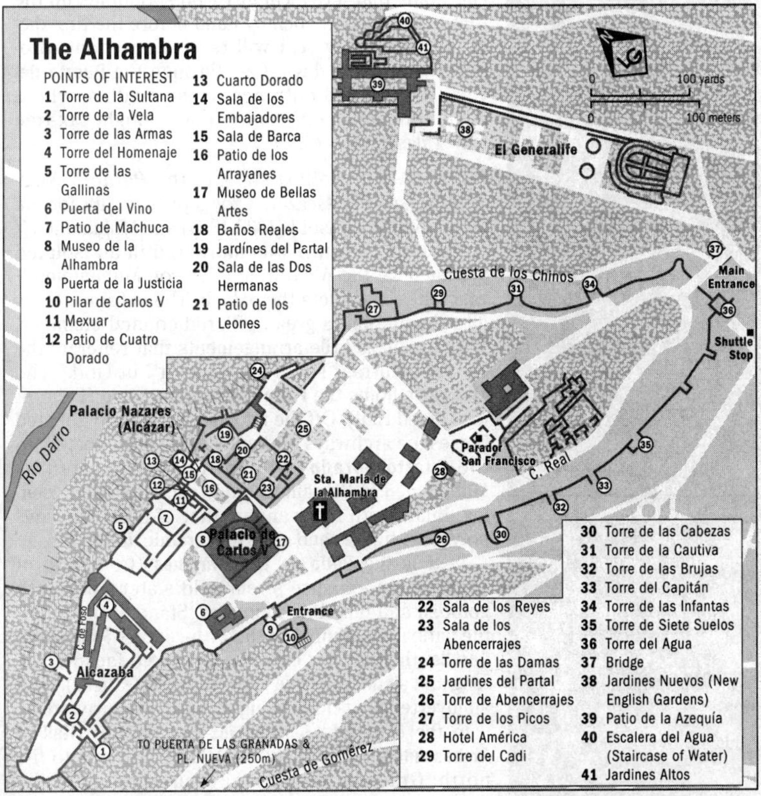

piece of architecture; one that magically unites water, light, wood, stucco, and ceramics to create a fortress-palace of rich aesthetic and symbolic grandeur. Celebrated by poets and artists throughout the ages, the Alhambra continues to inspire those who visit with its timeless beauty. The age-old saying holds true: *"Si has muerto sin ver la Alhambra no has vivido"* (If you have died without seeing the Alhambra, you have not lived).

THE ALCAZABA. The Christians drove the first Nasrid King Alhamar from the Albaicín to this more strategic hill, where he built the series of rust-colored brick towers which form the Alcazaba, or fortress. A dark, spiraling staircase leads to the **Torre de la Vela** (watchtower), where visitors get a great 360° view of Granada and the surrounding mountains. The tower's bells were rung to warn of impending danger and to coordinate the Moorish irrigation system. Every January 1st, during the annual commemoration of the Christian conquest of Granada, an old legend holds that any local girl who scrambles up the tower and rings the bell by hand before the first day of the actual new year will receive a wedding proposal within 365 days. Exit through the **Puerta del Vino,** the original entrance to the medina, where inhabitants of the Alhambra once bought tax-free wine (alas, no more).

THE ALCÁZAR. Follow signs to the *Palacio Nazaries* to see the Alcázar, a royal palace built for the Moorish rulers Yusuf I (1333-1354) and Muhammed V (1354-1391). Yusuf I was murdered in an isolated basement of the Alcázar, and his son Muhammed V was left to complete the palace. The entrance leads into the **Mexuar,** a great, pillared council chamber. Note the glazed tile arrangements that reiterate the Nasrid mantra: "There is no victor but God." The Mexuar adjoins the **Patio del Cuarto Dorado** (Patio of the Gilded Hall). Off the far side of the patio, foliated horseshoe archways of diminishing width open onto the **Cuarto Dorado** (Gilded Hall), decorated by Muhammed V. Its painstakingly carved wooden ceiling, inlaid with ivory and mother-of-pearl, displays polygonal figures and colorful ceramic *dados*.

Next is the **Patio de los Arrayanes** (Courtyard of Myrtles), an expanse of emerald water filled with goldfish and bubbling fountains. Stand at the top of the patio for a glimpse of the 14th-century **Fachada de Serallo,** the palace's elaborately carved facade. The long and slender **Sala de la Barca** (Boat Gallery), with an inverted boat-hull ceiling, flanks the courtyard.

In the elaborate **Sala de los Embajadores (Hall of Ambassadors),** adjoining the Sala de la Barca to the north, Granada was formally surrendered to the

FROM THE ROAD

A WALK IN THE PARK

Any local will tell you that the Parque Natural de las Sierras de Cazorla, Segura, y las Villas cannot be fully appreciated in a week, a month, or even a year. The average traveler doesn't have that much time, so here's the best way to see the highlights of the park in just one day, via public transportation.

From the Pl. Constitucion catch the Carcesa bus in the morning (M-Sa; Sept.-May 5:45am, June-Aug. 6:30am June-Aug.; €3 one-way.) It takes about 1¼hr. to descend the windy mountain road into the park, and you must ask to be dropped off at **Torre del Vinagre Centro de Interpretacion**—the main visitor's center (the bus itself continues on to Coto Ríos, deeper within the park). Since the center doesn't open until 10am, make sure you bring a map, a sack lunch, bottled water, sunscreen, sturdy hiking shoes, and a windbreaker. The hike is not very strenuous and can be completed at a leisurely pace.

From the visitor's center, cross the road and bear left, heading downhill in the direction towards which the sign "Central Eléctrica" points. At the bottom of the hill you'll cross the Guadalquivir river, which at this point, is nothing more than a stream. Continue down this road for about 2km, passing the *piscifactoria* (trout hatchery) on your left, until you come to a parking lot beside the swift and cold Río Borosa. Pass the lot and head toward the unpaved road—this is where the marked trail begins.

Catholic Monarchs, and Fernando and Columbus discussed finding a new route to India. Every surface of this magnificent square hall is intricately wrought with symbolic inscriptions and ornamental patterns. The Mozarabic dome, carved of more than 8000 pieces of wood and inlaid cedar, depicts the seven skies of paradise mentioned in the Qur'an. From the Patio de los Arrayanes, the Sala de los Mozárabes leads to the **Patio de los Leones** (Courtyard of the Lions), the grandest display of Nasrid art in the palace, where a rhythmic arcade of marble columns borders the courtyard, and a fountain supported by 12 marble lions babbles in the middle. Some believe that this fountain originally belonged to one of the sultan's Jewish advisors, but was transferred to this patio and redecorated with Muslim motifs.

Moving counter-clockwise around the courtyard, the next room is the **Sala de los Abencerrajes.** Here, Boabdil had the throats of 16 sons of the Abencerrajes family slit after one of them had allegedly had amorous encounters with his concubine Zorahayda. The rust-colored stains in the basin are said to mark the indelible traces of the butchering; evidently none of this bothered the Emperor Charles V, who dined here during the construction of his neighboring *palazzo*. Light bleeds into the room through the intricate domed ceiling, which features an eight-pointed star—a design said to represent terrestrial and heavenly harmony.

Through stalactite archways, at the far end of the courtyard from the Patio de los Leones, lies the **Sala de los Reyes** (Hall of Kings). Fixed to the walls with bamboo pins, detailed sheepskin paintings depict important assemblies and hunts. On the remaining side of the courtyard, the resplendent **Sala de las Dos Hermanas** (Chamber of the Two Sisters) has a honeycombed Mozarabic dome comprised of thousands of tiny cells. From here a secluded portico, **Mirador de Daraxa** (Eyes of the Sultana), overlooks the Jardines de Daraxa.

Passing the room where American author Washington Irving resided in 1829, a courtyard leads to the 14th-century **Baños Reales** (Royal Baths), the center of court social life. Light shining through star-shaped holes in the ceiling once refracted through steam, creating indoor rainbows. Unfortunately, the baths are currently closed during summer for conservation studies and archaeological bubble baths.

TOWERS AND GARDENS. Just outside the east wall of the Alcázar in the **Jardines del Partal,** lily-studded pools stand beside rose-laden terraces. The **Torre de las Damas** (Ladies' Tower) soars above it all. A series of six additional towers traverses the area between the Alcazaba and El Generalife.

Walk along the trail—which follows the Borosa—for about 30min. If the weather is warm, stop for a dip in the refreshingly cool river pools designated as *Sitio de baño* on your right. Soon you will come to a fork in the trail—take the path that goes in the direction of *Laguna de Valdeazores*. With the Borosa to your left, you will continue for another 30min. towards a gorge—here you might spot some of the park's wildlife, including *jabali* (wild boar), *ibex*, and *mouflon* (varieties of sheep). Again, you will come to another fork in the path—take the right side of the trail marked *Cerrada de Elias*. Shortly you will enter a very narrow part of the gorge—you have reached the *cerrada* itself. This beautiful 30min. section along catwalks that are attached to the limestone cliff takes you above inviting pools and dramatic cascades in what is perhaps the most memorable part of the Borosa's course. After passing through this point, you may choose to continue the trail for another hr. to reach the artificial *Laguna de Aguas Negras* (a reservoir) and the *Laguna de Valdeazores* (a natural lake). Or you can head back towards Torre del Vinagre, stopping along the way for another dip in the river, or a refreshing drink from one of the many fountains which dot the trail.

Since the last bus back to Cazorla leaves Torre del Vinagre at 4:30pm, allow 2½hr. to get to *Cerrada de Elias* and back (10km), and 3½hr. to get to the lakes and back (15km). Those who wish to camp in the park should contact the visitor's center in advance to check the availability and accessibility of the campsites located in the area which are open to the public.

EL GENERALIFE. Over a bridge, across the **Callejón de los Cipreses** and the shady **Callejón de las Adelfas,** are the vibrant blossoms, towering cypresses, and streaming waterways of El Generalife, the sultan's vacation retreat. In 1313 Arab engineers changed the Darro's flow by 18km and employed dams and channels to prepare the soil for Aben Walid Ismail's design of El Generalife. Over the centuries, the estate passed through private hands until it was finally repatriated in 1931. The two buildings of El Generalife, the **Palacio** and the **Sala Regia,** connect across the **Patio de la Acequia** (Courtyard of the Irrigation Channel), embellished with a narrow pool fed by fountains that form an aquatic archway. Honeysuckle vines scale the back wall, and shady benches invite long rests. An old oak tree stands here at the place where the sultana Zorahayda apparently had several amorous encounters with a nobleman from the Abencerrajes tribe.

PALACIO DE CARLOS V. After the *Reconquista* drove the Moors from Spain, Fernando and Isabel restored the Alcázar. Little did they know that two generations later Emperor Charles V would demolish part of it to make way for his Palacio, a Renaissance masterpiece by Pedro Machuca (a disciple of Michelangelo). Although it is incongruous with the surrounding Moorish splendor, scholars concede that the palace is one of the most beautiful Renaissance buildings in Spain. A square building with a circular inner courtyard wrapped in two stories of Doric colonnades, it is Machuca's only surviving design. Inside, the **Museo de La Alhambra** contains the only original furnishings remaining from the Alhambra. *(☎958 22 62 79. Open Tu-Sa 9am-2:30pm. Free.)* Upstairs, the **Museo de Bellas Artes** displays religious sculptures and paintings of the Granada School dating from the 16th century to the present. *(☎958 22 48 43. Open April-Sept. Tu 2:30-6pm, W-Sa 9am-6pm, Su 9am-2:30pm; Oct.-March Tu 2:30-7:45pm, W-Sa 9am-7:45pm, Su 9am-2:30pm. €1.50.)*

IN THE CATHEDRAL QUARTER

CAPILLA REAL. Downhill from the Alhambra's Arab splendor, through the Puerta Real off Gran Vía de Colon, on C. Oficios, the Capilla Real (Royal Chapel), Fernando and Isabel's private chapel, exemplifies Christian Granada. During their prosperous reign, the Catholic Monarchs funneled almost a quarter of the royal income into the chapel's construction (which lasted from 1504 to 1521) to build a proper burial place. Their efforts did not go unrewarded; intricate Gothic masonry and meticulously rendered figurines, as well as **La Reja,** the gilded iron grille of Master Bartolomé, grace the couple's resting place. Behind La Reja lie the almost lifelike marble figures of the royals themselves. Fernando and Isabel are on the right, when facing the altar; beside them sleeps their daughter Juana la Loca (the Mad) and her husband Felipe el Hermoso (the Fair). Much to the horror of the rest of the royal family, Juana insisted on keeping the body of her husband with her for an unpleasantly long time after he died. The lead caskets, where all four monarchs were laid to rest, lie directly below the marble sarcophagi in a crypt down a small stairway on the left. The smaller, fifth coffin belongs to the hastily buried child-king of Portugal, Miguel, whose death allowed Charles V to ascend the throne.

SACRISTY. Next door in the sacristy, Isabel's private **art collection,** the highlight of the chapel, favors Flemish and German artists of the 15th century. The glittering **royal jewels**—the queen's golden crown and scepter and the king's sword—shine in the middle of the sacristy. Nearby are the Christian banners which first fluttered in triumph over the Alhambra. *(☎958 22 92 39. Capilla Real and Sacristy both open M-Sa 10:30am-1pm and 4-7pm, Su 11am-1pm and 4-7pm; €2.50.)*

CATHEDRAL. Behind the Capilla Real and the Sacristy is Granada's cathedral. Construction of the cathedral began after *la Reconquista* upon the smoldering

THE HEADLESS MOORISH HORSE In 1829, after an undistinguished legal career and a brief stint as United States Ambassador to Spain, Washington Irving traveled to Granada, where he stayed for several months in the Alhambra as a guest of the royal governor. Enchanted by his surroundings, Irving later published a collection of short stories entitled *Tales of the Alhambra* (1832). Particularly memorable is the legend of the eerie but innocuously headless Moorish horse who "issues forth in the dead of the night and scours the avenues of the Alhambra and the streets of Granada." In later years, Irving again took up the theme of phantasmagorical decapitation, although he was no less inspired by the beauty of the Andalucian countryside. A girl's transformation into womanhood, he wrote, "is like passing from the flat, bleak, uninteresting plain of La Mancha, to the voluptuous valleys and swelling hills of Andalucía." Perhaps it's time the regional tourism board adopt a new slogan. Tales of the Alhambra *is available at El Corte Inglés (€3.90) and countless souvenir shops throughout Granada. If you're willing to risk an encounter with the headless Moorish horse,* ***tours of the Alhambra under moonlight*** *are romantic and unforgettable. June-Sept. Tu, Th, Sa 10-11:30pm; Oct.-May Sa 8-10pm (€7).*

embers of Granada's largest mosque and was not completed until 1704. The first purely Renaissance cathedral in Spain, its massive Corinthian pillars support a 45m vaulted nave. *(☎958 22 29 59. Open Apr.-Sept. M-Sa 10:45am-1:30pm and 4-7pm, Su 4-7pm; Oct.-Mar. M-Sa 10:30am-1:30pm and 3:30-6:30pm, Su 11am-1:30pm. €2.50.)*

THE ALBAICÍN. A labyrinth of steep streets and narrow alleys, the Albaicín was the only Moorish neighborhood to escape the torches of the *Reconquista* and remains a key stop in Granada. After the fall of the Alhambra, a small Muslim population remained here until being expelled in the 17th century. Today, with its abundance of North African cuisine, outdoor bazaars blasting Arabic music, teahouses, and the presence of a mosque near Pl. San Nicolás, the Albaicín attests to the persistence of Islamic influence in Andalucía. Spectacular sunsets over the surrounding mountains can be seen from C. Cruz de Quirós, above C. Elvira. Although generally safe, the Albaicín is disorienting and should be approached with caution at night. *(Bus #12 runs from beside the cathedral to C. Pagés at the top of the Albaicín.)*

The best way to explore this maze is to proceed along Carrera del Darro off Pl. Santa Ana, climb the Cuesta del Chapiz on the left, then wander through Muslim ramparts, cisterns, and gates. On Pl. Santa Ana, the 16th-century **Real Cancillería** (or **Audiencia**), with its beautiful arcaded patio and stalactite ceiling, was the Christians' Ayuntamiento. Farther uphill are the 11th-century **Arab baths.** *(Carrera del Darro, 31. ☎958 02 78 00. Open Tu-Sa 10am-2pm. Free.)* The **Museo Arqueológico** showcases funerary urns, classical sculpture, Carthaginian vases, Muslim lamps, and ceramics. *(Carrera del Darro, 41. ☎958 22 56 40. Open Tu 3-8pm, W-Sa 9am-8pm, Su 9am-2:30pm. €1.50, free for EU members.)* The **mirador** (lookout terrace) adjacent to **Iglesia de San Nicolás** in the heart of the Albaicín affords the city's best view of the Alhambra, especially in winter when snow adorns the Sierra Nevada behind it. From C. Elvira, go up C. Caldereria Nueva to C. San Gregorio and continue uphill on this street past Pl. Algibe Trillo, where it becomes Cta. Algibe de Trillo. At Pl. Camino, make a left on Cta. Tomasa and another left on Atarazana Cta. Cabras. The mirador will be on your right.

OTHER SIGHTS. The 16th-century **Hospital Real** is divided into 4 tiled courtyards. Above the main staircase, the Mudéjar-coffered ceiling echoes those of the Alhambra. *(Av. Hospicio. Open M-F 9am-2pm. Free.)* The 14th-century **Monasterio de San Jerónimo** is around the corner. Though badly damaged by Napoleon's troops, it has since been restored. *(☎958 27 93 37. Open Apr.-Sept. M-Sa 10am-1:30pm and 4-7pm, Su 11am-1:30pm; Oct.-Mar. M-Sa 10am-1pm and 3-6:30pm, Su 11am-1:30pm. €2.10.)*

NIGHTLIFE

Entertainment listings are at the back of the daily paper, the *Ideal*, under *Cine y Espectáculos;* the Friday supplement lists bars and special events. The *Guía del Ocio*, sold at newsstands (€0.85), lists clubs, pubs, and cafes.

FLAMENCO AND JAZZ

The most "authentic" flamenco performances, which change monthly, are advertised on posters around town. A list of the nightly *tablaos* is available at the tourist office. A smoky, intimate setting awaits at **Eshavira,** C. Postigo de la Cuna, in a very secluded alley off C. Azacayes, between C. Elvira and Gran Vía. This joint is *the* place to go for flamenco, jazz, or a fusion of the two. Photos of Nat King Cole and other jazz greats plaster the walls. Those with musical talent who wish to stage their own impromptu concerts can pick up the guitar or sit down at the piano which the owner has provided specifically for this purpose. (☎958 29 08 29. Min. 1 drink. Call for schedule, or pick up a flier at the tourist information office.)

PUBS, BARS, AND CLUBS

Pubs and bars spread across several neighborhoods, genres, and energy levels. The most boisterous crowds hang out on C. Pedro Antonio de Alarcón, running from Pl. Albert Einstein to Ancha de Gracia, while hip new bars and clubs line C. Elvira from Cárcel to C. Cedrán. A few gay bars cluster around Carrera del Darro, while a more openly gay scene can be found at the Parque del Triunfo and the Paseo del Salón. A full list of gay establishments is available at the tourist office, or by calling Juvenos, an organization for gay youth.

Camborio, Camino del Sacromonte, 48 (☎958 22 12 15), a 20min. walk uphill from Pl. Nueva. Gypsies and highwaymen once roamed the caves of Sacromonte, now the domain of scantily-clad clubbers. Pop music echoes through labyrinthine dance floors to the rooftop terraces above. Striking view of the Alhambra at sunrise. Can seem empty on Tu and W. €4.20 cover on F and Sa. Beer €1.80-3. Open Tu-Sa 11pm-dawn.

Granero, Pl. Luis Rosales (☎958 22 89 79), near Pl. Isabel Católica. A New Age barn loft bulging with Spanish yuppies. Still groovin' early in the week. Salsa and Spanish pop pervade. Beer €2.40, mixed drinks €3-4.20. Open daily 10pm-dawn.

Planta Baja, C. Horno de Abad, 11 (☎958 25 35 09). Live bands play regularly within the concrete confines of this techno dance club. Wildly popular with students. Beer €1.80. Cover €3. Open from fall until early July, Th-Sa 10pm-6am.

Granada 10, C. Carcel Baja, 3 (☎958 22 40 01). Movie theater by evening, raging dance club by night. Perhaps the most opulent disco you'll ever see (at least in Granada). Best for after hours on weekends. Open daily. €6 cover Th-Sa includes one drink.

Gustav Klimt, C. Imprenta, 3. Post-impressionist decor with posters of "The Kiss" on all the walls make this a popular "pick-up" place. Bars on 1st and 2nd floors cater to a sophisticated crowd. Flamenco performances on some Th each month. Beer €2, mixed drinks €4 and up. Open daily 4pm-4am.

Kasbah, C. Caldereria Nueva, 4 (☎958 22 79 36). Relax amidst the comforts of this candlelit cafe. Silky pillows and romantic nooks abound. Arab pastries and an exhaustive selection of Moroccan teas (€1.80). Open daily 3pm-3am.

Fondo Reservado, Cuesta de Sta. Inés, off Carrera del Darro. A popular gay bar with a mixed crowd that parties hard. Beer €2.40, mixed drinks €3.60. Opens daily at 11pm.

El Angel Azul, C. Lavadero de las Tablas, 15. Well established gay bar with a basement dance floor and curtained booths. Monthly drag shows and striptease contests. Beer €2.40. Open daily midnight-5am.

ENTERTAINMENT

Festivals sweep Granada in the summer. The **Corpus Christi** celebrations, processions, and bullfights in May are world famous. That same month, avant-garde theater groups from around the world make a pilgrimage to Granada for the **International Theater Festival** (☎958 22 93 44). The **Festival Internacional de Música y Danza** (mid-June to early July) sponsors open-air performances of classical music, ballet, and flamenco in the Alhambra's Palacio de Carlos V and other outdoor venues. (☎958 22 18 44. Tickets €6-36, senior and youth discounts available.)

DAYTRIP FROM GRANADA

GUADIX

From the station on C. Santa Rosa, Maestra buses (☎958 66 06 57) depart for: Almería (1½hr., 3 per day 8am-6pm, €6.20); Granada (1hr.; M-Sa 11 per day 6:45am-6:45pm, Su 6 per day 9:45am-8:30pm; €3.60); and Jaén (1½hr.; 11am, 6pm; €6.25). The tourist office, on Av. Mariana Pineda, is several blocks to the left when your back is to Guadix's cathedral. (☎958 66 26 65. Open M-F 8am-3pm.) The bus station provides luggage storage (daily until 6pm).

Dug (literally) into the rock basin of what was once a prehistoric lake, Guadix has been populated for thousands of years. But what distinguishes Guadix from other cities in Spain and the rest of the world is that almost half of its residents (10,000 people) live in *cueva-casas* (cave houses). The **zona de cuevas** is a 10min. walk uphill from the cathedral; signs point the way up winding streets. One well-preserved cave serves as the **Museo de Alfarería,** C. San Miguel, 47. (☎958 66 47 67. Open M-F 10am-2pm and 4-8pm, Sa-Su 10am-noon. Adults €1.80, children €0.60.) More preserved rock formations can be seen at the **Cueva Museo,** on the right off C. Canada de las Perales. (Open M-F 10am-2pm and 4-8pm, Sa-Su 10am-noon. Adults €1.25, children €0.65.) The best way to visit the **zona de cuevas** itself is to simply wander the city's streets or to splurge on a **burro taxi,** a scenic donkey ride through the higher portion of the caves. The burro taxi stand is by the Cueva Museo in the Pl. de la Hermita Nueva (☎958 66 25 30; €1.20-6). Ride that ass to the **Mirador Cerro de la Bala,** a lookout point which affords a magnificent 360 degree view of the snow-capped Sierra Nevadas in the distance, and the *zona de cuevas*, the Alcazaba Arabe, and the Cathedral below. Back in town, the *casco antiguo* begins at the impressive **Catedral.** Up any of the slanting side streets to the left, you'll find the **Alcazaba Arabe,** built of 11th-century turrets that command an amazing view of the town and its surroundings. (Currently closed for archaeological excavations.)

Despite Guadix's impressive attractions, the city remains relatively untouristed: accommodations are scarce but prices are reasonable. Experience cave living at **Chez Jean & Julia ❷,** Ermita Nueva, 67, in the *barriada cueva*. Groups can rent mini-cave apartments complete with kitchen and bath. (☎958 66 91 91. Cave quads €48, for 6 people €60. Regular, cave-less doubles and triples €30.) Those who prefer more modern comforts should check out **Hotel Mulhacen ❸,** Av. Buenos Aires, 43, on the highway towards Murcia. Most rooms are handicapped-accessible. (☎958 66 07 50. June-Aug. singles €31.10; doubles €39.67. Sept.-May €25.54/€32.76.) For a great food option, dine outdoors with a view of the cathedral at **Cafe-Bar Los Arcos ❷,** Pl. de las Palomas, 21. (☎958 66 62 99. Open daily 9am-1am.)

LAS ALPUJARRAS

The *pueblos blancos* (white villages) of Las Alpujarras are scattered along the southern slopes of the Sierra Nevada, an area known as *la falda* (the skirt). Although the roads are now paved and the towns well-traveled, a medieval Berber influence is still evident in the region's architecture; the low-slung houses rendered from earth and slate quite closely resemble those in Morocco's Atlas Mountains. With the fall of Granada in 1492, the Berbers relocated to the Alpujarras and Christian-Muslim conflict continued until 1610, when John of Austria finally ousted the Moors. The legacy of Moorish defiance lives on every June during Trevélez's Fiestas de Moros y Cristianos. Settlers from Galicia made the Alpujarras their home after the Moors were expelled, and they brought with them Celtic and Visigothic traditions found nowhere else in Andalucía.

Although tourists have recently discovered the beauty of these settlements and the region's numerous hiking trails, Las Alpujarras remain one of Spain's poorest areas. Nevertheless, the villages' slow-paced lifestyle, well-preserved beauty, and rooted cultural traditions make for a refreshing visit. For the more active tourist, the mountains themselves offer plenty of climbing and hiking opportunities.

Las Alpujarras can be best appreciated by car, but for those without wheels, Alsina Graells buses travel from Granada to many of the high-altitude towns. Bus drivers will often stop to let travelers off at intermediate points. (Buses leave Granada at 10:30am, noon, and 5:15pm for the villages, and return from the farthest town, Alcutar, at 5am and 5pm.) The buses trace switchback after unnerving switchback, hugging the scenic road. Some hard-core visitors hike from place to place, and the locals, well aware of the transportation problem, often sympathize with hitchers. *Let's Go* does not recommend hitchhiking.

PAMPANEIRA

As the road winds in serpentine curves up to the high Alpujarran villages, the landscape quickly becomes harsh. A sign at the entrance to Pampaniera (pop. 360) nevertheless encourages visitors: *Quédate a vivir con nosotros*—"stay and live with us." Pampaneira (1059m) is the first in a trio of hamlets overlooking the **Poqueira Gorge,** a massive ravine cut by the Río Poqueira; the town makes a great springboard for climbing to **Bubión** (30min.) and **Capileira** (1¾hr.). The trail to both begins from behind the church at the very top of town; a sign points the way. For more info on the region's natural wonders, visit the local organization **Nevadensis** in the main square; in addition to arranging rural accommodations, hiking tours of the Sierra Nevada, and horseback riding, they serve as the town's main tourist information center. (☎958 76 31 27; fax 958 76 33 01; www.nevadensis.com. Open Tu-Sa 10am-2pm and 4-6pm, Su-M 10am-3pm.) Standing atop the hill above Pampaneira is the small Tibetan Buddhist meditation center **Osel Ling** (Place of Clear Light). Those looking to find their inner peace can access the center from a small road called 'Ruta Pintoresca' which branches off the main highway 5km below Pampaneira. The center's six monks are more than happy to show you the grounds if you call in advance for opening hours (☎958 34 31 34). **Hostal Pampaneira ❷,** C. Jose Antonio, 1, just off the highway in front of the bus stop, has large rooms with private baths. (☎958 76 30 02. Singles €20; doubles €28; triples €36. MC/V.) The hostel **restaurant ❷** tends to be busy when other eating establishments aren't, and the food is simple, hearty, no-nonsense fare. (Entrees €3.90-7.20. MC/V.)

BUBIÓN

Bubión, a steep 3km (30min.) hike on a dirt trail from Pampaneira, is resplendent with Berber architecture, village charm, and enough *artesanía* (typical arts and crafts) to make your head spin. For tourist info, stop by **Rustic Blue,** Barrio La

Ermita. The helpful staff organizes excursions and rural lodging. (☎958 76 33 81; fax 958 76 31 34. English and French spoken. Open M-F 10am-2pm and 5-8pm, Sa 11am-2pm.) **Las Terrazas ❷,** Pta. Sol, has several flower-filled terraces and cozy rooms that overlook the valley. (☎958 76 30 34. Singles €19; doubles €25.25.) A pleasant meal can be had at **Restaurante La Artesa ❷,** on the main road in front of the bus stop. (☎958 76 30 82. *Menús* €6.60-9. Open daily 1-4pm and 8-11pm.)

CAPILEIRA

Capileira (1436m), perched atop the Poqueira Gorge (2½hr. from Granada and a 1hr. hike on the trail or a 20min. walk on the road from Bubión), makes a good base for exploring the neighboring villages and the back side of *la Falda*. Looming peaks tower over cobblestone alleys, with the distant valley below. Enjoy small luxuries in the tiled **Hostal Paco Lopez ❷,** Ctra. de la Sierra, 5, with balconies, TVs, and bathrooms in every room. (☎958 76 30 11. Singles €18; doubles €30.) A filling *menú* (€6-9) is served at **Restaurant Poqueira ❷,** C. Dr. Castillo, 6. (Open Tu-Su for lunch and dinner.)

TREVÉLEZ

Jamón serrano, and lots of it, distinguishes Trevélez, continental Spain's highest community (1476m). The town is best known for its cured pork, whose special qualities will probably elude all but the true connoisseur. The ham gets its unique flavor from being cured in the cool, dry winter and sweated in the hot summer. Nearly everything in this tiny town revolves around the ham industry, but it still has its share of history and charm. Steep roads weave through three *barrios*, and water rushes through Moorish irrigation systems still intact from 1000 years ago.

Trevélez is a logical base for the ascent to **Mulhacén** (3479m), one of the highest peaks of the Sierra Nevada. Every August, throngs of locals climb to pay homage to the **Virgen de las Nieves** (Virgin of the Snow). Summit-bound travelers should head north on the trail leaving the upper village from behind the church; avoid the trail that follows the swampy Río Trevélez. Continue past the Cresta de los Postreros for a good 4-5hr. until you reach the **Cañada de Siete Lagunas** (the largest lake, Laguna Hondera, should be directly in front of you); go right to see **Cueva del Cura,** a famous cave refuge. To reach Mulhacén, go up the ridge south of the refuge (3-4hr. farther). Since both itineraries take a considerable amount of time, it is not advisable to hike Mulhacén the same day you visit the lake. Regardless of which trail you choose, you should purchase a **map** and hiking guide of the Sierra Nevada, available in any souvenir shop in town. **Alpina** publishes a good one (€5.48).

Budget beds aren't hard to find in Trevélez. **Hostal Gonzalez ❶,** Pl. Francisco Abellán, behind the restaurant of the same name, has perfectly comfortable, clean rooms waiting past the grungy exterior. (☎958 85 85 31. Singles €12; doubles €21.) If you like ham, you're in luck—nearly every **restaurant** in town either advertises ham specials or has the meat hanging from the ceiling. Any one of the restaurants in the main plaza by the bus station serves up a variety of tasty local dishes, most often made of pork products. Non-pork entrees exist as well (though in less abundance), and the *menú* options (around €6.60) tend to include them.

JAÉN

Spain's "olive-oil capital" is more of a transportation hub than a destination, but half a day waiting for a bus to Baeza can be profitably spent among the winding hillside streets and crowded shopping avenues. Popular with Andalucian tourists as well as those from farther afield, Jaén is a fine place for an afternoon stroll.

TRANSPORTATION. Trains (☎902 24 02 02) depart from Po. Estación at the bottom of the slope and run to: **Córdoba** (1½hr., 8am, €7.21); **Madrid** (4-5hr., 3 per day 6am-5pm, €19); **Sevilla** (3hr., 8am, €14). **Buses,** Pl. Coca de la Piñera (☎953 25 50 14), head to: **Baeza** (1hr., 12 per day 8:30am-8:45pm, €2.70); **Cazorla** (2hr., noon and 4:30pm, €6); **Granada** (1½hr., 14 per day 7:30am-9pm, €5.56); **Málaga** (3hr., 3 per day 7:30am-4:30pm, €13); **Úbeda** (30min., 12 per day 8:30am-8:45pm, €3.50).

ORIENTATION AND PRACTICAL INFORMATION. Jaén centers around **Plaza de la Constitución.** From the plaza, **C. Bernabé Soriano** leads uphill to the cathedral and the old section of town. **C. Maestra,** home to the tourist office, is up several blocks to the right. To reach the town center from the bus station, exit from the depot and follow Av. Madrid uphill to Pl. de la Constitución (5min.). From the train station, turn right on Po. Estación, which becomes C. Roldán y Marín. If you're not up for the 25min. walk, take the #1 bus along Po. Estación (€0.55) or take a taxi (€3). The **tourist office,** C. Maestra, 13, is near the cathedral and has a very helpful staff. (☎/fax 953 24 26 24. Open July-Aug. M-F 10am-8pm, Sa-Su 10am-1pm. Sept.-June M-F 10am-7pm, Sa-Su 10am-1pm.) Other services include: **Santander Central Hispano,** Pl. de la Constitución (☎902 24 24 24; open June-Sept. M-F 8:30am-2pm, Sa 8:30am-1pm; Oct.-May same hours except closed on Sa); **luggage storage** at the bus station (€1.80 for 24hr.); **emergency** ☎112; **police** ☎953 21 91 05. **Internet access** is available at **Cu@k Internet,** Adarves Bajos, 24. From Pl. de la Constitución, turn left onto C. Ignacio Figueroa, and continue past the church of San Ildefonso until it becomes C. Vicente Montuno. Make a right on Adarves Bajos; it's on your left. (☎953 19 06 16. €2 per hr. Open M-F 11am-2:30pm and 5:30pm-3am, Sa 11am-3pm and 6pm-12:30am, Su 12-3pm and 6pm-midnight.) The **post office,** Pl. de Jardinillos, s/n, is next to the pedestrian street Miguel de Priego, which becomes Jardinillos when it hits the plaza. From Pl. de la Constitución, turn right on C. San Clemente until you reach Pl. de Jardinillos. (☎953 24 78 00. Open M-F 8:30am-2:30pm, Sa 9:30am-1pm.) **Postal code:** 23004.

ACCOMMODATIONS AND FOOD. Most of Jaén's accommodations lie close to the cathedral and along Av. de Madrid. The central location of **Hostal Carlos V ❷,** Av. de Madrid, 4, 2nd fl., downhill from Pl. de la Constitución, makes up for its tiny rooms. All six rooms share a single hallway and bathroom with shower. (☎953 22 20 91. Singles €16.25; doubles €28.25; triples €38.25.) Those seeking more modern rooms with TV, phone, bath, elevator—some even have body-massaging showerheads—should head to **Hotel Europa ❸,** Pl. de Belen, 1. Walking downhill on Av. de Madrid from the Pl. de la Constitución, turn right on Av. de Granada and then left on Cuesta de Belen. Walk halfway up the hill; the hotel is on your left. (☎953 22 27 00. Singles €32.85; doubles €52.11; triples €58.83.) The extensive menu at **Colon Cafetería ❶,** C. Navas de Tolosa, 7, along the main pedestrian walkway, includes everything from *churros* (€0.55-0.75) to *batidos helados* (frappes; €1.50-3), and a wide variety of other dishes. Prices are slightly higher at outside tables. Delicious Andalucian fare can be found at **Restaurante La Abadía ❸,** Melchor Cobo Medina, 19, where hearty portions are served in a cozy rustic setting. Try the three-course meal (€30). Heading toward Pl. de la Constitución on Av. de Madrid, turn left on C. Dr. Sagaz Zubelzu and veer to the right. The restaurant is on your right just before the street intersects with C. Teodoro Calvache. (☎953 24 50 38. Open daily 1-6pm and 8:30pm-1am.)

SIGHTS AND ENTERTAINMENT. The Renaissance **Catedral de Santa María,** on C. Bernabé Soriano uphill from Pl. Constitución, was designed by Andrés de Vandelvira. (☎953 23 42 33. Open M-Sa 8:30am-1pm and 5-8pm, Su 8:30am-1pm and 6-8pm. Free.) The **Museo de la Catedral** displays sundry objects of interest, among them candlesticks by Maestro Bartolomé. (☎953 22 46 75. Open daily 10am-1pm and afternoons when the cathedral is open. €1.20.) Jaén's most imposing and least accessible sight is the 13th-century stone **Castillo de Santa Catalina,** a 5km climb from the center of town. Those preferring to avoid a sweaty walk may take a taxi (€5.40) from the bus station. Though the castle itself is closed for restoration until the summer of 2004, the spectacular view from the promontory of the city and its surrounding olive groves is well worth the trek. The Renaissance **Palacio de Villardompardo,** in Pl. Santa Luisa Marillac, at the end of C. Maestra, contains incredible 11th-century Moorish baths—Spain's largest—and an art museum which houses the second-largest collection of *Narif* artwork in the world. Follow C. Maestra from the cathedral to C. Martínez Molina. (☎953 23 62 92. Open Tu-F 9am-8pm, Sa-Su 9:30am-2:30pm. Free.) Uphill from the cathedral, **Peña Flamenca Jaén,** C. Maestra, 11, serves up drinks and flamenco. Try the *manzanillo*, Andalucía's specialty apple liquor. (☎953 23 17 10. Open M-F noon-4pm and 8pm-1am, Sa-Su noon-1am. €1.50 for a beer, which includes a *tapa* of your choice. Mixed drinks €3 and up.) If you want to take a break from *el tapeo*, hire a taxi to drive you to **Moët** (like the champagne), Av. Andalucia, 10, near the train station. This ultra-hip bar attracts an effervescent crowd of local students and professionals in their 20's. On the weekends, it turns into a disco, with a DJ spinning the latest in Spanish pop. (☎953 27 30 94. Open M-W 4pm-4:30am and Th-Sa 4pm until the last customer stumbles out the door. Beer €1.80, mixed drinks €4 and up.)

BAEZA

If you're looking for a taste of quintessential old Spain, look no further. A former Roman, Visigothic, and Moorish capital and among the first Andalucian towns to fall to the armies of Ferdinand III during the *Reconquista*, Baeza (pop. 17,000) flaunts its Renaissance heyday with well-preserved monuments, still unspoiled by modern life. Nearby Úbeda may have similar architecture and attractions, but Baeza's overall small-town feel makes it a more desirable destination. Antonio Machado, a poet who taught at Baeza's old university, immortalized the village in his works when he wrote, *"Campo de Baeza, soñaré contigo cuando no te vea"* ("Countryside of Baeza, I shall dream of you when I see you no more").

TRANSPORTATION. **Trains** leave from **Estación Linares-Baeza** (☎902 24 02 02), 13km out of town on the road to Madrid (which can be reached by bus from the bus station in Baeza, 15 min., 8 per day 7:45am-9pm, €0.85), for **Madrid** (3hr., 5 per day 7am-6pm, €16) and **Málaga** (4hr.; 2:45, 5pm; €18). At the top of Av. Alcalde Puche Pardo, as it becomes C. Julio Barrel, the **bus station** (☎953 74 04 68) offers service to: **Cazorla** (1½hr.; 1, 5:30pm, €3.30); **Granada** (2-3hr., 7 per day 7:55am-6:55pm, €8.40); **Jaén** (1hr., 11 per day 7:10am-6:55pm, €2.85); and **Úbeda** (15min., 15 per day 8:20am-9pm, €0.65).

ORIENTATION AND PRACTICAL INFORMATION. Marking the center of town, **Pl. de España** leads downhill to **Paseo de la Constitución.** To get to Pl. de España from the bus station, follow C. Julio Burrel to C. San Pablo, and continue to the plaza. The **tourist office,** Pl. del Pópulo, offers guided tours of the town; inquire within for times, prices, and availability. (☎953 74 04 44. Open M-F 9am-2pm and 5-7:30pm, alternating Sa 10am-1pm.) Services include: **emergency** ☎112; **police,** C. Cardenal Benavides, 5 (☎953 74 06 59); **Centro de Salud Comarcal,** Av. Alcalde Puche Pardo, s/n, past the bus station (☎953 74 29 00). For **Internet access** try **Microware,** Po. Tundidores, 13, in Pl. Constitución. (☎953 74 70 10. €1.80 per hr.

Open Tu-Su 10:30am-2pm and 5-10pm.) The **post office** is on C. Julio Burell, 19. (☎953 74 08 39. Open M-F 8:30am-2:30pm, Sa 9am-1pm.) **Postal code:** 23440.

ACCOMMODATIONS AND FOOD. Baeza's hostels are hidden throughout the city. **Hostal El Patio ❶,** C. Romanones, 13, has the cheapest rooms in town and a location in the middle of the *barrio monumental* that's hard to beat. (☎953 74 02 00. Singles €9, with shower €12; doubles €18, with bath €24; triples with bath €33.) Directly uphill from Pl. de España, **Hostal Comercio ❷,** C. San Pablo, 21, has cozy rooms, all with private bathrooms. (☎953 74 01 00. Singles €15; doubles €27.) Several bars and restaurants line Po. de la Constitución, and almost all serve *comida típica.* Of these, **Meson Restaurante La Gondola ❸,** Portales Carboneria, 13, offers the most extensive menu, with a fine selection of meat, seafood, and the tasty local specialty, *perdiz* (partridge) cooked in a garlic-based vegetable stew. (☎953 74 29 84. Entrees €9-15. Open daily 9am-3pm.) A popular choice with locals is the bar **Guadalquivir ❶,** C. San Pablo, 44. (☎953 74 15 29. *Bocadillos* €1.65-2.10, *raciones* €4.80-6. Open daily noon-4pm and 8:30pm-midnight.)

SIGHTS. Baeza's main attraction is the **Barrio Monumental.** With your back to the tourist office, walk up the stairs to your right, then take a left on C. Romanones; at the street's end stands the **Antigua Universidad** (founded in 1595), whose courtyard served as an outdoor classroom where poet Antonio Machado taught French. (Open every day except W 10am-1:30pm and 4-6:30pm. Free.) Further down C. Romanones stands the 13th-century **Iglesia de Santa Cruz,** Baeza's oldest church, which contains frescoes of La Virgen, Santa Catalina, and the martyr San Sebastián. (Open M-Sa 11am-1pm and Su noon-2pm.) Next door to the church is a small **museum** which houses old church documents and ornate artifacts from the annual procession of the religious brotherhood of Santa Vera-Cruz in Baeza, held during *Semana Santa.* (Open daily 11am-1:30pm and 4:30-7pm. Free.) On the other side of the Pl. Santa Cruz, adjacent to the imposing 15th-century **Palacio Jabalquinto** (which is currently closed for restoration), the **seminario's** facade bears the names of some egotistical graduates and a caricature of an unpopular professor, rumored to be painted in bull's blood. Across the Pl. Santa María from the seminary towers, the **Santa Iglesia Catedral,** houses *La Custodia de Baeza,* Spain's second-most important Corpus Christi icon after Toledo's. (Open daily June-Aug. 10:30am-1pm and 4:30-6:30pm; Sept.-May 10:30am-1pm and 4:15-6pm.) Fabulous views of the olive-carpeted Guadalquivir Valley unfold from the park atop the old city wall, which can be reached by walking along Po. Murallas.

ÚBEDA

Úbeda is a city of two faces: the cobbled streets of its monument district dip between the ivied medieval walls of old churches and palaces, while modern sprawl envelops the rest of the city. A stop on the crucial 16th-century trade route linking Castilla to Andalucía, the town (pop. 56,000) prospered from American gold. Today, the *barrio antiguo* stands as one of the best-preserved gems of Spanish Renaissance architecture, attracting visitors from around the world.

TRANSPORTATION. There is **no train service** to Úbeda; the nearest station is **Estación Linares-Baeza** (☎953 65 02 02), 40min. northwest by bus. **Buses** leave Úbeda from C. San José, 6 (☎953 75 21 57). **Alsina Graells** travels to: **Baeza** (15min., 17 per day 7am-7:30pm, €0.65); **Cazorla** (1hr., 4 per day 10am-6pm, €2.85); **Estación Linares-Baeza** (30min., 8 per day 7:45am-9pm, €1.65); **Granada** (2-3hr., 7 per day 7:45am-6:45pm, €9); and **Jaén** (1hr., 13 per day 7am-6:45pm, €3.50). **Bacoma** buses go to **Córdoba** (2½hr., 6 per day 5am-8:40pm, €8.56) and **Sevilla** (5hr., 6 per day 5am-8:40pm, €16.53).

ORIENTATION AND PRACTICAL INFORMATION. Úbeda centers around **Plaza de Andalucía.** To reach the plaza from the **bus station,** bear right from the front of the station, walk downhill one block, then turn left on C. Obispo Cobos, which turns into C. Mesones, and continue to the plaza (5min.). From the plaza, the **barrio antiguo** stretches downhill along C. Doctor Quesada (which leads to C. Real) and surrounding streets. The main **tourist office** is in the **Palacio Marqués de Contadero,** C. Baja del Marqués, 4. From Pl. Andalucía, head down C. Rastro and make a left on Av. Medina. Turn right immediately onto C. Narvaez and then left on C. Corazón de Jesús. Make another immediate left onto C. Baja del Máarquez; the tourist office is on the left. (☎953 75 08 97; fax 953 79 26 70. Open M-F 8:30am-7:30pm, Sa-Su 10am-2pm.) There is also a small tourist information kiosk in the Pl. del Ayuntamiento (in the *barrio antiguo*) which has the same operating hours as the main office. **Santander Central Hispano,** Pl. Andalucía, 13, has an **ATM.** (☎953 75 04 43. Open May-Sept. M-F 8:30am-2pm, Oct.-Apr. M-F 8:30am-2pm and Sa 8:30am-1pm.) Local services include: **luggage storage** at the bus station (€1.80 per day); **emergency** ☎112; **police** ☎953 75 00 23; **Centro de Salud,** C. Esplanada (☎953 75 11 03), off Av. Ramón y Cajal; and the **post office,** C. Trinidad, 4, along the Hospital de Santiago. (☎953 75 00 31. Open M-Sa 9am-2pm.) **Postal code:** 23400.

ACCOMMODATIONS AND FOOD. Indulge at **Hostal Victoria ❷,** C. Alaminos, 5, 2nd fl. From the bus station, walk down C. Mesones past Hospital de Santiago and turn right off C. Sagasta, then left on C. Alaminos. Glistening private bathrooms, color TVs, and A/C make for a pleasant stay. (☎953 75 29 52. Singles €15-17; doubles €28-30.) One of the city's best restaurants is **Restaurante Meson Gabino ❷,** Fuente Seca, 4, below the old outer walls of the *barrio antiguo*. Located in a cave which hid Republican fighters and ammunition from Franco's forces during the Spanish Civil War, the restaurant serves a quality selection of typical Andalucian meat, poultry and fish dishes (€9-15) in a rustic and dimly lit setting. (☎953 75 75 53. Open daily 11am-2pm and 4-11pm.) The **market** is down C. San Fernando from Pl. Andalucía. (Open M-Sa 7am-2:30pm.)

SIGHTS AND ENTERTAINMENT. A walk through historic Úbeda begins right out of the bus at the **Hospital de Santiago,** adjacent to the station, which houses a modern art museum. (☎953 75 08 42. Open M-F 8am-3pm; evening hours 5:30-10pm in summer, 4:30-10pm in winter, Sa 8am-3pm. €1.65, children and seniors €0.45.) Every year from the first week in May to the first week in June, the Hospital hosts the **Festival Internacional de Musica y Danza** with classical music and dance performances by artists from around the world. (Performances every Sa and Su at 9pm. Tickets (€7-16) per person can be purchased at the ticket counter in the Hospital de Santiago or by calling the hospital's number listed above.) From Pl. Andalucía, C. Real leads downhill to C. Juan Montilla, which then continues to **Plaza de Vázquez de Molina** and the center of Úbeda. Two stone lions guard the **Palacio de las Cadenas,** now the Ayuntamiento. Across the way is the Gothic **Colegiata de Santa María de los Reales Alcázares,** its side chapels embellished with wrought-iron grilles; you can't enter, but the facade alone is worth the visit. Uphill from Pl. Vásquez de Molina and along C. Juan Ruíz Gonzales, Pl. 1 de Mayo runs in front of **Iglesia de San Pablo** (open 7-9pm and during Mass). The **Museo Arqueológico,** C. Cervantes, 6, uphill from the church, narrates Úbeda's history through prehistoric, Roman, Moorish, and Castilian times. (☎953 75 37 02. Open Tu 3-8pm, W-Sa 9am-8pm, Su 9am-3pm. €1.50, EU citizens free with passport.) In the basement of the Ayuntamiento, the small but charming **Museo de Alfarería** (*artesanía* or handcrafts), displays pottery and local arts. (Open Tu-Sa 10:30am-2pm and 5:30-8pm. €1.60.) A walk downhill along C. Baja del Salvador leads to a stunning view of the olive-laden **Guadalquivir Valley.** Kick back, relax, and enjoy a *cerveza* at **Casablanca Café,** on the corner of C. Redonda de Santiago and Av. Ramón y Cajal. (☎953 79 27 88. Open daily 4pm-3am. Beer €1.05, mixed drinks €3 and up.)

CAZORLA ☎953

Nestled between foreboding cliffs and two ancient castles, Cazorla (pop. 9000) keeps quietly to itself, paying little heed to the trickle of tourists passing through on their way to the **Parque Natural de las Sierras de Cazorla, Segura, y las Villas** (1hr. away), the source of the Guadalquivir river. With over 210,000 densely forested hectares of protected mountains and waterways, the national park offers some of the best hiking, mountain biking, and horseback riding in Andalucía, and the abundant wildlife makes it a veritable paradise for animal lovers. However, for those not interested in exploring the natural park, the town of Cazorla itself provides a tranquil place for a weekend getaway.

ORIENTATION AND PRACTICAL INFORMATION. The center of Cazorla clusters around two plazas—**Pl. de Corredera** and **Pl. Constitución.** To reach **Pl. de Corredera** from the bus stop, face the peaks and walk down the narrow C. Dr. Muñoz to the right. Farther downhill past Pl. de Corredera are Pl. Santa María and the **barrio antiguo. Alsina Graells buses** (☎953 75 21 57) depart from Pl. Constitución for: **Granada** (4hr.; M-Sa 7am and 5:30pm, Su 8am and 5:30pm; €12); **Jaén** and **Úbeda** (2hr., 4 per day 7am-5:30pm, €6.25 and €2.84). Buy tickets in the tiny office across from the plaza bus depot (open daily 6:30am-5:30pm). The **tourist office,** Po. Santo Cristo, 17, is up a garden-lined walkway from Pl. Constitución. (☎953 71 01 02; fax 953 72 00 60. Open M-F 10am-2pm and 5-9pm.) Services include: **emergency** ☎112; **police** on Pl. Corredera (☎953 72 01 81); **Centro de Salud,** Av. Ximénez de Rada, 1 (☎953 72 10 61); and the **post office,** C. Mariano Extremera, 2, uphill from Pl. Corredera. (☎953 72 02 61. Open M-F 8:30am-2:30pm, Sa 9am-1pm.) **Postal code:** 23470.

ACCOMMODATIONS AND FOOD. From the far end of Pl. Corredera, walk uphill on C. Carmen to reach the **Albergue Juvenil Cazorla (HI) ❶,** Pl. Mauricio Martínez, 6. This hostel has a TV lounge, basketball/soccer court, and a heaven-sent pool, although it's only open for swimming mid-June through mid-Sept. (☎953 72 03 29; fax 953 72 02 03. 24hr. Security guard. Breakfast included; sheets provided. HI members Oct.-May €8.50, over 26 €11.50; June-Sept. €10.90/€15.20.) **Hostal Betis ❶,** Pl. Corredera, 19, has incredible views of the valley from most rooms. (☎953 72 05 40. Singles with bath €10-11; doubles €22, with bath €23.) To the left side of Pl. Corradera if you are heading down C. Doctor Munoz is the impeccable **Hotel Guadalquivir ❸,** C. Nueva, 6. Spacious and airy rooms with marble floors and private bathrooms, plus an attentive staff make this a very comfortable place to crash after a long day of hiking. (☎/fax 953 72 02 68. Singles €30; doubles €36.06; triples €38.58.) Open-air bar/restaurants serving traditional platters such as *rinran* (a cold soup of potatoes, red peppers, olives, and fish) line Pl. Corredora and Pl. Santa María. Perhaps the best bargain in town is **La Taberna ❶,** C. Nueva, s/n, on a side street off Pl. Corredera (across from Hotel Guadaliquivir), where brightly tiled walls and a casual environment attract a range of patrons. (☎953 71 01 22. *Tapas/raciones* €4.81-7.21. Open every day except Tu noon-4:30pm and 7:30pm-midnight.) For a romantic, candlelit dinner at the foot of the **Castillo de la Yedra,** and in front of the enchanting ruins of the 13th-century **Iglesia de Santa Maria,** head to **Asador Plaza Vieja ❷,** C. La Hoz, 2 in the Pl. de Santa Maria. House specialties include *patata a lo pobre* (potato sautéed with onion, green pepper, and egg; €5.50) and *jabali al horno* (roast wild boar; €9). The restaurant's rustic mountain decor gives it a very cozy feel, but if the weather is nice, get a table outside and watch the sun go down behind the *castillo*. (☎953 72 12 25. Open daily noon-4:30pm and 6-11pm.) The **market** is at Pl. Mercado, downstairs from C. Dr. Muñoz (open M-F 9am-noon), and a larger **supermarket** sits in Pl. Corredera. (Open M-F 9am-noon and 6-9pm, Sa 9am-noon.)

SIGHTS AND HIKING. The majority of visitors to Cazorla come for the **Parque Natural de las Sierras de Cazorla, Segura y las Villas.** The truly adventurous can take a 9hr. round-trip hike from Cazorla to the park; stop by the tourist office for a map. Rising majestically above the town is the medieval **Castillo de la Yedra.** Begun by Roman builders, the castle provides a lovely view of town from its solitary turrets. (☎953 71 00 39. Open Tu 3-8pm, W-Sa 9am-8pm, Su 9am-3pm. €1.50. EU citizens free.) For information on longer or guided excursions by 4x4 vehicle through the park, stop by **Quercus,** C. Juan Domingo, 2. Tours can be arranged with an English-speaking guide. Also inquire here for jeep rentals if you prefer to drive yourself. (☎953 72 01 15. Open daily 9am-2pm and 5-9pm, holidays 10am-2pm and 6-9pm. Map €2.25. Half-day tours €17-36. Jeep rental prices and availability subject to change.) **Carcesa Buses** run from Cazorla to the park, but service is subject to change. (1¼hr.; June-Aug. M-Sa 6:30am and 2:40pm, Sept.-May 5:45am and 3pm; €3 one-way, purchase tickets on the bus.) Buses depart Pl. Constitución for the **Torre del Vinagre Visitor Center,** near the trailhead of the popular **Sendero Cerrada de Elias/Río Borosa,** from which 4 or 12km trails lead up the river canyon. (☎953 71 30 40. Open M-Sa 10am-2pm and 4-7pm, hours vary slightly Sept.-May. Call ahead to make sure when the center is open.) Five hundred meters down the road from the center is the **Picadero "El Cortijo"** stable, where **horses** can be rented. (☎649 32 40 38. €12 per hr.) Those with a car can drive farther into the park along the autoroute A-319 to the source of the **Río Guadalquivir,** where breathtaking waterfalls and scenic trails wind alongside the river. The last bus back to Cazorla leaves Torre del Vinagre at 4:30pm; buy tickets on the bus.

PDAs
&
Travel
LET'S GO
(it's not what you're thinking)
Let's Go City Guides
are now available for
Palm OS™ PDAs.
Download a free trial at
http://mobile.letsgo.com
AMSTERDAM BARCELONA BOSTON LONDON PARIS ROME NEW YORK CITY SAN FRANCISCO WASHINGTON D.C.
Palm OS is a registered trademark of Palm, Inc. Let's Go is a registered trademark of Let's Go Publications, Inc. Guidewalk is a registered trademark of Guidewalk LLC.

VALENCIA AND MURCIA

VALENCIA

With a coastline of popular beaches and a rolling interior, Valencia is something of a natural wonder. The farmlands are a patchwork of orange orchards and vegetable fields, all fed by Moorish irrigation systems. Bordering the lush heart of Valencia, the 466km of Mediterranean shoreline alternate between soft dunes and jagged promontories. Valencia's natural beauty has found a place even in its cities, where carefully landscaped gardens display ornate fountains and exotic plants.

Valencia's past is a tangle of power struggles between the whole cast of usual suspects: Phoenicians, Carthaginians, Greeks, Romans, and Moors. The region first fell under Castillian control when El Cid expelled the Moors in 1094; he ruled it in the name of Alfonso VI until his death in 1099. Without El Cid's powerful influence, the region again fell to the Moors, remaining an Arab stronghold until 1238. In the 1930s, Valencia was again besieged, this time by Franco's troops. The *valencianos* resisted with characteristic strength; Valencia was the last region incorporated into Franco's Spain. In 1977, with the reinstitution of the monarchy, the region finally regained its autonomy.

Valenciano, the regional language spoken sparingly in the north and inland, is a dialect of Catalan. Although Valencia's regionalism is not as intense as Cataluña's, the Generalitat's recent mandate that all students enroll in one course of *valenciano* reflects a resurgence of regional pride. Valencia's festivals are some of the wildest in Spain, and its culinary heritage has had a pronounced impact on Spanish cuisine: *paella*, now considered a quintessential Spanish dish, was first concocted somewhere in the region's rice fields, and Valencian oranges are widely accepted as the best in the nation, if not the world.

VALENCIA ☎963

Though Valencia's population (750,000) makes it the third largest city in Spain, it has very little of the ugly urban sprawl which characterizes many of the country's other big cities. An architectural wonder, Valencia is among the few places in Europe where ultra-modern styles are successfully blended with the traditional. It is a city of great contrasts, from the white-sand beaches of its coast, to the multitude of parks which lie in the dried-up bed of the Río Turia, to its palm tree-lined avenues and thoroughfares. Despite its cosmopolitan modernity, Valencia still manages to retain a certain small-town charm that enchants all those who visit.

TRANSPORTATION

Flights: Airport (☎961 59 85 00), 8km from the city. **Cercanías** trains run between the airport and train station (30min.; M-F every 30min., Sa-Su every hr. 7:03am-10:03pm; €1). Many flights to the Balearic Islands. **Iberia,** C. La Paz, 14 (☎963 52 75 52 or 24hr. info and reservations 902 40 05 00). Open M-F 9am-2pm and 4-7pm.

Trains: Estación del Nord, C. Xàtiva, 24 (☎963 52 02 02), 3 blocks down Av. Marqués de Sotelo from Pl. Ayuntamiento. Ticket windows open 7:30am-9:30pm. **RENFE** (24hr. ☎902 24 02 02) to: **Alicante** (2-3hr., 9 per day 10am-9pm, €8.58-25); **Barcelona** (3hr., 12 per day 6:35am-8:05pm, €31); **Madrid** (3½hr., 9 per day 6:45am-8:15pm, €28); **Sevilla** (8½hr., 11:30am, €34). **Cercanías** trains run at least twice an hour to: **Gandía** (1hr., €3.15); **Játiva** (45min., €2.43); **Sagunto** (30min., €2.01).

Buses: Estación Terminal d'Autobuses, Av. Menéndez Pidal, 13 (☎963 49 72 22), across the riverbed, a 25min. walk from the city center. Municipal bus #8 (€0.78) runs between Pl. Ayuntamiento and the bus station. **Auto Res** (☎963 49 22 30) goes to **Madrid** (4hr., 13 per day 7am-3am, €20.82). **ALSA** (☎902 42 22 42) to: **Alicante** via the **Costa Blanca** (4½hr., 13 per day 6:30am-6pm, €12); **Barcelona** (4½hr., 15 per day 1am-10pm, €19); **Granada** (8hr., 5 per day 1-10:30pm, €31); **Málaga** (11hr., 5 per day 1-10:30pm, €38); **Sevilla** (11hr., 4 per day 2:45-10:30pm, €40).

Ferries: Trasmediterránea, Estació Marítima (☎902 45 46 45). Take bus #4 from Pl. Ayuntamiento or #1 or 2 from the bus station. Ferries run to Mallorca and Ibiza (1-2 per day, €30-69, depending on speed of ferry and class). There is one 15hr. ferry to Menorca each week. (Sa 11:30pm, prices vary). Buy tickets at a travel agency or at the port on the day of departure. Ask a travel agent about **Balearia** (☎902 16 01 80) Denia-Eivissa service. See **By Boat,** p. 337.

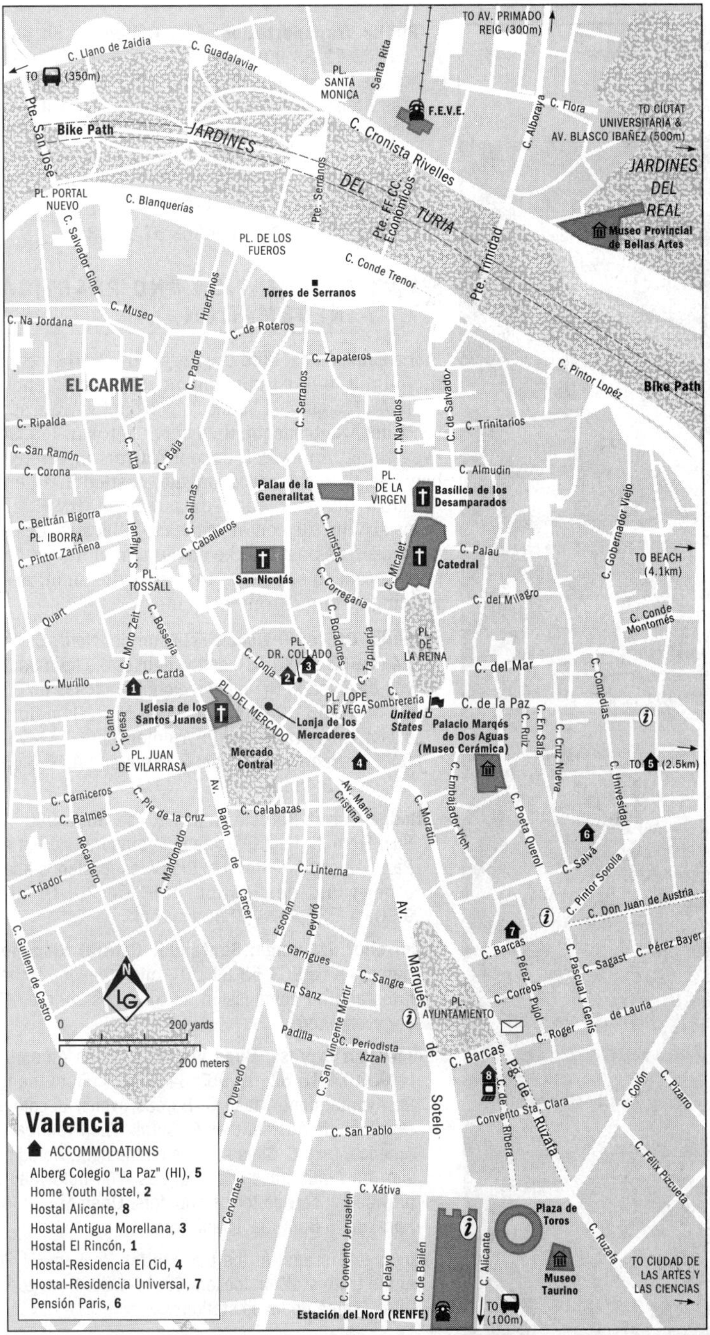
Valencia
ACCOMMODATIONS
Alberg Colegio "La Paz" (HI), 5
Home Youth Hostel, 2
Hostal Alicante, 8
Hostal Antigua Morellana, 3
Hostal El Rincón, 1
Hostal-Residencia El Cid, 4
Hostal-Residencia Universal, 7
Pensión Paris, 6
TO AV. PRIMADO REIG (300m)
TO (350m)
TO CIUTAT UNIVERSITARIA & AV. BLASCO IBAÑEZ (500m)
JARDINES DEL TURIA
JARDINES DEL REAL
Museo Provincial de Bellas Artes
Bike Path
F.E.V.E.
PL. SANTA MONICA
PL. PORTAL NUEVO
PL. DE LOS FUEROS
Torres de Serranos
EL CARME
Palau de la Generalitat
PL. DE LA VIRGEN
Basílica de los Desamparados
Catedral
San Nicolás
PL. TOSSALL
PL. IBORRA
PL. DE LA REINA
PL. DR. COLLADO
PL. LOPE DE VEGA
United States
Iglesia de los Santos Juanes
Lonja de los Mercaderes
Mercado Central
PL. DEL MERCADO
PL. JUAN DE VILARRASA
Palacio Marqués de Dos Aguas (Museo Cerámica)
TO BEACH (4.1km)
TO (2.5km)
PL. AYUNTAMIENTO
Plaza de Toros
Museo Taurino
Estación del Nord (RENFE)
TO (100m)
TO CIUDAD DE LAS ARTES Y LAS CIENCIAS
0 200 yards
0 200 meters
C. Llano de Zaidia
C. Guadalaviar
Santa Rita
C. Flora
C. Alboraya
C. Cronista Rivelles
Pte. San José
Pte. Serranos
Pte. FF.CC. Económicos
Pte. Trinidad
C. Blanquerías
C. Conde Trenor
C. Salvador Giner
C. Museo
C. Na Jordana
Huerfanos
C. de Roteros
C. Zapateros
C. Pintor Lopéz
C. Padre
C. Serranos
C. Navellos
C. de Salvador
C. Trinitarios
C. Ripalda
C. San Ramón
C. Corona
C. Alta
C. Baja
C. Almudin
C. Salinas
C. Beltrán Bigorra
C. Pintor Zariñena
S. Miguel
C. Caballeros
C. Juristas
C. Micalet
C. Palau
C. Gobernador Viejo
C. Corregaria
C. del Milagro
C. Conde Montornés
Quart
C. Moro Zeit
C. Bossería
C. Boradores
C. Tapinería
C. Lonja
C. Murillo
C. Carda
C. Sombrerería
C. del Mar
C. Comedias
C. de la Paz
C. En Sala
C. Ruiz
C. Cruz Nueva
C. Santa Teresa
C. Universidad
C. Carniceros
C. Balmes
C. Pie de la Cruz
Av. Barón de Carcer
C. Calabazas
Av. María Cristina
C. Moratín
C. Embajador Vich
C. Poeta Querol
C. Salvá
Recardero
C. Maldonado
C. Triador
C. Linterna
C. Pintor Sorolla
C. Don Juan de Austria
C. Guillem de Castro
Escolan
Peydró
Av. Marqués de Sotelo
C. Barcas
Pérez Pujol
C. Pascual y Genís
C. Sagast
C. Pérez Bayer
Garrigues
C. Sangre
En Sanz
C. San Vincente Mártir
C. Correos
Padilla
C. Periodista Azzah
C. Roger de Lauria
C. Quevedo
Pg. de Ruzafa
C. de Ribera
Convento Sta. Clara
C. Colón
C. Pizarro
C. San Pablo
C. Félix Pizcueta
C. Xátiva
Cervantes
C. Convento Jerusalén
C. Pelayo
C. de Bailén
C. Alicante
C. Ruzafa

FROM THE ROAD

GOING SOLO

"Traveling by yourself in Spain is like going to the movies alone. Yes, you might enjoy the picture, but you have no one to put your arm around during the romantic parts, no one to hold during the scary parts, and when it's over, no one with whom you can discuss what you've just seen."

Don Carlos, the quintessentially Spanish owner of a hostel in Alicante, wasn't the first person in Spain with whom I'd discussed that most sensitive of subjects: traveling alone. Most of the Spaniards I spoke with seemed utterly appalled at the thought of journeying solo around their country.

"Only anti-social people do that," one young Spanish woman told me. After I mentioned that I myself was a solo traveler, she altered her opinion only slightly. "Well, I guess it's for sociable people, but only those who are trying to escape something," she conceded.

Perhaps because they are a gregarious and social people, the Spanish don't seem to understand the benefits of eating, sunbathing, or traveling on your own. Still, I was surprised and humored to hear what one German traveler, as gregarious and social as the Spaniard, had to say about it. "Traveling alone is great because it offers you an escape from your normal life and the things that bother you—you can eat, go to the beach, and do whatever you want at your own pace," he said. I couldn't help but laugh at the irony: the aspects of traveling alone that made the experience negative for one person were precisely the same aspects that made it positive for someone else.

Public Transportation: EMT Office, C. En Sanz, 4 (☎963 52 83 99). Open M-F 8am-2pm. Bus #8 runs to the bus station. Buses #10, 21, 22, and 23 go to Las Arenas and Malvarrosa along Po. Marítimo. Buy tickets (€0.78) on board; 10-ride ticket (€4.44) or 1-day pass (€3) available at newsstands. Service stops at 10:30pm. Late-night buses go through Pl. Ayuntamiento (every 45min. 11pm-1:38am).

Taxis: ☎963 70 33 33 or 963 57 13 13.

ORIENTATION AND PRACTICAL INFORMATION

Since **Estación del Nord** lies very close to the center of the city, it is most convenient to enter Valencia by train. **Av. Marquéz de Sotelo** runs from the train station to **Pl. del Ayuntamiento,** the center of town. Just about everything of interest, except for the university and beaches, is in the **casco antiguo,** nestled in a bend of the now-diverted Río Turia, whose dry riverbed loops around the center of the city. Because of Valencia's size, it's best to take advantage of the extensive bus system to see more than just the small area in walking distance from the center.

Tourist Office: Regional, Estación del Nord, C. Xàtiva, 24 (☎963 52 85 73), on the right of the train tracks as you disembark. The main regional **branch** is on C. Paz, 46-48 (☎963 98 64 22). Open M-F 10am-6pm, Sa 10am-2pm. **City office,** Pl. Ayuntamiento, 1 (☎963 51 04 17). Open M-F 8:30am-2:15pm and 4:15-6:15pm, Sa 9am-12:45pm.

Budget Travel: Barceló Viajes: C. Paz, 38 (☎963 51 47 84). From Pl. Reina, facing the cathedral, go left on C. Paz. Can organize travel to the Balearic Islands and any other world destination. ISIC €4.20. Open M-F 9:30am-1:30pm, Sa 9:30am-1pm.

Currency Exchange: Santander Central Hispano, C. Barcas, 8 (☎963 53 81 00), offers decent exchange rates and no commission on traveler's checks. **ATMs** are everywhere.

American Express: Duna Viajes, C. Cirilo Amorós, 88 (☎963 74 15 62; fax 963 34 57 00). From the tip of Pl. Ayuntamiento, take C. Barcas, which becomes C. Don Juan de Austria, then C. Sorní. When you reach Pl. América, take C. Cirilo Amorós on the right. No commission on AmEx traveler's cheques. Will hold mail and provide fax service for cardholders. Open M-F 9:30am-2pm and 5-8pm, Sa 10am-1pm.

Luggage Storage: At the **bus station,** lockers €1.80-3. At the **train station,** lockers €2.40-4.50. Both good for 24hr., same hours as stations.

El Corte Inglés, C. Colón and C. Pintor Sorilla (☎963 51 24 44). Open M-Sa 10am-10pm.

Laundromat: Lavandería El Mercat, Pl. Mercado, 12 (☎963 91 20 10). Full-service wash and dry in 2-3hr. for €9. Open M-F 10am-2pm and 5-9pm, Sa 10am-2pm.

Emergency: ☎112. **Ambulance:** ☎085.

Late-Night Pharmacy: Rotates daily. Check listing in the local paper *Levante* (€0.75) or check the *farmacias de guardia* schedule posted outside any pharmacy.

Hospital: Hospital Clínico Universitario, Av. Blasco Ibañez, 17 (☎963 86 26 00), at the corner of C. Dr. Ferrer. Take bus #41, 71, or 81 from Pl. Ayuntamiento. An English-speaking doctor is often on duty.

Internet Access: Fundación Bancaixa, Pl. Tetuán, 23 (☎963 87 58 64). Free 1hr. per day on somewhat slow computers. Passport or student ID required. Open M-F 9am-2pm and 4-9pm, Sa 9am-2pm. **Confederación,** C. Ribera, 8 (☎963 94 03 11), off Pl. Ayuntamiento. 46 ultra-modern computers. €1.80 per 30min., €3 per hr. **Ono,** C. San Vicente, 22 (☎963 28 19 02), around the corner from the farthest end of the Pl. Ayuntamiento headed toward Pl. del Mercado, has the latest in Internet technology. €1.20 per hr. Open daily 9am-1am.

Post Office: Pl. Ayuntamiento, 24 (☎963 51 67 50). Open M-F 8:30am-8:30pm, Sa 9:30am-2pm. **Postal Code:** 46080.

ACCOMMODATIONS

Hostels may clutter Valencia's streets, but during weekends, especially in summer, finding a room isn't always easy—it's best to call in advance. Reservations are especially necessary during the *papier-mâché* orgy of *Las Fallas* (Mar. 12-19). The best deals cluster around **Plaza del Ayuntamiento** and **Plaza del Mercado.**

NEAR PLAZA DEL AYUNTAMIENTO

Hostal-Residencia El Cid, C. Cerrajeros, 13 (☎/fax 963 92 23 23). From the train station, pass Pl. Ayuntamiento and take the 2nd left off C. Vicente Mártir. Room quality varies–some have TVs and A/C, others just a fan. Singles €12; doubles €22, with shower €26, with bath €30. AmEx/MC/V. ❶

Pensión Paris, C. Salvá, 12 (☎963 52 67 66). From Pl. Ayuntamiento, turn right at C. Barcas, left at C. Poeta Querol, and take the 2nd right onto C. Salvá. 13 spotless rooms with balconies. Singles €16; doubles €24, with shower €28; triples €34/€39. ❷

Obviously, the experience is entirely what you make of it. With the right attitude, it can be incredibly satisfying, but be aware that at times, it can be difficult even for the most self-assured. I'll admit there were instances when I became unbearably conscious of the fact that I was traveling alone. They all happened to occur on the same day: all the hostels in Alicante had only double rooms available; the mouth-watering *paella* I saw at an outdoor restaurant was made for two; there was a 2-for-1 deal on sangria at one of the bars I visited, but only if you brought someone else with you. And for some reason, the scooter-rental agency I passed had only 2-seater models available.

Though traveling alone can be trying at times, remember this: the splendors of the Alhambra can only be appreciated in the eyes of the one who beholds them, and the purity of the Guadalquivir River can only be sensed by the individual who makes the trek to its source in the Parque de Cazorla and bathes in its waters. Though *paella* and sangria are meant to be enjoyed in the company of others, one of the most gratifying aspects of going solo is being able to say "no" when that beautiful person on the Costa Blanca asks you if anyone is sitting in the only unoccupied beach chair, the one right beside you.

Don Carlos was right. Traveling alone in Spain is exactly like going to the movies by yourself. The only difference is that in your travels, you can determine what the ending will be like.

–Josh Ludmir

Hostal Alicante, C. Ribera, 8 (☎963 51 22 96), on the pedestrian street off Pl. Ayuntamiento. As central as it gets, with clean, well-lit rooms and firm beds. Hugely popular with backpackers. Singles €19, with bath €24; doubles €27, with bath €36. MC/V. ❷

Hostal-Residencia Universal, C. Barcas, 5 (☎963 51 53 84), off Pl. Ayuntamiento. Clean rooms, large windows, and quilted bedspreads make up for the slightly dingy hallway showers. No curfew. Singles €17; doubles €26, with shower €29; triples €34. ❷

NEAR PLAZA DEL MERCADO

Home Youth Hostel, C. Lonja, 4 (☎963 91 62 29), directly behind the Lonja, on a side street off Pl. Dr. Collado. In this popular communal dwelling, road-weary guests take time to exchange travel stories and phone numbers. Coed hall baths with showers. Internet €0.50 for 15min. Laundry service €4 for wash and dry. Bike rental €6 per day. Dorms €14 per person; singles €21; doubles €30; triples €43; quads €54. ❷ Those who wish to crash in Valencia for an extended period of time can stay at the hostel's other location, **C. Cadirers, 11** (☎963 92 40 63; www.likeathome.net), past Pl. Mercado, about 1 block from the main hostel. Rooms €120-150 per month. ❶

Hostal Antigua Morellana, C. En Bou, 2 (☎/fax 963 91 57 73), past Pl. Dr. Collado, in the small streets behind the Lonja. Brightly lit, quiet, and comfortable rooms with bath, A/C, TV, and phone. Caters to an older crowd. Singles €29; doubles €42. ❸

Hostal El Rincón, C. Carda, 11 (☎963 91 79 98). From Pl. Ayuntamiento, Pl. Mercado extends past the market and continues as C. Carda. Bright hallways lead to bare-walled but clean rooms. Singles €10, with bath €13; doubles €18, with bath €24. MC/V. ❶

NEAR THE BEACH

Alberg Colegio "La Paz" (HI), Av. Puerto, 69 (☎96 369 01 52), nearly halfway between the city and the port. Take bus #19 from Pl. Ayuntamiento (next to Citibank) and get off at the 8th stop on Av. Puerto (20min. walk to the beach). 2-4 people and a bathroom in every room. Breakfast included. Sheets €3. Reception daily 3pm-2am. Open July-Sept. 15. Dorms €12, over 26 €9.61. ❶

FOOD

Paella may be the most famous, but it is actually just one of 200 Valencian rice dishes. Other specialties include *arroz a banda* (rice and fish with garlic, onion, tomatoes, and saffron), *all i pebre* (eels fried in oil, paprika, and garlic), *fideua* (same as *paella*, but made with noodles instead of rice), and *sepia con salsa verde* (cuttlefish with garlic and parsley). Valencia's restaurants are generally cheap and perfect for people on the run. Bushels of fresh fish, meat, and fruit are sold at the **Mercado Central,** on Pl. Mercado (open M-F 7am-3pm). For **groceries,** stop by **El Corte Inglés,** C. Colón (basement level) or C. Pintor Sorilla (5th fl.). (☎963 51 24 44. Open M-Sa 10am-10pm.)

El Rall, Tundidores, 2 (☎963 92 20 90), between the Lonja and Pl. Negrito. Excellent *paellas* (€7.50-10) and other seafood dishes served outdoors in a small, pleasant square. Open daily 1-4pm and 8-11pm. ❷

Restaurante Pruvi Hoy Paella, C. Cerrajeros, 3. Good, homestyle *paella* served in a no-frills setting. *Menu del día* €7.21. Open daily 1-11pm. ❷

La Pappardella, C. Bordadores, 5 (☎963 91 89 15). Facing the cathedral, the restaurant is on the left. 2 floors of pasta bliss. Vast selection of dishes ranging from basic spaghetti, oil, and garlic to exotic pastas complemented by fresh vegetables, meats, and seafood (€3.50-6). *Menú* €7.20. Open daily 2-4:30pm and 9pm-midnight. ❶

La Lluna (☎963 92 21 46), C. Sant Ramón, in El Carme district. From Pg. Guillém de Castro, take C. Corona, then the 1st left onto C. Beneficia; C. Sant Ramón is on the right. A veggie restaurant to moon over. Serves a 4-course *menú* (€5.40) weekday afternoons. Entrees €2.40-3.90. Open M-Sa 1:30-3:30pm and 9-11:30pm. ❶

SIGHTS

Touring Valencia on foot is a good test of stamina. Most of the sights line the now-diverted Río Turia or cluster near Pl. Reina, which is linked to Pl. Ayuntamiento by C. San Vicente Mártir. EMT bus #5, dubbed the **Bus Turistic** (☎963 52 83 99), makes a loop around the old town sights (€0.78; 1-day pass €3 for all buses).

CIUDAD DE LAS ARTES Y LAS CIENCIAS. Modern, airy, and thoroughly fascinating, Valencia's latest urban creation dedicated to the arts and sciences has raised quite a stir. Built on the dried-up bed of the Río Turia, this mini-city has already become the fourth-biggest tourist destination in Spain. The complex is divided into four large attractions, all surrounding a vast reflecting pool. Designed by renowned Spanish architect Santiago Calatrava, the complex is nothing short of stunning. Even the parking garage is a work of art, with a garden terrace, **L'Umbracle,** on the roof. **L'Hemisfèric,** a sleek glass and steel capsule, wows the eyes with its IMAX theater, laser shows, and planetarium. **L'Oceanografic,** which is currently under construction with no set opening date, will recreate diverse aquatic environments in an underground water-world. The enormous **Palau de les Arts,** which is scheduled to be completed by 2004, will house stages for opera, theater, and dance. The **Museu de Les Ciencies Principe Felipe,** the gleaming centerpiece, is packed with students and tourists learning through hands-on exhibits on science and technology. Visitors come as much for the building's extraordinary design as for the museum itself. *(Heading toward the beach along the riverbed off C. Alcalde Reig, bus #35 runs from Pl. Ayuntamiento. ☎902 10 00 31; www.cac.es. IMAX shows €6.60, M-F children and students €4.80. Museum open M-F and Su 10am-8pm, F-Sa 10am-9pm. €6, M-F children and students €4.21.)*

CATHEDRAL. Begun in the 13th century and completed in 1482, this magnificent cathedral is the region's most impressive building. The three different entrances display a melange of Romanesque, Gothic, and Baroque architectural styles. Incredible views of Valencia's skyline can be seen from atop the **Miguelete** (the cathedral tower). French novelist Victor Hugo once counted 300 bell towers in the city from this vantage point. The interior is lined with altars, each with its own design and character. The **Museo de la Catedral** squeezes a great many treasures into three tiny rooms—one for the Gothic period, one for the Renaissance, and the last for Mannerism. Check out the overwrought tabernacle made from 1200kg of gold, silver, platinum, emeralds, and sapphires, plus a Holy Grail, two Goyas, and the Crucifijo de Marfil statues, which depict "man's passions." *(Pl. Reina. Cathedral ☎963 91 01 89. Open daily 8am-2pm and 5-8pm. Closes earlier in winter. Free. Tower open daily 10am-1pm and 4:30-7pm. €1.20. Museum ☎963 91 81 27. Open Mar.-May and Oct.-Nov. M-F 10am-1pm and 4:30-6pm, June-Sept. 10am-1pm and 4:30-7pm, Dec.-Feb. 10am-1pm. Sa-Su open 10am-1pm year-round. €1.20.)*

MUSEU PROVINCIAL DE BELLES ARTES. One of Valencia's finer attractions, this museum features a wide array of paintings, with one floor dedicated to 14th- to 16th-century Valencian art and another to more recent works. The museum has been named one of Spain's premier art galleries. The collection also includes works by Spanish and foreign masters, including El Greco's *San Juan Bautista*, Velázquez's self-portrait, Ribera's *Santa Teresa*, and a slew of Goyas. Check out the sculpture pavilion. *(C. Sant Pius V, near the Jardines del Real. ☎963 60 57 93. Open Tu-Sa 10am-2:15pm and 4-7:30pm, Su 10am-7:30pm. Free.)*

PYROMANIAC'S PARADISE If you can choose any time of year to come to Valencia, make it March 12 to 19, when Valencia's most illustrious event, *Las Fallas*, grips the city. The city explodes with festivity, including parades, bullfights, fireworks, and street dancing. Neighborhoods compete to build the most elaborate and satirical *papier-mâché* effigy; over 300 such enormous *ninots* spring up in the streets. On the final day—*la nit del foc* (fire night)—Valencians burn all the *ninots* simultaneously in one last, clamorous inferno meant to bring luck for the agricultural season and exorcize the social ills satirized by the *papier-mâché* giants.

INSTITUT VALENCIÁ D'ART MODERN (IVAM). See everything from classic avant-garde to 1970s clash. IVAM is also home to a collection of abstract works by 20th-century sculptor Julio González, among others. The rotating temporary exhibits are extremely popular. *(C. Guillém de Castro, 118, west across the old river. Bus #5 stops right in front. ☎963 86 30 00. Open Tu-Su 10am-7pm. €2.10, students €1.05; Su free.)*

PARKS. Manicured parks surround the city center. Horticulturists will marvel at the **Jardín Botánico,** a university-maintained garden that cultivates 43,000 plants of 300 international species. *(C. Quart, 80, on the western end of Río Turia near Gran Vía Fernando el Católico. ☎963 91 16 57. Open Tu-Su 10am-9pm, closes earlier in winter. €0.30.)* One block farther, a series of well-kept recreation areas line the banks and bed of the Río Turia. Next to the Museu Provincial de Bellas Artes, off C. San Pio V, is the popular **Jardines del Real,** home to ponds, caged birds, fountains, and greenhouses.

OTHER SIGHTS. The elliptical **Basílica Virgen de los Desamparados** houses a resplendent golden altar. *(Behind the cathedral on Pl. Virgen. Open for Mass M-F 7am-2pm and 5-9pm, Su 7:30am-2:30pm and 5-9:30pm. Free.)* The old **Lonja de la Seda (Silk Exchange)** is one of the foremost examples of Valencian Gothic architecture and a testament to Valencia's prominence in the medieval silk trade. *(Pl. Mercado. ☎963 52 54 78. Open Tu-Sa 9:15am-2pm and 5:30-9pm, Su 9am-1:30pm. Free.)*

FESTIVALS

Valencia's most famous festival is **Las Fallas,** March 12-19 (see **Pyromaniac's Paradise,** p. 316). During **Semana Santa,** the streets clog with monks enacting Biblical scenes and children performing the miracle plays of St. Vincent Ferrer. **Corpus Christi** follows soon after with its display of *rocas* (huge carriages symbolizing Biblical mysteries). The **Festiu de Juliol** (Festival of July) brings fireworks, riverside concerts, bullfights, and a *batalla de flores*—a violet skirmish in which flowers are tossed between parade-goers and girls on passing floats.

NIGHTLIFE

Use your siesta wisely—Valencia's nightlife will keep you drinking and dancing until sunrise. Bars and pubs in **El Carme,** just beyond the market, start up at 11:30pm. Follow Pl. Mercado and C. Bolsería (bearing right) to Pl. Tossal, where outdoor terraces, upbeat music, and *agua de Valencia* (orange juice, champagne, and vodka) energize the masses. Many bars can also be found along **C. Caballeros** in El Carme district. One of the most popular establishments here is **Carmen Sui Generis,** C. Caballeros, 38, an upscale lounge with eclectic decor and chic clientele set in an 18th-century palace. (☎963 92 52 73. Cocktails €5-6. Open W-Sa 11pm-3am.) Popular with locals is **Cafe Negrito,** Pl. del Negrito, 1, off C. Caballeros, a loud bar and cafe which prides itself on its *agua de Valencia* (€6 for a pitcher) and outdoor tables. (☎963 91 42 33. Open daily 10pm-3am.) Fans of house music flock to **Circus,**

C. Alta, 11, a hip bar with brightly painted walls and disco balls. (☎963 91 38 16. Beer €4.50. Open daily 11pm-3am.) An older crowd fills the spacious bar **Fox Congo,** C. Caballeros, 35. (☎963 92 55 27. Beer €3.60, mixed drinks €5.40. Open daily 7pm-3:30am.) Sip martinis (€4-6) to the soothing sounds of classic jazz at **Jimmy Glass,** an ultra cool bar on C. Baja, 28, not far from Circus. American students frequent **Finnegan's,** at Pl. Reina, 19, an Irish pub in front of the cathedral. (☎963 91 05 03. Pints of beer €3. Open Su-Th 12:30pm-1am, F-Sa 12:30pm-3am.)

Discos, which normally don't draw a crowd until at least 3am, dominate the university area, particularly on **Av. Blasco Ibañez.** Among these is **Rumbo 144,** Av. Blasco Ibanez, 144, which spins Spanish pop and house and is popular among local students and foreigners alike. (☎963 71 00 25. Cover €6-8. Open F-Su midnight-7am.) There are a few smaller discos in El Carme district, most of which are popular with both gay and straight patrons. A lively and popular gay club is **Venial,** C. Quart, 34 (☎963 91 73 56), by the Jardín Botánico. In summer, some of the best places to be seen are the outdoor discos at Playa de Malvarrosa. **Caballito de Mar,** C. Eugenia Viñes, 22 (☎963 71 07 63), is the most popular and heats up with a psychedelic tunnel and huge outdoor deck. For more info, consult the *Qué y Dónde* weekly magazine (€0.90) or the weekly entertainment supplement, *La Cartelera* (€0.75), both available at newsstands.

BEACHES

Sand-seekers can join the topless by bouncing down to the expansive and packed beaches on Valencia's coast. The sand and water quality are less than spectacular, but the blistering heat converts everyone into sea-lovers. The most popular beaches are **Las Arenas** and **Malvarrosa,** connected by a bustling boardwalk. Buses #20, 21, 22, and 23 all pass by the sands. Equally crowded but more attractive is **Salér,** a pine-bordered strand 14km from the city that divides a lagoon from the sea. Cafeterias and snack bars line the shore. **Autobuses Buñol** (☎963 49 14 25) go to Salér (on the way to El Perello) from the intersection of Gran Vía de Germanías and C. Sueca. To get to the bus stop, exit the train station, and take the street to the right (between the station and the bullring) to Gran Vía Germanías. The bus stop is one block down (25min., every 30min. 7am-10pm, €0.90).

DAYTRIPS FROM VALENCIA

SAGUNTO (SAGUNT)

Frequent Cercanías trains (☎962 66 07 28) from Valencia (C-6 line) stop in Sagunto (30min.; M-F 37 per day 6:10am-10:30pm, Sa-Su 15 per day 7:20am-10:30pm; M-F €2.07, Sa-Su €2.16), as do ALSA buses (☎964 66 18 50; 45min., every 30min. 7am-10:15pm, €1.74).

The residents of Sagunto are thought to be the most courageous in Spain. This reputation dates back to the 3rd century BC, when the citizens of Phoenician-controlled Sagunto (called Saguntum) held out for an eight-month siege by Hannibal's Carthaginians. Some sources say that on the brink of annihilation, Sagunto's women, children, and elderly threw themselves into a burning furnace; others insist that the residents chose starvation over defeat.

The architectural medley of Sagunto's monuments reflects a long list of conquering forces. The highlight of the old town is its refurbished **medieval castle,** declared a national monument in 1931. (Open June-Sept. Tu-Sa 10am-8pm, Su 10am-2pm; Oct.-May Tu-Sa 10am-2pm and 4-6pm, Su 10am-2pm. Free.) Along the way into town is the **Roman Theater,** which has survived a controversial restoration process to become an impressive modern performance stage, built entirely on the skeleton of the original Roman structure. Ask at the **tourist office** in Pl. Cronisto Chabret, at the far end from the Ayuntamiento, for a list of performances. (☎962 66 22 13; www.sagunt.com/turismo. Open M-Th 8am-3pm and 4:30-7pm, F 8am-3pm and 4-6:30pm, Sa 8:45am-1:45pm.) By the port (4km from the town center), Sagunto's **beaches** attract summer travelers. **Puerto de Sagunto** bears the EU's *bandera azul.* **Buses** to the beaches leave from Av. Santos Patronos next to the tourist office (every 30min. 7am-9:30pm, €0.60).

L'ALBUFERA

Autobuses Buñol buses (☎963 49 14 25) depart from the intersection of Gran Vía de Germanías and C. Sueca in Valencia, stopping in L'Albufera en route to El Perello (40min., every 30min., €1.05). To catch the return bus, walk with your back to the lagoon and cross the bridge on your right.

Spain's largest lagoon, L'Albufera, 15km south of Valencia, and the surrounding **Parc Natural de L'Albufera,** are a nature lover's paradise. Trails for biking and hiking ring the lake, while small fishing boats hide amid tall wetland reeds. L'Albufera, one of the wettest regions on the Iberian peninsula, is a prime spot for bird watching—over 250 migrant species make temporary camp along its shores. Ask at a Valencia tourist office for information on boat tours or cultural excursions.

JÁTIVA (XÀTIVA)

Trains are the best way to get in and out of Játiva. RENFE (☎963 52 02 02) runs from Valencia to Játiva (1hr., every 30min. 6am-10pm, €2.61). From Játiva, trains run to Valencia (6am-10pm) and Alicante (1hr., 6 per day, €15). To reach the old village from the train station, walk straight up Baixada de L'Estació and turn left at its end.

Once the second most populated city in Valencia, Játiva, a mecca of palaces and churches, was burned to the ground by Felipe V in the 18th century. Today it is simply a quiet town with little to offer other than its impressive castle and its annual festival. Held since 1250, Játiva's **Fira festival** storms the city August 15-20 with live music, bullfights, and pulling (tug-of-war) contests. **Alameda de Jaume I** divides the town into the new and the old villages, starting from the foot of a hill topped by an awe-inspiring castle. The **castle** above has two sections: the **castell machor,** on the right as you enter, and the pre-Roman **castell chicotet.** The former, used from the 13th through the 16th century, bears the scars of siege and earthquake. Its vaulted **prison** has held some famous wrongdoers, including King Fernando el Católico and the Comte d'Urgell, would-be usurper of the Aragonese throne. The Comte is now buried in its chapel. To get there, it's a 30min. walk uphill. A tourist train chugs up to the castle at 12:30 and 4:30pm. (Open Tu-Su 10am-7pm; in winter Tu-Su 10am-6pm. €1.50, students and seniors €0.75.) The **tourist office,** Alameda Jaume I, 50, is across from the Ayuntamiento. (☎962 27 33 46. English spoken. Open June 15-Sept. 15 Tu-F 10am-2:30pm and 5-7pm, Sa-Su 10am-2pm; Sept. 16-June 14 Tu-F 9am-2pm and 4-6pm, Sa-Su 10am-2pm.)

MORELLA ☎964

Rising majestically above the fertile valley below, the medieval fortress town of Morella (pop. 2000) is an isolated gem for the traveler, located in the northernmost extremes of the Comunitat Valenciana. With picturesque cobblestone streets, impressive medieval walls, and a castle crowning its highest point, the town offers soothing vistas for those who wish to get away from the hustle and bustle of Barcelona or the Costa Blanca. Tourists are only the latest in a long line of people who have been drawn to Morella, as the town has also played host to the Celts, Romans, and Moors at various times throughout its history.

PRACTICAL INFORMATION. Morella is hard to reach. Most visitors arrive via Valencia, though the city is also accessible from Barcelona. Travelers must make a connection at **Castelló,** on the **Cercanías train** line from Valencia (1hr.; M-F 36 per day 6:10am-10:30pm, Sa-Su 15 per day 7:20am-10:30pm; M-F €3.15, Sa-Su €3.30). From Barcelona, the **RENFE** Mediterranean goes to Castelló (2½hr., 17 per day 8am-9pm, €14-23). **Autos Mediterráneo buses** (☎964 22 00 54 or 964 22 05 36) depart from the bus stop outside of Castelló's train station for **Morella** (2½hr.; to Morella M-F 7:30am and 3:45pm, Sa 3:45pm; returns M-F 7:30am and 4pm, Sa 4pm; €7.20). The bus from Castelló doesn't originate at the bus stop, however, and only stops there briefly, so keep an eye out for it. Morella's **tourist office,** Pl. San Miguel, 3, is right by Puerta San Miguel, the enormous arched entrance to the city. (☎964 17 30 32; fax 964 17 30 32; www.morella.net. Open July-Aug. daily 10am-2pm and 4-7pm, Sept.-June Tu-Sa 10am-2pm and 4-6pm.) In an **emergency,** dial ☎112. For **medical assistance,** call ☎964 16 09 62.

ACCOMMODATIONS. Once you pass through the Moorish archways of Morella, you may never want to leave. **Hostal La Muralla ❷,** C. Muralla, 12, has rooms with TV and private bath. (☎964 16 02 43. Breakfast €2.40. Singles €19; doubles €27. MC/V.) Live royally (on budget) at **Hostal El Cid ❷,** Port Sant Mateu, 3, 1 block to the right of the bus stop when facing the city wall. Gigantic rooms come with TV, phone, and bathtub; some have balconies. (☎964 16 01 25. Singles €20-25; doubles €33-35. V.) Those seeking a touch of elegance will find it in the comfortable rooms of **Hotel Cardenal Ram ❸,** Cuesta Suner, 1, built in a 15th-century palace at the end of the colonnade on Av. Don Blasco de Alagon. All rooms with large bath, TV, phone, and heat. (☎964 17 32 18. Singles €35; doubles €55.)

FOOD. The town's gourmet cuisine is filled with *trufas* (truffles) dug up from under the local turf. Specialties include *paté de trufas* (truffle pâté) and *cordero relleno trufado* (lamb with truffle stuffing). Eating out in Morella is somewhat pricey, and options are limited—most eateries are located on shop-lined Don Blasco de Alagón, Morella's main street. For an unforgettable meal, make reservations at **Restaurante Marques de Cruilles ❸,** C. de l'Hospital, s/n, in front of the Castell de Morella. Set in the rose-covered courtyard of a 14th-century house, the restaurant serves local specialties like rabbit or chicken marinated in garlic (€6.95) and steak (€11.25)—no truffles, though. (☎964 16 09 90. Open daily 1-4pm and 8:30-11pm.) **Restaurante Cardenal Ram ❷,** Cuesta Suner, 1, in the hotel and off C. Don Blasco de Alagón, serves delicious local favorites, including hen, quail, rabbit, and truffle-stuffed lamb (€6.60-9.60) in a beautiful dining room with views of the countryside. (☎964 17 30 85. *Menú* €25. Open daily 1:30-3:15pm and 8:30-10:15pm. MC/V.) Those looking to escape the truffle madness run to **Restaurante Lola ❶,** Blasco de Alagón, 21, for the best Italian cuisine in town. (☎964 16 03 87. Entrees €4.20-6. Open M-Sa noon-4:30pm and 8:30pm-2am.)

SIGHTS. Perched atop a massive rock, the **Castell de Morella** dazzles even the most seasoned of castle-goers. Celts, Romans, and Moors have all defended Morella's walls as their own. El Cid stormed the summit in 1084, and Don Blasco de Aragón took the town in the name of Jaume I in 1232. Civil wars in the 19th century and an internal explosion have damaged the castle, but the resulting craters only add to the intrigue. Artillery walls surround the exterior, with openings just wide enough for the sights of battling archers or the lens of your Nikon. Inspect the **Cadro guardhouse** and the **Catxo dungeon,** where the prince of Vienna was imprisoned in the 15th century. (☎964 17 31 28. Entrance on C. Hospital, uphill from the basilica and through the Convent of St. Frances. Open M-F 10:30am-2pm and 4-7:30pm, Sa-Su 10:30am-7:30pm; in winter until 6:30pm. €1.80, students €1.20.) In Pl. Arciprestal, on the way to the castle, the ceiling of Gothic **Basílica Santa María la Mayor** hovers over a winding stairwell, an overgrown organ, and the ghostly statue of Nuestra Señora de la Asunción. Bracketed by golden chandeliers, the altar is almost as breathtaking as the Basílica's original 14th-century stained glass windows. (Open June-Aug. daily 11am-2pm and 4-7pm; Sept.-May noon-2pm and 4-6pm. Mass M-F 7pm; Sa 8:15pm; Su 10am, 5, 6:30pm. Basílica free. Museum €0.90.) Exit the city from Pta. de San Miguel, turn left, and walk five minutes to the remnants of the Gothic **aqueduct,** whose arches once spanned 16 towers and six gates. Knights, jesters, minstrels, and tourists flock to the town on the first weekend in July for the **Medieval Fair.** Activities include concerts, medieval banquets, and craft shows. Ask the tourist office for more information.

ALICANTE (ALACANT) ☎965

Few cities blend beach life, nightlife, and city life as well as Alicante (pop. 285,000), a place where anyone can find activities catering to their tastes. History and art buffs get lost in the streets of the *casco antiguo*, peruse the modern art museum, and check out the castle overlooking the entire city. Beach bums catch rays on the crowded shores mere blocks away from the city center, or find refuge on a secluded stretch of coastline just a bus ride away. Partiers marvel at the center's array of pubs, bars, and port-side discos. Every facet of Alicante's vibrant energy crescendoes for one wild week at the end of June when the city celebrates the festival of Sant Joan with a world-famous *fiesta*.

TRANSPORTATION

Flights: Aeroport Internacional El Altet (☎966 91 90 00), 10km from town. **Iberia** (24hr. ☎902 40 05 00) and **Air Europa** (☎902 24 00 42) have daily flights to Madrid, Barcelona, and the Balearic Islands, among other destinations. **Alcoyana** (☎965 16 79 11) bus C-6 runs to the airport from Pl. Luceros (every 40min., €0.85).

Trains: RENFE, Estació Término (☎902 24 02 02), on Av. Salamanca, at the end of Av. Estación. Info open daily 7am-midnight. To: **Barcelona** (4½-6hr., 9 per day 6:55am-6:30pm, €36-62.40); **Elche** (30min., every hr. 6:05am-10:05pm, €1.47-1.56); **Madrid** (4hr., 9 per day 7am-8pm, €33.60-51.60); **Murcia** (1½hr., every hr. 6:05am-10:05pm, €3.45-3.60); **Valencia** (1½hr., 10 per day 6:55am-10:20pm, €8.58-31.80). **Ferrocarriles de la Generalitat Valenciana,** Estació Marina, Av. Villajoyosa, 2 (☎965 26 27 31), on Explanada d'Espanya. Service along the Costa Blanca (see **Costa Blanca,** p. 325). In summer the **Trensnochador** (night train; ☎965 26 27 31) runs to beaches near **Alicante,** including Altea and Benidorm, with some continuing to Dénia (July-Aug. F-Sa every hr. 9pm-5am, Su-Th 4 per night 9pm-5am; €0.90-4.20).

Buses: C. Portugal, 17 (☎965 13 07 00). To reach Explanada d'Espanya from the station, turn left on C. Italia and continue walking; the street will turn into C. San Fernando. Any right turn runs directly to the waterfront. **ALSA** (☎965 13 06 73) to: **Altea** (1hr., 18 per day 6:30am-7:30pm, €3.36); **Barcelona** (7hr., 11 per day 1am-10:30pm, €28); **Calpe** (1½hr., 17 per day 6:30am-7:30pm, €3.99); **Dénia** (2½hr., 10 per day 6:30am-8pm, €6.39); **Granada** (6hr., 7 per day 1:15am-10:45pm, €21); **Jávea** (2hr., 7 per day 8am-9pm, €5.58); **Madrid** (5hr., 9 per day 8am-midnight, €20-30); **Málaga** (8hr., 7 per day 1:15am-10:45pm, €28); **Sevilla** (10hr., 6 per day, €36); **Valencia** (2½hr., 10 per day 7am-9pm, €11.88). **Mollá** (☎965 13 08 51) to **Elche** (30min.; M-F 2 per hr. 7am-10pm, Sa every hr. 8am-10pm, Su 8 per day 9am-9:30pm; €1.38).

Ferries: Balearia Eurolines Maritimes (☎902 16 01 80) departs from nearby Dénia (see p. 330).

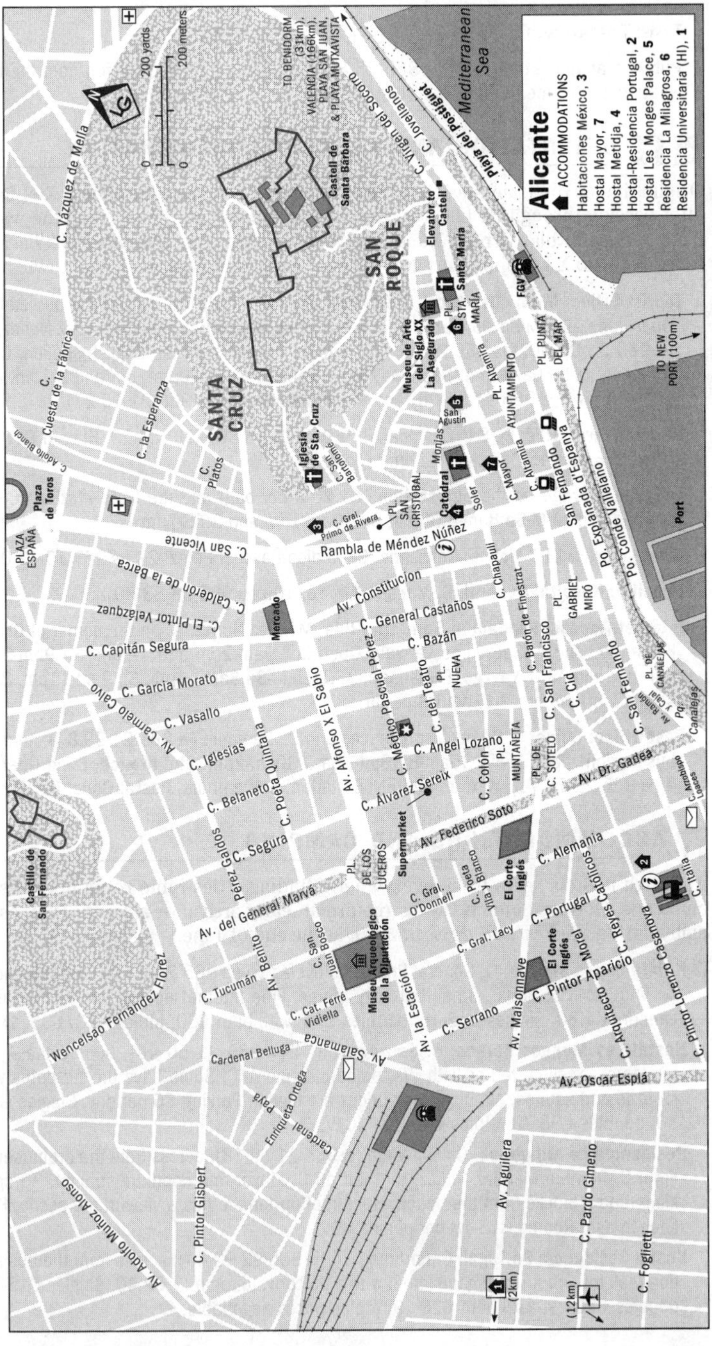
Alicante
ACCOMMODATIONS
Habitaciones México, 3
Hostal Mayor, 7
Hostal Metidja, 4
Hostal-Residencia Portugal, 2
Hostal Les Monges Palace, 5
Residencia La Milagrosa, 6
Residencia Universitaria (HI), 1
Mediterranean Sea
Playa del Postiguet
TO BENIDORM (31km), VALENCIA (166km), PLAYA SAN JUAN, & PLAYA MUTXAVISTA
200 yards
200 meters
Castell de Santa Bárbara
SAN ROQUE
SANTA CRUZ
Elevator to Castell
Santa María
PL. STA. MARÍA
FGV
Museu de Arte del Siglo XX La Asegurada
Iglesia de Sta. Cruz
Catedral
San Agustín
PL. SAN CRISTÓBAL
PL. PUNTA DEL MAR
AYUNTAMIENTO
TO NEW PORT (100m)
Port
C. Vázquez de Mella
C. Cuesta de la Fábrica
C. la Esperanza
C. Platos
C. Adolfo Blanch
Plaza de Toros
PLAZA ESPAÑA
C. San Vicente
C. Calderón de la Barca
C. El Pintor Velázquez
C. Capitán Segura
C. Garcia Morato
Av. Carmelo Calvo
C. Vasallo
C. Iglesias
C. Belaneto
C. Poeta Quintana
C. Segura
Pérez Galdos
Mercado
Rambla de Méndez Núñez
C. Gral. Primo de Rivera
Av. Constitución
C. General Castaños
C. Bazán
PL. NUEVA
C. del Teatro
C. Médico Pascual Pérez
Av. Alfonso X El Sabio
C. Angel Lozano
C. Álvarez Sereix
C. Colón
PL. MUNTAÑETA
Supermarket
PL. DE LOS LUCEROS
Av. Federico Soto
Av. Dr. Gadea
PL. DE C. SOTELO
C. San Francisco
C. Barón de Finestrat
PL. GABRIEL MIRÓ
C. Cid
C. Chapauli
C. Altamira
C. Mayor
PL. Altamira
Soler
Monjas
C. Virgen del Socorro
C. Jovellanos
San Fernando
Explanada d'Espanya
Po. Conde Vallellano
C. San Fernando
PL. DE CANALEJAS
Av. Ramón y Cajal
Pq. Canalejas
C. Arzobispo Loaces
Castillo de San Fernando
Av. del General Marvá
C. Gral. O'Donnell
C. Poeta Vila y Blanco
El Corte Inglés
C. Alemania
C. Portugal
C. Reyes Católicos
C. Italia
Av. Benito
C. San Juan Bosco
Museu Arqueològic de la Diputació
C. Tucumán
C. Cat. Ferré Vidiella
Av. la Estación
C. Gral. Lacy
C. Serrano
Av. Maisonnave
C. Pintor Aparicio
Morel
C. Arquitecto Morel
C. Pintor Lorenzo Casanova
Wencelsao Fernandez Florez
Av. Salamanca
Cardenal Belluga
Enriqueta Ortega
Cardenal Payá
Av. Oscar Esplá
Av. Aguilera
C. Pardo Gimeno
C. Foglietti
C. Pintor Gisbert
Av. Adolfo Muñoz Alonso
(2km)
(12km)

Taxis: Teletaxi ☎965 25 25 11.

Public Transportation: TAM (☎965 25 82 82). Buses #21 and 22 run from the train station in Alicante to Playa San Juan. €0.75.

ORIENTATION AND PRACTICAL INFORMATION

Originating at the train station, **Av. de la Estación** becomes **Av. Alfonso X el Sabio** after passing through Pl. Luceros. **Explanada d'Espanya** stretches along the waterfront between Rbla. Méndez Núñez and Av. Federico Soto; the two reach back up to Av. Alfonso X El Sabio. This grid of streets constitutes the center of town.

Tourist Office: Main city office, C. Portugal, 17 (☎965 92 98 02), at the bus station. Open June-Aug. M-Sa 9am-2pm and 4-8pm. **Regional office,** Rbla. Méndez Nuñez, 23 (☎965 20 00 00; fax 965 20 02 43). Info on the entire coast. English spoken. Open June-Aug. M-F 10am-8pm; Sept.-May M-F 10am-7pm, Sa 10am-2pm and 3-7pm. Also at the **airport** (☎966 91 91 00) and the **Ayuntamiento** (☎900 21 10 27).

Budget Travel: TIVE, Pl. San Cristóbal, 8 (☎965 21 16 86). ISIC €4.20. HI card €10.80. Open M-F 9am-1:30pm and 5-8pm.

Luggage Storage: At the **bus station** (€1.20-3 per bag) and the **train station** (€2.40 per bag). Open M-Sa 8am-8:30pm, Su 10am-1pm and 3:45-7pm.

Emergency: ☎112. **Police:** Comisaría, C. Médico Pascual Pérez, 27 (☎965 10 72 00).

Hospital: Hospital General, C. Maestro Alonzo, 109 (☎965 93 83 00).

Internet Access: Fundación BanCaja, Rbla. Méndez Nuñez, 4, on the corner of C. San Fernando, 2nd fl. Sometimes a wait. Open M-F 9am-2pm and 4-9pm, Sa 9am-2pm. 1hr. free with ISIC. **Yazzgo,** Explanada, 3. Open M-Sa 8am-11pm, Su 9am-11pm. 8am-4pm €1.50 per hr.; 4-11pm €3 per hr.

Post Office: Corner of C. Arzobispo Loaces and C. Alemania (☎965 21 99 84), near the bus station. Open M-F 8:30am-8:30pm, Sa 9:30am-2pm. **2nd branch,** Bono Guarner, 2 (☎965 22 78 71), next to the RENFE Station. Same hours. **Postal Code:** 03070.

ACCOMMODATIONS AND CAMPING

Although hostels seem to be everywhere, finding a desirable room may pose a challenge. Good accommodations require an early arrival or a reservation, especially during the *Festival de Sant Joan* at the end of June.

Habitaciones México, C. General Primo de Rivera, 10 (☎965 20 93 07), off the end of Av. Alfonso X El Sabio. Small but cozy rooms. Free Internet access and kitchen use. Laundry €4.80. Singles €12-15; doubles €27, with bath €30; triples €33/€36. ❶

Hostal Les Monges Palace, C. San Agustín, 4 (☎965 21 50 46), behind the Ayuntamiento. Excellent rooms with TVs, paintings, and A/C. Some have private baths with jacuzzis and saunas, although their prices are higher. Parking €6 per day. Singles €18-30; doubles €33-78; triples €42-90. MC/V. ❷

Residencia La Milagrosa, C. Villa Vieja (☎965 21 69 18), across from the art museum. From C. Rambla Méndez Nuñez, turn left on C. Mayor and continue straight. 30 sparkling rooms blocks from the beach. Huge rooftop terrace has a view of the castle. Free kitchen use. Rooms €15-18 per person. ❷

Hostal-Residencia Portugal, C. Portugal, 26 (☎965 92 92 44), across from the bus station. Ask for a room facing the street with a balcony. In-room TV €2.40. Singles €15-16; doubles €23-29, with bath €28-29; triples prices negotiable. ❷

Hostal Metidja, Rbla. Méndez Nuñez, 26 (☎965 14 36 17), right next door to Havana Café. Ultra-clean rooms with hallway baths that smell like baby powder. All rooms with TV and A/C. Singles €21-26; doubles €36-45; triples €54-67. ❷

Hostal Mayor, C. Mayor, 5 (☎965 20 13 83), 2 blocks up from the waterfront. Centrally-located with simple, brightly painted rooms and clean hallway baths. Since it's close to the beach, Rbla. Méndez Nuñez, and the bars of the *casco antiguo*, rooms can get noisy at night. Sept.-May singles €12; doubles €24. Jun.-Aug. €20/€35. ❷

Residencia Universitaria (HI), Av. Orihuela, 59 (☎965 11 30 44). Take bus #03 (€0.75). Shared rooms with bath and A/C, snack bar, big-screen TV, free laundry, and foosball. 3-day max. stay. Dorms €4.80, with breakfast €5.40, with 3 meals €11.40; over age 26 dorms €6.60, with breakfast €8.40, with 3 meals €14. Open July-Sept. ❶

Camping: Playa Mutxavista (☎965 65 45 26), right by the beach, a few km north of the city center. Hop on bus #21 (€0.75) to get there. Restaurant and supermarket on site. June-Sept. €3.42 per person, €11.07 per tent; Oct.-May €2.10/€7.50. ❶

FOOD

Most visitors refuel along the main pedestrian streets; prices are reasonable despite the crowds of tourists. The numerous Turkish and Lebanese *kebap* restaurants are the best bargains in the city. Smaller, cheaper, family-run *bar-restaurantes* in the old city have less visitors but also less variety. The **market** is near Av. Alfonso X el Sabio (open M-Sa 8am-2pm). Buy basics at **Supermarket Mercadona,** C. Alvarez Sereix, 5, off Av. Federico Soto. (☎965 21 58 94. Open M-Sa 9am-9pm.)

Kebap, C. Italia, 2 (☎965 22 92 35), near Av. Dr. Gadea. Mouth-watering Middle Eastern cuisine. *Kebaps* (pitas with meat or veggies; €2.34) are the most popular dish. Heaping entrees (€5.70-6). Open daily 1-4pm and 8pm-midnight. ❶

La Taberna del Gourmet, C. San Fernando, 10 (☎965 20 42 33). Traditional restaurant which specializes in a *menú* for 2, which includes a wide selection of *paella*, fish, and meat dishes (€16.53-19.53). Other entrees €6-10. Open daily 1-4pm and 7-11pm. ❸

Restaurante El Buen Comer, C. Mayor, 8 (☎965 21 31 03). Fabulous *menú* options (€7.70). Entrees are pricey. Open daily 10am-midnight. ❷

Cafetería Mediterráneo, C. Altamira, 8 (☎965 14 08 40), 2 blocks from the Explanada. A cafe bursting with locals at all hours of the day. Chrome bar displays an array of raw fish. 4-course *menú* €6. Open M-Sa 7am-10pm. ❶

Restaurante O'Pote Gallego, Pl. Santísima Faz, 6 (☎965 20 80 84), in the square behind the Ayuntamiento. Galician and Valencian specialties served in a pleasant outdoor setting. Meat and fish entrees €7-12.95. Open daily 1-4pm and 5-11pm. ❷

SIGHTS AND BEACHES

With drawbridges, dark passageways, and hidden tunnels, the **Castell de Santa Bárbara** keeps silent guard over Alicante's beach. Built by the Carthaginians, the 200m high fortress boasts a dry moat, dungeon, and ammunition storeroom. The *Albacar Vell*, or lower zone, constructed during the Middle Ages, holds a vast sculpture garden with exhibits of Spanish greats. A paved road from the old section of Alicante leads to the top, although most people opt for the **elevator** rising from a hidden entrance on Av. Jovellanos—just across the street from Playa Postiguet, near the white crosswalk. (☎965 26 31 31. Castle open Apr.-Sept. 10am-7:30pm; Oct.-Mar. 9am-6:30pm. Free. Elevator €2.40.) The **Museu de Arte del Siglo XX La Asegurada,** Pl. Santa Maria, 3, at the eastern end of C. Mayor, showcases modern art pieces, including several works by Picasso and Dalí. The museum offers free guided tours if reserved in advance. (☎965 14 07 68. Open May 15-Sept. 14 M-F 10am-2pm and 5-9pm, Sa-Su 10:30am-2:30pm; Sept. 15-May 14 M-F 10am-2pm and 4-8pm, Sa-Su 10:30am-2:30pm. Free.)

Alicante's **Playa del Postiguet,** just meters to the left of the New Port, is perpetually packed with sunbathers, volleyball players, and children on the loose. For more peaceful shores, the 6km of **Playa de San Juan** and **Playa del Mutxavista** are the nearest options. Both **Playa del Postiguet** and **Playa de San Juan** wave the EU *bandera azul* for great waters and beautiful sands. The **Costa Blanca's** gorgeous shores extend to the north along the Alicante-Dénia train line. (To San Juan, take TAM buses #21, 22, or 31. For Mutxavista, take #21. Each departs every 15min., €0.75. The Alicante-Dénia train leaves from the main station every hr., €0.75.)

ENTERTAINMENT AND NIGHTLIFE

The discos and port-side pubs of Alicante make for a vibrant and varied nightlife. Most night owls kick off the evening with bar-hopping in the *casco antiguo*, though there are enough watering-holes in this area to keep even the most alcohol-tolerant of partygoers busy until morning. **Pl. San Cristóbol,** one block toward the castle from Rbla. Méndez Nuñez, offers several popular bars; others line the streets behind the cathedral and heading down toward the water. For a famous *mojito* (lemon, rum, mint, and sugar; €2.10), head to **Coscorrón,** C. Tarifo, 3, open since 1936 and claiming status as the oldest bar in Alicante. (Open Su-Th 10:30pm-2:30am, F-Sa 11pm-4:30am.) Other bars and disco-pubs nearby include the surf-themed, hole-in-the-wall **Marea;** the upscale **Astronomo,** featuring mean bouncers and a large, outdoor terrace; **Nepal,** which attracts well-dressed Spanish yuppies; **Cafe Directo,** boasting four differently-themed dance floors, each with its own bar; and **Celestial,** a small but beautifully-decorated locale that caters to an older, mixed gay-straight crowd. Those seeking to take a break from the bar madness head to the rooftop terrace at **Hanoi 27,** Pl. Quijano, 13-14, which is peaceful, despite the raucous dance floor below. (Mixed drinks €4.50 and up.) A self-consciously sophisticated crowd sips martinis (€5) and discusses art to the sounds of St. Germain at the eclectically decorated cafe-bar **Do-Desafinado,** Santo Tomas, 6. (☎670 40 82 36. Open Th-Su 10pm-4:30am.) Away from the *casco* antiguo, American and British exchange students hang out and hook up at the lively Irish pub **O'Connell's,** Av. Constitucion, 14, parallel to Rbla. Méndez Nuñez in the direction of the train station. (☎965 14 05 84. Beer €3. Open daily 4pm-4am.)

Alicante's **main port** houses a complex of bars overlooking the water. These tend to fill up a bit later than the bars in town. A dance-happy crowd fills the discos on the **Puerto Nuevo,** to the left when facing the water. None of these charge cover, though there is sometimes a drink minimum. The most lively spots are **Puerto Di Roma,** with a well-dressed mixed-age crowd, and **Cafe Directo,** a more upscale version of its sister-bar in the *casco antiguo*. If English is your language of choice, **Coyote Ugly** is right next door. Like in the movie, the bartenders here are hot, but the crowd is uninspiring (and mostly British). The truly elite clubbers in Alicante head to the ultra-modern **Z-Klub,** where top quality DJs spin house all night long for a mixed gay-straight crowd. Coming off Rbla. Méndez Nuñez, make a right on Po. de la Explanada, and walk for two blocks; the club is on your right on a small side-street. (Cover €12-15, includes 1 drink. Open Th-Sa 12-6am.) For yet wilder nightlife, **Benidorm** (see p. 326), 45min. away, rocks out with several huge *discotecas*, all accessible from July to August by FGV's special **Trensnochador** (see **Trains,** p. 322).

During July and August, la Playa de San Juan becomes a stage for **ballet and musical performances,** part of the *Plataforma Cultural* series. (Open nightly until 9pm. Cover from €9.) From June 20-29, hedonism rules during the **Festival de Sant Joan**, culminating on the 24th (see **We Like to Party,** below). The **Verge del Remei**

WE LIKE TO PARTY Everyone knows that Spain loves partying. During the rollicking **Festival de Sant Joan** (June 20-29), Alicante takes it to the next level. Only Pamplona's running of the bulls even comes close. During the *fiesta*, streets are more packed at 5am than 5pm as young and old fill the streets from midnight 'til dawn, dancing and drinking in one dizzying outdoor fiasco—for one week straight. Huge papier-maché *fogueres* (satiric effigies) are erected around the city, only to be burned on the 24th in a ceremony known as *la Cremà*. Firefighters then proceed to soak everyone nearby during *la Banya*, and the party continues until dawn—wet.

procession begins in Alicante on August 3rd; pilgrims then trek to the monastery of Santa Faz the following Thursday. Alicante honors *La Virgen del Demedio* all summer during the **Fiestas del Verano,** when numerous concerts and theatrical performances are held in the new open-air theater on the port.

DAYTRIPS FROM ALICANTE

ELCHE (ELX)

RENFE ***trains*** *run from Alicante every hr. 6:05am-10:05pm, €1.47-1.56.* ***Mollá buses*** *(☎965 13 08 51) leave Alicante M-F 2 per hr. 7am-10pm, Sa every hr. 8am-10pm, Su 8 per day 9am-9:30pm; €1.38.*

A lush oasis of a city, 23km from Alicante and surrounded by one of Europe's only palm forests, Elche is a refreshing change from the monochrome cities lining the rest of the *Costa Blanca*. Elche's parks make for a great daytrip; heading to nearby beaches is also an option, although better beaches lie farther north. At the corner of Av. Ferrocarril and Po. Estación begins the **Parque Municipal,** where palm trees, grassy promenades, and playgrounds make for a cheerful, family-oriented park. (Open daily June-Aug. 7am-midnight; Sept.-May 7am-9pm.) Of Elche's parks and public gardens, by far the most beautiful is **Hort del Cura** (Orchard of the Priest), where magnificent trees shade colorful flower beds. (Open June-Aug. 9am-9pm, Sept.-May 9am-6pm. €1.80.) Both the **train station** (Estación Parque) and the **bus station** (☎965 45 58 58), are located along Av. Libertat. To get to the town center from the bus and train stations, bear left when leaving either station, then left again on Po. Estación. The **tourist office** is on Pl. Parc, at the end of Po. Estación. (☎965 45 27 47. Open M-F 10am-7pm, Sa 10am-2:30pm, Su 10am-2pm.)

ISLA TABARCA

Cruceros Kon Tiki (☎965 21 63 96) departs daily from the dock on Explanada d'Espanya to Tabarca. (High-speed 30min., regular 1hr. July-Aug. 11am, 12:30, 2:30pm; Sept.-June. 11am. Ferries return July-Aug. 2, 5:30, 6:30, 7:30pm; Sept.-June 5pm. Round-trip €13.)

Still a quiet fishing village, this tiny island 15km south of Alicante offers an old fort, several fresh seafood restaurants, a rocky beach with beautiful turquoise water, and several coves with tide pools perfect for a refreshing dip in the sea. Despite its petite proportions, tourists have begun to make the island a choice daytrip destination. The only **beach** is straight ahead when you come off the dock; rent beach chairs and umbrellas from an attendant (chairs €4.80 per day, 2 chairs and umbrella €9.60). To the left, the remnants of the tiny **fort,** once a jail for Spanish exiles, overlooks the Mediterranean on three sides. To find the tide pools, head to the right past the beach when you come off the dock, and proceed down the main street through the town until you reach a large stone gate. Walk through the gate to find several tide pools and small, rocky coves. Seafood **restaurants** line the narrow strip between the fort and the beach—all serve delicious *comida típica* with *menús* ranging from €7.20-9. For **tourist info** and the **police** call ☎965 96 00 58.

COSTA BLANCA

You could spend a lifetime touring the charming resort towns of the Costa Blanca. The "white coast" that extends from Dénia through Calpe to Alicante takes its name from the fine white sand of its shores. A varied terrain of hills blanketed with cherry blossoms, jagged mountains, lush pine-covered slopes, and natural lagoons surrounds densely populated coastal towns. Altea, Calpe, Dénia, and especially Jávea offer relief from the disco droves that energize Alicante and Benidorm, although even these towns are not tourist-free.

COASTAL TRANSPORTATION

TRAINS. Ferrocarrils de la Generalitat Valenciana (☎965 92 02 02, in Alicante 965 26 27 31) hits almost every town and beach along the coast with its Alicante-Dénia line. Trains run from Alicante to: **Altea** (1½hr., every hr. 6am-10pm except noon, €3.48); **Benidorm** (1hr., every hr. 6am-10pm, €2.16); **Calpe** (1¾hr., 8 per day 6am-9pm, €4.32); **Dénia** (2¼hr., 8 per day 6am-9pm, €6.30). From Dénia and Calpe, trains return to **Alicante** every 2hr. (6:25am-7:25pm), while from Altea and Benidorm trains depart every hour (6:24am-10:24pm). **Trensnochador** (☎965 26 22 33), the night train from Alicante, runs July-Sept. to **Altea, Benidorm, Calpe,** and **Dénia** (F-Sa every hr. to Altea and Benidorm, 3 per night to Calpe and Dénia; Su-Th 4 per night to Altea and Benidorm, 3 per night to Calpe and Dénia; 10:20pm-6am).

BUSES. ALSA (☎902 42 22 42) runs **buses** between Alicante and Valencia, stopping in towns along the Costa Blanca. Buses are the easiest and most cost-efficient way to get around the Costa Blanca. From **Valencia** buses run to: **Alicante** (4½hr., 13 per day 6:30am-6pm, €12); **Benidorm** (4hr., 12 per day 7:55am-9:20pm, €9.60-10.35); **Altea** and **Calpe** (3-3½hr., 12 per day 6:30am-6pm, €7.89-8.52); **Dénia** (2hr., 9 per day 6:30am-9:15pm, €6.42); **Gandía** (1hr., 13 per day 6:30am-9:15pm, €4.41); **Jávea** (2hr., 7 per day 8am-9:15pm, €6.48). From **Alicante** buses run to: **Altea** (1¼hr., 18 per day 6:30am-9pm, €3.36); **Benidorm** (1hr., 20 per day 7:40am-10:15pm, €2.40); **Calpe** (1½hr., 18 per day 6:30am-9pm, €4.05); **Dénia** (2½hr., 10 per day 6:30am-8pm, €6.29); **Jávea** (2½hr., 7 per day 8am-9pm, €5.58); **Valencia** (4-4½ hr., 10 per day 6:30am-6pm, €12).

BENIDORM ☎965

A carnival-like beach culture abounds in Benidorm, from the countless rows of sandal and sunglass shops along Playa del Levante to the heart of the *casco antiguo*, where hordes of sunburnt tourists crowd the streets 24 hours a day. Thousands of visitors from the British Isles, Holland, and Belgium come to Benidorm every summer, some merely to sunbathe on the city's 5km of white-sand beaches. Those wishing to own a piece of the madness settle down in the numerous apartment buildings that dot the skyline. If it's the quintessential tranquility of the Costa Blanca that you seek, bypass Benidorm and head north toward the calmer towns of Altea and Jávea. But if you want to party, Benidorm's unbelievable nightlife will keep you going from dusk till dawn, every day of the week.

ORIENTATION AND PRACTICAL INFORMATION. The **train station** (☎965 85 18 95) is located on C. Estación, at the top of a small hill above the city. Local bus #7 departs from the train station for the city center. (☎965 85 43 22. Every 30min. 6:30am-9:50pm. €0.60.) For **taxis** call ☎965 86 26 26. The **bus stop** (there's no real bus station) is on Av. Europa, about 4 blocks inland from the beach, close to the city center. Benidorm is divided into two sections by the *casco antiguo*, which forms the center of the city. To the north, along the boardwalk **Av. D'Alcoi,** is the main beach, **Playa de Levante,** as well as the larger streets where most of the big hotels and apartment buildings are located. To the south is the seaside **Parque de Elche,** and a more secluded beach, **Playa de Poniente.** To get to the main **tourist office,** C. Martinez Alejos, 16, from the bus stop, continue down Av. Europa toward the beach, make a right at Av. del Mediterraneo, and continue until you hit **Pl. de La Hispanidad.** Veer left onto C. Dr. Perez Llorca, and make a left on Av. Martinez Alejos. The office will be half a block down on the left. (☎965 85 32 24. Open M-F 9:30am-1:30pm and 4:30-7:30pm, Sa 10am-1:30pm and 4:30-7:30pm.) **Banks** and **ATMs** line C. Dr. Perez Llorca and the pedestrian street that leads to the boardwalk, Av. Martinez Alejos. **Internet access** is at **Cybercat Cafe,** on the bottom floor of the arcade/cafeteria complex of **El Otro Mundo de Jaime,** C. Ruzafa, 2, near the *casco antiguo.* (☎965 86 79 04. €0.50 for 15min. Open daily 10am-midnight.) In an **emergency,** call ☎112. The **post office** is located at Pl. Dr. Fleming, 1. (☎965 85 34 34. Open M-F 8:30am-8:30pm, Sa 9:30am-1pm.) **Postal code:** 03500.

VALENCIA AND MURCIA

ACCOMMODATIONS AND FOOD. Though Benidorm has an abundance of upscale hotels and resorts, it has little to offer in terms of affordable lodging for the budget traveler. The most reasonably priced accommodations are found in the *casco antiguo.* A few blocks up the street from the tourist office is **Hostal Tabarca ❷,** C. Ruzafa, 9, with narrow, spartan rooms and clean hallway baths. (☎965 85 77 08. Singles €15; doubles €24-30; triples €30-36.) If you continue on C. Ruzafa, more comfortable rooms can be found at **Pensión La Orozca ❸,** C. Ruzafa, 37. (☎965 85 05 25. All rooms with bath. Singles €25-30; doubles €35-50.) Those seeking peace and quiet will find it in the cheerful, modern rooms of **Hotel La Santa Faç ❹,** C. La Santa Faç, 18. (☎965 85 40 63. All rooms with bath, A/C, TV, and phone. Singles €42; doubles €61-72.) The main **supermarket** and **produce market** are on Vía Emilio Ortuno, in the *casco antiguo.* **Restaurants** are found every few meters along **C. Esperanto** and **C. Gerona,** and consist mainly of pizzerias, a couple of Indian and Turkish restaurants, and eateries whose neon signs and huge, illuminated outdoor menus offer "international cuisine"—more varieties of pizza. If you seek *comida típica,* **Restaurante Albufera ❷,** on the corner of C. Gerona and C. Dr. Orts Llorca, has a huge menu and hearty portions of Spanish fare at reasonable prices. (☎965 86 56 61. Most entrees €7-10. Open daily 1pm-midnight.) Look for the giant *paella* on the sign outside the **Restaurante Aitona ❷,** C. Ruzafa, for excellent *paella* dishes (€7.81-8.41). Call ahead for reservations, especially on weekends. (☎965 85 30 10. Open daily 1pm-midnight.) If you're in the mood to eat a filling meal with the locals, try **La Tasca del Pueblo ❷,** Marques de Comillas, 5, which has a huge selection of meat and fish dishes for €7-10. (☎966 80 63 12. Open daily 1pm-midnight.)

SIGHTS AND ENTERTAINMENT. It's difficult to find many remnants of Benidorm's historic past, since most of what was once the old city is now enveloped by modern high-rises and wide roadways. Tucked within the narrow streets of the *casco antiguo,* however, are the ruins of the **Castillo-Mirador de Benidorm,** Pl. del Castell, at the end of **El Carerer dels Gats,** the old main street. Built in the 14th century to protect the city from attacks by Berber pirates, the castle now affords excellent views of Playa del Levante to the north and Playa de Poniente to the south, as well as **Benidorm Island,** the enormous slanted rock formation that lies in the water directly in front of the main beach. Spectacular sunsets can be seen from the castle's famous **mirador,** known as "The Balcony of the Mediterranean." Any visit to Benidorm is not complete without a stroll along the 2080m long **Paseo Maritimo de la Playa de Levante.** Dotted with hip cafes and bar, this expansive boardwalk is the place to see and be seen, and the beautiful (and the not so beautiful) traverse its length at all hours of the day and night. Benidorm has a small **Moros y Cristianos Festival** every October, but the city is best known for its international music festival, **Festival de la Canción de Benidorm,** held every year in late summer.

NIGHTLIFE. Nightlife in Benidorm usually follows an expensive, exhaustive, but hedonistically fulfilling pattern, every night of the week in July and August and on weekends during the rest of the year. Locals and tourists alike begin their party trek through the city around midnight in the various bars and taverns in the *casco antiguo.* Wildly popular among locals is **Andale Andale,** on C. Alameda, which serves mixed drinks (€4 and higher) to well-dressed Spanish yuppies who like to rock out to the latest in Spanish pop. Closer to the Ayuntamiento, off C. Alameda is **La Sal,** Costera del Barco, 5. Located in an old, half-timbered house, this small establishment is packed on the weekends with an ultra-hip crowd of mainly Spanish and German patrons. (☎966 87 34 94. Beer €4.80. Open daily 10:30pm-4am.)

When most bars close or start winding down (generally around 3am), partygoers head toward the beach, as some of the craziest disco-pubs in Benidorm line the Po. Marítimo de la Playa de Levante. A mixed gay-straight crowd grooves to house at **Ku,** while young and old party to a variety of music at **KM** and **Richard's New Look.** If all you want to do is dance (particularly on top of bars and pool tables), head to **Penelope,** whose multiple bars and packed dance floor make it one of the hippest venues on the beach. Most disco-pubs are open nightly in summer and on weekends during the rest of the year 11pm-5am. None charge cover, but drinks can get expensive (beer €5-6). Keep an eye out for club promoters standing outside entrances, as they often give out coupons for free shots at the bars or free admission to bigger discos on the outskirts of the city on **Av. de la Communitat Valenciana.**

Around 4am, the party shifts from the beach to the huge disco gardens on Av. de la Communitat Valenciana. These places tend to be far away, and you may not be in a state to walk, so it is best to take a **taxi** (€3.20). Once there, numerous discos line both sides of the street. **Racha** is a cavernous locale specializing in Spanish pop. See the big sisters of the beach clubs at **Ku, KM,** and **Penelope. Pachá,** Spain's largest disco chain, has a venue here that is hugely popular with tourists. **Manssion** is a palatial venue that plays hardcore house for a sophisticated crowd. Most head to **Space** around 6 or 7am to watch the sunrise over the city. The majority of these clubs are open every night in the summer midnight-6am, and on the weekends throughout the rest of the year. Covers run €6-7. Mixed drinks are €6 and up.

ALTEA

Unlike the majority of towns lining the Costa Blanca, Altea's coastline betrays little of its growing tourism industry. Restaurants remain modest (but not necessarily cheap), daily life appears uninterrupted, and huge hotels have yet to spring up. A long jetty with a charming walkway protects Altea's calm stretch of shoreline from waves, and serene, pebbly beaches fan out from one end of town to the other. From the beach, narrow cobblestone streets wind up to **Pl. de la Iglesia.** Shaded by the cobalt dome of the church of the **Virgen del Consuelo,** the square commands breathtaking views of the Mediterranean. The main thoroughfare, **Comte d' Altea,** is filled with snack shops and beachware. During the last week of September the city erupts with music, gunpowder, and dance for the **Fiestas de Moros y Cristianos.**

Both **trains** and **buses** stop at the foot of the hill on C. La Mar (head left to go toward the center). If you're arriving by bus from Alicante, get off at the first stop; if arriving from Valencia, get off at the second stop. The **tourist office** sits on C. Sant Pere, 9, parallel to C. La Mar, right by the water. From the train station or the bus stop, walk toward the sea to C. Sant Pere. (☎965 84 41 14; fax 965 84 42 13. Open June-Aug. M-Sa 10am-2pm and 5-8:30pm; Sept.-May M-Sa 10am-2pm and 5-7:30pm.)

Services include: **emergency** ☎112; **police** ☎965 84 05 25; and **ambulance** ☎965 84 35 32. **Internet access** is available at **Red Attack,** C. Garganes, 9. (☎966 88 12 91. €1.20 per 30min. Open June-Aug. M-F 11am-2pm and 6pm-2am, Sa-Su 6pm-2am; Sept.-May M-F 10am-2am, Sa-Su noon-2am). The **post office** is at C. Jaime I, 13. (☎965 84 01 74. Open M-F 8:30am-2:30pm, Sa 9:30am-1pm.) **Postal code:** 03590.

Budget accommodations are hard to find in Altea. Among the cheapest options available is **Habitaciones La Mar, 82 ❷,** C. La Mar, 82, close to the train station. The rooms are small and clean with hallway baths, but those overlooking the street can be noisy. (☎965 84 30 16. Singles €18; doubles €24-30.) **Hostal Paco ❸,** C. Jaime I, 7-A, just off Comte d'Altea, provides A/C, full baths, TVs, and wide windows. (☎965 84 05 41. Singles €30; doubles €48.) For breakfast Altea has many pastry shops and bakeries along Comte d'Altea, near the Pl. del Ayuntamiento. For lunch or dinner, head to C. Jaime I, parallel to the water, and its sidestreets—here you'll find seafood restaurants, pizzerias, and even some Chinese restaurants with entrees ranging €7-10. Try **La Liebre ❷,** Po. Mediterraneo, 39, which specializes in typical Spanish fare. Don't miss the banana split for €2.40. (☎965 84 57 79. *Menú* €8.45. Open daily 1pm-midnight.) Though there are a number of bars on the waterfront, they usually cater to an older crowd and close early, as local and foreign partygoers head to Benidorm and Alicante for nightlife and entertainment.

CALPE (CALP)

With t-shirt stores lining the streets and beaches packed with foreigners, Calpe seems the classic tourist trap—yet the flocks of visitors descend for good reason. The Peñó d'Ifach (327m), a massive, flat-topped rock formation whose precipitous face edges right on the sea, towers above the beach and town. Farther north, from the cliffs and caves above Calpe, Ibiza can be seen in the distance on a clear day. Calpe's beaches, the town's main draw, lure visitors with kilometers of white sand.

Calpe's main avenue, Gabriel Miró, descends to the blue-flagged (EU-praised) **Platja Arena-Bol.** Beyond the Peñó, both **Platja Levante** and the cove of **Calalga** bear the same *bandera azul.* To hike to the **Peñó d'Ifach** (2½hr. round-trip), walk past the tourist office, then turn right on Av. del Port, and left on C. Isla Formentera, following the signs. **ALSA buses** (☎965 83 90 29) stop 2km from the beach at C. Capitán Pérez Jorda (see **Transportation,** p. 326). From the station, set out straight down Av. Masnou (toward the rotary), which curves around to the left before turning into C. Goleta and leading ultimately into Pl. Constitución. From the plaza to the water, turn right down **Av. Gabriel Miró,** and follow the smell of the sea. Taking the **Autobuses Ifach bus** past the bus station to the beach is a less strenuous option (1 per hr., €0.70). If all else fails, call a **taxi** (☎965 83 78 78).

With your back to the bus station, turning right will lead you downhill to a neighborhood of gorgeous Mediterranean architecture. A 20min. beach walk along the street running from the old town leads to the main **tourist office,** Av. Ejércitos Españoles, 62. (Open June-Aug. M-Sa 9am-9pm, Su 10:30am-2pm; Sept.-May M-F 9am-2pm and 4-8pm, Sa 9am-2pm.) The **police,** Av. Ejércitos Españoles (☎965 08 90 00), are several doors down. **Internet Center Perlamar,** C. Benidorm, 1, is right off Gabriel Miró, three blocks from the beach. (☎965 83 93 83. Coin-operated computers €1.20 for 30min. Open daily 10am-midnight.) For a comfortable bed, try the tiny **Pensión Céntrica ❶,** Pl. Ifach. All rooms have sinks, but the toilets are relegated to hallway bathrooms. (☎965 83 55 28. €9 per person.) Other affordable lodging options are located in the narrow streets of the *casco antiguo,* above **Pl. de la Constitución** off Gabriel Miró. Among these is **Hostal El Parque ❶,** C. Portalet, 4, with simple, clean rooms with bath. (☎965 83 07 70. Singles €12; doubles €24.) The most reasonably priced restaurants in Calpe can also be found in the *casco antiguo.* **Casa Florencia ❷,** C. del Mar, 21, serves delicious seafood *paellas* and other rice dishes for two or more people for €8.50-10.90. (☎965 83 35 84. Open daily 1-11pm. Call ahead for reservations.) A number of small bars can be found behind Pl. de la Constitución and along the beach headed toward the Peñó d'Ifach, but for a wilder scene, your best bet is to go to Benidorm or Alicante for the night.

DÉNIA ☎966

Set halfway between Valencia and Alicante along the Golfo de Valencia, Dénia (named by the Greeks for Diana, goddess of the hunt, the moon, and purity) is an upscale family resort. Though the town has little to offer budget travelers in the way of bargains, its beautiful beaches, water-sports, and tasty restaurants are enough to tempt even the most thrifty to splurge. Dénia's harbor serves as an important ferry connection to the Balearic Islands. Come summertime, the town erupts in celebration with several wild festivals.

ORIENTATION AND PRACTICAL INFORMATION. The **train station** (☎965 78 04 45) is on C. Calderón. The **bus station** is on Pl. Arxiduc Carles. For train and bus schedules, see **Transportation,** p. 326. Local buses (☎966 42 14 08) depart from the tourist office for nearby beaches. Take the bus marked "Marina" or "Calma" for the best beaches; the bus marked "Rotas" heads in the opposite direction. (Marinas and Rotas depart every hr. 8am-8pm, Calma 6 per day 9am-9pm; €0.65.) To reach the Balearics by sea, consult **Balearia Eurolinies Maritimes,** in Pl. Oculista Buigues, next to the tourist office. (☎902 16 01 80; www.balearia.com.) Ferries run from Dénia to **Palma** and **Ibiza** (€38-60). For full ferry info, see **By Boat,** p. 337. For **taxis,** call ☎965 78 65 65. Local services, including local **buses, trains, ferries,** and the **post office,** are located on **C. Patricio Fernández,** which runs straight to the port. The **tourist office** sits on Pl. Oculista Buigues, 9, 30m inland from Estació Marítima. (☎966 42 23 67; www.denia.net. Open M-Sa 9:30am-1:30pm and 4:30-7:30pm, Su 10am-2pm.) To get to the tourist office from the bus depot, turn left out of the plaza onto C. Patricio Fernandez; from the train station, go straight ahead, then veer right. Three blocks from C. Patricio Fernández, shop- and restaurant-lined **C. Marqués de Campo** is the main tourist strip. In an emergency, contact the **police** ☎092. **Internet access** is available at **CiberDeni@,** C. Senija. From C. Patricio Fernández take C. Sagunto; C. Senjira is the second left. (☎966 43 14 81. €2.88 per hr.)

ACCOMMODATIONS AND FOOD. Dénia certainly doesn't cater to budget travelers, especially in the lodging department. Be prepared to shell out €30 or more for a single room in the summer. **Hostal L'Anfora ❷,** Explanada de Cervantes, 8, has some of the most inexpensive rooms in town. (☎966 43 01 01. Deposit required. Oct.-June singles €21; doubles €36. July-Sept. €30/€48. MC/V.) With A/C, TVs, and private baths, **Hostal Comercio ❸,** C. de la Vía, 43, may appear more of a hotel than a hostel. (☎/fax 965 78 00 71. June singles €30; doubles €47. July-Sept. €32/€49. Oct.-May €23/€29. MC/V.) Other relatively inexpensive accommodations can be found along **Av. del Cid** at the foot of the hill leading to the *castillo*. **Hostal Cristina ❷,** Av. del Cid, 5, has small, cozy rooms with bath, A/C, and TV. (☎966 42 31 58. Singles €20-24; doubles €24-36.) **Camping Las Marinas ❶,** C. Les Bovetes Nord, 4, is a 3km bus ride (€0.75) from Platja Jorge Joan. Hot water, supermarket, restaurant, and beach-side locale are all added bonuses. (☎966 47 41 85 or 966 75 51 88. €4.14 per person and per tent. Open year-round.) **Restaurants** line C. Marqués de Campo and the Explanada de Cervantes, though most cater to the hyper-tourist. Cheaper eateries sit merely a block or two away off the main streets. Despite its portside location, **Khyber I ❶,** Pl. Fontanella, 4, serves up reasonably priced and authentic curries and other Indian cuisine. (☎965 78 56 04. Entrees €4.60-6. Open daily 1-4pm and 9-11pm.)

Right next door is **Clima ❷,** Pl. Drassanes, 5. With a huge menu consisting of everything from *paellas* (€7-9) to pizza (€7-10) to sandwiches (€4-6), this restaurant caters to a wide array of culinary tastes. (☎965 78 10 54. Open daily 1pm-midnight.) The **supermarket,** C. Carlos Senti, 7, is just off C. Patricio Fernández. (☎965 78 22 61. Open M-Sa 9am-8:30pm.)

SIGHTS. An 18th-century **castle** sprawls across the hill overlooking the marina. James II enforced the 1304 separation between the town below and the castle above by displacing all of Dénia's inhabitants to the *villa vella*, or old town, beyond the castle walls. (☎966 42 06 56. Open daily Nov.-March 10am-1pm and 3-6pm; April-May 10am-1:30pm and 3:30-7pm; June 10am-1:30pm and 4-7:30pm; July-Aug. 10:30am-1:30pm and 7-8:30pm; Sept. 10:30am-1:30pm and 5-8pm; Oct. 10am-1pm and 3-6:30pm. €1.80.) A tourist train chugs to the castle from the tourist office (every 30min. 10am-1pm and 5-8pm, €3 includes entrance to the castle), or you can walk by way of the stairs next to the town hall. Dénia's biggest attraction, however, is its 14km of pristine **beaches.** Windsurfers skip over the waves off **Playa Els Molins** (north of the port on the "Marina" bus), while scuba divers explore the depths off **Las Playas Area de Las Rotes** (south of the port on the "Rotas" bus). Beyond beaches, **Montgó Natural Park** (☎966 42 32 05) has plenty of trails.

FESTIVALS. Dénia holds a miniature **Fallas festival** March 16 to 20, burning effigies on the final midnight. During **Festa Major** (early July), locals prove they're just as gutsy as their fellow countrymen in Pamplona—bulls and fans dive as one into a pool of water, a feat known as **Bous a la mar.** In mid-July, the **Fiestas de la Santísima Sangre** feature street dances, concerts, mock battles, and fireworks over the harbor. The parades and religious plays of the **Fiesta de Moros y Cristianos** celebration also take place between August 14 and 17.

JÁVEA (XÀBIA)

Jávea's harbors shelter tranquil waters free from tourists—while British families venture here in summer, backpackers head to younger, more popular destinations.

Inconvenient transportation has spared the town from heavy tourist loads. **ALSA buses** stop at C. Príncipe de Asturias, but arrive only five times per day (see **Transportation,** p. 326). To get to the port, take the **municipal bus.** (☎966 42 14 08. June-Sept. every 30min., Oct.-May every hr., 8am-2pm and 4-10pm. €0.66.) If you don't feel like waiting, continue on Av. Alicante, which runs to the port (20min.). **Autocarres Carrió** (☎965 58 10 36) run between Denia and Jávea (15min., 6 per day 8am-7pm, €0.84). Jávea has three tourist offices—most convenient are those near the port, Pl. Almirante Bastarreche, 24 (☎965 79 07 39), or by the Ayuntamiento, Pl. de la Iglesia, 6 (☎965 79 43 56). All are open M-F 9am-2pm and 5-9pm, Sa 10am-2pm and 5-9pm, Su 10am-1pm. Jávea's location may necessitate an overnight stay. **Pensión La Favorita ❷,** C. Magallanes, 4, is as good as it gets; follow signs to the tourist office. (☎965 79 04 77. Singles €18; doubles €24-37, with bath €30-40.) **Restaurants** line C. Andrés Lambert, and consist mainly of pizzerias and seafood *freidurías.*

Although the municipal bus runs from the port through a long stretch of pebbled bathing spots, Jávea's real beauties—its secluded beaches, coves, and cliffs—are not well served by public transportation. A number of secluded coves also line the coast south of the port. Jávea's most popular beaches, **Playa La Granadella, Playa de Ambolo,** and **Playa La Barraca,** can best be reached by car, about 5km south of the port along Ctra. del Cabo de la Nao. Ask the tourist office for a map and driving directions. The **Fiesta de Moros y Cristianos** erupts during the second half of July; fireworks jolt wide-eyed tourists roaming among costumed Moors and Christians.

GANDÍA

Five centuries before the EU began blue-flagging beaches, the powerful Borjas family of Valencia had already discovered Gandía and transformed it into a center of noble beach bumming. Today, Gandía still gets most of its income from visitors seeking the peace of a seaside retreat. Fine sands stretch for kilometers, so not surprisingly, the most popular activity here is sunbathing. Departing from the tourist office, **La Marina buses,** Marqués de Campo, 14, run to the **beach** along Pg. Marítimo (every 15min.; last bus 1am in summer, 11:30pm in winter; €0.87).**RENFE trains** (☎902 24 02 02) run from **Valencia** (1hr., every 30min. 6am-10pm, €3.30). **ALSA,** C. Magistrado Catalán, 3 (☎962 96 50 66), runs **buses** to **Valencia** (1hr., 9-12 per day, €4.41) and **Alicante** (3hr., 9-12 per day, €7.41). Buses to Alicante stop in **Altea** (€4.05), **Calpe** (€3.36), and **Dénia** (€2.01).

The majority of services in Gandía are located near the train station on **Marqués de Campo;** everything else is by the beach. The **tourist office,** Marqués de Campo, is across from the train station. (☎962 87 77 88. English spoken. Open June-Aug. M-F 9:30am-1:30pm and 4:30-7:30pm, Sa 10am-1:30pm; Sept.-May M-F 9:30am-1:30pm and 4-7pm, Sa 10am-1pm.) Services include: **emergency** ☎112; **police** ☎962 87 88 00; and **Internet** at **Cibercafé,** C. Cibeles, 46. (☎962 84 00 97. €1.80 per hr. Open daily 10am-1am.) The **post office,** Pl. Jaume I, 7, is a few blocks behind the Ayuntamiento. (☎962 87 10 91. Open M-F 8:30am-2:30pm.) **Postal code:** 46700.

Gandía is full of expensive hotels; those who want to stay cheaply here should make reservations. **Habitaciones Rosmar ❷,** C. Cullera, 8, has the cheapest rooms and is a 3min. walk from the beach. (☎962 84 31 96. Singles €19; doubles €33. Open Apr.-Sept.) **El Nido ❸,** C. Alcoy, 22, is right off the beach but is pricier. (☎962 84 46 40. Sept.-June doubles €36, July €42, Aug. €48.) Most restaurants are located along the beach and in the pedestrian streets near the train station. Among these is **Tasca Mediterráneo ❷,** Parc de l'Estacio, 21, which serves hearty grilled fish dishes and *paellas* from €7.50-10. (☎962 87 35 07. Open Th-Tu 1pm-midnight.) Stock up on groceries at **Supermarket Macedona,** C. Perú. (Open M-Sa 9am-9pm.)

NEAR GANDÍA: PLATJA DE PILES

Just 10km south of Gandía, Platja de Piles offers seemingly endless stretches of tranquil, white-sand beaches. From Gandía, **La Amistad buses,** Av. Marqués de Campo, 9 (☎962 87 44 10), runs to and from Platja de Piles (M-Sa 4-5 per day 8:45am-8:30pm, €0.75). Buses depart from outside the train station, across from the supermarket. While in Platja, spend the night at **Alberg Mar i Vent (HI) ❶,** C. Dr. Fleming. Walk down the street from the bus stop, then follow the signs to the hostel. The beach is out the back door. The owner organizes **bike** (€6 per day) and **kayak rental,** as well as **windsurfing** lessons. The hostel will be closed for renovations until Feb. 1, 2003. (☎962 83 17 48 or 962 83 17 25. 3-day max. stay, flexible if uncrowded. Curfew weeknights 2am, Sa 4am. Closed in Dec. and Jan. Breakfast, lunch, and dinner €4.85-5.10. Sheets €1.80. Dorms €6-7.20, over 26 €9-10.20.) Reasonably priced **restaurants** and **bars** serving everything from *paella* to pizza are found below the apartment buildings in the *urbanizaciones* surrounding the hostel—most are usually open daily from midday until midnight.

MURCIA

The tiny province of Murcia, bordered by Valencia to the north, the Mediterranean to the east, and Andalucía to the west, may be in the shadow of more touristed regions, but its sunny, warm climate, tiny beach resort towns, and thriving capital city give it more than its share of character. Four centuries ago, a bizarre wave of plagues, floods, and earthquakes wreaked havoc throughout Murcia. Along with the utter destruction of some areas, the earthquakes uncovered a rich supply of minerals and natural springs. Today, thermal spas, pottery factories, and paprika mills pepper the lively coastal towns, and orange and apricot orchards bolster Murcia's reputation as the "Huerta de Europa" (Europe's Orchard).

MURCIA

Residents of Murcia will tell you that their city is a pleasant place to visit from fall until spring, when the city thrives off the energy of its university. In summer, from mid-July to mid-September, Murcia becomes a ghost town; even the most patriotic of residents flee the oppressive heat of the city for the nearby Mediterranean. Though much of Murcia is characterized by modern parks, cafes, and tree-lined avenues, the winding lanes of its old quarters reveal the Moorish heart of the city of *Mursiya*, as it was once called by Abderramán II when he founded it in AD 825.

TRANSPORTATION. **Aeropuerto San Javier** (☎968 17 20 00) has flights to Barcelona, Madrid, and London. **RENFE trains** (☎902 24 02 02), at Pl. Industria, head to: **Alicante** (1½hr., 9-17 per day, €3.60); **Barcelona** (7-10hr., 2 per day, €39); **Lorca** (1hr., every hr., €3.33); **Madrid** (4-5hr., 3 per day, €33); **Valencia** (3½hr., 3 per day, €12-21). **Buses** (☎968 29 22 11) leave from C. San Andrés, behind the Museo Salzillo, to: **Alicante** (1½hr., 7 per day 8:15am-8:15pm, €3.60); **Almería** (3½hr., 9 per day 5:30am-8:30pm, €14); **Barcelona** (8½hr., 11 per day, €32); **Denia** (3½hr., 4 per day 2am-9:10pm, €9.05); **Granada** (4-5hr., 5 per day 8:30am-10pm, €15); **La Manga de Mar Menor** (1hr.; Sept.-June 2 per day, July-Aug. every hr.; €2.30); **Lorca** (1½hr., 12 per day 7am-9pm, €3.33); **Madrid** (5-6hr., 12 per day 7am-midnight, €20); **Málaga** (6hr., 6 per day 2:30am-11pm, €24); **Sevilla** (7-9hr., 3 per day 11:30am-10pm, €29); **Valencia** (3¾hr., 4-12 per day 8am-9:30pm, €11.40). Municipal buses (€0.70) cover the city and outskirts; bus #9 runs past the train and bus stations.

ORIENTATION AND PRACTICAL INFORMATION. The **Río Segura** divides the city, with sights and services to the north half and the train station to the south (take bus #9 or 11 between the two). The cathedral is in **Pl. Cardenal Belluga,** at C. Trapería's end, while the bus station is a 10min. walk to the west of town. **Gran Vía** is the main thoroughfare, connecting to Pl. Circular, home to the post office. The **tourist office,** C. San Cristóbal, 6, is in Pl. Romea. (☎968 36 61 00. Open M-F 9am-2pm and 5-7pm.) The bus station provides **luggage storage** (€1.80 per day). **Emergency** (☎112); **police** on Av. San Juan de la Cruz (☎968 26 66 00); and **Hospital Morales Meseguer,** Av. Marqués de Vélez, 22 (☎968 36 09 00). For **Internet** access, visit **Cyber Forum,** C. Vinader, on the pedestrian path off the street behind Pl. Santa Isabel. (☎968 90 18 04. €1.20 per 30min., €2.10 per hr. Open M-Sa 10:30am-4:30pm and 4pm-12:30am, Su 4pm-12:30am.) The **post office,** on Pl. Circular, 8a, is located where Av. Primo de Ribera connects to the plaza. (☎968 24 10 37. Open M-F 8:30am-8:30pm, Sa 9:30am-2pm.) **Postal code:** 30008.

ACCOMMODATIONS AND FOOD. When Murcia steams up and empties out in summer, finding a room is the only breeze in town; it is a considerably more difficult task in winter. One of the few decent budget options is **Hostal-Residencia Murcia ❷**, C. Vinader, 6, off Pl. Sta. Isabel; take bus #11 from the train station. Rooms have TVs, phones, and A/C. (☎968 21 99 63. Singles €18, with bath €21; doubles €36/€42.) Another reasonable option with a central location is **Hotel Hispano I ❷**, C. Traperia, 8, just before the cathedral. (☎968 21 61 52. Singles €22, with bath €25; doubles €30/€34.) Although ice cream shops and outdoor cafes seem to be everywhere, finding a decent meal is a bit harder. The area around **Pl. San Juan,**

near the river, is home to a good number of popular restaurants and *tapas* bars. Enjoy Italian food at **Restaurante Pizzeria Vía Apostolo ❶**, C. Los Apostoles, 22, behind the cathedral. An extensive selection of pizzas and pasta (€5-7) to satisfy every taste. Outdoor tables in summer make for a pleasant dinner. (☎968 21 23 79. Open daily 1:30-4pm and 8pm-midnight.) **Foster's Hollywood ❷**, Pl. Santa Catalina, 4, one block off Gran Vía, serves up globalized favorites and has a *menú* for €7.50. (Open M-Th 1-5pm and 8:30pm-midnight, F-Su 1-5pm and 8:30pm-12:30am.) Sample the Murcian harvest at the **market** on C. Verónicas. (Open M-Sa 9am-1pm.)

SIGHTS. The palatial **Casino de Murcia** (a.k.a. Casino Cultural), C. Trapería, 18, began as a gentlemen's club for the town's 19th- and 20th-century bourgeoisie. Current members have use of all the building, from its lounges to its libraries. The rooms were each designed according to a theme, including the Versailles ballroom, English billiard room, Arabic patio, and Oxford library. Several of these magnificent rooms are open to the public. (☎968 21 22 55. Open daily 10am-9pm. €1.20.) Murcia's **Museo de Bellas Artes,** C. Obispo Frutos, 12, is the region's largest art museum, with over 1000 works and an extensive collection of local art. (☎968 23 93 46. Open M-F 9am-2pm and 5-8pm, Sa 10am-2pm. €1.20.) The **Museo Taurino,** C. Alfaro, 6, displays bullfighting memorabilia, matador costumes, and mounted bulls' heads that pay homage to particularly valorous beasts. Of particular importance is the shrine to José Manuel Calvo Benichon's shredded, bloody shirt, worn the day he was gored to death in Sevilla by his 598kg opponent. (☎968 28 59 76. Open June-Aug. M-F 10am-2pm and 5-8pm; Sept.-May 10am-2pm and 5-8pm, Su 11am-2pm. Free.) Just outside of Murcia, the Río Espuña courses through the mountains, pines, and sagebrush of the **Parque Natural Sierra Espuña.** The flowers explode into dazzling color in springtime, the best season to visit the park. The park is best accessed from **Lorca** (see Daytrips from Murcia below), but there is no public transportation from here to the park—having a car is a necessity. Stop by the tourist office for bike routes, hiking trail maps, and practical info about the park.

ENTERTAINMENT AND NIGHTLIFE. Much of Murcia's nightlife centers around the city's numerous plazas. The *tapas* bars in Pl. San Juan, two blocks from the river by Pl. Cruz Roja, are great places for starting the night. **Café-Pub Pura Vida,** Pl. Periodista Jaime Campmany, a left off C. Isidoro de la Cierva, is one of the more popular spots. (Mixed drinks €3-3.60. Open M-Sa 4pm-2:30am.) Most clubs are clustered around **Parque Atalayas,** the large park off Ronda Levante, a main thoroughfare in the city. Others lie near the university, along C. Doctor Fleming and Pl. Universidad, and they are most lively Th-Sa nights when students are off for the weekend. If you're up for sensory overload, stop by the huge **Zig Zag** complex of clubs and bars. Take Av. Juan Carlos I from Pl. Circular and make a left on C. Auditorium. The building is on your left past a large sports stadium. There is no cover charged for any of the ten bars and clubs on the complex's three terraced floors. For bowling, head up to the top floor. (Beer €2.10. Open daily 10pm-4am.) On the day before Easter, the **Fiesta de Primavera** starts a week-long harvest celebration that brings jazz and theater performances to the city.

DAYTRIPS FROM MURCIA

ÁGUILAS

RENFE Cercanías trains (☎902 24 02 02) leave from Lorca (5 per day, €0.80) and from Murcia (€4.45). Buses from Murcia via Lorca (9 per day, €5.10).

EU blue-flagged beaches line the shores of Águilas, the easternmost town along *la Costa Cálida,* and frequent buses and trains make it the most accessible beach getaway from Murcia. Águilas's beaches and turquoise waters are the main draw, though the **Torre de Cope** and **Castillo de San Juan de las Águilas,** featuring incredible views of the coast, are popular stops in the city's *casco antiguo.* **Playa de Levante Puerto,** the closest *bandera azul* beach to town, is to the left of the port when facing the water. At the next cove over, **Playa Delicias** is cleaner and more popular. **Pl. de España,** the center of town, is halfway between the bus and train stations. To get there from the bus station, head toward the ocean and take your second left; from the train station, head toward the beach, take a right by the water, and another right at the pier onto C. Coronel Pareja. *Paella* is the beachfront favorite, and any number of cafes and restaurants along the water serve steaming platters of it. Head back to Murcia for the night, as accommodations are limited and expensive. The **tourist office,** C. Coronel Pareja, is a block toward the water from the plaza. (☎968 41 33 03. Open M-F 9am-2pm and 6-8pm, Sa 10am-2pm.)

LORCA

RENFE Cercanías trains (☎902 24 02 02) run to Lorca Sutullena Station, Av. Estació (1hr., every hr. 6:45am-9:45pm, €3.46). The bus station (☎968 46 92 70) sends buses to Murcia (every hr., €3.33) and Águilas (30min.; M-F 9 per day, Sa-Su 2-3 per day; €1.75).

A stroll through Lorca, from the modern train station to the crumbling medieval castle, leads you through centuries of architectural variety. Medieval ghettos, Renaissance artistry, post-Franco urban expansion, and contemporary elitism all flavor the town's neighborhoods. Ancient and medieval battles left Lorca without the orchards that extend through the rest of the region. Yet each conquering force left its own peculiar imprint on the **castillo** atop Lorca's central hill, a 20min. walk from Pl. España. The castle itself is being converted into a pricey hotel, but the facade is the real attraction. The Moors built the **Torre Espolón** shortly before the city fell to Alfonso X el Sabio of Castilla, who in a fit of self-adulation ordered the construction of the **Torre Alfonsín.** The ruins of the **Ermita de San Clemente,** deteriorate at the castle's eastern edge. When Granada fell in 1492, inhabitants moved to the bottom of the slope, leaving in their wake three idyllic churches—**Santa María, San Juan,** and **San Pedro.** Starting anew, Lorcans erected six monasteries and the **Colegiata de San Patricio.** One of many well-preserved private residences, the **Casa de Guevarra,** features a pre-19th-century pharmacy. (Open M-F 11am-1pm and 5-7pm. Free.) Enjoy lunch at **Don Jamón ❶,** C. Museo Valiente, 2, off C. Juan Carlos I, where *tapas* start at €1.50. (☎968 47 07 89. Open M-Sa noon-4pm and 8pm-1am, Su 8pm-1am.) Other restaurants serving *comida típica* can be found around Pl. España. The **tourist office** is just before the Casa de Guevarra on C. Lópes Gisbert. (☎968 46 61 57. Open M-F 9am-2pm and 5-7:30pm, Sa 11am-2pm.) **Luggage storage** is available in the bus station (€1.80 per day).

BALEARIC ISLANDS

Dreaming of the vast fortunes to be made in the 21st-century tourist industry, nearly every culture with boats and colonists to spare has tried to conquer the Balearic Islands. Spain won this race centuries ago; today, foreign invasion continues, as 2 million tourists flood the islands' discos and beaches each year.

While all four of the islands—Mallorca, Ibiza, Formentera, and Menorca—share fame for their gorgeous beaches and landscapes, each has its own special character. Mallorca, home to the islands' capital of Palma, absorbs the bulk of high-class, package tour invaders. With its museums and nightlife, Palma competes with Ibiza City as the Balearics' cultural hub. Mallorca also harbors natural beauty, albeit in the shadows of urbanization. Ibiza, a counter-cultural haven since the 1960s, is the style center of the islands. With its monstrous discos and a stronghold of crazy, beautiful party-goers, Ibiza affords the best nightlife in all of Europe. Formentera, Ibiza's little sister, is more peaceful with unspoiled sands and unpaved roads, while Menorca, wrapped in green fields and stone walls, leads a private life of empty white beaches, hidden coves, and mysterious Bronze Age megaliths.

Summers are hot, dry, crowded, and fun; winters are chilly. Spring and autumn can be sumptuous, but the beaches remain cool; nightlife doesn't heat up until early July. Most hours, schedules, and prices listed are for summer months only. Off-season prices at hotels can drop by up to 50%, and hours are often cut back.

GETTING TO THE ISLANDS

Flying to the islands is cheap and faster than a ferry. Those under 26 can receive discounts from **Iberia/Aviaco Airlines** (☎902 40 05 00 in Barcelona; www.iberia.com). **SOM** (Servicios de Ocio Marítimo; ☎971 31 03 99) lines up bus companies, ferry lines, and *discotecas* for packages to Ibiza designed for disco fiends who seek transportation and an all-night party but have no use for lodging. Book tickets through a travel agency in Barcelona, Valencia, or on any of the islands.

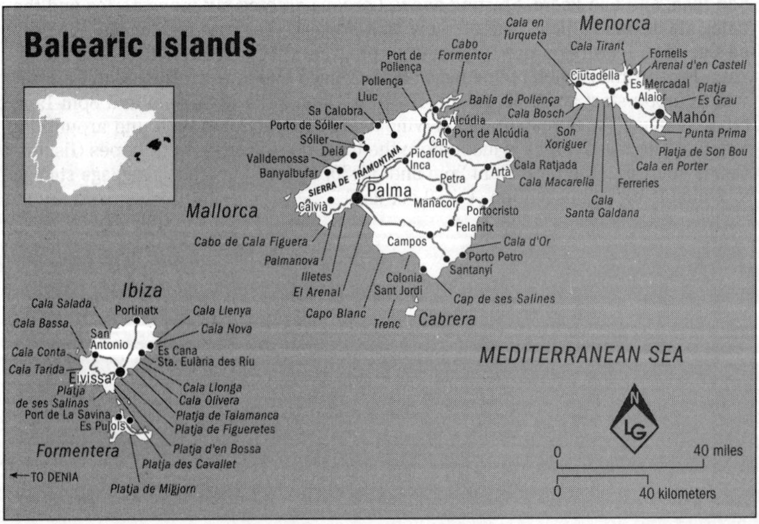

BY PLANE

Scheduled flights are the easiest to book and flights from Spain to any of the islands won't break the bank. Frequent flights soar from cities in Spain and throughout Europe (including Frankfurt, London, and Paris). On **Iberia** (☎902 40 05 00), many daily flights connect Palma de Mallorca and Ibiza to Madrid, Barcelona, and Valencia. Service from Alicante and Bilbao exists too, but is less frequent.

Iberia offers student fares (with an ISIC 26) on flights from Barcelona (40min., €60-120) and Madrid (1hr., €150-180). **Air Europa** (☎902 24 00 42) and **Spanair** (☎902 13 14 15; www.spanair.com) also offer inexpensive flights to the islands. Schedules and prices are subject to change. Another option is **charter flights,** which can be the cheapest and quickest means of travel. Most deals entail a stay in a hotel, but some companies (called *mayoristas*) sell unoccupied seats on package-tour flights. The leftover spots ("seat only" deals) can be found in newspaper ads or through travel agencies (check TIVE and other budget travel havens in any Spanish city). Prices during summer and *Semana Santa* are higher than in off-season (Oct.-May). Off-season, tickets are easy to get a week or so before departure. Those traveling in July or August should reserve several weeks in advance.

BY BOAT

Ferry service is considerably less expensive than flights, but longer in duration. On-board discos and small swimming pools on some boats ease the longer ride. Ferries run from Barcelona and Valencia to Palma (on Mallorca) and Eivissa (on Ibiza); ferries also run from Dénia (in Alicante) to Ibiza. Seats may be available up to an hour before departure, but it's best to reserve tickets a few days in advance.

Trasmediterránea (☎902 45 46 45; www.trasmediterranea.com) departs daily from Barcelona's Estació Marítima Moll and Valencia's Estació Marítima. Boats from both cities go to Mallorca, Menorca, and Ibiza. Fares from the mainland to the islands are €43 slowpoke, €58 fast boat. Fares between the islands range from €23 slow to €37 fast.

Balearia (☎902 16 01 80; www.balearia.com) runs ferries out of Estació Marítima in Dénia (in the province of Alicante). A short trip between Dénia and Ibiza (2-4½hr., 3 per day, from €25), continuing on to Palma (from €41).

Pitra Car Ferries (Dénia ☎971 19 10 68) run from Denía to Formentera via Eivissa and to San Antonio de Portmany (4hr.; 2 per day; €33, children €17, cars €90).

Buquebus (☎902 41 42 42 or 934 81 73 60) has super-fast catamaran service between Barcelona and Palma (4hr.; 2 per day; €49, cars €112).

Umafisa Lines (☎902 19 10 68) has service between Barcelona and the islands 3 times per week. €43, some economy tickets available for €37.

TRANSPORTATION

INTER-ISLAND TRANSPORT

Flying isn't always the best way to go between islands. **Iberia** flies between Palma and Ibiza (45min., 5 per day, €54-80) and between Palma and Mahón, Menorca (35min., 4 per day, from €54). **Air Europa** (☎902 24 00 42) and **Spanair** (☎902 13 14 15) connect the islands at similar prices. Youth discounts are often available.

A cheaper option is to take **ferries** between islands. Prices and times are constantly changing; consult the tourist office or a travel agent. Ferries to and from Mahón are lengthy (6½hr.), but "fast ferries" now make the journey between the other three islands in under three hours. **Trasmediterránea** (☎902 45 46 45) sails between Palma and Mahón (6½hr., Su only, €23) and between Palma and Ibiza (fast 2½hr., 1 per day at 7am from Palma, 7:45am from Ibiza, €37; slow 4½hr., 3 per week,

€23). There is no direct Mahón-Ibiza connection. **Trasmapi** (☎971 31 20 71) links Ibiza and Formentera (fast ferry 25min., 12 per day). **Umafisa Lines** (☎971 31 45 13) runs car ferries on the same route. **Iscomar Ferries** (☎902 119 128) runs between Menorca's Port de Ciutadella and Mallorca's Port d'Alcudia for day trips.

INTRA-ISLAND TRANSPORT

The three major islands have extensive **bus** systems, although transportation nearly comes to a halt on Sundays in most locations, so check schedules. Mallorca has two narrow-gauge **train** systems that are more of a tourist attraction than a major mode of getting around. Intra-island travel is reasonably priced—bus fares between cities range €1.20-6 each way. While it's possible to visit any of the islands without renting a vehicle, cars and mopeds are a great way (if you can afford it) to explore remote areas not accessible by bus service. In Mallorca and Menorca, cars are the best option, while in Ibiza, a moped is more than adequate. On Formentera, bicycles are a great way to get around. A tiny standard-transmission **car** costs around €36 per day including insurance. **Mopeds** are around €18 and **bicycles** a mere €6-10. Prices drop in the off-season and for long-term rentals.

MALLORCA

Mallorca has long been attracting the rich and famous. The site of the scandalous honeymoon of Polish pianist Frédéric Chopin and French novelist George Sand, Mallorca is also the choice vacation spot for Spain's royal family. Today, European package tourists have converged on the island, often suffocating the coastline.

Nevertheless, there are legitimate reasons for such Mallorca lust. To the northwest, white beaches and olive trees adorn the jagged Sierra de Tramontana. To the east, expansive beaches sink into calm bays, while to the southeast, caves mask underground treasure. Inland, towns retain their unique culture, where windmills drawing water for almond trees power a thriving agricultural economy. Although the coastline has been sacrificed to developers, even the most jaded of travelers sigh at the expanses of sea, sand, and rock that sprawl across much of this island.

PALMA

A stroll along Palma's (pop. 323,000) streets can be a dizzying, but at the same time thoroughly satisfying experience. Wander through the expansive maze of twisting lanes in the old quarter and you seem to forget that you are on an island. After a visit to the various department and designer stores near Pl. Espanya, it becomes hard to imagine that the city was once a devotional retreat for Fernando and Isabel. Head to the beach, and you suddenly feel as though you're no longer in Spain, given the abundance of German and British tourists sunbathing on the white sands. Nevertheless, despite the fairly recent foreign invasion and the city's growth as a major urban center in the last few years, Palma still retains a genuinely local flavor. In its many cafes and traditional *tapas* bars, where the native dialect of *mallorquín* is the only language that can be heard, it becomes quite clear why Palma reigns as the undisputed cultural capital of the Balearics.

TRANSPORTATION

Flights: Aeroport Son San Juan (☎971 78 90 00), 8km from downtown Palma. Bus #17 and 25 go to and from Pl. Espanya (€1.80). **Iberia** (☎902 40 05 00), **Air Europa** (☎902 24 00 42), foreign carriers, and a host of charter operators all offer service to Palma. See **By Plane,** p. 337 or **Inter-Island Transport,** p. 337.

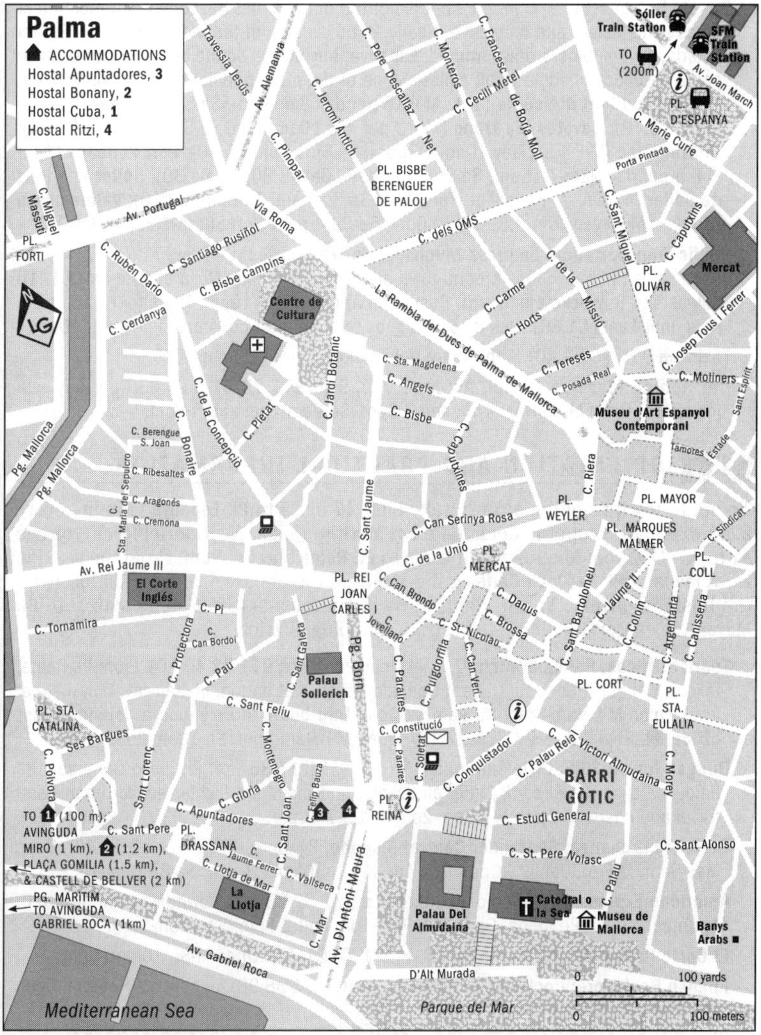

Ferries: Trasmediterránea, Estació Marítim, 2 (☎902 45 46 45). Ferries dock at Moll Pelaires (south of the city). Bus #1 goes through Pg. Marítim. Tickets sold M-F 9am-1pm and 5-7pm, Sa 9am-noon. Tickets and info also available at travel agencies. Daily ferries to Barcelona, Ibiza, and Valencia. **Balearia** (☎902 16 01 80) sends ferries to Dénia. See **By Boat,** p. 337, or **Transportation,** p. 337.

Trains: Ferrocarril de Sóller (☎971 75 20 51), Pl. Espanya. Runs to **Sóller** (1hr., 5 per day 8am-8:05pm, €2.40). Avoid the 10:40am "tourist train" when prices inflate to €4.80 for a 10min. stop in Mirador del Pujol d'en Banya. **Servicios Ferroviarios de Mallorca (SFM),** Pl. Espanya, 6 (☎971 75 22 45), departs to **Inca** (35min., 22 per day 5:45am-10pm, €1.80).

Buses: Bus travel to and from Palma is not too difficult, but travel between most other areas is inefficient and restrictive. Nearly all buses stop at the main stop on C. Eusebi Estada, several blocks down from Pl. Espanya; buy tickets on the bus. The tourist office has a detailed schedule of all buses. Some of the more popular destinations include: **Alcúdia** and **Port d'Alcúdia** (1hr.; M-F 16 per day 8am-9pm, Sa-Su 5 per day 9:30am-9pm; €3.70); **Covetes/Es Trenc** (M-F 3 per day 10am-5pm, Sa-Su 10:30am; €3.84); **Cuevas Drac** (M-F 4 per day 10am-1:30pm, Sa-Su 10am; €5.40); **Port Pollenca** (1hr.; M-F 5 per day 9am-7:15pm, Sa-Su 3 per day 10am-8:30pm; €4.30); **Sóller** and **Port de Sóller** (45min.; M-F every hr. 7am-7pm, Sa-Su 1 and 4:30pm; €2.10); **Valldemossa** (30min.; M-F every 2hr. 7:30am-7:30pm, Sa-Su 4 per day 8:30am-7:30pm; €1.20).

Public Transportation: Empresa Municipal de Transportes (EMT; ☎971 75 22 45). Pl. Espanya is the hub. Stops around town and as far as Palma Nova and Arenal. €1, 10 tickets €9. Buy tickets onboard. Buses run approx. 6am-10pm. The airport bus, #17, runs until 1am (€1.80). Bus #25 also goes to the airport but stops running at 10pm.

Taxis: (☎971 75 54 40). Airport fare from center of town is about €15.

Car Rental: Mascaro Crespi, Av. Joan Miró, 9 (☎971 73 61 03). €30 per day with insurance. Open M-Sa 8am-1pm and 3-8pm, Su 9am-1pm and 5-8pm.

ORIENTATION AND PRACTICAL INFORMATION

To get to town from the airport, take bus #17 or 25 to **Pl. Espanya** (15min., every 20min., €1.80). From the dock, take Pg. Marítim (a.k.a. Av. Gabriel Roca), or bus #1 to Av. D'Antoni Maura, which leads to **Pl. Reina** and **Pg. Born.** From the sea, Pg. Born leads to **Pl. Rei Joan Carles I,** the center of the old town, and **Av. Rei Jaume III,** the business artery. To the right, C. de la Unió leads (after some stairs) to **Pl. Mayor,** the center of Palma's pedestrian shopping district.

Tourist Offices: Palma branch, C. Sant Dominic, 11 (☎971 72 40 90). From Pl. Reina, take C. Conquistador until C. Sant Dominic; office is at bottom of stairway, below street level. Open M-F 9am-8pm, Sa 9am-1:30pm. **Info booth** in Pl. Espanya. **Island tourist office,** Pl. Reina, 2 (☎971 71 22 16). Open M-F 9am-8pm, Sa 10am-2pm.

Budget Travel: TIVE, C. Jeróni Antich, 5 (☎971 71 17 85), off Pl. Bisbe Berenguer de Palou. ISIC cards, HI cards, Interrail tickets, and mainland flights. Not for inter-island travel and charters. Open M-F 9am-2pm and 5-7:30pm.

Currency Exchange: Santander Central Hispano, Pg. Born, 17 (☎971 72 51 46). Open May-Sept. M-F 8:30am-2:30pm; Oct.-Apr. M-F 8:30am-2:30pm, Sa 8:30am-1pm.

American Express: Av. Antonio Maura, 40 (☎971 72 23 44), downtown right next to C. Apuntadores, off Pl. Reina. Open M-F 9am-1pm and 2-8pm, Sa 10am-2pm.

El Corte Inglés: Av. Rei Jaume III, 15 (☎971 77 01 77). Open M-Sa 10am-10pm.

English Bookstore: Book Inn, C. Horts, 20 (☎971 71 38 98), right off La Rambla. Open M-F 10am-1:30pm and 4:30-8pm.

Women's Center: Centro de Derechos Mujeres, Galería, 4 (☎971 77 49 74; 24hr. hotline 900 19 10 10). Rape crisis assistance available. Open M-F 9am-2pm.

Laundromat: Lavandería Fast, Joan Miró, 5 (☎971 45 46 14). €9 for 5kg. Open M-Sa 10am-2pm and 4-8pm. **Coronet Lavandería,** corner of C. Annibal and C. Argentina. A block from Hostal Cuba. €8.40 for 5kg. Open M-Sa 8am-1pm and 4-8pm.

Emergency: ☎112. **Police:** Av. Sant Ferrá (☎091 or 092).

Late-Night Pharmacy: Rotates daily; see listings in local paper, the *Diario de Mallorca.*

Medical Services: Clínica Juaneda, C. Son Espanyolet, 55 (☎971 73 16 47), and **Femenía,** Av. Camilo José Cela, 20 (☎971 45 23 23). **Clínica Rotger,** C. Santiago Russinyol, 9 (☎971 71 66 00), is more centrally located. All open 24hr.

Internet Access: La Red, C. Concepció, 5 (☎971 71 35 74), 2 blocks off of Av. Jaume III near the intersection of Pg. Born. €2.40 for 30min. Open daily 10am-midnight. **Cyber Central,** C. Soletat, 4 (☎971 71 29 27), in Pl. Reina. €4.80 per hr., students €3.60 per hr. Open M-Sa 9am-10pm, Su noon-8pm.

Post Office: C. Constitució, 5 (☎902 19 71 97), 1 block off Pl. Reina. Parcels upstairs. **Fax** service. Open M-F 8:30am-8:30pm, Sa 9:30am-2pm. **Postal Code:** 07080.

ACCOMMODATIONS

This resort town has few *hostals* or bargains. Call in advance for summer stays.

Hostal Ritzi, C. Apuntadores, 6 (☎971 71 46 10), conveniently situated above "Big Byte" cybercafe. Centrally located *hostal* with rooms overlooking an interior patio which can get noisy at night. Laundry €7. Singles €23; doubles €34, with bath €49. ❷

Alberg Platja de Palma (HI), C. Costa Brava, 13 (☎971 26 08 92), in El Arenal. Take bus #15 from Pl. Espanya (every 8min., €1), and get off at C. Costa Brava. 4-person dorms with shower. HI card required. Breakfast included. Sheets €2.40. Laundry €6. Reception 8am-3am. Curfew midnight. Dorms €9-12, over 26 €10.20-14. ❶

Hostal Apuntadores, C. Apuntadores, 8 (☎971 71 34 91), in a great, central location. Rooms are airy and bright. Dorms €12; singles €18; doubles €30, with shower €33. ❷

Hostal Cuba, C. San Magí, 1 (☎971 73 81 59), at C. Argentina. From Pl. Joan Carles I, turn left and walk down Av. Jaume III, cross the river, and turn left on C. Argentina. Look for the "Restaurant Cuba" sign several blocks down. 1st floor rooms are more basic than 2nd floor. Singles €15-18; doubles €30-33. ❷

Hostal Bonany, C. Almirante Cervera, 5 (☎971 73 79 24), in a wealthy residential area 3km from the town center. Take bus #3, 20, 21, or 22 from Pl. Espanya to Av. Joan Miró and walk up C. Camilio José Cela. Take the 1st right, then the 1st left. Spacious rooms with bath and balcony. Singles €26; doubles €40. ❸

FOOD

Palma's multi-ethnic restaurants are paradise for those sick of *tapas*. Pricey but popular outdoor restaurants fill **Pl. Mayor** and **Pl. Llotja,** but budget eaters head to the side streets off **Pg. Born,** to the cheap digs along **Av. Joan Miró,** or to the pizzerias along **Po. Marítimo.** Make sure to try the *ensaimadas* (pastries smothered in powdered sugar) and the *sopas mallorquinas* (a pizza-like snack of stewed vegetables over brown bread). Two **markets** vie for customers: one is in Pl. Olivar off C. Padre Atanasio, the other is across town at the corner of C. Pou and C. Dameto. For **groceries,** try **Servicio y Precios** on C. Felip Bauzá, near C. Apuntadores and Pl. Reina (open M-F 8:30am-8:30pm, Sa 9am-2pm), or the supermarket in **El Corte Inglés,** Av. Rei Jaume III, 15. (☎971 77 01 77. Open M-Sa 10am-10pm.)

Bon Lloc, C. San Feliu, 7 (☎971 71 86 17), a left off C. Born, heading away from water. Ultra-hip vegetarian restaurant. Menu features salads (€5.70), falafel (€7.20), and dishes like basmati rice with Chinese-style sauteed vegetables (€9.60). Midday *menú* €9.60. Open M-Tu 1-4pm, W-Sa 1-4pm and 9-11:30pm. MC/V. ❷

Pizzeria Restaurante Vecchio Giovanni, C. San Juan, 3 (☎971 72 28 79), right off C. Apuntadores. Lively family restaurant with excellent pizzas (€5-8) and pastas (€7-10). Gets crowded for dinner, especially on weekends. Open daily 5pm-midnight. ❷

Cellar Montenegro, C. Montenegro, 10, off C. Apuntadores. Heaping portions of *comida típica* in a family setting. *Menú* €9. Open M-F 1-4pm and 8:30pm-midnight. MC/V. ❷

Cantina Mariachi, C. Ramon y Cajal, 2 (☎971 73 30 33), across the river (and Pg. Mallorca) from the old quarter, off Av. de l'Argentina. Inexpensive Mexican food served in a lively locale. Tacos €7.50, fajitas (chicken or lamb) €10. Open daily 8pm-midnight. ❷

SIGHTS

Palma's architecture is a medley of Arabic, Christian, and Modernist styles: a reflection of the island's multicultural past and present. Many of its landmarks are nestled amidst the narrow streets of the Barri Gòtic (Gothic quarter).

CATEDRAL O LA SEA. This Gothic giant towers over Palma and its bay. The cathedral, dedicated to Palma's patron saint San Sebastián, was begun in the 1300s, finished in 1601, and then modified by Gaudí in Modernist fashion in 1909. Now the interior and the ceiling ornamentation blend smoothly with the stately exterior. Its southern facade, perhaps the most impressive, overlooks a reflective pool and the ocean. *(C. Palau Reial, 29, off Pl. Reina. ☎971 72 31 30. Cathedral and museum open Apr.-Oct. M-F 10am-6pm, Sa 10am-2pm; Nov.-Mar. M-F 10am-3pm. €3.)*

PALAU DEL'ALMUDAINA. Built by the Moors, this imposing austere palace was at one point a stronghold of *los Reyes Católicos*, Fernando and Isabel. Guided tours, which pass through the museum, are given in numerous languages. The pleasant garden off Pl. Reina directly in front of the palace also merits a visit. *(C. Palau Reial, just off Pl. Reina. ☎971 72 71 45. Open M-F 10am-6:30pm, Sa 10am-2pm. Guided visits €3.91, unguided €3.16. Students and children €2.25. EU citizens free on W.)*

CASTELL DEL BELLVER. Overlooking the city and bay, Castell de Bellver was a summer residence for 14th-century royalty; it also housed Mallorca's most distinguished prisoners. Castle contains a municipal museum and models of archaeological digs. *(Bus #3, 21, or 22 from Pl. Espanya. ☎971 73 06 57. Castle and museum open Apr.-Sept. M-Sa 8am-8:30pm, Su 10am-5pm; Oct.-Mar. M-Sa 8am-7:15pm, Su 10am-5pm. €1.68.)*

MUSEU D'ART ESPANYOL CONTEMPORANI. Now part of the March Foundation, this mansion-turned-museum displays modern art, including works of the 20th century's most iconic Spanish artists—Picasso, Dalí, Miró, Juan Gris, and Antoni Tápies. *(C. Sant Miquel, 11. ☎971 71 35 15. Open M-F 10am-6:30pm, Sa 10am-1:30pm. €3.)*

OTHER MUSEUMS. Inaugurated in December 1992, **Fundació Pilar i Joan Miró** displays the works from Miró's Palma studio at the time of his death. (C. Saridakis, 29. From Pl. Espanya, take buses #3, 21, or 22 to C. Joan Miró. ☎971 70 14 20. Open May 16-Sept. 14 Tu-Sa 10am-7pm, Su 10am-3pm; Sept. 15-May 15 Tu-Sa 10am-6pm, Su 10am-3pm. €4.20.) **Fundació "la Caixa"** hosts a collection of Modernist paintings in Doménech's Modernist Gran Hotel. (Pl. Weyler, 3. ☎971 17 85 00. Open Tu-Sa 10am-9pm, Su 10am-2pm. Free.) The **Casal Solleric** houses modern art. (Pg. Born, 27. ☎971 72 20 92. Open Tu-Sa 10:30am-1:45pm, Su 10am-1:45pm. Free.) **Centre de Cultura "Sa Nostra"** features rotating exhibits and cultural events such as lectures, concerts, and movies. (C. Concepción, 12. ☎971 72 52 10. Open M-F 10:30am-9pm, Sa 10am-1:30pm.) **Museu de Mallorca** is ideal for travelers interested in archaeology or medieval painting. (C. Portella, 5. ☎971 71 75 40. Open Apr.-Sept. Tu-Sa 10am-2pm and 5-8pm; Oct.-Mar. Tu-Sa 10am-1pm and 4-8pm, Su 10am-2pm. €1.80.) For those fed up with being inside, there's the **Poble Espanyol,** a small village with replicas of famous Spanish architecture. (C. Poble Espanyol, 39. Buses #4 and 5 pass on C. Andrea Doria. ☎971 73 70 75. Open daily 9am-8pm; Dec.-Mar. 9am-6pm. €4.80.)

BEACHES. Mallorca is a huge island, and many of the best beaches are a haul from Palma. Still, several picturesque (albeit touristy) stretches of sand are accessible by city bus. The beach at **El Arenal** (Platja de Palma, bus #15), 11km to the southeast (toward the airport), is the prime stomping grounds of Mallorca's most

YO QUIERO BAILAR... In the words of Spanish disco-pop queen Paulina, the next phrase would run "toda la noche." But for the disco-pub owners in Palma, Mallorca, the song would more accurately end "hasta las tres"—at least in the city's *casco antiguo*, Palma's traditional bar-hopping center. For years locals and tourists alike have let loose at the numerous bars crowding the streets near C. Apuntadores, drinking and dancing 'til dawn. But with the advent of a new city law aimed at maintaining a high-class image and controlling rowdiness, establishments in Palma proper must now stop serving alcohol by 2am, and close their doors by 3am. The end result of the new regulation hasn't meant an end to Palma's nightlife, but instead a migratory shift toward the port along Po. Marítimo—great for the huge clubs and *bares-musicales* that line the water, but the end of an era for the traditional hotspots.

sunburnt German tourists. The waterfront area is full of German signs for restaurants, bars, and hotels—think *Frankfurt am Mediterranean*. The beach is one of the longest and most crowded in the area, but with white sands and turquoise water, it's enough to make even the Germans smile. Other beaches close to Palma include **Palma Nova** (bus #21), 15km southwest, and **Illetes** (bus #3), 9km southwest, which are smaller than El Arenal, but equally popular. The tourist office distributes a list of 40 nearby beaches—take your pick and remember to say *danke*.

NIGHTLIFE AND ENTERTAINMENT. Entertainment *à la Mallorca* has a Spanish flavor often missing in the other isles, but still well documented for visitors. The tourist office keeps a list of sporting activities, concerts, and exhibits. Every Friday, *El Día del Mundo* (€0.75) publishes an entertainment supplement with listings of bars and discos, and *La Calle* offers a monthly review of hotspots.

In the past, Pl. Reina and La Llotja were the place for bar-hoppers, but a recent law requiring bars to close by 3am has shifted the action to the waterfront. Nevertheless, many partiers still start their night in the *casco viejo*. **La Bodeguita del Medio,** C. Vallseca, 18, plays Cuban rhythms. (Open Th-Sa 8pm-3am, Su-W 8pm-1am.) Follow the Aussies to **Bar Latitude 39,** C. Felip Bauza, 8, a "yachtie" bar. (Beer €1.50. "Twofer nights"—2 for the price of 1—Tu, Th, and Sa 9-10pm. Open M-Sa 7pm-3am.) **Barcelona,** C. Apuntadores, 5, jams with live music from midnight to 3am. (Cover €1.80 for live concerts. Open daily 11pm-3am.)

Palma's clubbers start the night in the *bares-musicales* on the **Po. Marítimo** strip. Each mini-disco boasts different tunes, but Spanish pop dominates. Come 2am, head to the salsa-happy **Made in Brasil,** Po. Marítimo, 27 (mixed drinks €3.60-4.80; open daily 8pm-4am), and dance-crazy **Salero,** Po. Marítimo, 31 (open daily 8pm-6am). Several clubs and bars are centered on Pl. Gomilia and along C. Joan Miró—but take caution here at night, as there have been a number of reported instances of petty crime occurring here in recent years. The bars and clubs around **El Arenal** are German-owned, German-filled, and German-centric. But if you don't mind partying with Deutschland, quite possibly the best deal for entertainment in Palma is here at **Riu Palace,** one block in from the beach. Two huge rooms, one playing techno and the other spinning hip-hop, fill nightly with hip, young, fashion-conscious German disco-fiends. All guests receive free t-shirts, "Rapper caps," necklaces, and coupons for free food at a nearby beer garden. Themed parties every weekend. (Cover €15; open bar, all you can drink. Open daily 10pm-6:30am.)

When the bar scene fades at 3am, partiers migrate to Palma's *discotecas*, which attract more locals than tourists. **Tito's Palace,** Po. Marítimo, is Palma's hippest disco, with two floors of house in an indoor colosseum of mirrors and lights. (Cover €15-18. Open daily 11pm-6am.) **Pachá,** Av. Gabriel Roca, is a toned-down version of the Ibiza landmark, but this little sibling has a massive dance floor, tropical terrace, and enthusiastic patrons. (Cover €12-18. Open daily 11pm-6:30am.)

Mallorcans use any and every occasion as an excuse to party. One of the more colorful bashes, **Día de Sant Joan** (June 24), brings singing, dancing, and drinking to Parc del Mar. The celebration begins with a fireworks display the night before.

WESTERN MALLORCA

The west coast of Mallorca has some of the most beautiful landscapes in the Mediterranean. It has inspired a range of creative minds, from lovers Chopin and George Sand to writer Robert Graves and actor Michael Douglas. Ten minutes beyond the modern roads and white highrises of Palma, the road enters a ravine (the island's first cave dwellers sheltered here) and rises in tight, narrow curves. On the north road beyond Valldemossa, olive groves pitch steeply toward the sea.

VALDEMOSSA

Valldemossa's tiny, shaded streets huddle beneath the slopes of the Sierra de Tramontana. Quaint and peaceful, little in this village hints at the passion that scandalized the townsfolk in the winter of 1838 when Frédéric Chopin and George Sand stayed in the 14th-century monastery **Cartoixa Reial** (see **A Winter of Nocturnes,** p. 345). The Chopin memorabilia includes the piano which he carried up the mountain in several pieces. Piano recitals try to recapture the magic in summer. (☎971 61 21 06. Recitals every hr. on the half hr. Open M-Sa 9:30am-6pm, Su 10am-1pm. €9. Includes entrance to the Museu Municipal and the **Palau del Rei Sancho,** where folk dances take place M and Th 11am-1:30pm.) **Nord Balear buses** (☎971 49 06 80) to **Valldemossa** leave Palma at C. Arxiduc Salvador, 1 (30min., 7 per day 7:30am-7:30pm, €1.20). Cafes around the main square serve simple fare—linger over your meal because once the few stores and sights close, there's nothing else to do.

SÓLLER

Thirty kilometers up the coast from Valldemossa, Sóller basks in a fertile valley. Oranges and tomatoes are the principal crops, and every plot of land is lined with citrus groves or sunburnt tourists. The town, with a backdrop of spectacular mountains and quaint squares, is a pleasant change from Palma's touristy beaches. In July, the Ajuntament hosts a **Festival of Folk Dancing.** The old-fashioned Palma-Sóller **train,** run by Ferrocarril de Sóller, C. Castanyer, 7, is a highlight. The bravehearted ride between cars as they pass through orchards and tunnels. (☎971 63 03 01, Palma 971 75 20 51. 5 per day 8am-8:05pm. €2.40.) Sóller's **tourist office,** in an old trolley car in Pl. d'Espanya, downstairs from the train station, has accommodations listings and maps. (☎971 63 02 00. Open M-F 9:30am-1:30pm and 3-6:30pm, Sa-Su 10am-1pm. Info posted in front of the church in Pl. Constitució if the office is closed.) Restaurants fill Pl. Constitució, but if you don't need a full meal, try the *coca mallorquina*, a cold pizza-like snack (about €1.80) in local bakeries.

PUERTO DE SÓLLER

From Sóller it's a 30min. walk (or a short ride on the Nord Balear bus) to Puerto de Sóller, where a pebbly beach lines the bay. Trolleys also connect the two (every 30min. 7am-9pm, €0.75). The **tourist office,** C. Canonge Oliver, 10, has quality maps. (☎/fax 971 63 30 42. Open M-F 10am-1pm and 3-6:30pm, Sa 10am-1pm.) The popular restaurant downstairs serves a €6.60 *menú.* Two **grocery stores** are on C. Jaume Torrens, and **restaurants** line the beach. The surrounding area's famous **coves** are most easily explored by **boat.** On the port near the last trolley stop, **Tramontana** and **Barcos Azules** sail to the dramatic cove of **Sa Calobra,** most visitors' final destination. (May-Oct. 15 3-5 per day, round-trip €15.) Nord Balear "tunnel express" **buses** link Puerto de Sóller to **Palma** (1hr., every hr. 7am-9pm, €2.10).

A WINTER OF NOCTURNES, PRELUDES, AND THE PAINS OF LOVE Mallorca has always attracted rich and famous vacationers, from Michael Douglas to the Spanish Royal Family. Nevertheless, the most widely recognized of its visitors are the Polish musician Frédéric Chopin, and his lover, the French novelist George Sand (the pen name for Aurore Dupin), who spent 98 days here in the winter of 1838-39. Though it was intended to be a honeymoon of sorts for the two lovers, the vacation was doomed from the outset. Chopin suffered from tuberculosis at the time, constantly in pain and prone to black moods. Sand, a passionate free-thinker, felt trapped on the island, as is evident in her writings. The couple's presence (particularly the fact that Sand had her two children from a previous marriage with her at the time) caused a stir among the townsfolk, who tormented the couple through the windows of cells #2 and 4 of the Cartoixa Real, which they occupied during their stay. Sand documents these incidents in the book she wrote while on the island, *Un Hiver a Majorque* (A Winter in Mallorca), and refers to the local villagers as "barbarians and monkeys." Despite these less than ideal circumstances, Chopin produced some of his greatest pieces while on the island. Sadly, Chopin and Sand's love affair came to an end when the two realized their personalities were too divergent, and nothing could eliminate their differences. Thus, in February of 1839, they boarded the same ship which had taken them to Mallorca less than four months before, and after reaching the Spanish mainland, parted ways forever.

SA CALOBRA

Like a serpent, the road to Sa Calobra writhes over 10 nail-biting kilometers while dropping 1000m to the sea. The boat from Puerto de Sóller is easier on the nerves. (5 per day from Puerto de Sóller 10am-3pm, return 4 per day 10:45am-5pm. €9 one way.) **Torrent de Pareis,** a spectacular cove which leads into a ravine with freshwater pools, is a 15min. hike from the bottom of the road and a popular photo opportunity (look for a landing packed with tourists). Sa Calobra itself is a smooth pebble beach, bordered by cliffs. Like the rest of the island, its beauty is marred by an infestation of tourist restaurants, tourist gift shops, and tourists themselves.

NORTHERN MALLORCA

Known for their long beaches and rocky coves, the northern gulfs of Mallorca are popular among the older, package-tour crowd; much of the coast is swamped beyond belief. The drive can be stunning, and though the region's coves and beaches are far from secluded, they are among the most beautiful on the island.

PUERTO DE ALCÚDIA

Puerto de Alcúdia is far from undiscovered. The beaches along the shallow bay are packed with hotels, bars, and pizzerias. The excessive number of arcades and ice cream stands testify to Puerto de Alcúdia's popularity among families with children of the little-and-screaming variety. Despite its tourist infestation, Puerto de Alcúdia makes a nice base for exploring the stunning beaches of the northeastern coast. If you have a car, take the road towards **Arta** and then **Capdepera** from town. About 20km from Puerto de Alcúdia, you will see signs leading to **Cala Torta** along a bumpy dirt road. Cala Torta itself is the most touristed of the three arid coves which make up the northeastern corner of the island. If you hike from this beach over the cliffs to the west, you come to **Cala Mitjana,** a beautiful cove with crashing waves and tide pools filled with seaweed. (Beach chairs and umbrellas €2.) Past Cala Mitjana is **Es Matzoc,** a pleasant white-sanded beach which is not entirely overrun by tourists. If you're looking for more than a beach, visit Alcúdia's old town with **14th-century ramparts, Roman remains** dating from 2 BC, and town walls from a series of medieval razings and rebuildings. (15min. walk; buses depart every 15min. from C. dels Mariners.) The **Museu Pollentia** documents archaeological discoveries on Mallorca. (☎971 54 70 04. Open M-F 10am-2pm and 5-7pm, Sa-Su 10:30am-1pm. €1.20.) **Parc Natural de L'Albufera,** walking distance from the beach, is filled with marshes, flowers, and dunes. (Open daily 10am-7pm, in winter until 5pm. Free.) The tourist office has a brochure of 10 hiking/biking excursions.

Hostal Calma ❸, C. Teodoro Canet, 25, offers pleasant rooms with private bath. (☎971 54 85 85. Singles €27; doubles €35.) **Alberg Victoria (HI) ❶,** Ctra. Cap Pinar, 4, lies 100m from a beach on the Bahía de Pollença. From the town center, signs lead 4km to Malpas and point to the hostel. (1hr. walk or €6.60 taxi ride.) Reserve in advance. (☎971 54 53 95. Breakfast included. HI members only. €9, over 26 €10.) For food, hit up one of the **restaurants** along the port, or head to **Supermercats Aprop,** C. Mariners, 14, to get groceries (open M-Sa 9am-10pm, Su 9am-8pm).

Buses, leaving from Pl. Espanya in Palma (☎971 54 56 96), run to Alcúdia (€3.57) and Puerto de Alcúdia (€3.69) from Pl. Espanya in Palma (1hr.; M-Sa 16 per day 8am-9pm, Su 5 per day 9:30am-9pm). The bus to Port Pollença and Cap de Formentor leaves from C. dels Mariners. The **tourist office** is on Pg. Marítim, in a small plaza at the far end of the beach, on your left as you face the water. (☎971 54 72 57. Open M, W-Sa 9:30am-8pm; Tu 9:30am-1:30pm and 4-8pm.) **Police:** ☎971 54 50 78.

PORT POLLENÇA (PUERTO POLLENSA)

Calmer and classier than its neighboring beach towns, Port Pollença features a beautiful man-made beach along a crescent-shaped bay. Popular among British and northern Europeans, cafes, restaurants, and pubs cater to a more refined crowd of middle-aged tourists, though the town isn't particularly expensive. The **tourist office,** C. Monges, is one block from the bus stop. (☎971 86 54 67. Open M-F 8am-3:30pm, Sa 9am-1pm.) **Hostal Corro ❷,** C. Joan XXIII, 68, offers air-conditioned rooms blocks from the beach. (☎971 86 50 05. Singles €24; doubles €30; triples €36.) **Rent March,** C. Joan XXIII, 89, rents bikes and mopeds. (☎971 86 47 84. Open Mar.-Nov. M-Sa 9am-1pm and 3-8pm, Su 9am-2:30pm. Bikes €4.20 per day; mopeds €18-19.80 per day.) The area hosts a **music festival** July-Sept. A complete schedule of events and list of ticket vendors is available at the tourist office (tickets €6-30). **Autocares Mallorca buses** connect Alcúdia and Pollença (20min., every 15min. 8:30am-1:30pm and 3-8pm, €0.90). **Autocares Villalonga** (☎971 53 00 57) goes to Palma (1hr., 5 per day 7:15am-5:30pm, €4.30). Buses stop at the rotary at the end of Pg. Saralegui. In an emergency, dial ☎112 or the **police** (☎971 53 04 37).

CAP DE FORMENTOR

A trek to Cap de Formentor, 15km northeast of Port Pollença, leads to dramatic seaside cliffs. Before the final kilometer, the road drops to **Platja Formentor,** where a canopy of evergreens seems to sink into the water. If you have your own transportation, head downhill from the lighthouse to the bottom of the road for two of the most beautiful coves in Mallorca. On your right is the small dirt parking lot for **Cala Figuera,** a cove surrounded by jagged cliffs which is a popular anchorage for private yachts. Across the road to your right is a small wooden sign pointing in the direction of **Cala Murta,** perhaps the only secluded cove on the island. From the road, follow the dirt path indicated by the sign until you come to a small electrical station. Bear right and you will see the tiny pebbly beach and turquoise water which characterize the cove. **Buses** drop you off at a road 6km away from the end of Cap de Formentor, where a lighthouse, a spectacular view, and dozens of tourist families await. **Autocares Villalonga,** San Isidro, 4 (☎971 53 00 57), sends one bus daily from Palma

(10:15am, returns 3:30pm; €4.80). **Autocares Mallorca** buses (☎971 54 56 96) leave from Port Pollença (2 per day 9am-2:15pm, €2.40). A **boat** (☎971 86 40 14) goes to Platja Formentor from Port Pollença's Estació Marítima (every hr. 10am-4pm, returns every hr. 10:30am-5:30pm; round-trip €5.85).

SOUTHEAST MALLORCA

Signs along the highway of Mallorca's southeast coast might as well read "Welcome tourist hordes," as much of the area has been built up by developers. On the coast, east of Cap de Salinas, Mallorca's southernmost point, scalloped fringes of bays are the developers' most recent discovery. Still, the breathtaking scenery and intriguing caves remain relatively unspoiled.

CUEVAS DRACH. The Cuevas Drach, near Porto Cristo, are among the island's most dramatic natural wonders, with their red and pink stalagtites. A 30min. walk into the depths of the cave is one of the largest underground lakes in the world. The performances given by classical musicians boating across the lake are classified somewhere between absurd and bizarre; audience members can take free boat rides at the concert's end. *(A bus runs from Palma to the caves, leaving from the main station by Pl. Espanya. 1hr.; M-Sa 4 per day 10am-1:30pm, Su 10am; €5.40.)*

ES TRENC. West of Cap de Salinas and east of Cap Blanc sprawls one of Mallorca's best beaches, Es Trenc. In most cases, a 1-2km walk is usually enough to put plenty of sand between you and the thickest crowds. *(Buses run to Es Trenc in the summer from Pl. Espanya in Palma. M-Sa 3 per day 10am-5pm, Su 10:30am; €3.84.)*

MENORCA

Menorca's beaches, rustic landscape, and picturesque town draw ecologists, sun worshippers, and photographers. In 1993, UNESCO declared the island a biosphere reserve; since then, administrators have put effort into preserving Menorca's natural harbors, pristine beaches, rocky northern coast, and network of farmlands. The act has also encouraged protection, excavation, and study of Menorca's stone burial chambers and homestead complexes, remnants of a mysterious Talayotic stone-age culture dating from 1400 BC. Since its incorporation into the Catalan kingdom in 1287, Menorca (pop. 71,617) has endured a succession of foreign invaders—Arab, Turkish, French, and British. After occupying the island several times during the 18th century, the Brits have returned to dominance as tourists, with children and German neighbors in tow. Quieter and more upscale than the other Balearics, Menorca attracts wealthy young families in search of a peaceful beach vacation and has less to offer budget travelers than its larger neighbors. Most families that come here tend to stay in resorts and apartments along the beaches; the towns themselves sometimes offer reasonable prices. Students make their appearance here before the real tourist season starts, usually in the spring, while everyone else arrives full-force come August. Menorca's main cities, Mahón and Ciutadella, serve as gateways to the island's real attractions.

MAHÓN (MAÓ)

Atop a steep bluff, Mahón's (pop. 25,000) whitewashed houses overlook a well-trafficked harbor. The British occupied the city for most of the 18th century, leaving Georgian doors, brass knockers, and wooden shutters in their wake. Two centuries later, the predominance of British tourists testifies to their continuing influence. Most people clear out during the day, using the town as a jumping off point for the numerous beaches nearby; public buses go to some of the more popular stretches of sand. Others spend their hours window-shopping along Mahón's pedestrian streets. The city comes alive in early evening when sunburnt visitors return from the beaches. Despite the presence of bars and clubs, Mahón's nightlife is more centered around lingering over dinner than all-night partying.

TRANSPORTATION

Flights: Airport (☎971 15 70 00), 7km out of town. **Iberia/Aviaco** (☎971 36 90 15); **Air Europa** (☎971 24 00 42 or 971 15 70 31); **SpanAir** (☎971 15 70 98). In summer advance booking is essential. See **By Plane,** p. 337, or **Inter-Island Transport,** p. 337.

Ferries: Estació Marítima, on Moll Andén de Ponent (☎971 36 60 50). Open M-F 8am-1pm and 5-7pm, Sa 8am-noon, Su 8-10:30am and 3:30-5:15pm. **Trasmediterránea** (☎971 36 29 50) sends ferries daily to Barcelona and weekly to Valencia and Palma. For more info, see **By Boat,** p. 337, or **Inter-Island Transport,** p. 337.

Buses: Check the tourist office or the newspapers *Menorca Diario Insular* and *Menorca* for schedules. There is no central bus station; buses stop around Pl. s'Esplanada. **Transportes Menorca (TMSA),** C. José M. Quadrado, 7 (☎971 36 03 61), off Pl. s'Esplanada. To: **Ciutadella** via **Ferreries** and **Es Mercadal** (1hr., 6 per day 8am-7pm, €3.51); **Es Castell** (every 30min. 7:45am-8:45pm, €0.87); **Platja Punta Prima** (9 per day 8:30am-7:30pm, €1.02); **Son Bou** (7 per day 8:45am-7pm, €1.65). Some depart from Pl. s'Esplanada, some from nearby C. Quadrado; check signs at the bus stop. Tickets available when boarding the bus or at office on C. Quadrado. **Autobuses Fornells Roca Triay** (☎971 37 66 21) buses depart from C. Vassallo, off Pl. s'Esplanada. To: **Arenal d'en Castell** (7 per day 9:30am-7pm); **Es Grau** (4 per day 10am-6:15pm); **Fornells** (4 per day 11am-7pm); **Son Parc** (3 per day 1-7pm). Buy tickets on board.

Taxis: Main stop at Pl. s'Esplanada (☎971 36 12 83), or **Radio Taxi** from anywhere on the island (☎971 36 71 11). To: **airport** (€7.80); **Cala Mesquida** (€7.80); **Cala'n Porter** (€11.40); **Es Castell** (€4.80).

Car Rental: Autos Menorsur, C. Luna 23 (☎971 36 56 66), off C. Hannóver. July-Aug. €36 per day, €180 per week; substantial discounts in low season. English spoken. Open M-F 9am-2pm and 5-9pm, Sa-Su 9am-2pm.

Bike and Scooter Rental: Motos Menorca, Moll de Levante, 35-36 (☎971 35 47 86), Puerto de Mahón. Bicycles €9 per day, €37-42 per week. Scooters €21-27 per day, €93-150 per week. Open Apr.-Sept. daily 9:30am-1:30pm and 5-7:30pm.

ORIENTATION AND PRACTICAL INFORMATION

Take a taxi (€7.80) between the **airport** and Mahón. To get to the heart of the city from the **ferry station,** go left (with your back to the water) about 150m, then turn right at the steps that cut through the serpentine **Costa de ses Voltes.** The steps end between Pl. Conquesta and Pl. Espanya. To reach **Pl. de s'Esplanada,** take Portal de Mar to Costa de Sa, which becomes C. Hannóver and C. Ses Moreres, and continue to the plaça. To reach **Pl. de la Miranda,** walk through Pl. Espanya and Pl. Carme; when you reach Pl. Príncep, turn left, and Pl. Miranda is 100m ahead.

Tourist Office: Sa Rovellada de Dalt, 24 (☎971 36 37 90; fax 971 36 74 15). From Pl. s'Esplanada, head down C. Ses Moreres 1 block, and take the 1st left. English spoken. Open M-F 9am-1:30pm and 5-7pm, Sa 9am-1pm. Summer office at the airport (☎971 15 71 15) provides similar materials. Open daily Mar.-Oct. 8:30am-10:30pm.

Currency Exchange: Banks with 24hr. **ATMs** line C. Hannóver and C. Nou.

Emergency: ☎112. **Police: Municipal,** Pl. Constitució (☎971 36 39 61).

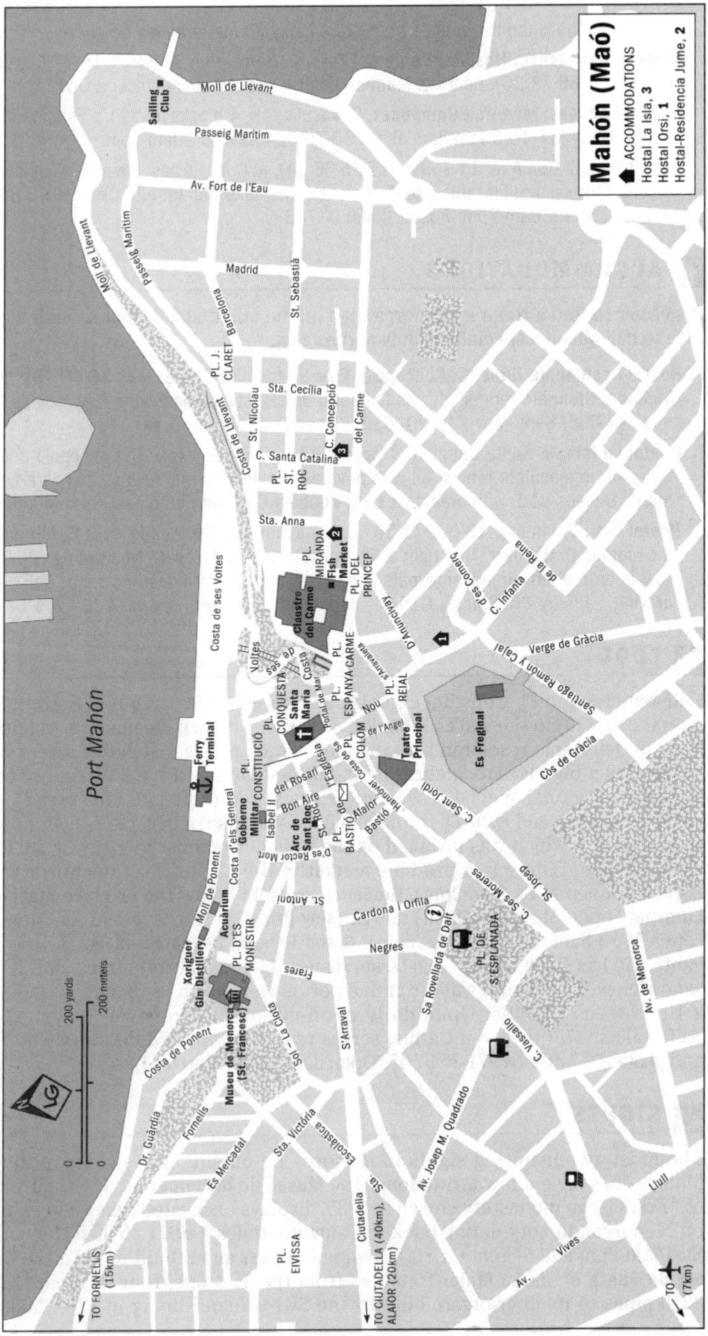
Mahón (Maó)
ACCOMMODATIONS
Hostal La Isla, 3
Hostal Orsi, 1
Hostal-Residencia Jume, 2
Port Mahón
200 yards
200 meters
0
Sailing Club
Moll de Llevant
Passeig Marítim
Av. Fort de l'Eau
Madrid
Barcelona
St. Sebastià
PL. J. CLARET
Sta. Cecília
St. Nicolau
C. Concepció
del Carme
Costa de Llevant
C. Santa Catalina
PL. ST. ROC
Sta. Anna
PL. MIRANDA
Fish Market
PL. DEL PRÍNCEP
Claustre del Carme
Costa de ses Voltes
Costa de ses Voltes
PL. ESPANYA
CARME
PL. CONQUESTA
Santa Maria
Portal de Mar
s'Arravaleta
D'AnunciVay
d'es Comerç
de la Reina
C. Infanta
Verge de Gràcia
Santiago Ramón y Cajal
PL. REIAL
Nou
de l'Àngel
Ferry Terminal
PL. CONSTITUCIÓ
PL. COLOM
Costa de sa l'Església
Teatre Principal
Es Freginal
Còs de Gràcia
Gobierno Militar
Isabel II
del Rosari
Bon Aire
Hannover
Arc de Sant Roc
St. Roc
PL. BASTIÓ
de Alaior
Bastió
C. Sant Jordi
Costa d'els General
D'es Rector Mort
Moll de Ponent
Acuarium
Xoriguer Gin Distillery
PL. D'ES MONESTIR
St. Antoni
Cardona i Orfila
Negres
Frares
Sa Rovellada de Dalt
PL. DE S'ESPLANADA
C. Ses Moreres
St. Josep
C. Vassallo
Av. de Menorca
Museu de Menorca (St. Francesc)
Costa de Ponent
Sol – La Clota
S'Arraval
Dr. Guàrdia
Fornells
Es Mercadal
Sta. Victòria
Escolàstica
Sta.
Av. Josep M. Quadrado
Ciutadella
PL. EIVISSA
TO FORNELLS (15km)
TO CIUTADELLA (40km), ALAIOR (20km)
Av. Vives
Llull
TO (7km)

Pharmacy: Check the list outside of any pharmacy for the *farmacia de guardia.*

Medical Assistance: Hospital Verge del Toro, C. Barcelona, 3 (☎971 15 77 00; emergency 971 36 77 26), near Pg. Marítim. English spoken. Ambulance: ☎061.

Internet Access: Menorca Compunet, C. Vasallo, 48, 4 blocks from Pl. s'Esplanada. €3 per hr. Open M-F 10:30am-2pm and 4:30-7:30pm, Sa 10:30am-1pm.

Post Office: C. Bon Aire, 11-13 (☎971 35 66 34), at C. Esglésias. From Pl. s'Esplanada, take C. Moreres until it turns into C. Hanover, then take the 1st left. Open M-F 8:30am-8:30pm, Sa 9:30am-2pm. **Postal Code:** 07703.

ACCOMMODATIONS

It's easier to find a room in Menorca than on the other islands, but it's still a good idea to call ahead, especially in July and August.

Hostal-Residencia Jume, C. Concepció, 6 (☎971 36 32 66; fax 971 36 48 78), off Pl. Miranda. Standard rooms, all with full bath. Breakfast included. June-Aug. singles €18; doubles €35. Sept.-May €17.20/€32. Closed Dec. 15-Jan. 5. ❷

Hostal La Isla, C. Santa Catalina, 4 (☎/fax 971 36 64 92). Take C. Concepció from Pl. Miranda. Immaculate rooms, all with private bath. Restaurant downstairs has a typical *menú*. Singles €15, with breakfast €18; doubles €30, with breakfast €34. MC/V. ❷

Hostal Orsi, C. Infanta, 19 (☎971 36 47 51). From Pl. s'Esplanada, take C. Moreres as it becomes C. Hanover. Turn right at Pl. Constitució and follow C. Nou through Pl. Reial; Orsi is on the left. American expats keep clean rooms. Breakfast included. Call before arriving. Laundry €6. Singles €15-21; doubles €26-35, with shower €30-42. MC/V. ❷

FOOD

Cafe-bars around Pl. Constitució, Reial, and s'Esplanada serve *platos combinados* (€2.70-5.10) to sidewalks of hungry customers, though the majority of tourists head to the scenic restaurants on the port, where prices match the atmosphere. Seafood is a big hit among chefs here, but restaurants serve a myriad of other favorites. Regional specialties include *sobrassada* (soft sausage spread), *crespells* (biscuits), and *rubiols* (turnovers filled with fish or vegetables). *Mahónesa* (mayonnaise), which was invented on the island, is popular in many of the more exotic dishes. There is a produce **market** in the cloister of the church in Pl. Espanya (open M-Sa 9am-2pm). **Groceries** are sold below the produce market at **Eurospar** (open M-Sa 8am-8pm) and at **Miny Prix,** C. J.A. Clavé and Av. Menorca (open M-Sa 8am-2pm and 5-8:30pm). **Grand General Delicatessen ❶,** Moll de Llevant, 319, has fresh, cheap vegetarian dishes, fish and meat entrees, and Italian sandwiches. The 20min. walk from the port is well worth it. (Sandwiches €1.50-2.10, entrees €3.90-6. Open daily noon-midnight.) In town, **La Oca ❷,** C. Sa'Ravaleta, 27, off Pl. del Carme, serves reasonably priced pizzas (€5.65-7.50) and pastas (€7-10). (☎971 35 37 45. Open daily 1-4pm and 6-11pm.)

SIGHTS

The most awe-inspiring sights in Menorca lie outside of its cities, although Mahón does have a few attractions. The **Museo de Menorca,** Av. Dr. Guàrdia, an old Franciscan monastery closed in 1835, displays excavated items and exhibits on Menorcan history dating back to Talayotic times. (☎971 35 09 55. Open Tu-Su 10am-2pm and 5-8pm. €1.80.) Founded in 1287 and rebuilt in 1772, the **Església de Santa María La Major** trembles from the 51 stops, four keyboards, and 3210 pipes of its über-organ, built by the Swiss Juan Kilburz in 1810. Mahón's

Festival de Música de Maó in July and August showcases the instrument. (Pl. Constitució. Festival concerts start at 9:30pm; see tourist office for upcoming events. Seat "donation" €3.) The **Arc de Sant Roc,** up C. Sant Roc from Pl. Constitució, the last fragment of the medieval wall built to defend the city from Catalan pirates, straddles the streets of Mahón. Get sauced off free liquor samples at the **Xoriguer Gin Distillery** on the port. Through glass windows at the back of the store, visitors watch their drinks bubble and froth in large copper vats. (☎971 36 21 97. Open M-F 8am-7pm, Sa 9am-1pm.) Mahón is close to numerous **archaeological sites,** including prehistoric caves, settlements, and monuments, but they are only accessible by car; see tourist office for info on a self-guided driving tour. Perhaps the most famous of these monuments is **Torre d'en Galmes,** off the road to Platges de Son Bou from Alaior. Atop a hill overlooking the island's interior, this Talayotic city dates from 1400 BC, and served as both a religious and commercial center for Menorca's original inhabitants. Though many of the monuments have yet to be fully excavated and seem to be nothing more than piles of disorganized rubble, of special interest is the eerie **Sala Hipostila,** a prehistoric house whose roof is suspended by columns which are narrower at their bases than at their crowns. (Open daily 10am-8pm. €1.80.)

NIGHTLIFE AND ENTERTAINMENT

Mahón is not known for its nightlife. Weekdays are quiet except in August. A string of *bares-musicales* line the **Costa d'els Generals,** near the water. The colorful, lively **Tse Tse Bar,** Moll de Ponent, 14, fills nightly with energetic 18-20 year-olds eager to take advantage of the ample dance floor. An upstairs *terraza* has an unbeatable view of the harbor. (Beer €2.40, mixed drinks €4.80. Open daily 10pm-4am, in winter Th-Sa 10pm-4am.) One of the more fashionable places on the strip is **Akelarre,** a spacious, trendy bar and dance club. Occasional free jazz concerts start earlier. A mixed straight-gay crowd fills the dance floors upstairs around midnight. (Open daily June-Oct. 8am-5am; Nov.-May 7:30pm-4am. Live music W-Th 11pm-2am. No cover.) Away from the port, **Discoteca Sí,** C. Virgen de Grácia, 16, turns on the strobelight only after midnight, while **Nou Bar,** C. Nou, 1, 2nd fl., serves drinks to a calm, older crowd. (Open daily noon-3pm and 7:30pm-3am.)

From May to September, merchants sell shoes, clothes, and souvenirs in **mercadillos** held daily in various town squares (Tu and Sa Mahón; F and Sa Ciutadella; Th Alaior; Su Mercadal; Tu and F Ferrerias; M and W Es Castell). On July 16, Mahón's **Verge del Carme** celebration brings a colorfully trimmed armada into the harbor.

NEAR MAHÓN

The coves and beaches near Mahón are best explored with a rental car and the *Let's Go to the Beach* brochure and map available at the tourist office. Though the highway from Mahón to Ciutadella is straight and well-maintained, the local roads are curvy, pot-holed, and oftentimes unpaved. Take caution if driving here at night.

THE NORTH SHORE

ARENAL D'EN CASTELL. Breathtaking views, calm water, and packed sands make this tiny cove a popular destination for daytrippers from Mahón and the vacationing families who populate the upscale resorts and condos that dot the slope above the beach. From Arenal, a tourist train, "Arenal Na Macaret Express," makes the short trip from the bus stop in Arenal across a narrow strip of land to **Macaret,** a tiny fishing village with an even tinier beach. *(Autocares Fornells buses leave from C. Vasallo in Mahón. 30min.; M-Sa 7 per day 9:30am-7pm, Su 11am and 7pm; €1.59.)*

ES GRAU. A large natural reserve, Albufera Es Grau entices visitors with lagoons, pine woods, and farmland, as well as diverse flora and fauna. Recreational activities include hiking to the coves across the bay. Some of the best swimming areas are across from the main lagoon and uphill from the town, along a series of bluffs that form secluded coves where only the sound of the clear water lapping at the rocks can be heard. **Illa d'en Colom,** a tiny island with more beaches, is a boat ride away. **Viajes Isla Colom,** sends four boats per day (☎971 35 98 67; 10:30am-5pm, last boat returns at 7pm) from the marina on the lagoon in Es Grau to the island. *(Autocares Fornells buses leave from C. Vasallo in Mahón. 20min., 4 per day 10am-6:15pm, €1.02.)*

CAP DE CAVALLERIA. Off the main road to Fornells, along a lonely, windswept highway that is more frequently used by goats than tourists, is the breathtaking landscape of Cap de Cavalleria. Bearing a striking resemblance to parts of the British Isles, the green hills dotted with medieval ruins that characterize this cape lead to a series of white limestone cliffs crowned by a beautiful lighthouse overlooking the deep blue water below. Though there are several beaches along the cape, it is best to come here for a relaxing picnic on the seaside bluffs or to watch the sun dip down into the sea from the lighthouse. To get to the lighthouse of Cap de Cavalleria, you must pass a gate which warns against trespassing. Disregard this sign (it is merely to deter the tourist hordes from ruining the pristine, rugged beauty of the place), and remember to close the gate behind you as you enter or exit.

THE SOUTH SHORE

PLATGES DE SON BOU. The longest beach on the island, Son Bou offers 4km of sand on the southern shore, covered with throngs of sunburned tourists. As the most popular of Menorca's beaches, it's also the most visitor-friendly, with frequent bus service to and from Mahón and Ciutadella, endless beach chairs and umbrellas for rent, cafes, and even *discotecas* only two blocks from the sand. Be aware, though, that part of the beach is also for nudists, and the farther away from the commercial center you walk, the more naked it gets. *(Transportes Menorca buses leave from C. Josep Quadrado, on the corner of Pl. s'Esplanada in Mahón to the beaches. 30min., 7 per day 8:45am-7pm, €1.65.)* For those who choose to stay late, **Disco/Bar Copacabana,** in the Nuevo Centro Comercial, on the left when heading away from the water, is the best place to rock your evening, all the while with a great view of the water. *(No cover. Open May-Oct. daily 11pm-3:30am.)* If you're just in the mood for a relaxing frozen drink, head across the street to the big rattan chairs and couches of **Bou Hai Hawaiian Bar,** serving margaritas and daiquiris for €5.50. *(Open daily 4pm-3am.)* If you do choose to stay late, make sure you have a rental car or a place to stay—there is no public transportation back to Mahón until the morning.

CALEN PORTER. Expansive and touristy, Calen Porter greets thousands of visitors each summer with its whitewashed houses, orange stucco roofs, and red sidewalks. Its small but well-used beach lies at the bottom of a steep, bouldered hillside, but pedestrian access is easy via the main road and a marked staircase. *(TMSA buses run to and from C. Josep Quadrado, on the corner of Pl. s'Esplanada in Mahón. 7 per day 9:30am-7:30pm, €1.02.)* A 10min. walk away, the **Covas d'en Xoroi** caves dominate cliffs high above the sea. Inhabited by a network of bars by day, and a popular disco (which attracts a largely young British crowd) by night. (☎971 37 72 36. Bars open Apr.-Oct. daily 10:30am-9pm, disco open nightly at 11pm. Foam parties every Th. Cover for bars €3.50, includes 1 drink. Cover for disco €15.)

PUNTA PRIMA. While this beach may not be as secluded or expansive as some of the island's others, it draws a crowd with its proximity to Mahón and local atmosphere. A lighthouse on a strip of land across from the beach overlooks the coastline. *(TMSA buses run to and from Pl. s'Esplanada in Mahón. 8 per day 9:30am-7:30pm. €1.02.)*

ES CANUTELLS. Situated off the road from Mahón to Cala en Porter (15min. drive from Mahón), Es Canutells is a pleasant and secluded cove with calm, turquoise waters good for swimming and snorkeling. A couple bars and restaurants lie on the road above the cove. Es Canutells cannot be reached by public transportation.

CALASCOVES. Past Es Canutells and off the road from Mahón to Cala en Porter (20min. drive from Mahón) is this pristine serpentine cove with rocky cliffs and a small beach perfect for a refreshing swim. Equally refreshing is this area's lack of tourists. Since Calascoves cannot be reached by public transportation, leave your car at the top of the hill, and continue down the dirt path for about 20min. until you reach the rocky part of the cove. The beach is over the cliffs to your right.

CALA MITJANA AND CALA MITJANETA. On the main highway from Mahón to Ciutadella, head toward Ferreries, and then take the road to Santa Galdana. Directly on your left before reaching the roundabout above the town is the dirt road that leads to **Cala Mitjana** (a 30min. drive from Mahón). Park your car in the small dirt lot and continue on foot to the small beach overlooking a dramatic cove bordered by white limestone cliffs that plunge into the turquoise sea. Though this beach is not totally secluded, if you climb the staircase on your right upon entering the cove and head down the dirt path for about 5min., you get to **Cala Mitjaneta,** a smaller cove which affords even more dramatic views of the limestone cliffs and the wide expanse of the Mediterranean beyond the inlet. While some wade into the water here, others prove their bravery (or recklessness) by diving from the rocks.

CIUTADELLA (CIUDADELA)

Ciutadella's (pop. 15,000) narrow, cobblestoned paths weave between neighborhoods nearly undisturbed by tourists, while only blocks away, restaurants, shops, and postcard vendors compete for attention in the crowded plazas. There is a seductive charm to the city's ancient streets, broad *plaças*, and winding port.

TRANSPORTATION

Buses: Transportes Menorca buses leave from C. Barcelona, 8 (☎971 38 03 93), and go to Mahón (6 per day, €3.51). **Autocares Torres** (☎971 38 64 61), offers daily service from the front of the ticket booth in Pl. s'Esplanada to surrounding beaches, all of which are 15-30min. away. To: **Cala Blanca** (15 per day 9am-11pm, €0.96); **Cala Blanes, Los Delfines,** and **Cala Forcat** (23 per day 7am-11:35pm, €0.96); **Cala Bosch** and **Son Xoriguer** (24 per day 7am-midnight, €0.96); **Sa Caleta** and **Santandria** (18 per day 7am-11pm, €0.96).

Ferries: Iscomar de Ferrys (☎902 11 91 28) runs between Ciutadella and **Alcúdia, Mallorca** (2½hr.; M-F 11:30am, 8pm, Sa-Su 8pm; €28.80). **Cape Balear** (☎902 10 04 44) links Ciutadella to **Cala Ratjada, Menorca** (55min.; May-Oct. 9am, 9pm; €36).

Taxis: (☎971 38 28 96 or 971 38 11 97). Pl. s'Esplanada is a prime hailing spot.

Bike and Scooter Rental: Bicicletas Tolo, C. Sant Isidor, 28-34 (☎/fax 971 38 15 76), across the street from Hostal Oasis. Bike rental €4.21-5.41 per day, €20-26 per week. Scooters €35-66 for 2 days, €96-190 per week. Open M-F 9am-1pm and 4-7:30pm, Sa 9am-1pm and 6:30-7:30pm, Su 9:30-11am.

Car Rental: Europcar, Av. Jaume I, 59 (☎971 38 29 98). Min. age 21. Rental from €35 per day and from €210 per week. Open daily 9am-8pm.

ORIENTATION AND PRACTICAL INFORMATION

To get from the **bus station** to **Plaça de la Catedral** and the tourist office, head left half a block, take a left on Camí de Maó, go straight through Pl. d'Alfons III, and continue along C. de Maó as it turns into Quadrado (Ses Voltes) after crossing Pl. Nova. To get from Pl. Catedral to **Plaça de s'Esplanada** (also called Pl. Pins), exit the plaza on C. Major d'es Born with the cathedral behind you and to the right, cross P. Born on its right side, and bear diagonally across to the left. The **port,** and its accompanying street, C. Marina, lie below the rest of the city and can be reached via a stone stairway just off the corner of Pl. Born.

Tourist Office: Pl. Catedral, 3 (☎971 38 26 93). English, German, French, and Italian spoken. Open M-F 9am-1:30pm and 5-7pm, Sa 9am-1pm.

Banks: BBVA, Pl. Born, 14 (☎971 48 40 04). Open M-F 8:30am-2pm.

Emergency: ☎112. **Police:** Pl. Born (☎971 38 07 87).

Medical Emergencies: Clínica Menorca, Canonge Moll (☎971 48 05 05). Open 24hr.

Internet Access: Accesso Directo, Pl. s'Esplanada, 37 (☎971 38 42 15). €1.20 per 30min. Open M-Sa 9am-midnight, Su 3pm-midnight.

Post Office: Pl. Born (☎971 38 00 81). Open May-Oct. M-F 8:30am-8:30pm, Sa 9:30am-1pm; Nov.-Apr. M-F 8:30am-2:30pm, Sa 9:30am-1pm. **Postal Code:** 07760.

BALEARIC ISLANDS

ACCOMMODATIONS

Hostels are packed and pricey during peak season (June 15-early Sept.)—you can't usually find a double room for under €30. Always call ahead in the summer.

Casa de Huespedes Sa Posada, C. Ibiza, 14 (☎971 38 58 96 or 971 38 57 78), off Pl. s'Esplanada. Easy to miss, so look carefully for the small CH sign above the door. If you're lucky enough to score 1 of the 7 double rooms at this *hostal*, you'll be rewarded with some of the cheapest and comfiest accommodations in Ciutadella. Smallish rooms all have private baths. Aug. doubles €28. July and Sept. €24. Oct.-May €22. ❷

Hostal Residencia Oasis, C. Sant Isidre, 33 (☎971 38 21 97). From Pl. s'Esplanada, take Av. Capitá Negrete to Pl. d'Artrutx and C. Sant Isidre. A centrally located floral paradise. Gorgeous patio and dining area. Breakfast included. Doubles with bath €40. ❷

Hotel Geminis, C. Josepa Rossinyol, 4 (☎971 38 58 96; fax 971 38 36 83). Take C. Sud off Av. Capital Negrete from Pl. s'Esplanada; turn left onto C. Josepa Rossinyol. Rooms with phones, baths, fans, and TVs. Outdoor terrace has small pool. Mid-June to Sept. singles €33; doubles €55. Oct.-Mar. €21/€35. Apr. to mid-June €25/€43. ❸

FOOD

Most of Ciutadella's food options are fairly touristy. Nicer restaurants surround the port area, while more generic spots near Pl. s'Esplanada and along C. Quadrado offer cheaper fare. Shop at the **market** on Pl. Llibertat or **Supermercado Diskont,** C. Purísima, 6. (☎971 38 32 68. Open M-Sa 8:30am-2pm and 4-9pm.)

La Guitarra, C. Dolores, 1 (☎971 38 13 55). Take C. Major d'es Born off Pl. Born, then turn right onto Carres del Roser, which leads to C. Dolores. For traditional island cuisine, descend to this stone cave-turned-restaurant and sample the mysterious *sopa mallorquina*, a traditional meat and veggie soup (€4.95). *Menú* €9. Entrees €6.60-18. Open June-Sept. M-Sa 12:30-3:30pm and 7-11:30pm. MC/V. ❸

HOLD YOUR HORSES! Every last Thursday in June, Ciutadella celebrates *La Fiesta de San Juan,* a wild festival that rivals the infamous *San Fermines.* The party begins with the arrival of the *fabioler* (herald of the ceremony) on a white horse. Playing a drum and flute, he gallops through town for four hours with crowds of drunken Menorcans following close behind. At 6pm, village men ride 250 wild horses through town on their hind legs. Successfully bipedal horses are rewarded with cheers of *"Olé!"* and the rest charge into the crowd, often knocking over bystanders. In 1999, one off-balance horse crashed down on the mayor of Menorca, ending his term for good. *Note bene* for future office-holders: some P.R. opportunities just aren't worth it.

Restaurant Unger Madison, C. San Joan, 8 (☎971 38 15 63), around the corner from La Guitarra. Not-so-traditional fare served in a traditional setting. Smooth jazz playing in the background. Entrees €8.50-11. Open M-F 7pm-midnight and Sa 8pm-2am. ❷

Pizzeria Restaurant Raco d'es Palau, C. del Palau, 3 (☎971 38 54 02), in an alley off C. Major del Born. Pleasant indoor and outdoor seating complements great pizza (€5.15-6.35) and seafood dishes (€8-12). Open daily 4pm-midnight. ❷

SIGHTS AND ENTERTAINMENT

An interesting complement to Menorca's beaches are the remnants at Menorca's various archaeological sites. Dating from the Bronze Age, the **Naveta des Tudons,** one of the oldest structures in Europe, sits 4km from the city. These ruins of community tombs are the island's best preserved. **Torretrencada** and **Torrellafuda** were rounded towers that overlooked the countryside. Both protect Stonehenge-like *taulas,* formations that have stood for over 3000 years. Buses don't come near these sights, so consider **hiking** (about 5km) along C. Cami Vell de Maó. The descriptive *Archaeological Guide to Menorca* is available at the tourist office.

The Ciutadella community is one of early-to-bedders. **Asere,** C. de Curniola, 23, one block off Pl. Nova, spices things up a bit with a Cuban theme and frozen drinks (open F-Sa 8pm-midnight). From the first week in July to the beginning of September, Ciutadella hosts the **Festival de Música d'Estiu,** featuring some of the world's top classical musicians. Tickets (€9.60-21) are sold at **Foto Born,** C. Seminari, 14 (☎971 38 17 54), and at the box office (open daily 9:30am-1:30pm and 5-8pm). Concerts take place in the cloisters of the seminary. On the 22nd of June, even veteran partiers of Palma and Ibiza join locals as they burn gallons of midnight oil during the **La Fiesta de San Juan,** Menorca's biggest *fiesta.* A week before the festivities, which include jousting and equestrian displays, a man clad in a sheepskin carries a decorated lamb on his shoulders through the city.

BEACHES

The more popular Menorcan beaches, those accessible by bus from Mahón and Ciutadella, are located in somewhat touristy areas and are overrun by resort hotels, bars, restaurants, and postcard shops. Many Menorcan beaches are located in small coves, thus the more accessible ones can get fairly packed during the day. Never fear: because Menorca is home to over 80 beaches, with a car, moped, or a little legwork, endless stretches of less-crowded sands are easily accessible. The northern beaches are rocky but less crowded. Finer sands, however, are hidden under hundreds of tourists on the southern coast. Most of the beaches listed are accessible by bus; for a complete list of beaches you can access by car, request the *Let's Go to the Beach* pamphlet (no relation) at the tourist office.

NEAR CIUTADELLA

NORTH SHORE. The stretch east of Cala Morell is home to the most outstanding beaches on the island. **Platges d'Algaiarens** may be the superstar of the series, including Cala en Carabó, Penyal de l'Anticrist, Sa Falconera, and Cala del Pilar Ets Alocs. *(Cars can go only up to a few km from these beaches; from there you must walk.)*

CALA BOSCH. Five-star resorts provide the backdrop for this popular cove situated between jagged cliffs. Because of its proximity to Ciutadella, this is one of the more crowded beaches, but with fruit sellers and restaurants, it's worth visiting. *(Accessible by Torres bus from Ciutadella. 24 per day 7am-midnight, €0.96.)*

FORNELLS. A small fishing village known for its lobster farms, Fornells has only recently begun to attract tourists. Windsurfers zip around Fornells's long, shallow port, while beach gurus make excursions to **Cala Tirant** and **Binimella,** both only a few kilometers west. Fornells also serves as a calm base from which to explore coves and jagged cliffs by car or bike, as bus service is very limited. *(Autobuses Roca Triay buses run to Fornells from C. Vassallo in Mahón. 30min., 5 per day, €1.35.)*

SON XORIGUER. Just own the road from Cala Bosch, this beach isn't quite as hectic as its neighbor but is equally beautiful. *(Accessible by a Torres bus from Ciutadella. 24 per day 7am-midnight, €0.96.)*

IBIZA

Nowhere on Earth does style rule over substance (or does substance rule over style) more than on Ibiza (pop. 84,000). Once a 1960s hippie enclave, Ibiza has forgotten her roots in favor of a new age of decadence. Disco fiends, high-fashion gurus, movie stars, and party-hungry backpackers arrive in droves to debauch in the island's outrageous, sex- and substance-driven culture. However, not every night on the island has to be filled with such hedonism and glam; much of Ibiza's wild see-and-be-seen disco culture is just at a few megaclubs. It's not uncommon to see people arriving at discos in jeans or shorts, or to spend a night just chilling at a waterfront bar. A thriving gay community lends credence to Ibiza's image as a center of tolerance, but the island's high price tags preclude true diversity.

Surprisingly, there is more to Ibiza than spectacular nightlife; its beaches and mountains are some of the most spectacular in all the Balearics. The island's rich history has left its mark in the form of several ancient castles—the most prominent in Eivissa (Ibiza City). Since the Carthaginians retreated to Ibiza from the mainland in 656 BC, the island's list of conquerors reads like a "Who's Who of Ancient Western Civilization." Perhaps the most famous was the 1235 invasion by the Catalans, who brought Christianity and built the walls that still fortify Eivissa.

EIVISSA (IBIZA CITY)

Eivissa (pop. 35,000) is the world's biggest 24hr. party. The town itself is like Dr. Jekyll and Mr. Hyde. During the day, families meander and sightsee through the walled Dalt Vila, and the city streets remain tranquil while the majority of visitors sleep off hangovers, tanning at nearby beaches. In natural light, Eivissa could easily be mistaken for any other seaside village in Spain. At night, however, there's no mistaking this town for any other. Flashy bars appear seemingly out of nowhere, filling street after street with neon lights, blasting music, and fast-talking club promoters; grab a front-row seat at the outdoor tables to enjoy the prime people-watching action. Come 3am, the scene migrates to the clubs, where parties last until dawn—and often well into the next day...then it all begins again.

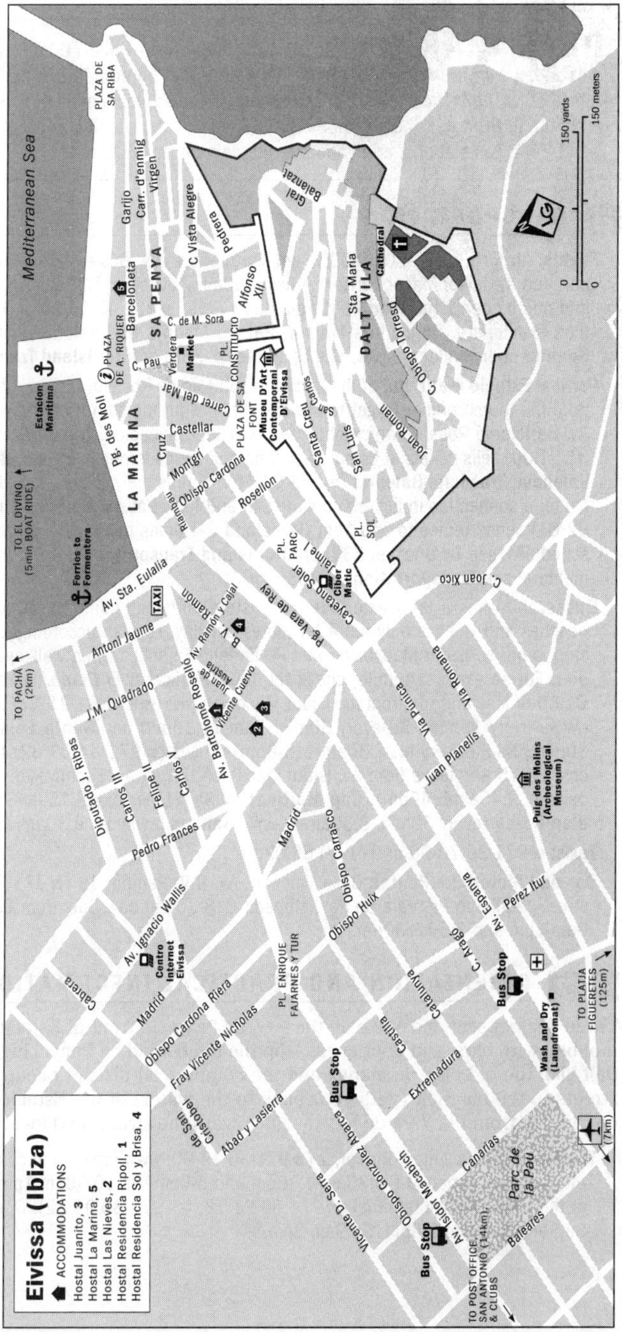
Eivissa (Ibiza)
ACCOMMODATIONS
Hostal Juanito, 3
Hostal La Marina, 5
Hostal Las Nieves, 2
Hostal Residencia Ripoll, 1
Hostal Residencia Sol y Brisa, 4
Mediterranean Sea
Estacion Maritima
Ferries to Formentera
TO EL DIVINO (5min BOAT RIDE)
TO PACHÁ (2km)
PLAZA DE SA RIBA
PLAZA DE A. RIQUER
LA MARINA
SA PENYA
DALT VILA
Market
Museu D'Art Contemporani D'Eivissa
Cathedral
Ciber Matic
Centro Internet Eivissa
Puig des Molins (Archeological Museum)
Bus Stop
Wash and Dry (Laundromat)
Parc de la Pau
TO PLATJA FIGUERETES (125m)
TO POST OFFICE, SAN ANTONIO (14km), & CLUBS
(7km)
PL. CONSTITUCIO
PLAZA DE SA FONT
PL. PARC
PL. SOL
PL. ENRIQUE FAJARNES Y TUR
Pg. des Moll
Av. Sta. Eulalia
Antoni Jaume
J.M. Quadrado
Diputado J. Ribas
Carlos III
Felipe II
Carlos V
Pedro Frances
Av. Bartolomé Rosello
Av. Ignacio Wallis
Cabrera
Madrid
Obispo Cardona Riera
Fray Vicente Nicholas
Abad y Lasierra
Cristobal de San
Vicente D. Serra
Obispo Gonzalez Abarca
Obispo Macabich
Av. Isidor Macabich
Canarias
Baleares
Extremadura
Castilla
Cataluña
C. Aragó
Av. España
Av. Perez Itur
Obispo Huix
Obispo Carrasco
Juan Planells
Via Punica
Via Romana
C. Joan Xico
Cayetano Soler
Pg. Vara de Rey
B. V. Ramon
Av. Ramon y Cajal
Juan de Austria
Vicente Cuervo
Rosellon
Obispo Cardona
Rambleu
Montgri
Cruz
Castellar
Carrer del Mar
C. Pau
Verdera
C. de M. Sora
Barceloneta
C Vista Alegre
Pedrera
Alfonso XII
Garijo
Carr. d'enmig
Virgen
Gral Balanzat
Sta. Maria
Santa Creu
San Carlos
San Luis
Joan Roman
C. Obispo Torres
150 yards
150 meters

DEAR DIARIO The local paper *Diario de Ibiza* (€0.75; www.diario-deibiza.es) has an *Agenda* page that lists essential information, including the bus schedule for the entire island, the ferry schedule, the schedule of all domestic flights to and from Ibiza, water and weather forecasts, info on the island's 24hr. pharmacies, a list of 24hr. gas stations, and important phone numbers.

TRANSPORTATION

Flights: Airport (☎971 80 90 00), 7km south of the city. Bus #10 runs between the airport and Av. Isidor Macabich, 20, in town (30min., every hr. 7:30am-10:30pm, €0.75). Info booth open 24hr. **Iberia,** Pg. Vara de Rey, 15 (☎902 40 05 00 or 971 30 03 00), flies to Alicante, Barcelona, Madrid, Palma, Madrid, and Valencia. **Air Europa** and **Spanair** offer similar options. See **By Plane,** p. 337, or **Inter-Island Transport,** p. 337.

Ferries: Estació Marítima, at the end of Av. Bartolomé Roselló. Directly across the street from the tourist office. To get to the city center and bus stop from the waterfront, take Av. Bartolomé Roselló, which becomes Av. Isidor Macabich. **Trasmediterránea** (☎971 31 51 00) sells tickets at Estació Marítima and sends ferries to **Palma, Barcelona,** and **Valencia. Trasmapi-Balearia** (☎971 31 40 05) runs daily to and from **Dénia,** near Alicante; a connection in Eivissa continues to and from **Palma. Umafisa Lines** (☎971 21 02 01) sends ferries to and from **Barcelona** 3-4 times per week. For rates, fares, and schedules, see **By Boat,** p. 337, or **Inter-Island Transport,** p.337. For transport to Formentera, see **Transportation,** p. 363.

Buses: Ibiza has a fairly extensive bus system, although some buses to more remote beaches and villages only run a few times per day, so plan accordingly. The main bus stop is on Av. Isidor Macabich, past Pl. Enrique Fajarines when walking away from the port. For an exact schedule, check the tourist office or *El Diario.* Intercity buses are €1.80 or less and run from Av. Isidor Macabich, 42 (☎971 31 21 17) to **San Antonio** (M-Sa every 15min., Su every 30min. 7am-11:30pm) and **Santa Eulária** (M-F every 30min., Sa-Su every hr. 7:30am-11:30pm). Buses (☎971 34 03 82) to the beaches cost €0.75 and leave from Av. Isidor Macabich, 20, or Av. Espanya to: **Cala Tarida** (5 per day 9:45am-5:45pm); **Cap Martinet** (M-Sa 11 per day 8:15am-8:15pm); **Platja d'en Bossa** (every 30min. 8:30am-11pm); **Salinas** (every hr. 9:30am-7:30pm).

Taxis: ☎971 30 70 00 or 971 30 66 02.

Car and Motorbike Rental: Casa Valentín, Av. B.V. Ramón, 19 (☎971 31 08 22), the street parallel to Pg. Vara de Rey. Mopeds €18-30 per day. Cars from €39. Open daily 9am-1pm and 3:30-8:30pm.

ORIENTATION AND PRACTICAL INFORMATION

Three distinct sections make up the city. **Sa Penya,** in front of Estació Marítima, is mobbed with bars, and boutiques. Atop the hill behind Sa Penya, high walls circle **Dalt Vila,** the old city. **Sa Marina** and the commercial district occupy the gridded streets to the far right (with your back to the water) of the Estació. **Av. Espanya,** continuing from Po. Vara de Rey, heads toward the airport and local beaches.

Tourist Office: C. Antoni Riquer, 2 (☎971 30 19 00; www.ibizaonline.com), across from the ferry port. Open M-F 9:30am-1:30pm and 5-8pm, Sa 10:30am-1pm. Also a **booth** at the airport arrival terminal (☎971 80 91 18; fax 971 80 91 32). Open May-Oct. M-Sa 9am-2pm and 3-8pm, Su 9am-2pm.

BALEARIC ISLANDS

Currency Exchange: You can change money at exchanges all over town, but stick to banks and ATMs, which offer better rates. **La Caixa,** Av. Isidor Macabich, has good exchange rates for cash and traveler's checks.

Laundromat: Wash and Dry, Av. España, 53 (☎971 39 48 22). Wash and dry €4.20 each. **Internet** access €5.40 per hr. Open M-F 10am-3pm and 5-10pm, Sa 10am-5pm.

Emergency: ☎112. **Police:** C. Vicent Serra (☎971 31 58 61).

Medical Assistance: Hospital, Barrio Can Misses (☎971 39 70 00), to the west of town. **Ambulance:** ☎971 39 32 32. **Hospital Nuestra Senora** (☎971 39 70 21).

Internet Access: Centro Internet Eivissa, Av. Ignacio Wallis, 39 (☎971 31 81 61). €3 per hr. Open M-Sa 10am-midnight, Su 5pm-midnight. **Ciber Matic,** C. Cayetano Soler, 3 (☎971 30 33 82). €1.80 per 30min., €3 per hr. Open M-Sa 10am-11pm.

Post Office: C. Isidor Macabich (☎971 31 43 23). With your back to the port, follow Av. Isidor Macabich to its end. **Lista de Correos.** Open M-F 8:30am-8:30pm, Sa 9:30am-2pm. **Postal Code:** 07800.

ACCOMMODATIONS

Decent, cheap *hostales* in town are rare, especially in the summer—but then again, who actually *sleeps* here anyway? Call several weeks in advance for summer stays, when prices climb and hostels fill fast. The letters "CH" *(casa de huespedes)* mark many doorways, but the owner can often only be reached by the phone number on the door. Eivissa has a relatively safe and up-all-night lifestyle, and owners offer keys for 24hr. entry. All prices listed below are for high-season and can drop by as much as €12 in the off-season. The tourist office offers an extensive list of all the lodging options available in the city.

Hostal Residencia Sol y Brisa, Av. B. V. Ramón, 15 (☎971 31 08 18; fax 971 30 30 32), parallel to Pg. Vara de Rey. Upstairs from Pizzeria da Franco. Clean and centrally located; rooms are hot in summer. Social atmosphere. Singles €21; doubles €36. ❷

Hostal La Marina, Puerto de Ibiza, C. Barcelona, 7 (☎971 31 01 72; fax 971 31 48 94), across from Estació Marítima and in the middle of the raucous bar scene. 4 buildings offer lodging ranging from stark to plush. The best (and most expensive) have TV, A/C, private bath, carpeting, and balcony. Singles €27-48; doubles €42-96. ❸

Hostal Residencia Ripoll, C. Vicente Cuervo, 14 (☎971 31 42 75). Fastidiously clean hallways and bathrooms and unusually large, fan-cooled rooms are among the best in town, though the singles are a bit pricey. July-Sept. singles €27; doubles €39; 3-person apartments with TV, patio, and kitchen €72. ❸

Hostal Juanito and Hostal Las Nieves, C. Juan de Austria, 17-18 (☎971 19 03 19). Run by the same owner, both hostels offer cheap housing in a central area. Rooms are basic and bare-walled, but more than adequate for sleeping off a hangover. Singles €21; doubles €42, with bath €45. ❷

Camping: Es Cana (☎971 33 21 17; fax 971 33 99 71). €3 per person, €1.80 per site, €2.70 per tent. Bungalow €14. Reserve via fax. **Cala Nova** (☎971 33 17 74). €3 per person, €2.85 per tent. Both sites close to Sta. Eulària del Río. ❶

FOOD

Inexpensive cuisine is hard to find; it's not uncommon to see budget travelers stocking up at grocery stores or chowing down at fast food joints to save their euros for the discos. Ibizan dishes include *sofrit pagès*, a deep-fried lamb and chicken dish; *flao*, a lush lemon- and mint-tinged cheesecake; and *graxonera*, cinnamon-dusted pudding made from eggs and bits of *ensaimada* (candied bread).

The **market,** at C. Extremadura and C. Canarias, sells meat, fruits, and vegetables (open M-Sa 7am-1pm). For **groceries,** try **Hiper Centro,** C. Ignacio Wallis, near C. Juan de Austria. (☎971 19 20 41. Open M-Sa 9am-2pm and 5-9pm.)

Mama Pat's Curry y Más, C. Espanya, 43. Not only does Mama Pat's have some of the cheapest food around, it also has some of the most creative. Authentic Caribbean cuisine or awesome chicken, veggie, and lamb curry entrees (€6-9). Vegetarian options. *Menú* €6. Open M-Sa 8am-3am, closed Su. ❷

Restaurante La Oliva, C. Santa Cruz, 2 (☎971 30 57 52), on a crowded street in the lower part of the Dalt Vila. Pricey but delicious Italian fare. Get a candlelit outdoor table and people-watch. Pasta €5-7, meat and fish entrees €9-18. Open daily 8pm-1am. ❸

Casa Alfredo, Pg. Vara de Rey, 16. Fish, meat, and heavenly desserts fill the *menú* (€6-9) that locals call the best in town. Open M-Sa noon-3pm, 8:30pm-midnight. ❷

BALEARIC ISLANDS

SIGHTS

Wrapped in 16th-century walls, the **Dalt Vila** (High Town) rises above the town. Its twisting streets lead to the 14th-century **cathedral,** built in several phases and styles. (Open daily 10:30am-1pm.) Next to the cathedral is the **Museu Arqueològic D'Eivissa,** home to a variety of regional artifacts. (Open Tu-Sa 10am-1pm and 5-10pm, Su 10am-2pm. €1.80, students €0.90.) Amid stone walls, the small **Museu D'Art Contemporani D'Eivissa** displays a range of art exhibitions. (C. Sa Carrosa, on the left when entering through Dalt Vila's main entrance. ☎971 30 27 23. Open M-F 10am-1:30pm and 5-8pm, Sa 10am-1:30pm. €1.20, students free.) The archaeological museum, **Puig des Molins,** Vía Romana, displays Punic, Roman, and Iberian artifacts. (Open M-Sa 10am-2pm and 5-8pm, Su 10am-2pm. €1.20.)

BEACHES

The power of the rising sun draws thousands of topless solar zombies to nearby tanning grounds. **Platja Figueretes,** a thin stretch of sand in the shadow large hotels, is the best foot-accessible beach from Eivissa. To get there, walk down Av. Espanya for about 10min., and take a left on C. Juan Ramón Jiménez. Farther down, **Platja d'en Bossa** is the liveliest of Ibiza's beaches, home to numerous beach bars, as well as throngs of sun-seeking tourists. **Platja des Duros** is tucked across the bay from Sa Penya and Sa Marina, just before the lighthouse. At **Platja de Talamanca,** the water—more an enclosed bay than open sea—is accessible on foot by following the road to the new port and continuing on to the beach (20min.). **Platja de ses Salinas** is one of Ibiza's most popular and famous beaches, although others are actually more scenic. Bask among the beautiful people, and groove to chilled- out house pulsating from **Sa Trincha** bar at the end of the beach. Neighboring **Platja des Cavallet** is decidedly clothing-optional and attracts a beautiful, largely gay crowd. To get to both, take the bus from Eivissa to Salinas; for Es Cavallet, get off at the stop before Salinas (look for the T-intersection to the left or just ask the bus driver) and walk to the beach (10min.) or just walk from Salinas (20min.).

More private coastal stretches lie in the northern part of the island and are accessible by car or scooter. Among these, the German enclave at **Cala de Sant Vicent** (past Santa Eularia on the road to St. Carles de Peralta) offers white sands and breathtaking views that are far from secluded but peaceful nonetheless. The small coves in the rocky northernmost point of the island (between Portinatx and St. Agnes de Corona) are worth visiting if you seek serenity or the company of modern-day flower children. **Cala Xarraca** is a beautiful EU *bandera azul* cove popular with families, who fight for spots on its small beach. The views from **Cap Rubio** are among the most dramatic on the island. On the road from Sant Miquel to

Sant Mateu, take the left fork up a semi-paved road; the road rises and then drops suddenly to a rocky path, which leads to impressive limestone cliffs. Hike down to any of the coves at the bottom of the paths next to the abandoned mine shafts, and you'll be rewarded with your own private swimming hole.

NIGHTLIFE

The crowds return from the beaches by nightfall, when even the stores dazzle with throbbing techno and flashing lights. Herds of men and women representing each club parade through the streets, advertising their disco and trying to outdo others. Meanwhile, seaport bars crawl with aggressive promoters. **Bars** in Eivissa are crowded between midnight and 3am and are everyone's first stop before hitting the discos. The scene centers around **C. Barcelona** and spins outward into the side-streets. **C. Virgen** is the center of gay nightlife and outrageous fashion. Cocktails cost as much as €10 and beer rings in at around €6, so if you plan on drinking a lot, either pre-game on your own or head to the cheaper bar scene in San Antonio.

The island's **discos** (virtually all have a mixed gay/straight crowd) are world-famous—veterans claim that you will never experience anything half as wild or fun. The best sources of information are disco-goers and the zillions of posters that plaster the stores and restaurants of Sa Marina and Sa Penya. There is something different each day of the week, and each club is known for a particular theme party—be sure to hit up a club on a popular night, or you'll end up shelling out a lot of money for a not-so-happening party. For listings, check out *Ministry in Ibiza* or *DJ* magazines, free at many hostels, bars, and restaurants. Drinks at Ibiza's clubs cost about €10 and covers start at €30. If you know where you're going ahead of time, buy your disco tickets from a promoter at or in front of the bars in town; you'll pay €6-18 less than what you would pay at the door, and it's completely legit—some tickets even include transportation and admission afterwards to Space, the beachfront after-hours club, although these deals are more commonly found in San Antonio. Generally, disco-goers bar-hop in Eivissa or San Antonio and jet off to clubs via bus or taxi around 3am. The **Discobus** runs to all the major hotspots (leaves Eivissa from Av. Isidoro Macabich every hr. 12:30am-6:30am, schedule for other stops available at tourist office and hotels, €1.50).

Privilege, on the Discobus to San Antonio or a €9 taxi. The world's largest club, according to the Guinness Book. This enormous complex packs in up to 10,000 with bars in the double-digits and a pool. *The* place to be on M for its infamous "Manumission" parties. Cover (€30-48) includes 1 drink. Open June-Sept. daily midnight-7am. V.

Pachá, 15min. walk from the port, 2min. in a cab. The most famous club chain in Spain, and the most elegant of Ibiza's discos. "Ministry of Sound" on F brings the biggest crowd. Pirati "Made in Italy" on Th is, not surprisingly, very popular with Italian clubbers. The only club in Ibiza open year-round. Cover €30-42. Open daily midnight-7:30am.

Amnesia, on the road to San Antonio; take the Discobus. Converted warehouse with psychedelic lights and movie screens has 2 gigantic rooms; a largely gay crowd congregates in the one to the left. Foam parties Su and W. Best known for "Cream" on Th, when London DJs play hard house or trance. Cover €30-42. Open daily midnight-7am.

Space, Platja d'en Bossa. Starts hopping around 8am, peaks mid-afternoon, and doesn't wind down until past 5pm. The metallic get-up and techno music is almost as hardcore as the dancers. An outdoor dance terrace has a more low-key atmosphere. Known for its Su morning show, Sa-Tu mornings are popular too. Hosts the official after-parties for "Ministry of Sound" at Pachá, "Manumission" at Privilege, and "La Troya Asesina" (the infamous drag-queen party) at Amnesia. Cover €30 and up.

BALEARIC ISLANDS

Eden, C. Salvador Espíritu, across from the beach in San Antonio. Gaining in popularity, Eden pulls out all the stops for "Judgement Sunday," when DJ Judge Jules attracts huge crowds. Popular among British visitors. Retro nights on Tu feature house from the past decade. Cover €30-42. Open daily midnight-7am.

El Divino, Puerto Ibiza Nueva. Small, energetic club on the water—worth coming just for the view, although the exotic dancers, thumping house, and lively crowd aren't too shabby either. El Divino fliers serve as free passes for the disco shuttle boat—otherwise, it costs €0.90 each way. Cover €30. Open mid-June to mid-Sept. daily midnight-6am.

Es Paradis Terrenal, C. Salvador Espiru, 20, in San Antonio, portside. Looks are deceiving: a classy environment hosts some not-so-classy behavior at water parties on Tu and Sa. Cover €36. Open midnight-6am.

SAN ANTONIO DE PORTOMANY (SANT ANTONI)

Every summer, masses of young Brits migrate to San Antonio. The rowdy nightlife and down-to-earth atmosphere combined with its proximity to some of the island's best beaches have turned the town into a 20-something enclave. With two clubs, plenty of bars, and cheaper food and accommodations than in Eivissa, San Antonio is the perfect budget alternative to its sister city's high prices and lifestyle.

TRANSPORTATION AND PRACTICAL INFORMATION. Buses run from from Pg. Mar. in San Antonio to: **Cala Bassa** (10min., 8 per day 9:30am-6:30pm, €1); **Cala Conta** (15min., 7 per day 9:10am-6pm, €1); **Cala Tarida** (10min., 8 per day 9:30am-6:30pm, €1); **Eivissa** (25min.; every 30min. M-Sa 7-9:30am and 10-11:30pm, every 15min. 9:45am-9:30pm, Su every 30min. 7:30am-10:30pm; €1.35); **Santa Eulária** (35min., M-Sa 4 per day 10:15am-6:45pm; €1). **Ferries** leave San Antonio for **Dénia** (see **Transportation,** p. 338). Smaller companies run daily **boats** to nearby beaches. Signs posted daily along the port have schedules. For a **taxi,** call ☎971 34 07 79. San Antonio is very easy to get around, as major streets lie on something of a grid. For **car** and **moped rental,** try **Motos Luis,** Av. Portmany, 5. (☎971 34 05 21. Mopeds €20 and up. Cars €38 and up. Open M-Sa 9am-2pm and 4-8pm, Su 9am-2pm.) The **tourist office** is a stone building in the middle of the pedestrian thoroughfare by Pg. Fonts. (☎971 34 33 63. Open M-F 9:30am-2:30pm and 3-8:30pm, Sa 9am-1pm, Su 9:30am-1:30pm.) In an **emergency,** call ☎112 or the **police,** Av. Portmany, km 14 (☎971 34 08 30). There is a **Centro de Salud** on C. Alicant (☎ 971 34 51 21).

ACCOMMODATIONS AND FOOD. *Hostales* in San Antonio are numerous, cheap, and full of Brits. Call well in advance for any summer stay; in the low season prices drop. **Hostal Residencia Roig ❷,** C. Progreso, 44, has gorgeous, clean rooms all with private bath. (☎971 34 04 83. Singles €21; doubles €42.) The large bedrooms, huge TV lounge, and great location make **Hostal Salada ❷,** C. Soletat, 34, one of the best bargains in town. Walk up C. Bartolomé Vicente Ramon from the port and turn left on to C. Soletat. (☎971 34 11 30. Singles €15; doubles €24; triples €30.) Another option is the more basic **Hostal Rita ❷,** C. Bartolomé Vicente Ramon, 17B. Doubles and triples have private baths; singles share common baths. (☎971 34 63 32. Singles €20; doubles €39; triples €53.) **Restaurants** are everywhere in San Antonio. A variety of choices are available at the outdoor cafes along Pg. Mar or on its sidestreets leading uphill. Of the more trendy beachfront establishments, **Terraza Kiwi Beach ❶,** Av. Doctor Fleming, 2-4, stands out. The orange building right on the water serves cheap sandwiches, salads, fruit drinks, milkshakes, and alcoholic favorites. (Entrees €2.40-4. Alcoholic milkshakes €5.40, non-alcoholic shakes and smoothies €2.70-4. Open daily 10am-4am.)

BEACHES AND NIGHTLIFE. The **beaches** near San Antonio are some of Ibiza's best and are fairly accessible. The town itself is situated on a long, narrow strip of sand, but better beaches are only a stone's throw away. Check out **Cala Bassa,** one of the more popular tanning spots, for a gorgeous (and sometimes nude) beach; accessible by bus. **Cala Gració,** 1½km from San Antonio, is easily reached by foot. **Santa Eulária** is more built up, but it's substantially larger than some of the other beaches nearby. Hoof it or bike to the small coves of **Es Pouet** and **Caló des Moro.** If you have a car or moped, head to **Cala Salada,** just a few kilometers north of town, for calm, beautiful waters and a picturesque hippie community. San Antonio's **nightlife** revolves largely around three main areas. The area on the far end of town, near the littered beach of Es Ganguil, has several waterfront bars. Crowds gather on the small beach to watch the **sunset** and chill to mellow house. **Café del Mar,** "the original sunset bar," serves overpriced drinks, the chic **Cafe Mambo** is a popular pre-party bar, and, much farther down toward Calo des Moro, **Kanya** offers a lively scene. The crowded streets of town are packed with low-key watering holes and drunk pre-partiers. The clubs **Eden** and **Es Paradis Terrenal,** beach bars (including the popular and upscale **M Bar**), and mini-discos facing the main beach round out the options. Compared to the competitive club scene of Eivissa, the nightlife options in San Antonio can be much more casual and relaxed.

FORMENTERA

The tiny island of Formentera is Spain's version of island paradise. Despite the recent invasions by bourgeois, beach-hungry Germans and Italians, the island's stunning beaches maintain a sense of hypnotic calm. Join Formentera's "save our island" spirit by hiking or renting a bike—the tourist office offers a comprehensive list of "Green Tours" for hikers and cyclists, and bike paths are plentiful. The island itself is pricey, and often is visited simply as a daytrip from Eivissa.

TRANSPORTATION. Ferries at Estació Marítima, near the Burger King in Eivissa, offer transportation. **Pitra** car ferries (☎971 19 10 88), **Trasmapi-Balearia** (☎971 31 20 70), and **Umafisa** car ferries (☎971 31 45 13) all run to and from Formentera. If you're in a hurry, choose **Línea Jet's** speedy ride (25min., 16 per day 7:45am-8:30pm, €13) or ride with the trucks on the cheaper, slower mothership (1hr.; M-Sa 9 per day 6:45am-8pm, Su 5 per day 9am-8pm; €7.95). For transport between Formentera and the mainland, see **By Boat,** p. 337.

ORIENTATION AND PRACTICAL INFORMATION. The main port, **La Savina,** is on the northern side of the island. The main artery runs from the port (km 0) to the eastern tip, **Punta D'Esfar** (km 20). The island's "capital," **San Francisco,** at km 3.1, has the basics but little else. **Es Pujols,** km 4, is the island's liveliest town. **Buses** run from La Savina to: **Es Pujols** (9 per day 8:30am-7:15pm, €1.05); **Platja de ses Illetes** (10:30am and 5pm, €0.85); **Platja Migjorn** (7 per day 9:45am-7:15pm, €1.05); **San Francisco** (12 per day 8:30am-7:15pm, €0.85). For a **taxi,** call ☎971 32 80 16. Car, scooter, and bike **rental booths** line the dock in La Savina. (Cars €30-36 per day. Scooters €18-21. Bikes €3-6.) **Autos Ca María** offers friendly service and advice on routes. (☎971 32 29 21. Cars €33. Scooters €18. Bicycles €3-6. Open daily 9am-9pm. MC/V.) All main roads have lanes for scooters to putter along with bicycles. The **tourist office,** Edificio Servicios La Savina, is at the port. (☎971 32 20 57. Open M-F 10am-2pm and 5-7pm, Sa 10am-2pm.) For the **police,** dial ☎971 32 20 22. For the **medical center,** dial 971 32 23 69. **Postal code:** 07870.

ACCOMMODATIONS AND FOOD. Formentera offers the top shelf of hostel-living—and prices certainly reflect it. There are virtually no budget options, so be prepared to either shell out or head back to Ibiza for the night. Almost all of the island's hostels are hotel-quality with attentive staff; the best of them are tucked away on their own stunning, deserted beaches. At **Hostal Costa Azul ❸,** Platja de Migjorn, km 7, serene rooms are complemented by a quiet beach. (☎971 32 80 24. Doubles before July 15 €41, after July 15 €58.) **Hostal Mayans ❹,** in Es Pujols, has spacious doubles with fridges, balconies, and large bathrooms, and believe it or not, they're some of the cheapest in town. (☎971 32 87 24. Breakfast included. Doubles €73.) Gobble down *paella* (€7.80) at **El Mirador ❷,** km 14.3, overlooking both the island and the water. (☎971 32 70 37. Open daily 12:30-4pm and 7-11pm.) Check out the varied restaurants in Es Pujols for both *comida típica* and more international cuisine. **Supermarkets** line all major roads on Formentera.

BEACHES. To bask on Formentera's best beaches, take Av. Mediterránea from the port, turn left at the sign pointing toward Es Pujols, and take another left onto the dirt road at the sign marking Verede de Ses Salines. Paths to the right lead to **Platja de Llevant,** a long strip of fine sand. Farther up the peninsula, roads to the left lead to **Platja de Ses Illetes,** with its more popular, but rocky, swimming holes. **Platja de Migjorn,** the longest beach on the island, is less crowded than the others. A tourist boat runs to Ses Illetes and Espalmador from La Savina (leaves La Savina 10:15, 11:45am, 1:15pm; returns 4:15, 5:30, 6:45pm; round-trip €9). For sailing, windsurfing, and canoe rental try **Wet 4 Fun** on Es Pujols beach. (☎971 32 18 09. Sailboats €35.60 per hr. Windsurfing €13 per hr. Canoes €5.40 per hr., €12 per half-day.) For stunning sightseeing, those with mopeds should drive through the mountainous regions of **La Mola** to the lighthouse at **Far de la Mola** and **Punta de Sa Ruda** on the easternmost extreme of the island, or cruise by the groves of olive trees to Cap de Barbaria just south of La Savina. Those seeking a less touristed beach should head to **Cala Saona,** a pleasant cove on the western part of the island.

BARCELONA

Barcelona loves to indulge in the fantastic. From the urban carnival that is Las Ramblas to its Modernista buildings with no straight lines; from wild festivals to even wilder nightlife; from bronzed nude beaches to a beloved white gorilla named Floquet, the city pushes the limits of style and good taste in everything it does, and does so with amazing results. As the center of the whimsical and daring *Modernisme* architectural movement, Barcelona boasts fairy-tale buildings like none other in the world. With artists like Salvador Dalí, Pablo Picasso, and the lovable Joan Miró, even Barcelona's world famous art is grounded in an alternate reality.

The time is now for Barcelona. In the quarter-century since Spain was freed from Franco's oppressive regime, Barcelona has led Cataluña in a resurgence of a culture so unique it puzzles even the rest of Spain. The city has given itself a complete makeover, which began as preparation for the Olympics in the early 1990s but was so successful that the image-obsessed *barceloneses* have kept it going. The result is a vanguard city squeezed between the mesmerizing blue waters of the Mediterranean and the green Tibidabo hills, flashing with such vibrant colors and intense energy that you'll see Barcelona long after you have closed your eyes.

Barcelona is a stunning gateway to Cataluña, Spain, the Mediterranean, and the Pyrenees. Pack your swimsuit and your skis, your art history book and your clubbing shoes, and don't worry if you don't speak Spanish—neither does Barcelona.

INTERCITY TRANSPORT

BY PLANE

Domestic and international flights land at **El Prat de Llobregat** airport (☎932 98 38 38; www.aena.es/ae/bcn/homepage), 12km southwest of Barcelona. The **Aerobus** links the airport to Pl. Catalunya, the center of Barcelona (approx. 40min.; every 15min. to Pl. Catalunya M-F 6am-midnight, Sa-Su 6:30am-midnight; to the airport M-F 5:30am-11:15pm, Sa-Su 6am-11:20pm; €3.30). RENFE Cercanías **trains** provide cheaper airport transport (24hr. info ☎934 91 31 83; 43min.; every 30min. 6:13am-11:15pm from the airport, 5:43am-11:24pm from Sants; €2.15). The most useful stops are **Estació Barcelona-Sants** and **Plaça Catalunya.** Tickets are sold at the red machines. In Sants, buy tickets at the "Aeroport" window (open 5am-11pm). After 11pm, get them from the ticket machines or the Recorridos Cercanías window.

The city **bus** offers the only inexpensive late-night service. Take bus #106 from the airport to Pl. Espanya (airport to Pl. Espanya every hr. 6:20am-10:15pm, then 11:35pm, 12:50, 2:05, and 3:20am; Pl. Espanya to airport 7:10am-3:15am with similarly erratic late-night service; €1). The stop in Pl. Espanya is on the corner of Gran Vía de les Corts Catalanes and Av. Reina Maria Cristina. A **taxi** ride between Barcelona and the airport costs €18-27.

AIRLINES

Spain's three national airlines serve all domestic and major international destinations. **Iberia/Aviaco,** Diputación, 258 (☎902 40 05 00; www.iberia.com), has extensive coverage and student discounts. **Air Europa** (☎902 40 15 01; www.aireuropa.com) and **Spanair** (☎902 13 14 15; www.spanair.com) often offer cheaper fares. All major international airlines serve Barcelona, including: **American** (902 115 570; www.aa.com), **British Airways** (☎902 11 13 33, airport ☎932 98 34 55, open 6am-7pm; www.ba.com), **Delta** (☎901 11 69 46; www.delta-air.com), and **Lufthansa** (☎902 220 101; www.lufthansa.com). **Easy Jet** (☎902 29 99 92; www.easyjet.com) also offers flights to Amsterdam, Geneva, Liverpool, and London.

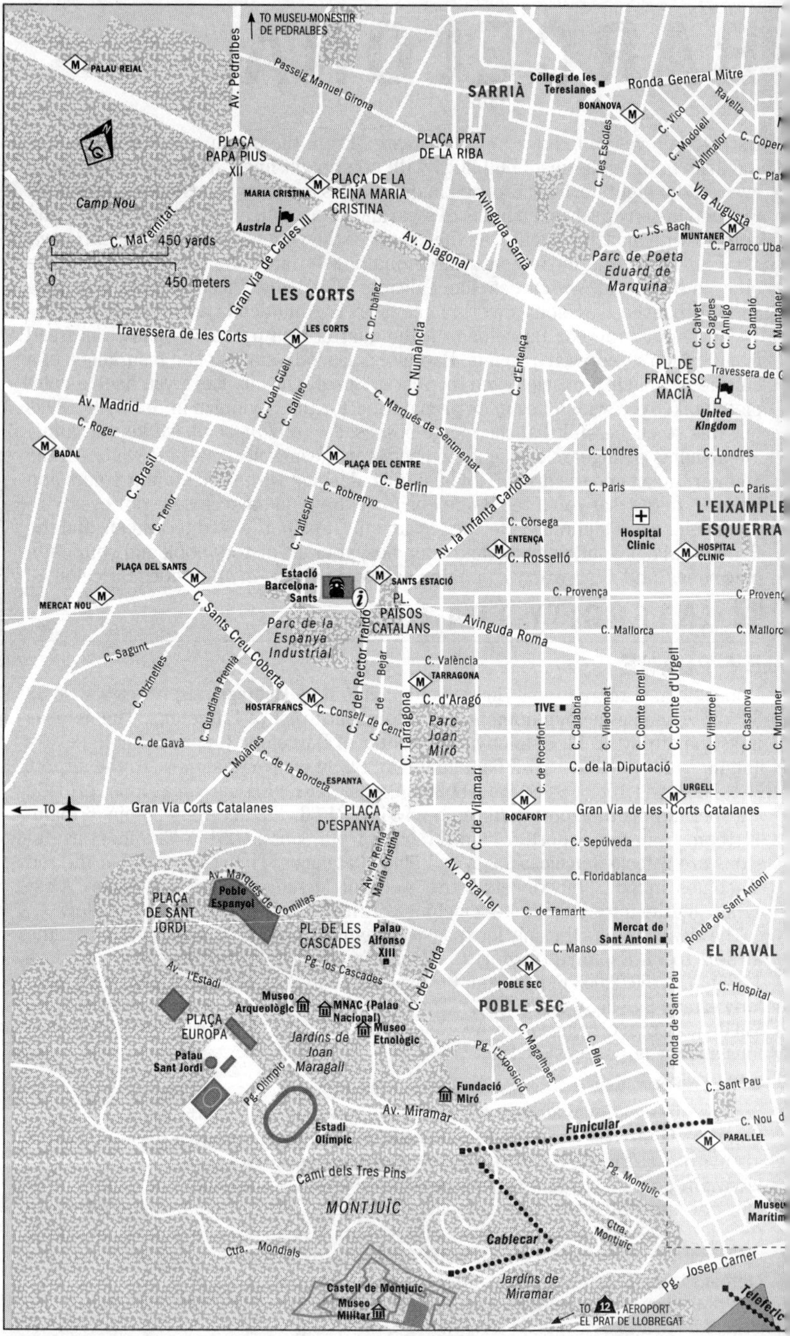
TO MUSEU-MONESTIR DE PEDRALBES
PALAU REIAL
Av. Pedralbes
Passeig Manuel Girona
SARRIÀ
Collegi de les Teresianes
Ronda General Mitre
BONANOVA
PLAÇA PAPA PIUS XII
PLAÇA PRAT DE LA RIBA
MARIA CRISTINA
PLAÇA DE LA REINA MARIA CRISTINA
Austria
Camp Nou
C. Maternitat
0 450 yards
0 450 meters
Gran Via de Carles III
Av. Diagonal
Avinguda Sarrià
C. les Escoles
C. Vico
C. Modolell
Vallmajor
C. Coper
Ravella
C. Plat
Via Augusta
C. J.S. Bach
MUNTANER
C. Parroco Uba
Parc de Poeta Eduard de Marquina
LES CORTS
C. Dr. Ibáñez
Travessera de les Corts
LES CORTS
C. Numància
C. d'Entença
C. Calvet
C. Sagues
C. Amigó
C. Santaló
C. Muntaner
PL. DE FRANCESC MACIÀ
Travessera de G
United Kingdom
Av. Madrid
C. Roger
BADAL
C. Joan Güell
C. Galileo
C. Marqués de Sentmenat
PLAÇA DEL CENTRE
C. Londres
C. Londres
C. Brasil
C. Tenor
C. Berlin
C. Robrenyo
C. Paris
C. Paris
Av. la Infanta Carlota
L'EIXAMPLE ESQUERRA
Hospital Clinic
C. Vallespir
C. Còrsega
ENTENÇA
C. Rosselló
HOSPITAL CLINIC
PLAÇA DEL SANTS
MERCAT NOU
Estació Barcelona-Sants
SANTS ESTACIÓ
PL. PAÏSOS CATALANS
C. Provença
C. Provenç
Parc de la Espanya Industrial
C. Sants Creu Coberta
C. del Rector Triadó
Avinguda Roma
C. Mallorca
C. Mallorc
C. Sagunt
C. Olzinelles
C. Guadiana Premià
Bejar
C. València
TARRAGONA
HOSTAFRANCS
C. Consell de Cent
C. d'Aragó
C. Tarragona
Parc Joan Miró
TIVE
C. de Rocafort
C. Calàbria
C. Viladomat
C. Comte Borrell
C. Comte d'Urgell
C. Villarroel
C. Casanova
C. Muntaner
C. de Gavà
C. Moianes
C. de la Bordeta
ESPANYA
C. de la Diputació
C. de Vilamarí
URGELL
ROCAFORT
TO
Gran Via Corts Catalanes
PLAÇA D'ESPANYA
Gran Via de les Corts Catalanes
Av. la Reina Maria Cristina
C. Sepúlveda
Av. Marquès de Comillas
Poble Espanyol
Av. Paral.lel
C. Floridablanca
PLAÇA DE SANT JORDI
C. de Tamarit
Ronda de Sant Antoni
PL. DE LES CASCADES
Palau Alfonso XIII
Mercat de Sant Antoni
C. Manso
EL RAVAL
Pg. los Cascades
Av. l'Estadi
C. de Lleida
POBLE SEC
POBLE SEC
C. Hospital
Museo Arqueològic
MNAC (Palau Nacional)
PLAÇA EUROPA
Museo Etnològic
Jardins de Joan Maragall
C. Magalhaes
C. Blai
Ronda de Sant Pau
Palau Sant Jordi
Pg. l'Exposició
Pg. Olímpic
Fundació Miró
C. Sant Pau
Av. Miramar
Estadi Olimpic
Funicular
C. Nou
PARAL.LEL
Pg. Montjuïc
Camí dels Tres Pins
MONTJUÏC
Museu Marítim
Ctra. Montjuïc
Cablecar
Ctra. Mondials
Pg. Josep Carner
Jardíns de Miramar
Castell de Montjuïc
Museo Militar
TO 12, AEROPORT EL PRAT DE LLOBREGAT
Teleferic

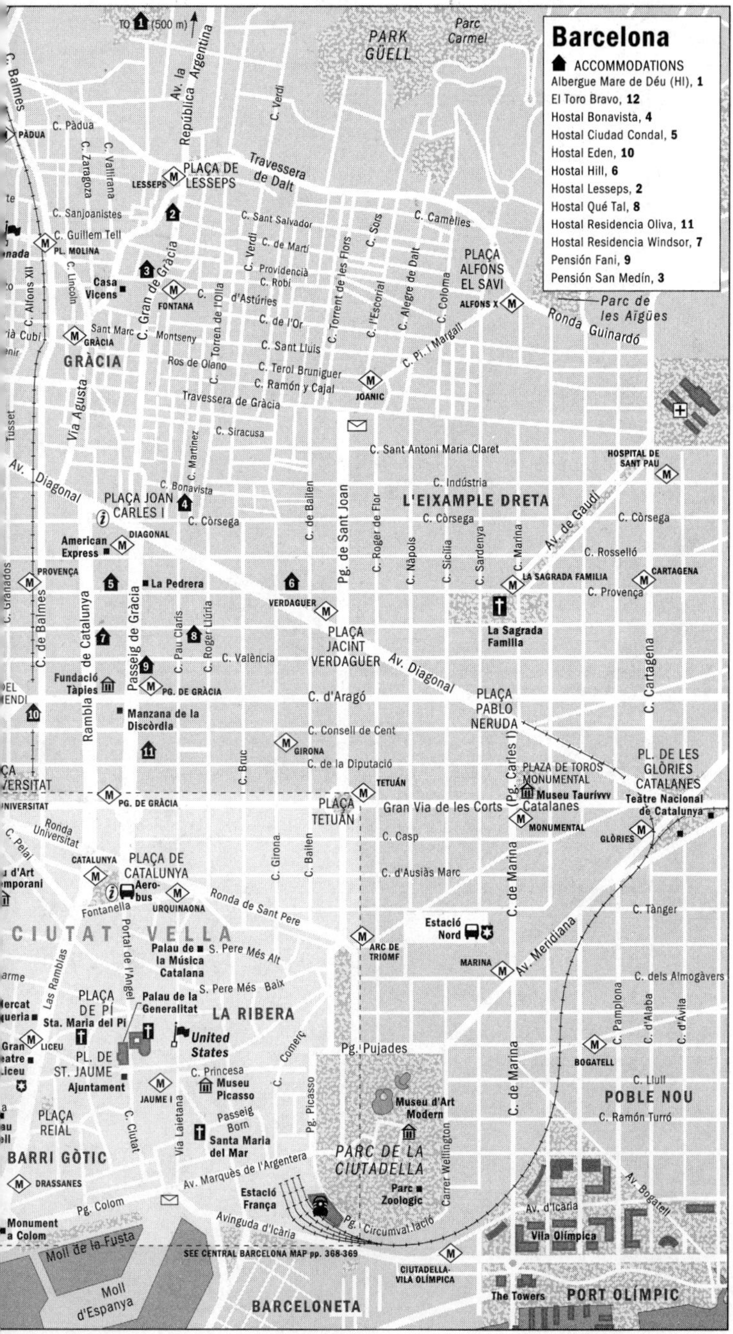
Barcelona
ACCOMMODATIONS
Albergue Mare de Déu (HI), 1
El Toro Bravo, 12
Hostal Bonavista, 4
Hostal Ciudad Condal, 5
Hostal Eden, 10
Hostal Hill, 6
Hostal Lesseps, 2
Hostal Qué Tal, 8
Hostal Residencia Oliva, 11
Hostal Residencia Windsor, 7
Pensión Fani, 9
Pensión San Medín, 3
TO 1 (500 m)
PARK GÜELL
Parc Carmel
Parc de les Aïgües
Ronda Guinardó
Av. la República Argentina
C. Verdi
C. Balmes
C. Pàdua
PÀDUA
C. Zaragoza
C. Vallirana
PLAÇA DE LESSEPS
LESSEPS
Travessera de Dalt
C. Sanjoanistes
C. Guillem Tell
PL. MOLINA
C. Sant Salvador
C. Camèlies
C. de Martí
Providència
C. Robí
C. Sors
C. Torrent de les Flors
C. Alegre de Dalt
C. Coloma
C. l'Escorial
PLAÇA ALFONS EL SAVI
ALFONS X
Casa Vicens
FONTANA
C. Gran de Gràcia
C. Lincoln
C. Alfons XII
C. d'Astúries
C. Torrent de l'Olla
C. de l'Or
C. Sant Lluís
Sant Marc
GRÀCIA
Montseny
GRÀCIA
Ros de Olano
C. Terol Bruniguer
C. Ramón y Cajal
C. Pi. i Margall
JOANIC
Travessera de Gràcia
Via Augusta
Tusset
C. Siracusa
C. Sant Antoni Maria Claret
HOSPITAL DE SANT PAU
C. Martínez
C. Indústria
Av. Diagonal
C. Bonavista
PLAÇA JOAN CARLES I
L'EIXAMPLE DRETA
C. Còrsega
C. de Bailen
Pg. de Sant Joan
C. Roger de Flor
C. Nàpols
C. Sicília
C. Sardenya
C. Marina
Av. de Gaudí
C. Rosselló
American Express
DIAGONAL
PROVENÇA
C. Granados
C. de Balmes
La Pedrera
VERDAGUER
LA SAGRADA FAMILIA
CARTAGENA
C. Provença
Rambla de Catalunya
Passeig de Gràcia
C. Pau Claris
C. Roger Llúria
PLAÇA JACINT VERDAGUER
La Sagrada Familia
C. València
C. Cartagena
Fundació Tàpies
PG. DE GRÀCIA
C. d'Aragó
PLAÇA PABLO NERUDA
Manzana de la Discòrdia
C. Consell de Cent
GIRONA
C. Bruc
C. de la Diputació
TETUÁN
C. Marina (Pg. Carles I)
PLAZA DE TOROS MONUMENTAL
Museu Taurívvv
PL. DE LES GLÒRIES CATALANES
Teatre Nacional de Catalunya
UNIVERSITAT
PG. DE GRÀCIA
PLAÇA TETUAN
Gran Via de les Corts Catalanes
MONUMENTAL
GLÒRIES
Ronda Universitat
C. Pelai
C. Casp
C. Girona
C. Bailen
CATALUNYA
PLAÇA DE CATALUNYA
C. d'Ausiàs Marc
Aero-bus
URQUINAONA
Fontanella
Ronda de Sant Pere
C. Tànger
CIUTAT VELLA
Portal de l'Àngel
Estació Nord
Palau de la Música Catalana
S. Pere Més Alt
ARC DE TRIOMF
Av. Meridiana
MARINA
C. dels Almogàvers
Las Ramblas
S. Pere Més Baix
PLAÇA DE PI
Palau de la Generalitat
LA RIBERA
Sta. Maria del Pi
United States
Comerç
C. Pampiona
C. d'Alaba
C. d'Àvila
LICEU
Pg. Pujades
PL. DE ST. JAUME
C. Princesa
BOGATELL
Ajuntament
Museu Picasso
C. Llull
JAUME I
Pg. Picasso
Museu d'Art Modern
POBLE NOU
PLAÇA REIAL
Via Laietana
C. Ciutat
Passeig Born
C. de Marina
C. Ramón Turró
Santa Maria del Mar
PARC DE LA CIUTADELLA
BARRI GÒTIC
Av. Marquès de l'Argentera
Carrer Wellington
DRASSANES
Estació França
Parc Zoologic
Av. Bogatell
Pg. Colom
Av. d'Icària
Monument a Colom
Avinguda d'Icària
Pg. Circumval.lació
Vila Olímpica
Moll de la Fusta
SEE CENTRAL BARCELONA MAP pp. 368-369
CIUTADELLA-VILA OLÍMPICA
Moll d'Espanya
BARCELONETA
The Towers
PORT OLÍMPIC

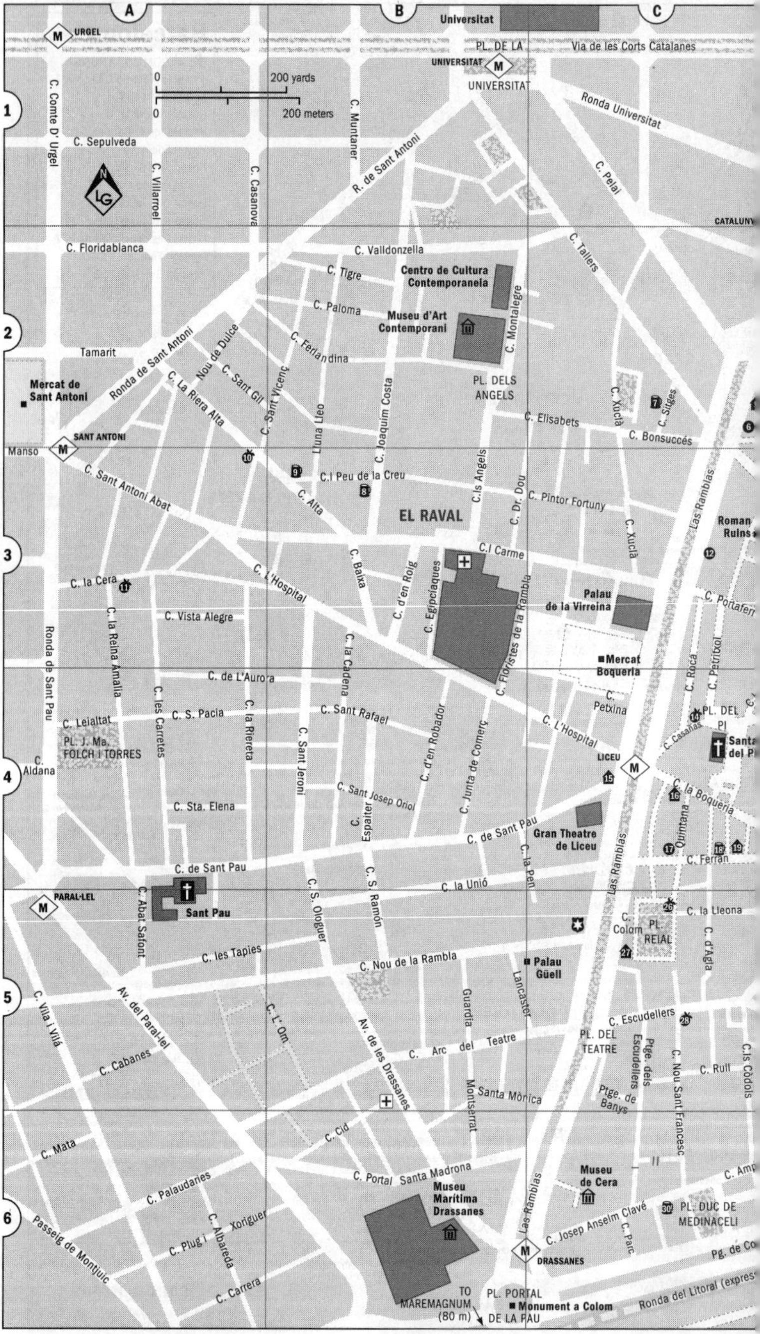
A
B
C
1
2
3
4
5
6
URGEL
Universitat
PL. DE LA
UNIVERSITAT
UNIVERSITAT
Via de les Corts Catalanes
0
200 yards
0
200 meters
C. Comte D' Urgel
C. Sepulveda
C. Villarroel
C. Casanova
C. Muntaner
R. de Sant Antoni
Ronda Universitat
C. Pelai
CATALUNY
C. Floridablanca
C. Valldonzella
C. Tallers
C. Tigre
Centro de Cultura Contemporaneia
C. Paloma
Museu d'Art Contemporani
C. Montalegre
Tamarit
Ronda de Sant Antoni
Nou de Dulce
C. Sant Gil
C. Feriandina
PL. DELS ANGELS
Mercat de Sant Antoni
C. La Riera Alta
C. Sant Vicenç
Lluna Lleo
C. Joaquim Costa
C. Xuclà
C. Sitges
C. Elisabets
C. Bonsuccés
SANT ANTONI
Manso
C.l Peu de la Creu
C. Sant Antoni Abat
C. Alta
C.ls Angels
C. Dr. Dou
C. Pintor Fortuny
Las Ramblas
EL RAVAL
C. Xuclà
Roman Ruins
C.l Carme
C. la Cera
C. L'Hospital
C. Baixa
C. d'en Roig
C. Egipciaques
C. Floristes de la Rambla
Palau de la Virreina
C. Portaferr
C. Vista Alegre
C. la Reina Amalia
Ronda de Sant Pau
C. la Cadena
Mercat Boqueria
C. Roca
C. Petritxol
C. de L'Aurora
C. les Carretes
C. Petxina
C. Leialtat
C. S. Pacia
C. la Riereta
C. Sant Rafael
C. d'en Robador
C. L'Hospital
PL. DEL PI
PL. J. Ma. FOLCH I TORRES
C. Sant Jeroni
C. Junta de Comerç
C. Casanas
Santa ... del P
C. Aldana
LICEU
C. Sant Josep Oriol
C. la Boqueria
C. Sta. Elena
C. Espalter
C. de Sant Pau
Gran Theatre de Liceu
Quintana
C. de Sant Pau
C. la Pen
C. Ferran
PARAL·LEL
C. Abat Safont
Sant Pau
C. S. Ologuer
C. S. Ramón
C. la Unió
C. la Lleona
C. Colom
PL. REIAL
C. les Tapies
C. Nou de la Rambla
Palau Güell
C. d'Agla
Lancaster
C. Vila i Vilá
Av. del Paral-lel
C. L' Om
Av. de les Drassanes
Guardia
C. Escudellers
C. Arc del Teatre
PL. DEL TEATRE
Ptge. dels Escudellers
C. Nou Sant Francesc
C.ls Codols
C. Cabanes
Montserrat
Santa Mònica
C. Rull
Ptge. de Banys
C. Mata
C. Cid
C. Palaudaries
C. Portal Santa Madrona
Museu Marítima Drassanes
Museu de Cera
C. Am
Passeig de Montjuic
C. Albareda
Xoriguer
C. Plug i
Las Ramblas
C. Josep Anselm Clavé
C. Parc
PL. DUC DE MEDINACELI
DRASSANES
Pg. de Co
C. Carrera
TO MAREMAGNUM (80 m)
PL. PORTAL DE LA PAU
Monument a Colom
Ronda del Litoral (expres

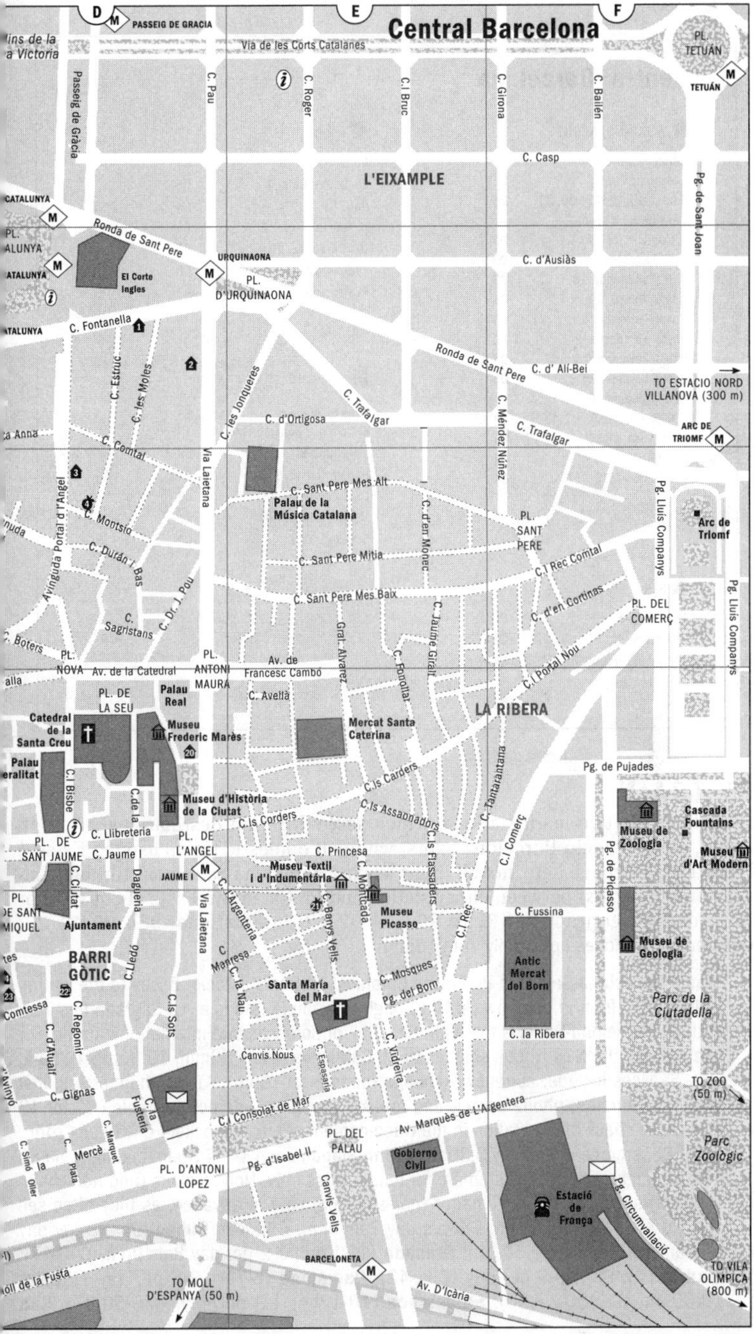
Central Barcelona
D
E
F
PASSEIG DE GRACIA
Via de les Corts Catalanes
PL. TETUÁN
TETUÁN
Passeig de Gràcia
C. Pau
C. Roger
C.l Bruc
C. Girona
C. Bailén
C. Casp
L'EIXAMPLE
Pg. de Sant Joan
CATALUNYA
Ronda de Sant Pere
URQUINAONA
El Corte Ingles
PL. D'URQUINAONA
C. d'Ausiàs
C. Fontanella
C. Estruc
C. les Moles
C. les Jonqueres
C. Trafalgar
Ronda de Sant Pere
C. d' Alí-Bei
TO ESTACIO NORD VILLANOVA (300 m)
C. d'Ortigosa
C. Méndez Núñez
C. Trafalgar
ARC DE TRIOMF
C. Comtal
Via Laietana
C. Sant Pere Mes Alt
Palau de la Música Catalana
C. d'en Monec
Pg. Lluís Companys
Arc de Triomf
Avinguda Portal d'Angel
C. Montsio
C. Durán i Bas
PL. SANT PERE
C.l Rec Comtal
C. Sant Pere Mitja
C. Dr. J. Pou
C. Sant Pere Mes Baix
C. d'en Cortinas
PL. DEL COMERÇ
Pg. Lluís Companys
C. Sagristans
C. Boters
PL. NOVA
Av. de la Catedral
PL. ANTONI MAURA
Av. de Francesc Cambó
Grat. Alvarez
C. Fonollar
C. Jaume Giralt
C.l Portal Nou
PL. DE LA SEU
Palau Real
C. Avellà
LA RIBERA
Catedral de la Santa Creu
Museu Frederic Marès
Mercat Santa Caterina
C. Tantarantana
Palau
C.l Bisbe
C. de la
Museu d'Història de la Ciutat
C.ls Carders
Pg. de Pujades
C.ls Corders
C.ls Assaonadors
C.l Comerç
Cascada Fountains
Museu de Zoologia
PL. DE SANT JAUME
C. Llibreteria
PL. DE L'ANGEL
C. Jaume I
C. Princesa
Museu d'Art Modern
JAUME I
Museu Textil i d'Indumentária
C. Montcada
C.ls Flassaders
Pg. de Picasso
C. Ciutat
Dagueria
C.l Argenteria
C. Banys Vells
Museu Picasso
C. Fussina
PL. DE SANT MIQUEL
Ajuntament
C.l Rec
Museu de Geologia
BARRI GÒTIC
C. Lledó
C. Manresa
C. la Nau
C. Mosques
Antic Mercat del Born
Comtessa
Santa María del Mar
Pg. del Born
Parc de la Ciutadella
C. Regomir
C. d'Atualf
C.ls Sots
C. la Ribera
Canvis Nous
C. Espasería
C. Vidreria
TO ZOO (50 m)
C. Gignas
C. la Fusteria
C.l Consolat de Mar
Av. Marquès de L'Argentera
C. Marquet
PL. DEL PALAU
Parc Zoològic
C. Simó Oller
la Mercè
C. Plata
Pg. d'Isabel II
Gobierno Civil
PL. D'ANTONI LOPEZ
Canvis Vells
Estació de França
Pg. Circumvallació
BARCELONETA
Moll de la Fusta
TO MOLL D'ESPANYA (50 m)
Av. D'Icària
TO VILA OLIMPICA (800 m)

Central Barcelona

ACCOMMODATIONS

Albergue de Juventud Kabul, 27	C5
Albergue Juvenil Palau, 23	D5
Casa de Huéspedes Mari-Luz, 24	D5
H.-R. Lausanne, 3	D3
H.-R. Rembrandt, 13	D3
Hostal Aviñyó, 29	D5
Hostal Fernando, 19	C4
Hostal Fontanella, 2	D2
Hostal Layetana, 20	D4
Hostal Levante, 25	D5
Hotel Toledano & H.-R. Capitol, 5	C2
Mare Nostrum, 15	C4
Pensión Aris, 1	D2
Pensión Dalí, 16	C4

SERVICES

Net Movil, 6	C2
Pharmacy, 12	C3
Tintorería Ferran, 17	C4

FOOD

Colibri, 10	A3
Els Quatre Gats, 4	D3
Irati, 14	C4
La Habana Vieja, 21	E5
Las Caracoles, 28	C5
Le Quinze Nits, 26	C5
Restaurante Can Lluís, 11	A3

NIGHTLIFE

Casa Almirall, 8	B3
El Cafe que pone Muebles Navarro, 9	B3
Harlem Jazz Club, 22	D5
La Oveja Negra, 7	C2
Margarita Blue, 30	C6
Schilling, 18	C4

BARCELONA

BY TRAIN

Barcelona has two main stations, which serve different destinations. When in doubt, go to Estació Barcelona-Sants; while all domestic trains leaving Estació França pass through here, not all trains leaving Barcelona-Sants pass through Estació França. A taxi between either station and Pl. Catalunya costs about €6. For information, contact **RENFE** (☎902 24 02 02; international 934 90 11 22; www.renfe.es; phones open daily 7am-10pm).

Estació Barcelona-Sants, in Pl. Països Catalans. M: Sants-Estació. Buses to the station include #30 from Pl. Espanya, #44 through L'Eixample (stops at La Sagrada Família), and N2. Barcelona-Sants is the main terminal for domestic and international traffic. For late arrivals, the N14 Nitbus shuttles to Pl. Catalunya (every 30min. 10:30pm-4:30am, €1). Services include: currency exchange (open 8am-10pm), ATMs, pharmacy, tourist office, restaurants, phone center, and touristy shopping. Internet available (€1 for 13 min.) in the back of the station in the video-game room. Large lockers €4.50 per 24hr., small €3; storage open daily 5:30am-11pm. Station open M-F 4:30am-midnight, Sa-Su 5am-midnight. The prices listed are for *turista* class only. Non-smokers (and non-chain-smokers) should buy a *no-fumador* (non-smoking) seat in advance, as they often sell out. To: **Alicante** (4½-5½hr., 7-8 per day 7am-6pm, €30-41); **Bilbao** (9hr., 3 per day 9:55am-10:30pm, €30.50-32); **Granada** (11-12hr., 1-2 per day 8am-9pm, €46-47); **Madrid** (6½-9hr., 6-7 per day, €31-42); **Pamplona** (6-7hr., 3-5 per day 7:30am-10:30pm, €26.50-27.50); **Salamanca** (10-12hr., 1-3 per day, €35.50-37); **San**

Sebastian (8-9hr., 1-2 per day 9:55am-10:30pm, €29.50-31); **Sevilla** (10-12hr., 3 per day 8am-10pm, €47-64); **Valencia** (3-4hr., 12-15 per day 7am-9pm, €27.50-32). International destinations include **Milan** (through **Figueres** and **Nice**) and **Montpellier** with connections to **Geneva, Paris,** and various stops along the French Riviera. 20% discount on round-trip tickets.

Estació França, Av. Marqués de l'Argentera (☎902 24 02 02). M: Barceloneta. Buses include #17 from Pl. Catalunya and N6. Open daily 7am-10pm. Serves regional destinations on RENFE, including Girona and Zaragoza, as well as international arrivals.

BY BUS

Most buses arrive at the **Barcelona Nord Estació d'Autobuses,** C. Ali-bei, 80 (☎902 30 32 22). The station has food, money exchange, and luggage storage. The building also houses an office of the **Guardia Urbana,** the local police. Bus #54 along Gran Vía (1 block from Pl. Catalunya) and N11 go to the station. A taxi from Pl. Catalunya costs about €4. Other buses, particularly **international buses,** arrive at the **Estació d'Autobuses de Sants** station, next to the train station in Pl. Països Catalans. The following companies operate out of Estació Nord:

Eurolines (☎902 40 50 40; www.eurolines.es). Numerous international destinations.

Sarfa (☎902 30 20 25; www.sarfa.com). Sarfa buses stop at many beach towns along the Costa Brava, north of Barcelona. Open daily 8am-9pm. To: **Cadaqués** (2½hr.; 11:15am, 8:25pm; €15.15); **Palafrugell** (2hr., 13 per day, €11.40); **Tossa del Mar** (1½hr., 10 per day 9am-9pm, €7.50).

Linebús (☎932 65 07 00). Open M-F 8am-8pm, Sa 8:30am-1pm and 5-8pm. To **Paris** (13hr., M-Sa 8pm, €80). Also has daily service to southern France and Morocco.

Alsa/Enatcar (☎902 42 22 42; www.alsa.es). To: **Alicante** (9hr., 3 per day, €32.46); **Madrid** (8hr., 13 per day, €22.08); **Valencia** (4hr., 16 per day, €20.46); **Zaragoza** (3½-4½hr., 20 per day, €17.74); **Naples** (24hr., 5:15pm, €113).

BY FERRY

Barcelona is an ideal gateway to the **Balearic Islands,** renowned for their beaches, raging clubs, and resorts. The main ferry station is **Estació Marítima** in Port Vell.

Trasmediterránea (☎902 45 46 45; fax 932 95 91 34), in Estació Marítima-Moll Barcelona, Moll de Sant Bertran. Summer only to: **Ibiza** (10-11hr., 1 per day M-Sa, €45.43); **Palma** (3½hr., 1 per day, €63); **Mahón** (10½hr., 1 per day, €45.43).

Turbocat (☎902 18 18 88; www.turbocatonline.com), in Estació Marítima-Moll Barcelona, Moll de Sant Bertran. Summer only to **Ciutadella** (3½hr., 1 per day, €65) and **Alcuida** (5hr., 1 per day, €62).

ORIENTATION

Barcelona's layout is simple. Imagine yourself perched on Columbus's head at the **Monument a Colom** (on **Passeig de Colom,** along the shore), viewing the city with the sea at your back. From the harbor, the city slopes upward to the mountains. From the Columbus monument, **Las Ramblas** (see p. 383), the main thoroughfare, runs from the harbor up to **Plaça Catalunya** (M: Catalunya), the city's center. The **Ciutat Vella** (Old City) is the heavily-touristed historic neighborhood, which centers around Las Ramblas and includes the Barri Gòtic, La Ribera, and El Raval. The **Barri Gòtic** is east of Las Ramblas (to the right, with your back to the sea), enclosed on the other side by **Vía Laietana.** East of Vía Laietana lies the maze-like neighborhood of **La Ribera,** which borders Parc de la Ciutadella and the Estació França train station. To the west of Las Ramblas (with your back to the sea) is **El Raval.**

Beyond La Ribera, (farther east, outside the Ciutat Vella) is the **Poble Nou** neighborhood and the **Vila Olímpica,** with its twin towers (the tallest buildings in Barcelona) and an assortment of discos and restaurants. Beyond El Raval (to the west) rises **Montjuïc,** crammed with gardens, museums, the 1992 Olympic grounds, Montjuïc castle, and other attractions. Directly behind the Monument a Colom is the **Port Vell** (Old Port) development, where a wavy bridge leads across to the ultramodern shopping and entertainment complexes **Moll d'Espanya** and **Maremàgnum** (see p. 398). Beyond the Ciutat Vella is **l'Eixample,** the gridded neighborhood created during the expansion of the 1860s, which runs from Pl. Catalunya toward the mountains. **Gran Vía de les Corts Catalanes** defines its lower edge and **Passeig de Gràcia,** l'Eixample's main street, bisects the neighborhood. **Avinguda Diagonal** marks the border between l'Eixample and the **Zona Alta** ("Uptown"), which includes **Pedralbes, Gràcia,** and other older neighborhoods in the foothills. The peak of **Tibidabo,** the northwest border of the city, offers the most comprehensive view of the city.

LOCAL TRANSPORT

MAPS

El Corte Inglés has a good free map, distributed in their stores (see p. 374) and at mobile and stationary info centers. The Barcelona **tourist office** (Pl. Catalunya or Pl. Sant Jaume) also has maps with a good enlarged inset of the Barri Gòtic. The *Guia d'Autobuses Urbans de Barcelona,* free at tourist offices and Metro stations, maps out the city's bus routes and five Metro lines; the *Guia Facil del Bus per Mour't per Barcelona,* also free, describes the routes in more detail.

METRO AND BUS

Barcelona's public transportation (info ☎010) is quick and cheap. If you plan to use public transportation extensively, there are several *abonos* (passes) available, all of which work interchangeably for the Metro, bus, urban lines of the FGC commuter trains, and the Nitbus. The **T-1 pass** (€5.60) is valid for 10 rides and saves you nearly 50% off the cost of single tickets. The **T-Día pass** (€4.20) is good for a full day of unlimited travel, the **3 Dies** (€10.80) gets you three days of unlimited travel, and the **5 Dies** (€16.50) is good for five days. These three save you money if you use the Metro more than three times per day.

Metro: (☎934 86 07 52; www.tmb.net). Vending machines and ticket windows sell passes. Red diamonds with the letter "M" inside mark stations. Hold on to your ticket until you leave the Metro–riding without one carries a fine of €40. Trains run M-Th 5am-midnight, F-Sa 5am-2am, Su and holidays 6am-midnight. €1 per *sencillo* (single ride).

Ferrocarrils de la Generalitat de Catalunya (FGC): (☎932 05 15 15; www.fgc.es). Commuter trains with main stations at Pl. Catalunya and Pl. Espanya. Blue symbols resembling 2 interlocking *V*s mark connections with the Metro. The commuter line charges the same as the Metro (€1) until Tibidabo. After that, rates go up by zone: zone 2 destinations €1.50, zone 3 destinations €2.10. Metro passes are valid on FGC trains. Information office at the Pl. de Catalunya station open M-F 7am-9pm.

Buses: Go just about anywhere, usually from 5am-10pm. €1.

Nitbus: (☎901 511 151). 16 different lines run every 20-30min. 10:30pm-4:30am, depending on the line; a few run until 5:30am. All buses depart from the Pl. Catalunya; a Metro pass is valid on the Nitbus. The buses stop in front of most of the club complexes and work their way through the Ciutat Vella and the Zona Alta. Maps are available at *estancos* (tobacco shops) and marked by signs in Metro stations.

Bus Turístic: The Bus Turístic stops at 27 sites along 2 routes (red for the north-bound buses, blue for south-bound); a ticket comes with an info guide in 6 languages. A full ride on both routes takes about 3½hr., but you can get on and off as often as you wish. The easiest place to hop on the Bus Turístic is Pl. Catalunya, in front of El Corte Inglés (see p. 374). Many sights are closed on Mondays. Purchase tickets on the bus, at the Pl. Catalunya tourist office, or at Estació Barcelona-Sants. Runs daily every 10-30min. 9am-9:30pm; 1-day pass €14, children aged 4-12 €8, 2-day pass €18.

TAXIS

On weekend nights, you may wait up to 30min. in some locations; long lines form at popular club spots like the Port Olímpic. A *lliure* or *libre* sign or a lit green light on the roof means vacant; yellow means occupied. To call a cab, try **RadioTaxi** (☎932 25 00 00), or **Servi Taxi** (☎933 30 03 00). Disabled travelers should call ☎934 20 80 88.

CAR RENTAL

Avis/Auto Europe, Casanova, 209 (☎932 09 95 33).

Budget, Av. Josep Tarradellas, 35 (☎934 10 25 08). 25+. **Branch** in El Prat de Llobregat airport (see p. 365).

Docar, C. Montnegre, 18 (24hr. ☎934 39 81 19). M: Les Corts. Open M-F 8:30am-2pm and 3:30-8pm, Sa 9am-2pm.

Hertz, C. Tuset, 10 (☎932 17 80 76; www.hertz.es). M: Diagonal or FCG: Gràcia. Open M-F 9am-2pm and 4-7pm, Sa 9am-2pm. **Branch** office at airport (☎932 98 36 37).

Tot Car, C. Berlín, 97 (☎934 30 01 98). Open M-F 8am-2pm and 3-8pm, Sa 9am-1pm.

MOPED RENTAL

Everyone who's anyone in Barcelona has a moped; it's probably the most popular method of transport. Be wary of speeding suits and grannies on *motos*.

Vanguard Rent a Car, C. Viladomat, 297 (☎934 39 38 80). Min. age 19. Mopeds start at €36.95 per day. More expensive 2-person *motos* also available. Includes insurance and helmet. Open M-F 8am-1:30pm and 4-7:30pm, Sa-Su 9am-1pm.

PRACTICAL INFORMATION

TOURIST AND FINANCIAL SERVICES

Tourist Offices: Informació Turística Plaça Catalunya, Pl. Catalunya, 17S (☎907 30 12 82), below the coner of Pl. Catalunya. M: Catalunya. Open daily 9am-9pm. **Informació Turística Plaça Sant Jaume,** Pl. Sant Jaume, 1, off of C. Ciutat. M: Jaume I. Open M-Sa 10am-8pm, Su 10am-2pm. **Oficina de Turisme de Catalunya,** Pg. de Gràcia, 107 (☎932 38 40 00; fax 932 92 12 70; www.gencat.es/probert). M: Diagonal. Open M-Sa 10am-7pm, Su 10am-2pm. **Estació Barcelona-Sants,** Pl. Països Catalans. M: Sants-Estació. Station open M-F 4:30am-midnight, Sa-Su 5am-midnight. **Aeroport El Prat de Llobregat** (☎934 78 05 65), international terminal. Open daily 9am-9pm. **Tourist Office Representatives** dot the city in the summer. Open July-Sept. 10am-8pm.

Tours: In addition to the Bus Turístic (see **Metro and Bus,** p. 372), the Pl. Catalunya tourist office offers walking tours of the Barri Gòtic Sa-Su 10am in English and noon in Catalan and Spanish. Tour group size is limited; buy tickets in advance. Call ☎906 301 282 for info. €6.60, children aged 4-12 €3.

Budget Travel: usit UNLIMITED, Ronda Universitat, 16 (☎934 12 01 04; fax 934 12 39 84; www.unlimted.es). Open M-F 10am-8:30pm and Sa 10am-1:30pm. **Centre d'Informació Assesorament per a Joves,** C. Ferrán, 32 (☎934 02 78 00; www.bcn.es/ciaj). M: Liceu. 1 block off Las Ramblas. No tickets for sale, but offers free advice and youth opportunities. Library of travel guides. Open M-F 10am-2pm and 4-8pm.

Currency Exchange: As always, **ATMs** give the best rates (with no commission). The next best rates are available at banks. General banking hours M-F 8:30am-2pm.

American Express, Pg. de Gràcia, 101 (☎933 01 11 66). M: Diagonal. Open M-F 9:30am-6pm, Sa 10am-noon. Also at Las Ramblas, 74 (☎933 01 11 66). Open daily 9am-8pm.

LOCAL SERVICES

Luggage Storage: Estació Barcelona-Sants. M: Sants-Estació. Large lockers €4.50 per 24hr. Open daily 5:30am-11pm. **Estació França.** M: Barceloneta. Open 7am-10pm.

El Corte Inglés: Pl. Catalunya, 14 (☎933 06 38 00). M: Catalunya. Behemoth department store. **Free map** of Barcelona at the information desk. Also has English books, salon, cafeteria, supermarket, and the *oportunidades* discount department. Open M-Sa and first Su of every month 10am-10pm. Branches: Portal de l'Angel, 19-20 (M: Catalunya); Av. Diagonal, 471-473 (M: Hospital Clinic); Av. Diagonal, 617 (M: Maria Cristina).

English Bookstores: Llibreria del Raval, C. Elisabets, 6 (☎933 17 02 93). M: Catalunya, in **El Raval,** off Las Ramblas. Books in Catalan, Spanish, English, and French. Catalan/Spanish and Catalan/English dictionaries (€6.60). Open M-F 10am-8:30pm, Sa 10am-2:30pm and 5-8pm. **LAIE,** Av. Pau Claris, 85 (☎933 18 17 39). M: Urquinaona. Small English book section with travel guides and a cafe. Bookstore open M-F 10am-9pm, Sa 10:30am-9pm. Cafe open M-F 9am-1am, Sa 10am-1am.

Libraries: Biblioteca Sant Pau, C. de l'Hospital, 56 (☎933 02 07 97). M: Liceu. Take C. de l'Hospital off Las Ramblas and walk down to a castle on your right. Walk to the far end of the courtyard; the library is on the left. Do not confuse it with the Catalan library you'll see first, which requires permission to enter. Open M, W, F 3:30-8:30pm; Tu, Th, Sa 10am-2pm and 3:30-8:30pm. **Institut d'Estudis Norteamericans,** Vía Augusta, 123 (☎932 40 51 10). Open Sept.-July M-F 9am-2pm and 4-7pm.

Religious Services: Comunidad Israelita de Barcelona (Jewish services), C. Avenir, 29 (☎932 00 61 48). **Comunidad Musulmana** (Muslim services), Mosque Toarek Ben Ziad, C. Hospital, 91 (☎934 41 91 49). Services daily at prayer times. **Església Catedral de la Santa Creu** (Catholic services), in Pl. Seu, up C. Bisbe from Pl. St. Jaume. M: Jaume I. Cloister open 9am-1:15pm and 4-7pm.

Gay and Lesbian Services: Antinous, C. J. Anselm Clavé, 6 (☎933 01 90 70; www.antinouslibros.com). M: Drassanes. On the right as you walk down C. Clavé from Las Ramblas. A large bookstore and cafe specializing in gay and lesbian books, including several guide books. Decent selection of books in English. Open M-F 11am-2pm and 5-9pm, Sa noon-2pm and 5-9pm. **Cómplices,** C. Cervantes, 2 (☎934 12 72 83). M: Liceu. From C. Ferran, take a left onto C. Avinyó and then the 2nd left. A bookstore with publications in English and Spanish and a decent selection of gay films. Also provides an **informative map** of Barcelona's gay bars and discos. Open M-F 10:30am-8:30pm, Sa noon-8:30pm.

Laundromats: Tintorería Ferrán, C. Ferrán, 11. M: Liceu. Open M-F 9am-8pm. **Tintorería San Pablo,** C. San Pau 105 (☎933 29 42 49). M: Paral.lel. Wash, dry, and fold €10; do-it-yourself €7.25. Open July-Sept. M-F 9am-2pm; Oct.-June M-F 9am-2pm and 4-8pm.

EMERGENCY AND COMMUNICATIONS

Emergency: ☎112. **Local Police:** ☎092. **National police:** ☎091. **Medical:** ☎061.

Police: Las Ramblas, 43 (☎933 44 13 00), across from Pl. Reial and next to C. Nou de La Rambla. M: Liceu. The department labeled "Tourist attention" is staffed by multilingual officers. Open 24hr., tourist assistance open 8am-2am. Other offices beneath the Pl. Catalunya on the Banco Nacional side, and at Barcelona-Nord bus station.

Crisis Lines: Oficina Permanente de Atención Social (24hr. toll-free ☎900 70 30 30).

24hr. Pharmacy: Check pharmacy windows for current listing of on-call pharmacies.

Hospitals: Hospital Clinic, Villarroel, 170 (☎932 27 54 00). M: Hospital Clinic. Main entrance at the intersection of C. Roselló and C. Casanova. **Hospital de la Santa Creu i Sant Pau** (☎932 91 90 00, emergency 932 91 91 91), at the intersection of C. Cartagena and C. Sant Antoni Moria Claret. M: Hospital de Sant Pau. **Hospital Vall d' Hebron** (☎932 74 60 00). M: Vall d'Hebron.

Internet Access:

Easy Everything, Las Ramblas, 31 (www.easyeverything.com). M: Liceu. €1.20 for about 40min. Price fluctuates according to the number of computers in use. Open 24hr. Also at Ronda Universitat, 35, right next to Pl. Catalunya.

bcnet (Internet Gallery Café), Barra de Ferro, 3 (☎932 68 15 07), down the street from the Picasso museum. M: Jaume I. €1.50 per 15min., €3.61 per hr.; 10hr. ticket available for €18. Open daily 10am-1am.

CiberOpción, Gran Vía, 602 (☎934 12 73 08), across from the Universitat building. M: Universitat. €0.60 per 30min. Open M-Sa 9am-1am, Su 11am-1am.

Cybermundo Internet Centre, Bergara, 3, and Balmes, 8 (☎933 17 71 42). M: Catalunya. Just off of Pl. Catalunya, behind the Triangle shopping mall. Allows uploading of disks. €1 per hr. Open M-F 9am-1am, Sa 10am-1am.

Internet Exchange, Las Ramblas, 130 (☎933 17 73 27). M: Catalunya. €0.06 per min., €12 for 5hr., €27 for 20hr.; students €15 for 10hr., €30 for 30hr.

Locutorio, Gran Vía, 820 (☎932 46 36 07), near the Monumental bullring, en route to Pl. Glòries, in l'Eixample. M: Monumental. Internet 3-11pm €2 per hr.; noon-3pm €1 per hr. Black-and-white printing €0.60 per page. Color printing €1 per page. Open daily noon-11pm. Cash only.

Telephones: Get phone cards at tobacco stores, tourist offices, and newsstands. **Private phone service** (☎/fax 934 90 76 50), at Estació Barcelona-Sants. M: Sants-Estació. Open M-Sa 8am-9:45pm. **Directory Assistance:** ☎1003 for numbers within Spain, 1008 for numbers within Europe, 1005 for numbers outside Europe.

Post Office: Pl. de Antoni López (☎902 19 71 97). M: Jaume I or Barceloneta. Fax and **lista de correos.** Open M-F 8:30am-9:30pm. **Postal Code:** 08003.

ACCOMMODATIONS

The area between Pl. Catalunya and the water—the **Barri Gòtic, El Raval,** and **La Ribera**—offers budget beds, but except for a few places that subsist on walk-ins, reservations are a must. Last-minute travelers can crash in **Gràcia** or **l'Eixample,** outer boroughs that typically have more vacancies.

LAS RAMBLAS

Las Ramblas is the heart of the city. Because of the prime location, you'll likely end up paying more for lower quality rooms than in other areas of the city.

Hostal Benidorm, Las Ramblas, 37 (☎933 02 20 54; www.barcelona-on-line.es/benidorm). M: Drassanes. A great value. Very clean rooms with phones, full baths, and balconies overlooking Las Ramblas. Singles €25-29; doubles €33-45; triples €50-60; quads €65-70; quints €75. ❸

Mare Nostrum, Las Ramblas, 67 (☎933 18 53 40; fax 934 12 30 69). M: Liceu. The swankiest hostel on the strip. All rooms have A/C and satellite TV. Breakfast included. High season doubles €57, with bath €67; triples €87; quads €107. ❹

Hotel Toledano/Hostal Residencia Capitol, Las Ramblas, 138 (☎933 01 08 72; www.hoteltoledano.com), off Pl. Catalunya. M: Catalunya. Rooms with cable TV and phones; some have balconies. Hotel rooms have full bath, hostel rooms don't. English-speaking owner. Wheelchair accessible. 4th-floor Hotel Toledano: singles €26, with bath €29; doubles with bath €50; triples with bath €63; quads with bath €71; small room for a couple with bath €40. 5th-floor Hostal Residencia Capitol: singles €22; doubles €34, with shower €39; triples €44/€49; quads €51/€56. AmEx/MC/V. ❷

Hostal Parisien, Las Ramblas, 114 (☎933 01 62 83). M: Liceu. 13 well-kept rooms with heat keep young guests happy. Balconies provide front-row seats to the street's daily pedestrian spectacle. Friendly multi-lingual owner. TV lounge. Quiet hours after midnight. Singles €30; doubles with bath €38; triples with bath €48. ❸

Hotel Internacional, Las Ramblas, 78-80 (☎933 02 25 66). M: Liceu. 60 standard rooms, all with private bath, safe, and telephone. Full breakfast included. High season singles €56; doubles €97; triples €127; quads €154; quints €184. ❺

LOWER BARRI GÒTIC

The following hostels are in the lower part of the Barri Gòtic, between C. Ferran and the water. Backpackers flock here to be close to hip Las Ramblas.

Hostal Levante, Baixada de San Miguel, 2 (☎933 17 95 65; www.hostallevante.com). M: Liceu. Walk down C. Ferran, turn right onto C. Avinyó, and take the 1st left onto Baixada de San Miguel (you'll see the sign from C. Avinyó). The best deal in lower Barri Gòtic. Singles €27; doubles €46, with bath €52. MC/V. ❸

Hostal Fernando, C. Ferran, 31 (☎/fax 933 01 79 93; www.barcelona-on-line.es/fernando). M: Liceu. On the left on C. Ferran coming from Las Ramblas. Fills almost entirely from walk-ins. Dorms with lockers. TV/dining room. High season dorms €17, with bath €18; doubles €40, with bath €54; triples with bath €60. MC/V. ❷

Casa de Huéspedes Mari-Luz, C. Palau, 4 (☎/fax 933 17 34 63). M: Liceu. From Las Ramblas, follow C. Ferran, go right on C. Avinyó, left on C. Cervantes, and then right on tiny C. Palau. Tidy dorm rooms for 4-6 people and a few comfortable doubles. Reservations require a credit card number. In summer dorms €16, doubles €37. MC/V. ❷

Hostal Avinyó, C. Avinyó, 42 (☎933 18 79 45; www.hostalavinyo.com). M: Drassanes. 28 rooms with couches, high ceilings, fans, in-room safes, and stained-glass windows. Singles €16; doubles €28, with bath €40; triples €42, with bath €60. Cash only. ❶

Albergue Juvenil Palau (HI), C. Palau, 6 (☎934 12 50 80). M: Liceu. A tranquil refuge in the Barri Gòtic. Kitchen (open 7-10pm), dining room, and 45 clean dorm rooms with lockers (3-8 people each). Breakfast included. Showers 8am-noon and 4-10pm. Linen €1.50. Reception 7am-3am. Curfew 3am. No reservations. Dorms €13. Cash only. ❶

Albergue de Juventud Kabul, Pl. Reial, 17 (☎933 18 51 90; www.kabul-hostel.com). M: Liceu. Head to the port on Las Ramblas, pass C. Ferrán, and turn left onto C. Colon Pl. Reial; Kabul is on the near right corner of the *plaça.* Legendary among European backpackers; the cramped co-ed dormitory rooms can pack in up to 200 frat boys at a time. The common area includes a satellite TV, restaurant/snack bar, free email for residents, a pool table, blaring pop music, and even beer and french-fry vending machines. Key deposit €10. Laundry €2.50. No reservations. Dorms €20. Cash only. ❷

UPPER BARRI GÒTIC

This section of the Barri Gòtic is between C. Fontanella and C. Ferran. **Portal de l'Angel,** a pedestrian avenue, runs through the middle. Rooms are pricier than in the lower Barri Gòtic but more serene. Early reservations are essential in summer.

Hostal Plaza, C. Fontanella, 18 (☎/fax 933 01 01 39; www.plazahostal.com). Super-friendly Texan owners, brightly painted rooms, and great location make this place unbeatable. The common room boasts black leather couches, a drink/coffee/breakfast bar, a kitchen, TV, phone, and Internet access with videophone. Laundry €9. 24hr. reception, but 10am-10pm preferred. Singles €52, with bath €65; doubles €58, with bath €67; triples €68, with bath €86. 12% discount Nov. and Feb. AmEx/MC/V. ❺

Hostal Campi, C. Canuda, 4 (☎/fax 933 01 35 45). From M: Catalunya, take the 1st left off Las Ramblas (bearing right at the fork). A great bargain for the quality and location. Reservations accepted 9am-8pm. Prices vary by season and availability, but generally doubles €40, with bath €48; triples €60. ❸

Hostal-Residencia Rembrandt, C. Portaferrissa, 23 (☎/fax 933 18 10 11). M: Liceu. Take the 2nd left off of Las Ramblas coming from Pl. Catalunya; the hostel is on the left. New owner is currently undertaking renovations to spruce up the already nice hostel. Ask for a room with a balcony. Fans €2 per night. Singles €25; doubles €42, with bath €50; triples €52, with bath €60. Cash only. ❷

Pensión Dalí, C. Boquería, 12 (☎933 18 55 90; fax 933 18 55 80). M: Liceu. C. Boquería intersects with Las Ramblas at the Metro. Designed as a religious house by Domènech i Montaner, Pensión Dalí retains the stained glass and gaudy iron doors of its early years. In the high season doubles €44.80, with bath €50.80; triples with bath €68.40; quads with bath €82.40. AmEx/MC/V. ❸

Hostal-Residencia Lausanne, Av. Portal de l'Angel, 24 (☎933 02 11 39). M: Catalunya. Main entrance framed by 2 Zara display windows; walk left past the grand staircase in front to the smaller stairs in back by the elevator. A single-hallway hostel with basic rooms and a posh living room overlooking one of Barcelona's most popular shopping streets. Doubles €45, with bath €55. Cash only. ❸

Hostal Fontanella, Vía Laietana, 71 (☎/fax 933 17 59 43). M: Urquinaona. Tastefully decorated and clean, with a floral waiting room, wood furniture, and fans in the 11 rooms. Safe available, as well as information on planning excursions. Singles €26, with bath €31; doubles €41, with shower €47, with bath €55; triples €57.40, with shower €65.80, with bath €65.80; quads €71.75, with shower €82.25. AmEx/MC/V. ❸

Hostal Malda, C. Pi, 5 (☎933 17 30 02). M: Liceu. Go down C. Casañas from Las Ramblas, walk through Pl. del Pi, and make a left on C. Pi; the stairwell up to the hostel is inside a shopping center. Malda offers 15 rooms of the same quality as elsewhere at half the price. Doubles with shower €24-26; triples with shower €36. Cash only. ❷

Hostal Layetana, Pl. Ramón Berenguer el Gran, 2 (☎/fax 933 19 20 12). M: Jaume I. A short walk from the Metro going up Vía Laietana toward the mountains. Look for the multinational flags on the 3rd-floor balcony in the *plaça.* A sophisticated, peaceful hostel. High season singles €22.60; doubles €37.80, with bath €48.70. MC/V. ❷

Hostal Palermo, C. Boquería, 21 (☎/fax 933 02 40 02). M: Liceu. Watch your head on the way up the stairs. Party-conducive rooms with green plaid bedspreads. Small TV room. Laundry €2.50, safe €1.50 per day. Reservations require a credit card number. Singles €39, with bath €47; triples with bath €93; quads with bath €120. MC/V. ❹

Pensión Aris, C. Fontanella, 14 (☎933 18 10 17). About 100m from Pl. Catalunya. 13 huge, clean, sparse rooms with fans. Basic hostel with prices that are unbeatable for the location. Laundry €9. Singles €18; doubles €36, with bath €45. Cash only. ❷

LA RIBERA

Hostal de Ribagorza, C. Trafalgar, 39 (☎933 19 19 68). M: Urquinaona. With your back to Pl. Urquinaona, walk down Ronda Sant Pere and turn right on C. Méndez Núñez. *Hostal* is 1 block down on the corner. 12 rooms in an ornate Modernista building complete with marble staircase and tile floors. Rooms have TVs and fans. Doubles only. Oct.-Feb. €26.50, with bath €38.50; Mar.-Sept. €35.50/€47.50. ❷

Hostal Orleans, Av. Marqués de l'Argentera, 13 (☎933 19 73 82). From M: Barceloneta, follow Pg. Joan de Borbó and turn right on Av. Marqués de l'Argentera. Spotless, newly renovated hostel with comfortable common area. Singles with TV €31, with bath €39.50; doubles €53, with A/C €54; triples €60-67; quads €80. ❸

Pensión Ciutadella, C. Comerç, 33 (☎933 19 62 03). M: Barceloneta. 6 spacious rooms, each with fan, TV, and balcony. Family feel. Doubles only. Oct.-May €37, with bath €42; June-Sept. €39/€48. Each additional person (up to 4) €9. Cash only. ❷

Hostal Nuevo Colón, Av. Marqués de l'Argentera, 19 (☎933 19 50 77). M: Barceloneta. Follow Pg. Joan de Borbó and turn right on Av. Marqués de l'Argentera. Newly renovated hostel with very clean, modern rooms and a large common area with TV and balcony. Singles €27; doubles €36, with bath €48. 6-person apartments with kitchens €110. ❸

Pensión Lourdes, C. Princesa, 14 (☎933 19 33 72). M: Jaume I. Cross Vía Laietana and follow C. Princesa. Popular backpacker destination. 32 no-frills rooms with phones. Common area with TV. Singles €23; doubles €33, with bath €42. Cash only. ❷

EL RAVAL

Be careful in the areas nearer to the port and farther from Las Ramblas.

Pensión L'Isard, C. Tallers, 82 (☎933 02 51 83; fax 933 02 01 17). M: Universitat. Take the C. Pelai Metro exit, turn left at the end of the block, and then left again at the pharmacy. A simple, elegant, and unbelievably clean find. Ask for a room with a balcony. Singles €19; doubles €33, with bath €42; triples €48. ❷

BARCELONA

Hostal Opera, C. Sant Pau, 20 (☎933 18 82 01). M: Liceu. Off Las Ramblas. Recently renovated, making its sunny rooms feel like new. All rooms come with bath, telephone, and A/C. Handicapped accessible. Singles €31; doubles €50. MC/V. ❸

Pensión 45, C. Tallers, 45 (☎933 02 70 61). M: Catalunya. From Pl. Catalunya, take the 1st right off Las Ramblas onto C. Tallers. Old paintings and photographs don the walls of its 25 charming rooms. Singles €20; doubles €33, with bath €40. Cash only. ❷

Hotel Peninsular, C. Sant Pau, 34 (☎933 02 31 38). M: Liceu. Off Las Ramblas. This venerable building, now one of the 50 sights on the Ruta del Modernisme (see **Sights,** p. 383), served as the monastery for the Augustine order of priests in the mid-1800s. A fabulous inner patio with a bright skylight and numerous hanging plants. The 80 rooms all come with telephones and A/C, and most have baths. Breakfast included. Singles €25, with bath €45; doubles €45, with bath €65; triples with bath €80. MC/V. ❸

L'EIXAMPLE

Pensión Fani, València, 278 (☎932 15 36 45). M: Catalunya. Just off Pg. de Gràcia on the left (facing Pl. Catalunya). This long-term *pensión* oozes with quirky charm. Rooms are rented by the month but can be used for a single night if available. 3 shared baths, full kitchen, dining room/TV room, laundry. Singles €276 per month; doubles €490; triples €760. 1-night stay €20 per person. Payment due 1st of each month. Cash only. ❶

Hostal Ciudad Condal, C. Mallorca, 255 (☎932 15 10 40). M: Diagonal. Just off Pg. de Gràcia, 2 blocks from La Pedrera. Prices reflect the generous amenities and prime location. All 11 rooms have full bath, heat, TVs, and phones; A/C soon to come. 24hr. reception with beer and soda. Must reserve with a credit card. Wheelchair accessible. Singles €65; doubles €90. Prices often drop in winter. MC/V. ❺

Hostal Residencia Oliva, Pg. de Gràcia, 32 (☎934 88 01 62). M: Pg. de Gràcia. At the intersection with C. Diputació. Elegant bureaus, mirrors, and a light marble floor give this hostel a classy ambiance. All 16 rooms have color TVs, and some overlook the Manzana de la Discòrdia. Reservations a must. Laundry €12. Singles €24; doubles €45, with bath €52; triple with bath €72. Cash only. ❷

Hostal Eden, C. Balmes, 55 (☎934 52 66 20; www.eden.iberica.com). M: Pg. de Gràcia. From the Metro, walk down C. Aragó past Rambla de Catalunya to C. Balmes and turn left. Modern, well-kept rooms have TVs, lockboxes, and fans; most also have big, new bathrooms. Free Internet available in the lounge. May-Oct. singles €29, with bath €39; doubles €39, with bath €55. Nov.-Apr. €23/€32/€29/€45. AmEx/MC/V. ❸

Hostal Hill, C. Provença, 323 (☎934 57 88 14), between C. Girona and C. Bailen. M: Verdaguer. Funky furniture and fans in the rooms. Guests get keys. Reservations with a credit card number. Singles €25, with bath €32.50; doubles €41, with bath €49. V. ❷

Hostal Qué Tal, C. Mallorca, 290 (☎/fax 934 59 23 66; www.hotelsinbarcelona.net/hostalquetal), near C. Bruc. M: Pg. de Gràcia or Verdaguer. High-quality gay- and lesbian-friendly hostel. 14 carefully decorated rooms have their own distinctive colors and personality. Morning coffee included. Singles €35; doubles €55, with bath €66. Cash only. ❸

Hostal Residencia Windsor, Rambla de Catalunya, 84 (☎932 15 11 98). M: Pg. de Gràcia. On the corner with C. Mallorca. With carpeted hallways, gilded mirrors, and a plush TV room, this hostel lives up to its royal name. Rooms come equipped with comfy sleep sofas and heat in winter (no A/C). Singles €31, with bath €37; doubles €47, with sink and shower €51, with bath €55; extra beds €10 each. Cash only. ❸

GRÀCIA

Gràcia is Barcelona's "undiscovered" quarter, but natives have definitely discovered its lively nightlife. Last-minute arrivals may find vacancies here.

Hostal Lesseps, C. Gran de Gràcia, 239 (☎932 18 44 34). M: Lesseps. Spacious, classy rooms sport red velvet wallpaper. All 16 rooms have a TV and bath, 4 have A/C (€5.60 extra per day). Singles €34; doubles €52; triples €70; quads €90. MC/V. ❸

Pensión San Medín, C. Gran de Gràcia, 125 (☎932 17 30 68; fax 934 15 44 10; www.sanmedin.com). M: Fontana. Family-run *pensión*. Common room with TV. Owner speaks English. Singles €30, with bath €39; doubles €48, with bath €60. MC/V. ❸

Hostal Bonavista, C. Bonavista, 21 (☎932 37 37 57). M: Diagonal. Head toward the fountain at the end of Pg. de Gràcia and take the 1st right; the hostel is just off the traffic circle. 9 well-kept rooms with sinks. TV lounge. Showers €1.50. No reservations. Singles €18; doubles €25, with bath €34. Cash only. ❷

THE INSIDER'S CITY

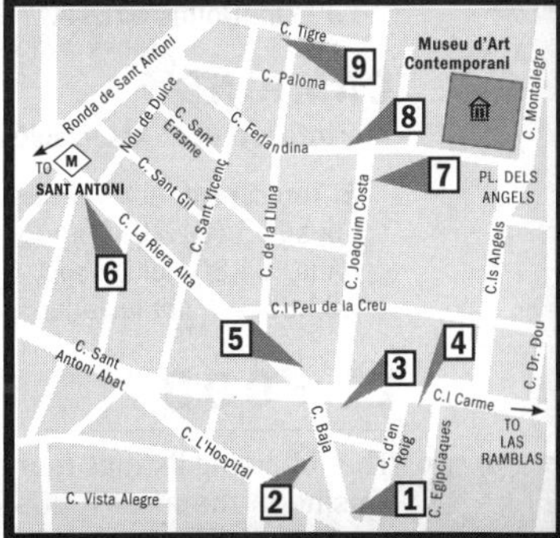

REVELS IN RAVAL

In the northwestern corner of El Raval lies a quiet but eclectic neighborhood filled with quirky shops, old-style bars, and great restaurants. From M: Sant Antoni walk down C. Riera Alta; from Las Ramblas, walk down C. Carme

1. Gear up for battle with the fashion police at **G.I. Joe Surplus** (☎933 29 96 52).
2. Think the New Kids on the Block are washed up? Think again at **Discos Edison** (☎934 41 96 74).
3. Indulge in South Asian spice at **Shalimar** (☎933 29 34 96).
4. Ponder the good life over a drink at **Muy Buenas** (☎934 42 50 53).
5. Relax, lounge, and snuggle in huge colorful sofas at **Muebles Navarro.**
6. Take someone special out for an unforgettable dining experience at **Colibri** (☎934 43 23 06).
7. Satiate any hunger without denting your wallet at **Restaurant Riera** (☎934 42 32 93).
8. Down *absenta* and watch everything around you dissolve into the 19th century at **Casa Almirall.**
9. Hit the dance floor running at **La Paloma.**

Albergue Mare de Déu de Montserrat (HI), Pg. Mare de Déu del Coll, 41-51 (☎932 10 51 51; www.tujuca.com), beyond Park Güell. Bus #28 from Pl. de Catalunya and Nitbus N4 stop across the street from the hostel. This 180-bed government-sponsored hostel is gorgeous. Restaurant, Internet access, and multiple common spaces. HI members only. Breakfast included. Sheets €2.10. Flexible 3-day max. stay. Reception 8am-3pm and 4:30-11:30pm. Lockout 10am-1:30pm. Midnight curfew, but doors open every 30min. Dorms €15, over 25 €19.23; prices drop €5 in the winter. AmEx/MC/V. ❶

CAMPING

For info, contact **Associació de Càmpings de Barcelona,** Gran Vía, 608 (☎934 12 59 55).

El Toro Bravo, Autovía Castelldefells, km11 (☎936 37 34 62; fax 936 37 21 15). Take bus L95 (€1.20) from Pl. Catalunya. Reception 8am-7pm. Electricity €3.65. June 15-Aug. €4.80 per person, €5.10 per site, €4.80 per car. Sept.-June 14 €4.55/€4.85/€4.55. IVA not included. AmEx/MC/V.

FOOD

The following listings represent a variety of regional, vegetarian, and international cuisine in the most touristed areas. As always, the *Guía del Ocio* (available at newsstands) is an invaluable source of additional suggestions. The following is a breakdown of what's hot in neighborhoods without listings: Barceloneta, Port Vell, and Port Olímpic are great places to head for seafood; Las Ramblas has plenty of good and visible, albeit touristy and expensive options. The restaurants on C. Aragó by Pg. de Gràcia, have delicious lunchtime *menús*, and the Pg. de Gràcia has beautiful outdoor dining. Gràcia's Pl. Sol and La Ribera's Santa Maria del Mar are the best places to head for *tapas* (if you don't mind standing), while the other northern areas like Sarrià and Horta have authentic Catalan cuisine.

BASICS

If you want to live cheap and do as *barceloneses* do, buy your food fresh at a *mercat* (marketplace), and hit up a grocery store for other essentials.

Markets: La Boquería (Mercat de Sant Josep), off Las Ramblas. M:Liceu. Wholesale prices for fruit, cheese, and wine. **Mercat de la Concepi,** on C. València between C. Bruc and C. Girona. M: Girona. Smaller version of La Boquería.

Supermarkets: Champión, Las Ramblas, 113. M: Liceu. Open M-Sa 9am-9pm. **El Corte Inglés,** Pl. Catalunya, 14. M: Catalunya. Supermarket in basement. Open M-Sa and 1st Su of month 10am-10pm.

LOWER BARRI GÒTIC

Restaurants are scattered on C. Escudellers and C. Clave. Lively hangouts surround Santa Maria del Pi.

Les Quinze Nits, Pl. Reial, 6 (☎933 17 30 75). M: Liceu. A very popular restaurant in Barcelona, with quick-moving lines at night. Delicious Catalan entrees at great prices (€3-7). No reservations. Open daily 1-3:45pm and 8:30-11:30pm. MC/V. ❶

Irati, C. Cardenal Casañas, 17 (☎933 02 30 84). M: Liceu. An excellent Basque restaurant that attracts droves of hungry *tapas*-seekers. Bartenders pour Basque *sidra* behind their backs. Starters €9. Entrees €15-18. Open daily noon-1am. AmEx/MC/V. ❹

Los Caracoles, C. Escudellers, 14 (☎933 01 20 41). M: Drassanes. What started as a snail shop in 1835 is now a full Catalan restaurant. Dishes taste as good as they look; specialties include, of course, the *caracoles* (snails; €7.21), half of a rabbit (€10.22), and chicken (€9.02). Expect a wait. Open daily 1pm-midnight. AmEx/MC/V. ❸

Mi Burrito y Yo, Paso de la Enseñanza, 2 (☎933 18 27 42). M: Jaume I. To the left off C. Ferran after Pl. St. Jaume. Lively restaurant/*bodega*. Nightly live music at 9:30pm. Starters €8. Entrees €10-20. Open daily 1-4pm and 6:30-11:30pm. AmEx/MC/V. ❹

L'Antic Bocoi del Gòtic, Baixada de Viladecols, 3 (☎933 10 50 67). M: Jaume I. From C. Jaume I coming from Pl. del Angel, take a left onto C. Dagueria, and follow it to the end (through 3 name changes). Formed in part by a 1st-century Roman wall. Salads, pâtés, and sausages around €6. Open M-Sa 8:30pm-midnight. AmEx/MC/V. ❷

UPPER BARRI GÒTIC

Els Quatre Gats, C. Montsió, 3 (☎933 02 41 40). M: Catalunya. Take the 2nd left off Av. Portal de l'Angel. Picasso's old Modernista hangout; he designed a personalized menu (on display at Museu Picasso; see p. 392). Reproductions of his works adorn the walls. Food is expensive (entrees €12-15); *tapas* are the way to go (€2-4). Live piano and violin 9pm-1am. Open M-Sa 9am-2am, Su 5pm-2am. Closed Aug. AmEx/MC/V. ❸

Betawi, C. Montsió, 6 (☎934 12 62 64). M: Catalunya. Take the 2nd left off Portal de l'Angel coming from the Metro. A peaceful Indonesian restaurant; the food verges on gourmet. *Menú* €7.81. Open M 1-4pm, Tu-Sa 1-4pm and 8-11pm. AmEx/MC/V. ❷

Govinda, Pl. Vila de Madrid, 4 (☎933 18 77 29). M: Catalunya. Just off Las Ramblas on C. Canuda. Vegetarian Indian food served a few feet from a row of 2000-year-old Roman tombs. Salad bar €4-6. M-F *menú* €8. Entrees around €7. Open daily 1-4pm, for dinner Tu-Th 8-11pm and F-Sa 8-11:45pm. AmEx/MC/V. ❷

Xaloc, C. de la Palla, 13-17 (☎933 01 19 90). M: Liceu. Classy delicatessen has a restaurant right next to the butcher counter. Salads (€3.40-6) and sandwiches on baguettes (€2.90-7.30). *Tapas* €0.80-6. Open daily 9am-midnight. MC/V. ❶

La Colmena, Pl. de l'Angel, 12 (☎933 15 13 56). M: Jaume I. After more than 120 years in the Pl. de l'Angel, this absolutely divine pastry and candy shop has more than earned its prime location. Most pastries €1-3. Open daily 9am-9pm. AmEx/MC/V. ❶

LA RIBERA

East of Vía Laietana, La Ribera is home to numerous bars and small restaurants. The few tourists who walk over are well rewarded. The area around Santa María del Mar and the Mercat del Born is crawling with *tapas* bars.

La Habana Vieja, Carrer dels Banys Vells, 2 (☎932 68 25 04). M: Jaume I. Cuban music sets the mood for large portions, great for sharing. Cuban rice €4-5; meat dishes €10-12. Open M 10am-4:30pm and 8:30-11pm, Tu-Su 10am-4:30pm and 8:30pm-1am. ❷

Xampanyet, C. Montcada, 22 (☎933 19 70 03). M: Jaume I. Cross Vía Laietana, walk down C. Princesa, and turn right on C. Montcada. Xampanyet is just past the Museu Picasso. The house *cava* (champagne) is served at a colorful bar. Glasses €1. Bottles €5 and up. Open Tu-Sa noon-4pm and 7-11:30pm, Su 7-11:30pm. Closed Aug. MC/V. ❶

Va de Vi, C. Banys Vells, 16 (☎933 19 29 00). From M: Jaume I, walk down C. Princesa, turn right on C. Montcada, right on C. Barra de Ferro, and left on C. Banys Vells. Romantic, medieval wine bar in a 16th-century building. Wine €1.60-4 per glass, cheeses €3-7.20, *tapas* €2.70-5.40. Open Su-W 6pm-1am, Th 6pm-2am, F-Sa 6pm-3am. ❷

Tèxtil Café, C. Montcada, 12 (☎932 68 25 98). M: Jaume I. Set in the picturesque courtyard of the Museu Tèxtil i d'Indumentària. Weekday lunch *menú* €8.75. Wine and *cava* €1.50-2.10 per glass. Sandwiches €2-5. Open Tu-Su 10am-midnight. ❶

Gades, C. L'Esparteria, 10 (☎933 10 44 55). M: Jaume I. Relax within romantic stone walls at this fondue heaven. Open M-Th 10:30pm-12:30am, F-Sa 10:30pm-1:30am. ❷

EL RAVAL

Students and blue-collar workers congregate in Catalan joints west of Las Ramblas. Restaurants are fairly inexpensive; most have simple decor, basic food, and lots of noise, although trendier places have started to move in as well.

Bar Ra, Pl. Garduña (☎933 01 41 63), behind Las Ramblas' Boqueria market. M: Liceu. A mixture of traditional Spanish and trendy California cuisine. Duck magret with mango-pumpkin sauce (€9.50). Open M-Sa 1:30-4pm, 9:30pm-2am. Dinner by reservation. ❷

Colibri, C. Riera Alta, 33-35 (☎934 43 23 06). M: Sant Antoni. From the Metro, head down C. Riera Alta; it will be on your right. Fresh ingredients and divinely flavored dishes. The pistachio vinaigrette sea bass filet (€25.09) is unbelievable. Call ahead for reservations. Open M-F 1:30-3:30pm and 8:30-11:30pm. ❺

Restaurante Can Lluís, C. Cera, 49 (☎934 41 11 87). M: Sant Antoni. From the Metro, head down Ronda S. Pau and take the 2nd left on C. Cera. Succulent baby goat ribs (€9.80), grilled squid (€8.90), and fresh-grilled asparagus (€5.40). Dinner *menú* €19.90. Entrees €8.90-18.60. Open M-Sa 1:30-4pm and 8:30-11:30pm. V. ❸

Pla dels Angels, C. Ferlandina, 23 (☎934 43 31 03). The funky decor of this colorful, inexpensive eatery is fitting for its proximity to Barcelona's contemporary art museum. Entrees around €6. Open M-Th 1-3:30pm and 9-11:30pm, F-Sa 9-11:30pm. ❷

Silenus, C. Angels, 8 (☎933 02 26 80). From M: Catalunya, a right off C. Carme. Entrees include fish, meat (€11-19) and the exotic *filete de kangoo*—yep, kangaroo (€16.20). Open M-Th 11am-11:30pm, F 11am-midnight, Sa 1pm-midnight. MC/V. ❹

L'EIXAMPLE

L'Eixample is full of places to spend a long, enjoyable dinner, but restaurants are spread out widely. Most tourists never make it past the Pg. de Gràcia, which caters to a wealthy clientele. Be prepared to pay well for the food and atmosphere.

El Racó d'en Baltá, C. Aribau, 125 (☎934 53 10 44), at the intersection with C. Rosselló. M: Hospital Clínic. Eccentric, colorful restaurant offers creative and flavorful Mediterranean-style dishes. Fish and meat entrees €9.90-15.50. Wine and *cava* €4-15.45 per bottle. Open M 9-10:45pm, Tu-Sa 1-3:45pm and 9-10:45pm. AmEx/MC/V. ❸

Comme-Bio, C. Gran Vía, 603 (☎933 01 03 76), at the intersection with Rambla de Catalunya. M: Catalunya or Universitat. Serves fresh salad, tofu, yogurt, and juice, as well as pasta and veggie pizzas (€6). Open daily 9am-11:30pm; dinner starts at 8pm. ❶

Thai Gardens, C. Diputació, 273 (☎934 87 98 98). M: Catalunya. A wooden bridge entrance, lush greenery, and colorful pillows. Weekday lunch *menú* €10.80. Pad thai €6. Entrees €9-13.50. Wheelchair accessible. Open Su-Th 1:30-4pm and 8:30pm-midnight, F-Sa 1:30-4pm and 8:30pm-1am. ❸

Laie Llibreria Café, C. Pau Claris, 85 (☎933 18 17 39; www.laie.es). M: Urquinaona. An ultra-cool lunch spot; offers a fresh buffet lunch (€8.90) in an open, bamboo-draped room with a glass ceiling. Grab a praline cappuccino (€2.30) at the bar on the way out. Vegetarian dinner *menú* €14.90. Open M-F 9am-1am, Sa 10am-1am. AmEx/MC/V. ❷

Mandalay Café, C. Provença, 330 (☎934 58 60 17). M: Verdaguer. Exotic pan-Asian cuisine served in sultanesque luxury. F-Sa night trapeze artist around 11pm; variable extra cover for show. Entrees €10-18. Open Tu-Sa 9-11pm. MC/V. ❸

Txapela (Euskal Taberna), Pg. de Gràcia, 8-10 (☎934 12 02 89). M: Catalunya. This Basque restaurant is a godsend for the *tapas*-clueless traveler who wants to learn. *Tapas* €1.05. Wheelchair accessible. Open M-Th 8am-1:30am, F-Su 10am-2am. ❷

GRÀCIA

La Buena Tierra, C. Encarnació, 56 (☎932 19 82 13). M: Joanic. Follow C. Escorial for 2 blocks, turn left on C. Encarnació. Vegetarian dishes and a backyard terrace. Entrees €4.50-7. Open Tu-F 1-4pm and 8-11pm, F 1-4pm and 8pm-midnight, Su 1-4pm. D. ❷

La Gavina, C. Ros de Olano, 17 (☎934 15 74 50), at the corner of C. St. Joaquím. Funky Italian pizzeria complete with a life-size patron saint. Pizzas €7.50-16. Open Tu-Su 2pm-1am, F-Sa 2pm-2am. Wheelchair accessible. ❸

NUT, C. Verdi, 2 (☎932 10 86 40), at Pl. Revolució Setembre de 1868. M: Fontana. Egyptian cuisine. Entrees €5-9. Open daily 12:30-5pm and 8:30pm-1am. ❷

Restaurant Illa de Gràcia, C. Sant Domenec, 19 (☎932 38 02 29). M: Diagonal. Follow Gran de Gràcia for 5 blocks and make a right onto C. Sant Domenec. Huge vegetarian menu with tons of well-balanced options. Entrees €2.55-4.11. Open Tu-F 1-4pm and 9pm-midnight, Sa-Su noon-4pm and 9pm-midnight. Closed Aug. D/MC/V. ❶

SIGHTS

Architecturally, Barcelona is defined by its unique Modernista treasures. Las Ramblas—a bustling avenue smack in the city center—and the Barri Gòtic, Barcelona's "old city," are the traditional tourist areas. But don't neglect vibrant La Ribera and El Raval, the upscale avenues of l'Eixample, the panoramic city views from Montjuïc and Tibidabo, Gaudí's Park Güell, or the harbor-side Port Olímpic.

RUTA DEL MODERNISME

For those with a few days in the city and an interest in seeing all the biggest sights, the Ruta del Modernisme is the cheapest and most flexible option. The Ruta del Modernisme isn't a tour precisely, in the sense that it doesn't offer a guide or organized transportation; it's a ticket which gives discounted entrance to Modernista sites, to be used at the owner's discretion. Passes (€3; students, over 65, and groups over 10 people €2) are good for a month and give holders a 25-30% discount on entrance to **Palau Güell** (see p. 386), **La Sagrada Família** (p. 387), **Casa Milà** (La Pedrera; p. 387), **Palau de la Música Catalana** (p. 385), **Casa-Museu Gaudí, Fundació Antoni Tàpies, Museu d'Art Modern** (p. 393), **Museu de Zoologia** (p. 112), a tour of **El Hospital de la Santa Creu i Sant Pau** (p. 388), tours of the facades of **La Manzana de la Discòrdia** (Casas Amatller, Lleó Morera, and Batlló; p. 388), and other attractions. The pass comes with a map and a pamphlet that gives a history of the movement and prioritizes the sites. Purchase passes at **Casa Amatller,** Pg. Gràcia, 41 (☎934 88 01 39; www.rutamodernisme.com; M: Pg. de Gràcia) near the intersection with C. Aragó. As many of these sights have mandatory hour-long tours, visiting all of them on the same day is virtually impossible.

LAS RAMBLAS

Las Ramblas' pedestrian strip is an urban carnival, where street performers dance, human statues pose, vendors peddle birds, and artists draw caricatures—all for the benefit of droves of tourists and all, of course, for a small fee. The wide, tree-lined thoroughfare dubbed Las Ramblas is actually composed of five distinct *ramblas* (promenades) that together form one boulevard, about 1km long.

The first segment, by Pl. Catalunya, is **La Rambla de les Canaletes,** named for the **Font de les Canaletes,** recognizable by its four faucets and the Catalan crest. Legend has it that visitors who sample the water will fall in love with the city and are bound to return to Barcelona. Because of its central location in the city, La Rambla de les Canaletes sees a fair deal of political demonstrations.

You'll hear the squawking from next section of Las Ramblas, **La Rambla dels Estudis,** before you see it. This stretch, which extends to C. Carme and C. Portaferrissa, is also called La Rambla dels Ocells—the **Rambla of the Birds.** Stalls here sell birds of nearly every kind: roosters, parrots, doves, and even baby emus. Other caged critters are also available. The official name of this stretch of *rambla* comes from the university that used to be located here; *"estudis"* is Catalan for "studies."

Screeching bird stalls lead to the roses of **La Rambla de Sant Josep,** a.k.a. **La Rambla de les Flors** (the Rambla of the Flowers). In April, flower stands are joined by book vendors for the **Día de Sant Jordi** (April 24), a Catalan holiday when couples exchange flowers and books. The stone building at C. Carme is the Església de Betlem, a Baroque church burned during the Civil War. Farther down is the traditional market, **La Boquería,** and the infamous **Museu de l'Eròtica** (see p. 393). The Boquería market is officially named **El Mercat de Sant Josep.** At Pl. Boquería, before the Liceu Metro station, you'll walk across Joan Miró's circular mosaic, a popular meeting point. The mosaic marks **La Rambla dels Caputxins.** Across from the **Liceu** opera house (see below), restaurants with outdoor seating offer unremarkable and fairly expensive food on prime people-watching terraces.

The last stretch of *la rambla* could be nicknamed *La Rambla de las Prostitutas;* instead, it's called **La Rambla de Santa Mónica.** After nightfall, women of the night patrol this area by the port, beckoning with kissing noises. During the day, the street distinguishes itself with skilled practitioners of a different art. Roving artists sell landscapes, caricatures, and portraits. La Rambla de Santa Monica is also home to the **Centre d'Art de Santa Mónica** and the **Museu de Cera.** Las Ramblas ends at the seafront-end of La Rambla de Santa Monica with one very visible statue. *(M: Catalunya, Liceu, or Drassanes. Low numbers addresses lie toward the port; for higher numbers head toward Pl. Catalunya.)*

BARCELONA

MONUMENT A COLOM. Ruis i Taulet's Monument a Colom towers at the port end of Las Ramblas. Nineteenth-century Renaixença enthusiasts convinced themselves that Columbus was Catalan, from a town near Girona. The fact that Columbus points proudly toward Libya, not the Americas, doesn't help the claim; historians agree that Columbus was from Italy. Take the elevator for a stunning view. *(Portal de la Pau. M: Drassanes. Elevator open June-Sept. 9am-8:30pm; Oct.-Mar. M-F 10am-1:30pm and 3:30-6:30pm, Sa-Su 10am-6:30pm; Apr.-May 10am-2pm and 3:30-7:30pm, Sa-Su 10am-7:30pm. €1.80, children and over 65 €1.20, groups of more than 15 €1.50 per person.)*

LA BOQUERÍA. One of the cheapest ways to get food in the city, la Boquería is a traditional Catalan market located right on Las Ramblas. Specialized vendors sell their goods—produce, dairy, meat—from independent stands. A wonderland of fresh foods for wholesale prices; butcher displays are not for the faint of heart. *(Las Ramblas, 95. M: Liceu, Mercat exit. Open M-Sa 8am-8pm.)*

GRAN TEATRE DEL LICEU. Once one of Europe's leading stages, the Liceu has been ravaged by anarchists, bombs, and fires. It is adorned with palatial ornamentation, gold facades, sculptures, and grand side rooms—a Spanish hall of mirrors. *(Las Ramblas, 51-59, by C. Sant Pau. Office open M-F 2-8:30pm and 1hr. before performances. ☎934 85 99 13. Guided tours M-F 10am, reservation only. €5.)*

PALAU DE LA VIRREINA. This 18th-century palace houses temporary photography, music, and graphics exhibits. Also on display are the 10-15ft. tall dolls who have been in the city's *Carnaval* celebrations since 1320. The imposing couple Jaume and Violant, dressed in regal robes, are the undisputed king and queen of the *Carnaval* parade. The cultural institute here, **ICUB,** serves as information headquarters for Barcelona's cultural festivals. Be sure to also check out the famous rainbow stained-glass facade of the **Casa Beethoven** next door at no. 97, now a well-stocked music store. *(Las Ramblas, 99, on the corner of C. Carme. M: Liceu. ☎933 16 10 00. Open Tu-Sa 11am-8:30pm and Su 11am-3pm. Free.)*

BARRI GÒTIC

The Barri Gòtic offers everything that Barcelona's Modernista architecture and l'Eixample do not. Its narrow, winding streets were not the products of careful planning and rapid execution, but have developed out of centuries of architectural and cultural mixing, from the early Roman through the medieval Romanesque and Gothic periods. This area is best enjoyed by wandering slowly and paying close attention to your surroundings; nearly every street has at least a few interesting historical sights and an endless array of shops, eateries, and cafes. The Barcelona tourist office leads professional walking tours of the Barri Gótic; buy tickets there or at the Ajuntament in Pl. St. Jaume. *(For walking tours, call ☎906 301 282. Sa-Su at 10am in English and noon in Catalan and Spanish. Buy tickets in advance. €7, children under 12 €3.)*

ESGLÉSIA CATEDRAL DE LA SANTA CREU. La Catedral de la Santa Creu is one of Barcelona's most popular monuments. Three separate buildings have existed on the site: a 4th-century basilica, an 11th-century Romanesque church, and the present Gothic cathedral, begun in 1298. The facade comes from another era; it was tacked on to the main structure by architect Josep Mestres in 1882. Upon entering, you'll first see the **choir.** Beyond the choir are the altar with the bronze **cross** designed by Frederic Marès in 1976, and the sunken **Crypt of Santa Eulalia,** one of Barcelona' s patron saints. Completed in 1334, the crypt holds a marble sarcophagus which depicts scenes from the saint's martyrdom at age 13. Also at rest is **Saint Olegario,** who died in 1137. His preserved body, in full regalia, is visible through glass by the **Chapel of El Santo Cristo de Lepanto.** Outside of the sacristy are the **tombs** of Ramon Berenguer I and his wife. To the right of the tombs is the **cloister,** home to 13 white geese, reminders of Sta. Eulalia's age at her death. At the right corner of the cloister you'll find the **cathedral museum,** whose most notable holding is Bartolomé Bermejo's *pietà*, the image of Christ dying in the arms of his mother. On Sundays after Mass at noon and 6:30pm, *barceloneses* gather in front of the cathedral to dance the **sardana.** *(M: Jaume I. In Pl. Seu, up C. Bisbe from Pl. St. Jaume. Cathedral open daily 8am-1:30pm and 4-7:30pm. Cloister open 9am-1:15pm and 4-7pm. Elevator to the roof open M-Sa 10:30am-12:30pm and 4:30-6pm; €1.35. Choir area open M-F 9am-1pm and 4-7pm, Sa-Su 9am-1pm; €0.90. Audioguides in English €1.)*

PLAÇA DE SANT JAUME. Plaça de Sant Jaume has been Barcelona's political center since Roman times. Two of Cataluña's most important buildings have dominated the square since 1823: the **Palau de la Generalitat,** the headquarters of Cataluña's autonomous government, and the **Ajuntament,** the city hall. *(Palau open 2nd and 4th Su of every month 10:30am-1:30pm. Closed Aug. Mandatory tours in Catalan, Spanish, or English every 30min. starting at 10:30am. Free. Ajuntament open Su 10am-1:45pm. Free.)*

LA RIBERA

As the stomping ground of fishermen and merchants, La Ribera has always had a plebeian feel; recently, the neighborhood has evolved into Barcelona's bohemian nucleus, with art galleries, chic eateries, and exclusive bars.

PALAU DE LA MÚSICA CATALANA. In 1891, the Orfeó Catalan choir society commissioned Modernista Lluís Domènech i Montaner to design this must-see concert venue. The hall glows with stained-glass, an ornate chandelier, marble reliefs, intricate woodwork, and ceramic mosaics. Concerts given at the Palau include all varieties of symphonic and choral music in addition to more modern pop and jazz. *(C. Sant Francesce de Paula, 2. ☎932 95 72 00; www.palaumusica.org. M: Jaume I. Off Vía Laietana by Pl. Urquinaona. Entrance only with tour; in English on the hr., in Spanish on the half-hr. During high season, reserve 1 day in advance. Purchase tickets inside the Palau. Open daily Aug. 10am-6pm, Sept.-July 10am-3:30pm. Box office open M-Sa 9:45am-3pm,*

Su from 1hr. prior to the concert. No concerts in Aug.; check the Guía del Ocio *for listings. €5, students and seniors €4; with Ruta del Modernisme pass €2.50. Concert tickets €9-125. MC/V.)*

SANTA MARÍA DEL MAR. Built in the 14th century in a quick 55 years, Santa María del Mar (Mary of the Sea) was important to the growing population of sailors living in La Ribera at the time. At a distance of 13m apart, the supporting columns span a width greater than any other medieval building in the world. A fascinating example of the limits of Gothic architecture—were it 2ft. higher, it would collapse from structural instability. Church holds classical, gospel, and folk concerts. *(Pl. Santa Maria, 1. M: Jaume 1. ☎933 10 23 90. Open M-Sa 9am-1:30pm and 4:30-8pm, Su 9am-2pm and 5-8:30pm. Free. For concert info, call ☎933 19 05 16.)*

PARC DE LA CIUTADELLA. Barcelona's military resistance to the Bourbon monarchy in the early 18th century convinced Felipe V to quarantine Barcelona's influential citizens in the Ciutadella, a large citadel on what is now Pg. Picasso. The city razed the fortress in 1868 and replaced it with the peaceful promenades of Parc de la Ciutadella. Host of the 1888 Universal Exposition, the park now harbors several museums, well-labeled horticulture, the wacky **Cascada** fountains, a pond, and a zoo. Buildings of note include Domènech i Montaner's Modernista **Castell dels Tres Dragons** (now **Museu de Zoología**), the **geological museum,** and Josep Amergós's **Hivernacle.** Expo '88 also inspired the **Arc de Triomf,** just across Pg. Pujades from the park. *(M: Barceloneta or Arc de Triomf.)*

PARC ZOOLÒGIC. Quarters are cramped for the zoo's residents, but the zoo still draws park-goers young and old. Stately and saucy **Floquet de Neu** (Snowflake), the world's only white gorilla, titillates tourists of all ages, although the elephants, hippos, and seals also draw crowds. The zoo also features an aquarium, petting zoo, and the famous **Senyoreta del Paraigua** sculpture. *(M: Ciutadella. Follow C. Wellington out of the Metro to a separate entrance. Inside the park, the entrance is next to the Museu d'Art Modern. ☎932 25 67 80. Open Nov.-Feb. 10am-5pm; Mar. and Oct. 10am-6pm; Apr. and Sept. 10am-7pm; May-Aug. 9:30am-7:30pm. €10, children ages 3-12 €6.50, seniors over 65 €5.80. May-Sept. after 5pm €6.50, children €4, and seniors €3.60.)*

OTHER SIGHTS. Museums, art galleries, and palaces of 16th-century bureaucrats crowd **C. Montcada.** The **Museu Picasso** (see p. 392) inhabits several such mansions, and the **Galería Maeght** (C. Montcada, 26), an art gallery, was once a medieval manor. Also worth a look is Antoni Tàpies's **Homenatge a Picasso,** a sculpture on Pg. Picasso in front of the Museu Geologia. The 1983 jumble of wood and steel was inspired by Picasso's comment that "A picture is not something to decorate a sitting room, but a weapon of attack and of defense against the enemy."

EL RAVAL

PALAU GÜELL. Gaudí's Palau Güell (1886)—the haunting Modernista residence built for patron Eusebi Güell—has one of Barcelona's most spectacular interiors. Güell and Gaudí spared no expense. The 20 unique rooftop chimneys display Gaudí's first use of *trencadis*—the covering of surfaces with irregular shards of ceramic. *(C. Nou de La Rambla, 3-5. ☎933 17 39 74; fax 933 17 37 79. 2 blocks from Opera Liceu, off Las Ramblas. M: Liceu. Visits by tour only, every 15min. Open Mar.-Oct. Su 10am-2pm, M-Sa 10am-8pm, last tour 6:15pm; Nov.-Dec. M-Sa 10am-6pm. €3, students €1.50.)*

L'EIXAMPLE

The Catalan Renaissance and the growth of Barcelona during the 19th century pushed the city past its medieval walls and into modernity. Ildefons Cerdà drew a plan for a new neighborhood which called for a grid of squares, softened by octagonal intersections with cropped corners. Cerdà envisioned both an escape from

SYMBOL MINDS Gaudí was a religious man, and his plans for La Sagrada Família called for elaborate and deliberate symbolism in virtually every decorative element. The cypress tree on the **Nativity Facade,** according to one theory, symbolizes the stairway to heaven (cypress trees do not put down deeper roots with time but only grow taller); the tree is crowned with the word "Tau," the Greek word for God. Similarly, the top of each of the eight finished towers carries the first letter of one of the names of the apostles (and the words "Hosanna" and "Excelsis" spiral up the sides of the towers). Inside, on the **Portal of the Rosary,** references to modern life lurk among more traditional imagery: the Temptation of Man is represented in one carving by the devil handing a bomb to a terrorist and in another by his waving a purse at a prostitute.

Suberachs, the famous Catalan sculptor, continued the religious symbolism in his **Passion Facade.** To the left a snake lurks behind Judas, symbolizing the disciple's betrayal of Jesus. The 4x4 box of numbers next to Him contains 310 possible combinations of four numbers, each of which adds up to 33, Christ's age when He died. The faceless woman in the center of the facade, **Veronica,** represents the Biblical woman with the same name and the miraculous appearance of Christ's face on the cloth she compassionately wiped His face with. Suberachs even hid a statue of Gaudí himself among the Biblical figures, a nod to the original architect.

the stress that had festered in the overcrowded Barri Gòtic as well as a new city where people of all social classes could live side by side. He called each 10-block area a *massa* (neighborhood) and allotted each its own school, market, and park. However, l'Eixample (luh-SHOMP-luh) did not thrive as a utopian community but rather as a playground for the bourgeois. Today it's home to some of the city's most upscale shopping and famous Modernista buildings. If you plan on seeing a lot of the sights in l'Eixample, get a **Ruta del Modernisme** pass (see p. 383) and allow more than just an afternoon; two days can be consumed with sightseeing here.

LA SAGRADA FAMÍLIA. Although Antoni Gaudí's unfinished masterpiece is barely a shell of the intended finished product, La Sagrada Família is without a doubt the world's most visited construction site. Despite the fact that only eight of the church's 18 planned towers have been completed (and those the shortest) and the church still doesn't have an "interior," millions of people make the pilgrimage to witness its work-in-progress majesty. Of the three proposed facades, only the Nativity Facade was finished under Gaudí. A furor has arisen over recent additions, especially sculptor Josep Subirachs's Cubist Passion Facade on C. Sardenya, which is criticized for being inconsistent with Gaudí's plans. The **museum** displays artifacts relating to the building's construction as well as the plans for the outrageous final product. *(C. Mallorca, 401. ☎932 07 30 31. M: Sagrada Família. Open Oct.-Mar. daily 9am-6pm, elevator open 9:30am-5:45pm; Apr.-Sept. 9am-8pm, elevator open 9:30am-7:45pm. Guided tours Apr.-Sept. daily 11am, 1, 3, and 5:30pm; Oct. 11am, 1, and 3pm; Nov.-Mar. F-M 11am and 1pm. €3. (Buy tickets right inside the Sardenya entrance.) Entrance €6, students and those with the Ruta pass €4. Cash only.)*

CASA MILÀ (LA PEDRERA). *Modernisme* buffs argue that the spectacular Casa Milà apartment building, an undulating mass of granite popularly known as *La Pedrera* (the Stone Quarry), is Gaudí's most refined work. Note the intricate ironwork around the balconies and the irregularity of the front gate's egg-shaped window panes—there is not a single straight line on the entire facade. The roof sprouts chimneys that resemble armored soldiers, one of which is decorated with broken champagne bottles. Rooftop tours provide a closer look at the "Prussian helmets" (spiral chimneys inspired by the helmets worn in Wagner's operas). The winding brick attic (recently restored along with the rooftop in a multi-million-*peseta* project) has been transformed into the **Espai Gaudí,** a multimedia presentation of Gaudí's life and works. A refurnished and restored apartment awaits one floor below, as an example of the fine, captivating interior of Gaudí homes. *(Pg. Gràcia, 92. ☎934 84 59 95. Open daily 10am-8pm. €6, with Ruta del Modernisme pass €4.20; students and over 65 €3. Free guided tours in English M-F 4pm, Sa-Su 11am.)*

LA MANZANA DE LA DISCÒRDIA. A short walk from Pl. Catalunya, the odd-numbered side of Pg. Gràcia between C. Aragó and Consell de Cent is popularly known as *la manzana de la discòrdia* (block of discord), referring to the stylistic clashing of the three buildings. Regrettably, the bottom two floors of **Casa Lleó i Morera,** by Domènech i Montaner, were destroyed to make room for a leather store, but you can buy the **Ruta del Modernisme pass** (see p. 383) there. Puig i Cadafalch opted for a geometric, Moorish-influenced pattern on the facade of **Casa Amatller** at #41. Gaudí's balconies ripple like skulls, and tiles sparkle in blue-purple glory on **Casa Batlló,** #43. The most popular interpretation of Casa Batlló is that the building represents Cataluña's patron Sant Jordi (St. George) slaying a dragon; the chimney plays the lance, the scaly roof is the dragon's back, and the bony balconies are the remains of his victims. Also of interest is **Fundació Tàpies** (see p. 394), designed by Domènech i Montaner, around the corner from *la manzana.*

HOSPITAL DE LA SANTA CREU I SANT PAU. Designated a UNESCO monument in 1997, the Modernista Hospital de la Santa Creu i Sant Pau was Domènech i Montaner's masterpiece. In 1905, Domènech i Montaner designed pavilions that would serve only 28 patients. The interior is painted in shades of green and is full of natural light. Domènech i Montaner studied wind patterns and put infectious wards at the back of the hospital, at the end of the current. He also built underground tunnels for staff, to keep the grounds feeling as unlike a hospital as possible. The most interesting attraction is the main administrative building, which is steeped in symbolism. The sculptured figures on the front facade represent faith, hope, charity, and work, and the multi-domed ceiling of the entrance foyer is covered with symbols of Cataluña. *(Entrance at corner of C. Cartagena and C. St. Antonia Maria Claret. ☎934 88 20 78. M: Hospital de St. Pau. Hospital grounds open 24hr. 50min. guided tours Sa-Su 10am-2pm every 30min., in Catalan, Spanish, or English as needed. Last tour leaves 1:30pm. €4.21, students and over 65 €3.01. Cash only.)*

AROUND THE PORT

Barcelona's drive to refurbish its seafront for the 1992 Olympics resulted in the expansion of Port Vell, the port complex, and the waterfront area near Monument a Colom, clamoring with seaside eateries, loud discos, and overpriced shops. After moving the coastal road underground, the city opened **Moll de la Fusta,** a pedestrian zone leading down to the docks past the **Museu d'Història de Catalunya** (see p. 394). **Rambla de Mar** links Moll de la Fusta with the **Maremàgnum** mall (see p. 398).

L'AQUÀRIUM DE BARCELONA. This aquarium—the largest in Europe—is an aquatic wonder, featuring copious amounts of octopi and a plethora of penguins. The highlight is an 80m-long glass tunnel through an ocean tank of sharks, sting rays, and one two-dimensional fish. *(Moll d'Espanya, next to Maremàgnum. M: Drassanes. ☎932 21 74 74. Open daily July-Aug. 9:30am-11pm; Sept.-June 9:30am-9pm. €11, under 12 and seniors €7.70, students 10% off.)*

TORRE SAN SEBASTIÀ. One of the easiest and best ways to view the city is on the cable cars that span Port Vell, connecting beachy Barceloneta with mountainous Montjuïc. The full ride, which takes about 10min. each way and offers a stop at the Jaume I tower near Colom, gives an aerial perspective of the entire city. *(Pg. Joan de Borbo. M: Barceloneta. In Port Vell, as you walk down Joan de Borbo and see the beaches to the* *left, stay right and look for the obvious high tower. ☎934 41 48 20. Open daily 11am-8pm. To Jaume I 1-way or round-trip €7.50, to Montjuïc 1-way €7.50, round-trip €9.50.)*

VILA OLÍMPICA. The Vila Olímpica was built to house athletes and entertain tourists for the 1992 Summer Olympics. Today it is home to parks, a mall, and offices. Toward the Mediterranean, **Port Olímpic** is an L-shaped complex flaunting twin towers, a metallic fish sculpture by Frank Gehry, docked sailboats, and upscale discos and restaurants. **Barceloneta's** (see p. 401) mediocre beaches—good for a tan—stretch out from the port. *(From M: Ciutadella/Vila Olímpica, walk along the waterfront on Ronda Litoral toward the 2 towers.)*

MONTJUÏC

Throughout Barcelona's history, whoever controlled Montjuïc (Hill of the Jews) controlled the city. Dozens of despotic rulers have modified the **fortress,** built atop the ancient Jewish cemetery; Franco made it one of his "interrogation" headquarters. Somewhere in the recesses of the structure, his *beneméritos* (honorable ones) shot Cataluña's former president, Lluís Companys, in 1941. The fort was not available for recreation until Franco rededicated it to the city in 1960. A huge stone monument expresses Barcelona's (forced) gratitude for the return of the fortress. Since reacquiring the mountain, Barcelona has made it a tourist attraction, and it was chosen as the site of the 1992 Olympics. To get to **Parc de Montjuïc,** take the Metro to Pl. Espanya (M: Espanya) and catch bus #50 either at Av. Reina María Cristina (flanked by 2 large brick towers) or as it heads up the hill (every 10min.). Outdoor escalators lead up to Montjuïc from the Palau Nacional.

BARCELONA PAVILION. Designed by German architect Mies van der Rohe for the 1929 International Exposition and rebuilt in 1986, the Barcelona Pavilion is a modernist dream come true. Composed of glass, travertine, and steel, its simple, elegant design inspires a sense of serenity. *(To the right of the fountain at the end of Av. Reina Maria Cristina. Open daily 10am-8pm.)*

FONTS LUMINOSES. The "Illuminated Fountains" run along Av. Reina Maria Cristina and are dominated by the central **Font Mágica**. View the fountains from Pl. Espanya or from the hilltop **Palau Nacional** (home of MNAC; see **Museums,** p. 393). On weekends, lights and music bring the fountains to life in a spectacular display. *(Shows June-Sept. Th-Su every 30min. 9:30pm-12:30am; Oct.-May F-Sa 7-8:30pm. Free.)*

ANELLA OLÍMPICA. Barcelona inaugurated the "Olympic Ring" area with the **Estadi Olímpic de Montjuïc** in 1929 in its failed bid for the 1932 Games. Over 50 years later, architects Federic Correa and Alfons Milà finished the esplanade in preparation for the 1992 Olympics. *(☎934 26 20 89. Open daily 10am-8pm. Free.)* Designed by Japanese architect Arata Isozaki, the **Palau d'Esports Sant Jordi** is the most technologically sophisticated of the Olympic structures. *(☎934 26 20 89. You must call in advance to visit.)* Test your swimming mettle in the **Olympic pools** (see p. 401) or visit the **Galeria Olímpica** exposition at the south end of the stadium. *(☎934 26 06 60. Open M-F 10am-2pm and 4-6pm. €2.40, students €2.10, seniors €1.10.)* The soaring telecommunications tower was designed by renowned Spanish architect Santiago Calatrava.

POBLE ESPANYOL. Built for the International Exhibition in 1929, this tourist-oriented "town" features replicas of sights from every region of Spain. During the day, Poble Espanyol is a souvenir bazaar with mediocre restaurants, but at night the disco scene brings new meaning to the word "party." *(On Av. Marqués de Comillas, to the right when facing the Palau Nacional. M: Espanya, up the escalators. ☎935 08 63 00. Open M 9am-8pm, Tu-Th 9am-2am, F-Sa 9am-4am, Su 9am-midnight. €7, students and seniors €4.40, children 7-12 €3.60. Guided tours in English daily 1:30 and 3:30pm; €3. MC/V.)*

CASTELL DE MONTJUÏC. A visit to this fortress and its **Museum Militar** is a great way to get an overview of the city—both its layout and its history. Enjoy coffee at the cafe while cannons stare you down. *(From M: Paral.lel, take the funicular to Av. Miramar and then the Teleféric de Montjuïc to the castle. Teleféric open M-Sa 11:15am-9pm. 1-way €3.20, round-trip €4.50. Alternatively, walk up the steep slope on C. Foc from the funicular station. Castle open Mar. 21-Nov. 14 Tu-Su 9:30am-7:30pm; Nov. 15-Mar. 20 Tu-Su 9:30am-5pm.)*

GRÀCIA

PARK GÜELL. Eusebi Güell commissioned the Gaudí to fashion a garden city in the tradition of Hampstead Heath in England; the English spelling of "park" is a nod to the Anglo gardens. Intended by Güell as a housing development, the park was to have 60 houses; only three houses went up before Gaudí passed away.

As a housing development, it was a failure; as a park, it is fantastic. Combining natural influences with Catalan and religious symbolism, Park Güell is dreamy and whimsical, organic and tactile. The most eye-catching structures are by the entrance on C. Olot. The entrance's **Palmetto Gate** is flanked by two dwarfish buildings, inspired by *Hansel and Gretel,* with the spire-topped hut belonging to the children and the other, crowned with a red poisonous mushroom, belonging to the witch. Up the double staircase, tourists jostle for a photo with the gaping **lizard** fountain, drooling into the basin below. The stairs lead to the **Hall of One Hundred Columns (Teatro Griego),** which actually only has 86 columns (but who's counting?). The hall's multicolored medallions, designed by Gaudí's right-hand man Josep Marià Jujol, are made with bits of mirror, glasses, and even porcelain dolls. Stairs next to the hall lead up to the **Pl. de la Naturalesa,** surrounded by the **Serpentine bench,** the longest park bench in the world. The shape of the bench is not only aesthetic, but comfy. The park's summit commands tremendous views of the city.

To the right of the lizard fountain when walking up the stairs, follow the wide path past the flower beds and continue to the right as smaller paths branch off and the path twists uphill to the pink **Casa-Museu Gaudí.** Farther ahead, the **Pont dels Enamorats** offers views of the city all the way to the sea. Along the left-hand side, Gaudí's **stone trees**—tall columns topped with plants—are interspersed with benches which seem to hang in midair. Around the next curve is **Casa Trias** (1905), which is owned by Trías Domènech's family. *(Bus #24 from Pl. Catalunya stops at the upper entrance. From M: Vallarca, walk down Av. l'Hospital Militar for 4 blocks, turn left onto Baixada de la Glòria, and take the escalators to the park's back entrance. Park ☎932 19 38 11. Open daily May-Sept. 10am-9pm; Mar.-Apr. and Oct. 10am-7pm; Nov.-Feb. 10am-6pm. Free.)*

PLAÇAS. Gràcia has several notable *plaças.* The first of these is **Plaça Rius i Taulet,** home to the **Torre del Reloj** (Clocktower), an emblem of the Revolution of 1868. **Plaça del Diamant,** on nearby C. Astúries, was made famous by Catalan author Mercè Rodoreda's novel of the same name. **Plaça del Sol** is full of cafes and bars and crowded with locals at night. Protest graffiti fills the *plaça,* touching on everything from Catalan independence to the Zapatista uprising in Chiapas, Mexico.

CASA VICENS. One of Gaudí's earliest projects, Casa Vicens was designed for a local tile manufacturer, is fittingly decorated with blocks of cheerful ceramic tiles. The *casa* illustrates the influence of Arabic architecture and a rigidness that is uncharacteristic of Gaudí's later works. The hard lines contrast with Gaudí's trademark fluid ironwork on the balconies and facade. *(C. Carolines, 24-26. Walk uphill on Gran de Gràcia and turn left onto C. Carolines. M: Fontana.)*

ELSEWHERE IN THE ZONA ALTA

MONESTIR DE PEDRALBES. The artistic high-water of this Gothic church and 14th-century cloister is in the **Capella Sant Miguel,** where murals by Ferrer Bassa depict the seven joys of Mary, as well as several of her sorrows. The monastery

THE WONDERFUL WORLD OF JOAN MIRÓ

Tourists on the Spanish art circuit tend to run into each other frequently because they are all clamoring to see the same great Spanish masters in two weeks or less. Somehow, between mad dashes to the Prado, the Picasso Museum, and the Teatre-Museu Dalí, not everyone pauses to take note of the works of one of the most innovative artists and endearing characters of 20th-century Spain—Joan Miró.

Miró is often overlooked by travelers, written off as eccentric and inaccessible; his popularity in Spain and his native Cataluña is regarded as peculiar rather than intriguing. Yet commanding an appreciation of his life and of his works is one of the most enriching ways to experience Barcelona, Cataluña, and Spain, for his works chronicle the region's recent turbulent history, and look forward from Franco with a generous, yet distinctly Catalan optimism.

Born in Barcelona in 1893, Joan Miró displayed a strong sense of Catalan nationalism his whole life. In Paris he was exposed to Cubist art but rejected its emphasis on the visual and spatial elements; he made a conscious decision to try to go beyond these plastic elements of painting and sculpture. On returning to Barcelona, Miró produced a series of works that treated everyday Catalan life as subjects. Throughout the 1920s and early 1930s, Miró's works became increasingly intuitive; while his paintings always represent objects and are therefore never abstract (as they are so often mislabeled), the spaces he represents become increasingly simplified and free of gravity, and as the object he paints float away, some of them become difficult to recognize on the simply colored background. His paintings from this world invoke the intuitive world of childhood, not quite yet part of reality or reason.

With Franco's rise to power in 1936, Spain became a dangerous place for artists and intellectuals; Republican Miró retreated into a deep depression and a self-imposed exile on the Balearic islands. His works from the 1940s are moving in the way that they detail not only his depression, but the depression of Cataluña. The backgrounds of his works turned a dark brown, and the focus of his painting became nightmarish creatures with gaping maws, or deformed and perverse characters. *A Man and a Woman in front of a pile of Excrement*, which represents a deformed man and woman celebrating their recent bowel movement (a distinctly Catalan theme), is one such work from this period that clearly provides a dark, satiric commentary on the state of Cataluña under Franco.

Although Miró refused to sign the Surrealist manifesto, he is Spain's first Surrealist painter, for appreciation of his art depends not on how well he copies objects in the "real world," but on how the observer responds to his infantile interpretation. Although he was not appreciated in his native Spain until the 1970s, he was lauded in Paris throughout the Franco era. As the dictatorship weakened and eventually ended, Miró returned to a brighter and more joyful style of painting in his old age, using white backgrounds and primary colors. He also, for the first time, displayed a sense of Spanish nationalism, which he no longer saw as necessarily in conflict with his Catalan nationalism; his *España* is famous for its bright colors, playful style, and proud declaration of nationalism. It is a forceful and optimistic commentary on his hopes for post-Franco Spain.

Apart from appreciating Miró's art, one also has to admire his activist spirit and presence in Barcelona and Spain. After the fall of the dictatorship, Miró sprinkled every corner of Barcelona with public works of art to try to beautify and re-energize his then-battered city. His mural at the airport is a welcome homecoming for Catalan residents, and his ceramic mural in the center of Las Ramblas is one of the most popular meeting places in the city. His greatest donation to Barcelona is, of course, the Fundació Miró. Rather than creating a museum that was a self-aggrandizing monument to himself (see the **Teatre-Museu Dalí**, p. 215), Miró created this foundation to foster interest in and appreciation of modern art, which had never had a space to display itself safely under Franco. Miró died on Mallorca in 1983, but he is one of the most present artists in Barcelona; his art reaches outside museums and self-referential buildings and lives alongside residents and travelers, in the city itself.

Sarah Kenney was editor of Let's Go: Barcelona 2002. *She lived in Barcelona for a year, where she learned to speak Spanish and Catalan. She is currently editing for a Spanish-language publishing company in Boston and teaching English for a non-profit organization. She is an avid fan of Floquet de Neu.*

also received a part of the Thyssen-Bornemisza collection in 1993. *(Baixada del Monestir, 9. FGC: Reina Elisenda. A 10min. walk down Pg. Reina Elisenda. ☎932 03 92 82. Open daily 10am-2pm. Church open M-Sa 11am-1pm, Su 11am-12:30pm. €3.50, students 16-25 €2, under 16 free. Combined ticket with art collection €4.80, students 16-25 €3, under 16 free.)*

PARC DE COLLSEROLA. People come to these 16,000 acres of greenery to hike, bike, and horseback ride. Before entering the park, be sure to stop at the **Centre d'Informació,** which has loads of info on all the park's attractions. The park is full of natural and man-made sights worth tracking down. Numerous lookout points in the park offer good views of the city and surrounding hills, especially the **Mirador de Vila Paula.** Take the FGC train from Pl. Catalunya to the Peu del Funicular stop, walk up the hill from the station on Av. de Vallvidrera, follow it along the tight, immediate left turn, then a right turn, and then a few smaller twists and curves (about 15min.); it will be up the hill on your right. Also inside the park are more than 50 notable archaeological finds. The **Cova de l'Or,** the oldest cave dwelling in the park, dates back to the Neolithic period, 6000 BC. The terraced remains of a 4th-to-6th century BC Laietana dwelling can be seen on **La Penya del Moro** hillside. **Castellciuró,** a castle built in the 14th century over 12th-century remains, doubles as a particularly good lookout point. *(Take the FGC train to Baixador de Vallvidrera and follow the steps at the top of the stop for 10min. Tourist office at Carretera de l'Església, 92. ☎932 80 35 52. Open daily 9:30am-3pm except Dec. 25-26 and Jan. 1 and 6.)*

MUSEUMS

When I was a child, my mother said to me, "If you become a soldier, you'll be a general. If you become a monk, you'll end up as the Pope." Instead, I became a painter and wound up as Picasso.
—Pablo Picasso

Barcelona has always been on the cutting edge of defining what can be included in the category of "art"; the city's museums range from Surrealist and classical masterpieces to historical exhibits and one-of-a-kind curiosities. Culture vultures should invest in the **Articket,** which gives half-price admission to five of Barcelona's premier art centers, including the **Museu Nacional d'Art de Catalunya** (MNAC; see p. 394), the **Fundació Miró** (see p. 392), the **Fundació Tàpies** (see p. 394), the **Centre de Cultura Contemporània de Barcelona** (CCCB; see p. 394), and the **Museu d'Art Contemporani** (MACBA; see p. 393). The ticket, available at tourist offices (see p. 373) and at the museums, goes for €15, and is valid for three months.

MUSEU PICASSO. This incredible museum traces the development of Picasso as an artist, with a collection of his early works that weaves through five connected mansions. Although the museum offers little from Picasso's well-known middle years, it boasts the world's best collection of work from his formative period in Barcelona. The collection also includes lithographs and pencil sketches by an 11-year-old Picasso, and an excellent display of the artist's Cubist interpretations of Velázquez's *Las Meninas*. *(C. Montcada, 15-19. ☎933 19 63 10. M: Jaume I. Walk down C. Princesa from the Metro, and turn right on C. Montcada. Open Tu-Sa 10am-8pm, Su 10am-3pm. €4.80, students and seniors €2.40, under 16 free. First Su of each month free.)*

FUNDACIÓ MIRÓ. Designed by Miró's friend Josep Lluís Sert and tucked into the side of Montjuïc, the Fundació links interior and exterior spaces with massive windows and outdoor patios. Skylights illuminate an extensive collection of statues, paintings, and tapestries from Miró's career, including the stunning Barcelona Series, which depicts Miró's personal reaction to the Spanish Civil War and several paintings from Miro's *Las Constelaciones* series, a reaction to Nazi invasion during

WWII. His best-known pieces in the museum include *El Carnival de Arlequin, La Masia,* and *L'or de L'azuz.* Room 13 displays experimental work by young artists. The Fundació also sponsors music recitals and film festivals. *(Av. Miramar, 71-75. ☎934 43 94 70; www.bcn.fjmiro.es. Take the funicular from M: Paral.lel. Turn left out of the funicular station; the museum is a 5min. walk up on the right. Open July-Aug. Tu-W and F-Sa 10am-8pm, Th 10am-9:30pm, Su 10am-2:30pm; Oct.-June Tu-W and F-Sa 10am-7pm, Th 10am-9:30pm, Su 10am-2:30pm. €7.20, students and seniors €3.90.)*

MUSEU D'ART MODERN. This museum houses paintings, sculptures, and furniture by 19th-century Catalan artists. Works include Ramon Casas's *Plein Air*, Josep Llimona's *Desconsol*, Isidre Nonell's paintings of Gypsy women, and a room of Josep Clará's *Noucentiste* sculptures. Of note are furniture designed by Gaudí for Casa Battló and two early Dalí portraits, the only in Barcelona. *(Pl. D'Armes. M: Arc de Triomf. Follow Pg. Til.les to the statue of General Prim at the roundabout and turn left toward Pl. D'Armes; signs point the way. ☎933 19 57 28. Open Tu-Sa 10am-7pm, Su 10am-2:30pm. €3, students and children €2. Free entrance 1st Th of every month.)*

MUSEU D'ART CONTEMPORANI (MACBA). The MACBA was a collaboration between Barcelona's mayor and the Catalan government to make El Raval a cultural center. Architect Richard Meier created a building whose sparse decor would allow the art to speak for itself. The MACBA has received acclaim for its focus on avant-garde art between the two World Wars; exhibits focus on three-dimensional art, photography, and video. *(Pl. dels Angels, 1. M: Catalunya. ☎934 12 08 10. Open July-Sept. M, W, and F 11am-8pm, Th 11am-9:30pm, Sa 10am-8pm; Su 10am-3pm. Oct.-June M and W-F 11am-7:30pm, Sa 10am-8pm, Su 10am-3pm. €6, students €4, 16 and under free.)*

MUSEU D'HISTORIA DE LA CIUTAT. Exhibits display the history of Barcelona, from its Roman foundations in the 1st-century BC through the 6th-century Visigoth takeover and medieval development to the modern day. The history of the city unfolds as you descend to the original Roman ruins in the basement and continue on toward former royal palaces. The upper floors are home to the **Capella de Santa Agueda,** which stored the king's holy relics. *(In Pl. del Rei. M: Jaume I. Walk up C. Jaume I and take the 1st right. Enter on C. Verguer. ☎933 15 11 11. Open June-Sept. Tu-Sa 10am-8pm, Su 10am-2pm. Oct.-May Tu-Sa 10am-2pm and 4-8pm, Su 10am-2pm. Closed Jan. 1, May 1, June 24, and Dec. 25-26. €3.50, students €2; exhibition €3, students €1.50; combined museum and exhibition €5.50, students €3.50.)*

MUSEU NACIONAL D'ART DE CATALUNYA. Inside the **Palau Nacional,** the MNAC houses the world's finest collection of Catalan Romanesque art and Gothic altarpieces from Cataluña's medieval churches. The museum's Gothic art corridor displays murals from homes in Mallorca. *(M: Espanya, walk up Av. Reina María Cristina to the escalators. ☎936 22 03 60. Open Tu–Sa 10am-7pm, Su 10am-2:30pm. €4.80, €6 with temporary exhibits; students and seniors €3.30/€4.20. Free 1st Th of every month.)*

MUSEU DE L'ERÒTICA. This museum examines the anthropological and sociological insights gleaned from erotica. Um, yeah, okay. Exhibits include vintage porn flicks from the 1930s and saucy international sculptures and sketches, depicting more sexual acrobatics than thought humanly possible. Wince at the rather medieval-looking "pleasure chair" and giggle at the sex phones. *(Las Ramblas, 96. ☎933 18 98 65. Open June-Sept. 10am-midnight; Oct.-May 11am-9pm. €7, students €6.)*

MUSEU DEL FÚTBOL CLUB BARCELONA. A close second to the Picasso Museum as Barcelona's most visited museum, the FCB museum merits all the attention it gets. Sports fans will appreciate the storied history of the team. Enter the stadium and take in the enormity of Camp Nou (see p. 400). *(C. Aristides Maillol, next to the stadium. M: Collblanc. Enter through access gates 7 or 9. ☎934 96 36 08. Tours run every 15min.*

Open M-Sa 10am-6:30pm, Su 10am-2pm. Museum entrance €4.80, children under 13 €3.50; with 45min. stadium tour €8.90, children under 13 €3.50.)

FUNDACIÓ TÀPIES. Tàpies's wire sculpture atop Domènech i Montaner's red brick building announces this collection of abstract art. Tàpies's art is characterized by his use of unconventional materials like sand and glue to show the eloquence inherent in simplicity. Most of his works include a "T" in some form. The symbolism of the "T" has been variously interpreted: as a religious cross, sexual penetration, and his own signature. Most of his works are interpreted as protests against the dictatorship and its urban alienation. The other floors feature exhibits of other modern artists. *(C. Aragó, 255, around the corner from the Manzana de la Discòrdia. M: Pg. Gràcia. ☎934 87 03 15. Open Tu-Su 10am-8pm. €4.20, students and seniors €2.10.)*

MUSEU DEL ARQUEOLÒGIA DE CATALUNYA. The exhibits cover prehistoric times up to the constitution of Cataluña. Several rooms feature a collection of Carthaginian art from Ibiza and excavated relics from the Greco-Roman city of Empúries. *(Pg. Santa Madrona, 39-41. ☎934 23 21 49. From M: Espanya, take bus #55 up the hill to the Palau Nacional. When facing the Palau Nacional, the museum is to the left. Open Tu-Sa 9:30am-7pm and Su 10am-2:30pm. €2.40; students and seniors €1.80.)*

BARCELONA

MUSEU D'HISTÒRIA DE CATALUNYA. This high-tech, hands-on museum guides visitors through Cataluña's history, from Roman times through the 20th century. Computer screens, original film clips, and music stations help narrate the region's tumultuous past. *(Pl. Pau Vila, 3, on the waterfront. M: Drassanes. ☎932 25 47 00. Open Tu-Sa 10am-7pm, W 10am-8pm, Su 10am-2:30pm. €3; students, seniors, and children €2.10.)*

MUSEU DE CERA (WAX MUSEUM). 300 wax celebrities and legends will keep visitors guessing which figures are wax and which are just creepy-looking tourists. *(Las Ramblas, 4, on the left as you face the port. M: Drassanes. ☎933 17 26 49. Open M-F 10am-2pm and 4-8pm, Sa 11am-2:30pm, Su and holidays 4:30-9pm. €6.65, children 5-11 €3.75.)*

CENTRE DE CULTURA CONTEMPORÀNIA DE BARCELONA (CCCB). This cultural center investigates modern urban design and sponsors temporary exhibits, dance performances, concerts, workshops, and lectures; check the *Guía del Ocio* for a schedule. *(Casa de Caritat, C. Montalegre, 5, next to the MACBA. ☎933 06 41 00. M: Catalunya. Open Tu-Su 11am-8pm. €4, students €3, children under 16 free.)*

MUSEU TAURÍ. This dense collection commemorates the tradition of bullfighting, with pictures of fights and fighters, old posters and stamps, a colorful exhibit on the evolution of the bullfighter's costume throughout time, and a good handful of stuffed bulls' heads on the walls. For tickets to a bullfight, see p. 401. *(Gran Vía de les Corts Catalanes, 749. ☎932 45 58 04. M: Monumental. Open M-Sa 11am-2pm and 4-8pm, Su 11am-2pm, fight days 10:30am-1pm. €4, children €3.)*

ART GALLERIES

One of the capitals of cutting-edge art, Barcelona showcases many of the latest artistic trends. Many private showings display the works of both budding artists and renowned masters. Most of Barcelona's galleries are located in **La Ribera** around C. Montcada. Three of the best-known in the La Ribera area include: **Gallery Surrealista, Galeria Maeght,** and **Galeria Montcada.** For more in-depth gallery info check the *Guía del Ocio*. The **Palau de la Virreina** also has information on cultural events. *(Las Ramblas, 99. Between La Boquería market and C. Carme. ☎933 01 77 75. M: Liceu. Open Tu-Sa 11am-8:30pm and Su 11am-3pm.)*

NIGHTLIFE

The whole world knows that Madrid sleeps less than any other city in Europe. Clearly, whoever's counting forgot to take their survey to Barcelona; as in Madrid, nightlife here begins with a 5pm stroll and doesn't wind down until nearly 14 hours later—if even then. Following the afternoon *siesta*, the masses stroll to their favorite *tapas* bars, crowded *plaças*, or outdoor cafes for drinks or a snack with friends. Most people dine between 9 and 11pm, the bar scene picks up around 10pm, and discos start to fill around 2am. Places on Las Ramblas tend to be tourist-dominated, as do the Maremàgnum Mall and most portside establishments. L'Eixample is famous for its gay nightlife, and Poble Nou (the neighborhood inland from Port Olímpic) has a good alternative music scene.

BARRI GÒTIC

Here, cookie-cutter *cervecerías* and *bar-restaurantes* can be found every five steps. Nightlife in the Barri Gòtic is perfect for chit-chatting your night away, sipping sangría, or scoping out your next dance partner.

Schilling, C. Ferran, 23 (☎933 17 67 87). M: Liceu. The fancy exterior conceals a surprisingly diverse and chill bar. Mixed gay and straight crowd. Excellent sangría (pitcher €13.40). Mixed drinks €4.90. Beer €1.70. Open 10am-2:30am. Cash only.

Jamboree, Pl. Reial, 17 (☎933 19 17 89), in the corner of the plaza. M: Liceu. This former convent is one of the city's most popular music venues. Jazz or blues performances daily M-F (€6 with 1 drink, Sa-Su €9-12). Open daily 11pm-1am. Upstairs, **Tarantos** hosts flamenco shows (€25). Open M-Sa 9:30pm-midnight.

Vildsvin, C. Ferran, 38 (☎933 17 94 07). M: Liceu. This Norwegian bar specializes in oysters (half dozen €7.20; 1 dozen €13.20). Wide selection of international beers (€4-7.50). Mixed crowd of tourists and locals. *Tapas* €3-5, desserts €3.50-10, entrees €8-26.50. Open 9am-2am, F-Sa 9am-3am.

El Bosq de les Fades (☎933 17 26 49). M: Drassanes. Walk to the Wax Museum and then make a right. From the maniacal geniuses who brought you the wax museum, the Forest of Fables is a fairy-tale world, complete with gnarly trees, waterfalls, gnomes, a small bridge, and plush side rooms. Open M-Th until 1:30am, F-Sa until 2:30am.

Molly's Fair City, C. Ferran, 7 (☎933 42 40 26). M: Liceu. Boasts blaring music, fast-flowing imported beer, and a prime location next to Pl. Reial. Head to Molly's to meet fellow English-speakers. Guinness on tap €4.90. Mixed drinks €6. Open M-F 8pm-2:30am, Sa-Su 7pm-3am. Cash only.

Dot Light Club, C. Nou de Sant Francesc, 7 (☎933 02 70 26). M: Drassanes. Take the 2nd right off C. Escudellers. Look for the "DOT" sign above the door. Futuristic 2-room bar/club. Nightly indie films at 10:30pm. Beer €2.70, mixed drinks €5.40. Open Tu-Th and Su 10:30pm-2:30am, F-Sa 10:30pm-3am. Cash only.

Margarita Blue, C. J. A. Clavé, 6 (☎933 17 71 76). M: Drassanes. Off Las Ramblas, 1 block from the port. This Mexican-themed 80s bar draws a 20- and 30-something crowd of locals and tourists. Blue margaritas €3. Beer €3.45. Tu magic shows, W drag performances (11:30pm-midnight). Open Su-W 7pm-2am, Th 7pm-2:30am, F-Sa 7pm-3am.

New York, C. Escudellers, 5 (☎933 18 87 30), right off Las Ramblas. M: Drassanes. Once a strip joint, now the biggest club in the Barri Gòtic. Crowds don't arrive until well after 3am. Cover 11:30pm-2am €5.40 (includes 1 beer); 2-5am €11.40, (includes any drink). Open Th-Sa midnight-5am. Cash only.

Fonfone, C. Escudellers, 24 (☎933 17 14 24). M: Liceu or Drassanes. Another futuristic bar/club mix. Music includes lounge, house, free style, garage, and more. Beer €3. Mixed drinks €6. Open Su-Th 9:30pm-2:30am, F-Sa 9:30pm-3am. Cash only.

Café Royale, C. Nou de Zurbano, 3 (☎934 12 14 33). M: Liceu. On a tiny street leading from the corner of Pl. Reial. The self-proclaimed "only" place to chill out to soul and funk. Arrive by midnight—later, the wait can be up to 1hr. Mixed crowd of 20- and 30-somethings. Beer €3.50, mixed drinks €4.80-6. Open Sa-Th 8pm-2:30am, F 8pm-3am.

Glaciar Bar, Pl. Reial, 3. M: Liceu. In the near left corner coming from Las Ramblas. A hidden treasure in a sea of indistinguishable tourist bars. Beer €1.50-2. Mixed drinks €4. Liter of sangría €10. Open M-Sa 4pm-2:30am, Su 8am-2:30am. Cash only.

Harlem Jazz Club, C. Comtesa de Sobradiel, 8 (☎933 10 07 55). M: Liceu. Between Pl. Reial and Vía Laietana. Live blues, jazz, reggae, flamenco, and acoustic rock. 2 sessions per night: Tu-Th and Su 10:30pm and midnight, F-Sa 11:30pm and 1am. F-Sa cover €5 (includes 1 drink). Open daily 10pm-4am; closed either M or Tu. Cash only.

Barcelona Pipa Club, Pl. Reial, 3 (☎933 02 47 32). M: Liceu. Decidedly unmarked; look for the small name plaque on the door to the left of Glacier Bar (on your left as you enter the *plaça* from Las Ramblas) and ring the doorbell to be let in. This private smokers' club opens daily. Occasional activities like tango classes and poetry readings. No entrance after 4am. Cocktails €5.50. Beer €3. Cash only. Open daily 11pm-5am.

Hook Bar, C. Ample, 35 (☎92 442 09 84). M: Drassanes. From Las Ramblas turn down C. J. A. Clavé, which turns into C. Ample; the bar is near the end of the street. If Peter Pan ever does grow up, this is where he'll come to drink. In 1809, Catalan revolutionaries plotting against the Bourbon monarchy were hanged here; the hook is still visible in the ceiling. Beer €2.50-3.50. Cocktails €5. *Tapas* €3-5. Open Tu-Th and Su 7:30pm-2am, F-Sa 7:30pm-3am. Cash only.

LA RIBERA

In La Ribera, the name of the game is *tapas* bars, where crowds gather to soak up artsy flavor. La Ribera is more of a place to mingle—you may want to brush up on your Spanish or Catalan before giving one of these bars a try.

Plàstic Café, Pg. del Born, 19 (☎933 10 25 96). M: Jaume I. Follow C. Princesa, turn right on C. Comerç, and right again on Pg. del Born. "Café" is a misnomer for this hyper-trendy bar. Mix of international, house, and 80s pop spinning in the background. Beer €2.40-3, mixed drinks €3 and up. Open Su-Th 10pm-2:30am, F-Sa 10pm-3am.

El Copetin, Pg. del Born, 19. M: Jaume I. Cuban rhythm infuses everything in this casual yet peppy nightspot. Grab a *mojito* (€4) and enjoy live Cuban music. Open Su-Th 6pm-2am, F-Sa 6pm-3am.

Palau Dalmases, C. Montcada, 20 (☎933 10 06 73). A self-labeled "Baroque space" in a 17th-century palace decorated with oil paintings, candelabras, and statues. Romantic candle-lit tables complete the atmosphere. Live opera performances Th at 11pm (€20, includes 1 drink). Mixed drinks €5.40-9. Open Tu-Sa 10pm-2am, Su 6-10pm.

Pitin Bar, Pg. del Born, 34 (☎933 19 50 87). Chill beneath tiny blue lights, or people-watch from one of the intimate upstairs tables. Trippy lounge music may put you in the mood for absinthe (€2.10). Mixed drinks €4.50-8. Open daily 6pm-2am.

EL RAVAL

Though traditionally El Raval has been home to a local, unpretentious set of bars, this neighborhood to the west of Las Ramblas is rapidly becoming a hotspot for funky new lounge-style hangouts.

La Oveja Negra, C. Sitges, 5 (☎933 17 10 87). M: Catalunya. From Pl. Catalunya, walk down Las Ramblas and take the 1st right onto C. Tallers; C. Sitges is the 1st left. The most touristed tavern in town. Gossip (in English) about your European backpacking romp over foosball and huge pitchers of beer or sangría (€6.90). Open M-Th 9am-3am, F 9am-3:30am, Sa 5pm-3:30am, Su 5pm-3am.

(El Café que pone) Muebles Navarro, Riera Alta, 4-6, a right off C. Carme. A mature local crowd is drawn here by a mellow ambiance ideal for conversation. Beer and wine €2.50, mixed drinks €3.60-9. Open Tu-Th 6pm-2am, F-Sa 6pm-3am.

London Bar, C. Nou de la Rambla, 34 (☎933 18 52 61). M: Liceu. Off Las Ramblas. Rub shoulders with unruly, fun-loving expats at this smoky Modernista tavern, founded in 1910. Live music nightly at 12:30am, usually rock or blues. Beer €3, wine €2; absinthe €3. Open Su and Tu-Th 7:30pm-4:30am, F-Sa 7:30pm-5am.

Sant Pau 68, C. Sant Pau, 68 (☎934 41 31 15). M: Liceu. Follow C. Sant Pau off Las Ramblas past Marsella Bar. Popular among locals, Sant Pau 68 is one of the hippest, newest bars in El Raval. Beer (€1.80), wine (€1.20), mixed drinks (€4.20-6). Open Tu-Th 8pm-2:30am, F-Sa 8pm-3am.

Lupino, C. Carme, 33 (☎934 12 36 97). M: Liceu. Ultra-chic restaurant and lounge with a cool aqua color scheme. Cocktails €5.50. Restaurant open Su-W 8:30pm-midnight, Th-Sa 8:30pm-1am. Lounge open Su-Th noon-2:30am, F-Sa noon-3am.

Casa Almirall, C. Joaquim Costa, 33. M: Universitat. Take the C. Pelai Metro exit, turn left at the end of the block, and turn again at the 2nd left. Laid-back Casa Almirall is Barcelona's oldest bar, founded in 1860. The staff will walk you through your 1st glass of *absenta* (absinthe; €4.50)–and cut you off after your 2nd. Beer €1.90, mixed drinks €5. Open Su-Th 7pm-2:30am, F-Sa 7pm-3am.

L'EIXAMPLE

L'Eixample has upscale bars and the some of the best gay nightlife in Europe.

La Fira, C. Provença, 171 (☎658 84 04 15). M: Hospital Clinic or FGC: Provença. A bar like no other, La Fira is a hodgepodge of funhouse and circus castaways. Bartenders pour drinks for a hip crowd dangling from carousel swings. DJs spin a mix of funk, disco, and oldies. Open M-Th 10pm-3am, F-Sa 10pm-4:30am, Su 6pm-1am.

Buenavista Salsoteca, C. Rosselló, 217 (☎932 37 65 28). FGC: Provença. This over-the-top salsa club manages to attract a laid-back, mixed crowd. The dancers are not shy. Free salsa and merengue lessons W and Th at 10:30pm. F-Sa cover €9 (includes 1 drink), Su-Th free. Open W-Th 11pm-4am, F-Sa 11pm-5am, Su 8pm-1am.

Dietrich, C. Consell de Cent, 255 (☎934 51 77 07). M: Pg. de Gràcia. A rather unflattering painting of Marlene Dietrich in the semi-nude greets a mostly gay crowd. Bartenders are scantily clad, and at 1:30am you can see the nightly drag/strip/dance show. Beer €3.50. Drinks €5-8. Open Su-Th 10:30pm-2:30am, F-Sa 10:30pm-3am.

Fuse, C. Roger de Llúria, 40 (☎933 01 74 99), between C. Gran Vía and C. Diputació. M: Tetuán or Pg. de Gràcia. A cutting-edge Japanese-Mediterranean restaurant, cocktail bar, dance club, and Internet cafe. Mixed gay and straight crowd. Beer €2.40, mixed drinks €6. Restaurant open M-Sa 8:30pm-1am. Bar/club open Th-Sa 1-3am. MC/V.

Les Gens que J'Aime, C. València, 286 (☎932 15 68 79), just off Pg. de Gràcia. M: Pg. de Gràcia. Travel back to Gaudí's time in this intimate bar dripping with chandeliers, mirrors, old paintings, plush corner sofas, and arm chairs. Beer €3, mixed drinks €5. Mini-bottles of wine €8.10. Open daily 7pm-2:30am. Cash only.

The Michael Collins Irish Pub, Pl. Sagrada Família, 4 (☎934 934 59 19 64). M: Sagrada Família. Directly across the *plaça* from the church. 100% Irish, from the wait-staff to the smoky, wooden decor. TVs play American and European sports. Live music Th-Su after 11pm (Irish, local guitarists, covers of American rock). Pints €3.80. Bottled beer €2.90, mixed drinks €5. Open daily 2pm-3am. Cash only.

berlin, C. Muntaner, 240 (☎932 00 65 42). M: Diagonal. A slice of streamlined German style in Barcelona. Corner bar with marble accents and huge, naked light bulbs attracts area hipsters, hordes of l'Eixample yuppies, and Barcelona's most beautiful people. Beer €1.80-2.40, mixed drinks €3.61-4.80.

Luz de Gas, C. Muntaner, 246 (☎932 09 77 11). M: Diagonal. Chandeliers, gilded mirrors, and deep red walls set the mood in this hip, uptown club. Live music every night. After 1am, the chairs are folded up and the luxurious club becomes a high-class disco. Beer €5, mixed drinks €8. Live music concerts €15. Open M-Sa 11pm-5am.

POBLE NOU

Poble Nou is the place to be for the untouristed alternative scene in Barcelona. **DIXI 724** boasts cheap beer, a bizarre shark-turned-airplane hanging from the ceiling, and tons of space (C. Pallars, 97; open F-Su 6pm-3am). **Bar Coyote & Co.** offers a Western twist (C. Pere IV, 68; open F-Su 6pm-3am). **Q3** blasts heavy metal (C. Pere IV, 49; open F-Sa 6pm-6am), while **Bóveda** is a club with dance beats (C. Pallars, 97; open F-Sa 6-10pm and midnight-6am, Su 6-10pm). On the same street, **Garatge Club** hosts rock concerts (C. Pallars, 195).

La Ovella Negra (Megataverna del Poble Nou), C. Zamora, 78 (☎933 09 59 38). From M: Marina, walk 2 blocks along C. Almogàvers and turn right on C. Zamora. This cavernous warehouse turned medieval tavern is the brother of La Oveja Negra in El Raval and is *the* place to come for the 1st few beers of the night. *Tapas* and *bocadillos* €2-4. Kitchen open until 12:30am. Open Th-Su 5pm-3am; disco open Sept.-May.

Razzmatazz, C. Pamplona, 88 (☎933 20 82 00), 2½ blocks from M: Marina following C. Almogàvers. Another huge warehouse turned entertainment complex. A 2-in-1 club: choose the front entrance for 3 rooms *or* the back entrance for 2; the venues are not connected. Cover €8, includes 1 drink. Open F, Sa, and holidays 1-5am. MC/V.

PORT OLÍMPIC

Port Olímpic caters to tourists with money to burn. A long strip of glitzy clubs fling open their doors at night, and the walkway becomes a carnival of scantily-clad dance fiends and late-night eaters and drinkers. Mixed drinks are expensive (€6-7). **Pachito** attracts clubbers, while the **Kennedy Irish Sailing Club** is popular with those who prefer pubbing. The complex is open 5pm-6am. Other options line Pg. Marítim.

Luna Mora (☎932 21 61 61). C. Ramón Trias Fargas, on the corner with Pg. Marítim. This planetarium-like disco with a more mature crowd is one of the best places for late-night dancing on the beach. The mostly local crowd doesn't arrive until 3am. Beer €5, mixed drinks €8. Cover €12. Open F midnight-6am, Sa midnight-6:30am.

El El, Pg. Marítim, 36 (☎932 25 92 00). From the beach, hidden behind the Greek restaurant Dionisos; enter from above. Colored strobe lights, fog machines, and techno beats entrance the wild crowd at this lively dance club. Beer €4, mixed drinks €7. Cover (includes 2 drinks) Th-F and Su €12, Sa €15, free if you eat dinner at Dionisos. Open July-Aug. daily midnight-6am; Sept.-June Th-Su midnight-6am. MC/V.

MAREMÀGNUM

Like Dr. Jekyll, Barcelona's biggest mall has more than one personality. At midnight, the complex turns into a tri-level maze of clubs, complete with escalators to cut down on navigating effort. Each club plays its own music for international students, tourists, and the occasional Spaniard. This is not the most "authentic" experience in Barcelona, but it is an experience. None of the clubs charge cover; they make their money from exorbitant drink prices. Good luck catching a cab home.

MONTJUÏC

Lower Montjuïc is home to Barcelona's epic "disco theme park," Poble Espanyol.

La Terrrazza/Discothèque (☎934 23 12 85), in Poble Espanyol on Av. Marqués de Comillas. M: Espanya. Enter to the right of the front gates of Poble Espanyol and shake it until the early morn in the outdoor *plaça*. La Terrrazza heads indoors from Oct.-May and becomes Discothèque. Drinks €4-8. Cover (includes 1 drink) Th and Su €12.15, F-Sa €15. Open Sept.-June Th-Su midnight-6am; July-Aug. Su only.

Torres de Ávila (☎934 24 93 09). M: Espanya. Next to the main entrance of Poble Espanyol. The height of club chic when it was built in the 80s, Torres is still going strong as one of the city's hottest clubs, complete with glass elevators, 7 different bars, and a rooftop terrace with gorgeous views of the city. DJ spins house and techno. Drinks €5-10. Dress to impress. Cover €18, includes 1 drink. Open Th-Sa midnight-6:30am.

Tinta Roja, C. Creu dels Molers, 17 (☎934 43 32 43). From M: Poble Sec, walk down Av. Paral.lel and turn right on C. Creu dels Molers. This converted factory showcases spectacular Argentinian delights by tango gurus Hugo and Carmen. Tango shows €3-8. Take tango lessons from Hugo himself (Tu 9-10:30pm, €14 per lesson or €96 for 2 months). Candlelit bar. Call ahead for show reservations. Open July-Aug. Tu-Th 7pm-1:30am, F-Sa 8pm-3am; Sept.-June Tu-Th and Su 7pm-1:30am, F-Sa 8pm-3am.

ZONA ALTA

The area around C. de Marià Cubí has an eclectic mix of bars and clubs. They are all a substantial walk from FCG: Muntaner (take a taxi). For fun in more accessible Gràcia, head to Pl. Sol.

Otto Zutz, C. Lincoln, 15 (☎932 38 07 22; www.ottozutz.com). FGC: Pl. Molina. Walk downhill on Vía Augusta and take C. Lincoln when it splits off to the right. Groove to house, hip hop, funk, and rap beats while Japanimation lights up the top floor. Beer €5, mixed drinks €8. Cover €15 (includes 1 drink). Open Tu-Sa midnight-6:30am.

D_Mer, C. Plató, 13 (☎932 01 62 07). FCG: Muntaner. Walk uphill on C. Muntaner for 2 blocks and turn right on C. Plató. A blue-hued heaven for lesbians of all ages to chat it up or get down on the dance floor to fun pop tunes. A touch of class, and a ton of fun. Cover €6 (includes 1 drink). Beer €3.50, mixed drinks €6. Open Th-Sa 11pm-3:30am.

Bar Fly, C. Plató, 15 (☎934 14 00 32). FGC: Muntaner. Same directions as D_Mer (see above). More popular in winter. Grab a drink at one of the 2 bars, hit the red-tinted dance floor, or shoot some pool in back. DJs spin rap, hip-hop, and funk. Drinks €6. No cover. Open Th-Sa midnight-3:30am.

Gasterea, C. Verdi, 39 (☎932 37 23 43). M: Fontana. Follow C. Astúries for several blocks and make a right on C. Verdi. Yellow walls cast a warm glow in this table-less bar. Grab a seat at one of the counters and dig into Gasterea's selection of fresh *tapas* (€1.05) like eggplant with goat cheese. Su-Tu and Th 7:30pm-1am, F-Sa 7:30pm-2am.

ENTERTAINMENT

Barcelona has everything from outdoor sports and bullfights to shopping and films. Consult the oh-so-informative **Guía del Ocio,** available at newsstands, for info on movies, live concerts, nightlife, and cultural events.

MUSIC, THEATER, AND DANCE

Barcelona offers many options for theater aficionados, though most performances are in Catalan (*Guía del Ocio* lists the language of the performance). Reserve tickets through **Tel Entrada** (24hr. ☎902 10 12 12; www. telentrada.com) or any branch of **Caixa Catalunya** bank (open M-F 8am-2:30pm). The **Grec** summer festival turns Barcelona into an international theater, music, and dance extravaganza from late June to the end of July (www.grec.bcn.com). For info about the festival, which takes place in venues across the city, ask at the tourist office, stop by the booth at the bottom of Pl. Catalunya for the duration of the festival, or swing by the **Institut de Cultura de Barcelona (ICUB),** Palau de la Virreina, Ramblas, 99. (☎933 01 77 75.

Open Tu-Sa 11am-8:30pm, Su 11am-3pm. Grec ticket sales M-Sa 10am-9pm. Most performances €24.10.) Another resource for tickets is www.travelhaven.com/activities/barcelona/barcelona.html, providing 10% discounts for performances at Palau de la Música Catalana, Gran Teatre del Liceu, and L'Auditori.

Palau de la Música Catalana, C. Sant Francesc de Paula, 2 (☎932 95 72 00; www.palaumusica.org). M: Jaume I. Off Vía Laietana near Pl. Urquinaona. Box office open M-Sa 9:45am-3pm, Su from 1hr. prior to the concert. No concerts in Aug.; check the *Guía del Ocio* for listings. Concert tickets €9-125. MC/V.

Centre Artesá Tradicionàrius, Tv. de Sant Antoni, 6-8 (☎932 18 44 85; www.personal4.iddeo.es/tramcat), in Gràcia. M: Fontana. Catalan folk music concerts Sept.-June F 10pm. Tickets €10. Open M-F 11am-2pm and 5-9pm. Closed Aug.

Gran Teatre del Liceu, Las Ramblas, 51-59 (☎934 85 99 13; www.liceubarcelona.com. 24hr. ticket sales ☎902 33 22 11), on Las Ramblas. M: Liceu. Founded in 1847, destroyed by fire in 1994, and recently reopened, Liceu has regained its status as the city's finest venue. Tickets start at €7and rise fast. Reserve tickets well in advance.

L'Auditori, C. Lepanto, 150 (☎932 47 93 00; www.auditori.com), between M: Marina and Glòries, in l'Eixample. The Auditori is home to the city orchestra. Concerts from late Sept. to mid-July, with performances F at 7pm, Sa at 9pm, and Su at 11am. Tickets €9.80-44.80 (Su is cheapest). Available by phone, through ServiCaixa, or at ticket windows (open M-Sa noon-9pm, Su 1hr. before show starts and 1hr. after it has begun).

El Patio Andaluz, C. Aribau, 242 (☎932 09 33 78), in Gràcia. M: Diagonal. From the Metro, turn left on Diagonal and right on C. Aribau. Lively Andalucian-themed restaurant showcases traditional Spanish flamenco. Show and 1 drink €29.96. Daily shows at 9:30pm and midnight. Call 9am-7pm for reservations. El Patio's red-paneled bar, Las Sevillanas del Patio, stays open until 3am for drinks and dancing.

El Tablao de Carmen (☎933 25 68 95; www.tablaodecarmen.com), on Av. Marqués de Comillas, inside Poble Espanyol. M: Espanya. Restaurant with flamenco shows. Dinner and show €51, drink and show €27. Open Tu-Su from 8pm; shows Tu-Th and Su 9:30pm and 11:30pm, F-Sa 9:30pm and midnight. Call ahead for reservations. MC/V.

FILM

Most screens display the latest Hollywood features, some in the original English. The *Cine* section in the *Guía del Ocio* denotes subtitled films with *V.O. subtitulada (versión original);* other foreign films are dubbed *(doblado),* usually in Catalan. Many theaters have a discount day (usually Monday). **Cine Malda,** C. del Pi, 5, is the only theater in the city which lets you see two movies with one ticket. (☎933 17 85 29. M: Liceu. Tickets M €4, Tu-F €5, Sa-Su €5.25. Cash only.) **Filmoteca,** Av. Sarrià, 33, screens classic, cult, and otherwise exceptional films. (☎934 10 75 90. M: Hospital Clínic. €2.70.) **Méliès Cinemas,** Villarroel, 102, shows classics. (☎934 51 00 51. M: Urgell. Tu-Su €4, M €2.70.) **Icària-Yelmo,** C. Salvador Espira, 61, in the Olympic Village, boasts 15 screens and *V.O.* (☎932 21 75 85. Tu-Su €5.50, M matinees €4.) The new **IMAX Port Vell** on the Moll d'Espanya next to the aquarium and Maremàgnum, has an IMAX screen, an Omnimax 30m in diameter, and 3-D projection. Get tickets at the door, through **ServiCaixa** machines, or by phone. (☎932 25 11 11. Tickets €9.60, matinee €6.60. Showtimes 10:30am-12:30am.)

FÚTBOL

For the record, the lunatics covered head to toe in red and blue didn't just escape from an asylum—they are **F.C. Barcelona** fans. Grab some face paint and head to **Camp Nou,** which has a box office on C. Aristedes Maillol, 12-18. Get tickets early. **R.C. Deportivo Espanyol,** a.k.a. *los periquitos* (parakeets), Barcelona's second professional soccer team, spreads its wings at **Estadi Olímpic,** Pg. Olímpic, 17-19.

This team isn't as renowned as the FCB, but the games are great fun, and they're **free.** Get tickets from Banca Catalana or by calling TelEntrada (24hr. ☎902 10 12 12).

RECREATIONAL SPORTS

The tourist offices can provide info about swimming, cycling, tennis, squash, sailing, hiking, scuba diving, white-water rafting, kayaking, and most other sports.

Piscines Bernat Picornell, Av. Estadi, 30-40 (☎934 23 40 41), to the right when facing the stadium. Test your swimming in the Olympic pools–2 gorgeous facilities nestled in stadium seating. €4.40 for outdoor pool, €8 for workout facilities including sauna, massage parlor, and gym. Outdoor pool open M-Sa 9am-9pm, Su 9am-8pm. Workout facilities open M-F 7am-midnight, Sa 7am-9pm, Su 7:30am-8pm. **Club Sant Jordi,** C. París, 114 (☎934 10 92 61). M: Sants. Passes available for other facilities including sauna, weights, and stairmaster. Bring your passport. Pool €3.50 per hr. Open M-F 7am-9:45pm, Sa 8am-6pm, Su and holidays 9am-2pm. Closed 1st week in Aug.

Beaches: The entire strip between Vila Olímpica and Barceloneta is a long public beach accessible from M: Ciutadella or Barceloneta. The closest and most popular is **Platja Barceloneta,** off Pg. Marítim. Beware (or be aware) of nudity on **Platja San Sebastià.** The southernmost section of the beach is primarily gay.

BULLFIGHTS

Although the best bullfighters rarely venture out of Madrid, Sevilla, and Málaga, Barcelona's **Plaza de Toros Monumental,** Gran Vía de les Corts Catalans, 743, is an excellent facility, complete with Moorish influences. (☎932 45 58 04. M: Monumental.) Bullfights take place during the summer tourist season, since tourists are about the only people who go (June-Oct. Su at 7pm; doors open at 5:30pm). Tickets are available at travel agencies or ServiCaixa ("la Caixa" banks; ☎902 33 22 11; €15-69). The box office also sells tickets before the start of the fight. The cheapest seats are in the *Andanada* section, in the sun.

FESTIVALS

Festas abound in Barcelona. The city celebrates **Carnaval** February 27 to March 5, but many head to even more raucous celebrations in Sitges and Vilanova i la Geltrù. Also in February is the **Festa de San Medir,** when neighbors gather at the base of Tibidabo to be showered with candy by men riding down the mountain on horses. Soon thereafter, the **Festa de Sant Jordi** (St. George), April 24, brings feasts in honor of Cataluña's patron saint. This is Barcelona's St. Valentine's Day; men give women roses, and women give men books. **Setmana Santa** is a huge festival complete with grand processions; *barceloneses* pour into the streets to celebrate. On May 10-11, the **Fira de Saint Ponç,** a traditional market of aromatic and medicinal herbs and honey, sets up in Carrer Hospital, close to Las Ramblas. Barcelona erupts on June 23, the night before **Día de Sant Joan.** Bonfires roar throughout the city, unsupervised children play with firecrackers, and the fountains of Pl. Espanya and Palau Reial light up in anticipation of fireworks over Montjuïc. On August 15-21, city folk jam at Gràcia's **Fiesta Mayor.** Lights blaze in the plazas and streets, and rock bands play all night. On September 11, the **Fiesta Nacional de Catalunya** brings traditional costumes, dancing, and Catalan flags hanging from balconies. The **Feria de Cuina i Vins de Catalunya** draws wine and *butifarra* (sausage) producers to Rambla Catalunya. For one week you can sample fine food and drink for a small fee. From October through November, the **Festival Internacional de Jazz** hits the city's streets and clubs. The beginning of November also marks the **Fiesta del Sant Çito,** when locals and tourists alike roll up their sleeves and party on Las Ramblas.

SHOPPING

Many of Barcelona's stores are out of the budget range, but there's nothing wrong with window shopping. Expensive designer shops line **Passeig de Gràcia, Rambla de Catalunya,** and **Portal de l'Angel.** For off-the-runway style, Barcelona's signature stores include **Zara** (Pg. de Gràcia) and **Mango** (Pg. de Gràcia). Fashion-snobs can be found roaming the avenues of **l'Eixample** while the fashion-smart go for some of the smaller boutiques hidden in side streets off **Las Ramblas.** Funky art and jewelry can be found all over **La Ribera.** Barcelona's most unique jewelry shop is probably **Locura Cotidiana,** Pl. Rius i Taulet, 12, in Gràcia. Antiques get their 15 minutes of fame on **C. Rosa** and **C. Banys Nous** (off Pl. Pi). For more of a mall experience, try **El Corte Inglés,** in Pl. Catalunya, and **Maremàgnum,** at Port Vell.

Bargains abound if you know where to go. One place to try is **Calle Girona,** between C. Casp and Gran Vía, in **l'Eixample,** where you'll find a small line-up of discount shops offering girl's clothing, men's dress clothes, shoes, bags, and accessories, and even a coveted Mango outlet. (M: Tetuán. Walk two blocks down Gran Vía and take a left on C. Girona.) Another area to try for discounts is the **Mercat Alternatiu** (Alternative Market) on C. Riera Baixa in **El Raval.** (M: Liceu. Take C. de l'Hospital—a right off Las Ramblas if you're facing the ocean—and follow it to C. Riera Baixa, the 7th right, shortly after the stone hospital building.) This street is crammed with second-hand and thrift stores. The area around C. Banys Nou (M: Jaume I), in **La Ribera,** is a great place to look for antiques. Flea markets are a mess of shopping deals. Hold your wallet in **Fira de Bellcaire** and visit **El mercado de Sant Antoni.** (M: Sant Antoni. Visit M,W, F, or Sa for the best selection.)

NEAR BARCELONA

MONTSERRAT

A 1235m peak protruding from the Río Llobregat Valley with a colorful interplay of limestone, quartz, and slate stone, Montserrat (Sawed Mountain) inspires poets, artists, and travelers. A millennium ago, a wandering mountaineer had a vision of the Virgin Mary; as story spread, pilgrims flocked to the mountain. The monastery to the Virgin, founded in 1025 by the opportunistic Bishop Oliba, is today tended by 80 Benedictine monks. During the Catalan *Renaixença* (renaissance) of the 19th century, politicians and artists like poets Joan Maragall and Jacint Verdaguer turned to Montserrat as a source of Catalan legend and tradition. Under Franco, it became a center for Catalan resistance. Today, the site attracts devout worshipers and tourists who come to see the Virgin of Montserrat, her ornate basilica, the art museum, and the panoramic views of the mountain's stunning rocks.

TRANSPORTATION. FGC (☎932 05 15 15) line R5 runs to Montserrat from M: Espanya in Barcelona (1hr.; every hr. 8:36am-5:36pm; round-trip including cable car €11.30); get off at Aeri de Montserrat, not Olesa de Montserrat. From there, catch the **Aeri cable car** to the monastery. (July-Aug. daily every 15min. 9:25am-6:35pm, Mar. and Oct. 9:25am-1:45pm and 2:20-6:45pm; price included in FCG fare or €6 by itself. Schedules change frequently; call ☎938 77 77 01 to check.) **Autocars Julià** buses run to the monastery, from near Estació Sants. (Leaves Barcelona daily at 9am and returns at 5pm. Call ☎933 17 64 54 for reservations. €10. MC/V.) If you plan to use the funiculars to hike, consider the **Tot Montserrat** available at tourist offices or in M: Espanya; it includes tickets for the FGC, cable car, mountain funiculars, Museu de Montserrat (see below), and a meal, all for €34 (€20 if you buy it at Montserrat without the FCG fare). Call ☎938 35 03 84 for a **taxi.**

PRACTICAL INFORMATION. Montserrat is not a town, but a monastery with adjacent lodging and food for religious and camera-toting pilgrims. Visitor services are in Pl. Creu, the area straight ahead from the top of the Aeri cable car steps. The **info booth** in Pl. Creu provides free maps, schedules of religious services, and advice on mountain navigation. (☎938 77 77 77. Open July-Sept. daily 9am-7pm; Oct.-June M-F 9am-5pm, Sa-Su 9am-7pm.) For more detailed information, buy the *Official Guide to Montserrat* (€6.40) or the guide to the museum (€6.30). Services include: **ambulance** or the **mountain rescue team** (☎904 10 55 55); **ATMs;** and a **post office** (open daily 10am-1pm).

ACCOMMODATIONS AND FOOD. For room reservations, contact the **Central de Reserves i Informació** (☎938 77 77 01; fax 938 77 77 24; www.abadiamontserrat.net). The apartment administration office, **Administració de les Delles,** is in the corner of the *plaça.* (Open daily 9am-1pm and 2-6pm; after 6pm they're at the Hotel Abat Cisneros reception. 2-day minimum stay, 7-day July-Aug.) **Abat Marcet** ❷ has rooms with bath, TV, heat, and a kitchen. (Singles €11.50-30.10; doubles €23.60-38.60, students €19.20-32.) The **Hotel Abat Cisneros** ❷**,** next to the basilica, has comfortable bedrooms. (Breakfast included. Singles €24.15-43.75; doubles €40.70-76.30.) The **campsite** ❶ is a 5min. walk uphill from the Sta. Cova funicular. (☎938 35 02 51. Open Apr.-Oct. Office open daily 8am-9pm. €2.50 per person, under 12 €2; €2.25 per tent. No fires allowed.) Pick up some food for your hike at **Queviures supermarket** in Pl. Creu. For a quick meal, **Bar de la Plaça** ❶ is next to the supermarket (*bocadillos* and hamburgers €2.60-3.60; open M-F 9:30am-5pm, Sa 9:30am-4:40pm). The **self-service cafetería** ❷ for *Tot Montserrat* card-holders is up the hill to the right from the cable car steps (open Feb.-Dec. daily noon-4pm), as is **Restaurant de Montserrat** ❷**.** (*Menú* €12, kids €5.40. Open Mar. 15-Nov. 15 daily noon-4:30pm. MC/V.) The **Restaurant Hotel Abat Cisneros** ❺ offers an expensive *menú* (€23.30) in a nice setting. (Open daily 1-4pm and 8-10pm. AmEx/MC/V.)

SIGHTS. Above Pl. Creu, the **basilica** looks onto Pl. Santa Noría. Next to the main chapel, a route through side chapels leads to the 12th-century Romanesque **La Moreneta** (the black Virgin), an icon of Mary. (Walkway open Nov.-June M-F 8-10:30am and noon-6:30pm, Sa-Su 8-10:30am and noon-6:30pm; July-Sept. daily 8-10:30am and noon-6:30pm.) Legend has it that St. Peter hid the figure, carved by St. Luke, in Montserrat's caves. The solemn little statue is now showcased in a silver case. For luck, rub the orb in Mary's hand. If you can, catch a performance of the renowned **Escalonia boys' choir** in the basilica. (Daily at 1pm and 7:30pm, except late June and July.) Also in Pl. Santa María, the **Museo de Montserrat** has a variety of art, from a mummified Egyptian to Picasso's *Sardana of Peace,* painted for Montserrat. The Impressionist paintings are its highlights; Ramon Casas's *Madeline Absinthe* is one of the evocative portraits. (Open Nov.-June M-F 10am-6pm, Sa-Su 9:30am-6:30pm; July-Sept. M-F 10am-7pm, Sa-Su 9:30am-7pm. €4.50, students and over 65 €3.50, children ages 10-14 €3, under 10 free.)

WALKS. Some of the most beautiful areas of the mountain are accessible only on foot. The **Santa Cova funicular** descends from Pl. Creu to paths which wind to ancient hermitages. (Apr.-Oct. daily every 20min. 10am-6pm; Nov.-Mar. Sa-Su only 10am-5pm. Round-trip €2.50.) Take the **St. Joan funicular** for inspirational views of Montserrat. (Apr.-Oct. daily every 20min. 10am-6pm; Nov.-Mar. M-F 11am-5pm, Sa-Su 10am-5pm. Round-trip €6.10; joint round-trip ticket with the Sta. Cova funicular €6.90, over 65 €6.20, ages 10-14 €3.50.) The dilapidated **St. Joan monastery** and **shrine** are only a 20min. tromp from the highest station. The real prize is **Sant Jerónim** (the area's highest peak at 1235m), with its views of Montserrat's mystical rocks.

The serrated outcroppings are named for human forms, including "The Bewitched Friars" and "The Mummy." The hike is about 2½ hours from Pl. Creu or a one-hour trek from the terminus of the St. Joan funicular. The paths are long and winding but not difficult—after all, they were made for guys wearing long robes. En route, take a sharp left when, after about 45min.; you'll come to a little old chapel—otherwise, you're headed straight for a helicopter pad. On a clear day the hike offers views of Barcelona and surrounding areas. For **guided visits** and hikes, call ☎938 77 77 01 two weeks in advance. (Hiking tour in English €6.50, museum tour €5, joint tour €14. In Spanish, hiking and museum tour €4 each, joint tour €7.) For rock climbing and athletic hiking in the area, call Marcel Millet at ☎938 35 02 51 or stop by his hiking/climbing office next to the Montserrat campsite.

SITGES

Forty kilometers south of Barcelona, beachy Sitges deserves its self-given title "Jewel of the Mediterranean," with prime tanning grounds, lively festivals, and a atmosphere of tolerance. A thriving gay community mingles with daytripping Spaniards, tourist families, and 20-something partiers, all in search of sun and fun. The climate, with over 300 sunny days a year, sees to the former, while a vibrant nightlife helps with the latter. Through it all, Sitges has not fallen into the commercial traps of typical resort towns; despite booming tourism, the old town somehow has kept traces of its fishing village past, with narrow cobblestoned streets and 19th-century architecture. Sitges is the ideal daytrip when Barcelona's crowded city beaches just aren't cutting it and is well worth a couple of days' stay.

TRANSPORTATION. **Cercanías trains** (☎934 90 02 02) run from Estació Barcelona-Sants to Sitges (40min., every 15-30min. 5:27am-11:52pm, €2.15) and continue on to **Vilanova** (7min.; every 15-30min., last train from Sitges at 12:44am; €1). The last train from Sitges returns to Barcelona at 10:26pm. Rent a car in Sitges at **Europcar** (☎938 11 19 96), on the 1st fl. of the Mercat next to the train station. For a **taxi,** call ☎938 94 13 29. A taxi between Barcelona and Sitges costs €40-45.

ORIENTATION AND PRACTICAL INFORMATION. The train station is on Av. Carbonell, a 5min. walk from the center of town. Take a right as you leave the station, and then the third left onto C. Sant Francesc, which leads to the old town, and C. Parellades, the main commercial path, parallel to the ocean. From here, all streets lead to water; Pg. Ribera runs along the main beaches. For a free map, stop by the **tourist office,** Sínia Morera, 1. From the station, turn right onto C. Carbonell and take the first big right. The office is across the street, to the left—look for the sign with the big "i." (☎938 94 50 04. Open July-Aug. daily 9am-9pm; Sept.-June W-M 9am-2pm, and 4-6:30pm.) In summer, a smaller branch opens by the museums on C. Fonollar. (☎938 94 42 51. Open W-F 10:30am-1:45pm, Sa 11am-2pm and 4-7pm, Su 11am-2pm.) **Super Avui,** C. Carbonell, 24, is a supermarket across from the train station. (Open M-Sa 9am-2pm and 5-8pm.) Services include: **medical** (☎938 94 64 26) and **emergency assistance** (☎938 94 39 49). **Internet access** and **fax** service are available at **Sitges Internet Access,** C. Espanya, 7. (☎938 11 40 03. €1.20 per 15min., €4.50 per hr. Open daily 11am-1am.) The **post office** is in Pl. Espanya. (☎938 94 12 47. Open M-F 8:30am-2:30pm, Sa 9:30am-1pm. No packages Sa.) **Postal code:** 08870.

ACCOMMODATIONS AND FOOD. Rooms are expensive and scarce on summer weekends, so reserve early. **Hostal Parellades ❷,** C. Parellades, 11, is close to the beach and offers standard rooms that are dirt cheap for Sitges. (☎938 94 08 01. Singles €20; doubles €32, with bath €38; triples with bath €45.) **Hotel El Cid ❸,** C. Sant Josep, 39, is one of the best deals in town. (☎938 94 18 42. Su-Th singles €29;

doubles €37.30. F-Sa singles €34; doubles €47.60.) **Hostal Internacional ❸,** C. Sant Francesc, 52, off Carbonell, has bright rooms. (☎938 94 26 90. Doubles €36, with bath €42.) **Izarra ❶,** C. Mayor, 24, behind the museum area, is a Basque *tapas* bar for a quick food fix before a night of club-hopping. (*Tapas* €1. Entrees €4 and up. Open daily 1:30-4pm and 8:30-11pm.) **Restaurante La Oca ❷,** C. Parellades, 41, roasts chickens that attract lines of hungry tourists. Try the *half-pollo al ast* (roasted chicken) for €5. (Open Su-F 1pm-midnight, Sa 1pm-1am.)

SIGHTS AND BEACHES. The pedestrian street **C. Parellades,** which features shopping, eating, and drinking galore, is the central attraction. Cultural activities may seem as undesirable as rain to some beachgoers, but Sitges has some can't-miss attractions, including Morell's whimsical **Modernista clock tower,** Pl. Cap de la Vila, 2, above Optica at the intersection of Parellades and Sant Francesc. Behind it, on C. Fonollar, the **Museu Cau Ferrat** (☎938 94 03 64) hangs over the water's edge. Once home to Catalan Modernista Santiago Rusinyol and a meeting point for young Catalan artists Pablo Picasso and Ramon Casas, the building is a shrine to Modernista iron work, glass work, and painting. Next door, the **Museu Maricel del Mar** (☎938 94 03 64) has a selective collection of Romanesque and Gothic painting and sculpture. Farther into town, the **Museu Romàntic,** C. Sant Gaudenci, 1, off C. Parellades, is a 19th-century bourgeois house filled with period objects like music boxes and 17th- to 19th-century dolls. (☎938 94 29 69. All 3 museums open in summer Tu-Su 10am-2pm and 5-9pm; rest of the year Tu-F 10am-1:30pm and 3-6:30pm, Sa 10am-7pm, Su 10am-3pm.) Across the street from the museums, the stately **Palau Maricel,** on C. Fonollar, built in 1910 for American millionaire Charles Deering, wows visitors with its sumptuous halls and rich gardens. Guided tours are available on summer nights and include a glass of *cava* (champagne); Friday through Sunday, a piano and soprano concert complete the evening. Call ahead for reservations. (☎938 11 33 11. M-Th €5.40; F-Su €7.20.)

Plenty of soothing sand accommodates hordes of sunworshippers on hot summer days. At **Platja de la Fragata,** the beach farthest to the left as you face the sea, sand sculptors create new masterpieces every summer day. By midday, the beaches closest to downtown can become almost unbearably crowded. The best beaches, with calmer water and more open space, are a kilometer or two walk further down, at **Platja de la Barra** and **Platja de Terramar.** Rocks shield the beach here from waves, creating a shallow ocean swimming pool ideal for children. Showers and Red Cross stations abound. For those desiring more private sunbathing, there are two gorgeous, secluded coves surrounded by cliffs a kilometer out of town. Facing the water, turn right and follow Pg. Ribera to its end. Continue walking past Club Atlàntida and follow the footpath that leads away from the parking lot. The first cove is a mixed nude beach. The second is gay; look for the rainbow flags.

NIGHTLIFE AND FESTIVALS. The place to be at sundown is **Carrer Primer de Maig** (which runs directly from the beach and Pg. Ribera) and its continuation, **Carrer Marquès Montroig,** off C. Parellades. Bars and clubs line the small street, blasting pop and house from 10pm until 3am. The clubs here are wide-open with a mixed crowd. Beers go for about €3, mixed drinks €6. Even crazier is the "disco-beach" **Atlàntida,** in Sector Terramar (☎938 94 26 77; foam parties on Th and Su nights), and the legendary **Pachá,** on Pg. Sant Didac in nearby Vallpineda (☎938 94 22 98). Buses run all night on weekends to the two discos from C. Primer de Maig.

Sitges shines especially bright in its gay nightlife scene. **Parrot's Pub** on C. Primer de Maig is a place to relax with a drink before hitting the clubs. Ask for the **plano gay,** the free map of gay establishments in Sitges. **Mediterráneo,** C. Sant Bonaventura, 6, off C. Sant Francesc, shakes every summer night with two floors of drinking and dancing (open 10pm-3:30am). After hours, **Trailer,** C. Angel Vida, 36, is the hottest disco party in town, with foam parties W and Su (opens at 2am).

Sitges celebrates holidays with all-out style. During the **Festa de Corpus Christi** in June, townspeople collaborate to create intricate fresh-flower carpets. For *papier-mâché* dragons, devils, and giants dancing in the streets, visit during the **Festa Major,** held August 22-27 in honor of the town's patron saint, Bartolomé. Nothing compares to the **Carnaval,** a preparation for Catholic fasting during the first week of Lent (Feb. 27-Mar. 5). Spaniards crash the town for a frenzy of dancing, outrageous costumes, and vats of alcohol. The last night is the wildest, as hundreds parade through the streets dressed in drag. On the first Sunday in March, a pistol shot starts the **Rally de Coches de Época,** an antique car race from Barcelona to Sitges. June brings the **International Theater Festival** (€9-21 per show), and July and August the **International Jazz Festival** (€10.20 per concert). From September 12 to 14, competitors trod on fresh grapes on the beach for the annual **Grape Harvest.** October 1-12 brings the world-famous **Festival Internacional de Cinema de Catalunya.**

DAYTRIP FROM SITGES: VILANOVA I LA GELTRÙ

Cercanías trains (RENFE) run from Vilanova to Sitges (7min., every 15-30min., €1), and continue to Barcelona (50min., €2.15). Mon Bus (☎938 93 70 60) connects Vilanova to Sitges (€1.20), Vilafranca (€1.60), and Barcelona (€2.90). The bus station is in the plaza in front of the train station. A taxi (☎938 933 2 41) from Sitges costs about €9-12.

Vilanova i la Geltrù are actually two cities in one: an industrial center and a well-groomed beach town. There is little in the uptown area except for old churches and stone facades; most visitors spend the day on the beach (10min. from the train station). In the evening, Vilanovans generally forego late-night madness for beach volleyball or soccer at Parc de Ribes. To get to the **beaches,** exit the station, turn left on C. Forn de Vidre, take the third left onto Rambla de la Pau, head under the overpass, and follow the *rambla* all the way to the port. Grab a **map** at the **tourist office,** about 100m to the right, off Pg. del Carme in a small park called **Parc de Ribes Roges.** (☎938 15 45 17. Open July-Aug. M-Sa 10am-8pm, Su 10am-2pm; Sept.-June 10am-2pm and sometimes 4-7pm.) The wide **Platja de Ribes Roges** is past the tourist office; to the left is the smaller **Platja del Far.**

If you decide to stay in town, the popular **Can Gatell ❸,** C. Puigcerdà 6-16, has clean rooms and full baths. With your back to the station, head down C. Victor Balaguer; at the end, turn right onto La Rambla and then take the first left. (☎938 93 01 17. Singles €28; doubles €45, with A/C €51. Extra bed €10.) The hostel's *menú* (€8, served M-F) is popular with locals. (Open daily 7-10:30am, 1-5pm, and 8:30-10pm.) Numerous restaurants serving fresh seafood line Pg. del Carme, but they can be quite pricey. A less expensive alternative is **Supermarket Orangutan,** Rambla de la Pau, 36, on the way to the beach. (Open M-Sa 9:30am-2pm and 5:30-9pm.)

CATALUÑA (CATALUNYA)

From rocky Costa Brava to smooth Costa Dorada, the lush Pyrenees to chic Barcelona, Cataluña is a vacation in itself. It has also been graced with many of the nation's richest resources, making it the most prosperous region in Iberia. *Catalanes* are famous for their resourcefulness and work ethic. As the saying goes, *"El Català de les pedres fa pa"* (a Catalan can make bread out of stones).

Colonized first by the Greeks and the Carthaginians, Cataluña was later one of Rome's favored provinces. Only briefly subdued by the Moors, Cataluña's counts achieved independence in AD 987. Cataluña grew powerful as she joined the throne of Aragón in 1137; while this union empowered Cataluña to pursue her own empire for a time, it ultimately doomed her to be subjugated to subsequent Spanish rule. King Felipe V was finally able to fully suppress Cataluña in the early 18th century when the Catalans sided against him in the War of Spanish Succession (1702-1714). In the late 18th century, the region's fortunes revived when it developed into one of Europe's premier textile manufacturers, opening trade with the Americas. Nineteenth-century industrial expansion nourished arts and sciences, ushering in an age known as the Catalan Renaixença (Renaissance). The 20th century gave birth to the Modernist movement and an all-star list of artists and architects, including Picasso, Miró, Dalí,

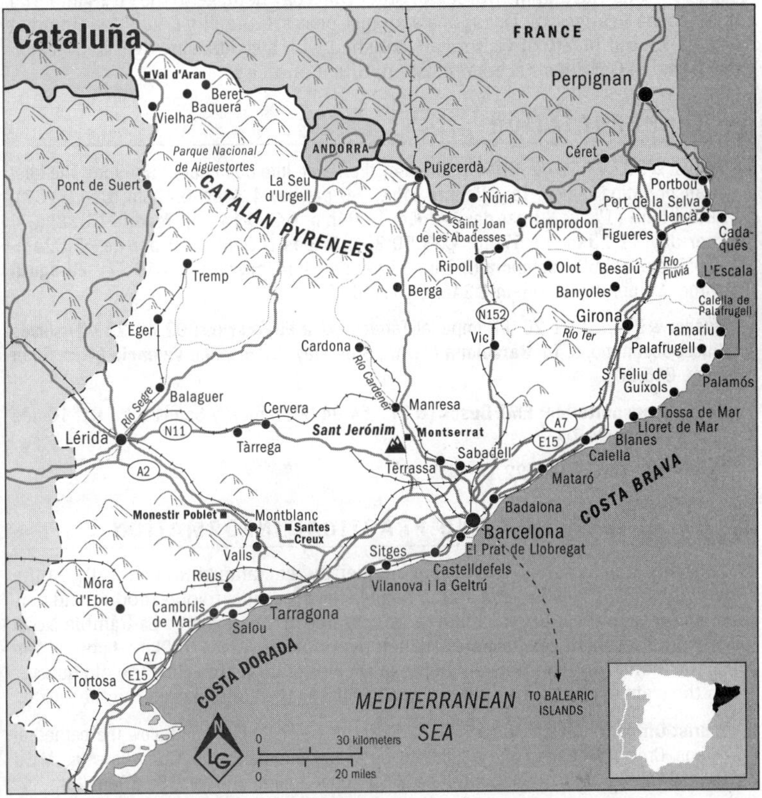

Antoni Gaudí i Comet, Lluís Domènech i Montaner, and Josep Puig i Cadafalch. Home to staunch opponents of the Fascists during Spain's Civil War, Cataluña lost its autonomy in 1939. During his regime, Franco suppressed Catalan language instruction (except in universities) and limited Catalan publications.

Since Cataluña regained regional autonomy in 1977, Catalan media and arts have flourished. Today, Catalan is once again the region's official language. While some worry that the use of the regional dialect will discourage talented Spaniards from working or studying in Cataluña, effectively isolating the region, others argue that extensive regional autonomy has generally led to progressive ends. Many *catalanes* will answer inquiring visitors in Catalan, even if asked in Castilian. Lauded throughout Spain, Catalan cuisine boasts *pa amb tomaquet* (bread smeared with olive oil, tomato, and garlic), and *ali-oli* (a garlic and olive oil sauce).

COSTA DORADA

TARRAGONA

Tarragona's strategic position made the city a provincial Roman capital under Augustus; today an amphitheater and other ruins pay homage to the city's imperial days. These vestiges of Tarragona's august past are the city's most compelling attractions, but plenty of visitors are satisfied with a sightseeing-light and beach-heavy stay in Cataluña's second most important port city.

TRANSPORTATION

Trains: ☎902 24 02 02. On Pl. Pedrera by the water. Info open daily 6am-9pm. The best transportation option. To: **Alicante** (4hr., 7-9 per day 4:34am-6:49pm, €24.50-37); **Barcelona** (1¼hr., 30 per day 5:15am-11:04pm, €4.55-14.50); **Madrid** (6½-8hr., 4 per day 11:23am-11:57pm, €28.50-39); **Sitges** (45min., 20 per day 5:52am-10:21pm, €2.60); **Valencia** (2-3hr., 15 per day 4:34am-9:49pm, €18-27); **Zaragoza** (4hr., 10 per day 10:04am-1:24am, €17.50-22).

Buses: ☎977 22 91 26. Pl. Imperial Tarraco. **Alsa Enatcar** (☎902 42 22 42) serves most destinations. To: **Barcelona** (1½hr., 8 per day, €7.50) and **Valencia** (4hr., 6 per day, €15.20).

Public Transportation: EMT Buses (☎977 54 94 80) run daily 6am-11pm. €1, 10-ride *abono* ticket €4.70.

Taxi: Radio Taxi (☎977 22 14 14).

ORIENTATION AND PRACTICAL INFORMATION

Most sights are clustered on a hill, surrounded by remnants of Roman walls. At the foot of the hill, **La Rambla Vella** and **La Rambla Nova** (parallel to one another and perpendicular to the sea) are the main thoroughfares of the new city. La Rambla Nova runs from **Passeig de les Palmeres** (which overlooks the sea) to **Plaça Imperial Tarraco,** the monstrous rotunda and home of the bus station. To reach the old quarter from the train station, turn right and walk 150m to the stairs parallel to the shore.

Tourist Office: C. Major, 39 (☎977 24 52 03; fax 977 24 55 07), below the cathedral steps. Crucial **free map** and a guide to Tarragona's Roman ruins. Open July-Aug. M-Sa 9am-9pm, Su 10am-2pm; Sept.-June M-Sa 10am-2pm and 4-7pm, Su 10am-2pm.

Tourist Information booths: Pl. Imperial Tarraco, at the bottom of La Rambla Vella, just outside the bus station; another at the intersection of Av. Catalunya and Vía de l'Impera Romi; a 3rd at the corner of Vía Augusta and Pg. Sant Antoni. Open July-Sept. daily 10am-1:30pm and 4:30-8pm; Nov.-June Sa-Su 10am-2pm.

Luggage Storage: At the train station 4:30am-midnight; €3.

Emergency: ☎091. **Police: Comisaria de Policía,** Pl. Orleans (☎977 24 98 44). From Pl. Imperial Tarraco on the inland end of La Rambla Nova, walk down Av. Pres. Lluís Companys, and take the 3rd left to the station.

Medical Assistance: Hospital de Sant Pau i Santa Tecla, La Rambla Vella, 14 (☎977 25 15 70). **Hospital Joan XXIII,** C. Dr. Mallafré Guasch (☎977 29 58 00).

Internet Access: Ciberspai.net, C. Estanislao Figueras, 58 (☎977 24 57 64), off the Imperial Tarraco rotunda. €0.75 per 15min., €1.80-2.40 per 1hr. Open M-F 9am-midnight, Sa-Su 10am-midnight. **Biblioteca Pública,** C. Fortuny, 30 (☎977 24 05 44). Public library; free use of the computers with passport.

Post Office: Pl. Corsini, 12 (☎977 24 01 49), below La Rambla Nova off C. Canyelles. Open M-F 8:30am-8:30pm, Sa 9:30am-1pm. **Postal Code:** 43001.

ACCOMMODATIONS AND CAMPING

Most of the city's accommodations are two- to four-star hotels near the center. Pl. Font in the old quarter (parallel to La Rambla Vella) is filled with quality lodging.

Hostal Noria, Pl. de la Font, 53 (☎977 23 87 17), in the heart of the historic town. Enter through the restaurant. 24 clean and bright rooms with pretty-in-pink bathrooms. Singles with bath €22, doubles with bath €39. ❷

Hostal Forum, Pl. de la Font, 37 (☎977 23 17 18), upstairs from the restaurant. Clean rooms and bathrooms don't leave space for spreading out, but it's a decent place to sleep for the night. Singles with bath €19; doubles with bath €37. ❷

Camping: Several campgrounds line the road toward Barcelona (Vía Augusta or CN-340) along the northern beaches, especially around km 1.17. Take bus #9 (every 20min., €1) from Pl. Imperial Tarraco. **Tarraco** (☎977 29 02 89) is the closest, at Platja de l'Arrabassada. Well-kept facilities near the beach. 24hr. reception. €3.50 per person, per car, and per tent. Open Apr.-Sept. ❶

FOOD

Pl. Font and Las Ramblas Nova and Vella are full of cheap *menús* (€5-7.50) and greasy *platos combinados*. Tarragona's indoor **Mercado Central** (market) takes place in Pl. Corsini next to the post office. (☎977 23 15 51. Open M-W and Sa 8am-2pm, Th-F 7am-2pm and 5:30-8:30pm. Flea market Tu and Th.) For **groceries,** head to **Champión,** C. Augusta at Comte de Rius, between Las Ramblas Nova and Vella. (Open M-Sa 9am-9:15pm.) **El Serrallo,** the fisherman's quarter right next to the harbor, has the best seafood. Try your food with Tarragona's typical *romesco* sauce, simmered from red peppers, toasted almonds, and hazelnuts.

Restaurant Les Coques, Nou Patriarca, 2 (☎977 22 83 00), off Pl. La Seu near the cathedral. Les Coques offers a peaceful refuge from the world and serves traditional specialties. Entrees €10-32. Open M-Sa 1:15-3:45pm and 9-10:45pm. ❹

La Teula, C. Mercería, 16 (☎977 23 99 89), in the old city near Pl. del Fórum. Great salads (€3-4.50) and toasted sandwiches with Catalan veggie/meat combos (€6-9). Lunch *menú* €6.60. Open daily noon-4pm and 8pm-midnight. MC/V. ❷

SIGHTS AND BEACHES

Tarragona's status as provincial capital transformed the small military enclosure into a glorious imperial port. Countless Roman ruins stand silently amid 20th-century hustle and bustle, all just minutes from the beach.

ROMAN RUINS. Below Pg. Palmeres and set amid gardens above Platja del Miracle beach is the **Roman Amphitheater** (☎977 44 25 79), where gladiators once killed wild animals and each other. In AD 259, the Christian bishop Fructuosus and his two deacons were burned alive here; in the sixth century, these martyrs were honored with a basilica built in the arena.

Next to the Museu Nacional Arqueològic in Pl. Rei is the entrance to the **Pretori I Circ Romans** (☎977 24 19 52), which houses the **Praetorium Tower,** the former administrative center of the region, and the **Roman Circus,** the site of chariot races and other spectacles. Visitors descend into the long, dark tunnels that led fans to their seats, and see a model reconstruction of what the complex looked like. The Praetorium was the governor's palace in the first century BC. Rumor has it that the infamous hand-washer Pontius Pilate was born here.

The scattered **Fòrum Romà,** with reconstructed Corinthian columns, lies near the post office on C. Lleida. Once the center of the town, its distance clearly demonstrates how far the walls of the ancient city extended. To see what remains of the second-century BC walls, stroll through the **Passeig Arqueològic.** The walls originally stretched to the sea and fortified the entire city. *(All ruins open May-Sept. Su 9am-3pm, Tu-Sa 9am-9pm; Oct.-Apr. Tu-Su 9am-7pm. Admission to each €1.87, students €0.62.)*

MUSEUMS. The **Museu Nacional Arqueològic,** across Pl. Rei from the Praetorium, displays ancient architecture, utensils, statues, and mosaics, and offers descriptions of daily life in the Roman Empire. *(☎977 23 62 09. Open June-Sept. Tu-Su 10am-8pm; Oct.-May Tu-Su 10am-1:30pm and 4-7pm. €2.40, students €1.20; includes admission to the necropolis.)* The early Christian burial site at the **Museu i Necròpolis Paleocristians,** Av. Ramón y Cajal, 78, has yielded a rich variety of urns, tombs, and sarcophagi, the best of which are in the small museum. *(☎977 21 11 75. Open June-Sept. Tu-Sa 10am-8pm, Su 10am-2pm; Oct.-May Su 10am-2pm, Tu-Sa 10am-1:30pm and 4-7pm. €2.40, students €1.20; Tu free; includes admission to Museu Arqueològic.)* If you've had too much Roman roamin', descend the steps in front of the cathedral and take the third right onto C. Cavellares to the **Casa-Museu Castellarnau.** It housed the Viscounts of Castellarnau in the 18th century. *(☎977 24 22 20. Open May-Sept. Tu-Sa 9am-9pm, Su 9am-3pm; Oct.-Apr. Tu-Su 9am-7pm. €1.87, students €0.62.)*

CATALUÑA

OTHER SIGHTS. The **Pont del Diable** (Devil's Bridge), a Roman aqueduct 10min. outside of the city, is visible on the way in and out of town by bus. Take municipal bus #5 (every 20min., €1) from the corner of C. Christòfer Colom and Av. Prat de la Riba or from Pl. Imperial Tarraco. Lit by octagonal rose windows flanking the transept is the gigantic Romanesque-Gothic **cathedral,** which dates from 1331 and is one of the most magnificent cathedrals in Cataluña. The stunning interior holds the tomb of Joan d'Aragó. The adjoining **Diocesian Museum** showcases religious relics from the last 700 years. *(Entrance to both on C. Claustre, near Pl. La Seu. Open mid-Mar. to May M-Sa 10am-1pm and 4-7pm; mid-June to Oct. M-Sa 10am-7pm; mid-Oct. to mid-Nov. M-Sa 10am-5pm; mid-Nov. to mid-Mar. M-Sa 10am-2pm. €2.40, students €1.50.)*

BEACHES. The hidden access to **Platja del Miracle,** the town's main beach, is along Baixada del Miracle, starting off Pl. Arce Ochotorena, beyond the Roman theater. Walk away from the theater until you reach the underpass, under the train tracks, to the beach. Though not on par with the region's other beaches, it's not bad for a few hours of relaxation. A bit farther away are the larger beaches, **Platja l'Arrabassada** and **Platja Llarga.** *(Take bus #1 or 9 from Pl. Imperial Tarraco or any of the other stops.)*

NIGHTLIFE AND FESTIVALS

Weekend nightlife in Tarragona is on a much smaller scale than that of Sitges and Barcelona. Between 5 and 9pm, Las Ramblas Nova and Vella (and the area in between) are packed with strolling families. After 9pm, the bars liven up; around 10pm on Saturdays in summer, fireworks brighten the skies. The place to be is **Port Esportiu,** a portside plaza full of restaurant-bars and mini-discos. Heading up La Rambla Nova away from the beach, take a left onto C. Unió; bear left at Pl. General Prim and follow C. Apodaca to its end. Cross the tracks; the fun will be to the left.

The end of July ushers in the **Fiesta de Tarragona,** which goes through the first week of August (☎977 24 47 95; tickets 24hr. 902 33 22 11). Pyromaniacs shouldn't miss the first week of July when fireworks light up the beach in **El Concurso Internacional de Fuegos Artificiales.** On even-numbered years, the first Sunday in October brings the **Concurs de Castells,** a competition of tall human towers, as high as seven to nine "stories," called *castells. Castells* also appear amid beasts and fireworks during the annual **Fiesta de Santa Tecla** (Sept. 23). If you're unable to catch the *castellers* in person, don't miss the monument to the *castellers* on La Rambla Nova.

COSTA BRAVA ☎972

Skirting the Mediterranean Sea from Barcelona to the French border, the Costa Brava's jagged cliffs and pristine beaches draw throngs of European visitors, especially in July and August. Early June and late September can be remarkably peaceful; the water is already warm and the beaches much less crowded. In the winter Costa Brava lives up to its name, as fierce winds sweep the coast, leaving behind tranquil, near empty, beach towns. The rocky shores have traditionally attracted romantics and artists, like Marc Chagall and Salvador Dalí, a Costa Brava native. Dalí's house in Cadaqués and his museum in Figueres display the largest collections of his work in Europe.

CATALUÑA

TOSSA DE MAR

Falling in love in (or with) Tossa de Mar is easy. In 1934, French artist Marc Chagall commenced a 40-year love affair with this seaside village, deeming it "Blue Paradise." When *The Flying Dutchman* was filmed here in 1951, Ava Gardner fell hard for Spanish bullfighter-turned-actor Mario Cabrera, much to the chagrin of Frank Sinatra, her husband at the time. (A statue of the actress in Tossa's old city commemorates her visit.) Like many coastal cities, Tossa (pop. 4000) suffers from the usual tourist industry blemishes: souvenir shops, inflated prices, and crowded beaches. That said, it resists a generic beach town ambiance, drawing from its historical legacy and cliff-studded landscape to preserve a unique small-town feel.

TRANSPORTATION

Buses: Av. Pelegrí (☎972 34 09 03), at Pl. de les Nacions Sense Estat. Ticket booth open 7am-12:40pm and 2:20-8:10pm. **Pujol i Pujol** (☎610 50 58 84) goes to **Lloret del Mar** (20min.; June-Aug. every 30min., Sept.-May every hr. 8am-9:10pm; €1.05). **Sarfa** (☎972 34 09 03) goes to **Barcelona** (1½hr., 18 per day 7:25am-8:10pm, €7.55) and **Girona** (1hr.; in summer 2 per day, offseason 1 per day; €4).

Car Rental: Viajes Tramontana, Av. Costa Brava, 23 (☎972 34 28 29; fax 972 34 13 20). **Avis** (☎902 13 55 31), and their affiliates **Olimpia** (☎972 36 47 10) and **SACAR** (☎972 36 60 16), operate from the same storefront. Min. age 21. Expect to be asked for a major credit card, driver's license (international driver's license required for longer rentals), and passport. 1-day rentals €34.16-103.88. Open daily July-Aug. 9am-9pm; Apr.-June and Sept.-Nov. 9am-3pm and 4-8pm.

Bike and Moped Rentals: Jimbo Bikes, La Rambla Pau Casals, 12 (☎972 34 30 44). Staff gives bike route information. Bring license for moped rental. Mountain bikes €3.50-4.50 per hr., €17-22 per day. Open M-Sa 9am-9pm, Su 9:30am-2pm and 4-8pm. AmEx/MC/V.

Boat rentals: Kayaks Nicolau (☎972 34 26 46), on the beach at Mar Menuda, offers 1½hr. kayak excursions to Cala Bona (10am, noon, and 4pm; €10.30). Kayak rental €5 per hr., paddle boats €7. Open Apr.15-Oct.15 daily 9am-6pm.

Taxis: ☎972 34 05 49. Wait outside the bus station.

ORIENTATION AND PRACTICAL INFORMATION

Buses arrive at **Pl. de les Nacions Sense Estat** where **Av. del Pelegrí** and **Av. Ferrán Agulló** meet; the town slopes down from there to the waterfront. Walk away from the station down Av. Ferrán Agulló and turn right on Av. Costa Brava; as it turns into Pou de la Vila, take a right on any of the side streets and continue until your feet get wet (10min. total). **Pg. del Mar,** to the right at the end of Av. Costa Brava, curves along the **Platja Gran** (Tossa's main beach) to the old quarter, **Vila Vella.**

Tourist Office: Av. Pelegrí, 25 (☎972 34 01 08; fax 972 34 07 12; www.infotossa.com), in the bus terminal at Av. Ferrán Agulló and Av. Pelegrí. Grab a free map. English spoken. Provides advice on hiking trails and tourist sights, and posts a schedule of upcoming events. Offers guided hikes and walks on weekends (€6-9). Open June 15-Sept. 15 M-Sa 9am-9pm, Su 10am-2pm and 5-8pm; Apr.-May and Oct. M-Sa 10am-2pm and 5-8pm, Su 10:30am-1:30pm; Mar. and Nov. M-Sa 10am-1pm and 5-7pm; Dec.-Feb. M-F 10am-1pm and 5-7pm, Sa 10am-1pm.

Bank: Santander Central Hispano, Av. Ferrán Agulló, 2 (☎972 34 10 65). Open Apr.-Sept. M-F 8:30am-2pm; Oct.-Mar. M-F 8:30am-2:30pm, Sa 8:30am-1pm.

Police: Municipal Police, Av. Pelegrí, 14 (☎972 34 01 35), down the street from the tourist office. English spoken.

Medical Services: Casa del Mar, Av. de Catalunya (☎972 34 18 28). Primary health care and immediate attention. The nearest hospital is in Blanes, 30min. south.

Internet Access: Tossa Bar Playa, C. Socors, 6 (☎972 34 09 22), off the main beach. €1 per 14min. Open May-Oct. 15 daily 9:30am-midnight. **Scuba Libre,** Av. Sant Raimón de Penyafort, 11 (☎972 34 20 26). Several Internet terminals. €3.60 per hr. Open daily May-Oct. 8am-2am; Nov.-Apr. Sa-Su 10am-6pm.

Post Office: C. Maria Auxiliadora, 4 (☎972 34 04 57), down Av. Pelegrí from tourist office. Open M-F 8:30am-2:30pm, Sa 9:30am-1pm. **Postal Code:** 17320.

ACCOMMODATIONS

Tossa is a seasonal town; many hostels, restaurants, and bars are open only from May to October. During July, August, and festivals, Tossa fills quickly; make reservations in advance. The **old quarter** hotels are the only ones really worth considering. The tourist office website (www.infotossa.com) also lists rooms.

Fonda/Can Lluna, C. Roqueta, 20 (☎972 34 03 65; fax 972 34 07 57). From Pg. del Mar, turn right onto C. Peixeteras, veer left onto C. Estalt, walk up the hill until the dead-end, then turn left. Immaculate single, double, and triple rooms with private baths. Breakfast included. Rooftop terrace. Laundry €6. Book months in advance in summer. Oct.-Mar. and July-Aug. €16 per person. Mar.-June and Sept. €12. Cash only. ❷

Pensión Carmen Pepi, C. Sant Miguel, 10 (☎972 34 05 26). Turn left off Av. de Pelegrí onto Maria Auxiliadora and veer to your immediate right through the Pl. de l'Antic Hospital and onto C. Sant Miguel. Traditional house with a small courtyard. All rooms have private bath. Breakfast €1.50. July-Aug. singles €19.50; doubles €39. May-June €17/€34. Sept.-Apr. €14.50/€29. Cash only. ❷

L'Hostalet de Tossa, Pl. de l'Església, 3 (☎972 34 18 53; fax 972 34 29 69; www.tossa.com/hostalettossa), in front of the Sant Vicenç church. Hotel-quality doubles with baths. Breakfast included. Foosball, pool table, and TV. In-room TV €4 per day. Doubles July-Aug. and *Semana Santa* €25.50, with balcony €27. June and Sept. €19.50/€21.50. Apr.-May and Oct. €15/€18.50. MC/V. ❸

Pensión Moré, C. Sant Telmo, 9 (☎972 34 03 39). Large doubles and triples with views of the old quarter. July-Aug. €12 per person. Sept.-June €10. Cash only. ❶

Camping: Can Martí (☎972 34 08 51; fax 972 34 24 61), at the end of La Rambla Pau Casals, off Av. Ferrán Agulló. 15min. from the bus station, this is the closest camping site, on the fringes of a wildlife reserve. Hot showers, telephones, pool, and restaurant. June 20–Aug. €5.50 per person, €6 per tent, €3.50 per car. May 12-June 19 and Sept. 1-16 €4.50/€5/€2.70. Traveler's checks or cash only. ❶

FOOD

The old quarter has the best cuisine and ambiance in Tossa. Restaurants catering to tourists serve up *menús* at reasonable prices; most specialize in local seafood. If you need groceries, head to **Megatzems Palau,** C. Enric Granados 4. (☎972 34 08 58. Open daily June-Sept. 8am-9pm.)

Restaurant Santa Marta, C. Francesco Aromi, 2 (☎972 34 04 72), just inside the old fortress off C. Portal. The contemporary cuisine is a delectable contrast to the medieval building. Entrees €10-27. Open daily 12:30-4pm and 7:30-11:30pm. AmEx/MC/V. ❸

La Taberna de Tossa, C. Sant Telm, 26 (☎972 34 14 47). In the heart of the old quarter, right off La Guardia. Serves traditional *tapas* (€1.65-3.16) and provincial meat and fish specialities (sandwiches €2.61-3.46). *Menús* €7.18-8.38. Open Apr.-Sept. daily 1-4pm and 7pm-1am. Oct.-Mar. F-Su 1-4pm and 7pm-1am. V. ❷

Restaurant Marina, C. Tarull, 6 (☎972 34 07 57). Outdoor seating for prime people-watching. Features pizza, meat, fish, and lots of *paella*. Entrees €3.75-12.30. *Menús* €8.50 and €10.50. Open *Semana Santa* to Oct. daily 11:30am-11:30pm. MC/V. ❷

SIGHTS AND BEACHES

Inside the walled fortress of the Vila Vella, a spiral of medieval alleys leads to tiny Pl. Pintor J. Roig y Soler, where the **Museu Municipal** has a collection of 1920s and 1930s art, including one of the few Chagall paintings still in Spain. Tossa's Roman mosaics (dating from the 4th-1st century BC), and other artifacts from the nearby Vila Romana are displayed in 12th-century palace turned museum. (☎972 34 07 09. Open June 1-15 and Sept. 16-30 M-F 11am-1pm and 3-5pm, Sa-Su 11am-6pm; June 16-Sept. 15 daily 10am-8pm; Oct. M-F 11am-1pm and 3-5pm, Sa-Su 11am-5pm. €3, students and seniors €1.80.)

Tossa's main beach, **La Platja Gran,** is surrounded by cliffs and the dreamy Vila Vella, and draws the majority of beach-goers. To escape the crowds, visit some of the neighboring *calas* (small coves), accessible by foot. The tiny **Es Codolar** sits just under the tower of the Vila Vella palace, hugged by precipices cloaked in foliage. To get there, follow C. Portal to the end. Snorkeling and diving are popular sports; pick up gear at **Andrea's Diving Center,** C. San Raimon de Penyafort, 11 (☎972 34 20 26). Well-marked hiking and mountain-biking paths also criss-cross the **Massif of Cadiretes** wildlife reserve and offer impressive views of the coastline. For less strenuous activity, several companies, like **Fonda Cristal,** send glass-bottomed boats to nearby beaches and caves, where you can sometimes jump in for a swim. Tickets are available at booths on the Platja Gran. (☎972 34 22 29. 1hr.; 17 per day; €7.50 per person, children €5.) **Club Aire Libre,** on the highway to Lloret, organizes various excursions and rents equipment for water sports. (☎972 34 12 77. Canoeing and kayaking €13, water skiing €26 for 2 lessons, scuba diving €264 for 5-day certification course, sailing €11 per hr., windsurfing €10.30 per hr.)

NIGHTLIFE

Bars line the streets of the old quarter and occasionally offer live music. At **Bar Trinquet,** C. Sant Josep, 9, flirt over dripping candles under romantic chandeliers or enjoy the stars in the ivy-covered interior courtyard. **Bar El Pirata,** C. Portal, 32, and its companion bar **Piratín,** C. Portal, 30, have outdoor tables overlooking the sea at Es Codolar. (☎972 34 14 43. Open Apr.-Oct. daily 11pm-3am.) DJs spin jazz and house on weekend nights. (☎616 38 55 87. Open Apr.-Oct. daily 9pm-3am.) For live music try **Don Pepe,** C. Estolt, 6, a small bar which hosts a flamenco guitarist every night. (☎972 34 22 66. Open Apr.-Oct. daily 9:45pm-4:30am.)

PALAFRUGELL ☎972

In 988, inhabitants of the beach town of Llafranc founded inland Palafrugell, seeking refuge from the constant plundering of Mediterranean pirates. Today, budget travelers come here to flee the wallet plundering of seaside hotels and restaurants. Forty kilometers east of Girona, Palafrugell serves as a base for trips to the nearby beach towns Calella, Llafranc, and Tamariu, that cater to wealthy Europeans whose idea of budget accommodation is any hotel that doesn't leave mints on the pillow. To save some euros, stay in bland and beachless Palafrugell and daytrip to the beaches, connected by the Camino de Ronda footpaths.

TRANSPORTATION

Buses: Sarfa, C. Torres Jonama, 67-79 (☎972 30 06 23). Prices rise on weekends. To: **Barcelona** (2hr.; 17 per day, last bus 8:30pm; €11.40); **Calella** and **Llafranc** (15min.-20min.; 12-24 per day, in winter months 4-5 per day; €1); **Figueres** (1½hr., 3-4 per day, €5.65); **Girona** (1hr., 18 per day, €3.75).

Taxis: Radio Taxi (☎972 61 00 00). 24hr. service throughout the area.

ORIENTATION AND PRACTICAL INFORMATION

To get from the bus station to the center of town, turn right and walk down C. Torres Jonama to C. de Pi i Maragall. Turn right and walk past the Guardia Civil and the market until you hit **Pl. Nova,** the main square of the town, off which are C. San Sebastià and C. Cavallers. On your way you'll pass the **Pl. l'Església** on the right. To get to the nearby beach towns of Calella, Llafranc, and Tamariu, take a bus (see above), or speed away on a moped or mountain bike.

Tourist Office: Can Rosés, Pl. l'Església (☎972 61 18 20; fax 972 61 17 56). 1st right off C. Cavallers walking away from Pl. Nova. Ask for the indispensable *Guía Municipal.* A **larger branch** is at C. Carrilet, 2 (☎972 30 02 28; fax 972 61 12 61). From the bus station, go left on C. Torres Jonama, left again at the traffic circle. Both open May-Sept. M-Sa 10am-1pm and 5-8pm, Su 10am-1pm; Oct.-Apr. M-Sa 10am-1pm and 4-7pm, Su 10am-1pm. Carrilet branch also open July-Aug. M-Sa 9am-9pm, Su 10am-1pm.

Currency Exchange: Banesto, C. Torres Jonama, 43 (☎972 30 18 22), at the corner of C. l'Estrella. **ATM.** Open M-F 8:30am-2pm.

Emergency: ☎112. **Police:** ☎092. **Municipal police:** Av. Josep Pla and C. Cervantes (☎972 61 31 01).

Medical Services: Centro de Atención Primaria, C. d'Angel Guimerà, 6 (☎972 61 06 07; emergencies/ambulance 972 30 00 23). Open 24hr.

Internet Access: Internet Papereria Palé, C. Cavallers, 16 (☎972 30 12 48). €1 per 15min. Open July-Sept. Su 10am-1pm, M-Sa 9am-1pm and 5-9pm.

Post Office: C. Barris i Buixó, 23 (☎972 30 06 07). **Lista de Correos.** Open M-F 8:30am-2:30pm, Sa 9:30am-1pm. **Postal Code:** 17200.

ACCOMMODATIONS

Though options are few, accommodation prices are reasonable and room quality high in Palafrugell. Be sure to call ahead on summer weekends.

Fonda l'Estrella, C. Quatre Cases, 13-17 (☎972 30 00 05), at the corner of C. La Caritat, a right off C. Torres Jonama. High-ceilinged, well-lit rooms with sinks surround a Moorish courtyard. Gorgeous common baths. Breakfast €4. Singles €24 (available only Apr.-May and Sept.); doubles €37; triples €54. Open Apr.-Sept. ❷

Hostal Plaja, C. Sant Sebastià, 34 (☎972 30 05 26), off Pl. Nova. Grand, frescoed foyer gives way to a broad courtyard surrounded by spotless rooms, all with balconies, bathrooms, TVs, bottled water, clotheslines, and new beds. Singles €24; doubles €44. ❷

Residencia Familiar, C. Sant Sebastià, 29 (☎636 26 36 03), off Pl. Nova. Clean rooms with sinks. No private baths. Singles €18.50; doubles €37. Less for longer stays. ❷

Camping: Moby Dick, C. Costa Verda, 16-28 (☎972 61 43 07). Take the Sarfa bus to Calella and ask to be let off. No white whale in sight, but it is close to the water. €4.20 per adult, €3.30 per child; €4.20 per tent; €4.20 per car. Open May-Sept. ❶

FOOD

Restaurants near the beach are predictably expensive, making meals in Palafrugell proper a wiser option. For some reason, the town has a disproportionately high number of pizzerias and Italian restaurants. Shrugs one local, "We just really like pizza." **L'Arcobaleno ❷,** C. Mayor, 3, offers a delicious, all-inclusive lunchtime *menú* (€8) including everything from lasagna to roast chicken. (☎972 61 06 95. Open Apr.-Sept. 14 daily 11am-4pm and 6:30pm-12:30am; Sept. 15-Mar. closed M. AmEx/MC/V.) **Pizzeria Vapor ❷,** C. de les Botines, 21, serves the requisite pizza (€4.50-5.50) plus a fresh *menú* for €7. (☎972 30 57 03. Entrees €4.50-10. Open June-Aug. daily noon-4pm and 8pm-midnight; Sept.-May Tu-Su noon-4pm and 8pm-midnight.) Ice cream shops and restaurants with terraces dominate **Pl. Nova.**

SIGHTS AND ENTERTAINMENT

In addition to nearby beaches, Palafrugell boasts one of the world's few cork museums. The **Museu del Suro,** C. Tarongeta, 31, has everything you ever (never?) wanted to know about cork. (☎972 30 78 25. Open June 15-Sept. 15 daily 10am-2pm and 4-9pm; Sept.16-June 14 Tu-Sa 10am-1pm and 5-8pm, Su 10:30am-1:30pm. €1.20, students and seniors €0.60. English explanations available.)

A Palafrugell Friday evening stroll ends up at the *plaça,* where young and old often dance the traditional Catalan *sardana* around 10:30pm in July and August. The tourist office prints a monthly bulletin of upcoming events; also check the *Guía Municipal.*

The town's biggest party takes place July 19-21, when the dance-intensive **Festa Major** bursts into the streets. Calella honors **Sant Pere** on June 29 with lots of *sardana* dancing, and Tamariu celebrates on August 15, coinciding with the Assumption of the Blessed Mother. The **Festivals of the Hanaveres** (Spanish-Cuban sea songs) come to town the first Saturday of every July.

DAYTRIPS FROM PALAFRUGELL

CALLELA, LLAFRANC, AND TAMARIU

Take a Sarfa bus from Palafrugell to Calella (15min., 12-24 per day, €1). From Calella, follow the Camino de Ronda (see below) and walk 20min. to Llafranc. From Llafranc, Tamariu is a 2hr. walk farther along the path. Tourist Office at Tamariu, C. Riera. ☎972 62 01 93. Open June-Sept. M-Sa 10am-1pm and 5-8pm, Su 10am-1pm.

The three beaches grow quieter the farther you walk from Callela; Tamariu is the most peaceful. In Callela, **Jardí Botànic de Cap Roig,** the botanical garden in front of Hotel Garbí, provides an excellent view of the coast. (☎972 61 45 82. Open daily June-Aug. 9am-8pm; Sept.-May 9am-6pm. €1.80.) Russian Nicolas Voevodsky built the garden's **seaside castle** after fleeing the Bolshevik Revolution. He and his wife planted the splendid maze of paths and flower beds with their own hands. The first sign for the castle points to the right at the fork of Av. Costa Daurada and C. Consolat del Mar—it also hosts the **Festival de Jazz de la Costa Brava** in July and August. Callela's **tourist office,** C. Voltes, 6, provides maps of walking paths that criss-cross the area, including the **Camino de Ronda,** a popular climb along the coast from Callela to Llafranc. (☎972 61 44 75. Open daily July-Aug. 10am-1pm and 5-9pm; Apr.-June and Sept.-Oct. 12 M-Sa 10am-1pm and 5-8pm, Su 10am-1pm.)

CATALUÑA

GIRONA ☎972

Girona (pop. 70,000) is a world-class city that the world has yet to notice. A Roman settlement and then an important medieval center, Girona was one of the few Spanish cities where Christians, Arabs, and Jews were able to peacefully coexist—for a time. Girona was the founding place of the renowned *cabalistas de Girona*, a group of 12th-century rabbis who created an oral tradition called the *Kabbala* based on numerological readings of the Torah (see **The Jewish Sepharad,** p. 420). The city is divided by the Riu Onyar, which separates the medieval alleys and Romanesque buildings of the old quarter from the Spanish dwellings of the new.

TRANSPORTATION

Trains: RENFE (☎972 24 02 02), in Pl. Espanya. Open daily 6:30am-10pm. To: **Barcelona** (1½hr.; 6:12am, 9:29pm; €4.90); **Figueres** (30-40min., 23 per day 6:15am-10:44pm, €2.05); **Madrid** (10½hr., 8:21pm, €31); **Paris** (11hr.; 10:17pm; €85-106).

Buses: Next to the train station. **Sarfa** (☎972 20 17 96). Open daily 8am-8:30pm. All fares €3-5, 10% discount for students; cash only. To: **Palafrugell** (1hr., 17 per day), for connections to Begur, Llafranc, Calella, and Tamariu and **Tossa de Mar** (40min.; July-Aug. 2 per day, Sept.-June 1 per day). **Teisa** (☎972 20 02 75). Open M-F 9am-1pm and 3:30-7:15pm, Sa-Su 9am-1pm. Cash only. To: **Olot** (1¼hr., 9 per day, €4.30); and **Ripoll** (2hr., 3 per day, €7.50). **Barcelona Bus** (☎972 20 24 32). Open M-F 6:30-10am, 11am-2:25pm, and 4:30-7:10pm. MC/V. Express buses to **Barcelona** (1¼hr.; M-F 6 per day, €10; Sa-Su and holidays 3 per day, €11.45) and **Figueres** (50min.; M-F 6 per day, €3.95; Sa 2 per day, €4.55; Su and holidays 3 per day, €4.55).

Taxis: ☎972 22 23 23 or 972 22 10 20. Try Pl. Independència or Pont de Pedra.

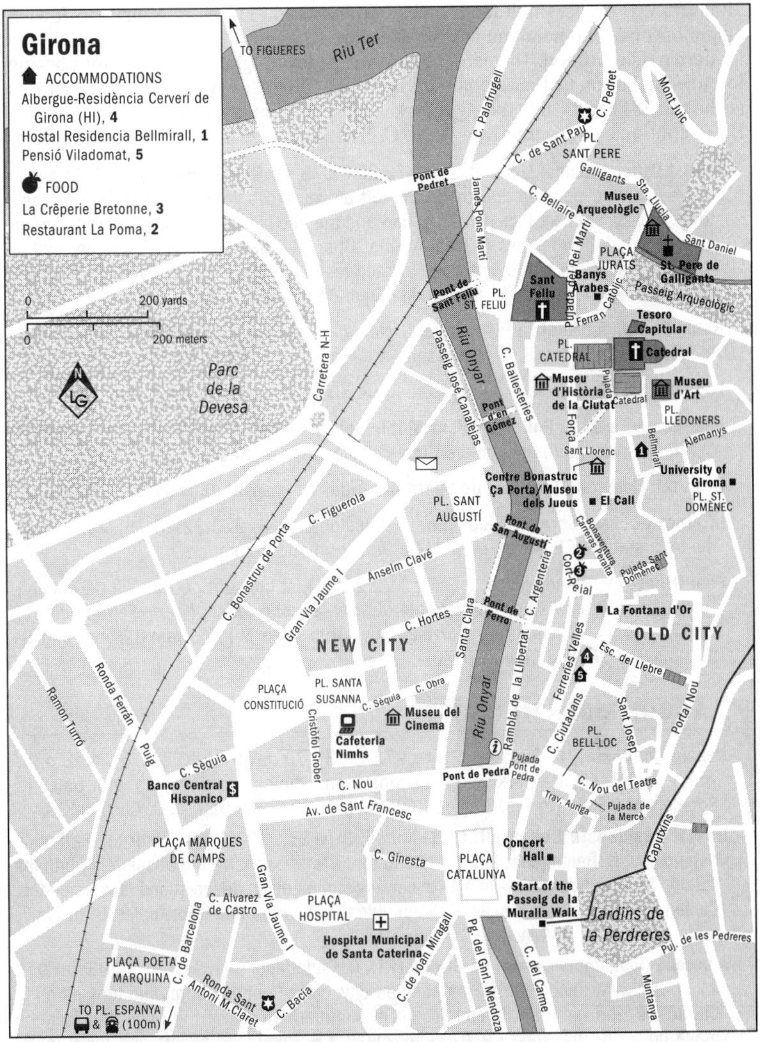

Car Rental: Europcar is inside the train station. Other companies cluster around C. Barcelona, right outside. Must be 21+ and have had a license for at least 1-2 years. **Avis** is also inside the train station. 23+, and must have had a valid licence for at least 1 year. €16.63 per day. Surcharge of €6 per day for those under 25. Open M-Sa 8am-9pm. AmEx/MC/V; credit cards only.

ORIENTATION AND PRACTICAL INFORMATION

The **Riu Onyar** separates the new city from the old. The **Pont de Pedra** bridge connects the two banks and leads into the old quarter by way of C. Ciutadans, C. Peralta, and C. Força, which lead to the cathedral and **El Call,** the historic Jewish neighborhood. The **train** and **bus terminals** are situated off C. de Barcelona, in the modern neighborhood. To get to the old city, head straight out through the parking lot, turning left on C. Barcelona. Follow C. Barcelona for two blocks until it forks at the traffic island. Take the right fork via C. Santa Eugenia to Gran Vía de Jaume I, and continue across the Gran Vía to C. Nou, which leads to the Pont de Pedra.

Tourist Office: Rambla Llibertat, 1 (☎972 22 65 75; fax 972 22 66 12), in an American cheese-colored building directly on the left as you cross Pont de Pedra from the new town. English spoken. Pick up a free map and the free bi-weekly *La Guía,* in Catalan but with easy-to-follow listings of local events. Open M-F 8am-8pm, Sa 8am-2pm and 4-8pm, Su 9am-2pm. Another **branch** located nearby in Plaça del Vi. Open in winter M-F 9am-7pm, Sa 9am-2pm; in summer M-F 9am-3pm, Sa 9am-2pm.

Bank: Santander Central Hispano, at C. Nou and Gran Vía, has an **ATM.** Open Oct.-Mar. M-F 8:30am-2:30pm, Sa 8:30am-1pm; Apr.-Sept. M-F 8:30am-2:30pm.

Luggage Storage: Lockers in train station €4.50 per 24hr. Open M-F 6:30am-10pm.

Emergency: ☎112. **Police: Policía Municipal,** C. Bacià, 4 (☎092). From Santander Central Hispano, turn right on the Gran Vía, then right on Bacià.

Hospital: Hospital Municipal de Santa Caterina, Pl. Hospital, 5 (☎97 218 26 00).

Internet Access: Corado Telephone, C. Barcelona, 31 (☎972 22 28 75), across from the train station. €2 per hr. Open M-Sa 9am-2pm and 5-9pm.

Post Office: Av. Ramón Folch, 2 (☎972 22 21 11), at the start of Gran Vía de Jaume I. Turn right on Gran Vía coming from the old city. **Second office,** Ronda Ferrán Puig, 17 (☎972 22 34 75). **Lista de Correos** only. Both open M-F 8:30am-8:30pm and Sa 9:30am-2pm. **Postal Code:** 17070.

ACCOMMODATIONS

Pensió Viladomat, C. Ciutadans, 5 (☎972 20 31 76; fax 972 20 31 76), next to the youth hostel. Light, sparkling clean rooms and dining/reading area with balcony. Rooms with bath have TVs. Singles €16; doubles €31, with bath €50. Cash only. ❷

Hostal Residencia Bellmirall, C. Bellmirall, 3 (☎972 20 40 09). With the cathedral behind you, C. Bellmirall is straight ahead to the left. Expensive but absolutely worth the splurge for delightful rooms in a 14th-century stone house. Reservations recommended. Closed Jan. 6-Feb. 28. Singles €32; doubles €49, with bath €56; triples €75; family room (for 4) €96 (IVA included). Cash only. ❸

Albergue-Residència Cerverí de Girona (HI), C. Ciutadans, 9 (☎972 21 80 03; fax 972 21 20 23; www.tujuca.com). From the new city, cross Pont de Pedra, and turn left on C. Ciutadans. The furniture is reminiscent of summer camp, but the price and location make up for it. Breakfast €2.70; other meals €5. Combined sheets and towel rental €3. Laundry €3. Internet €1.20 per hr. HI members only, but HI cards for sale. Reserve at the Barcelona office (☎934 83 83 63). Dorms €11.57; over 25 €15.63. MC/V. ❶

FOOD

Girona's specialties are its *botifarra dolça* (sweet sausage made with pork, lemon, cinnamon, and sugar) and *xuixo* (sugar-sprinkled pastries filled with cream). The best place to find good, cheap food is on C. Cort Reial, at the top of C. Argenteria. La Rambla is home to tourist cafes with ubiquitous terrace seating. In summer, an open **market** can be found near the Polideportivo in Parc de la Deversa (open Tu and Sa 8am-3pm). Get your **groceries** at **Caprabo,** C. Sequia, 10, a block from C. Nou off the Gran Vía. (☎972 21 45 16. Open M-Sa 9am-9pm.)

La Crêperie Bretonne, C. Cort Reial, 14 (☎972 21 81 20). This popular crepe joint combines a funky atmosphere with cheap prices. *Menú* €9. Crepes €2.25-5.65. Unusual salads €5.56-6.31. Open Su 8pm-midnight, Tu-Sa 1-4pm and 8pm-midnight. ❷

Restaurante La Poma, C. Cort Reial, 16 (☎ 972 21 29 09). Internationally-influenced sandwiches, crepes, pasta, pizza, and salads at unbelievable prices. Salads and pasta €3.90-4.50. Pizza €4. Crepes €3-3.40. Open W-M 7:30pm-midnight. Cash only. ❶

Café Le Bistrot, Pujada Sant Domènech, 4 (☎972 21 88 03), a right off C. Ciutadans. Provides an elegant atmosphere, with a view of one of the old city's slanted streets. Pizzas €3.60-4.20. Crepes €3-4.20. Lunch *menú* €12. Terrace 10% extra. Open M-Th 1-4pm and 8pm-1am, F-Sa 1-4pm and 7pm-2am, Su 1-4pm and 8pm-midnight. ❶

SIGHTS

The narrow, winding streets of the medieval old city, interspersed with steep stairways and low arches, are ideal for wanderers. Start your self-guided historical tour at the **Pont de Pedra** and turn left at the tourist office down tree-lined **Rambla de la Llibertat.** Continue on C. Argenteria, bearing right across C. Cort Reial. Up the flight of stairs, C. Força begins on the left.

EL CALL. The part of the old town around C. Força and C. Sant Llorenç was once the center of Girona's medieval Jewish community ("call" comes from *kahal,* for "community" in Hebrew). The site of the last synagogue in Girona now serves as the **Centre Bonastruc Ca Porta,** named for Rabbi Moshe Ben-Nahman (Nahmanides), a scholar of Jewish mysticism (*Kabbala*) and the oral tradition (see **The Jewish Sepharad,** p. 420). The center includes the **Museu d'Història dels Jueus Girona,** notable for its detailed wooden model of the original Call, as well as its collection of inscribed Hebrew tombstones. *(The entrance to the center is off C. Força, about halfway up the hill. ☎972 21 67 61. Center and museum open May-Oct. M-Sa 10am-8pm, Su 10am-3pm; Nov.-April M-Sa 10am-6pm, Su 10am-3pm. Museum €2, students and over 65 €1, under 16 free. The tourist office offers guided tours of El Call in July and Aug. €6 during the day, €12 at night.)*

CATHEDRAL COMPLEX. Farther uphill on C. Força and around the corner to the right, Girona's imposing Gothic **cathedral** rises a record-breaking 90 steps (its stairway is the largest in Europe) from the *plaça.* The **Torre de Charlemany** (bell tower) and **cloister** are the only structures left from the 11th and 12th centuries; the rest of the building dates from the 14th through 17th centuries. The world's widest Gothic **nave** (22m) is surpassed in sheer size only by St. Peter's in Rome. A door on the left leads to the trapezoidal cloister and the **Tesoro Capitular** (treasury), home to some of Girona's most precious possessions. The *tesoro's* (and possibly Girona's) most famous piece is the **Tapis de la Creació,** an 11th-century tapestry depicting the story of creation. *(Tesoro ☎972 21 44 26. Cathedral and Tesoro open July-Sept. Tu-Sa 10am-2pm and 4-7pm, Oct.-Mar. Tu-Sa 10am-2pm and 4-6pm, Mar.-June Tu-Sa 10am-2pm and 4-7pm; open Su-M and holidays 10am-2pm year-round. Tesoro and cloister €3.)*

WALKS. Girona's renowned **Passeig de la Muralla,** not for the faint of heart, begins at the bottom of La Rambla in Pl. de la Marvà. Take the steps up to the guard's rampart atop the old Roman defense walls and follow them around the entire eastern side of the old town. The walk ends behind the cathedral, where the equally beautiful **Passeig Arqueològic** begins. Partly lined with cypresses and flower beds, this path skirts the northeastern medieval wall and also overlooks the city. (Passeig de la Muralla is open daily 8am-10pm.) For the less athletically inclined, a small trolley gives a 30min. guided tour of the main sights of the old town, includ-

THE JEWISH SEPHARAD Though Girona has a reputation for tolerance, the Jews of Girona were still victims of discrimination, ostracism, and eventual expulsion. Despite it all, they contributed ineradicably to the city's culture. The *aljama* (Jewish quarter) in Girona, once populated by 300 people, became a leading center for the study of the **Kabbala,** a mystical reading of the Torah in which number values are assigned to each Hebrew letter and numerical sums are interpreted to reveal spiritual meaning. Operating like a tiny, independent country within the city (inhabitants answered to their King, not the city government), El Call was protected by the crown of Catalunya in exchange for financial tribute. Until the 11th century, Christians and Jews coexisted peacefully, even intermarrying. Unfortunately, this did not last. Historical sources cite attacks and looting of the Jewish quarter in eight separate years, the first in 1276 and the last in 1418. Eventually, almost every entrance to El Call was blocked off. The reopening of the streets of El Call began only after Franco's death in 1975. In recent years, eight Spanish mayors have created a network called *Caminos de Sepharad,* an organization aimed at restoring Spain's Jewish quarters and fostering a broader understanding of the Sephardic legacy.

ing the town hall, cathedral, St. Feliu church, El Call, and the walls. *(In summer, leaves daily every 20-25min. from the Pont de Pedra, 10am-8pm or so. In winter, it runs less frequently, sometimes only weekends; check in the tourist office. Available in English. €3.)*

MUSEU DEL CINEMA. This unusual collection documents the rise of cinema from the mid-17th to the 20th centuries, with a few pieces from as early as the 11th century (Chinese shadow theater). It walks you through the chronological development of the camera obscura (9th-12th century), magic lantern (1659), panorama (1788), diorama (1822), Edison's kinetoscope (1891), and more, with several hands-on displays and a short film at the end. *(C. Sèquia, 1, one block north of C. Nou off C. Santa Clara. ☎ 972 41 27 77. Open Oct.-Apr. M-F 10am-6pm, Sa 10am-8pm, Su 11am-3pm; May-Sept. daily 10am-8pm. €3, students and over 65 €1.50, under 16 free. AmEx/MC/V.)*

CATALUÑA

OTHER MUSEUMS. The remarkably well-done **Museu d'Història de la Ciutat,** C. Força 27, showcases 2000 years of Girona's history, from the first settlers in Cataluña to the present day. *(☎ 972 22 22 29. Open Tu-Sa 10am-2pm and 5-7pm, Su and holidays 10am-2pm. Some descriptions in English. €2, under 16 free.)* To get to the **Banys Arabs** from the cathedral, with your back to the stairs, take a right on C. Ferrán Catòlic. Inspired by Muslim bath houses, the graceful 12th-century structure once contained saunas and baths of varying temperatures; now they occasionally host outdoor art exhibits. *(☎ 972 21 32 62. Open Apr.-Sept. M-Sa 10am-7pm, Su 10am-2pm; Oct.-Mar. daily 10am-2pm. €1.50, students €0.75.)* The **Museu Arqueològic,** past the Banys Arabs through Pl. Jurants, complements its archaeological displays with detailed booklets on the area's history. *(☎ 972 20 26 32. Open Tu-Sa 10:30am-1:30pm and 4-7pm, Su 10am-2pm. €1.80, students €1.40, under 16 free.)* The **Museu d'Art,** next to the cathedral, holds medieval and modern art. *(☎ 972 20 38 34. Open Mar.-Sept. Tu-Sa 10am-7pm, Oct.-Feb. Tu-Sa 10am-6pm; Su and holidays 10am-2pm. €1.80, students or over 65 €1.40.)*

ENTERTAINMENT AND NIGHTLIFE

During the latter half of May, government-sponsored **flower exhibitions** spring up all over the city; local monuments and pedestrian streets swim in blossoms, and the courtyards of Girona's fine old buildings are open to the public. Summer evenings often inspire spontaneous *sardana* dancing in the city *plaças*. Girona lights up for the **Focs de Sant Joan** on June 24, an outdoor party of fireworks and campfires.

Nightlife concentrates in **Pl. de l'Oli,** the old quarter, and in summer, the expansive, impeccably designed **Parc de la Devesa,** which explodes with *carpas*, temporary outdoor bars. (Across the river from the old town, several blocks to the left. Open June-Sept. 15 Su-Th 10pm-3am and F-Sa 10pm-4:30am. Drinks €4.20-5.40.) The bars and cafes in the old quarter are particularly mellow and relaxing, a good way to start the evening. **Platea,** behind the post office on C. Fontclara, is a popular early morning dance spot on weekends. **Café la Llibreria,** C. Ciutadans, 15, serves cocktails (€3.60), beer (€1.40), and *tapas* (€2.10-2.70) to chic intellectual types, or those who think they are. (Open M-Sa 8:30am-1am, Su 8:30am-midnight. MC/V.)

FIGUERES (FIGUERAS) ☎972

In 1974, the mayor of Figueres (pop. 35,000) asked native Salvador Dalí to donate a painting to an art museum the town was planning. Dalí refused to donate a painting; he was so flattered by his hometown's recognition that he donated an entire museum. With the construction of the Teatre-Museu Dalí, Figueres was catapulted to international fame; ever since, a multilingual parade of Surrealism fans has been awed and entranced by Dalí's bizarre perspectives and erotic visions. Though it is a beachless sprawl, Figueres hides other quality museums and some pleasant cafes. If you choose to extend your visit beyond Dalí's spectacle, the town's lovely Rambla is a good place to start for food, accommodations, and further sightseeing.

TRANSPORTATION

Trains: ☎902 24 02 02. To: **Barcelona** (2hr., 23 per day 6:11am-8:59pm, €8.05) and **Girona** (30min., 23 per day 6:11am-8:59pm, €2.40).

Buses: All buses leave from the **Estació Autobuses** (☎972 67 33 54), in Pl. Estació. **Sarfa** (☎972 67 42 98; www.sarfa.com) runs to **Cadaqués** (1¼hr.; July-Aug. 5 per day, Sept.-June 2-3 per day; €3.45) and **Llançà** (25min.; July-Aug. 4 per day, Sept.-June 2 per day; €2). **Barcelona Bus** (☎972 50 50 29) drives to **Barcelona** (2¼hr., 2-6 per day, €12.90) and **Girona** (1hr., 2-6 per day, €3.40).

Taxis: ☎972 50 00 08 or 972 50 50 43. Taxis line La Rambla and the train station.

Car Rental: Hertz, Pl. Estació, 9 (☎902 40 24 05). All-inclusive rental from €44 per day. 24+. Open M-F 8am-1pm and 4-8pm, Sa 8am-1pm and 5-8pm. AmEx/D/MC/V.

ORIENTATION AND PRACTICAL INFORMATION

Trains and buses arrive at **Plaça de Estació** on the edge of town. Cross the plaza and bear left on C. Sant Llàtzer, walk several blocks to Carrer Nou, and take a right to get to Figueres's tree-filled Rambla. To reach the **tourist office,** walk up La Rambla and continue on C. Lasauca straight out from the left corner. The blue, all-knowing "**i**" beckons across the rather treacherous intersection with Ronda Frial.

Tourist Office: Main office, Pl. Sol (☎972 50 31 55). Good map and free list of accommodations. Open Apr.-June and Oct. M-F 9am-3pm and 4:30-8pm, Sa 9:30am-1:30pm and 3:30-6:30pm; July-Aug. M-Sa 9am-8pm, Su 9am-3pm; Sept. M-Sa 9am-8pm; Nov.-Mar. M-F 9am-3pm. 2 **branch offices** in summer, one at Pl. Estació (open July-Sept. 15 M-Sa 10am-2pm and 4-6pm), and the other in a yellow mobile home in front of the Dalí museum (open July-Sept. 15 M-Sa 9am-8pm, Su 9am-3pm).

Currency Exchange: Santander Central Hispano, Rambla, 21. **ATM.** Open Apr.-Sept. M-F 8:30am-2pm; Oct.-Mar. M-F 8:30am-2pm, Sa 8:30am-1pm.

Luggage Storage: At the train station, large lockers €3.60. At the bus station €1.80. Bus station open daily 6am-10pm; train station open daily 6am-11pm.

Emergency: ☎112. **Police:** Ronda Final, 4 (☎972 51 01 11).

Internet Access: Tele Haddi, C. Joan Reglá, 1 (☎972 51 30 99). €1 per 15min., €1.80 per 30min., €3 per hr. Open daily 9am-1am.

Post Office: C. Santa Llogaia, 60-62 (☎972 50 54 31). Open M-F 8:30am-2:30pm, Sa 9:30am-1pm. **Postal Code:** 17600.

ACCOMMODATIONS

Most visitors to Figueres make the journey a daytrip from Barcelona, but affordable accommodations in Figueres are easy to find. Most tend to be on the upper floors of small bars or restaurants. Some cluster on **C. Jonquera,** around the Dalí museum; others are located closer to **La Rambla** and **C. Pep Ventura.** The tourist office has an annually updated list of all pensions and hostels.

Hostal La Barretina, C. Lasauca, 13 (☎972 67 64 12 or 972 67 34 25). From the train station, walk up La Rambla to its end; look for C. Lasauca directly ahead. A luxury experience—each room has TV, A/C, heat, and bath. Reception in the restaurant downstairs. Reservations recommended. Singles €22.50; doubles €38.60. AmEx/MC/V. ❷

Hostal San Mar, C. Rec Arnau, 31 (☎972 50 98 13). Follow C. Girona off La Rambla and continue as it becomes C. Jonquera; take the 5th right onto C. Isabel II, then take the 2nd left. Enter through the bar. The long walk is rewarded with clean, modern rooms with bath and TV. Singles €13; doubles €26. Cash only. ❶

Pensión Mallol, C. Pep Ventura, 9 (☎972 50 22 83). Follow La Rambla toward the tourist office, turn right on Castell at its end, and take the 2nd left. Look for the "Habitaciones-Chambres" sign. Spacious and simply decorated rooms with shared bathrooms. A very good value. Singles €14.50; doubles €24.50. Cash only. ❶

FOOD

Restaurants near the Dalí museum serve overcooked *paella* to the masses; better choices surround La Rambla on smaller side streets. The **market** is at Pl. Gra. (Open Tu, Th, Sa 5am-2pm. Widest selection on Th.) Buy groceries at **Bonpreu,** Pl. Sol, 5. (☎972 51 00 19. Open M-Th 9am-2pm and 5-9:30pm, F-Sa 9am-9:30pm. MC/V.)

Hotel Duran Restaurant, C. Lasauca, 5 (☎972 50 12 50). From the train station, walk up La Rambla to its end and look for C. Lasauca directly ahead. Serves traditional Catalan cuisine with a distinctive French influence. Lunch *menú* €10.25. Meat and seafood entrees €11.15-40.85. Open daily 1-3:30pm and 8:30-10:30pm. ❹

La Llesca, C. Mestre Falla, 15 (☎972 67 58 26), just beyond Pl. Sol. Specializes in *llesques,* toasted sandwiches topped with just about anything (€3.35-10.25). *Menú* €7.20; salads €2.70-4. Open M-Sa 8am-midnight, Su 6pm-midnight. AmEx/MC/V. ❷

La Churraskita, C. Magre, 5 (☎972 34 11 71). Hammocks and handweavings adorn the colorful walls of this popular Argentinian restaurant. A romantic terrace hides out back. Wide selection of grilled meats (€4.70-15) and plenty of vegetarian options like pizza and salads (€3.50-6.60). Open Tu-Su 1-4pm and 8pm-midnight. AmEx/MC/V. ❷

SIGHTS AND ENTERTAINMENT

TEATRE-MUSEU DALÍ. Welcome to the world of the Surrealist master. This building was the municipal theater for the town of Figueres before it burned down in 1939—hence the name Teatre-Museu ("theater-museum") Dalí. When Dalí decided to donate a museum to Figueres, he insisted on using the ruins of the old

HELLO DALÍ From an early age, Salvador Dalí was plagued by nightmares and insecurities. By age 15, he already had high hopes for himself: "I'll be a genius and the world will admire me." Although Dalí appeared to be confident in his talents, he was not equally confident in other aspects of his life. Sexually inexperienced until a late age, Dalí was sexually ambiguous and had a fear of close contact and impotence. This fear was one of the two central subjects of his work; the other, interestingly enough, was landscapes. Dalí was also influenced by Sigmund Freud, and sought to connect the unconscious with the conscious in his paintings. Surrealism itself attempted to explore the language of dreams in order to tap the unconscious. Although Dalí's paintings can be confusing at first, aspects of their symbol-language are consistent enough to be translated. Here a few examples:

–Look carefully at Dalí's **women.** Those that are portrayed in a cubist style are that way because they pose no threat to Dalí.

–Most of Dalí's **landscapes** are of the rocky shores of Cadaqués.

–A rotting **donkey** or **fish** is Dalí's symbol of the bourgeoise.

–The **crutches** propping up bits of soft flesh are symbols of masturbation.

–The **grasshopper** is a symbol of terror, as Dalí had a great fear of the insect.

–**Staircases** are a Freudian image, representing the fear of intercourse.

–A **melting candle** is a symbol of impotence.

–**Lions** represent animal aggression and **knives** are meant to be phallic symbols.

–A **fish hook** (found in Dalí's head) is a symbol of his entrapment.

–When asked about the **clocks** he said, "the famous soft watches are nothing else than the tender, extravagant, solitary, paranoia-critical Camembert of time and space." (*Conquest of the Irrational,* 1969.)

theater, which was where he showed his first exposition as a teenager. The resulting homage to his first gallery is the reconstructed theater, covered in sculptures of eggs and full of Dalí's painting, sculptures, other creations, and his own tomb.

Despite his reputation as a Fascist self-promoter, Dalí's personally designed mausoleum/museum/monument to himself should be approached as a multimedia experience, an electrifying tangle of sculpture, painting, music, and architecture. It's all here: Dalí's naughty cartoons, his dramatically low-key tomb, and many paintings of Gala, his wife and muse. The treasure trove of paintings includes, among others, the remarkable *Self Portrait with a Slice of Bacon, Poetry of America, Galarina,* and *Galatea of the Spheres.* There is also a small offering of works by other artists selected by Dalí himself, including pieces by El Greco, Marcel Duchamp, and the architect Peres Piñero. *(☎972 67 75 00; fax 972 50 16 66; www.salvador-dali.org. From the Rambla, take C. Girona from the end farthest from the tourist office. Follow C. Girona past Pl. Ajuntament as it becomes C. Jonquera. Steps by a Dalí statue to your left lead to the pink and white, egg-covered museum. Open Oct.-June daily 10:30am-5:15pm; July-Sept. daily 9am-7:15pm. €9, students and seniors €6.50. Call ahead about night hours during the summer.)*

OTHER SIGHTS. Delight once again in the wonders of your favorite childhood toys at the **Museu del Joguet,** winner of Spain's 1999 National Prize of Popular Culture. The colorful collection features antique dolls, board games, comics, rocking horses, toys for the blind, caganers, and more. *(Sant Pere, 1, off La Rambla. ☎97 250 45 85; www.mjc-figueres.net. Open June-Sept. M-Sa 10am-1pm and 4-7pm, Su 11am-1:30pm and 5-7:30pm; Oct.-May Tu-Sa 10am-1pm and 4-7pm, Su 11am-1:30pm. €4.70, students and children under 12 €3.80.)* Ten minutes from the Museu Dalí, the 18th-century **Castell de Sant Ferran** commands a view of the countryside and is the largest stone fortress in

Europe at 12,000 square meters. *(Av. Castell de Sant Ferrán; follow Pujada del Castell from the Teatre-Museu Dalí. ☎972 50 60 94. Open July-Sept. 15 daily 10:30am-8pm; Nov.-Feb. daily 10:30am-2pm; Mar.-July and Sept. 16-Oct. daily 10:30am-2pm and 4-6pm. €2.10.)*

FESTIVALS. In September, classical and jazz music flood Figueres during the **Festival Internacional de Música de l'Empordà.** (Tickets available at Caixa de Catalunya. Call ☎972 10 12 12 for info.) From September 10 through 14, the **Mostra del Vi de L'Alt Empordà,** a tribute to regional wines, brings a taste of the local vineyards to Figueres. Around May 3, the **Fires i Festes de la Santa Creu** sponsors cultural events and art exhibitions. Parties and general merrymaking can be expected at the **Festa de Sant Pere,** held June 28 to 29, which honors the town's patron saint.

CADAQUÉS AND PORT LLIGAT

The whitewashed houses and small bay of Cadaqués (pop. 2000) have attracted artists, writers, and musicians ever since Dalí built his summer home in neighboring Port Lligat in the 1930s. Cadaqués is the bigger of the two overlapping towns (Port Lligat is basically just Dalí's house). The rocky beaches and dreamy landscape attract their share of tourists, but Cadaqués preserves a pleasantly laid-back atmosphere. If you're traveling to Cadaqués from September to May, it's best to make it a daytrip, as most food and entertainment options close in the off season.

TRANSPORTATION AND PRACTICAL INFORMATION. Cadaqués has no train station, but Sarfa **buses** (☎972 25 87 13) run to: **Barcelona** (2½hr.; 11:15am, 4:15pm; €15.20); **Figueres** (1hr., 5-7 per day, €4.30); and **Girona** (2hr., 1-2 per day, €7). Bus stop to the right of the Sarfa office. With your back to the Sarfa office, walk downhill on Av. Caritat Serinyana to the waterfront square, **Plaça Frederic Rahola,** where a signboard map with indexed services and accommodations will orient you. The **tourist office,** C. Cotxe, 2, off Pl. Frederic Rahola, is opposite the *passeig*. (☎972 25 83 15. Open July-Aug. M-Sa 9:30am-1:30pm and 4-8pm, Su 10:30am-1:30pm; Sept.-June M-Sa 9am-2pm and 4-7pm.) **Santander Central Hispano** is at C. Caritat Serinyana, 4. (☎972 25 83 62. Open Oct.-Mar. M-F 8:30am-2:30pm, Sa 8:30am-1pm; Apr.-Sept. M-F 8:30am-2:30pm.) Services include: **local police,** Pl. Frederic Rahola (☎972 15 93 43), by the promenade; **medical assistance** (☎972 25 88 07); and the **post office,** on Av. Rierassa off C. Caritat Serinyana. (☎972 25 87 98. Open M-F 9am-2pm, Sa 9:30am-1pm.) **Postal code:** 17488.

CATALUÑA

ACCOMMODATIONS AND FOOD. As Cadaqués is a beach town, many accommodations are open only during the summer. **Hostal Cristina ❸,** C. Riera, is right on the water, to the right of Av. Caritat Serinyana. Cristina offers bright, newly renovated rooms and a rooftop terrace overlooking the water. (☎972 25 81 38. Summer prices include breakfast. May-Sept. singles €26; doubles €40, with bath €52, with TV €57. Oct.-Apr. €20/€27/€38/€50. MC/V.) **Pensión Ranxo ❸,** Av. Caritat Serinyana, 13, is on the right as you walk down from the bus stop. Potted plants and whitewashed hallways lead to clean and comfortable rooms. (☎972 25 80 05. July-Sept. 15 singles €26; doubles €49.50. Sept. 15-June €20/€43. Traveler's checks accepted. MC/V.) **Camping Cadaqués ❶,** Ctra. Portlligat, 17, is 100m from the beach on the way to Dalí's house; follow the signs for Hotel Port Lligat. The campground is popular and crowded, but still relatively clean. (☎972 25 81 26. Open Apr.-Sept. €4 per person, €5 per tent, €4 per car.)

Cadaqués harbors the usual slew of overpriced, unexciting waterfront tourist restaurants—wander into the back streets for more interesting options. **Groceries** can be purchased at **Super Auvi,** C. Riera. (Open July 15-Aug. M-Sa 8am-2pm and 4:30-9pm, Su 8am-2pm; Sept.-July 14 M-Sa 8:30am-1:30pm and 4:30-9pm.) **Can Tito**

❷, C. Vigilant, 8, is an exceptional historical and culinary experience. The stone archway at the entrance to this elegant restaurant is one of five portals dating back to AD 1100 when Cadaqués was still a fortified village at the mercy of roving pirates. Three-course lunchtime *menú* €12. (Fish and meat entrees €4.80-14. Open daily Mar.-Jan. 1:30-3pm and 8-10:30pm. MC/V.) **Restaurant Vehí ❸,** C. de l'Església, 6, serves traditional Catalan seafood. (Menú €10.50-12. Open Mar.-Oct.)

SIGHTS AND ENTERTAINMENT. **Església de Santa María,** is a 16th-century Gothic church with a Baroque altar. Nearby, the **Museu de Cadaqués,** C. Narcis Monturiol, 15, displays rotating exhibits, often with a Dalí theme. (☎972 25 88 77. Open daily mid-June to Sept. 10:30am-1:30pm and 3-8pm. €4.50; students €3.) From the museum, it's a pleasant walk (30min.) to **Casa-Museu Salvador Dalí,** in Port Lligat, the house where Dalí and his wife Gala lived until her death in 1982. With your back to the Sarfa station, take the right fork and follow the signs to Port Lligat until Casa de Dalí signs appear. At C. President Lluís Companys, where signs point to the house in two different directions, follow the one to the right. This modest fisherman's abode was transformed to meet the artist's eccentric needs. Though only two (unfinished) Dalí originals remain in the house, the decorating is a work in itself. (☎972 25 10 15. Open June 15-Sept. 15 daily 10:30am-9pm; Sept. 16-Nov. and Mar. 15-June 14 Tu-Su 10:30am-6pm. Tours are the only way to see the house; make reservations 1-2 days in advance. Ticket office closes 45min. before closing. €7.80; students, seniors, and children €4.80.) **Boat rides** in his *Gala* depart from the front of the house on the hour for a 55min. trip to Cap de Creus. (☎617 46 57 57. Open daily 10am-7pm. €9.) On the beach, **Escola de Vela Ones** rents kayaks, sailboats, and windsurfing gear. (☎937 53 25 12. Open daily July-Sept. 15 10am-8pm.)

CATALAN PYRENEES

While beach-goers and city-dwellers flock to Barcelona and the Costa Brava, Cataluña's portion of the Pyrenees draws a different breed of tourist. Bikinis are tossed aside for slightly better insulation as hikers and high-brow skiers, mostly from Spain and France, come for the refined ski resorts and some of Spain's wildest mountain scenery. Meanwhile, history and architecture buffs, notebooks in hand, eagerly explore the tranquil mountain towns filled with well-preserved Romanesque buildings. Early June to late September is the best time for trekking in the Pyrenees; any earlier, avalanches are a potential danger, and it can get prohibitively cold later. Tourist offices distribute pamphlets with information on scenic areas and outdoor activities. Skiers will find the *Snow in Catalonia* or *Ski España* guides most useful, and the website www.pirineo.com is a fantastic general planning resource (for skiing and hiking both) for those who can read Spanish. The Pyrenees are best explored with a car, as public transportation links are few and far between. Either way, entry from the east begins in Ripoll.

RIPOLL

Although the sleepy town of Ripoll (pop. 11,000) may be trapped in a permanent time-warp, it continues to attract visitors in search of Spain's Romanesque architectural legacy; the elaborately carved portal of the Monasterio de Santa María is one of the most famous in all of Spain. Ripoll also serves as a convenient base for excursions to the nearby town of Sant Joan de las Abadesses.

TRANSPORTATION. RENFE, Pl. Mova, 1 (☎972 70 06 44), runs **trains** to **Barcelona** (1¾hr., 9-12 per day 6:32am-6:31pm, €4.90) and **Puigcerdà** (1hr., 6 per day 8:56am-8:54pm, €2.51). The bus station (across a small park from the train station) sends **Teisa buses** (☎972 20 48 68) to: **Barcelona** (4hr., 12 per day, €10.80); **Girona** (2hr., 1 per day, €6.60) via Olot; **Sant Joan de las Abadesses** (15min., 8-10 per day, €1.10).

PRACTICAL INFORMATION. The **tourist office,** next to the monastery on Pl. Abat Oliba, gives out free maps. (☎972 70 23 51. Open M-Sa 9:30am-1:30pm and 4-7pm, Su 10am-2pm and 4-7pm.) Connect to the **Internet** at **Xarxtel,** Pl. d'Espanya, 10. The **public library,** C. de les Vinyes, 6, offers free use of their computers. (Open M-Tu and Th-F 4-8:30pm, W 9am-1:30pm, Sa 10am-1:30pm.) Other services include: **emergency** ☎112; **police,** Pl. Ajuntament, 3 (☎972 71 44 14); and the **post office,** C. d'Estació, facing the tree-lined park. (☎972 70 07 60. Open M-F 8:30am-2:30pm, Sa 9:30am-1pm.) **Postal code:** 17500.

ACCOMMODATIONS AND FOOD. Ripoll is an ambitious daytrip; consider sleeping at the luxurious and friendly **Fonda La Paula ❷,** C. Berenguer, 4, on Pl. Abat Oliba alongside the tourist office, which has comfortable beds, TVs, and spacious, tiled bathrooms. (☎972 70 00 11. Singles €21.40; doubles €36.38; triples €50.29; quads €64.20. V.) The few other accommodations in town are pricey. From the monastery's plaza, follow C. Sant Pere for two blocks to **Hostal del Ripollès ❷,** Pl. Nova, 11, which provides small but well-furnished rooms with TV, phone, and full bath. (☎972 70 02 15. Breakfast included. Doubles €48.)

Restaurants surround Pl. Gran. Follow C. Bisbe Morgades and take a right before the river on C. Mossen; the *plaça* is to the left. If you are looking for fancy Catalan fare, try **Reccapolis ❸,** Ctra. Sant Joan, 68, about a 10-15 minute walk down Ctra. Sant Joan from Pl. Ajuntament. (☎972 70 21 06. Entrees €10.82-16.83. Open Th-Tu 1-4pm and 8:30-10:30pm, W 1-4pm.) At **La Piazzetta ❷,** Pl. Nova, 11, the ambiance and menu may be Catalan, but the food is Italian; same owners and location as the Hostal del Ripollès. (☎972 70 02 15. Pizzas €5.10-8.75, pasta €5.35-7.25. Open M-Sa 1-3:15pm and 8:15-11:30pm, Su 8:15-11:30pm.) Stock up on **groceries** at the supermarket across from the bus station, **Champión,** C. Progress, 33-37. (☎972 70 26 32. Open M-Th 9am-9pm, F-Sa 9am-9:30pm, Su 10am-2pm. AmEx/MC/V.)

SIGHTS. Most visitors to Ripoll come to see the incredibly intricate 11th-century portal of the **Monasterio de Santa María.** To reach the monastery, take a left on C. Progrés from the train and bus stations, following it until it merges with C. Estació. Take the first left after the colorful modern "metal dancers" onto Pont d'Olot, cross the river, then continue straight on C. Bisbe Morgades to the Pl. Ayuntament and Pl. Abat Oliba. Founded in AD 879 by Count Guifré el Pelú (Wilfred the Hairy), the Santa María monastery was once the most powerful in all of Cataluña. The curved doorway, nicknamed the "Stone Bible," depicts survival scenes from the Old and New Testaments as well as a hierarchy of the cosmos and a 12-month calendar. Panels (in Catalan) attempt to decode the doorway. Adjoining it is a beautiful two-story Romanesque and Gothic **cloister.** (Church open daily 10am-1pm and 3-7pm. €2, with student card €1; includes entrances to the cloister.)

PUIGCERDÀ

A challenging name for foreigners, Puigcerdà (pop.7000; Pwee-chair-DAH) has become a popular town by virtue of its stunning location in the mountainous Cerdanya region. Puigcerdà's view of the valley is beautiful, and the town serves as a cheap base for hiking, biking, or skiing the surrounding hillsides. Puigcerdà is perhaps best known for appearing in the 1993 *Guinness Book of World Records* for the world's longest *butifarra* (sausage), a Freudian nightmare measuring 5200m.

TRANSPORTATION

RENFE trains (☎972 88 01 65) run to: **Barcelona** (3hr., 6 per day 6:33am-6:50pm, €7.05) and **Ripoll** (1¼hr., 6 per day 6:33am-6:50pm, €2.60). **Alsina Graells buses** (☎973 35 00 20) run to **Barcelona** (3¼hr., 2-4 per day, €12) and **La Seu d'Urgell** (1hr., 7 per day, €4). Buses depart in front of the train station and from Pl. Barcelona; purchase tickets on board. See the schedule in Bar Estació, to the right in the train station. Taxis (☎972 88 00 11) wait on Pl. Cabrinetty. For **bike rental,** try **Sports Iris,** Av. de França, 16. (☎972 88 23 98. Bikes €9 per half day, €15 per day. MC/V.)

ORIENTATION AND PRACTICAL INFORMATION

Puigcerdà's center sits at the top of its own hill. Off the main plaza, **Plaça Ajuntament** is nicknamed *el balcón de Cerdanya* for its commanding view of the valley. The less picturesque **train station** is at the foot of the western slope. Buses stop at the train station and then Pl. Barcelona; get off at the second stop. To reach Pl. Ajuntament from the inconvenient train station, walk past the stairs in the station's *plaça* until you reach the first real flight of stairs (between 2 buildings). Turn right at the top, then look for the next set of stairs on your left, just before a sign for C. Hostal del Sol. Turn left at the top onto C. Raval de les Monges where the final set of stairs winds up to the right (make sure not to take the prior set). From the *plaça* walk one block on Carrer Alfons I to **Carrer Major,** the principal commercial street. Turn left on C. Major to Pl. Santa María. From Pl. Santa María with your back to the bell tower, head out diagonally to the left to Pl. Barcelona.

Tourist Office: C. Querol, 1 (☎/fax 972 88 05 42), off Pl. Ajuntament. Open M-Tu and F-Sa 9am-2pm and 3-8pm, W-Th 10am-1:30pm and 4:30-7:30pm, Su 10am-2pm.

Bank: Santander Central Hispano, on Pl. Cabrinetty. Open Oct.-Mar. M-F 8:30am-2pm, Sa 8:30am-1pm; closed Sa Apr.-Sept. 24hr. **ATM** available.

Emergency: ☎091. **Municipal police,** Pl. Ajuntament, 1 (☎972 88 19 72). **Hospital: Hospital de Puigcerdá** in Pl. Santa María (☎972 88 01 50), behind the *campanari.*

Internet: Punt Com, C. d'Espanya, 10 (☎972 88 31 55). €1.20 per 30min. Open daily 10am-1pm and 4-8pm.

Post office: Av. Coronel Molera, 11 (☎972 88 08 14). Located 1½ blocks down Av. C. Molera from Pl. Barcelona (look for the pink movie theater). Open M-F 8:30am-2:30pm, Sa 9:30am-1pm. **Postal code:** 17520.

ACCOMMODATIONS AND CAMPING

Rooms in Puigcerdà come easily, if not cheaply. Most less-expensive *pensiones* lie off Pl. Santa Maria, in the old town.

Alfonso Habitaciones, C. Espanya, 5 (☎972 88 02 46), a left off C. Alfons I. Dimly lit rooms with TVs and baths. Singles €21; doubles €42. Cash only. ❷

Hotel Avet Blau, Pl. Santa Maria, 14 (☎972 88 25 52), right next to the bell tower. Has 6 spacious and comfortable doubles. Rates vary by season from €71-97. ❺

Mare de Déu de les Neus (HI), on Ctra. Font Canaleta (☎972 89 20 12; reservations 934 83 83 63). Modern facilities and a great location just 500m from the La Molina train station and 4km from the slopes. In winter, buses run to the slopes. Breakfast included. Sheets €2. Reserve in high season. Dec.-Oct. dorms €14, over 25 €18; Jan.-Nov. €12/€16. Doubles and triples available, same price per person. MC/V. ❷

Camping Stel (☎972 88 23 61), 1km from Puigcerdà on the road to Llivia. Full-service camping with a chalet-style restaurant-bar/lounge. Site with tent and car €15, €4.45 per person. Electricity €3. Open Sa-Su only June 1-Sept. 30 and Oct. 27-May 1. ❷

FOOD

The neighborhood off C. Alfons I is filled with markets and restaurants. For fresh produce, try the weekly **market,** at Pl. 10 d'Abril (Su 6am-2pm). Get **groceries** at **Bonpreu,** C. Colonel Molera, 12, the small supermarket diagonally across from the post office. (Open M-Th 9am-1:30pm and 5-9pm, F-Sa 9am-9pm, Su 10am-2pm. MC/V.) **El Pati de la Tieta ❷,** C. dels Ferrers, 20, serves large portions of pasta and pizzas (€6-9.60) and heavenly desserts in an ivy-covered outdoor patio. (☎972 88 01 56. Fish and meat entrees €11.50-17. Open daily 1-3:30pm and 8-11:30pm. MC/V.) At **Cantina Restaurant Mexicà ❷,** Pl. Cabrinetty, 9, kick back with a margarita and enjoy excellent tacos, fajitas, and quesadillas. (☎972 88 16 58. Entrees €4-15. Open M 9-11:30pm, Tu-W and F-Su 2-4pm and 9-11:30pm. MC/V.)

SIGHTS AND SLOPES

Between ski runs and cycling, dash over to the **campanario,** the octagonal bell tower in Pl. Santa Maria. This 42m high 12th-century tower is all that remains of the **Església de Santa Maria,** an eerie reminder of the destruction wreaked by the Civil War. Climb to the top for 360° views of Puigcerdà and the Pyrenees. (Open July-Aug. M-F noon-2pm and 5-8pm; Sa-Su 11am-noon and 5-8pm. Free.) The 13th-century **Església de Sant Domènec,** on Pg. 10 d'Abril, contains several Gothic paintings considered to be among the best of their genre. (Open 9:30am-8pm. Free.) Puigcerdà's picturesque **Lake Estany,** a 2min. walk up C. Pons i Gasch from Pl. Barcelona, was created in 1380 for irrigation purposes. It now serves the town well as a lovely place to rent a boat (€2 per person per 30min.; inquire at the cafe).

Puigcerdà calls itself the "capital of snow." **Ski** in your country of choice (Spain, France, or Andorra) at one of 19 ski areas within a 50km radius. The closest and cheapest one on the Spanish side is **La Molina** (☎972 89 20 31; www.lamolina.com). Nearby **Masella** (☎972 14 40 00; www.masella.com) offers the longest run in the Pyrenees at 7km. For cross-country skiing, the closest site is **Guils** (☎972 19 70 47). A little farther out, try **Lles** (☎973 29 30 49) or **Aransa** (☎973 29 30 51). The Puigcerdà area is also popular for **biking;** the tourist office has a map with 17 routes. La Molina opens trails for biking in the summer months and provides rentals for €12.62 per day. You can also navigate the trails on horseback for €12 for an hour-long excursion. **Club Poliesportiu Puigcerdà,** on Av. del Poliesportiu, has a pool, tennis courts, basketball courts, and a skating rink. (☎972 88 02 43. Open M-F 11am-10pm, Sa 11am-9:30pm, Su 11am-8pm. €3.80 per sports facility or €6 per day.)

CATALUÑA

PARC NACIONAL D'AIGÜESTORTES

The full name of Cataluña's only national park is actually Parc Nacional d'Aigüestortes i Estany de Sant Maurici. The **Estany de Sant Maurici**, in the east, is the park's largest lake; in the west, the wild tumbling of the Riu de Sant Nicolau through its own valley has earned it the nickname "Aigües Tortes" ("Twisted Waters"). On a sunny spring day, flocks of sheep roam the park's wildflower-dusted meadows as golden eagles soar above its snow-capped peaks. With more than 100 glacial lakes and over 10,000 hectares to explore, the park merits at least two days—using public transportation, it's hard to do it in fewer than three.

Free maps and itineraries from the tourist office list well-defined itineraries, but the explorer may want to drop the extra cash to buy a better, more detailed map (€5.45-6.05 in the office; also available in area stores for a bit more). The red *Editorial Alpina* guides, one each for Montardo, Vall de Boí, and Sant Maurici, are also a useful option (€3). Trail accessibility and difficulty varies by season. One particularly popular hike is the east-west traverse from Espot to Boí (see below for more on the towns themselves). From **Espot** to the **Estany de Sant Maurici** (April-Nov.; moderate difficulty due to duration) is 8km (2hr.). From the lake, a path climbs 2.5km to the **Portarró d'Espot,** the gateway between the park's two halves and a prime spot for viewing the scenery (June-Oct.; low difficulty, moderate if you choose to continue up to the peak of **Portarró**). Those with a car may opt for half the hike by parking in the last public access lot inside the park. From the pass it is nearly 2km to the **Estany Llong** and the **Aigüestortes** themselves (about 3½hr. from the Estany de Sant Maurici; June-Oct., moderate difficulty). Near the western tip of the Estany Llong lies the park's first *refugio*, also called **Estany Llong** (☎973 69 61 89. Open mid-June to mid-Oct. and winter weekends. €9.10 per person.) Finally, to get to the western park entrance from the Estany Llong is a 3.5km hike, and to **Boí** itself another 6½km (May-Nov.; moderate difficulty due to duration). The entire hike takes around 9hr. but can be shortened by taking a jeep from Espot to the Sant Maurici lake or a taxi from the western entrance to Boí.

For more detailed hiking info, contact the park **tourist offices** (in Espot ☎973 62 40 36; in Boí 973 69 61 89). The park's five *refugios* (€8-10 per person) and *Casas de Pagés* (pension-like lodging in private homes) are good options for those planning multi-day treks. The mountains appear calm from afar, but the region's notoriously unpredictable weather can be quite dangerous, especially in winter. Casual wandering is not recommended. Though the main trails are clearly marked, it is easy to become lost should one stray into the mountainsides.

CATALUÑA

ESPOT AND ESTANY DE SANT MAURICI

The official gateway to the eastern half of the park, and the best point of entrance from the direction of Barcelona, the tiny town of **Espot** is comprised of mostly rustic restaurants and quiet accommodations for the weary hiker. Espot is a good 4½km from the actual entrance of the park, but the walk to it is quite scenic.

TRANSPORTATION. A four-wheel-drive **jeep service** (Dec.-Mar. 9am-5pm, July-Sept. 15 9am-8pm, 9am-7pm during the rest of the year) next to the tourist office navigates the bumping mountain back roads from Espot to: **Amitges** (round-trip €13 per person), a view-blessed site near the park's biggest and best **refugio** (see below), **Estany Negre de Pegura** (€16.20 per person, a much less frequented area of the park), **Estany de Ratera** (€10 per person, dropping off passengers to hike down to the waterfall, then picking them up below), and **Estany Sant Maurici** (each way €4 per person). Unfortunately for those relying on public transportation, the **Alsina Graells bus** (☎973 26 85 00) from Barcelona (3hr., M-Sa 1:30pm, €20)—the only mass transit in the area—only comes within 7km of Espot, on Highway C-147 at the La Torrassa crossing. Ask to be dropped off in **la Guingueta d'Aneu,** where you can call the jeep service for pickup. (☎973 62 41 05. €12 for the ride to Espot. Jeeps are operated by a driver and seat 7-8.)

PRACTICAL INFORMATION. The bustling **park information office,** on Espot's main road (on the right as you enter town), provides brochures and trekking advice. (☎973 62 40 36. Open daily Apr.-Oct. 9am-1pm and 3:30-7pm; Nov.-Mar. M-Sa 9am-2pm and 3:30-6pm.) Police ☎085. In medical **emergency** call ☎973 62 10 05.

ACCOMMODATIONS AND CAMPING. You'll find the best deals in the many local residences that take in travelers. The tourist office has a listing of such lodging possibilities. Safety should not be an issue; the locals are honest and content, with no motive to steal or cause harm (and nowhere to go if they do). The intrepid wanderer who happens upon one of the many shepherd's huts that dot the park may find adequate shelter within. Be warned: safety and comfort are not assured with this option. Cross the main bridge over to **Residència Felip ❸** for comfortable rooms with a down-home touch. Follow the bridge road for two blocks, and then take a left; the Residència is just behind Hotel Roya. (☎973 62 40 93. Oct.-June doubles €24.04, with bath €30. July-Sept. and holidays prices jump €6.) In the park proper is **Refugi d'Amitges ❶.** (☎973 25 00 07 or 973 25 01 09. Open Feb. 10-25, Apr. 7-16, Apr. 29-May 1, June-Sept., Oct. 12-14, Nov. 1-4, and Dec. 6-9.)

Those devoted to the ascetic life may be disappointed by the camping in Espot; all locations provide food, games, water, showers, and a selection of other amenities as well. **Casa Peret de Peretó ❶** and **Camping Solau ❶** (☎973 62 40 68) run a joint establishment, offering spacious, sunny rooms inside and 22 campsites outside on the sprawling front yard. This is one of the more rustic camping sites in the park. (Rooms €16 per person. Campsites €3 per person, per tent, and per car.). Located 1.3km down the park entrance road on the right, **Camping Vora Parc ❶** offers the closest camping to the park, with sites along the riverbank. The stone entryway and manicured lawn are indicative of the carefully maintained sites. (☎973 62 41 08. €4.10 per person, per tent, per car. MC/V.) **Càmping de la Mola ❶** (☎973 62 40 24) and **Càmping Sol i Neu ❶** (☎973 62 40 01), both on the way to Espot, provide comparatively cushy camping with laundry, market, and bar. (Open June 1-Sept. 30 and *Semana Santa*. €4 per person, per tent, per car; electricity €4.10. MC/ V.)

AIGÜESTORTES AND VALL DE BOÍ

The village of Boí is the most convenient base from which to explore the western half of the park. **Public transportation** from the east to the medieval village is difficult but possible through **Vielha,** or through **Lleida** via Pont de Suert. If you have no other options, it's worth a try. From Lleida, catch the Alsina Graells 9am bus from Barcelona on its way to Pont de Suert. From July-Sept. 15, catch the daily 11:15am connecting bus from Pont de Suert to Boír; in winter, a school bus makes the run W, F at 2pm and M-Tu, Th at 5:30pm. From Boí's main *plaça* it's an easy taxi ride to the park. (☎973 69 63 14, in winter ☎629 20 54 89. €4 per person.) Boí's **park info office** is near the bus stop on the *plaça.* (☎973 69 61 89. Open daily Apr.-Oct. 9am-1pm and 3:30-7pm, Nov.-Mar. M-Sa 9am-2pm and 3:30-6pm.) Reach the **Guardia Civil** at ☎973 69 12 01. **Police** ☎085. In an **emergency** call ☎112 or 973 69 11 59.

Despite the nearby ski resort in **Taüll,** Boí hasn't lost its country charm. The village's cobblestone streets wind their way through low arches and mini-plazas. Green RCPs (Residencias Casa de Payés) indicate the many local residences offering traveler accommodation. Although very safe, most of these private residences do not accept credit cards, have very limited space (usually only 1-2 rooms), and change hours each week depending on the whim of the host. Inquire at the tourist office for a comprehensive price listing of local hostels and houses.

The owners of **Can Guasch ❶** let simple rooms and welcome visitors to use their kitchen. Exit the plaza through the stone arch, turn right through the next arch, then bear left and turn left again where the street ends; the entrance is on the left. (☎973 69 60 42. Doubles €24.08.) For a more reliable option, visit **Hostal Fondevila ❷,** to the right of the main road through Boí. Palatial rooms have bath. (☎973 69 60 02; fax 973 69 60 11. Singles €20; doubles €38; triples €54. MC/V.)

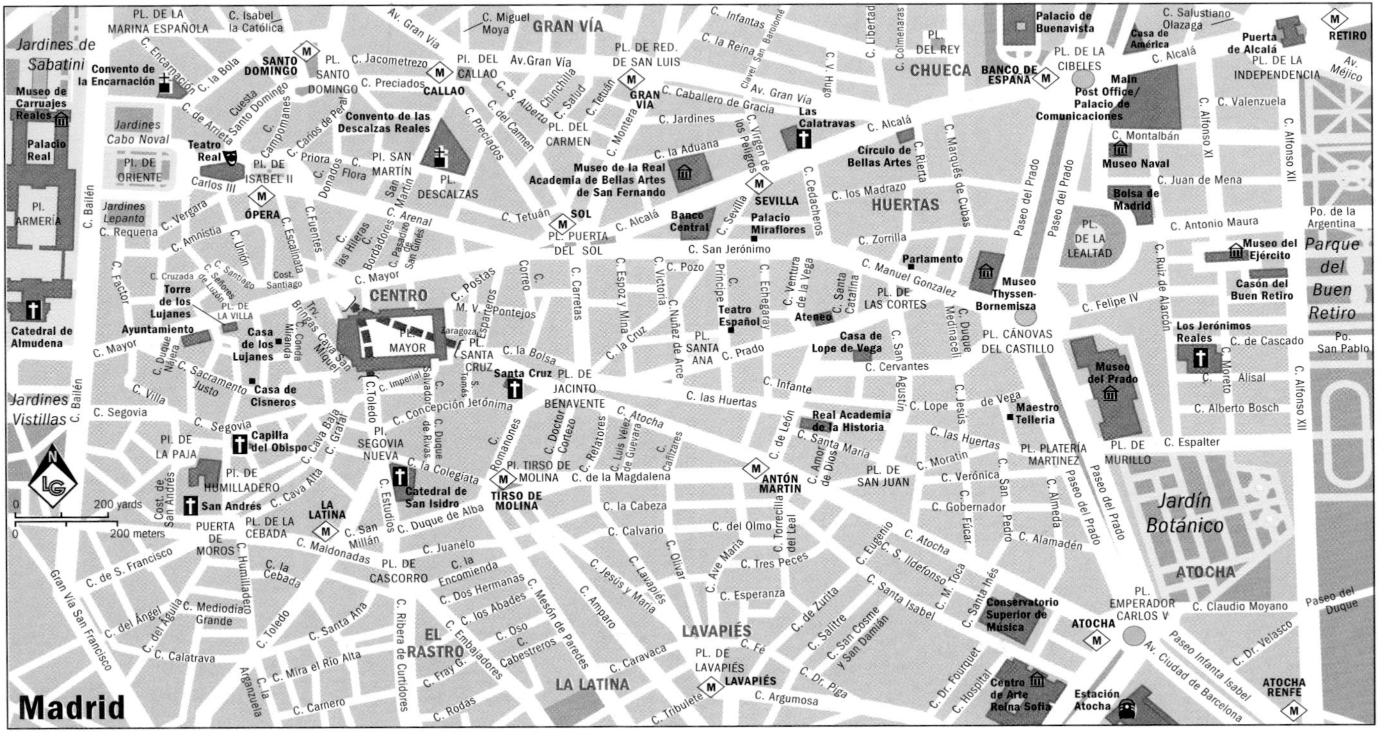

Madrid
GRAN VÍA
CHUECA
HUERTAS
CENTRO
LAVAPIÉS
LA LATINA
EL RASTRO
ATOCHA
Jardines de Sabatini
Jardines Cabo Noval
Jardines Lepanto
Jardines Vistillas
Jardín Botánico
Parque del Buen Retiro
Museo de Carruajes Reales
Palacio Real
PL. ARMERÍA
Catedral de Almudena
Convento de la Encarnación
PL. DE LA MARINA ESPAÑOLA
PL. DE ORIENTE
Teatro Real
PL. DE ISABEL II
ÓPERA
SANTO DOMINGO
PL. SANTO DOMINGO
Convento de las Descalzas Reales
PL. DESCALZAS
PL. SAN MARTÍN
CALLAO
PL. DEL CALLAO
PL. DEL CARMEN
PL. DE RED. DE SAN LUIS
GRAN VÍA
Museo de la Real Academia de Bellas Artes de San Fernando
SOL
PL. PUERTA DEL SOL
Banco Central
SEVILLA
Palacio Miraflores
Las Calatravas
Círculo de Bellas Artes
PL. DEL REY
BANCO DE ESPAÑA
Palacio de Buenavista
PL. DE LA CIBELES
Main Post Office/ Palacio de Comunicaciones
Casa de América
Puerta de Alcalá
PL. DE LA INDEPENDENCIA
RETIRO
Museo Naval
Bolsa de Madrid
PL. DE LA LEALTAD
Museo del Ejército
Casón del Buen Retiro
Los Jerónimos Reales
Museo Thyssen-Bornemisza
PL. CÁNOVAS DEL CASTILLO
Museo del Prado
PL. DE MURILLO
Parlamento
PL. DE LAS CORTES
Ateneo
Casa de Lope de Vega
Teatro Español
PL. SANTA ANA
Torre de los Lujanes
PL. DE LA VILLA
Ayuntamiento
Casa de los Lujanes
Casa de Cisneros
PL. MAYOR
PL. SANTA CRUZ
Santa Cruz
PL. DE JACINTO BENAVENTE
Real Academia de la Historia
Maestro Telleria
PL. PLATERÍA MARTINEZ
PL. DE SAN JUAN
ANTÓN MARTIN
PL. TIRSO DE MOLINA
TIRSO DE MOLINA
PL. SEGOVIA NUEVA
Catedral de San Isidro
Capilla del Obispo
PL. DE LA PAJA
PL. DE HUMILLADERO
San Andrés
PUERTA DE MOROS
PL. DE LA CEBADA
LA LATINA
PL. DE CASCORRO
PL. DE LAVAPIÉS
LAVAPIÉS
Conservatorio Superior de Música
Centro de Arte Reina Sofía
ATOCHA
PL. EMPERADOR CARLOS V
Estación Atocha
ATOCHA RENFE
C. Bailén
C. Encarnación
C. la Bola
C. Isabel la Católica
Av. Gran Vía
C. Miguel Moya
C. Jacometrezo
C. Preciados
Cuesta Santo Domingo
C. de Arrieta
C. Campomanes
C. Caños de Peral
C. Priora
C. Donados
C. Flora
C. San Martín
Carlos III
C. Vergara
C. Requena
C. Amnistía
C. Unión
C. Escalinata
C.Fuentes
C. las Hileras
C. Bordadores
C. Pasadizo de San Ginés
C. Arenal
C. Tetuán
C. del Carmen
C. S. Alberto
C. Chinchilla
C. Salud
C. Montera
Av.Gran Vía
C. Infantas
C. la Reina
C. Clavel
C. San Bartolomé
C. Caballero de Gracia
C. Jardines
C. la Aduana
C. Virgen de los Peligros
C. V. Hugo
C. Libertad
C. Colmenaras
C. Alcalá
C. Sevilla
C. Cedacheros
C. los Madrazo
C. Marqués de Cubas
C. Riería
Paseo del Prado
C. Salustiano Olazaga
C. Valenzuela
C. Alfonso XI
C. Alfonso XII
C. Montalbán
C. Juan de Mena
C. Antonio Maura
Po. de la Argentina
Po. San Pablo
Av. Méjico
C. Ruiz de Alarcón
C. Felipe IV
C. de Cascado
C. Moreto
C. Alisal
C. Alberto Bosch
C. Espalter
C. Zorrilla
C. Manuel Gonzalez
C. San Jerónimo
C. Pozo
C. Victoria
C. Espoz y Mina
C. Carretas
C. Correo
C. Postas
M. V. Pontejos
C. Esparteros
C. Mayor
Cost. Santiago
C. Cruzada
C. Santiago
C. Señores de Luzón
C. Factor
C. Duque Nájera
C. Sacramento
Justo
C. Villa
C. Segovia
Trv. Bringas
Cava San Miguel
C. Conda Miranda
Zaragoza
C. Imperial
C.Toledo
C. Salvador
C. Duque de Rivas
C. Concepción Jerónima
S. Tomás
C. la Bolsa
C. la Cruz
C. Nuñez de Arce
C. Príncipe
C. Prado
C. Echegaray
C. Ventura de la Vega
C. Santa Catalina
C. Cervantes
C. San Agustín
C. Duque Medinaceli
C. Infante
C. las Huertas
C. Lope de Vega
C. Jesús
C. de León
C. Santa María
C. Amor de Dios
C. Moratín
C. Verónica
C. San Pedro
C. Gobernador
C. Fúcar
C. Almeda
C. Alamadén
C. Atocha
C. Doctor Cortezo
C. Relatores
C. Luis Vélez de Guevara
C. Cañizares
C. Romanones
C. la Colegiata
C. de la Magdalena
C. Estudios
C. Duque de Alba
C. Cava Baja
C. Grafal
C. Cava Alta
C. San Millán
C. Maldonadas
C. Juanelo
C. la Encomienda
C. Dos Hermanas
C. los Abades
C. Oso
C. Cabestreros
C. Embajadores
C. Mesón de Paredes
C. la Cabeza
C. Calvario
C. del Olmo
C. Torrecilla del Leal
C. Olivar
C. Jesús y María
C. Lavapiés
C. Amparo
C. Ave María
C. Tres Peces
C. Esperanza
C. Eugenio
C. S. Ildefonso
C. M. Toca
C. Santa Inés
C. Santa Isabel
C. de Zurita
C. Salitre
C. San Cosme y San Damián
C. Dr. Piga
C. Fe
C. Caravaca
C. Argumosa
C. Tribulete
C. Dr. Fourquet
C. Hospital
C. Claudio Moyano
Paseo del Duque
C. Dr. Velasco
Paseo Infanta Isabel
Av. Ciudad de Barcelona
C. de S. Francisco
Gran Vía San Francisco
C. Humilladero
C. la Cebada
Cost. de San Andrés
C. del Ángel
C. del Águila
C. Mediodía Grande
C. Toledo
C. Santa Ana
C. Calatrava
C. Mira el Río Alta
C. la Arganzuela
C. Carnero
C. Ribera de Curtidores
C. Fray G.
C. Rodas
0
200 yards
200 meters
N
LG

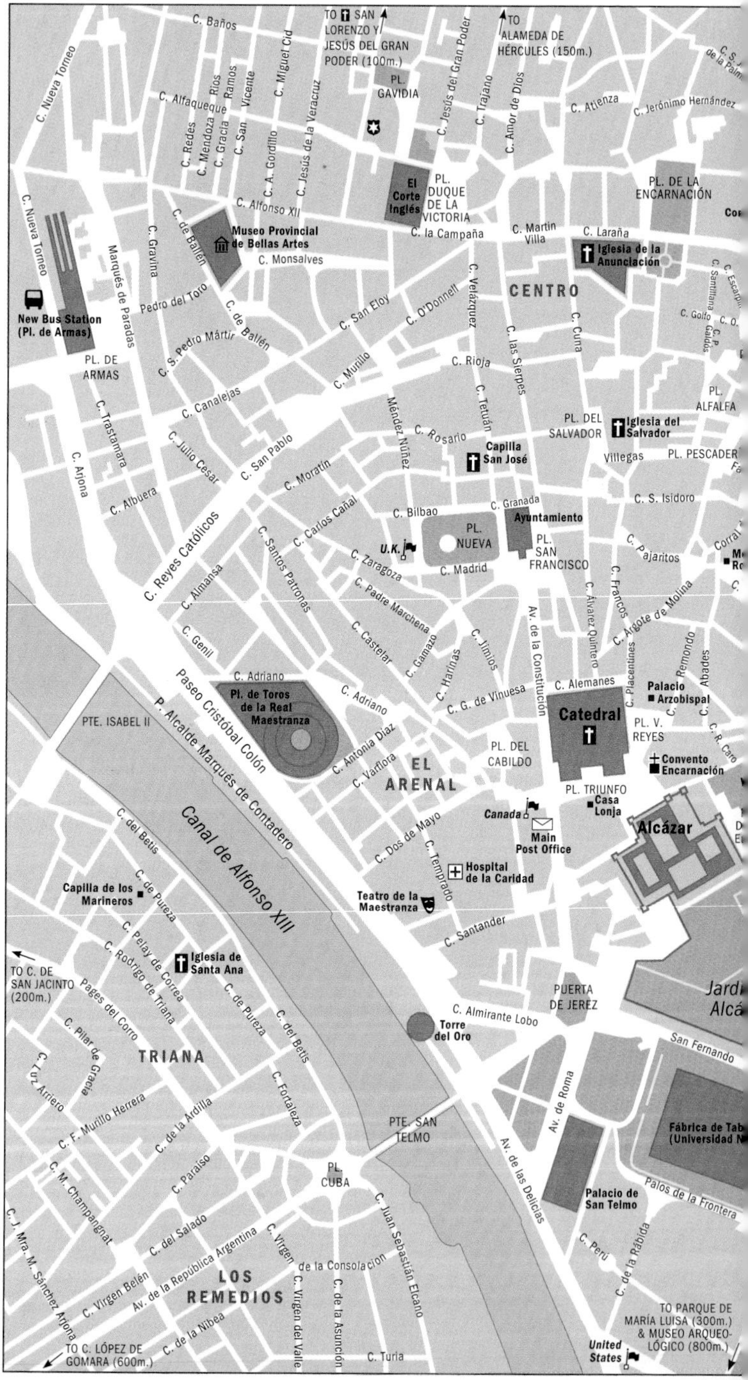

C. Baños
TO SAN LORENZO Y JESÚS DEL GRAN PODER (100m.)
TO ALAMEDA DE HÉRCULES (150m.)
C. Nueva Torneo
C. Alfaqueque
C. Redes
C. Mendoza Ríos
C. Gracia Ramos
C. San Vicente
C. Miguel Cid
C. A. Gordillo
C. Jesús de la Veracruz
PL. GAVIDIA
C. Jesús del Gran Poder
C. Trajano
C. Amor de Dios
C. Atienza
C. Jerónimo Hernández
El Corte Inglés
PL. DUQUE DE LA VICTORIA
PL. DE LA ENCARNACIÓN
C. Alfonso XII
C. de Bailén
C. Gravina
Marqués de Paradas
Museo Provincial de Bellas Artes
C. Monsalves
C. la Campaña
C. Martín Villa
C. Laraña
Iglesia de la Anunciación
CENTRO
New Bus Station (Pl. de Armas)
Pedro del Toro
C. de Bailén
C. S. Pedro Mártir
C. San Eloy
C. O'Donnell
C. Velázquez
C. las Sierpes
C. Cuna
C. Golfo
PL. DE ARMAS
C. Murillo
C. Rioja
C. Trastamara
C. Canalejas
Méndez Núñez
C. Tetuán
PL. ALFALFA
PL. DEL SALVADOR
Iglesia del Salvador
C. Rosario
Capilla San José
Villegas
C. Arjona
C. Julio César
C. San Pablo
C. Moratín
C. S. Isidoro
C. Albuera
C. Bilbao
C. Granada
Ayuntamiento
C. Reyes Católicos
C. Carlos Cañal
C. Santos Patronas
U.K.
PL. NUEVA
PL. SAN FRANCISCO
C. Pajaritos
C. Zaragoza
C. Madrid
C. Almansa
C. Padre Marchena
Av. de la Constitución
C. Álvarez Quintero
C. Francos
C. Argote de Molina
C. Genil
C. Castelar
C. Gamazo
C. Jimios
C. Harinas
C. Placentines
C. Remondo
C. Abades
C. Adriano
Paseo Cristóbal Colón
Pl. de Toros de la Real Maestranza
C. Adriano
C. G. de Vinuesa
C. Alemanes
Palacio Arzobispal
PTE. ISABEL II
P. Alcalde Marqués de Contadero
Catedral
PL. V. REYES
C. Antonia Díaz
C. Varflora
EL ARENAL
PL. DEL CABILDO
Convento Encarnación
PL. TRIUNFO
Casa Lonja
Canada
Alcázar
Canal de Alfonso XIII
C. del Betis
C. Dos de Mayo
Main Post Office
C. Temprado
Hospital de la Caridad
Capilla de los Marineros
C. de Pureza
Teatro de la Maestranza
C. Santander
C. Pelay de Correa
Iglesia de Santa Ana
C. Rodrigo de Triana
TO C. DE SAN JACINTO (200m.)
Pages del Corro
C. de Pureza
PUERTA DE JEREZ
C. Almirante Lobo
Torre del Oro
C. del Betis
C. Pilar de Gracia
San Fernando
C. Luz Arriero
TRIANA
C. Fortaleza
C. F. Murillo Herrera
C. de la Ardilla
Av. de Roma
PTE. SAN TELMO
C. M. Champagnat
C. Paraíso
PL. CUBA
Av. de las Delicias
Palos de la Frontera
Palacio de San Telmo
C. J. Mra. M. Sánchez Arjona
C. del Salado
C. Juan Sebastián Elcano
C. Perú
C. de la Rábida
Av. de la República Argentina
C. Virgen de la Consolación
LOS REMEDIOS
C. Virgen Belén
C. Virgen del Valle
C. de la Asunción
TO PARQUE DE MARÍA LUISA (300m.) & MUSEO ARQUEOLÓGICO (800m.)
C. de la Nibea
TO C. LÓPEZ DE GOMARA (600m.)
C. Turia
United States

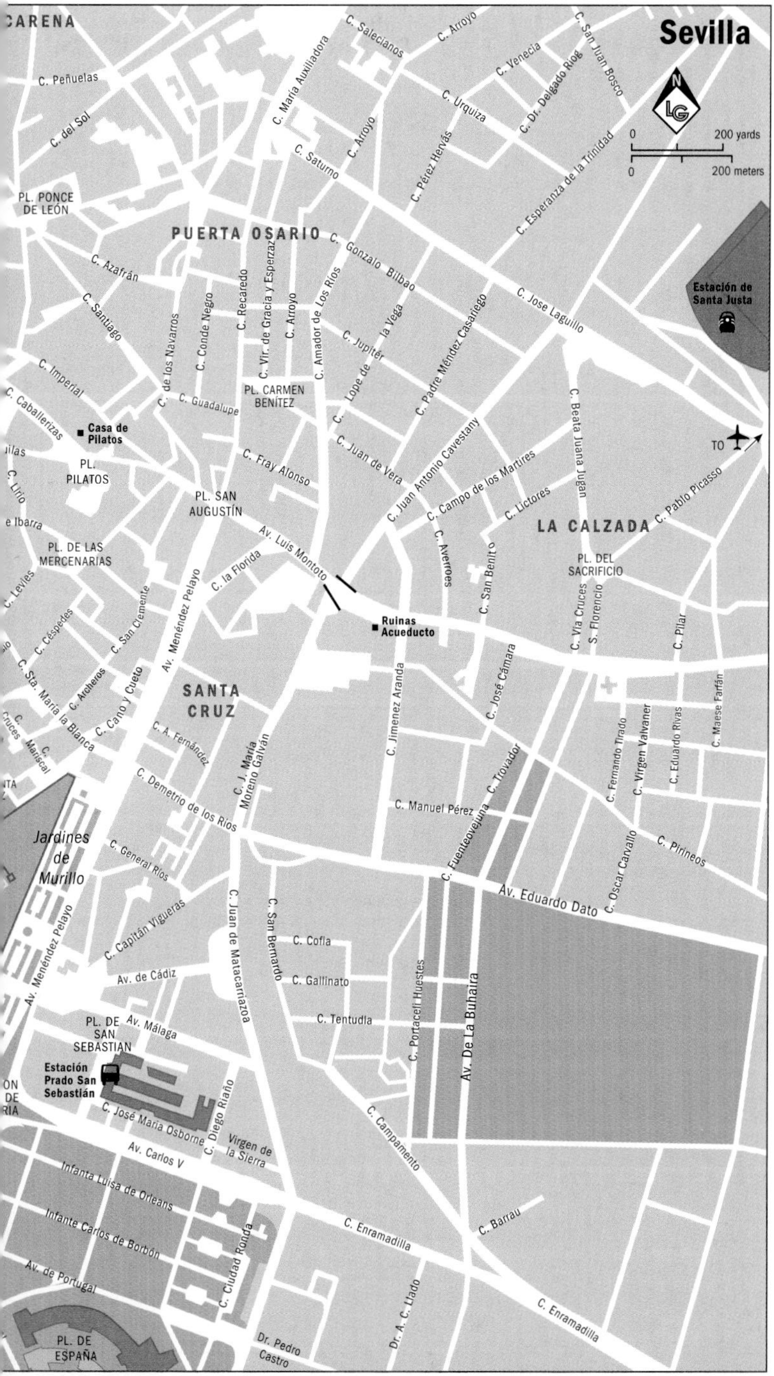

Sevilla
N
LG
0
200 yards
0
200 meters
ARENA
C. Peñuelas
C. del Sol
PL. PONCE DE LEÓN
PUERTA OSARIO
C. María Auxiliadora
C. Salecianos
C. Arroyo
C. Venecia
C. San Juan Bosco
C. Dr. Delgado Ríos
C. Urquiza
C. Saturno
C. Arroyo
C. Pérez Hervás
C. Esperanza de la Trinidad
Estación de Santa Justa
C. Gonzalo Bilbao
C. Jose Laguillo
C. Azafrán
C. Santiago
C. de los Navarros
C. Conde Nego
C. Recaredo
C. Vir. de Gracia y Esperaz
C. Arroyo
C. Amador de Los Ríos
C. Lope de la Vega
C. Júpiter
C. Padre Méndez Casariego
C. Imperial
C. Caballerizas
Casa de Pilatos
C. Guadalupe
PL. CARMEN BENÍTEZ
C. Beata Juana Jugan
TO
PL. PILATOS
C. Lirio
C. Fray Alonso
C. Juan de Vera
C. Juan Antonio Cavestany
C. Campo de los Martires
C. Lictores
C. Pablo Picasso
PL. SAN AUGUSTÍN
LA CALZADA
Ibarra
PL. DE LAS MERCENARIAS
Av. Luis Montoto
C. la Florida
C. Averroes
C. San Benito
PL. DEL SACRIFICIO
C. Levíes
Av. Menéndez Pelayo
C. San Clemente
Ruinas Acueducto
C. Vía Cruces
S. Florencio
C. Pilar
C. Céspedes
C. Sta. María la Blanca
C. Archeros
C. Cano y Cueto
SANTA CRUZ
C. Jimenez Aranda
C. José Cámara
C. Maese Farfán
C. A. Fernández
C. Cruces
C. Mariscal
C. J. María Moreno Galván
C. Trovador
C. Fernando Tirado
C. Virgen Valvaner
C. Eduardo Rivas
C. Demetrio de los Ríos
C. Manuel Pérez
Jardines de Murillo
C. General Ríos
C. Fuenteovejuna
C. Oscar Carvallo
C. Pirineos
Av. Eduardo Dato
Av. Menéndez Pelayo
C. Capitán Vigueras
C. Juan de Matacarriazoa
C. San Bernardo
C. Cofla
Av. de Cádiz
C. Gallinato
C. Portaceli Huestes
Av. De La Buhaira
PL. DE SAN SEBASTIAN
Av. Málaga
C. Tentudla
Estación Prado San Sebastián
C. José Maria Osborne
C. Diego Riaño
Virgen de la Sierra
C. Campamento
Av. Carlos V
Infanta Luisa de Orleans
Infante Carlos de Borbón
C. Barrau
C. Enramadilla
Av. de Portugal
C. Ciudad Ronda
Dr. A. C. Llado
C. Enramadilla
PL. DE ESPAÑA
Dr. Pedro Castro

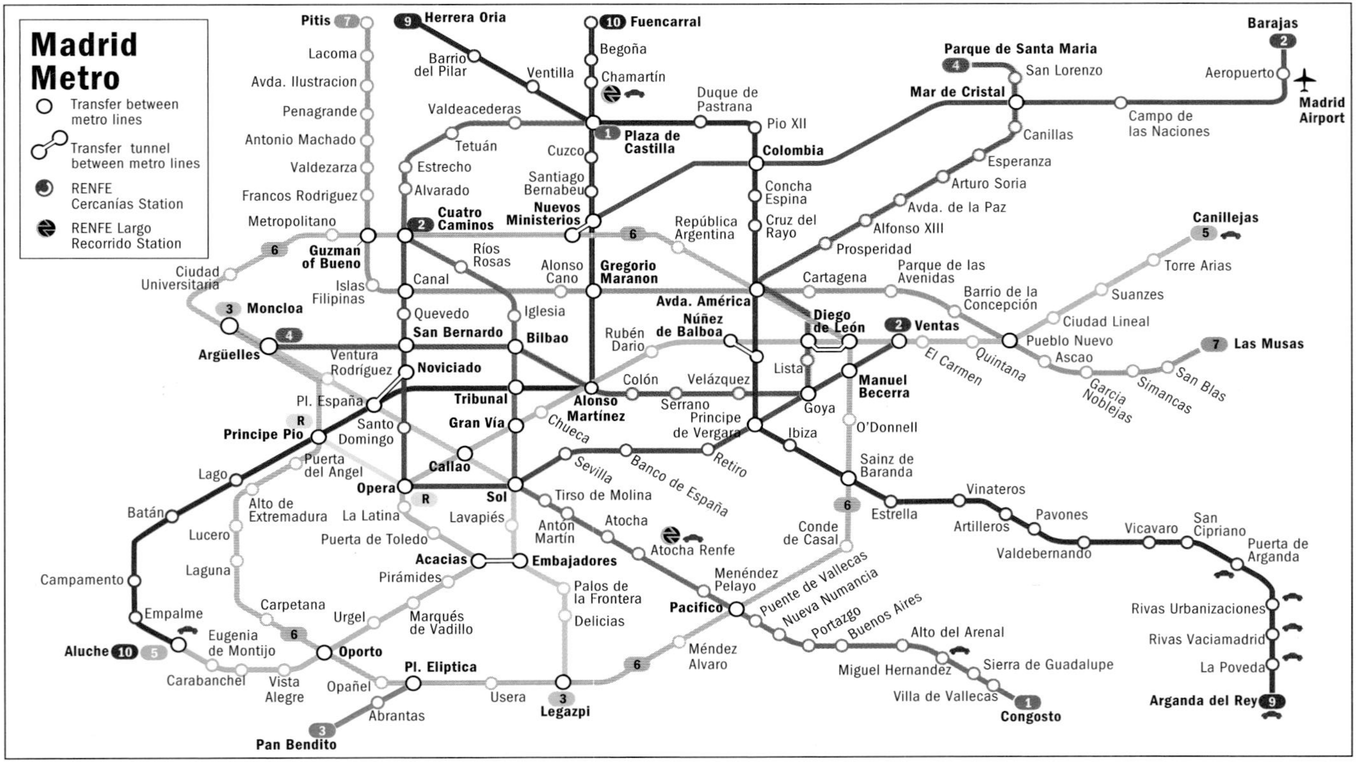

Madrid Metro
Transfer between metro lines
Transfer tunnel between metro lines
RENFE Cercanías Station
RENFE Largo Recorrido Station
Pitis
Lacoma
Avda. Ilustracion
Penagrande
Antonio Machado
Valdezarza
Francos Rodriguez
Metropolitano
Guzman of Bueno
Ciudad Universitaria
Islas Filipinas
Moncloa
Argüelles
Herrera Oria
Barrio del Pilar
Ventilla
Valdeacederas
Tetuán
Estrecho
Alvarado
Cuatro Caminos
Ríos Rosas
Canal
Quevedo
San Bernardo
Iglesia
Bilbao
Ventura Rodríguez
Noviciado
Pl. España
Tribunal
Principe Pio
Santo Domingo
Gran Vía
Callao
Puerta del Angel
Lago
Batán
Opera
Sol
Alto de Extremadura
La Latina
Lavapiés
Lucero
Puerta de Toledo
Acacias
Embajadores
Laguna
Pirámides
Campamento
Empalme
Carpetana
Urgel
Marqués de Vadillo
Aluche
Eugenia de Montijo
Oporto
Carabanchel
Vista Alegre
Opañel
Pl. Eliptica
Usera
Legazpi
Abrantas
Pan Bendito
Fuencarral
Begoña
Chamartín
Plaza de Castilla
Cuzco
Santiago Bernabeu
Nuevos Ministerios
Alonso Cano
Gregorio Maranon
Alonso Martínez
Chueca
Tirso de Molina
Antón Martín
Atocha
Atocha Renfe
Sevilla
Banco de España
Palos de la Frontera
Delicias
Duque de Pastrana
Pio XII
Colombia
Concha Espina
Cruz del Rayo
República Argentina
Avda. América
Rubén Dario
Núñez de Balboa
Colón
Serrano
Velázquez
Lista
Principe de Vergara
Retiro
Goya
Diego de León
Ibiza
Menéndez Pelayo
Pacifico
Méndez Alvaro
Conde de Casal
Puente de Vallecas
Nueva Numancia
Portazgo
Buenos Aires
Alto del Arenal
Miguel Hernandez
Sierra de Guadalupe
Villa de Vallecas
Congosto
Barajas
Aeropuerto
Madrid Airport
Parque de Santa Maria
San Lorenzo
Mar de Cristal
Campo de las Naciones
Canillas
Esperanza
Arturo Soria
Avda. de la Paz
Alfonso XIII
Prosperidad
Cartagena
Parque de las Avenidas
Barrio de la Concepción
Canillejas
Torre Arias
Suanzes
Ciudad Lineal
Pueblo Nuevo
Ventas
El Carmen
Quintana
Ascao
Garcia Noblejas
Simancas
San Blas
Las Musas
Manuel Becerra
O'Donnell
Sainz de Baranda
Estrella
Vinateros
Artilleros
Pavones
Valdebernando
Vicavaro
San Cipriano
Puerta de Arganda
Rivas Urbanizaciones
Rivas Vaciamadrid
La Poveda
Arganda del Rey

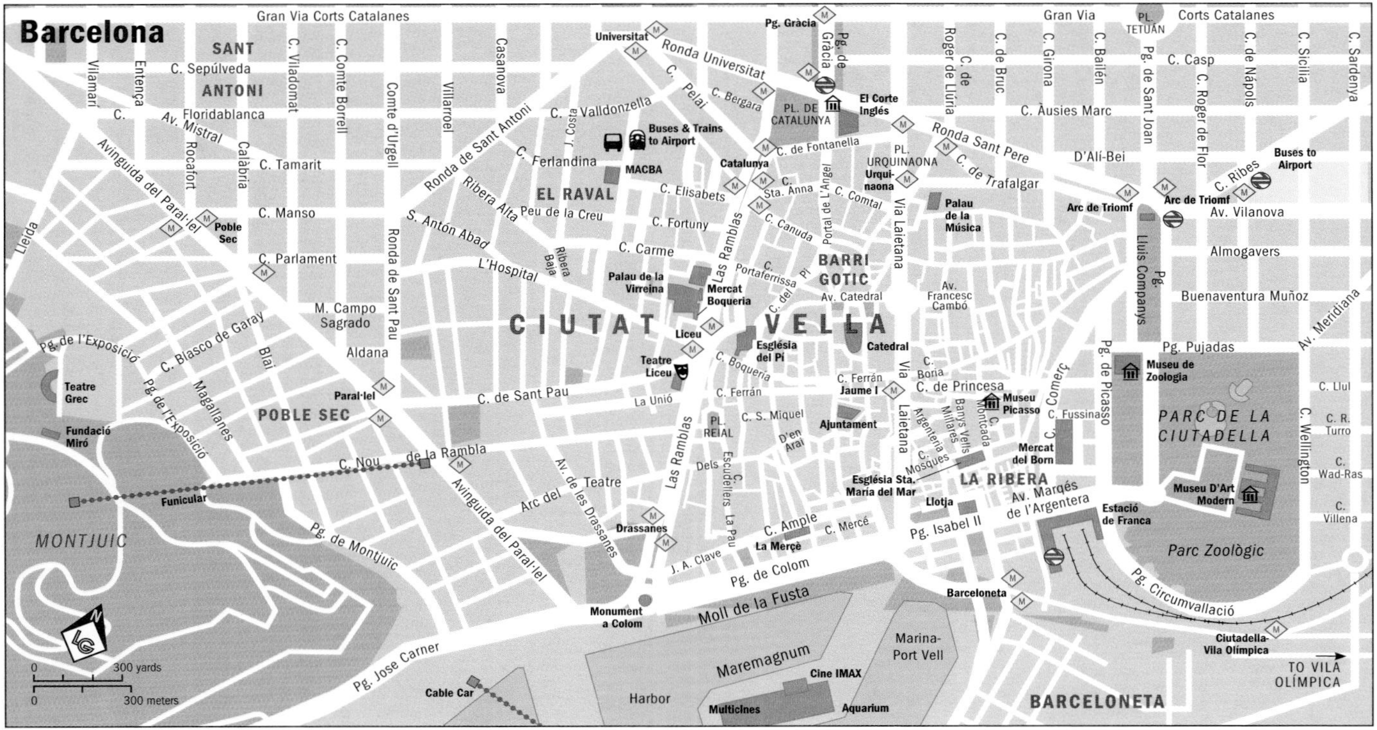
Barcelona
SANT ANTONI
EL RAVAL
CIUTAT VELLA
BARRI GOTIC
LA RIBERA
POBLE SEC
BARCELONETA
MONTJUIC
PARC DE LA CIUTADELLA
Parc Zoològic
Gran Via Corts Catalanes
Gran Via
Corts Catalanes
PL. TETUÁN
C. Sepúlveda
Floridablanca
Av. Mistral
C. Tamarit
C. Manso
C. Parlament
Vilamarí
Entença
Rocafort
Calàbria
C. Viladomat
C. Comte Borrell
Comte d'Urgell
Villarroel
Casanova
Ronda de Sant Antoni
Ronda de Sant Pau
Ronda Universitat
C. Pelai
C. Bergara
C. Valldonzella
J. Costa
C. Ferlandina
Ribera Alta
Peu de la Creu
S. Antón Abad
L'Hospital
Ribera Baja
C. Elisabets
C. Fortuny
C. Carme
Las Ramblas
C. Sta. Anna
C. Canuda
C. Portaferrissa
C. del Pi
Portal de L'Àngel
C. Comtal
C. de Fontanella
PL. DE CATALUNYA
PL. URQUINAONA
Via Laietana
Av. Catedral
Av. Francesc Cambó
C. Boqueria
C. Ferrán
C. S. Miquel
D'en Arai
PL. REIAL
Dels Escudellers
La Pau
La Unió
C. de Sant Pau
C. Nou de la Rambla
Av. de les Drassanes
Arc del Teatre
J. A. Clave
C. Ample
C. Mercé
Pg. de Colom
Moll de la Fusta
Pg. Jose Carner
Pg. de Montjuïc
Avinguida del Paral·lel
Pg. de l'Exposició
C. Blasco de Garay
Blai
Magallanes
M. Campo Sagrado
Aldana
Lleida
C. Boria
C. de Princesa
C. Montcada
Banys Vells
Millares
Argenteria
C. Mosques
C. Comerç
C. Fussina
Pg. Isabel II
Av. Marqués de l'Argentera
Pg. Circumvallació
Pg. de Picasso
Pg. Pujadas
Pg. Lluis Companys
Ronda Sant Pere
C. de Trafalgar
D'Alí-Bei
Av. Vilanova
Almogavers
Buenaventura Muñoz
Av. Meridiana
C. Ribes
C. Àusies Marc
C. Casp
C. Roger de Flor
Pg. de Sant Joan
C. Bailén
C. Girona
C. de Bruc
C. de Roger de Llúria
Pg. de Gràcia
C. de Nápols
C. Sicília
C. Sardenya
C. Wellington
C. Llul
C. R. Turro
C. Wad-Ras
C. Villena
Universitat
Pg. Gràcia
Catalunya
Urquinaona
Liceu
Jaume I
Drassanes
Barceloneta
Ciutadella-Vila Olímpica
Arc de Triomf
Paral·lel
Poble Sec
El Corte Inglés
Buses & Trains to Airport
Buses to Airport
MACBA
Palau de la Virreina
Mercat Boqueria
Església del Pi
Catedral
Teatre Liceu
Ajuntament
Palau de la Música
Museu Picasso
Mercat del Born
Església Sta. Maria del Mar
Llotja
La Mercè
Museu de Zoologia
Museu D'Art Modern
Estació de Franca
Monument a Colom
Marina-Port Vell
Maremagnum
Cine IMAX
Aquarium
Multicines
Harbor
Cable Car
Funicular
Teatre Grec
Fundació Miró
TO VILA OLÍMPICA
N
0 300 yards
0 300 meters

TO MUSEU-MONESTIR DE PEDRALBES
PALAU REIAL
Av. Pedralbes
Pg. Manuel Girona
SARRIÀ
Col.legi de les Teresianes
Ronda General Mitre
BONANOVA
C. Vico
Ravella
C. Modolell
Vallmajor
C. les Escoles
PL. PAPA PIUS XII
PL. PRAT DE LA RIBA
MARIA CRISTINA
PL. DE LA REINA MARIA CRISTINA
Via Augusta
Camp Nou
Austria
C. Maternitat
Avinguda Sarrià
C. J.S. Bach
MUNTANER
C. Parroc
Av. Diagonal
Parc de Poeta Eduard de Marquina
Gran Via de Carles III
LES CORTS
C. Dr. Ibáñez
LES CORTS
Tv. de les Corts
C. Numància
C. d'Entença
C. Calvet
C. Sagues
C. Amigó
C. Santaló
PL. DE FRANCESC MACIÀ
Tv. de Gràc
C. Joan Güell
C. de Galileo
Av. Madrid
C. Marqués de Sentmentat
United Kingdom
C. Roger
BADAL
PL. DEL CENTRE
C. Londres
C. Londres
C. Brasil
C. Berlin
C. Paris
C. Robrenyo
Av. la Infanta Carlota
L'EIXAM
ESQUER
C. Tenor
C. Vallespir
C. Còrsega
Hospital Clinic
ENTENÇA
HOSPITAL CLINIC
C. Rosselló
PL. DEL SANTS
Estació Barcelona-Sants
SANTS ESTACIÓ
MERCAT NOU
C. Provença
PL. PAÏSOS CATALANS
C. Sants Creu Coberta
Parc de la Espanya Industrial
C. del Rector Triadó
Avinguda Roma
C. Mallorca
C. dels Jocs Florals
C. Sagunt
C. Olzinelles
Bejar
C. València
TARRAGONA
C. Comte d'Urgell
C. Guadiana Premià
HOSTAFRANCS
C. Consell de Cent
C. d'Aragó
TIVE
C. de Rocafort
C. Calabria
C. Viladomat
C. Comte Borrell
C. Villarroel
C. Casanova
C. Tarragona
Parc Joan Miró
C. de Gavà
C. Moianes
C. de la Bordeta
C. de la Diputació
ESPANYA
URGELL
C. de Vilamarí
ROCAFORT
TO
Gran Via Corts Catalanes
PL. D'ESPANYA
Gran Via de les Corts Catalanes
C. Sepúlveda
Av. la Reina Maria Cristina
Av. Paral.lel
C. Floridablanca
Av. Marqués de Comillas
Poble Espanyol
PL. DE SANT JORDI
C. de Tamarit
PL. DE LES CASCADES
Palau Alfonso XIII
Mercat de Sant Antoni
Ronda de Sant Antoni
C. Manso
EL RAV
C. de Lleida
Pg. los Cascades
Av. l'Estadi
POBLE SEC
POBLE SEC
C. Hospit
Museo Arqueològic
MNAC (Palau Nacional)
PL. EUROPA
Museo Etnològic
Jardins de Joan Maragall
C. Magalhaes
C. Blai
Ronda de Sant Pau
Pg. l'Exposició
Palau Sant Jordi
Pg. Olimpic
Fundació Miró
C. Sant Pau
Av. Miramar
Funicular
PARAL.L
Estadi Olimpic
Camí dels Tres Pins
Pg. Montjuïc
MONTJUÏC
Ctra. Montjuïc
Cablecar
Ctra. Mondials
Pg. Josep Carner
Jardíns de Miramar
0
450 yards
0
450 meters
Castell de Montjuïc
Museo Militar
TO AEROPORT EL PRAT DE LLOBREGAT

Barcelona
PARK GÜELL
Parc Carmel
Av. la República Argentina
C. Verdi
C. Pàdua
C. Zaragoza
C. Vallirana
PL. DE LESSEPS
LESSEPS
Travessera de Dalt
C. Sanjoanistes
C. Guillem Tell
PL. MOLINA
C. Lincoln
Casa Vicens
C. Gran de Gràcia
FONTANA
C. Sant Salvador
C. de Martí
C. Providència
C. Robí
C. d'Astúries
C. Torrent de l'Olla
C. de l'Or
C. Sant Lluís
C. Terol Bruniguer
C. Ramón y Cajal
Tv. de Gràcia
C. Torrent de les Flors
C. Sors
C. l'Escorial
C. Alegre de Dalt
C. Camèlies
C. Coloma
PL. ALFONS EL SAVI
ALFONS X
Parc de les Aigües
Ronda Guinardó
C. Pi. i Margall
JOANIC
Sant Marc
GRÀCIA
Montseny
Ros de Olano
Via Augusta
C. Siracusa
C. Martínez
C. Sant Antoni Maria Claret
HOSPITAL DE SANT PAU
C. Indústria
L'EIXAMPLE DRETA
Diagonal
C. Bonavista
PL. JOAN CARLES I
C. Còrsega
DIAGONAL
C. de Bailen
Pg. de Sant Joan
C. Roger de Flor
C. Nàpols
C. Sicília
C. Sardenya
C. Marina
Av. de Gaudí
C. Rosselló
CARTAGENA
PROVENÇA
La Pedrera
LA SAGRADA FAMILIA
C. Provença
C. de Balmes
Rambla de Catalunya
Pg. de Gràcia
C. Pau Claris
C. Roger Llúria
VERDAGUER
La Sagrada Familia
PL. JACINT VERDAGUER
C. València
Av. Diagonal
C. Cartagena
Fundació Tàpies
PG. DE GRÀCIA
C. d'Aragó
PL. PABLO NERUDA
Manzana de la Discòrdia
C. Consell de Cent
GIRONA
C. de la Diputació
C. Bruc
(Pg. Carles I)
PL. DE LES GLÒRIES CATALANES
TETUÁN
Plaza de Toros Monumentales
PG. DE GRÀCIA
PL. TETUÁN
Gran Via de les Corts Catalanes
Teatre Nacional de Catalunya
MONUMENTAL
Ronda Universitat
C. Casp
GLÒRIES
Auditori Municipal
CATALUNYA
PL. DE CATALUNYA
C. Girona
C. Bailen
C. d'Ausiàs Marc
C. de Marina
Aerobus
URQUINAONA
Ronda de Sant Pere
Fontanella
C. Tànger
Portal de l'Àngel
ARC DE TRIOMF
Estació Nord
CIUTAT VELLA
Palau de la Música Catalana
S. Pere Més Alt
MARINA
Av. Meridiana
Las Ramblas
PL. DE PÍ
S. Pere Més Baix
C. dels Almogàvers
Palau de la Generalitat
LA RIBERA
Sta. Maria del Pi
United States
C. Comerç
C. Pamplona
C. d'Alaba
C. d'Àvila
LICEU
PL. DE ST. JAUME
Pg. Pujades
BOGATELL
C. Princesa
Ajuntament
Museu Picasso
C. Llull
JAUME I
Pg. Picasso
Museu d'Art Modern
POBLE NOU
PL. REIAL
C. Ciutat
Pg. Born
C. Ramón Turró
Via Laietana
Santa Maria del Mar
PARC DE LA CIUTADELLA
C. Wellington
BARRI GÒTIC
Av. Marquès de l'Argentera
DRASSANES
Estació França
Parc Zoologic
Av. Bogatell
Pg. Colom
Av. d'Icària
Monument Colom
Av. d'Icària
Pg. Circumval.lació
Vila Olímpica
Moll de la Fusta
CIUTADELLA-VILA OLIMPICA
Moll d'Espanya
The Towers
PORT OLÍMPIC
BARCELONETA

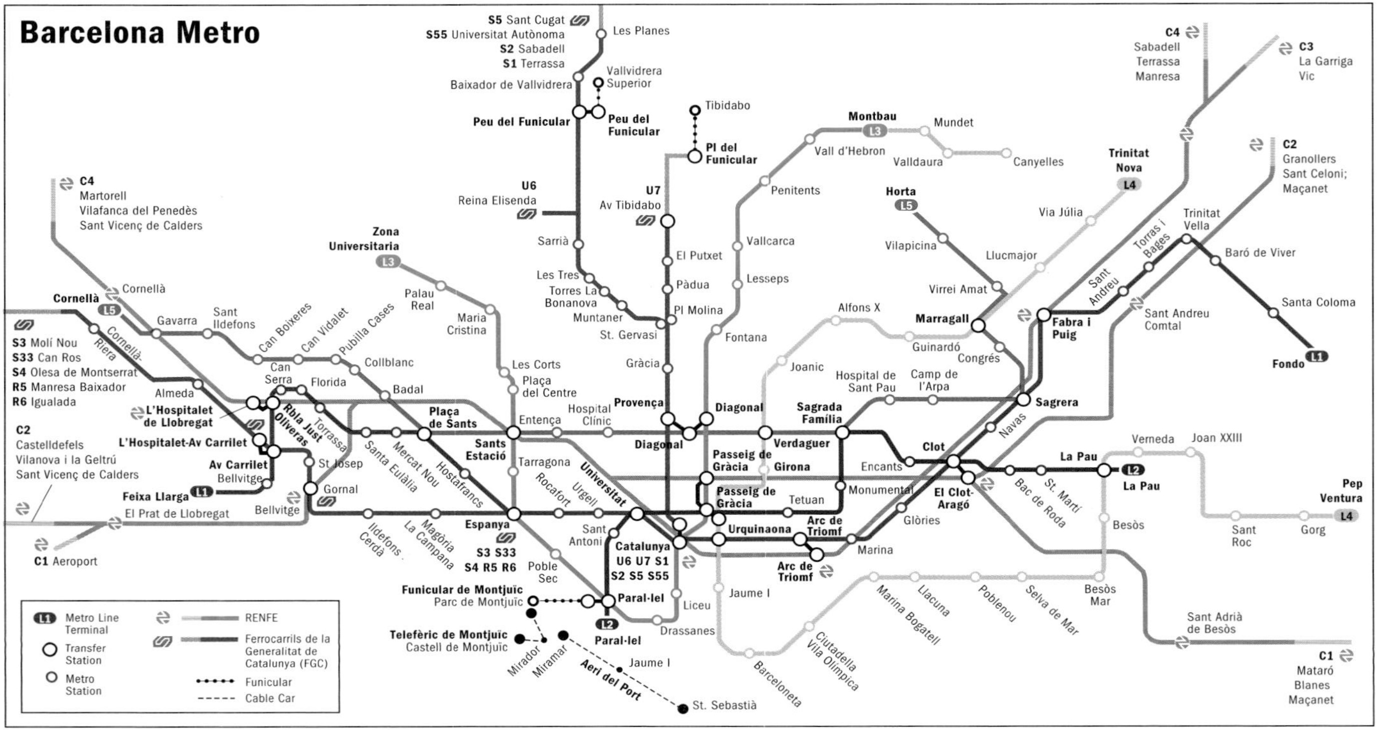

Barcelona Metro
S5 Sant Cugat
S55 Universitat Autònoma
S2 Sabadell
S1 Terrassa
Les Planes
Baixador de Vallvidrera
Vallvidrera Superior
Peu del Funicular
Peu del Funicular
Tibidabo
Pl del Funicular
Montbau
L3
Mundet
Vall d'Hebron
Valldaura
Canyelles
C4
Sabadell
Terrassa
Manresa
C3
La Garriga
Vic
C2
Granollers
Sant Celoni;
Maçanet
Trinitat Nova
L4
C4
Martorell
Vilafanca del Penedès
Sant Vicenç de Calders
U6
Reina Elisenda
U7
Av Tibidabo
Penitents
Horta
L5
Via Júlia
Trinitat Vella
Zona Universitaria
L3
Sarrià
El Putxet
Vallcarca
Vilapicina
Torras i Bages
Baró de Viver
Palau Real
Les Tres Torres
La Bonanova
Pàdua
Lesseps
Llucmajor
Maria Cristina
Muntaner
Pl Molina
Virrei Amat
Sant Andreu
Santa Coloma
Cornellà
Cornellà
L5
Gavarra
Sant Ildefons
St. Gervasi
Alfons X
Marragall
Fabra i Puig
Sant Andreu Comtal
Can Boixeres
Can Vidalet
Pubilla Cases
Fontana
Guinardó
Congrés
Fondo
L1
Cornellà-Riera
S3 Molí Nou
S33 Can Ros
S4 Olesa de Montserrat
R5 Manresa Baixador
R6 Igualada
Can Serra
Florida
Collblanc
Les Corts
Gràcia
Joanic
Hospital de Sant Pau
Camp de l'Arpa
Almeda
Badal
Plaça del Centre
Hospital Clínic
Provença
Diagonal
Sagrada Família
Sagrera
L'Hospitalet de Llobregat
Rbla Just Oliveras
Torrassa
Plaça de Sants
Entença
Verdaguer
Navas
C2
Castelldefels
Vilanova i la Geltrú
Sant Vicenç de Calders
L'Hospitalet-Av Carrilet
Santa Eulàlia
Mercat Nou
Sants Estació
Diagonal
Clot
Verneda
Joan XXIII
La Pau
L2
La Pau
Tarragona
Av Carrilet
Bellvitge
St Josep
Hostafrancs
Universitat
Passeig de Gràcia
Girona
Encants
Feixa Llarga
L1
Gornal
Rocafort
Urgell
Passeig de Gràcia
Tetuan
Monumental
El Clot-Aragó
Bac de Roda
St. Martí
Pep Ventura
L4
El Prat de Llobregat
Bellvitge
Ildefons Cerdà
Magòria La Campana
Espanya
Sant Antoni
Urquinaona
Arc de Triomf
Glòries
Besòs
Sant Roc
Gorg
C1 Aeroport
S3 S33
S4 R5 R6
Poble Sec
Catalunya
U6 U7 S1
S2 S5 S55
Arc de Triomf
Marina
Jaume I
Funicular de Montjuïc
Parc de Montjuïc
Paral·lel
Liceu
Marina Bogatell
Llacuna
Poblenou
Selva de Mar
Besòs Mar
Sant Adrià de Besòs
L2
Paral·lel
Drassanes
Telefèric de Montjuïc
Castell de Montjuïc
Mirador
Miramar
Jaume I
Aeri del Port
St. Sebastià
Barceloneta
Ciutadella Vila Olímpica
C1
Mataró
Blanes
Maçanet
L1 Metro Line Terminal
Transfer Station
Metro Station
RENFE
Ferrocarrils de la Generalitat de Catalunya (FGC)
Funicular
Cable Car

VAL D'ARAN

Some of the Catalan Pyrenees's most dazzling peaks cluster around green Val d'Aran, Cataluña's northernmost valley. Val d'Aran's main river flows into France and is hemmed in tightly by the highest peaks in the eastern range; consequently, the area's original native language is not Catalan but Aranese, a dialect close to *langue d'oc,* the medieval Romance language spoken in southern France. Today, modern transportation and the tourist industry have made substantial inroads into the valley's unique isolation, but it is still well worth exploring.

SWM SEEKING... Tall, dark, handsome, rich, famous, powerful, and searching for life partner. Enjoys water sports (competed on the Olympic sailing team). Educated at Georgetown. Looking for that special someone—attractive, charismatic, and preferably of noble lineage—to share interests and raise a family. His name is Felipe, the Prince of Asturias and heir to the Spanish throne. With his 30th birthday just behind him and his two elder sisters recently married, all eyes are on Felipe. Whom will he choose to be his queen when he takes over one of Europe's few powerful monarchies? The competition is fierce. Lovely ladies from wealthy families are stalking the streets of Madrid and the slopes of the Val d'Aran, but so far there are no front-runners. Cross your fingers and pack something nice—you could be the next queen of Spain.

BAQUIERA-BERET

Baquiera-Beret is Spain's most chic ski resort; after all, the Spanish royal family's favorite slopes are here. Currently, about 80 alpine trails and a few cross-country ones wind down the surrounding peaks. Although budget accommodations have disappeared at the ski station itself, the town of **Salardú,** a few kilometers away, has an enormous youth hostel, the **Albérja Era Garona (HI) ❶.** The hostel is accessible in the high season by shuttle bus from Vielha and offers dorms of four and six beds, as well as bike and ski rentals through the reception desk. (☎973 64 52 71. Breakfast included. Sheets €2.10. Dorms Jan.-Apr. €15.03, over 25 €19.23. May-Nov. €11.57/€15.63. Dec. €12.92/€17.43.) Upstairs above the umbrella tables of Bar Montanha, the rooms of **Pensión Montanha ❷,** C. Major, 8 offer a bit more privacy. With your back to the central pizzeria, head up the front-facing side street, keeping an eye out for signs pointing for Bar Montanha. (☎973 64 41 08. Singles €18, with bath €25; doubles €25/€30.) While in town, don't miss Salardú's 13th-century church of **Sant Andreu,** and its incredible garden view. The town of Vielha is only 12km from Bacquiera-Beret, and the two are connected by a shuttle bus in July and August. Check at the tourist office for schedules. For skiing info and reservations, contact the **Oficeria de Baquiera-Beret** (☎973 64 44 55; fax 973 64 44 88).

Upscale restaurants abound in Baquiera-Beret and Salardú, but you haven't really eaten in style until you've hit **Eth Bot ❹,** which lies just beyond **Pensión Montanha** in Pl. Major. As soon as you set foot within the stone walls of this restaurant-tavern and see the iron oven looming in the corner, you know you're going to enjoy your meal. The back dining hall, decked with barrels, glass jugs, and woven baskets, harkens to an age when social drinking meant toasts and ribaldry rather than martinis and handshakes. Nowhere else will you feel more of an urge to charge your glass and drink to the old days. To really treat yourself, order the hearty surf 'n turf (mar y montaña) *menú* €22. Less expensive options include salads, ham, and fish for €4.50-10. (☎973 64 42 12. Open daily 11am-2am. MC/V.)

VIELHA

The biggest town in the Val d'Aran, Vielha (pop. 7000) combines the warmth of its small old quarter with the bustling activity of the main commercial thoroughfare. From its prime location, Vielha welcomes hikers and skiers to its lively streets with every sort of service the outdoorsy-type might desire.

PRACTICAL INFORMATION. **Alsina Graells** (☎973 27 14 70 or 932 65 68 66) runs buses from Vielha to **Barcelona** (5½hr.; 5:30am, 1:30pm; €23). For a Cardona **taxi** call ☎973 64 22 60. The **tourist office,** C. Sarriulèra, 8, is one block up-river from the Plaça de la Iglesia (look for the bright yellow sign.) Staff assists hikers, skiers, and Romanesque-seekers alike. (☎973 64 01 10; fax 973 64 03 72. Open daily 9am-9pm.) **ATMs** pepper main Av. Castiéro, which intersects the river before turning into Av. Pas d'Arró. Services include: **emergency** ☎112; **police** ☎973 64 09 72; **Internet access** at **CCV Informática,** C. Aneto, 7a. (☎973 64 12 88. Open M-F 9:30am-1:30pm and 4:30-8:30pm, Sa 9:30am-1:30pm. €4.21 per hr. MC/V.) The **post office,** C. Sarriuléra, 6, is by the tourist office. (☎973 64 09 12. Open M-F 8:30am-2:30pm, Sa 9:30am-1pm.) **Postal code:** 25530.

ACCOMMODATIONS AND FOOD. Budget travelers in need of a treat can put their feet up at the elegant, yet homey **Hotel El Cierco ❷,** Pl. San Orencio, 3. Standing on the bridge with your back to the tourist office, head downhill to the left. Upon entering the plaza, turn left to face the hotel's light green, mural-bedecked exterior. (☎973 64 01 65; fax 973 64 20 77. Apr.-Oct. singles €18.03; doubles €33.36. Dec.-Mar. €24.04/€42.07. Closed for Nov. and the last two weeks in June. Several other inexpensive *pensiones* also fill the end of Camin Reiau, off Pg. Libertat (which intersects Av. Casteiro at Pl. Sant Antoni). **Casa Vicenta ❷,** C. Reiau, 3, with its great mattresses and modern furnishings, comes highly recommended. (☎973 64 08 19. Singles €22; doubles €38. Closed Oct. and Nov.)

Quiet your rumbling stomach with a sampling of every tortilla under the sun at the inviting **Restaurant Basteret ❷,** C. Mayor 6A, tucked into a corner facing the tourist office, just across the river. Friendly staff and a well-priced daily *menú* (€8.50, including a glass of wine) make this a great spot. (☎973 64 07 14. Open daily June 1-Sept. 15 1-4:30pm and 8-11pm. Closed the last two weeks of Oct. and M from Sept.16-May. MC/V.) **Eth Breç ❶,** Av. Castiero, 5, beneath the green Fujifilm sign along the main road, serves incredible pastries and a selection of teas. (☎973 64 00 50. Open daily 8am-2pm and 4-8:30pm. MC/V.) **Taverna deth Gascon ❶,** Pl. Sant Orenc, 1 (☎973 64 22 87) is a refreshing change from the many *cervecerías*. Pick up tasty toast dishes (€3) or *bocadillos* (€2.40-3.30). Open daily 10am-10pm.

SIGHTS AND ENTERTAINMENT. The **Iglesia de San Miguel,** a simple 12th-century Romanesque church, houses the intricate *Crist de Mijaran*. The church is to your left in the plaza as you face the tourist office. (Open daily 11am-8pm.) Also in Vielha is the **Museu de Val d'Aran,** on C. Mayor, whose ethnographic collection sheds light on Aranese culture. (☎973 64 18 15. Open Tu-Sa 10am-1pm and 5-8pm, Su 10am-1pm. €1.40.) Vielha is also a good base for all sorts of outdoor activities. **Camins,** Av. Pas d'Arro, 5, in the shopping gallery, is a great place to start planning. Staff can answer questions, organize **treks** into the Aigüestortes National Park and the surrounding mountains (starting at €20), lead **rafting** and **horseback trips,** and rent **mountain bikes.** Ask about the popular half-day bike trip (26km one-way) to Camino Real/Vielha-Les, which promises a great workout and spectacular views. (Bikes half-day €15.30, full-day €20.) In conjunction with the **Escola Snowboard Val d'Aran,** Camin can also teach you how to **snowboard** (Escola: ☎973 64 51 26; fax 973 64 41 54. Open M-F 9am-1pm and 4-8:30pm; try calling on weekends.)

When the sun goes down, the ready-to-rage of all ages run to **Eth Clót,** a self-proclaimed *bar musical.* Warm up at the side tables below before heading to the upstairs dance floor (most drinks €2.) A smaller bar sits on the second floor for refueling. A number of foosball tables are scattered both levels. (Just beyond Hotel El Cierco near Pl. San Orencio. Open daily 10:30pm-3am except Su in Oct.)

LÉRIDA (LLEIDA)

Lérida (pop. 120,000) doesn't attract tons of tourists, but even so, a fair number of camera-toting visitors pass through this industrious but unassuming city to see the impressive cathedral of Seu Vella. Alongside the Río Segre, Lérida's modern avenues run around its exterior, while narrow streets surround the cathedral.

TRANSPORTATION. RENFE trains (☎902 24 02 02), Pl. Berenguer IV. Trains to: **Barcelona** (2-4hr., 18 per day 5am-8:51pm, €7.91-18.66); **Huesca** (2hr., 7 per day 7:30am-9:30pm, €6.60); **Madrid** (5hr., 3 per day 8:41am-1:25am, €33-44); **Tarragona** (1½-2hr., 10 per day 2:48am-5:55pm, €4.15); and **Zaragoza** (2-4hr., 16 per day 8:41am-2:49am, €14.16-19.16). **Central Buses** (☎973 26 85 00) stop one block from Av. Madrid near the intersection with Av. Catalunya. Buses to: **Barcelona** (2¼-2¾hr., 11 per day 6am-7:30pm, €14.05); **Girona** (3½hr.; Sept.-June 3 per day 6am-6:30 pm, July-Aug. 6am and 5:30pm; €15.30); **Tarragona** (2hr.; M-F 6 per day 7:30am-9:15pm, Sa-Su 9:30am and 9:15pm; €3.70); **Zaragoza** (2¼hr., 5 per day 8am-6pm, €17.57). Yellow **city buses** (☎973 27 29 99) run throughout the city; the tourist office has a map and schedule. The most useful are the "Exterior" bus (#10) from the train station to the center, which stops along Av. Madrid, and #15 between the train station and Seu Vella (€0.66). For a **taxi,** call **Radio Taxi** (☎973 20 30 50).

ORIENTATION AND PRACTICAL INFORMATION. Bordered by the Río Segre, Lérida sprawls up the hill toward Seu Villa. **C. Major,** one block inland from the river, is the city's principle commercial street. Major banks and the post office line **Rbla. Ferran,** near the train station. Av. Madrid, Av. Catalunya, Rambla d'Aragó, and Seu Villa frame the center of the city. Pl. Sant Joan, at the end of C. Major, is for all practical purposes the tourist's center, with several hostels. Lérida has two main **tourist offices.** For city information, head to the office at C. Major, 31, the street parallel to the river and one block inland. (☎973 70 03 19. Open M-F 11am-8pm, Sa 10am-8pm, Su 10am-1:30pm.) The office at Av. Madrid, 36, around the corner from the bus station, has regional information. (☎973 27 09 97; fax 973 27 09 49. Open June-Sept. M-F 9am-2pm and 3-8pm, Sa 9am-2pm; Oct.-May M-F 9am-2pm and 3-7pm, Sa 10am-2pm.) **Banks** with 24hr. **ATMs** line Rbla. Ferran and are scattered throughout the city. Other services include: **luggage storage,** at the train station (€4.50 for 24hr.), but none at the bus station; **emergency,** ☎112; **police,** Gran Passeig de Ronda, 52 (☎973 26 47 99); **Arnan de Vilanova Hospital,** Av. Alcalde Rovira Roure, 80 (☎973 24 81 00); **Cafetó Internet,** C. Bonaire, 8. (☎973 72 51 48; €2.50 per hr.; open M-F 9am-2pm and 3:30pm-1am, Sa 9am-2pm and 4pm-2am, Su 4pm-midnight); and the **post office,** C. Rambla Ferran, 16, toward town from the train station. (☎973 24 70 00. M-F 8:30am-8:30pm, Sa 9:30am-2pm.) **Postal code:** 25007.

ACCOMMODATIONS. Most of Lérida's budget accommodations (including those listed) double as student housing, so term-time (Oct.-June) space is limited. Dimly-lit rooms at the central **Hostal Mundial ❶,** Pl. Sant Joan, 4, provide abundant floor space, even with large beds. Ask for one with a balcony overlooking the plaza. (☎973 24 27 00; fax 973 24 26 02. Singles with bath or shower €13; doubles with shower €20, with bath €25. Breakfast €3. M-F *menú* €6. Parking 9pm-9am €3.60.) **Alberg Sant Anastasi (HI) ❶,** Rbla. d'Aragó, 11, offers clean, 4-person rooms,

CATALUÑA

free Internet, two TV lounges, and a game room. The halls can be noisy during the day but are more subdued as bedtime approaches. (☎973 26 60 99. Under 21 €12.92; over 21 €17.43.) **Hotel Goya ❷,** C. Alcalde Costa, 9, 1½ blocks up C. Catalunya from the river, provides comfortably-sized rooms with squeaky-clean bathrooms and framed posters. Each *habitación* comes with a desk, dresser, and small TV. (☎973 26 67 88; fax 973 26 69 22. Singles €20; doubles €33; triples €45.)

FOOD. Lérida's local specialty is *caragoles* (snails), and the city manages to consume over 12 slimy tons of them each year, most notably during their popular May gastronomic festival, *Aplec del Caragol.* The tourist office has a list of restaurants that serve a special *menú Xec Caragol* (€24) composed entirely of various snail dishes—some of the more popular dishes are snails cooked on a *llauna* (grill), served with *alioli* (mayonnaise and garlic), cooked with veggies on a stone tile, and *a la gormanta* (fried with seasonings). For those who would prefer to chop off one of their less important fingers than to eat snails, the area surrounding C. Bonaire provides basic food, and the area around Seu Vella has a variety of tiny hole-in-the-wall establishments that serve African cuisine.

A prime escargot-free location is **l'Escala ❷,** C. Académia, 34, off Gran Passeig de Ronda, which boasts everything from *bocadillos* (€2.10-3.60) to pizza and hamburgers (about €4) to salmon dishes (€5). Grab a quick bite up front or go to the more formal back dining room for the superb *menú del día* for €12. (☎973 27 04 06. Open daily except Sa 8am-2am; dining room 5-12pm. MC/V.) For a tasty eye-opener, visit **Topkati ❶,** C. Ballester, 19, at the end of C. Bisbe Torres off C. Catalunya. Popular for breakfast on the go, this bustling cafe serves scrumptious pastries and snacks, but the real draw is its varieties of gourmet coffee (€0.80-1.60). Add a drop or two of whiskey for a nice morning buzz. Add more for a nice afternoon hangover. (☎973 26 85 97. Open daily 8am-11pm.) To satisfy your sweet tooth, head to **Crêpes & Gofres ❶,** C. Camp de Mart, 1, for delightful dessert crepes. (Crepes €1.50-2.10. Open Su-M 6-10:30pm, Th-Sa 6pm-3:30am.)

SIGHTS. High above the city, **Seu Villa,** Lérida's amazing 14th-century cathedral and cloister was built upon the grounds of a Muslim mosque. When the city was conquered by Felipe V, whose plans to destroy the Seu Villa were going swimmingly until he died, both the mountaintop and Seu Villa itself were overtaken as a defensive fort. Military occupation lasted until 1947. Fine examples of architecture from the school of Lleida and 14th-century sarcophagi remain. For an excellent historical/architectural account of Seu Villa, get the audio tour for an additional €0.60. The long climb up to the **bell tower** is worth every step. Two of its seven bells are Gothic originals from the 15th century. To reach the cathedral, take bus #15 from the stop at the end of the plaza opposite the train station (30min.), or take the stairs or escalator up from Pl.Sant Joan; the elevator (€0.40) to your left takes you to La Seu. (☎973 23 06 53. Open daily June-Sept. 10am-1:30pm and 4-8pm, Oct.-May 10am-1:30pm and 3-5:30pm. Bell tower closes 30min. before rest of complex. €2.40, over 65 and under 21 €1.80. Tu free.)

Lérida's intricate Romanesque Ayuntamiento, the **Palau de la Paeria,** houses a small basement museum dedicated to the art and archaeology of the city. (C. Major. Museum open M-Sa 11am-2pm and 5-8pm, Sa 11am-2pm. Free.) The tiny and free **Museu d'Arte Jaume Morera** houses a rotating display of 19th- and 20th-century works; the permanent collection includes paintings by Morera himself. (C. Cavallers, 15, 2nd fl. ☎973 27 36 65. Open June 15-Sept. 15 Tu-Sa 10am-1pm and 6-9pm, Su 10am-1pm; Sept. 15-June 15. Tu-Sa 11am-2pm and 5-8pm, Su 11am-2pm.)

ANDORRA

Welcome to Andorra (pop. 65,800; 464 sq. km), the forgotten European nation, where stunning landscapes vie for attention with a neon-lit capital. While a drive through any of its only four main highways may make duty-free shoppers salivate and most others wince, outdoors folk swear by the many off-road biking, skiing, and climbing adventures the country has to offer. Behind this conflation of the tacky and the tantalizing is a rich history. According to legend, Charlemagne founded Andorra in 784 as a reward to the valley's inhabitants for having led his army against the Moors. For the next 12 centuries, the country played the rope in a game of tug-o'-war between the Spanish Counts of Urgell, the Church of Urgell, and the French King. Not until 1990 did the country create a commission to draft a democratic constitution, adopted on March 14, 1993. Andorra today is far less progressive than other western European nation. In the 1993 election, only the 10,000 native Andorrans (out of 65,000 total inhabitants) were granted the vote; women have only had suffrage since 1970.

Sandwiched between France and Spain, Andorra's citizens are comfortably trilingual, though Catalan is the official language. Now on the Euro system with the rest of the EU, all establishments were once required to accept both *pesetas* and *francs*. Currency seems to flow like water, as the absence of a sales tax (and the abundance of duty-free shops) draws consumers from all over Europe. Excellent skiing and biking opportunities, as well as frequent soccer matches, lure sports buffs across the border. With Andorran towns mere minutes apart and an extensive local bus system, a single day can include wading through aisles of duty-free perfume, hiking through a pine-scented valley, and relaxing in a luxury spa.

TRANSPORTATION

The only way to get to Andorra is by car or bus. All traffic from Spain enters through the town of **La Seu d'Urgell;** the gateway to France is **Pas de la Casa.** Upon exiting Andorra, you must stop at customs for a brief and rubber-glove-less search.

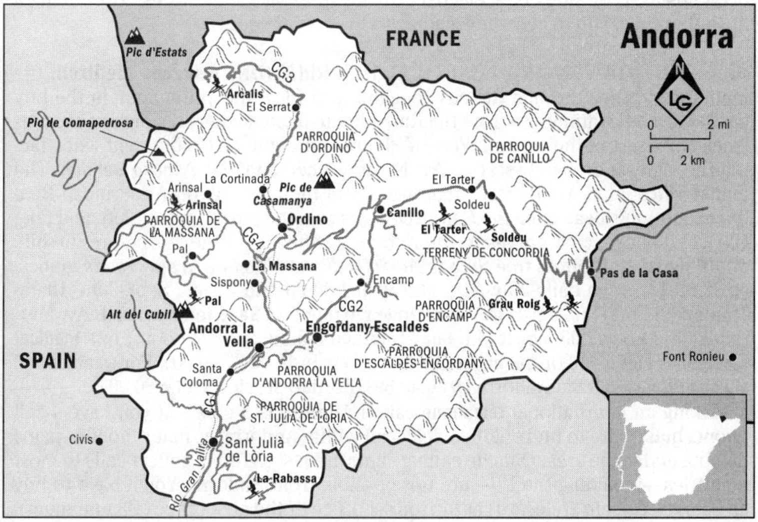

BY BUS

Andor-Inter/Samar buses (in Madrid ☎914 68 41 90; in Toulouse ☎561 58 14 53; in Andorra 82 62 89) run from Andorra la Vella to **Madrid** (9hr.; Tu, F-Su 11am; W-Th, Su 10pm, €33) as does **Eurolines** (Andorra ☎80 51 51; Madrid ☎915 06 33 60; Tu-Th, Su 11:30am; F and Su 10pm, €33). **Alsina Graells** (Andorra ☎82 65 67) runs to **Barcelona** (4hr.; daily 6:30, 7:30, 10:30am, 3, 6pm; €17.25), as does **Eurolines** (3¼ hr., daily at 6, 11am, 4, 6, and 8pm; €18.50). Buses arrive at and depart from **Estació d'Autobusos,** C. Bonaventura Riberaygua, in **Andorra la Vella.** To get to the station from Pl. Princep Benlloch, follow Av. Meritxell past the tourist office to the other side of the river. Make an immediate right after crossing the river, then an immediate left. Take the fourth right and go straight for four to five blocks (20min.). To go anywhere in Spain other than Madrid or Barcelona, first go to the town of La Seu d'Urgell on a **La Hispano-Andorra** bus (☎82 13 72; 30min., 5-7 buses per day, €2.50), departing from Av. Meritxell, 11. From La Seu, Alsina Graells buses continue into Spain via Puigcerdà (1hr., 2 per day, €3.50) and Lérida (2½hr., 2 per day, €10).

BY CAR

Driving in Andorra la Vella is an adventure for some, a nightmare for others. Motorcycles curve through the avenues with ease; larger vehicles must squeeze their way around tight and confusing streets with little help from any map. It's best to simply follow signs and park the car as soon as possible. Efficient intercity buses connect the villages along the three major highways that converge in Andorra la Vella. Since most towns are only 10min. apart, cities can be seen in a day via public transportation. Bus stops are easy to find, and rides are €0.60. All buses make every stop in the city, so don't worry about finding the right bus—just ask the driver to alert you at your stop.

ANDORRA LA VELLA

Andorra la Vella (pop. 23,000), the country's capital, is little more than Spain and France's shopping mall. Virtually a single cluttered road flanked by shop after duty-free shop, this city is anything but *vella* (old); most of the old buildings have been upstaged by shiny new electronics and sporting goods stores. After doing a little shopping, you're best off escaping to the countryside.

ORIENTATION AND PRACTICAL INFORMATION. Avinguda Meritxell, the main artery, runs through the city, beginning at Pl. Princep Benlloch in the tiny **barri antic** and continuing across the Riu Valira to become the main highway to parishes northeast of the capital. West of Pl. Princep Benlloch (to the right when facing the Eglésia de Sant'Esteve), Av. Meritxell becomes **Av. Princep Belloch.** The **tourist office** is on Av. Doctor Villanova. From the bus stop on Av. Princep Benlloch, continue away from the *Espanya* signs past the *plaça* on your left, and take C. Dr. Villanova, as it curves to the right; the office is on the left before the hill. Multilingual staff offers free *Sports Activities* and *Hotels i Restaurants* guides. (☎82 02 14. Open daily July-Aug. M-F 9am-1:30pm and 3-7pm; Sept.-June 10am-1pm and 3-7pm, Su 9am-1pm.) Exchange currency at **Banc Internacional,** Av. Meritxell, 32. (☎88 47 05. Open M-F 9am-1pm and 3-5pm, Sa 9am-noon.) In a **medical emergency** call ☎116 or the **police,** Prat de la Creu, 16 (☎87 20 00). For **weather and ski conditions,** call Ski Andorra (☎86 43 89). For **taxi** service, call ☎86 30 00.

Making an international **telephone call** in Andorra is a chore. If you have a cell phone, make sure to find out if you can call within Andorra, as many mobiles plans do not service the area. Outside calling cards are just as futile; collect calls to most countries—including the US—are not possible from Andorra. You'll have to buy an STA *teletarjeta* (telecard) at the tourist office or the post office (€3 minimum).

For directory assistance dial ☎111 or 119 (international). The **country code** is **376.** The **post office,** Carrer Joan Maragall, 10, is across the river from Pl. Princep Benlloch. (☎902 19 71 97. **Lista de Correos** upstairs. Open M-F 8:30am-2:30pm, Sa 9:30am-1pm.) **Internet** is available at **Future@Point**, C. de La Sardana, 6, on your right down the street from the corner bus station. (☎82 82 02. €0.90 for 15min., €1.80 for 30min., €3.05 for 1hr. Open daily 10am-11pm. MC/V.)

ACCOMMODATIONS AND FOOD. There are no singles in **Hotel Viena ❶,** C. de la Vall, 3, but its sunny doubles are a steal. From C. Major off of C. Princep Benlloch, turn left onto C. de la Vall; the hotel is on the left. (Breakfast €3 per person. Doubles €30. MC/V.) To reach the inviting, capacious rooms of **Hostal del Sol ❶,** Pl. Guillemó, take a left onto C. Les Canals after the Pyrenees department store on the main road, then follow the signs for Spain until you reach the plaza with a water fountain. (☎82 37 01. €12 per person. MC/V.) You don't exactly rough it at shaded **Camping Valira ❶,** Av. Salou, behind the Estadi Comunal d'Andorra la Vella, which has video games, hot showers, and an indoor pool. (☎82 23 84. €4 per person, per tent, and per car. Call ahead. Handicap accessible.) Check out one of the three-story supermarket monstrosities in nearby Santa Coloma, or the **Grans Magatzems Pyrénées,** Av. Meritxell, 11, the country's biggest department store, where an entire aisle is dedicated to chocolate bars. (Open Sept.-July M-F 9:30am-8pm, Sa 9:30am-9pm, Su 9:30am-7pm; Aug. and holidays M-Sa 9:30am-9pm, Su 9:30am-7pm.)

Casa Teresa ❸, C. Bonaventura Armengol, 11, with elegant table settings and bow-tied waiters, makes you feel important. Try the house pizza with a fried egg in its center. Choose something from the diverse wine list to accompany the wide selection of fish and meats (€7-15). Pizzas run €5.25-5.85 and the daily *menú* is €7.55. (☎82 64 76. Open daily 8am-4pm, and 8-10:30pm; closed June 24-July 12.)

EXCURSIONS. The best thing to do in Andorra la Vella is drop your bags in a hostel and get out. The **Caldea-Spa,** in nearby **Escaldes-Engordany,** offers luxurious treatments and prices to match. (☎80 09 95. Open daily 10am-11pm. €22.80 for 3hr., plus fees for each service.) The parish of **Ordino** bucks the Andorran trend of "bigger is better" with its quirky **Microminiature Museum,** Edifici Margada. Using yogic breathing to steady his hand, Nikolai Siadristy has created amazingly small, often microscopic objects, including the tiniest inscription ever made. (☎83 83 38. Open Tu-Sa 9:30am-1:30pm and 3:30-7pm, Su 9:30am-1:30pm. €1.80.) If you have no patience for the miniscule, visit **Canillo** for some fun in the colossal **Palau de Gel D'Andorra,** a recreational complex with swimming pool, ice-skating rink ("ice disco" by night), and squash courts. (☎80 08 40. Open daily 10am-11:30pm; each facility has its own hours. €5 each or €10 for all in 1 day. Equipment rental €2.50.)

HIKING AND THE OUTDOORS. An extensive network of hiking trails traverses Andorra. The free, multilingual, and extremely helpful tourist office brochure *Sports Activities* includes 52 suggested itineraries and bike rental locations, as well as cabin and refuge locations within the principality. La Massana is home to Andorra's tallest peak, **Pic Alt de la Coma Pedrosa** (2946m). For organized hiking trips, try the **La Rabassa Sports and Nature Center** (☎32 38 68), in the parish of Sant Juliàde Lòria. In addition to *refugio*-style accommodations, the center has mountain biking, guided hikes, horseback riding, archery, and field sports.

SKIING. With five outstanding resorts, Andorra offers skiing opportunities galore during the Nov.-Apr. months; lift ticket prices range from €30-40. **Pal** (☎73 70 00; fax 83 59 04), 10km from La Massana, is accesible by bus from La Massana (5 per day, last returning at 5pm; €1.50). Seven buses run daily from

La Massana to nearby **Arinsal,** the last returning at 6:45pm (€1). On the French border, **Pas de la Casa Grau Roig** (☎80 10 60) offers 600 hectares of skiable land, lessons, two medical centers, night skiing, and 27 lifts serving 48 trails for all levels of ability. **Soldeu-El Tarter** (☎89 05 00 or 89 05 01) occupies 840 hectares of skiable area between Andorra la Vella and Pas de la Casa. **Free buses** pick up skiers from their hotels in Canillo. The more horizontal **La Rabassa** (☎32 38 68) is Andorra's only cross-country ski resort, offering sleighing, skiing, horse rides, and a children's snow park. Andorra's tourist office publishes a winter edition of *Andorra.* Call **SKI Andorra** (☎86 43 89; www.skiandorra.ad) or the tourist offices with any questions.

ARAGÓN

A striking collage of semi-deserts and lush mountain peaks, Aragón's landscape reflects the influence of both Mediterranean and Continental climates. In the south lies a sun-baked assemblage of hardworking towns and flaxen plains, scattered with fine examples of ornate Mudéjar architecture. In the center, prosperous and industrious Zaragoza is Aragón's capital and the fifth-largest city in Spain. To the north, the stunning snow-capped peaks of the Pyrenees peer down at tiny medieval towns filled with Romanesque architecture. The Ebro, Spain's largest river, carves between these vastly different terrains.

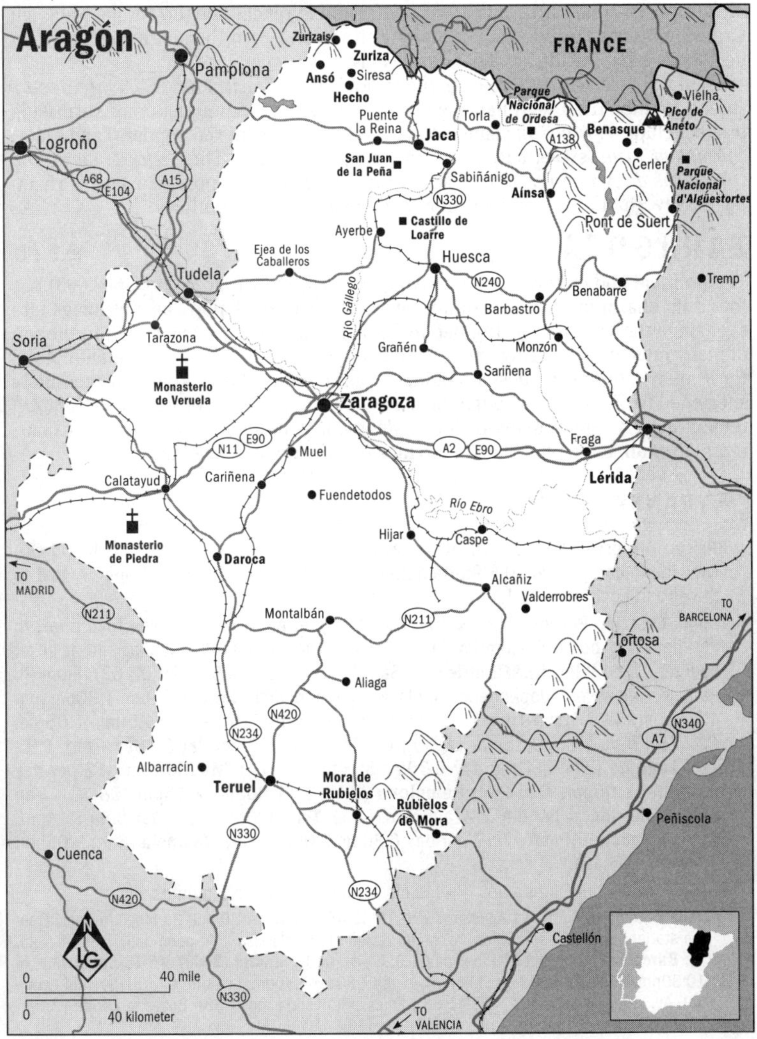

Aragón's harsh climate, coupled with the region's strategic location, has produced a predominantly martial culture. Established as a kingdom in 1035, and united with enterprising Cataluña in 1137, Aragón forged a far-flung Mediterranean empire. But when Felipe II marched into Zaragoza in 1591, he brought the region to its knees. Economic decline followed political humiliation; as eyes turned to the New World, people (and capital) moved to the coast in search of wealth. Today, Aragón is back on its feet economically and, having gained autonomy in 1982, continues to expand its political influence. While the region's more bucolic areas continue to celebrate their traditional and popular festivals, its urban museums, parks, and historical sites have recently undergone massive restoration to improve their accessibility and attractiveness. Still, Aragón remains relatively tourist-free. Only some areas of the rural Pyrenees and the Parque Nacional Ordesa y Monte Perdido attract many visitors, and even those are mostly urban neighbors escaping the city heat during July and August.

Aragón's hearty cuisine reflects the region's varied character. *Migas de pastor* (bread crumbs fried with ham) and lamb chops are ubiquitous; more surprising treats include *chilindrón* (lamb and chicken stewed with red peppers) and *melocotones al vino* (sweet native peaches steeped in wine). The *Guía de servicios turísticos de Aragón*, available at any tourist office in the province, makes roaming easy, with information on accommodations and tourist offices.

ZARAGOZA ☎976

The political and cultural nexus of Aragón, beautiful Zaragoza (pop. 603,000) has found its charm in its relative international obscurity. A popular pilgrimage site ever since the Virgin Mary dropped in for a visit, it is just now making it to the top of many must-see lists. Augustus founded the city in 14 BC as a retirement colony for Roman veterans, modestly naming it Caesaraugusta; the name was eventually shortened to 'Zaragoza.' Though the narrow, winding streets of the *casco antiguo* remain largely intact, many of the city's major plazas and leafy *paseos* are currently torn up, to be reworked in the image of the grand Plaza Pilar.

TRANSPORTATION

Flights: Airport (☎976 34 90 50). **Iberia,** C. Canfranc, 9 (24hr. ☎902 40 05 00; www.iberia.com). Open M-F 9:30am-2pm and 4-7pm, Sa 9:30am-1:30pm. A **taxi** to the airport costs about €12.

Trains: Estación Portillo (24hr. ☎976 21 11 66), at Av. Anselmo Clavé. Take a taxi to Pl. Pilar (€3); bus #21 from Po. María Agustín also stops at Pl. España. Info at ticket counter. Open 24hr. **RENFE office,** C. San Clemente, 11 (☎976 28 02 02). From Pl. Paraíso, follow Po. Independencia 4 blocks, then turn right. Open M-F 9am-1:30pm and 4:30-8pm, Sa 9:30am-1pm. Trains to: **Barcelona** (4hr., 15 per day 1:50am-7:05pm, €22-28); **Jaca** (3hr., 2:15pm, €8.50); **Lérida** (1½hr., 10 per day 2:30am-7pm, €15-19); **Logroño** (2¼hr., 4 per day 6:30am-8:14pm, €8.71); **Madrid** (3hr., 12 per day 2:40am-11:05pm, €21-27); **Pamplona** (2¼hr.; 11:30am, 4:15pm; €8-13); **San Sebastián** (4hr., 4 per day 2:22am-5pm, €21); **Teruel** (3hr., 3 per day 8am-7:14pm, €7.45); **Tudela** (45min., 7-17 per day 6:30am-9:05pm, €3); **Valencia** (6hr.; 8:05am, 3:45pm; €15.45).

Buses: Various bus companies dot the city, each with private terminals.

Agreda Automóvil, Po. María Agustín, 7 (☎976 43 45 10). Bus #20 and 21 stops in front. From the station, turn right and follow Po. María Agustín to Pl. Paraíso. Info open daily 7:30am-9pm. To: **Barcelona** (3½hr., 16-21 per day 1-9:30pm, €10); **Madrid** (3½hr., 15-18 per day 1:15-10:30pm, €11); **Soria** (2½hr.; M-Sa 5 per day 7:30am-4:30pm, Su 9am; €7.95). **Second Terminal,** Av. Valencia, 20 (☎976 55 45 88.) Enter on C. Lérida (bus #38). Buses to **Lérida** (2½hr.; M-Sa 4 per day 6:45am-6:30pm; €7.50).

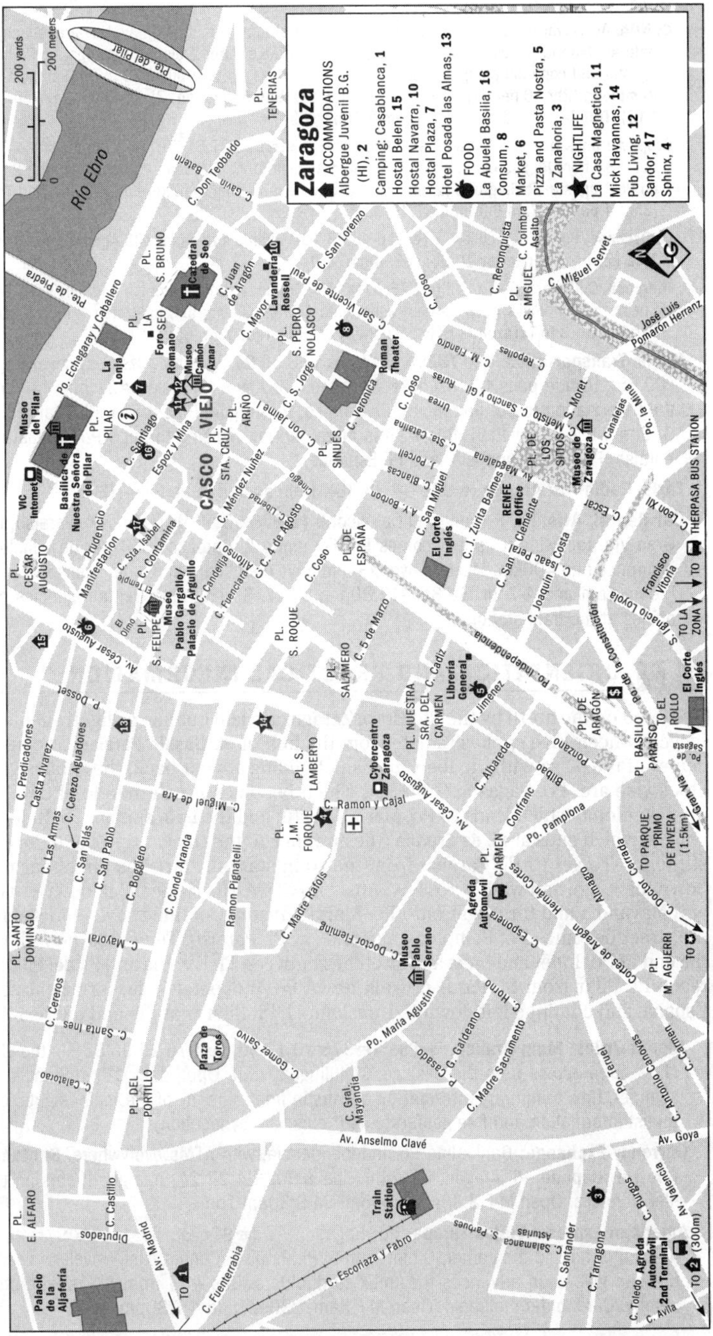
Zaragoza
ACCOMMODATIONS
Albergue Juvenil B.G. (HI), 2
Camping: Casablanca, 1
Hostal Belen, 15
Hostal Navarra, 10
Hostal Plaza, 7
Hotel Posada las Almas, 13
FOOD
La Abuela Basilia, 16
Consum, 8
Market, 6
Pizza and Pasta Nostra, 5
La Zanahoria, 3
NIGHTLIFE
La Casa Magnetica, 11
Mick Havannas, 14
Pub Living, 12
Sandor, 17
Sphinx, 4
0 200 yards
0 200 meters
Río Ebro
Pte. del Pilar
Pte. de Piedra
Po. Echegaray y Caballero
Museo del Pilar
Basílica de Nuestra Señora del Pilar
La Lonja
Catedral de Seo
Foro Romano
Museo Camón Aznar
CASCO VIEJO
Roman Theater
El Corte Inglés
RENFE Office
Museo de Zaragoza
PL. DE LOS SITIOS
PL. DE ESPAÑA
PL. DE ARAGÓN
Po. Independencia
Po. de la Constitución
Av. César Augusto
Museo Pablo Gargallo/ Palacio de Arguillo
VIC Internet
Cybercentro Zaragoza
Librería General
Agreda Automóvil
Museo Pablo Serrano
Plaza de Toros
Av. Anselmo Clavé
Av. Goya
Train Station
Palacio de la Aljafería
Av. Madrid
Agreda Automóvil 2nd Terminal
THERPASA BUS STATION
TO LA ZONA
TO EL ROLLO
TO PARQUE PRIMO DE RIVERA (1.5km)
Gran Vía
Po. María Agustín
Po. Pamplona
C. San Vicente de Paul
C. Coso
C. Miguel Servet
José Luis Pomarón Herranz
Lavandería Rossell

ARAGÓN

CONDA, Av. Navarra, 81 (☎976 33 33 72). From the station, turn right on Av. Navarra, bearing left onto Av. Madrid. Cross highway on the pedestrian bridge. After 2 blocks, turn right on Po. María Agustín and continue along Po. Pamplona to Pl. Paraíso. Or take bus #25 to Po. Pamplona. To: **Pamplona** (2hr., 6 per day 7:15am-8:30pm, €10); **San Sebastián** (3¼hr., 3 per day 7am-7pm, €16); **Tudela** (1hr., 6 per day 7:15am-8:30pm, €5).

Grupo Autobús Jiménez, C. San Juan Pablo Bonet, 13 (☎976 27 61 79). To get to the station, take bus #33 from Pl. España and watch for the road sign for C. San Juan Pablo Bonet after 2 stops on Po. Sagasta. To: **Logroño** (2½hr.; 6-8 per day 7am-7:15pm, Sa 7am-9pm; €8.25) and **Teruel** (3hr., 4 per day 7am-6:30pm, €7.45).

La Oscense, Po. María Agustín, 7 (☎976 43 45 10). Shares a terminal with Agreda Automóvil. To **Jaca** (2¼hr., 3-4 per day 10:55am-9:40pm, €9).

Therpasa, C. General Sueiro, 22 (☎976 30 00 45). From the station, turn left and follow C. General Sueiro for 1½ blocks, then turn left again onto C. San Ignacio; turn right after 2 blocks into Pl. Paraíso. Goes to **Tarazona** (1½hr., 6 per day 10:30am-6:30pm, €5).

Public Transportation: Red **TUZSA buses** (☎976 59 27 27; www.tuzsa.es) cover the city (€0.55; 10-ride pass €3.30; tickets available at any kiosk). Bus #21 runs from near the train station to Po. Pamplona, Pl. Paraíso, Pl. Aragón, Pl. España, Pl. Pilar, and up C. San Vincente de Paúl. Bus #33 is more central, passing through Po. Sagasta, Pl. Paraíso, Po. Independencia, and Pl. España.

Taxis: Radio-Taxi Aragón (☎976 38 38 38). Train station to Pl. Pilar (€3).

Car Rental: Avis, Po. Fernando El Católico, 9 (☎976 55 50 94). From Pl. Paraíso, take Gran Vía, following it as it becomes Po. Fernando El Católico. €84 per day, includes insurance and 400km. Must be over 23 and have credit card and valid license. Open M-F 8am-1pm and 4-7pm, Sa 8am-12:30pm. MC/V. Several other rental agencies have offices at the train station.

ORIENTATION AND PRACTICAL INFORMATION

Bordered on the north by the Río Ebro, Zaragoza is laid out like a slightly damaged bicycle wheel. Five spokes radiate from the hub of **Pl. Basilio Paraíso.** Facing the center of the plaza with the IberCaja bank building at your back, the spokes going clockwise are: Po. Sagasta; Gran Vía, which becomes Po. Fernando el Católico; Po. Pamplona, which leads to Po. María Agustín and the **train station;** Po. Independencia, which ends at **Pl. de España** (the entrance to the *casco viejo*); and Po. Constitución. To get to Pl. Paraíso from the train station, start upstairs, bear right down the ramp, and walk across Av. Anselmo Clavé. Head one block down C. General Mayandía and turn right onto Po. María Agustín. Continue seven blocks until the street becomes Po. Pamplona and ends at Pl. Paraíso. The *casco viejo* lies at the end of Po. Independencia and stretches between Pl. España and **Pl. del Pilar**. To reach Pl. Pilar from Pl. Paraíso, walk down Po. Independencia, turn right at Pl. España, and continue left down C. Don Jaime I; Pl. Pilar is at the end on the left.

Tourist Office: Main Branch, Pl. Pilar (☎976 20 12 00; fax 976 20 06 35), in the black glass cube across from the basilica. Multilingual staff. Open daily 10am-8pm. In the summer, tiny, temporary **information booths** in front of many of the major sights, offer tourist information and free guided tours (hours vary by location).

Currency Exchange: Banks line Po. Independencia, with **ATMs** everywhere. **Santander Central Hispano,** Pl. Aragón, 6, (24hr. line ☎902 24 24 24) has good rates on traveler's checks. Open M-F 8:30am-2:30pm, Sa 8:30am-1pm.

American Express: Viajes Turopa, Po. Sagasta, 47 (☎976 38 39 11; fax 976 25 42 44). Enter around the corner, 6 blocks from Pl. Paraíso. Cannot cash traveler's checks, but can give cash advances for AmEx cardholders. Bus #33 from Pl. España stops nearby. Cardholder mail held. Open M-F 9am-1:30pm and 4-7:30pm.

El Corte Inglés: Po. Sagasta, 3 (☎976 21 11 21), and a smaller store at Po. Independencia, 11 (☎976 23 86 44). Open M-Sa 10am-10pm.

Luggage Storage: At the **train station** (small €2.40, large €3). Open 24hr. At **Agreda Automóvil** bus station, Po. María Agustín, 7 (€1.20). Open M-F 10am-1:30pm and 4-7:30pm, Sa 10am-1:30pm. At the other **Agreda Automóvil,** Av. Valencia, 20 (€0.60 per piece per day). Open M-F 10am-2pm and 4:30-7:30pm, Sa 9am-noon. At **Therpasa** bus station (€0.60). Open M-F 9am-1pm and 4:15-7:30pm, Sa 9am-12:45pm.

Bookstore: Librería General, Po. Independencia, 22 (☎976 22 44 83; fax 976 22 89 48). Under the rainbow awning. 5 levels of tightly-packed shelves. Open June 15-Aug. M-F 9:30am-1:30pm and 4:30-9pm, Sa 10am-2pm; Sept.-June 14 M-F 9:30am-1:30pm and 4-8:30pm, Sa 10am-2pm and 3-9pm. AmEx/MC/V.

Laundromat: Lavandería Rossell, C. San Vicente de Paul, 27 (☎976 29 90 34). From Pl. España, turn right onto C. Coso, continue 4 blocks, and head left on C. San Vicente for another 4½ blocks. Wash and dry small €6, medium €8.40, large €11.40. Open M-F 8:30am-1:15pm and 4:45-8pm, Sa 9am-1:30pm.

Emergency: ☎112. **Police:** ☎091 or 092, on Domingo Miral.

Medical Services: Hospital Miguel Servet, Po. Isabel La Católica, 1 (☎976 35 57 00).

Emergency: Ambulatorio Ramón y Cajal, Po. María Agustín, 12 (☎976 43 41 11).

Internet Access: Cybercentro Zaragoza, C. Ramón y Cajal (☎976 46 96 10). From Pl. Aragón, walk toward Pl. España, take a left on C. Ibareda, then a right at the big intersection on Av. César Augusto. Bear left onto C. Ramon y Cajal and look for the yellow awning on your right. (€1.50 for 1hr. Open daily 10am-2pm and 4-10:30pm.) **VIC Internet and Change Station,** C. Florenco Jardiel, 3, conveniently located on the street to the left of the Basílica. English spoken. (☎976 29 76 25. €0.90 for 15min., €1.20 for 30min., €2.10 for 1hr., €3.60 for 2hr. Open daily 11:30am-2:30pm and 5-10pm.)

Post Office: Po. Independencia, 33 (☎976 23 68 68; www.correos.com), 1 block from Pl. Aragón on the right. **Fax** and **Lista de Correos** downstairs. Open M-F 8:30am-8:30pm, Sa 9:30am-2pm. Another **branch** next to the train station at C. Clavé. Open M-F 8:30am-8:30pm, Sa 9:30am-1pm. **Postal Code:** 50001.

ACCOMMODATIONS AND CAMPING

Small hostels and *pensiones* pepper the narrow streets of the central *casco viejo*, especially within the rectangle bounded by C. Alfonso I, C. Don Jaime I, Pl. España, and Pl. Pilar, along **C. Madre Sacramento,** perpendicular to Av. Anselmo Clavé, and near the train station. Be wary the week of October 12, when Zaragoza celebrates the *Fiesta de la Virgen del Pilar*. Make reservations as early as possible and expect to pay as much as double the rates listed below. *Ferias* (trade shows) are held from February through April (www.feriazaragoza.com), during which advance reservations are essential.

Hostal Belen, C. Predicadores, 2, 2nd fl. A and B. (☎976 28 09 13). This place is stocked: TV, A/C, sink, toilet, and built-in radio in every room. Doubles €24, with shower €28. IVA included. ❸

Hostal Plaza, Pl. Pilar, 14 (☎976 29 48 30 or 976 28 48 39; fax 976 39 94 06). Glistening modern bathrooms, TV, and phone in cozy but thin-walled rooms; interior rooms have A/C. Unbeatable location. July-Aug. singles with shower €27; doubles with shower €42, with bath €48. Sept.-June €24/€30/€36. V. ❸

Hotel Posada de las Almas, C. San Pablo, 22 (☎976 43 97 00 or 976 43 96 22; fax 976 43 91 43). Turn left onto C. San Pablo as you head up Av. Caesar Augusto and walk 1 block. Plain but comfortable rooms come with TV, bath, and shower. Check out an impressive tile rendering of the Basílica as you head up the lobby stairs. Affiliated restaurant next door. Singles €24; doubles €36; triples €50. MC/V. ❷

Albergue Juvenil Baltasar Gracián (HI), C. Franco y López, 4 (☎976 30 66 90). Take bus #22 from the train station. On foot, turn right out of the station onto Av. Clavé, take the 2nd right onto C. Burgos, following it for 6 blocks as it becomes C. Obispo Covarrubias, then turn right onto C. Franco y Lopez. It's just past the basketball court on the corner. 50 beds in rooms of 2, 4, and 6. Quite out of the way, but a real deal. Sheets and breakfast included. Midnight curfew. Dorms €8.60, over 26 €11.56. ❶

Hostal Navarra, C. San Vicente de Paul, 30 (☎976 29 16 84 or 976 39 10 44). Comfortable rooms, some with balconies. TV lounge. Singles €16, with bath €19; doubles €25, with shower €28, with bath €30. ❷

Camping: Casablanca (☎976 75 38 70), Barrio Valdefierro, down Ctra. Madrid. Bus #36 from Pl. Pilar or Pl. España to the suburb of Valdefierro. Ask driver to let you off at the campsite, as it's difficult to find. Supermarket, bar, restaurant, and pool open in summer. Water and showers included. July-Aug. €4 per person, per tent, and per car. ❶

FOOD

Zaragoza considers itself Spain's unofficial *tapas* capital. (Check out the tourist office-provided pamphlet, *Guía de Tapas*.) The side streets flanking C. Don Jaime I and the *tapas* bar-laden zone known as *El Tubo* (bordered by C. Mártires, C. Cinegio, C. 4 de Agosto, and C. Estébanes) are traditional dinner areas. More expensive and varied restaurants fill the streets branching off from Po. Independencia. The freshest fruits and vegetables are stashed in the **market,** a long green building on Av. César Augusto off Pl. Pilar, but you first have to get past the crowds. (Open M-F 9am-2pm and 5-8pm, Sa 9am-2pm.) Famed *frutas de Aragón*, chocolate-dipped and candied fruits in colorful wrappers, are available at almost any candy shop, souvenir store, or *carnicería*. Stock up at **Consum** C. San Jorge, 22, the continuation of C. Merdeo Núñez (open M-Sa 9am-9pm), or at the supermarket in **El Corte Inglés** (see **Practical Information,** above).

La Zanahoria, C. Tarragona, 4 (☎976 35 87 94). From Pl. Paraíso, start down Gran Vía, turn right onto Av. Goya, then take the 1st left after crossing Av. Teruel/Valencia. Popular with locals and college students. Excellent salads and vegetable quiches (€3.70-5.70). *Menú* €6.30. Entrees €6. Open daily 1:30-4pm and 9-11:30pm. MC/V. ❶

La Abuela Basilia, C. Santiago, 14 (☎976 39 05 94), next to Pl. Pilar. A huge, log-fueled oven rests beside the serene facade of a country cottage in the back dining section of La Abuela. The clay oven cooks juicy lamb (€16) and pork (€14.50). Few vegetarian options. Open Tu-F 11am-4pm and 8pm-1am, Su 11am-4pm. MC/V. ❸

Pizza and Pasta Nostra, C. Marqués de Casa Jiménez, 8 (☎976 15 85 04). Pizzas and freshly made pasta dishes are leaps and bounds above competitors. Pizzas €5.70-8.60. Pasta dishes €5.90-10.10. Open daily 1-4pm and 8pm-midnight. MC/V. ❷

SIGHTS

PLAZA DEL PILAR

A vast square surrounded by a unique fusion of architectural styles, Plaza del Pilar alone offers enough to satisfy any traveler. The beautiful *Basílica*, flanked on one side by a dignified Goya statue and a glimmering modern fountain on the other, presides over the central square. The plaza is the perfect place to begin a city tour or simply to sit and feed the pigeons all day.

SAINTLY SOUVENIR Although she is frequently overshadowed by the amazing deeds of her internationally acclaimed son, the original Madonna had some adventures of her own. The blue-clad Virgin is said to have hiked from Jerusalem to Spain, arriving in the Roman city of Caesaraugustus (present-day Zaragoza) on January 2, AD 40. Mary carried with her the sacred pillar that still stands, encased in silver, in Zaragoza's awe-inspiring cathedral. The people of Aragón proudly sing that "she did not do anything like this with any other nation," reminding others that her visit was an actual "coming" rather than a mere spiritual apparition.

BASÍLICA DE NUESTRA SEÑORA DEL PILAR. This massive Baroque structure (begun in 1681, though a few of the towers weren't completed until the mid-20th century) is Zaragoza's defining landmark. The interior walls feature frescoes by Goya, González Velázquez, and Francisco Bayeau. Two bombs (now on display) were dropped on the basilica during the Spanish Civil War in 1936 but failed to explode, purportedly due to the divine intervention of the Virgin. Thank her with a kiss; there's a spot to lay lips on a pillar that was supposedly graced with her own sacred smooch. The **Museo del Pilar** exhibits the glittering *Joyero de la Virgen* (Virgin's jewels) and preliminary paintings of the ceiling frescoes. Don't miss the breathtaking panorama of Zaragoza from one of the towers. *(Open daily 5:45am-9:30pm. Free. Museum ☎976 29 95 64. Open daily 9am-2pm and 4-6pm. €1.50. Elevator open June-Aug. Sa-Th 9:30am-2pm and 4-7pm; Sept.-May Sa-Th 9:30am-2pm and 4-6pm. €1.50.)*

OTHER SIGHTS. On the left as you exit the *basílica* is Zaragoza's **Ayuntamiento.** Next door is the Renaissance **La Lonja,** host to occasional cultural exhibits (art, photography, etc.) and featuring the intricately vaulted ceiling of many a Zaragoza postcard. *(☎976 39 72 39. Open Tu-F 10am-2pm and 5-9pm, Su 10am-2pm. Free.)* In front of La Lonja, statues portray scenes from Goya's paintings. On the other side of C. Don Jaime I, a large marble-and-glass cube houses the entrance to the **Foro Romano,** one of three nearby museums dedicated to Zaragoza's classical past. Excavated ruins from 1 BC-AD 1 await underground. The **Museo de las Termas Públicas de Caesaraugusta,** San Juan y San Pedro, 3-7, and the **Caesaraugusta River Port Museum,** Pl. San Bruno, 8, display archaelogical remains of baths and buildings from the same time period. *(Main office for all three at Pl. La Seo, 2. ☎976 39 97 52. Open Tu-Sa 10am-2pm and 5-8pm, Su 10am-2pm. Prices include admission to all three museums. Guided visits begin on the hr. €3.80, students €2.50, over 65 and under 8 free.)*

BEYOND PLAZA DEL PILAR

PALACIO DE LA ALJAFERÍA. Following the Muslim conquest of the Iberian Peninsula in the 8th century, a crisis over succession smashed the kingdom into petty tributary states called *taifas*. Weighty renovations have somewhat encumbered the building's original grace, but its awesome stone exterior and refined interior are still impressive. The ground floor has a distinctly Moorish flavor that bears stark contrast with the Gothic second floor. The fortified tower imprisoned *el trovador* in García Gutierrez's drama of the same name, the inspiration for Verdi's opera *Il Trovatore. (C. Castillo. Take bus #21 or 33. Or head left on C. Coso from Pl. España; facing the casco viejo, continue onto Conde Aranda, make a right onto Pl. Maria Agustín, then a left onto C. Aliaferia. ☎976 28 96 85. Open daily Apr. 15-Oct. 15 10am-2pm and 4:30-8pm; Oct. 16-April 14 M-Sa 10am-2pm and 5-8pm except Tu and F mornings, Su 10am-2pm. €1.80, students and seniors €0.90, under 12 free.)*

MUSEO DE ZARAGOZA. Archaeology buffs will love the extensive collection of artifacts that fill the museum's ground floor. The second story exhibits Aragonese painting. The room dedicated to Goya is the most popular, though many of the others are more impressive. *(Pl. Los Sitios, 6. From Pl. España, follow Po. Independencia about 4 blocks, turn left on C. Joaquín Costa and continue 3 more blocks; the museum is on the left after Pl. Los Sitios. ☎976 22 21 81. Open Tu-Sa 10am-2pm and 5-8pm, Su 10am-2pm. Free.)*

MUSEO PABLO GARGALLO. Dedicated to one of the most influential Aragonese sculptors of the 1920s, the Museo Pablo Gargallo houses a small collection of his works in the graceful **Palacio de Arguillo,** built in 1670. The thirty-years-in-the-making *Gran Profeta* (Great Prophet) showcases Gargallo's use of empty space as a fundamental sculptural element. These holey works are a testament to the man's immense talent as both metallurgist and artist. *(Pl. San Felipe, 3. ☎976 72 49 23. From Pl. España, walk down C. Don Jaime I and turn left on C. Menéndez Nuñez. The museum is 5 blocks down in Pl. San Felipe. Open Tu-Sa 10am-2pm and 5-9pm, Su 10am-2pm. Free.)*

MUSEO PABLO SERRANO. This modern building houses bronze sculptures by the fascinating Pablo Serrano (1908-1985). Look for *Gran Pan Partido* (Big Bread Parted) and sculptural reinterpretations of works by Picasso, Velázquez, and Goya. Smaller halls feature exhibits of modern sculpture and paintings. *(Po. María Agustín, 20. ☎976 28 06 59. Open Tu-Sa 10am-2pm and 4-8pm, Su 10am-2pm. Free.)*

MUSEO CAMÓN AZNAR. If the permanent Goya exhibit isn't enough of a draw, visit for a crash course in art history; on display is an eclectic selection of works from various schools of artistry throughout the 15th-20th centuries. The 16th-century building, typical of Aragonian Renaissance architecture, is named after its main donor. (*C. Expoz y Mina, 23. ☎976 39 73 28 or 976 39 73 87. Open Tu-F 9:15am-2:15pm and 6-9pm, Sa 10am-2pm and 6-9pm. €0.60. Passport required for entrance.)*

NIGHTLIFE AND FESTIVALS

The Zaragozan nightlife scene is almost strictly limited to weekends; even the most popular of *tapas* bars don't see more than a trickle of visitors before Friday night. But before you think Zaragoza is a dead city, just wait until Saturday night; the young and beautiful emerge from hibernation. Most locals begin their nights in **La Zona**—the streets bounded by Po. Constitución, C. León XIII, Po. Damas, and Camino de las Torres. You can gulp beer from *litros* (about €2.50) around **El Rollo,** the area bounded by C. Moncasi, C. Bonet, and C. Maestro Marquina at the southern end of Po. Sagasta. University students storm Po. Sagasta and its offshoot, C. Zumalacárregui; party-goers crowd around Pl. San Felipe.

Gay bars and discos center around the west side of the *casco viejo;* mixed gay and straight crowds let loose on the small dance floor of **Sphinx,** C. Ramón y Caja, one block down from C. Conde Aranda. (Cover F-Su €12. Open daily 11pm-5am.) The purely gay **Mick Havannas,** C. Ramon Pignatelli, 7, hosts a range of guys from late teens on up with its zebra-striped wall-paper, long bar, and numerous television screens. Many start the night here before heading to Sphinx. (☎976 28 44 50. Open daily 5pm-5am.) **Sandor,** C. Loscos, 2, off of C. Alfonso I, provides a less frenetic setting for the gay crowd. The undecorated but popular bar hosts occasional drag shows. (Beer €3. Mixed drinks €4-7. Open midnight-5am.)

Partiers craving flashing lights and thumping music should head over to C. Espoz and Mina off of C. Don Jaime I for a buffet of venues. There's lots of space for dancing at **Pub Living.** Alternatively, go to its neighbor, **La Casa Magnética,** to booze under the eerie glare of a large, veiny eye. Don't worry, Big Brother isn't watching. Magnets adorn the walls, and a classy record turntable sits behind the bar. (Beer €2. Mixed drinks €4.50. Open Tu-Su 7pm, weekends 8pm.) **La Casa del Loco,** C. Mayor, 10-12, frequently has concerts and plays a range of music for its international crowd. (No cover. Open daily 10pm-5am.)

The city erupts for a week of unbridled craziness around October 12 in honor of **La Virgen Santa del Pilar,** one of the few remaining full-blown autumn *fiestas* in Spain; a schedule of events is available at the tourist office. City patrons San Valero and San Jorge are celebrated on January 29 and April 23, respectively.

DAYTRIPS FROM ZARAGOZA

Ask at the Zaragoza tourist office for info on excursions like the *Ruta del Vino* (wine route) and the *Ruta de Goya*. Students of the Romanesque should inquire about visits to the **Cinco Villas** (5 villages).

MONASTERIO DE PIEDRA

Aragón Tours buses, C. Almagro, 18 (☎976 21 93 20), leave from Zaragoza and return the same evening (2hr.; July-Oct. 15 Tu, Th, Sa, Su 9am, return 5pm; €14 round-trip).

Waterfalls drop onto the dry plains surrounding the Monasterio de Piedra, about 110km southwest of Zaragoza. The main attraction is the surrounding park and the Río Piedra, which tumbles through the valley. (Park open daily 9am-8pm.) The monastery, founded in 1195 by an order of Cistercian monks from Tarragona but abandoned under government orders in 1835, is now a three-star hotel. This was the first monastery kitchen in Europe to serve hot chocolate. (€7.50 for monastery and park.) The 12th-century **Torre del Homenaje,** the only part of the existing building that hasn't since been restored, towers over the valley. (☎976 84 90 11; www.monasteriopiedra.com. Open daily 9am-8pm.)

TARAZONA

Buses run from the Therpasa bus station (☎976 30 00 45) on C. General Sueiro in Zaragoza. 4-7 per day 8am-8:30 pm; €5. Tarazona station (☎976 64 11 00) on Av. Narvarra.

Tarazona (pop. 10,750) is known as the "Mudéjar City." Some even liken the winding streets of its medieval quarter to those in Toledo. The town makes a nice daytrip from Zaragoza, especially during *Las Fiestas de Cipotegato* (Aug. 27-Sept. 1). The festivities begin when the jester, clad in a psychedelic getup of red, green, and yellow, is released into the crowds at noon on the 27th. After being pelted with tomatoes, he makes his way through the city with the help of his friends. Not until he successfully completes his route is the jester's identity triumphantly revealed to the people. The next six days are ablaze with activities, including *encierros*, bullfights, concerts, and dances honoring San Atilano, Tarazona's patron saint.

Tarazona's 13th- and 15th-century **cathedral** is closed for restorations. The towers, belfry, lantern, and plasterwork in the inner cloister are fine examples of Mudéjar work. From the cathedral, follow signs for Soria/Zaragoza down C. Laureles, then take your first right and pass through the arch to the octagonal **Pl. de Toros Vieja.** Built in the 18th century, the plaza included private residences with built-in balconies for the express purpose of watching *corridas*. Tarazona was also the seasonal residence of Aragonese kings until the 15th century. Their Alcázar has since served as the **Palacio Episcopal.** Though now the Bishop's home and closed to visitors, the exterior is still worth a peek. From the Pl. Toros Vieja, walk left 1 block, then up the stairs of the Recodos and Rúa Baja. Opposite the Palacio Episcopal, in the heart of **El Cinto** (the medieval quarter), rises the **Iglesia de Santa Magdalena** and its Mudéjar tower. To enter, take a left up Cuesta del Palacio from the Palacio Episcopal and then another left.

The **tourist office,** Pl. San Francisco, 1, is on the right side of the building in front of the church. (☎976 64 00 74. Open M-F 9am-1:30pm and 4:30-7pm, Sa-Su 10am-1:30pm and 4:30-7pm. July-Aug. office open Sa-Su until 8pm.) **Santander Central Hispano,** in Pl. San Francisco (open M-F 8:30am-2pm, Oct.-Mar. Sa 8:30am-1pm as well), offers no commission and a **24hr. ATM.** There is **luggage storage** at the Therpasa Bus Station (open daily 6:30am-1pm and 2-10pm; free).

STAR-CROSSED LOVERS The tombs of Diego de Marcilla and Isabel de Segura in the **Mausoleo de los Amantes** are the source of Teruel's nickname: *Ciudad de los Amantes* (City of Lovers). The story began when Diego left Teruel to make his fortune and prove his worth to Isabel's affluent family. Five years later, he returned a rich man, just in time to watch Isabel marry his childhood rival. Diego begged for one last kiss but was refused; he immediately died of grief. At the funeral, Isabel kissed the corpse and, overcome with sorrow, died herself. Plaques scattered about the city recall the tragic love story in moving verse. At the mausoleum, the lovers are commemorated with life-size statues, reaching out to touch each other. For a peek at the lovers' remains, duck down near their heads. (From Pl. Torico, take the alleyway to the left of the purple Modernista house. Stairs lead directly to the mausoleum. Open M-Sa 10am-2pm and 5-7:30pm, Su 10:30am-2pm and 5-7:30pm. €0.30.)

NEAR TARAZONA: MONASTERIO DE VERUELA

Travelers with cars can visit the walled monastery of Veruela, which slumbers in the Sierra de Moncayo, 15km south of Tarazona. Its golden stone walls guard a Romanesque-Gothic church and a peaceful cloister. Nineteenth-century poet Gustavo Adolfo Bécquer wrote his *Cartas Desde Mi Celda* (Letters from My Cell) here. (☎976 64 90 25. Open Apr.-Sept. Tu-Su 10am-2pm and 4-7pm; Oct.-Mar. Tu-Su 10am-1pm and 3-6pm. €1.80.) Buses run to Vera de Moncaya, about 400m from the monastery; ask the tourist office for more information.

TERUEL

The small capital of southern Aragón, Teruel (pop. 29,300) seduces visitors with its history of tragic love and rich cultural exchange. Lively and welcoming, this little town's narrow streets and old plazas belie its cosmopolitan past. From the 12th to the 15th centuries, Muslims, Jews, and Christians lived here in cultural collusion. The resulting Mudéjar architecture blends Arab patterns with Gothic and Romanesque touches. The town retains an intoxicating charm without the hordes of tourists that plague similar Andalucian destinations. An easy stopover between Valencia and Zaragoza, Teruel doesn't reach its prime until July, when citizens celebrate the resilience of their *torico* (iron bull) in an 168-hour liquor fest.

TRANSPORTATION. **Trains** depart from Camino de la Estación, 1 (☎902 24 02 02), down the stairs from Pl. Ovalo to: **Valencia** (2¾hr., 3 per day 7:55am-6:36pm, €6.90) and **Zaragoza** (2½hr.; 6:40, 11:53am; €8.60). **Buses** depart from the new **station,** Ronda de Ambeles (☎978 61 07 89), only a few blocks from the *casco viejo*. **La Rápida** (☎978 60 20 04) goes to **Barcelona** (5½-6½hr., M-Sa 12:30pm, €20) and **Cuenca** (3hr., M-Sa 11:45am, €7.30). **Samar** (☎978 60 34 50) goes to **Madrid** (4½-5hr.; 4 per day M-Sa 7:30am-5pm, Su 3 per day 7:30am-5pm; €15.20) and **Valencia** (2-2½hr.; 5 per day M-Sa 7:15am-7pm, Su 8am-7pm; €7.30). **Jiménez** goes to **Zaragoza** (M-Sa 6 per day 7am-7pm, Su 4 per day 7am-7pm; €7.20). To rent a car, call **BMW** (☎978 60 65 36; €60 per day plus IVA).

ORIENTATION AND PRACTICAL INFORMATION. A small valley spanned by connecting bridges separates the *casco viejo* from its more modern mate. The center of the *casco* is **Pl. de Carlos Castell,** affectionately known as **Pl. del Torico.** To reach the plaza from the train station, take the staircase from the park and follow signs to the *centro*. To Pl. Torico from the new bus station, turn right out of the station and take your first left into Pl. Judería, then take zig-zagging C. Hartzenbusch to Pl. del Torico. The **tourist office** is at C. Tomás Nogues, 1. From Pl. Torico, follow C. Ramón y Cajal and take the first left; the office is one block away on the right, at the corner. (☎978 60 22 79. Open M-Sa 10am-2pm and 5-8pm, Su 10am-2pm.) Services include: **Santander Central Hispano,** Pl. Torico, 15 (☎978 60 11 35; open M-F 8:30am-2pm; Oct.-May also Sa 8:30am-1pm); **luggage storage,** at the train station (lockers €3) or bus station (€0.60 per day; both open daily 6:30am-10:30pm); **emergency** ☎112; and the **post office,** C. Yagüe de Salas, 19 (☎978 60 11 90 or 978 60 11 92; open M-F 8:30am-8:30pm, Sa 9:30am-2pm). **Postal code:** 44001.

ACCOMMODATIONS. Lodgings are scarce during August and *Semana Santa* and even more difficult to find during the *fiestas* of early July. Directly between the cathedral and the main plaza, **Hostal Aragón ❷,** C. Santa María, 4, features simple rooms, some with TV. From Pl. Torico, head away from the Torico and take the first left as you exit the plaza. (☎978 61 18 77. Singles €16.05, with bath €21.40; doubles €24.60, with bath €36.40; triples with bath €48.15.) Thought to be the oldest hostel in all of Spain, **Fonda el Tozal ❸,** C. Rincón, 5, features typical Mudéjar design, including stunning and spacious tiled bathrooms. (☎978 60 10 22. Doubles €27; triples €38.) As you exit the train station, look to your right for **Hostal Ovidio ❷,** Camino de la Estación, 6, a convenient nightspot with small, neatly-kept rooms. (☎978 60 28 66. Singles €16, with bath €22; doubles €27, with bath €40; triples €40.) Just off of Pl. Torico lies **Hostal Alcazaba ❷,** C. de Joaquín Costa, 38. Though the tidy rooms only come with a bed and folding chair, the private bathrooms make this hostel a sweet deal. (☎978 61 07 62. Singles €18; doubles €30.)

FOOD. Teruel is famous for its flavorful cured ham, *jamón de Teruel*, featured in the *tapas* bars of Pl. Torico. The streets leading away from Pl. Torico are home to most of the town's restaurants, many of which serve nearly identical fare. **Restaurante La Parrilla ❷,** C. Estebán, 2, off C Abodía two blocks uphill from the tourist office, has a magnificent *menú* (€10) with succulent meats grilled in a stone fireplace. (☎978 60 59 17. Open M-Sa noon-4:30pm and 8-midnight, Su noon-4:30pm. MC/V.) For a change from the typical *tapas* selections, take a right at the street on the end opposite the Cathedral in the Pl. Catedral and walk half a block to **Aquí Teruel ❶,** C. de Yagüe de Salas, 4. Enjoy assorted ham delicacies (€7.81, half portion €5.41) and more veggie-friendly options, amidst soothing music in the colorful modern interior. Try the lunch special of wine, salad, and half *bocadillo* for only €2.70. (☎978 61 89 50. Open daily 9am-12:30pm and 2:30pm-1am. MC/V.)

SIGHTS. The mother of all Teruel's Mudéjar monuments is the 13th-century **Catedral de Santa María de Mediavilla.** The vast difference between the chapels is noteworthy—the gilding of the *Capilla de la Inmaculada*, dating from the 19th century is brilliant in comparison to the more subdued carvings of the 16th-century *Retablo Mayor*. The cathedral itself has three naves, the most recent of which wasn't finished until the late 1800s. (Open daily 11am-2pm and 4-8pm. €1.80 with mandatory guide.) Muslim artisans built the brick-and-glazed-tile **Torres Mudéjares** between the 12th and 15th centuries, after a Christian church adapted the Almohad minarets to their own purposes. The most intricately designed of the towers is the 13th-century **Torre de San Salvador,** on C. Salvador; it is the only tower open to visitors. Climb 122 steps through several chambers to the panoramic bell tower. (Open daily 11am-2pm and 5-8pm. €1.50.) Teruel's Romeo and Juliet love story is kept alive at the **Mausoleo de los Amantes,** where the 1217 tragedy is immortalized. (See **Star-crossed Lovers,** p. 448. Open M-Sa 10am-2pm and 5-7:30pm, Su 10:30am-2pm and 5-7:30pm. €0.30.) Behind the cathedral, the **Museo Provincial,** devoted mainly to archaeological and ethnographic pursuits, rests in the 16th-century **Casa de la Comunidad,** a leading example of the "Aragonese Renaissance" style. Don't miss the reproduction of an

FROM THE ROAD

ROAD FLOCK

The sheep, I told myself, would move. They had to: I was the one with the 2000-pound, 16-valve Vectra; all they could claim was a twelve-year-old shepherd boy and an abundance of wool.

But now that almost 300 of the animals surrounded my car, I found that I'd been a bit hasty in trying to drive through the flock. These creatures didn't seem to care what kind of itinerary I had to keep or that my patience level was quickly dropping. They were content to rock me left to right as they pressed up against the sides of the previously unblemished rental. Nothing would stop them from feasting on the curbside grass, even if it meant working around the large metallic box in the middle of the road. So while they ate, I sat.

What irked me wasn't that the sheep wouldn't move, but that this was the second time I had been flock-blocked. This road trip was going to take a lot more fortitude than I'd thought; sheep aren't the only nuisances Spanish driving has to offer. Cows, horses, aggressive hitchhikers and narrow roads lined with precipitous drops-I dealt with them all.

Worst of all were mopeds-or, as I came to call them, highway mosquitoes. Zipping dangerously close to me, the tiny, buzzing machines infest Spanish city streets and sidewalks, blithely oblivious to traffic lights and lane lines. In the city, there's no way to escape them; head to the Pyrenees countryside, where fewer exist.

Chugging up mountain roads in my clunky rental, I found other solutions to the problems posed by Iberian driv-

18th-century chemist's shop. Rotating temporary exhibits complement the permanent collection. (Pl. Fray Anselmo Polanco. ☎978 60 01 50. Open Tu-F 10am-2pm and 4-7pm, Sa-Su 10am-2pm. Free.)

ARAGONESE PYRENEES

Aragón claims 90 km of Pyrenean grandeur, bracketed by the Río Gallego in the west and the Río Nobuera in the east. Within these two frontiers, alpine meadows and twenty crystalline glaciers are tucked between gorges and jagged cliffs. Such terrain has had its use—founded in the mid-9th century upon these fortifying slopes, the Kingdom of Aragón was left unconquered by northern enemies. The most popular entry point for the Aragonese Pyrenees is Jaca, from which most head to the spectacular Parque Nacional de Ordesa. In the east, Benasque draws hardcore mountaineers with its access to the highest peaks in the Pyrenees, while the western valleys of Ansó and Hecho are ideal for less strenuous mountain rambling. Ski resorts await demanding downhillers in Astún, Panticosa, Cerler, and Candanchú. For details on winter in Aragón, get the free tourist office pamphlets *Ski Aragón* or *El Turismo de Nieve en España.*

JACA ☎974

Now much more than a mere overnight stop, Jaca (pop. 14,000) used to serve as a refuge for weary-worn pilgrims crossing the Pyrenees to Santiago. Though the city also had a brief stint as capital of Aragón (1035-1095), for centuries it had little to offer in the way of diversion. At present, Jaca provides not only the perfect base for organizing excursions into the Pyrenees and nearby ski resorts but also holds many festivals of its own, most notably the *Fiestas de Santa Orosia y San Pedro* (June 23-29). During these *fiestas*, the city is awash in various concerts and plays, as well as both formal processions like *La Comparsa de Gigantes*—a company of characters in oversized costumes—and numerous *ad hoc* parades, which usually occur under the influence of many a malted beverage.

TRANSPORTATION. RENFE trains (☎974 36 13 32; www.renfe.es; ticket booth open 10am-noon and 5-7pm) to: **Madrid** (7hr.; M-F, Su 1:45pm; €24); **Zaragoza** (3hr.; daily 7:36am, 6:46pm; €8.41). **La Oscense buses** (☎974 35 50 60) to: **Pamplona** (2hr., 1 per day, €5.41);

Sabiñánigo (20min., 4-6 per day, €30); **Zaragoza** (2hr., 3-4 per day, €9.45). From Sabiñánigo, **Empresa Hudebus** (☎974 21 32 77) connects to **Torla** (11am), near Ordesa and Aínsa. **Josefa Escartín** (☎974 36 05 08) buses go to **Ansó** (1½hr., M-Sa 6:30pm, €3) via **Hecho** (55min., €2.40) and **Siresa** (1hr., €2.55). Catch **taxis** (☎974 36 28 48) at the intersection of C. Mayor and Regimiento Galicia.

ORIENTATION AND PRACTICAL INFORMATION. Buses drop passengers on Av. Jacetania, at the edge of the city center. From the station, walk through the plaza to C. Zocotín and continue straight ahead for two blocks to **C. Mayor.** The green city bus runs from the **train station** to the center of town. To walk, take Av. Juan XXIII to its end, turn left onto Av. de Francia, continue straight as it becomes C. Primer Viernes de Mayo, and then make a left onto C. Mayor. The staff at the **tourist office,** Av. Regimiento de Galicia, 2, at the end of C. Mayor, speaks English. (☎974 36 00 98. Open July-Aug. M-F 9am-2pm and 4:30-8pm, Sa 9am-1:30pm and 5-8pm, Su 10am-1:30pm; Sept.-June M-F 9am-1:30pm and 4:30-7pm, Sa 10am-1pm and 5-7pm.) **Alcorce,** Av. Regimiento Galicia, 1, organizes hiking, rock climbing, spelunking, and rafting trips. (☎974 35 64 37; www.alcorceaventura.com. Guided hiking trips from €21 per person per day; rafting from €35; ski and snowboard rentals €15 per day. Open June-Sept. M-Sa 9:30am-1:30pm and 5:30-9pm; Oct.-May M-Sa 9:30am-1:30pm. MC/V.) Ski season is Dec.-Apr. For ski conditions, call **Teléfono Blanco** (☎976 20 11 12). Local services include: **Santader Central Hispano,** C. Primer Viernes de Mayo (open Apr.-Sept. M-F 8:30am-2pm; Oct.-Mar. M-F 8am-2:30pm, Sa 8:30am-1pm); **police,** C. Mayor, 24 (☎091 or 092); **Centro de Salud,** Po. Constitución, 6 (☎974 36 07 95). For **Internet access,** try **Ciber Santi,** C. Mayor, 42-44, inside La Tienda Mayor to the right. (☎974 35 68 69. €1.80 per 30min., €2.85 per hr. Open M-Sa 10:30am-1:30pm and 5-8:30pm.) **Ciber Civa** is two stores down from the tourist office on Av. Regimiento de Galicia. (☎974 36 4408. €1.90 per hr. Open M 5-9pm, Tu-Su 4:30-11pm.) The **post office** is at C. Correos, 13. (☎974 35 58 86. Open M-F 8:30am-2:30pm, Sa 9:30am-1pm.) **Postal code:** 22700.

ACCOMMODATIONS AND FOOD. Jaca's hostels and *pensiones* cluster around C. Mayor and the cathedral. Lodgings are scarce only during the semiannual *Festival Folklórico* in late July and early August. To reach the large, ancient rooms of **Hostal Paris ❷,** San Pedro, 5, from the bus station, cross the park and head right, circling around the church to the next plaza; look for the sign straight ahead.

ing. Having nearly driven for half a kilometer in complete darkness, I found that locating the switch for the headlights as soon as you pick up your vehicle saves you from any frantic fumbling that may occur when you realize how few tunnels in Spain are lit. I also learned to be cautious when approaching bridges, as many are built for only one vehicle. Furthermore, contrary to my—quite reasonable, I thought—assumptions, the apex of the triangles painted on roads point away from the direction of traffic, not towards it.

But before I could employ my new knowledge, all roadway complications seemed to fade away. I began to notice the grandeur of the Pyrenees, the sense of freedom involved in dodging crags and cutting through cavernous tunnels. I started to enjoy the tight and meandering mountain traversals. I even came to appreciate the floods of fleece that occasionally inundated the roadways; waiting and watching was a nice break.

Sitting in my unmoving vehicle among a cacophony of bells, munching, and baas, I realized that to truly appreciate the Pyrenees transportation system, you must adopt one of two strategies: tear along the narrow highways etched into rocky cliffs, or slowly glide under the snow-capped peaks while admiring gossamer morning mists rising from glacial lakes.

To enjoy this country via car, I learned, you have to either floor it or brake; there is no in-between.

—Nate Gray

(☎974 36 10 20. July 15-Sept. 15 and *Semana Santa* singles €16; doubles €26; triples €35. Rest of the year €15/€23/€32. The *casa rural* **El Arco ❷,** C. San Nicolas is a pleasant option. Coming from the bus station, cross the park and head away from the church; the *casa* is to the left of the barber shop. (☎974 36 44 48. Breakfast €2.10-3.60. €18 per person.) **Albergue Juvenil de Escuelas Pias (HI) ❶,** Av. Perimetral, 6, offers rows of two-bunk bungalows. From C. Mayor, turn left onto C. Regimiento de Galicia, then left again onto Av. Perimetral; turn off onto the driveway marked *Alburgue Juvenil* immediately before the skating rink. (☎974 36 05 36. Breakfast included. Quads €9.05 per person, over 25 €10.85, without HI €12.)

Bocadillos fill the menus on Av. Primer Viernes de Mayo. **Restaurante Vegetariano El Arco ❷,** C. San Nicolás, 4, in El Arco *casa rural*, serves an all-veggie *menú* for €9. (Open M-Sa 1-3pm and 8:30-11:30pm.) For *menús* and *tapas*, follow your nose along C. Mayor and stop at **El Canigó ❶,** C. Mayor, 5. Within its unostentatious exterior lies a small and bustling hideout which has occasional deals on great sangria (€4.81) and a huge selection of other fare including pizza, sandwiches, and combinations. (☎974 36 40 78. Entrees €2-9. *Menú* €7.25. Open 10am-4pm and 6pm-midnight. MC/V.) **Supermercado ALDI,** C. Correos, 9, is next to the post office. (Open M-Sa 9:30am-2pm and 5:30-8:30pm. V.)

DAYTRIPS FROM JACA

MONASTERIO DE SAN JUAN DE LA PEÑA

Taxis (☎974 36 28 48) will make the journey for €36, with a 1hr. wait before bringing you back. If you are driving, park at the lot above the monastery; a shuttle transports visitors every 30min. The adventurous can catch a bus from Jaca to Pamplona and ask to be dropped at Santa Cruz de La Seró (C.N. 240, 295 km). From there, it's a 9km hike to the monastery.

Without a car, the spectacular **Monasterio de San Juan de la Peña** is difficult to reach—it was designed that way. The Holy Grail was supposedly concealed here for three centuries. Determined hermits hid the original monastery in a canyon 22km from Jaca and maintained such extreme privacy that both church and cup were kept safe from invading Moors. It's worth a visit, both for the 10th-century underground church carved directly into the rock and the 12th-century cloister wedged under a massive boulder. The carved capitals of the cloister's arcade are not to be missed. Don't confuse the monastery with the uninteresting 17th-century *monasterio nuevo*, 1km up the hill in the open field. A **snack bar ❶** next to the parking lot sells *bocadillos* €2-2.70, and other items. (☎974 35 51 19 or 974 35 51 45; www.monasteriosanjuan.com. Open June-Aug. daily 10am-2:30pm and 3:30-8pm; Mar. 16-May and Sept.-Oct. 15 daily 10am-2pm and 4-7pm; Oct. 16-Mar. 15 Tu-Su 11am-2pm and 4-5:30pm. €3.50 includes entrance to church in Santa Cruz de la Seró, €4.50 includes shuttle from the parking lot.)

CASTILLO DE LOARRE

Only serious hikers and those with cars can reach the castle. La Oscense (☎974 35 50 60) sends 1 bus from Jaca to Loarre, 5km from the castle (1hr., M-F 7:15am, €4.70); the return bus (5pm, €3.91) stops only in Ayerbe, 7km away from Loarre. Trains run only to Ayerbe (1½hr.; departs Jaca daily at 7:36am and 6:11pm, returns at 8:58am and 5:18pm; €3.16). From there, you take a taxi or trek the 2hr. to Loarre and then another 5km uphill to the castle.

The power and magnificence of **El Castillo de Loarre** is visible for kilometers in each direction. Every inch of this fortress is open to exploration; visitors are free to investigate on their own or go on the guided tour (€2). Though you may want to spend your time admiring the vast countryside below, the castle's history is fascinating. In the 11th century, King Sancho Ramírez built the castle in an effort to protect the Western Pyrenees from a Moorish invasion. He succeeded—sharp cliffs at its rear and 400m of thick walls to the east make it nearly impenetrable. A crypt, which opens to the right of the steep entrance staircase, holds the remains of Demetrius, the French saint who died in Loarre. You can go up to the battlements of both towers, but be careful when climbing the wobbly steel rungs to the roof or descending into the dark basement. (Open July-Aug. daily 10am-8pm; Mar.-June and Sept. Tu-Su 10am-1:30 and 4-7pm; Oct.-Mar W-Su 11am-2:30pm. Free.)

VALLE DE HECHO

The craggy Valle de Hecho and its picturesque hamlets, 40km west of Jaca, are an almost-forgotten wilderness, and offer some of the most undiscovered hiking opportunities in Aragón. Under the humid influence of the Atlantic, these western slopes and glacial valleys encourage dense forest growth, including the lush *Selva de Oza* filled with beech and fir trees. The valley is best visited during the summer, as it is extremely quiet during the rest of the year. A **Josefa Escartín** bus (☎974 36 05 08) leaves Jaca M-Sa at 6:30pm, stopping at **Hecho** (7:30pm) and **Siresa** (7:40pm) before continuing to **Ansó** (8:10pm). Every morning except Su the bus returns from **Ansó** (6am) via **Siresa** (6:30am) and **Hecho** (6:45am) on its way to **Jaca** (7:40am).

HECHO (ECHO)

Hecho (pop. 670) is the valley's geographical and administrative center, a serious title that doesn't suit the small and inviting town. The Ayuntamiento in Pl. Conde Xiquena (next to Pl. Alta, off of C. Mayor) houses a small **tourist office** in the summer months. (☎974 37 55 05. Open July-Sept. 15 M-Sa 10am-2pm and 5-7pm, Su 10am-2pm.) Someone upstairs in the office (M-F 8am-3pm) or downstairs in the library (M-F 5-7pm) will happily answer questions during the rest of the year. The hiking experts of **Compañía de Guías Valle de Echo** on C. Lobo lead trips and rent cross-country skis. (☎974 37 52 18. Call ahead.) A **bank** with **24-hr. ATM** is on Pl. Alta, off of C. Mayor. (Open Apr.-Oct. M-F 8:15am-2:30pm; Nov.-May M-W and F 8:15am-2:30pm, Th 8:15am-1:45pm and 5:15-7:30pm. MC/V.) **Supermercado Alvi,** is on C. Mayor. (Open July-Sept. M-Sa 9:30am-2pm and 5-8pm, Su 10am-2pm; Oct.-June M-Sa 10am-2pm and 5-8pm.) In an **emergency,** call ☎112. The **Guardia Civil** number is ☎974 37 50 04. The **post office,** Pl. Alta, is also off C. Mayor. (Open M-F 8:30am-2:30pm, Sa 9:30am-1pm.)

For somewhere to stay, look for any of a number of *casas rurales* which provide enjoyable company in an intimate atmosphere. Follow signs toward the *centro de salud* to the tall, white **Casa Blasquico ❷,** Pl. Fuente 1. After one night, you're part of the family. Enjoy the familiarity or escape into your beautifully decorated, flower-patterned room. The restaurant provides all you need for a tasty, balanced meal. (☎974 37 50 07. Breakfast €3.50. *Menú* €10.22. Doubles €45, with living room €48. IVA not included. MC/V.) At half the price, try the small rooms of the central but unmarked **Casa Marina ❶,** C. Medio, 12, which is located on the right, just up the cobblestone street from the center and across from Bar Archer. (☎974 37 50 77. Doubles €21.) At the entrance to Hecho from Jaca, the well-kept sites and *albergue* bunks of **Camping Valle de Hecho ❶** are just a short walk from town. (☎/fax 974 37 53 61. €3.35 per person, per tent, per car. Bunks €6.61. IVA not included. MC/V.) For nourishment, **Serbal ❷,** C. Mayor, 6, boasts a menu with more than just predictable pork, including salad (€4.69) and chicken (€8.65). Choose from indoor dining or, during the night hours, a romantic terrace overlooking the countryside. (☎974 37 53 35. Open daily 1:30-4pm and 8:30-11pm. MC/V.)

VALLE DE ANSÓ

Farther down the road from Jaca, the little town of Ansó is set in one of the most appealing valleys in the Pyrenees, a lush growth of oak and pine trees. You might see the very last of Pyrenean bears; they only reside in this particular valley. Like Hecho, the Valle de Ansó lives for July and August, when the bulk of its visitors pour in over the mountain ridges. Visitors stop in cobblestoned Ansó before heading farther up the valley to Zuriza, the departure point of the valley's best hikes.

ANSÓ

Peacefully resting just east of Navarra, tiny Ansó's (pop. 530) cobblestone streets and matching houses immediately expose its gentle warmth. At the **Museo de Etnología** inside the **Iglesia de San Pedro,** antique chorus books are displayed beside mannequins modeling traditional dress. (☎974 37 00 22. Open July-Sept. 15 M-F 10:30am-1pm and 4-7pm; during the rest of the year, the priest living in the stone house across from church can open it for you. €1.50.) A fairly easy 4.8km roundtrip hike that begins in Ansó will take you along the paved road to a weather-sculpted rock formation called *El Fraile y la Monja* (The Monk and the Nun). Start at the town's southern edge next to the sign pointing towards Huesca and walk along its highway, heading out of town. It's then 2km downhill to the Hecho-Huesca fork. Going towards Hecho, march along the 0.4km traversal up the hill until you come to the first tunnel. There you can admire the striking crimson pinnacles of *El Fraile y la Monja.*

Posada Magoria ❸, C. Chapitel, 8, the corner house just below the church, beckons you to relax; after loosening up with a massage (€10-15), rinse off in their modern showers. Vegetarian meals with home-grown produce are also offered. (☎974 37 00 49. Singles €30; doubles with 1 bed €43, with 2 beds €50. MC/V.) The more impersonal **Hostal Aisa ❷,** just beside the post office, offers rooms with private baths. (☎974 37 00 09. Singles €22; doubles €40. MC/V.) The most affordable lodging is 3km out of town at *refugio*-style **Borda Changalé ❶,** Ctra. Ansó, on the way to Zuriza. Be cautious crossing the narrow bridge at the entrance. (☎974 37 02 46. Breakfast included. *Menú* at the restaurant €8.20. July-Aug. 6-8 bunk rooms. €36 for 4, each additional person €6. Sept.-June €9 per person.) The **tourist office** is in Pl. Domingo Miral. (☎974 37 02 25. Open July-Aug. daily 10am-2pm and 5-8pm.) Next door is the **post office.** (☎ 974 37 02 25. Open M-Sa 9am-2pm.)

ZURIZA AND ENVIRONS

In the northern part of the Valle de Ansó (15km north of Ansó itself) lies Zuriza, which consists of little more than a single camping location, **Camping Zuriza.** Surrounding terrain alternates between the shallow **Hona La Solana** (Hole of Solana) and the steep summit of southwest **Ezcaurri.** Many hikers use the area as a base for the arduous trek to **Sima de San Martín,** a gorgeous trail along the French border. To get there, drive from Zuriza 12km towards Isaba until you come to the Isaba-Belagua crossroads. Take the road to Belagua, heading north along the Belagua river. After about 12km of smooth terrain and then a gentle 2km ascent, you'll near the French border and will see signs for the trail. **Camping Zuriza ❶** lies along the banks of a stream running between Ezcaurri and Hondonada. It's a great spot for fishing, hiking, and kayaking (Apr.-May). The campground also provides a **supermarket, hostel,** and **pub/restaurant** where you can get info and maps (€6.65) of nearby trails. (☎974 37 01 96 or 974 37 00 77. Breakfast €2.60. Hot showers included. Campsite €3.30 per person, per tent and per car; IVA not included. Hostel doubles €27, with bath €36. Year-round bunks €7.50. MC/V.) From the campground, it's a mild and well-marked day hike (5hr.) to the **Mesa de los Tres Reyes** (2444m), a series of peaks close to the borders of France, Navarra, and Aragón.

PARQUE NACIONAL DE ORDESA

The beauty of Ordesa invites you to spend a week as a vagabond. After staying the night in a crowded *refugio*, extremely well-maintained trails draw you through the park, cutting across forest, rock face, snow-covered peak, and river. No luxury living here: you sleep where you are and eat what you carry. Ordesa is located just south of the French border, and includes the canyons and valleys of Ordesa, Añisclo, Escuaín, and Pineta. The park offers trails for all levels and attracts huge crowds in July and August. It is easiest to enter Ordesa through the village of **Torla.**

TRANSPORTATION. All **trains** along the Zaragoza-Huesca-Jaca line stop in Sabiñánigo. **La Oscense** (☎974 35 50 60) also runs a **bus** between Sabiñánigo and **Jaca** (20min., 2-3 per day 8am-5:15pm, €1.08.) From there, **Compañía Hudebus** (☎974 21 32 77) runs to **Torla** (55min.; July-Aug. daily 11am, 6pm; Sept.-June daily 11am; €2.40.) In summer, a shuttle runs between Torla and **Ordesa** (15min.; June 30-Aug. 6am-7pm, Sept. 6am-6pm, Oct. 7am-6pm; €1.80). When the shuttle is running, from late May-Oct., cars are prohibited from entering the park. Park in Torla for €0.50 per hr. from 9am-8pm or €3.95 per day; overnight parking is free. In the off-season, those without a car will have to either hike the 8km to the park entrance or catch a **Bella Vista taxi** (☎974 48 61 53; €12). To exit the park area, catch the bus as it passes through Torla at 3:30pm on its way back to Sabiñánigo.

PRACTICAL INFORMATION. The **visitors center** is on the left 1.8km beyond the park entrance. (Open Apr. daily 9am-2pm and 3:30-6pm; May-Oct. daily 9am-2pm and 4:30-7pm.) The **park info center** in Torla, across the street from the bus stop, takes over in low season (mid-Sept.-May). (Open M-F 8am-3pm; July-Sept. M-F 8am-3pm, Sa-Su 9am-2pm and 4:30-7pm.) The indispensable *Editorial Alpina* guide (€7.50) is available in town. Across from the pharmacy on C. a Ruata, **Compañía Guías de Torla** organizes rafting, canyoning, and year-round mountaineering expeditions. (☎974 48 64 22; www.guiasdetorla.com. Open daily May-June 15 and Oct.-Nov. 5-9pm; late June-Sept. 8:30am-1:30pm and 5-10pm; Dec.-Apr. available by phone. MC/V.) In an **emergency,** call ☎112. Local services include: **Guardia Civil** (☎974 48 61 60), and the **post office,** on C. a Ruata at Pl. de la Constitutión (open M-Sa 9-11am). **Postal code:** 22376.

ACCOMMODATIONS. Hotels and higher-end accommodations are located beside the highway before entering Torla; a few lie along the road closer to Ordesa. Torla offers the greatest number of budget accommodations, but it tends to fill up fast in July and August—reserve ahead. Don't worry about oversleeping here; the reliable town rooster sounds daily at 7:30am. Go to **Refugio L'Briet ❶** for the most comfortable bunks local *refugios* have to offer. Ascend C. a Ruata, following the sign across the street to the left of the bus stop pointing to "Centro Población," then continue 1 block uphill. (☎974 48 62 21. *Menú* €9. Bunks €7. Private rooms available. MC/V.) Across the street, **Refugio L'Atalaya ❶,** C. a Ruata, 45, and the adjoining restaurant are hippie-hiker heaven. A small kitchen is available for use. (☎974 48 60 22. Open *Semana Santa*-Oct. 11. *Menú* €8.60. Loft mats €7 per person. MC/V.) **Camping Río Ara ❶** is located along the river just outside of Torla and offers a supermarket and bar. (☎974 48 62 48. Open *Semana Santa*-Oct. €3.20 per person, per tent, and per car. IVA not included.) Closer to the park, **Camping San Antón ❶** rents 4-person bungalows. (☎974 48 60 63. Open *Semana Santa*-Sept. €3.40 per person, per tent, per car. Bungalows €73.) Midway between these two, the pool, tennis courts, and bar of **Camping Ordesa ❶** sit in the shadow of the enormous Hotel Ordesa. (☎974 48 61 25. Open *Semana Santa*-Oct. 15. €3.90 per person, €4.10 per tent and per car. 30% off in low season. AmEx/MC/ V.)

FOOD. For those staying overnight in Torla, most accommodations serve a very filling dinner (€13-15) and simple breakfast (included). To pick up your own food, **Supermercado Torla,** on C. a Ruata, is a few buildings down from Refugio L'Atalaya on the opposite side of the street. (☎974 48 63 88. Open May-Oct. daily 9am-2pm and 5-8:30pm. Nov.-Apr. closed Su. MC/V.) Up C. a Ruata, **Restaurante Bar El Rebeco ❸** serves a satisfying *menú* (€12) in its informal but elegant dining room; lower-priced entrees range from €4.81-12. (☎974 48 60 68. Open May-Oct. daily 1-3:30pm and 8-10:30pm. MC/V.) **Bar Restaurante Taillon ❷,** C. a Ruata, has sandwiches (€3), a *menú* (€10.25) and an impressive view of Mt. Mondaruego. (☎974 48 63 04. Open May-Oct. daily 7:30am-1am.)

HIKING. If you have only a day to spend in Ordesa, the **Soaso Circle** is the most practical hike, especially for inexperienced mountaineers. Frequent sign-posts along the wide trail clearly mark the 5hr. (1-way) journey up to **Refugio Góriz.** The trail passes the **Gradas de Soaso** waterfall along the way. Check weather fore-casts (☎906 36 53 22 or 906 36 53 80) before starting out; heavy snow makes the trail impassable in winter and spring, and paths becomes dangerous in the rain. Less intrepid travelers may want to reduce the hike to 2hr. (1-way), by turning around at the **gradas.** The views from **Cascada del Cueva** (Cave Falls) and especially from **Cascada del Estrecho** (Wide Falls) make this hike well worth it. Try to arrive early, especially July-Aug., as the park is often flooded with visitors by noon.

AÍNSA (L'AINSA)

Romantic, if slightly touristy, the village of Aínsa is the ideal stop for less rugged travelers, 1hr. drive from Ordesa. From the friendly souvenir shops along its main intersection, Ainsa leads the visitor up a winding cobblestone staircase to its perfectly preserved medieval quarter. A thousand years ago Aínsa was the capital of the Kingdom of Sobrarbe (incorporated into Aragón in the 11th century), and the ruins of its 11th-century **castle** on Pl. Mayor remind visitors of its past prominence. In 1181, priests consecrated the **Iglesia de Santa María,** across the plaza from the castle, whose spiraling tower steps can be climbed for €1. An incredible view of the Parque Nacional de Ordesa's peaks awaits at its top. For those exhausted from the uphill hike to the plaza, a stairless view can be found just behind the church.

TRANSPORTATION AND PRACTICAL INFORMATION. Compañía Hudebus (☎974 21 32 77) runs daily buses from **Sabiñánigo** to Aínsa, stopping in **Torla** along the way (2hr.; 11am, returning at 2:30pm; €5). **Compañía Cortés** (☎974 31 15 52) runs from Aínsa to **Barbastro** (1hr., M-Sa 7am, €4), where buses make the connection to **Benasque.** The **tourist office,** Av. Pirenáica, 1, is at the highway crossroads. (☎974 50 07 67. Open July-Aug. daily 9am-9pm; May-June and Sept. M-Sa 10am-2pm and 4-8pm, Su 10am-2pm; Oct.-Apr. Tu-Sa 10am-2pm and 4-8pm.) The **post office** is located on Av. Sobrarbe, down the street across from the tourist office. (☎974 50 00 71. Open M-F 9am-2pm and Sa 9am-12:30pm.) **Internet** is available at **Casa Cheliz,** Av. Sobrarbe, 11, across the street from the post office. (☎974 40 06 11. €3 per hr., €1.80 per 30min. Open July-Sept. daily 10am-2pm and 4:30-8:30pm; Oct.-June M-F 10am-2pm and 4:30-8:30pm.) Although Aínsa is not as well situated for hiking as are Torla or Benasque, companies surrounding the tourist office can arrange countless outdoor activities. **Intersport** (☎974 50 09 83) and **EKM** (☎974 51 00 90) rent out bikes and lead backpacking trips; **Aguas Blancas** (☎974 51 00 80) does rafting and kayaking excursions.

ACCOMMODATIONS AND FOOD. Casa Rural El Hospital ❷, C. Sta. Cruz, 3, is a converted stone house in the medieval quarter. No outside sign marks the residence; you'll find reception in the corner boutique. (☎974 50 07 50. June 16-

FAR TREK On your way to Berlin? A *Gran Recorrido* (Great Hike) trail will get you there—eventually. One of the most beautiful and rugged stretches of the pan-European *Gran Recorrido* network treks east to west just below the French-Spanish border. Strung together by old mountain roads, animal tracks, and forest paths, the Aragonese portion of **GR-3** passes by clear mountain lakes and under, over, and through snow-covered peaks (the highest being Mt. Aneto, at 3404m). Though some parts of GR-3 are pretty gentle, the full trek across Aragon requires hiking experience. The border-to-border route takes eight to ten days. For detailed info on this and other GR trails, consult tourist offices in the area and the **Federación Aragonesa de Montañismo** at C. Albareda, 7 (☎976 22 79 71) in Zaragoza, and ask for the detailed and trail-specific *Topoguía* guide. The extremely useful *Editorial Alpina* provides a good route map.

Sept. singles €21; doubles with bath, TV, and A/C €36. Oct.-June 15 €24/€30. MC/V.) While more luxurious establishments line the main road and aren't difficult to locate, less expensive options surround the bus stop in the new part of town. Outside of the center is **Camping Aínsa ❶,** Ctra. Aínsa-Campo, km 1.8. (☎974 50 02 60. €4.50 per person, per car, per tent. Open *Semana Santa*-Oct. 15. MC/V.) Essential groceries, as well as a few delicacies, can be picked up at **Alimentación M. Cheliz,** Av. Ordesa. (☎974 50 00 62. Open July-Sept. daily 8:30am-9pm; Oct.-June M-Sa 8:30am-2:30pm and 4-8:30pm, Su 8:30am-2:30pm. MC/V.) The **Restaurante Brasería ❹,** located near the *castillo* end of Pl. Mayor, offers large portions and a soothing refuge from the hot sun. The selection of *menús* cost between €14.40-21. (☎974 50 09 81. Open June-Oct. daily 10am-midnight. MC/V.)

VALLE DE BENASQUE: BENASQUE

The Valle de Benasque is a haven for no-nonsense hikers, climbers, and skiers. Countless trails wind through the mountains, and the area teems with *refugios*, allowing for longer expeditions. With its many excursion companies and nearby trailheads, mellow **Benasque** (pop. 1100) is an excellent base for outdoor activities. Casual hikers are often scared off by the valley's reputation for serious mountaineering—the Pyrenees's highest peaks, including the awe-inspiring Mt. Aneto (3404m), are here—but relaxing nature walks are within every visitor's reach.

TRANSPORTATION AND PRACTICAL INFORMATION. La Alta Aragonesa (☎974 21 07 00) runs buses to **Huesca** (3hr.; M-Sa 6:45am, 3pm; Su 3pm; €10). July-Aug., the shuttle bus **Pirineos 3000** makes frequent runs from the town to the trailhead parking lots Senarta and La Besurta. To get to the **tourist office,** face the Hotel Aragüells at the main bus stop and walk one block down the alley between the BBVA and the building bearing the KHURP sign. (☎/fax 974 55 12 89. Open daily 10am-2pm and 5-9pm; July and Aug. 9am-2pm and 4-9pm.) In an **emergency,** call ☎608 53 68 82. For the **Guardia Civil,** call ☎974 55 10 08. The **post office** is in the Ayuntamiento across from the church. (☎974 55 20 71. Open M-F 9am-noon, Sa 10:30am-noon.) **Postal code:** 22440.

ACCOMMODATIONS AND FOOD. Both the spacious wooden rooms of **Hotel Aneto ❷** and the smaller, less expensive alternatives in the adjoining **Hostal Valero ❶** provide a comfortable night's rest for the travel-weary. The two share a modest pool, gym, and tennis court. (Both ☎974 55 10 61. July-Aug. and Dec.-Mar. hotel singles €31; doubles €47; triples €68. *Hostal* singles €17; doubles €30. Apr.-June, Sept.-Nov. hotel €25/€35/€52. *Hostal* €12/€23. MC/V.) Another reasonably-priced lodging option is **Fonda Barrabés ❶,** C. Mayor, 5. With your back to the bridge, take a left onto the main road into town, passing Hotel Aragüells; Barrabés is 200m ahead on the left, inside the restaurant named **Fonda de Vescelia.** (☎974 55 16 54. Bunks €7.21; singles €19.63; doubles €23; triples €32. MC/V.) About 3km uphill from the town center, **Camping Aneto ❶** offers a convenient starting point for a day's hike. (☎974 55 11 41. Open year-round. €3.60 per person, per tent, and per car; kitchen access available. IVA not included.) Signs from C. Ministro Cornel off of Pl. Ayuntamiento will lead you to **Restaurante-Crêperie Les Arkades ❷,** a piece of town history occupying an old stone building built in 1647. (☎974 55 12 02. *Menú* €10.22. Restaurant open June 22-Oct. 12 daily 1-4pm and 8-11pm. Bar open daily 5:30pm-3:30am.) At the end of the street crossing in front of Fonda de Vescelia is **Bardanca ❷,** C. las Plazas, a casual eatery away from the noise of the town's center. Either snappy indoor or laid back outdoor service is available. Excellent chicken and spaghetti *menú* choices €7.90. Combination plates €5-6. (☎974 55 13 60. Open daily 10am-4pm and 8-11pm.) For fresh produce, **Fruta Albá,** C. San Pedro, is hidden in an unmarked warehouse down the alleyway just to the left of the tourist office. (Open July-Aug. daily 8:30am-1pm and 5-9pm, closed Su Sept.-June.)

HIKING. Experienced hikers can start out early from Benasque and can hike uphill 8km on the valley road, following signs towards France. After passing the first parking area, turn onto the trail off the main road and climb up, up, and away, following the falls of the Río Cregueña. The sometimes steep but not yet technical ascent winds through glens, but never strays far from the river's edge. Four arduous hours later, you'll reach **Lago de Cregueña** (2657m), the largest and highest lake in the surrounding area. This trail is sometimes impassable in the winter months, so ask at the tourist office before putting on your hiking boots. Those wishing to scale **Mount Aneto** (3404m), the highest of the Pyrenees, can pick up some gear and head out at 5am with the experts from the **Refugio de la Renclusa ❶.** To reach the *refugio*, take the main road (again, follow the signs to France) north 14km until the paved road ends; from there it's a 45min. hike. (☎974 55 21 06. Open June 22-Sept. 24. Bunk and kitchen access €5, with breakfast €6.) Many companies in Benasque organize trips. For less strenuous nature-wandering, head in the opposite direction, down the main road and follow the signs to **Forau de Aigualluts,** a lovely pond at the base of a waterfall (40min.).

LA RIOJA AND NAVARRA

From the rustic Pyrenean *pueblos* on the French border, south through bustling Pamplona, and to the dusty villages in the south, you can sense the immense history behind the peaceful monuments and ruins of La Rioja and Navarra. Bordered by the País Vasco to the west and Aragón to the east, La Rioja and Navarra's ensconced villages greet tourists with open arms and a toast of wine.

Navarran cities are somewhat of an oddity. Though subdued, quiet, picturesque, and conservative, they throw the country's wildest parties—Pamplona's outrageous *San Fermines* (July 6-14) is undoubtedly the most famous. But there hasn't always been reason to celebrate. In the 13th century, the Kingdom of Navarra was divided into six districts (Pamplona, Tudela, Estella, Sangüesa, Olite, and Ultrapuertos) and since then, Navarra has long experienced the difficulties of Spain's on-again/off-again regionalism. It gained regional autonomy in 1512, only to see it revoked in 1833. To avoid another devastating loss, Navarrans sided with the "winners" in the 20th century, allying themselves with Franco's Nationalist forces in the Spanish Civil War. Unfortunately, they found themselves under a regime with no tolerance for regional differences. Despite all this, Navarra's spirit has remained relatively unchanged. It has continued to support regionalist causes,

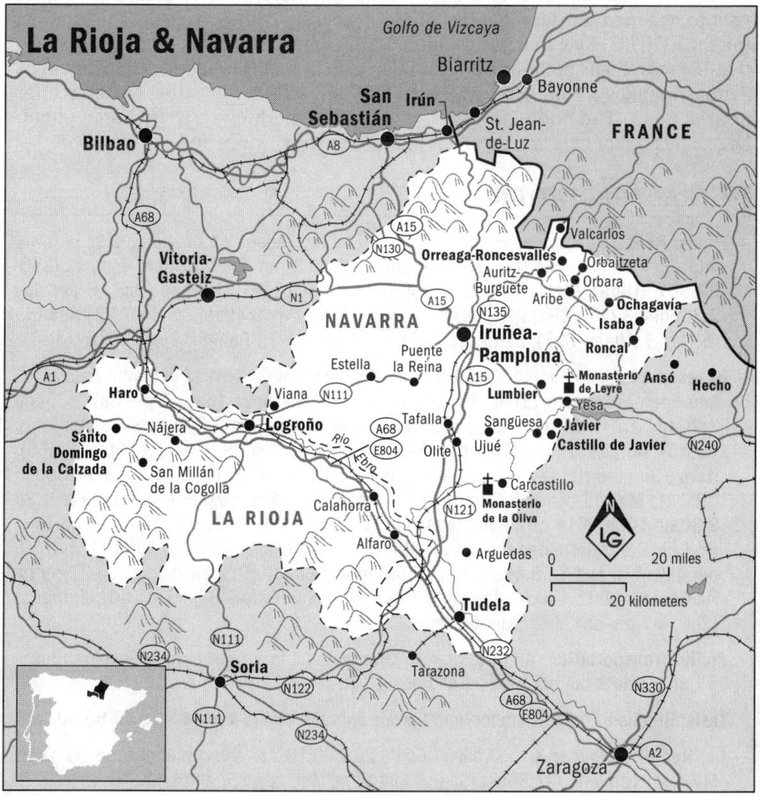

especially the re-establishment of provincial autonomy in 1983. Many of the region's northern inhabitants identify themselves as Basque, and some are concerned with separation from the País Vasco and the Basque independence efforts.

Just south of Navarra, La Rioja and "great wine" are literally synonymous. "Rioja" is an internationally acclaimed wine classification with an 800-year tradition; both the 1994 and 1995 grapes received the highest ratings possible, and, since 1991, its wine has been the only in Spain to earn the coveted *Calificada* rating. The region's name derives from the Ebro tributary Río Oja, whose waters trickle through the vineyards. When ordering wine, asking for *"vino"* will get you the wine of the year, ordering *"crianza"* delivers higher-quality wine at least three years old, while a request for *"gran reserva"* brings the *crème de la crème* (and you'll pay for it). The best *bodegas* (wine cellars) draw from the lands in western Rioja Alta, around Haro. The Camino de Santiago (see **These Boots Were Made for Walking,** p. 533) passes through much of La Rioja, and tourist offices can provide useful info on the route. The mountainous Sierra region, with tranquil fields at the feet of towering peaks, lines La Rioja's southern border.

LOGROÑO ☎941

The best entry point into the vineyard towns of La Rioja, Logroño (pop. 135,000) has always cared about its *bodegas*; in 1635, the mayor banned carts from streets next to wineries "for fear that the vibration caused by these vehicles might affect the must." The city's tourist brochure, with characteristic hyperbole, proclaims that Logroño feeds both the body and the soul. In reality, although the Camino de Santiago makes a stop here, your soul will find little but bustling commerce for nourishment. The body, however, will have something to write home about. Logroño is full of bars serving the region's renowned wines and savory *tapas*.

TRANSPORTATION

Trains: RENFE Pl. Europa (☎902 24 02 02), off Av. España on the south side of town. Info open daily 7am-11pm. To: **Barcelona** (7hr., 3 per day 12:38pm-4am, €26.50-27.50); **Bilbao** (4hr., 3 per day 3:46pm-4am, €13.60); **Burgos** (2hr., 5 per day 2:30pm-4:32am, €9.05-14); **Haro** (45min., 3 per day 6:40am-6pm, €7.80); **Madrid** (5½hr., 7:20am, €27); **Zaragoza** (2-2½hr., 4 per day 7:20am-8:10pm, €9.05-14).

Buses: Av. España (☎941 23 59 83), on the corner of C. General Vara and Av. Pío XII. Info open M-Sa 6am-11pm, Su 7am-11pm. To: **Barcelona** (6hr., 5 per day 2:15pm-2:20am, €24); **Bilbao** (2hr.; 3-5 per day M-Sa 8:30am-7:30pm, Su 11am-9pm; €9.85); **Burgos** (2hr.; 4-7 per day, M-Sa 8:30am-7:30pm, Su 11am-9:45pm; €5.65); **Haro** (1hr.; 3-6 per day M-F 7:30am-8pm, Sa 10:15am-7:15pm, Su 10:15am-8:30pm; €2.23); **Madrid** (4hr.; 5-6 per day M-Th and Sa 6:45am-7pm, F 6:45am-8pm, Su 9:30am-10pm; €16.55); **Pamplona** (2hr.; 3-5 per day M-Sa 7am-7pm, Su 10am-7pm; €6.05); **Santo Domingo de la Calzada** (1hr., 3-9 per day, €2.32); **Soria** (1½hr.; 5-6 per day M-Th and Sa 6:45am-7pm, F 6:45am-10pm, Su 9:30am-10pm; €5.27); **Vitoria-Gasteiz** (2hr.; 4-6 per day M-Sa 10am-8pm, Su 10am-9:30pm; €7.60); **Zaragoza** (2hr., 4-7 per day M-Sa 7am-6:30pm, €8.56).

Public Transportation: All buses run to Gran Vía, 1 block from Parque Espolón. Buses #1 and 3 pass the bus station. All rides €0.51.

Taxis: Stands at the bus station and Parque Espolón. **Radio Taxi** (☎941 50 50 50).

Car Rental: Europcar, C. de Chile, 1 (☎941 28 60 73), on the corner of Gran Vía. Open M-F 9am-1pm and 4-7:30pm, Sa 9:30am-1pm. Min. age 25. AmEx/MC/V.

ORIENTATION AND PRACTICAL INFORMATION

Both the old and new towns radiate from the **Parque del Espolón,** a tree-lined set of gravel paths with a fountain at the center. The **casco antiguo** stretches between the park and the Río Ebro, on the far north side of the city. To reach the park from the **train station,** cross the major traffic artery **Avenida de Lobete** and angle left on Av. España. At the **bus station** (the next major intersection), turn right onto C. General Vara de Rey, which leads north to the park (8min.) and the *casco antiguo.*

Tourist Office: Po. Espolón (☎941 29 12 60; fax 941 29 16 40), in Parque Espolón facing C. General Vara de Rey, in the large rotunda. English, French, and German spoken. Open June-Oct. M-F 9am-9pm, Sa 10am-2pm and 5-8pm, Su 10am-2pm; Nov.-May M-Sa 10am-2pm and 4-8pm, Su 10am-2pm.

Currency Exchange: Santander Central Hispano, on C. General Vara at the corner of Parque Espolón. **ATM.** Open M-F 8:30am-2:30pm; Oct.-Mar. also Sa 8:30am-1pm.

Luggage Storage: At the **bus station** (€2 per locker; large bags can be left in one of the shops; ask at info desk). Open M-Sa 6am-11pm, Su 7am-11pm. At the **train station** (€3). Open daily 7am-11pm.

Emergency: ☎112. **Police:** C. Ruavieja (☎091 or 092), near Iglesia de Palacio.

Medical Services: Hospital San Millán, Av. de la Autonomía de la Rioja (☎941 29 45 00). Follow Av. de La Paz away from the *casco antiguo*; go right on Av. de la Autonomía.

Internet Access: Centro MAIL, Av. Dr. Múgica, 6 (☎941 20 78 33). English-speaking video game store with a dozen computers in the back. €0.75 per 15min. Open M-Sa 10am-2pm and 5-9pm, Su noon-2pm and 5-9pm.

Post Office: Pl. San Agustín (☎941 22 00 66), between C. San Agustín and C. Portales. Open M-F 8:30am-8:30pm, Sa 9:30am-2pm. **Postal Code:** 26070.

ACCOMMODATIONS AND CAMPING

The *casco antiguo* brims with budget *pensiones* and *hostales.* Try C. San Juan, the second left past Parque Espolón from the stations, or C. San Agustín and C. Laurel. Reservations are crucial for the *fiesta* week around September 21.

Fonda Bilbaína, C. Capitán Eduardo Gallarza, 10, 2nd fl. (☎941 25 42 26). Take C. Sagasta into the *casco antiguo,* turn left on C. Hermanos Moray and then right on C. Capitán Gallarza. Bright rooms with high ceilings, shiny floors, good beds, and sinks. Rooms €18, with shower €21, with bath €24. ❷

Hostal Sebastián, C. San Juan, 21 (☎941 24 28 00). From C. de Sagastá, off Parque Espolón, turn right onto C. Hermanos Moroy, then continue onto C. San Juan. Comfy beds and small sinks. Doubles €30. ❷

Residencia Universitaria (HI), C. Caballero de la Rosa, 38 (☎941 26 14 30 or 941 26 14 22). From the train and bus stations, turn right from C. General Vara onto Mura de Cervantes, which becomes Av. Paz. After 7 long blocks, turn left on C. Caballero de la Rosa and walk 3½ blocks. Public phone and 2 common rooms with TV. University dorms during the school year; used by athletic teams in summer. Doubles with bunks and private bath; rooms usually not shared. No curfew. Breakfast €1.80. HI card not required. Bunks €6, with obligatory sheets €8.11. Open July-Sept. 15. Closed Sept. 16-30. ❶

FOOD

Logroñeses take their grapes seriously; wine is the beverage of choice with everything. C. Laurel and C. San Juan brim with bars and cafes. The market, **Mercado de San Blas,** is in a concrete building on C. Capitán Eduardo Gallarza, off C. Mura de la Francisco de la Mata along the park (open M-F 7:30am-1:30pm and 4-7:30pm, Sa 7:30am-1:30pm). For **groceries,** head to **Champión,** Av. La Rioja, left off C. Miguel Villanueva past the tourist office. (☎941 22 99 00. Open M-Sa 9am-9:30pm.)

Bar Soriano, Travesía de Laurel, 2 (☎941 22 88 07), where C. Laurel turns. No indoor seating. The specialty is *champiñones con gambas* (mushrooms with shrimp; €0.75), washed down with a shot of *vino* (€0.45). Open daily 11am-3am. ❶

Joshua, C. Laurel, 10, off of C. Capitán Gallarza, on the right. Find a tasty take on Middle Eastern cuisine at this quick, informal spot. Don't worry; their special *tortuga* (turtle) pita wraps (€2-3) are only shaped like the animals. Try their succulent chicken and pistachio balls (€1). Baklava €1. Th-M noon-4pm and 7pm-midnight, W noon-4pm, Tu closed. ❶

Pata Negra, C. Laurel, 24 (941 21 36 45), on the corner of Tr. de Laurel. You never knew pork had so many names until you've seen the menu of this *jamonero*. Specialty cheeses €9.60. Ham and meat dishes €5.40-7.80. Pâté €5.40. Open Tu-Su 7pm-midnight. ❷

SIGHTS AND ENTERTAINMENT

In a Baroque palace, the **Museo de la Rioja** has a collection of art spanning the last eight centuries, which came from the 1835 state seizure of regional monasteries' and convents' artwork. (Pl. San Agustín, 23, along C. Portales and next to the post office. ☎941 29 12 59. Open Tu-Sa 10am-2pm and 4-9pm, Su 11:30am-2pm. Free.) The towers of the **Catedral de Santa María de la Redonda** dominate the Pl. Mercado in the *casco antiguo*. (From C. General Vara turn left on C. Portales; the cathedral is 2 blocks away on the right. Open M-Sa 7:45am-1:30pm for Mass and 6:30-10pm, Su 8:15am-1:15pm and 6:30-9pm. Free.) The grassy knolls along the **Río Ebro** make for a nice walk; a pedestrian path runs by the **Puente de Hierro** and **Puente de Piedra.**

Logroño **nightlife** begins in the *casco antiguo* along C. Laurel and after midnight moves to C. Mayor along Pl. Mercado, C. Sagasta, and, on weekends, C. Carnicerías. The **Fiestas de San Bernabé** (June 11) bring revelry and fireworks. The biggest party in town takes place the week of Sept. 21 for the **Fiesta de San Mateo.** That same week, locals celebrate the grape harvest with the **Fiestas de la Vendimia,** in which they make a ceremonial offering of crushed grapes to the Virgin of Valvanera. Participants crush the grapes with their bare feet in the Parque de Espolón.

DAYTRIP FROM LOGROÑO

HARO

RENFE trains (☎941 31 15 97) connect Logroño to Haro (35min.; daily 6:40am, 6pm; also M, W, F 2:30pm; €3.01; additional train F 7:04pm, €8.66). Buses from Logroño (1hr.; 3-6 per day M-F 7:30am-7:15pm, Sa 10:15am-7:15pm, Su 10:15am-10:30pm; €2.45) arrive at the Haro station (☎941 31 15 43).

Rubi, Paternina, Rioja Santiago, Carlos Serres: these are the names of just a few of Haro's 17 *bodegas*. Awash with the warming drink, Haro (pop. 10,000) serves as the heart of La Rioja's wine industry and should be a priority stop for anyone who fancies themself a wine connoisseur, or simply a wine-lover. Most *bodegas* offer free tours of their facilities in English and Spanish between 9am and 2pm, although reservations are almost always required. **Bodegas Muga,** across the river and under the train tracks, can be visited during the week without calling ahead. (☎941 31 04 98. Tours M-F 11am in English and noon in Spanish. €3.) **Bodegas Bilbaínas,** located across the river but before the train tracks, can be visited by appointment. (☎941 31 01 47. Free.) If you're interested in buying some of Haro's wine, try the **wine shops** on C. Santo Tomás. Most charge €1.35-3 per bottle, but *jarreros* (nickname given to Haro locals) insist that any bottle less than €2.80 should not be drunk. In the Estación Enológica, the **Museo**

THE EGGS OF WRATH A visit to one of the many *bodegas* in Haro will make any visitor appreciate the art of wine-making. After the grape juice has been gathered and put into 18,000-liter barrels, workers must ensure that all the grape leftovers are removed from the juice. One man breaks between 1000 and 2000 eggs, separating the whites from the yolks. These egg yolks are then poured into the barrel (about 540 eggs per barrel), creating a thick film on the top. This film slowly begins to sink, and after 35 days it has removed any grape debris. The yolks are then donated to neighborhood bakeries to be used in cakes.

del Vino has sleek exhibits in Spanish on everything you could possibly want to know about wine. (☎941 31 05 47. Open M-Sa 10am-2pm and 4-8pm, Su 10am-2pm. €2. W free.) Join the locals and *ir de vinos* ("go for wines") in the evening in **La Herradura,** the area around C. Santo Tomás, off Pl. Paz. Ask for *vino* and you'll get the vintage of the year (€0.35); for higher quality, order *crianza,* wine that is more than three years old (€0.75). Haro breaks out in festivities June 24-29, culminating in the **Batalla del Vino** (June 29), when participants spray wine at innocent bystanders.

To reach **Pl. Paz** from the **train station,** take the road downhill, turn right and then left across the river, and follow C. Navarra uphill to the plaza (15min.). From the **bus station,** follow signs to *centro ciudad* along C. Ventilla, continuing 2 blocks past the Consum supermarket. Head diagonally left across Pl. Cruz onto C. Arraball, which leads straight into Pl. Paz. **Luggage storage** is available in the bus station (lockers €2). The **tourist office,** Pl. Monseñor Florentino Rodríguez, provides information on all the wine routes. Take C. Vega from the corner of Pl. Paz; the office is in the plaza to the left around the bend, located in the corner of the large stone building across from Hotel Los Augustinos. (☎941 30 33 66. Open July-Sept. M-Sa 10am-2pm and 4:30-7:30pm, Su 10am-2pm; Oct.-June Tu-F 10am-2pm and 4-7pm, Su 10am-2pm.) **Santander Central Hispano,** C. Vega, 20, offers **currency exchange** with no commission and a **24hr. ATM.** (☎941 31 11 84. Open Apr.-Sept. M-F 8:30am-2pm; Oct.-Mar. M-F 8:30am-2pm, Sa 8:30am-1pm.)

PAMPLONA (IRUÑA) ☎948

El encierro, la Fiesta del San Fermín, the Running of the Bulls, utter debauchery: call it what you will, the outrageous festival of the city's patron saint is the reason people come to Pamplona (pop. 200,000). *San Fermines* is rightly touted as the biggest and craziest festival in all of Europe. Though the city's parks, museums, and monuments await exploration, it is the famous *encierro,* the focal point of the July 6-14 celebration, that draws visitors from the world over. Ever since Ernest Hemingway immortalized the *San Fermines* chaos in *The Sun Also Rises,* hordes of visitors have come to witness and experience the legendary running. At the bullring, a bust of Hemingway welcomes fans to the eight-day extravaganza of dancing, dashing, and of course, drinking—no sleeping allowed.

Although *San Fermines* may be the city's most irresistible attraction, Pamplona's lush parks, Gothic cathedral, massive citadel, and winding *casco antiguo* entertain those who show at up other times. Despite being the capital of Navarra, Pamplona's roots are truly Basque; the area was settled by the Basque long before the Roman "founders" arrived and named the city after Pompey the Great.

TRANSPORTATION

Flights: Aeropuerto de Noaín (☎948 16 87 00), 6km from the center. Accessible only by taxi (about €7.50). **Iberia** (☎902 40 05 00) to **Barcelona** (2-4 per day) and **Madrid** (4-6 per day).

Trains: Estación RENFE, Av. San Jorge (☎902 24 02 02). Take bus #9 from Po. Sarasate (20min., €0.70). Info open daily 6am-10pm. **Ticket office,** C. Estella, 8, is located near the bus station. (☎948 22 72 82. Open M-F 9am-1:30pm and 4:30-7:30pm, Sa 9:30am-1pm.) Pamplona's rail connections aren't the most reliable. To: **Barcelona** (6-8hr., 3-4 per day 12:28pm-12:57am, €27); **Madrid** (5hr.; 7:15am, 6:10pm; €33.50); **Olite** (40min.; M-Sa 4 per day 7:25am-8:05pm; Su 1:25, 8:05pm; €2.30); **Tudela** (1½hr., Su-F 6:50pm, €6.50); **Vitoria-Gasteiz** (1¼hr.; M-Sa 8:40am, 4:39, 7:35pm; Su 4:39, 7:35pm; €4); **Zaragoza** (2hr.; 12:28, 5:10pm; €13).

Buses: Estación de Autobuses, at the corner of C. Conde Oliveto and C. Yanguas y Miranda. **La Tafallesa** (☎948 22 28 86) to: **Olite** (50min.; M-F 7 per day 8:15am-8:30pm, Sa 6 per day 9:30am-8:30pm; €2.25); **Roncal** (2hr.; M-F 5pm, Sa 1pm; €6.50). **La Roncalesa** (☎948 22 20 79) runs buses to: **Jaca** (1¾hr.; M-Sa 8:30am, F and Su 3:30pm; €5.41); **San Sebastián** (1hr.; M-Sa 9 per day 7am-11pm, Su 7 per day 8:15am-11pm; €5.10). **Conda** (☎948 22 10 26) to: **Madrid** (5hr.; 4-7 per day M-Th and Sa 7am-6:30pm, F and Su 7am-9:30pm; €21.38); **Tudela** (1½hr., 5-8 per day 7:15am-8:45pm, €5.97); **Zaragoza** (2-3hr., 6-8 per day 7:15am-8:30pm, €10.92). **La Burundesa (ALSA)** (☎948 22 17 66) to: **Bilbao** (2hr.; M-Sa 4-6 per day 7am-8:30pm, Su 11am-8pm; €10.13); **Vitoria-Gasteiz** (1½hr.; M-Sa 8-11 per day 7am-8:30pm, Su 5 per day 9am-7pm; €5.50). **Bilman** (☎948 22 09 97) to **Barcelona** (5½hr.; 8:35am, 4:40pm, 12:45am; €18.55). **La Estellesa** (☎948 22 22 23) to **Logroño** (1hr., 4-5 per day 7:30am-7pm, €5.95).

Public Transportation: (☎948 42 32 42). Bus #9 runs from Po. Sarasate to the train station (20min., every 15min. 6:30am-10:15pm, €0.70). 24hr. during *San Fermines*.

Taxis: (☎948 23 23 23 or 948 23 23 00), cluster at Pl. Castillo and Taconera.

Car Rental: Europcar, Hotel Blanca Navarra, Av. Pío XII, 43 (☎948 17 60 02). Take bus #15, 4-1 or 4-2 from Po. Sarasate and get off after the traffic circle on the way out of town. 21+. Open M-F 8:30am-1pm and 4-7:30pm, Sa 9am-1pm.

ORIENTATION AND PRACTICAL INFORMATION

The **casco antiguo,** in the northeast quarter of the city, contains almost everything of interest in Pamplona. **Plaza del Castillo** is Pamplona's center. To reach it from the **bus station,** turn left onto Av. Conde Oliveto; at the traffic circle on Pl. Príncipe de Viana, take the second left onto Av. San Ignacio, follow it to the end of the pedestrian thoroughfare Po. Sarasate, and bear right. From the **train station,** take bus #9 (€0.70) to the last stop; cut across Po. Sarasate, and walk diagonally left to Pl. Castillo. North of Pl. Castillo, the Baroque **Casa Consistorial (Ayuntamiento)** is a marker in the swirl of medieval streets.

Tourist Office: C. Hilarión Eslava, 1 (☎948 20 65 40; fax 948 20 70 34; www.pamplona.net). From Pl. Castillo, take C. San Nicolás, turn right on C. San Miguel, and walk straight through Pl. San Francisco. Minute-by-minute guides to the festivities. Open during *San Fermines* daily 8am-8pm; July-Aug. M-Sa 10am-2pm and 4-7pm, Su 10am-2pm; Sept.-June M-F 10am-2pm and 4-7pm, Sa 10am-2pm.

Currency Exchange: Santander Central Hispano, Pl. Castillo, 21 (☎948 20 86 00), has an **ATM.** Open May-Sept. M-F 8:30am-2:30pm; Oct.-Apr. M-F 8:30am-2:30pm, Sa 8:30am-1pm; *San Fermines* 9am-1pm.

Luggage Storage: At the **bus station.** Bags €2 per day, large packs €3 per day. Open M-Sa 6:15am-9:30pm, Su 6:30am-1:30pm and 2-9:30pm. Closes for *San Fermines*, when the **Escuelas de San Francisco,** the big stone building at one end of Pl. San Francisco opens instead. Lines are long, and you must have a passport or ID. €2 per day and each time you check on your luggage. Open 24hr.

Laundromat and Public Baths: Casa de Baño, C. Hilarión Eslava (☎948 22 17 38), at the corner of C. Jarauta. No full service during *San Fermines.* 4.5kg wash €5, dry €7.25. Open Tu-Sa 8:30am-8pm, Su 8:30am-12:30pm. Freshen up in its **showers** (€0.80). Towel €0.25, soap €0.25. Open daily during *San Fermines* 8am-9pm.

Public Toilets: Squat **toilet booths** are set up for *San Fermines,* but the permanent bathrooms in the **Jardines de Taconera** (beyond Hotel Tres Reyes) are more comfortable.

Emergency: ☎112. **Municipal Police:** C. Monasterio de Irache, 2 (☎092).

Pharmacy: FarPlus, C. San Nicolás, 76 (☎948 21 07 04). Open M-F 9am-1:30pm and 5-8pm, Sa 9:30am-1:30pm. **Late-night pharmacy** changes daily. All pharmacies post info for that evening's location, or call ☎948 22 21 11.

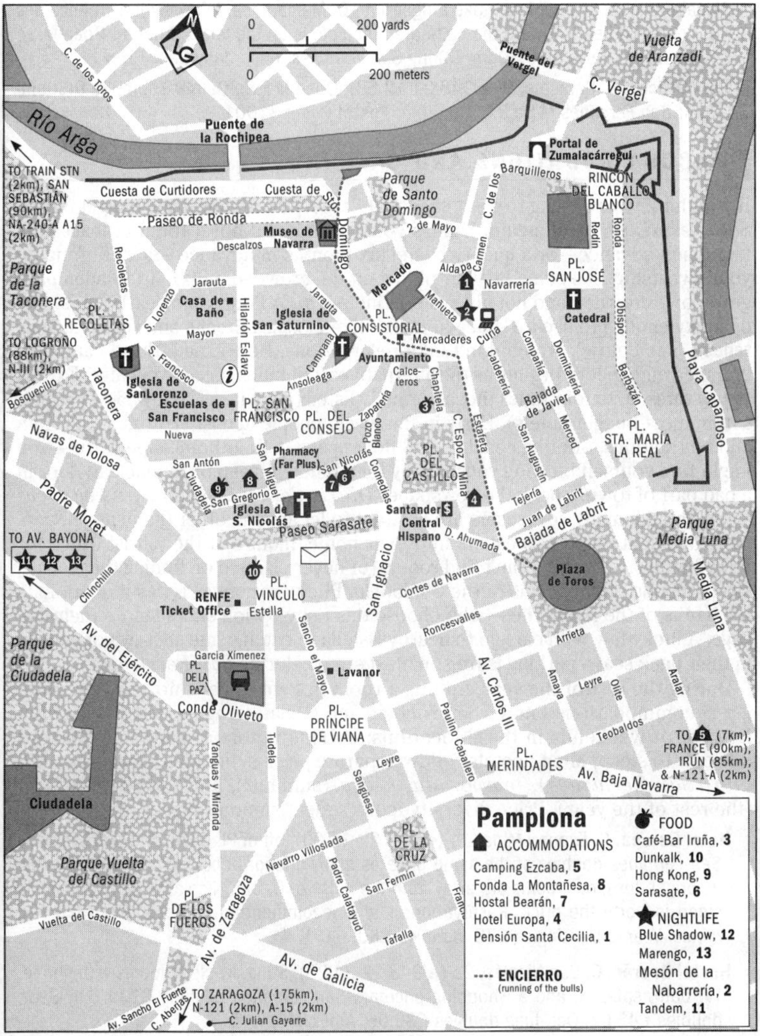

While Pamplona is usually a very safe city, assaults and muggings skyrocket during *San Fermines*. Apparently, some characters come with shadier intentions, more interested in tourist cash than *fiesta* excitement. Do not roam alone at night, and be extremely cautious in the parks and dark streets of the *casco antiguo*. If they aren't careful, revelers in parks and along riverbanks can say good-bye to their wallets and money belts

Medical Services: Hospital de Navarra, C. Irunlarrea (☎948 42 21 00). The **Red Cross** also sets up stands at the bus station and the *corrida* during *San Fermines.*

Internet Access: Kuria.Net, C. Curia, 15 (☎948 22 30 77). Convenient *casco antiguo* location. From C. Chapitela, take a right onto C. Mercaderes, following it as it becomes C. Curia and heads toward the cathedral; the cafe is on the left. €3 per hr. Open M-Sa 10am-10pm, Su 4:30-9:30pm. During *San Fermines*, open daily 9am-11pm.

Post Office: Po. Sarasate, 9 (☎948 21 12 63). Open M-F 8:30am-8:30pm, Sa 9:30am-2pm; *San Fermines* M-Sa 8:30am-2pm. **Postal Code:** 31001.

ACCOMMODATIONS AND CAMPING

If you think you're going to get a good night's sleep on a shoestring budget during *San Fermines*, think again. Unless you've booked a hotel room at least nine months in advance—or a quality hostel six months in advance—start fluffing up your sweatshirt: it's going be your pillow on the crowded, noisy, litter-laden park grass, or a crowded and not-always-pristine *pensión* floor. Some early birds may be lucky enough to secure space in places like **Camping Ezcaba** and **Fonda La Montañesa** (see below), which don't take reservations. Be warned: these can be as cramped and uncomfortable as the alternatives, but much more expensive. Expect to pay rates up to four times those normally listed (anywhere from €36-54 per person in most budget hotels). Early in the week, people accost visitors at the train and bus stations, offering couches and floor space in their homes. Be wary— you might find yourself blowing your money for a blink of sleep on an unclean floor in a bad part of town. Check the newspaper *Diario de Navarra* for *casas particulares*, though many advertisers are hesitant to let anyone other than native Spaniards or fluent Spanish speakers into their home. Inquire at the tourist office for other listings. Many who can't find rooms (or never planned on finding them at all) sleep outside on the lawns of the Ciudadela, Pl. Fueros, and Pl. Castillo, or along the banks of the river. Those who choose this risky option should store their luggage. A lucky few with cars go to nearby Estella to catch some shut-eye or snooze in their back seat—parking is free on most streets during *San Fermines*.

During the rest of the year, finding a room in Pamplona is no problem. Budget accommodations line C. San Nicolás and C. San Gregorio off Pl. Castillo. Beware of weekends in these locations; outside rabble-rousing may make it difficult to sleep. Most hostels follow separate price schedules for *temporada alta (San Fermines)*, *temporada media* (summer), and *temporada baja* (the rest of the year). Price diversity icons reflect summer prices.

Hotel Europa, C. Espoz y Mina, 11 (☎948 22 18 00), off of Pl. Castillo. Offers luxurious *San Fermines* doubles at the same price as many inferior *pensiones* during the week. Its bright, luxurious rooms are away from the noise of C. San Nicolás. One good night's sleep is worth the price. Reservations highly recommended, especially for *San Fermines*. Year-round singles €70; doubles €80. MC/V. ❺

Hostal Bearán, C. San Nicolás, 25 (☎948 22 34 28). Squeaky-clean rooms with phone, TV, bath, safebox, and a whopping pricetag. *San Fermines* doubles €109. July-Sept. doubles €42.07. Oct.-June doubles €36.06. AmEx/MC/V. ❷

Pensión Santa Cecilia, C. Navarrería, 17 (☎948 22 22 30). From C. Chapitela (off Pl. Castillo), take the 1st right onto C. Mercaderes, then left onto C. Navarrería. 18th-century mansion. Comfy rooms with winter heating. July-Aug. singles €20; doubles €30; triples €35. *San Fermines* €45 per person. Rest of the year €15/€20/€30. MC/V. ❷

Fonda La Montañesa, C. San Gregorio, 2 (☎948 22 43 80), down C. San Nicolás. Older rooms, but adequate when space is tight. Ask for a room on a higher floor during the festival. No reservations. *San Fermines* €40 per person; rest of year €13. ❶

Camping Ezcaba (☎948 33 03 15), in Eusa, 7km down the road to Irún. City bus line 4-1 runs to the campground from Pl. de las Merindades (4 per day; €0.70). Hop off at the final gas station stop. Fills fast during *San Fermines.* No reservations. *San Fermines* €8.25 per person, per tent, and per car. Rest of the year €3.50. AmEx/MC/V. ❶

FOOD

Tiny neighborhood cafes advertise hearty *menús:* try the side streets near Pensión Santa Cecilia, C. Jarauta, C. Descalzos, near Po. Ronda, and the area above Pl. San Francisco. C. Navarrería and Po. Sarasate are lined with numerous *bocadillo* bars. The *barracas políticas* (bars organized by political interest groups that don't expect any interest in their platforms), next to the amusement park in the Ciudadela, offer cheap drinks. Many cafes and restaurants close for one to two weeks after *San Fermines* to recover. The **market,** C. Mercado, is to the right of Casa Consistorial's facade, down the stairs. (Open M-Sa 8am-2:30pm.) **Vendi Supermarket** is at the corner of C. Hilarión Eslava and C. Mayor. (Open M-F 9am-2pm and 5:30-7:30pm, Sa 9am-2pm; *San Fermines* M-Sa 9am-2pm. MC/V.)

Restaurante Sarasate, C. San Nicolás, 19 (☎948 22 57 27), above a seafood store. Organic vegetarian dishes. Lunchtime *menú* €8. Open M-Sa 1:15-4pm, Su 9-11am. ❷

Café-Bar Iruña, Pl. Castillo. Hemingway's favorite haunt and the backdrop for much of *The Sun Also Rises.* A delicious *menú* (€9.60) draws an older crowd. Open M-Th 8am-11pm, F 8am-2am, Sa 9am-2am, Su 9am-11pm. MC/V. ❸

Dunkalk, C. Alhodiga, 13, off of Po. Sarasate. This pub/eatery overflows with boomerangs, crocodile barstools, and murals of a kangaroo-filled outback. An inexpensive menu with a selection of beers. Large *bocadillos* €2.70-4.20. *Menú* 9.60. Chicken and other entrees €3-6. Open 10am-2pm and 5pm-midnight. ❶

Hong Kong, C. San Gregorio, 38 (☎948 22 66 35). Look for the red balcony. For the Spanish take on Chinese food, split a 2-, 3-, 4-, or 5-person *menú* (€16-42) or try the 3-course *menú* for one (€6). Open daily noon-4pm and 8pm-midnight. MC/V. ❷

SIGHTS

CATHEDRAL AND CHURCHES. Pamplona has a rich architectural legacy. The recently restored 14th-century **Gothic cathedral** houses an alabaster mausoleum, where Carlos III and his wife Queen Leonor are entombed. Off the cloister is a five-chimneyed kitchen, one of four of its kind in Europe. *(At the end of C. Navarrería. ☎948 21 08 27. Open M-F 10am-1:30pm and 4-7pm, Sa 10am-1:30pm. Guided tours €3.20.)* The 13th-century **Iglesia de San Saturnino** is near the Ayuntamiento, and **Iglesia de San Nicolás,** in Pl. San Nicolás. *(Both open daily 9am-12:30pm and 6-8:30pm. Free.)* For a peek at the legendary San Fermín and his wolven comrade, head to **Iglesia de San Lorenzo,** next to the tourist office. *(C. Mayor, 74. Open daily 8am-12:30pm and 6:30-8pm.)*

CIUDADELA. The pentagonal Ciudadela was built by Felipe II in an effort to secure the city's safety. Today, it's part of a grassy park that hosts an amazing *San Fermines* fireworks display and free exhibits and concerts in the summer. Its impressive **walls** even scared off Napoleon, who refused to launch a frontal attack and staged a trick snowball fight instead; when Spanish sentries joined in, the French entered the city through its gates. For a scenic walk to the **Ciudadela** from the old quarter, pick up C. Redín at the far end of the cathedral plaza. A left turn follows the walls past the **Portal de Zumalacárregui** and along the Río Arga. Bear left through the gardens of **Parque de la Taconera**—where deer, swans, and peacocks roam—until reaching the Ciudadela. *(To get to the intimidating walls from Pl. Castillo, follow Po. Sarasate to its end, then take a right on Navas de Tolosa. Take your next left on C. Chinchilla; you'll see the massive entrance at the end of the street, 2 blocks down. Av. Ejército. ☎948 22 82 37. Open daily 7:30am-10pm; closed during San Fermines. Free.)*

MUSEO DE NAVARRA. The Museo de Navarra shelters 4th-century Roman mosaics, murals from all over the region, and a collection of 14th- to 20th-century paintings, including Goya's portrait of the Marqués de San Adrián. *(Up C. Santo Domingo from Pl. Consistorial. ☎948 42 64 92. Open Tu-Sa 9:30am-2pm and 5-7pm, Su 11am-2pm; San Fermines Tu-Su 11am-2pm. €1.80, students €0.90. Sa afternoons and Su mornings free.)*

ENTERTAINMENT

There *is* (night)life after *San Fermines*, and it's not difficult to find. **Plaza de Castillo** is the social heart of Pamplona. High school students gather at bars in the *casco antiguo* to demonstrate their vocal abilities; singing, shouting, and any other type of loud carousing are *de rigueur*. C. San Nicolás and C. San Gregorio are nighttime favorites, as are C. Calderería, C. San Agustín, and C. Jaruata. A great spot to chat with friends over drinks, **Mesón de la Nabarrería,** C. Navarrería draws crowds day and might. (☎948 21 31 63. Open Su-Th 10:30am-midnight and F-Sa 11am-2:30am.) Claustrophobes escape the cramped streets of the *casco antiguo* to the bars of Barrio San Juan on Av. Bayona. **Alakarga,** Pl. Monasterio Azuelo draws a hip late-night crowd. (☎948 26 60 05. Beers €3; mixed drinks €4.80. Open Th-Sa midnight-7am; Su-W 10:30pm-6am; ring the bell to enter.)

You'll find the university crowd at **Travesia de Bayona,** a small plaza of bars and *discotecas* off Av. Bayona, just before it forks into Monasterio de Velate. At places like **Blue Shadow** and **Tandem,** Tr. de Bayona, 3 and 4, most scoff at signs prohibiting drinks from leaving the bar; here, the party is outside. (Beer €3. Mixed drinks €5. Both open Th-Sa 6pm-6am.) Av. Bayona also boasts the most popular and pricey of nightspots. Half a block from Pl. Juan XXIII, the enormous **Marengo,** Av. Bayona, 2, needs five doormen to

FROM THE ROAD

GRABBING THE BULL BY THE HORNS

Cheers and cries of *olé* floated through the window of my dilapidated *pensión* room in Pamplona's *casco antiguo*, but I was already awake. I checked my watch: July 7th, 6am. Two hours until the running of the bulls. I'd been waiting for this event for years.

I stepped outside, clad in the requisite *San Fermines* garb—all white except for the red *faja* encircling my waist and red *pañuelo* around my neck. Thousands of eager spectators were already planted on, under, and between the wooden fences lining the path to the *plaza del toros*. I ducked under one of the gates and made my way up the final stretch of the run, toward the bulls' holding pen.

I continued up the cobblestone path. Fences to jump over or, if need be, roll under, were nearby. Failing that, I told myself that the *capótico de San Fermín*, (San Fermín's cape) would shield me; legend has it that it is responsible for a few miraculous escapes each year. I had no idea how much I would really need such protection.

Eight o'clock neared. Police passed, dragging under-18 wannabe runners out of the way; last-minute doubters scaled the sides of storefronts, clambering for a balcony's safety; the mass slowly drifted away from the holding pen, deciding they'd start a bit closer to the finish line. I began to stampede-proof myself, slipping the loose end of my *faja* into a pocket, and scuffing my tennis shoes on the ground as best I could to

guard its threshold from sneaky fun-seekers. A ticket and appropriate dress (clubbing gear) are required for entrance. (☎948 26 55 42. Tickets €8. Beer €4. Mixed drinks €6. Open Th-Sa 11pm-6am.)

LOS SAN FERMINES (JULY 6-14)

No limits, no lethargy, and no liability make Pamplona's **Fiestas de San Fermín**—known to most as "The Running of the Bulls"—Europe's premier party. At no other festival will you witness mayhem quite like this eight-day frenzy of parades, bullfights, parties, dancing, fireworks, concerts, wine, and more wine. Pamplonese, clad in white with red sashes (*fajas*) and bandanas (*pañuelos*), throw themselves into the merry-making, displaying obscene levels of physical stamina and alcohol tolerance.

Around 9am on July 6, the whole city crowds around the Ayuntamiento, in anticipation of the mayor's noon appearance. As the midday hour approaches, the mass sings and chants *"San Fermín!,"* as they display their *pañuelos*, raised high above their heads. Don't commit the faux pas of wearing your *pañuelo* before the first rocket blast (*chupinazo*); tie it around your wrist to keep it safe. Also, the plaza can get unbearably packed; wear closed-toed shoes and prepare to get up close and personal with hundreds of fellow revelers. As the mayor emerges and fires the awaited *chupinazo* from the balcony, a howl explodes from the sea of expectant *sanferministas* in the plaza below. Champagne rains (beware of flying corks) along with eggs, ketchup, wine, flour, and yellow *pimiento*. Within minutes the streets of the *casco antiguo* flood with improvised singing and dancing troupes. The *peñas*, societies more concerned with beer than bullfighting, lead the hysteria. At 5pm on the 6th and at 9 or 9:30am every other day, they are joined by the *Comparsa de Gigantes y Cabezudos*, a troupe of *gigantes* (giant wooden monarchs) and *zaldikos* (courtiers on horseback). *Kilikis* (swollen-headed buffoons) run around chasing little kids and hitting them with play clubs. These misfits, together with church and town officials, escort San Fermín on his triumphant procession through the *casco antiguo*. The saint's 15th-century statue is brought from the Iglesia de San Lorenzo at 10am on July 7, the actual day of *San Fermín*. (Note: virtually everything closes on the 7th; hours listed for the festival refer only to the 6th and the 8th through 14th.)

THE RUNNING OF THE BULLS

The running of the bulls, the *encierro*, is the highlight of *San Fermines*. The ritual dates back to the

prevent slipping on the champagne- and urine-slicked cobblestone. Murmurs of anticipation resonated in the chill morning air.

Seconds before a signal, a wave of about 50 men who must have seen the starter ready the rocket rushed toward me, clawing past my startled frame and diving in between the wooden fences. Not a moment later, two blasts shot through the air. I turned and ran.

About halfway through the 7min. 6sec. ordeal, I heard the trampling gait of a particular beast not far behind. Desperate to escape his onslaught, I tore past the frightened mob in front of me, drilling through the clog of bodies any way I could: I kicked, I grabbed, I spit, I punched. And so did anyone else who valued his health. This was every man for himself.

My mad scrambling was to no avail. The *toro* easily advanced up alongside me. It jerked its body around and bucked back its head into my left hip, lifting me off the ground. Airborne, I felt something brush against my leg, but was too busy readying myself for the fall that I didn't notice the horn shredding my left pant leg and just nicking the shin. As a knee hit the ground, I performed my best sprinter-start away from the animal, whose attack had rendered my knee momentarily incapacitated. His hooves had slipped out from under him, tossing him sidelong to the ground. It wasn't until the next day, when I saw photographs of myself contending with the bull in the local and international newspapers, that I realized how much danger I'd been in.

My head ached, my lungs burned, and the vinegary aftertaste of last night's *kalimotxo* burned my throat, but I had never felt better.

—Nate Gray

14th century, when it served the practical function of getting the bulls from their corrals to the bullring. These days, the first *encierro* of the festival is at 8am on July 7 and is repeated every day for the next seven days. Hundreds of bleary-eyed, hung-over, hyper-adrenalized runners flee from large bulls as bystanders cheer from barricades, windows, and balconies

A rocket marks the release of the bulls into the 825m course. Six to nine animals are released from their pens as runners scurry away. If you want to participate in the bullring excitement without the risk of running with the beasts, you can line up by the Pl. Toros well before 7:30am and run in *before* the bulls are even in sight (though such a "cowardly" act will bring booing from the locals). Three to six steers accompany the bulls—watch out, they have horns, too. Both the bulls and the mob are dangerous. Runners, all convinced the bull is right behind them, flee for dear life and act without concern for those around them. Experienced runners, many of whom view the event as an athletic art form, try to get as close to the bull as possible. The course has three sharp turns, which the bulls have difficulty cornering; when their legs slide out from under them, they falter, creating a pile of bull. Runners should avoid the outside of corners to avoid getting crushed under said pile, and should be especially careful at the Mercaderes-Estafeta corner.

After cascading through a perilously narrow opening (where a large proportion of injuries occur), the run pours into the bullring, amid shouts and cries from appreciative spectators. After the bulls have been safely rounded into their pens inside the Pl. Toros, younger, less dangerous bulls with covered horns are released to "play" with the mass of 350 people. The safer alternative is to follow Hemingway's example: don't run—watch the *encierro* from the bullring instead. Music, waves, chanting, and dancing pump up spectators until the headline entertainment arrives. Bullring spectators should arrive around 6:45am. Tickets for the *Grada* section of the ring are available at 7am (M-F €3.60, Sa-Su €4.20). You can watch for free, but the free section is overcrowded, and it can be hard to see and breathe.

To watch one of the actual bullfights, you must wait in the line that forms at the bullring around 8pm every evening; earlier is always better. (Tickets range from €15-70.) As one bullfight ends, tickets go on sale for the next day. Cheaper, more subdued spectacles occur in the days preceding and following *San Fermines*—bargain with the scalpers outside the bullring for the best price (€4-12). Though the *sol* section can get hot, it is cheaper, closer, and generally more fun.

THE REST OF THE DAY

Once the running is over, the insanity spills into the streets, gathering steam until nightfall, when it explodes with singing in bars, dancing in alleys, spontaneous parades, and a no-holds-barred party in Pl. Castillo, which quickly becomes a huge open-air dance floor. The attire for this dance-a-thon includes sturdy, closed-toed shoes (there's glass everywhere), a white t-shirt (which will soon be wine-soaked), a red *pañuelo* (bandana), and a cheap bottle of champagne (to spray, of course; don't pay more than €2). English speakers often congregate where C. Estafeta hits Pl. Toros, at an outdoor consortium of local *discotecas*. A word to the wise: avoid the fountain-jumping (you'll know it when you see it). It is *not* a traditional part of the festivities; it was inaugurated by Americans, Aussies, and Kiwis, and several people have died in recent years. The truly inspired partying takes place the first few days of *San Fermines*. After that, crowds thin, and the atmosphere goes from dangerously crazed to mildly insane. The party begins (or ends) each day at 6am, when bands march down the streets, waking everyone for the running. The city eases the transition with concerts, outdoor dances, and a host of other performances. The festivities culminate at midnight on July 14 with the singing of *Pobre de mí: "Pobre de mí, pobre de mí, que se han acabado las Fiestas de San Fermín"* (Poor me, poor me, the festivals of San Fermín have ended).

RUN FOR YOUR LIFE So, you're going to run with the bulls. Partaking in the *encierro* gives you a lifetime of bragging rights, but those who decide to run should seriously consider the risks involved. Some have been gored to death (the last fatality was an inexperienced American in 1995), and each day, gruesome newspaper photos of injuries are posted for all to behold. To prevent ending up on evening news programs around the world, heed a few words of *San Fermines* wisdom:

—Research the *encierro* before you run. The tourist office dispenses a pamphlet that outlines the exact route of the 3min. run and offers tips for inexperienced runners. It's a long course, and running the whole thing safely is nearly impossible. Most runners start at the Ayuntamiento, midway through the course. You should also watch it once on TV to get a glimpse of what you're in for, and then once in person, if possible.

—Do not stay up all night carousing. Not surprisingly, hung-over foreigners have the highest rate of injury. Experienced runners get a good night's sleep before and arrive at the course no later than 7am. Many locals arrive at 6am. The course closes at 7:30am.

—Wear proper clothing (nothing loose or baggy) and appropriate shoes. Do not carry anything with you (especially a backpack or video camera).

—Give up on getting near the bulls and concentrate on getting to the bullring in one piece. Although some whack the bull with rolled newspapers, runners should never distract or touch the animals; anyone who does is likely to anger the bull and locals alike.

—Try not to cower in a doorway; people have been trapped and killed this way.

—Be particularly wary of isolated bulls—they seek company in the crowds.

—If you fall, **stay down.** Curl up into a fetal position, lock your hands behind your head, and **do not get up** until the clatter of hooves has passed.

Attending all eight days of the festivities is a challenge. Noisy crowds and increasingly disturbing street odors drive many away after only a few days. But if you want more, nearby towns sponsor *encierros:* **Tudela** has its festival the week July 24, **Tafalla** during the week of Aug. 15, and **Sangüesa** during the second week of Sept. Many Pamplonese take part in a festival less touristed than their own.

DAYTRIPS FROM PAMPLONA

Though the following daytrips are actually closer to small towns in the Pyrenees, especially Sangüesa, their only public transportation runs from Pamplona.

LUMBIER GORGES

Río Irati buses (☎948 30 35 70) run to Lumbier from Pamplona (1hr.; M-F 1, 6, 7pm, Sa 1:30, 6pm; return to Pamplona M-F 8am and 2:30pm, Sa 2:30pm; €2.40-3.50). From Lumbier to Iso, it's a 12km walk, drive, or taxi ride. Pedro Iso taxi ☎636 48 58 50. Parking at Foz de Lumbier is €1.50.

Two fantastic gorges cut into the mountains near Pamplona. Outside the little town of Lumbier, the **Foz de Lumbier** (Lumbier Gorge) drops 50m down to the Río Irati, and a path alongside leads through old railway tunnels. Take the path to the left at the entrance (following the N-113 signs) for an easy 5.5km nature walk that circumnavigates the gorges. For an astounding view, stop along the mostly flat, well-marked path at Corral de Atzuela (1.2km) to take in an astounding view, and at Puente de Diablo (Devil's Point, 4km) to examine its ruins. Just before the town of Iso, 12km down the road, the even more impressive **Foz de Arbayún** cuts a chasm to the river below. A lookout above affords glimpses of swooping griffin vultures, while a small footpath below follows the Río Salazar toward its source.

CASTILLO DE JAVIER

La Tafallesa (☎948 22 28 86) runs a bus from Pamplona to Javier (1hr.; M-F 5pm, Sa 1pm; €3.30). Buses return M-Sa at 8am. You can also take a taxi (☎669 93 69 57) from Sangüesa for about €8 round-trip plus the wait.

Near the entrance to the small village of Javier lies the majestic **Castillo de Javier,** the birthplace of San Francisco Javier (Xavier). This picture-perfect castle on the border between Navarra and Aragón has changed hands numerous times over the last millennium, landing finally in the Jesuits' possession. Its **Chapel of the Holy Christ** houses a 14th-century effigy that is said to have suffered a spontaneous blood-sweating fit at the moment of San Francisco Xavier's death. (Open daily 9am-1pm and 4-7pm; last entrances at 12:40 and 6:40pm. Occasional tours in Spanish. Free, but donations requested.)

SANGÜESA

Though it was founded in AD 1122 by King Alfonso I the Rowdy, the people of Sangüesa (pop. 4600) are anything but. This hushed, dusty town is yet another night's stop on the pilgrim road to Santiago. Those with cars also stay in Sangüesa, as it is a great excursion base; the city is closer to many of the Pamplona daytrips than Pamplona itself. Rumors surrounding subdued Sangüesa about each of its streets holding a monument are not incorrect, but may be misleading. Only the **La Iglesia Santa María la Real** and **Iglesia de Santiago** are worth the trip to the city. The former boasts a Gothic silver-plated sculpture of the Virgin Mary in the impressive central apse. The Romanesque exterior is the only aspect of the latter that can be admired without a tour or mass attendance. Guided visits allows you a glimpse of the magnificent San Aloy altarpiece and admittance to its tower. (Iglesia de Santa María: ☎620 11 05 81. Open 10am-2pm and 8-9pm. €1.65. Iglesia de Santiago: Mass M-Sa 8:30pm; Su noon, 7pm. City-run guided visits to Palacio de Ongay and Iglesias Santa María and Santiago €2.55, to 4 more city monuments €3.30.)

Veloz Sanguesina runs **buses** from **Pamplona** to Sangüesa (M-Sa 3 per day 1-8pm, Su 8:15pm) and back (M-Sa 3 per day 8am-6:30pm, Su 7:15 pm; €2.65 each way). **Legarre taxis** (☎669 93 69 57) also run between the two cities. The **tourist office,** C. Mayor, 2, is just past the bridge. (☎948 87 14 11. Open M-Sa 10am-2pm and 4-7pm, Su 10am-2pm.) Sangüesa's best low-cost accommodation is **Hostal Asador ❷,** C. Alfonso el Batallador, 7, near the tourist office off C. Mayor. Cozy rooms come with complete bath. (☎948 87 00 77. Singles €16; doubles €32.50.) Many a small *tapas* bar line C. Mayor, but for greater sustenance, devour a tender sirloin (€15) at **Restaurante Ciudad de Sangüesa ❸,** C. Santiago, 4, off C. Mayor. (☎948 87 10 21. *Menú* €7.50, July-Sept only. Fish €8-12. Open daily 12:30-4pm and 8:30-11pm.)

NAVARRAN PYRENEES

The Navarran Pyrenees are not for the sedentary; only pilgrims, athletes, and wanderlust-stricken journeyers can appreciate its well-preserved forests and topographical diversity. Forbidding peaks dominate the eastern Valle de Roncal, while the mountain slopes to the west allow easy access to the area's streams, waterfalls, and green meadows. Mist and fog obscure visibility at high altitudes to create a dreamy atmosphere—or nerve-racking driving conditions—depending on your point of view. While most inhabitants log or raise cattle, tourism is becoming a booming business. The French portion of El Camino de Santiago (see **Pilgrim's Progress,** p. 531) crosses the border at Roncesvalles and winds down through Pamplona on its way to Santiago de Compostela in Galicia. Many free and cheap *refugios* cater to modern-day pilgrims along the way, as well as others who don't mind sleeping beside a few scruffy travelers. Navarra's *casa rurales* (rural lodging houses) are particularly beautiful.

Pick up a free copy of the *Guía de alojamientos de turismo rurales* in any of Navarra's tourist offices. As a rule, these homes are welcoming places to stay and great budget options; doubles usually run between €21-29. For reservations, call the multilingual tourist office at ☎948 20 65 40. Pamplona is a sensible base for those dependent upon public transportation; you can head east toward Valle de Roncal, or north toward Roncesvalles. Buses are one-a-day affairs throughout most of the area.

RONCESVALLES AND AURITZ-BURGUETE

The first stop in Spain on the Camino de Santiago pilgrimage path, Roncesvalles's mist-enshrouded 10-odd buildings rest amid miles of thickly wooded mountains. The devout aren't the only ones who pass through this itty-bitty town (pop. 31); folklore buffs come in search of the remains of Roland, Charlemagne's favorite solder. Just up the hill from Roncesvalles in AD 778, was where Roland was supposedly slain, and Puerto Ibañeta (1057m), less than 2km up the main road from the monastery, supposedly marks the spot where Roland breathed his final breath. The heavily restored Capilla de Sancti Spiritus stands over the remains of the bone heap (courtesy of dead soldiers and pilgrims), where his tomb is thought to be. (The chapels can only be visited by guided tours; see below.)

Inside the **Colegiata,** up the driveway from the *capilla*, the tombs of King Sancho El Fuerte (the Strong) and his bride rest in solitary splendor, lit by the huge stained-glass windows of the **Capilla de San Agustín.** (☎948 79 04 80. Chapel and cloister open daily 10am-1:30pm and 3:30-6:30pm. €2; students, seniors, and pilgrims €1.40.) In the decisive battle of the Navas de Tolosa, Sancho reputedly broke the chains protecting the Arab king Miramomolin with his own hands, then promptly decapitated him. The heavy iron chains hanging from the walls of the chamber are represented in Navarra's flag. The monastery's lovely French Gothic **church,** endowed by Sancho and consecrated in 1219, is its main attraction. (Call ☎948 76 00 00 for more info. Open M-Sa 10am-8pm, Su 7am-8am. Free. Guided visits including all monuments and the Roncesvalles museum, €3.20.)

PRACTICAL INFORMATION. **La Montañesa buses** (☎948 22 15 84) run to and from **Pamplona** to Roncesvalles. (1¼hr.; M-F 6pm, Sa 4pm; €3.91. Return bus leaves Roncevalles M-Sa 6:50am.) The bus stops in **Burguete** each way. A **tourist office** in the mill behind **Casa Sabina Hostería** offers maps and guides to the sites of Roncevalles and the Camino de Santiago. (☎948 76 03 01. Open M-Sa 10am-2pm and 4-7pm, Su 10am-2pm.) For **Santander Central Hispano** (open Apr.-Sept. M-F 8:30am-2:30pm; Oct.-Mar. M-F 8:30am-2:30pm, Sa 8:30am-1pm), **supermarkets,** and **restaurants,** head to nearby Burguete (2km south).

ACCOMMODATIONS AND FOOD. The **monastery ❶** in Roncesvalles has free lodging for pilgrims—enter the door to the right as you face the monastery. To attain "official pilgrim" status, you'll have to make an €1 symbolic payment and obtain proper credentials: a stamped piece of paper that verifies your sacred mission. The attached **Oficina de Peregrinos** (☎948 76 00 00) provides this service. But don't become official just to get free lodging; true pilgrims look down upon such vagrancy, and you won't be able to use the credentials until the next stop on the path. Behind the monastery is **Albergue Juvenil Roncesvalles (HI) ❶,** a somber building that served as a pilgrims' hospital in the 18th century. Rec rooms are in the basement. (☎948 76 03 64. Meals are only available for large groups. Members only. HI cards for sale. 4- to 11-bed dorms €7 per person, with meals €16; over 26 €9/€20. Call ahead for reservations June-Aug.) Accommodations, including several *casas rurales*, are plentiful in nearby **Burguete.** Those following the **Camino de Hemingway** can check out the **Hostal Burguete ❸,** San Nikolas, 71, est. 1880. With its springy beds and old-fashioned rooms, not much has changed since the novelist made a stop here himself; Ernest did some resting and writing here on his way back to Paris from *San Fermines*. (☎/fax 948 76 00 05. Breakfast €3. *Menú* €11. All rooms have private bath. Aug. singles €35.45; doubles €45.10. Sept.-July €29.44/€37.86. Open *Semana Santa*-Dec. 10. AmEx/MC/V.) Roncesvalles's lone restaurant, **Casa Sabina Hostería ❶**, offers a *menú* for €8 M-F and €9 Sa-Su.

VALLE DE SALAZAR: OCHAGAVÍA

At the confluence of the Ríos Anduña, Zatoia, and Salazar sits Ochagavía (pop. 600), a picturesque mountain village typical of Navarran Pyrenee *pueblos* in appearance if not in population. Forty kilometers from Pamplona, the Valle de Salazar's largest town spans both sides of the cheerful Río Anduña. Ochagavía's whitewashed houses and cobbled streets lead to forested mountains great for hiking, trout fishing, and cross-country skiing. The 12th-century **Hermito de Muskilda,** the spiritual and cultural nexus of the town, is a 45min. hike away; follow the path from behind the church, or take the road toward the town of **Izalzu** and look for the stone cross. (☎948 89 00 38. Open May-June and Oct. M-F 4-7pm, Sa-Su 11am-2pm and 4-8pm; July-Sept. daily 11am-2pm and 4-8pm; Nov.-Apr. Sa-Su 11am-2pm and 4-7pm.) Local dances featuring elaborate costumes are performed at the sanctuary on September 8, the first day of Ochagavía's annual **festival.** Hikers will find the climb up the **Pico de Orhy** (2021m) a breeze. The 1hr. trail leaving the parking lot at **Puerto de Larrau,** 9km north of Ochagavía along the highway to France, leads to panoramic views of the valley. A second lengthy but smooth hike (20km; 6hr. 1-way) follows the Río Irati past the **Embalse de Irabia** lake and through the **Selva de Irati** forest to the town of **Orbaitzeta;** hikers should leave their cars at the **Ermita de las Nieves,** 24km north of Ochagavía and head west along the river. **Cross-country skiers** can also enjoy two circuit trails originating farther down the same highway.

TRANSPORTATION AND PRACTICAL INFORMATION. Río Irati (☎948 22 14 70) runs buses to **Pamplona** (1½hr., M-Sa 7am, €5.50), which continue on to **Ochagavía** (M-Th and Sa 3:30pm, F 7pm). The **tourist office,** on the main road (C. Aísaba), is in the same building as a nature center and offers a free lodging guide, *Guía de Alojamientos Turísticos*. (☎948 89 06 41; fax 948 89 06 79. Office open *Semana Santa*-Oct. M-Sa 10am-2pm and 4:30-7:30pm, Su 10am-2pm; Nov.-*Semana Santa* M-F and Su 10am-2pm, Sa 10am-2pm and 4-7pm.) Several **ATMs** are located on the main road. In an **emergency,** call ☎112. The **pharmacy** is at C. Urrutia, 31 (☎948 89 05 06; open M-F 10am-2pm and 5-7:30pm, Sa 10am-2pm), and the **post office** is on C. Labaria, near the Ayuntamiento. (☎948 89 04 52. Open M-Sa 9-10am.)

ACCOMMODATIONS. A left down the street just beyond the post office will take you to the door of the warm and welcoming **Casa Ñavarro ❷,** which rents large, immaculate rooms with balconies. Look for a corner building with a wide entryway. (☎948 89 03 35. Breakfast €3. Reservations recommended. Singles €20; doubles €24, with bath €29.) Across the river from the main road, **Hostal Orialde ❸,** C. Urrutia, 6, has attractive, spacious rooms. (☎948 89 00 27. *Menú* €12.10. Singles €26.35; doubles €37.35, with bath €42.25.) Ask at the tourist office or look for the "CR" signs advertising one of the town's 25 *casas rurales*. **Camping Osate ❶,** at the entrance to town (turn right at the large green and blue recycling bins), provides a campsite on the river with supermarket, bar, and mountain bike rentals. (☎948 89 01 84. Bikes €18, €12 per half day. *Menú* €9. 2-6 person bungalows €60-90 per day. Camping €3.50 per person and per car, €3.35 per tent. MC/V.)

VALLE DE RONCAL

Carved by the Río Esca, Valle de Roncal is a handsome valley stretching south from the French border. Its darling towns, inviting *casas rurales*, and prime hiking trails demand that Valle de Roncal is not to be missed.

RONCAL ☎948

Smack in the center of the Valle de Roncal, the diminutive town of **Roncal** (pop. 300) prides itself on two things: its famed *queso Roncal*, a sharp, sheep's milk cheese, and its world-renowned tenor, Julián Gayarre (1844-1889). **Casa Museo Julián Gayarre,** on C. Arana, occupies the singer's birthplace, showcasing his belongings and assorted memorabilia. (☎948 47 51 80. Open Apr.-Sept. Tu-Su 11:30am-1:30pm and 5-7pm; Oct.-Mar. Sa-Su 11:30am-1:30pm and 4-6pm. €1.80, seniors free). **La Tafallesa buses** (☎948 22 28 86) run to **Pamplona** (2hr., M-F 7am, €6). The **tourist office** on Roncal's main road, Po. de Juliana Gayarre, has info on hiking and *casas rurales*. (☎948 47 52 56; fax 948 47 53 16. Open June 15-Sept. 15 M-Sa 10am-2pm and 4:30-8:30pm, Su 10am-2pm; Sept. 16-June 14 M-F 10am-2pm, Sa 4:30-7:30pm.) Services include: **emergency** ☎112; **Guardia Civil** ☎948 47 50 05; and a **pharmacy,** next door to the tourist office (open July-Sept. M-F 10am-2pm and 5-8pm, Sa 10am-2pm; Oct.-June M-F 10am-2pm and 5-7:30pm, Sa 10am-2pm). Go to the *panadería* down the path next to Caja Navarra bank for some wine and a taste of the oft-lauded Roncal cheese. If you spend the night, head to **Casa Villa Pepita ❶,** Po. Julián Gayarre, 4, across from a playground just before the bridge. (☎948 47 51 33. Breakfast €2.40, meals €9. Singles €11.42; doubles €23, with bath €31.)

ISABA AND ENVIRONS

North of Roncal, Isaba (pop. 550) draws hikers and skiers eager to explore the surrounding mountains. A stunning hike climbs from Isaba to **Zuriza** in the Valle de Hecho (5-6hr.). The ascents from Collado Argibiela to **Punta Abizondo** (1676m) and **Peña Ezkaurre** (2050m) are shorter but steeper. For more routes, ask at the tourist office. Ski trails run north of Isaba, at the **Estación de Ski Larra-Belagna,** km 18 of NA-1370, the highway towards France (call tourist office: ☎948 89 32 51). A village **festival,** featuring stone-throwing contests and a local variation of polo, runs July 25-28 in honor of Santiago. Isaba comes to life with dancing and general merriment on Sept. 16, in honor of San Cipriano.

Isaba's **tourist office,** C. Bormapea, 5, is located on the right as you enter town, just before the boardwalk. (☎948 89 32 51. Open *Semana Santa*-Oct. 12 M-Sa 10am-2pm and 4:30-7:30pm, Su 10am-2pm; rest of the year M-F 10am-2pm, Sa 4:30-7:30pm.) **Telephones** and **ATMs** can be found just uphill from the tourist office. Isaba doesn't provide anything luxurious in the way of lodging, but try **Hotel Isaba ❸,** C. Bormapea, 51, before the tourist office, if you're looking for something less rugged than the typical *refugio*. Restaurant below hotel serves a *menú* (€12). All rooms have full bath. (☎948 89 30 00. Singles €27.50; doubles €46. IVA not included. MC/V.) **Albergue Oxanea ❶,** C. Bormapea, 47, offers wooden bunks and a TV lounge. (☎948 89 31 53. Breakfast €2.30. Meals €7.20. Dorm €6, with sheets €7.80. Open Oct.-Dec. 15 and Apr.-June Sa-Su nights only.) **Camping Asolaze ❶,** 6km up the road toward France, offers a restaurant, store, and bunkbeds in addition to campsites. (☎948 89 30 34. Closed for Nov. Sheets €2.55. Dorm €8.11. Camping €3.75 per person, per tent, per car. MC/V.) The mountains open into the **Valle de Belagua,** 8km north of Isaba, where **Refugio Angel Olorón ❶** offers bunks year-round. The refuge is at km19 on the highway toward France. (☎/fax 948 39 40 02. Breakfast €2; meals €9.50. Dorms €7; *Federación de Montaña* and *Carnet Jovens* members €4.) Those venturing into the wilderness can hoard food for the trail at **Vendi Supermercado** on C. Mendigatxa (☎948 89 31 91). Bedraggled backpackers returning from the great green yonder should try **Restaurante Ezkaurre ❷,** located next to the Isaba parking lot. Weary hikers appreciate the down-home feel and the generous portions. (☎948 89 33 03. *Menú* €9.90, €4.50 per course for other meals. MC/V.)

PAÍS VASCO (EUSKADI)

As the Basque saying goes, "Before God was God and the rocks were rocks, the Basques were Basque." The País Vasco is officially composed of the provinces Guipuzcoa, Alava, and Vizcaya, but those who identify themselves as Basque are not restricted by boundaries. The Basque country is often thought to expand into Navarra and southwestern France. The varied landscape of the País Vasco resembles a nation complete unto itself, with cosmopolitan cities, verdant hills, industrial wastelands, and quaint fishing villages. The people are bound by their deep attachment to the land and immense cultural and national pride.

Many believe that the Basques are the native people of Iberia, as their culture and language are untraceable to any known source. Today's nationalistic sentiment stems from the 18th-century abolition of the Basque *fueros* (ancient rights of self-government), the Basques' military defeat in the late 19th-century Carlist wars, and Franco's heavy repression of Basque identity. The organization Euskadi ta Askatasuna ("Basque Country and Freedom"; ETA) began an anti-Spanish terrorist movement that has lasted over 30 years and killed over 800 people. A short-lived 1998 cease-fire between the Spanish government and ETA did little to quell the group's violence; European Union summits and tourist areas have been the

group's most recent targets, the last successful of which was a small car-bomb incident in 2002. Anti-ETA sentiment is now quite strong among País Vasco natives—posters, banners, and demonstrations denouncing the organization line streets and hang from buildings throughout the region—but many argue that the government's attempted ETA suppression/extermination undermines free speech.

Most Basques share a strong desire to preserve their cultural identity. Although Castilian Spanish is the predominant language, Basque *(euskera)* has enjoyed a resurgence of popularity since Franco's death. Other regional traditions like *cesta punta* or *pelota vasca* (known outside of Spain as *jai-alai*) continue to thrive. Basque cuisine is some of Iberia's finest, including *bacalao a la vizcaína* (salted cod in a tomato sauce) and dishes *a la vasca* (in a parsley-steeped white wine sauce). *Tapas*, considered regional specialties, are called *pintxos* (PEEN-chos); locals wash them down with *sidra* (cider) and the local white wine, *txakoli*.

SAN SEBASTIÁN (DONOSTIA) ☎943

Glittering on the shores of the Cantabrian Sea is San Sebastián (pop. 180,000). An elaborate ivory boardwalk and wide white-sand beaches give the city an air of gentility—Queen Isabel II made it her summer residence—but belie the 21st-century edge found in its boutiques, surf-shops, and nightclubs. Such international catering doesn't interfere with the city's strong sense of regional culture. Residents and posters offer constant reminders: you are not in Spain, you are in Basque Country.

In the early 19th century, San Sebastián stood as one of Spain's great ports, but much of it was destroyed during the 1813 Peninsular War. The ruined walls were finally torn down in 1863, and construction of a new city began, one whose popularity has been increasing ever since. Foreigners and land-locked Spaniards journey to San Sebastián for its world-famous beaches, bars, and scenery.

TRANSPORTATION

Flights: Airport in Hondarribia (☎943 66 85 00), 20km east of the city. **Interurbanos buses** to Hondarribia pass by the airport (45min., every 15-20min, €1.25). A **taxi** costs €25. Flights to **Madrid** (1¼hr., 3-6 per day) and **Barcelona** (1¼hr., 1-4 per day). **Iberia** (☎902 40 05 00) has an office at the airport.

Trains: San Sebastián has 2 train stations, Estación del Norte and Estación de Amara. **RENFE, Estación del Norte,** Po. Francia (☎902 24 02 02), on the east side of Puente María Cristina. Info open daily 7am-11pm. To: **Alicante** (12hr., daily 1:37pm, €45); **Barcelona** (9hr.; Su-F 10:45am, 10:59pm; €30); **Burgos** (3½hr.; 7 per day Su-F 8:32am-10:37pm, Sa 9:02am-10:37pm; €17-22); **Madrid** (8hr., Su-F 10:37pm, €19-22); **Pamplona** (2hr., daily 10:45am, €11); **Paris** (8-11hr.; Su-F 7am, 8:55pm; Sa 7am, 8:25pm; €72-80); **Salamanca** (10hr., daily 1:37pm, €26); **Vigo** (12hr., daily 9:02am, €35); **Vitoria-Gasteiz** (1¾hr.; 8-9 per day 6:57am-10:37pm, Su 8:32am-10:37pm; €7-22); **Zaragoza** (4hr., daily 10:45am, €19).

Buses: PESA, Av. Sancho el Sabio, 33 (☎902 10 12 10), to **Bilbao** (1¼hr.; every 30min. M-F 6:30am-10:30pm, Sa-Su 7:30am-10:30pm; €7.50). **Continental Auto,** Av. Sancho el Sabio, 31 (☎943 46 90 74) to: **Burgos** (3-3½hr., 7 per day 9am-12:30pm, €12); **Madrid** (6hr., 7-9 per day 7:15am-12:30am, €25); **Vitoria-Gasteiz** (2hr.; M-F 8 per day 7:15am-12:30am, Su 9 day 7:15am-12:20pm; €5.90). **La Roncalesa,** Po. Vizcaya, 16 (☎943 46 10 64) to: **Pamplona** (1hr., 9 per day 7am-10pm, €5.50). **Vibasa,** Po. Vizcaya, 16 (☎943 45 75 00) to: **Barcelona** (7hr.; 7:20am, 3:30, 11:20pm; €22.15). **Turytrans,** Po. Vizcaya, 16 (☎943 46 23 60) to: **Paris** (11hr.; Tu, Th, Sa 8pm; €53). **Interbus** (☎943 64 13 02) to: **Hondarribia** (45min., every 15min. 7:25am-11:25pm, €1.25); **Irún** (35min., every 15-30min., €1).

THE DEVIL'S TONGUE Linguists still cannot pinpoint the origin of *euskera*. Its commonalities with Caucasian and African dialects suggest that prehistoric Basques may have migrated from the Caucasus mountains through Africa. Referred to by other Spaniards as *la lengua del diablo* (the devil's tongue), *euskera* has come to symbolize cultural self-determination. Only half a million natives speak the language, chiefly in País Vasco and northern Navarra. During his regime, Franco banned *euskera* and forbade parents to give their children Basque names (like Iñaki or Estibaliz). Since his death, there has been a resurgence of everything from *euskera* TV shows to *ikastolas* (Basque schools), and the language is frequently used for street signs and menus in the País Vasco.

Public Transportation: (☎943 28 71 00). Each trip €0.80. **Bus #16** goes from Alameda del Boulevard to the campground and beaches.

Taxis: Santa Clara (☎943 36 46 46), **Vallina** (☎943 40 40 40), or **Donostia** (☎943 46 46 46). Taxis to **Pamplona** take about 45min., and cost around €78.

ORIENTATION AND PRACTICAL INFORMATION

Street and plaza signs are usually in both *castellano* and *euskera*. The street guide on the tourist office map gives both versions, so don't despair when you encounter the ubiquitous "kalea" and "tx." The **Río Urumea** splits San Sebastián. The city center, most monuments, and the two most popular beaches, **Playa de la Concha** and **Playa de Ondaretta,** line the peninsula on the west side of the river. The tip of the peninsula is called **Monte Urgull.** On the east side of the river, **Playa de la Zurriola** attracts a younger surfing and beach crowd. Inland lies the **parte vieja** (old city), San Sebastián's restaurant, nightlife, and budget accommodation nexus, where you'll find most tourists. South of the *parte vieja*, at the base of the peninsula, is the commercial district. The **bus station** is south of the city on Pl. Pío XII, while the **RENFE station, Barrio de Gros,** and **Playa de la Zurriola** are east of the city. The river is spanned by four bridges: Puentes Zurriola, Santa Catalina, María Cristina, and de Mundaiz (listed north to south). To get to the *parte vieja* from the train station, head straight to Puente María Cristina, cross the bridge, and turn right at the fountain. Continue four blocks north to Av. Libertad, then left and follow it to the port; the *parte vieja* fans out to the right, and Playa de la Concha to the left.

Tourist Office: Municipa, Centro de Atracción y Turismo, C. Reina Regente, 3 (☎943 48 11 66; fax 943 48 11 72), in front of the Puente Zurriola. From the train station, turn right immediately after crossing Puente María Cristina, and continue until reaching Puente Zurriola; the office is on the left. From the bus station, start down Av. Sancho el Sabio. At Pl. Centenario, bear right onto C. Prim and follow the river until the 3rd bridge, Puente Zurriola, look to the plaza at your left. Open June-Sept. M-Sa 8am-8pm, Su 10am-2pm; Oct.-May M-Sa 9am-1:30pm, 3:30-7pm, Su 10am-2pm.

Hiking Information: Club Vasco de Camping, San Marcial, 19 (☎/fax 943 42 84 79), 1 block south of Av. Libertad. Organizes excursions. Open M-F 6-8:30pm. **Izadi,** C. Usandizaga, 18 (☎943 29 35 20), off C. Libertad. Sells hiking guides and maps, some in English. Open M-F 10am-1pm, 4-8pm, Sa 10am-1:30pm, 4:30-8pm.

Luggage Storage: Train station (€3 per day; buy tokens at the ticket counter). Open daily 7am-11pm.

Laundromat: Lavomatique, C. Iñigo, 14 (☎943 42 38 71), off C. San Juan in the *parte vieja*. 4kg wash €3.75, 6kg wash €5.55 (cold water only), €2.70 dry. Soap €0.45. Open M-F 9:30am-2pm and 4-8pm, Sa-Su 10am-2pm.

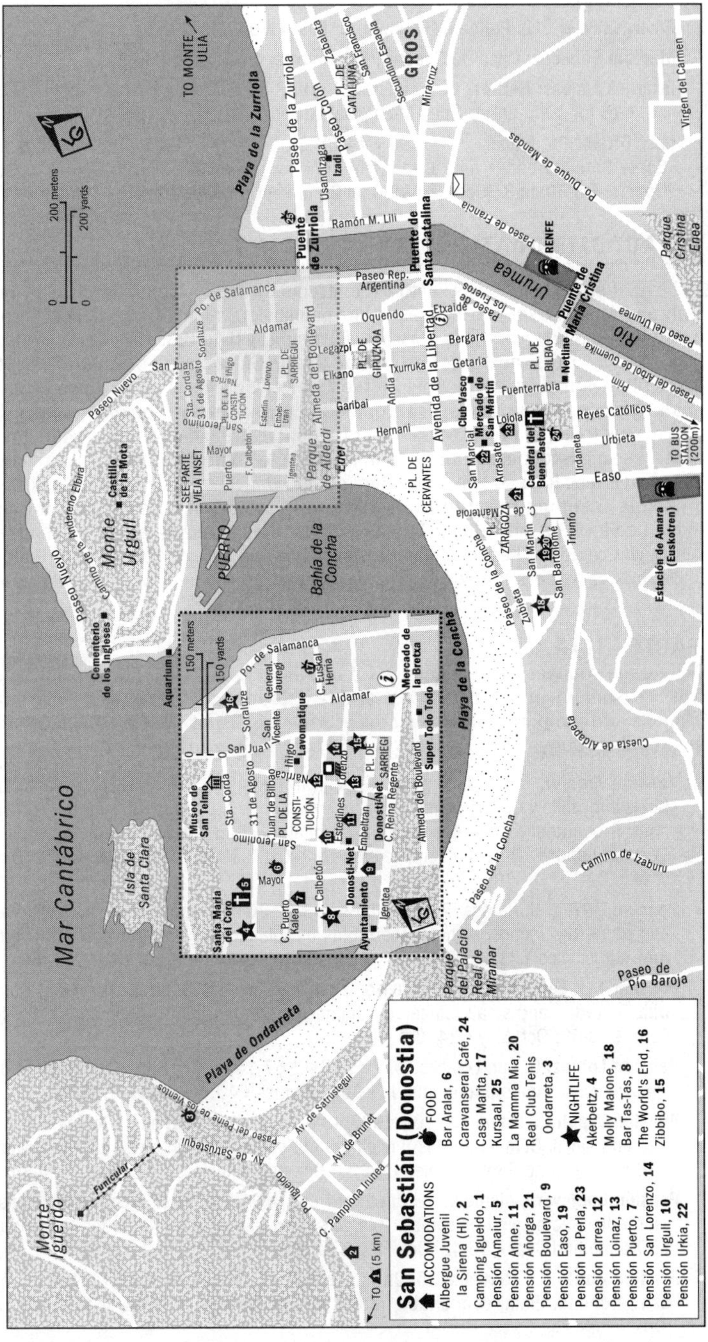
San Sebastián (Donostia)
ACCOMODATIONS
Albergue Juvenil la Sirena (HI), 2
Camping Igueldo, 1
Pensión Amaiur, 5
Pensión Anne, 11
Pensión Añorga, 21
Pensión Boulevard, 9
Pensión Easo, 19
Pensión La Perla, 23
Pensión Larrea, 12
Pensión Loinaz, 13
Pensión Puerto, 7
Pensión San Lorenzo, 14
Pensión Urgull, 10
Pensión Urkia, 22
FOOD
Bar Aralar, 6
Caravanserai Café, 24
Casa Marita, 17
Kursaal, 25
La Mamma Mia, 20
Real Club Tenis Ondarreta, 3
NIGHTLIFE
Akerbeltz, 4
Molly Malone, 18
Bar Tas-Tas, 8
The World's End, 16
Zibbibo, 15
Mar Cantábrico
Isla de Santa Clara
Monte Urgull
Castillo de la Mota
Cementerio de los Ingleses
Aquarium
Monte Igueldo
Funicular
Playa de Ondarreta
Playa de la Concha
Bahía de la Concha
Playa de la Zurriola
PUERTO
GROS
Río Urumea
RENFE
Estación de Amara (Euskotren)
TO BUS STATION (200m)
TO MONTE ULIA
SEE PARTE VIEJA INSET
Museo de San Telmo
Santa María del Coro
Ayuntamiento
Mercado de la Bretxa
Super Todo Todo
Lavomatique
Donosti-Net
Catedral del Buen Pastor
Mercado de San Martín
Club Vasco
Netline
Izadi
Puente de Zurriola
Puente de Santa Catalina
Puente de María Cristina
Avenida de la Libertad
Parque Alameda del Boulevard
Parque del Palacio Real de Miramar
Paseo de la Concha
Paseo Nuevo
Paseo de la Zurriola
PL. DE GIPUZKOA
PL. DE CERVANTES
PL. DE BILBAO
PL. ZARAGOZA
PL. DE CATALUÑA
PL. DE LA CONSTITUCIÓN
PL. DE SARRIEGI
200 meters
200 yards
150 meters
150 yards

Emergency: ☎112. **Police: Municipal,** C. Easo (☎943 45 00 00).

Medical Services: Casa de Socorro, Bengoetxea, 4 (☎943 44 06 33).

Internet Access: Netline, C. Urdaneta, 8 (☎943 44 50 76). €1.80 per 30min., €3 per hr., €18 for 10hr. ticket. Open M-Sa 10am-10pm.

Post Office: Po. Francia, 13 (☎943 44 68 26), near the RENFE station, just over the Santa Catalina bridge and to the right; look for the yellow trim on left side of street. Open M-F 8:30am-8:30pm, Sa 9:30am-2pm. **Postal Code:** 20006.

ACCOMMODATIONS AND CAMPING

A bevy of small *pensiones* scatter the streets throughout the *parte vieja*, but in July and August *"completo"* signs—the Spanish equivalent of "no vacancy"—begin to appear in many *pensión* doorways. Particularly tight times are during *San Fermines* (July 6-14) and *Semana Grande* (starts Su the week of Aug. 15); September's film festival (starts just before the last week of Sept.) is not much better. To make matters worse, many *pensiónes* don't take reservations in summer. Solo travelers should be prepared to pay for a double if unable to find a willing roommate, as single rooms are virtually impossible to come by. Late-night arrivals will have even less luck. Adept bargainers should put their skills to work as often as possible, keeping in mind that hostel owners often take pity on the more wretched-looking individuals. You haven't truly mastered the art of haggling if you think you're above begging. The tourist office has lists of accommodations, and most hostel owners know of *casas particulares*. Owners of these *casas* often solicit guests at the RENFE station—be wary, this is illegal.

PARTE VIEJA

Where the younger backpackers go for a night's rest, the *parte vieja* is brimming with reasonably-priced *pensiones* and restaurants. Its proximity to Playa de la Concha and the port makes this area a prime nightspot; scores of places offer a night's sleep above loud *pintxos (tapas)* bars. Call in advance for reservations.

Pensión Amaiur, C. 31 de Agosto, 44, 2nd fl. (☎943 42 96 54). From Alameda del Boulevard, follow C. San Jerónimo to its end, turn left, and look for the low, obscured front. 9 beautiful rooms, each with a personal touch. 5 common baths. July-Aug. and *Semana Santa* €24 per person. May-June and Oct. €18. Sept. and Nov.-Apr. €13. MC/V. ❷

Pensión Larrea, C. Narrica, 21, 2nd fl. (☎943 42 26 94). Spend some time with *mamá* and *papá,* the friendly owners. The rooms are plain, but comfortable and welcoming. July-Aug. singles €21; doubles €34; triples €45. Sept.-June €18/€30/€45. ❷

Pensión San Lorenzo, C. San Lorenzo, 2 (☎943 42 55 16), off C. San Juan. Doubles with TV, radio, and small refrigerator. Immaculate baths. July-Aug. doubles €45. June, Sept. €30-42. Oct.-May €24. ❷

Pensión Loinaz, C. San Lorenzo, 17 (☎943 42 67 14), off C. San Juan. English-speaking owners. Common bathrooms. July-Aug. doubles €40. Sept.-June €25. ❷

Pensión Urgull, C. Esterlines, 10 (☎943 43 00 47), on the 3rd floor. Rooms with balconies and sinks. Common baths. Prices are not set, so bargain away. July-Aug. doubles €36-42. June and Sept. doubles €24-27. Oct.-May singles €15; doubles €24-30. ❷

Pensión Boulevard, Alameda del Boulevard, 24 (☎943 42 94 05). Spacious rooms, all with radios, some with balconies. 2 large shared baths for 8 rooms. July-Aug. doubles €50. June and Sept €36-42. Oct.-May €30. ❸

Pensión Anne, C. Esterlines, 15, 2nd fl. (☎943 42 14 38), between C. Narrica and C. San Jerónimo. Plain, comfortable rooms in a convenient location. 4 to a bathroom;

€12 extra for a bath inside the room. 10% discount with *Let's Go*. July-Aug. singles €36; doubles €45; triples €60. Sept.-June €18/€24/€34. ❹

Pensión Puerto, C. Puerto, 19, 2nd fl. (☎943 43 21 40), off C. Mayor. Spotless rooms with comfy beds. July-Aug. €30 per person. June and Sept. €20-22. Oct.-May €18. ❸

OUTSIDE THE PARTE VIEJA

Most of these places tend to be quieter than those elsewhere yet are still close to the port, beach, bus and train stations, and no more than 5min. from the old city. This area is also home to the city's most elegant boulevards and buildings.

Pensión La Perla, C. Loiola, 10, 2nd fl. (☎943 42 81 23), on the street directly ahead of the cathedral. English spoken. Private baths and TVs. July-Sept. singles €30; doubles €46. Oct.-June €24/€32. ❸

Pensión Easo, C. San Bartolomé, 24 (☎943 45 39 12). Head toward the beach on C. San Martín, turn left on C. Easo, and right on C. San Bartolomé. Huge windows and mirrored rooms. July-Sept. 15 singles €32.45, with bath €48; doubles €40.90, with bath €60. June and Sept. €27/€40/€33/€45. Oct.-May €25/€33/€30/€40. MC/V. ❸

Pensión Urkia, C. Urbieta, 12, 3rd fl. (☎943 42 44 36), on C. Urbieta between C. Marcial and C. Arrasate and borders the Mercado de San Martín. Rooms with full bath and TV. July-Sept. singles €30; doubles €39; triples €54. Oct.-June €24/€30/€40. ❸

Pensión Añorga, C. Easo, 12 (☎943 46 79 45), at C. San Martín. Shares entryway with 2 other *pensiones.* Spacious rooms have shiny wood floors and comfy beds. July-Aug. singles €25; doubles €32, with bath €43. Sept.-June €19/€25/€32. ❷

Albergue Juvenil la Sirena (HI), Po. Igueldo, 25 (☎943 31 02 68; fax 943 21 40 90), a light-pink building 3min. from the beach at the west end of the city. Buses #24 and 27 run from the train/bus stations to Av. Zumalacárregui (in front of the San Sebastián Hotel). From Av. Zumalacárregui, take Av. Brunet and turn left at its end. Clean rooms, multilingual staff. HI members and ISIC-carriers only. Laundry. Kitchen available 8am-10pm. Breakfast included. Sheets €2.53. Curfew Sept.-May Su-Th midnight, F-Sa 2am. July-Aug. €12.95, over 25 €14.61 (3-night max. stay if full). May 6-Jun. 7 and Apr. 8-31 €11.77/€13.80. Rest of year €10.70/€12.95. MC/V. ❶

Camping Igueldo (☎943 21 45 02), 5km west of town. The 268 spots fill quickly. Beautiful views of the ocean make the drive worth it. Bus #16 ("Barrio de Igueldo-Camping") runs between the site and Alameda del Boulevard (every 30min., €0.80). *Parcelas* June-Aug. and *Semana Santa* €11, extra person €3.20. Sept.-May €9/€3. MC/V. ❶

FOOD

Pintxos (tapas), chased down with the fizzy regional white wine, *txakoli,* are a religion here; bars in the old city spread an array of enticing tidbits on toothpicks or bread. In the harbor, many places serve tangy sardines with slightly bitter *sidra* (cider). Custom demands pouring it with arm extended to aerate the *sidra* and release its full flavor. It is also customary to pour just enough for one or two sips at a time. Restaurants and bars clamor for attention on C. Fermín Calbetón, in the old quarter. The underground shopping center located between Alameda del Boulevard and C. San Juan houses the clean and modern **Mercado de la Bretxa** selling everything from fruits and vegetables to *pintxos* (open M-Sa 9am-9pm, though most vendors take lunch from 3-5pm). The local market, **Mercado de San Martín,** on C. San Marcial between C. Loiola and C. Urbieta, sells fresh local meats, fish, and produce (open M-F 7:30am-2pm and 5-7:30pm, Sa 7:30am-2pm). For **groceries,** stop by **Super Todo Todo,** Alameda del Boulevard, 3, across the street from the Mercado de la Bretxa. (☎943 42 82 59. Open M-Sa 8:30am-9pm, Su 10am-2pm. MC/V.)

PARTE VIEJA

Kursaal, Po. Zurriola, 1 (☎943 00 31 62), in an ultra-modern building across the river from the Old City. Treat yourself to an elegant lunch on their breezy patio. The chef is a legend among locals. *Menú* M-F 1-3:30pm €10.50, Sa-Su €14, plus IVA. MC/V. ❷

Casa Marita, C. Euskal Herria (☎943 43 04 43), off Po. Salamanca. The talented kitchen staff uses only fresh, natural ingredients. Try the homemade lasagna (€7.50) or smoked salmon (€7). *Menú* €15. Open daily 8-11pm, except W. MC/V. ❷

Bar Aralar, C. Puerto Kalea (☎943 42 63 78). Fresh, tasty *pintxos* (€1.50) and sandwiches (€1-2). An excellent place to try local cuisine. Open Su-Th 11am-midnight, F-Sa 11am-2:30am. Closed 3 weeks in Nov. and May. MC/V. ❶

La Cueva, Pl. Trinidad (☎943 42 54 37), off 31 de Agosto. A cavernous restaurant serving traditional seafood cuisine prepared by an all-female staff. M-F *Menú* €15. Grilled tuna, cod, and squid entrees €6-12. Open Tu-Su 1-3:30pm and 7:30-11pm. MC/V. ❸

PARTE NUEVA

Real Club de Tenis Ondarreta, Po. Peine de los Vientos (☎943 31 11 50 or 943 31 41 18), on along Playa de Ondarreta. Escape the crowded *parte vieja to* mingle with San Sebastián's preppies. *Menú* M-Sa €9.35, Su €15. Entrees €10-15. Open M-Sa 1-3:30pm and 9-11pm, Su 1-3:30pm. Call ahead for reservations. AmEx/MC/V. ❸

La Mamma Mia, C. San Bartolomé, 18 (☎943 46 52 93). Freshly-made pastas (€5.75-6.50). M-F luncheon *menú* €7. Open daily 1:30-4pm and 8:30pm-12:30am. MC/V. ❷

Caravanserai Café, C. San Bartolomé, 1 (☎943 47 54 18), along the right side of the cathedral when facing its front doors. Chic and artsy, without the pretentious prices. Fabulous vegetarian options. Entrees €5-7. Open M-Th 8am-midnight, F-Sa 8am-1am, Su 10:30am-midnight. MC/V. ❷

SIGHTS

San Sebastián's best sight is the city itself—parks, grandiose buildings, and attractive hillsides crowd San Sebastián's bay and the pleasant island of Santa Clara.

MONTE IGUELDO. Though the views from both of San Sebastián's mountains are spectacular, those from Monte Igueldo are superior. By day, the countryside meets the ocean in a line of white and blue; by night, Isla Santa Clara seems to float in a halo of light. The sidewalk toward the mountain ends just before the base of Monte Igueldo with Eduardo Chillida's sculpture *El Peine de los Vientos* (Wind's Comb). The walk up is not strenuous, but the funicular is great on warmer afternoons. A small amusement park at the top has bumper cars, water rides, and trampolines, but the magnificent view is the real entertainment. *(☎943 21 02 11. Open daily June-Sept. 10am-9pm; Oct.-Feb. Sa noon-6pm, Su 11am-7pm; Mar.-June Sa 11am-8pm, Su 11am-9pm. Funicular runs every 15min.; €0.80 1-way, €1.50 round-trip.)*

MONTE URGULL. Across the bay from Monte Igueldo, the gravel paths on Monte Urgull wind through shady woods, monuments, and stunning vistas. The overgrown **Castillo de Santa Cruz de la Mota** tops the summit with 12 cannons, a chapel, and the statue of the *Sagrado Corazón de Jesús* blessing the city. *(4 pathways lead up to the summit from Po. Nuevo; a convenient one is located next to the Museo de San Telmo. Castillo open daily May-Sept. 8am-8pm; Oct.-Apr. 8am-6pm. Free.)*

PASAJES DE SAN JUAN. Thirty minutes from the town center lies the town of Pasajes de San Juan, overlooking a bay filled with colorful *chalupas* boats. The charming fishing village's wood-balconied homes create an enchanting time warp. The house where Victor Hugo once lived is to the right when exiting the ferry. *(The H-1 Herribus runs from Pl. Gipúzkoa to Pasajes de San Juan every 20-30min. for €0.85.)*

BASQUE-ET BALL The Basque sport known as *cesta punta,* or *jai alai,* is the world's fastest ball game. In this unique form of handball, burly players fling balls at a walled court (called a *frontón*) at speeds up to 200km per hour. The traditional game is played with bare hands, but the faster version incorporates *txisteras,* hand-held baskets of sorts. Local teams often play in public *frontones;* watch for the trademark white uniforms with red or blue sashes. Spreading beyond its homeland, *jai alai* now exists in more than 20 variants, 14 of them at the world championship level. The sport has even caught on in such far-flung places as Cancún, Cuba, and Connecticut, but sorry ladies: so far only men have played.

MUSEO DE SAN TELMO. The Museo de San Telmo resides in a Dominican monastery. The serene, overgrown cloister is strewn with Basque funerary relics, and the main museum beyond the cloister displays a fascinating array of pre-historic Basque artifacts, a few dinosaur skeletons, and a piece of contemporary art. *(Po. Nuevo. ☎943 42 49 70. Open Tu-Sa 10:30am-8:30pm, Su 10:30am-2pm. Free.)*

PALACES. When Queen Isabel II started vacationing here in the mid-19th century, fancy buildings sprang up like wildflowers. **El Palacio de Mirama** has passed through the hands of the Spanish court, Napoleon III, and Bismarck; it now serves as the País Vasco University, but anyone can stroll through the grounds and contemplate the views of the bay. *(Between Playa de la Concha and Playa de Ondarreta. Open daily June-Aug. 9am-9pm; Sept.-May 10am-5pm. Free.)* The other royal residence, **Palacio de Ayete,** is also closed to the public, but surrounding trails aren't. *(Head up Cuesta de Aldapeta or take Bus #19. Grounds open June-Aug. 10am-8:30pm; Sept.-May 10am-5pm. Free.)*

AQUARIUM. On rainy days, the aquarium, one of Europe's most modern, is worth a visit. *(Arrows point the way from the port; its huge sign can be seen from the far end of the beach. Open summer daily 10am-10pm; rest of the year 10am-8pm. Adults €6, children €4.)*

BEACHES AND WATER SPORTS

The gorgeous **Playa de la Concha** curves from the port to the **Pico del Loro,** the promontory home to the Palacio de Miramar. The virtually flat beach disappears during high tide. Sunbathing crowds jam onto the smaller and steeper **Playa de Ondarreta,** beyond Miramar, and surfers flock to **Playa de la Zurrida,** across the river from Mt. Urguel. Picnickers head for the alluring **Isla de Santa Clara** in the center of the bay, either by rented rowboat or public motorboat ferry (5min., June-Sept. every 30min., round-trip €1.95). Check at the portside kiosk for more info.

Several sports-related groups offer a variety of activities and lessons. For **windsurfing** and **kayaking,** call the Real Club Náutico, C. Igentea, 9, located on the water and shaped like a small cruise ship. (☎943 42 35 75. Open 10am-1pm and 4-6:30pm. Day courses €30-48.) For **parachuting,** try Urruti Sport, C. José María Soroa, 20 (☎943 27 81 96). **Surfers** can check out the Pukas Surf Club, C. Mayor, 5, for info on lessons and a large variety of gear. (☎943 42 72 28. Open M-Sa 10am-1:30pm and 4-8:30pm. AmEx/MC/V.) For general information on all sports, pick up a copy of the *UDA-Actividades Deportivas* brochure at the tourist office.

NIGHTLIFE

The *parte vieja* pulls out all the stops in July and August, particularly on C. Fermín Calbetón, three blocks in from Alameda del Boulevard. During the year, when students outnumber backpackers, nightlife tends to move beyond the *parte vieja.* Keep an eye out for discount coupons on the street.

The World's End, Po. de Salamanca, 14 (☎/fax 943 42 09 63), 1 block outside of the *parte vieja* in the direction of the beach. Rapidly becoming a fixture on the backpacker circuit. Great pub ambiance, frequent live music, and tasty snacks (€3-4.25). Open Su-Th 2pm-2:30am, F-Sa 2pm-3:30am. Closed M.

Zibbibo, Pl. Sarriegi, 8 (☎943 425 334). The usual stop en route from World's End to Tas-Tas. Plays a blend of top 40 and techno tunes. Popular *"grande"* sangría €4.50. Happy Hour Su-Th 10:30-11:30pm. Open daily 2pm-4am. MC/V.

Bar Tas-Tas, C. Fermín Calbetón, 35 (☎943 43 06 12). A notorious hotspot for international beach-goers, particularly surfers. Drink to American pop hits during Happy Hour (Su-Th 8-11:30pm). Assorted music ranging from salsa to disco. "Big" sangria €8.50. Open daily June-Sept. 3pm-4am; Oct.-May 3pm-3am. AmEx/MC/V.

Akerbeltz, C. Koruko Andra Mari, 10. Face the Iglesia de Santa María on the C. 31 de Agosto, take a left and go up the stairs; it's in the corner at the road's end, just before the port. A tiny, sleek, cavernous bar. Open M-Th 3pm-2:30am; F-Sa 3pm-3:30am.

Molly Malone, C. San Martín, 55 (☎943 46 98 22), right off the Po. de la Concha, outside of the *parte vieja*. An Irish pub with impressive brew selections and a mellow upstairs loft. Beer €1.50-4.50. Open June-Aug. Su-Th 8pm-3am.

NEAR SAN SEBASTIÁN

HONDARRIBIA ☎943

Less than 1hr. east of San Sebastián by bus, Hondarribia (pop. 15,000) is a charming miniature of its popular neighbor. Stretching along the Txingudi Bay, the suburbanized beach town boasts old wharfs, new shops, and carefully-landscaped parks along a golden sand beach. Compared to chic San Sebastián, Hondarribia is refreshingly small and simple, but not old-fashioned. In the peak days of summer, the beach can become ridiculously crowded with vacationers from Madrid and Barcelona, but it's usually pleasantly calm through June.

PRACTICAL INFORMATION. Interurbanos buses (☎943 64 13 02) to **San Sebastián's** Pl. Guipuzcoa stop in front of the post office; pay on-board (45min.; every 20min. M-Sa 7:30am-10:35pm, Su 7:45am-9:45pm; €2). **AUIF buses** (☎943 63 31 45) go to **Irún** (10min., 10am-8pm, €0.75). The **airport,** C. Gabarrari Kalea (☎902 40 05 00), is within walking distance of the town center. The **tourist office, Bidasoa Turismo,** C. Javier Ugarte, 6, is right off Pl. San Cristóbal; from the bus stop walk around to the other side of the building. English is spoken. (☎943 64 54 58. Open July-Sept. M-Sa 10am-2pm and 3-8pm. Oct.-June M-F 9am-1:30pm and 4-6:30pm, Sa 10am-2pm). Local services include: **emergency** ☎112; **police,** C. Mayor, 10 (☎943 64 43 00). **Internet** access at Itsasargi Kalea, 2. (☎943 94 54 35. €2 per 30min., €3 per hr. Open M-F 10am-1pm and 8-9pm.) **Post office,** Pl. San Cristóbal, 1. (☎943 64 12 04. Open M-F 8:30am-2:30pm and Sa 9:30am-1pm.) **Postal code:** 20280.

ACCOMMODATIONS. Reservations are a good idea in the summer. **Casa Hostal Txoko Goxoa ❷,** C. Murrua, 22, lies in the other direction from Pl. San Cristóbal. From the tourist office, head up C. Javier Ugarte, take the second right onto C. Juan Laborda, and follow the street uphill until it ends at the city's old walls. Take a right; the hostel is half a block on your left. The friendly English-speaking owner will greet you. (☎/fax 943 64 46 58. Private baths. Breakfast €3.20. July-Sept. doubles €43.33. Oct.-June €24.50/€38.50. MC/V.) **Hostal Alvarez Quintero ❸,** C. Bernat Etxepare, 2, is on a small driveway across from the post office. Convenient rooms with large private baths. Tennis courts and swimming pool. (☎943 64 22 99. Breakfast €4.10. July-Sept. singles €32; doubles €41. Oct.-June €26/€34.

Reception closed midnight-8am. MC/V.) **Albergue Juan Sebastián Elcano (HI) ❶**, Ctra. Faro, sits on a hillside overlooking the beach and mountains. From the last bus stop, head to the beach on C. Itsasargi, bearing left at the coast, and continue straight for several long blocks. At the traffic circle, turn left and follow signs up the steep hill. The hostel has a TV room and tennis and basketball courts. (☎943 64 15 50; fax 943 64 00 28. Breakfast included. 3-night max. stay when full. Reception daily 9am-noon and 4-8pm. Sometimes closed in Dec. and Jan. so call ahead. Curfew midnight, but doors open at 1 and 2am. Members only; HI cards €6-10. Sheets €1. Dorms €8.40, over 30 €13. MC/V.) **Camping Jaizkibel ❶** is 2km from town on Ctra. Guadelupe toward Monte Jaizkibel and can only be reached by car or foot. Campground has hot water showers, cafeteria, restaurant, and self-service laundry. Bungalows come with full bath and kitchenette. (☎943 64 16 79; fax 943 64 26 53. Reception daily 9am-10pm. €3.70 per person, per tent, and per car. Bungalows for 1-2 people €45-60, for 3-4 €60-78. Open year-round.)

FOOD. Several **markets** spill onto C. San Pedro, 3 blocks inland from the port. Stock up at **Charter,** C. Santiago 19. (☎943 64 15 40. Open M-F 8:30am-1:30pm and 5-7:30pm, Sa 8:30am-1:30pm. Sept. 16-June M-F open until 7:30pm. MC/V.) The lunch *menú* (M-F €6) at **Kantabriko ❸,** Bernat Etxepare, 4, has a great selection of shrimp and squid for €8-20. (☎943 64 52 57. Open M-Sa 1-3:30pm and 8-10:30pm.)

SIGHTS AND EXCURSIONS. The gorgeous stone-and-timber **casco antiguo,** centered around Carlos V's imposing palace in Pl. Armas (now a *parador nacional*—peek inside to catch a glimpse of the luxury hotel), provides a welcome relief from Coppertone fumes. The **Parroquia de Nuestra Señora de la Asunción,** also in Pl. Armas, is a lovely 15th-century church where Louis XIV of France married, by proxy, the Spanish Habsburg María Teresa. (Open only for Mass daily at 7pm and tours; check at the front desk. €3.) There are several possible excursions from Hondarribia. **Monte Jaizkibel,** 6km up Av. Monte Jaizkibel, guards the **Santuario de Guadalupe.** Hiking the mountain—the highest on the Costa Cantábrica—affords incredible views of the coast; on a clear day you can see as far as Bayonne, France. **Jolaski Boats** (☎943 61 64 47) shuttle travelers 5km to **Hendaye,** a French town with a bigger beach. The boats leave from the pier at the end of C. Domingo Egia, off La Marina (every 15min.; €1.40).

IRÚN ☎943

Irún (pop 50,000) is far from pleasant. Visitors are usually in a hurry to get somewhere else—the city is little more than a dirty, crowded transportation hub. **RENFE trains,** C. Estación (☎902 24 02 02), run through Spain and to the French border, connecting frequently to **San Sebastián** (25min., every 30min. 6:53am-11:23pm, €1). The station has **currency exchange** and **luggage lockers** (€3; open daily 7am-11:15pm). The **Ayuntamiento (SAC office),** C. Juan de la Cruz, 2, on Pl. Zabaltza off Po. Colón, serves as the tourist office. (☎943 64 92 00. Open M-F 8:30am-2pm and 4:30-7:30pm, Sa 9:30am-1pm. Closed afternoons in Aug.) Local services include: **emergency** ☎112; **police,** in Pl. Ensanche (☎092); **Internet** at **Tulocutorio.es,** C. Estación, 8. (€1 per 15min., €3 per hr. Open daily 10am-10pm.)

If you're forced to spend a night in Irún, affordable hostels line C. Estación in front of the station. A popular option is **Hostal Residencia Lizaso ❶,** C. Aduana, 5. Follow C. Estación, bear right on Po. Colón, and take the first right. All rooms have TV. (☎943 61 16 00. Doubles €28.10, with shower €34.70, with bath €37-39.) **Pensión Bidasoa ❷,** C. Estación, 14, on the left from the train station, just past the church. Rooms share common baths, and some have balconies. (☎943 61 99 13. July-Aug. singles €20, with bath €25; doubles €25, with bath €35. Sept.-June €12/

€18/€18/€24. MC/V.) **Yong Feng ❷,** C. Fermín Calbeton, 3, across Pl. San Juan from the Ayuntamiento, serves savory Chinese noodles, shrimp, and duck. This restaurant is a nice alternative to the crowded, dirtier spots near the train station. *Menú* €6.50. (☎943 62 87 94. Open daily noon-4pm and 8pm-midnight.)

BILBAO (BILBO) ☎944

Bilbao (pop. 370,000) is a city transformed; thanks to the past decade's efforts, it has made a technological, cultural, and aesthetic turnaround. The economic engine of the Basque country and major shipbuilding center since the 1700s, Bilbao, known affectionately as "Botxo" to its Basque inhabitants, was an important trade link between Castile and Flanders. But what was once all industry—bourgeois, business-minded, and ugly—is now new, avant-garde, and futuristic. Careful investment and 20th-century success showered the city with wide boulevards lined by grandiose buildings, a gleaming new subway system, an overhauled international airport, a stunning new bridge, and a stylish riverwalk, all designed by renowned international architects. But it is the shining Guggenheim Museum that has most powerfully fueled Bilbao's rise to international prominence.

TRANSPORTATION

Flights: Airport (☎944 86 93 00), 8km from Bilbao. To reach the airport take the **Bizkai Bus** (☎944 48 40 80) marked **Aeropuerto** from P. Moyua, in front of the Hacienda building (20min., M-F every 30 min. 6:30am-9pm, €0.95; Sa-Su every hr. 7am-9pm, €1). Buses return from the airport to Pl. Moyua (M-F every 30min. 6:45am-10:45pm, Sa-Su every hr. 6:30am-10:30pm). **Taxis** about €17. **Iberia,** C. Ercilla, 20 (info ☎902 40 05 00). Open daily M-F 9:15am-1:30pm and 3-6pm, Sa 9:15am-1:30pm.

Trains: Bilbao has 3 train stations.

RENFE: Estación de Abando del Norte, Pl. Circular, 2 (☎944 23 86 23). Info open 7am-9pm. To: **Barcelona** (8¾-10½hr.; Su-F 10:05am, 10:45pm; €30.66-32.16); **Madrid** (5½-8½hr.; Su-F 4:30, 11:05pm; Sa 9:50am; €28.16-35.66); **Salamanca** (5½hr., 2:05pm, €23.16).

FEVE: Estación de Santander, C. Bailén, 2 (☎944 25 06 33). From Pl. Circular, walk down C. Navarra toward the river and take a right before the bridge; it's the gilded building on the water. Info open M-F Jun.-Sept. 15 9am-2pm and 4-7pm; Sept. 16-May 7am-10pm. To **Santander** (2½hr.; 9:35am, 1:35, 6:35pm; €5.90).

Ferrocarriles Vascongados/Eusko Trenbideak (FV/ET): Atxuri Station, Cl. Atxuri, 8 (☎902 54 32 10). Follow the river south from Pl. Arriaga. Trains to **San Sebastián** via **Guernica.** Currently closed for renovation; expected to reopen in late 2002.

Buses: The following companies are based at the **Termibús terminal,** C. Gurtubay, 1 (☎944 39 52 05; M: San Mamés), on the west side of town. The station's **information booth** (☎944 39 50 77) is open M-F 7am-10pm, Sa-Su 8am-9pm. To get to Pl. Arriaga from the Termibús station, take the Metro to Casco Viejo, exiting at Pl. Unamuno. Take a right on C. Sombrería and the 1st right onto C. Correo. A bus to **Guernica** leaves daily from **Estación de Abando del Norte** (45min.; M-F every 15min. 6:15am-10pm, Sa every 30min. 6:30am-10:30pm, Su every 30min. 7:30am-10:30pm; €2-2.05).

Continental Auto: (☎944 27 42 00). To **Burgos** (2hr.; 7-10 per day M-Sa 6:30am-10:30pm, Su 8:30am-10:30pm; €9.62) and **Madrid** (4-5hr.; M-F 10-18 per day 7am-1:30am, Su 8am-1:30am; €21.75).

PESA: ☎902 10 12 10. To **San Sebastián** (1¼hr.; M-F every hr. 6:30am-10:30pm; Sa-Su every hr. 7:30am-8pm, every 30min. 8-10:30pm, except no 2pm departure on Sa; €7.45).

La Unión: ☎944 27 11 11. To: **Haro** (1hr., 3-5 per day 8:30am-7:30pm, €7); **Logroño** (1¾hr., 3-5 per day 8:30am-7:30pm, €9.85); **Pamplona** (2hr.; July-Aug. 4-6 per day M-Sa 7:30am-8:30pm, Su 11am-8pm; Sept.-June M-Th and Sa 7:30am-7pm, F 7:30am-8pm, Su 11am-8pm; €10.55); **Vitoria-Gasteiz** (1hr.; 11-22 per day M-F 6:35-10pm, Sa 7:30am-10pm, Su 8:30am-9:30pm; €4.50).

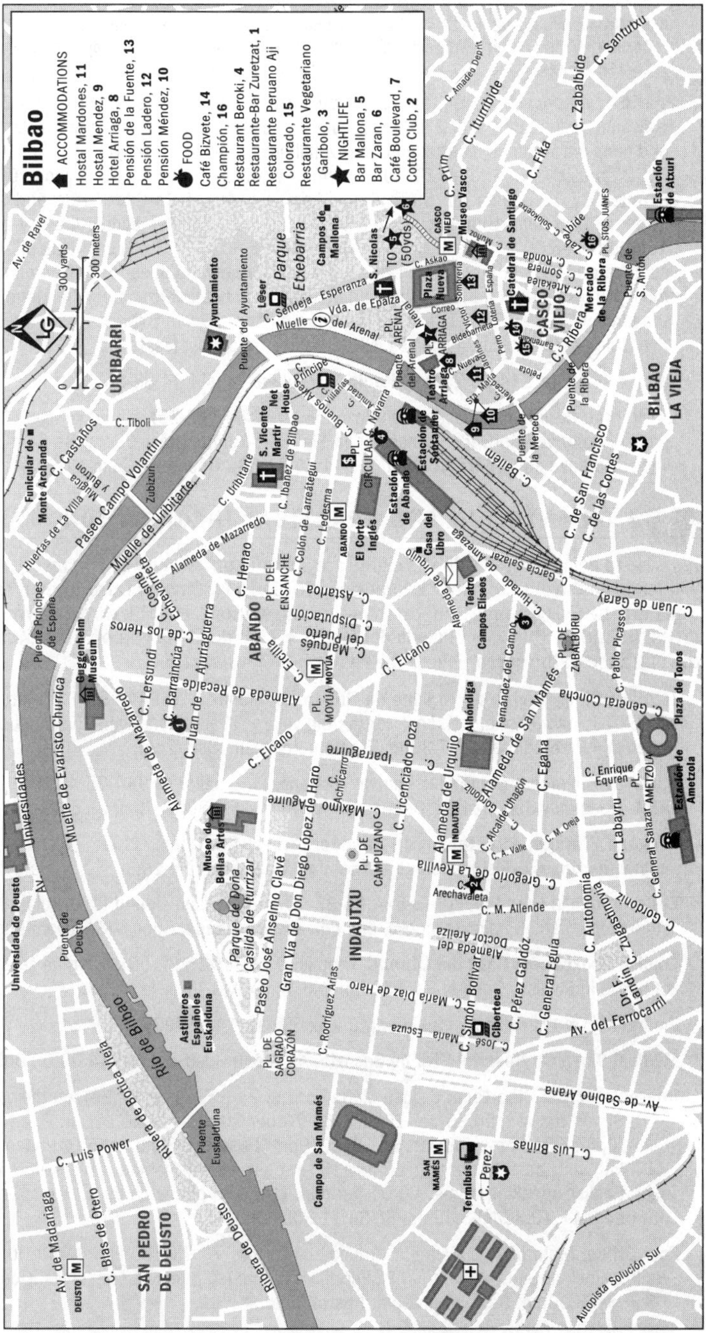

Bilbao
ACCOMMODATIONS
Hostal Mardones, 11
Hostal Mendez, 9
Hotel Arriaga, 8
Pensión de la Fuente, 13
Pensión Ladero, 12
Pensión Méndez, 10
FOOD
Café Bizvete, 14
Champión, 16
Restaurant Beroki, 4
Restaurante-Bar Zuretzat, 1
Restaurante Peruano Aji Colorado, 15
Restaurante Vegetariano Garibolo, 3
NIGHTLIFE
Bar Mallona, 5
Bar Zaran, 6
Café Boulevard, 7
Cotton Club, 2
0 300 yards
0 300 meters
URIBARRI
Ayuntamiento
Parque Etxebarria
Campos de Mallona
TO 5 (50yds)
CASCO VIEJO
Museo Vasco
Catedral de Santiago
Plaza Nueva
Mercado de la Ribera
Estación de Atxuri
BILBAO LA VIEJA
Puente de S. Antón
Puente de la Ribera
Puente de la Merced
Estación de Santander
Estación de Abando
Teatro Arriaga
S. Vicente Martir
Net House
L@ser
Funicular de Monte Archanda
Paseo Campo Volantín
Muelle de Uribitarte
Alameda de Mazarredo
ABANDO
El Corte Inglés
Casa del Libro
Teatro Campos Elíseos
Guggenheim Museum
Puente Príncipes de España
Muelle de Evaristo Churrica
Alameda de Recalde
PL. MOYÚA
Alhóndiga
Alameda de Urquijo
Alameda de San Mamés
PL. DE ZABALBURU
Plaza de Toros
Estación de Ametzola
Museo de Bellas Artes
Parque de Doña Casilda de Iturrizar
Gran Vía de Don Diego López de Haro
INDAUTXU
PL. DE CAMPUZANO
Universidad de Deusto
Puente de Deusto
Río de Bilbao
Astilleros Españoles Euskalduna
Puente Euskalduna
PL. DE SAGRADO CORAZÓN
Ciberteca
Campo de San Mamés
Termibús
Av. de Sabino Arana
Av. del Ferrocarril
Autopista Solución Sur
SAN PEDRO DE DEUSTO
Ribera de Deusto
Ribera de Botica Vieja
C. Luis Power
C. Blas de Otero
Av. de Madariaga

ALSA Grupo: info ☎902 42 22 42. To: **Barcelona** (7¼hr.; 4 per day 6:30am-11pm; €33.60); **La Coruña** (5½hr.; 10am, 1:45am; €37.57); **Santander** (1¼hr., 13 per day 6:30am-11pm, €5.41); **Zaragoza** (4hr.; 4-10 per day M-F 6:30am-8:15pm, Su 6:30am-9pm; €16.24).

Public Transportation: Bilbao sports an ultra-modern **Metro** (☎944 25 40 25; www.metrobilbao.net) with 2 lines. Look for 3 interlocking red circles to find entrances, and hang onto your ticket after entering—you'll need it again to exit. Travel within 1 zone €1, 2 zones €1.10, 3 zones €1.20. 10-trip ticket within 1 zone €5.50, 2 zones €6.50, 3 zones €7.50. Trains run Su-Th 6am-11pm, July-Aug. F-Sa 6am-11pm and every 20min. 11pm-6am. **Bilbobús** (☎944 48 40 80) runs 23 lines across the city (6am-11:30pm; M-F €0.81, Sa-Su €0.90). **Bizkai Bus** (☎902 22 22 65) connects Bilbao to suburbs and the airport. You can buy a pre-paid **Creditrans pass** for any amount you think you'll spend on transport that can be used in Bilbobús, Bizkaibus, the Metro, and the funicular. 20% off rides that are less than an hour (except Bilbobús) with the card. Available at Metro ticket machines, ONCE booths, and most kiosks.

Taxis: Teletaxi (☎944 10 21 21). **Radio Taxi Bilbao** (☎944 44 88 88).

Car Rental: Europcar, C. Licenciado Poza, 56 (☎944 42 22 26). Minimum age 21 with passport and valid driver's license. Open M-F 8am-1pm and 4-7:30pm, Sa 9am-1pm. They also have an **airport location** (☎944 71 01 33). Open daily 7am-11:30pm.

ORIENTATION AND PRACTICAL INFORMATION

It's wise to get a map, as Bilbao's sights are spread out. The city's main artery, **Gran Vía,** leads east from the oval Pl. Federico Moyúa to **Pl. Circular** (also known as Pl. España), the axis for many important stops and stations. Past Pl. Circular, you will cross the Río de Bilbao on **Puente del Arenal,** which deposits you on **Pl. de Arriaga,** the entrance to the **casco viejo** to the right of the tourist office.

Tourist Office: Oficina de Turismo de Bilbao, Pl. Arenal, 1 (☎944 79 57 60; fax 944 79 57 61; www.bilbao.net). Look for the big yellow "i" along the river. English spoken. Open M-F 9am-2pm and 4-7:30pm, Sa 9am-2pm, Su 10am-2pm.

Currency Exchange: Santander Central Hispano, Pl. Circular (☎944 25 48 00). 24hr. **ATM.** Open May-Sept. M-F 8:30am-2pm, Oct.-Apr. M-F 8:30am-2pm, Sa 8:30am-1pm.

Luggage Storage: At **Estación de Abando,** lockers €3. Open 7:30am-11pm. In **Termibús,** lockers €1. Inside storage €1 per bag. Open M-F 7am-10pm, Sa-Su 8am-9pm.

El Corte Inglés: Gran Vía, 7-9 (☎944 25 35 00), on the east side of Pl. Circular. Dept. store, supermarket, haircuts, books, and **currency exchange.** Open M-Sa 10am-9pm.

English Bookstores: Casa del Libro, C. Urquijo, 9 (☎944 15 32 00). A terrific selection of books in English. Open M-Sa 9:30am-9pm. AmEx/MC/V.

Emergency: ☎112. **Police: Municipal,** C. Luis Briñas, 14 (☎092).

Medical Services: Hospital Civil de Basurto, Av. Montevideo, 18 (☎944 00 60 00).

Internet Access: Ciberteca, C. José Maria Escuza, 23 (☎944 27 82 26), on the corner of C. Simón Bolívar. €0.60 per 10min., €1.20 per 30min., €2.10 per hr. Open M-Th 8am-10pm, F-Sa 8am-midnight, Su 10am-10pm. **L@ser,** C. Sendaja, 5 (☎944 45 35 09). With your back to the tourist office, take a left. Located about a block up on the right. English-speaking owner. €0.05 per min. Also sells phone cards, €12 per 2hr. to US. Open M-F 10:30am-3:30am, Sa-Su 11:30am-3:30am.

Post Office: Main office, Alameda Urquijo, 19 (☎944 70 93 38; fax 944 43 00 24). Walk 1 block down Gran Vía from Pl. España and turn left after El Corte Inglés. Open M-F 8:30am-8:30pm, Sa 8:30am-2pm. **Postal Code:** 48008.

ACCOMMODATIONS

During **Semana Grande** (August 17-25) rates are higher than those listed below. As for the rest of the year, it shouldn't be hard to find a reasonably priced room if you arrive before noon. **Pl. Arriaga** and **C. Arenal** have budget accommodations galore, while nice hotel options line the river or farther into the new city off **Gran Vía.**

Hotel Arriaga, C. Ribera, 3 (☎944 79 00 01; fax 944 79 05 16). Crossing the Pte. Arenal heading toward the *casco viejo,* take a left after the theater and walk 200m. Large, lavish rooms, many with a view of the river. All with private baths, TV, A/C, and telephones. Garage and elevator. Singles €39; doubles €60; triples €72. AmEx/V. ❹

Pensión Méndez, C. Santa María, 13, 4th fl. (☎944 16 03 64). From Pte. Arenal, take C. Bidebbarrieta; after 2 blocks go right onto C. Perro, and right on C. Sta. María. Many rooms have sinks and balconies. Common baths. Singles €25; doubles €33; triples €45. ❷ On the 1st floor of the same building is the affiliated and more comfortable **Hostal Méndez.** Rooms have full bath and TV. Singles €36-39; doubles €48-50. ❹

Pensión Ladero, C. Lotería, 1, 4th fl. (☎944 15 09 32). From Pte. Arenal, take C. Correo; after 3 blocks turn right onto C. Lotería. Modern common baths, rooms with TVs, and winter heating. Singles €18; doubles €30. ❷

Hostal Mardones, C. Jardines, 4, 3rd fl. (☎944 15 31 05). From Pte. Arenal, take C. Bidebarrieta, then take the 1st right onto C. Jardines; hostel is on left towards the end. Some rooms with balconies, all with marble sinks. Singles €29, with bath €36; double with 1 bed €32, with 2 beds €39, with bath €38-45; triples with bath €45-50. ❸

Pensión de la Fuente, C. Sombrería, 2 (☎944 16 99 89). From Pte. Arenal, turn right on C. Correo, follow it 2 blocks past Pl. Nueva, and then turn left. Heating and TV €3. Singles €16; doubles €25-30, with bath €35. ❷

Albergue Bilbao Aterpetxez (HI), Ctra. Basurto-Kastrexana Errep., 70 (☎944 27 00 54; fax 944 27 54 79) Take bus #58 from Pl. Circular or Pl. Zabalburu. 142 beds. Internet, currency exchange, bike rental, and laundry services. July-Sept. singles €16, over 25 €18; bed in a double or triple €14, over 25 €16. Oct.-June €1 cheaper. MC/V. ❶

IN RECENT NEWS

YOU CAN'T SPELL "THREAT" WITHOUT ETA

One of Europe's longest-running guerrilla rebellions—that of Basque terrorists against the Spanish government—shows no sign of ending anytime soon. Since 1968, the Basque separatist group ETA (Euskadi ta Askatasuna) has been blamed for more than 800 deaths, most of them among members of the Spanish government. Most Spaniards are fed up with the violence. Vigils have been held nationwide, and in July 2001, more than half a million people marched in Madrid to protest ETA violence. Prime Minister José María Aznar has declared that he simply will not negotiate with terrorists.

On the other side, Arnaldo Otegi, spokesman for Batasuna, the radical nationalists seen as ETA's political wing, has said that violence will not end until the Basques have an independent state. But by no means does the entire País Vasco support this stance. Surveys show that only about 30% of Basques hope for complete sovereignty.

Despite a series of bombs launched in summer 2002 to coincide with the European Union summit, tourists haven't been deterred from visiting Spain. The Spanish government continues to aggressively fight the ETA, using the courts, the political structures, and the police.

FOOD

Restaurants and bars in the *casco viejo* offer a wide selection of local dishes, *pintxos*, and *bocadillos*. The new city has more variety but less ambiance. **Mercado de la Ribera,** down C. Ribera past Pte. Ribera on the river bank, is the biggest indoor **market** in Spain; it's worth a trip even if you're not eating. (Open M-Th, Sa 8am-2:30pm; F 8am-2:30pm and 4:30-7:30pm.) Pick up **groceries** at **Champión,** Pl. Santos Juanes, past the Mercado de la Ribera. (Open M-Sa 9am-9:30pm. MC/V.)

Restaurante Vegetariano Garibolo, C. Fernández del Campo, 7 (☎944 22 32 55). Right off C. Hurtado de Amézaga, about 5 blocks past Estación de Abando. Serves up delicious and creative vegetarian fare. *Menú* €9.75. Open M-Sa 1-4pm. MC/V. ❷

Restaurante Beroki, Pl. Circular, 2 (☎944 24 85 36), next to Estación Abando. Spreads of flowers, wine bottles, and clay pots decorate the bright and very elegant upstairs dining room. Great creamy chowder (€7.81). Lunchtime *menú* €9. Other entrees €9-15.50. Open Su-Th 1-4pm, F-Sa 1-4pm and 9-11:30pm. V. ❸

Restaurante Peruano Ají Colorado, C. Barrencalle, 5 (☎944 15 22 09), in the *casco viejo*. Specializes in *ceviche* (marinated raw fish salad; €9.65-11.40). M-F luncheon *menú* €12. Open Tu-Sa 1:30-3:30pm and 9-11:30pm, Su 1:30-3:30pm. MC/V.

Restaurante Bar Zuretzat, C. Iparraguirre, 7 (☎944 24 85 05), near the Guggenheim. High-quality seafood. Don't miss the incredibly sweet cinnamon rice pudding (€3.20). Open M-Sa 7am-11pm, Su 8am-11pm. MC/V. ❷

Café BiZVETE, Pl. Santiago, 6 (☎944 16 29 45), in the peaceful courtyard of the Cathedral de Santiago. Sandwiches €1.90-3.80, entrees €4-6. 10% surcharge for outside dining, but well worth it. Open M-Sa 8am-9pm. ❶

SIGHTS

THE GUGGENHEIM. Frank O. Gehry's Guggenheim Museum Bilbao can only be described as breathtaking. Lauded in the international press with every superlative imaginable, it has catapulted Bilbao straight into cultural stardom. Visitors are greeted by Jeff Koons's "Puppy," a dog composed of 60,000 flowers and standing almost as tall as the museum. The main attraction is undoubtedly the undulating shapes and flowing forms of the building itself. Sheathed in titanium, limestone, and glass, the US$100 million building is said to resemble an iridescent scaly fish or a blossoming flower. The amazingly light, dramatically spacious interior features a towering atrium and a series of non-traditional exhibition spaces, including a colossal 130m by 30m hall. Don't be surprised if you are asked to take your shoes off, lie on the floor, walk through mazes, or even sing throughout your visit to the various eccentric exhibits. The museum currently hosts rotating exhibits drawn from the Guggenheim Foundation's collection. A cafe on the ground floor serves snacks and drinks; the restaurant on the second floor provides a more decadent dining experience and is a work of modern art in itself. *(Av. Abandoibarra, 2. ☎944 35 90 00; www.guggenheim-bilbao.es. Handicap accessible. Audio tour €3.61. Guided tours in English Tu-Su 11am, 12:30, 4:30, and 6:30pm. Sign up 30min. before tour at the info desk. Open daily July-Aug. 9am-9pm; Sept.-June Tu-Su 10am-8pm. €8.40, students and seniors €4.20, under 12 free.)*

MUSEO DE BELLAS ARTES. Although it can't boast the name-recognition of the Guggenheim, the Museo de Bellas Artes wins the favor of locals, who claim it to be the superior attraction. Hoarding aesthetic riches behind an unassuming facade, the museum boasts an impressive collection of 12th- to 20th-century art, featuring excellent 15th- to 17th-century Flemish paintings, works by El Greco, Zurbarán, Goya, Gauguin, Francis Bacon, Velázquez, Picasso, and Mary Cassatt, as well as canvases by Basque painters. The sculpture garden in back is perfect for a relaxing stroll. *(Pl. Museo, 2. Take C. Elcano to Pl. Museo, or take bus #10 from Pte. Arenal. ☎944 39 60 60. Guided visits ☎944 39 61 37. Audio guides €2. Open Tu-Sa 10am-8pm, Su 10am-2pm. €4.50, seniors and students €3, under 12 free. W free.)*

MUSEO VASCO. Dip into Basque culture and history at the Museo Vasco, in the old city. Housed in a 17th-century building with a beautiful cloister, its exhibits cover a variety of topics, including weaving, blacksmiths, pastoral life, and the sea. *(Pl. Miguel de Unamuno, 4. From the Pte. Arenal take C. Correo, to the left of Café Boulevard, for 2 blocks, turn left onto C. Sombrería, following it to the end; museum is on the right side of the plaza. ☎944 15 54 23. Open Tu-Sa 11am-5pm, Su 11am-2pm. Also open Tu-Su 5-8pm for temporary exhibit viewing only. €3; students, seniors, and under 12 free. Th free.)*

OTHER SIGHTS. The best view of Bilbao's surrounding landscape and the perfect place for a picnic is at the top of **Monte Archanda,** north of the old town and equidistant from both the *casco viejo* and the Guggenheim. *(Funicular to the top every 15min. M-F 7:15am-10pm, Sa-Su 8:15am-10pm, July-Aug. until 11pm on the weekends. €0.69. Handicap accessible, lift €0.25. With your back to the new town, turn left from Pl. Arenal and follow the riverside road past the Ayuntamiento. On Po. Campo de Volantín, turn right on C. Mugica Y Butrón and continue until Pl. Funicular.)* A short Metro ride to the north (5-20min.) leads to various **beaches,** including **Getxo, Sopelana,** and **Plencia (Plentzia).** For Getxo, get off at any stop near Neguri or Algorta, then walk ½km to the beach. Along with Sopelana, Getxo attracts a surfer crowd and lies just a little nearer to the Bay of Biscay; its illuminated **Puente Colgante** (a suspension bridge constructed over 100 years ago) spans the river, leading to a plethora of all-night bars.

ENTERTAINMENT AND NIGHTLIFE

Bilbao has a thriving bar scene. In the *casco viejo*, revelers spill out into the streets to sip their *txikitos* (chee-KEE-tos; small glasses of wine), especially on C. Barrencalle (Barrenkale), one of the original "seven streets" from which the city of Bilbao has grown. Teenagers and 20-somethings fill C. Licenciado Poza on the west side of town. The **Cotton Club,** C. Gregorio de la Revilla, 25 (entrance on C. Simón Bolívar), decorated with over 30,000 beer caps, draws a huge crowd on Friday and Saturday nights while the rest of the week is a little more low-key. DJ spins W-Th at 11pm and F-Sa at 1pm. Over 100 choices of whiskey for €4.50 per *copa*. (☎944 10 49 51. Beer €2-3.50. Cash only. Open M-Th 4:30pm-3am, F-Sa 6:30pm-6am, Su 6:30pm-3am.) For a mellower scene, munch on *pintxos* (€0.90-1.20) and people-watch at Bilbao's oldest coffee shop (est. 1871), **Café Boulevard,** C. Arenal, 3. This Art Deco cafe was once an important site for literary meetings and one of Miguel de Unamuno's favorite haunts. Put on your dancing shoes and get ready to tango on Fridays at 11pm. (☎944 15 31 28. Open M-Th 7:30am-11pm, F-Sa 8am-2am, Su 11am-11pm. MC/V.) Climb your way to a peaceful drink at **Bar Zaran,** C. Calzadas de Mallona, 18, towards Campos de Mallona. Ascend the long stone stairway next to the *casco viejo* Metro entrance. Take your drink outside for great views of Bilbao. (Beer €1.35, red wine €0.35, cigars €0.40-1. Open daily 8am-12:30am.) A bigger scene can be found three doors uphill at **Bar Mallona.**

The massive fiesta in honor of *Nuestra Señora de Begoña* takes place during **Semana Grande,** a nine-day party beginning the Saturday after August 15 with fireworks, concerts, theater—you name it. The tourist office has a schedule of events. Documentary filmmakers from all over the world gather for a week in October or November for the **Festival Internacional de Cine Documental de Bilbao.** During the summer, there are free **concerts** every Sunday morning at the bandstand in Parque Arenal. Pick up a *Bilbao Guide* from the tourist office for event listings.

GUERNICA (GERNIKA)

On April 26, 1937, the Nazi "Condor Legion" released an estimated 29,000kg of explosives on Guernica (pop. 15,600), obliterating 70% of the city in three hours. The tragedy marked the first mass civilian aerial bombing attack, and the nearly 2000 people who were killed have been immortalized in Pablo Picasso's stark masterpiece *Guernica*, which now hangs in Madrid's Museo Reina Sofía. The small, reconstructed city is not much of an attraction in itself, but for those interested in learning more about Basque history and the infamous event that occurred here, Guernica is a rewarding daytrip.

PRACTICAL INFORMATION. **Trains** (☎902 543 210; www.euskotren.es) connect Guernica to **Bilbao** (45min.; every 45min. M-F 5:50am-10:15pm, except 9:45pm; Sa-Su every 30 min. 8:15am-10:15pm, except 8:45am; €2). **Bizkai Bus** (☎902 222 265) sends more convenient and more frequent **buses** between Guernica and **Bilbao's Estación Abando** (45min.; M-F every 30min. 6:15am-9:45pm, Sa every hr. 7am-10pm, Su every hr. 9am-10pm; €2-2.05, with Creditrans card €1.50). To reach Guernica's English and French-speaking **tourist office,** C. Artekalea, 8, from the train station, walk three blocks up C. Adolfo Urioste and turn right on C. Artekalea. At the first crosswalk on the road, take a right into the alleyway and the office will be on your right. (☎946 25 58 92; fax 946 25 32 12; www.gernika-lumo.net. Open July-Sept. M-Sa 10am-7:30pm, Su 10:am-2:30pm; Oct.-June M-Sa 10am-1:30pm and 4-7pm, Su 11am-2pm.) The **post office,** C. Iparragirre, 26, is slightly to the left as you exit the train station. (☎946 25 03 87. Open M-F 8:30am-2:30pm, Sa 9:30am-1pm.) The **postal code** is 48300.

ACCOMMODATIONS AND FOOD. Although Guernica's main attractions can be seen in a daytrip from Bilbao, **Akelarre Ostatua Pensión ❸,** C. Barrenkale, 5, offers a delightful place to stay. From the train station walk 2 blocks up C. Adolfo Urioste and take a right onto C. Barrenkale. (☎946 27 01 79; fax 946 27 06 75. *Semana Santa* and July-Aug. 20 singles €28; doubles €35, with bath €40. Rest of the year singles €18-22; doubles €25-28, with bath €30-34. Prices go down by €3 with a stay of 2 nights or more. MC/V.) For a restaurant with a family feel, head to **Restaurante Zallo Barri ❷,** C. Juan Calzada, 79. After exiting the train station, walk up C. Urioste and take the second left; look for a cream-colored awning and marble front several blocks down on the left. This place dishes out a tasty luncheon *menú* (€8.15) with several fish, meat, and dessert choices. (☎946 25 18 00. Open daily 8:30am-11pm; *menú* offered M-F 1-3:30pm only. AmEx/MC/V.) Another excellent dining choice is **Restaurante Boliña ❷,** conveniently located on C. Barrenkale, 3, on the left just before Akelarre Ostatua Pensión. This classy bar/restaurant with dark woods and mellow yellow walls draws in a large local crowd. Friendly waitstaff and large portions of delicious foods make for a delightful lunch. (☎946 25 03 00. *Menú* M-F 1-3:30pm €8. *Pintxos* €1-1.20. Open daily 8am-1:30am. MC/V.)

SIGHTS. The emotional focus of Guernica is **El Arbol,** inside the gates of the **Casa de Juntos.** Encased in stone columns, the 300-year-old "Old Tree" (an oak) marks the old political center of the País Vasco, the place where medieval Basques gathered to debate community issues and Castilian monarchs ritually swore their respect for the autonomy of the local government. Next to the oldest tree grows an oak that was planted in 1860, and behind that, a "sapling" only 30 years old. The Casa de Juntos is the meeting place of the Vizkaya (Basque) General Assembly. (☎946 25 11 38. Open daily June-Sept. 10am-2pm and 4-7pm; Oct.-May 10am-2pm and 4-6pm. Free.) There are two sights worth seeing in Guernica's **Parque de los Pueblos de Europa.** Eduardo Chillida's dramatic sculpture **Gure aitaren etxea** (Our Father's

THE TRAGEDY OF GUERNICA Founded on April 28, 1366, Guernica was virtually erased from the map on April 26, 1937. It was a Monday market day when the church bell rang three times to warn the small town of an aerial attack. The German Condor Legion began to bomb the small town at 4:30pm and didn't stop until 7:45pm. Heavy bombs and hand grenades were first dropped from small planes in order to create a panic and a stampede. Next, low-flying planes machine-gunned those running on foot or hiding in the fields. These planes forced the townspeople into buildings, which were then wrecked and burned by 12 bombers. The entire center city was effectively destroyed. Strangely, the Casa de Juntos and the oak tree were untouched, as was Franco's war-material factory a few kilometers down the road. Guernica was far behind the lines; the destruction was fueled solely by a desire to rob the anti-Fascist Basque people of their desire to fight.

Many pictures, sketches, and paintings have attempted to capture this day. In a painting now at the Gernika Museoa, Sofía Gandarias depicted clocks stopped at 4:30, women holding dead children, and the words "*y del cielo lloría sangre*" (and the sky cried blood). But it was Pablo Picasso who brought the town's tragedy to international fame. The still-republican Spanish government had commissioned the artist to paint a mural for the Universal Exhibition in Paris in 1937, and he used the bombing for inspiration. In 10 days he had 25 sketches; he finished the painting–his largest work–in only one month. After much controversy, *Guernica*, Picasso's masterpiece, now resides in Madrid's Reina Sofía (see p. 123). When asked about the meaning of the painting as a whole, he replied, "Let them interpret as they wish." Picasso was even approached by a German ambassador who asked of the painting, "Did you do this?" Picasso simply answered, "No, you did."

House), a peace monument, was commissioned for the 50th anniversary of the city's bombing, and it stands alongside Henry Moore's voluptuous 1986 **Large Figure in a Shelter,** which suggests a female form and symbolizes rebirth. To get to the park from the bus station, follow C. Adolfo Urioste as far as it goes. At the top follow the arrow to the right and enter the park on the corner. (Open daily June-Aug. 10am-9pm; Sept.-May 10am-7pm. Free.) The modest **Museo de la Paz de Gernika,** Pl. Foru, 1, just across the main street, C. Artekalea, from the tourist office, is currently undergoing major renovations, and is expected to re-open in August 2002. Paintings and artifacts on display inside the **Museo de Euskal Herria,** C. Allende Salazar, 5, document Basque history. (☎946 25 54 51. Guided tours in English. Tu-Sa 10am-2pm and 4-7pm, Su 11am-3pm. Free.) The tourist office offers a **historic tour** of the city's principal attractions July-Sept. M-Sa at 11am (€4); during the rest of the year call ahead and the office will gladly arrange one (minimum of 2 people). To go at your own pace, you can buy a Guernica guide in English or French (€4). The city holds a **fiesta** on the first Saturday of June to October.

VITORIA-GASTEIZ ☎945

Vitoria-Gasteiz (pop. 220,000) boasts greenery galore and an impressive newly-opened contemporary art museum. Packed with avenues and parks, Vitoria-Gasteiz possesses a charm that belies its status as a sleek cosmopolitan center. The city's hyphenated name testifies to its regional loyalty; renamed Villa de Nueva Vitoria by the King of Navarra in 1181, the Basques re-incorporated the city's original name upon recovering regional autonomy in 1979. Spray-painted road signs with "Vitoria" crossed out are evidence of its continuing Basque pride. Plenty of hiking and biking opportunities await visitors, and for those spending some time in the País Vasco, it is a worthwhile place to visit.

TRANSPORTATION

Flights: Aeropuerto Vitoria-Foronda (☎945 16 35 00), 9km out of town. Accessible only by car or taxi (about €15). Info open M-F 8am-2:15pm. **Iberia** (☎945 16 37 38). Info open 6am-midnight.

Trains: RENFE Pl. Estación (☎902 24 02 02). From the city center, follow C. Eduardo Dato, off C. Postas, to the very end, walking away from the old city. Info open 7:30am-10:30pm. To: **Barcelona** (8-14½hr., 1-3 per day 10:40am-12:33am, €29.66); **Burgos** (1½hr.; 10-15 per day M-Sa 7:30am-12:33am, Su 11:40am-6:05pm; €6.66-12.16); **Madrid** (4½-7hr.; 8-9 per day M-F 7:30am-12:33am, Su 10:08am-12:33am; €26.66); **Pamplona** (1hr.; M-Sa 1-4 per day 7:40am-7:05pm; Su 3:25, 7:05pm; €3.71); **San Sebastián** (2hr., 8 per day 6:37am-4:58am, €7.46-12.16); **Zaragoza** (3hr., change in Pamplona; 2-4 per day M-Sa 7:40am-7:05pm, Su 3:25-7pm; €13.10-16.66).

Buses: C. Herrán, 50, on a traffic island east of the old city. General info (☎945 25 84 00) open M-F 8am-8pm, Sa-Su 9am-7pm. **ALSA** (☎945 25 55 09; www.alsa.es) goes to: **Barcelona** (6½-7hr.; M-Th 7:30am, 3:30pm; F-Su 7:30am, 3:30, 11:15pm, €30.19); **Pamplona** (1½hr.; 6-11 per day M-Sa 7am-8:30pm, Su 9am-9pm; €5.98); **Zaragoza** (3hr.; 5-7 per day M-Th and Sa 7:30am-9:15pm, F and Su 7:30am-10pm; €27.45). **La Unión** (☎945 26 46 26) goes to **Bilbao** (1hr.; 12-21 per day M-F 6:35am-10pm, Sa 7:30am-10pm, Su 8:30am-9:30pm; €4.50). **Continental Auto** (☎945 28 64 66) to: **Burgos** (1½hr.; 7-9 per day M-Th 6:45am-2:05am, Sa-Su 10:45am-2:05am; €6.03); **Madrid** (4½-5hr.; 9-10 per day M-Sa 6:45am-2:05am, Su 8:45am-2:05am; €18.83-27); **San Sebastián** (1½hr.; 8-10 per day 5am-11:30pm, F and Su 5am-1:30am; €6.13).

Public Transportation: Tuvisa Buses (☎945 16 10 54) cover the metropolitan area and suburbs (7am-10pm, €0.60); the main bus stops are on C. Monseñor Cadenay Eleta (in front of the new cathedral) and C. La Paz (in front of El Corte Inglés). Bus #2 goes from the bus station to C. Florida, but it is probably easier to walk.

Taxis: Radio-Taxi (☎945 27 35 00). 24hr. service to Vitoria and surrounding areas.

Car Rental: Europcar, Adriano VI, 29 (☎945 20 04 33). Minimum age 21. Open 9am-1pm and 4-7:30pm, Sa 9am-1pm. Also an airport office open M-F 1:30-2:45pm.

ORIENTATION AND PRACTICAL INFORMATION

The medieval **casco viejo** is the almond-shaped center of Vitoria-Gasteiz. At its base, **Plaza de la Virgen Blanca** marks the center of town. From the **train station,** follow C. Eduardo Dato to its end, turn left on C. Postas, and head straight to the plaza. To get to the center of town from the **bus station,** a glass building on C. Herrán between C. Prudencio María Verástegui and C. Arana, exit left on C. Herrán, then make an immediate right onto C. Verástegui. Follow C. Verástegui to its end and turn left on C. Francia. Follow C. Francia for four blocks as it becomes C. Paz and turn right onto C. Postas, which leads straight to Pl. Virgen Blanca.

Tourist Office: Pl. General Loma, 1 (☎945 16 15 98; fax 945 16 11 05; www.vitoria-gasteiz.org/turismo), just across from the park. From the train station, follow C. Eduardo Dato, take the 4th left onto C. General Alava, and walk 1 block. From the bus station, cross Pl. Virgen Blanca to Pl. del General Loma. Open daily 9am-1pm and 3-7pm.

Currency Exchange: Santander Central Hispano, Pl. del Arca, 13. Open M-F 8:30am-2pm, Oct.-Apr. also Sa 8:30am-1pm. Also has a 24hr. **ATM.**

Luggage storage: At the **train station** (€3 for a locker). Buy tokens at the ticket counter 6am-1am. At the **bus station** (€0.63 per piece the 1st day, €0.52 each additional day). Open M-Sa 8am-8pm, Su 9am-7pm.

El Corte Inglés: On the corner of C. Paz and C. Independencia (☎945 26 63 33), 1 block past C. Postas coming from bus station. Supermarket. Open M-Sa 10am-10pm.

Emergency: ☎112. **Police:** C. Aguirrelande, 8 (☎091 or 092).

Medical Services: Hospital General de Santiago, C. Olaguíbel, 29. (☎945 00 76 00). From the bus station, go left 1 block after C. Francia becomes C. Paz. **Osakidetza Servico Vasco de Salud,** Av. Santiago, 7 (☎945 24 44 44), off C. Paz. Open M-F 5pm-midnight, Sa 2pm-midnight, Su 9am-midnight. Free medical attention; passport required.

Internet Access: Nirv@na, C. Manuel Iradier, 11 (☎945 14 06 60), down 1 block and to the left as you come from the train station. €0.60 per 15min. Open M-Sa 10:30am-2:30pm and 5-10pm, Su 5-10pm. **Cuatro Azules,** C. Postas, 28 (☎945 13 45 13), across from the post office. A convenient Internet kiosk near the entrance of the large bar/disco-pub–beware drunken emails. Gets noisy after 11pm. €0.50 per 7min., €1 per 30min. Open Su-Th 12:30pm-2:30am, F-Sa 12:30pm-4am.

Post Office: C. Postas, 9 (☎945 15 46 92; fax 945 23 37 80), on the pedestrian street leading to Pl. Virgen Blanca. Open M-F 8:30am-8:30pm, Sa 9:30am-2pm. For **Lista de Correos,** walk to the C. Señora del Cabello side of the building. **Postal Code:** 01008.

ACCOMMODATIONS AND CAMPING

Vitoria-Gasteiz has only a handful of cheap *pensiones*, although more deluxe hostels abound. If you plan to come during the jazz festival (3rd week of July) or the *Fiestas de la Virgen Blanca* (Aug. 4-9), make reservations in advance.

Hotel Iradier, C. Florida, 49 (☎945 27 90 66; fax 945 27 97 11), 2 blocks to the right of C. Eduardo Dato coming from the train station. Ring buzzer to enter. Cozy blue and yellow rooms, some with balconies, have bathroom, TV, and phone. Reservations recommended, especially during the jazz festival. Singles €28; doubles used as a single €40; doubles €46; triples €66. IVA included. MC/V. ❸

Pensión Araba, C. Florida, 25 (☎945 23 25 88). On the road to the tourist office from the bus station; from the train station, turn right onto C. Florida. Attractive rooms have sinks and TV (some with VCRs). Elevator and parking (€6 per night). Singles €24, with bath €28; doubles €30, with bath €36; triples €40, with bath €48. ❷

Hostal-Residencia Nuvilla, C. Fueros, 29, 3rd fl. (☎945 25 91 51). From the bus station, on C. Herrán, follow directions to Pl. Virgen Blanca (see **Orientation,** p. 494) but take the 1st left off C. Postas. Common baths. All have balconies and marble sinks. Singles €20.25; doubles €29; triples €41. ❷

Camping Ibaya (☎945 14 76 20), 3km from town toward Madrid. Follow Portal de Castilla west from the new cathedral. Supermarket, restaurant, hot showers, and laundry. Open year-round. €3.46 per person, per tent, and per car. IVA included. MC/V. ❶

FOOD

You can't go wrong in the *casco viejo* and the surrounding streets. The streets around Pl. España have *pintxos* galore. Buy groceries at **Champión,** C. General Alava, 10 (open M-Sa 9am-9:30pm), or at the huge **Consum,** C. Pio XII, 11, next to Pl. Santa Bárbara (open M-Sa 9am-9pm).

Museo del Organo, C. Manuel Iradier, 80 (☎945 26 40 48), on the corner, just before the Pl. de Toros. A favorite among locals, with fresh, filling vegetarian cuisine. M-F 4-course *menú* €8.50, Sa €11.50. Open M-F 1-4pm, Sa 1:30-3:30pm. MC/V. ❷

Restaurante Argentino La Yerra, C. Correría, 46 (☎945 26 57 59), in the *casco viejo*. Good beef entrees (€11-18) and enticing pasta dishes (€7.25). M-F luncheon *menú* (€8). Open Su and Tu-W 1:30-4pm, Th-Sa 1:30-4pm and 9:30pm-midnight. MC/V. ❷

La Taberna de Los Mundos, C. Independencia, 14 (☎945 13 93 42). Serves excellent and affordable sandwiches (€3-4). Fish and *cerdo* entrees €8-11. Open M-W 9am-midnight, Th 9am-1am, F-Sa 10:30am-2am, Su noon-midnight. ❷

El Siete, C. Cuchillería, 3 (☎945 27 22 98). Popular with locals in search of a traditional food–and a lots of it. *Menú* served M-F 1-4pm (€8.20). 38 varieties of sandwiches (€2.50-3.60). Open Su-Th 9am-12:30am, F-Sa 10am-3am. ❶

SIGHTS

The tree-lined pedestrian walkways of the new city and steep narrow streets of the *casco viejo* make for pleasant wanderings. **Plaza de la Virgen Blanca** is the focal point of the *casco viejo* and site of Vitoria-Gasteiz's *fiestas*. Beside Pl. Virgen Blanca is the broad, arcaded **Plaza de España,** marking the division of the old town from the new. **Los Arquillos,** a series of arches that rise above Pl. España, were designed by architect Justo Antonio de Olaguíbel from 1787 to 1802 to connect the *casco viejo* with the rapidly growing new town below.

MUSEUMS AND PALACIOS. The permanent collection at **Artium,** the recently opened (summer 2002) contemporary art museum, boasts multimedia works and paintings by 20th-century greats such as Dalí, Picasso, Miró, and Arroyo. Unconventional and macabre rotating exhibits grace two of its galleries. This museum alone is worth a trip to Vitoria-Gasteiz. *(C. Francia, 24. ☎945 20 90 20. Open Tu-F 11am-8pm, Sa-Su 10:30am-8pm. Adults €3; students, seniors, and under 18 €1.50; under 14 free; W "you decide." Audio guides €2.)* Many of the *casco viejo*'s Renaissance palacios are open to the public as museums. The gorgeous **Palacio Augustín** houses the **Museo de Bellas Artes,** with works by regional Basque artists. *(Po. Fray Francisco de Vitoria. Open Tu-F 10am-2pm and 4-6:30pm, Sa 10am-2pm, Su 11am-2pm. Free.)* The 15th-century **Casa del Cordón,** hosts changing exhibitions, many featuring student art. *(C. Cuchillería, 24. ☎945 25 96 73. Open Tu-F 10am-2pm and 4-6:30pm, Sa 10am-2pm, Su 11am-2pm. Free.)*

CATHEDRALS. Construction of the Gothic **Catedral de Santa María** (also known as the *Catedral Vieja*, or Old Cathedral), at the top of the *casco viejo*, began in the 12th century; today it flaunts two especially expressive doors. Though it is currently closed for a €24 million restoration and is scheduled to reopen in 2010, English tours of the restoration process and archaeological studies are offered. *(☎945 25 51 35. Tours Mar.-Sept. €2 per person, under 12 free.)* The 20th-century neo-Gothic **New Cathedral** is in the new town. The apse hosts the **Diocesan Museum of Sacred Art,** a collection from Basque churches, including a canvas by El Greco. *(C. Monseñor Cadena y Eleta. Cathedral open M-Sa 11am-2pm. Free. Museum ☎945 18 19 18. Open Tu-F 10am-2pm and 4-6:30pm, Sa 10am-2pm, Su 11am-2pm.)*

ENTERTAINMENT AND NIGHTLIFE

For info on **theater** and special events, pick up the weekly *Kalea* (€1.40) from tobacco stands or newsstands. World-class jazz grooves into the city the second or third week of July for the week-long **Festival de Jazz de Vitoria-Gasteiz.** Tickets for big name performers cost €10-35, but there are plenty of free performances on the street. Call or visit the **Asociación Festival de Jazz de Vitoria,** C. Florida, 3, for specific info (☎945 14 19 19; www.jazzvitoria.com). On July 24-25, *Los Blusas* or "the blouses" hold their own festival with wine, music, and games. The blue shirts represent the old shepherds that used to live in Vitoria. Rockets mark the start of the **Fiesta de la Virgen Blanca** (Aug.4-9) at 6pm on the 4th in Pl. Virgen Blanca.

After nightfall, the *casco viejo* lights up. Bars line C. Cuchillería ("La Cuchi"), C. Herrería ("La Herre"), C. Zapatería ("La Zapa"), and C. San Francisco; check out **Bar Carajo,** C. Mateo Moraza, 11, for an all-out *fiesta*. Try a *marchacado* (slammer) for €1.20. (Beer €1.35. Open July-Sept. Th-Sa 7pm-2am; closes 30min. earlier in winter.) Dancing types can head to **Mana,** C. Florida, 39. Music starts thumping at 1am, and it's packed with 20-somethings until 6am. (Open F-Sa. Cover €6, includes 1 drink.) For a pint of English Real Ale brewed on site (€3) try **The Man in the Moon,** C. Manual Iradier, 7, just in front of Iglesia Carmen. Catch the Thursday night jam session (starts around 10pm) or test your knowledge on Wednesdays at their weekly trivia quiz (in English). Not much Spanish spoken here (in fact, the locals come to practice their English), but it's a fun place to mingle with locals and travelers alike. (☎945 13 43 27. Open daily 8am-3am.) For more intimate socializing, **Sherezade,** C. Correría, 42, offers a sumptuous Moroccan tea room with small tables, embroidered cushions, and an intoxicating ambiance. Sip a kiwi shake (€1.80) or hot tea with fresh herbs blended to order (€1.50) and let your creative juices flow—crayons and paper are provided. (☎945 25 58 68. Open Su-Th 4:30-11pm, F 4:30pm-midnight, Sa 4:30pm-1am. July-Sept. opens daily at 6pm.)

ASTURIAS AND CANTABRIA

Jagged cliffs and precipitous ravines lend an epic scope to the tiny lands of Asturias and Cantabria, tucked between the País Vasco and Galicia. Though connected by location and landscape, Asturias and Cantabria have distinct provincial personalities. With its world-class resort towns of Santander and Comillas, Cantabria appeals to Spain's vacationing elite. Asturias instead draws hearty mountaineers looking to conquer the peaks of its national parks, including the Picos de Europa and the Parque Natural de Oyambre.

Agricolar Moors had little use for the region's rough terrain, enabling the Christians to make the land their northern stronghold. *La Reconquista* officially began in the small Picos town of Covadonga, the only region never to fall to the Moors thanks to the impassable peaks of the Cordillera Cantábrica. Today, Spain's heir to the throne is titled the Príncipe de Asturias, in honor of the region's preservation of the 'true' Spain during Moorish invasions. During the Civil War this legendary spirit of defiance found outlet in the blue-collar resistance to the Fascists. Mountainous terrain has still limited the number of rail lines through the region, leaving lone roads to wind along its steep mountain sides and scalloped shores.

Asturias is famous for its apples, cheeses, wholesome fresh milk, and *arroz con leche* (rice pudding). *Sidra* (cider) and *fabada asturiana*, a hearty bean-and-sausage stew, grace menus everywhere. True Asturians can be recognized by the way they take their cider, poured from several feet above the glass and downed immediately. Cantabrian cuisine draws from the mountains and the sea, adding anchovies, tuna, and sardines to the mix. Local favorites include *cocido montanés* (bean stew) and *marmita* (tuna, potato, and green pepper stew).

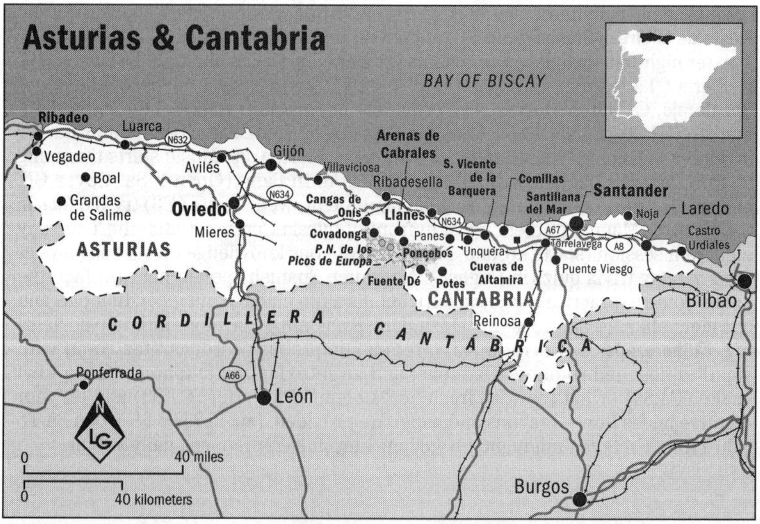

ASTURIAS

Impenetrable peaks and dense alpine forests define the Asturian landscape, as well as its history. Thanks to the foreboding mountains of the Picos de Europa, Asturias never fell to the bands of marauding Moors in the 8th century. The mountains have, however, finally succumbed to invasion, this time by tourists reveling in the endless outdoor activities in the Picos de Europa National Park. Although it is better known for its peaks, Asturias also has a popular coastline. Not the swaths of sand and raging waves of Cantabria, Asturian beaches are more often quiet, rocky coves where tropical and alpine vegetation commingle with mountaineers.

OVIEDO ☎958

Oviedo's name comes from the Latin word for city *(ovetum)*, and for a few centuries, it really was *the* city in Spain. As one of the few places to ward off Moorish attacks, it became the epicenter of *la Reconquista.* Oviedo (pop. 200,000) was made the capital of the Kingdom of Asturias as early as 810, but the city has since faded into the background of Spanish life. The city center is pleasant enough, with an immense park, lively street musicians, beloved *churrerías*, and the promise of mountains on the horizon. Yet beyond its provincial art museum and miles of pedestrian shopping streets, there's not much to see or do in Oviedo. It is, however, the only way to access the western gateways to the Picos de Europa.

TRANSPORTATION

Flights: Aeropuerto de Ranón/Aeropuerto Nacional de Asturias (☎985 12 75 00), in Áviles, 28km northwest of Oviedo. **Prabus,** C. Marqués de Pidal, 20 (☎985 25 47 51), runs frequent buses from the ALSA station to the airport. **Aviaco** (☎985 12 76 03) and **Iberia** (☎985 12 76 07) fly to Madrid, Barcelona, and London.

Trains: Both RENFE and FEVE serve Oviedo from **Estación del Norte,** Av. de Santander, uphill from the center of town at the end of C. Uría.

RENFE (☎985 24 33 64 or 985 25 24 02), on the 1st fl. of the train station. Pay attention to the type of train; a slow local train through the mountains can double your travel time. Info open daily 7:45am-11:15pm. To: **Barcelona** (12-13½hr.; 10:57am, 7:48pm; €38.50-51) via **Burgos** (5-6hr., €20.50-27); **Gijón** (30min., every 30min. 5:18am-11:28pm, €1.90); **León** (2-2½hr.; M-F 7 per day 7:30am-11pm, Sa-Su 6 per day 1-11pm; €12-16); **Madrid** (6-9hr.; 9:15am, 4:25, 11pm; €32-36) via **Valladolid** (4hr., €22-25).

FEVE (☎985 29 76 56), on the 3rd fl. of the train station. Info open daily 9am-10pm or until last train. To: **Bilbao** (7hr., 9:08am, €16.70); **Ferrol** (6½hr.; 7:47am, 2:47pm; €15.70); **Llanes** (2hr., 4 per day 9:08am-6:33pm, €5.65); **Ribadeo** (4hr.; 7:47am, 2:47pm; €8.15); **Santander** (4½hr.; 9:08am, 3:48pm; €10.65).

Buses: There are 2 major bus lines: **ALSA** (national) and **Económicos/ENSA** (regional).

ALSA, Pl. General Primo de Rivera, 1 (☎985 96 96 96 or 902 42 22 42), unmarked, on the lower level of the white shopping building between C. Fray Ceferino and Av. General Elorza. Ticket office at C. Uría across the street from El Corte Inglés. Open M-F 9:30am-2pm and 4-8pm, Sa 9:30am-2pm. To: **Barcelona** (12hr., 8pm, €69.14); **Burgos** (4¼hr.; 10:45am, 8pm; €12.48); **La Coruña** (4½-6¾hr., 3 per day 10:45am-8pm, €20.49); **León** (1½hr., 12 per day 7:30am-10:30pm, €6.65); **Madrid** (5hr.; M-F 12 per day, Sa 10 per day, Su 14 per day 6:30am-12:30am; €47.75); **Santander** (3-4hr., 8-10 per day 7am-8:30pm, €10.71-18.25); **Santiago** (5½-7hr.; 6:45, 8am, 4pm, Su also at 7pm; €24-28); **Vigo** (7-9hr.; 6:45am, 3pm; €28.93); **Valladolid** (4hr., 5 per day 7:30am-12:30am, €14.12).

Económicos (EASA), C. Jerónimo Ibrán, 1 (☎985 29 00 39). To: **Arenas de Cabrales** (2hr.; M-F 4 per day 9:30am-6pm, Sa-Su 9:30am, 6pm; €6.70); **Cangas de Onís** (1-1½hr.; M-F 10 per day 8am-9:30pm, Sa-Su 7 per day 8am-9:30pm; €4.70); **Covadonga** (1¾hr.; M-F 4 per day 6:45am-5:30pm, Sa-Su 9:30am, 12:30, 3:30pm; €5.40); **Llanes** (1½-2hr., 7 per day 7am-8:30pm, €7).

Public Transportation: TUA (☎985 22 24 22) runs **buses** 8am-10pm (€0.77). All stops have bus maps. #4 runs from the bus and train stations up C. Uría, turning off just before Campo San Francisco. #2 runs from all of the stations to the youth hostel and hospital. #2, 3, 5, and 7 run from the RENFE station along C. Uría to the old city.

Taxis: Radio Taxi (☎985 25 00 00 or 985 25 25 00). 24hr. service.

Car Rental: Avis, C. Ventura Rodríguez, 12 (☎985 24 13 83). From Campo San Francisco, walk up C. Uría toward the train station, turn left on C. Gil de Jaz and right onto C. Ventura Rodríguez. Another branch is in the train station, but keeps irregular hours. From €58 per day. Weekend specials. Min. age 25, with credit card in driver's name. Open M-F 9am-1pm and 4pm, Sa 9am-1pm.

ORIENTATION AND PRACTICAL INFORMATION

At Oviedo's city center is the **Campo San Francisco,** a massive park on the slope of a hill. At its downhill base is **C. Uría,** the city's main thoroughfare, running from the train station past the Campo. The **cathedral** lies down C. San Francisco from C. Uría. From the **train station,** exit onto Av. de Santander and C. Uría will be directly in front of you. The bus station and EASA bus stop lie a little farther out off **Pl. General Primo Rivera,** but **C. Fray Ceferino** connects them to C. Uría. From the **EASA bus stop** on C. Jerónimo Ibrán, walk to Pl. General Primo Rivera and follow the rotary to the right; C. Fray Ceferino will be the second street on the right. From the ALSA station, follow the rotary to the left; C. Fray Ceferino will be the second street. Walk uphill on C. Fray Ceferino, and take the third left onto C. Uría.

Tourist Office: C. Uría, 64 (☎985 21 33 85). 1 block off the train station. Offers a good number of brochures of Oviedo and Asturias, including hiking trail routes in the Parque Nacional Picos de Europa. English spoken. Open M-F 10:30am-2pm and 4:30-7:30pm. **Municipal Office,** Marqués de Santa Cruz, 1 (☎/fax 985 22 75 86), corner of C. Uría, in front of the Campo San Francisco. Open M-F 10:30am-2pm and 4:30-7:30pm; Sa-Su 11am-2pm.

Currency Exchange: Santander Central Hispano, Pl. La Escandalera, s/n (☎902 24 24 24), across from the Campo San Francisco. Open Apr.-Sept. M-F 8:30am-2:30pm; Oct.-Mar. M-F 8:30am-2:30pm, Sa 8:30am-1pm.

Luggage Storage: Lockers (€1.80; open daily 7am-11pm) at the **RENFE station.**

English-Language Bookstore: Librería Cervantes, C. Doctor Casal, 9 (☎985 20 77 61). A left off C. Uría when walking toward the park from the train station. Huge selection, from Shakespeare to Byron. Open M-F 9am-1:30pm and 4-8pm, Sa 9am-2pm.

Emergency: ☎1006. **Police: Policía Municipal** (☎092 or 985 11 56 57), **Guardia Civil** (☎062 or 985 28 02 04). Both are in the municipal building on C. Quintana, s/n.

24hr. Pharmacy: Farmacia Nestares, C. Uría, 36. Across the street from El Corte Inglés.

El Corte Inglés: C. Uría, 33. 2 blocks from the train station. Open M-Sa and the 1st Su of every month 10am-10pm.

Medical Services: Hospital Central de Asturias, C. J. Clavería, s/n (☎985 10 61 00), near the Plaza de Toros. **Ambulance:** ☎985 10 89 00.

Internet Access: Laser Internet Center, C. San Francisco, 9 (☎985 20 00 66). Open daily 24hr. €3 per hr.

Post Office: C. Alonso Quintanilla, 1 (☎985 21 41 86 or 902 19 71 97). From C. Uría, with your back to the train station, turn left onto C. Argüelles, then left onto C. Alonso Quintanilla. Open M-F 8:30am-8:30pm, Sa 9:30am-2pm. **Postal Code:** 33060.

ACCOMMODATIONS

Pensiones, *hostales*, and *hoteles* pack the new city on C. Uría, C. Campoamor (with the RENFE station behind you, walk 1 block to the left), C. Nueve de Mayo (2 blocks to the left of the station), and C. Jovellanos (near the cathedral).

Residencia Juvenil Ramón Menéndez Pidal, C. Julián Clavería, 14 (☎985 23 20 54), just off Pl. Toros. Walk down C. Uría from the RENFE station, take a right on Conde de Toreno, walk through 2 plazas past the Pl. Toros, and turn left on C. J. Clavería (25min.). Or take bus #2 (dir.: Hospital) from Pl. Primo de Rivera or C. Uría. TV room, library, and dining room. Rooms vary in size from 4-12 bunks, but all have sinks. Only a few available in winter. Curfew 1am. Dorms €4.69, with breakfast €5.66; over 26 €6.41, with breakfast €8. AmEx/MC/V. ❶

Pensión Martínez, C. Jovellanos, 5 (☎985 21 53 44). A modern apartment building with clean rooms with sinks. Pristine communal bathrooms. Singles €18; doubles €21. ❷

Pensión Riesgo, C. Nueve de Mayo, 16, 1st fl. (☎985 21 89 45). From the bus stations, walk up C. Fray Ceferino and take the 1st left onto C. Nueve de Mayo; from the train station, walk up C. Uría and turn right onto C. Fray Ceferino, taking the 2nd right onto C. Nueve de Mayo. A pleasant *pensión* on a pedestrian street in the city center. Singles €13; doubles €20, with shower €27. ❶

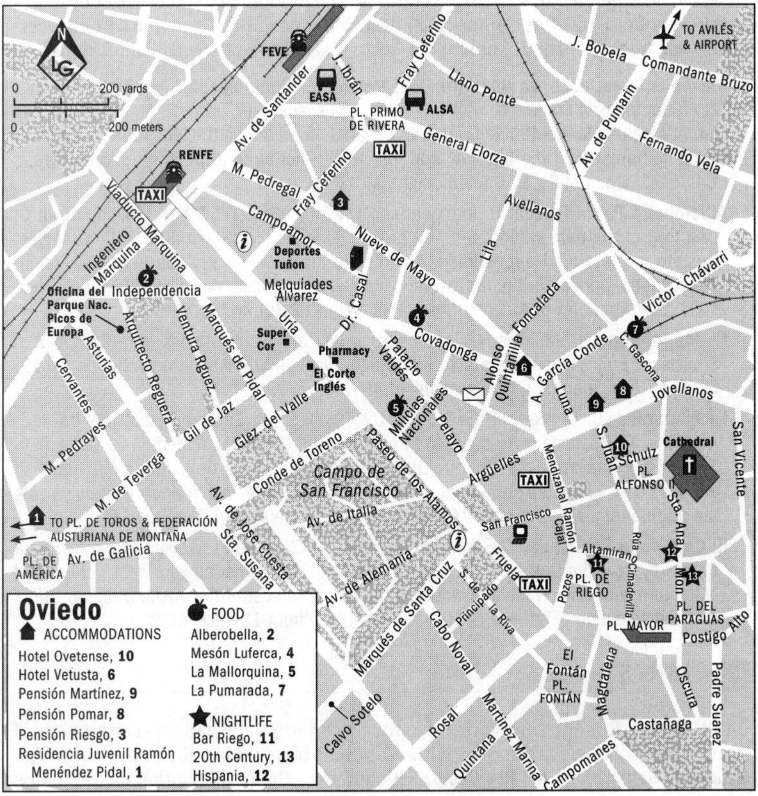

Pensión Pomar, C. Jovellanos, 7 (☎985 22 27 91). From the bus and train stations, a left off C. Uría at Pl. La Escaladera and the Teatro Campoamor. Spacious, old building has 20 rooms with large windows. Communal bathrooms are somewhat dingy. Singles €12; doubles €18-24; triples €27. ❶

Hotel Ovetense, C. San Juan, 6 (☎985 22 08 40; fax 985 21 62 34). From the train station, take C. Uría, turn left on C. Jovellanos, and C. San Juan will be the 2nd right. Comfortable rooms in a noisy neighborhood. Only a few steps away from the cathedral. Singles €25-31; doubles €37-43; triples €46-57; quads €61-73. AmEx/MC/V. ❸

Hotel Vetusta, C. Covadonga, 2 (☎985 22 22 29; fax 985 22 22 09). From the train station, walk down C. Uría; C. Melquíades Alvarez will be the 2nd street on your left and will become C. Covadonga. A modern 3-star hotel, Vetusta offers jacuzzis and saunas in half of its rooms. Singles €50.50-70; doubles €73-96. AmEx/MC/V. ❺

FOOD

If you only have enough euros for one drink in Oviedo, be sure to try *sidra* (cider) by the bottle (€1.50-3.60). It goes fast, and much of it ends up on the floor due to the unconventional pouring method. For the best *sidra* experience, head to the wooden-beamed, ham-hung **sidrerías,** where waiters pour from above their heads and expect you to swallow in one huge gulp. Cheap restaurants line C. Fray Ceferino between the bus and train stations. The indoor **market** on Pl. El Fontán, is at the end of C. Uría after Campo San Francisco (open M-Sa 8am-3pm). For groceries try **Supercor,** C. Uria, 15, next to El Corte Inglés (open M-Sa 9:30am-9:30pm).

Mesón Luferca, a.k.a. **La Casa Real del Jamón,** C. Covadonga, 20 (☎985 21 78 02). From Campo San Francisco, walk across Pl. La Escandalera, down C. Argüelles, veering left at Alcalde Manuel García Conde; C. Covadonga will be on the left. You'll see a lot of hanging hams; feed the big bad wolf inside you—huffing and puffing optional. *Tapas* €4.75-21. Open M-Sa 8:30am-midnight. MC/V. ❷

Alberobella Pasta Fresca, C. Independencia, 22 (☎985 27 57 15). Walking down C. Uría toward the train station, turn left onto C. Independencia just after El Corte Inglés. Despite the fast food appearance, Alberobella makes delicious and authentic Italian concoctions, perfect for the *tapas*-weary traveler. Huge pasta dishes €5.20-7.60. Open M-F 11am-4pm and 6:30-11:30pm, Sa-Su 11am-11:30pm. MC/V. ❷

La Mallorquina, C. Milicies Nacionales, s/n, just off C. Uría across from Campo San Francisco. Sunny pastry cafe also offers light, vegetarian-friendly fare. Salads €6-12. *Menú* €7.50. Open daily 10am-midnight. ❷

La Pumarada, C. Gascona, 8 (☎985 20 02 79). From C. San Francisco walk down C. Argüelles; C. Gascona is on the right hand side after C. Luna. Located on *La Calle de la Sidra,* La Pumarada is both a popular restaurant offering delicious meat and fish entrees (€13-17) and a starting point for Oviedo's nightlife, with friendly waiters serving the traditional glasses of *sidra* (€1.95 per bottle). Open Tu-Su 9am-2am. ❹

El Café de la Encimada, C. San Antonio, 3 (☎985 20 33 17). Walking down C. Santa Ana away from the Cathedral, C. San Antonio is the 1st street on your right. A beautiful restaurant with brick walls and wooden floors in the midst of the *casco antiguo*. Offers a varied selection of entrees (€10-40). Open daily from 10am-2am. ❺

SIGHTS

CATHEDRAL. Recent renovation restored Oviedo's cathedral to its original beauty. Two chapels are roofed with a brilliant blue ceiling above the altar. The **Capilla de Santa María del Rey Casto,** which houses the royal pantheon (the tombs

> **TOWER OF BABLE** Galicians have Gallego, Catalans have Catalan, and Asturians have...Bable? It's not an official language, but the dialect has returned full-force with the sweeping post-Franco reassertion of regional tradition, and it's now taught to children in school. The codification of a hodgepodge of more than 10 distinct traditional dialects originating in different corners of Asturias, Bable's grammar borrows from many but belongs to no one. As a result, almost no one is fluent in the tongue (you probably won't hear it on the street) and grandmothers tend to express bewilderment at their grandchildren's bable-ing.

of important members of the Asturian monarchy), was chosen by Alfonso II el Casto, in 802 to house the remains of Asturian monarchs and Christian relics rescued from the Moors. An intense metal relief sculpture in the unusual **Capilla de San Pedro** depicts Simon Magnus dropped from the sky by hideous demons. The cathedral complex also includes an 80m **tower** with great views of the city's rooftops, a *cámara santa* (holy chamber), a **cloister,** and a church **museum.** *(Pl. Alfonso II. Standing on C. Uría in front of Campo San Francisco, cross Pl. La Escaladera and walk up C. San Francisco to the cathedral. ☎985 22 10 33. Cathedral open daily 10am-8pm. Free. Cámara Santa €1.25. Museum ☎985 20 31 17. Museum, Cámara, and cloister open M-Sa 10am-2pm and 4-8pm. €2.50, seniors €1.80, children €0.90. Th free.)*

MUSEO DE BELLAS ARTES. The two buildings of the **Museo de Bellas Artes** in the **Palacio de Velarde** display a wide range of Asturian art and a small collection of 16th- to 20th-century Spanish works. While the upper floors display devotional art on loan from Madrid's Prado, the ground floor has a permanent collection of astonishing modern works by local artists. In addition to the Klimt-esque work of Herme Anglada Camaresa, the highlight is undoubtedly José Ramón Zaragoza's triptych of the myth of Prometheus. *(C. Santa Ana, 1, and C. Rúa, 8, just up C. Santa Ana from Pl. Alfonso II. ☎985 21 30 61. Open Tu-Sa 11am-2pm and 4:30-8:30pm; Sa 11:30am-2pm and 5-8pm; Su 11:30am-2:30pm. Free.)*

OTHER SIGHTS. Behind the cathedral is the **Museo Arqueológico-Antiguo Monasterio de San Vicente** and the **Iglesia de San Vicente,** the original urban center of medieval Oviedo. *(C. San Vicente, 3. Standing in front of the Campo San Francisco on C. Uría, cross Pl. La Escandalera and walk up C. Argüelles; follow it as it becomes C. Jovellanes, then turn right onto C. San Vicente. Museum ☎985 21 54 05. Open Tu-Sa 10am-1:30pm and 4-6pm; Su 11am-1pm. Church ☎985 21 18 70. Open Tu-Sa 10am-1pm and 4:30-7pm; Su 11am-1pm. Both free.)* The **Centro de Arte Moderno** hosts temporary exhibits of regional and national cutting-edge artists. *(C. Alonso Quintanilla, 2, opposite the post office. Walk up C. Argüelles from C. Uría and take the 1st left onto C. Pelayo; C. Alfonso Quintanilla is the 1st right. Open M-F 5-9pm, Sa 11:30am-2:30pm and 5-9pm, Su 11:30am-2:30pm. Free.)* Asturian Pre-Romanesque was the first European attempt to blend architecture, sculpture (including human representations), and mural painting since the fall of the Roman Empire. The style was developed under Alfonso II (789-842) and refined under his son Ramiro I, for whom the *Ramirense* style is named. Two beautiful examples, **Santa María del Naranco** and **San Miguel de Lillo,** lie 4km outside Oviedo on **Monte Naranco.** *(☎985 25 72 08. Both open May-Sept. M-Sa 9:30am-1pm and 3-7pm, Su 9:30am-1pm; Oct.-Apr. Su-M 9:30am-1pm, Tu-Sa 9:30am-1pm and 3-7pm. €1.50, children €0.75. M free.)*

HIKING

Though not the best base for hiking in the Picos de Europa National Park (see p. 509), Oviedo is definitely the place to stock up on gear and supplies, as shops within the park and in its gateway towns can be prohibitively expensive.

Federación Asturiana de Montaña, C. de Julián Clavería (☎985 25 23 62), near the bullring, a 30min. walk from the city center. Or take bus #2 (dir.: Hospital) from C. Uría. If you walk, you'll need the full-sized map of the city from the tourist office. Organizes excursions and provides guides, weather conditions, and advice on the best hiking routes. Instructors for everything from paragliding to kayaking. Open M-F 8am-8pm.

Oficina Parque Nacional de los Picos de Europa, C. Arquitecto Reguera, 13, 2nd fl. (☎985 24 14 12). Heading toward the train station on C. Uría, turn left onto C. Gil de Jaz then right onto C. Arquitecto Reguera. Excursions, camping, and trail info. Open M-F 8am-3pm and 5-7pm. The office in **Cangas de Onís,** Av. Covadonga, 35 (☎985 84 91 54), is the best place to get detailed (free) information on the Picos.

Deportes Tuñon, C. Campoamor, 7. From C. Uría heading toward the train station, turn right onto C. Doctor Casal, then left onto C. Campoamor. Extensive selection of camping and rock-climbing gear, long underwear, and a few maps. Open M-F 10am-1:30pm and 4:30-8:30pm, Sa 10am-1:30pm. AmEx/MC/V.

ENTERTAINMENT

The streets south of the cathedral, especially C. Mon and the areas around Pl. Riego, Pl. El Fontán, and Pl. El Paraguas, teem with noisy *sidrerías* and clubs. Stylish **Bar Riego,** on Pl. Riego, serves tasty *batidos* (milkshakes; €1.80-3.60) on a breezy *terraza.* (Open M-Sa noon-4pm and 8pm-2am.) After a few *chupitos* and *copas*, most students head to one of the several clubs in the area. **20th Century,** C. Mon, 12, and **Hispania,** C. Altamirano, 1, are both very popular among locals and tourists and play mostly pop music. (Mixed drinks €2-3. Open midnight-8am.) Wine connoisseurs follow **la ruta de los vinos** from *bodega* to *bodega* along C. El Rosal; walk up C. Uría away from the train station to its end, and C. El Rosal will be on the right. (*Copas* €1.80-3.60.) On C. La Luna, between Alcalde García Conde and C. Jovellanos, **Danny's Jazz Café,** C. La Luna, 11, hosts a variety of acts. (☎985 21 14 83. Beers €1.80. Mixed drinks €3.60. Open daily 8pm-4am.) From Sept. 19-21, Oviedo celebrates its **fiesta patronal** in honor of San Mateo.

LLANES

Wedged on a narrow ledge between the heights of the Picos de Europa and the cliffs plummeting into the Bay of Biscay, Llanes seems like an apparition. While the small, rocky beaches here are crowded, this is no resort town; rather, it's a small Asturian village—complete with cows, ruins, and winding streets—rising above the frothing teal sea.

TRANSPORTATION. ALSA-Turytrans runs **buses** from C. La Bolera, s/n (☎985 40 23 22; info open M-F 8:30am-7:30pm, Sa-Su 8:30am-2pm and 3:15-8pm) to: **Bilbao/San Sebastián** (5-7hr.; 10:30am, 1:15, 4:30pm; €17); **La Coruña/Pontevedra/Santiago de Compostela/Vigo** (6-11hr., 4:55am, €26-35); **Oviedo** (1-1½hr.; M-F 10 per day 6:30am-8:30pm, Sa-Su 7-8 per day 8:45am-8:15pm; €7); **Santander** (2¼hr., 5 per day 10:30am-9pm, €5). To reach the town center from the bus station, take a left onto C. La Bolera, and veer to the right as it becomes C. Cueto Bajo; at the post office, turn left onto C. Les Barqueras, which leads to the Ayuntamiento and tourist office. **Trains** chug from the FEVE station, C. Alonso Vega, s/n (☎985 40 01 24) to **Oviedo** (2½hr., 5 per day 8:05am-8pm, €5.65) and **Santander** (2hr.; 11:27am, 6:13pm; €5.15). To get to the tourist office from the train station, walk up C. Román Romano, turn left onto C. Manuel Romano, and then right onto C. Nemesio Sobrino. For a **taxi** call 24hr. ☎985 40 11 77.

PRACTICAL INFORMATION. The **tourist office** is in a 13th-century tower on C. Alfonso IX, directly behind the yellow Ayuntamiento on C. Castillo Meraderes. (☎985 40 01 64. Open July-Aug. M-Sa 10am-2pm and 5-9pm, Su 10am-3pm; Sept.-June M-F 10am-2pm and 4-6:30pm, Sa 10am-1:30pm and 4:30-6:30pm.) For adventure activities, stop by **Centro de Información de Turismo de Aventura,** C. Posada Herrera, s/n, next to the tourist office. (☎985 40 05 41. Open daily 10am-2pm and 4-10pm.) Services include: **emergency** ☎1006; **municipal police,** C. Nemesio Sobrino, s/n (☎985 40 18 87); **Farmacia Mariano Ruiz,** Pl. Parres Sobrino, 1 (open M-F 9:30am-1:30pm and 4:30-8pm; Sa 10:30am-1pm; **late-night pharmacy** location is posted in the window, though it may be a few towns over); **health center,** Av. de San Pedro, s/n (☎985 40 36 15). For **Internet Access,** head to **Cyber Spacio,** C. La Paz, 6. With the Ayuntamiento on your right, walk down C. Alfonso IX and make a right on C. Nemesio Sobrino, which later becomes C. Egidio Gavito and then C. La Paz. (☎985 40 03 44. €3 per hr. Open M-F 8am-midnight.) **Post office,** C. Pidal, s/n (☎985 40 11 14. Open M-F 8:30am-2:30pm; Sa 9:30am-1pm.) **Postal code:** 33500.

ACCOMMODATIONS AND FOOD. Rooms fill early in summer, making reservations a necessity. **Casa del Río ❷,** Av. San Pedro, 3, a restored mansion near the beach, has wonderful rooms with large windows, some with balconies. Facing the Ayuntamiento, walk left on C. Nemesio Sobrino, and turn right onto San Pedro. (☎985 40 11 91. Reception 24hr. Doubles €30-36, with bath and TV €38-50.) The spacious and bright rooms of **Pensión La Guía ❷,** Pl. Parres Sobrino, 1, are right in the center of town. (☎985 40 25 77. Check-out 2pm. Reservations accepted. Doubles with bath €38-50. MC/V.) **Albergue de la Estación ❶,** C. Alonso Vega, s/n, at the FEVE station, is Llanes's only hostel, frequented by Spanish teens enjoying a beach weekend. The owners arrange outdoor excursions in the Picos. (☎985 40 14 58 or 610 52 81 11. Lockout 1:30-5pm. 4- to 8-bed dorms €12. MC/V.) On a small bluff, **Camping Entreplayas ❶,** off Av. de Toro between Playas de Puerto Chico and Toro, is wildly popular, if not for its scenic views, then for the neighboring bar, where campers laze away their days with bikinis and beer. (☎985 40 08 88. €2.40 per person, per tent, and per car; electricity €1.80. IVA not included.)

Cafes and *sidrerías* line C. Las Barqueras, C. Castillo de Marqueres, and C. Nemsio Sobrino; near the beaches, Av. de Toro and C. Marqués de Argüelles have many local eateries. **Café Bitácora ❶,** C. Las Marqueras, 1 (☎985 40 03 88) serves salads (€2-5) and entrees (€5-6) in a quiet setting close to the river. However, the most interesting fare in town is undoubtedly served at **Sabor Latino ❷,** C. Venezuela, 1. From the Ayuntamiento, walk up C. Nemesio Sobrino, turn right on Av. San Pedro, and then left onto C. Genaro, which becomes Av. de Méjico and brings you to the C. Venezuela. This tropical cantina serves all the Mexican favorites, including guacamole, enchiladas, and fajitas. (Bar open daily 10am-2am daily; restaurant 8pm-2am. Entrees €3-10.82.) For groceries, go to **El Arból,** C. Manuel Romano, 3, at the intersection with C. Román Romano. (Open M-Sa 9am-9pm.)

BEACHES. Though some of the most popular beaches in Asturias, these are not the wide swaths of sand that jump to one's mind. Rather, Llanes's beaches are tucked into coves and inlets along the coast, made all the more idyllic by the occasional rocky outcropping in the water. As these are protected waters, the sea is calm (and rather seaweedy). The compact **Playa de Sablón,** in the center of town, is the most popular—and the most crowded. From the Ayuntamiento, turn right onto C. Alonso IX, which runs straight to the beach. **Playa de Toro** is by far Llanes's prettiest and most swimmable beach, though it's still fairly crowded. It's also the only beach with any semblance of waves. From the Ayuntamiento, walk up C. Castillo Mercaderes across the river, and turn left onto Av. de la Guía at the post office, which turns into Av. de Toro. **Playa de Puerto Chico** will please those looking for total seclusion, but only if they can stand the mountains of seaweed and their accompanying stink. Follow the directions to Playa del Sablón, above, and take the steps up the hill to the **Paseo de San Pedro,** a grassy strip running along the edge of the cliffs above the sea. Plenty of benches, shade trees, and chameleons share the wide open and breezy sea views.

CANGAS DE ONÍS

During the summer months, when the streets are packed with mountaineers and vacationing families, it can seem like Cangas's (pop. 6285) sole purpose is to help travelers spelunk and hang glide. While it's true that most visitors come to Cangas to get closer to the Picos de Europa National Park (see p. 509), Cangas is, if not thrilling, a relaxing, history-rich town. Its few sights highlight the town's Paleolithic and Celtic legacies, but the rest of this busy mountain town is devoted to the outdoors. Cangas is not the most central base for exploring the Picos, but it does have plenty of less hard-core outdoor opportunities.

TRANSPORTATION. ALSA, Av. Covadonga, 18 (☎985 84 81 33), in the Pícaro Inmobiliario building across from the tourist office, runs **buses** to: **Arenas de Cabrales** (30min.; M-F 4 per day 11am-7:30pm, Sa-Su 11am; €2); **Oviedo** (1½-2hr.; M-F 9 per day 6:15am-8:15pm, Sa-Su 6 per day 9:15am-8pm; €4.70); **Madrid** (7hr., 2:35pm, €24.68) via **Valladolid** (5hr., €14); **Covadonga** (30min.; M-F 10 per day 8:30am-7:40pm, Sa-Su 8 per day 9:15am-7:40pm; returns to Cangas 10:30am-8pm; €1.50). For a taxi call **Radio Taxi** (24hr. ☎985 84 87 97 or 84 83 73) or wait in front of the Ayuntamiento.

PRACTICAL INFORMATION. The main street in Cangas de Onís is **Av. Covadonga.** The **tourist office,** Jardines del Ayuntamiento, 2, is just off Av. Covadonga across from the bus stop. (☎985 84 80 05. Open May-Sept. daily 10am-10pm; Oct.-Apr. daily 10am-2pm and 4-7pm.) Park information is available at the **Picos de Europa National Park Visitors' Center,** Av. Covadonga, 43, in the **Casa Dago.** The office has a list of mountain *refugios*, maps, hike suggestions, and a fantastic, three-dimensional model of the park. From the bus stop, walk up Av. Covadonga toward the large church. (☎/fax 985 84 86 14. Open daily 9am-2pm and 5-6:30pm.) Services include: **Santander Central Hispano,** Av. Covadonga, 6 (☎985 84 87 84; open Apr.-Sept. M-F 8:30am-2:30pm, Oct.-Mar. also Sa 8:30am-1pm); **emergency** ☎112; **municipal police** in the Ayuntamiento, Av. Covadonga, 21 (☎985 84 85 58); **pharmacy,** Av. Castilla, 24, just off Av. Covadonga near the Puente Romano (open 9am-2pm and 4:30-7:30pm); **health center,** C. de la Cárcel, s/n (☎985 84 85 71), down C. Emilio Laria from Av. Covadonga; and the **post office,** Av. Constantino González, s/n, a right off Av. Covadonga when heading toward the Puente (☎985 84 81 86; open M-F 8:30am-2:30pm, Sa 9:30am-1pm). **Postal code:** 33550.

ACCOMMODATIONS AND FOOD. A few clean *pensiones* along Av. Covadonga will gladly accept your euros. Hospedaje Principado ❷, Av. Covadonga, 16, 3rd fl., is a tiny, immaculate *pensión* with a TV in every room. Walking down Av. Covadonga toward the Puente Romano, Av. Castilla is the last street on the left before the bridge. (☎985 84 83 50 or 667 98 31 88; fax 985 84 83 15. Singles €15-18; doubles €20-27, with bath €33-39.) El Chofer ❶, C. Emilio Laria, 10, has clean rooms, firm beds, Oriental rugs, and hall baths. C. Emilio Laria is the street directly in front of the tourist office across Av. Covadonga. (☎985 84 83 05. Winter heating. Reception in El Chofer restaurant around the corner. Singles €9-12; doubles €20-22.) Camping Covadonga ❶, in Soto de Cangas, 4km up the road toward Arenas de Cabrales (5-7 buses per day), has a cafeteria, bar, supermarket, and showers. (☎985 94 00 97. €3.76 per adult, €3.16 per child; €3-4 per tent; €5-6.43 per car. Open *Semana Santa* and June-Sept. 20.) Restaurant Pizzería Eladia ❷, next to the bus stop, serves pizzas (€6-7), entrees (€7-9), and three course *menús* (€9). (Open daily 9am-midnight.) Choose from sandwiches, *pinchos*, *tapas*, and even hamburgers (€2-5) at Cafetería Reconquista ❶, C. Covadonga, 6. (☎985 84 82 75. Open daily 8am-11pm.) For a do-it-yourself-meal, try Alimerka Supermercado, Av. Covadonga, 15. (Open Su-M 9am-2pm, Tu-Sa 9am-9pm.)

SIGHTS AND EXCURSIONS. At the far end of Av. Covadonga is the **Puente Romano,** a medieval bridge with an ornate golden cross hanging from the middle. From the bridge, following Av. Covadonga into town, turning left onto C. Constantino González, and crossing the river brings you to the **Capilla de Santa Cruz.** This Romanesque chapel, built in AD 737, sits atop the town's oldest monument, a Celtic *dolmen* (monolith) dating from 3000 BC, which can be seen from the chapel's cave. (Open daily 10am-1pm and 3-6:30pm.) Also of interest is **Cueva del Buxu** (BOO-shoo), whose walls are adorned by 15,000-year-old paintings by Cangas's paleolithic residents. To reach the cave, follow the main road to Covadonga for 3km until the signs for the *cueva* and Cardes, the closest town, directs you left. From here, it's a gradual 1km climb past pastures to the easily missed sign to the caves, by Bar Cueva El Buxu. **Buses** to Covadonga, Llanes, and Arenas (see **Transportation,** above) run near the cave; ask to be dropped off at the **Cruce de Susierra.** Come early, as only 25 people are allowed in each day. (☎985 94 00 54. Open Apr.-Sept. W-Su 9:30am-1pm and 4-6:30pm; Oct.-Mar. W-Su 9:30am-1pm and 3-5pm. €1.32. W free.) Those with wheels will want to head south from Onís along Río Sella. This route winds through Santillan, Sames, and finally to the **Desfiladero de los Beyos,** a 11km gorge filled with wet rocks and blossoming beech trees.

ADVENTURE TOURISM. Cangas de Onís is the perfect place to arrange outdoor activies, but it is imperative to reserve ahead of time, especially June-Aug. **Aventura,** Av. Covadonga, 23 (☎985 84 92 61; fax 985 84 85 61), sets up various expeditions, including hiking (only in the low season), white-water rafting, *espeleología* (spelunking), *barranquismo* (canyoning, swimming, and spelunking), canoeing, horseback riding, 4-wheeling, and bungee jumping. Prices range €19-42 per person depending on the activity, time of day, and size of the group. Prices include equipment, a guide, transportation to and from Cangas, and sometimes a bagged lunch. Discounts are offered for large groups and/or multiple activities. Call for departure times and destinations. **Monteverde,** C. Alférez Provisional, 5 (☎985 84 80 79; www.hotel-monteverde.com) offers the same activities led by very friendly instructors (€22-36 per person). **Los Cauces,** Av. de Covadonga, 23, offers most of the same activities for similar prices. (☎985 94 73 18 or 985 84 01 38. €18-33 per person. Open daily 9:30am-9:30pm.) The tourist office lists other agencies.

ARENAS DE CABRALES

Some say the small town of Arenas de Cabrales (pop. 800) sits "as close to the sky as to the ground," and that's not so far from the truth. This one-street hamlet rests on several craggy peaks. The fog, wandering mountain goats, and breathtaking vistas make Arenas seem almost like a mountain mirage, drawing outdoor enthusiasts eager to take advantage of the excellent hiking and climbing just 6km away in the Picos de Europa National Park (see p. 509).

TRANSPORTATION. **ALSA buses** (☎902 42 22 42) head to **Oviedo** (2½hr.; M-F 4 per day 7:25am-5:50pm, Sa-Su 8:35am, 5:50pm; €6.37) via **Cangas de Onís** (50min., €2)

THE CHEESE STANDS ALONE It's an odd selling point, but somehow Cabrales has become famous by emphasizing the unbridled moldy funkiness of its blue cheese. To produce the cheese, locals arduously empty cow, goat, and ewe udders into large tin bins. After allowing the mix to "mature," cheese-makers drain the extra liquid, add a pinch of cow afterbirth and a twist of lamb fetus, store the mush inside cabbage leaves and let them stew in mountain caves in humid darkness. Half a year later the speckled brown wheels rolls out onto the sidestreets of every tourist destination in Asturias. Brave tasters rave about the pungent flavor, the creamy texture, and the "knock you to the floor and have you begging for yo' *madre*" kick.

and to **Poncebos** (20min.; M-F 6 per day 10:15am-7:15pm, Sa-Su 7:15am; €0.75). Buses to Poncebos depart from the tourist hut; the others leave from across the street in front of the small park (look for the ALSA sign). For a **taxi,** call Joaquín (☎985 84 64 87 or 689 38 06 03), who claims "un cliente, un amigo" and will go just about anywhere in the Asturian Picos.

PRACTICAL INFORMATION. The **tourist office,** in a hut on the main road just before the bridge, is small but helpful. (☎985 84 64 84. Theoretically open July-Sept. 20 Tu-Su 10am-2pm and 4-8pm, but in reality has no set hours.) Services include: **emergency** ☎112; **Guardia Civil,** on the main road toward Cangas near the post office (☎985 84 50 04); **Consultorio Médico** (☎985 84 55 04), uphill on the main road across the street from the **ATM** and the pharmacy; the **pharmacy** (☎985 84 50 16), next to Cajastur; and the **post office,** near the bus stop but towards Cangas (open M-Sa 9-11am). **Postal code:** 33554.

ACCOMMODATIONS AND FOOD. Since many of Arenas's visitors opt for camping, the town has few reasonably priced hotels. **El Castañeu ❶,** down C. Pedro Niembro directly across from the tourist office, offers decent doubles and triples with breathtaking views of the Picos. (☎985 84 65 73. Reserve 2 months ahead. Winter heating. Doubles with bath €24-30.) Family-style **Pensión Covadonga ❶,** next door to El Castañeu, offers similarly spotless rooms with incredible mountain views. (☎985 84 68 10. Reserve 2 months ahead. Doubles €24-27.) **Hotel Picos de Europa ❸,** Arenas de Cabrales, s/n. With your back to Cangas, walk down the main road from the bus stop, and the hotel will be on your right. Hotel Picos de Europa offers ample, fully equipped, and comfortable rooms. (☎985 84 64 91. Reservations 1 month ahead required for July and Aug. €36-65, depending on the time of the year.) **Naranjo de Bulnes Camping ❶,** 1km east on Crta. AS-14, has campsites and cabins, as well as a cozy TV room, a cafeteria, a bar, and shower facilities. (☎/fax 985 84 65 78. Camping €4.18 per person, €3.86-5.14 per tent, €3.70 per car. Cabins 1-2 people €33; each additional person €6.)

Of the few eateries in Arenas, **Restaurant La Panera ❸** is by far the best. Atop a small hill to the left of Banco Bilbao Vizcaya and behind La Jueya Restaurant, this restaurant has the look and the feel of an intimate alpine lodge, complete with a romantic balcony and outdoor terrace with astounding views of the surrounding peaks. From the tourist office, walk uphill on the main road; after the curve, look to the left for the restaurant's sign. (Entrees €11-17.) For a traditional Spanish *cafetería*, head down the main road to **Cafetería Santelmo ❷,** beside Hotel Picos de Europa, which offers a wide variety of dishes (€7-9) and *tapas* (€2-6). (Open daily noon-4pm and 8pm-midnight. AmEx/MC/V.) The **Casa Tres Palacios** store is opposite the tourist office. (Open daily 6:30am-7pm.)

ADVENTURE TOURISM. Novedades Cendón, across the street from the tourist office, sells basic gear and maps. (☎985 84 64 74. Open daily 10am-1pm and 3-7pm.) **PicoSport,** next door to El Castañeu, also sells gear and arranges expeditions. (☎667 64 68 60. Activities €18-42.) **Pico Urrielly** (☎985 85 67 70), outside of town toward Panes on AS-114, arranges hiking expeditions, spelunking, canoeing, and horseback-riding. Prices range from €12-48, depending on the activity, the length of the trip, the size of the group, and the day of the week.

PICOS DE EUROPA

Three hundred million years ago, Mother Nature flapped her limestone bedsheet and erected the Picos de Europa, a mountain range of curious variation and chaotic beauty. This accident of nature created a formidable border between the Asturias and Cantabria region and the rest of Spain. In fact, this jagged barrier is one of the main reasons Asturias never fell to the Moors, instead finding protection and divine inspiration in this otherwise impenetrable range. Although the mountains and towns here often feel as isolated as they were centuries ago, they are now actually part of the very civilized Picos de Europa National Park. Founded in 1918 as the National Park of Covadonga, Spain's first foray into the national park scene, Covadonga grew into the largest national park in Europe, spanning three massifs and three provinces (Asturias, Cantabria, and Castilla y León).

The ancient crags and summits shelter some of Europe's most elusive and endangered species, including wild horses, boars, bears, and *chamois* (a goat-type animal), as well as long-eared owls, Egyptian vultures, songbirds, and eagles. The scrub-spotted peaks lure thousands of outdoor enthusiasts, who come to explore the myriad caves and caverns carved out by centuries of glacial abuse. Gorges and rivers criss-cross the floor of the park, and silent alpine meadows sway in the breeze high above.

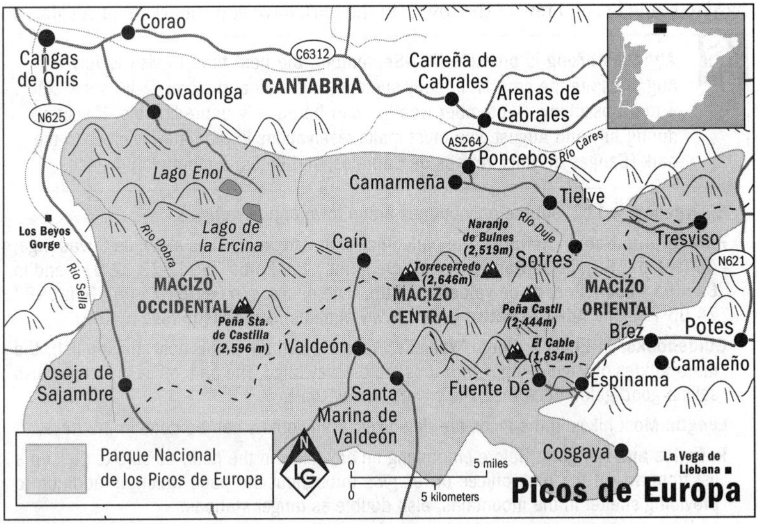

ORIENTATION

Part of the larger Cordillera Cantábrica range, the Picos de Europa consist of three mountainous massifs: the **Occidental** (Cornión), the **Central** (Urrieles), and the **Oriental** (Ándara), with the highest peak **Torrecerredo** (2646m) rising out of the Central massif. Several rivers wind through the floor of the park; the three largest are the Sella, Dobra, and Cares. The **Garganta del Cares** (Cares Gorge), which cuts a dramatic border between the Central and Oriental massifs, holds the park's most popular trails and most famous peaks: the life-claiming Peña Vieja (2613m) and Pico Tesorero (2570m), the stark Llambrión (2642m), and the mythic **Naranjo de Bulnes** (Picu Urriellu; 2519m). Serious hikers interested in multi-day treks use **Arenas de Cabrales** (see p. 507) as their base; those interested more in day hikes and guided adventure tourism start in **Cangas de Onís** (see p. 506) and **Potes** (see p. 523). Although independent adventures are definitely possible, most visitors opt for guided hikes and expeditions instead of setting out on their own.

TRANSPORTATION

Getting to the Picos is relatively easy—it's the getting around once there that's difficult. **ALSA buses** link **Cangas de Onís** (see p. 506) and **Arenas de Cabrales** (see p. 507), the gateways in the west and the north, with the towns lying just inside the park's borders, the most important of which are Covadonga and Poncebo; **La Palomera buses** link **Potes,** the gateway in the east, with Fuente Dé. It is, however, much more efficient to travel by car as buses run infrequently on weekdays and service is severely limited on weekends. Route **AS-114** runs along the north edge of the Picos from **Cangas de Onís** (10km north of **Covadonga**) through **Arenas de Cabrales,** and on to **Panes,** where it intersects Route N-621. N-621 runs 50km south and west to **Potes,** where a branch leads to **Fuente Dé.**

PRACTICAL INFORMATION

The key to hiking in the Picos is planning ahead. Water sources and campsites are hard to come by, and few of the towns in the park have supermarkets or ATMs.

> Although hiking is possible May-September, the best time to visit is July and Aug., despite the crowds. In early summer, it is cold and stormy, with snow still a real possibility; September weather can be equally unpredictable. If visiting during July and August, you must make reservations in the gateway cities to the park (Cangas de Onis, Arenas de Cabrales, and Potes) a month in advance.

Emergency: ☎112, but the only phones are in town and at *refugios*.

Park Information: In **Asturias,** the park office is in Cangas de Onís at Av. de Covadonga, 43 (see p. 506); in **Cantabria:** Fuente Dé in the Ctra. Potes (☎942 73 32 01); and in **Castilla y León:** Posada de Valdeón at Ctra. Cordinanes, s/n (☎987 74 05 49; fax 987 74 05 79). The **Administrative Office** (www.mma.es) is in Oviedo (see p. 499).

Guidebooks: In English, Robin Walker's *Picos de Europa* is the best. In Spanish, the many guides of Miguel Angel Andrados are the way to go. The park office in Cangas also sells a good guide book that lists several hiking trails.

Length: Most hikes in the Picos are day hikes. Many others can be done in 2-3 days.

Refugios and Rangers: Before embarking on any hikes in the park, be sure to pick up a list from any of the park offices of *refugios* throughout the park, which, in addition to providing shelter in the mountains, also double as ranger stations.

Gear: Basic amenities and hiking gear are available in all of the gateway towns, but **gear** is cheapest in Oviedo (see p. 499). Inside the park, **food and water** are scarce, even in the towns of Poncebos, Covadonga, and Fuente Dé, none of which have supermarkets. Only in Oviedo are **water purification** packets available. The free **maps** of the park provided by tourist offices are insufficient for hiking. Extensive trail maps can be purchased in just about every store in Cangas de Onís, Arenas de Cabrales, and Potes.

Tours and Guided Hikes: For information on **adventure tourism** outings see Cangas de Onís and Potes. There are no outfitters in Arenas de Cabrales. The park service offers **free guided hikes** daily, all departing between 9:30 and 10:30am from Los Lagos, Covadonga, Poncebos, and Fuente Dé, in addition to other towns throughout the park. For a complete list of hikes and departure locales, visit one of the park offices.

ACCOMMODATIONS

The easiest accommodations are in Cangas de Onís, Arenas de Cabrales, and Potes; however, these limit one to day hiking. For multi-day hikes, the 15 **refugios** (usually cabins with bunks but not blankets) scattered throughout the park are the best option (6 in the Macizo Occidental, and 9 in the Macizo Central). All of the park offices have a complete list of the Picos's 15 *refugios*. There are only five **campgrounds** in the park and all are in towns (Buferrera, Cain, Santa Marina, Caldevilla, and Fuente Dé). Other lodging options include **albergues** (hostels, usually in ancient, unheated buildings with bunks and cold water) and **casas** (buildings with bunks, hot water, and wood stoves); these, however, are also only in or near towns. In all cases you should bring a sleeping bag. Prices range €3-6 per person, and reservations are usually not accepted, though it's wise to call ahead to see if space is available before you set out. Towns within the park also have *pensiones* and rooms in private residences; look for *camas* and *habitaciones* signs.

HIKING AND EXCURSIONS

For multi-day routes, consult one of the Picos de Europa park offices. In addition to the following suggested day hikes, there are numerous free guided hikes arranged through the park offices. The following hikes are listed according to the nearest trailhead or town. Before embarking on any hike, secure a good map that has all trails clearly marked. The following are merely suggestions; be sure to gather more information before departing.

COVADONGA

Covadonga is accessible only from Cangas de Onís and Oviedo. ALSA buses (☎902 42 22 42) from Cangas (30min.; M-F 6 per day 8:30am-6:45pm, Sa-Su 4 per day 10am-4:40pm; €0.90) and Oviedo (1¾hr., 9:30am, €5) grace Covadonga with two stops, one at the Hospedería and one uphill at the basilica.

SUGGESTIONS FOR HIKERS Always consider the difficulty level and length of route when planning your hike. If you don't get a guide or hike with someone that knows the area, stay only on clearly marked trails. Never start a hike without a compass and a map of the area (minimum scale 1/25000). Before you start hiking, tell someone where you are heading and when you expect to come back. The best guides are the people you will find during your hikes; don't hesitate to ask them for any information you might need. If you want to spend the night in the *refugios* scattered throughout the park, call ahead and make sure they're open. In case of fog, it is better to sit down and wait rather than walk around without knowing where you are.

SKY HIGH While the mountaineers in the Picos tend to shy away from Spain's usual party life, they do indulge every once in a while. The biggest Picos party is the **Fiesta del Pastor** (July 25th) in Vega del Enol, near the glacial lakes of Ercina and Enol. Called the *Romería cerca del cielo* ("feast near the sky") for its mountainous location, the party starts at 8am, when most of the town starts the trek up to the lakes. Competitions like the Escalada a la Porre de Enol (a type of local alpinism race), the bareback horse race, and the town tug-of-war are serious affairs; the winners of the last 12 years are listed in local newspapers.

"This little mountain you see will be the salvation of Spain," prophesied Don Pelayo, the first king of Asturias, to his Christian army in 718, gesturing to the rocky promontory above what is now Covadonga. The mountain soon became the site of the first successful rebellion against the Moors, although legend claims that it was not geography but the intervention of the Virgin Mary that made victory possible. Don Pelayo became the first king of Asturias, and out of this battle grew *la Reconquista.* Covadonga was also the center of the first national park in Spain, the precursor to the Picos de Europa established in 1918. Visitors come to Covadonga to see the cliffside basilica, and the cave where the Virgin is said to have appeared to Don Pelayo. Nearly 1300 years ago he prayed to the Virgin for help in defeating the Moors from atop a waterfall in the **Santa Cueva.** Today, pilgrims and tourists crowd the quiet, candlelit sanctuary where the Virgin appeared to him. (Open daily 9am-9pm, in winter 9am-7pm. Free.) The **Santuario de Covadonga,** a neo-Gothic basilica built in 1901, towers above the town. (Open daily 9am-9pm, in winter 9am-7pm. Free.) The **Museo del Tesoro,** across from the basilica, displays the *Corona de la Virgen,* a gold-and-silver crown studded with 1109 diamonds and 2000 sapphires; below it lies a sparkling crown crafted to honor Jesus. (Open daily 11am-2pm and 4-7:30pm. €1.20, children €0.60.) On Wednesdays, the park service offers a moderately difficult **hike** through the mountains around Covadonga (3hr., departs at 10am from Escolania).

Covadonga's **info office,** on the main road near the Hospedería, has details on local accommodations and sights. (☎985 84 60 35. Open daily May-Oct. 10am-2pm and 3-7pm; Nov.-Apr. 11am-2pm and 3-5pm.) Cangas offers cheaper accommodations, but it's hard to resist the friendly atmosphere and stunning views of the mountains at the **Hospedería del Peregrino ❸,** on the main highway. (☎985 84 60 47; fax 84 60 51. €20-35, depending on room and season. AmEx/MC/V.) **Hotel Pelayo ❹,** (☎985 84 60 61), near the Santa Cueva, offers comfortable rooms with astounding views of the Picos. Singles €30; doubles €62. For a quick meal, visit **Merendero Covadonga ❶** (☎985 84 60 67), right where the main highway meets the road to the Lagos. Enjoy a wide variety of sandwiches (€2), *raciones* (€4), *platos combinados* (€6), and *paellas* (€8) on the outdoor terrace. (Open daily 9am-9pm, or later if there are enough customers.) The only **groceries** in town arrive for Hospedería guests twice a week (W and Sa) by truck—buy them from the driver at the hostel.

LOS LAGOS DE ENOL Y ERCINA

These tarns, or mountain lakes, are accessible from Cangas de Onis and Covadonga (see above). ALSA buses (☎902 42 22 42) run from Cangas past Covadonga, continuing to the lakes (45min.; July-Aug. M-F 6 per day 8:30am-6:45pm, Sa-Su 4 per day 10am-4:40pm; Sept.-June 2 per day; €1.62). In Covadonga, buses leave from the basilica to follow a frightening but spectacular road lined with cliffs and precipitous pastures; the right side of the bus has the best en route views. It's not worth the trip on cloudy days.

Perhaps the most impressive site in the park, the ice-cold **Lagos de Enol y Ercina** sparkle silently among limestone slopes and open valleys. Free guided hikes around the lakes depart from the Buferrera parking lot (3hr., M-F 10:30am). Slightly more difficult hikes are offered W at 9:30am (5hr.) and F at 10am (4hr.). The first recommended hike goes from the Buferra parking lot around Lago Enol, on to the **Mirador del Príncipe** and the **Mina de Buferrera,** an old abandoned mine. After the *mina*, the trail leads to the Lago Ercina, the **Monte Palomberu,** and ends up in the parking lot. This is an easy hike that takes 2-3hr. to complete.

Two especially good hikes from the lakes take travelers east to the **Vega de Ario,** which offers a panoramic view of the Urrieles mountains (8-9hr. round trip, medium to high level of difficulty), or south to the **Mirador de Ordiales,** a vantage point overlooking the Pico de las Vidriosas, Río Pomperi, and a frightening gorge (7-8hr. round-trip, rated as a difficult hike). Alternatively, head west (2km) to the **Mirador de Rey** lookout point, then wander among the beeches of the **Bosque de Pome** (4-5hr.). Both lookouts are accessible by car driving from Covadonga to Los Lagos. The **Refugio de Vega de Ario** (1630m) sits just off the trails leading from the lakes, 300m past the intersection and behind the **free Buferrera campgrounds.** The refuge has 40 spots year-round and provides meals and guides. To get there by car, follow highway C-6312 (the Cangas de Onís-Panes highway), take the *desvío* (exit) for Covadongas y Lagos, go right at Lago Enol, and continue straight to the refugio. (☎639 81 20 69. No reservations accepted. €3.)

PONCEBOS

Poncebos is only accessible from Arenas de Cabrales. ALSA buses run from Arenas de Cabrales (20min.; July-Sept. M-F 6 per day 10:15am-7:15pm, Sa-Su 7:15am; €0.75). By car, take AS-114 to Las Arenas, then turn across the river onto AS-264 to town.

Poncebos is actually the starting point for Arenas's hiking trails 6km away. The walk to the trailhead threads through the feet of surrounding mountains; tight, winding roads make some corners dangerous. For those interested in spending the night, **Hostal Poncebos ❷** (☎985 84 64 47) and **Hostal-Restaurante-Bar Garganta del Cares ❷** (☎985 84 64 63) have comfortable rooms. (Singles in both €18-24; doubles €36.) Check with the tourist office about **refugio** options.

Poncebos marks the start of one of the Picos's most famous trail, the 12km **Ruta del Cares.** Chiseled out of the mountains, the gorge's vertical walls drop 200m down to the Río Cares below. The Ruta del Cares is an easy hike that starts in Poncebos and ends in **La Posada del Valdeón.** However, it is possible to walk for only a couple of hours from Poncebos to **Caín** and take a taxi or bus from there to the Posada del Valeón. The whole trail takes approximately 6hr., but only 3hr. to get to Caín. The **Poncebos-Bulnes** route follows the Río Tejo to Bulnes, a small village that is seemingly frozen in time. This is also an easy hike and takes approximately 3hr. Consider tucking in at the **Albergue de Bulnes ❶,** which has 20 beds in three rooms, a bar, library, showers, guides, and meals. (☎985 84 59 43. Reservations suggested. €9 per person, with breakfast €12.) The park service offers free guided hikes to Bulnes on Tuesday and Saturday (4hr.; departs at 10am from the small information hut on Poncebos's main highway). The **Poncebos-Invernales de Cabao-Naranjo de Bulnes** route, a killer 17km hike (10-12hr.), crawls first to Invernales de Cabao and then inches 9km farther to the Picos's most famous mountain, **Naranjo de Bulnes,** named for its unmistakable sunburnt orange face. From here you can see the major *picos* in the area and the dancing blue waves of the Bay of Biscay in the distance. Most climbers start the hike in **Sortes** and continue from there (9-10hr.). There are two *refugios* in the Naranjo de Bulnes area: **Refugio Vega de Urriellu** (☎985 94 50 24; 96 beds; €3 per person) and **Refugio Jou de Los Cabrones** (☎985 36 69 32; 24 beds; €3). If the trail is open, it's worth going beyond the **Poncebos-Camareña** path, up a rocky slope, to **Puertos de Ondón,** where the view is incomparable.

FUENTE DÉ

Fuente Dé is accessible only from Potes on ALSA buses (☎902 42 22 42; 45min.; July-Sept. M-F 8:15am, 1, 8pm, Sa-Su 1pm; €3.91), which stop right at the cable car base.

Only 23km from Potes, the **Teleférico de Fuente Dé** is well worth an excursion. The mind-blowing, goosebump-inducing *teleférico*, the third largest cable car in the world, jets 750m to the mountain top (1834m) in less than 4min. (☎942 31 89 50. Open July-Aug. daily 9am-8pm; Sept.-June 10am-6pm. €6, round-trip €9; under 10 round-trip €4.50.) A zig-zagging trail ascends just left of the cable (3hr.). At the top, there are many safe routes along four-wheel-drive tracks. If you're feeling ambitious, take the northern trail to **Sortes.** Another good, less demanding Fuente Dé trek starts and ends at the cable car's lower station (11½km; 4½hr.). The **Somo Waterfall Route** swings through the Berrugas cattle sheds, the soft Bustantivo meadows, and on to the Somo waterfall. From the top of the *teleférico*, it's a 4km walk to **Refugio de Aliva** ❹ (1666m), the most expensive and luxurious 'refuge' in the park. All rooms come with full baths and heat in winter; there is also a cafe on site. (☎/fax 942 73 09 99. Doubles €45. MC/V.) To return to road-level, retrace your steps to the *teleférico* or walk (3hr.) to **Espinama,** where **Habitaciones Sebrango** ❷ offers respite from the Picos. (☎942 73 66 15. Singles €24; doubles €30.)

CANTABRIA

From the spectacle of Santander's *El Sardinero* beaches to the pristine provincial park of Oyambre, it's the shore that makes Cantabria famous. Though they have yet to see the resort build-up of Spain's more famous southern coasts, the region's beach towns are by no means untouched or secluded. The beach scene, particularly in Santander, is what lures visitors, but Cantabria also has some of the world's cleanest surfing waters, hikes in the Picos de Europa, Paleolithic cave drawings, and renowned architecture like Gaudí's *El Capricho.*

SANTANDER ☎942

Welcome to Vacationland, Spanish-style. Here in Santander (pop. 185,000), palm trees rub shoulders with pines, pasty Brits bake on the beach next to well-bronzed Spaniards, and the grime of the city center is easily forgotten on the walk down *El Sardinero's* bougainvillea-filled boardwalks. Santander has been destroyed three times by natural and not-so-natural disasters—a fire at the beginning of the 15th century incinerated everything in sight, an explosion on a dynamite ship in 1893 leveled the city, and in 1941 another fire gutted the peninsular town. The most recent incarnation of Santander has resulted in the "ideal city," complete with surf, sand, and sometimes sun. Those looking to get away from it all should avoid Santander, as it is "all" and then some. Those willing to share their beach space with a thousand other sun-starved bodies will, however, reap great rewards. The mountainous horizon with cliff-top lighthouses is the Bay of Biscay at its best.

TRANSPORTATION

Flights: Aeropuerto de Santander, Av. de Parayas (☎942 20 21 00), in nearby Camargo 4km away. Serviced by Iberia only. Accessible only by taxi (€10). **Iberia,** Po. Pereda, 18 (☎942 22 97 00). Open M-F 9am-1:30pm and 4-7pm.

Trains: Both the FEVE and RENFE stations are at Pl. de las Estaciones, s/n. **RENFE** (☎942 28 02 02) serves only a few destinations, as Santander is the terminus of a rail line; to head elsewhere, you'll need to take a slower FEVE train to larger cities east or west of

Santander. Info open 7:30am-11pm. To: **Madrid** (7hr.; M-Th 8:10am, 3:45, 11pm; F-Sa 8:10am, 3:45pm; Su 8:10am, 3:45, 5:15, 11pm; €41.16); **Palencia** (2¼hr., 5 per day 8:10am-11pm, €9.66-18.66); **Valladolid** (5hr., 5 per day 8:10am-11pm, €12.31-21.16). **RENFE ticket office,** Po. Pereda, 25 (☎942 21 23 87). Open M-F 9am-2pm and 5-7pm, Sa 9am-1:30pm.

Buses: Navas de Tolosa, s/n (☎942 21 19 95), across C. Rodríguez from the train station. Info open M-F 8am-10pm, Sa 8am-1pm. To: **Barcelona** (10hr.; daily 9am, 1:45, 9:30pm; €39.45); **Bilbao** (1½hr., 25 per day 6am-9pm, €5.43); **Burgos** (4hr.; daily 10:30am, 4:30, 8pm; €18); **León** (3½hr.; M-Sa 9am, 4pm; €10); **Oviedo** (3½hr.; M-F and Su 9 per day, Sa 7 per day 6:30am-7:30pm; €20.35); **Madrid** (6hr., 4 per day 10:30am-7pm, €21-27); **Salamanca** (6hr.; 9am, 4, 8pm; €13.27).

Ferries: Brittany Ferries, Estación Marítima, s/n (☎942 36 06 11; www.brittany-ferries.com), near the Jardines de Pereda. To **Plymouth, England** (2 per week, €81-219, plus €6 for seat reservation). Info M-F 9am-3:30pm and 4:30-7:30pm. In summer reserve 2 weeks ahead. **Los Reginas,** Embarcadero, s/n (☎942 21 66 19), by the Jardines de Pereda. Tours of the bay (45min., June 6-Sept. 1 3-6 per day, €3).

Public Transportation: Municipal buses (info ☎942 20 07 71) run frequently throughout the city (every 15min.; July-Aug. 6am-midnight, Sept.-June 6am-10:30pm; night buses run every hr. midnight-6am; €0.90). Buses #1, 3, 4, 5, 7, and 9 run from the Ayuntamiento stop (buses heading east stop in front of the plaza; buses heading west stop in front of Foot Locker) to El Sardinero along Po. de Pereda and Av. de la Reina Victoria, stopping at Pl. Italia and Jardines de Piquío. Stops are usually not marked with route numbers, but the tourist office offers bus route maps.

Taxis: Radio Taxi (☎942 33 33 33). 24hr. and service to greater Santander. Taxis wait outside the train stations, on C. Vargas and near the Ayuntamiento.

Car Rental: Avis, C. Nicolás Salmerón, 3 (☎942 22 70 25). Min. age 25, must have had driver's license for at least 1yr. and a credit card in the renter's name. From €54 per day. Open M-F 8am-1pm and 4-7:30pm, Sa 9am-1pm.

ORIENTATION AND PRACTICAL INFORMATION

Santander sits on a peninsula in the Bay of Biscay; its southern shores form the Bay of Santander. There are two main sections to the city: **the center,** around the train and bus stations and the Jardines de Pereda in the east, and **El Sardinero** in the west. The main thoroughfare starts at the Ayuntamiento in the center as **Avenida Calvo Sotelo,** and runs along the shore to the Jardines de Piqui in El Sardinero, changing its name to **Paseo de Pereda** and **Avenida de la Reina Victoria** along the way. At the western tip of Santander is **La Peninsula de la Magdalena,** the city's famed park. Santander is surprisingly large; the best way to get around is by city bus.

Tourist Office: Jardines de Pereda (☎942 20 30 00). From any of the stations, walk up C. Calderón de la Barca into the park; the office is off Po. de Pereda on the left just before the rotary. Bus and city maps. Open July-Sept. daily 9am-9pm; Oct.-June M-F 9am-1:30pm and 4:30-7:30pm, Sa 9am-1:30pm. **Branches** in the ferry station, Pl. Porticada, and El Sardinero across from Pl. Italia; all open July-Sept. daily 10am-9pm.

Budget Travel: TIVE, C. Canarias, 2 (☎942 33 22 15). Take eastbound bus #5 from the Ayuntamiento 6 stops to C. Camilo Alonso Vega, 22. ISIC €5. HI card €10. Open M-F 9am-2pm.

Currency Exchange: Santander Central Hispano, Av. Calvo Sotelo, near the post office. Open May-Sept. M-F 8:30am-2:30pm; Oct.-Apr. M-F 8:30am-2:30pm, Sa 8:30am-1pm.

Luggage Storage: Lockers at the **RENFE train station,** by the ticket window (€3 per day). Open daily 7am-11pm. Lockers at the **bus station** on the bottom level near *pasaje* 16 (€3 per day). Open daily 7:30am-10:30pm.

Emergency: ☎112. **Police:** Pl. Porticada, s/n, and Av. del Deporte (☎942 20 07 44).

Hospital: Hospital Universitario Marques de Valdecilla, Av. de Valdecilla, s/n (☎942 20 25 20). **Ambulances:** (☎942 31 30 00, 942 27 30 58, or 942 32 06 05).

Pharmacy: Lda. Isabel Ochoa, C. Castilla, 15, around the corner from the train station. Open M-F 10am-2pm and 4-9pm, Sa 10am-3pm. In El Sardinero, Rosio Castanedo Pfeiffer, Av. de los Castros, 75. Open M-F 10am-2pm and 4-8pm, Sa 10am-2pm. For late-night pharmacies, call ☎942 22 02 66 to find the pharmacist on call. Every pharmacy also posts the weekly schedule of on-call pharmacies.

Internet: Divernet Informática, C. Cisneros, 25 (☎942 24 14 25). €1.80 per hr. Open M-Th 9am-2pm and 4-10pm, Sa 9am-2pm and 4pm-1am, Su 4-10pm.

Post Office: Av. Alfonso XIII, s/n (☎942 21 26 73). Open M-F 8:30am-8:30pm, Sa 9:30am-2pm. **Branch** in El Sardinero on Av. Las Cruces, s/n. Open M-F 8:30am-2pm. **Lista de Correos, fax** only at Av. Alfonso XIII branch. **Postal Code:** 39080.

ACCOMMODATIONS AND CAMPING

In summer and on weekends, all rooms are booked over a week in advance; showing up in town without a reservation will most definitely leave you homeless. The train and bus stations are loaded with *pensión* hawkers, but beware: this is illegal, and the rooms are often far from the beaches. The highest hotel densities are near the market on Pl. Esperanza, across from the train station on C. Rodríguez, and along elegant Av. Castros in El Sardinero.

EL SARDINERO

Everyone wants to stay in El Sardinero, and for good reason: it's lined with beaches and promenades. Unfortunately, its popularity means rooms are expensive and hard to come by. From the Ayuntamiento stop in the city center, take bus #1, 3, 4, 5, 7, or 9 to Piquío (Hotel Colón); Av. de los Castros is directly to your left.

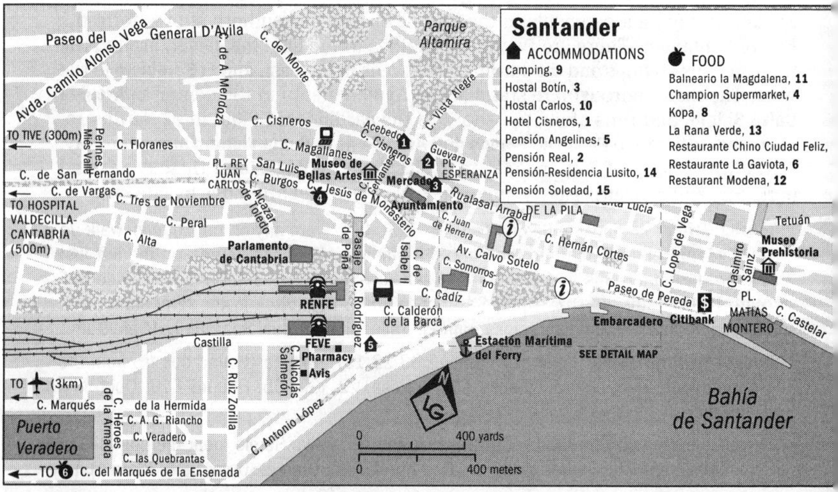

Pensión-Residencia Luisito, Av. Castros, 11 (☎942 27 19 71). The garrulous owner will tend to your every need. Airy rooms sport flowered sheets, terraces, sinks, and sloping ceilings. TV room on 1st fl. Breakfast €1.50. Open July-Sept. Doubles €30. ❷

Pensión Soledad, Av. Castros, 17 (☎942 27 09 36), next door to Luisito. 16 large rooms with sinks and good views. Breakfast €1.35. Singles €18; doubles €30 (IVA not included). Open July-Sept. ❷

Hostal Carlos, Av. de Reina Victoria, 135 (☎942 73 00 15; fax 942 73 04 05). Big, sunny rooms across from El Sardinero beach. English and German spoken. June 16-June 30 singles €37; doubles €51. July 1-Sept. 15 €48/€63. Mar. 16-June 15 and Sept. 16-Nov. 4 €31/€44. MC/V. ❹

Camping: 2 sites lie on the scenic bluff of Cabo Mayor, 2km from Primero and Segundo Playas. From the Ayuntamiento, take bus #8 or 9 to Av. del Faro, 7 stops after Piquío. From the bus stop, turn left onto Av. del Faro and follow it into the Cabos; the campgrounds are a 10min. walk. Alternatively, head north along coastal Av. de Castañeda, bear right at the roundabout with the park on your left, and then turn left onto G. Marañon; Av. del Faro is on the right.

Camping Municipal Bellavista, Av. del Faro, s/n (☎942 39 15 30), is a 1st-class site just minutes from Playa de Matalenas. Reception daily 8am-midnight. €0.60 per person and per car. ❶

Camping Cabo Mayor, Av. del Faro, s/n (☎942 39 15 42). Pool and tennis courts. Slightly pricier option than Bellavista. Reception daily 8am-11pm. €10 per person and per car, €6 per tent. Open July 15-Sept. 30. ❶

CITY CENTER

Although the area is loaded with cheap accommodations, only out of desperation should one stay near the stations. By day, the area is grimy, noisy, and far from the beach; by night, it's unsettling. The area north of the Ayuntamiento and Av. de Calvo Sotelo is a far more pleasant area in the center. While the beaches are a bus ride away, this neighborhood is packed with restaurants, shops, and bars.

Hostal Cisneros, C. Cisneros, 8, 1st fl. (☎942 21 16 13). From the Ayuntamiento plaza, walk 3 blocks up C. Cervantes. A clean, comfortable option. All rooms have TVs, beautiful wooden headboards, sunny terraces, and bathrooms. Reservations with 1st night's payment required. Doubles €36. Open June-Sept. Cash only. ❷

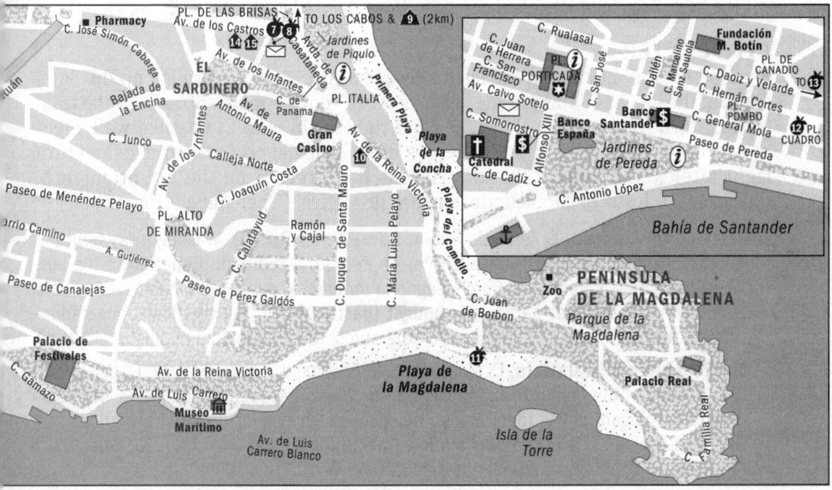

Pensión Angelines, C. Rodríguez, 9, 2nd fl. (☎942 31 25 84). Immaculate rooms with huge windows and winter heating. Strong shower. TV lounge. July-Aug. singles €18; doubles €27. Sept.-June €12/€21. ❷

Pensión Real, Pl. Esperanza, 1, 3rd fl. (☎942 22 57 87), in the peach building at the end of C. Isabel II. Communal baths, but all rooms have sinks. No reservations. June-Sept. doubles €30-36; Oct.-May €24. ❷

Hotel Picos de Europa, C. Arco Iris, 3 (☎942 37 10 15; fax 942 37 10 35). Facing the Ayuntamiento, follow C. Jesús de Monasterio to your left until you reach Pl. Rey Juan Carlos; C. Arco Iris will be on your left. Fully equipped rooms with TV, bathroom, and telephones in Santander's commercial district. Singles €25; doubles €40. MC/V. ❸

Hostal Botín, C. Isabel II, 1, 1st fl. (☎942 21 00 94 or 630 49 26 06). Crazy 80s comforters keep guests warm. Balconies overlook the bustling market. 25% discount on the public parking lot (100m away). Reservations accepted with pre-pay. Singles €13; doubles 21-37; triples €28-48; quads €37-63. ❶

FOOD

EL SARDINERO

The best grocery option is **Alimentación Different,** C. Joaquín de la Costa, 18, in the Hotel Sartena shopping complex. (Open M-Sa 9:30am-2:45pm and 5:45-9:30pm, Su 10am-3pm. AmEx/MC/V.)

Restaurante Chino Ciudad Feliz Iruña, C. Las Brisas, s/n (☎942 27 32 30). This seaside restaurant serves all the Westernized Chinese staples. Alas, no fortune cookies, but plenty of other post-meal gifts to make your family a happy one. Lunch *menú* €9.20. Entrees €5.75-9. Open daily 1-4pm and 7pm-midnight. MC/V. ❷

Cafetería Kopa, C. Las Brisas, s/n, in the same building as Ciudad Feliz. Though not the most exciting fare, Kopa has what most restaurants in El Sardinero lack: good food at reasonable prices. *Menú del día* €9. Open daily 10am-2pm. ❷

Balneario La Magdalena, C. La Horadada, s/n (☎924 03 21 07), on Playa La Magdalena. A quiet restaurant on the beach with a decent selection of entrees (€7-10). The best place for a late afternoon beer. Open daily 10am-midnight. ❷

CITY CENTER

Seafood restaurants crowd the **Puerto Pesquero** (fishing port), grilling up the day's catch at the end of C. Marqués de la Ensenada. From the main entrance of the train station, turn right onto C. Rodríguez and right again onto C. Castilla; walk eight blocks down and turn left on C. Héroes de la Armada; cross the tracks and turn right after about 100m (20min.). Across the street from the Ayuntamiento, **Champión,** C. Jesús de Monasterio, s/n, has groceries. (Open M-Sa 9:15am-9pm.)

Restaurante Modena, C. Eduardo Benot, 6 (☎942 31 33 71). Walking away from the tourist office and the post office on Po. de Pereda, C. Eduardo Benot is on the left. Delectable Italian standards, from lasagna to *tortellini al quattro formaggio,* served in a sleek dining room. Not particularly budget (pasta €6-10), but the filling, vegetarian-friendly fare and *tiramisú* are worth the extra euros. Open M-Sa 1pm-midnight. MC/V. ❷

Bar Restaurante La Gaviota, C. Marqués de la Ensenada, s/n (☎942 22 11 32 or 942 22 10 06), at the corner of C. Mocejón in the *barrio pesquero* (fishermen's neighborhood). An elegant dining room hidden behind a rough exterior. Try the fresh grilled sardines (12 for €3.60) or the *paella mixta* (*ración* for €3.60). *Menú* €7.50. Open daily 11:30am-4:15pm and 7:30pm-midnight. MC/V. ❷

La Rana Verde, Daoiz y Velarde, 30 (☎942 22 24 02). The biggest collection of frog figurines you'll ever see and tasty *patatas* (€2-3) set this place apart from the countless fast-food joints in Santander. Sandwiches €2.30-3.40. Open daily noon-midnight. ❶

SIGHTS

While Santander is proud of its few official architectural sights and museums, skip them in favor of its beaches and parks unless it rains (which is very likely), in which case Santander's amusing—and free—museums are worth a perusal. The tourist office has a list of one- to two-hour walking tours, the best way to get to know the city and feel like you actually did something during the day.

PENÍNSULA DE LA MAGDALENA. Although it can feel a bit like an amusement park at times, La Magdalena is Santander's prime attraction and one of the most beautiful parts of the city. The entire peninsula is filled with palms and pines and ringed by bluffs plunging into the sea and slender, calm beaches. The park's centerpiece is the *palacio*, the 20th-century, neo-Gothic mansion that was Alfonso XIII's summer home. Today, the palace houses the elite Universidad Internacional Menéndez Pelayo summer sessions on oceanography. The peninsula also shelters a mini-zoo (polar bears, penguins, and sea lions only), sports several models of mermaids and ships, and offers a free trolley ride around the park. Walking, however, is the best way to explore, and the 2km path ends with nourishment: *churrerías* flank the park's entrance. *(Península de La Magdalena. ☎942 27 25 04. Park open daily June-Sept. 8am-10pm; Oct.-May 8am-8:30pm. The palace has no scheduled visiting hours.)*

LOS CABOS. Just north of the El Sardinero beaches are more peninsular parks. While Cabo Menor and Cabo Mayor lack the attractions and action of La Magdalena, their bluffs and vistas are even more scenic. Cabo Menor, the more southern of the two, houses Santander's golf course and another mini-zoo; it also has postcard-worthy views of Cabo Mayor's 19th-century lighthouse. *(From Pl. Italia, walk up Av. de Castañeda past Pl. Glorieta Doctor Fleming, and turn right onto Av. de Pontejos, which turns into Av. del Faro and takes you up onto the cabos.)*

MUSEO DE BELLAS ARTES. Devoted to the works of local artists, Santander's Museo de Bellas Artes is surprisingly impressive. Art history buffs will enjoy the collection of 20th-century pieces, many of which mimic the

IN RECENT NEWS

CAVING IN

In 1879, 8-year old Maria Sanz de Sautuola stumbled on a 15,000-year-old art gallery. Paleolithic man's murals of deer, horses, wild boar, and bison charmed the world, and by the 1970s, 3000 visitors a day were heading to Altamira to marvel at them.

The moisture from their breath and their body heat took their toll on the cave paintings, and in 1982, officials limited the number of visitors to 20 per day, in an effort to preserve the historical treasures. The waiting list is now three years long, and staff say that many cry from happiness when finally allowed to enter the cave.

Unfortunately for them, and for anyone who dreams of visiting *La Cueva de Altamira*, the cave will be closed for an undetermined amount of time. In 2002, a sample of reddish pigment from a bison found Acidobacterium, which may be contributing to the decay of the cave paintings. A team of microbiologists of the University Clinic of Vienna has been assembled to work in the cave and try to identify the numerous microorganisms.

Luckily, a new $20 million replica of the cave stands just 100 yards away, at the **Museo de Altamira.** Over 2000 people a day can visit these caves, which are accurate down to the bump.

styles and trends of the time: much of the sculpture could easily be mistaken for Giacometti, and an entire room is devoted to forays into Cubism (and apparently Juan Gris imitation). The lower two floors feature special exhibitions of more well-known Spanish artists like Picasso and Miró. *(C. Rubio, 6. ☎942 23 94 85. From the Ayuntamiento, walk up C. Jesús de Monasterio and turn right onto C. Florida; the museum is on the right. Open July 15-Sept. 15 M-F 10:30am-1pm and 5:30-8pm, Sa 10:30am-1pm; Sept.16-June14 M-F 10am-1pm and 5-8pm, Sa 10am-1pm. Special exhibitions open until 9pm. Free.)*

CATEDRAL DE SANTANDER. Built in the Middle Ages, Santander's Gothic cathedral is often called the city's first monument. The heads of martyred Roman soldiers Emeterio and Celedonio are kept inside the ruins of an oven once used to heat Roman baths; occasionally they are taken out for religious processions. After dropping into the guillotine basket in AD 300 in La Rioja, they were brought to Santander in the 8th-century for safekeeping during the Moorish invasion. *(On Pl. Somorrostro, just behind the post office and Banco España. ☎942 22 60 24. Open M-F 10am-1pm and 4-7:30pm, Sa 10am-1pm and 4:30-8:45pm, Su 8am-2pm and 4:30-9pm. Free tours in Spanish at 10:30, 11:30am, 12:45, 4:30, 5:45, 6:30, and 7:30pm daily. Cathedral free.)*

MUSEO MARÍTIMO DEL CANTÁBRICO. The top floors of the Museo Marítimo chart the evolution of regional fishing-boats, while the bottom floor highlights the sea's living creatures. *(C. San Martín de Bajamar, beyond the Puerto Chico. ☎942 27 49 62. Open mid-June to mid-Sept. Tu-Sa 11am-1pm and 4-7pm, Su 11am-2pm; mid-Sept. to mid-June M-Sa 10am-1pm and 4-6pm, Su and holidays 11am-2pm. Free.)*

BEACHES

In Santander, every day is a beach day: rain or shine (but most often rain), locals flock to the beach as soon as work gets out and spend the late afternoon and evening soaking up the last rays of sun. It's easy to understand why, as Santander's beaches, particularly those in El Sardinero, are wide swaths of powdery sand. The water, however, can get very rough; it's not uncommon for five-foot breakers to crash into the beach. The water is calmer and the beaches rockier on the bay side. The best and most popular beaches are undoubtedly **Playas Primero y Segundo** in El Sardinero. Not only does the soft sand go on forever, but the waters have been named one of the eight cleanest beaches in the world. Primero and Segundo are also the hangout of Santander's surfing crowd, which comes out during and after rain. Calmer waters but no fewer bodies line the southern shore of La Magdalena. Rock-framed **Playa de Bikinis,** on the peninsula itself, is the most secluded and the haunt of Santander's guitar-playing teens; **Playa de la Magdalena** and **Playa de Los Peligros,** stretching from the peninsula to below Av. de la Reina Victoria, are virtually waveless and therefore very popular with families. To escape the beach-going hordes, either head across the bay to **Playas Puntal, Somo,** and **Loredo** lining a narrow peninsula of dunes, or hoof it up to the remote beaches of Los Cabos where **Playa de Matalenas** and **Playa de Los Molinucos** await you sans the throngs.

ENTERTAINMENT AND NIGHTLIFE

The August **Festival Internacional de Santander** brings crowds of people and myriad music and dance recitals to town, culminating in the **Concurso Internacional de Piano de Santander.** For more info, contact the **Oficina del Festival,** Palacio de Festivales de Cantabria (☎942 21 05 08), on C. Gamazo. The **Baños de Ola** is a turn-of-the-century style celebration of Alfonso XIII's discovery that, lo and behold, playing in the waves is fun. The festival takes place in the third week of July on the El Sardinero promenades, with bathers clad in antique swimming suits. That same week, the *barrio pesquero* celebrates the patron of fishermen, **Santiago.**

Exhausted from sunbathing, everyone in Santander seems to hit the sack early. In **El Sardinero,** cafes and bars line the promenade along Playas Primero and Segundo, with street performers offering live entertainment to families and teenagers. Others spend their evenings blowing euros at the **Gran Casino,** Pl. Italia, s/n. Passport, proper dress (pants and shoes), and a minimum age (18 to gamble) are required. (Open 24hr.) In the city center, university students and older couples *tapas*-hop around Pl. Cañadío, C. Daoíz y Velarde, and C. Pedrueca; facing Banco Santander from the tourist office, walk up C. Las Infantes, which runs into C. Pedrueca. Around 2 or 3am, crowds flood **C. Río de la Pila** and **C. Casimiro Sainz.**

DAYTRIPS FROM SANTANDER

CUEVAS DE ALTAMIRA

The Altamira caves are just outside of Torrelavega on the way to Santillana del Mar. La Cantábrica (☎942 72 08 22) sends buses from Pl. Estaciones, s/n, in Santander to Torrelavega (30min.; M-F 7 per day 9am-9:30pm, Sa-Su 5 per day 10:30am-9:30pm; €1.65). Ask the bus driver to let you off near the caves.

Bison roam, horses graze, and goats butt heads on the ceilings of the limestone **Cuevas de Altamira,** dubbed the "Sistine Chapel of Paleolithic Art." The large-scale polychrome paintings are renowned for their scrupulous attention to naturalistic detail and resourceful use of the caves' natural texture. Unfortunately, excessive tourism has caused substantial damage, and now only 20 people per day are allowed to visit. **To see the caves yourself, you must be at least 13 years old and must write to request permission at least one year in advance.** Rumor has it there's a three-year waiting list, but if you do write, include a photocopy of your passport and address the request to the **Centro de Investigación de Altamira,** Santillana del Mar, Cantabria, Spain 39330 (☎942 81 80 05; fax 942 84 01 57). For those not fortunate enough to get a ticket to the caves, the **Museo de Altamira** offers a replica of the original cave and plenty of information about the archaelogical treasures of Altamira. (☎942 81 80 05. Open June-Sept. Tu-Sa 9:30am-7:30pm, Su 9:30am-5:30pm. €2.40, Sa afternoon and all day Su free.)

SANTILLANA DEL MAR

Santillana del Mar is on the Santander-San Vicente de la Barquera line. La Cantábrica (☎942 72 08 22) sends buses from Navas de Tolosa, s/n, in Santander (45min.; M-F 7 per day 9am-9:30pm, Sa-Su 5 per day 10:30am-9:30pm; €1.70). In Santillana, buses stop on C. Santo Domingo in front of the Museo Diocesano; the return bus stops in front of the stairway across the street.

French philosopher Jean-Paul Sartre proclaimed Santillana del Mar (pop. 4000) to be the most beautiful town in Spain, and perhaps it is: atop a hill in northern Cantabria, the town is a perfectly preserved collage of tangled stone streets and architecture dating back to the Middle Ages. Alas, Santillana's beauty is no secret to others, and the town seems entirely devoted to the hundreds of tourists who pass through daily. If you dislike crowds and commercialism, avoid Santillana altogether.

The town doesn't owe its name to either its flatness (*llana*) or its seaside perch *(del mar)*, as it has neither of these; it is named for the **Colegiata de Santa Juliana,** a 12th-century Romanesque church founded by Turkish monks that holds the remains of Juliana, a woman martyred for not renouncing her virginity or faith in God. The sepulchre guards her relics and the gorgeous high altarpiece is a 15th-century Spanish-Flemish painting depicting the saint's martyrdom. From the bus stop in front of the steps on C. Santo Domingo, walk uphill into town, and veer to the right at the first fork onto C. Cantón, which turns into C. del Río and leads directly to the church.

(Open daily 10am-1:30pm and 4-7:30pm. €2.40, which also gets you into the Museo Diocesano.) From the front of the Colegiata, heading back up C. del Río leads to the **Museo del la Tortura y de la Inquisición.** This small museum reveals the dark side of Christianity with an exhibit of terrifying torture methods used during the Spanish Inquisition. The most frightening is the vaginal pear, an expanding device that, when inserted, will gouge out and burst all the abdominal organs. (☎942 84 02 73. Open daily 10am-9pm. €3.60.) The **Museo Diocesano,** across the street from the stop on C. Santo Domingo in the Monasterio Regina Coeli, has a mediocre collection of religious relics and artwork. Most interesting is the collection of over 300 miniature figurines of the crucifixion. (Open daily 10am-1:30pm and 4-7:30pm. €2.40, includes admission to the Colegiata.)

The **tourist office** is in **La Casa del Aguila y la Parra** on Pl. Ramón Pelayo. From the bus stop, walk uphill on C. Santo Domingo and veer left at the first fork; this leads directly onto Pl. Ramon Pelayo. (☎942 81 82 51. Open daily 9am-1pm and 4-6pm.) The **post office** is next door to the tourist office on Pl. Ramón Pelayo. (☎942 81 80 40. Open M-F 8:30am-2:30pm, Sa 9:30am-1pm.) **Postal code:** 39330.

COMILLAS

Comillas lies on the Santander-San Vicente de la Barquera bus route. La Cantábrica buses (☎942 72 08 22 or 942 72 08 22) run from Santander, Navas de Tolosa, s/n (M-F 7 per day 9am-9:30pm, Sa-Su 5 per day 10:30am-9:30pm; €3).

The beaches of Comillas (pop. 2500) are intoxicating. From desolate and calm inlets to the wind-swept swaths of sand directly on the Bay of Biscay, Comillas's beaches are its main attraction, and drawing everyone from Spanish nobles to foreign visitors for their summers. Everyone shuttles serenely to the beaches, amazed to simply have access to the splendor of Comillas. This small resort town's central beach, **Playa Comillas,** is a vast expanse of silky sand and raging waves; on windy days, 10-foot breakers pound the shores. From the bus stop follow up C. Marqués de Comillas uphill into town. Pass through Pl. del Generalísimo and veer left onto Cuesta General Mola; after another small square, Corro San Pedro will be on the right. From this street, turn left onto C. La Moria, and then follow the footpath downhill to the beach (10min.). Heading in the opposite direction on C. Marqués de Comillas from the bus stop will bring you, 4km later, to **Playa Oyambre,** another expansive beach. It's easier to take the La Cantabria bus toward San Vicente and ask the driver to let you off at Oyambre.

Comillas is equally proud of its architectural attractions. Most notable—and amusing—is **El Capricho,** Gaudí's summer palace. While it's not possible to tour the building, most visitors are content to see the bright swirling turrets and gingerbread-esque windows outside. Standing at the bus stop, you can see the colorful palace on the hill; follow the footpath across the street for a closer view. For a look inside El Capricho, it is possible to eat a meal in the house's dining hall. (Reservations ☎924 72 03 65. Entrees €12-13. Open daily 1-4pm and 9-11:30pm.) Next to El Capricho on the same hill are the neo-Gothic **Palacio de Sobrellano** and the **Capilla-Pantheon,** containing furniture designed by Gaudí. (Hours vary; check with the tourist office before venturing over.) From July 15-18, Comillas's **fiestas** go up in a blaze of fireworks, pole-walking, goose-chasing, and dancing in the plaza.

The **tourist office** is at C. María del Piélago, 2. From the bus stop follow C. Marqués de Comillas past the turn-off for the beach, through the plaza, and uphill one block, then follow the signs to the office. (☎942 72 07 68. Open May-Sept. M-Sa 10am-1pm and 5-9pm, Su 11am-1pm and 4:30-7pm.) The **post office** is at C. Antonio López, 6, on the main road uphill from the tourist office turn-off. (☎942 72 00 95. Open M-F 8:30am-2:30pm, Sa 9:30am-1pm.) **Postal code:** 39520.

POTES

The Potes (pop. 2000) tourist brochure prophesies "...*Y Volverás*" (you'll return) and it's probably right; visitors tend to fall in love with this town in the shadow of the mountains. In addition to making a great base for outdoor activities in the Picos de Europa National Park (see p. 509), Potes itself can captivate for days.

TRANSPORTATION. **Palomera buses** (☎942 88 06 11 or 942 50 30 80) travel to and from **Fuente Dé** (45min.; M-F 8:15am, 1, 8pm; Sa-Su 1pm; €1.50) and **Santander** (2½hr.; M-F 7, 9:45am, 5:45pm; Sa-Su 10:30am, 5:45pm; €5.80). There is no bus station in Potes; all buses stop at the small hut on C. Fonfría near the tourist office, across from the municipal parking lot and in front of the supermarket. For a **taxi** call ☎942 73 04 00. They cluster in Pl. de la Serna.

PRACTICAL INFORMATION. The **tourist office,** C. Independencia, 30, in the old church, has a list of suggested trails and *refugios* with contact info. Free tours of Potes are given daily at noon and 6pm. There are two bus stops in Potes; get off at the second one. From the bus stop, walk up C. Fonfría toward town to Pl. de la Serna, where you'll see signs on the left for the **tourist office.** (☎/fax 942 73 07 87. Open W-Su 10:30am-1:30pm and 4-6pm.) Services include: **Banco Santander,** C. Doctor Encinas, s/n, at the corner of C. San Marcial (☎902 11 22 11; open M-F 8:30am-2pm); **Guardia Civil** (☎942 73 00 07) on C. Obispo off C. Doctor Encinas; **Farmacia F. Soberón,** C. Cántabra, s/n (☎942 73 00 08; open daily 9am-9pm); **health center** (☎942 73 03 60) on C. Eduardo García de Enterría, inside the **Cruz Roja** (Red Cross) building (☎942 73 01 02); **post office,** Pl. de la Serna, s/n (open M-F 8:30am-2:30pm, Sa 9:30am-1pm). **Postal code:** 39570.

ACCOMMODATIONS AND FOOD. Several hostels are scattered on C. Dr. Encinas and on C. Cantábra, a side street. The cheapest rooms fill early in the day, so make reservations. The palatial rooms at **Casa Cayo ❸,** C. Cántabra, 6, a right off C. Dr. Encinas when walking into town from the bus stop, have in-room TVs, phones, bathrooms, and a cozy lounge with an even bigger TV. (☎942 73 01 50. Singles €30; doubles €40. MC/V.) **Hostal Lombraña ❶,** C. el Sol, 2, has small, bright rooms with beautiful views of the mountains. Walking into town from the bus stop, it's on the right just before the bridge; look for the sign. (☎942 73 05 19. Doubles €23-26. IVA not included.) Closer to Panes off C. Dr. Encinas, **Fogón de Cus ❷,** C. Capital Palacios, 2, has sunny, ample rooms. Walking from the bus stop along C. Dr. Encinas into town, the hotel is up a stairway on the right. (☎942 73 00 60. Singles €15; doubles €24, with bath €25. AmEx/MC/V.) Even closer to Panes on C. Dr. Encinas is **Hotel Rubio ❷,** where the friendly English-speaking staff will help you with info on the best hiking trails and food options in town. (☎924 73 00 15. Singles €18-24; doubles €36-42. MC/V.) There are also several *casas de labranza* (farm houses for rent) in the area; ask at the tourist office for details. The closest camping site is the first-class **Camping La Viorna ❶,** about 1km up the road to Monasterio Santo Toribio, which helps organize excursions and has a restaurant, supermarket, and pool. (☎942 73 20 21 or 73 21 01. €3.60 per person, car, and tent. Open *Semana Santa*-Oct. 30.)

Potes can feed plenty of hungry hikers; C. Dr. Encinas, C. Cántabra, and C. San Cayetano are packed with restaurants, *tapas* bars, and cafeterias. **Restaurante El Fogón de Cus ❷** serves hearty mountain fare on white tablecloths; for a livelier atmosphere, ask for a table in the back room with the TV. The restaurant is next door to the *pensión* of the same name. (☎942 73 00 60. *Menú* €11. Open daily 1:30-4pm and 8:30-11pm. AmEx/MC/V.) Another delicious dining option is riverside **Restaurante La Caseta II ❷,** C. Cántabra, 8, next door to Casa Cayo, where veal, lamb, and game are the specialties. (☎/fax 942 73 07 13. *Menú* €11, entrees €7-10. Open daily 1-4pm and 8pm-midnight.) **Restaurante La Serna ❷**, next to the bus stop, offers delicious salads (€4-6), tasty pizzas (€4-6), and the typical three-course *menú* (€7.80) in a sunny terrace. (☎942 73 10 44. Open daily noon-midnight.) **Supermercado Ugari,** C. Dr. Encinas, 6, stocks the basics. (Open M-F 9am-2pm and 4:30-8:30pm, Sa 9am-2pm.)

ADVENTURE TOURISM AND HIKING. The streets of Potes are lined with outfitters specializing in the latest outdoor fads. The tourist office has a list of all the outfitters in town. In the summer, it is necessary to book several days in advance for expeditions. **Picos Aventura,** C. Cervantes, 3, organizes horseback riding, mountain-biking, paragliding, and canyoning. The office is at the base of the bridge on C. Dr. Encinas. (☎942 73 21 61; fax 985 73 21 45. Prices range €15-51. Open daily 10am-2pm and 4-8pm. Closed Su Nov.-May. MC/V.) **La Liebana,** C. Independencia, 4, organizes similar outings. The office is behind the gazebo on the river on C. Dr. Encinas. (☎942 73 10 21; fax 942 73 10 00. Prices range €18-48.) The best horseback riding and paragliding trips are organized through **La Cabaña,** C. La Molina, s/n. (☎942 73 00 50; fax 942 73 00 51. Tandem paragliding €51 per flight. Horseback riding €18.03-28.24.) For those wanting to explore on their own, **Bustamente,** C. Dr. Encinas, 10, sells maps and guidebooks.

Urdón, 15km north of Potes on the road to Panes, is the start of a challenging 6km (4hr.) hike to **Treviso,** a tiny town where chickens outnumber human inhabitants. Trail details are on posters all over Potes. Another option for outings from Potes is **Peña Sagra,** about 13km east (2hr.) of the towns of **Luriezo** or **Aniezo.** From the summit, you can survey the Picos and the sea, 51km away. On your way down, visit **Iglesia de Nuestra Señora de la Luz,** where the beautifully carved patron saint of Picos lives 364 days a year. The Virgin, known affectionately as *Santuca* (tiny saint), is removed from the church and honored on May 2.

GALICIA (GALIZA)

If, as the old Galician saying goes, "rain is art," then there is no gallery more beautiful than the misty skies of northwestern Spain. Galicia looks and feels like no other region of the country. Often veiled in a silvery drizzle, it is a province of fern-laden eucalyptus woods, slate-roofed fishing villages, and seemingly endless white beaches. Rivers wind through hills and gradually widen into estuaries that empty into the Bay of Biscay and Atlantic Ocean.

A rest stop on the Celts' journey to Ireland around 900 BC, Galicia harbors enduring Celtic influences. Ancient *castros* (fortress-villages), inscriptions, and bagpipes testify to this Celtiberian past, and lingering lore of witches, fairies, and buried treasures have earned Galicia a reputation as a land of magic. The rough terrain has historically hampered trade, but ship building, auto manufacturing, and even renowned fashion labels are contributing to the region's gradual modernization and development. Tourists have begun to permeate even the smallest of towns, and Santiago de Compostela, the terminus of the Camino de Santiago, continues to be one of the world's most popular backpacking destinations.

Galicians speak *gallego*, a linguistic missing link of sorts between Castilian and Portuguese. While newspapers and street signs alternate between languages, most conversations are conducted in Spanish. Regional cuisine features *caldo gallego* (a vegetable broth), *vieiras* (scallops, the pilgrim's trophy), *empanadas* (turnovers stuffed with assorted fillings), and *pulpo a gallego* (boiled octopus). Regionalism in Galicia doesn't cause quite the stir it does in the País Vasco or Catalunya, but you still may see graffiti calling for *"liberdade."*

SANTIAGO DE COMPOSTELA ☎981

Santiago (pop. 130,000) is a city of song. From the impromptu orchestra concerts on Rúa Vilar to the thumping of all-night discos, from the roving bands of *gaita* players to the cathedral's morning chimes, every street and plaza is filled with musical celebration. Perhaps these are the chords of weary pilgrims, elated to have, at long last, reached the apostle's tomb. Or perhaps these are the tunes of the Apostolo, the city's extravagant 10-day fiesta in honor of its namesake. But more likely, these are just the sounds of joy at waking up to another day in Santiago, where narrow, Baroque streets empty into vast plazas, where relaxers and revelers spill out of the myriad cafes and bars, and where every day in this sun-blessed (and perhaps Apostle-blessed) city is worthy of celebration.

TRANSPORTATION

Flights: Aeropuerto Lavacolla (☎981 54 75 00 or 981 54 75 01), 10km away on the road to Lugo. A bus goes to Santiago, stopping at the bus and train stations and C. General Pardiñas, 26 (8 per day 8am-10pm, €0.75). Schedule in the daily *El Correo Gallego* (€0.75), available at newsstands. **Iberia,** C. General Pardiñas, 36 (☎981 57 20 28 or 981 57 20 24). Open M-F 9:30am-2pm and 4-7:15pm.

Trains: R. Horreo, s/n (☎981 52 02 02 or 981 24 02 02). To: **Bilbao** (10¾hr., 9:04am, €32.50) via **León** (6½hr., €23) and **Burgos** (8hr., €28.50); **La Coruña** (1hr.; M-F 20 per day 6:30am-10:26pm, Sa-Su 14 per day 7:12am-10:26pm; €3.20-11); **Madrid** (8hr.; M-F 1:47 and 10:25pm, Sa 10:30pm, Su 9:52, 1:47am, 10:30pm; €36); **Vigo** (2hr.; M-F 20 per day 6:30am-10:05pm, Sa-Su 14 per day 7:33am-10:05pm; €4.90-6.25) via **Pontevedra** (1½hr., €3.20-4.05).

Buses: Estación Central de Autobuses, R. de Rodríguez, s/n (☎981 58 77 00), a 20min. walk from downtown. From Pl. Galicia walk down Fonte de Santo Antonio and follow it through its multiple name changes until you get to R. de San Pedro; turn right and keep on walking. R. de San Pedro becomes R. dos Concheiros and later becomes R. de Rodríguez; the bus station will be on your left. Bus #10 and bus C Circular leave from the R. Montero Ríos side of Pr. Galicia for the station (every 15-20min. 6:30am-10pm, €0.66). Info open daily 6am-10pm.

ALSA (☎981 58 61 33, reservations 902 42 22 42). Open daily 7:30am-9:30pm. To: **Bilbao** (11¼hr., 9am and 9:30pm, €39); **Madrid** (8-9hr., 4 per day 8am-9:30pm, €31); **San Sebastián** (13½hr., 8am and 5:30pm, €44).

Castromil (☎981 58 90 90 or 902 10 44 44). To: **El Ferrol** (2hr.; M-F 6 per day 9:15am-9pm, Sa-Su 4 per day 9:15am-9pm; €6.31); **La Coruña** (1½hr.; M-F every hr. 7am-10pm, Sa every hr. 9am-10pm, Su every hr. 9:15am-10:30pm; €5.25); **Noia** (1hr.; M-F 15 per day 8am-10:15pm, Sa 10 per day 8am-8pm, Su 8 per day 8am-8:30pm; €3); **Vigo** (2hr.; M-F every hr. 6am-10pm, Sa every hr. 8am-9pm, Su every hr. 9am-9pm; €5.85) via **Pontevedra** (1½hr., €4.05).

Arriva/Finisterre (☎981 58 85 11) to **Finisterre** (2½hr.; M-F 7 per day 8am-7:30pm, Sa 4 per day 8am-7:30pm, Su 3 per day 8am-6:15pm; €9.30).

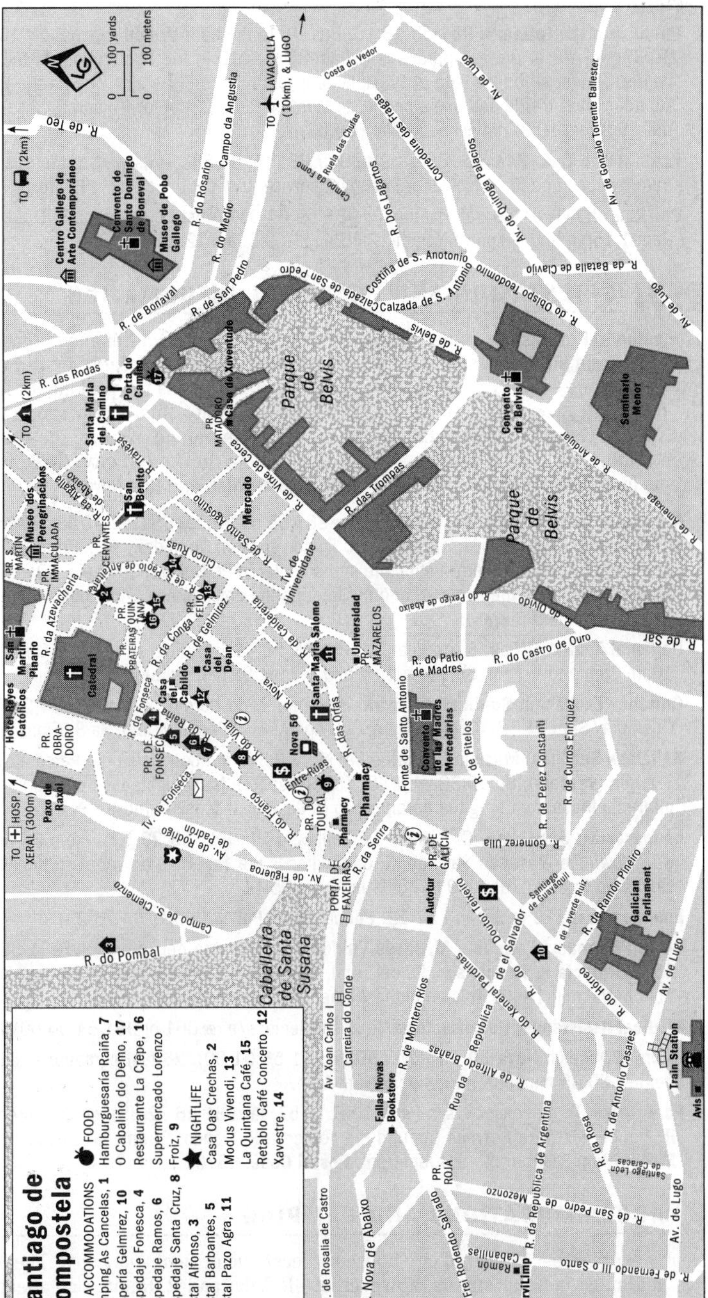
Santiago de Compostela
ACCOMMODATIONS
Camping As Cancelas, 1
Hespería Gelmírez, 10
Hospedaje Fonesca, 4
Hospedaje Ramos, 6
Hospedaje Santa Cruz, 8
Hostal Alfonso, 3
Hostal Barbantes, 5
Hostal Pazo Agra, 11
FOOD
Hamburguesaría Raiña, 7
O Cabaliño do Demo, 17
Restaurante La Crêpe, 16
Supermercado Lorenzo
Froiz, 9
NIGHTLIFE
Casa Oas Crechas, 2
Modus Vivendi, 13
La Quintana Café, 15
Retablo Café Concerto, 12
Xavestre, 14
Catedral
Hotel Reyes Católicos
San Martín Pinario
Museo dos Peregrinacións
San Benito
Santa María del Camino
Porta do Camino
Casa de Xuventude
Mercado
Parque de Belvis
Convento de Belvis
Seminario Menor
Centro Gallego de Arte Contemporáneo
Convento de Santo Domingo de Boneval
Museo de Pobo Gallego
Universidad
Santa María Salome
Casa del Dean
Casa del Cabildo
Nova 50
Pharmacy
Convento de las Madres Mercedarias
Paxo de Raxoi
Autotur
Galician Parliament
Train Station
Avis
Fallas Novas Bookstore
ServiLimp
Caballeira de Santa Susana
TO LAVACOLLA (10km), & LUGO
TO HOSP. XERAL (300m)
100 yards
100 meters

GALICIA

Public Transportation: ☎981 58 18 15. Bus #6 to the train station (open daily 10am-10:30pm), #9 to the campgrounds (10am-8pm), #10 to the bus station. In the city center, almost all buses stop at Pr. Galicia, where there are 2 stops, one on the R. do Doutour Teixeiro side and one along R. de Montero Ríos. Except for #6 and 9, buses run daily 6:30am-10:30pm every 20min. (€0.66).

Taxis: Radio Taxi (24hr. ☎981 58 24 90 or 981 59 84 88). Taxis wait at the bus and train stations and Pr. Galicia. For late-night service, try near the clubs in Pl. Roxa.

Car Rental: Avis at the train station (☎981 59 61 01). Must be at least 25. Open M-F 9am-1:15pm and 4-7pm, Sa 9am-12:45pm, Su 9:30am-12:30pm.

ORIENTATION AND PRACTICAL INFORMATION

The **cathedral** marks the center of the old city, which sits on a hill above the new city. The **train station** is at the far southern end of town. To reach the old city, either take bus #6 to Pr. Galicia or walk up the stairs across the parking lot from the main entrance, cross the street, and bear right onto Rúa do Horreo, which leads to Pr. Galicia. The **bus station** is at the far northern end of town; the walk is over 20min., so instead take bus #10 to Pr. Galicia. In the old city, three main streets lead to the cathedral: **Rúa de Franco, Rúa de Vilar,** and **Rúa Nova.**

GALICIA

Municipal Tourist Office: R. do Vilar, 63 (☎981 55 51 29; fax 981 55 47 48; www.santiagoturismo.com). English, German, and French spoken. Open daily 9am-9pm. Another **branch** is in a little Modernist structure in the center of Pr. Galicia. Open M-F 10am-2pm and 5-8pm. During the summer, another information office opens at the bus station (M-F 10am-2pm and 5-8pm).

Regional Tourist Office: R. do Vilar, 43 (☎981 58 40 81). English spoken. Open M-F 10am-2pm and 4-7pm, Sa 11am-2pm and 5-7pm, Su and holidays 11am-2pm.

Currency Exchange: Santander Central Hispano, R. do Hórreo, 20 (☎902 24 24 24). Open May-Sept. M-F 8:30am-2:30pm; Oct.-Apr. M-F 8:30am-2:30pm, Sa 8:30am-1pm.

Religious Services: Mass in the cathedral M-Sa 9:30am, noon (Misa del Peregrino), 6, 7:30pm (vespers); Su 10:30am, 1, 5, 7pm (vespers). Most nights also offer a special **pilgrim's Mass,** featuring the *botafumeiro* (a gigantic incense burner).

Laundromat: ServiLimp, C. Ramón Cabanillas, 16 (☎981 59 29 52). From Pr. Roxa, walk down Frei Rosendo Salvado; R. Cabanillas is the 1st street on your left. ServiLimp cleans up to 4.5kg (about 9 lb.) of laundry for €5.11.

Emergency: ☎112 or 900 44 42 22. **Police: Local Police** (☎981 54 23 23).

24hr. Pharmacy: Farmacia M. Jesús Valdés Cabo, Cantón del Toral, 1 (☎981 58 58 95). **Farmacia R. Bescanses,** Pl. del Toral, 1 (☎981 58 59 90), also stays open 24hr. Built in the mid-1800s, it is an old-fashioned establishment worth seeing.

Medical Assistance: Hospital Xeral, R. das Galeras, s/n (☎061 or 981 54 00 00).

Internet Access: Nova 50, R. Nova, 50 (☎981 56 01 00). 26 fast computers. €1.20 per hr., €0.45 minimum. Open daily 9am-1am.

Post Office: Tr. de Fonseca, s/n (☎981 58 12 52; fax 981 56 32 88), on the corner of R. Franco. **Lista de Correos** (around the corner at R. Franco, 6) and **fax** service. Open M-F 8:30am-8:30pm, Sa 9:30am-2pm. **Postal Code:** 15701.

ACCOMMODATIONS AND CAMPING

Nearly every street in the old city houses at least one or two *pensiones.* The liveliest and most popular streets, however, are R. Vilar and R. Raíña. Call ahead in winter when university students occupy most rooms.

Hospedaje Ramos, C. Raíña, 18, 2nd fl. (☎981 58 18 59), above O Papa Una restaurant. In the center of the *ciudad vieja,* Ramos has small, simple rooms with clean shared baths. Winter heating. Checkout 11am. Reservations recommended. Singles €11.75, with bath €13; doubles €21.60, with bath €23.50. ❶

Hostal Barbantes, R. do Franco (☎981 58 17 93). Big, sunny rooms with bath. Ask for the room in the restaurant downstairs. Singles €26; doubles €39. ❸

Hostal Pazo Agra, R. da Caldeirería, 37 (☎981 58 35 17). From Pr. Toural walk down Cantón do Toural, take your 1st left onto Rúa Nova and then a right onto C. Salomé which runs into Rúa de Caldeirería. Nice rooms with bath, winter heating. Some have TV. July-Sept. singles €17; doubles €26. Oct.-June €23/€33. ❷

Hostal Alfonso, R. Pombal, 40 (☎981 58 56 85). With your back to the cathedral, exit Pr. de Obradeiro through the Costa do Cristo, which will lead to R. das Hortas. When you get to Campo das Hortas, R. Pombal will be on your left. This quiet *hostal* across from a park offers the perfect place to relax after a day of walking or a month of pilgrimage. Breakfast included. Singles June-Sept. €45; doubles €54. Oct.-May €30/€42. ❹

Hespería Gelmirez, C. Hórreo, 92 (☎981 56 11 00; fax 981 55 52 81). If you find a small fortune during your pilgrimage, head to Gelmirez. Marble floors and top-notch rooms will comfort the most exhausted travelers. Singles €81.15; doubles €99.70. ❺

Hospedaje Santa Cruz, R. Vilar, 42, 2nd fl. (☎981 58 28 15). Clean rooms near many bars and restaurants. Winter heating. Singles €15; doubles €25, with bath €30. ❷

Hospedaje Fonseca, R. Fonseca, 1, 2nd fl. (☎981 57 24 79). Colorful, sunny rooms. Open July-Sept. Singles, doubles, triples, and quads all €12 per person. ❶

Camping As Cancelas, R. 25 de Xullo, 35 (☎981 58 02 66), 2km from the cathedral on the north side of town. Take bus #6 or 9 from the train station or Pr. Galicia. Laundry, supermarket, and pool. €3.60 per person, €3.90 per car and per tent, electricity €3. ❶

FOOD

Tapas-weary budget travelers will appreciate Santiago's selection of restaurants. Bars and cafeterias line the streets with a variety of remarkably inexpensive *menús;* most restaurants are on R. Vilar, R. Franco, R. Nova, and R. Raíña. In the new city, look near Pl. Roxa. End your meal with a *tarta de Santiago*, rich almond cake emblazoned with a sugary St. James cross. Santiago's **market,** between Pl. San Felix and Convento de San Agustín, is a sight in its own right. (Open M-Sa 7:30am-2pm.) **Supermercado Lorenzo Froiz,** Pl. Toural, is one block from Pr. Galicia. (Open M-Sa 9am-3pm and 4:30-9pm, Sa 9am-3pm and 5-9pm. MC/V.)

O Cabaliño do Demo, R. Aller Ulloa, 7 (☎981 58 81 46). Walk to Porta Do Camino, where R. Cerca meets R. San Pedro; R. Aller Ulloa is the last stretch of R. Cerca before the Porta. Enjoy a variety of global vegetarian entrees–from Middle Eastern to Ethiopian–in this chic orange-walled restaurant. *Menú* €6.65. Open M-Sa 2-4pm and 9pm-midnight. Cafe downstairs open 8am-midnight. ❷

Hamburguesería Raiña, C. Raiña, 18. An oasis for the starving, money-lacking traveler with huge hamburgers for €1-2.15, entrees €3.80-€4.25, and a *menú* for only €4.30 that includes bread and wine. Open daily 1-4pm and 8pm-1am. ❶

Restaurante Le Crêpe, Pr. de Quintana, 1 (☎981 57 76 43), across from the cathedral. Santiago's hipsters dine on perfectly thin crepes in this airy, techno-filled eatery with a beautiful terrace. Open daily 1-4pm and 8pm-midnight. ❷

Mesón La Cigala d' Oro, C. Franco, 10 (☎981 58 29 52). Specializes in seafood. The *mariscada* (€55) serves 2 and contains every kind of seafood imaginable. 3-course *menú* €18.75. Open daily 1-3:30pm and 8-11:30pm. AmEx/MC/V. ❸

SIGHTS

THE CATHEDRAL. Santiago's cathedral has four facades, each a masterpiece from a different era, with entrances opening to four different plazas: Praterías, Quintana, Inmaculada, and Obradoiro. From the southern **Praza das Praterías** (with the spitting sea horse), enter the cathedral through the Romanesque arched double doors. The **Torro de Reloxio** (clock tower), Pórtico Real, and Porta Santa face the **Praza da Quintana,** to the west of the cathedral. To the north, a blend of Doric and Ionic columns grace the **Praza da Inmaculada,** combining Romanesque and Neoclassical styles. Consecrated in 1211, the cathedral later acquired Gothic chapels (in the apse and transept), a 15th-century dome, a 16th-century cloister, and the 18th-century Baroque **Obradoiro facade** with two towers that soar above the city. This facade faces the west and **Praza do Obradoiro,** an immense plaza scattered with souvenir hawkers and *tunas* (young lute-strumming men in medieval garb).

Many consider the Maestro Mateo's **Pórtico de la Gloria,** encased in the Obradoiro facade, the crowning achievement of Spanish Romanesque sculpture. This unusual 12th-century amalgam of angels, prophets, saints, sinners, demons, and monsters forms a compendium of Christian theology. Unlike most rigid Romanesque statues, those in the Pórtico seem to smile, whisper, lean, and gab. Galician author Rosalía del Castro once remarked, "It looks as if their lips are moving…might they be alive?" The revered **remains of St. James** (Santiago) lie beneath the high altar in a silver coffer, while his bejeweled bust, polished by the embraces of thousands of pilgrims, rests above the altar. The **botafumeiro,** an enormous silver censer intended to overpower the stench of dirty pilgrims, swings from the transept during high Mass and liturgical ceremonies. Much older than the towers that house them, the **bells** of Santiago were stolen by Moorish invaders and transported to Córdoba on the backs of Christian slaves. Centuries later, when Spaniards conquered Córdoba, they took their bells right back and completed their revenge by forcing some unlucky Moors to carry them. (☎981 58 35 48. Open daily 7am-7pm.)

MUSEUM AND CLOISTERS. Inside the museum are several gorgeous, intricate 16th-century tapestries and two unusual statues of the pregnant Virgin Mary. The museum also houses manuscripts from the *Codex Calixtinus* and Romanesque remains from one of many archaeological excavations conducted in the cathedral. There is also a room dedicated to the stone choir that once stood inside the cathedral. This impressive structure was built by Maestro Mateo and was intended to represent the "New Jerusalem that descends from heaven" as written in the Apocalypse. The 12th-century *Codex*, five volumes of manuscripts on the stories of the Apostle James, includes travel information for early pilgrims. *(☎981 58 11 55. Museum open June-Sept. M-Sa 10am-1:30pm and 4-7:30pm, Su and holidays 10am-1:30pm; Oct.-Feb. M-Sa 11am-1pm and 4-6pm, Su and holidays 11am-1pm; Mar.-June M-Sa 10:30am-1:30pm and 4-6:30pm, Su 10:30am-1:30pm. Museum and cloisters €3.)*

MUSEO DAS PEREGRINACIÓNS. This three-story Gothic building is chock-full of creatively displayed historical info about the *Camino*, including exhibits on the rites and rituals of pilgrimage, the iconography of St. James, and statues of the Virgin as a baby-Jesus-toting pilgrim. *(Pl. San Miguel. ☎981 58 15 58. Open Tu-F 10am-10pm, Sa 10:30am-1:30pm and 5-8pm, Su 10:30am-1:30pm. €2.40, children and seniors €1.20, free when there are special expositions and during most of the summer.)*

CENTRO GALLEGO DE ARTE CONTEMPORÁNEO. The expansive galleries and rooftop *terraza* of the sparkling Centro Gallego de Arte Contemporáneo (CGAC) house cutting-edge exhibitions of boundary-bending artists from around the world. *(R. Ramón del Valle Inclán, s/n. Next door to the Museo de Pobo Gallego. ☎981 54 66 19; www.cgac.org. Open Tu-Su 11am-8pm. Free.)*

PILGRIM'S PROGRESS Pilgrims are easily spotted by their crook-necked walking sticks, sunburnt faces, and shells tied onto weathered backpacks. True *peregrinos* (pilgrims) must cover 100km on foot or horse or 200km on bike to receive *La Compostela,* an official certificate of the pilgrimage issued by the cathedral. A network of *refugios* and *albergues* (shelters) offer free lodging to pilgrims on the move and stamp the "pilgrims' passports" to provide evidence of completion of the full distance. For more information and free guides to the Camino de Santiago, contact the Oficina de Acogida del Peregrino, R. Vilar, 1 (☎981 56 24 19), in the Casa del Deán. At a rate of 30km per day, walking the entire French route (from Roncesvalles in the Pyrenees to Santiago de Compostela; 750-870km), takes about a month and places you in the ranks of such illustrious pilgrims as royal couple Fernando and Isabel, St. Francis de Assisi, Pope John Paul II, and Shirley MacLaine.

MUSEO DE POBO GALLEGO. Find out everything you have ever wanted to know about traditional Galician living. Documentary exhibits on ship building, pottery, house construction, and *gaitas* (the Galician bagpipe) are the highlights, but the museum also includes exhibits dedicated to Galician painting. *(Just past the Porto de Camino, inside the Gothic Convento de Santo Domingo de Boneval. ☎981 58 36 20. Open June 7-Mar. 2 M-Sa 10am-1pm and 4-7pm; Mar. 3-June 6 M-Sa 10am-2pm and 4-7pm. Free.)*

PAZO DE RAXOI. The majestic facade of the former Pazo de Raxoi shines with gold-accented balconies and monumental Neoclassical columns. Once a royal palace, it now houses the Ayuntamiento and the office of the president of the Xunta de Galicia (Galician government). At night, floodlights illuminate the remarkable bas-relief of the Battle of Clavio. *(Across Pr. do Obradoiro, facing the cathedral.)*

MONASTERIO DE SAN MARTÍN PINARIO. Once a religious center almost as powerful as the cathedral, the monastery is a mixture of Romanesque cloisters, Plateresque facades, and Baroque sculpture. Its composite style makes it the most outstanding architectural example of its kind in Santiago. *(In Pr. de San Martín, across from the cathedral in Pl. Inmaculada.)*

ENTERTAINMENT AND NIGHTLIFE

At night, crowds looking for post-pilgrimage consumption and debauchery flood cellars throughout the city. To boogie with local students, hit the bars and dance joints off Pr. Roxa (take R. Montero Ríos). Clubs are open roughly from midnight to 6am. The local newspaper *El Correo Gallego* (€0.75) and the free monthly *Compostela Capital* list art exhibits and concert information. Consult any of three local monthlies, *Santiago Días Guía Imprescindible*, *Compostelán*, or *Modus Vivendi*, for updates on the live music scene. The city celebrates the **Día de Santiago** (July 25) for a full two weeks, from July 15 to 31, in a celebration called Apostolo; on the night of the 24th, a Pontifical Mass with incense is held in the cathedral during **Las Vísperas de Santiago.**

Casa oas Crechas, Vía Sacra, 3 (☎981 56 07 51), just off Pr. da Quintana. A smoky stone-and-wood pub with a witchcraft theme. Renowned for its Galician folk concerts. Beer €1.50-1.95. Open M-F noon-2am, Sa-Su noon-4am.

Xavestre, Rua de San Paolo de Antaltares, 31. Get to know some *santiaguinos* up close and personal in this crowded bar. Packed with 20-somethings, Xavestre plays the latest hits in Spanish pop music. Mixed drinks €5. Open daily at midnight.

La Quintana Café, Pr. Quintana, 1. Set in a dark stone-walled basement, Quintana attracts Santiago's students on weekends to dance to popular Spanish and English songs. Mixed drinks €4, beer €3-5. Open daily 11pm-late.

SEX-ED Although most passersby don't notice it, Praza do Toural houses one of Santiago's most important–and infamous–sculptures: at the top of the Pazo da Bendana is a rendition of Atlas lifting up the world. University legend says that Atlas will drop the granite globe on the first female student to walk by who successfully manages to graduate a virgin. Perhaps afraid of getting crushed, Santiago's female students have yet to relieve Atlas of his burden. And they say this is a holy city...

Retablo Cafe Concerto, R. Vilar, 13. Minimalist decor and low prices keep tourists and students coming back to Retablo. Its eclectic music selections include techno, pop, and house. Drinks start at €2. Open daily from noon until the last *santiaguino* leaves.

Modus Vivendi, Pr. de Feijo, 1, near the cathedral. Santiago's oldest pub, and a clubhouse for revolutionary Galician youths in the 1970s. Today, it houses Santiago's alterna-youth into the wee hours of the night. Beer €2, drinks €4. Open daily 4pm-4am.

DAYTRIPS FROM SANTIAGO DE COMPOSTELA

The northern parts of the Rías Baixas harbor undiscovered hamlets frequented only by pilgrims. These small towns make good daytrips from Santiago, but buses in this area tend to stop frequently, making travel times quite lengthy. Unless you have a car, your time may be better spent in Santiago.

CABO FINISTERRE

Arriva/Finisterre buses make daily trips from Santiago to Finisterre (2½hr.; M-F 7 per day 8am-7:30pm, Sa 4 per day 8am-7:30pm, Su 8am, 12:15, 6:15pm; €9.10) and back (M-F 4 per day 7:50am-4:45pm, Sa 3 per day 7am-4pm, Su 1:45 and 6:45pm). The bus stop is in front of the fishing center in the harbor.

Jutting out precariously from the infamously rocky Costa de Muerte ("Coast of Death"), Cabo Finisterre was once considered Europe's westernmost point, and for centuries it was a crucial port for all naval trade along the Atlantic. But Finisterre's (*Fisterre* in Gallego) greater claim to fame has to do with the ancient belief that it was off these shores that the world ended, hence its name: *finis* (end), *terre* (earth). Even today, it feels like the end of the earth, with the desolate town and the seemingly endless bus ride out to a lonely, wind-swept peninsula.

The hour and a half hike from the port to the **Monte San Guillermo** is long, but those who complete it are rewarded with incredible views of the tumultuous sea and Finisterre's famous bed-shaped **fertility rocks.** Couples having problems conceiving are advised to make a go of it on the rocks under a full moon (harvest moons are even better). On another hill on the Monte are **As Pedras Santas,** two fairly large rocks which cannot be lifted by themselves, but which slide effortlessly side-to-side if you press the right spot. Try it yourself—the contact point is well marked. Four kilometers out from town stands the **lighthouse** that has beckoned ships for years. To reach the **beach,** climb uphill from the statue at the port past C. Carrasqueira, then turn right at the first dirt road. After 50m, turn left onto the seaward path at the white house. The best beach in Finisterre, however, is on the flat and narrow isthmus that connects the peninsula with the mainland. The sands are powdery and wide and the waters calm but frigid. Either walk the four kilometers along the road to Santiago, or take the bus and ask the driver to stop.

For maps, brochures and tourist info, try the **Albergue de Peregrinos,** C. Real, 2, behind the bus stop/fishing building. (☎981 74 07 81. Open M-F 9:30am-1pm and 7-11pm, Sa-Su noon-2pm and 7-11pm.) If you are forced to spend the night in Cabo Finisterre, the **Hospedaje López ❶,** C. Carrasqueira, 4, has 18 cheap, immaculate, light-filled rooms. (☎981 74 04 49. Singles €9-12; doubles €18-21; triples €27.)

THESE BOOTS WERE MADE FOR WALKIN'

One night in 813, a hermit trudged through the hills on the way to his hermitage. Suddenly, miraculously, bright visions flooded his senses, revealing the long-forgotten tomb of the Apostle James. Around this *campus stellae* (field of stars) the cathedral of Santiago de Compostela was built, and around this cathedral a world-famous pilgrimage was born. Since the 9th century, thousands of pilgrims have traveled the **Camino de Santiago.** Many have made the pilgrimage in search of spiritual fulfillment, most as true believers, some to adhere to a stipulation of inheritance, a few to absolve themselves of sin, and at least one to find romance (the wife of Bath in Chaucer's *Canterbury Tales* sauntered to Santiago in bright red stockings to find herself a husband). Clever Benedictine monks built monasteries to host pilgrims along the *camino*, giving rise to the world's first large-scale international tourism and helping make Santiago's cathedral the most frequented Christian shrine in the world. In the 12th century, an enterprising French monk added a book to the *Codex Calixtinus*, a collection of stories about the apostles, that was filled with information on the quality of water at various rest stops and descriptions of villages and monuments along *La Ruta Francesa* (beginning near the French border in Roncevalles, Navarra); in essence, the world's first travel guide. The scallop shell was acquired by pilgrims who visited the site of Santiago's landing after visiting the cathedral; although only pilgrims on their way home used to carry the shell, it has now become a symbol of the Camino de Santiago.

O CASTRO DE BAROÑA

To reach O Castro de Baroña, you'll need to make a connection in Noia. Castromil (☎981 58 90 90) runs buses from Santiago to Noia (1hr.; M-F 15 per day 6:15am-8pm, Sa 10 per day 7am-8pm, Su 8 per day 8am-8:30pm; €3). From Noia, Hefsel buses stop at O Castro de Baroña (in front of Café-Bar O Castro) en route to Riveira (30min.; M-F 14 per day 6:50am-9:30pm, Sa 7 per day 8am-9pm, Su 11 per day 8am-10pm; €1.50). Be sure to tell the bus driver where you're going. From the bus stop, follow the signs to the castro. Catch the bus home across the road from Café-Bar O Castro.

Nineteen kilometers south of Noia lies one of Galicia's best-preserved coastal Celtic villages, **O Castro de Baroña.** The seaside remains of a 5th-century Celtic **fortress** cover the neck of the isthmus, ascending to a rocky promontory above the sea and then descending to a crescent **beach** where clothing is optional. For those who need a shower, **Café-Bar O Castro ❶,** Lugar Castro de Baroña, 18, in **Porto do Son** (the O Castro bus stop), offers spotless rooms. (☎981 76 74 30. Doubles €21-27. Open June-Aug.) The nearest town, **Baroña,** 1km north, has a supermarket, restaurant, and bus stop. Should you get stuck in **Noia** on the way back to Santiago, several hotels are a short walk from the bus station on R. de Galicia. **Hospedaje Marico ❶,** R. de Galicia, s/n, has plain but comfortable rooms. From the bus station, walk uphill on R. Pedra Sartaña, turn right onto R. Rosalía de Castro and then left onto R. de Galicia. (☎981 82 00 09. Singles €12; doubles €15, with bath €18.)

RÍAS BAJAS (RÍAS BAIXAS)

According to Galician lore, the Rías Baixas (Low Estuaries) were formed by God's tremendous handprint, with each *ría* stretching like a finger through the land. These deep, navy blue bays, countless sandy coves, and calm cool waters have lured vacationing Spaniards for decades. Only recently have foreign tourists caught on to the area's unique charm, and they now arrive at the beaches in droves every summer. While not nearly as cool or rainy as their Galician neighbors (the

Rías Baixas are, after all, the sunniest part of the northern Spanish coasts), the ocean wind and mildly hot summer days are still a refreshing break from the scorching heat (and hordes of tourists) of central and southern Spain.

VIGO ☎986

José María Alvarez once wrote that "Vigo does not end, it goes on into the sea." Often called Spain's door to the Atlantic, Vigo (pop. 300,000) began as a small, unobtrusive fishing port; with the arrival of the Citröen manufacturing factory, it exploded into the biggest city in Galicia. While Vigo isn't the place to go for an escape from city life, the nightlife and shopping are among the best in the region. The city is also a good base for visiting nearby daytrip villages and beaches.

GALICIA

TRANSPORTATION

Flights: Aeropuerto de Vigo on Av. Aeropuerto (☎986 26 82 00), 15km from the center of Vigo. Daily flights to **Barcelona, Bilbao, Madrid,** and **Valencia.** The local R9 bus runs regularly from R. Urzáiz near R. Colón to the airport (€0.80). **Iberia** (☎986 26 82 28) and **Air Europa** (☎986 26 83 10) have offices at the airport.

Trains: RENFE, Pr. de la Estación, s/n (☎986 43 11 14), downstairs from R. Urzaiz. Open daily 7am-11pm and runs trains to: **La Coruña** (2½hr.; M-F 14 per day 5:45am-8:55pm, Sa 9 per day 5:45am-8:55pm, Su 12 per day 5:45am-8:55pm; €10); **Madrid** (8-9hr.; Su-F 9:20am and 10:20pm, Sa 10:20pm; €36-55); **Pontevedra** (20min.; M-F 20 per day 5:45am-10:05pm, Sa 14 per day 5:45am-10:05pm, Su 17 per day 5:45am-10:05pm; €1.05-2.10); **Santiago de Compostela** (2hr.; M-F 17 per day 5:45am-9:35pm, Sa 11 per day 5:45am-9:35pm, Su 14 per day 5:45am-9:35pm; €4.90-6.55).

Buses: Estación de Autobuses, Av. de Madrid, s/n (☎986 37 34 11), on the corner of R. Alcalde Gregorio Espino. **Castromil** (☎986 27 81 12) buses run to: **La Coruña** (2½hr., every hr. 7am-8:30pm, €10.95); **Pontevedra** (45min., every 30min. 7:30am-8:30pm, €1.95); **Santiago de Compostela** (1¼hr., every 30min. 7:30am-8:30pm, €5.85). For **ATSA buses** (☎986 61 02 55), buy tickets onboard. To: **Bayona** (50min.; every 30min. M-Sa 7am-10pm, Su 8am-11pm; €1.70); **La Guardia** (1½hr., every 30min. 7:30am-9pm, €3.90); **Túy** (45min.; M-F every 30min. 7:30am-9pm, Sa every hr. 8:30am-8:30pm; €2.90). **Auto Res, S.A.** (☎986 27 19 61) runs to **Madrid** (9hr., 6-7 per day 8:30am-11:30pm, €27.67-30.66).

Ferries: Estación Ría, R. As Avenidas, s/n (☎986 22 52 72), past the nautical club on the harborside walkway, runs ferries to: **Cangas** (20min.; M-F every 30min. 6:30am-10pm, Sa every hr. 6:30am-10:30pm, Su every hr. 8:30am-9:30pm; €1.56); **Islas Cíes** (50min.; Oct.-May 3 per day 11am-4pm, June-Sept. 4 per day 11am-7pm; round-trip €13.25); and **Moaña** (30min.; M-Sa every hr. 6:30am-10:30pm, Su every hr. 8:30am-10:30pm; €1.29).

Car Rental: National, R. Urzáiz, 84 (☎986 41 80 76). Min. age 21. Must have had a license for at least 1yr. Open M-F 8:30am-1:30pm and 4:30-7:30pm, Sa 9am-1pm.

ORIENTATION AND PRACTICAL INFORMATION

Gran Vía is Vigo's main thoroughfare, stretching south to north from Pr. América, through Pr. España, and ending at the perpendicular **Rúa Urzáiz.** A left turn (west) onto R. Urzáiz leads to Pta. do Sol and into the **casco antiguo;** most of the city's action is here in the old city and along the waterfront. As you exit the **train station** onto R. Urzáiz (up the stairs from the main entrance), go right two blocks to reach the central Gran Vía. Keep walking on Avenida Urzáiz for 10min. to reach the waterfront.

The city center is a 25min. trek from the **bus station.** Exit right uphill along busy Av. Madrid. Eventually, a right on Gran Vía at Pr. España leads to the intersection with R. Urzáiz. It's easier to just take the R4, 7, or 12 buses from Av. Madrid in front of the bus station to Gran Vía, R. Urzáiz, or R. Colón (€0.80).

Tourist Office: R. Canovás de Castillo, s/n (☎986 43 05 77). From the train station, turn right on R. Urzáiz and follow it to R. Colón, where you'll veer to the right. When R. Colón reaches the water, turn left onto R. Montero Ríos. The office is on the left as the name changes to R. Canovás de Castillo and moves left. English spoken. Open June-Sept. M-F 9:30am-2pm and 4:30-7pm, Sa-Su 10am-2pm and 5-8pm; Oct.-May M-F 9:30am-2pm and 4:30-6:30pm, Sa 10am-12pm.

Currency Exchange: Santander Central Hispano, R. Urzáiz, 20 (☎902 24 24 24). Open Apr.-Sept. M-F 8:30am-2:30pm; Oct.-Mar. M-F 8:30am-2:30pm, Sa 8:30am-1pm.

Luggage Storage: At the train station (€3). Open daily 7am-9:45pm. At the bus station (€2.40). Open M-F 9:30am-1:30pm and 3-7pm, Sa 9am-2pm.

Emergency: ☎112. **Police:** Pr. do Rei, s/n (☎986 43 22 11).

Late Night Pharmacy: C. Príncipe, 27, left off R. Urzáiz just before it turns into R. Colón. Open 9am-1pm and 4-7pm. All pharmacies post a rotating list of late-night pharmacies.

Medical Assistance: Hospital Xeral, R. Pizarro, 22 (☎986 81 60 00). **Ambulances:** ☎061, 986 41 62 26, 986 34 42 29, or 986 81 60 62.

Internet Access: CiberStation, C. Príncipe, 22, ground floor (☎986 11 36 01), a left off R. Urzáiz just before it turns into R. Colon. €1.80 per hr. Open 10am-1am.

Post Office: Pr. Compostela, 3 (☎986 43 81 44), a left off R. Colón. **Lista de Correos** and **fax.** M-F 8:30am-8:30pm, Sa 9:30am-2pm. **Postal code:** 36201.

ACCOMMODATIONS

Vigo's inexpensive rooms make the city a logical base for exploring surrounding areas. Most accommodations are clustered in the area around the train station on R. Alfonso XIII (to the right upon exiting the train station) and its side streets.

Hospedaje La Estrella, Martín Codax, 5 (☎ 986 22 50 35), a left off R. Alfonso XII, three blocks down from the station. Unadorned but large rooms, complete with TVs and clean, spacious bathrooms. Singles €12, €18 with private bathroom; doubles €30. ❶

Hostal Ría de Vigo, R. Cervantes, 14 (☎986 43 72 40), a left off R. Alfonso XIII 4 blocks from the station. Cheerful rooms with private bathrooms and TVs, and balconies overlooking busy R. Cervantes. Check-out 11am. Singles €15; doubles €21. Cash only. ❷

Hostal Atlántico, García Barbón, 35 (☎ 986 22 05 30). From the train station follow R. Alfonso XII until you get to García Barbón; Atlántico will be on your right. In a central location near the *casco antiguo,* this hostal offers comfortable beds and spacious rooms for tired travelers. Singles €24; doubles €36; triples €48. ❷

Hotel Celta, C. México, 22 (☎986 41 46 99; fax 986 48 06 56). From the train station, walk up the stairs to R. Urzáiz and make a right; the first street on your left is C. México. A two-star hotel in center of the restaurant area. Private baths, phone, TVs, and friendly service. July-Sept. Singles €38; doubles €48. Oct.-June Singles €32; doubles €45. ❹

FOOD

For groceries, hit **Supermercado Froiz,** R. do Uruguai 14. (Open M-Sa 9am-2pm and 5-9pm.) Gran Vía and C. Venezuela, four streets uphill from R. Urzáiz off Gran Vía, are brimming with bright *cafeterías* and *terrazas.*

FROM THE ROAD

LIFE'S A SPORT: DRINK UP

Every four years, Spaniards put everything on hold and gather in front of TV screens at local bars to watch the world's biggest sporting event: the World Cup. The second match of the 2002 World Cup (between Spain and Paraguay) caught me in a little Galician town called La Guardia. I didn't want to miss this national event, so I went into a *cafetería,* asked for a *Cola Cao,* and waited.

After Paraguay scored the first goal, makeshift coaches throughout the bar loudly voiced their opinion on what was wrong with the Spanish team while blowing cigar smoke and munching tortillas. The man next to me asked for my opinion in *gallego*, and the only thing I could say was "*sí claro hombre, tienes razón*" (yes, man, you're right), because I had no idea what he was talking about.

When Spain scored, the man forgot about my lack of expertise, embracing me and buying me a beer. When Spain scored a second time, the entire community of La Guardia, most of whom were in the cafeteria by now, exploded into a single cheer: "*España! España!*"

And there I was, singing and laughing along with them, eating free *bocadillos*, drinking sangría, and forgetting for a moment that my team, the Chileans, didn't even make it to the World Cup. I didn't know if Spain would win, but I knew that no matter what, the hospitality, friendliness, and enthusiasm of the Spanish people would remain untouched.

—Sebastian Brown

Cafetería El Coral, on the corner of C. Ecuador and C. Cuba (☎986 41 07 19). From R. Urzáiz, take a left onto Gran Vía and a left again on C. Ecuador. El Coral is on your left. Whether you want an early breakfast or a cheap dinner, El Coral is the place for *cocina gallega.* Entrees €4.50-6 and 3-course *menú* €6. Open daily 6:30am-midnight. ❶

Restaurante Curcuma Vegetariano, C. Brasil, 4 (☎986 41 11 27). Serves immense portions of Mediterranean veggie dishes, like *mousakka* and *couscous.* Entrees €5-6. Open M-Sa 1-4pm and 8pm-midnight. ❶

Tapas Areal, C. México, 36 (☎986 41 86 43). A typical Spanish *tapería* that specializes in fish and seafood. Delicious food and a broad selection of wines in a very traditional setting. Entrees €3-10, *tapas* start at €2.50. Open daily 1pm-12:30am. ❷

ENTERTAINMENT AND NIGHTLIFE

In honor of its notorious past as a haven for witches, Vigo hosts **Expomagia,** a celebration of all things occult, in mid-June. Watch for the magical **Fiesta de San Juan (Xuan)** on June 23rd, when neighborhoods light huge cauldrons of *aguardiente* (firewater) to make an infusion called *la queimada.* The potent potable consists of *aguardiente,* coffee, lemon, and sugar; the sweet mixture is passed around for all to drink and revel in traditional song and dance. A final summer festival, **Romería Vikinga,** in the seaside town of Catoira, is held the first week in August, when locals reenact the Viking landing, complete with period ships and costumes.

There isn't much to see or do in Vigo besides party. Starting in the late afternoon, students pack the *casco antiguo,* where cafes, bars, and discos abound. The area around **R. Areal** and **R. Concepción Arenal** is jam-packed with discos, nightclubs, and bars playing the latest Spanish hits for trendy 20-somethings.

20th Century Rock American Classic Bar, R. Areal, 18. A bar/Americana museum. With a full size Cadillac, Harley Davidson motorcycle, and the Statue of Liberty adorning its halls, your beer (€3) or mixed drink (€5) is only an excuse to gaze at the collection.

Posada de las Almas, Pr. de Compostela 19. A luscious mix of medieval castle and theater, this club, with its red silk curtains and crystal chandeliers, attracts a chic crowd in its thirties. Music is mostly pop. Drinks €6.

Versus, R. Areal, 22. Break out your most stylish ensemble for this upscale club. The numerous video screens and dim lighting create a decadent techno-minimalist ambiance. The latest pop songs get well-dressed crowds moving as they sip their €6 drinks.

Saborhabana, Rosalía de Castro, 48. For a little taste of Cuban spice in Vigo, head to Saborhabana. Practice your *acento cubano* and dance to salsa, merengue, and cumbia in this unique bar. Don't miss the *mojitos* (€3) and other sundry Cuban specialities.

VIP, R. Areal, 20. Frequented by scooter-riding teens sporting tight tops and dark sunglasses, VIP is a mecca of techno music. Different DJs perform in this 2-story club daily.

The area around the train station—R. Cervantes, R. Lepanto, and R. Churruca, in particular—is filled with trendsetting bars and clubs. For the latest hotspots, check the posters hanging around town advertising discos and techno music.

Black Ball, Churruca, 8. The perfect bar for anyone who lived through the feathered hair and leisure suits of the 70s. With an incredible collection of vintage kitsch and groovin' music from the likes of James, Jimi, and Janis, Black Ball offers a great atmosphere and cheap mixed drinks (€2.50) to start the night. Opens daily at 11pm.

La Bola de Cristal, Churruca, 12. Like its neighbor Black Ball, La Bola de Cristal specializes in the fab 1970s. Come for the retro decor; stay for the funk and disco. A mixed-age crowd dances to the beat of The Jackson 5 and Gloria Gaynor late into the night.

GALICIA

DAYTRIPS FROM VIGO

ISLAS CÍES

Four ferries per day make the trip to and from the island, sometimes more in nice weather. Though fairly expensive, the trip is worth every Euro. (40min.; daily June-Sept., Sa-Su only the rest of the year; 11am, 1, 5, and 7pm; returning noon, 2, 6, and 8pm; €13.25 round-trip, free for children under 12 years old.)

The Romans called them the "Islands of the Gods," and one can hardly doubt that Jupiter had at least a villa in the Islas Cíes. Guarding the mouth of the Ría de Vigo and 14km from the city, the three islands—**Illa de Monte Agudo** o del Norte, **Illa do Medio** o del Faro, and **Illa do Sur** o de San Martiño—offer irresistible beaches and cliff-side hiking trails for travelers. The islands were declared a natural park in 1980; only 2200 people are allowed in per day, ensuring wide stretches of uncrowded beach. **Playa de Figueiras** and **Playa de Rodas** gleam with fine sand and sheltered waters. For smaller, wavier, and more secluded spots, walk along the trail beyond Playa de Figueiras, which leads to a plethora of coves and rocky lookouts. A 4km hike to the left of the dock on the main "road" leads to a bird conservatory, two lighthouses, and breathtaking views. On the same trail is a camping site, a restaurant, and a supermarket that sells bottles of water, which will come in handy once you get to *o faro grande* (the big lighthouse). Watch out for territorial seagulls that dive-bomb hikers walking too close to the birds' spotted chicks.

CANGAS

Ferries run from the Estación Ría (☎986 22 52 72) in Vigo to Cangas (20min.; M-F every 30min. 6:30am-10pm, Sa every hr. 6:30am-10:30pm, Su every hr. 8:30am-9:30pm; €1.56). From Cangas, an equal number return (M-F every 30min. 6am-9:30pm, Sa every hr. 6am-10pm, Su every hr. 8am-9pm).

Just across the bay from Vigo, tiny Cangas's main draw is its placid, nearly deserted beach, **Praia de Rodeira.** With your back to the ferry terminal, turn right onto Po. Marítimo, the pedestrian waterside walkway, which brings you to the beach (10min.). The cobalt waters here are virtually waveless, perfect for actual swimming. While there are no snack bars near the beach, restaurants lurk near the ferry station. The most popular is undoubtedly **Restaurante-Bar Celta ❷,** R. Alfredo

Saralegui, 28, which serves endless seafood tapas to the hungry hordes gathered at long tables on the street. With your back to the ferry terminal, cross the street and head up the stairs to your left; the restaurant is at the top. (*Tapas* €0.75-9.50. Fish entrees €5-10. Open daily 10am-midnight.) On Fridays, Cangas attracts crowds from the surrounding towns for its extravagant **market** in the harborside gardens, immediately to the left of the ferry terminal.

LA GUARDIA (A GUARDA)

Buses run to and from La Guardia from Vigo (1½hr., every 30min. 7:30am-9pm, €3.90) and stop in La Guardia at the corner of C. Domínguez Fontela and C. Concepción Arenal. The bus office is open 9am-9pm.

Between the mouth of the Río Miño and the Atlantic Ocean, La Guardia (pop. 10,000) thrives on an active fishing industry and the 500,000 tourists who descend annually on its little beach and large mountain. The town itself is a sleepy, pastel-colored maze overlooking a bay; most visitors skip the town and head instead to its two attractions. To reach the majestic **Monte Santa Tecla** from the bus stop, turn right onto C. Domínguez Fontela and then right onto C. José Antonio. From C. José Antonio, bear right uphill onto C. Rosalía de Castro, which continues to the top (6km). Alternatively, hike 5min. up the road and look for the steps off to the left that mark the start of a shorter, steeper pedestrian pathway through the woods (3km). The mountain's highlight are the ruins of a Celtic castro that lie three-quarters of the way up the mountain. The interlocking circles of the foundations of this ancient fortress village overlook frothy seas, moss-laden mountains, and the glimmer of La Guardia below. Near the peak is a chapel dedicated to Santa Tecla, the patron saint of headaches and heart disease. The wax body parts inside (hearts, heads, and feet) are gifts to Santa Tecla from cured worshippers. To reach La Guardia's small beach from the bus station, follow the signs.

TÚY (TUI)

An ATSA bus (☎986 61 02 55) from Vigo stops on C. Calvo Sotelo at Hostal Generosa and returns to Vigo from the other side of the street (45min., every 30min. 7:30am-9pm, €2.90). Trains (☎986 60 08 13) run from Vigo to Túy, then on to Valença and Viana do Castelo, Portugal (2 per day 9:59am and 10pm, €2.90). The train station in Túy, however, is far from the center of town and the border.

While the medieval border town of Túy (pop. 16,000) offers the novel opportunity of walking into Portugal, it's more notable for its beautiful *casco antiguo* and its views of the Río Miño valley and Portugal. The centerpiece of the old city is the **cathedral;** constructed in 1120, it was the first piece of Gothic architecture in Iberia. It now houses the relics of San Telmo, patron saint of sailors, and boasts an impressive organ. One ticket gets you into the cathedral's **museum** and the **Museo Diocesano** as well. (Museo Diocesano ☎986 60 36 00. Cathedral and museums open daily July-Aug. 9am-9pm; Sept.-Dec. daily 9:30am-1:30pm and 4-8pm; Dec.-May daily 9:30am-1:30pm and 4-7pm. €2.40.) A 1km metal walkway over the Río Miño extends to Portugal's Valença do Minho. To get to the **tourist office** on Puente Tripe, s/n, follow Av. de Portugal from the International Bridge until you approach the little wooden cottage on your left. (☎986 60 17 89. Open July-Sept. daily 9:30am-2pm, 4:30-8pm; Oct.-June M-F 9:30am-1:30pm and 4-6pm.)

BAYONA (BAIONA)

ATSA buses run to Vigo (50min.; every 30min. M-Sa 7am-10pm, Su 8am-11pm; €1.65).

Twenty-one kilometers southwest of Vigo, in its own mini-estuary, Bayona (pop. 10,000) was the first European town to receive word from the New World when Columbus returned to port in March 1493. The town even boasts a reconstructed version of the famous globe-trotting ship **La Caravela Pinta** in the harbor and reenacts the landing every March. (Open W-M 8:30am-8:30pm. €0.75.) While this is Bayona's main historic attraction, most visitors skip the sight and head straight to its blustery Atlantic beaches, where brightly colored fishing boats lurk off shore and only the bravest dare to swim in the icy blue waves of the open sea. The golden sand, however, is perfect for lounging among myriad other sun worshippers. Those who get bored at the beach explore the grounds of the 16th-century **Fortress of Monte Real,** now a *parador nacional*, which stands just above the beaches. The 2km *paseo peatonal* Alfonso IX loops around the grounds along the shore. As you get off the bus, walk along Alfonso IX to your right to get to **Praia Santa Marta** and **Praia Ladeira.** To your left, the path will take you to the Fortress of Monte Real, the calm **Praia de los Frailes,** and the breezy **Praia Cruncheira.**

PONTEVEDRA ☎986

According to legend, Pontevedra (pop. 74,000) was founded by the Greek archer Teucro as a place to convalesce after his Trojan War exploits. Today, it continues the tradition of providing a place to crash by offering reasonably priced beds for visitors flitting about the various high-priced coastal towns. Although it makes a good base, Pontevedra on the whole is not the most interesting town, and the new city is a bit of an eyesore. The old city, however—filled with palm trees, flowering balconies, stately cathedrals, and squares lined with traditional arcaded *gallego* buildings—is pleasant and inviting, making for a surprisingly enjoyable stay.

TRANSPORTATION

Trains: Alféreces Provisionales, s/n (☎902 24 02 02 or 986 85 13 13), a 20min. walk southwest of the old city. Info open daily 6am-11pm. To: **La Coruña** (3hr.; M-F 14 per day 7:05am-6:21pm, Sa 9 per day 7:05am-6:21pm, Su 12 per day 7:05am-6:21pm; €6.80, express €8); **Madrid** (11hr.; Su-F 12:35pm and 9:30pm, Sa 8:45am and 9:30pm; €36); **Santiago** (1½hr.; M-F 18 per day 6:16am-10:14pm, Sa 12 per day 6:16am-10:14pm, Su 15 per day 6:16am-10:14pm; €3.20-4.05); **Vigo** (20min.; M-F 21 per day 8:19am-10:56pm, Sa 14 per day 8:19am-10:56pm, Su 17 per day 8:19am-10:56pm; €1.60-8.50).

Buses: Alféreces Provisionales, s/n (☎986 85 24 08), across the street from the train station. Info open daily 9am-9:30pm. To: **Cambados** (1hr.; 12 per day M-F 7:55am-8:35pm, Sa 11:15am-8:35pm, Su 3 per day 12:30-8:35pm; €1.90); **El Grove/La Toja** (1hr., every 30min. 7:45am-10pm, €3.05); **La Coruña** (2½hr.; M-F every hr. 7:30am-9pm, Sa every hr. 8am-9pm, Su every hr. 9am-8pm; €9.95); **Madrid** (8hr., 6 per day 9am-11pm, €27.67); **Santiago** (1hr.; M-F every hr. 9am-9pm, Sa every hr. 9am-9pm, Su every hr. 9am-7pm; €4.05); **Vigo** (1hr.; M-F every hr. 8am-9:30pm, Sa-Su every hr. 8am-8pm; €4.95).

Taxis: Radio Taxi (☎986 85 12 85). 24hr. €2.40 from the stations to town.

Car Rental: Avis, C. Peregrina, 49 (☎986 85 20 25). 1-day unlimited mileage €72. Must be 23 and have had a license for at least 1 yr. Open M-F 9am-1:15pm and 4-7pm, Sa 9am-12:45pm.

ORIENTATION AND PRACTICAL INFORMATION

Six streets radiate out from **Pr. Peregrina,** the main plaza connecting the new and old cities. The main streets are R. Oliva, R. Michelena, R. Benito Corbal, and R. Peregrina. **Pr. de Galicia** is a 5min. walk from Pr. Peregrina; from Pr. Peregrina, head down R. Peregrina and veer right at the first fork onto R. A. Muruais. The **train** and **bus stations,** located across from each other, are about 1km from the old city. To get to the city center, turn left onto Av. Calvo Sotelo from the bus station entrance; from the train station, walk straight out onto Av. Calvo Sotelo after crossing the highway. Continue on Av. Calvo Sotelo for 10-15min. as it changes to Av. de Vigo and then R. Peregrina before depositing you in Pr. Peregrina.

Tourist Office: Main office, R. General Mola, 3 (☎/fax 986 85 08 14). From Pr. Peregrina, walk up R. Michelena and take the 1st left onto R. General Mola. Tons of brochures and maps. English spoken. A **second office** opens in summer on Pr. de España in a small hut. Both open June-Aug. M-F 10am-2pm and 5-7:30pm, Sa-Su 10am-2pm and 5-6:30pm; Sept.-May M-F 9:30am-2pm and 4:30-6:30pm, Sa 10:30am-12:30pm.

Emergency: ☎112. **Police:** C. Joaquín Costa, 19 (☎091 or 986 85 38 00).

Pharmacy: R. Peregrina, 3. Open 9am-1pm and 4-8pm. Rotating list of all late-night pharmacies are posted in all pharmacy windows.

Hospital: Hospital Provincial, C. Doctor Loureiro Crespo, 2 (☎061 or 986 85 21 15).

Internet Access: Ciber Las Ruinas, R. Riestra, 21, 2nd fl. (☎986 86 63 25), just off Pr. de España. €1.50 per hr. Open M-F 10am-2:30pm and 5pm-2am, Sa 11am-2:30pm and 4pm-2am, Su 5pm-2am.

Post Office: C. Oliva, 21 (☎986 84 48 64). **Lista de Correos** and **fax service** available. Open M-F 8:30am-8:30pm, Sa 9:30am-2pm. **Postal Code:** 36001.

GALICIA

ACCOMMODATIONS

Hotel Madrid, C. Andrés Mellado, 5 (☎/fax 986 86 51 80). Follow the directions from the stations (see above), but turn left onto R. Andrés Mellado before you reach Pr. Peregrina. This 7-year-old hotel offers fully equipped rooms and a friendly staff. Check-out 11am. Singles €24-30; doubles €40-50. Extra bed €12. MC/V. ❸

Hotel México, Andrés Muruais, 10 (☎986 85 90 06). Follow the directions from the stations (see above), but turn left onto R. Andrés Muruais before you reach Pr. Peregrina. Carpeted rooms, laundry service and a cafeteria. Singles €24-31; doubles €36-47. ❸

Casa Alicia, Av. de Santa María, 5, 1st floor (☎986 85 70 79). From Pr. Peregrina, walk up R. Michelina through Pr. de España, and turn right onto R. Mestre Mateo. Av. de Santa María will be on the right. Winter heating. Reservations recommended. Doubles €18-21; quads €27. ❷

Casa Maruja, Av. de Santa María, 2 (☎986 85 49 01), across the street from Casa Alicia. Small, homey rooms in this family-run pension have pleasant views. Some rooms have TV. Singles €12, with private bath €14; doubles €18, with private bath €24. ❶

FOOD

Pontevedra prides itself on seafood. In the evenings, locals crowd tiny bars in the streets around Pr. Peregrina. C. Figueroa, Pr. da Lena, and C. San Sebastián harbor some of the most popular *marisquerías* and *tapas* bars. For groceries, there's **Supermercado Gadis,** C. Benito Corbal, 34. (Open M-Sa 9am-2pm and 5-9pm.)

Bodegón Micota, R. Peregrina, 4 (☎986 85 59 17). This basement bodega serves Spanish takes on global classics like fajitas (€6.60), shishkabobs (€6.90-11.12), and fondue (€6.60-12). €5.70 *menú del día*. Open daily noon-4:30pm and 8pm-1am. ❷

Restaurante Chipe, R. Peregrina, 3 (☎986 84 58 80). Offers a wide range of typical *gallego* dishes. These northwestern Spanish dishes are a trademark attraction of Pontevedra. Meat entrees €7-21. Fish €5-13. Open daily 9am-midnight. ❸

Mesón La Peregrina, R. Peregrina, 16 (☎986 86 27 50). This *restaurante típico* specializes in seafood and fish. Try the three course *menú* for €9 or any of the delicious seafood (€3-10) or fish (€5-13) entrees. Opens from 1-4pm and 8pm-midnight. ❷

SIGHTS AND ENTERTAINMENT

Pontevedra's primary sight is the extensive **Museo Provincial,** with exhibits covering everything from traditional Galician cooking to contemporary art. From Pr. Peregrina, walk up Po. de Antonio Odriozola, which runs between the gardens and Pr. de Ferrería; this leads to the museum on Pr. de Leña. (R. Pasantería, 10. Museum open June-Sept. Tu-Sa 10am-2:15pm and 5-8:45pm, Su 11am-2pm; Oct.-May 10am-1:30pm and 4:30-8pm. €3, EU members free.) In Pr. de España sit the 13th-century Gothic **Ruinas de Santo Domingo.** With moss encrusted sepulchres and the sun filtering through cracks in what remains in the structure, the ruins are an eerie time warp in the midst of the new city. (Ruins open June 1-Sept. 30 Tu-F 10am-2pm. Free.) The **Basílica de Santa María a Maior** features a golden Plateresque door, constructed in the 16th century, depicting several sculptures of Mary; at night, it's illuminated by flood-lights. From Pl. España take Av. Santa María, on the left of the Ayuntamiento. (☎986 86 61 85. Open daily 10am-1pm and 5-9pm.)

Sunny days are sure to bring a crowd to the white-sand **beaches** of nearby Marín. Monbus buses make the journey from the outer corner of Pr. Galicia on Av. Augusto García Sánchez. (30min., every 15min., €0.90.) From the bus stop in Marin, facing the water, head left on C. Angusto Miranda around the track and up the hill. To reach **Playa Porticelo,** turn right on C. Tiro Naval Janer, continue for 15min., and bear right where the road splits. Another 10min. on foot brings you to the larger **Playa Mogor.** The festivals of **Santiago de Burgos** (July 25) and **La Peregrina** (2nd Su in Aug.) bring city-wide celebration.

DAYTRIPS FROM PONTEVEDRA

The following towns are perfect daytrips from Pontevedra, as the Monbus lines run frequently or can be reached quickly from Santiago.

CAMBADOS

Plus Ultra buses run from Pontevedra to the new bus station in Cambados near Pr. Concello (1hr., 9 per day 9am-7pm, €2.10) and Santiago (1½hr.; M-F 8 per day 7am-7pm, Sa 8am, 3, 7pm, Su 9am and 7pm; €3.70).

Offering a glimpse of small-town life and a glass of good wine, harborside Cambados (pop. 14,000) makes for a quiet daytrip from Pontevedra, just 26km away. The lack of a beach has left Cambados out of the tourist loop, but the town's other attractions warrant a visit. On a quiet hill 15min. from the center, the beautiful ruins of the **Iglesia Santa María** watch over the town's cemetery. The small **park** up the steps to the left of the ruins offers a lovely view of the town and the *ría*. The **Torre de San Sadorniño** also offers a privileged view of the *ría*. Facing the waterfront, walk left for about 10 minutes to see the remains of this 12th-century fortification standing on an island off the coast of Cambados. The **Pazo de Fefiñanes,** an attractive 16th-century palace-turned-*bodega*, brims with gigantic, sweet-smelling barrels of wine; the bars and restaurants in the Pr. de Fefiñanes serve this prized beverage of Cambados. A new **tourist office** serves the town and gives good free maps. With your back to the bus station, head left to the Pr. do Concello. The tourist office will be on your left. (Open M-Sa 10am-1:30pm and 4:30-7pm.)

EL GROVE (O GROVE) AND LA TOJA (A TOXA)

Monbus (☎902 15 87 78) runs buses from Pontevedra to El Grove (1hr.; June-Sept. every 30min. 7:45am-10pm, less in winter; €3.05); an equal number return (every 30min. 6:30am-9pm). There is no bus station in El Grove; all buses stop on the waterfront at the corner of R. Beiramar and R. Pablo Iglesias. Schedules are posted at the bus stop.

Every July and August, affluent Europeans come in Land Rovers and BMWs to the fishing town of El Grove (pop. 11,000) and its swanky island partner, La Toja. Sea-saturated El Grove, on a tranquil strait west of Pontevedra, is lined with mussel farms, colorful boats, and clam-diggers. The waterfront is the main attraction, although there's no beach in town and few on-the-water activities; instead, tourists gawk at fishermen bringing their catches to the local restaurants and peruse the wares at the Friday morning market. From July to mid-October the El Grove **tourist office,** Plaza do Corgo, 1, has an office in the square near the bus stop. (☎986 73 14 15. Open July-Oct. 15 M-Sa 10am-2:30pm and 4:30-9pm, Su 11am-2:30pm.)

GALICIA

LA LANZADA

Some Monbuses (☎902 15 87 78) en route to El Grove stop at La Lanzada (1hr.; 3 per day 8:30am-10pm; €2.80).

Ten kilometers toward Pontevedra from El Grove, La Lanzada's beach—arguably the best in Galicia—seduces bathers with its fine white sands and irresistible waves. This mile-long beach is protected by a dunes and rocky promontories jutting into sea. While most bathers come to relax and lounge in the Atlantic, quite a few come seeking the elusive "Ninth Wave"; according to pagan legend, women who swim in exactly nine waves at moonlight will forever be cured of infertility.

RÍAS ALTAS

Thick fogs and misty mornings have kept the Rías Altas secret from most visitors. With the exception of La Coruña, the area's busy capital, the Rías Altas seem to have been nearly forgotten, and that's the very reason to visit: isolated highways and the tiniest of coastal towns mean that the visitors who actually make it here have miles of green estuaries and secluded beaches all to themselves.

LA CORUÑA (A CORUÑA) ☎981

Unlike most of its Galician neighbors, La Coruña (pop. 255,000) is a *big* city, complete with high rises, expressways, and urban sprawl. Somehow, though, La Coruña manages to preserve the feel of an old-time fishermen's port. The streets in the center are a maze of tangled, narrow alleys, teeming with raucous bars and popular *marisquerías*. The harborside walks echo with Galician legend and lore: the lighthouse was supposedly built by Hercules and the city's nickname, the Crystal City, was earned for the blinding effect of a sunset on its rows of tightly packed windows. As any proud *coruñese* will tell you, Santiago might be the northwest's most popular city, but La Coruña is the *real* Galicia.

TRANSPORTATION

Flights: Aeropuerto de Alvedro (☎981 18 72 00), 9km south. Served by **Air Europa** (☎981 18 73 08), **Iberia** (☎981 18 72 59), and **ERA** (☎981 18 72 86). Daily charters to Paris via Barcelona and London.

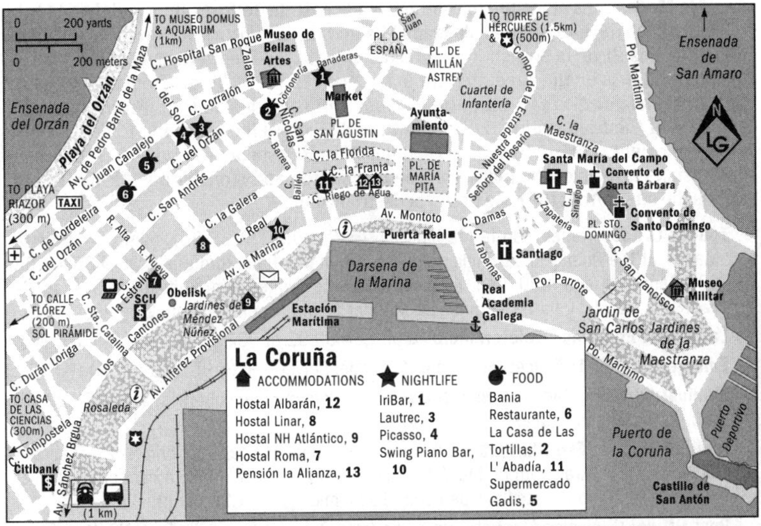

Trains: Estación San Cristóbal, Pr. San Cristóbal, s/n (☎902 24 02 02). Info open daily 7am-11pm. To: **Barcelona** (15-16hr.; 7:10am, 6:05pm; €39.50-50); **Madrid** (8½-11hr.; Su-F 12:55, 10:22pm; Sa 12:55pm; €38); **Santiago** (1hr.; M-F 20 per day 5:55am-10:01pm, Sa 13 per day 5:55am-9:20pm, Su 16 per day 5:55am-10:01pm; €3.88-18); **Vigo** (2-3hr.; M-F 13 per day 6:15am-8:40pm, Sa 8 per day 8:25am-8:40am, Su 10 per day 8:25am-8:40pm; €2.60-10) via **Pontevedra.**

Buses: C. de Caballeros, s/n (☎981 23 96 44 or 981 23 90 99). **ALSA-Intercar** (☎981 15 11 00 or 902 42 22 42). To: **Oviedo** (4½-6¾hr., 5 per day 7am-7pm, €20.49); **Madrid** (8½hr., 5-6 per day 7:30am-10:30pm, €38.08); **San Sebastián** (14hr.; 9am, 5:45pm; €42.56) via **Santander** (10hr., €31.61). **Castromil** (☎981 24 91 92 or 981 23 92 41) to **Santiago** (50min.-1½hr.; M-F 2 per hr. 7am-10pm, Sa-Su every 1-2hr. 8am-10pm; €5.25) and **Vigo** (2-2½hr., every hr. 8am-8pm, €10.95) via **Pontevedra** (1½-2hr., €9.15). **IASA-Arriva** (☎981 23 90 01) to **Betanzos** (40min.; M-F every 30min., Sa-Su every hr. 6:30am-10:30pm; €1.65) and **Vivero** (3½hr.; M-Sa 6 per day, Su 4 per day 6:30am-7:30pm; €10.90) with stops at **El Ferrol** and **Betanzos.**

Public Transportation: Red **Compañía de Tranvías de la Coruña** buses (☎981 25 01 00) run frequently (7am-11:30pm; €0.77). Buy tickets onboard. In the city center, the main stop is the Puerto Real, just across the street from the tourist office on Av. de la Marina. Buses #1 and 1a run between the bus station and the city center; bus #14 connects the center with the museums and monuments along Po. Marítimo.

Taxis: Radio Taxi (☎981 24 33 33). **TeleTaxi** (☎981 28 77 77). Both 24hr. With the tourist office and ocean to the right, walk along the sidewalk to the taxi stand.

Car Rental: Autos Brea, Av. Fernández Latorre, 110 (☎ 981 23 86 45 or 689 53 94 86). Min. age 21; must have had license for 1yr. From €30 per day with unlimited mileage. 3-day min. rental. Open M-F 9am-1pm and 4-7pm, Sa 9am-2pm.

ORIENTATION AND PRACTICAL INFORMATION

La Coruña sits on a narrow peninsula between the Atlantic Ocean and the Ría de A Coruña. The new city stretches across the mainland; the peninsula contains the *ciudad vieja* (old city). Beaches are on the Atlantic side and the harbor is on the river.

Av. de la Marina runs along the harbor and leads past the tourist office and the obelisk to **Puerta Real,** the entry into **Pl. de María Pita** and the *ciudad vieja.* From the bus station, take bus #1 or 1a straight to the **tourist office** at the Puerta Real stop; the stop at the bus station is on the street in front of the main entrance. To get from the train station to the *ciudad vieja,* take the city bus from the bus station. From the main entrance of the train station on Pr. San Cristóbal, cross the plaza and R. de Outeiro, then walk right on R. de Outeiro. Turn left onto R. Estaciones and then follow the pedestrian paths over the highway. The bus station and stop for bus #1 and 1a are across the street from the base of the pedestrian stairs.

Tourist Office: Dársena de la Marina, s/n (☎/fax 981 22 18 22), right off Av. de la Marina at the Puerta Real. English spoken. Open M-F 9am-2pm and 4:30-6:30pm, Sa 10:30am-1pm and 4:30-7pm. **Turismo A Coruña,** Núñez, s/n, Edificio Atalaya, 1st fl. (☎981 21 61 61), in the Jardines de Méndez Núñez. Open M-F 9am-2pm and 4-8pm.

Late-Night Pharmacy: Telefarmacia (☎981 56 09 92 or 902 13 41 34). 24hr. service.

Emergency: ☎061. **Police: Municipal,** C. Miguel Servet, s/n (☎981 18 42 25).

Medical Services: San José Health Center, C. Comandante Fontanes, 8 (☎981 22 63 35). **Ambulances,** dial ☎061.

Internet Access: Estrella Park, C. Estrella 12. Speedy connections and nice flat screen monitors. Walk away from Pl. María Pita on C. Riego de Agua. Make a right on R. Nueva, then turn left onto C. Estrella. Open daily 11am-midnight. €1.20 per hr.

Post Office: C. Alcalde Manuel Casas, s/n (☎902 19 71 97), past Teatro Colón off Av. Marina, between the Puerta Real and the Jardines de Méndez Núñez. **Lista de Correos** and **fax** service. Open M-F 8:30am-8:30pm, Sa 9:30am-2pm. **Postal Code:** 15070.

ACCOMMODATIONS

Most accommodations are located near the old city. Bed-hunters should head to C. Riego de Agua and R. Nueva. Reservations are only necessary in August during the city's month-long festival.

Hostal Roma, R. Nueva, 3 (☎981 22 80 75). From Puerta Real, walk down Av. de la Marina toward the city center; turn left at the obelisk onto R. Nueva. Common room with TV and tables; no kitchen. Reception 24hr. Singles €24-30; doubles €36-45. MC/V. ❸

Pensión la Alianza, C. Riego de Agua, 8, 1st fl. (☎981 22 81 14). Small but comfortable rooms near the *ciudad vieja.* Be sure to ask for a *cuarto* with a window, as a few rooms have none. Spotless bathroom. Singles €15; doubles €25. ❷

Hostal Albarán, Riego de Agua, 14 (☎981 22 65 79). Tiny rooms with bath. 1st floor common room with sofas and a big screen TV. Singles €23-24; doubles €33-37. ❷

Hostal Linar, General Mola, 7 (☎981 22 10 92). Walk away from Pl. María Pita through Riego de Agua; General Mola is 1 block before R. Nueva. Comfortable rooms with bath. This *hostal* is well known for its Brazilian restaurant on the 1st floor. July-Aug. singles €25; doubles €40. Sept.-June €18/€27. MC/V. ❸

Hotel NH Atlántico, Jardines Méndez Núñez, s/n (☎981 22 65 00; fax 981 20 10 71). Atlántico has everything you need and more. Your stay will be a memorable experience, both for you and your checking account. Rooms €104 plus tax. AmEx/MC/V. ❺

FOOD

The streets around C. Estrella, C. Franja, and C. La Galera teem with cheap *marisquerías* and other restaurants. The area around C. Rubine off Playa de Raizor is fancier. The **market** is in the oval building on Pr. San Agustín, near the old town; from Pl. de María Pita, walk up C. de la Florida and then turn left on C. Trompeta, which brings you to the market. (Open M-Sa 8am-3pm.) For groceries, stop by **Supermercados Gadis,** C. Orzán, 86. Walk away from Pl. María Pita on Riego de Agua three blocks to C. Torreiro and make a right; C. Orzán will be the third street on your left. (Open daily 9:30am-9:30pm.)

Bania Restaurante Vegetariano, C. Cordelería, 7 (☎981 22 13 01). Fresh, creative vegetarian cuisine served in a sunny environment. Immense salads €3.70-6.40. Open M-Sa 1:30-4pm and 9-11:30pm. ❶

La Casa de las Tortillas, R. Orzán, 5 (☎981 22 67 18). In a warm, homey setting, La Casa offers dozens of creative varieties of *tortilla española*, one of the country's most famous and delicious dishes (€5-7). Opens Su-Th 8pm-12:30am, F-Sa 8pm-2am. ❷

L'Abadía, Riego de Agua, 44 (☎981 22 97 02). A typical *taberna* with a wide variety of beers, *tapas*, sandwiches, and entrees. The huge dishes of meat and eggs are complemented by exotic salads that include pineapple and bananas. Delicious food and reasonable prices. Entrees €4.65-5.10; salads €4.80. Open daily 11am-1am. ❶

SIGHTS

While La Coruña lacks many of the historic monuments of other Galician towns, it has a phenomenal series of attractions along the Po. Marítimo. To visit all of these in one afternoon, start from the Playa del Orzán and follow the waterside Po. Marítimo, which brings you to the major museums and the Torre de Hércules. Trolleys also follow the Po. Marítimo with stops at all the museums and the Torre. The route begins at the start of the Paseo Marítimo, near the Puerta Real, and ends at Playa del Orzán. (Trolleys daily noon-7pm every 30 min., €0.75.)

LAS TRES CASAS CORUÑESAS

A €7 bono ticket allows same-day admission to all 3 museums: the Aquarium Finisterrae, Domus, and Casa de las Ciencias and Planetarium. www.casaciencias.org.

AQUARIUM FINISTERRAE. Also known as **Casa de los Peces,** this aquarium is La Coruña's magnificent homage to the sea. Over 200 species of local marine life are displayed in vast aquariums while the downstairs room features exhibitions on marine ecosystems the world over. *(On the Po. Marítimo at the bottom of the hill from La Torre de Hércules. Also reached by bus #14 from Puerta Real. ☎981 22 72 72. Open daily July-Aug. 11am-10pm; Sept.-June M-Sa 10am-7pm, Su 10am-8pm. €6, children and seniors €3.)*

MUSEO DOMUS. The Domus, also called **Casa del Hombre** (House of Man), is an anthropology, natural history, and science museum rolled into one, featuring interactive, high-tech exhibits on the human body and cultures. Watch "blood" spurt at 50kph from a model heart; hear "Hello, I love you" in over 30 languages (sadly, from a computer); and spend hours playing with microscopes, computers, and other fun gizmos. *(Santa Teresa, 1, on Po. Marítimo, between the Aquarium and Playa Orzán. ☎981 21 70 00. Open July-Aug. daily 11am-9pm; Sept.-June daily 10am-7pm. €2, children and seniors €1. IMAX supplement €1.20; check at ticket booth for schedule.)*

CASA DE LAS CIENCIAS. The smallest of the Casas Coruñesas, Casa de las Ciencias is an interactive science museum designed for kids to learn by doing rather than reading. This four-story building features a giant Foucault pendulum and a planetarium. *(Parque Sta. Margarita. ☎981 18 98 46. Open July-Aug. daily 10am-7pm, Sept.-June daily 11am-9pm. €2, children and seniors €1. Planetarium €1, check show schedules.)*

TORRE DE HÉRCULES. La Coruña's tourist magnet, the 2nd-century Torre de Hércules towers over rusted ships at the peninsula's end. Legend has it that Hercules erected the tower, the world's oldest working lighthouse, upon the remains of his defeated enemy Geryon. The long climb to the top is rewarded with stunning views of the city and bay. *(On Po. Marítimo, a 20min. walk from Puerta Real. From the Puerta, walk through Pl. de María Pita; from behind the Ayuntamiento, walk uphill on C. Millán Astray. Turn left onto C. de Orillamar, which turns into Av. de Navarra and brings you to the tower. Open July-Aug. Su-Th 10am-8:45pm, F-Sa 9am-11:45pm; Apr.-June and Sept. daily 10am-6:45pm; Oct.-Mar. daily 10am-5:45pm. €2, children and seniors €1.)*

MUSEO DE BELLAS ARTES. In a renovated convent, this museum displays classic Spanish, French, Italian, and Flemish art as well as local *gallego* artists. Don't miss the Goya display. *(C. Zalaeta, 2. With the tourist office behind you, cross the street into and take C. Bailén until it becomes C. San Nicolás, which runs into C. Zalaeta and the museum. ☎981 22 37 23. Open Tu-F 10am-8pm, Sa 10am-2pm and 4:30-8pm. Su 10am-2pm. €2.40.)*

CASTILLO DE SAN ANTÓN. This fort serves as La Coruña's archaeological museum, with displays of Galician fortresses, as well as artifacts from the Roman, Bronze, and Megalithic Ages. *(Puerto Deportivo, on Po. Marítimo. From the tourist office follow Dársena de la Marina away from the port. Once you reach the paseo, walk for 10min.; it's on the thin peninsula. ☎981 20 59 94. Open July-Aug. Tu-Sa 10am-7:30pm, Su 10am-2:30pm; Sept.-June Tu-Sa 10am-7pm, Su 10am-3pm. €2, children and seniors €1.)*

GALICIA

BEACHES

La Coruña's best beaches are the long, narrow **Playa de Riazor** and **Playa del Orzán,** which flank Paseo Marítimo on the Atlantic side of the peninsula and are separated from one another only by a small walkway. On the weekends, these calm waters are packed with bodies, but during the week they're nearly deserted. Small, secluded beaches hide farther down Po. Marítimo, including **Playas del Matadero, de Las Amorosas,** and **das Lapas,** although these tend to be rockier and seaweedier.

FESTIVALS

Although it is celebrated in many parts of Europe, La Coruña greets **La Noche de San Juan** (June 23) with particular fervor since it coincides with the opening of sardine season. Locals light the traditional *aguardiente* bonfires before spending the night leaping over the flames and gorging on sardine flesh. Contrary to what you might assume, the rite is supposed to ensure fertility. If you drop an egg white in a glass of water on this night, it will supposedly assume the form of your future spouse's occupation. The city's main festival is **Las Fiestas de María Pita,** which lasts for the entire month of August. Party-hardy *coruñeses* spend the month celebrating with various concerts, parades, and a mock naval battle to honor María Pita, the woman who single-handedly rallied a defense against the invading army of Sir Francis Drake after the town's men had fled from the port in fear.

NIGHTLIFE

In the early evening, *coruñeses* linger in Celtic pubs throughout the old city, bar-hopping around C. Orzán, C. del Sol, and the mess of streets near C. Franja and C. La Florida. **IriBar,** C. Panaderas, 34, is La Coruña's sleekest and most cosmopolitan lounge. (Open daily 9pm-4am.) When bars die down around 2am, **discos** pick up along the two beaches and on C. Juan Florez. **Sol Pirámide,** C. Juan Florez, 50 (☎981 27 61 57), plays dance music loud enough to rouse the dead, while **Picasso,** C. del Sol, 21, and **Lautrec,** C. del Sol, 12, across the street, attract house-music lovers. (All open daily midnight-5am.) For a more sophisticated (and pricier) scene, *coruñeses* head to the **Swing Piano Bar,** Av. de la Marina, 32, where smoky singers and Benny Goodman tunes entertain martini drinkers. (Open daily 10pm-3am.)

THE BEAUTY OF THE BEASTS It is estimated that more than 100,000 wild horses roam the Galician hills, and records indicate that they have been there for nearly 4000 years. No longer useful as cart-pullers, few of these animals are domesticated today, but the ancient branding rituals are still celebrated every July during *La Rapa das Bestas* ("Raping of the Beasts").

"Here, we fight horses for tradition," says one rider, a sweaty, blood-speckled bandana across his hairline. The blood may not be his; for the past two hours he's straddled, head-locked, tail-pulled, herd-surfed, tackled, branded, been kicked and bitten, and most importantly, sheared numerous feisty steeds. Consistent with one of the central themes of Spanish culture—man versus beast—*La Rapa* gives a new face to the traditional noble bull-Matador dynamic. Before the festival begins, Spanish Marlboro men comb the mountains and valleys gathering wild horses. No one animal can be picked out of the writhing sea of horseflesh, but brave souls wielding scissors fight their way into the crowd, wrestle one horse at a time to submission, and send thick crops of shiny hair flying to the ground—to be collected later by children as souvenirs. By the end of the three-day festival, horses may be shaken by the unsolicited crew-cut, but unlike the unfortunate fallen bull, they will most definitely be ridden again.

THE NORTHERN COAST

The northern estuaries of Galicia are among the cleanest, loveliest, and emptiest in all of Spain. To explore the Rías Altas often means spending hours on quiet coastal roads in the misty rain; if you want to escape the beaten path, coming here may be the answer. Public transportation is reliable, but renting a car is more convenient.

Eighty-four kilometers northeast of La Coruña, **Cedeira** has Spain's highest coastline and is home to thriving pagan cults with rituals involving worship of the *hierba de enamorar* (love herb). Cedeira hosts the annual **Pantín Classic** surfing competition at its famous **Playa de Pantín** and goes crazy for its annual horse-shearing festival (see **The Beauty of the Beasts,** above) every July. To reach the **tourist office,** C. Ezequiel López, 22, walk to the main street outside the bus station at Pr. Estación, s/n, and take a right. Follow the street to the small river, cross the bridge, and turn left onto C. Ezequiel López. (☎981 48 21 87. Open Apr.-Sept. M-F 10:30am-1:30pm and 5-8pm, Sa 10am-2pm, Su and holidays noon-2pm.) **IASA buses** run to **El Ferrol** (1hr., 7-9 per day 7:15am-7:15pm, €2.64), where connections can be made to **La Coruña** (2hr., 6 per day 8:30am-7:30pm, €6.85).

A tiny, beautiful old city poised between forest and sea, **Viveiro** is known throughout Spain for its beaches, peaceful atmosphere, and July *fiestas*, especially **Las Rapas das Bestas.** Vivero's **tourist office,** C. Benito Galcerán, s/n, posts info on accommodations. (☎982 56 08 79. Open daily June 15-Sept. 15 10am-2pm and 5:30-8:30pm; *Semana Santa* daily 11am-2pm and 4:30-8:30pm.) **IASA buses** connect to: **El Ferrol** (2¼hr., 4-6 per day 6:30am-7:30pm, €6.85); **Ribadeo** (1½hr., 9:15am and 3:45pm, €4.20); and **La Coruña** (4hr., 5 per day 6:30am-7:30pm, €10.75).

The official boundary between Galicia and Asturias, **Ribadeo** lays claim to one of the most beautiful beaches in Spain, the **Praia As Catedrais.** Natural rock archways droop into the sea, and low tide reveals caverns, coves, and warm lagoons perfect for exploring and swimming. The town itself has a quiet, almost ghostly air. The **tourist office,** Pl. España, s/n, is in the Parque de San Francisco. (☎982 12 86 89. Open M-F 10am-2:30pm and 4:40-8:30pm, Sa-Su 10am-8pm.) **IASA buses** to: **La Coruña** (2½-3½hr.; M-Sa 7:15, 8:45am, 1:30, 6:15pm; €10.90); **Santiago de Compostela** (3¼hr., 6pm, €12.50); **Viveiro** (1½hr.; M-Sa 9, 11:30am, 6pm; Su 2:45, 6pm; €3.76).

CANARY ISLANDS

From the snowy peak of Mount Teide to the fiery volcanos of Timanfaya, the Canary Islands have enchanted humanity since the beginning of time. Homer and Herodotus often referred to them as gardens of astounding beauty, and the lost civilization of Atlantis was said to have left behind these seven islands when it sank into the ocean. Since then, the Canaries have been known as the "Fortunate Isles" for their incomparable natural beauty—from volcanic deserts in the east, to wind-swept dunes in the south, to misty forests in the north. Beyond these natural treasures, however, the Canaries could easily leave the average traveler reflecting on a paradise lost. The concrete wastelands and 80s architecture that mark a great deal of the coastal landscape detract from the mystique of the Canaries. In most touristed parts, Spanish culture and language are overtaken by German and British tourists flocking to the islands year-round. The coastal towns of the Canary Islands are an eclectic mix of craft stalls, surf shops, fruit stands, and high-priced resorts, but their inland hamlets remain largely unchanged. Beyond tourism, the islands are blessed with incredible national parks and stunning Atlantic vistas.

The Spanish in the Canaries bears stronger resemblance to the Spanish of Cuba or Puerto Rico than that of mainland Spain, while Canarian fare is marked by a heavy Mediterraneran influence. Remnants of pre-Spanish Guanche culture—names such as Tenerife, for example—stand as reminders of the island pre-Spanish conquest in 1496 and the subsequent development of plantation economies.

When properly informed and guided, a trip to the Canaries can be unforgettable. The vast majority of travel to the Canaries comes in the form of budget tour packages sold throughout travel agencies in Europe. Browse windows of agencies within Spain, England, and Germany for advertisements of 8 day/7 night packages to the Canaries, including hotel and flight, for €300-400. You won't be staying at the Ritz, but expect much more than your average budget hostel. These packages usually restrict you to a specific part of an island; for wanderers or backpackers looking to explore, a packaged tour is not the best option. For island adventure, purchase your tickets to and from the mainland to opposite sides of the Canaries, hop from island to island by boat, make your way through island interiors with cheap rental cars, and stay in rural houses, beach-side apartments, or *hostals*.

GETTING TO THE ISLANDS

Located off the western coast of Morocco, the Canaries make for a long haul by boat (15hr. from Cádiz, Spain), but a relatively quick flight (2½-3½hr.) from mainland Spain. Competitive fares and quick flights make flying the best option. Many airlines fly direct from Spain, Portugal, Morocco, and northern Europe. Flights from Madrid are the cheapest and most frequent. European tourists, primarily Germans and Brits, flock to the islands in January and February, when the warm temperatures of the Canaries provide a retreat from the harsh winter up north; airfares during this time are the most expensive. Still, as long as you plan ahead, getting to the Canary Islands does not have to be expensive. Prices are the same whether you purchase your tickets in Spain or abroad. However, buying your tickets from consolidators can cut your costs in half (www.travelocity.com provides good deals). A one-way ticket in the summer should cost no more than €115.

Iberia (24hr. ☎ 902 40 05 00; www.iberia.com) flies from Madrid and Barcelona to Gran Canaria, Fuerteventura, Tenerife, and Lanzarote (round-trip €170-350).

Air Europa (24hr. ☎ 902 24 00 42; www.aireuropa.com) and **Spanair** (☎ 902 13 14 15; www.spanair.com) fly to the islands at cheaper rates (round-trip €150-360).

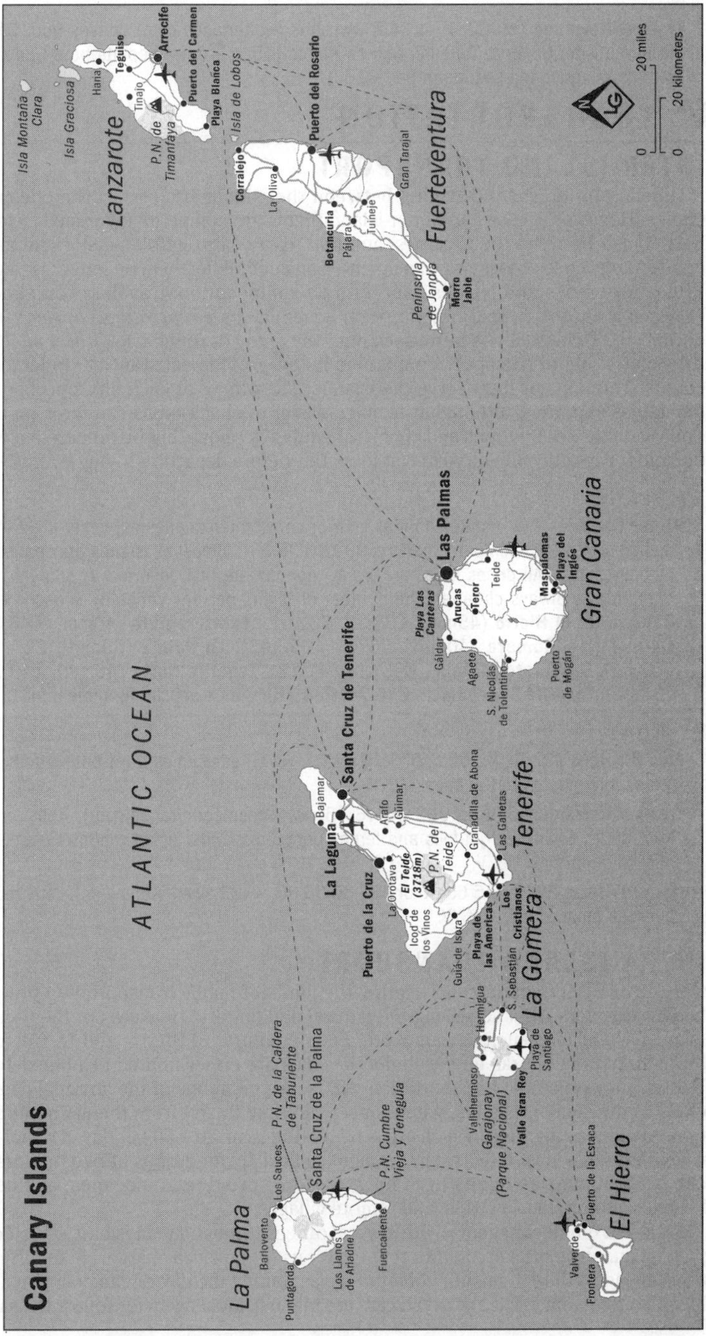

CANARY ISLANDS

Trasmediterránea (☎902 45 46 45; www.trasmediterranea.com) cruises from Cádiz, Spain to Gran Canaria, Tenerife, and La Palma (15hr.-2 days; departs from Cádiz Sa, returns W; round-trip with dorm bed €360).

TRANSPORTATION

INTER-ISLAND TRANSPORT

If time is not an issue, traveling between the islands by ferry is the cheapest choice. However, jet-foils and inter-island flights are competitively priced to facilitate transit between the Canaries, and both carry cars. Jetfoils, faster and more comfortable, cost almost twice as much—consider taking them on longer voyages. Prices for ferries and jetfoils vary with accommodation; travelers can choose between a *butaca* (a seat like those on buses) and a *camarote a compartir* (a dorm bed). Tickets can be purchased one-way *(ida)* or round-trip *(ida y vuelta)*. All Canary Island transport companies listed provide substantial student discounts. Three major lines serve the islands. The offices at each city's ports offer timetables and fares, although it is much easier to check times and fares on-line. You can make reservations and check schedules by phone, but be prepared to wait on hold for roughly 30min. Arrive at least 1hr. before departure to buy your ticket.

BY PLANE

Binter Canarias (www.bintercanarias.com or www.bintercanarias.es; verify flight information with parent company **Iberia** ☎902 40 05 00). Almost all islands are connected by daily flights. All prices listed are 1-way, normal fare first, followed by student rate; round-trip is always cheaper. The number of flights per day varies by season. **Gran Canaria** to: **El Hierro** (45min., €73.32/€62.51); **Fuerteventura** (40min., €48.08/€40.87); **La Gomera** (40min., €67.61/€58.90); **La Palma** (50min., €67.61/€57.50); **Lanzarote** (45min., €55.29/€47.18); **Tenerife Norte** (40min., €40.26/€34.26); **Tenerife Sur** (35min., €40.26/€34.26). Check website for more info.

BY BOAT

Fred Olsen (☎922 62 82 00 or 902 10 01 07; www.fredolsen.es) runs both jetfoils and ferries throughout the Canaries. MC/V.

Trasmediterránea (24hr. ☎902 45 46 45; www.trasmediterranea.com). Runs ferries from Cádiz, Spain and jet-foils and ferries between islands. Ticket windows open 1hr. prior to departure. MC/V.

Naviera Armas (☎902 45 65 00 or 928 30 06 00; www.naviera-arms.com). Ferry routes between most islands. MC/V.

INTRA-ISLAND TRANSPORT

Outside of Gran Canaria and Tenerife, the limits of public transportation prevent budget travelers from accessing the natural and cultural treasures of the Canary Islands. On islands such as Lanzarote, Fuerteventura, El Hierro, and La Gomera, buses to national parks and secluded beaches are either limited or nonexistent. Dependency on public transportation will leave you in one of the abysmal capital cities of the smaller islands, where buses run only to and from the main bus station. Avoid wasting time in such areas by renting a car. At €30 per day, a rental car is an invaluable, cost-effective investment, especially for groups of two or more. A car in the Canaries opens up a new world of pristine landscapes, secluded beaches, mountain-top vistas, and remote villages.

Choose a rental car agency with several offices throughout an island, so you can pick up and drop off a car in different locations for no extra charge. Make reservations ahead of time to ensure good prices, as renting the day of can cost you double. Also remember that almost all cars are manual. Most agencies follow the same time schedule (9am-1pm and 5-8pm); cars must be picked up and dropped off during these times. Prices quoted are per day (based on 1-2 day rental), including tax, insurance, and unlimited mileage. Prices drop significantly when renting for longer periods of time. Minimum age for rental is 21, and you must have a driver's license, though it need not be an international one. Some agencies allow you to take the car from island to island (via ferry), but this comes with a hefty fee.

CICAR (Canary Islands Car) is the best option for car rental on all islands. The company has 27 offices throughout the Canaries. Reservations must be made through the main office (☎928 82 29 00). Certain offices arrange for a representative to pick you up upon arrival and take you to the car rental office, free of charge. Economy cars are available for €29 per day. Other reliable companies include: **Auto-Reisen** (☎922 63 59 78 or 922 39 22 16, €26 per day); **Avis** (☎ 902 13 55 31, €35 per day); **Betacar/Europcar** (☎922 37 28 82, €35 per day); **Felycar** (☎900 21 10 40, €28 per day); and **Hertz** (☎902 14 37 89).

ORIGIN	DESTINATION	LENGTH	FREQUENCY	TIME	PRICE
Arrecife	Las Palmas	8hr.	Tu, Th, Sa	1pm	€27.50
Arrecife+	Las Palmas	8hr.	W, F	noon	€26.52
Arrecife+	Puerto del Rosario	45min.	W, F	10:15am	€11.40
Arrecife+	S.C., Tenerife	10hr.	W, F	10:15am	€32.30
Corralejo+	Playa Blanca	45min.	5-6 per day	8am-8pm	€11.40
Corralejo*	Playa Blanca	45min.	5 per day	9am-7pm	€12.30
Las Palmas	Arrecife	8hr.	1 per day	Su-F midnight; Sa 2:30pm	€26.52
Las Palmas+	Arrecife	10hr.	M, W, F	11:50pm	€27.50
Las Palmas	Morro Jable	1½hr.	1 per day	M-Sa 10, 11:30am; Su noon, 3pm	€47.72
Las Palmas+	Morro Jable	4hr.	1 per day	M-Sa 7:10am; Su 1:30pm	€25.30
Las Palmas	Puerto Rosario	8hr.	M, W	midnight	€26.52
Las Palmas+	Puerto Rosario	8hr.	Tu, Th	11:50pm	€27.50
Las Palmas	Santa Cruz, La Palma	8½hr.	Th	11:30pm	€34.92
Las Palmas	Santa Cruz, Tenerife	2hr.	2-3 per day	8am, 5pm	€47.72
Las Palmas+	Santa Cruz, Tenerife Santa Cruz, Tenerife	3½hr.	M-F 2 per day; Sa-Su 1 per day	M-F 6:45am, 3:30pm; Sa-Su 7am	€15.10
Las Palmas* (bus to Agate)		1½hr.	M-F 6 per day; Sa-Su 2 per day	M-F 7am-8:30pm; Sa-Su 9am-7pm	€25.96
Los Cristianos	San Sebastián	1½hr.	1-3 per day	daily 8:30am; M-F 2pm; W, F, Su 7pm	€14.52
Los Cristianos*	San Sebastián	40min.	5 per day	8am-8:30pm	€17.69
Los Cristianos*	Santa Cruz, La Palma	5hr.	1 per day	Su-F 7am; Sa 8am	€21.82
Los Cristianos	Valverde, El Hierro	5hr.	1 per day	Su-F 7pm; Sa 8:30am	€20.52
Los Cristianos*	Valverde, El Hierro	5hr.	Su-F 1 per day	8am	€18.39
Morro Jable	Las Palmas	1½hr.	1 per day	5pm	€47.72
Morro Jable+	Las Palmas	4hr.	1 per day	7pm	€25.30
Playa Blanca+	Corralejo	45min.	5-6 per day	7am-7pm	€11.40
Playa Blanca*	Corralejo	45min.	4-5 per day	8am-6pm	€12.30
Puerto del Rosario	Las Palmas	8hr.	Tu, Th, Sa	1pm	€26.52
Puerto del Rosario+	Las Palmas	8hr.	M, W, F, Sa	M, W, F 1pm; Sa 3pm	€27.50
Puerto del Rosario+	Santa Cruz, Tenerife	12hr.	W, F	2:30pm	€32.30
San Sebastián	Los Cristianos	1½hr.	1-3 per day	M-F 11:45am; M, Tu, Th 5:10pm	€14.52
San Sebastián*	Los Cristianos	40min.	5 per day	7am-6:30pm	€17.69
San Sebastián	Valverde, El Hierro	3hr.	1 per day	M, Tu, Th 5:10pm; W, F, Su 8:45pm; Sa 10:30am	€20.52

ORIGIN	DESTINATION	LENGTH	FREQUENCY	TIME	PRICE
Santa Cruz, LP+	Arrecife	19hr.	Tu, Th	1pm	€32.30
Santa Cruz, LP*	Los Cristianos	5hr.	1 per day	Su-F 11:55pm; Sa 4:30pm	€21.82
Santa Cruz, LP+	Puerto del Rosario	19hr.	Tu, Th	1pm	€32.30
Santa Cruz, LP+	Santa Cruz, Tenerife	8hr.	Tu, Th, Su	Tu, Th 1pm, Su 5pm	€25.50
Santa Cruz, Tenerife+	Arrecife	10hr.	Tu, Th	10:30pm	€32.30
Santa Cruz, Tenerife+	Las Palmas	3½hr.	1-2 per day	M-F 11:10am, 8:10pm; Sa-Su 7:30pm	€15.10
Santa Cruz, Tenerife+	Puerto del Rosario	10hr.	Tu, Th	10:30pm	€32.30
Santa Cruz, Tenerife+	Santa Cruz, La Palma	8hr.	Tu, Th, Sa	1am	€25.50
Valverde	Los Cristianos	8hr.	1 per day	Su-F midnight, Sa 2pm	€20.52
Valverde*	Los Cristianos	8hr.	1 per day	1:30pm	€18.39
Valverde	San Sebastián	3hr.	1 per day	Su-F midnight, Sa 2pm	€20.52

Unless otherwise noted, ferries are run by Trasmediterránea. * denotes Fred Olsen. + denotes Naviera Armas.

CANARY ISLANDS

GRAN CANARIA

Often called the "miniature continent," Gran Canaria sports a wide range of landscapes, from the small pockets of forest in the north to the rolling dunes of Maspalomas. The incredible weather and beautiful beaches of the south, tucked behind miles of Saharan sand, are the main draw for European tourists. The island provides your typical beach vacation, with some attractive museums in the capital city and remote mountain towns in the interior. Though advertised as the Canaries' "party island," bar- and club-hopping here are mediocre at best. Come to Gran Canaria in the winter, when the Canaries serve as Europe's sun savior.

LAS PALMAS

The urban mecca of the Canaries, Las Palmas (pop. 365,000) features all the qualities of any normal big city—shopping, decent eating, theater, cafes, and bars. The city boasts a quaint historic district in the south, equipped with some of the Canaries' best museums, and some mediocre but famous beaches in the north, along Playa de las Canteras. The city can be viewed in less than one day, allowing time to head south to the beach towns of Playa del Ingles and Maspalomas.

TRANSPORTATION

Flights (24hr. ☎928 57 90 00). **Buses** *(guaguas)* run from Parque San Telmo's Estación de Guaguas to the airport (#60, 45min., every hr. 6:30am-1:30am, €1.60). **Iberia** (☎928 57 95 38). **Air Europa** (☎928 57 95 84). **Spanair** (☎928 57 94 07).

Buses: Estación de Guaguas (☎928 36 83 35; info 928 36 86 35), on the sea side of Parque San Telmo. Office open M-F 6:30am-8:30pm. **Líneas Global** (☎902 38 11 10; www.globalsu.net) connects Las Palmas to the rest of the island. For those exploring extensively by bus, the blue **tarjeta insular** pass (€12.20) works on municipal and island-wide buses with a 20% discount on all fares. Bus schedules change on weekends, especially on Su. To: **Arucas** (#205, 209, 210, and 234; every 30min.-1hr. 6am-2am; €1.30-1.60); **Maspalomas-Playa de Inglés** (#5 and 30; 30min.; every 20min. 5:20am-3am; Playa Inglés €3.90-4.40, Maspalomas €4.60); **Puerto Mogan** (#1, 20min., every 20min. 5:40am-7pm, €6.10); **Puerto Rico** (#91, every hr. 6am-8:15pm, €5.25); **Teror** (#216, every 30min. 6am-11pm, €1.60).

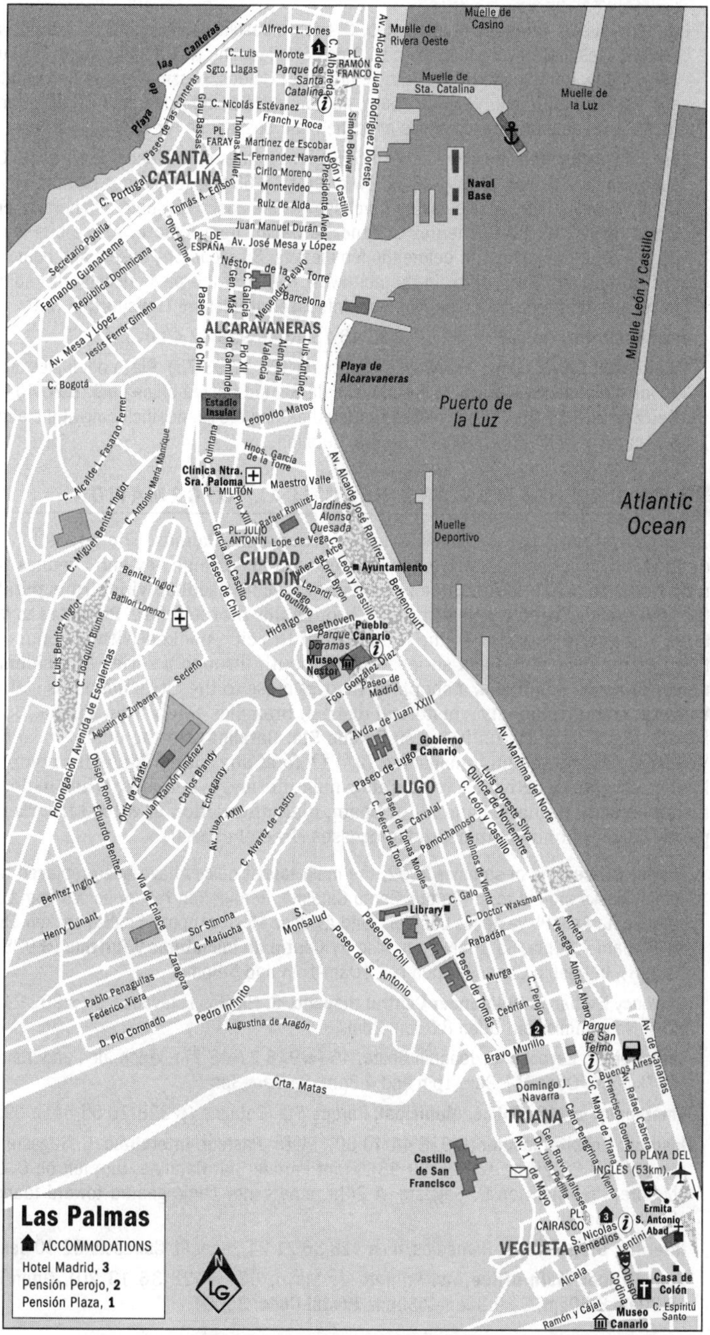

CANARY ISLANDS

Inter-city buses: Guaguas Municipales, C. León y Castillo, 330 (☎928 44 65 00), are yellow buses that travel within the city. Stops are frequent. Bus #1 runs north to south, 24hr. a day, from Puerto de la Luz to Teatro Pérez Galdós, passing Parque San Catalina and Parque San Telmo. When in doubt, hop on bus #1. Individual ride €0.80; 10-ride *"bono"* available at tobacco shops or at the main bus station for €5.

Ferries: Trasmediterránea (☎928 26 56 50) runs jetfoils from *Muelle* (Port) Santa Catalina. **Naviera Armas** (☎928 26 77 00 or 902 45 65 00) ferries depart from Muelle León y Castillo. Ferry tickets can be purchased at the docks 1hr. before departure. **Fred Olsen** (☎922 62 82 00) ferries to **Tenerife** depart from **Agaete.** A free bus leaves Parque Santa Catalina 1hr. before the ferry leaves. Buy your ferry tickets and board the bus at the Fred Olsen office in the northwest corner of the park. Tickets also sold at travel agencies for a small fee. For more info, see **Inter-Island Transport,** p. 550.

Taxi: Radio Taxi (☎928 46 22 12, 928 46 18 18, or 928 42 43 00).

Car Rental: CiCAR Gran Canary airport office (☎928 57 93 78). Playa del Inglés office, Av. de Italia, 13 (☎928 76 76 54). Muelle de Santa Catalina office (☎928 26 40 89). **Hertz** (☎928 57 95 77) has offices scattered around the island, including at the airport and in the Jetfoil office at Muelle de Sta. Catalina.

ORIENTATION AND PRACTICAL INFORMATION

The bus system is the easiest way to get around Las Palmas. The city is loosely divided into a series of districts, connected by a major highway and avenues running north to south along the east coast. **Av. León y Castillo,** which runs parallel through the city center. Bus #1 passes through this thoroughfare. **Playa de Las Canteras** and **Puerto de la Luz** frame the north of the city, packed with accommodations, bars, discos, and sex shops. Farther south through a series of residential neighborhoods lies **Triana,** a shopping district close to the city's main bus station. **Vequeta,** home to the city's historical district, branches south from Triana. Buses #1, 12, 13, 15, and 41 run between **Parque Sta. Catalina** and the quaint, beautiful Vequeta. Pick up the mini-magazine *Info Ocio* at any tourist kiosk for complete listings of cultural activities, restaurants, nightlife, and cybercafes. When in doubt, throughout the Canaries and all of Spain, dial information at ☎1003 from a pay phone to get phone numbers and addresses (free of charge).

Tourist Offices: As of summer 2002, the main tourist offices have been replaced by 5 small kiosks around town (Parque Santa Catalina, Parque San Telmo, across from Catedral Santa Ana, Playa de las Canteras, and Av. Jose Mesa y Lopez). English spoken. Open M-F 10am-7:30pm, Sa 10am-3pm. Also try **Centro de Iniciaturas y Turismo** (☎928 24 35 93), in Pueblo Canario. Open M-F 10am-1pm and 5-8pm.

Currency Exchange: Santander Central Hispano, C. Nicolás Estévanez, 5 (☎902 24 24 24). No commission. Open 8:30am-2pm.

Laundromat: Lavasec, C. Joaquín Costa, 46 (☎928 27 46 17). Wash, dry, and iron (up to 7kg) €6. Open M-F 9am-1pm and 4-8pm, Sa 9am-3pm.

Emergency: ☎112. **Police: Municipal,** Parque Sta. Catalina (☎928 26 05 51 or 092).

Hospital: Hospital Insular (☎928 44 40 00), Pl. Dr. Pasteur. **Interclinic,** C. Sagasta, 62 (☎928 27 88 26 or 928 26 90 98). From Parque Sta. Catalina, turn left on C. Luis Morote, then right on C. Sagasta. A 24hr. emergency clinic geared toward tourists. English spoken.

Internet: Dragonbit, C. Remedios, 4 (☎928 36 21 24), near Pl. Cairasco. €2.10 per hr.

Post Office: Main office, Av. Primero de Mayo, 62 (☎928 36 13 20). Open M-F 8:30am-8:30pm, Sa 9:30am-2:30pm. **Postal Code:** 35007.

ACCOMMODATIONS

Without advance notice, it's nearly impossible to find lodging during high season (Dec.-Feb., especially during *Carnaval*). If the places listed below are full, try calling the **Reservations Center** (☎928 38 46 46 or 928 38 47 47; after hours fax 928 38 48 48) and ask for Sr. Cabrera.

Hotel Madrid, Pl. Cairasco, 4 (☎928 36 06 64; fax 928 38 21 76), in the Triana-Vegueta district, inland from C. Lentini; enter through Café Madrid on the plaza. Elegantly-furnished rooms retain historical feel. Franco stayed in #3 the night before the Civil War began. Singles €24, with bath €30; doubles €30, with bath €36. ❷

Pensión Perojo, C. Perojo, 1 (☎928 37 13 87), inland from the Estación de Guaguas off C. Bravo Murillo. Lots of street noise, but these simple, spare rooms are a short walk from the old city. Communal bathrooms. Singles €15; doubles €24; triples €30. ❶

Pensión/Residencia Plaza, C. Luis Morote, 16 (☎928 26 52 12), facing Parque Sta. Catalina. Location makes up for negligible water pressure. Laundry €7. 24hr. reception. Singles €17, with bath €20; doubles €23, with bath €25. Extra beds €6. ❷

FOOD

Las Palmas's cuisine is as international as its fluctuating population, and most restaurants cater to tourists. The *Info Ocio* has a complete listing of all restaurants in Las Palmas. For **groceries, Mercado de Vegueta,** C. Mendizábal, near Teatro Perez Galdos, is a sensory parade of fresh fruit, dairy, fish, and olive stands. (Open daily 6am-2pm.) **Hipócrates ❷,** C. Colón, 4 (☎928 31 11 71), across from Casa-Museo Colón in Vegueta, offers vegetarian dining with a *menú* for €9.20. (Open daily 1-4pm and 8:30pm-midnight, closed Su evenings and M afternoons.) **Casa Montesdeoca ❸,** toward the sea from Casa de Colón, serves Spanish entrees (€7-14) in a 16th-century courtyard. (☎928 33 34 66. Open M-Sa 12:30-4pm, 8pm-midnight.)

SIGHTS AND ENTERTAINMENT

A tour of Las Palmas's sights can be accomplished in a single day. Begin in the south in Las Palmas's **historic neighborhood;** its colonial and Neoclassical architecture and open markets make for a sweet respite from the new city's commercial buildings. A plethora of small side-streets renders maps difficult to follow; from the bus station, head down C. Triana and cross C. Lentini to enter the historical neighborhood. For history buffs, the **Museo Canario,** C. Verneau, 2, off Dr. Chil, provides a comprehensive background on the Canaries' pre-conquest history. Peruse the extensive collection of Cro-Magnon skulls and mummies, documenting the evolution of man and Guanche society. (☎928 33 68 00; fax 928 33 68 01. Open M-F 10am-8pm, Sa-Su 10am-2pm. Guided tours run every 45min. 10am-2pm, and at 6 and 7pm. €3, students €1.20.) The 16th-century Gothic **Catedral de Sta. Ana** houses the **Diocesan Museum of Religious Art,** C. Espíritu Santo, 20. From the bus stop, go left up C. Cavo Sotello and left on C. Obispo Cobina. José Luján Pérez, the Canaries' favorite sculptor, designed the Neoclassical facade. (☎928 31 49 89. Open M-F 10am-4:30pm, Sa 10am-1:30pm. €3.) Columbus is said to have stayed several times in the old-style **Casa de Colón,** C. Colón, 1, as a last stop before landing in the New World. The museum contains various artifacts of early transatlantic voyages and investigations of pre-Colombian cultures. (From Pl. Santa Ana, follow C. Espíritu Santo. ☎928 31 23 86 or 928 31 23 84; www.casadecolon.com. Open Tu-F 9am-7pm, Sa-Su 9am-3pm. Free.) In the white-washed **Pueblo Canario** (Canarian Village), dedicated to the dissemination of Canarian culture, resides the **Museo Néstor,** a stunning collection of painter Néstor

CANARY ISLANDS

Martín-Fernández de la Torre's celebration of body and spirit. As per Néstor's request, on Sunday mornings, Pueblo Canario is filled with traditional Canarian folk dance and music from 11:30am-1pm. (In Dorames Park, to the left when facing the hotel. Take bus #1, 15, or 41. ☎928 24 51 35. Open Tu-F 10am-8pm, Su 10:30am-2:30pm. €0.90, students free.) The city's new pride and joy, the **Museo Elder de la Ciencia y la Tecnología,** on the port side of Parque Sta. Catalina, is a state-of-the-art exploration of topics from energy to transport. It also houses a space station, science workshop, and IMAX theater. (☎828 01 18 28; www.museoelder.org. Open Tu-Su 10am-8pm. €3.)

A new walking path frames the **Playa de Las Canteras,** one of Europe's most famous beaches. The cafe-lined beach is packed with tanners, scuba divers, surfers, and windsurfers. From Parque de Sta. Catalina, take a left on C. Luis Morote, and follow it to the end. **Medusa Sub,** Bernardo de La Torre, 33, specializes in diving, instructional courses, and equipment rental and sales. (☎928 26 27 86. Open M-F 11am-2pm and 5-9pm, Sa 11am-1pm and 6-8pm.)

Nightlife in Las Palmas is nothing remarkable. Most popular spots (including karaoke bars) are located near the Parque Sta. Catalina—be careful at night. Take advantage of year-round outdoor terraces on Pl. España and along Po. Canteras. **Palacio Latino,** C. Luis Morote, 51, is your standard *discoteca,* while **Pequeña Habana,** C. Fernando Guanarteme, 45, sizzles with salsa until 4am on weekends.

DAYTRIPS FROM LAS PALMAS

MASPALOMAS

Buses run to and from the airport (#66, 40min., every 30min. 6:30am-9pm, €2.45); Las Palmas (#5 and 30, 1hr., every 15min. 5am-2:30am, €3.90-4.60); Puerto Mogan (#32 and 61, 30min., schedule varies 8:30am-8:30pm, €2.90); and Puerto Rico (#32, 39, 61; 30min.; schedule varies 7am-8:30pm; €1.90).

Located on the southern tip of Gran Canaria, the 17km of Maspalomas's shoreline offer the best beaches in the Canary Islands. The famed **Playa del Inglés** offers parasailing, surfing, jet-skiing, scuba diving, and deep-sea fishing. The secret has long been out, and planeloads of European tourists swarm the coast every year. The crowds are worth putting up with, though, to see the awesome, wind-swept **Dunas de Maspalomas** beyond the beach, a subtle reminder that the Canaries share their latitude with the Sahara. To get to the dunes, follow Av. Tirajana towards the ocean until you reach the Hotel RIU Palace. Follow the main hotel pathway towards the water, and within minutes, you're immersed in the dunes. Climb the dunes until you reach the beach, roughly 30min. Alternatively, take a taxi to the lighthouse *(faro)*, make a left at the water, and follow the signs toward the nude beach. In 20min., you will be at the spectacular sand mounds.

Other good beaches include the flawless, quieter **Playa de Maspalomas** and the rocky **Playa de la Mujer** and **Playa las Meloneras. Water Sports Center,** in the Kabash shopping center, rents jetskis (☎928 76 66 83; €30-36 for 20min.); **Tortuga** (☎928 77 02 18; www.sunsub.com) offers diving trips and provides equipment (€19-28). **Happy Biking,** in the Yumbo Center, rents bikes, equipment, guides, and picnic supplies. (☎928 76 68 32. €9-24 per day.) Beyond the fantastic beaches, most people come to Playa del Inglés and Maspalomas to eat, drink, and party. The frequent nightbus between Las Palmas and Maspalomas makes nighttime entertainment that much easier. **Yumbo Centrum,** located between Av. Tirajana and Av. España and facing Av. de EEUU, houses an entire block of restaurants, gay and straight bars, clubs, Internet shops, laundromats, and grocery stores.

Residencia San Fernando ❶, C. La Palma, 16, is the only budget accommodation in town, though nicer hotels are affordable through tour packages. Follow Av. Tirajana uphill away from the beach; La Palma is the second right after the highway. The hostel is across from Centro San Fernando. The dunes and beach are easily accessible, but rooms are bare and bathrooms are often unclean. (☎928 76 39 06. Singles €12; doubles €18.) Dining in Maspalomas is quite awful. Hustlers lure you to tourist-themed restaurants serving over 120 generic entrees. The town's culinary savior is the dirt-cheap **Pepe Chiringo ❶,** at Av. Tirajana and Av. Francia, with heaping portions of chicken breast covered in homemade alioli (€3). Cement buildings and market bazaars house the town's **nightlife.** Once you get over the ostentatious party atmosphere, marvel at the sparkler in your drink, accompanied by a plastic frog and token orange slice.

The **tourist office** is on the corner of Av. España and Av. EEUU, next to the Yumbo Centrum. (☎928 77 15 50. Open in summer M-F 9am-2pm and 3-8pm, Sa 9am-1pm; in winter M-F 9am-9pm, Sa 9am-1pm.)

ARUCAS

Buses #205, 209, 210, and 234 travel from the Las Palmas station to Arucas (every 30min.-1hr. 6am-11pm, €1.30-1.60).

Arucas, a delightful mountain town set on a dormant volcano, has a stunning neo-Gothic church and a genuine, relaxed atmosphere. An enjoyable daytrip from Las Palmas or any point on the island, it is worth tearing yourself away from the beach to take in the town's splendor. Overlooking a set of gardens, the **Church of San Juan Bautista** is a magnificent structure mostly constructed by local stonemasons and artisans between 1909 and 1977. (Open daily 9am-1pm and 4-7pm. Free.) A short walk up out of town leads to the **Montaña de Arucas,** which features breathtaking panoramic views of the island. Tourist kiosks in Las Palmas and tourist offices in Maspalomas can provide maps and guides for the city of Arucas. There is one (and only one) place to stay in Arucas: a little *albergue* called **La Granja Escuela Anatol ❷,** C. Ruz de Pineda, 5, which provides a home for scholars—and for you, too, if you reserve in advance. (☎/fax 928 60 55 44. €21 per person.)

TEROR

Ultinsa buses #216 run from Las Palmas to Teror (every 30min. 6am-11pm, €1.60). Bus #215 connects Arucas and Teror (every hr. 8am-9pm, €0.90).

Gran Canaria's patron saint, **La Virgen del Pino,** once resided in **Teror,** a picture-perfect village tucked away in the mountains. The town's church was built on the spot where 17th-century conquistador Don Juan de Frías saw a vision of the Virgin. On September 8, the entire island pays its respects to their founding saint in a rousing celebration. In the plaza facing the church lies a small museum, **Casa Museo de los Patrones de la Virgen,** the preserved 17th-century summer home of Manrique de Lara filled with historical Canarian photos, furniture, tapestries, and paintings. (Pl. del Pino. M-Sa 11am-6pm, Su 10am-2pm. €2.40.)

TENERIFE

The volcanic peak of El Teide (3718m) jets into the blinding blue sky, peering down on Tenerife's diverse landscapes and tranquil serenity. Though Tenerife stands as the Canaries' second most inhabited island, the land is dotted with countless solitary walking trails less than 10 minutes outside of the capital. The microclimates of the island have generated a land of ever-changing flora and terrain, best characterized by the verdant gardens of the north, the rocky beaches of the south, and the mesmerizing mountainous and volcanic spectacles of the interior. Though the beauty of the island lies more in its people and spectacular vistas than beaches, sun-worshippers can still get their fix down south. Nature-lovers, adventurous backpackers, and families will find Tenerife a rewarding travel destination, a peaceful outlet from the urban sprawl of mainland Europe. For those in search of even greater seclusion, the island provides transportation to the more untouched westernmost islands of La Gomera, La Palma, and El Hierro. Cheap flights from Madrid and Barcelona make Tenerife easily accesible from Iberia.

SANTA CRUZ DE TENERIFE

The capital of Tenerife, Santa Cruz was home to the first shots of the Spanish Civil War, commanded by the Canaries' General-in-Chief, none other than Francisco Franco. Today, with more than 250,000 residents, the small port city is a pedestrian's utopia, with endless *ramblas*, quaint historical houses, *zumerías*, and lush parks. Santa Cruz de Tenerife has a strong sense of Spanish and Canarian culture that is somehow lost in the capitals of the easterly islands.

TRANSPORTATION

Flights: There are 2 airports on Tenerife. The majority of national flights land at the northern airport, **Los Rodeos** (☎922 63 56 35; www.aena.es/ae.tfn), 6km west of Santa Cruz. From Los Rodeos, buses #102, 107, 108, and 109 run to town (20min., every 20min. 6am-midnight, €1.05). International flights dominate the south's larger **Reina Sofía** airport (☎922 75 92 00 or 922 75 90 00; www.aena.es/ae.tfs). From Reina Sofía, buses #111 and 341 head to town (every hr. 5am-1:30am, €4.67). **Iberia** (☎922 33 58 79), **Spanair** (☎922 63 58 13), **Air Europa** (☎922 63 59 55), and **Binter Canarias** (☎922 63 56 44) all fly to the island.

Buses: TITSA (24hr. ☎922 53 13 00 or 922 21 56 99; www.titsa.com) serves all towns from **Estación de Guaguas,** Av. Tres de Mayo, 57, down C. José Antonio Rivera from Pl. España. Some lines do not run during the summer; call ahead or check online for information. To **Los Cristianos/Playa de América** (#110 and 111; 1hr., every 30min.-1hr. 6:15am-8:15pm, €5.71-6.01) and **Puerto de la Cruz** (#102 has stops, #103 runs direct; 1hr.; every 30min.-1hr. 6:50am-9:50pm, then 11pm, 12:45, 3:15, 4:45am; €3.30). Those planning to explore the island by bus should invest in the **bonobus** ticket/Card Titsa (€12). The amount deducted from the card is 31% less than the cost of individual tickets on short rides and 50% for distances greater than 20km.

Ferries: Trasmediterránea (☎922 24 30 11). **Fred Olsen** (☎922 62 82 00) runs a **free bus** from the main station to Los Cristianos for departures to La Gomera and El Hierro 90min. prior to departure. See **Inter-Island Transport,** p. 550.

Car Rental: See **Intra-Island Transport,** p. 550. Local offices include **CiCar** (☎922 63 59 25), **Auto-Reisen** (☎922 26 22 02), **Avis** (☎922 25 87 13).

Taxis: ☎922 25 88 06.

ORIENTATION AND PRACTICAL INFORMATION

Despite its extensive bus system, Santa Cruz is easily navigable on foot. The port city branches out from **Plaza de España.** C. Castillo runs perpendicular to the water into the commercial district. Av. José Antonio Primo de Rivera and Av. Anaga originate in Pl. España and run along the waterfront, separating the port and the city. To get to Pl. España from the **ferry terminals,** turn left onto Av. Anaga, sometimes identified as Av. Francisco la Roche, and follow it to the plaza (10min.). From the **bus station,** head right down Av. Tres de Mayo towards the water, then take a left on Av. José Antonio Primo de Rivera, continuing on to the plaza (15min.).

FLOCK OF SEAGULLS The most important workers at Tenerife's airports wear their wings permanently—21 intensively trained hawks patrol the skies above Los Rodeos and Reina Sofía, killing and scaring off seagulls and pigeons. The wayward gulls have caused near-wrecks in the past as they are sucked into plane engine turbines. With an attractive landfill nearby, they flock in by the thousands. Fortunately, the hawks—especially the females—have carried out quite an effective anti-gull campaign. The best part? The search-and-destroy superstars only require wages of €0.80 a day in food. Handlers report that the hawks would never attack humans. Hitchcock would beg to differ.

Tourist Office: Pl. España, s/n (☎922 23 95 92 or 922 22 98 11), on the corner of Av. José Antonio Primo de Rivera. Facing the monument, it's in the far right corner. Open July-Sept. M-F 8am-5pm, Sa 10am-1pm; Oct.-June M-F 8am-6pm, Sa 9am-1pm.

Police: Av. Tres de Mayo, 72 (☎922 60 60 92). Follow Av. Tres de Mayo past the intersection with Av. de La Salle; the station is on the right.

Pharmacy: Many are located along C. Castillo and its extensions. To reach a large one in **Pl. San Francisco** (☎922 24 72 11), take a right onto C. San Francisco from C. Castillo. Open M-F 9am-1pm, 5-7pm, Sa 9am-1pm. MC/V.

Hospital: In an **emergency** dial ☎112. In La Laguna, north of Santa Cruz, **Hospital Universitario de Canarias,** Urb. Ofra s/n (☎922 67 80 00 or 67 82 83). Take bus #014 or 015. **Red Cross,** C. San Lucas, 60 (☎922 28 29 24). From C. Castillo, turn right onto C. San Lucas; it's across from the church.

Internet Access: El Navegante, C. Combate, 12 (☎922 24 15 00). Follow C. Béthencourt Alfonso and its continuation, C. Pérez Galdós; turn right onto C. Combate. A bar-cum-email kiosk. €1.80 per 30min. Open M-Th 9am-10:30pm, F-Sa 10:30am-11pm.

Post Office: Av. Benito Pérez Armas, 2 (☎922 24 20 02). Follow Av. de San Sebastián past the stadium; take the 1st left onto C. Heliodoro Rodríguez López. Follow its continuation, C. Tome Cano Heliodoro, and turn right onto C. Fragata Danmark. Open M-F 8:30am-8:30pm, Sa 9:30am-2pm. **Postal code:** 38007.

ACCOMMODATIONS

Budget accommodations in Santa Cruz tend to be overshadowed by one- and two-star hotels. Beyond the lodgings listed below, several affordable places to spend the night are scattered along C. Castillo and C. Béthencourt Alfonso. The tourist office has lists of accommodations, and their map marks the hotels; make use of their free 2min. phone calls to reserve a room.

Hotel Horizonte, C. Sta. Rosa de Lima, 11 (☎922 27 19 36; fax 922 24 36 79). From Pl. España, take C. La Marina, turn left onto C. Emilio Calzadilla, then right onto C. Sta. Rosa de Lima. The spacious, flower-filled rooms are spotless and all have private baths. Superb service. Singles €24; doubles €42; triples €48. ❷

Pensión Casablanca, C. Viera y Clavijo, 15 (☎922 27 85 99). Take C. Béthencourt Alfonso, which becomes C. Pérez Galdós and then C. de Viera y Clavijo. Funky rooms are cramped but alive with pink, blue, or green color schemes. Common baths. Reservations highly recommended as the rooms are few. Singles €15; doubles €21. ❶

Hotel Anago, C. Imeldo Serís, 19 (☎922 24 50 90; fax 922 24 56 44). Take C. General Gutiérrez, and turn right on C. Imeldo Seris. Basic rooms, many with balconies. Singles with shower €25.50, with bath €32; doubles with shower €42, with bath €53. ❸

FOOD

Eating is a cheap and delicious activity in Santa Cruz. The numerous *zumerías* and sandwich shops lining the city streets serve over 50 combinations of fresh fruit juices and shakes for around €1.60. The best in town, **Zumería Tropicana ❶**, C. Portlier, 71, specializes in vegetarian food (like pumpkin burgers) and drinks made from fruits and vegetables. (☎929 84 44 90. Open 5pm-midnight.) Cafes, restaurants, and bars crowd Pl. España, but **Av. Anaga** has better deals (*menús* €6) and chic *terrazas*. **La Hierbita,** C. Clavel, 19, offers Canarian specialties. From Pl. España, take C. General Gutiérrez, a right onto C. Imeldo Serís, and another right onto C. Cruz Verde; Clavel is your first left. (☎922 24 46 17. Open M-Sa 11am-4pm and 7-11pm.) The **Mercado de Nuestra Señora de Africa,** across the river and one block inland from the Museo de la Naturaleza, sells meat and produce.

SIGHTS AND ENTERTAINMENT

The greatest sights of Santa Cruz lie outside the city limits along lookout points off the main highway and smaller side roads. Renting a car allows you to explore the hidden treasures that encircle the city. Within the city itself, the social plazas and beautiful parks are perfect for coffee sipping, people-watching, and deep thoughts. Besides **Pl. España,** the **Pl. Weyler** is the most popular plaza in the city and a gateway to the great **shopping** that lies southward. The **Parque García Sanabria** doubles as an impressive garden and an open-air sculpture museum with avant-garde works by Pablo Serrano, Rafael Soto, and Gustavo Torner. The **Museo de la Naturaleza y el Hombre,** C. Fuente Morales, s/n, off C. San Sebastián, transports you to the Canaries' archaeological past, detailing everything from pre-historic marine biology to Guanche burial practices in Lanzarote and La Palma. On the lighter side, have a go at sculpting your own ceramic pots in the museum's classroom. (☎922 20 93 20. Open Tu-Su, 10am-7pm. €2.40, students €1.20. 50% discount with *bono-bus* pass. Su free.) The intricate woodwork of the 16th-century **Iglesia de la Concepción** is worth the architectural pilgrimage. To reach the Pl. de la Iglesia, turn left onto C. Bravo Murillo from the tourist office. (☎922 24 23 84. Mass M-F 9am, 7:30pm; Sa 6, 7:30pm; Su 9, 11am, noon, 1, 6, 8pm. Open M-F 8am-7:30pm.) A different variety of splendor can be found in the breathtaking frescoes of the 17th-century **Iglesia de San Francisco** in Pl. San Francisco. From Pl. España, turn right onto C. Cruz Verde, follow it for two blocks to Pl. San Francisco. (Mass M-Sa 8am; Su 8, 10am, 8pm. Open M-Sa 8am-7pm.)

BEACHES AND NIGHTLIFE

Many flock to Tenerife for a beach holiday. Though the beaches are not spectacular, the black sand of **Almáciga** (bus #246), **Benijo** (bus #246), and **Las Gaviotas** (bus #245), and the artificial golden sand of **Las Teresitas** (bus #910), all lie near Santa Cruz, accessible by frequent buses departing from the central bus station.

In Tenerife, warm summer **nights** beckon Latin lovers of both sexes. Exploding from Av. Anaga's bar-discos at 4am, the drunken parade of stilettos marches to the sizzling **terrazas del verano** running down Av. José Antonio Primo de Rivera's waterfront. A night at **El Primero,** one of three adjoining outdoor clubs, goes by in a blur of booze promotions, seductive platform dancers, and bursting sequined halters until dawn. (Open 11pm until dawn.) The young'uns of Santa Cruz take a pause to down cheap vodka-colas in the plaza since drinks in the clubs run €4.80. **Camel Bar,** Av. Anaga, 41, is a virtual shrine to the phallic-nosed mascot of the tobacco giant, sporting old posters and advertisements urging readers to smoke.

Trendy music and a long bar keep the local crowd dancing (open daily 9pm-5am). The party at disco-bar **Noctua Anaga,** Av. Anaga, 35, spills out to its streetside tables until dawn. (☎922 29 04 61. Open 10am-5am.) For more nightlife and a variety of gay bars, head north to the student town of **La Laguna.**

LOS CRISTIANOS AND PLAYA DE LAS AMÉRICAS

The white prenumbral sand of Playa de las Américas is the first hint of what awaits visitors to Tenerife's main southern attractions: from the frat-boy nightlife to the fast food chains, just about everything here quivers with a flavor of modern kitsch. Brought in from the Sahara desert, the sand is a tasteful contrast to the nearby gray-sanded Los Cristianos beach. Exploding into full-fledged resorts in the 1960s and 70s, these two popular island towns probably have more sub-par five-star hotels than natives. Shying in comparison with the beaches of Fuerteventura, Las Américas and Los Cristianos can still serve as useful bases for exploring other shores in the south, including **Playa del Médano,** one of Tenerife's best and a windsurfing mecca. Most importantly, ferries to La Gomera depart from Los Cristianos.

TRANSPORTATION. Although Playa de las Américas and Los Cristianos are actually two separate towns and municipalities (accounting for the high taxi fare between the two, about €3.60), they are considered one by tourists and tourist offices alike. The pedestrian **Paseo Marítima** connects Los Cristianos to its northern neighbor, Playa de las Américas. **Ferries** leave from Los Cristianos, connecting Tenerife to the western islands. **Fred Olson** (☎922 79 05 56) and **Trasmediterránea** (☎902 45 46 45) run ferries to **Santa Cruz, San Sebastián,** and **Valverde** (see **Inter-Island Transport,** p. 550). **Buses** run from stops on Av. Juan Carlos in Los Cristianos to **Puerto de la Cruz** (#343, 4 per day 9am-5:45pm, €8.40), the **Reina Sofía airport** (#487, every hr. 7:20am-9:20pm, €1.80), **El Teide** (#342, 9:15am, €3.90), and **Santa Cruz** (#110, 111; every 30min. 6am-10pm, then 11:15pm, 12:30, 4:30am; €5.40). In Playa de las Américas, buses stop along Av. Puig Lluvina. Buses #342, 487, 467, 470, 442, 487, and 441 link Playa de las Américas and Los Cristianos, stopping frequently along the shore. Buses from Santa Cruz run directly from Los Cristianos along the outer highway to Costa Adeje's bus station. To get to Pl. Américas, get off at Los Cristianos and take one of the above buses.

PRACTICAL INFORMATION. To reach the **tourist office** from Los Cristianos bus stop, walk downhill on Av. Juan Carlos and take a right onto Av. de Amsterdam; it's on your left in the Centro Cultural. (☎922 75 71 37. Open M-F 9am-4pm.) Services include: **banks,** centered around Pl. Carmen and Av. General Franco in Los Cristianos (most open M-F 9am-1pm and 4-7pm); **police,** on Av. Valle Menéndez, in Los Cristianos (☎922 79 78 50); **Internet access** at **Atlantis Net,** C. General Franco, 36 (☎922 75 37 17; €3.60 for 30min., €6 per hr.); and the **post office** on C. Sabandenos, just follow yellow *correos* signs from Pl. Carmen. (☎922 79 10 56. Open M-F 8:30am-2:30pm, Sa 9:30am-1pm.) **Postal code:** 38650.

ACCOMMODATIONS AND FOOD. Pl. Américas is full of resorts, but unless you want to splurge, stick to C. General Franco or C. Paloma in Los Cristianos. Although there are many *pensiones*, they are almost always full; be sure to call ahead. One option is **Pensión La Playa ❷,** C. Paloma, 9. From Av. General Franco, turn uphill onto C. Estocolmo; C. Paloma is the first left. The basic rooms boast aqua decor and lush plant life. (☎922 79 22 64. Communal bathrooms. Singles €20; doubles €25.) **Pensión Corisa ❷,** C. Amalia Alayón, 18. From Pl. Carmen, bear right onto Amalia Alayón, parallel to C. General Franco; across from the gas station. The neat furniture forges comfort out of small rooms. The common baths are spotless, and the price is right. (☎922 79 07 92. Singles €16; doubles €25.) **Food** in both towns caters to international tastes and big budgets but is marginally better in Los Cristianos, away from the beachfront. For groceries, go to **Supermercado Carolina,** C. General Franco, 8. (☎922 79 30 69. Open M-Sa 8am-8:30pm. V.)

BEACHES AND NIGHTLIFE. Playa de las Américas makes for a picture-perfect postcard, but **Playa Vistas** in Los Cristianos is more appealing if heavy crowds aren't your style. Either way, break out the bronzer. Kiosks and parked info-vans fortify the beaches, full of fliers for **water sports** and **scuba diving.** For **fishing,** booths on the far end of Los Cristianos beach offer daily excursions for €12. **Water Sports & Charters** (☎922 71 40 34; booking office open 10am-4:30pm) monopolizes the water sports centers on several beaches around Playa de las Américas; parasailing is €21 for 10min. If the tourists on the beach aren't enough for you, **Odyssey 3** leaves Los Cristianos for multilingual whale-watching. (☎922 75 24 16. Cruises leave 10:30am, 12:30, and 2:45pm; €10.85.) Nightlife centers on Playa Américas, where a pastiche of vibrant lights, bikini contests, and beer (€2.40) awaits. A battery of two-story discos hawking 2-for-1 drink promotions to thirsty foreigners, ensuring that the city's nightlife stays charged and energetic. The **Verónicas** complex offers an imitation Ministry of Sound and your standard Shamrock Pub. Down C. Rafael Puig Lluvina, near Hotel Conquistador, stands **Metrópolis,** where a classier local crowd bounces to Spanish pop hits.

PUERTO DE LA CRUZ

Filled with a wholesome energy in its colorful streets, this port town (pop. 25,000) is one of the most enjoyable urban spots in the islands. Once a capital of the wine trade and an important 17th-century connection to the New World, Puerto de la Cruz draws an assorted mix of sailors and visitors; the steep streets are filled with African vendors, Spanish fishermen, tanned Europeans, and some unusually large lizards. Puerto de la Cruz serves as a base for exploring the Orotava region and Teide National Park, as frequent buses depart from this western destination.

ORIENTATION AND PRACTICAL INFORMATION. From the main bus station on C. Pozo, 1 (☎922 38 18 07), buses leave for: **El Teide** (#348, 1½hr., 9:15am, €4.01); **La Orotava** (#350, 352, 345, 101, 353; 25min.; every 30min.-1hr. 6:30am-1:10am; €0.90); **Playa de las Américas** (#343, 1hr., 4 per day 9am-5:45pm, €9.30); and **Santa Cruz** (#101, 102, and 103; 1-2hr.; every 30min. 6:15am-9:40pm, then 11pm, 12:45, 3:15, and 4:45am; €3.30). Puerto de la Cruz expands from Playa San Telmo past **Plaza del Charco,** ultimately reaching the sands of Playa Jardín. To get to Pl. Charco from the bus station, turn right on C. Pozo as you exit, continue onto C. Dr. Ingram, and turn left on C. Blanco (10min.). The **tourist office** sits on Pl. Europa. From Pl. Charco, head toward the port on C. Blanco, and turn right on C. Santo Domingo; the office is on the left at the far end of the plaza. (☎922 38 60 00. Open July-Sept. M-F 9am-7pm, Sa 9am-noon; Oct.-June M-F 9am-8pm, Sa 9am-1pm.) Services include: **emergency** ☎112; **police,** on Pl. Europa (☎922 37 84 48); and the **post office,** C. Pozo, 14, across from the bus station. (☎922 38 58 02. Open M-F 8:30am-2:30pm, Sa 9:30am-1pm.) **Postal code:** 38400.

ACCOMMODATIONS AND FOOD. *Pensiones* are comfortable and plush in Puerto de la Cruz—reserve in advance if you don't want to pay hotel prices. The tourist office has an extensive list of accommodations. An excellent option is **Pensión los Geranios ❷**, C. Lomo, 14. From Pl. Charco, turn left on C. Felipe, right on C. Pérez Zamora, and left on C. Lomo. Marble floors, great location, comfortable rooms, and a friendly owner all add to the charm of this *hostal.* (☎922 38 28 10. Doubles €22.85-24.) **Cafes** line Pl. Charco. For something a little more refined, try **La Rosa de Bari ❷**, C. Lomo, 23, featuring fresh pastas and other Italian fare. (☎922 36 85 23. Entrees €4-9. Open Tu-Su 12:30-2:45pm and 6:30-11pm.)

SIGHTS AND ENTERTAINMENT. The parade of flowers, tourists, bathing suits, and palm trees makes Puerta de la Cruz a sight in itself. **Loro Parque** houses the world's largest penguinarium, marine mammal shows, and great ape exhibits. (www.loroparque.com. Free shuttle from Playa Martiáñez. Open daily.) The small **Museo Arqueológico,** C. Lomo, 9, features exhibits on the processes and ceremonies used by the prehistoric natives to produce pots, urns, jewelry, and decorations. (☎922 37 14 65. Open Tu-Sa 10am-1pm and 5-9pm, Su 10am-1pm. €0.90, students €0.45.) Far more interesting are the city's **botanical gardens,** C. Retama, 2. To reach them, climb from Playa San Telmo on C. de la Hoya and continue onto C. Calzada Martiánez until you reach Av. del Marqués Villanueva del Prado. Follow the road past the Canary Centre; the gardens are on your left. Buses to Orotava and Santa Cruz pass by as well. (☎/fax 922 38 35 72. Open daily Apr.-Sept. 9am-7pm, Oct.-Mar. 9am-6pm. Free.) For beaches, **Playa Jardín** is preferable to the smaller **Playa Martiáñez.** The amusing **Lago Martiánez** is a nature-based water park designed by Cesar Manrique. (Open daily 10am-7pm. €3.30.)

Party-primed locals and tourists mix in Puerto's nightlife. **Azúcar,** at the intersection of C. Dr. Ingram and C. Blanco, is a Cuban-themed bar and a local favorite. (Open daily 7:30pm until late. Drinks €2.40-3.60.) Tourists are also drawn to the **Fiestas de Julio,** two weeks of live performances and festive meals centered around July 16th's **Fiesta de la Virgen del Carmen,** in which an image of the fisherman's saint is paraded through town and out into the ocean.

DAYTRIPS FROM PUERTO DE LA CRUZ

EL TEIDE NATIONAL PARK

From Puerto de La Cruz, bus #348 departs from the main station at 9:15am and returns from the Parador de Turismo of El Teide at 4pm. From Playa de las Americas, bus #342 departs from Torviscas at 9:15am, passing by Los Cristianos at 9:30am, on its way to the park (1½hr., €3.90). The bus returns to Playa and Cristianos at 3:15pm from El Portillo, 3:40pm from the Teleférico, and 4pm from the Parador de Turismo. Renting a car provides flexibility and allows exploration of the wildly different but equally beautiful views of the eastern (from the Puerto de la Cruz) and western (from Los Cristianos) access roads.

Towering 3718m over Tenerife, Spain's highest peak presides over a vast, unspoiled wilderness. El Teide itself forms the northern ridge of a much larger volcano that erupted millions of years ago; the remaining 17km-wide crater, the **Caldera,** only hints at the size of the explosion. El Teide shadows peaceful fields of the most vibrant wildflower fields on earth. In 1798, during the last major eruption, lava seeped down the slopes of **Pico Viejo** (3102m), creating a stunning, 800m crater. **Las Cañadas,** comprised of collapsed craters, is another product of the sinking process. Though dormant, the area's volcanic activity has not yet ceased. Among the 400 species that inhabit the diverse terrain, watch out for the large **Lagarto Tizón,** a stone-camouflaged lizard, lurking in the park.

The park is accessible by **bus** from Puerto de La Cruz or Playa de las Américas. The buses stop first at **El Portillo Visitors Center,** which offers comprehensive park maps and a brief, but excellent, video on the history and geology of El Teide. (☎922 35 66 00 or 922 29 01 29. Open daily 9am-4:30pm.) The bus then continues to the **teleférico** (cable car), which climbs the final 1000m to El Teide's peak.

(Daily 9am-5pm; €18.50, children €9.) The bus stops last at the **Parador de Turismo/ Cañada Blanca,** which has free brochures, maps, and a restaurant, but is less helpful than the visitors center at El Portillo. (☎922 37 33 91. Open 9:15am-4:15pm.)

By calling the national park information service in Santa Cruz (☎922 29 01 29 or 922 29 01 83, open M-F 9am-2pm), you can reserve a spot on one of the **free guided hikes** that depart daily or inquire about the most scenic routes for the day. Nine **unguided hiking trails** allow for independent pacing and meandering. The Parador occupies an idyllic setting next to the emblematic **Roques de García** (2140m), rock chimneys and remnants of volcanic eruptions that face their creators, Mt. Teide and Pico Viejo. An enjoyable 3hr. hike circles the huge formations of **Guajara's** peak and leaves plenty of time to spare for bus-riders. Hikes to El Teide's peak require strong legs and an ample start to complete in a day, though it is possible. Alternatively, walkers spend the night at **Refugio Altavista,** past the Montaña Blanca, and hike the last hour up the mountain to catch the early-morning sunrise. To reserve a spot, contact the office in Santa Cruz. (☎922 23 98 11. Open M-F 9am-2pm. €12 per person.) The summit is difficult to reach in the winter, especially as the refuge is only open from March to October.

LA OROTAVA

Buses #350, 101, and 353 run from Puerto de la Cruz's main bus station (30min., at least every 30min.-1hr. 6:30am-1:25am, €0.90).

Named after the lush valley that spreads out below its balconies, the small town of La Orotava warrants a daytrip from Puerto de la Cruz. Nobility resided here in the 17th and 18th centuries, leaving a number of elegant squares, streets, and churches renowned for their facades. If you intend to visit the sights, plan a weekday for the jaunt—most establishments here are closed on weekends.

The tourist office map cites over 15 sights; though it would take forever to see them all, the following walking-tour should take 2hr. From the tourist office, turn left down C. Tomás Zerolo to find **Iglesia de Santo Domingo,** whose chapel houses several notable paintings and a museum examining handicrafts of Spain and Latin America. (Church open during Mass. Free. Iberoamerican Museum, C. Tomás Zerolo, 34. ☎922 32 33 76. Open M-F 11am-1pm and 5-7pm. €2.10.) Next up, **Iglesia de la Concepción,** off C. Cologón, is a National Artistic Monument and perhaps the Canaries' most graceful Baroque building. Rebuilt in the late 18th century after earthquakes ravaged it, the church has a marble dome over the altar and its myriad works. Especially delicate is Angelo Olivari's rendition of the Concepción. Check out the church's collection of jewels from the Americas. (Open M-Sa 9am-1pm and 4-8pm. Free.) From the church, go uphill on C. Tomás Pérez and right on C. Carrera to the neo-classical **Palacio Municipal** and the **Pl. del Ayuntamiento.** The cobblestones in the plaza are the result of regal egotism—Alfonso XIII ordered the streets paved before he visited. (Open 9am-2pm. Free.) Just up C. Tomás Perez, the sensory explosion of **Hijuela del Botánico,** behind iron gates, offers celestial walkways through displays of tropical flora. (Open M-F 8am-2pm. Free.) From the bus station, head downhill on C. Tejar and take a left onto C. Calvario to the **tourist office,** C. Carrera del Escultor Estévez, 2. (☎922 32 30 41. Open M-F 8:30am-6pm.)

FUERTEVENTURA

Named Fuerteventura after the strong winds that whip along the western coast, the second largest island in the archipelago is a varied physical and cultural landscape. The island is home to the Canaries' best stretch of beach in the south, the Canaries' most abysmal city in the east, and some decent beaches in the north.

Outside coastal towns, Fuerteventura is quite undeveloped, providing mountainous serenity. Like Lanzarote, car rental is a must for those venturing to Fuerteventura on their own. For more information, see **Intra-island Transport,** p. 550.

PUERTO DEL ROSARIO

Until 1957, Fuerteventura's whitewashed capital was known as Puerto de Cabras (Goats' Harbor) for its abundance of billy-goats-gruff. The goats knew what was good for them when they migrated out of the city, which has since become the armpit of the Canaries. Unless you long for a depressing vista of dilapidated and crumbling cement buildings, use Puerto del Rosario (pop. 21,000) only as a transportation hub, and make a beeline for the south.

TRANSPORTATION **Trasmediterránea** (☎928 85 00 95) and **Naviera Armas** (☎928 85 15 42) run ferries to and from Las Palmas; see **Inter-Island Transport,** p. 550. **Tiadhe buses** (☎928 85 21 66 or 928 85 21 62) run to: **airport** (#3 Caleta de Fuste bus, 20min., 13 per day 7am-9pm, €0.95); **Corralejo** (#6, 45min., every 30min. 7am-10pm, €2.40); **Morro Jable** (#1; 2hr.; every 1½hr. M-Sa 8 per day 7am-7pm, Su 4 per day; €6.80). For a **taxi,** dial ☎928 85 00 59.

ORIENTATION AND PRACTICAL INFORMATION. **C. León y Castillo** is the main thoroughfare of Puerto del Rosario, running downhill to the port and ferry station. **Av. Primero de Mayo,** which runs perpendicular to C. León y Castillo and parallel to the water, is the town's commercial drag. The **tourist office,** Av. Constitución, 5, down the street from the bus station and two blocks from Av. Primero de Mayo, has a handy map of Fuerteventura's major towns. (☎928 53 08 44. Open M-F 8am-2pm.) In an **emergency,** dial ☎112 or the **police,** C. 23 de Mayo, 16 (☎928 85 51 00). Fuerteventura's main **hospital** (☎928 86 20 00) is on Ctra. Aeropuerto. A **pharmacy** is on Av. Primero de Mayo, 43. (☎928 53 17 21. Open M-F 9am-1pm and 5-7pm.) A back room of the **S.O.S. market** has two brand new computers offering **Internet access** (€1.20 per 30min.). The office is off Av. Primero de Mayo on C. el Rosario. The **post office** can be found at C. Primero de Mayo, 58. (☎928 85 04 12. Open M-F 8:30am-8:30pm, Sa 9:30am-1pm.) **Postal code:** 35600.

ACCOMMODATIONS AND FOOD. Unprepared budget travelers may find themselves stuck in Puerto del Rosario for a night until accommodations in more scenic towns open up. Pray that this doesn't happen, or better yet, plan ahead. Most budget accommodations are at the end of C. León y Castillo and its continuation past the port, C. Almirante Lallermand. **Hostal Tamasite ❷,** C. León y Castillo, 9, has clean rooms on the waterfront. Though few have a view, all have TV and phones. (☎928 85 02 80. Singles €21; doubles €35.) Food in Puerto del Rosario is equally basic; *cafeterías* are scattered along Av. Primero de Mayo and C. León y Castillo. *Tapas* suggestions from the friendly owners at **Getaría Taberna ❷,** C. Guise, 3, are a standout in the generic *cafetería* scene. It's located on a small alley next to Hostal Tamasite. (☎928 85 94 11. Open M-Sa 10am-4pm and 7pm-1am.)

CORRALEJO

Corralejo's center is a zoo of northern European families, car rental shops, and restaurants. To the south, however, those in search of water sports will appreciate the protected sand dunes, which unfold into a silent, crystal ocean. Daily ferries to Playa Blanca in Lanzarote make Corralejo a necessary stop for island hoppers.

TRANSPORTATION. Fred Olsen and **Naviera Armas** run daily **ferries** to **Playa Blanca, Lanzarote** (see **Inter-Island Transport,** p. 550). To reach the center from the **port,** take C. Bral García Escamez and turn left onto C. la Milagrosa, then turn left to reach the end of **Av. General Franco** (20min.). **Tiadhe** runs **buses** from the **station** on Av. Juan Carlos Primero (☎928 85 21 66), off C. Lepanto, to **Puerto del Rosario** (#6, 45min., every 30min. 7am-10pm, €2.20). For a **taxi,** call ☎928 86 61 08 or hail one next to Supermercado Los Corales.

ORIENTATION AND PRACTICAL INFORMATION. All activity extends from **Avenida General Franco,** where tourists walk from the southern sand dunes to their hotels in the north, by the port. The **tourist office** is in Pl. Pública, off the end of Av. General Franco nearest the port. (☎928 86 62 35. Open in summer M-F 8am-2:30pm, Sa 9am-noon.) Services include: **emergency,** ☎112; **police,** Po. Atlántico (☎928 86 61 07), near the intersection with Av. General Franco; **pharmacy,** at Av. General Franco, 46 (☎928 86 60 20; open M-F 9am-1:30pm, 5-9pm); **Internet access** at **Coolers Internet and Wine Bar,** C. La Milagrosa, 31, behind the tourist office (☎928 86 63 35; €2.50 per hr.; open M-F 9:30am-2:30pm and 7:30pm-2am, Sa-Su 9:30am-2am, W closed); and the **post office,** C. Isaac Peral (☎928 53 50 55; open M-F 8:30am-2:30pm, Sa 9:30am-1pm). **Postal code:** 35660.

ACCOMMODATIONS AND FOOD. Apartments and hotels line the beach, but budget accommodations are rare. With a convenient and quiet beachfront location, **Hotel Corralejo ❷,** C. la Marina, 1, is the choice for very simple rooms with ocean views. (☎/fax 928 53 52 46. Singles €25; doubles €25-31; triples €38.) The English-speaking crew at **Hostal Manhattan ❷,** C. Gravina, 24, a left off Av. General Franco when heading toward the port, offers plain, cool rooms, all with bath. (☎928 86 66 43. Singles €22; doubles €30. MC/V.) Unfortunately, **food** in Corralejo is not much better than anywhere else on the islands. Restaurants line Av. General Franco; breakfast deals abound. For standard supplies, try **Los Corales Supermarket,** Av. General Franco, 40. (☎928 86 70 43. Open M-Sa 9am-9:30pm, Su 2-9pm.)

ENTERTAINMENT AND BEACHES. The Fiestas del Carmen, beginning July 16 and lasting for two weeks, make for a lively visit. During the festival, such decidedly unholy events as volleyball competitions and outdoor dances help celebrate the town's patron saint before she is led on a watery parade through the port. Nightlife in Corralejo is a parade of tipsy tourists and leering locals. Bars tend toward the cliché, with surf or pub themes; most of them are found along Av. General Franco and in the connecting shopping centers. The **Caleta Dorada Complex** and **Centro Commercial Atlántico** are filled with various second-rate bars and pubs.

The main attraction in Corralejo is the **Parque Natural de Corralejo y Lobos,** which contains protected and rugged sand dunes. Adventure companies compete for business along Av. General Franco, catering to all athletic tastes and abilities. **Dive Centre Corralejo,** C. Nuestra Señora del Pino, 36 (☎928 53 59 06), offers dive trips, lessons, and equipment rental. **Catamaran Celia Cruz** rigs daily trips on glass-bottomed catamarans. (☎646 53 10 68. €7.50-9 per person.) **Ventura Surf,** in the Apartamentos Hoplaco complex on Av. General Franco, rents windsurfing equipment (€24 per day) and offers a 3hr. (€66) beginner's course and an 8hr. (€120) course for those wanting extra assistance. (☎928 86 62 95. Open daily 10am-6pm.)

BETANCURIA

An escape from the touristed coast line, Fuerteventura's amber interior reveals rocky villages, fallen windmills, and small farms. Betancuria, named by the self-effacing Jean de Béthencourt, was built along the side of a dormant volcano.

Shady palms and pockets of lush vegetation rise out of the dry, rocky mountains. Betancuria's tranquil state makes it a restful, low-key daytrip. From the bus stop it's an easy walk to the central **Iglesia de Santa María.** Betancuria's tranquil state offers a restful night's stay (especially if you miss the only bus back to Puerto Rosario). **Vicente Ruiz Méndez ❶,** Roberto Trondán, 2, on the opposite side from the Museo Arquelógico, is a sometimes-pension that might be able to put you up if you're stranded in town. It's run by a charming Civil War veteran whose wife was supposedly the first female mayor in Spain (☎928 97 80 95; €12). Though a bus goes to and from Betancuria, it is impossible to complete the daytrip using public transportation due to ill-fated bus schedules. Two **buses** (#2; 45min.; 11am, 2:30pm; €2.45) run M-Sa from Puerto del Rosario, and **only one bus runs back** (12:30pm), so plan your trip wisely. The only real way to get here is by car.

MORRO JABLE/PENINSULA DE JANDÍA

Expanding 30km across the south of Fuerteventura, the Peninsula de Jandía and its crystal blue beaches along Playa de Sotavento and Playa de Barlovento are the top reason for visiting the island. The heavenly white sands and turquoise waters that frame the southern coast have transformed the former fishing village of Morro Jable into a mecca for accommodations, food, and transport.

TRANSPORTATION. Though there is no designated bus station in town, **Tiadhe** buses (☎928 85 21 66) stop at the Centro Commercial de Jandía before terminating on C. Gambuesas (across from the post office) in Pueblo Morro Jable. **Buses** run to **Costa Calma** (#5, 1hr., 11 per day 8:30am-9pm, €2.40-3) and **Puerto del Rosario** (#1, 2hr., 8 per day 6am-7pm, €6.60). **Taxis** (☎928 54 12 57) stand at the port in Morro Jable. A ride to one of the two main *playas* of Jandía costs €2.50. In addition to the normal rental cars, **Orlando,** in Apartamentos El Matorral, rents four-wheel-drive vehicles for navigating the peninsula's rough dunes. (☎928 54 04 09. Min. age 21. Rates start at €33 per day. AmEx/V.)

ORIENTATION AND PRACTICAL INFORMATION. Morro Jable hugs the beach across vast expanses of sun and sky, most notably the **Playa de la Cebada** and the **Playa del Mattoral. Av. Jandía,** which becomes **Av. del Saladar,** connects the east and west sides of the city center. Most hotels and restaurants line these two streets. Most of the town's roads inevitably lead to the beach. The **tourist office,** Av. Saladar, is in the Centro de Comercial de Jandía, local 88. (☎928 54 07 76; www.rcanaria.es/pajara. Open M-F 9am-3:30pm.) Services include: **emergency,** ☎112; the **police,** C. Hibisco, 1 (☎928 54 10 22); **pharmacy,** C. Senador Cabrera, 23 (☎928 54 10 12; open M-F 9am-1pm and 5-7pm, Sa 9am-1pm); the **Centro Médico Jandía,** at the Jandía Beach Center, Urb. Solana. (☎928 54 04 20 or 928 54 15 43; open 24hr.); Internet access at **Internet Café Jandía,** Centro Comercial Jandía, location 14a (open M-Tu, Th-F 10am-noon and 2-9pm; W, Sa-Su 6-9pm; €3 per 30min.); and the **post office** on the corner of C. Buenavista and C. Gambuesa. (☎928 54 03 73. Open M-F 8:30am-2:30pm, Sa 9:30am-1pm.) **Postal code**: 35625.

ACCOMMODATIONS AND FOOD. Budget accommodations cluster around the city center, most notably along C. Maxorata and C. Senador Velázquez Cabrera. **Hostal Maxorata ❷,** C. Maxorata, 31, has fresh and airy double rooms, some with views of the beach. (☎928 54 10 87. Singles €20; doubles with bath €26.) Have an experience down the street at **Hostal Omahy ❷,** C. Maxorata, 47. (☎928 54 12 54. Call ahead for reservations. Singles €20; doubles with bath €25.) **Restaurants** in the area are tailored to the tourist crowds; Italian bistros, dime-a-dozen seafood joints, and German *konfiterias* line the beach. For a calm seaside escape, try

Morro Jable's best, near the port. **Av. del Mar ❷,** Av. del Mar, 1, at the end of the string of restaurants, offers fresh fish (€9) served to you on a fabulous patio. (☎928 84 43 35. Open daily 10:30am-11pm.)

BEACHES AND ENTERTAINMENT. The main attractions on the Peninsula and in Morro Jable are fierce tanning and water sports in the welcoming turquoise waters. Morro Jable's **beaches** are lined with bodies in various states of undress from early morning to late night. The most pristine beaches of the peninsula are those in the south along Playa de Sotavento, followed by the those in Playa de Barlovento and Playa del Mattoral (close to the city center). The beaches are ideal for reflective walks and adventurous drives (where cars are allowed to enter the beach). Blessed with the islands' calmest waters and lushest sea life, Morro Jable offers excellent opportunities to practice **water sports.** Stiff breezes off the peninsula's southern tip justify the innumerable **windsurfing** schools who set up camp on the beach (the coast hosted last year's world freestyle competition in July). **Barakuda Club,** Av. Saladar, offers **scuba diving** and equipment rental. (☎928 54 14 18. Dives Su-F 9:30am, 2:30pm. €30 per dive; €24 with your own equipment.) Sparse **nightlife** revolves around the resorts along Av. Saladar. Start the night with drinks in one of the many bars of the **Centro Comercial de Jandía,** and continue the night in the city's two *discotecas,* **La Cara Disco** and **Stella Discoteque,** two blocks away.

LANZAROTE

Having avoided the construction of the high-rises and resorts that mar its western neighbors, Lanzarote is only beginning to blemish its landscape. Outside of port and tourist cities, Lanzarote is a precious natural phenomenon covered in a blanket of volcanic rock and ash. Volcanic activity from nearly 300 years ago has left the land barren and dry, with an unusual landscape resembling the surface of the moon. Driving through the island can best be described as inspirational, most notably en route to the unique Parque National Timafaya. Beyond the volcanic rhapsody, the architecture of César Manrique dots the island, with unprecedented homes, museums, and restaurants built directly into the volcanoes themselves. When visiting the island, do not rely on public transportation—the vast majority of the islands' sights can be accessed only by car. Rent a car, pick up an island map at any tourist office, and start exploring.

ARRECIFE

Meaning "rocky reef," Arrecife, Lanzarote's hamlet capital (pop. 31,000), resides on the island's eastern coast, fringed with blackened lava and yellow sands. The city has little to offer beyond an interesting art museum and a few good bars. Travelers should only stay overnight in Arrecife as a last resort.

TRANSPORTATION. **Lanzarote Airport** (☎928 84 60 00) is the main entry point from other islands and mainland Spain. Over seven car rental agencies are located in the airport. Bus #4 runs between the airport and Arrecife (20min., every 30min.-1hr. 8:20am-7:20pm, €0.90), stopping at the end of Av. Fred Olsen; follow it along the water to Av. Gen. Franco. **Naviera Armas** (☎928 82 49 30) and **Trasmediterránea** (☎928 81 10 19) run frequent ferries to **Las Palmas** (on Gran Canaria) and less frequent service to **Santa Cruz de Tenerife.** Trips to **Corralejo** or **Puerto Rosario** (on Fuerteventura) depart from **Playa Blanca** in the south of Lanzarote; **Fred Olsen** runs a free bus to Playa Blanca from their office in Puerto del Carmen at 9am and 5pm. For more info, see **Transportation,** p. 550. The **bus station**

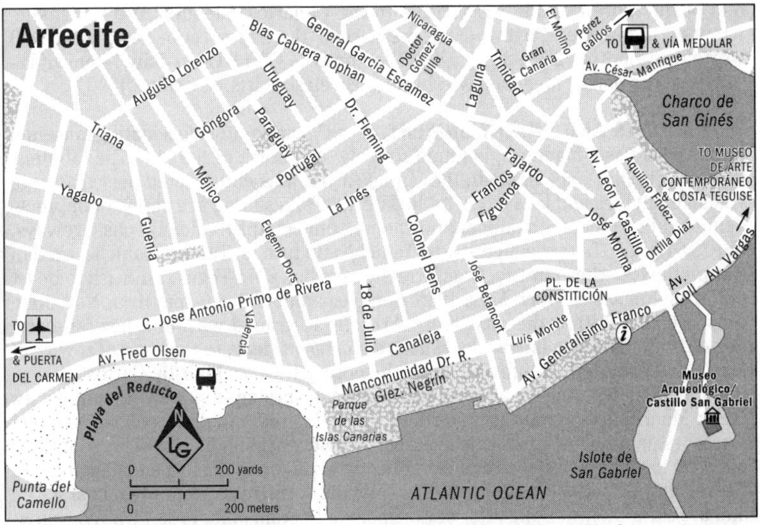

(☎928 81 15 22), C. Vía Medular, is open daily 8am-10pm. Note that buses run very infrequently on weekends. During the week, buses run to: **Costa Teguise** (#1, every 20min. 6:40am-11:40pm, €0.95); **Maguez** (#7, 4 per day 11:45am-8pm, €2.10); **Playa Blanca** (#6, 6 per day 6am-8:15pm, €2.60); **Puerto del Carmen** (#2, 40min., every 20min. 6:20am-11:20pm, €0.85); and **Teguise** (#7, 9, and 10; 7 per day 7:40am-8pm; €0.90). **Taxis** (☎928 80 31 04) can be found at each end of Av. León y Castillo.

ORIENTATION AND PRACTICAL INFORMATION. Arrecife is easy to navigate on foot, though poorly marked streets can prove frustrating. **Av. Generalísimo Franco** hugs the coast while its numerous continuations spread from the **port** to the west and the Playa Reducto to the east. The **tourist office** (☎/fax 928 81 18 60; open M-F 8am-2pm, Sa 9am-2pm) is on Av. Generalísimo, near its intersection with **Av. de León y Castillo,** the main pedestrian thoroughfare, which runs perpendicular to the ocean. The other tourist office in the airport is equally sufficient, and the staff is incredibly friendly. In an **emergency,** call ☎112 or dial the **police,** Av. Coll, 5. (☎928 81 13 17. For **medical emergencies,** dial ☎061.) There is a **pharmacy** on Av. de León y Castillo, 41. (☎928 81 10 72. Open M-F 9am-1pm, 5-8pm.) Check your email at **Servi Computer,** C. Coronel Bens, 14; take a left off Av. Generalísimo Franco, from Av. de León Castillo. (☎928 80 50 36. €1.20-1.50 per hr. Open daily 10am-2pm, 4:30-10pm.) Send letters home at the **post office** on Av. Generalísimo Franco, 8. (☎928 80 06 73. Open M-F 8:30am-8:30pm, Sa 9:30am-1pm.) **Postal code:** 35500.

ACCOMMODATIONS AND FOOD. While the other towns in Lanzarote often have only one *pensión*, Arrecife has a few more options. The tourist office has a massive list of accommodations with phone numbers and addresses, but no prices. *Apartamientos* tend to be cheaper than hotels, but rural houses in the countryside are the way to go in Lanzarote. If you have to spend a night in Arrecife, head to **Residencia Cardona ❸**, C. 18 de Julio, 11, which boasts huge rooms with pay-TV, telephones, and gleaming bathrooms. From the tourist office, turn left on Av. Generalísimo Franco and right on C. 18 de Julio. Reserve well in advance. (☎/fax 928 81 10 08. Singles €26; doubles €32; triples €38.) **Castillo de San José Restaurante and Bar ❸**, Pto. de Naos, beneath the modern art museum outside of town, is one of the more upscale restaurants in the Canaries. Blended into the castle, wrapped in glass, and overlooking the harbor, the dining room has a view well worth the price. (☎928 81 23 21. *Tapas* and entrees €5-14. Open daily 1-4pm and 8-11:30pm; bar open 11am-1am. No shorts, sleeveless shirts, or t-shirts.)

SIGHTS AND ENTERTAINMENT. The Canaries' most fascinating museum, **Fundacion César Manrique,** is found roughly 6km north of the city. The fabulous two-story house, once home to the famous artist, was constructed over five large volcanic bubbles and lava caves in the late 1960's, resulting in a series of unprecedented subterranean chambers and rooms connected by volcanic passageways. (☎928 84 31 38. Take the highway to Tahiche and turn on Taro de Tahiche, off San Bartolome Rd. Alternatively, from Arrecife take bus #7 to Teguise and ask to be let off at the Funacion. Open M-Sa 10am-6pm year-round, Su 10-3pm from Nov.-June only. €6.50.) Within the city itself, Arrecife is graced with another fantastic museum, the **Museo Internacional de Arte Contemporáneo,** to the west of town, off Av. Naos. The original building, an 18th-century fortress built by Carlos III, was intended to defend the island from pirate attacks. Its simple stonework epitomizes César Manrique's revitalization of the island's history and architecture. Exhibits rotate frequently, but geometric and abstract works (including those by Manrique himself) form part of the permanent collection, affixed to the fort and hanging into the restaurant below. (☎928 81 23 21. A 40min. walk; taxis from town cost €2.60 and are safer than walking after dark. Open daily 11am-9pm. Free.) On Av. Generalísimo Franco, next to the tourist office, the **Castillo de San Gabriel** houses the **Museo Arqueológico** (☎928 80 28 84; closed until Dec. 2003).

C. José Antonio fills Arrecife's **nightlife** quota with small, rambunctious bars, restaurants, and a few dance spots. On weekends, the street is a sea of bar-hopping. The most popular joint is **Tambo Bar,** C. Luis Morote, 24, just past C. Jose Antonio near the start of Av. Generalismo Franco. **El Convento,** C. José Antonio Ribera, 76, **Goa Goa Bar,** C. José Antonio, 61, and **Sunami,** C. José Antonio, 59, are also packed.

PUERTO DEL CARMEN

Primarily British tourists flock to Puerto del Carmen, packaged and lobster-tied by one of many tour companies. As Lanzarote's largest tourist destination, the area provides typical beach fare and decent sun-bathing spots. **Avenida de las Playas** squeezes in endless restaurants, bars, and bazaars. Offshore reefs offer some of the islands' best **scuba diving.** For more information try the **Delfín Club,** Av. Playas, 38, in the Centro Aquarium, which runs four dives a day (10am-3:30pm). (☎928 51 42 90. €33 for a beginner's course; €25 for certified divers needing equipment; €19 if you have your own. Open M-Sa 9am-6pm.)

Bus #2 runs between Arrecife and Puerto del Carmen and stops along Av. Playas (40min., every 20min. 6:20am-11:20pm, €1.20). **Fred Olsen** (☎922 62 82 31) and **Naviera Armas** (☎928 51 79 12) also run buses to Playa Blanca to meet their ferry departures. The **tourist office** is at Av. las Playas near the beach. (☎928 51 33 51; fax 928 51 56 15. Open M-F 10am-5pm.) To explore the island to its fullest, rent a car—there are good deals along Av. Playas. **Lanzauto,** Av. Playas, 19, rents from €24 per day, insurance and unlimited mileage included. (☎928 51 06 18. Min. age 21. Open M-F 8:30am-1pm and 4-8pm, Sa-Su 8:30am-1pm and 6-8pm.)

PARQUE NACIONAL DE TIMANFAYA

Known as **Montañas de Fuegos** (Fire Mountains), the barren landscape of Lanzarote's national park erupts with evidence of the six-year explosion that began in 1730. Resembling the surface of the moon, copper *hornitos* (mud-volcanos) and blackened folds of solidified lava carve their way into the loose soil; only lichen seem to survive in the scorching ground. The winding roads leading to the national park entrance provide countless photographic opportunities. Note that no public transportation runs to the park; you need your own car. Exploration of the park itself is achieved through a tri-lingual 30min. bus tour (sit on the right for better views). Buses leave from the main parking lot, in front of El Diablo Restaurant. (☎928 84 00 56. Park open daily 9am-5:45pm. €6.10.) The magic tricks of **Islote de Hilario's** geothermal heat are the tour's highlight. Legend has it that the hermit Hilario, who lived here with his lone camel, planted a fig tree whose fruit was consumed by the underground fires. Similar spectacles are performed by park employees to demonstrate the effects of the 300°C temperatures below the earth. The **El Diablo** ❹ restaurant that now occupies the *islote* was designed by César Manrique and constructed using only stone, metal, and glass (due to the high temperatures). Volcanic heat seeping from the earth powers the kitchen's grill. The panoramic view from the dining room is the best on the island, extending from the arid mountains to the azure sea. (☎928 84 00 57. Open daily noon-3:30pm.)

Self-exploration of the national park is prohibited, but free walking tours can be arranged through the Spanish National Park State Network. The 3½km Termesana trail in English or Spanish gives tourists a rare opportunity to explore the natural volcanic beauty by foot (M, W, F 10am from Visitor's Center in Mancha Blanca). Walking tours must be arranged ahead of time by phone or in person at the **Visitor's Center in Mancha Blancha.** (☎/fax 928 84 08 39; www.mma.es/parques. 5min. from park main entrance. Take the road from Yaiza to Tinajo, km11.5. Open M-F 9am-3pm.) Tours by camel are run separately but do nothing more than go up a hill near the park entrance. The visitor's center can also provide detailed directions for exploring two spectacular and accessible craters outside the national park. They also host a challenging guided walk, called the *Ruta del Litoral*, along Lanzarote's northern coast, which last roughly 6hr. About 7km away, in the town of Tiagua, lies Lanzarote's quaintest accommodations, **La Casa Rural Molina** ❷. Turn into the driveway directly next to the km13 sign off the highway in the town of Tiagua. Lounge around the country house and sip on fresh juice in a quiet and secluded setting. The gay-friendly Molina is an ideal base for exploring the entire island. (☎928 52 92 66; www.casalamolina.com. Doubles €40, with private bath €56.) Head even further south towards Mozaga to dine at Lanzarote's most delicious restaurant, **Monumento al Campesino Restaurante** ❸, adjacent to the monument itself. Feast on the best *papas arrugadas* in all of the Canaries, drowned in homemade *mojos*. (☎928 52 01 36. *Tapas* and entrees €4-15.)

TEGUISE

Brushing the side of the Guanapays mountains (452m), Teguise is Lanzarote's prettiest village, perfect for wandering walks. Frequent buses run daily from Arrecife to Teguise (#7, 9, and 10; 6 per day 7:40am-8pm; €0.90), stopping in front of the Ayuntamiento. To get to the **Pl. de la Constitución,** the center of town, face the Ayuntamiento, turn right on C. Santo Domingo, right on C. Morales Lemes, then right into the plaza, the site of the **Sunday market.** Teguise is famous for its authentic Canary Islands cuisine, and food stands flood the town on market day. **Iglesia de la Virgen de Guadalupe** resides in the corner of the plaza.

A 5min. drive or 30min. walk from the Pl. Constitución, the 16th-century **Castillo Santa Bárbara** offers one of the island's best views. The castle houses the **Museo Etnográfico del Emigrante Canario,** whose centerpiece is a provoking ethnographic chronicle of the island's first 12 families to emigrate here. The collection, however, barely rivals the castle itself, with its views of the town and the lava landscape. (☎619 84 50 76. Exit Pl. Constitución on C. Herrera y Rojos; following the main highway, enter at the Castillo Santa Bárbara sign, up the mountain to the castle. Open Tu-F 10am-4pm, 3pm in summer; Sa-Su 10am-3pm, 2pm in summer. €3.)

Back in Teguise itself, across from the church's entrance lies the 18th-century **Casa Museo Palacio Spinola,** named after the wealthy local merchant. César Manrique oversaw renovations to restore the island's official museum. Old photos of festivals and Canarian customs fill the simple rooms. (☎928 84 51 81. Open M-F 9am-4pm, 3pm in summer; Sa-Su 9am-3pm, 2pm in summer. €3.)

PLAYA BLANCA

Island-hoppers will invariably end up at Playa Blanca, a beach town and transportation hub at the southern tip of Lanzarote, in the transit to Fuerteventura. Budget accommodations are limited in the area. If you need a place to stay, try **Apartamentos Gutierrez ❹,** Pl. Nuestro Senora del Carmen, 8. (☎928 51 70 89. Doubles €45-60.) A **tourist office** is located in the port (☎928 51 90 18 or 928 51 77 94).

LA GOMERA

Many believe the verdant island of La Gomera, with its terraced gorges and steep mountain passes, to be the most blessed of all the Canaries. La Gomera's relative isolation and small, stony beaches keep the droves of tourists at bay. Surrounded by banana and avocado plantations, and freshened by a constant breeze, the island's main town, San Sebastián, is refreshingly provincial, unscarred by day-trippers from Tenerife. La Gomera's crown jewel, however, is the spectacular Garajonay National Park, the largest refuge of laurisilva forests, which died out elsewhere millions of years ago and remain only in the western Canary Islands.

SAN SEBASTIÁN DE LA GOMERA

Heading off to find the mythical Middle Passage to India, Christopher Columbus dropped anchor here for a few days. He gathered water from the well, prayed at the church, and fell in love with a girl before "discovering" the Americas. May your stay be as storied. These days most explorers breeze through this charming town on their way to the beaches in the south. Still, as a transportation hub filled with affordable accommodations, good restaurants, and a welcoming feel, San Sebastián makes an excellent base for discovering the rest of La Gomera.

TRANSPORTATION

Flights: Though most people arrive in La Gomera via ferry from Tenerife, the island's new **airport** (☎922 87 30 00) is home to a few daily flights from Tenerife and Gran Canaria.

Buses: The main bus stop is by the ferry station on the port. 3 lines start in the port and branch out across the island (€4.15). Not all buses actually stop at the **bus station,** Vía de Ronda, on the corner of Av. Colón (☎922 14 11 01), so the port is your best bet. Line 1 to **Valle Gran Rey** with stops in the **Parque de Garajonay** (M-Sa 10:30am, 2, 5:30, 9:30pm; Su 10:30am, 5:30pm). Line 2 to **Vallehermoso** with stops in **Agulo** and **Hermigua** (M-Sa 10:30am, 2, 5:30, 9:30pm; Su 10:30am, 5:30pm). Line 3 to **Playa Santiago** and **Alajero** (M-Sa 10:30am, 2, 5:30, 9:30pm; Su 10:30am, 5:30pm). Line 5 to the island's new **airport** (M-Sa 8:15am, 2:45pm).

Ferries: Trasmediterránea (☎920 87 08 02) and **Fred Olson** (☎922 87 10 07) run daily ferries to **Los Cristianos** and **El Hierro.** See **Inter-Island Transport,** p. 550.

Car Rental: Hertz (☎922 87 00 28), in the port terminal. Min. age 21. Open M-F 9am-1pm and 4-7pm, Sa 9am-1pm. AmEx/MC/V.

Taxis: ☎922 87 05 24.

ORIENTATION AND PRACTICAL INFORMATION

Navigating San Sebastián is a breeze. From the port, **Av. Fred Olsen** becomes **Av. de los Descubridores** and runs along the entire coast, intersected midway by **C. del Medio,** the town's main drag, at **Pl. Américas.** To get to the plaza from the **port,** turn left on Av. Fred Olsen; the plaza is on the right (5min.). If you arrive after dark, consider taking a quick taxi into town (€2), as the streets aren't clearly named and are difficult to maneuver in the dark. **Buses** stop at the port, meeting most ferries (though they're quick to leave once the ferry has arrived). If you've rented a **car,** turn right on C. Vía de Ronda and left on C. Sur to head out of town toward Valle de Gran Rey. Use extreme caution driving the island; blind corners on narrow mountain passes and wide-turning buses can be treacherous—honk that horn.

Tourist Office: C. Real, 4 (☎922 14 15 12 or 922 87 02 81; fax 922 14 01 51; www.gomera-island.com), behind Pl. Américas on the corner of C. Medio. Open M-Sa 9am-1pm and 4-6pm, Su 10am-1pm. **Park Service,** C. Sur, 6 (☎922 87 01 05 or 922 80 09 03). Go left on Av. Colón from C. Medio, and continue across the bridge following signs to Valle Gran Rey; the office is on the right at the 2nd bend. Open M-F 8am-3pm.

Currency Exchange: Banks line Pl. Américas. Open M-F 8:30am-2pm, Sa 8:30am-1pm. **BBVA** is on C. Medio. Open M-F 9am-1:30pm.

Laundromat: Lavandería HECU, C. Medio, 76 (☎922 14 11 80). Open M-F 8:30am-1:30pm and 5-8pm, Sa 8:30am-1:30pm. €4.20 wash, €4.20 dry.

Emergency: ☎112.

Pharmacy: Pl. Constitución, 14 (☎922 14 16 05). Next to the tourist office in Pl. Américas. Open M-F 9am-1:30pm and 5-8pm, Sa 9-1:30pm.

Hospital: Nuestra Sra. de Guadalupe (☎920 14 02 02). From Pl. Américas, walk away from the port, turn right on C. Vía Ronda, left across the bridge, and take the 1st right.

Internet Access: Pedalán Informática, C. Medio, 79 (☎922 87 20 17). €4.50 per hr. Open M-F 9:30am-1pm and 4:30-8pm, Sa 10am-2pm.

Post Office: C. Medio, 60 (☎922 87 10 81). Open M-F 8:30am-2:30pm, Sa 9:30am-1pm. **Postal code:** 38800.

ACCOMMODATIONS

San Sebastián's budget accommodations are more affordable than anywhere in the Canaries. *Pensiones* offer double rooms in old Canary-style homes; most have communal baths. For longer stays, *apartamentos* are a better option. *Pensión* signs hang out of windows on C. Medio. Pricier hotels reside on C. Ruiz de Padrón.

Pensión Victor-Leralita, C. Medio, 23 (☎670 51 75 65 or 670 81 32 01). A renovated 250-year-old house with flower beds and vines along the outdoor patio. High wood-beamed ceilings and common baths. Ask for the room with the terrace. Noisy restaurant downstairs has tasty sandwiches (€1.20). Singles €16; doubles €20. ❷

Apartamentos San Sebastián, C. Medio, 20 (☎922 14 14 75 or 653 96 21 66; fax 922 87 13 54). Breezy and newly furnished apartments with 2 twin beds, a kitchen, TV, and living room. Reception is in the currency exchange office to the right when facing the entrance. Open 8:30am-1pm and 4-8pm. Multi-day stays for 2 people €35; 1 person €30. 1-night stays €37. ❸

Pensión Colón, C. Medio, 59 (☎/fax 922 87 02 35). Tiled floors and austere rooms surround a quiet courtyard. Avoid the few rooms without windows; they can get stuffy. Singles €16, negotiate €13 for multi-day stays; doubles €23. ❶

FOOD

San Sebastián is filled with authentic Canarian restaurants and cheap *tapas* joints. Nicer options surround Pl. Constitución, and typical bars and *mesones* line C. Ruiz de Padrón and C. Medio. At **Gomera Garden ❷,** C. Medio, 12, carefully-prepared local fare graces candlelit tables in a romantic interior garden. (☎922 14 12 63. Entrees €5-9. Open daily noon-4pm and 6:30-11pm.) **Bar-Restaurant Cubino ❷,** C. Virgen de Guadalupe, 2, off Pl. Constitución, serves delicious seafood and meat dishes in healthy portions to a local crowd. (☎922 86 03 83. Entrees €4-9. Open W-M 9am-4pm and 7pm-midnight.) For a meal on the run, try **Supermercado Brito,** Pl. Constitución, 14. (☎922 14 18 18. Open M-Sa 8am-2pm and 4-10:45pm, Su 8am-1:30pm. MC/V.) A **produce market** fills the plaza on Wednesdays and Saturdays.

SIGHTS

The few sights in San Sebastián are centered on a foreigner: Columbus. C. Medio's only church (down the street from the Columbus Casino) is the **Iglesia de la Asunción,** where Columbus prayed before he left. The carved woodwork adorning the simple church is typical of Canarian architecture. Nearby, the **Casa de Colón,** C. Medio, 56, hosts a small and unimpressive exhibit on the explorer's life. Don't miss the religious icon made out of pure sugar. (Open M-F 4-7pm. Free.) The **Torre del Conde,** a small 15th-century fort, looms over the beach. In 1488, the wife of the murdered governor Hernán Peraza bolted herself inside as she watched the citizens take control of the port. Now it displays Gomeran cartography. (Open Tu-F 10am-1pm.) The tourist office is located inside **La Casa de la Aguada,** which features the well from which Columbus drew water to "baptize the Americas."

No Canarian city would be complete without a **beach.** Although there is a small patch of black sand in front of Pl. Américas, **Playa de la Cueva** is a better alternative with more sand, calmer waters, caved cliffs, and a view of Tenerife. From Pl. Américas, follow Av. Fred Olsen toward the port and curve away from the wharf.

GARAJONAY NATIONAL PARK

Take the bus (line #1) to Valle Gran Rey and get off at Pajarito; if you bear right, the trailhead is 1km up the road. A car greatly facilitates exploration of the park, but several of the best trails are reachable by bus.

Blanketed in thick mist and fog that produces a "horizontal rain" year-round, the Garajonay National Park sustains some of the last **laurisilva forest** on earth. Once ubiquitous in the Mediterranean basin, these moss-filled forests fell victim to the Ice Age millions of years ago. Hikers in Garajonay wade through lush ferns, myriad streams, and dripping plants to reach a stunning mountaintop view of the other islands. The park maintains numerous trails and **three self-guided paths,** most originating from **Contadero.** Remnants of volcanic activity, **Los Roques,** line the roadside. Strangely, the **visitors center** (☎922 80 09 93) is in **Agulo,** 9km outside of the park (open daily 9:30am-4:30pm). To get to the visitors center take bus #3 from San Sebastián (45min., 4 per day 10:30am-9:30pm) and get off at the Las Rosas stop. The **Park Service,** Ctra. General de Sur, 20, in San Sebastián, has the same info. (☎922 87 01 05 or 922 80 09 03. Open M-F 8am-2:30pm.) Either office can make the reservations required for the **free guided tours** (Sa 10am, meet in La Laguna Grande; tour in Spanish only), and both carry the booklet whose descriptions corresponds to the numbered wooden signs on the park trails.

JUST GIVE A WHISTLE No, it's not the moped alarm and probably not that sleazy guy across the street; that piercing noise you just heard is a demonstration of **El Silbo,** the Guanche whistle language. This is not just your average whistle; "speakers" make full use of both hands to manipulate the sound. The language, which has a complete alphabet, developed in order to communicate over long distances across the island's rough terrain. During the Spanish conquest, El Silbo dwindled, and today it is only used to garner a few euros from amazed tourists.

VALLE GRAN REY

Green terrace farms step back from sandy beaches into the deep gorge of the "Valley of the Great King." The mellow shores keep the tourist population content with sunbathing, cliff-exploring, and water sports, while farmers work the peaceful valley. Because of its beaches, Valle Gran Rey is probably the nicest place to base a stay in La Gomera, but it can be slightly expensive.

Bus #1 runs from San Sebastián to the Valle Gran Rey's three small villages: **La Calera, La Playa,** and **Vueltas,** in that order. (2hr.; M-F 5 per day 5am-6:30pm, Su 8:30am and 3pm; €4.20.) La Caleras sits up higher in the valley, while La Playa and Vueltas cover the shores below. The three are geographically aligned in a triangular form less than a kilometer long. Street signs are nonexistent, but the area is easy to navigate—for help, stop at the **tourist office** in La Playa on C. Noria. From the La Playa bus stop, face the beach, head right on the main road, and turn left on C. Noria. (☎/fax 922 80 54 58. Open in winter M-Sa 9am-1:30pm and 4-6:30pm, Su 10am-1pm; in summer M-Sa 9am-1pm and 4-6pm, Su 10am-1pm.)

The most popular beaches are **Playa de Aruga** and **Playa las Américas,** a short walk left of Vueltas when facing the beach. The sandy **Playa de Calera** and **Playa de Puntilla,** which stretch left from La Playa, have calm waters. **Playa del Inglés** features more waves, nearby cliffs, and naked bodies, a 10min. walk from La Playa. With your back to the tourist office turn right, take your first right, and follow the road, as it becomes dirt, to the beach.

Valle Gran Rey's charm and scenery are best experienced with an overnight stay. The few *pensiones* in the area solely offer doubles. *Apartamentos* provide more creature comforts; one place to inquire is the **San José** ❷ restaurant, just to the right of the tourist office in La Playa. (☎922 80 53 31. Single apartment €17; double apartment €25.) **Casa Bella Cabellos** ❶ on C. La Alameda in La Calera offers great views from modern, balconied apartments, as well as simple wooden doubles in an antique home. From the bus stop, head back up the valley and take the first left (almost an uphill U turn), follow the road past the San Sebastián bar, then bear right at the "do not enter sign," and follow the road up the hill until it flattens out. It's on the left. (☎922 80 51 82. 3 night minimum. House rooms €16. Double with fridge €23; quad with kitchen €41.) Also in La Calera, **Pensión Parada** ❶ offers simple doubles (a bath for every 2 rooms) right next to the bus stop and a 10min. walk from the beach. (☎922 80 50 52; fax 922 28 13 10. Doubles €19.)

EL HIERRO

The smallest of the Canary Islands, El Hierro was thought by Ptolemy to be the edge of the world. Even now, few come to its scattered villages and jagged coastline. Those who do will be dutifully rewarded: with a horizon free of high-rise resorts but full of jagged juniper trees, El Hierro offers visitors an opportunity to explore traditional interior towns and small fishing ports.

The port town and tourist center **La Restinga** is renowned for its scuba diving. Farther north is **El Pinar,** a series of small villages encircled by pine forests. To the east emerges **Malpaso** peak (1501m), El Hierro's zenith. Unfortunately, beaches are scarce and rockier than the golden stretches on Gran Canaria and Fuerteventura. On the western coast, the sun-addicted can get their fix at **Playas del Verodal** and **Arenas Blancas.** To the northeast, the capital city of **Valverde** serves as little more than a bridge to the ferry stations and airport. The main **tourist office,** C. Doctor Quintero, 4 (☎922 55 03 02), is located here. El Hierro is most accessible by ferry from Los Cristianos. **Trasmediterránea** sails to San Sebastián de Gomera and Los Cristianos; **Fred Olsen** sails to Los Cristianos on Tenerife. The island also has a small **airport** (☎922 55 07 25) with a few daily flights to Gran Canaria, Tenerife, and La Palma. (See **Inter-Island Transport,** p. 550, for more info.)

LA PALMA

Painted green and lush by heavy rainfalls, it's easy to see the origins of La Palma's nickname, *"isla bonita."* Although the island was an important transatlantic port during colonial days, today relatively few visitors sail into the capital of **Santa Cruz.** With colonial houses and carved balconies lining the streets, the port city retains the Old World charm of its glory days. Sharp coastlines and cliffs trace the island and dissuade sunbathers, but hikers will discover a mountainous paradise, as La Palma is the world's steepest island. **La Caldera de Taburiente,** a volcanic crater almost 10km wide, commands the center of the island. Thick Canarian pines cover the rest of the **Parque National de la Caldera de Taburiente,** and a world-renowned observatory caps the **Roque de los Muchachos.** Although the northern town of **Los Llanos de Ariadne** has a stunning botanical garden in the Pueblo Parque La Palma, the volcanos to the south offer more opportunities for hiking. The views from **Volcán Teneguía** and **San Antonio** stretch to the neighboring eastern islands. Contact the **tourist office** (☎922 41 21 06) in Santa Cruz for details on exploring the island. Due to its distance from the other islands, La Palma is not easily accessible by boat. **Fred Olsen** runs ferries between Los Cristianos and Santa Cruz, while **Naviera-Armas** does long haul trips to the island from the other islands. Most people fly into La Palma's airport (☎922 41 15 40). **Binter Canarias** has daily flights from La Palma to Tenerife and Gran Canaria. (See **Inter-Island Transport,** p. 550, for more info.)

PORTUGAL

EUROS (€)

US $1 = €1.02	€1 = US $0.98
CDN $1 = €0.65	€1 = CDN $1.54
UK £1 = €1.56	€1 = UK £0.64
AUS $1 = €0.56	€1 = AUS $1.79
NZ $1 = €0.48	€1 = NZ $2.09
ZAR 1 = €0.09	€1 = ZAR 3.73
MOR 1DH = €0.09	€1 = MOR 10.50DH

Country Code: 351. **International dialing prefix:** 00.

LIFE AND TIMES

A place where rows of olive trees give way to ancient castles and working docks are flanked by trendy nightclubs, Portugal is a destination overflowing with diversity and contradictions that will delight any traveler. Today's Portugal is a product of its varied history that ranged from ruling over one of the most glorious trading empires in the world to being vassals of the Moors, the Spanish, and the French. The relics of that history are a major reason to come to Portugal, but modern Portugal hosts comparable attractions of its own, from Lisbon's nightlife to the hiking trails in the pristine mountains of Trás-Os-Montes. Preserved from much of the modernizing forces of the 20th century by an oppressive fascist dictatorship, Portugal is emerging from the shadows with a unique mix of the cosmopolitan and the traditional. That mixture makes Portugal a colorful and worthwhile choice for those tired of the more conventional travel spots in Europe.

OFFICIAL NAME: Portuguese Republic.

GOVERNMENT: Parliamentary democracy.

CAPITAL: Lisbon.

LAND AREA: 91,951 sq. km.

GEOGRAPHY: Mountainous in the north, rolling plains in the south.

CLIMATE: Maritime temperate.

MAJOR CITIES: Coimbra, Lisbon, Porto.

POPULATION: 10,066,253.

LANGUAGES: Portuguese.

RELIGIONS: Roman Catholic (94%).

AVERAGE INCOME PER CAPITA: US$15,800.

MAJOR EXPORTS: Textiles, cork, wine, machinery, chemicals, fish.

HISTORY

In the 14th and 15th centuries, Portugal was one of the most powerful nations in the world, ruling a wealthy empire that stretched from America to Asia. Although the country's international prestige declined by 1580, Portuguese pride did not. Over the following centuries, Portugal struggled to assert its national identity and its uniqueness from Spain. Modern Portugal, with its stable democracy and fast-growing economy, has proven the strength of its national character.

Portugal
50 kilometers
30 miles
Valença do Minho
Vila Nova de Cerveira
Rio Minho
Parque Nacional da Peneda-Gerês
Caminha
Viana do Castelo
MINHO
Rio Lima
Serra do Gerês
Caldas de Gerês
Parque Natural de Montesinho
Bragança
Rio Cávado
Barcelos
Braga
Guimarães
TRÁS-OS-MONTES
Rio Tamega
COSTA VERDE
Serra do Marão
Amarante
Vila Real
Porto
DOURO LITORAL
DOURO ALTO
Espinho
Rio Douro
ATLANTIC OCEAN
Ovar
BEIRA ALTA
Aveiro
BEIRA LITORAL
Viseu
Rio Mondego
Luso
Buçaco
Guarda
Coimbra
Serra da Estrêla
COSTA DA PRATA
Figueira da Foz
Conimbriga
Rio Zêzere
Serra da Gardunha
Leiria
BEIRA BAIXA
Nazaré
Batalha
Castelo Branco
São Martinho do Porto
Fátima
Ilhas Berlengas
Alcobaça
Tomar
Cabo Carvoeiro
Caldas da Rainha
Serra de Aire
Óbidos
Peniche
Rio Tejo
Castelo de Vide
Serra de São Mamede
ESTREMADURA
Vila Franca de Xira
Santarém
Marvão
Crato
Portalegre
SPAIN
Ericeira
RIBATEJO
Mafra
Sintra
Queluz
Cascais
Estoril
Lisbon
ALTO ALENTEJO
Estremoz
Elvas
Parque Nacional de Arrabida
Setúbal
Évora Monte
Évora
Cabo Espichel
Tróia Peninsula
Rio Sado
Serra de Ossa
Sesimbra
COSTA AZUL
Sines
Santiago do Cacém
Beja
BAIXO ALENTEJO
Rio Guadiana
COSTA DOURADA
Rio Mira
Mértola
Serra de Monchique
Silves
ALGARVE
Lagos
Portimão
Albufeira
Tavira
Cabo de São Vicente
Sagres
Faro
Olhão
Vila Real de Santo António
Golfo de Cádiz

PORTUGAL

EARLY HISTORY. The settlement of Portugal began around 5500 BC when neolithic cultures entered from Andalucia. Other than some banging of stones, their impact was negligible, leaving the real work of settling Portugal to be done hundreds of years later. Several tribes inhabited the Iberian Peninsula during the first millennium BC, including the **Celts,** who began to settle in northern Portugal and Spanish Galicia in the 9th and 8th centuries BC, and the **Phoenicians,** who founded several fishing villages along the Algarve and ventured as far north as modern-day Lisbon. The **Greeks** and **Carthaginians** soon followed, settling the southern and western coasts. After their victory over Carthage in the Second Punic War (218-201 BC) and their defeat of the Celts in 140 BC, the **Romans** gained control of Portugal, integrating the region into their Iberian province of Lusitania. Six centuries of Roman rule, which introduced the *Pax Romana* and "Latinized" Portugal's language and customs, also paved the way for Christianity.

VISIGOTHS AND ARABIAN KNIGHTS (469-1139). When the Roman Empire declined in the 3rd and 4th centuries AD, the Iberian Peninsula felt the effects. By AD 469, the **Visigoths,** a tribe of migrating Germanic people, had crossed the Pyrenees, and for the next two centuries they dominated the peninsula. In AD 711, however, the Muslims (also known as the **Moors**) invaded Iberia, toppling the Visigoth monarchy. Muslim communities settled along Portugal's southern coast, an area they called the *al-Gharb* (now the Algarve), and after nearly four centuries of rule, the Muslims left a significant legacy of agricultural advances, architectural landmarks, and linguistic and cultural customs.

THE CHRISTIAN RECONQUISTA AND THE BIRTH OF PORTUGAL (1139-1415). Though the *Reconquista* officially began in 718, it didn't pick up steam until the 11th century, when Fernando I united Castilla and León and provided a strong base from which to reclaim territory. In 1139, **Afonso Henriques** (Afonso I), a noble from the frontier territory of Portucale (a region centered around Porto), declared independence from Castilla and León. Soon thereafter, he named himself the first King of Portugal, though the papacy did not officially recognize the title until 1179.

With the help of Christian military groups like the Knights Templar, the new monarchy battled Muslim forces, capturing Lisbon in 1147. By 1249, the *Reconquista* defeated the last remnants of Muslim power with successful campaigns in the Alentejo and the Algarve. The Christian kings, led by **Dinis I** (Dom Dinis, 1279-1325), promoted use of the Portuguese language (instead of Spanish) and with the **Treaty of Alcañices** (1297) settled border disputes with neighboring Castilla, asserting Portugal's identity as the first unified, independent nation in Europe.

THE AGE OF DISCOVERY (1415-1580). The reign of **João I** (1385-1433), the first king of the House of Aviz, ushered in unity and prosperity never before seen in Portugal. João increased the power of the crown, thereby establishing a strong base for future Portuguese expansion and economic success. The Anglo-Portuguese alliance, which he secured with the **Treaty of Windsor** (1386), would come to influence Portugal's foreign policy well into the 19th century.

The 15th century was one of the greatest periods in the history of maritime travel and naval advances. Under the leadership of João's son, **Prince Henry the Navigator,** Portugal established itself as a world leader in maritime science and exploration. Portuguese adventurers captured the Moroccan city of Ceuta in 1415, discovered the Madeiras Islands in 1419, happened upon the uninhabited Azores in 1427, and began to exploit the African coast for slaves and riches a few years later.

Bartolomeu Dias changed the world forever when he rounded Africa's Cape of Good Hope in 1488. Dias opened the route to the East and paved the way for Portuguese entrance into the spice trade. The Portuguese monarchs may have turned down **Christopher Columbus,** but they funded a number of momentous voyages. In

IF GILLIGAN HAD BEEN SO LUCKY Paradise on earth? Start with water, water, everywhere. Add some volcanic eruptions, plus hearty, friendly, and pleasingly relaxed inhabitants. Pepper it with astounding beauty, alluring beaches, and filter out pollution, persecution, and stress. Voilà!—you have Portugal's Atlantic islands, the **Azores** and **Madeiras,** considered by many to be the world's most beautiful and most serene. The **Madeiras**—Madeira, Porto Santo, and Desertas—rise abruptly from the ocean off Africa's northwestern coast. Once an important stop-over for explorers, today their climate, colorful fauna, tropical fruits, and luxurious hotels make them a strong contender for the ideal resort spot. Immortalized in *Moby Dick*, the nine islands of the **Azores** boast rolling hills, lush fauna, cavernous lakes, glimmering seas, and friendly inhabitants. Tranquil and tempting, the Azores will leave the particularly melodramatic to muse (as does one brochure), "Is this the home of God?"

1497, they supported **Vasco da Gama,** who led the first European naval expedition to India; successive expeditions added numerous East African and Indian colonies to Portugal's empire. Three years after da Gama's voyage, **Pedro Álvares Cabral** claimed Brazil for Portugal, and Portugal established a far-flung empire. Portugal's monarchy peaked with **Manuel I the Fortunate** (1495-1521) on the throne. Known as "the King of Gold," Manuel controlled a spectacular empire. Competition from other commercial powers took its toll, however, and the House of Aviz lost it predominance in 1580.

THE HOUSES OF HABSBURG AND BRAGANÇA (1580-1807). In 1580, Habsburg King of Spain **Felipe II** claimed the Portuguese throne, and the Iberian Peninsula was briefly ruled by one monarch. For 60 years, the Habsburg family dragged Portugal into several ill-fated wars, including the Spanish-Portuguese Armada's crushing loss to England in 1588. Inattentive King Felipe didn't even visit Portugal until 1619, and by the end of Habsburg rule, Portugal had lost its once vast empire. In 1640, during a rebellion against King Felipe IV, the **House of Bragança** engineered a nationalist rebellion. After a brief struggle they assumed control, once again asserting Portuguese independence from Spain. To secure its independence, the Bragança dynasty went to great lengths to reestablish ties with England. Nearly half a century later, **João V** (1706-1750) had restored a measure of prosperity, using newly discovered Brazilian gold and diamonds to finance massive building projects, including the construction of extravagant palaces. The momentous **Earthquake of 1755** devastated Lisbon and southern Portugal, killing over 15,000 people. Despite the damage, dictatorial minister **Marquês de Pombal** was able to rebuild Lisbon while instituting national economic reforms.

NAPOLEON'S CONQUEST AND ITS AFTERMATH (1807-1910). Napoleon took control of France in 1801 and set his sights on the rest of Europe. When he reached Portugal, his army encountered little resistance. The Portuguese royal family fled to Brazil. **Dom João VI** returned to Lisbon in 1821, only to face an extremely unstable political climate. Amidst turmoil within the royal family, João's son **Pedro** declared independence for Brazil the following year, becoming the country's first ruler. The **Constitution of 1822,** drawn up during the royal family's absence, had severely limited the power of the monarchy, and after 1826, the **War of the Two Brothers** (1826-1834) between constitutionalists (supporting Pedro, the new king of Brazil) and monarchists (supporting Miguel, Pedro's brother) reverberated through Portugal. Eight gory years later, with Miguel in exile, Pedro's daughter **Maria II** (1834-1854) ascended to the throne at a mere 15 years old. The next 75 years brought continued tensions between liberals and monarchists.

FROM THE "FIRST REPUBLIC" TO SALAZAR (1910-1974). Portugal spent the first few years of the 20th century trying to recover from the political discord of the previous century. On October 5, 1910, 20-year-old King **Manuel II** fled to England. The new government, known as the **First Republic,** earned worldwide disapproval for its expulsion of the Jesuits and other religious orders, and the conflict between the government and labor movements heightened tensions at home. Portugal's decision to enter **World War I** (even though on the side of the victorious Allies) proved economically fatal and internally divisive. The weak republic wobbled and eventually fell in a 1926 military coup. General **António Carmona** took over as leader of the provisional military government, and in the face of financial crisis, he appointed **António de Oliveira Salazar,** a prominent economics professor, his minister of finance. In 1932, Salazar became prime minister, but he soon evolved into a dictator. His *Estado Novo* (New State) granted suffrage to women, but did little else to end the country's authoritarian tradition. While Portugal's international economic standing improved, the regime laid the cost of progress squarely on the shoulders of the working class, the peasantry, and colonial subjects in Africa. A terrifying secret police (PIDE) crushed all opposition to Salazar's rule, and African rebellions were quelled in bloody battles that drained the nation's economy.

REVOLUTION AND REFORM (1974-2000). The slightly more liberal **Marcelo Caetano** dragged on the unpopular African wars after Salazar's death in 1970. By the early 70s, international disapproval of Portuguese imperialism and the army's dissatisfaction with colonial entanglements had led General António de Spinola to call for decolonization. On April 25, 1974, a left-wing military coalition calling itself the Armed Forces Movement overthrew Caetano in a quick coup. The **Revolution of the Carnations** sent Portuguese dancing into the streets; today every town in Portugal has its own Rua 25 de Abril. The Marxist-dominated armed forces established a variety of civil and political liberties and withdrew Portuguese claims on African colonies by 1975, resulting in a flood of over 500,000 refugees into the country.

The socialist government nationalized several industries and appropriated large estates in the face of substantial opposition. The country's first elections in 1976 put the charismatic socialist Prime Minister **Mario Soares** into power. When a severe economic crisis exploded, Soares instituted "100 measures in 100 days" to shock Portugal into economic shape. Through austere reforms, he helped stimulate industrial growth. The landmark year 1986 brought Portugal into the European Community (now the European Union), ending its age-old isolation from more affluent northern Europe. Despite challenges by the newly formed Social Democratic Party (PSD), Soares won the elections in 1986, becoming the nation's first civilian president in 60 years. Soares was eventually replaced by the Socialist former mayor of Lisbon, **Jorge Sampaio,** in 1995.

CURRENT EVENTS

The European Union declared Portugal a full member of the EU Economic and Monetary Union (EMU) in 1999, and the nation continues in its quest to catch up economically with the rest of Western Europe. In 1999, Macau, Portugal's last overseas territory, was ceded to the Chinese. Portugal and Indonesia have agreed to cooperate over the reconstruction of East Timor, an ex-Portuguese colony which Indonesia invaded in 1975, with Portugal as an intermediary between the EU and Indonesia in their mutual efforts to promote stability and democracy in the former colony. Jorge Sampaio returned to the Presidency after the January 2001 parliamentary elections, but Socialist Prime Minister Antonio Guterres resigned in December of 2001 after his party suffered heavy losses in Parliamentary elections. President Sampaio then appointed Jose Manuel Durao Barroso as Prime Minister to represent the newly merged parties.

LANGUAGE

Thanks to the Romans, who colonized Iberia in the late third century BC, practiced Romance speakers will find Portuguese an easy conquest (though pronunciation may be difficult). Although this softer sister of Spanish is closely related to the other Romance languages, modern Portuguese is an amalgam of diverse influences. A close listener will catch echoes of Italian, French, Spanish, Arabic, and even English and Slavic. Portugal's global escapades spurred the spread of its language. Today, Portuguese (the world's 6th-most-spoken language) binds over 200 million people worldwide, most of them in Portugal, Brazil, Mozambique, and Angola. Prospective students of the language should note the differences between Brazilian and continental Portuguese, mainly in pronunciation and usage.

Some may be heartened to know that English, Spanish, and French are widely spoken throughout Portugal, especially in tourist-oriented locales. Look to the *Let's Go* glossary in the back of this book for terms (or their Castilian cousins) that are used in this guide (see **Glossary,** p. 795).

RELIGION

Though constitutional freedom of religion mandates no state religion in Portugal, it might as well; roughly 94% of the Portuguese population practices Roman Catholicism. Composing the remaining 6% are Protestants, Jehovah's Witnesses, and Mormons, along with 35,000 Muslims and a mere 700 Jews. A major force in the shaping of Portugal's history, the Catholic Church is a respected and powerful influence in modern-day Portugal as well; attendance is high at Sunday masses, and festivals honoring patron saints (*romarias*) are celebrated everywhere.

CULTURE

FOOD AND DRINK

TYPICAL FARE

The Portuguese season their dishes with the basics: olive oil, garlic, herbs, and sea salt. Despite their historic role in bringing Eastern flavorings to Europe, they use relatively few spices. The geography of Portugal means miles of coastlines; seafood forms the core of Portuguese cuisine and is usually prepared as simply as possible to emphasize freshness. Seafood lovers will enjoy *chocos grelhados* (grilled cuttlefish), *linguado grelhado* (grilled sole), and *peixe espada* (swordfish), to name a few. The more adventurous should try the *polvo* (boiled or grilled octopus), *mexilhões* (mussels), and *lulas grelhadas* (grilled squid). Meat is treated in the opposite manner from seafood; the taste is extensively embellished and even masked by heavy sauces. Pork, chicken, and beef appear on most menus and are often combined in *cozida à portuguesa* (boiled beef, pork, sausage, and vegetables). True connoisseurs add a drop of *piri-piri* (mega-hot) sauce on the side. An expensive delicacy is freshly roasted *cabrito* (baby goat). No matter what you order, leave room for *batatas* (potatoes), prepared countless ways—including *batatas fritas* (french fries)—which accompany each meal.

The widespread availability of excellent produce means that **sopas** (soups) are usually made from local vegetables. Tasty and substantial, soups can serve as a cheap alternative to a full meal. Common soups are *caldo de ovos* (bean soup with hard-boiled eggs), *caldo de verdura* (vegetable soup), and the tasty *caldo verde* (a potato and kale mixture with a slice of sausage and olive oil). **Sandes** (sandwiches) such as the *bifana* or *prego no pão* (meat sandwich) may be no more than a hunk of meat on a roll. Cows, goats, and ewes please the palate by providing raw material for Portugal's renowned **queijos** (cheeses). Vegetarians should accustom themselves to the cheese sandwich and Portugal's delectable bread.

Portugal's favorite dessert is **pudim,** or *flan*, a rich, caramel custard similar to *crême bruleé.* Satisfy your sweet tooth with marzipan made with almonds from the groves of the Algarve. For something different, try *pêras* (pears) drenched in sweet port wine and served with raisins and hazelnuts on top. Most common are countless varieties of inexpensive, high-quality **sorvete** (ice cream)—look for vendors posting the colorful, ubiquitous "Olá" sign. *Pastelarías* (bakeries) are in most towns, and tasty **pastries** make for a cheap breakfast.

MEALS AND DINING HOURS

Portuguese eat their hearty midday meal—*almoço* (lunch)—between noon and 2pm and *jantar* (dinner) between 9pm and midnight. Both meals entail at least three courses. There are no greasy lumberjack breakfasts to be found in Portugal—a pastry from a *pastelaría* (bakery) and coffee from a café suffices for *pequeno almoço* (breakfast). If you get the munchies between 4 and 7pm, snack bars sell **sandes** (sandwiches) and sweet cakes. It is advisable to make reservations when dining in some of the more upscale city restaurants.

EATING OUT

A full meal costs €6-15, depending on the restaurant's location and quality. **Meia dose** (half portions) cost more than half-price but are often more than adequate—a full portion may satisfy two. The ubiquitous **prato do dia** (special of the day) and **ementa** *(menú)* of appetizer, bread, entree, and dessert will stifle the loudest stomach growls. The **ementa turística** (tourist *menú*) is usually not a good deal—restaurants with menus translated into multiple languages are more likely to charge exorbitant prices. Standard pre-meal bread, butter, cheese, and pâté may be dished without your asking, but these pre-meal munchies are not free (€1-3 per person). You may appreciate them, however, since chefs only start cooking after your order; be prepared to wait. In restaurants (but not cafés), a service charge of 10% is usually included in the bill. When service is not included, it is customary to leave about 5 to 10% as a tip. Vegetarians may find themselves somewhat in the cold in Portugal, but given the availability and high quality of fresh produce, making special requests to chefs may prove fruitful. Smoking is still generally accepted in most establishments, although there has been a recent move in Parliament to institute no smoking zones in some areas.

DRINK

The exact date marking the birth of Portuguese wine is unknown, though 5000 BC is often used as an estimate. Though it does not quite rival the internationally renowned French and German wines, the quality and low cost of Portuguese *vinho* (wine) is truly astounding; the reds are perhaps the best known. The pinnacle, **vinho do porto** (port), pressed (by feet) from the red grapes of the Douro Valley and fermented with a touch of brandy, is a dessert in itself. Chilled, white port can be a snappy aperitif, while ruby or tawny port makes a classic after-dinner drink. A six-month-long heating process gives **Madeira** wines their unique "cooked" flavor. Try the dry Sercial and Verdelho before the main course, and the sweeter Bual and Malmsey after. Sparkling *vinho verde* is picked and drunk young; it comes in red and white versions. The red may be a bit strong but the white is deliciously brash by any standard. The latter is exported rather than consumed, and is classified as a semi-sparkling wine. The Adega Cooperatives of Ponte de Lima, Monção, and Amarante produce the best of this type. Excellent local table wines include Colares, Dão, Borba, Bairrada, Bucelas, and Periquita. If you can't decide, experiment with the **vinho de casa** (house wine); either the *tinto* (red) or the *branco* (white) is a reliable standby. Tangy **sangría** comes filled with fresh orange slices and makes even a budget meal festive at a minimal expense (usually around €2.50 for a half-pitcher). Your Portuguese drinking vocabulary should contain the following terms: *adega*: a cellar or winery, *branco*: white wine, *claro*: new wine, *doce*: sweet wine, *espumante*: sparkling wine, *garrafa*: a bottle, *rosado*: a rosé wine, *seco*: dry wine, *vinho de mesa*: table wine, and *vinho verde:* a young wine. Bottled Sagres and Super Bock are excellent beers. If you don't ask for it *fresco* (cool), it may come *natural* (room temperature). A tall, slim glass of draft beer is a **fino** or an **imperial,** while a larger stein is a **caneca.** To sober up and wake up, order a **bica** (cup of black espresso), a **galão** (coffee with milk, served in a glass), or a **café com leite** (coffee with milk, served in a cup).

CUSTOMS & ETIQUETTE

Portuguese are generally friendly, easygoing, and receptive to foreign travelers. Even if your Portuguese is a little rusty, a wholehearted attempt at speaking the native tongue will be appreciated.

TABOOS. Be cautious of shorts and flip-flops; they may be seen as disrespectful in some public establishments or in more rural areas, even during a heat wave. Though dress in Portugal is obviously more casual in the hot summer months than in the cold of winter, strapless tops on women and collarless t-shirts on men are generally unacceptable. Skimpy clothes are always a taboo in churches, as are tourist visits during masses or services.

PUBLIC BEHAVIOR. On any list of Portuguese values, politeness would be at the top. Be sure to address Portuguese as *senhor* (Mr.), *senhora* (Mrs.), or *senhora dona* followed by the first name (for older and respected women). To blend in, it is a good idea to be as formal as possible upon a first meeting. Introduce yourself in detail, giving more than just your name. You'll be welcomed openly and made to feel at home if you mention who you are, where you're from, and what you are doing in Portugal. Don't be surprised if you get pecked on both cheeks by younger Portuguese, but handshakes are generally the standard introductory gesture.

THE ARTS

ARCHITECTURE

Portugal's signature **Manueline** style celebrates the prosperity and imperial expansion of King Manuel I's reign (see **The Age of Discovery,** p. 579). Manueline works routinely merge Christian images and maritime motifs. Their rich and lavish ornaments reflect a hybrid of Northern Gothic, Spanish Plateresque, and Moorish influences. The Manueline style found its most elaborate expression in the church and tower at **Belém,** built to honor Vasco da Gama. Close seconds are the **Mosteiro dos Jerónimos** in Belém and the **Abadia de Santa Maria de Vitória** in Batalha.

Though few Moorish structures survived the Christian *Reconquista*, their style influenced later Portuguese architecture. One of Portugal's most beautiful traditions is the colorfully painted ceramic tiles which grace many walls and ceilings. Carved in relief by the Moors, these ornate tiles later took on Italian and northern European designs. Though many of these tiles are blue, their name doesn't come from *azul* (the Portuguese word for blue), but rather from the Arabic word *azulayj*, meaning little stone. Numerous museums showcase collections of *azulejos*, including Lisbon's Museu do Azulejo and Coimbra's Museu Machada do Castro.

PAINTING AND SCULPTURE

The Age of Discovery (1415-1580) was an era of vast cultural exchange with Renaissance Europe and beyond. Flemish masters such as **Jan van Eyck** brought their talent to Portugal, and many Portuguese artists polished their skills in Antwerp. King Manuel's favorite, High Renaissance artist **Jorge Afonso,** created realistic portrayals of human anatomy. Afonso's best works hang at the Convento de Cristo in Tomar and Convento da Madre de Deus in Lisbon. In the late 15th century, the talented **Nuno Gonçalves** led a revival of the primitivist school.

Portuguese Baroque art featured even more diverse styles and themes. Woodcarving became extremely popular in Portugal during the Baroque period. **Joachim Machado** carved elaborate crèches in the early 1700s. On canvas, portraiture was head and shoulders above other genres. The prolific 19th-century artist **Domingos António de Sequeira** depicted historical, religious, and allegorical subjects using a technique that would later inspire French Impressionists. Porto's **António Soares dos Reis** brought Romantic sensibility to 19th-century Portuguese sculpture.

In the 20th century, Cubism, Expressionism, and Futurism trickled into Portugal despite Salazar-inspired censorship. More recently, **Maria Helena Vieira da Silva** has won international recognition for her abstract works, and the master **Carlos Botelho** has become world-renowned for his wonderful vignettes of Lisbon life.

LITERATURE

Portugal's literary achievements, mostly lyric poetry and realist fiction, can be traced back to the 12th century, when the lyrical aspects of Portuguese were standardized by poet-king **Dinis I.** Dinis made Portuguese the region's official language (one of the first "official" non-Latin Romance vernaculars). **Gil Vicente** (1465-1537), court poet to Manuel I, is considered Portugal's equivalent to Shakespeare with his dramas about peasants, nature, and religion. The witty realism of his *Barcas* trilogy (1517-1519) influenced contemporaries Shakespeare and Cervantes.

Portuguese literature blossomed during the Renaissance, most notably in the letters of **Francisco de Sá de Miranda** (1481-1558) and the lyrics of **António Ferreira** (1528-1569). An explorer during the Age of Discovery, the humanist **João de Barros** (1496-1570) penned *Décadas da Ásia*, a history of Portuguese conquest in Goa. Influenced by the *Décadas*, the writer **Luís de Camões** (1524-1580) celebrated Vasco de Gama's sea voyages to India in Portugal's greatest epic, *Os Lusíadas* (*The Lusiads*, 1572), modeled on the *Aeneid* (see **Ladies' Man,** p. 608).

Spanish hegemony, intermittent warfare, and imperial decline conspired to make the literature of the 17th and 18th centuries somewhat less triumphant than that of past eras. The 19th century, however, saw a dramatic rebirth with poet **João Baptista de Almeida Garrett** (1799-1854) and historian **Alexandre Herculano** (1810-1877), who were both exiled because of their liberal political views. Garrett, whose most famous play *Frei Luís de Sousa* (*Brother Luís de Sousa*, 1843) marks him as a reviver of drama, and Herculano integrated Portuguese literature with the Romantic school of fiction they encountered while in exile.

When political thinkers dominated the rise of the literary intelligentsia in the **Generation of 1870,** literature shifted from romantic to realist. The most visible figure to influence this shift was novelist and life-long diplomat (residing almost always outside Iberia) **José Maria Eça de Queiroz.** He conceived of a distinctly Portuguese social realism, and he documented 19th-century Portuguese society, sometimes critical of its bourgeois elements. His best works were *O Crime do Padre Amaro (The Sin of Father Amaro)* and *Os Maias (The Mayas)*.

Fernando Pessoa (1888-1935), Portugal's most famed writer of the late 19th and early 20th centuries, wrote in English and Portuguese under four different names: Pessoa, Alberto Caeiro, Ricardo Reis, and Alvaro de Campos. His semi-autobiography, *Livro* *do Desassossego (The Book of Disgust)* is his only prose work, posthumously compiled and viewed as a modernist classic. Other influential writers of the 20th century include **Aquilino Ribeiro,** author of *O Homem que Matou o Diabo (The Man Who Killed the Devil)*, and **José Maria Ferreira de Castro,** widely known for his realist fiction, especially his novel *A Selva (The Jungle)*.

Contemporary writers like **Miguel Torga** have gained international fame for their wonderfully satirical novels. **José Saramago,** winner of the 1998 Nobel Prize for literature, is perhaps Portugal's most important living writer. His work, written in the realist style and laced with irony, has achieved new acclaim in the post-Salazar era. After Salazar's reign, female writers have emerged with a vengeance. In **Novas Cartas Portuguesas** *(New Portuguese Letters)*, the "Three Marias" expose the mistreatment of women in a male-dominated society. Other acclaimed post-Salazar authors include **António Lobo Antunes** and **José Cardoso Pires.** Antunes has achieved the status of Saramago but with a different style, one known for its scattered form and psychoanalytic themes. Pires' works often comment on the repression of the Salazar regime, and his novel *Balada da Praia dos Cães (Ballad of Dogs' Beach)* exposes the terror of Salazar's secret police.

MUSIC

Named after fate, **fado** is a musical tradition unique to Portugal, identified with a sense of *saudade* (yearning or longing) and characterized by tragic, romantic lyrics and mournful melodies. Solo ballads, accompanied by the acoustic *guitarra* (a flat-backed guitar, like a mandolin), appeal to the romantic side of Portuguese culture. **Amalia Rodrigues** (1920-1999) is often associated with the tradition; in her lifetime, she became an internationally known star as a singer of *fado* and Portuguese folk music. For more information on *fado*, see **Sweet Sorrow,** p. 616.

Apart from its folk tradition, the music of Portugal has yet to achieve international fame. Portuguese opera peaked with **António José da Silva** (1705-1739), a victim of the 1739 Inquisition. The Renaissance in Portugal led to the development of pieces geared for solo instrumentalists and vocals. Coimbra's **Carlos Seixas** thrilled 18th-century Lisbon with his genius and contributed to the development of the sonata form. **Domingos Bomtempo** (1775-1842) introduced symphonic innovations from abroad and helped establish the first Portuguese Sociedade Filarmónica, modeled after the London Philharmonic, in Lisbon in 1822.

Although the Civil War decreased patronage and stifled experimentation, folk music and dancing are still popular in rural areas. In the late 19th century, Joly Braga Santo led a modern revival of Portuguese classical music. The Calouste Gulbenkian Foundation in Lisbon has also kept Portuguese music alive, sponsoring a symphony orchestra since 1962, and hosting local folk singers (including Fausto and Sérgio Godinho), ballets, operas, and jazz festivals. The Teatro Nacional de São Carlos, with its own orchestra and ballet company, has further bolstered Portuguese music. The Teatro has spawned a group of talented young composers, including Filipe Pires, A. Vitorino de Almeida, and Jorge Peixinho, all of whom have begun to make their mark in international competitions.

THE MEDIA

Portugal's most widely read daily newspapers are *Público* (www.publico.pt), *Diário de Notícas* (www.dn.sapo.pt), and *Jornal de Notícas* (www.jn.sapo.pt). If you haven't mastered Portuguese, check out *The News*, Portugal's only online English language newspaper, at www.the-news.net. Those interested in international news stories can also pick up day-old foreign papers at larger newsstands.

Portuguese TV offers four main channels: the state-run Canal 1 and TV2, and the private SIC (Sociedade Independente de Communicação) and TVI (TV Independente). Couch potatoes can also enjoy numerous cable channels, most of which air Brazilian and Portuguese soap operas and subtitled foreign sitcoms.

SPORTS

Futebol (soccer to Americans) is the game of choice for just about all Portuguese sports fans. Team Portugal has had its moments in the sun—at the 1996 European Championships, the national team ousted Denmark en route to the semifinals, and the team garnered a third-place finish in 2000 at the UEFA European Championship in Belgium with the help of 2001 FIFA World Player of the Year, Luis Figo—but has also fallen short at crucial moments, such as the World Cup '98 qualification matches. Games create a crazed fervor throughout Portugal, and fans will be rewarded as Portugal hosts the European Championships in 2004. Lisbon's **Benfica** possesses some of the best players in the world. Native Portuguese have also made names for themselves in long-distance running, where marathon-queen **Rosa Mota** dominated her event for a number of years. For recreation other than jogging and pick-up soccer, native Portuguese often turn to the sea. **Windsurfers, body-surfers,** and **surfers** make waves along the north coast; **snorklers** and **scuba divers** set out on mini-explorations in the south and west.

RECOMMENDED READING

FICTION: PORTUGUESE AND FOREIGN. For Portuguese classics in most every genre, check out **Literature** (p. 585). The more famous works have been translated into English. *Selected Letters and Journals*, by Lord Byron, narrates the days Byron spent in Portugal. The classic *The Lusiads*, by Luís de Camões, chronicles Portuguese exploration during the Age of Discovery. *The Last Kabbalist of Lisbon*, by Richard Zimler, is a fantastic murder mystery exploring the world of Portugal's 16th-century Jewish mystics. *Baltasar and Blimunda* and *The Stone Raft* are some of the finest works by Noble Prize-winning José Saramago.

HISTORY AND CULTURE. David Birmingham's *A Concise History of Portugal* (1991) packs an amazing quantity of historical and cultural information in one handy volume. Elanea Brown's *Roads to Today's Portugal: Essays on Contemporary Portuguese Literature, Art, and Culture* (1983) provides a good introduction to 20th-century Portuguese culture. Though somewhat outdated, A.H. de Oliveira Marques's *History of Portugal* is among the most comprehensive Portuguese history texts available. *Modern Portugal* (1998), edited by António Costa Pinto, covers 20th-century Portuguese history from the rise of Salazar to the evolution of the nation's resilient democracy. *Europe's Best-Kept Secret: An Insider's View of Portugal* (1997), by Costa Matos, is a witty account of Portuguese culture and history, including amusing anecdotes about peculiar Portuguese personalities.

ESSENTIALS

The information in this section is mostly designed to help travelers get their bearings once they are in Portugal. For information about general **travel preparations** (including passports, money, health, packing, and more), consult the **Essentials** chapter (p. 8), which also has important info for those with specific concerns: **women travelers** (p. 50); **older travelers** (p. 51); **bisexual, gay, and lesbian travelers** (p. 52); **travelers with disabilities** (p. 52); **minority travelers** (p. 53); **travelers with children** (p. 53); and travelers with **dietary concerns** (p. 54). See **Alternatives to Tourism** for info about working and studying in Portugal (p. 56).

ENTRANCE REQUIREMENTS

Passport. Required for all citizens of Australia, Canada, Ireland, New Zealand, South Africa, the UK, and US.

Visa. Required only for citizens of South Africa.

Work Permit (p. 58) Required for all foreigners planning to work in Portugal.

Driving Permit (p. 45). Recommended for those planning to drive.

EMBASSIES AND CONSULATES

Embassies and consulates are usually open Monday through Friday, mornings and late afternoons, with *siestas* in between—call for specific hours.

Australian Embassy: Av. da Liberdade, 200, 2nd fl., 1250-147 **Lisbon** (☎213 10 15 00; fax 213 10 15 55).

British Embassy: R. São Bernardo, 33, 1249-082 **Lisbon** (☎213 92 40 00; fax 213 92 41 85). **Consulates:** Av. da Boavista, 3072, 4100-120 **Porto** (☎226 18 47 89; fax 226 10 04 38); Lgo. Francisco A. Mauricio, 7, 1st fl., 8500-355 **Portimão** (☎282 41 78 04; fax 282 41 78 06).

Canadian Embassy: Av. da Liberdade, 198-200, 3rd fl., 1269-121 **Lisbon** (☎213 16 46 00; fax 213 16 46 92). **Consulate:** R. Frei Laurenço do Santa Maria, 1, 1st fl., 8000 **Faro** (☎289 80 37 57; fax 289 88 08 88).

Irish Embassy: R. da Imprensa à Estrela, 4th fl., Ste. 1, 1200 **Lisbon** (☎213 92 94 40; fax 213 97 73 63).

New Zealand Embassy: Refer to New Zealand Embassy in Spain: Pl. de la Lealtad 2-3rd fl., 28014 **Madrid** (☎ 915 23 02 26; fax 915 23 01 71). **Consulate:** R. do S. Felix, 13-2nd fl., 1200 **Lisbon** (☎213 50 96 90; fax 215 72 004).

South African Embassy: Av. Luis Bivar, 10, 1069-024 **Lisbon** (☎213 19 22 00; fax 213 53 57 13). **Consulate:** R. Antonio José Da Costa, 78-1st fl., 4150-090 **Porto** (☎226 07 60 10; fax 226 09 98 20).

US Embassy: Av. das Forças Armadas, 1600-081 **Lisbon** (☎217 27 33 00; fax 217 27 91 09). **Consulate:** same address (☎/fax 217 27 23 54).

TRANSPORTATION

Portugal is easily accessible by plane from the US and Europe. Long-distance trains run from **Madrid** (p. 86) to Lisbon, and buses run from **Sevilla** (p. 213) to Lagos. Closer to the border, trains run from **Huelva** (easily accessible from Sevilla, p. 234) and **Cáceres** (p. 197) to Portugal. Trains and buses run from **Badajoz** (p. 208), only 6km from the border, to Elvas and elsewhere. **Ciudad Rodrigo** (p. 177) lies only 21km from the border. In the north, trains run from **Vigo** (p. 534) to Porto; from **Túy** (p. 539), you can walk across the Portuguese border to Valença do Minho.

BY PLANE

Most major international airlines serve Lisbon; some serve Porto, Faro, and the Madeiras. **TAP Air Portugal** (in US and Canada ☎800-221-7370; in UK 845 601 09 32; in Lisbon 218 43 11 00; www.tap.pt) is Portugal's national airline, serving all domestic locations and many major international cities. **Portugália** (www.pga.pt) is a smaller Portuguese airline that flies between Porto, Faro, Lisbon, all major Spanish cities, and other Western European destinations. Call centers are located in Portugal (☎218 42 55 59) and the UK (☎087 075 500 25).

BY TRAIN

Caminhos de Ferro Portugueses (www.cp.pt) is Portugal's national railway, but for long-distance travel outside of the Braga-Porto-Coimbra-Lisbon line, the bus is much better. The exception is around Lisbon, where local trains are fast and efficient. Most trains have first- and second-class cabins, except for local and suburban routes. When you arrive in town, go to the station ticket booth to check the departure schedule; trains often run at irregular hours, and posted schedules *(horarios)* aren't always accurate. Unless you own a Eurailpass, the return on **round-trip tickets** must be used before 3am the following day. Don't ride without a ticket; if you're caught *sem bilhete*, you'll be fined exorbitantly. Children under four travel free; ages four to 11 pay half-price. **Youth discounts** are only available to Portuguese citizens. Though there is a Portugal Flexipass, it is not worth buying.

BY BUS

Buses are cheap, frequent, and connect just about every town in Portugal. **Rodoviária** (national info ☎213 54 57 75), the national bus company, has recently been privatized. Each company name corresponds to a particular region of the country, such as Rodoviária Alentejo or Minho e Douro, with notable exceptions such as EVA in the Algarve. Private regional companies also operate, among them **AVIC, Cabanelas,** and **Mafrense.** Be wary of non-express buses in small regions like Estremadura and Alentejo, which stop every few minutes. Express coach service *(expressos)* between major cities is especially good; inexpensive city buses often run to nearby villages. Schedules *(horarios)* are usually printed and posted, but double-check with the ticket vendor to make sure they are accurate.

Portugal's main **Euroline** affiliates are Internorte, Intercentro, and Intersul. **Busabout** coach stops in Portugal are at Porto, Lisbon, and Lagos. Every coach has a guide to answer questions and make travel and hostel arrangements en route.

BY CAR AND THUMB

Portugal has the highest rate of automobile accidents per capita in Western Europe. The new highway system (IP) is quite good, but off the main arteries, the narrow, twisting roads are difficult to negotiate. Speed limits are ignored, recklessness is common, and lighting and road surfaces are often inadequate. Buses and trucks are safer options. Moreover, parking space in cities borders on nonexistent. **Gas** comes in super (97 octane), normal (92 octane), and unleaded. Gas prices may be high by North American standards—US$0.60-0.90 per liter. Portugal's national automobile association, the **Automóvel Clube de Portugal (ACP),** R. Rosa Araújo, 42, 1250 **Lisbon** (☎123 18 01 00), provides **breakdown** and **towing service** (M-F 9am-5pm) and **first aid** (24hr.).

In Portugal, **hitchhikers** are rare. Beach-bound locals occasionally hitch in summer but otherwise stick to the inexpensive bus system. Rides are easiest to come by between smaller towns. Best results are reputedly at gas stations near highways and rest stops. *Let's Go* does not recommend hitchhiking (see p. 50).

MONEY

Official **banking hours** are Monday through Friday 8:30am to 3pm, but play it safe by giving yourself extra time. For more information on money, see p. 14. **Taxes** are included in all prices in Portugal and are not redeemable like those in Spain and Morocco, even for EU citizens. **Tips** are customary only in fancy restaurants or hotels. Some cheaper restaurants include a 10% service charge; if they don't and you'd like to leave a tip, round up and leave the change. Taxi drivers do not expect a tip unless the trip was especially long. **Bargaining** is not customary in shops, but you can give it a shot at the local *mercado* (market) or when looking for a *quarto*.

SAFETY AND HEALTH

EMERGENCY	Dial ☎ **112** for police, medical, or fire.

In Portugal, the highest rates of crime have been in the Lisbon area, especially on buses, in train stations, and in airports. Exercise the most caution in the Alfama district, the Santa Apolonia and Rossio train stations, Castelo de São Jorge, and in Belém. The towns around Lisbon with the most reported crimes in recent years are Cascais, Sintra, and Fátima. Thieves try to distract people by staging loud arguments, passing a soccer ball back and forth on a crowded street, asking for directions, pretending to dance with their victim, or spilling something on their victim's clothing. Motorists should be wary of "Good Samaritans" who have been known to help ailing motorists by the side of the road and then steal their cars.

Portugal poses no particular health risks to travelers. For general **health** information, see p. 20. The public health system in Portugal is quite good, and many doctors speak English. A private clinic might be worth the money for convenience and quick service; most travel insurance providers will pick up the tab. For small medical concerns, Portuguese *farmacías* offer basic drugs and medical advice and are easy to find in most towns.

ACCOMMODATIONS

YOUTH HOSTELS

Movijovem, Av. Duque de Ávila, 137, 1069 Lisbon (☎707 20 30 30; fax 217 23 21 02; www.pousadasjuventude.pt), the Portuguese Hostelling International affiliate, oversees the country's HI hostels. All bookings can be made through them. A bed in a *pousada da juventude* (not to be confused with plush *pousadas*) costs €10-15 per night and slightly less in the off-season (breakfast and sheets included). Lunch or dinner usually costs €4.50, snacks around €1. Rates may be higher for guests 26 and older. Though often the cheapest option, hostels may lie far from the town center. Check-in hours are 9am to noon and 6pm to midnight. Some have lockouts 10:30am to 6pm, and curfews might cramp club-hoppers' style. The maximum stay is eight nights unless you get special permission. An **HI card** is usually mandatory to stay in an affiliated hostel. Although they are sold at Movijovem's Lisbon office, it is more convenient to get an HI membership before leaving home. To reserve a bed in the high season, obtain an **International Booking Voucher** from Movijovem (or your country's HI affiliate) and send it from home to the desired hostel four to eight weeks in advance. In the off-season (Oct.-Apr.), double-check to see if the hostel is open. Large groups should reserve through Movijovem at least 30 days in advance. For more info, see **Youth Hostels,** p. 26.

PENSÕES AND HOTELS

Pensões, also called **residencias,** are a budget traveler's mainstay. They're far cheaper than hotels and only slightly more expensive (and much more common) than crowded youth hostels. Like hostels, *pensões* generally provide sheets and towels and have common rooms. All are rated on a five-star scale and are required to visibly post their category and legal price limits. (If you don't see this information, ask for it.) During high season, many *pensões* do not take reservations, but for those that do, booking a week ahead is advisable.

Hotels in Portugal tend to be pricey. Room prices typically include showers and breakfast, and most rooms without bath or shower have a sink. When business is weak, try bargaining in advance—the "official price" is just the maximum allowed. **Pousadas,** like Spanish *paradores,* outperform standard hotel expectations (and, unfortunately, rates). They are castles, palaces, or monasteries converted into luxurious, government-run hotels. "Historical" *pousadas* play up local crafts, customs, and cuisine and may cost as much as expensive hotels. Most require reservations. Priced less extravagantly are *regional pousadas,* situated in national parks and reserves. For info, contact **ENATUR**, Av. Santa Joana Princesa, 10, 1749-090 Lisbon (☎ 218 44 20 01; fax 218 44 20 85; www.pousadas.pt).

ALTERNATIVE ACCOMMODATIONS

Quartos are rooms in private residences, similar to *casas particulares* in Spain. These rooms may be your only option in less touristed, smaller towns, or the cheapest one in bigger cities. The tourist office can usually help you find a *quarto.* When all else fails, ask at bars and restaurants for names and addresses, but try to verify the quality of the rooms. Prices are flexible and can drop with bargaining.

CAMPING

In Portugal, over 150 **official campgrounds** *(parques de campismo)* feature amenities and comforts. Most have a supermarket and cafes, and many are beach-accessible. Given the facilities' quality and popularity, happy campers are those who arrive early; urban and coastal parks may require reservations. Police are cracking down on illegal camping, so don't try it. Tourist offices stock *Portugal: Camping and Caravan Sites,* a free guide to official campgrounds. Otherwise, write the **Federação Portuguesa de Campismo e Caravanismo,** Av. Coronel Eduardo Galhardo, 24D, 1199-007 Lisbon (☎218 12 68 90; fax 218 12 69 18; www.fpcampismo.pt).

PORTUGAL

KEEPING IN TOUCH

Most useful communication information (including **international access codes, calling card numbers, country codes, operator** and **directory assistance,** and **emergency numbers**) is listed on the **inside back cover.**

TELEPHONES. Portugal's national telephone company is **Portugal Telecom.** Though phone offices exist in most cities, all services are available in phone booths on the street and in post offices. Pay phones are either coin-operated or require a phone card. The country uses the **Credifone** and **Portugal Telecom** systems. For both systems, the basic unit for all calls (and the price for local ones) is €0.10. Telecom phone cards, using "patch" chips, are most common in Lisbon and Porto and increasingly elsewhere. Credifone cards, with magnetic strips, are sold at drugstores, post offices, and locations posted on phone booths, and are most useful outside these two big cities. Private calls from bars and cafes cost whatever the proprietor decides; a posted sign usually indicates the rates. City codes all have a two before them, and local calls do not require dialing the city code.

Calling cards probably remain the best method of making international calls (see p. 32 for more details). The numbers to access major calling card services (including AT&T, MCI, Canada Direct, BT Direct, Ireland Direct, Telstra Australia, Optus Australia, Telecom New Zealand, and Telkom South Africa) are listed on the **inside back cover.** To **call home with a calling card,** contact the operator for your service provider in Portugal by dialing the appropriate toll-free access number (see p. 32).

MAIL. Mail in Portugal is somewhat inefficient—**Air mail** *(via aerea)* can take from one to two weeks (or longer) to reach the US or Canada. It is slightly quicker for Europe and longer for Australia, New Zealand, and South Africa. **Surface mail** *(superficie)*, for packages only, takes up to two months. **Registered** or **blue mail** takes five to eight business days (for roughly 3 times the price of air mail). **EMS** or **Express Mail** will probably get there in three to four days for more than double the blue mail price. **Stamps** are available at post offices *(correios)* and at automatic stamp machines outside post offices and in central locations around cities. Also at post offices, **fax** machines are available for public use.

EMAIL. Cybercafes are common in cities and most smaller towns, and are listed in the **Practical Information** section. When in doubt, try the library, where there is often at least one computer equipped for Internet access.

NATIONAL HOLIDAYS

The following table lists the national holidays for 2003.

DATE	FESTIVAL
January 1	New Year's Day
January 6	Epiphany
March 4	Carnival
April 13-20	Holy Week
April 17	*Senhor Ecce Homo* (Maundy Thursday)
April 18	Good Friday
April 20	Easter
April 25	Liberation Day
May 1	Labor Day
June 22	Corpus Christi
June 10	Portugal Day
August 15	Feast of the Assumption
October 5	Republic Day
November 1	All Saints' Day
December 8	Feast of the Immaculate Conception
December 25	Christmas
December 31	New Year's Eve

LISBON (LISBOA)

Rich history, good restaurants, fine art, and diverse nightlife combine to make Lisbon the primary destination for those heading to Portugal. Although Lisbon is the capital and the largest city in Portugal, it remains compact enough for travelers to experience a majority of the city's attractions in less than a week. Lisbon is modernizing through extensive building and restoration efforts, but the old charm of this very European city has not worn off.

Many ancient civilizations claim to have settled Lisbon. Officially, Lisbon is thought to have been inhabited for over 3000 years by Phoenicians, Greeks, and Carthaginians in turn, until the Romans arrived in 205 BC. Under Julius Caesar's reign, Lisbon became the most important city in Lusitania; in 1255, it was made the capital of the kingdom of Portugal. The city and the Portuguese empire reached their apex at the end of the 15th century when Portuguese navigators pioneered explorations of Asia, Africa, and South America. A huge earthquake on November 1, 1755, touched off the nation's fall from glory—close to one-fifth of the population died in the catastrophe and two-thirds of Lisbon crumbled. Under the authoritarian leadership of Prime Minister Marquês de Pombal, the city recovered with the construction of magnificent new squares, palaces, and churches.

Lisbon saw more than its share of changes over the course of the 20th century. During WWII, Portugal's neutrality and Atlantic connections made the city a frequent rendezvous spot for spies on both sides. In 1974, when Mozambique and Angola won independence, hundreds of thousands of refugees converged on Lisbon. Today, Portuguese of African, Asian, and European origin coexist in the capital city. In 1998, the World Expo descended upon Lisbon, providing the impetus for massive construction projects and a citywide face-lift while helping to renew Lisbon's seat at the forefront of European culture. The revival continues today, with more tourist hotspots and cultural sites constantly emerging.

INTERCITY TRANSPORTATION

BY PLANE

All flights land at **Aeroporto de Lisboa** (☎218 41 35 00), on the city's north edge. Walk out of the terminal, turn right, and follow the road around the curve to the bus stop. From here take **bus** #44 or 45 (15-20min., every 12-15min., €0.90) to Pr. Restauradores and Rossio (#44 runs to Pr. Restauradores weekdays only); the bus stops in front of the tourist office at Pr. Restauradores. Or take the express **Aero-Bus** to the same locations (bus #91; 15min., every 20min. 7am-9pm, €2.30); it's a better option during rush hour. A **taxi** from downtown costs about €11, plus a €1.50 luggage fee. Ask at the tourist office located inside the airport about the **voucher** program, which allows visitors to buy pre-paid vouchers for cab rides from the airport, avoiding potential problems with fare dishonesty. Major airlines have offices at Pr. Marquês de Pombal and along Av. Liberdade.

TAP Air Portugal, Aeroporto de Lisboa, Ed. 19, Rua C, ground level (☎218 41 50 00; www.tap.pt). Open M-F 9am-6pm.

Iberia, R. Barata Salgueiro, 28, 6th fl. (☎213 55 81 19; www.iberia.com).

Portugália, Aeroporto de Lisboa, Ed. 70, Rua C (☎218 42 55 00; www.pga.pt).

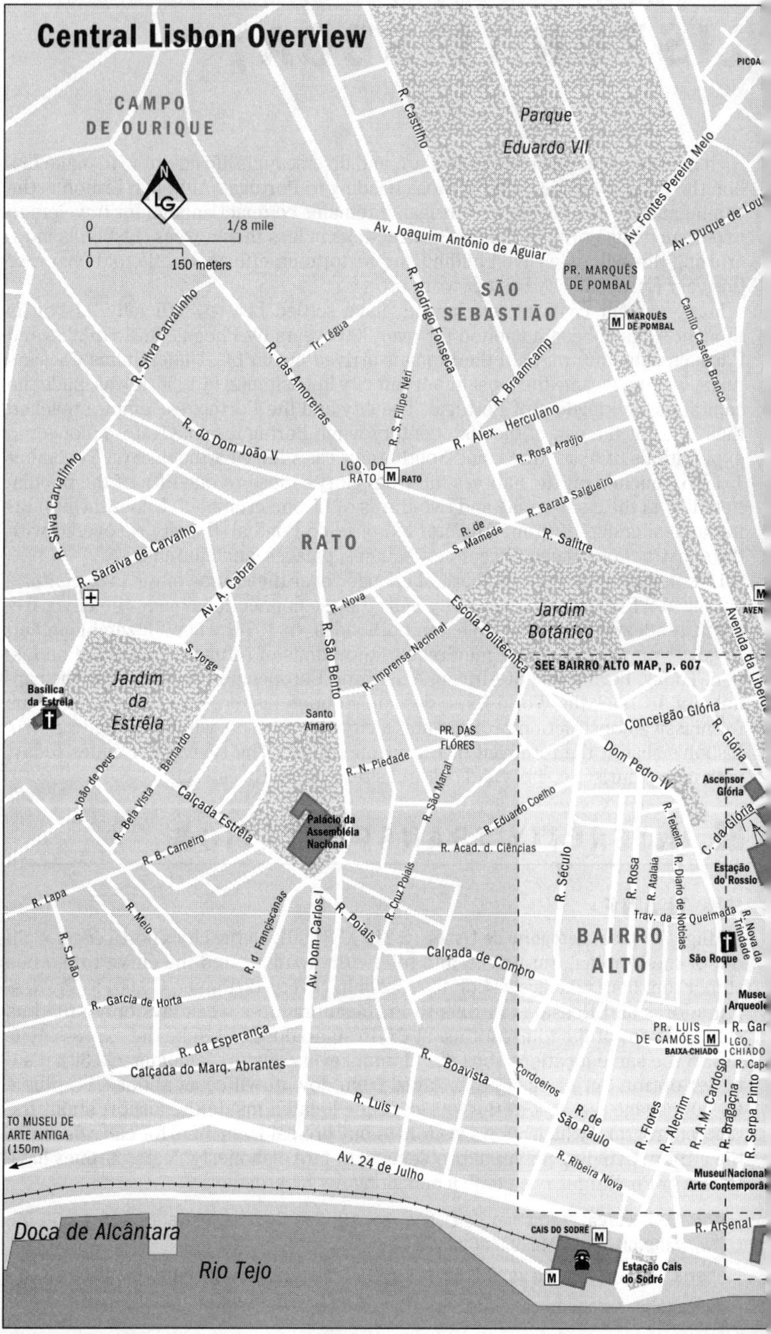
Central Lisbon Overview
CAMPO DE OURIQUE
0
1/8 mile
0
150 meters
Parque Eduardo VII
R. Castilho
PICOA
Av. Fontes Pereira Melo
Av. Duque de Lou
Av. Joaquim António de Aguiar
PR. MARQUÊS DE POMBAL
MARQUÊS DE POMBAL
SÃO SEBASTIÃO
R. Rodrigo Fonseca
Camilo Castelo Branco
R. Silva Carvalinho
Tr. Légua
R. das Amoreiras
R. S. Filipe Néri
R. Braamcamp
R. Alex. Herculano
R. Rosa Araújo
R. do Dom João V
LGO. DO RATO
RATO
R. Barata Salgueiro
R. Silva Carvalinho
R. Saraiva de Carvalho
RATO
R. de S. Mamede
R. Salitre
Av. A. Cabral
R. Nova
R. São Bento
Escola Politécnica
Jardim Botânico
AVEN
Avenida da Liberd
S. Jorge
R. Imprensa Nacional
SEE BAIRRO ALTO MAP, p. 607
Basílica da Estrêla
Jardim da Estrêla
Santo Amaro
PR. DAS FLÔRES
Conceição Glória
R. Glória
Dom Pedro IV
R. João de Deus
Bernardo
R. N. Piedade
Ascensor Glória
R. Bela Vista
Calçada Estrêla
R. São Marçal
R. Eduardo Coelho
R. Teixeira
C. da Glória
Palácio da Assembléia Nacional
R. Acad. d. Ciências
R. B. Carneiro
R. Século
R. Rosa
R. Atalaia
R. Diário de Notícias
Estação do Rossio
R. Lapa
R. Melo
R. d Franciscanas
Av. Dom Carlos I
R. Poiais
R. Cruz Poiais
Trav. da Queimada
R. Nova da Trindade
R. S. João
Calçada de Combro
BAIRRO ALTO
São Roque
R. Garcia de Horta
Museu Arqueol
R. da Esperança
PR. LUIS DE CAMÕES
BAIXA-CHIADO
R. Gar
LGO. CHIADO
R. Cap
Calçada do Marq. Abrantes
R. Boavista
Cordoeiros
R. Luis I
R. de São Paulo
R. Flores
R. Alecrim
R. A.M. Cardoso
R. Bragança
R. Serpa Pinto
TO MUSEU DE ARTE ANTIGA (150m)
Av. 24 de Julho
R. Ribeira Nova
Museu Nacional Arte Contemporâ
Doca de Alcântara
CAIS DO SODRÉ
R. Arsenal
Rio Tejo
Estação Cais do Sodré

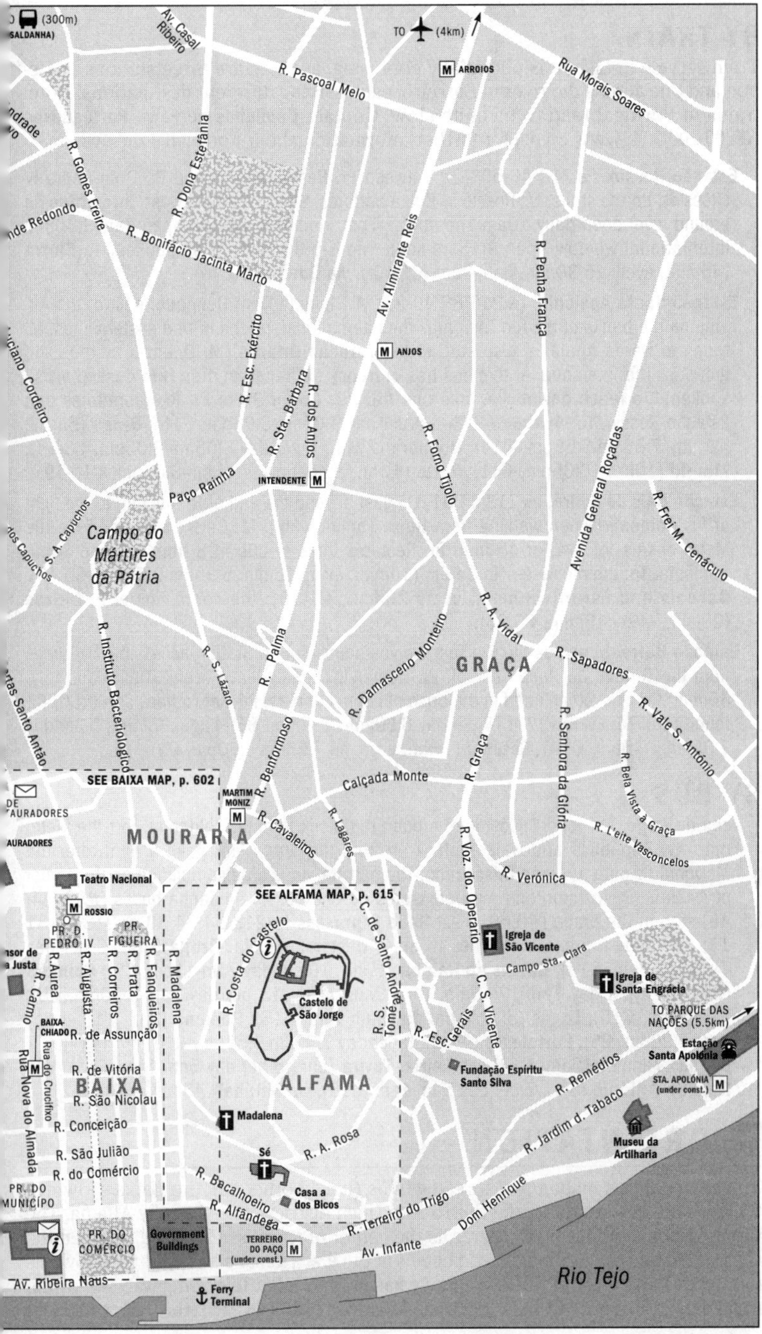
(300m)
Av. Casal Ribeiro
R. Pascoal Melo
TO (4km)
ARROIOS
Rua Morais Soares
R. Gomes Freire
R. Dona Estefânia
R. Bonifácio Jacinta Marto
Av. Almirante Reis
R. Penha França
R. Esc. Exército
ANJOS
R. Sta. Bárbara
R. dos Anjos
R. Forno Tijolo
Avenida General Roçadas
INTENDENTE
Paço Rainha
R. Frei M. Cenáculo
S. A. Capuchos
Campo do Mártires da Pátria
R. A. Vidal
R. Instituto Bacteriologico
R. S. Lázaro
R. Palma
R. Damasceno Monteiro
GRAÇA
R. Sapadores
R. Vale S. António
R. Benformoso
R. Graça
R. Senhora da Glória
SEE BAIXA MAP, p. 602
Calçada Monte
MARTIM MONIZ
R. Bela Vista à Graça
R. Cavaleiros
R. Lagares
MOURARIA
R. L'eite Vasconcelos
R. Voz. do. Operario
R. Verónica
Teatro Nacional
SEE ALFAMA MAP, p. 615
ROSSIO
C. de Santo André
PR. D. PEDRO IV
PR. FIGUEIRA
R. Costa do Castelo
Igreja de São Vicente
Campo Sta. Clara
R. Aurea
R. Augusta
R. Correiros
R. Prata
R. Fanqueiros
R. Madalena
Igreja de Santa Engrácia
R. Carmo
Castelo de São Jorge
R. S. Tomé
C. S. Vicente
TO PARQUE DAS NAÇÕES (5.5km)
BAIXA-CHIADO
R. de Assunção
R. Esc. Gerais
Estação Santa Apolónia
Rua do Crucifixo
Rua Nova do Almada
R. de Vitória
Fundação Espírito Santo Silva
R. Remédios
BAIXA
ALFAMA
STA. APOLÓNIA (under const.)
R. São Nicolau
R. Jardim d. Tabaco
Madalena
R. Conceição
R. A. Rosa
Museu da Artilharia
R. São Julião
Sé
R. do Comércio
R. Bacalhoeiro
Casa a dos Bicos
Dom Henrique
PR. DO MUNICÍPO
R. Alfândega
R. Terreiro do Trigo
PR. DO COMÉRCIO
Government Buildings
TERREIRO DO PAÇO (under const.)
Av. Infante
Rio Tejo
Av. Ribeira Naus
Ferry Terminal

BY TRAIN

Train service in Lisbon is potentially confusing, as there are three stations in Lisbon and one across the river in Barreiro, each serving different destinations. Note: trains in Portugal tend to be quite slow. Contact **Caminhos de Ferro Portuguêses** (☎800 200 904; www.cp.pt) for further information about Portugal's rail system.

Estação Rossio, (☎213 46 50 22), between Pr. Restauradores and Pr. Dom Pedro IV (Rossio), up the stairs. M: Rossio or Restauradores. Services points west. **Info office** on ground level open daily 10am-1pm and 2-7pm; domestic window open 7am-3:30pm; international window open 9:15am-noon and 1-5:30pm. English spoken. To **Sintra** (45min., every 15-30min. 6am-2am, €1.10.), via **Queluz** (€0.70).

Estação Santa Apolónia, (☎218 88 40 25), Av. Infante Dom Henrique, east of the Alfama on the banks of the Rio Tejo, runs the international, northern, and eastern lines. All trains to Santa Apolónia also stop at the **Estação Oriente** (M: Oriente) by the Expo grounds. The international terminal has **currency exchange** and an **info desk** (English spoken). To reach downtown, take bus #9, 39, 46, or 90 to Pr. Restauradores and Estação Rossio. To: **Aveiro** (3-3½hr., 4 per day 9:05am-8:05pm, €16); **Braga** (5hr., 2 per day 7:55am-5:55pm, €14); **Coimbra** (2½hr., 7 per day 8:05am-8:05pm, €8-13); **Madrid** (10hr., 10:05pm, €41); **Porto** (4½hr., 12 per day 7:55am-8:05pm, €10-19).

Estação Cais do Sodré, (☎213 47 01 81), just beyond the end of R. Alecrim, to the right of Pr. Comércio when walking from Baixa (5min. walk). M: Cais do Sodré. Take the Metro or bus #1, 44, or 45 from Pr. Restauradores or bus #28 from Estação Santa Apolónia. To: the monastery in **Belém** (10min., every 15min. 5:30am-2:50am, €0.70); **Cascais** and **Estoril** (30min., every 20min., €1.10); the youth hostel in **Oeiras** (20min., every 15min., €0.85).

Estação Barreiro, across the Rio Tejo, serves points south. Station accessible by ferries from the Terreiro do Paço dock off Pr. Comércio. Ferries leave every 30min. and take 30min.; ferry ticket included in the price of connecting train ticket (otherwise €0.50, €1 round-trip). To: **Évora** (2½hr., 7 per day 6:50am-11:50pm, €6); **Lagos** (5½hr., 5 per day 7:35am-7:45pm, €14); **Setúbal** (1½hr., every hr. 7:55am-6:50pm, €1).

BY BUS

Arco do Cego, Av. João Crisóstomo, around the block from M: Saldanha. Exit the Metro onto Av. República and walk 1 block up from the *praça*, and take a right after the McDonald's onto Av. João Crisóstomo. The bus station is a beige building on the corner of Av. João Crisóstomo and Av. Defensores de Chaves. All Saldanha buses (#36, 44, 45) stop in the *praça* (€0.60). Fast **Rede Expressos** (☎213 54 54 39 or 213 10 31 11; www.rede-expressos.pt) goes to many destinations. To: **Braga** (5hr., 6 per day 7am-12:15am, €13); **Caldas da Rainha** (1¼hr., 10 per day 7am-11pm, €5); **Coimbra** (2½hr., 16 per day 7am-12:15am, €9); **Évora** (2hr., 13 per day 7am-9:30pm, €8); **Faro** (5hr., €15); **Lagos** (5hr., 9 per day 5am-1am, €15); **Peniche** (2hr., 11 per day 7am-7:30pm, €5); **Portalegre** (4½hr., 8 per day 7:30am-9:55pm, €10); **Porto** (4hr., 7 per day 7am-12:15am, €12), via **Leiria; Tavira** (5hr., 5 per day 5am-1am, €13); **Vila Real St. Antonio** (6hr., 7 per day 5am-1am, €15), via **Setúbal** (45min., €4).

ORIENTATION

The city center is made up of three *bairros* (neighborhoods): the Baixa, (low district, resting in the valley), the Bairro Alto (high district), and the hilly Alfama. The **Baixa,** Lisbon's old business center, is the center of town, sandwiched between the Bairro Alto and the Alfama. Its grid begins at the **Praça Dom Pedro IV** (better known as the **Rossio**) and ends at the **Praça do Comércio** on the **Rio Tejo.** Once the site of the royal palace, Praça do Comércio was nicknamed **Terreiro do Paço** (the palace terrace) after it was destroyed in the 1755 earthquake. For tourists, Rossio is the center of the city. Adjacent to Rossio are **Praça dos Restauradores,** where buses from the airport stop and the main tourist office is located, and **Praça da Figueira.** Pr. Restauradores lies just above the Baixa, and from it the sprawling **Av. da Liberdade** runs uphill to the new business district centered around **Praça do Marquês de Pombal,** while Praça da Figueira extends towards the Alfama.

The **Bairro Alto** is a mix of narrow streets, parks, and Baroque churches. It is one of Lisbon's party districts; the streets are crowded until well past midnight. Other nightlife areas include the **Avenida 24 de Julho** and **Docas de Santo Amaro,** as well as the developments across from the **Santa Apolónia** station.

On the other side of the Baixa (to the right with your back to the river), is the Alfama, Lisbon's famous medieval Moorish neighborhood. Alfama, the lone survivor of the 1755 earthquake, is the city's oldest district. Alfama is made up of a labyrinth of narrow alleys and stairways beneath the Castelo de São Jorge. Expect to get lost. Without a detailed map, expect to get twice as lost. The twisting streets either change names every three steps or don't have street signs. Streets are labeled either *travessas* (side streets), *ruas* (streets), *calçadinhas* (walkways), or *escadinhas* (stairways). A street-indexed **GeoBloco Planta Turística de Lisboa** and the **Poseidon Planta de Lisboa** (including Sintra, Cascais, and Estoril) are good maps and well worth the money (both sold in Estação Rossio and at newsstands, €7.50).

LISBON

The areas stretching along the river from the Baixa's waterfront are some of the fastest growing parts of Lisbon. The former Expo '98 grounds, now called the **Parque das Nações** (Park of Nations), welcomes visitors both day and night, while the **Alcântara** and the Docas do Santo Amaro host Lisbon's late night party scene.

LOCAL TRANSPORTATION

Lisbon and its surrounding areas have an efficient public transportation system with subways, buses, trams, and funiculars, run by **CARRIS** (☎213 61 30 00; www.carris.pt). Use it to full advantage—no suburb takes longer than 90min. to reach. If you don't speak Portuguese, taxi drivers try to charge an exorbitant fare or keep your change. Make sure you know in advance what the fare should be.

Buses: Fare €0.90 within the city; pay on the bus. If you plan to stay for any length of time, consider a *passe turístico*, good for unlimited travel on all CARRIS transports. 1-, 3-, 4-, and 7-day passes available (€2.30, €5.50, €9, €13). Passes sold in CARRIS booths located in most network train stations and the busier Metro stations (e.g. Restauradores). Open daily 8am-8pm. You must show a passport to buy a tourist pass.

Subway: The Metro (☎213 55 84 57; www.metrolisboa.pt) covers downtown and the modern business district with 4 lines. A red "M" marks Metro stops. Tickets €0.55. Buy them at the ticket window or from vending machines. Book of 10 tickets €4.50. Trains run daily 6:30am-1am, though some stations close earlier.

Trams: Fare €0.90. Many date from before WWI. Line #28 is great for sight-seeing in the Alfama and Mouraria (stop in Pr. Comércio). Line #15 heads from Pr. Comércio or Pr. Figueira to Belém and the nightlife districts of Av. 24 de Julho and Docas Santo Amaro.

Funiculars: Fare €0.90. Funiculars link the lower city with the residential area on the hillsides. One goes up Ascensor Glória from Pr. Restauradores to the Bairro Alto.

Taxis: Rádio Táxis de Lisboa (☎218 11 90 00), **Autocoope** (☎217 93 27 56), and **Teletáxis** (☎218 11 11 00). Along Av. Liberdade and Rossio. Luggage €1.50.

Car Rental: If you're just planning on visiting Lisbon, a car is unnecessary. Agencies have offices at the airport and downtown; contact the agencies for specific locations. **Budget,** R. Castilho, 167B (☎213 19 55 55; fax 213 55 69 20); **Hertz,** R. Castilho, 72A (☎ 800 238 238 or 213 81 24 30; fax 213 87 41 64); **Avis,** R. Castilho (☎217 54 78 98; fax 217 54 78 52); **Mundirent,** R. Conde Redondo, 38A (☎213 13 93 60; fax 213 13 93 69); **Solcar,** R. São Sebastião da Pedreira, 51D (☎213 13 90 70; fax 213 56 05 04); **Alô Car,** R. Quirino da Fonseca, 22B/C (☎218 43 88 50; fax 218 46 00 64).

PRACTICAL INFORMATION

TOURIST AND FINANCIAL SERVICES

Tourist Office: Palácio da Foz, Pr. Restauradores (☎213 46 33 14; fax 352 57 89). M: Restauradores. The largest tourist office has information about the entire country. Open daily 9am-8pm. The **Welcome Center,** Pr. Comércio (☎210 31 28 10; fax 031 28 19) is the main office for the city. Sells tickets for sightseeing buses and the "Lisboa Card," which includes transportation and entrance to most sights for a flat fee (€11 for 24hr., €18 for 48hr., €23 for 72hr.; children €4.40/€6/€9). English spoken. Open daily 9am-8pm. An office at the **Aeroporto de Lisboa** (☎218 45 06 06), just outside the baggage claim area. English spoken. Open daily 6am-2am. Look for kiosks that read "Ask me about Lisboa" at Santa Apolónia, Belém, and other locations around the city.

Budget Travel: Movijovem, Av. Duque d'Ávila, 137 (☎213 59 60 00 or 213 52 40 72; www.pousadasjuventude.pt), at the bus stop, in the alley on the right. M: São Sebastião. Open daily 9am-7pm. V.

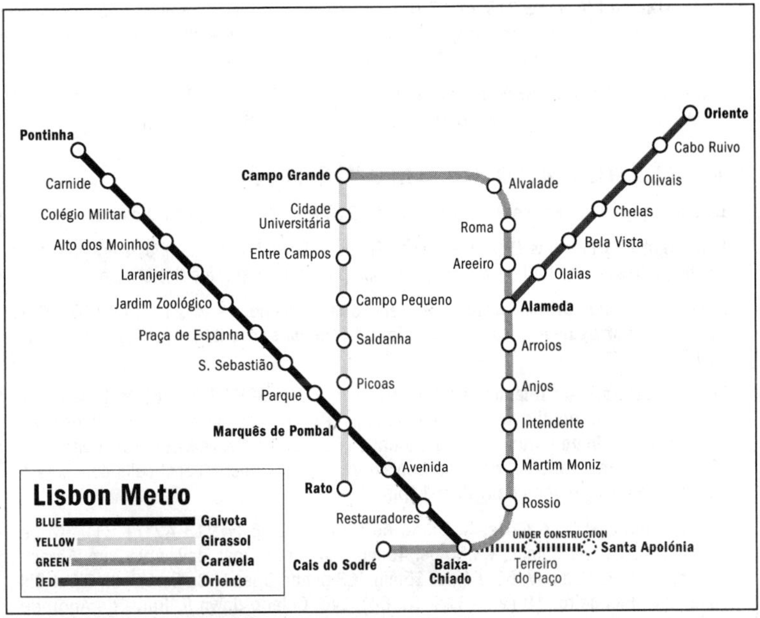

Embassies: see **Embassies and Consulates,** p. 587.

Currency Exchange: Banks are open M-F 8:30-3pm. **Cota Câmbio,** R. Áurea, 283 (☎213 42 52 32 or 213 47 00 73), 1 block off Pr. Dom Pedro IV in the Baixa. Open M-Sa 9am-8pm. The main post office, most banks, and travel agencies also change money. Exchanges line the streets of Baixa. Ask about fees first—they can be exorbitant.

American Express: Top Tours, Av. Duque de Loulé, 108 (☎213 19 42 90). M: Marquês de Pombal. Exit the Metro stop and walk up Av. Liberdade toward the Marquês de Pombal statue, then turn right; the office is 2 blocks up on the left side of the street. Handles all AmEx functions. English spoken. Open M-F 9:30am-1pm and 2:30-6:30pm.

LOCAL SERVICES

Luggage Storage: Estação Rossio. Lockers €3 for 48hr. Open daily 8:30am-11:30pm. Also available at Estação Sta. Apolónia.

English Bookstore: Livraria Británica, R. Luís Fernandes, 14-16 (☎213 42 84 72), in the Bairro Alto. Walk up R. São Pedro de Alcântara; keep going straight as it becomes R. Dom Pedro V and then R. Escola Politécnica. Turn left on R. São Marçal, then right after 2 blocks onto R. Luís Fernandes. Open M-F 9:30am-7pm. AmEx/MC/V.

Library: Biblioteca Municipal Central, Palácio Galveias (☎ 217 97 38 62). M: Campo Pequeno. Open M-Tu 10am-8pm, W-F 10am-7pm, Sa 10am-5pm.

Shopping Centers: Colombo, Av. Lusiada (☎217 11 36 36), in front of Benefica stadium. M: Colégio Militar-Luz. The largest shopping mall in Portugal, with over 500 shops, a 10-screen cinema, and a small amusement park. Open daily 10am-midnight. **Amoreiras Shopping Center de Lisboa,** Av. Duarte Pacheco (☎213 81 02 00 or 213 81 02 40), near R. Carlos Alberto da Mota Pinto. Take bus #11 from Restauradores. 383 shops including a huge **Pão de Açúcar** supermarket, English bookstores, and a 10-screen cinema. Open daily 10am-midnight. **Centro Vasco de Gama,** Av. Dom João II (☎218 93 06 01). M: Oriente. Open daily 10am-midnight. Portugal's first **El Corte Inglés,** Av. Antonio Augusto de Agular at Av. Duque D'Avila (☎213 71 17 00), has everything, including electronics, designer clothes, groceries, and the largest movie theater in Lisbon with 14 screens. M: São Sebastião. Open daily 9am-midnight.

Laundromat: Lavatax, R. Francisco Sanches, 65A (☎218 12 33 92). Wash, dry, and fold €5.50 per 5kg. Open M-F 8:30am-1pm and 3-7pm, Sa 8:30am-1pm.

EMERGENCY AND COMMUNICATIONS

Emergency: ☎112. **Police:** R. Capelo, 13 (☎213 46 61 41). English spoken.

Late-Night Pharmacy: ☎118 (directory assistance). Posted on the door of every pharmacy is the address of the next night's neighborhood pharmacy to provide this service.

Medical Services: British Hospital, R. Saraiva de Carvalho, 49 (☎213 95 50 67). **Cruz Vermelha Portuguesa,** R. Duarte Galvão, 54 (**ambulance** ☎219 42 11 11 or 217 71 40 00).

Telephones: Portugal Telecom, Pr. Dom Pedro IV, 68 (☎808 21 11 56). M: Rossio. Has pay phones and booths for international calls. Pay the cashier after your call or use a phone card. **Phone cards** come in 50 units (€3), 100 units (€6), or 150 units (€9). Buy them here or at neighborhood bookstores and stationers. Local calls consume at least 1 unit. Office open daily 8am-11pm. V.

Internet Access: Web C@fe, R. Diário de Notícias, 126 (☎213 42 11 81). €2 per 15min., €2.50 per 30min., €3.50 per 45min., €4 per hr. Open daily 4pm-2am. **Abracadabra,** Pr. Dom Pedro IV, 66. €1 per 15min., €3 per hr. Open M-Sa 8am-8pm. **Ciber Chiado,** Lgo. Picadeiro, 10 (☎213 22 57 64), Lgo. Chiado down R. Raiva de Andrade. Upstairs in the National Cultural Center building. Ring the bell to enter. €1.50 per 15min., €2 per 30min., €3 per 1hr., €4 per 2hr. Open M-F 4pm-midnight, Sa 8pm-midnight. **Cyber.bica,** R. Duques Bragança, 7 (☎213 42 11 00), further down the street from Ciber Chiado. €1 per 15min. Open M-F 9am-midnight, Sa 7pm-midnight.

Post Office: Marked by red *Correios* signs. **Main office,** Pr. Restauradores (☎213 23 89 71; fax 213 23 89 76). International express mail (EMS). Open M-F 8am-10pm, Sa-Su 9am-6pm. **Second office,** Pr. Comércio (☎213 22 09 21; fax 213 22 09 27). Open M-F 8:30am-6:30pm. Credit cards not accepted. **Postal Code:** 1100 for central Lisbon.

ACCOMMODATIONS

A price ceiling restricts the amount hostels can charge for rooms. The price list will be posted in the room or at reception. If the fee seems padded, request the printed price list. During low-season, prices generally drop—try bargaining. Many establishments have rooms with only double beds and charge per person. Expect to pay €15-25 for a single and €25-45 for a double, depending on amenities.

Most hotels are in the center of town on Av. Liberdade, while many convenient budget hostels are in the Baixa along the Rossio and on R. Prata, R. Correiros, and R. Ouro. Lodgings near the Castelo de São Jorge or in the Bairro Alto are quieter and closer to the sights. If central accommodations are full, head east to the hostels along Av. Almirante Reis. At night, be careful in the Baixa, the Bairro Alto, and especially the Alfama; many streets are isolated and poorly lit.

YOUTH HOSTELS

Pousada da Juventude de Lisboa (HI), R. Andrade Corvo, 46 (☎213 53 26 96; fax 213 53 75 41). M: Picoas. Exit the Metro station, turn right, and walk 1 block. HI card required. June-Sept. dorms €15; doubles with bath €33. Oct.-May €10/€25. MC/V. ❶

Pousada da Juventude de Parque das Nações (HI), R. de Moscavide, 47-101 (☎218 92 08 90; fax 218 92 08 91). M: Oriente. Exit the station and go left on Av. Dom João II, walking past the Parque das Nações until the street intersects with R. de Moscavide. The hostel is the striped building on the corner. Internet €0.50 for 15min. HI card required. June-Sept. dorms €11; doubles €26. Oct.-May €8.50/€22. ❶

Pousada da Juventude de Catalazete (HI), Estrada Marginal, 2780 (☎214 43 06 38), in the coastal town of Oeiras. Take a train from Estação Cais do Sodré to Oeiras (20min., every 15min. 5:30am-2:30am, €0.85). Exit through the train station underpass, go right and cross the street. Go straight (following the signs to Lisbon) as the street curves under a bridge and through a residential district. Keep going as the street becomes R. São Pedro de Ariero and then R. Cidade do Mendelo. It will become a miniature highway; turn left under the bridge at the INATEL sign. Follow the signs into the INATEL complex, past the apartments' reception building; continue straight on the only road in the complex. Turn left at the sign for apartments 84-142; the hostel is the big yellow building. June-Sept. dorms €11; doubles with bath €26. Oct.-May €8.50/€22. ❶

BAIXA

Dozens of hostels surround the three connected *praças* that form the heart of downtown Lisbon. Staying in this area is quite convenient as it makes a good base for visiting sights in and around the city. Most hostels, though, are on the top floors of buildings, often overlooking noisy streets; none are especially memorable, though they do differ in amenities. It's best to reserve at least a week ahead in summer, but it's usually possible to find a room somewhere.

Pensão Royal, R. do Crucifixo, 50, 3rd fl. (218 86 95 06). M: Baixa/Chiado. Take a right out of the station on R. Crucifixo; it's on the left before the intersection with R. Sao Nicolas. This new *pensão* has airy rooms with TVs and baths for the most reasonable prices in the Baixa. Offers convenient access to Baixa's historic districts and Bairro Alto's nightlife. May-Oct. dorms €15; singles €20; doubles €30. Nov.-Apr. €5 less. ❶

Pensão Estação Central, Calçada da Carmo, 17, 2nd-3rd fl. (☎213 42 33 08), a block from the central station, across Lgo. Duque Cadaval. M: Rossio. Small, plain rooms, but inexpensive and centrally located. TV lounge. Rooms without bath have shower. June-Sept. singles €15, with bath €20; doubles €30, with bath €35. Oct.-May €5 less. ❶

Residencial Duas Nações, R. Vitória, 41 (☎213 46 07 10), on the corner of R. Augusta, 3 blocks from M: Baixa-Chiado. Hotel-style lodging with large rooms that look out onto the main pedestrian street of Baixa. Breakfast included. May-Sept. singles €20, with bath €35; doubles €25, with bath €45; triples with bath €55. Oct.-Apr. €15/€30/€20/€40/€45. AmEx/MC/V. ❷

Residencial Florescente, R. Portas de Santo Antão, 99 (☎213 42 66 09), 1 block from Pr. Restauradores. M: Restauradores. Rooms with marble baths, French doors, small terraces, phone, and TV. June-Sept. singles €25, with bath €40; doubles €30, with bath €45-60; triples €45, with bath €60. Oct.-May €5 less. AmEx/MC/V. ❷

Hospedagem Estrela da Serra, R. dos Fanqueiros, 122, 4th fl. (☎218 87 42 51), at the end of R. São Nicolau, on the edge of the Baixa toward the Alfama. The rest of the old building that houses the *hospedagem* is under major repair, so construction can make it dusty and noisy during the day. Singles €15; doubles €20. ❶

Pensão Prata, R. Prata, 71, 3rd fl. (☎213 46 89 08), 2 blocks from Pr. Comércio near the corner of R. da Conceição; the entrance is to the right of the Pastelaria Flor da Prata. M: Baixa-Chiado. Basic rooms, some with small baths. July-Sept. singles €25, with bath €30; doubles €30, with bath €35; triples €35. Oct.-June €18-20/€20-25/€20/€25/€30. Must pay in advance. ❷

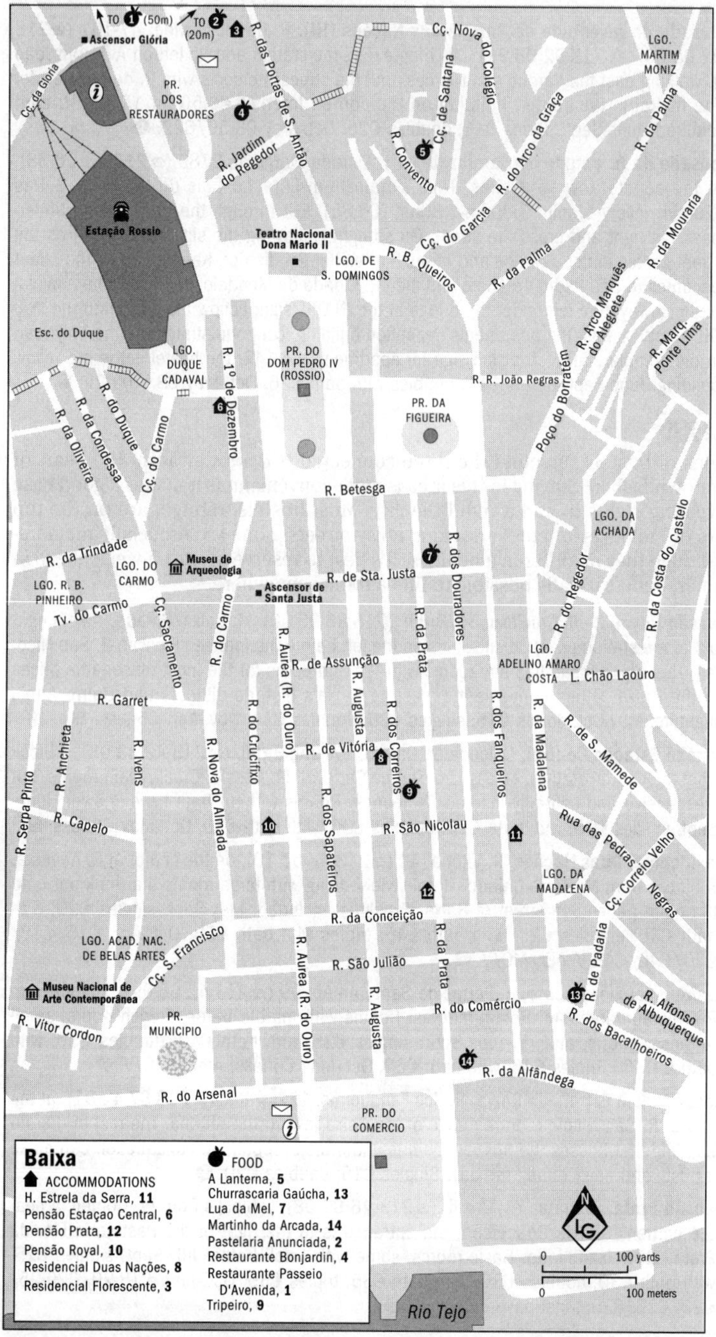
Baixa
ACCOMMODATIONS
H. Estrela da Serra, 11
Pensão Estaçao Central, 6
Pensão Prata, 12
Pensão Royal, 10
Residencial Duas Nações, 8
Residencial Florescente, 3
FOOD
A Lanterna, 5
Churrascaria Gaúcha, 13
Lua da Mel, 7
Martinho da Arcada, 14
Pastelaria Anunciada, 2
Restaurante Bonjardin, 4
Restaurante Passeio D'Avenida, 1
Tripeiro, 9
TO 1 (50m)
TO 2 (20m)
Ascensor Glória
Cç. da Glória
PR. DOS RESTAURADORES
R. das Portas de S. Antão
Cç. Nova do Colégio
LGO. MARTIM MONIZ
Cç. de Santana
R. Convento
R. Jardim do Regedor
R. do Arco da Graça
R. da Palma
Estação Rossio
Teatro Nacional Dona Maria II
LGO. DE S. DOMINGOS
R. B. Queiros
Cç. do Garcia
R. da Mouraria
R. Arco Marquês do Alegrete
R. Marq. Ponte Lima
Esc. do Duque
LGO. DUQUE CADAVAL
R. 1º de Dezembro
PR. DO DOM PEDRO IV (ROSSIO)
R. R. João Regras
PR. DA FIGUEIRA
Poço do Borratém
R. do Duque
R. da Condessa
R. da Oliveira
Cç. do Carmo
R. Betesga
LGO. DA ACHADA
R. da Trindade
LGO. DO CARMO
Museu de Arqueologia
R. de Sta. Justa
R. dos Douradores
R. da Costa do Castelo
LGO. R. B. PINHEIRO
Ascensor de Santa Justa
Tv. do Carmo
Cç. Sacramento
R. do Carmo
R. Aurea (R. do Ouro)
R. da Prata
R. do Regedor
R. de Assunção
LGO. ADELINO AMARO COSTA
L. Chão Laouro
R. Garret
R. Augusta
R. dos Correiros
R. dos Fanqueiros
R. da Madalena
R. de S. Mamede
R. Anchieta
R. Ivens
R. Nova do Almada
R. do Crucifixo
R. de Vitória
R. Serpa Pinto
R. Capelo
R. dos Sapateiros
R. São Nicolau
Rua das Pedras Negras
Cç. Correio Velho
LGO. DA MADALENA
R. da Conceição
LGO. ACAD. NAC. DE BELAS ARTES
Cç. S. Francisco
R. São Julião
R. de Padaria
Museu Nacional de Arte Contemporânea
R. do Comércio
R. Alfonso de Albuquerque
R. dos Bacalhoeiros
R. Vitor Cordon
PR. MUNICIPIO
R. da Alfândega
R. do Arsenal
PR. DO COMERCIO
N
LG
0
100 yards
100 meters
Rio Tejo

LISBON

IN AND AROUND THE BAIRRO ALTO

The Bairro Alto is harder to reach and has fewer budget accommodations than the Baixa, but it can be a good place to stay for views of the city and proximity to nightlife. If you have luggage, you may want to reach the Bairro by way of the Ascensor Glória from Pr. Restauradores; it's quite a hike up the stairways and steep streets from most public transportation.

Casa de Hóspedes Globo, R. Teixeira, 37 (☎/fax 213 46 22 79), on a small street across from the Parque São Pedro de Alcântara at the top of the funicular. From the park entrance, cross the street and go 1 block on Tv. da Cara, then turn right onto R. Teixeira. A popular spot for young travelers. All rooms newly renovated with phones, most with TV, and all but 2 with bath. Laundry €10 per load. Singles €15, with bath €25; double with bath €25-35; triple with bath €40. ❶

Residencial Camões, Tv. Poço da Cidade, 38, 1st fl. (☎213 47 75 10), off R. Misericórdia. From the top of Ascensor Glória, turn left onto R. São Pedro, which becomes R. Misericórdia; Tv. Poço da Cidade is the 5th right. In the heart of the party district–it may get noisy at night. TV lounge. Breakfast included. Singles €18, with bath €30; doubles €37.50, with bath €47.50; triples with bath €50. ❷

Pensão Londres, R. Dom Pedro V, 53, 2nd-4th fl. (☎213 46 22 03 or 213 46 55 23; www.pensaolondres.com.pt). From the top of the Ascensor Glória, turn right onto R. São Pedro de Alcantara; continue past the park as the road curves left and becomes R. Dom Pedro V; the *pensão* is on the corner of R. da Rosa. Rooms with phones, some with TVs and panoramic views of the city. Breakfast included. Singles €28, with bath €45; doubles €40, with shower €52, with bath €65; triples €76; quads €86. MC/V. ❸

ALFAMA

The Alfama has fewer accommodations options and less competition for prices, but staying here can be a nice change of pace (especially after the Baixa grid).

Pensão Ninho das Águias, R. Costa do Castelo, 74 (☎218 85 40 70), behind the Castelo. From Pr. Figueira take R. Madalena to Lgo. Adelino Costa, then head uphill to R. Costa do Castelo; climb the spiral staircase, then ring the bell to be let into the garden. Spectacular views of Lisbon. Best views from rooms #5, 6, 12, 13, or 14. Mostly double beds. All rooms with phones. English spoken. May-Aug. singles €25; doubles €38, with bath €40; one triple €50. Sept.-Apr. €25/€30/€33/€38. ❸

Pensão Estrela, R. dos Bacalhoeiros, 8 (☎218 86 95 06). An under-discovered option in the lower part of Alfama. Breezy rooms with the basic amenities look out onto the busy square below. Bargain for lower prices in winter. Checkout 11am. June-Sept. singles €20; doubles €30; one triple €45. Oct.-May €13-15/€20-25/€38. One floor up, the similar **Pensão Verandas** (☎218 87 05 19) has comparable rooms and prices. ❷

Pensão Beira Mar, Lgo. do Terreiro do Trigo, 16 (☎218 87 15 28). Probably the cheapest option in the Alfama for solo travelers. Some rooms with a view of the river cost a bit more. June-Aug. singles €15; doubles €30-40; quads €60. Oct.-May €10/€20/€40. Bargain for lower prices in winter. ❶

CAMPING

Although camping is popular in Portugal, campers are often prime targets for thieves. Info on campgrounds is available from the tourist office in the free booklet *Portugal: Camping and Caravan Sites*. There are 30 campgrounds within a 45min. radius of the capital; listed below is the only one in Lisbon proper.

Parque de Campismo Municipal de Lisboa (☎217 60 96 20; fax 217 60 96 33), on the road to Benfica. Take bus #43 to the Parque Florestal Monsanto. Pool and supermarket. Reception daily 9am-9pm. July-Aug. €4 per person and per tent, €2.50 per car. June and Sept. €3.60/€2.25. Oct.-May €2.80/€1.75. ❶

FOOD

Lisbon has some of the least expensive restaurants and best wine of any European capital. A full dinner costs about €9-11 per person and the *prato do dia* (special of the day) is often a great deal. One meal will probably be enough to keep you full all day. Until then, just snack on surprisingly filling, incredibly cheap, and sinfully delicious Portuguese pastries; *pastelarias* (pastry shops) are everywhere. In Lisbon, the closer to the industrial waterfront, the cheaper the restaurant. The south end of the Baixa, near the port, and the area bordering the Alfama are particularly inexpensive. In the Baixa, moving just a block off R. Augusta, the main pedestrian street, can save you at least a few euros. Lisbon abounds with seafood specialties such as *amêjoas à bulhão pato* (steamed clams), *creme de mariscos* (seafood chowder with tomatoes), and a local classic, *bacalhau cozido com grão e batatas* (cod with chick peas and boiled potatoes, doused in olive oil). For a more diverse food selection, head up to the winding streets of Bairro Alto, where restaurants specialize in everything from sushi to traditional Moroccan dishes. Belém offers world-famous pastries. Try **Antiga Confeitaria de Belém,** R. de Belém, 84-92 (☎213 63 80 77; fax 213 63 74 23). Ever since a monk from the nearby monastery brought the unique recipe of the world-famous *pastéis de Belém* to this pastry shop in 1837, the secret has been passed along with extreme care from generation to generation. Of the 100 people who currently work here, only three know the secret—these chosen few have signed notarized contracts, binding them to keep the treasured recipe in the shop where it belongs. Pastries €0.70, coffee €0.45.

SUPERMARKETS

Pingo Doce, 1 block off Rossio on the corner of R. 1 de Dezembro and Calçada de Carmo. A small branch of Portugal's major supermarket chain. Open M-Sa 10am-7pm.

Mercado Ribeira, Av. 24 de Julho (☎213 46 29 66), a vast market complex inside a warehouse, just outside the Estação Cais do Sodré. Accessible by bus #40 or tram #15. Go early for the freshest selection. Open M-Sa 6am-2pm.

Supermercado Pão de Açúcar, Amoreiras Shopping Center de Lisboa, Av. Duarte Pacheco (☎213 82 66 80). Take bus #11 from Pr. Restauradores or Pr. Figueira. Open M-Sa 10am-8pm, Su 10am-6pm.

LISBON

BAIXA

Although the Baixa is home to Lisbon's most tourist-oriented restaurants, it also has decent food at reasonable prices. Look for *pastelarias*—more than just pastry shops, they are less touristy and often have very good deals for lunch. On R. Portas de Santo Antão, seafood restaurants stack the day's catch in their windows; however, these places are aimed at tourists and the prices are somewhat inflated. Many of the cheaper and less aggressive eateries can be found a few blocks toward the Alfama, especially along Calçada de Santa Ana and R. dos Correeiros.

Lua da Mel, R. Prata, 242 (☎218 87 91 51), on the corner of R. Santa Justa. Caramelized everything draws crowds to this diner-style pastry shop. Pastries €0.55-1. Try the house specialty, also its namesake. Serves affordable meals (€5-7) and daily specials (€4-5). Open M-F 7:30am-9pm, Sa 7:30am-7pm. ❶

Restaurante Tripeiro, R. dos Correeiros, 70A (☎213 25 71 03). Busy during lunch, it specializes in fish. Large portions of non-seafood dishes are accompanied by piles of vegetables. Entrees €5-8. Open M-Sa noon-10pm. ❷

Pastelaria Anunciada, Lgo. da Anunciada, 1-2 (☎213 42 44 17), on the corner of R. de S. José. Specialties include *bacalhau à minhota* (codfish; €6.25). Open daily 6:30am-10pm, serves meals noon-10pm. ❷

Martinho da Arcada, Pr. do Comércio, 3 (☎218 87 92 59), at the back left corner of the *praça* when facing the river. Founded in 1782, this is the oldest restaurant in Lisbon. A bit expensive (entrees €11-15), but the **cafe** next door offers the best lunch deal in the Baixa from noon-3pm (€4). Open M-Sa 7am-10pm. AmEx/MC/V. ❸/❶

Restaurante Bonjardim, Tv. Santo Antão, 11 (☎213 42 43 89), off Pr. Restauradores. The self-proclaimed *rei dos frangos* (king of chicken) legitimately rules the roost with its savory roast chicken (€6.50). Open daily noon-11:30pm. AmEx/MC/V. ❷

Churrascaria Gaúcha, R. Bacalhoeiros, 26C-D (☎218 87 06 09), 1 block from the river towards the Alfama, near Pr. Comércio. South American-style *churrasco* (grilled meat) dishes. Most entrees €5-10. Open M-Sa 9am-2am. AmEx/MC/V. ❷

Restaurante Passeio D'Avenida, Av. Liberdade (☎213 42 37 55), just up from Pr. Restauradores. This cafe occupies the little park that separate the lanes of Av. Liberdade. Outdoor seating for coffee (€0.50-1.70) and sandwiches (€1.75-3). Also a restaurant inside, entrees €5.50-13. Open daily 9am-2am. AmEx/MC/V. ❷

A Lanterna, Calçada de Santa Ana, 99 (☎218 86 42 04), up the hill from R. Portas de Santo Antão, toward the Alfama. A pleasant escape from the tourist traps on the streets below. Entrees €3.50-5. Open M-Sa 9am-midnight, meals noon-3pm and 7-10pm. ❶

BAIRRO ALTO

The narrow streets of the Bairro Alto are lined with bars and restaurants; the prices range from modest to inflated, and the patrons follow accordingly.

Sul, R. do Norte, 13 (☎213 46 24 49). Dark wood paneling and candlelight give this restaurant and wine bar a romantic feel. Creative presentation on each plate served, and the food tastes as good as it looks. Fills up after 10pm when it converts into a bar. Spanish-themed entrees €7.50-13.50. Open Tu-Su noon-3pm, 7pm-1am. ❸

Restaurante Ali-a-Papa, R. da Atalaia, 95 (☎213 47 41 43). Serves generous helpings of traditional Moroccan food in a quiet atmosphere. Vegetarian options available. Entrees €7.50-12. Open M-Sa 7-11pm. ❸

Restaurante Calcuta, R. do Norte, 17 (☎213 42 82 95), near Lgo. Camões. Indian restaurant with wide selection of vegetarian options (€5-7). Meat entrees €6-8.50. *Menú* €12.50. Open M-Sa noon-3pm and 6:30-11pm. ❸

Hell's Kitchen, R. Atalaia, 176 (☎213 42 28 22), on the corner of R. Atalaia and Tv. da Cara; it has a big, black door. Entrees (€5.50-8), including vegetarian options. Falafel with salad €5.50. Open Tu-Su 8pm-12:30am. ❷

A Brasileira, R. Garrett, 120-122 (☎213 46 95 41). Considered by many to be "the best cafe in Portugal"; locals and tourists alike enjoy the after-dinner scene. Traditionally, a group of intellectuals gathers at the first 2 tables. Mixed drinks €5. The restaurant downstairs serves its specialty *bife à brasileira* (€11). Open daily 8am-2am. ❸

Rouge, Tv. dos Fieis de Deus (☎213 42 38 01), between R. Diario de Noticias and R. do Norte. Surrounded by statues of Buddhas, patrons enjoy Italian and Thai dishes in this classy new restaurant. Unique combinations and attentive to service. Entrees €8.50-15. Good sangría €11. Open Tu-Su 7pm-midnight. AmEx/MC/V. ❸

ALFAMA

The winding streets of the Alfama conceal a number of tiny, unpretentious restaurants, often packed with the neighbors and friends of the owners. Lively chatter echoes through the damp, narrow alleys. Watch the clock—the labyrinthine Alfama grows dangerously dark after nightfall.

Churrasqueira O Cofre, R. dos Bacalhoeiros, 2C-D (☎218 86 89 35), at the foot of the Alfama near Pensão Estrela. A display case at the entrance shows everything available for grilling. Outside seating in the summer. Entrees €6.50-11. Open daily 9am-midnight, meals noon-4pm and 7-11:30pm. AmEx/MC/V. ❷

O Eurico, Lgo. de S. Cristóvão, 3-4 (☎218 86 18 15), on C. do Marques de Tancos. Run by owner Eurico Ferreira for the past 32 years, this simple restaurant serves generous portions and is packed with workers at lunchtime. Entrees €4-8. Open M-Sa 9am-10pm, meals noon-4pm and 7-10pm. ❷

Costa do Castelo, Calçada Marquês de Tancos, 1-1B (☎218 88 46 36), just behind the Castelo in Alfama. This bar/cafe has a romantic view of the city from its outdoor patio. *Tapas* €2-2.50. Drinks €1.50-2.50. Open Tu-Su 12:30pm-2am. ❷

SIGHTS

BAIXA

Although the Baixa features few historic sights, a lively atmosphere surrounding the neighborhood's three main *praças* make it a monument in its own right.

AROUND THE ROSSIO. Begin your tour of Lisbon's 18th-century history in its heart—the **Rossio. Praça Dom Pedro IV,** the city's main square, was once a cattle market, a public execution stage, a bullring, and a carnival ground. The *praça* is now the domain of tourists and ruthless local motorists circling the statue of Dom Pedro IV. A statue of Gil Vicente—Portugal's first great dramatist (see **Literature,** p. 585)—peers from the top of the **Teatro Nacional de Dona Maria II** (easily recognized by its large columns) at one end of the *praça.* Adjoining the Rossio is the elegant **Pr. Figueira,** which lies on the border of the hilly streets of the Alfama district.

AROUND PRAÇA DOS RESTAURADORES. An obelisk and a bronze sculpture of the "Spirit of Independence" in **Pr. dos Restauradores,** just past the train station when walking from the Rossio, commemorate Portugal's independence from Spain (1640). The tourist office and numerous shops line the *praça* and C. Glória—the hill that leads to Bairro Alto. Pr. Restauradores is also the start of **Av. da Liberdade,** one of Lisbon's most elegant promenades. Modeled after the boulevards of 19th-century Paris, this mile-long thoroughfare ends at **Pr. do Marquês de Pombal;** from there an 18th-century statue of the Marquês overlooks the city.

AROUND PRAÇA DO COMÉRCIO. The grid of pedestrian streets on the other side of the Rossio from Pr. Restauradores caters to ice-cream eaters and window shoppers. After the earthquake of 1755, the Marquês de Pombal designed the streets to serve as a conduit for goods from the ports on the Rio Tejo to the city center. Built at the height of Enlightenment urban planning, each street was designated for a specific trade; *sapateiros* (shoemakers), *correeiros* (couriers), and *bacalhoeiros* (cod merchants) each had their own avenue. Two centuries later, the streets of the Baixa retain their commercial nature. From the streets of the Baixa, all roads lead to **Pr. do Comércio** on the banks of the Tejo. Also known as **Terreiro do Paço** (the palace terrace) ever since the royal palace which stood there was destroyed in the Earthquake of 1755, Pr. Comércio lies before the towering **statue of Dom João I,** cast in 1755 from 9,400 lbs. of bronze. The *praça* now serves as the headquarters of several Portuguese government ministries. Its center has been relegated to a less dignified use as a fairgrounds for concerts and other events.

BAIRRO ALTO

In the Bairro, pretentious intellectuals mix with teens and idealistic university students. It's the only place in Lisbon that never sleeps; there is as much to do here at night as there is to see during the day. At the center of the neighborhood is **Pr. Camões,** which adjoins **Largo Chiado** at the top of R. Garrett, a good place to rest and orient yourself while sightseeing. *(To reach R. Garrett and the heart of the chic Chiado neighborhood from the Rossio, take R. do Carmo uphill; R. Garrett is the 1st street on the right.)*

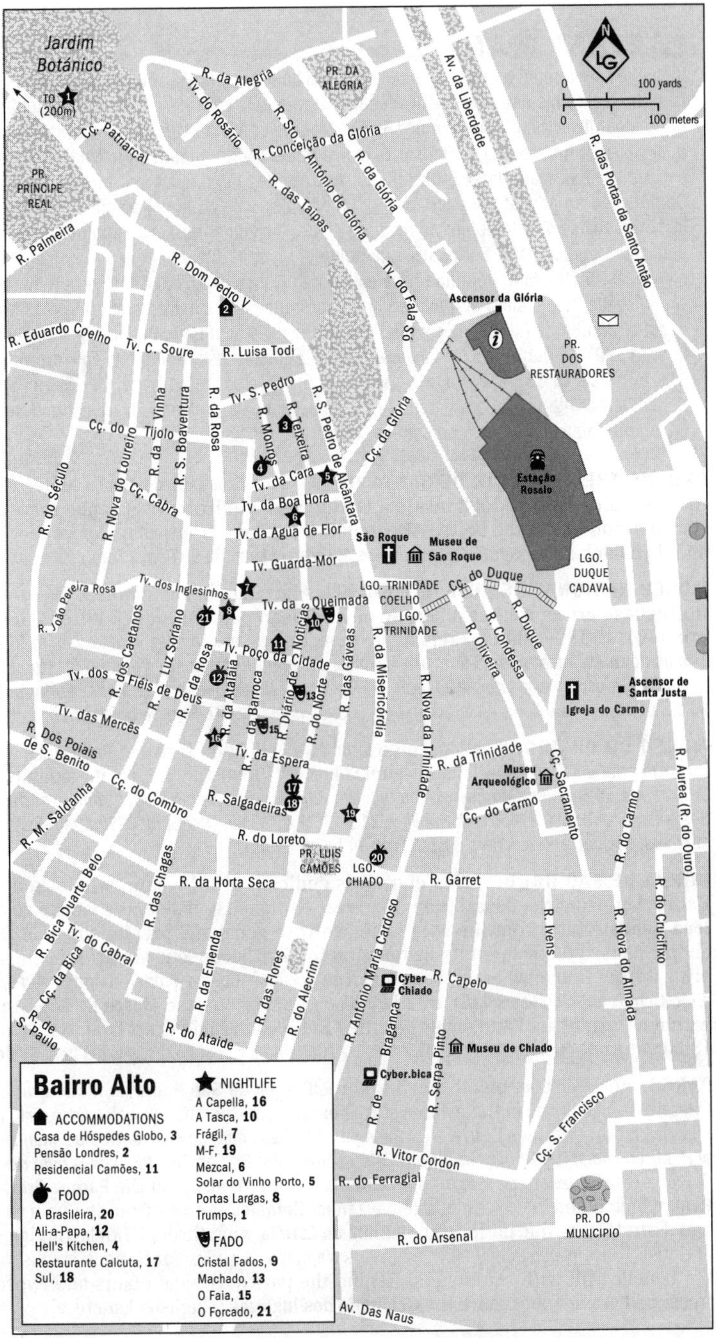
Bairro Alto
ACCOMMODATIONS
Casa de Hóspedes Globo, 3
Pensão Londres, 2
Residencial Camões, 11
FOOD
A Brasileira, 20
Ali-a-Papa, 12
Hell's Kitchen, 4
Restaurante Calcuta, 17
Sul, 18
NIGHTLIFE
A Capella, 16
A Tasca, 10
Frágil, 7
M-F, 19
Mezcal, 6
Solar do Vinho Porto, 5
Portas Largas, 8
Trumps, 1
FADO
Cristal Fados, 9
Machado, 13
O Faia, 15
O Forcado, 21
Jardim Botánico
TO 1 (200m)
PR. PRINCIPE REAL
PR. DA ALEGRIA
0 100 yards
0 100 meters
Ascensor da Glória
PR. DOS RESTAURADORES
Estação Rosaio
São Roque
Museu de São Roque
LGO. TRINIDADE COELHO
LGO. TRINIDADE
LGO. DUQUE CADAVAL
Ascensor de Santa Justa
Igreja do Carmo
Museu Arqueológico
PR. LUIS CAMÕES
LGO. CHIADO
Cyber Chiado
Cyber.bica
Museu de Chiado
PR. DO MUNICIPIO
R. da Alegria
Tv. do Rosário
Cç. Patriarcal
R. Sto. António de Glória
R. Conceição da Glória
R. da Glória
R. das Taipas
Av. da Liberdade
R. das Portas da Santo Antão
Tv. do Fala Só
R. Palmeira
R. Dom Pedro V
R. Eduardo Coelho
Tv. C. Soure
R. Luisa Todi
Tv. S. Pedro
R. S. Pedro de Alcântara
Cç. da Glória
Cç. do Tijolo
R. da Vinha
R. S. Boaventura
R. da Rosa
R. Monros
R. Teixeira
Tv. da Cara
Tv. da Boa Hora
Tv. da Agua de Flor
Tv. Guarda-Mor
R. do Século
R. Nova do Loureiro
Cç. Cabra
R. João Pereira Rosa
Tv. dos Inglesinhos
Tv. da Queimada
Cç. do Duque
R. Duque
R. Condessa
R. Oliveira
R. dos Caetanos
R. Luz Soriano
Tv. Poço da Cidade
R. Diário de Notícias
R. das Gáveas
R. da Misericórdia
R. Nova da Trinidade
Tv. dos Fiéis de Deus
R. da Atalaia
R. da Barroca
R. do Norte
Tv. das Mercês
R. Dos Poiais de S. Benito
Tv. da Espera
R. da Trinidade
Cç. Sacramento
R. Aurea (R. do Ouro)
Cç. do Combro
R. Salgadeiras
Cç. do Carmo
R. M. Saldanha
R. do Loreto
R. do Carmo
R. das Chagas
R. da Horta Seca
R. Garret
R. Bica Duarte Belo
Tv. do Cabral
R. Ivens
R. Nova do Almada
R. do Crucifixo
Cç. da Bica
R. da Emenda
R. das Flores
R. do Alecrim
R. António Maria Cardoso
R. Capelo
R. de S. Paulo
R. do Ataíde
R. de Bragança
R. Serpa Pinto
Cç. S. Francisco
R. Vitor Cordon
R. do Ferragial
R. do Arsenal
Av. Das Naus

LISBON

LADIES' MAN Pr. Camões, in the heart of the Bairro Alto off R. Garrettt, is marked by a monument to Luís de Camões. Camões, whose 16th-century *Os Lusíadas* chronicled his nation's discoveries in lyric verse, is considered Portugal's greatest poet. Most likely born in Lisbon in 1524 (accounts of his life vary slightly), this swashbuckling stud had so many affairs with ladies of the court that he fled to North Africa to escape their vengeful husbands (official sources say his politics got him banished). Camões led an adventurous life for a poet, enlisting as a common soldier in the army in 1547. His service took him all over the globe, including the Arab and Indian coasts and numerous stops in Portugal's expanding empire; all the while he was working on his verses. By the time he made his way back to Lisbon in 1570, Camões had lost an eye in battle, been jailed and injured in a sword duel, and survived a shipwreck off the coast of Cambodia (clutching his precious poetry the whole time, of course). Two years later (1572) he published *Os Lusíadas;* despite its success he died in poverty somewhere in Asia in 1580. Portugal was never able to recover his body, but Camões is remembered with an honorary tomb just outside Lisbon in Belém's Mosteiro dos Jerónimos and on streets across the country which bear his name.

AROUND THE ASCENSOR DE SANTA JUSTA. The **Ascensor de Santa Justa,** a historic elevator built in 1902 inside a Gothic wrought-iron tower, once served as transportation up to the Bairro Alto, but now just takes tourists up to see the view and then back down again. *(Elevator runs M-F 7am-11pm, Sa-Su 9am-11pm.)*

MUSEU NACIONAL DE ARTE ANTIGA. This museum hosts a large collection of Portuguese art as well as a survey of European painting, ranging from Gothic primitives to 18th-century French masterpieces. *(R. das Janelas Verdes, Jardim 9 Abril. 30min. down Av. Infante Santo from the Ascensor de Santa Justa. Buses #40 and 60 stop to the right of the museum exit. Tram #15, from Pr. Figueria or Pr. Comercio, also stops nearby. ☎213 91 28 00. Open Tu 2-6pm, W-Su 10am-6pm. €3, students €1.50. Free Su before 2pm.)*

LISBON

MUSEU DO CHIADO. The Museu do Chiado's collection features Portugal's most famous post-1850 artists. The museum is known for hosting important exhibits. *(R. Serpa Pinto, 4. From Pr. Camões, go through Lgo. Chiado and down R. Garrett, turn right onto R. Serpa Pinto, and walk 2 blocks downhill. ☎213 43 21 48. Open Tu 2-6pm, W-Su 10am-6pm. €3; students, seniors, and teachers €1.50. Free Su before 2pm.)*

IGREJA DE SÃO ROQUE. This church is dedicated to the saint who saved the Bairro Alto from the devastation of a great earthquake. Inside, the **Capela de São João Baptista** (4th from the left) is ablaze with gems and precious metals. The chapel caused a stir upon its installation in 1747 because it took three ships to bring it from Rome, where it was built. *(Lgo. Trinidade Coelho. From R. Carmo head uphill on R. Garrett until R. Misericórdia. ☎213 23 53 83.)* Next door, the **Museu de São Roque,** with its share of gold and silver, features European religious art from the 16th to 18th centuries. *(☎213 23 53 82. Open Tu-Su 10am-5pm. €1; students, seniors free. Su free.)*

PARKS. For a perfect picnic, head to the **Parque de São Pedro de Alcântara.** The Castelo de São Jorge in the Alfama stares back from the cliff opposite the park; the city of Lisbon twinkles below. *(On the right off R. São Pedro de Alcântara—the continuation of R. Misericórdia. It's a 5min. walk up R. Misericórdia from Pr. Camões; the park is right next to C. Glória.)* More greenery awaits uphill along R. Dom Pedro V at the **Parque Príncipe Real,** which connects to the extensive **Jardim Botánico.** Across from the church on Lgo. Estrela, the wide paths of the **Jardim da Estrêla** wind through flocks of pigeons and lush flora. *(Open 8am-9pm.)* Park walkways are popular for Sunday strolls, and the benches fill with smoochers. Behind the park's tropical plants and cypress trees, odd gravestones mark the **Cemitério dos Inglêses** (English Cemetery).

CHURCHES. For more neighborhood flavor, walk uphill through Pr. Camões and take R. Loreto, which turns into Calçada do Combro. Walk over the hill and down to where it levels out; turn right onto Tv. Convento de Jesús. Flowered balconies and hanging laundry frame the **Igreja das Mercês,** a handsome 18th-century Travertine building on a small *praça*. Back on Calçada do Combro, a few hundred meters ahead, is Lgo. António Sousa de Maced and a fork in the road. Follow the right fork onto R. Poiais de São Bento, which becomes Calçada da Estrêla and leads to more churches, including the **Basílica da Estrêla.** Built in 1796, the basilica's dome, poised behind a pair of tall belfries, dominates Lisbon's skyline. Half-mad Maria I, desiring a male heir, made vows promising God anything and everything if she were granted a son. When a baby boy was finally born, she built this church. Ask the sacristan to show you the 10th-century manger scene. *(On Pr. Estrela. Accessible by tram #28 from Pr. Comércio. ☎213 96 09 15. Open daily 8am-12:30pm and 3-7:30pm. Free.)*

ALFAMA

The Alfama, Lisbon's medieval quarter, was the lone neighborhood to survive the infamous 1755 earthquake. The area descends in tiers from the **Castelo de São Jorge** facing the Rio Tejo. Between the Alfama and the Baixa is the quarter known as the **Mouraria** (Moorish quarter), ironically established after Dom Afonso Henriques and the Crusaders expelled the Moors in 1147. Here, Portuguese grandmothers gossip and school boys play soccer amidst camera-toting tourists, all enjoying the enchanting ambiance of Alfama's streets. Watch out for muggers, especially at night; visit by day without handbags. Though the constant hike that defines sight-seeing in Alfama is half the fun, visitors can also hop on tram #28 from Pr. Comércio (€0.90), which winds up through the neighborhood past most of its sights.

THE LOWER ALFAMA. While any of the small uphill streets east of the Baixa lead to the Alfama's maze of streets, the least confusing way to see the neighborhood is by climbing up R. Madalena, which begins two blocks away from Pr. Comércio (take R. Alfandega from the *praça*). Veer right when you see the **Igreja da Madalena** in the Lgo. Madalena on the right. Take R. Santo António da Sé and follow the tram tracks to the small **Igreja de Santo António,** built in 1812 over the beloved saint's alleged birthplace. The construction was funded with money collected by the city's children, who fashioned miniature altars bearing images of the saint to place on doorsteps—a custom reenacted annually on June 13, the saint's feast day and Lisbon's largest holiday. *(☎218 86 91 45. Open daily 8am-7pm. Mass daily 11am, 5 and 7pm.)* In the square beyond the church is the solid 12th-century **Sé de Lisboa.** Although the interior of the cathedral lacks the excessive ornateness of the city's other churches, its sheer age and relic-filled treasury make it an intriguing visit. *(☎218 87 72 44. Open M 10am-5pm, Tu-Su 10am-6pm. Treasury open 10am-5pm. €2.)*

CASTELO DE SÃO JORGE. Near the top of the Alfama lies the **Castelo de São Jorge,** which offers spectacular views of Lisbon and the ocean. Built in the 5th century by the Visigoths and enlarged in the 9th century by the Moors, this castle was a playground for the royal family between the 14th and 16th centuries. Wander around the ruins, soak in the views, explore the ponds, or gawk at the exotic birds in the gardens. *(From the cathedral, follow the brown and yellow signs for the castle on a winding uphill walk. Castle open daily Apr.-Sept. 9am-9pm; Oct.-Mar. 9am-6pm. Free.)*

MUSEU DAS ARTES DECORATIVAS. The furnishings and ornamentation in this museum convey 18th-century palatial luxury. The bookstore has monographs on Portuguese art. *(Lgo. Portas do Sol, 2. Head up to the castle and turn right onto Lgo. Portas do Sol. ☎218 81 46 00. Open Tu-Su 10am-5pm. €2.50; seniors, children under 12 €1.25.)*

ALONG TV. SÃO VICENTE. On the far side of the castle, follow the tram tracks along Tv. São Tomé (which becomes R. São Vicente) to Lgo. São Vicente and the **Igreja de São Vicente de Fora.** Built between 1582 and 1629, it is dedicated to Lisbon's patron saint. Ask the church worker to see the *sacristia* with inlaid walls of Sintra marble. *(From the bottom of R. Correeiros in the Baixa, take bus #12 or tram #28; €0.90. Open Tu-Sa 9am-6pm, Su 9am-12:30pm and 3-5pm. Free. Chapel next door with scenic view €3.)* At the **Feira da Ladra** (flea market) in the church's backyard, the din of a lively social scene drowns out the cries of merchants hawking used goods. *(Tu and Sa 7am-3pm.)* The **Igreja de Santa Engrácia** (National Pantheon) is farther down toward the coast. The church and its dome took almost 300 years to complete. *(Walk along R. São Vicente and keep left as the road branches. Open Tu-Su 10am-5pm.)*

CONVENTO DA MADRE DE DEUS. A 16th-century convent houses the **Museu Nacional do Azulejo,** devoted to the art of the *azulejo* tile, which was first introduced by the Moors (see **Architecture,** p. 584). Through a Manueline doorway, the Baroque interior of the church is an explosion of oil paintings, *azulejos*, and gilded wood. The rapturous excess continues in the choir and the **Capela de Santo António.** *(R. Madre de Deus, 4. Follow Av. Infante Dom Henrique, which runs parallel to the Rio Tejo. The avenue leads to the Estação Santa Apolónia; from outside the station, take bus #13. ☎218 14 77 47. Open Tu 2-6pm, W-Su 10am-6pm. €2, students €1.)*

SALDANHA

Though most of Saldanha is dedicated to Lisbon's business affairs, this modern district has two excellent art museums.

MUSEU CALOUSTE GULBENKIAN. When oil tycoon Calouste Gubenkian died in 1955, he left his extensive art collection (some of it purchased from the Hermitage in St. Petersburg, Russia) to his beloved Portugal. Though the philanthropist was of Armenian descent and a British citizen, it was Portugal he chose to call home. The collection is divided into sections of ancient art—Egyptian, Greek, Roman, Islamic, and Oriental—and European pieces from the 15th to 20th centuries. Highlights include the Egyptian room, Rembrandts, Monets, Renoirs, and a Rodin. *(Av. Berna, 45. M: São Sebastião. Bus # 18, 46, 56. ☎217 82 30 00; www.gulbenkian.pt. Open Tu-Su 10am-5pm. €3, seniors €1.50, free for students and teachers.)*

MUSEU DO CENTRO DE ARTE MODERNA. Though not as famous as its neighbor, this museum houses an extensive modern collection. Most works are by Portuguese artists, but other notable 20th-century artists are also represented. Spend time in the sculpture gardens. *(R. Dr. Nicolau Bettencourt. M: São Sebastião. Bus #16, 31, 46. ☎217 95 02 41. Open Tu-Su 10am-5pm. €3, seniors €1.50, free for students and teachers.)*

BELÉM

To get to Belém, take tram #15 from Pr. Comércio (15min.), bus #28 or 43 from Pr. Figueira (15min.), or the train from Estação Cais do Sodré (10min., every 15min., €0.70). If taking the tram or the bus, get off at the stop "Mosteiro dos Jeronimos," one stop beyond the regular Belém stop. From the train station, cross the tracks, then cross the street and go left. The Padrão dos Descobrimentos is by the water, across the highway on your left (use the underpass), while the Mosteiro dos Jerónimos is to the right, through the public gardens.

Belém is more of an outlying suburb than a neighborhood of Lisbon, but its concentration of monuments and museums makes it a crucial stop on any tour of the capital. Belém is imperial glory at the service of culture; museums and historical sites showcase the opulence and extravagance of the Portuguese empire.

MOSTEIRO DOS JERÓNIMOS. Established in 1502 to give thanks for the success of Vasco da Gama's expedition to India, the Mosteiro dos Jerónimos was granted UN World Heritage status in the 1980s. The country's most refined celebration of the Age of Discovery, it showcases Portugal's native Manueline style combining Gothic forms with early Renaissance details. The main door of the church, to the right of the monastery entrance, is a sculpted anachronism; Prince Henry the Navigator mingles with the Twelve Apostles on both sides of the central column. The symbolic tombs of Luís de Camões (see **Ladies Man,** p. 608) and navigator Vasco da Gama lie in two opposing transepts. Inside the monastery, the octagonal cloisters of the courtyard drip with stone carvings, in contrast to the simplicity of the rose gardens in the center. *(☎213 62 00 34. Open Tu-Su 10am-5pm. €3, students €1.50. Free Su 10am-2pm. Cloisters open Tu-Su 10am-5pm. Free.)*

TORRE DE BELÉM. One of two well-known towers on Belém's waterfront, the Torre de Belém rises from the north bank of the Tejo and is surrounded by the ocean on three sides. Built under Manuel I from 1515-1520 as a harbor fortress, it originally sat directly on the shoreline; today, due to the receding beach, it is only accessible by a small bridge. Nevertheless, this symbol of Portuguese grandeur and member of the UN's World Heritage list offers panoramic views of Belém, the Tejo, and the Atlantic beyond. *(A 10min. walk along the water from the monastery in the opposite direction of Lisbon. Take the underpass by the gardens to cross the highway. ☎213 62 00 34. Open Tu-Su 10am-6pm. €3, students and seniors €1.50.)*

MONASTERY MUSEUMS. The **Museu da Marinha** displays the Portuguese prowess in the shipping business. Model ships and naval tools track the development of Portugal's constant attraction to the sea. *(At the far end of the monastery complex. ☎213 62 00 19. Open June-Aug. Tu-Su 10am-6pm; Sept.-May 10am-5pm. €3, students and seniors €1.50.)* The **Museu Nacional de Arquelogia** uses artifacts of various media to depict Portugal's history. *(From the monastery, go right; once inside the monastery complex, the entrance is around the corner. Open Tu 2-6pm, W-Su 10am-6pm. €2, students €1.)*

CENTRO CULTURAL DE BELÉM. Contemporary art buffs will bask in the glow of the luminous **Centro Cultural de Belém.** With four pavilions holding regular world-class exhibitions, several art galleries, and a huge auditorium for concerts and performances, the center provides modern entertainment amid a slew of imperial landmarks. *(Across the street from the monastery museums. ☎213 61 24 00; www.ccb.pt. Open daily 9am-10pm. Exhibitions 11am-7:15pm; prices vary.)*

PADRÃO DOS DESCOBRIMENTOS. Along the river is the Padrão dos Descobrimentos, built in 1960 to honor Prince Henry the Navigator. The great, white monument features Henry leading the centuries of Portuguese adventurers who set sail around the world under his inspiration. The view here is similar to that from the *torre*, but here an elevator (rather than stairs) transports visitors 50m up to a small terrace. The Padrão also hosts temporary exhibits. *(Across the highway from the monastery. ☎213 03 19 50. Open Tu-Su 9am-5pm. €2, students €1.)*

PALÁCIO NACIONAL DE AJUDA. Back toward the hub of Belém is the Palácio Nacional da Ajuda on Lgo. Ajuda, a short bus ride up the emerald hills overlooking Belém. Constructed in 1802, the 54 chambers are a telling display of decadence. *(Take tram #18 (Ajuda) to the palace back door, or walk up Calçada de Ajuda (20min). ☎213 63 70 95. Open Th-Tu 10am-4:30pm. €3, students €1.50.)*

PARQUE DAS NAÇÕES

The easiest way to reach the park from Lisbon is to take the Metro to the end of the red line (Linha Oriente, €0.55). The Oriente stop has escalators rising up to the park's main entrance at the Centro Vasco de Gama. Alternatively, city buses #5, 10, 19, 21, 25, 28,

44, 50, 68 and 114 all stop at the Oriente station (€0.90).

The **Parque das Nações** (Park of Nations; ☎218 91 93 33; www.parquedasnacoes.pt) inhabits the former Expo '98 grounds 6km from downtown. In the mid-1990s, the area was a muddy wasteland along the banks of the Tejo; in just a few years the city transformed the land, preparing the grounds for the millennium's last World Exposition. After Expo '98, the government took a risk, pumping millions of dollars into the land and converting it into the Parque das Nações. Fortunately, the gamble has paid off. Today, the park is packed day and night with people enjoying its futuristic yet graceful setting. If the proposed construction goes according to plan, the park will soon become a small city. The park entrance leads through the Centro Vasco de Gama **shopping mall** (☎218 93 06 01; open daily 10am-midnight) to the center of the grounds, where several information kiosks provide maps and offer free luggage storage (open 9:30am-8pm). For those who don't want to walk between attractions, cable cars connect one end of the park to the other (8min.; M-F 11am-7pm, Sa-Su 10am-8pm; €3, under 18 or over 65 €1.50).

The biggest attraction is the **Pavilhão dos Oceanos,** the largest oceanarium in Europe. The enormous new aquarium has interactive sections showcasing the four major oceans (down to the sounds, smells, and climates). All of these connect to the main tank, which houses fish, sharks, and other sea creatures. Visitors get within half a foot of playful sea otters and penguins. The multilevel design allows for unique views of sea life from underneath the tank. *(Open daily Apr.-Sept. 10am-7pm, Oct.-Mar. 10am-6pm. €9, under 18 or over 65 €5.)* Another solid draw is the **Pavilhão do Conhecimento** (Pavilion of Knowledge), an interactive science museum. *(☎218 91 71 12. Open Tu-F 10am-5pm, Sa-Su 11am-6pm. €5, under 18 or over 65 €2.50.)* Other **pavilions** scattered throughout the park, including the **International Fairgrounds,** accommodate rotating exhibits during the year. The **Atlantic Pavilion,** (site of many of Lisbon's big concerts), the **Virtual Reality Pavilion,** with a ride that challenges the senses, and the 145m **Torre Vasco de Gama** (the city's tallest building) grab visitors' attention with their striking, 21st-century architecture. The entire city can be seen from the observation tower. *(Open daily 10am-8pm. €2.50, under 18 or over 65 €1.25.)*

NIGHTLIFE

The Bairro Alto is the first place to go for nightlife. In particular, **R. Norte, R. Diário de Notícias,** and **R. Atalaia**

THE INSIDER'S CITY

LIVELY LISBON

The area around Av. 24 de Julho and Largo de Santos, a hot spot of Lisbon's thriving nightlife scene, is packed with clubs and bars that cater to a younger crowd. Clubs get crowded between 2 and 6am, while the bars are full a couple of hours earlier.

1. Grab a pre-club beverage at the dim and dark **A Paulinha** (☎213 96 47 83).
2. For an Art Deco, pre-clubbing drinking spot and great people watching, head to **Ruf Bar.**
3. Though it's nearly impossible for the common man to get in, the classy **Kaptial** promises a memorable night for the chosen ones inside (☎213 24 25 90).
4. House music blares for a young, attractive crowd at **Kremlin** (☎213 95 71 01).
5. Join the crowds of young late-night clubbers at the unpretentious **Litro e Meio** (☎213 95 05 26).

have many small bars and clubs packed into three short blocks, making club-hopping as easy as crossing the street. Most gay and lesbian establishments are between Pr. Camões and Tv. da Queimada, as well as in the **Rato** area near the edge of Bairro Alto past the Pr. Príncipe Real. There are plenty of options outside the Bairro as well; the **Docas de Santo Amaro** host a strip of waterfront bars, clubs, and restaurants while the **Av. 24 de Julho** and the **R. das Janelas Verdes** in the **Santos** area above have some of the most popular bars and clubs. Newer expansions include the area along the river across from the **Sta. Apolónia** train station, where the glitzy new club Lux is located. At clubs, jeans and sneakers are generally not allowed—some places have uptight fashion police at the door. Inside, beer runs €2-3. Some clubs also charge a cover (generally €5-10). There's no reason to show up at a club before midnight; crowds flow in around 2am.

DOCAS DE SANTO AMARO

Cosmos, Doca de Santo Amaro, Armazem 243 (☎213 97 27 47). Restaurant (open daily 11am-midnight) gives way to a Eurotrash techno scene. Torches welcome the crowd of trendy 20-somethings out on the patio while the music blasts inside. Cover €10, includes 4 beers or 2 mixed drinks. Disco open midnight-6am.

Salsa Latina, Gare Marítima de Alcântara (☎213 95 05 55), across the parking lot from the cluster at Doca de Santo Amaro. Sophisticated crowds come for the live salsa on weekends. Minimum consumption €10. Open M-Th 8-11pm, F-Sa 8pm-1:30am.

W.Disco, R. da Cozinha Economia, 11 (☎213 63 68 40). The newest disco in Docas plays house music attracting a young crowd with its fresh appeal. Cover €10, includes 2 drinks. Open Th-Sa 11pm-6am.

AVENIDA 24 DE JULHO AND SANTOS

Litro e Meio (1,5 LT.), R. das Janelas Verdes, 27 (☎213 95 05 26), in the Santos area above the clubs on Av. 24 de Julho. Unpretentious compared to other bars in the area. House and Latin music plays while young clubhoppers talk loudy. Steps lined with torches lead to a large, pleasant patio in back; there's a narrow upper level inside too. Most popular 1-2:30am before clubbing on the street below ensues. Minimum consumption usually €5. Beer €1.50, mixed drinks €3.50. Open M-Sa 10pm-4am.

Kapital, Av. 24 de Julho, 68 (☎213 24 25 90). The classiest club in Lisbon, with a ruthless door policy that makes admission a competitive sport. Don't expect to get in; for the best chance, go with Portuguese regulars and keep your mouth shut. 3 floors, with a nice terrace on top and a dance floor on the bottom. If you're still there at the 6am closing time, take the back tunnel directly into neighboring Kremlin to continue partying. Cover usually €15. Open M-Sa 11pm-6am.

Kremlin, Escandinhas da Praia, 5 (☎213 95 71 01), off Av. 24 de Julho next to Kapital. Run by the same management, but a more mixed crowd including Kapital rejects and the post-Kapital migration. Door policy is harsh but not impossible. Set in an old convent, Kremlin has giant fake statues and 3 rooms with throbbing house and dance music. Cover usually €5 for women and €10 for men, includes 1 drink. Open F-Sa midnight-9:30am, Th midnight-8am, Tu-W midnight-6am.

Indústria, R. do Instituto Industrial, 6 (☎213 96 48 41), just off Av. 24 de Julho across from the Outback Steakhouse. A happy alternative to the classy K's further up the street, Indústria is an old factory where the crowd is young enough to smile. Older clubbers may feel ancient here. Usually free for women and €10 minimum consumption for men. Open F-Sa (and eves of holidays) midnight-6:30am.

SANTA APOLÓNIA

Lux/Frágil, Av. Infante D. Henrique, A (☎218 82 08 90). Take a taxi to the area across from the Sta. Apolónia train station to get to this enormous 3 fl. complex. In a class and location all its own, Lux continues to be the hottest spot in Lisbon 3 years after opening. The top 2 levels are dominated by large bars and seating, while the subterranean level is dedicated to the mass of dancers. Minimum consumption €10. Open Tu-Sa 6pm-6am; arrive after 2am if you want company.

BAIRRO ALTO

Trumps, R. Imprensa Nacional, 104B (☎213 97 10 59), down R. Dom Pedro IV from the Bairro Alto, on the 5th street to the left after the Pr. Príncipe Real. Lisbon's biggest gay club, Trumps doesn't get going until after 1:30am. Enormous dance floor, lounge areas, pool tables, and live shows. Minimum consumption €5. Open F-Sa 11:30pm-6:30am, Tu-Th and Su 11:30pm-4:30am.

Clandestino, R. da Barroca, 99. Cavernous bar with messages from former patrons sprawled all over the rock walls. Groups of young people chat at low tables while rock plays in the background. Beers €2, small mixed drinks €4. Open Tu-Su 10pm-2am.

Portas Largas, R. Atalaia, 105 (☎213 46 63 79), at the end of Tv. da Queimada. The original rendezvous point for the Bairro's gay community, but also a popular bar for others (almost completely gay in summer, very mixed in winter). Portuguese music before midnight and techno afterwards. Open July-Sept. 7pm-3:30am, Oct.-June 8pm-3:30am.

A Tasca Tequila Bar, Tv. da Queimada, 13-15 (☎213 43 34 31). This classy Mexican bar is an ideal place for some after-dinner cocktails and schmoozing before heading off to the louder bars and discos. Cocktails €5. "Quickies" (specialized shots including Blow Job, Orgasmo, and Multi-Orgasmo) €2.50. Open daily 6pm-2am.

A Capella, R. Atalaia, 45 (☎213 48 91 49). A popular bar in the later hours. With gold walls and red velvet cushions, it offers more room and seats than many other bars in the district. Large beers €3, mixed drinks €5. Open daily 9pm-2am.

Mezcal, on the corner of Tv. Agua de Flor and R. Diario de Noticias. This tiny Mexican bar with the cheapest drinks in Bairro Alto is the perfect stop before hitting more upscale establishments. Sangria €1.75, caipirinhas €2.75, shots €2. Open daily 7pm-2am.

M-F (Mistura Fina), R. das Gáveas, 15 (☎213 42 08 49), just off Pr. Camões. Attracts an artsy mixed crowd. A big metal leg sculpture straddles the corner of the bar. Fills up after 12:30am. Open daily 4pm-2am.

Solar do Vinho do Porto, R. São Pedro de Alcântara, 45 (☎213 47 57 07), at the top of the steps through the large doorway. Product of a government institute created in 1933 to certify and promote port wine, Solar is a mature setting ideal for sipping the stuff, with plush red chairs and snooty air. Open M-Sa 2pm-midnight.

Frágil, R. Atalaia, 126 (☎213 46 95 78), across the street from Portas Largas. Once the best club in Lisbon, and still decent despite being well past its peak. Plays house music for a mostly gay crowd; different DJs nightly. Minimum consumption €15, or more at whim. Open M-Sa 11:30pm-4am.

ALFAMA

Restô, R. Costa do Castelo, 7. The huge outdoor patio has the best view of the city. Earlier in the afternoon and evening, the moderately priced restaurant serves steaks (€12), grilled gazelle (€15), and Spanish *tapas* (€4). By 10pm-midnight, Resto fills with a young crowd. Live Portuguese guitar F-Su. Caipirinha €4. Beer €1.25. Open daily 7:30pm-2am.

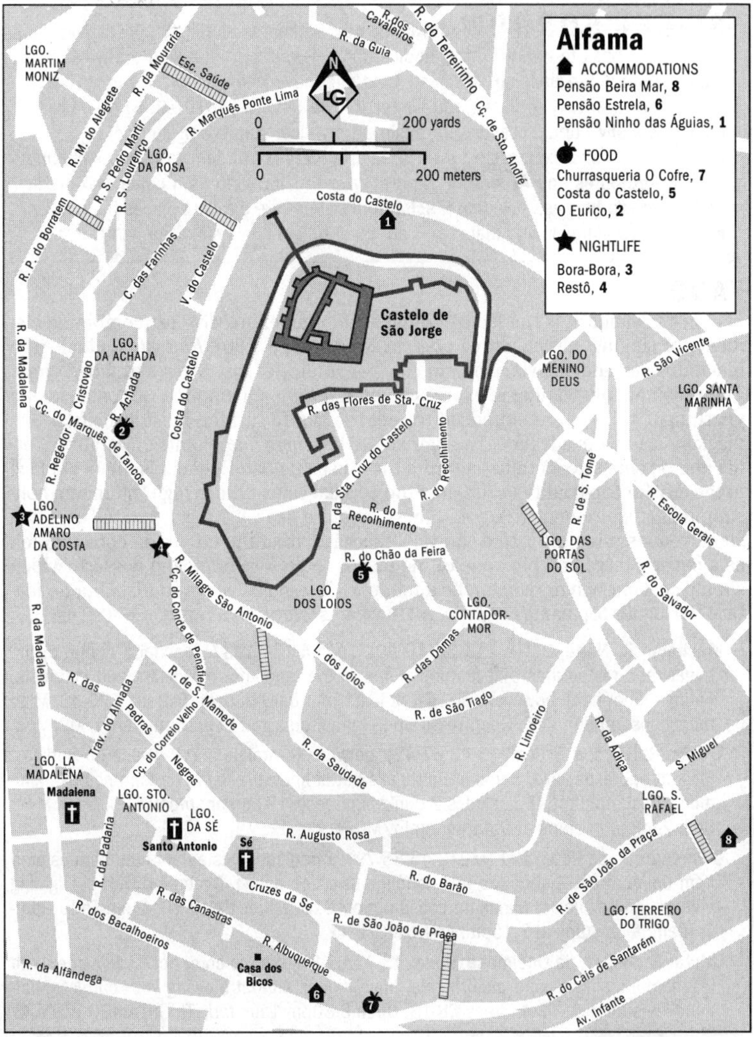

Bora-Bora, R. da Madalena, 201 (☎218 87 20 43). A Polynesian bar with a dark wood interior. Exotic cocktails served in extremely exotic cups (€5.25); most popular is the *pinho frio*. Open F-Sa 8:30pm-3am.

ENTERTAINMENT

Agenda Cultural and *Follow Me Lisboa*, free at kiosks in the Rossio, on R. Portas de Santo Antão, and at the tourist office, have information on concerts, movies, plays, and bullfights. They also have lists of museums, gardens, and libraries.

SWEET SORROW If your heart is broken, *fado* will not only captivate it but nurse it back to health. The melodies and lyrics of *fado* drip with the wrenching pain of unrequited passion. Although *fado* may have been rooted in African slave songs, the legendary *fadista* (*fado* singer) **Maria Severa** (1810-1836) made *fado* quintessentially Portuguese. Severa achieved mythical status with her moving lyrics, through which she expressed her own real-life dramas. Modern *fadistas*, including **Amália Rodrigues** and **Argentina Santos,** have secured *fado* as a cultural fixture in Portugal. *Fado* houses, including **Machado** in Lisbon, are the best places to enjoy an intimate *fado* moment with that significant other before they break your heart.

FADO

Lisbon's trademark is the heart-wringing *fado*, an expressive art combining elements of singing and narrative poetry (see **Music,** p. 586). *Fadistas*, cloaked in black dresses and shawls, perform emotional tales of lost loves and faded glory. Their melancholy wailing is expressive of *saudade*, an emotion of nostalgia and yearning; listeners are supposed to feel the "knife turning in their hearts." On weekends, book in advance. The Bairro Alto has many *fado* joints off R. Misericórdia and on side streets radiating from the Museu de São Roque; it's the best place in the city for top-quality *fado*. All of the popular houses have high "minimum consumption" requirements. To avoid these, explore nearby streets; various bars and small venues often offer free shows. Otherwise, treat the minimum consumption as a cover charge and pick one of the places to go for coffee and dessert (which should cost enough to rack up the minimum). These places are touristy but do feature Portugal's top names in *fado*. All have acts every 20 minutes.

Machado, R. Norte, 91 (☎213 22 46 40). Founded in 1937, Machado is one of the larger *fado* restaurants and features some of the best known *fadistas* and guitarists. Eating dinner here, however, will cost at least your daily budget. Entrees €20-68. Minimum consumption €15. Open Tu-Su 8pm-3am; *fados* start at 9:15pm. AmEx/MC/V. ❹

O Faia, R. Barroca, 56 (☎213 42 67 42), between R. Atalaia and R. Diário de Notícias. Elegant and expensive. Some of Portugal's better known *fadistas* perform nightly. Minimum consumption €18, includes 2 drinks. Entrees €18 and up; *menú* €35. Open M-Sa 8pm-2am; *fado* starts at 9:45pm. AmEx/MC/V. ❹

O Forcado, R. da Rosa, 221 (☎213 46 85 79). A traditional restaurant that features *fado* from Coimbra and Lisbon, as well as folk music and dance. Decorated with bullfighting pictures and *azulejos*. Minimum consumption €15. Entrees €18-20. Open Th-Tu 8pm-1:30am; *fado* starts at 9:15pm. AmEx/MC/V. ❹

Cristal Fados, Tv. da Queimada, 9 (☎213 42 67 87), on the corner of R. do Norte. With less famous singers and plain meals, have dinner without blowing your budget. Minimum consumption €8. Entrees €8-13. Open 8:30pm-1am; *fado* Th-Su. AmEx/MC/V. ❸

FESTIVALS

Those who love to mingle with the public will want to visit Lisbon in June. Open-air *feiras* (fairs)—smorgasbords of eating, drinking, live music, and dancing—fill the streets. After savoring *farturas* (Portuguese doughnuts) and Sagres beer, join in traditional Portuguese dancing. On the night of June 12, the streets become a haven for those who like to dance during the huge **Festa de Santo António:** banners are strung between streetlights, and confetti falls like snow during a parade along Av. Liberdade; young crowds absolutely pack the streets of the Alfama, and grilled sardines and *ginginha* are sold everywhere. Lisbon also has a number of commercial *feiras*. Bookworms burrow for three glorious weeks in the **Feira do Livro** (in the Parque Eduardo VII behind Pr. Marques Pombal from late May to early June). The **Feira Internacional de Lisboa,** which has moved to the Park of Nations, occurs every few months, while in July and August the **Feira de Mar de Cascais** and the **Feira de Artesania de Estoril** take place near the casino. Year-round *feiras* include the **Feira de Oeiras** (Antiques) on the fourth Sunday of every month and the **Feira de Carcanelos** for clothes (Th 8am-2pm). Packrats should catch the **Feira da Ladra** (flea market), held behind the Igreja de São Vicente de Fora in the Alfama neighborhood (Tu and Sa 7am-3pm). Take bus #12 or tram #28.

BULLFIGHTING

Portuguese bullfights (differing from the Spanish variety in that the bull is not killed) take place most Thursdays from the end of June to the end of September at **Praça de Touros de Lisboa,** Campo Pequeno (☎217 93 21 43. Open 10pm-2am). The Praça de Touros is due to re-open in May after a series of renovations, but call ahead or check at the tourist office to confirm that it's open before trekking out. Take the Metro to "Campo Pequeno" or bus #1, 44, 45, or 83.

FUTEBOL

Lisbon has two professional teams featuring some of the world's finest players: **Benfica** at the Stadium of Light (☎217 26 61 29. M: Colégio Militar Luz), and **Sporting** at Alvalade Stadium (☎217 56 79 14. M: Campo Grande). Check the ABEP kiosk in Pr. Restauradores or the sports newspaper *A Bola* for games. The European championship is scheduled to be played in Portugal in 2004.

THEATER AND MOVIES

The **Teatro Nacional de Dona Maria II,** Pr. Dom Pedro IV stages performances of classical Portuguese and foreign plays (☎213 47 22 26. €3.50-10, 50% student discount). At Lisbon's largest theater, the **Teatro Nacional de São Carlos,** R. Serpa Pinto, 9, near the Museu do Chiado in the Bairro Alto, opera reigns from late September through mid-June. (☎ 213 46 59 14. Open daily 1-7pm).

São Jorge movie theater (☎212 42 25 23) is at the corner of Av. Liberdade and Av. Condes, across the square from the Pr. Restauradores tourist office. 10-screen cinemas are also located in the **Amoreiras** (M: Marques Pombal) and **Colombo** (M: Colegio Militar Luz) shopping centers and on the top floor of the **Centro Vasco de Gama** (M: Oriente). The largest theater, with 14 screens, is part of the new **El Corte Inglés** shopping complex (M: Sao Sebastiao). American movies are shown with Portuguese subtitles.

DAYTRIPS FROM LISBON

The following coastal towns, many of them with beautiful beaches or sights, can be refreshing diversions from the city. Pay close attention to transportation links as you plan daytrips from Lisbon; many of these places lie en route to other destinations (including Sintra and Setúbal; see **Near Lisbon,** p. 621).

ESTORIL

Trains from Lisbon's Estação Cais do Sodré (☎213 42 48 93; M: Cais do Sodré) run to Estoril (30min., approximately every 20min. 5:30am-2:30am, €1) continuing to Cascais (also a pleasant 20min. walk along the beach from Estoril). Stagecoach bus #418 to Sintra departs from Av. Marginal, in front of the train station (35min., every hr. 6:10am-11:40pm, €2.30).

Even though Estoril is home to Europe's largest casino, the beaches, lined with bars and restaurants, are its best asset. One of the city's five beaches, **Praia Estoril Tamariz,** greets visitors upon arrival, and the palm-lined **Parque de Estoril** lies just across the street. To exit the train station, use the underpass; take a left to get to the beach or a right to go to the casino and the rest of the town. The **Casino Estoril** in Praça José Teodoro dos Santos is well worth a visit even for non-gamblers, offering free shows and concerts as well as a newly-renovated game room and over 1000 slot machines. A nightly laser show lights up the garden starting at 9:30pm, and shows in the casino's theater start at 11pm. Every Wednesday at 11:30pm in the Wonder-Bar, the *fado* concert features some of Portugal's most acclaimed singers. Be sure to reserve at least two days in advance. (☎214 66 77 00; www.casino-estoril.pt. Dress code: no sneakers, jeans, shorts, swimwear, or hats allowed anywhere in the casino; jackets required for the game room, but can be borrowed at the entrance if you leave an ID. Slots and game room 18+. Game room €5 per day, €7.50 per week. Passport required. Open daily 3pm-3am.)

The **tourist office,** on Arcadas do Parque, is across the street from the train station and to the left of the park. (☎214 66 38 13; fax 214 67 72 80. Wheelchair accessible. Open M-Sa 9am-7pm, Su 10am-6pm.) If you need a place to stay after the casino closes, the most convenient is **Residencial São Cristóvão ❹,** Av. Marginal, 7079. Facing the park, from the train platform, turn right, passing the gas station and continue up Av. Marginal for about two blocks. This *residencial* has bright, clean rooms, a large kitchen for the use of guests, and a common room with a TV. Breakfast included. (☎214 68 09 13; fax 214 64 92 86. 24hr. reception. Checkout noon. Reserve a month ahead in summer. Doubles €50, with bath €60; triples €78.) Those willing to spend their casino winnings a bit farther away from the beach will be rewarded by the lovely **Pensão Pica Pau ❹,** R. D. Afonso Henriques, 48. From the train station, take a left and walk past the tourist office, take the next right after the church onto R. Fausto Figueiredo. Walk up to the junction and take a right; you'll see the large, white building with a red-tiled roof. *Azulejo* tiles line all the hallways of this pension, which seems more like a posh beach resort hotel with bar and pool in the back. (☎214 66 71 40; fax 214 67 06 64. July-Sept. singles €40; doubles €60; triples €78. Apr.-Oct. €40/€50/€65. Nov.-Mar. €30/€40/€52.)

CASCAIS

To get to Cascais from neighboring Estoril, take a right onto the walkway at Praia Estoril Tamariz and walk along the coast about 20min. Trains from Lisbon's Estação Cais do Sodré (☎213 42 48 93; M: Cais do Sodré) head to Cascais via Estoril (30min., approximately every 20min. 5:30am-2:30am, €1.10). Stagecoach bus #417 leaves from outside the train station for Sintra (40min., every hr. 6:35am-7:08pm, €2.60). To visit Praia de Guincho, a popular windsurfing beach considered by many to be best of the coast, take the circular route bus #405/415 to the Guincho stop (22min., every 1-2 hr. 7:39am-5:34pm, €1.60). The last bus to Cascais is at 8:01pm.

Although the town is pleasantly serene during the off-season, the summer crowds seem to define the flavor of Cascais rather than spoil it. In balmy weather, the beaches, especially the **Praia da Ribeira,** the **Praia da Rainha**, and the **Praia da Duquesa,** are filled in balmy weather with tanners. To reach the Praia de Ribeira, simply take a right upon leaving the tourist office and walk down Av. Dos Combatantes de Grande Guerra until you see the water, while Praia da Rainha and the large Praia da Duquesa are a short walk out of town towards Estoril. Those in search of shade should head to the expansive **Parque Municipal da Gandarinha** (open daily 10am-6pm). About 1 km farther outside of Cascais, another 20 min. walk up Av. Rei Humberto de Itália, lies the **Boca de Inferno** (Mouth of Hell), so named because of the cleft carved in the rock by the Atlantic surf. As the sun sets, the pubbing picks up on **R. Frederico Arouca,** the main pedestrian street.

To get to the **tourist office,** Av. Dos Combatantes de Grande Guerra, 25, from the train station, cross the Largo da Estaçaõ square and take a right at the McDonald's onto Av. Valbom; the office is at the end of this shop-lined street. (☎214 86 82 04.

Open M-Sa 9am-7pm.) To spend the night, you might want to consider **Residencial Parsi ❷,** R. Afonso Sanches, 8, facing the Praia da Ribeira in the Largo 5 do Outubro, behind the big statue of D. Pedro. Ask for a room with a view of the ocean. (☎214 84 57 44; fax 214 81 82 22. Breakfast included. June-Sept. 15 singles €25; doubles €30, with bath €40-60. Sept. 16-May €15/€25/€35. AmEx/MC/V.)

QUELUZ

The best way to get to Queluz is by train. Take the Sintra line from Lisbon's Estação Rossio (M: Rossio) or Estação Sete Rios (M: Jardim Zoológico) and hop off at the Queluz-Belas (not Queluz-Massomá) stop (25min., every 15min., €0.80). To get to the palace, exit the train station through the ticket office and head left on Av. Antonio Ennes, continuing straight as the street becomes Av. República. Follow the signs until you see the expansive pink palace; the entrance is to the left of the statue of Dona Maria I.

Queluz itself is unexceptional, but the **Palácio Nacional de Queluz** makes it a worthwhile stop on the way to Sintra. In the mid-18th century, Dom Pedro III turned an old hunting lodge into this summer residence with the help of Portuguese architect Mateus Vicente de Oliveira and French sculptor Jean-Baptiste Robillon. While the well-ordered garden makes the palace feel like a miniature Versailles, the *azulejo*-lined canal is purely Portuguese. Highlights include the **Sala dos Embaixadores,** with its gilded thrones, marble floors, and Chinese vases and the **Quarto Piquenique's** gilded beehive-style ceiling. Of historical interest is the **Quarto Don Quijote** where Dom Pedro I, the first and last emperor of Brazil, drew his last breaths. (Open W-M 10am-5pm. Palace €3, garden €0.50. Seniors and students €1.50.)

MAFRA

Mafrense buses, labeled with a green and white "M," run from Lisbon's Campo Grande and stop in the square across from the palace; Mafrense buses serve Lisbon (1-1½hr., every hr. 5:30am-9:30pm, €2.75) and Ericeira (20min., every hr. 7:30am-midnight, €1.25). Don't take the train from Lisbon's Estação Santa Apolónia unless you're up for the 7km walk to Mafra; the station is out where cabs are rare.

An attractive stop on the way to Ericeira from Lisbon, Mafra is home to one of Portugal's most impressive sights and one of Europe's largest historical buildings, the **Palácio Nacional de Mafra.** Built by Dom João V to honor the birth of his first child, the building took 50,000 workers to build and includes a monastery, palace, library, and a large church. The monastery has its own hospital and infirmary, as well as a **Sala de Penitencia,** where the Franciscan monks punished themselves—note the whip on the wall and the skull above the bed. The palace on the third floor features two towers, one for the queen and one for the king. The **Throne Room,** where the king gave his speeches, is covered with murals representing his eight ideal virtues. Look for the **Music Room,** decorated with King Carlos's watercolors, and the **Game Room,** which contains billiard and lion-pocketed snooker tables. The most impressive space in the palace is the **biblioteca** containing 38,000 volumes from the 16th to 18th centuries, many of which were bound by the monks. Note the drawer-steps at the bottom of each Brazilian bookcase that allowed the monks to reach the top shelf. From the balcony of the **Sala de Bênção** (Blessing Room), king João V blessed the people of Mafra; the windows on the opposite wall look down into the church, allowing the royal family to view Mass from their quarters. The **Baroque church** below is renowned for its bell towers and its unique collection of six organs. For the tour of the palace and the monastery, enter through the door to left of the main steps of the palace. (☎261 81 75 50. Open W-M 10am-5:30pm, last entrance at 4:30pm. Daily 45min. tours in English 11am and 2:30pm. €3, students and seniors €1.5, under 14 free.)

To reach the **tourist office,** Av. 25 de Abril, take a right off the main steps of the palace onto Terreiro D. João and bear left, passing the post office on your left; the office will be on the right down the road, behind the fountain. (☎261 81 20 23. Open M-F 9am-7pm; Sa-Su 9:30am-1pm, 2:30-6pm.) If you get hungry after visiting the palace, try **Restaurante O Brasão ❷,** Tr. Manuel Esteves, 7, across the street from the Palácio Nacional. (☎261 81 56 87. Open daily 9am-midnight.)

ERICEIRA

Mafrense buses run from Lisbon's Campo Grande (1¼-1½hr., every hr. 6:30am-11:20pm, €3.80). Ask the driver to drop you at the stop nearest the center, or just get off at the bus station. Buses run to: Mafra (25min., every hr. 5:15am-9:05pm, €1.25); Sintra (50min., every hr. 6:30am-8:30pm, €2.50); Lisbon (1½hr., every hr. 5:15am-9:05pm, €3.80).

Ericeira is a pleasant fishing village whose beaches have been discovered by surfers. Despite its rising popularity, the town seems to have handled the attention responsibly, more or less holding onto its traditional flow of life while visitors come to play in the waves of the **Praça da República.** Beachgoers find their way along the coast to the nearby **Praia do Norte,** a long beach to the right of the port, and the **Praia do Sul** on the left. Surfers head beyond the Praia do Norte to the more pristine **Praia de São Sebastião,** or 3km farther to the **Praia da Ribeira d'Ilhas,** where the World Surfing Championships were held in 1994. The surf shop **Utilmar,** near the town center on R. 5 de Outubro, 25A, rents surfboards and bodyboards. (☎261 86 23 71. Surfboard or bodyboard €15 per day, €25 with wetsuit. AmEx/MC/V.)

To get to the **tourist office,** R. Eduardo Burnay, 46, from the bus station, cross the road (EN 247-2), turn left, and walk uphill. Take the second right onto Calçada do Rego and take a right at the fork onto R. Paróquia. After three short blocks take a left onto R. 5 de Outubro, which runs to the small Pr. República. The tourist office is the white building with blue trim on the opposite end of the square. The office rents out bikes during the summer. (☎261 86 31 22. Apr.-Sept. half-day 9:30am-2:30pm or 2:30-8pm, €2.50; full day 9:30am-8pm, €4.50. Open July-Sept. daily 9:30am-midnight; Oct.-June Su-M 9:30am-7pm, Sa 9:30am-10pm.) If you choose to stay or if you miss the last bus back to Lisbon (9:05pm), you might have trouble finding a cheap room in summer. Check with the tourist office for a list of rooms in private homes. One of the most suitable places to stay is **Residencial Fortunato ❹,** R. Dr. Eduardo Burnay, 7, a few blocks past the tourist office on the right side of the street. All rooms have bath and TV. (☎261 86 28 29. May-June singles €36; doubles €40. July-Sept. 15 €40-48/€45-55; Sept. 16-Oct. €35/€40; Nov.-Apr. €30/€35.) **Restaurante O Jogo da Bola ❷,** Travessa do Jogo da Bola, 3, just behind the tourist office, is a popular nightstop where you can sample local dishes. (☎261 88 46 46. Entrees €4.50-11; beer €0.60-0.85. Open Th-Tu noon-2am.) More seafood restaurants can be found along **R. Eduardo Burnay,** which runs from the Pr. de República to the right of the tourist office. In the evening, head over to **Neptuno Pub,** R. Mendes Leal, 12. After facing Praça da República from the tourist office, take a left onto Tr. do Jogo da Bola, and take the first left onto R. Mendes Leal. This friendly Irish pub offers live, traditional *fado* music every Friday night starting at 11pm. Their motto is, "A pleasant atmosphere, where one drink is not enough." (☎261 86 20 17. Open daily 7pm-2am. It sometimes opens at noon during the summer.)

SESIMBRA

To get to Sesimbra, take a Transtejo ferry from Lisbon to Cacilhas (10min., every 15min. 5:50am-9:30pm, €0.50) from the dock at Pr. Comércio and then catch a TST bus to Sesimbra (45min.-1hr., 15 per day 6:40am-12:40am, €2.40). Alternatively, Covas e Filhos and TST buses go directly to Sesimbra (1hr., 7 per day 8am-7:30pm, €2.90) from Lisbon's Pr. de Espanha (M: Pr. de Espanha), but heavy traffic can delay these buses. Covas e Filhos and TST buses leave from Sesimbra's main bus station on Av. Liberdade to: Cacilhas (45min.-1hr., 12 per day 5:40am-11pm, €2.50); Lisbon (1hr., 8 per day 6:30am-6:10pm, €2.90); Setúbal (45min., 9 per day 6:20am-6:50pm, €2.20).

The agenda in Sesimbra is refreshingly simple: go to the beach, gape at the **Moorish castle,** eat seafood, and relax. Come for a day and you'll feel welcome; spend the night and you'll feel like a local. For those who pride themselves on being outdoorsy, a steep hour-long hike above town to the Moorish castle rewards with a luminous view of the ocean and surrounding mountains. To reach the castle from the beach, follow the yellow and green signs and take R. Gen. Humberto Delgado to the marked path. (Castle open June-Sept. 7am-8pm, Oct.-May 7am-7pm. Free.)

To get to the **tourist office,** Lgo. da Marinha, 26-27, from the bus station take a left onto Av. Liberdade and walk downhill to the end, then take a right; the office is across the street from the beach. (☎212 23 57 43. Open daily June-Sept. 9am-8pm; Oct.-May 9am-12:30pm and 2-5:30pm.) Inexpensive rooms are difficult to find, especially in summer. Restaurants cluster in the plaza above the tourist office along Lgo. da Marinha. Don't miss **Casa Isaías ❷,** R. Coronel Barreto, 2, up the street from Lgo. do Município, at the end of the block on the right. Isaías grills fish (€4-8) in an outdoor brick oven. (☎914 57 43 73. Open M-F noon-10pm.)

NEAR LISBON

SINTRA ☎219

Called paradise by some, Sintra is indeed a lovely place to visit. Moorish sultans and Portuguese kings found Sintra a relaxing summer getaway for centuries, and today many daytrippers from Lisbon can find the same comfort among the town's geranium- and bougainvillea-lined streets and the surrounding hills. If you are hoping to get away from the frantic pace of Lisbon city life, a walk through this town will calm even the most weary of travelers. However, many visitors come to experience what the sultans and kings left behind—three palaces, one castle, and dozens of historic buildings that represent a huge spectrum of Portuguese history.

TRANSPORTATION

Trains: Estação de Caminhos de Ferro, Av. Dr. Miguel Bombarda (☎219 23 26 05). To **Lisbon's** Estação Rossio and Estação Sete Rios (45min., every 15min. 6:07am-2:07am, €1.10).

Buses: Stagecoach buses (☎214 83 20 55; fax 214 86 81 68), on Av. Dr. Miguel Bombarda just outside the train station, run to **Cascais** (#417, 40min., every hr. 7:20am-8:30pm, €2.60) and **Estoril** (#418, 40min., every hr. 6:50am-midnight, €2.20). **Mafrense** buses, just down the street from the Stagecoach buses, go to **Ericeira** (50min., every hr. 7:25am-8:25pm, €2).

ORIENTATION AND PRACTICAL INFORMATION

Situated 30km northwest of Lisbon and 10km north of Estoril, Sintra is split into three parts: the modern **Estefânia** around the train station, where most budget accommodations and banks are located; **Sintra-Vila,** where the historic sights settle on the mountainside; and **Portela de Sintra,** where shops and municipal offices cluster. To get to the old town from the train station (a 15min. walk), take a left out of the train station's ticket office, and turn right down the small hill at the next intersection. One block down the hill, turn left again at the fountain in front of the castle-like **Câmara Municipal,** following the road as it curves past the **Parque da Liberdade.** From there, head up the hill to the **Pr. da República;** the Palácio Nacional de Sintra is the large white building on the right.

Tourist Office: Sintra-Vila, Pr. República, 23 (☎219 23 11 57; fax 219 23 51 76), is in the historic center. From the Pr. República with the palace at your right, walk straight ahead 1 block; the tourist office is beyond the palace in a columned marble building on the far side of the *praça*. Open June-Sept. daily 9am-8pm; Oct.-May 9am-7pm.

Currency Exchange: Banco Totta e Açores, Sintra-Vila, R. Padarias, 4 (☎219 10 68 70; fax 219 10 68 71). On the popular uphill side street off the main *praça*. Open M-F 8:30am-noon, 1-3pm. **ATMs** also line Av. Heliodoro Salgado in modern Sintra.

Emergency: ☎112. **Police:** R. João de Deus, 6 (☎219 23 09 35), behind the end of the train tracks as you walk toward Sintra-Vila. **Local emergency service:** ☎219 10 69 00.

Medical Services: Centro de Saúde, R. Alfredo do Costa, 34, 1st fl. (☎219 23 21 22). **Hospital Fernando Fonseca (Amadora-Sintra)** in nearby Amadora (☎214 34 82 00).

Internet Access: Loja do Arco, R. Arco do Teixeira, 2 (☎219 10 61 51; fax 219 10 61 49; www.rigra.pt). €2.50 for first 30min., €1.25 for each additional 15min.

Post Office: Av. Movimento das Forças Armadas, 1 (☎219 23 91 51; fax 219 23 91 56). Internet access. Open M-F 8:30am-6pm. **Postal Code:** 2710.

ACCOMMODATIONS AND CAMPING

Sintra makes a good base for daytrips to surrounding historical sights and coastal towns, as accommodations are quite affordable. Be sure to make reservations, as some places can fill up months ahead in advance. If you're left without a hostel or hotel, a long list of rooms in private homes is available at the tourist office.

Pousada da Juventude de Sintra (HI), Santa Eufémia at S. Pedro de Sintra, (☎219 24 12 10; fax 219 23 31 76). Take bus #435 from the train station to São Pedro (15 min., €1.10), and then hike 2km, or hail a taxi in front of the train station (weekdays €9; weekends €10). Dining room, sitting room, TV with VCR, stereo, and winter heating. Breakfast included. HI membership required. June 16-Sept. 15 dorms €10.50 per person; doubles €24, with bath €25. Sept. 16-June 15 €8.50/€20/€24. MC/V. ❶

Casa Adelaide, R. Guilherme G. Fernandes, 11 (☎219 23 08 73). From the train station, head downhill toward Sintra-Vila, walk past the Câmara Municipal at Largo Dr. Virg Horten and turn left onto R. Guilherme Fernandes; half a block downhill on the left, enter through the back. Singles €25; doubles €25; triples €30. Ask for lower rates in winter. ❷

Pensão Economica, Pátio de Olivença, 6 (☎219 23 02 29). Take a right out of the train station, and walk up Av. Dr. Miguel Bombarda as it turns into Av. Heliodoro Salgado. Take the second right after Av. Salgado becomes a pedestrian street; the *pensão* is at end of this alley. Well-kept rooms with small low beds. One double and one triple available. Common bathroom. Singles €20, with TV €25; doubles €25; triples €30. ❷

Pensão Nova Sintra, Lgo. Afonso de Albuquerque, 25 (☎219 23 02 20; fax 219 10 70 33). From the train station, take a left; the *pensão* is the yellow building sitting atop a line of shops at the corner of R. Gomes Amorim and Av. Salgado. Offering space and luxury, all nine rooms of this two star hotel include TV, bath, and phone. The open patio of the hotel's restaurant and bar is a good place to relax. Singles €45; doubles €60. ❹

Camping: Parque de Campismo da Praia Grande, Av. Maestro Frederico de Freitas, 28 (☎219 29 05 81; fax 219 29 18 34), on the coast 12km from Sintra. Take bus #441 from Portela de Sintra to Praia Grande. Reception daily until 7pm. €3 per person. ❶

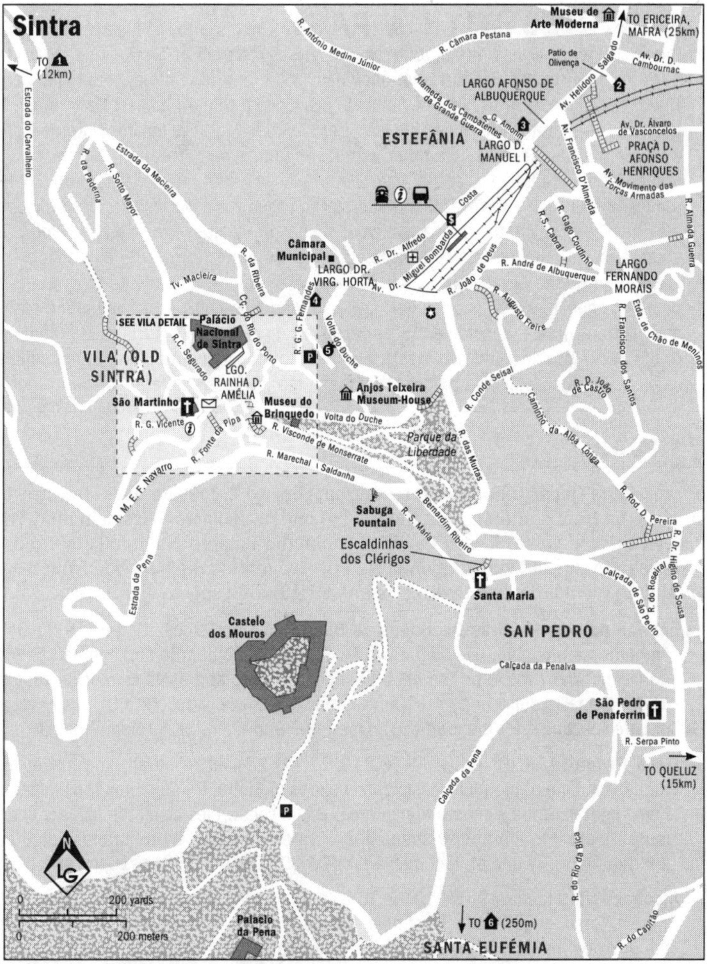

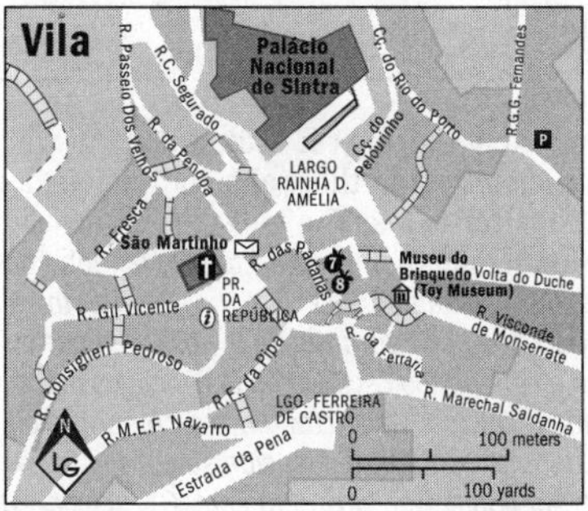

ACCOMMODATIONS

Camping, **1**
Casa Adelaide, **4**
Pensão Económica, **2**
Pensão Nova Sintra, **3**
Pousada da Juventude, **6**

FOOD

Alcobaça, **7**
Casa Piriquita, **8**
Fábrica das Verdadeiras Quijadas da Sapa, **5**

PASTRIES WITH A PAST There's a lot of history packed into those little cheese pastries proudly sold in the *pastelarias* of Sintra. *Queijadas* date back to the 13th century and were once used as a form of currency to pay landlords. The *queijada*'s ascent to fame began in 1756, when a woman named Maria made the pastries to sell at the entrance of town. After the railroad tracks linking Sintra to Lisbon were completed in 1887, famous writers began to pass through. Some were so impressed by the little sweet that it soon made its way into many classic works of Portuguese literature. Maria's descendants still run the oldest pastry shop in Sintra, and they have joined with the three prestigious names of the *queijada* tradition—Preto, Gregorio, and Piriquita—to form an association for the protection of the authenticity and integrity of *queijadas de Sintra*. All shops use the same ingredients to prepare the pastries: cheese, wheat flour, sugar, egg yolk, and cinnamon, in a shell made of flour and water. However, according to Francisco Barreto das Neves, the current grandfather of the Sapa tradition and self-proclaimed head of quality control, there are countless variables in the production process that make the *queijadas* different in every shop.

FOOD

Pastelarias (pastry shops) and restaurants crowd **R. João de Deus** (the street parallel to the train station across the tracks) and **Av. Helidoro Salgado** in modern Sintra. In the old town, **R. das Padárias** (near the Palácio Nacional) is lined with eateries. On the 2nd and 4th Sundays of every month, take bus #435 from the train station to the nearby São Pedro (15min., €1.10) for a spectacular **market.**

Fábrica das Verdadeiras Queijadas da Sapa, Volta do Duche, 12 (☎219 23 04 93). From the train station, head left down Av. Dr. Miguel Bombarda and bear left onto Volta do Duche; the shop is on the right. Founded in 1756 and at its current location since 1890, Sapa is still run by the same family. Try a *queijada* (€0.60) pastry or buy a *pacote* (package) for the road (€3). Open Tu-F 9am-6pm, Sa-Su 9am-7pm. ❶

Casa Piriquita, R. Padarias, 1 (☎219 23 06 26), up a small side street off Pr. República. One of the four classic pastry shops of Sintra, Piriquita has the advantage of being right in Sintra's central tourist area. Bright yellow tiles cover the facade, and *fado* music floats into the narrow street. The counter is flanked by a marble-floored coffee and tea room. Try one of their *queijadas* (€0.60). Open W-M 9am-10pm. ❶

Alcobaça, R. Padarias, 9 (☎219 23 16 51), up R. Padarias from Pr. República, and just beyond Casa Piriquita. Stacks of fresh seafood in the window. Shellfish lovers will enjoy the *arroz de marisco* (€8). Open daily noon-11pm. Closed Dec. 12-26. ❷

SIGHTS

CASTELO DOS MOUROS. You're not likely to forget a walk along the walls of this 8th century Moorish castle—or the views; from the walls and turrets, a panorama of sandy coast and mountains runs for miles. The view-struck are usually also sun-struck; a bottle of water is recommended. *(Bus #434 runs to the top from outside the tourist office. €3.60 for an all-day pass. If you want to walk (1-1½hr.), start at the Museu do Brinquedo off Pr. República and follow R. Visconde de Monserrate up the hill; continue straight as it becomes R. Bernardim Ribeiro, then take a right up the Escadinhas dos Clerigos and walk to the fork at the end. Turn left onto the Calçada da Santa Maria (toward the church), then right when you see a sign for Casa do Adro. Take another right at the first side street and follow it up the mountain to the Castelo. Open June-Sept. 9am-8pm, Oct.-May 9am-7pm. €3, seniors €1.)*

PALÁCIO NACIONAL DE SINTRA. Also known as the Paço Real or Palácio da Vila, the palace presides over Pr. República. Once the summer residence of Moorish sultans and their harems, the Paço Real and its gardens were built in two stages. Dom João I built the main structure in the 15th century; a century later, Dom Manuel I created the best collection of *azulejos* in the world. He added various wings to create a mix of Moorish, Gothic, and Manueline styles. The palace has more than 20 rooms, including the *azulejo*-covered **Sala dos Árabes** and the majestic **Sala dos Brasões.** You may notice a bird theme: doves symbolizing the Holy Spirit line the walls of the **Capela,** magpies cover the ceiling of the **Sala das Pegas,** and swans grace the ceiling of the **Sala dos Cisnes.** *(At Largo da Rainha Dona Amélia. ☎219 10 68 40. Open Th-Tu 10am-5:30pm. Closed holidays. Buy tickets by 5pm. €3; seniors, students €1.50.)*

PALÁCIO DA PENA. Built in the 1840s by Prince Ferdinand of Bavaria, the husband of Queen Maria II, this royal retreat palace embraces romantic and fantastic style with its excessive detail. The prince, nostalgic for his country, rebuilt and embellished the ruined monastery with the assistance of a Prussian engineer, combining the artistic heritages of both Germany and Portugal. The result is a Bavarian castle decorated with Arabic minarets, Gothic turrets, Manueline windows, and a Renaissance dome. Interior highlights include the chapel, a fully furnished kitchen, incredible views from the Queen's terrace, and her majesty's toilet—crafted entirely in *azulejos.* *(About 1km farther uphill from the Castelo dos Mouros. July-Sept. Tu-Su 10am-6:30pm; Oct.-June Tu-Su 10am-5pm. €5, seniors and students €1.50.)*

MUSEU DO BRINQUEDO (TOY MUSEUM). The toy museum, which grew out of the private collection of João Arbue's Moreira, displays a fascinating three-floor assortment of over 20,000 toys in Sintra's old fire station. According to Moreira, the unifying idea of his museum is to show the history of humanity by way of toys; this philosophy is what connects the pieces of his eclectic collection of cars, trains, LEGOs, dolls, lead soldiers, and many other items. The collection includes trinkets from all over the world as well as traditional Portuguese playthings. Especially intriguing is the second floor, which presents the entire history of war from the dawn of man to WWII. *(R. Visconde de Monserrate, 28. ☎219 10 60 16. Open Tu-Su 10am-6pm. €3, children under 3 and seniors €1.50.)*

SINTRA MUSEU DE ARTE MODERNA. This musuem houses contemporary works by Andy Warhol and Gerhard Richter, among others, in a 19th-century building. *(Past the train station in modern Sintra, on Av. Heliodoro Salgado. ☎219 24 81 70. Open Tu-Su 10am-6pm. €3, students €1.50, children under 10 free, seniors and under 18 free on W.)*

SETÚBAL ☎265

As a large port city located at the mouth of the Sado River, Setúbal maintains a cosmopolitan style while still preserving an old-fashioned charm; a historic pedestrian area links a series of whitewashed churches and *praças* in the city's center. Although factories and sprawling suburbs lie on the outskirts of this important industrial city, Setúbal's beauty is restored by tree-lined avenues and lively dock activity towards the banks of the Sado. With the city's fishing industry providing the daily catch to local restaurants, a 16th-century fort, a maze of *azulejo*-covered alleys, and its status as the departure point into the rural regions of the-Costa Azul, Setúbal warrants at least a day's visit from Lisbon.

TRANSPORTATION

Trains: leave from either the central **Estação Praça de Quebedo,** which is the most convenient to the city center, or **Estação de Setúbal** (☎265 23 88 02), in Pr. Brasil for **Faro** (4hr., 3 per day 9:20am-8:25pm, €10) and **Lisbon's** Estaçao Barreiro (50 min., every hr. 5am-1am, €1.10).

Buses: Setublanse, Av. 5 de Outubro, 44 (☎265 52 50 51). From the city tourist office, walk up R. Santa Maria to Av. 5 de Outubro and turn left; the station is about 2 blocks down on the right, in the building with the word "Rodoviaria" in big letters written vertically down the front. To: **Évora** (daily express bus 1¾hr., 10:20am, €7; other buses 2¼hr.-2½hr. 7 per day 6:30am-6:45pm, €4.90) and **Lisbon's** Praça de Espanha (1hr., every 30min. 7am-11:30pm, €2.90). **Covas & Filhos,** Av. Alexandre Herculano (☎212 23 31 03), a right 2 blocks past the Setublanse station, goes to **Sesimbra** (45min., 9 per day 7:20am-8pm, €2.10).

Ferries: Transado, Doca do Comércio (☎265 23 51 01), off Av. Todi at the east end of the waterfront. Trips run back and forth from Setúbal to **Tróia** (15min., every 15-45min. around the clock, €0.90. Children 5-10 €0.45, under 5 free.)

Taxis: (☎265 23 33 34), along Av. Todi and by the bus and train stations.

ORIENTATION AND PRACTICAL INFORMATION

Setúbal's spine is **Av. Luisa Todi,** a long boulevard parallel to the Rio Sado. Inland from the river and Av. Todi lies a dense district of shops and restaurants centered around **Pr. de Bocage.** Another major thoroughfare, **Av. 5 de Outubro,** runs along the opposite side from Av. Todi to Pr. de Bocage. Perpendicular to Av. 5 de Outubro, **Av. da Portela** runs past the train and bus stations.

Tourist Office: Posto de Turismo da Costa Azul, Tv. Frei Gaspar (☎265 53 91 30), just off Av. Luisa Todi near Lgo. Misericordia. Wheelchair accessible. Open May-Sept. Su 9:30am-12:30pm, M-Sa 9:30am-7pm; Oct.-Apr. M-Sa 9:30am-6pm.

Currency exchange: Av. Todi is lined with **banks.** All open M-F 8:30am-3pm. **Caixa Geral de Depositos**, Av. Todi (☎265 53 05 00).

Emergency: ☎112. **Police:** Av. Todi (☎265 52 20 22), at Av. 22 de Dezembro.

Medical Services: Hospital on R. Camilo Castelo Branco (☎265 52 21 33).

Internet Access: Ciber Centro, Av. Bento Gonçalves, 21A (☎265 23 48 00). 6 computers. €2.50 per 30min., €2.25 with student ID. Open M-F 9am-11pm.

Post office: Av. Mariano de Carvalho (☎265 52 86 20), at Av. 22 de Dezembro. **Posta Restante.** Open M-F 8:30am-6:30pm. **Postal code:** 2900.

ACCOMMODATIONS AND CAMPING

There are a few good, cheap *pensões* along **Av. Todi** and near the **Pr. de Bocage.** Alternatively, ask at the tourist office for a list of *quartos* in private houses.

Pensão Bom Amigo, R. Concelho, 7 (☎265 52 62 90), off Pr. Bocage and on a small street next to the Câmara Municipal. Airy rooms and tile-lined hallways. Some rooms with Praça views. July-Sept. rooms €30, with bath €30-45. Oct.-June €25/€30. ❸

Pensão O Cantinho, Beco do Carmo, 1-9 (☎265 52 38 99), in an alley off Av. Todi behind Lgo. do Carmo. The rooms above the restaurant are startlingly cheap. Reserve a month ahead in summer. Singles €10, with bath €15; double with bath €23. ❶

Camping: Get-away-from-it-all types will want to escape to **Parque Natural da Arrábida** or one of the smaller locations near Setúbal in Azeitão or Sesimbra. Closer to the center of town is **Toca do Pai Lopes,** on the riverbank of R. Praia da Saúde (☎265 53 18 20), past Doca dos Pescadores on the road to Outão. June-Aug. €1.50 per person, €1.30-€2.40 per tent, €1.30 per car. Sept.-May €1.10/€0.90-1.70/€1. ❶

FOOD

Setúbal is full of restaurants offering the town specialties (including grilled fish and fried calamari) at very affordable prices; there's no reason to pay more than €8 for a memorable meal. A row of seafood places line **Av. Todi** just up the street from Doca do Comercío; you can watch as they cut and fry your fish on grills set up along the sidewalk. Pick up **groceries** and fresh baked goods at **Pingo Doce,** Av. Todi, 249. (☎265 52 61 05. Open daily 8am-10pm.)

O Cantinho, Beco do Carmo, 1-9 (☎265 52 38 99), off Av. Todi in an alley behind Lgo. do Carmo. As indoor and outdoor tables fill with regulars, the lively atmosphere signals the quality of the grilled seafood. Excellent fish (€4-7.50); try the orgasmic *doce são marcos* dessert (€1.30). Open F-W 9am-11pm; meals served noon-3pm, 7-11pm. ❷

Casa de Santiago, Av. Todi, 92 (☎265 22 16 88), next to the Avis office. One of the better seafood places in town. Try the house specialty, *choco frito* (fried cuttlefish; €5). Meals served noon-3pm, 6:30-10pm. Open M-Sa 9:30am-3pm, 6:30-10pm. ❶

Saca Rohlas, Av. Todi, 388 (☎265 23 84 65). Stands out from neighboring establishment because of the generous portions and menu variety. With juicy pork and beef dishes (€7-8) and basic salads (€5), this place is a reprieve for non-fish lovers. Meals served with salad and a potato side dish. Open M-Sa noon-3pm, 7-10pm. MC/V. ❷

SIGHTS AND ENTERTAINMENT

The most impressive sight in town is not really *in* town. The 16th-century **Fortaleza de São Filipe** sits just outside the city. Designed by the Italian engineer Filipe Terzi, the fortress was built from 1582 to 1600 to complement the Fortaleza de Santiago at Outão. A phenomenal view of the Sado River rewards visitors. To reach the fortress, take Av. Todi to its end (towards the beaches), turn right onto Escadinhas do Castelo, then ascend R. Estrada do Castelo about 15min. It's a 40min. walk from the town center. During the last week of July and first week of August, the **Feira de Santiago** brings a carnival, bullfighting, and folk music to Setúbal.

DAYTRIPS FROM SETÚBAL

Outside of town are the beaches along the peninsula of **Tróia,** a brief ferry ride away from Doca do Comércio (15min.; every 15-45min; €0.90, children 5-10 €0.45, under 5 free). To the west of Setúbal is the **Parque Natural da Arrábida,** a large nature preserve that includes a variety of nature trails and the pristine **Praia da Figueirinha,** 9km from Setúbal. Also near Setúbal is the **Reservado Natural do Estuário do Sado**. Outdoor adventurers can contact **Mil Andanças,** Av. Todi, 121 (☎265 53 29 96), for somewhat pricey mountain biking, hiking, canoeing, and other nature trips. Before setting off on your own, check with **PNA,** Pr. da República for nature tourism information. (☎265 54 11 40. Open daily 9am-12:30pm and 2-5:30pm.)

ALGARVE

Behold the Algarve: a vacationland where happy campers from the world over bask in the sun. Nearly 3000 hours of annual sunshine have transformed this former fishermen's backwater into one of Europe's favorite vacation spots. In July and August, tourists mob the Algarve's resorts, packing bars and discos from sunset at 10pm until long after sunrise. Still, not all is excess in the Algarve. The region between Faro and the Spanish border remains untouched, and to the west of Lagos, towering cliffs shelter immaculate beaches. During the off-season, the resorts empty and wildlife of a different sort arrives, as roughly one-third of Europe's flamingos migrate to the wetlands surrounding Olhão.

With nearly a hundred miles of coastline, the Algarve has perfected the art of delicious seafood; local favorites include *sardinhas assadas* (grilled sardines), and *caldeirada* (seafood chowder). Almonds and figs also make their way into most regional cooking, especially the divine desserts like *figos cheios* (figs filled with a thick paste made of ground almonds, cacao, cinnamon, and lemon peel).

LAGOS ☎282

In the 17th century, travelers ventured here for the indigo and sugar markets; today they come for the meat market that is Lagos by night. Come for two days and you'll be tempted to stay a month. The Algarve's capital for almost 200 years, Lagos launched many of the caravels that brought Portugal power and fortune in the 15th and 16th centuries. A massive earthquake in 1755 destroyed most traces of Lagos's golden age, but no one's complaining—visitors swarm the town each summer in search not of history but legendary beaches and backpacker hedonism.

TRANSPORTATION

If you are trying to get to Lagos from northern Portugal, you must go through Lisbon; those coming from the east must transfer in Faro.

Trains: (☎282 76 29 87 or 282 79 23 61), across the river (over the pedestrian suspension bridge) from the main part of town. To: **Beja** (4hr.; 8:20am, 5:15pm; €7.10) via Faro; **Évora** (6hr.; 8:20am, 5:15pm; €10.20) via Faro; **Faro** (1¾hr., 9 per day 6:06am-10:30pm, €4); **Lisbon** (4-4½hr., 5-6 per day 6:55am-11:45pm, €12.60); **Silves** (40min., 9-12 per day 6:06am-11:45pm, €1.40); **Vila Real de Santo António** (4hr., 8-9 per day 6:55am-11:45pm, €5.40).

Buses: The **EVA** bus station (☎282 76 29 44), off Av. Descobrimentos, is just before R. Porta de Portugal (when walking into town) and across the channel from the train station and marina. To: **Albufeira** (1¼hr., 7 per day 7am-6pm, €3.40); **Faro** (2½hr., 6 per day 7am-5:15pm, €3.80); **Huelva, Spain** (4¾hr.; 7:30am, 2pm; €9.98); **Lisbon** (5hr., 12 per day 7:40am-1:30am, €14.50); **Portimão** (40min., 14 per day 7:15am-7:15pm, €1.90-2.50); **Sagres** (1hr., 17 per day 7:15am-8:30pm, €2.80).

Taxis: Lagos Central Taxi (☎282 76 24 69) 24hr. service to Lagos and environs.

Car Rental: Minimum age 21 for vehicles, 16 for motorbikes.

Marina Rent A Car, Av. Descobrimentos, 43 (☎282 76 47 89). July-Aug. cars start at €45 per day; May-June and Sept. €35; Oct.-Apr. €30; tax and insurance included. AmEx/MC/V.

Motoride, R. José Afonso lote 23-C (☎282 76 17 20), rents bikes (€10 per day) and scooters (€28 per day; min. age 16; must have license). Open daily 9am-7pm.

Hertz-Portuguesa, Rossio de S. João Ed. Panorama, 3 (☎282 76 98 09), behind the bus station off Av. Descobrimentos. Cars start at €45 per day, tax and insurance included. MC/V.

ORIENTATION AND PRACTICAL INFORMATION

Running the length of the channel, **Avenida dos Descobrimentos** is the main road that carries traffic to and from Lagos. From the **train station,** walk through the pastel pink marina and cross the channel over the pedestrian suspension bridge; turn left onto Av. Descobrimentos. Exiting the **bus station,** walk straight until you hit Av. Descobrimentos and turn right. After 15m, take another right onto R. Porta de Portugal to reach **Praça Gil Eanes,** the center of the old town. The local **tourist office** is on the corner of R. Lima Leitão, which extends from Praça Gil Eanes. A cornucopia of restaurants and accommodations surrounds the goofy statue of Dom Sebastião that presides over the square. From Praça Gil Eanes, bars and hostels line **R. Afonso Dalmeida, R. 25 de Abril,** and **R. Silva Lópes.** Follow R. Silva Lopes to R. General Alberto Silveira to reach the grotto-lined beach of **Praia Doña Ana.**

Tourist Office: Regional office, R. Vasco de Gama (☎282 76 30 31), an inconvenient 25min. walk from the bus station. Follow R. Vasco da Gama until it crosses Av. da República; from there it's another 150m on the right. Open daily 9:30am-12:30pm and 2-5:30pm. The **local office** (☎282 76 41 11) at Lgo. Marques de Pombal Square, on the corner of R. Lima Leitão, is more convenient. Open July-Aug. M-Sa 10am-10pm; June, Sept. M-Sa 10am-8pm; Oct.-May M-F 10am-6pm.

Currency Exchange: Cota Cambios, Pr. Gil Eanes, 11 (☎282 76 44 52). Open June-Sept. daily 8:30am-10pm; Oct.-May M-F 9am-7pm, Sa-Su 10am-7pm.

English Bookstore: Loja do Livro, R. Dr. Joaquim Telo, 3 (☎282 76 73 47). Small selection of English language books including best-sellers and travel guides. Open June-Aug. M-F 10am-1pm and 3-11pm, Sa 10am-1pm; Sept.-May M-F 10am-1pm and 3-7pm.

Laundromat: Lavandaria Miele, Av. Descobrimentos, 27 (☎282 76 39 69). Wash and dry €6.50 per 5kg. Open M-F 9am-1pm and 3-7pm, Sa 9am-1pm.

Emergency: ☎112. **Police:** R. General Alberto Silva (☎282 76 29 30).

Pharmacy: Farmácia Silva, R. 25 de Abril, 9 (☎282 76 28 59).

Medical Services: Hospital, R. Castelo dos Governadores (☎282 77 01 00).

Internet Access: The Em@il Box (Ciaxa de Correieo), R. Cândido dos Reis, 112 (☎282 76 89 50), has 5 computers. €1.25 per 15min., €3.50 per hr. Open M-F 9:30am-8pm, Sa-Su 10am-3pm. Several bars in Lagos have 1 or 2 computers; check along R. Lançarote de Freitas as well as at the youth hostel.

Post Office: R. Portas de Portugal (☎282 77 02 50), between Pr. Gil Eanes and the river. Open M-F 9am-6pm. **Postal Code:** 8600.

ACCOMMODATIONS

In the summertime, *pensãoes* (and the youth hostel) fill up quickly; reserve more than a week in advance. If full, the youth hostel will happily refer you to a *quarto* near the hostel (close to the nightlife) for about the same price. Locals trying to rent rooms in their homes will probably be wait to greet you at the station. Though these rooms are often inconveniently located, they can be the best deals in town, at €10-15 per person in summer. Haggle with owners; room quality varies greatly.

Pousada da Juventude de Lagos (HI), R. Lançarote de Freitas, 50 (☎282 76 19 70; fax 282 76 96 84; www.hostalbooking.com), off R. 25 de Abril. Friendly staff and lodgers congregate in the courtyard. Breakfast included. In summer, book through the central **Movijovem** office (☎213 59 60 00). June 16-Sept. 15 dorms €15; doubles with bath €42. Sept. 16-June 15 €10/€28. MC/V. ❶

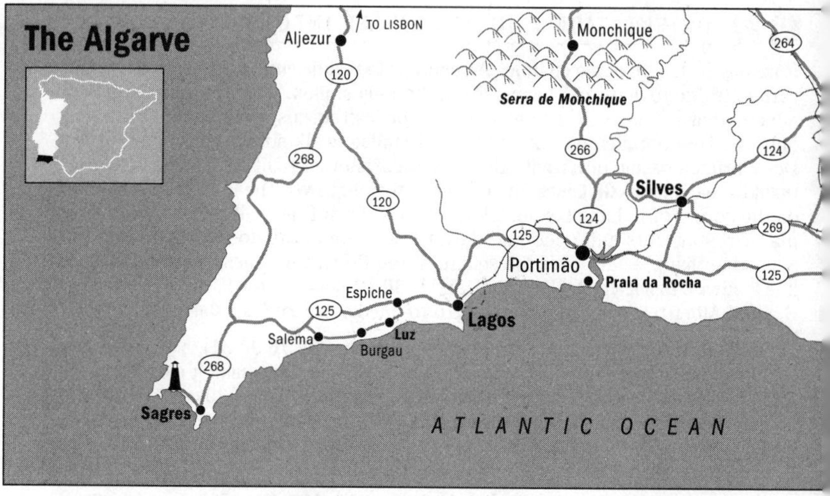

Olinda Teresa Maria Quartos, R. Lançarote de Freitas, 37, 2nd fl. (☎282 08 23 29), across the street from the youth hostel. Offers doubles or dorm rooms with shared kitchen, terrace, and bath. If the owner is not in, check at the youth hostel. June 16-Sept. 15 dorms €15; doubles €24. Sept. 16-June 15 €10/€30. ❶

Residencial Rubi Mar, R. Barroca, 70 (☎282 76 31 65; fax 282 76 77 49), off Pr. Gil Eanes toward Pr. Infante Dom Henrique. 8 centrally located rooms. Breakfast included. July-Oct. doubles €40, with bath €45; quads €75. Nov.-June €28/€33/€50. ❸

Residencial Lagosmar, R. Dr. Faria da Silva, 13 (☎282 76 37 22), up from Pr. Gil Eanes. Friendly 24hr. reception, and comfortable rooms all with bath, TV, and phone. July-Aug. singles €60; doubles €70; extra bed €22. June and Sept. €35/€40/€13. Nov.-Feb. €22/€25/€9. Mar.-May and Oct. €30/€35/€11. MC/V. ❺

Residencial Caravela, R. 25 de Abril, 8 (☎282 76 33 61), just up the street from Pr. Gil Eanes. 16 small and basic, but well-located rooms off a courtyard, some with balconies. Singles €24; doubles €32.50, with bath €36; triples €50. ❷

Camping: The way most Europeans experience the Algarve; sites are often crowded. **Camping Trindade** (☎282 76 38 93), just outside of town. Follow Av. Descobrimentos toward Sagres. €2.90 per person, €3.20 per tent, €3.50 per car. **Camping Valverde** (☎282 78 92 11), 6km outside Lagos and 1.5km west of Praia da Luz. Free showers. Grocery store, restaurant, and pool. €4.75 per person, €4.75 per tent, €4 per car. ❶

FOOD

Tourists can peruse multilingual menus around Pr. Gil Eanes and R. 25 de Abril, but the cheapest dining options in Lagos are the local produce **market,** on Av. Descobrimentos (5min. from the town center), or **Supermercado São Toque,** R. Portas de Portugal, 61. (☎282 76 28 55. Open July-Sept. M-F 9am-8pm, Sa 9am-7pm; Oct.-June M-F 9am-7:30pm, Sa 9am-7pm.) More expensive options are on R. Silva Lopes and R. 25 de Abril. Cheap seafood (€6-8) can be found near **Pr. Luis Camoes.**

Casa Rosa, R. Ferrador, 22 (☎968 37 71 15). A backpacker's culinary Mecca, this Lagos mainstay serves whopping portions for next to nothing. Gorge on a wide range of entrees with many vegetarian options (€3.50-7). Monday is all-you-can-eat spaghetti day (€5). Happy Hour 10-11pm. Open daily 6pm-midnight. ❶

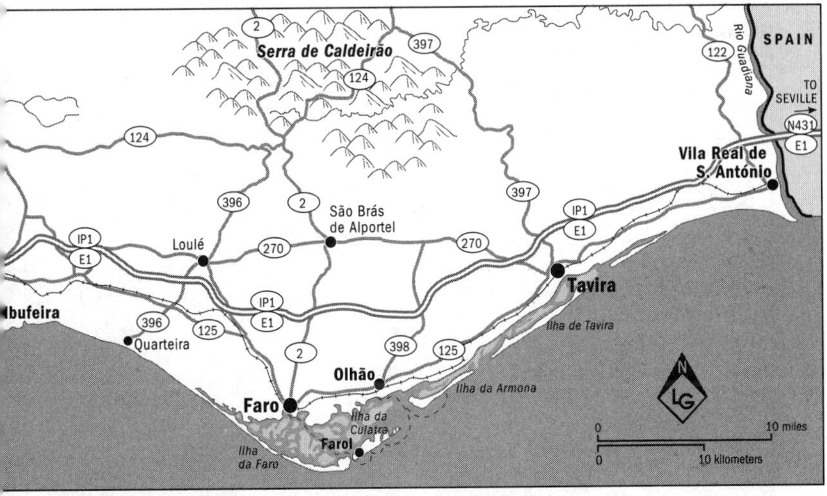

Mediterraneo, R. Senhora da Graça, 2 (☎282 76 84 76). Modern Mediterranean and Thai cuisine, including seafood and meat dishes, great salads and desserts. Indoor and outdoor dining. Entrees €9-13.50, vegetarian options. ❸

Snack-Bar Caravela, R. 25 de Abril, 14 (☎282 76 26 83), just off Pr. Gil Eanes. Well-touristed, but for good reason—it's a great place to people-watch and their pizza is the best in town. Outdoor seating. Pizzas and pasta €4.50-7.10. Open daily June-Sept. 9am-midnight; Oct.-Mar. 9am-10pm. AmEx/MC/V. ❷

A Vaca, R. Silva Lopes, 25-27 (☎282 76 44 31). Patrons savor traditional home-style Swiss dishes, including *roschti* (a potato dish), fondue, and crepes. Entrees €6.50-13.50. Open daily Apr.-Oct. noon-2am; Nov.-Mar. M-F noon-2am. MC/V. ❸

Restaurante O João, R. Silva Lopes, 15 (☎282 76 10 67). Great regional cuisine including traditional *cataplana* fish dishes, lamb in red wine sauce, and chicken in garlic sauce. Entrees €4.80-11, soups and salads €1.50-4.50. Open Th-Tu June-Sept. 12:30-2:30pm and 7-10pm. Oct.-May 12:30-2:30pm and 7-9pm. AmEx/MC/V. ❷

Adega Tipica, R. dos Ferreiros, 17. Few traditional Portuguese restaurants exist in Lagos, but locals swear by Adega, affectionately known as "Blue Door." Entrees €5.49-12.47. Open noon-3pm and 6:30-10pm. ❷

SIGHTS AND BEACHES

Although sunbathing and non-stop debauchery have long erased memories of Lagos's rugged, sea-faring past, most of the city is still surrounded by a nearly intact 16th-century wall. The **Fortaleza da Ponta da Bandeira,** a 17th-century fortress holding maritime exhibitions, overlooks the marina. (☎282 76 14 10. Open Tu-Sa 10am-1pm and 2-6pm, Su 10am-1pm. €1.85, students €1, children 13 and under free.) Also on the waterfront is the old **Mercado de Escravos** (slave market). Legend has it that the first sale of African slaves in Portugal took place here in 1441. Today the waterfront and marina offer jet-ski rentals, scuba diving lessons, sailboat trips, and motorboat tours of the coastal rocks and grottoes. Lagos's **beaches** are seductive any way you look at them. Flat, smooth, sunbathing sands (crowded during the summer, pristine in the off-season) line the 4km long **Meia Praia,** across the river from town. Hop on the 30-second ferry near Pr. República (€0.50 each way).

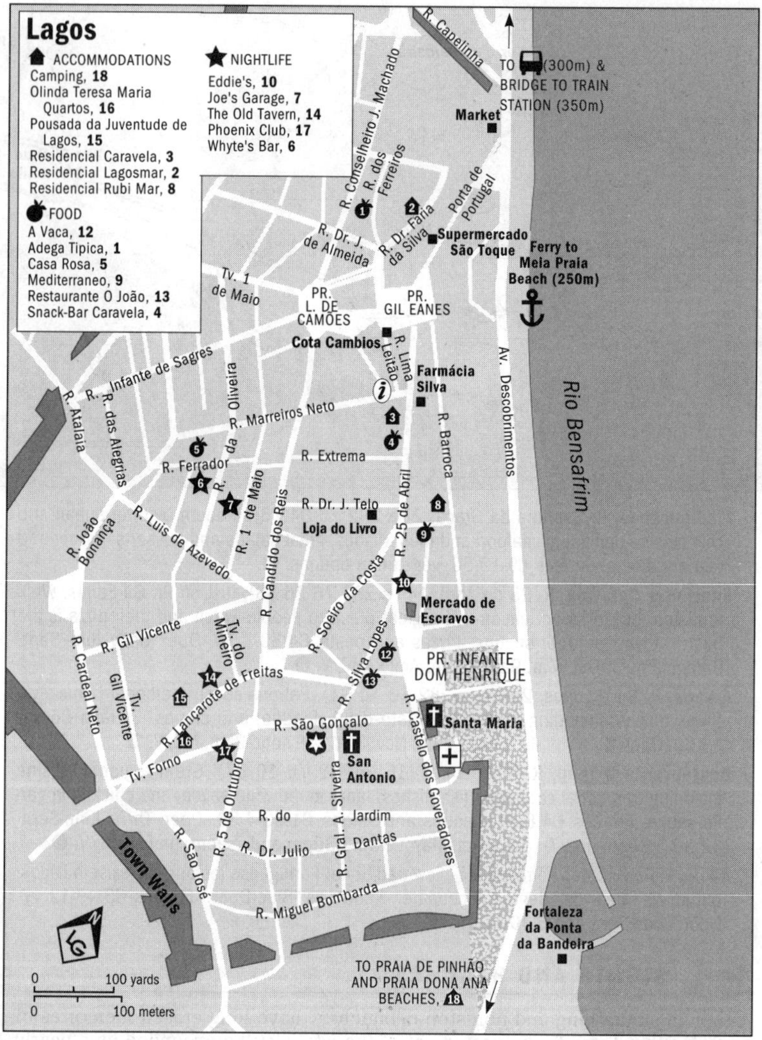

For cliffs that plunge into the sea hiding smaller, less-crowded beaches and caves, keep the ocean on your left and follow Av. Descobrimentos toward Sagres to **Praia de Pinhão** (20min.). Five minutes farther down the coast lies **Praia Dona Ana,** with sculpted cliffs and grottoes that appear on at least half of all Algarve postcards.

WATER SPORTS AND ACTIVITIES

If you're up for more than lazing on the beach, Lagos offers a wide variety of outdoor sports—from scuba diving, to surfing, to (booze) cruising.

Scuba Diving: Blue Ocean Diving Center (☎/fax 282 78 27 18; www.blue-ocean-divers.oe). About a 30min. walk out of the old city, at Motel Ancora, on the road to Porto de Mós. Medical license required for difficult dives. Lessons in English, French, German, and Portuguese. Half-day (in swimming pool) €25; full-day (in swimming pool and sea) €60. Open for reservations daily 8:30am-6pm.

Parasailing: Marina de Lagos (☎916 00 44 40). Diagonally to the left of the pastel pink building when facing the channel. Portuguese and English spoken. Group and family discounts. Parasailing €35; observing on the boat €15.

Grotto Boat Tours: Companies offering tours of the coastal cliffs and grottoes set up shop on Av. Descobrimentos. Most tours are 45min. and start at €25 for 2 people. Smaller boats are preferable, as they can maneuver into rock caves and formations.

Booze Cruise: This extremely popular cruise offers swimming, snorkeling, tours of the nearby grottoes, a live DJ, and, of course, cheap drinks. Cruises on Su, M, W, and F. €8-10, depending on the length of the cruise. For tickets call ☎963 01 26 92, or purchase them at the youth hostel.

Free Mountain Bike Tours: (☎182 76 83 29; www3.ns.sympatico.ca/freebike.) Highly recommended tours of the coast and the interior each ending with a complimentary beer at Eddie's bar. Different levels welcome. Also offers bike trips to Morocco €35 per day inclusive. Find guides at Eddie's or email coffeeinthedesert@hotmail.com.

Surfing:

Surf Experience: R. dos Ferreiros, 21 (☎282 76 19 43; www.surf-experience.com). 1 or 2 week surfing trips including lesson, transportation, and accommodations in Lagos. All levels welcome. Daytrips when space available. Apr.-Nov. 1 week €435; 2 weeks €747. Dec.-Mar. €388/€700. Board and wet suit rental €78 for 1 week; €117 for 2 weeks.

Surf Safari: R. Silva Lopes, 31 (☎282 76 47 34). Surfing trips including lesson, transportation, boards, and wet suit. All levels welcome. Local guide knows all the hidden spots. 1 day €25; 3 days €70; 5 days €100. Open Feb.-Oct. daily 10:30am-10:30pm.

NIGHTLIFE

You're tan, you're glam, now go find yourself a (wo)man. The streets of Lagos pick up as soon as the sun dips down. On alternate Sundays 4-10pm, **Bahia Beach Bar,** on Meia Praia Beach, hosts live music, volleyball, and a crowd packed with workers from Lagos's bars and restaurants. In town, the area between **Pr. Gil Eanes** and **Pr. Luis de Camões** is filled with cafes. **R. Cândido dos Reis, R. do Ferrador,** and the intersection of **R. 25 de Abril, R. Silva Lopes,** and **R. Soeiro da Costa** are packed with bars and clubs that rarely close until well past 5am.

Eddie's, R. 25 de Abril, 99. Friendly, easy-going bar popular with backpackers. Busy at night, but still comfortable. Beer €2. Open M-Sa 4pm-2am, Su 8pm-2am.

Taverna Velha (The Old Tavern), R. Lançarote de Freitas, 34 (☎282 76 92 31). Backpackers and expats mingle with the friendly staff. The only air-conditioned bar in Lagos, with free nightly showings of American movies at 5:30pm. Happy Hour with 2-for-1 drinks 9pm-midnight. Beer €1.25-2.50. Excellent strawberry-banana daiquiris (€7.50 per pitcher). Subs €3.50. Open M-Sa 4pm-2am, Su 8pm-2am. Closed 2nd week of Jan.-Mar.

The Red Eye, R. Candido Dos Reis, 63. 20-something Brits and Aussies flood in around midnight for classic rock and cheap liquor. Some dancing, but mostly a bar pick-up scene. Mixed drinks €2.50-3.50; 1½ pint coladas €4.50. Open daily 8pm-2am.

Joe's Garage, R. 1 de Maio, 78, 1 block from Whyte's Bar. With its sawdust-covered floor and table dancing patrons, Joe's is the rowdiest, and possibly raunchiest, bar in Lagos. Beer €2. 2-for-1 drinks 10pm-midnight. Open daily 10pm-2am.

Whyte's Bar, R. Ferrador, 7. A Lagos institution. Live DJ keeps this small bar packed all night long. Dancing on the basement level during the summer. Happy Hour nightly. Beer €2.50. Mixed drinks €2.50-3.50. Open daily Oct.-June 8pm-2am; July-Sept. 7pm-2am.

Phoenix Club, R. São Gonçalo, 29 (☎282 76 05 03). Rises from the early morning ashes for after-hours dancing. No dress code, but tight black outfits abound. Beer €2. Cover €6, includes 2 beers or 1 mixed drink. Open June-Sept. nightly midnight-7am, but the crowds don't arrive until 3:30am. Oct.-May F-Sa midnight-7am.

DAYTRIPS FROM LAGOS

PRAIA DA ROCHA

To reach Praia da Rocha from Lagos, take a bus to Portimão (40min., 14 per day 7:15am-8:15pm, €1.80), then switch to the Praia da Rocha bus, which stops in front of the nearby Portimão Honda dealership (10min., every 30min. 7:30am-8:30pm, €1.30).

A short jaunt from Lagos, this grand beach is perhaps the very best the Algarve has to offer. With vast expanses of sand, surfable waves, rocky red cliffs, and plenty of secluded coves, Praia da Rocha has a well-deserved reputation (and the crowds to match). The **tourist office,** at the end of R. Tomás Cabreina, offers maps and lists of accommodations and restaurants. (☎282 41 91 32. Open daily May-Sept. 9:30am-7pm; Oct.-Apr. M-F 9:30am-12:30pm and 2-5:30pm, Sa-Su 9:30am-12:30pm.)

LUZ, BURGAU, AND SALEMA

These towns are all accessible by the bus running from Lagos to Sagres (12 per day 7:15am-8:30pm). To reach Luz, get off at Espiche, 10min. away (€0.90); to Burgau, ride 20min. (€1.80); and to Salema 40min. (€1.60). Scootering oneself is a more windblown option (see Car Rental, p. 628). Be sure to check return bus schedules.

These three small towns on the way to Sagres make perfect daytrips from Lagos. Less "discovered" than their larger neighbor and a bit more charming than wind-swept Sagres, they offer a quiet escape from the crowds. All three towns feature lovely beaches (although Salema is less developed.) Try asking around for a *quarto* if you find yourself stranded at night. Fresh fruits, cheeses, and olives are sold by local farmers each morning at the main square in Salema, and decent bars and restaurants line the beachfront in all three towns.

SAGRES ☎282

Marooned atop a plateau at the most southwestern point in Europe, Sagres (pop. 2500) was for centuries considered the end of the world. Battered by ceaseless winds, the surrounding cliffs plunge hundreds of feet into the Atlantic. It was at Sagres that Prince Henry founded his school of navigation and organized voyages of exploration to the far reaches of the globe. Large tour groups and upscale vacationers are discouraged by the desolate location and relative lack of recreation, making Sagres a perfect destination for travelers in search of uncharted beauty.

TRANSPORTATION AND PRACTICAL INFORMATION. EVA buses (☎282 76 29 44) run from **Lagos** (1hr., 17 per day 7:15am-8:30pm, €2.80). Buses also run to to **Lisbon** (July-Sept. daily 4pm, €14.50). The friendly, English-speaking staff at the **tourist office** on R. Comandante Matoso, up the street from the bus stop, dispenses maps and information on Sagres's illustrious history. (☎282 62 48 73. Open Tu-Sa 9:30am-1pm and 2-5:30pm.) Local services include: privately-run **emergency** (☎112) in Pr. República; **police** in Cabo de São Vicente (☎282 63 91 12). At **Turinfo,** the energetic, English-speaking staff recommends accommodations, offers Internet access (€3 for 30min.), rents **bikes** (€9.50 per day, €6 per half-day), gives info on **jeep**

tours of a nearby nature preserve (€36, including lunch), provides **scuba** advice, and offers **currency exchange.** (☎282 62 00 03. Open daily 10am-1pm, 2-6:30pm.)

ACCOMMODATIONS AND FOOD. Finding a bed in Sagres is not hard; windows everywhere display multilingual signs for rooms, many in boarding houses with guest kitchens. Prices range €20-30 for singles and doubles; €25-40 for triples. Prices drop in the winter. Follow R. Comandante Matoso toward the tourist office and take a left on R. Patrão António Faustino to reach **Atalaia Apartamentos ❷.** The beautiful, fully-furnished rooms with bath, TV, and refrigerator, and apartments with kitchen, bath, living room, and terrace, are great deals. (☎282 62 46 81. Apartments: July-Sept. up to 3 people €50, for 4-6 people €80; Apr.-June €30/€60; Oct.-May €25/€50. Rooms: doubles July-Sept. €30; Apr.-June €25; Oct.-May €20.) Open-air **camping** is strictly forbidden, so head to the **Orbitur Campground ❶,** 2.5km on the way to Cabo de São Vicente, just off EN 268. (☎282 62 43 51; fax 282 62 44 45. June-Sept. €3-3.50 per person, €2.50-4.24 per tent, €1.75-2.24 per car. Oct.-May €2.50/€2-3/€1.25. Reception open daily June-Sept. 8am-11pm; Oct.-May 9am-7pm.) For groceries, try the **market** on R. Mercado, which intersects R. Comandante Matoso (open M-Sa 8am-9pm), or **Supermarket Alisuper,** on R. Comandente Matoso (☎282 62 44 87; open daily 9am-8pm). **O Dromedário Bistro ❷,** on R. Comandante Matoso, whips up innovative pizzas (€4.10-6.50) and vegetarian dishes (€4.80-7). The bar is a Sagres hotspot by night. (☎282 62 42 19. Open 10am-midnight; bar open until 2am. Closed Tu and Jan.-Feb.)

SIGHTS AND ENTERTAINMENT. Near town stands the **Fortaleza de Sagres,** the outpost where Prince Henry stroked his beard and founded his famous **school of navigation.** The pentagonal 15th-century fortress and surrounding paths yield vertigo-inducing views of the cliffs and sea. (Fortress open May-Sept. 10am-8:30pm; Oct.-Apr. 10am-6:30pm. Closed May 1 and Dec. 25. €3, under 25 €1.50.) Six kilometers farther west lies the desolate **Cabo de São Vicente,** which features the second most powerful lighthouse in Europe, a towering structure that overlooks the southwest tip of the continent and shines over 100km out to sea; tours are not available, though occasionally a caretaker can be persuaded to give one. On weekdays, take the bus from the bus station on R. Comandante Matos near the tourist office (10min.; 11:15am, 12:30, 4:15pm; €1). On weekends, you're on your own—it's an hour on foot, but is also accessible by bike (see **Turinfo,** above).

Several **beaches** fringe the peninsula, most notably **Mareta,** located at the bottom of the road from the town center. Rock formations jut into the ocean on both sides of this sandy crescent. Though not as picturesque or intimate as the coves of nearby Salema and Luz (see p. 634), Mareta is popular for its length and isolation, but can be windy. Just west of town are two of the best beaches for windsurfing, **Praia de Martinhal** and **Praia da Baleeira.** Praia de Martinhal is better, as Baleeira is closer to the shipyard and harbor. For a less windy option **Praia da Beliche** is located 3km outside of town, on the way to Cabo de São Vicente.

Although Sagres may seem dead on arrival, its pulse picks up around 10pm in the summer. At night, the young crowd fills the lively bar **Rosa dos Ventos** in Pr. República. (☎282 62 44 80. Beer €1. Mixed drinks €3. Open 10am-2am. Closed W.) Another hotspot is **Água Salgada,** on R. Comandante Matoso, 75m beyond the tourist office, going away from the fortress, which has an extensive drink menu. (☎282 62 42 97. Beer €1. Mixed drinks €4. Open 10am-2am. Closed W.) Next door is **O Dromedário** (see **Accommodations and Food,** above), where trendy young locals let loose and a request-taking DJ keeps the party raving. (☎282 62 42 97. Beer €1. Mixed drinks, including daiquiris and coladas, €3.50-5. Open daily 10am-2am.)

SILVES ☎282

Sleepy Silves was once the Moorish capital of the Algarve; from the mid-11th to mid-13th centuries it was larger than Lisbon, with a population of 30,000 and a bustling port. In 1189, however, English crusaders en route to the Holy Land sacked the city. Tortured and stripped of their possessions, the Moorish inhabitants managed briefly to regain control, but in 1249, Christian rule was reestablished permanently. River silting, earthquakes, and epidemics have done little to rejuvenate Silves over the past 700 years, although cork production brought an economic boom in the 1800s. Today, travelers venture to Silves to escape overcrowded beach towns and experience quirky local attractions, like the annual Beer Festival.

TRANSPORTATION. The train station, **Estação Cams Ferro** (☎282 44 23 10), is 1km out of town, so it's better to get to Silves by **bus.** If you do take a train, catch the "Estação" bus from the train station to town (10min., 6 per day 7:15am-7:40pm, €0.42). **Trains** run to: **Faro** (1hr., 6-11 per day 6:30am-11:16pm, €2.70); **Lagos** (40min., 10-13 per day 6:05am-12:15am, €1.40); **Lisbon** (4-5hr.; 9:25am, 11:03pm; €10-12.50) usually via **Funcheira; Portimão** (20min., 10-13 per day 6:05am-12:15am, €0.90). **Buses** depart from the bus stop next to the municipal market on route EN 124 for **Portimão** (30min., 11 per day 7:15am-6:10pm, €1.80) and the bus stop on the other side of the road, farther away from the castle for **Albufeira** (40min., 8 per day 6:40am-6:25pm, €2.70) and **Lisbon** (4hr., 4 per day 8:20am-6:20pm, €14).

ORIENTATION AND PRACTICAL INFORMATION. The **EVA bus office,** on R. Francisco Pablos, is just next to the municipal food market. (☎282 44 23 38. Open M-F 8am-noon and 2-6pm.) To get to the **tourist office,** R. 25 de Abril, 26-28, from Lgo. António Enes, follow R. Francisco Pablos to its intersection with R. 25 de Abril and continue up the steps; the office lies ahead. (☎282 44 22 55. May-Sept. open daily 9:30am-1pm and 2-5:30pm; Oct.-Apr. M-F 9:30am-1pm and 2-5:30pm.) Just uphill from the tourist office is **Rua da Sé,** with its old cathedral and municipal museum, and **Rua do Castelo,** which curves past the castle. The **Centro de Saúde,** is located just outside of town on R. Cruz de Portugal (☎282 44 00 20).

ACCOMMODATIONS AND FOOD. Inexpensive lodging is hard to come by in Silves. Ask at the tourist office or in any restaurant or bar for help in finding a private *quarto* (about €35 for a double). **Residencial Sousa ❶,** R. Samora Barros, 17, just down the steps from the tourist office, offers small, simple rooms. There is no reception desk; ask one of the cafe workers next door for assistance if the owner isn't around. (☎282 44 25 02. July-Aug. singles €15; doubles €30; triples €45. Sept.-June €12.50/€25/€36. Discounts for longer stays.) Camping is available in the neighboring town of Armação de Pera, accessible by bus (20-30min., 6 per day 7:50am-7:15pm, €1.80). For fresh fruits, vegetables, and fish, try the **mercado municipal** on Lgo. António Enes (open M-Sa 8:30am-2pm). For spectacular views of the town and tasty brick oven pizza, try **Café Inglês ❷,** R. do Castelo, 11, between the cathedral and the castle walls. During summer months, check out the roof-top bar. (☎282 44 25 85. Pizza and entrees, with many vegetarian options €6.50-11.75, salads €2.50-8, desserts €1.75-3.25. Open daily 9:30am-midnight, rooftop bar open June-Sept. 7pm-2am. AmEx/MC/V.) Other restaurants and cafes can be found along the river near the bus stop and the bridge.

SIGHTS AND ENTERTAINMENT. Start at the **Museu Municipal de Arqueologia,** R. das Portas de Loulé, 10, built around a 12th-century Moorish well (open M-Sa 9am-6pm, €1.50). From there head up R. da Sé to the **Sé Velha** (old cathedral). Thought to have been built in the 13th century on the site of a mosque, this small cathedral has undergone a series of renovations, most of them after the 1755 earthquake, but still has an impressive Gothic ceiling. (Open daily 8:30am-8:30pm. Mass M-F 9am, Su 8:30am, 10:15am, and noon. Free.) Just up the hill from the cathedral lies the **castelo.** The structure dates from the 12th century; archaelogical digs within the castle's walls continue to turn up artifacts. It offers great views and occasional art shows in a downstairs room. (☎282 44 56 24. July-Aug. open daily 9am-8pm; Sept.-June 9am-5:30pm. €1.25 for castle walls and garden. Art exhibits extra.) From the castle, turn left onto R. do Castelo and then right down R. Gregório Mascarenhas to get to the Fábrica do Inglês, which hosts the **Museu da Cortiça** (Cork Museum). Silves once served as the center of Portugal's cork industry, and this museum provides a look at both tradition and industrialization in Portugal, with photographs, machines, and plenty of cork in various processing stages. (☎282 44 04 80. Open daily June-Aug. 9:30am-12:45pm and 2-9:45pm; Sept.-May 9:30am-12:45pm and 2-6:15pm. €1.50, children 6-12 €1, under 6 free.) In the same complex as the cork museum, subdued Silves comes to life for 10 days in mid-June with the **Festival da Cerveja** (Beer Festival) when locals crowd the old mill to swig beers of every kind and color. (☎282 44 04 40. Held at the end of June and early July, usually open 6pm-1am. Tickets €8-10, includes 2 mugs of beer.)

ALBUFEIRA ☎289

When the clubs die down in the morning, the drilling begins. Dynamite and concrete have transformed the once pristine cliffs of Albufeira into an uncontainable expanse of high-rise hotels and condominiums. Sun, surf, and beer keep hordes of middle-aged northern Europeans coming on package tours; nary a Portuguese roams the cobblestone streets. A stroll through the old town or along the east edge of the beach hints at Albufeira's humble fishing origins.

TRANSPORTATION. **EVA buses** connect the **train station** (☎289 57 16 16) to the town center (10min., every hr. 7:05am-8:20pm, €1.20). To: **Faro** (45min., 9-14 per day 5:15am-11:52pm, €1.60); **Lagos** (1hr., 10 per day 7:45am-11:45pm, €2.80); **Lisbon** (4-5½hr., 5 per day 7:45am-7:10pm, €10.10-11.50); **Olhão** (1½hr., 6 per day 5:15am-11:55pm, €1.90); **Tavira** (2hr., 13 per day 5:15am-11:52pm, €3.30); **Vila Real de Santo António** (2¼hr., 6 per day 5:15am-11:55pm, €4). The EVA **bus station** (☎289 58 97 55) is in nearby Caliços. **Buses** head to: **Faro** (1hr., 9-15 per day 7:25am-7:30pm, €3.10); **Lagos** (1½hr., 7 per day 8:35am-6pm, €4.25); **Lisbon** (3½-4hr., 5 per day 6:45am-7:30pm, €14); **Tavira** (1½hr., 4 per day 8:45am-11:15pm, €4.30).

ORIENTATION AND PRACTICAL INFORMATION. Albufeira is spread along the Atlantic ocean with R. Latino Coelho, R. Bernardino Sousa, and R. da Bateria bordering the coast. **Av. De Outubro** and **Av. da Liberdade** run perpendicular to the ocean and separate the town's busy cafe- and bar-filled section to the east from a slightly more sedate area to the west. From the new "bus station," a parking lot in a field outside of the city, it is at least a 30min. trek to the town center. The EVA bus from the train station also dumps passengers here. Take the city bus marked "local" from the new bus station to Av. da Liberdade (every 20min., 9am-8pm, €0.55). To reach the **tourist office,** R. 5 de Outubro, 8, follow Av. da Liberdade downhill until reaching Tr. 5 de Outubro and take a right. Turn left when this small street intersects R. 5 Outubro and go straight for 50m. The English-speaking staff at the tourist office offers maps, a list of rooms, and brochures on water sports, including fishing and scuba diving. (☎289 58 52 79. June-Sept. open daily 9:30am-7pm; Oct.-May 9:30am-5:30pm.) Local services include: **taxis,** Radio Taxis (☎289 58 32 30); **banks,** surrounding the touristy Lgo. Eng. Duarte Pacheco; **laundromat,**

at the Bellavista Comercial building on Av. dos Descobrimentos (☎289 58 89 56) a short drive from town or 20min. walk; **emergency** ☎112; **police,** on Av. 25 de Abril (☎289 51 32 03); **pharmacy,** Farmácia Piedade on R. Joáo de Deus (☎289 58 75 50), also posts listing of on-call pharmacies; **Centro de Saúde,** in nearby Caliços (☎289 58 75 50). **Internet access** and **used books** can be found at **Windcafe.com,** in the Shopping Center California, R. Cândido dos Reis, 1. (☎289 58 54 51. Open June-Sept. M-F 10am-10pm, Sa-Su noon-10pm; Oct.-May closes at 8pm.) The **post office** is next to the tourist office on R. 5 de Outubro. (☎289 58 08 70; fax 289 58 32 30. Open M-F 9am-12:30pm, 2:30-6pm.) **Postal code:** 8200.

ACCOMMODATIONS AND FOOD. Most lodgings in Albufeira are booked solid by package tours from late June through mid-September. Fear not—with some luck, reasonably priced accommodations can be found. Ask for *quartos* at the tourist office or at any restaurant or bar. You will most likely be accosted by room renters at the bus and train stations as well. Don't be afraid to barter, but be sure to see the room before agreeing to pay. Most of these places are located at least 10min. from the beach. A single should cost around €15, a double €20; expect prices to rise in June and July. There are a few pensions closer to the center of town. **Pensão Dianamar ❸,** R. Latino Coelho, 36, is close to the beach, but removed from the commotion. It features a charming courtyard, guest kitchen, TV lounge, roof terrace with a gorgeous view of the sea, and clean and comfortable rooms all with bath and balconies, some with sea views. (☎289 58 78 01; www.dianamar.com. June and Sept. singles €25-30; doubles €38-40. July €28-33/€38-45. Aug. €30-35/€53-60. Apr.-May and Oct. €25/€30-33. Mar. €18/€20-23. Closed Nov.-Feb.) **Residencial Capri ❸,** Av. Da Liberdade, 83, offers basic white-walled rooms, many with verandas and all with TVs and bathrooms. Ask the owner for info on the hottest local clubs. (☎289 51 26 91. June-July singles €35; doubles €40; triples €45. Aug.-Sept. and Mar.-May €30/€35/€40. Closed Oct.-Feb.) Open-air camping is illegal, but weary travelers can pay for the ritz and glitz of **Parque de Campismo de Albufeira ❶,** 2km outside town on the road to Ferreiras. It's more like a shopping mall than a campground, with four swimming pools, three restaurants, tennis courts, and a supermarket. (☎289 58 76 29; fax 289 58 76 33. June-Sept. €4.67 per person, €4.17 per car, €4.37 per tent. Oct.-May 50% discount. AmEx/MC/V.) For fresh produce, check out the **mercado municipal** (open Tu-Su 8am-1pm; Th offers the most variety). Follow R. da Figueria from the main bus station and take a right on Es. Vale Pedras. Restaurants and cafes abound in Albufeira; head to **R. Cais Herculano** near the fisherman's beach to dine with a view of the sea.

BEACHES. Albufeira's spectacular slate of **beaches** ranges from the popular **Galé** and **São Rafael** (4-8km toward Lagos) to the chic **Falésia** (10km toward Faro), both accessible by car or taxi. To get to the centrally-located beach **Inatel** from the main square (Lgo. Eng. Duarte Pacheco), follow Av. 25 de Abril to its end and continue down R. Gago Coutinho until you hit sand. The beautiful but packed **Praia de Albufeira** awaits through the gate to the tourist office. It pays to explore beyond these popular options, as many small and uncrowded beaches await discovery.

ENTERTAINMENT. Bars and restaurants line all the streets of Albufeira; clubs blast everything from salsa to techno to *fado* as soon as the sun sets—and continue until it rises. **Classic Bar,** R. Cândido dos Reis, 10, is a popular spot with elaborately decorated drinks and a gaggle of tourists grooving to everything from pop and rock to disco and house. (☎289 51 20 75. Beer €1.75-2. Mixed drinks €5-6. Open daily June-Sept. noon-4am; Oct.-May noon-midnight.) **Café Latino,** R. Latino Coelho, 61, in the old town, is popular with young Portuguese youth and has a pool table, a terrace with a seaside view, and a grungy feel. (☎289 58 51 32. Beer €1.25.

Coffee €0.75. Open Tu-Su 10am-2am.) **Bar Bizzaro,** R. Dr. Frutuoso Silva, 30, offers a mellow vibe and spectacular views of the sea. (☎289 51 28 24. Beer €2.50. Open daily 9am-2am.) Small dance clubs, such as **Twist** and **Bleepers** line Tr. Candido dos Reis, but many of the hottest clubs are just outside of Albufeira (€3-6 by taxi), including **Locomia, IRS Disco,** or **Kiss Disco** (all open daily 2am-6am).

FARO ☎289

Many northern Europeans begin their holidays in Faro (pop. 55,000), the Algarve's capital and largest city, though few stay long enough to absorb its charm and local color. While Faro is primarily a transportation hub, it has a modern shopping district with a slick marina, a quiet historical neighborhood within the walls of the perfectly preserved old town, and calm beaches on the estuary's islands.

TRANSPORTATION

Flights: Aeroporto de Faro (☎289 80 08 00; flight info ☎289 80 08 01), 5km west of the city, has a **police station, bank, post office, car rental companies,** and **tourist info booth.** Open daily 10am-midnight. Buses #14 and 16 run from the street opposite the bus station to the airport (20min.; weekdays 24 per day 7:10am-9:40pm, weekends and holidays 20 per day 8am-9:40pm; €0.90).

Trains: Station, Lgo. Estação (☎289 80 17 26), near the center of town next to the bus station. To: **Albufeira** (45min., 6 per day 7:20am-11:15pm, €1.60); **Beja** (3hr.; 9:05am, 5:30pm; €7.10); **Évora** (5hr.; 9:05am, 5:30pm; €9.10); **Lagos** (2hr., 6 per day 8:05am-9:05pm, €4.10); **Lisbon** (5-6hr., 6 per day 7:20am-11:15pm, €12.30); **Vila Real de Santo António** (1½hr., 13 per day 6:15am-12:36am, €2.80).

Buses: EVA, Av. República (☎289 89 97 00). To: **Albufeira** (1hr., 8-17 per day 6:30am-6:45pm, €3.10); **Beja** (3-3½hr., 7 per day 7:45am-4pm, €8); **Lagos** (2hr., 8 per day 7:30am-5:30pm, €3.80); **Olhão** (20min., every 20-40min. 7:15am-7:30pm, €1.10); **Tavira** (1hr., 11 per day 7:15am-7:30pm, €2.25); **Vila Real de Santo António** (1½hr., 9 per day 7:15am-6:20pm, €3.25). **Renex,** Av. República (☎289 81 29 80), provides long-distance service to: **Braga** via Lisbon (8½hr., 9 per day 5:30am-1:30am, €20); **Lisbon** (4hr., 11-15 per day 5:30am-1:30am, €14); **Porto** via Lisbon (7½hr., 6-13 per day 5:30am-1:30am, €19). **Intersul** (☎289 89 97 70) runs to **Sevilla, Spain** (€15).

Taxis: Táxis Rotáxi (☎289 89 57 95). **Táxis Auto Faro** (☎289 89 22 75). Taxis gather near Jardim Manuel Bívar (by the tourist office) and at the bus and train stations. Look carefully, as they are not well marked.

ORIENTATION AND PRACTICAL INFORMATION

Faro's center hugs the **Doca de Recreio,** a marina lined with luxuriously apportioned ships and bordered by the Jardim Manuel Bívar and **Praça Dr. Francisco Gomes.** From the train or bus stations, follow Av. da República towards the harbor. Enter the old city through the **Arco da Vila,** a stone arch next to the tourist office, on the far side of the garden that borders Pr. Dr. Francisco Gomes.

Tourist Office: R. Misericórdia, 8 (☎289 80 36 04), at the entrance to the old town. From the bus or train station, turn right down Av. República along the harbor, then turn left past the garden. English spoken. Open June-Aug. daily 9:30am-7pm; Sept.-May daily 9:30am-5:30pm. The **regional tourism office** is on Av. 5 de Outubro, 18-20 (☎289 80 04 77). Open June-Aug. M-F 9am-7pm; Sept.-May M-F 9am-5:30pm.

Currency Exchange: Cota Cambios, R. Dr. Francisco Gomes, 26 (☎289 82 57 35), off Pr. Gomes. Open June M-F 8:30am-8pm, Sa-Su 10am-6pm; July-Sept. M-F 8:30am-9pm, Sa 10am-8pm, Su 10am-7pm; Oct.-May M-F 8:30am-6:30pm, Sa 10am-2:30pm.

Laundromat: Sólimpa, R. Batista Lopes, 30 (☎289 82 29 81), up R. 1 de Maio. Wash and dry €2 per kg, 4kg minimum. Open M-F 9am-1pm and 3-7pm, Sa 9am-1pm.

Emergency: ☎112. **Police:** R. Polícia da Segurança Pública (☎289 82 20 22).

Hospital: R. Leão Pinedo (☎289 89 11 00), just north of town.

Internet Access: Free at the **Instituto Português de Juventude,** next to the youth hostel. Open M-F 9am-7pm; 30min. limit. Also at the **Ciencia Viva** museum, R. Comandante Francisco Manuel (☎289 89 09 20), near the old city. From Pr. Gomes, walk through the gardens and turn right, heading toward the docks. €2, students €1. W 50% off. Open July-Sept. 15 Tu-Su 4-11pm; Sept. 16-June Tu-F 10am-5pm, Sa-Su 3-7pm.

Post Office: Lgo. Carmo (☎289 89 98 99), across from the Igreja de Nossa Senhora do Carmo. Open M-F 8:30am-6:30pm, Sa 9am-12:30pm. **Postal Code:** 8000.

ACCOMMODATIONS

Lodgings surround the bus and train stations. Most of the low-end budget *pensões* are plain but adequate.

Pousada da Juventude (HI), R. Polícia de Segurança Pública (☎/fax 289 82 65 21), opposite the police station. Sleep easy at the cheapest place in town. Bunk beds, sunny TV atrium, and kitchen. June 16-Sept. 15 dorms €9.50; doubles €23, with bath €26.50. Sept. 16-June 15 €7.50/€18/€21. AmEx/MC/V. ❶

Pensão-Residencial Central, Lgo. Terreiro Do Bispo, 12 (☎289 80 72 91), near the pedestrian area up R. 1 de Maio. Clean, bright, comfortable rooms, all with bath and TV, some with terraces. Doubles €30-50, depending on size and if it has a terrace. ❷

Residencial Madalena, R. Conselheiro Bivar, 109 (☎289 80 58 06; fax 289 80 58 07), close to the train and bus stations. Follow R. Gil Eanes to R. Infante Dom Henrique and take a right. 22 warmly-decorated rooms with dark wooden moldings and large windows. All have bath, phone, and TV. July-Sept. breakfast included. July-Sept. singles €43.50; doubles €57. Oct.-June €25-30/€35-40. ❹

Pensão São Filipe, R. Infante Dom Henrique, 55, 2nd fl. (☎/fax 289 82 41 82). From the train station, go up R. Ventura Coelho 3 blocks and turn right onto R. Infante Dom Henrique. Close to the center of town and only a 5min. walk from the train and bus stations, this place offers 10 charming rooms, all with TV and fans, some with bath. July-Sept. singles €35, with bath €40; doubles €40, with bath €50. Apr.-June €25/€30/€25/€35. Jan.-Mar. and Nov.-Dec. €20/€25/€20/€30.❸

Pensão-Residencial Oceano, R. Ivens, 21, 2nd fl. (☎289 82 33 49). From Pr. Gomes, head up R. 1 de Maio; it's 1 block up on the right. Rooms with bath, phone, and TV. Breakfast €2. July-Sept. singles €35; doubles €45; triples €60. Oct.-June €25/€35/€45. AmEx/MC/V. ❸

FOOD

Almonds and figs are native to the Algarve; local bakeries take good advantage of this and transform them into delicious marzipan and fig desserts. Faro has many cafes along **R. Conselheiro Bívar** and **Dr. Gomes.** At the **market,** away from the center in Lgo. Dr. Francisco Sá Carneiro, locals barter fresh seafood (open daily 8am-1:30pm). Stroll to R. Santo António, a pedestrian district where costly *marisqueiras* and credit cards reign, or shop at **Supermercado Minipreço,** Lgo. Terreiro do Bispo, 8-10. (☎289 80 77 34. Open M-Sa 9am-8pm.)

Sol e Jardim, Pr. Ferreira de Almeida, 22-23 (☎289 82 00 30). Great restaurant featuring pasta (€6.30-8.90), salads and soups (€1-7.40) and (what else?) fresh seafood (€4.70-9.50). Casual atmosphere hosts an international crowd. Traditional Portuguese music performed every F night (approx. 8:30pm). Open daily July 15-Sept. 15 10am-11pm, Sept. 16-July 14 M-Sa 10am-3pm and 6:30-11pm. AmEx/MC/V. ❷

Creperia, Pr. Ferreira d'Almeida, 27 (☎918 95 51 21), at the end of R. 1 de Maio. Delight in a variety of gourmet crepe options, from asparagus and cream to hot chocolate, kiwi, banana, and apple (€2-5.80). Open July-Sept. M-Tu 10am-10:20pm, W-Sa 10am-midnight, Su 6pm-midnight. Oct.-June daily 10am-8pm. ❶

La Pizza, R. Monte Gordo, 3 (☎289 806 023), parallel to R. Conselheiro Bivar. Excellent pizza and other Italian fare. Pizza €6.30-7.45, pasta €7.45-9.15, soups and salads €1.30-3.55, crepe desserts and *gelado* €1.85-3.10. 20% discount on take-out orders. Open daily noon-2pm and 7pm-midnight. ❷

SIGHTS

Faro's old town is a jewel—untouristed and traditional, it is a medley of ornate churches, museums, and shops selling local handicrafts. From Pr. Gomes, walk through the gardens to get to the entrance of the old town. Next to the tourist office, the early 19th-century **Arco da Vila** pierces the old city wall.

CAPELA DOS OSSOS. Step into **Igreja de Nossa Senhora do Carmo** to inspect the small Capela dos Ossos (Chapel of Bones), built from the remains of monks originally buried in the church's former cemetery. More than 1245 skulls and multitudes of bones are arrayed in geometric designs on the walls and ceiling. A sign above the door reads "Stop here and think if this fate will befall you." *(Lgo. Carmo. ☎289 82 44 90. Open May-Sept. 10am-1pm and 3-6pm; Oct.-Apr. M-F 10am-1pm and 3-5pm, Sa 10am-1pm. Church free, chapel €0.75.)*

MUSEU DA MARINHA. The Museu da Marinha displays three notable boat models: the boat that took Vasco da Gama on his journey to India in 1497, a boat used on a Portuguese expedition up the Congo River in 1482, and a boat that out-gunned several Turkish galleons in 1717. *(☎289 80 36 01. Open M-F 2:30-4:30pm. €1.)*

CATHEDRAL (SÉ). A narrow road leads through an Arab *portico* to the Renaissance cathedral, which stands in a deserted square. The **Capela do Rosário,** decorated with 17th-century *azulejos* and a red *chinoiserie* organ that interrupts the cathedral's understated Renaissance interior. Under the cathedral—a site once sacred to Romans, Visigoths, and Moors—lie traces of Neolithic civilization. The striking **cloister** is an ideal spot to relax with a book. *(Cathedral currently undergoing extensive renovations with no set completion date; check with the tourist office.)*

NIGHTLIFE AND BEACHES

Sidewalk **cafes** crowd the pedestrian walkways off the garden in the center of town, and several **bars** with young crowds liven R. Conselheiro Bívar and its side streets. Faro's sandy beach, **Praia de Faro,** hides on an islet off the coast with the **Parque National da Ria Formosa** on one side. Take bus #16 from the bus station or the stop in front of the tourist office, just across the garden from Pr. Gomes. (5-10min, every hr. 8am-8:40pm, €0.90.) Ferries go to nearby **Ilha do Farol,** a less crowded beach from June-Sept. (5 per day 9:30am-6pm. €3.60.)

OLHÃO ☎289

Olhão (ol-yow-n), 8km east of Faro, continues to be the largest fishing port in the Algarve. For hundreds of years, the few inhabitants of the area were fishermen, and modern locals have continued the tradition, helping to create one of Portugal's most productive fishing industries. Still, there is more to Olhão than tuna and cuttlefish. Beyond this no-frills town lie gorgeous beaches and the Parque Natural da Ria Formosa (see p. 643), with its numerous species of exotic birds.

TRANSPORTATION. The **train station** is on Av. Combatentes da Grande Guerra one block from Av. República. (☎289 70 53 78. Open daily 6:20-11am, 11:40am-7:30pm, 8:10-10:45pm.) **Trains** run to: **Faro** (10min., 17 per day 6:54am-10:39pm, €0.80); **Tavira** (30min., 6 per day 6:27am-12:45am, €1.20); **Vila Real de Santo António** (1¼hr., 6 per day 6:27am-12:45am, €2.10). The **bus station** is on R. General Humberto Delgado, one block from Av. República. (☎289 70 21 57. Open daily 7am-8pm.) **Eva buses** run to: **Faro** (20min., 11 per day 7:35am-7:50pm, €1.05); **Tavira** (40min., 11 per day 7:35am-7:50pm, €1.75); **Vila Real de Santo António** (1½hr., 9 per day 7:35am-6:40pm, €2.90).

ORIENTATION AND PRACTICAL INFORMATION. To reach the **port,** locate tree-lined **Av. República.** From the train station, turn left on Av. Combatentes da Grande Guerra and take a right on Av. República, after passing the Palace of Justice (10-15min.). From the bus station, turn right on R. General Humberto Delgado and then take another right onto Av. República (5-10min.). Once on Av. República, go straight until reaching Olhão's main church. Veer left on R. do Comercial and continue as far as possible. From the end of R. do Comercial, turn left on R. Olhanense and follow the street until it reaches Av. 5 de Outubro and the sea. The **tourist office** is on Lgo. Sebastião Martins Mestre, a small road that intersects with the end of R. Comércio. Its English-speaking staff has maps, ferry schedules, and sometimes free **luggage storage** during the day—ask nicely. (☎289 71 39 36. May-Sept. open Tu-Th 9:30am-7pm, F-M 9:30am-noon and 1-5:30pm; Oct.-Apr. open M-F 9:30am-noon and 1-5:30pm.) In an **emergency,** call ☎112. The **post office** is at Av. República, 17 (☎289 70 06 03; open M-F 8:30am-6pm). **Postal code:** 8700.

ACCOMMODATIONS AND FOOD. **Pensão Bela Vista ❷,** R. Teófilo Braga, 65-67, is off a side street around the corner from the tourist office. Nine comfortable rooms have TVs, and some come with baths. Exit the tourist office, follow Tr. da Lagoa to R. Teófilo Braga and turn right. (☎289 70 25 38. Singles €15, with bath €20; doubles €30, with bath €35-40.) **Pensão Boémia ❸,** R. Cerca, 20, from the train or bus station, take Av. República and turn right on R. 18 de Junho. After four blocks, turn left again. Boémia is away from the shore at the center of town but has all the modern amenities. Cheerful, sunny, and immaculate rooms, all with bath, TV, and A/C, some with large terraces. The friendly owner will give you all the info you need to explore the town and beaches. (☎/fax 289 71 45 13. Breakfast included. June-Aug. singles €30-35; doubles €45. Sept.-May €25-30/€35. AmEx/MC/V.) Olhão's highly recommended year-round campground is the **Parque de Campismo dos Bancários do Sul e Ilhas ❶.** It's off the highway outside of town and can be accessed by "Camara Municipal de Olhão" buses (9 per day 7:45am-7:15pm) which leave from in front of the gardens on R. 5 de Outubro. Amenities include a swimming pool, market, bar, and restaurant. (☎289 70 03 00; fax 289 70 03 90. Showers included. July-Aug. €3.50 per person, €2.35-5.50 per tent, €2.75 per car. June and Sept. €2.80/€2.05-4.65/€2.30. Oct.-May €1.70/€1.30-2.80/€1.40.)

Supermercado São Nicolau, R. General Humberto Delgado, 62, lies up the block from the bus station (open M-Sa 8am-8pm). The **market** is housed in two red brick buildings adjacent to the city gardens along the river, near Pr. Patrão J. Lopes (open daily 7am-1:30pm). Many eateries on Av. 5 de Outubro grill the day's catch. At the busy **Casa de Pasto O Bote,** Av. 5 de Outubro, 122, pick your slippery, silvery meal from the trays of fresh fish and watch it get charcoal-grilled right before your eyes. Meat dishes are also offered, but it's the seafood that draws the crowds. (☎289 72 11 83. Entrees €5.50-8. Open M-Sa 11am-3pm and 7-11pm).

DAYTRIPS FROM OLHÃO

ARMONA, CULATRA, AND FAROL

Ferries go to Armona from Olhão's dock (15min.; June and Sept. M-F 9 per day 7:40am-7:30pm, Sa-Su 11 per day 8am-7:30pm; July-Aug. 13 per day 7:30am-8pm; Oct.-May 8:30am, noon, 5pm; last return in June 8pm, July-Aug. 8:30pm; €0.95). Another fleet serves Culatra (30min.; June-Aug. every 2hr. 7am-7:30pm; Sept.-May 4 per day 7am-6:30pm; €0.95; last return June-Aug. 8pm) and Farol (45min.; June-Aug. every 2hr. 7am-7:30pm; Sept.-May 4 per day 7am-6:30pm; last return in June-Aug. 8:20pm, €1.20).

Long expanses of uncrowded, sandy beach and sparkling sapphire sea surround **Ilhas Armona** and **Culatra,** the two major islands off the coast of Olhão. Armona is the closest to reach, followed by Culatra, and then **Farol,** at the farthest end of Culatra; all three are easy daytrips from Olhão. The farther away you go, the quieter the beaches become, although they all have but a fraction of the human traffic of the rest of the Algarve. The islands and sandbars just offshore fence off the Atlantic, creating an important wetland habitat, the **Parque Nacional da Ria Formosa,** for birds, fish, and other creatures. During the winter, roughly one-third of Europe's flamingo population can be found here. If you miss the last ride back from Armona, bungalows are available at Orbitur's **campsite** ❺ on the central path, five minutes from the dock, but at €104 for a two night minimum stay, it's probably better not to find yourself stranded here. (☎289 71 41 73. Open May-Oct. July-Aug. 2 night minimum €104. No minimum rest of the year. June and Sept. €39, May and Oct. €33.)

TAVIRA ☎281

Tavira (pop. 12,000) is an inviting town with cobblestone streets and whitewashed houses, set along the Rio Gilão. Stunning nearby beaches bring tourists in the summer, but Tavira has managed to keep a calm and traditional feel. Much more than a beach town, Tavira offers a gentle place to spend time relaxing among the local fisherman, good restaurants, and welcoming atmosphere.

TRANSPORTATION

Trains (☎281 32 23 54; info ☎808 20 82 08) leave Tavira for: **Faro** (40min., 10-17 per day 6:26am-10:12pm, €1.61); **Olhão** (30min., 12-17 per day 6:26am-10:12pm, €1.20); **Vila Real de Santo António** (30min., 9-13 per day 6:55am-1:10am, €1.20). To get to **Albufeira** transfer in Faro; for **Lagos,** transfer in Faro and/or Tunes. **EVA buses** (☎281 32 25 46) leave from the station upriver from Pr. República for: **Faro** (1hr., 12-13 per day 6:50am-7:10pm, €2.25); **Olhão** (45min., 12-13 per day 6:50am-7:10pm, €1.75); **Vila Real de Santo António** (40min., 6-10 per day 6:55am-7:20pm, €2.10).

ORIENTATION AND PRACTICAL INFORMATION

From the **train station,** it's a short 5-10min. walk down Av. Dr. Teixeira de Azevedo to the town center. Alternatively, catch the local TUT bus to the town center (10min., every 30min. 8am-8pm, €0.80) or call a taxi (☎281 32 15 44; about €3.50). The **tourist office** on R. Galeria, 9 is staffed by English speakers. (☎281 32 25 11. Open daily July-Aug. 9:30am-7pm; Sept.-June Tu-Th 9:30am-5:30pm, F-M 9:30am-1pm and 2-5:30pm.) Rent **bikes** and **scooters** from **Loris Rent,** on R. Galeria next to the tourist office. (☎281 32 52 03 or 964 07 92 33. Mountain bikes €4-5 per day. Scooters €15-24 per day. Open M-F 9:30am-1pm and 3-6:30pm, Sa 9:30am-1pm and 3-5pm.) Local services include: **emergency** ☎112; **police** ☎281 32 20 22; **Centro de Saúde** ☎281 32 90 00. Free **Internet access** is available at **Sala Internet Camana Municipal de Tavira,** on the corner of R. da Liberdade and the Pr. da República. (Open M-F 10am-10pm, Sa 10am-8pm.) A faster connection is available across from the bus station at **Snack-Bar Bela Fria,** R. dos Pelames, 1. (Open daily 9am-2am. €1 per 15min.) The **post office,** is on R. Liberdade, 64, one block uphill from Pr. República (open M-F 9am-6pm). **Postal code:** 8800.

ACCOMMODATIONS AND FOOD

Like elsewhere in the Algarve, accommodations fill quickly in the summer; it's wise to call ahead for a reservation. **Pensão Residencial Lagôas Bica ❷,** R. Almirante Cândido dos Reis, 24, is highly recommended. Cross the pedestrian bridge from the side of town with the bus station and continue straight down R. A. Cabreira; turn right and go down one block. This *pensão*, run by a warm and hospitable woman, has well-furnished rooms, an outdoor patio, a lounge, washing facilities, and a fridge for guest use. (☎281 32 22 52. July-Sept. singles €18; doubles €28, with bath €38. €2.40 less in winter.) Back on the other side of the river, **Pensão Residencial Castelo ❹,** R. Liberdade, 22, has bright, spacious rooms all with bath, phones, A/C, and TV, and apartments with kitchenettes. (☎281 32 07 90; fax 281 32 07 99. Handicap accessible. Breakfast included. July singles €35; doubles €45; apartments €60 (4-person max.). Aug. €40/€50/€70. Sept.-June €25/€30/€45.) **Residencial Bela Fria ❺,** located across from the bus stop at R. dos Pelames, 1, has pleasant rooms all with bath, phones, TV, and A/C. Some rooms have a view of the river and/or a terrace. The pretty roof terrace affords river views for all guests. Internet access is available in the adjoining cafe. (☎/fax 281 32 53 75. Transportation to Faro airport €20. **Luggage storage** €0.75 per day. July singles €50; doubles €70; extra bed €18. Aug. €60/€90/€18. June and Sept. €35/€50/€15. Oct.-May €25/€40/€12.50. MC/V.)

ALENTEJO

The vast Alentejo region dominates the lower central section of Portugal and appeals to travelers desiring to escape the commotion of Lisbon or the wilds of the Algarve for a more historic Portuguese setting. Its arid plains stretch to the horizon, punctuated only by olive trees. The region is known for its wine and its cork—more than two-thirds of the world's cork comes from here. Évora, Elvas, and other medieval towns preserve their pristine state in the Alto Alentejo, while Beja remains the only major town on the seemingly endless Baixo Alentejo plain. The Alentejo is best in the spring; be prepared for fiery temperatures in summer.

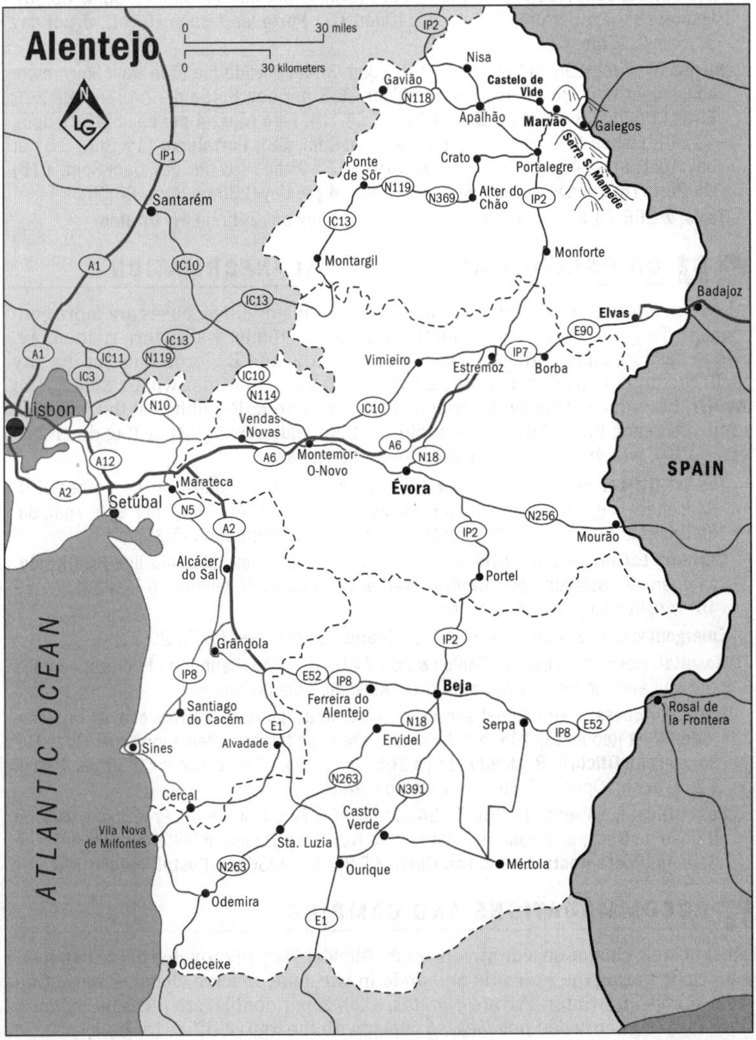

ÉVORA ☎266

Designated a World Heritage site by UNESCO, Évora (pop. 35,000) is the capital and largest city of the Alentejo region. The historic center is home to medieval palaces, churches, and Roman ruins. University of Évora (UÉ) students liven up the town, especially during the end of class celebration of *Queima das Fitas* (last week of May) when festivities culminate with the burning of graduation ribbons.

TRANSPORTATION

Trains: Av. dos Combatentes de Grande Guerra (☎/fax 266 70 21 25). To: **Beja** (2hr., 4 per day 7:35am-7:15pm, €4-5.50); **Faro** (5hr., 4 per day 7:35am-7:15pm, €8.20); **Lisbon** (3hr., 5 per day 5:15am-12:40am, €7) **Porto** via Lisbon (6½hr., 3 per day 5:15am-2:15pm, €13.20).

Buses: Av. Sebastião (☎266 76 94 10), about 300m outside the town wall. Much more convenient than trains. To: **Beja** (1-1½hr., 6-8 per day 8:45am-12:45am, €7.20); **Elvas** (1½-2hr., 3-5 per day 8am-9:05pm, €4.70); **Faro** (5hr., 4 per day 8:45am-6pm, €9.50); **Lisbon** (2-2½hr., every 1-1½hr. 6am-8pm, €8); **Portalegre** (1¾-2hr., 3-5 per day 10:15am-5:40pm, €4.70-6.70); **Braga** (7¾-9¾hr., 4-6 per day 6am-8pm, €15) via **Porto** (6-8½hr., €13.50); **Setúbal** (1¾hr., 4 per day 8:30am-8pm, €6.50).

Taxis: ☎266 73 47 34 or 266 73 47 35. Taxis hang out 24hr. in **Pr. Giraldo.**

ORIENTATION AND PRACTICAL INFORMATION

Although Évora is accessible by train from most major cities, buses are more convenient. To get to Pr. Giraldo from the **bus station** (10min. walk), turn right up Av. São Sebastião, and continue straight when it turns into R. Serpa Pinto at the city wall. No direct bus connects the **train station** to the center of town; to walk, go up Av. Dr. Baronha and continue straight as it turns into R. República at the city wall, until you reach **Pr. do Giraldo.** To avoid the hike, hail a taxi (€3) or flag down bus #6 (€0.70), which stops a short way down the tracks.

Tourist Office: Pr. Giraldo, 65 (☎266 70 26 71), in the plaza at the corner of R. Raimundo. Luggage storage. Wheelchair accessible. Open Apr.-Sept. M-F 9am-7pm, Sa-Su 9am-12:30pm and 2-5:30pm; Oct.-Mar. 9am-12:30pm and 2-5:30pm.

Currency Exchange: 24hr. **ATM** outside the tourist office. Several banks line **Pr. Giraldo,** all open M-F 8:30am-3pm. **Crédito Predial Português,** Pr. Giraldo, 67 (☎266 74 50 40) is right next to the tourist office.

Emergency: ☎112. **Police:** R. Francisco Soares Lusitano (☎266 70 20 22).

Hospital: Hospital do Espirito Santo (☎266 74 01 00), Lgo. Senhor da Pobreza, near the city wall and the intersection with R. Dr. Augusto Eduardo Nunes.

Internet Access: Free Internet access is available at **Instituto Portuguese da la Juventude,** R. da Republica, 105, but during the afternoon there is often a long line. Open M-F 9am-11pm. **Oficin@,** R. Moeda, 27 (☎266 70 73 12), off Pr. Giraldo. €0.50 per 10min. €2.50 per hr. Open Tu-F 8pm-3am, Sa 9pm-2am.

Post Office: R. Olivença (☎266 74 54 82; fax 266 74 54 86). From Pr. Giraldo, walk up R. João de Deus, take your 1st right onto R. Nova, the 1st left uphill, then right at Pr. de Sertória. **Posta Restante** and **fax.** Open M-F 8:30am-6:30pm. **Postal Code:** 7000.

ACCOMMODATIONS AND CAMPING

Most hostels cluster on side streets off **Pr. Giraldo.** They're crowded in the summer, especially during the *Feira de São João* in late June; reserve ahead. Prices often drop €2.50-5 in winter. Private *quartos*, €20-25 per double, are pleasant summer alternatives to crowded *pensões*, so check with the tourist office for listings.

Pousada da Juventude (HI), R. Miguel Bombarda, 40 (☎266 74 48 48; fax 266 74 48 43). From the tourist office, cross Pr. Giraldo and take a right on R. República, then bear left on R. Miguel Bombarda; the hostel is on the right. Lounge with pool table, kitchen, and laundry room. Luggage storage available. Breakfast included. Lockout 11am-3pm. In summer, reserve through **Movijem** (☎213 59 60 00; reserva@movijovem.pt). June 16-Sept. 15 dorms €12.50; doubles with bath €30. Sept. 16-June 15 €10/€25. €2 more per night without HI card. ❶

Casa Palma, R. Bernardo Matos, 29A (☎266 70 35 60). Take a right out of the tourist office and then the 1st right onto R. Bernardo Matos; the house is 3 blocks down on the left. This pleasant, well-kept house is over 100 years old, and each room has a unique, homey atmosphere. Singles €20, with bath and TV €25; doubles €30/€40. ❷

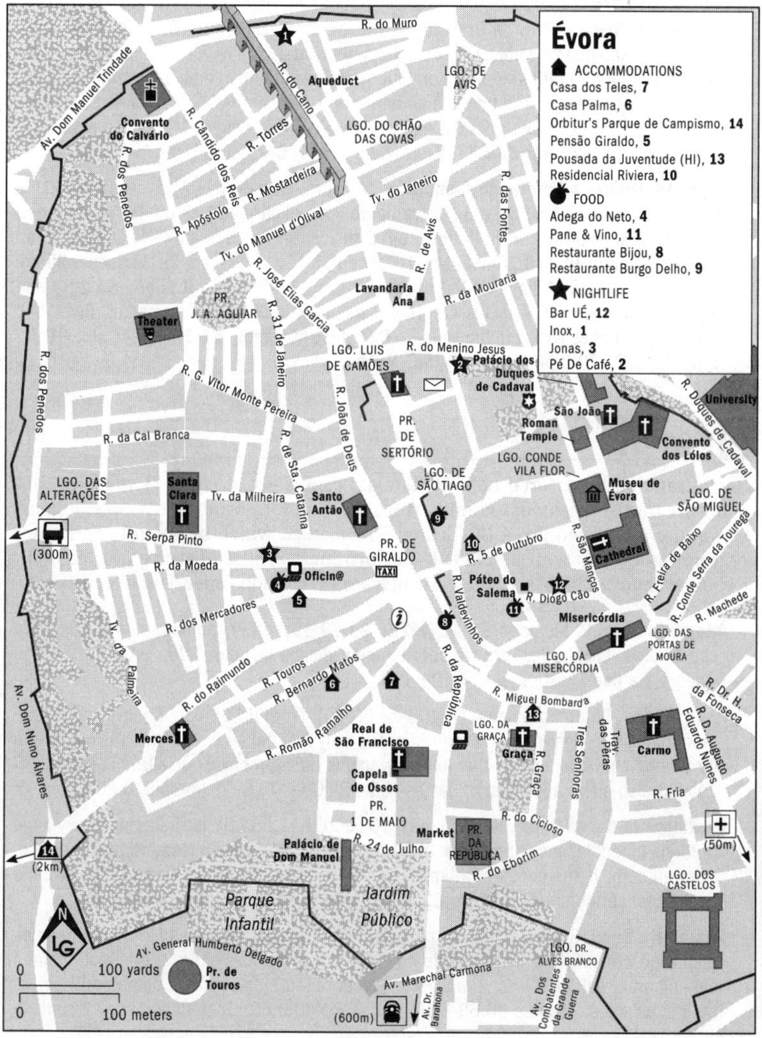

ALENTEJO

Casa dos Teles, R. Romão Ramalho, 31 (☎266 70 24 53). Take a right out of the tourist office and then another onto R. Romão Ramalho; it's 2 blocks down on the left. This unremarkable hostel with plain but clean rooms is often less crowded than other accommodations in Évora. June-Sept. singles €20-25, with bath €25-30; doubles €30-35, with bath €35-40; triples €35-40. Oct.-May €5-10 less. ❷

Pensão Giraldo, R. Mercadores, 27 (☎266 70 58 33). From the tourist office, turn left and walk 2 blocks, then turn left out of Pr. Giraldo onto R. Mercadores. All rooms have TVs. Reserve a week ahead, and show up within 15min. of your stated arrival time. 10% discount for 2 or more nights. July-Sept. singles €25, with bath €35; doubles €35, with bath €50; triples €55; quads €65. Mar.-June €22/€29/€25/€35/€40/€45. Oct.-Feb. €20/€28/€28/€33-35/€38/€40. AmEx/MC/V. ❷

Residencial Riviera, R. 5 de Octubro, 49 (☎/fax 266 73 72 10). Centrally located off Pr. Giraldo and near the university hang-outs, this hotel-style *residencial* has reasonable prices for its 4-star rating. Rooms combine traditional Alentejo motifs with modern comforts. Hardwood floors, soft beds, large bathrooms, TVs, and A/C complement the rustic decor. Included breakfast offers a large variety. May-Oct. singles M-Th €60, F-Su €70; doubles M-Th €67.50, F-Su €77.50. Nov.-April €40/€67.50/€57.50/€75. ❺

Camping: Orbitur's Parque de Campismo de Évora, Estrada das Alcáçovas (☎266 70 51 90; fax 266 70 98 30), a 3-star campground, which branches off at the bottom of R. Raimundo. A 30min. walk to town, but 2 buses run to the nearby Vila Lusitano stop from Pr. Giraldo: #5 (10-20min.; M-F 10 per day 7:45am-7:15pm, Sa 3 buses 8:25am-12:35pm) and #8 (15min.; M-F 6 per day 9:40am-5:45pm, Sa 9:25am, Su 2:50 and 7:05pm) Both €0.70. A taxi is €3. Has a washing machine and a market. Reception 8am-10pm. Prices vary with the season. €2-3.50 per person, €1-1.70 per child; €1.50-5 per tent; €1.70-3 per car. AmEx/MC/V. ❶

FOOD

Restaurants are scattered near **Pr. Giraldo,** especially along **R. Mercadores,** but many are tourist-oriented; to find Portuguese food for Portuguese people, it helps to wander a bit away from the center. The **market,** which sells crafts and other regional goods as well as cheese and produce, is just past the corner of R. República and R. Cicioso when walking from Pr. Giraldo (open Tu-Su 8am-1pm).

Adega do Neto, R. Mercadores, 46 (☎266 94 73 19), off Pr. Giraldo, across from Pensão Giraldo. Locals flock for typical Alentejan dishes for under €6. Entrees €3.50-5. Open M-Sa noon-3:30pm and 7-10pm. ❶

Pane & Vino, Páteo do Salema (☎266 74 69 60). From Pr. Giraldo, go up R. 5 de Outubro and take a right onto R. Diogo Cão. The only real Italian restaurant in Évora. Popular among students, who gather in the spacious dining room. Specializes in pizza (€5-11) but also offers a long list of pastas (€8-15). Open Tu-Su noon-3pm, 6:30-11pm. ❷

Restaurante Burgo Delho, R. de Burgos, 10 (☎266 22 58 58), is characterized by large portions of local dishes and above average service. In this small restaurant, a couple of extra euros buys the constant attentiveness of the friendly owner, attractive decor, and cool, quiet surroundings. Entrees €5-8.50. Open M-Sa noon-3pm, 7-10pm. ❷

Pastelaria Bijou, R. da República, 15, just off Pr. Giraldo. A variety of excellent pastries displayed beneath the long, marble countertop can be enjoyed in the air-conditioned seating area. Ask for a *briza* (pastry with sweet potato, almond, and cinnamon), one of their specialties. Pastries €0.60-1.40. Coffee €0.40-0.60. Open daily 7am-7:30pm. ❶

SIGHTS

CAPELA DOS OSSOS. The Capela dos Ossos (Chapel of Bones) warmly welcomes visitors: "*Nós ossos que aqui estamos, pelos vossos esperamos*" (We bones that are here are waiting for yours). In order to clear many local cemeteries and create needed space in town, three Franciscan monks used the remains of over 5000 people to build this chapel. Femurs, skulls, tibias, and pelvic bones line the wall and ceiling, while the bones of the three founders lie unexposed in stone sarcophagi to the right of the altar. *(Pr. 1 de Mayo. Follow R. República from Pr. Giraldo, then take a right into the Pr. 1 de Mayo; enter the chapel through the door of the Convento de São Francisco to the right of the church steps. ☎266 70 46 21. Open Apr. and June-Sept. M-Sa 9am-1pm and 2:30-6pm, Su 10am-1pm; May and Oct.-Mar. M-Sa 9am-1pm and 2:30-5:30pm, Su 10am-1pm. €1, photography permit €0.50.)*

ROMAN TEMPLE. Columns still stand in Lgo. Conde do Vila Flor as a reminder of Évora's long history as an important city. The small temple dates back to the time of Roman occupation in the 2nd and 3rd century.

CHURCH AND PALACE. Immediately facing the Roman temple is the Igreja de São João Evangelista (1485). The church and the ducal palace next door are owned by the Cadaval family, descendants of the dukes. The interior of the church is covered with dazzling *azulejos*. *(Lgo. Conde do Vila Flor. Open Tu-Su 10am-12:30pm and 2-6pm. €2.50 for church, €4.20 for church and exhibition hall in neighboring palace.)*

CATHEDRAL. With its asymmetrical towers, this 12th-century cathedral is darker and less ostentatious than other churches in Évora. The 12 Apostles adorning the doorway are masterpieces of medieval sculpture. The **cloister** was designed in the 14th-century Romanesque style, with stairs spiraling to the terrace. The **Museu de Arte Sacra,** in a gallery above the nave, houses the cathedral's treasury and a 13th-century ivory *Virgem do paraíso*. *(From the center of Pr. Giraldo, head up R. 5 de Outubro to the end. Cathedral open daily 9am-12:30pm and 2-5pm. Free. Cloisters open daily 9am-noon and 2-4:30pm. Museum open Tu-Su 9am-noon and 2-4:30pm. Cloisters and museum €2.50. July-Sept. 15 ticket includes visit to the tower. For just the cloister on M €1.50.)*

NIGHTLIFE

Évora's nightlife is fueled largely by the students from the university, who fill the bars after midnight and then move on to the clubs.

Jonas, R. Serpa Pinta, 67 (☎964 82 16 47), down the street from Pr. Firaldo. Orange textured walls give this bar a warm, cavernous feel, while the blue-lit room upstairs is made for chilling. The crowd, mostly 20- and 30-somethings, arrives after midnight. Popular Brazilian caipirinhas €2.50. Open M-Sa 10:30pm-3am.

Bar UÉ, R. Diogo Cão, 19 (☎266 74 39 24). From Pr. Giraldo go up R. 5 de Outubro and take a right onto R. Diogo Cão, then follow the road around to the left; UÉ is on left. Only students are allowed into this university bar. The place to meet people before deciding to head out elsewhere. Open Tu-Su noon-2am; serves food 1-3pm and 7:30-9:30pm.

Pé De Café, R. do Menino Jesus. Popular among a young, cell-phone toting crowd. Sit on the cafe's patio and enjoy a beer between dinner and clubbing. Open daily noon-1am.

Inox, R. do Muro, 3. Along the aqueduct and to the right. With its industrial look, Inox is the dominant player of the Évora clubbing scene. 20-something crowd gets going around 1am. Transitions from bar to disco at 3am. No cover during the week, €2.50 minimum consumption on weekends. Open Tu-Sa 10:30pm-5am.

ELVAS ☎268

Even if you're just stopping over in Elvas on your way elsewhere, a day here is not a wasted one. 12km from the Spanish border, the quiet hill town has a pleasant main square and steep streets that lead down to the fortified city walls. Although like many Alentejo towns, Elvas has cobblestone streets and a castle, the town's varied architecture is exceptionally well-preserved and uniquely integrated.

TRANSPORTATION. The nearest **train station** (☎268 62 28 16) is 3km away in the town of Fontainhas and has service to **Badajoz, Spain** (17min., 12:12pm, €0.80). A **taxi** (☎268 62 22 87) is the only transport from the train station to town (€5). **Buses** are the best transportation option from Évora, with a convenient **station** (☎268 62 28 75) and go to: **Albufeira** (5½hr., 6:40am, €11); **Beja** (3½hr., 6:40am, €8.50); **Caia,** on the border (30min.; 6:40am, 2pm; €1.20); **Évora** (1½hr., 3-4 per day 6:40am-4:25pm, €4.70); **Faro** (6½hr., 6:40am, €12); **Lisbon** (2¾-4hr, 5-7 per day 5am-6:30pm, €10.20); **Portalegre** (1½hr., M-F 7am, €4).

ORIENTATION AND PRACTICAL INFORMATION. Buses stop at the entrance to the walled center city. The **tourist office** is in Pr República. (☎268 62 22 36. Open Apr.-Sept. M-F 9am-6pm, Sa-Su 10am-12:30pm and 2-5:30pm; Oct.-Mar. daily 9am-5:30pm.) To get to the tourist office from the bus station (5min. walk), take a right and go through Lgo. da Misericordia; continue up to R. Cadeia, and after a series of fountains take a left into Pr. República—the *turismo* will be on the right. Trains arrive 3km away in Fontainhas; if you arrive at the train station and are prepared to do the 3km trek to the center on foot, take a right onto Estrada das Fontainhas and then take a left onto Estrada de Campo Maior at the traffic circle; continue straight and then take a right, passing under the giant Portas de Olivença, and go up R. Olivença until it reaches Pr. República. Services include: **emergency** ☎112; **police,** R. André Gonçalves (☎268 62 26 13); and the **hospital** (☎268 62 22 25). For **internet access,** check out **O Livreiro de Elvas,** R de Olivença, 4-A, a little bookstore with 2 computers in back. Watch your head as you enter the back room. (☎268 62 08 82. €0.80 for 15min., €1.40 for 30min. Open M-F 9:30am-1pm and 3:15-7:15pm, Sa 9:30am-1pm.) The **post office** is one block behind the tourist office. (☎268 62 26 96. Open M-F 9am-6pm.) **Postal code:** 7350.

ACCOMMODATIONS AND FOOD. António Mocisso e Garcia Coelho ❷, R. Aires Varela, 15. From the tourist office, take a right out of the *praça* (to the right of Banco Espirito Santo) and then your first left; go left at the end of the street and the reception will be on the right. Large rooms with TVs, private baths, and pinewood ceilings. Reservations recommended during the summer. (☎268 62 21 26. Singles €20; doubles €30; triples €40; quads €50.) Campers can try **Camping Torre Des Arcas ❶,** in an orchard 4km from Elvas accessible via the bus to Varche and a 10min. walk. (☎268 62 60 30. €2.50 per person, €1.75 per child under 12, €3-4 per car and tent. Owner also rents apartment-style rooms. Minimum rental €38 for 2, €40 for 3.) For fresh fish, fruits, and vegetables, try the **mercado municipal** on Av. São Domingos (open M-Sa 8am-1pm). Fans of roast meat will love **Canal 7 ❶,** R. Sapateiros, 16. Exit Pr. República on R. Sapateiros to the left of Banco Espirito Santo, and follow the curving road to the left toward the oven. Known around town for its excellent *frango assado* (roast chicken €3.50 for a ½ chicken). (☎268 62 35 93. Entrees €3.50-7. Open 11am-3pm, 6-10pm; Su take-out only.)

SIGHTS. Elvas's main sight, the **Aqueduto da Amoreira,** emerges from a hill at the entrance to the city. Begun in 1529 and finished almost a century later (1622), the colossal structure is Europe's largest aqueduct—its 843 arches span almost 8000m.

ALENTEJO

The **castelo,** above Pr. República, has a great view of the aqueduct and the infinite rows of olive trees on the horizon; a stairwell to the right of the entrance leads up to the castle walls. (Castle open 9:30am-5:30pm. €1.25; seniors and 14-25 €0.60, under 14 free.) The **Igreja de Nossa Senhora da Assunção** in Pr. República has *azulejos* and a beautifully ribbed ceiling. (Open M-F noon-1pm, 3-6:30pm. Mass Su 6pm.) Behind the cathedral and uphill to the right is the **Igreja de Nossa Senhora da Consolação dos Aflitos,** also known as **Freiras.** Its octagonal interior has beautiful geometric tiles. (Open Tu-Su 9:30am-12:30pm and 2:30-5:30pm.) In the three-sided *praça* stands the 16th-century **pelourinho,** an octagonal pillory (originally a medieval whipping post) culminating in a pyramid.

CASTELO DE VIDE

Situated 600m above sea level on the edge of the Serra de São Mamede, Castelo de Vide (pop. 4500) is a charming town of whitewashed houses and cobblestone streets. The **castelo,** completed in 1280, overlooks the historic center and offers stunning views. (Open daily July-Sept. 9am-6pm; Oct.-June 9am-5pm. Free.) The **medieval quarter** is Castelo de Vide's unique attraction. Located just below its castle, the old town consists of steep and narrow cobblestone alleys overflowing with potted plants, roses, and sunflowers. The town center surrounds the two 19th-century plazas, evidence of Castelo's popularity as a spa resort over 100 years ago. On weekends, the only way to get to **Marvão** is by taxi (€10). During the week, **buses** run from behind the tourist office to **Marvão** (25min., M-F 5:30pm, €0.80) and **Portalegre** (30min.; M-F 4 per day 8:05am-4:50pm, Sa-Su 8:05am and 4:50pm; €1.50-5), which offers frequent connections to larger cities. The **train station,** which lies 4km out of town, is accessible only by taxi (☎245 90 12 71; €3.74). Trains run to **Lisbon** (5hr.; 6:15am, 5:55pm; €13) and **Madrid.** The **tourist office,** R. Bartolomeu Alferes da Santa, 81, offers maps, helps find accommodations, and provides short-term **luggage storage.** (☎245 90 13 61. Open daily July-Sept. 9am-7pm; Oct.-June 9am-12:30pm and 2-5:30pm.) Services include: **emergency** ☎112; **police** on Av. Anamenha (☎ 245 90 13 14); the **health center** (☎245 90 11 05) behind the tourist office.

MARVÃO

The ancient walled town of Marvão (pop. 190) sits on a mountaintop, surrounded by the hills and meadows of the **Parque Natural de São Mamede.** Almost all of the town's whitewashed houses lie within the 17th-century walls. Marvão's 13th-century **castelo,** atop the ridge at the west end of town, hasn't been seized in 700 years. Prior to the castle's construction, however, Marvão passed through several different owners, among them the Romans, the Visigoths, and the Moors. Remnants of these early days are on display at the **Museu Municipal,** near the castle in the **Igreja de Santa Maria.** (Open daily 9am-12:30pm and 2-5:30pm. €1, students with ID €0.75.) **Buses** run to **Castelo de Vide** (25min., M-F 7:15am and 1:05pm, €0.80) and **Portalegre** (50min.; M-F 7:15am, 1:05pm; €1.60-5). Ask at the tourist office about express buses to **Lisbon** (5½hr., 7:30am, €12); buy tickets one day in advance. To get to the **train station** (☎245 99 22 88), 9km north of town in Beirã, with service to Lisbon and Madrid, take a taxi (☎245 99 32 72). Taxis are also a valid option to get to **Castelo de Vide** (€10). If you arrive by bus, you'll be dropped off just outside the town wall. Enter through one of the gates and proceed up R. Cima until you see the stone whipping-post in Pr. Pelourinho. From here, R. Espíritu Santo leads toward the *castelo* and the **tourist office.** (☎245 99 38 86. Open July-Sept. M-F 9am-6:30pm, Sa-Su 10am-12:30pm and 2-6:30pm; Oct.-June daily 9am-12:30pm and 2-5:30pm.) Services include: **emergency** ☎112 and **police** ☎245 99 36 17.

BEJA ☎284

Standing out amid the vast and monotonous wheat fields of the southern Alentejo, Beja is a relaxed, friendly town that is proud of its varied history and architecture. Its current name is a corruption of its original name, Pax Julia, given to Beja by the Romans in 48 BC to commemorate the peace with the Lusitanians. The city was then conquered by the Moors in 715 and proceeded to change ownership 13 times before becoming a Christian possession in 1232 under Dom Sancho II. The city maintains a medieval feel and a tranquility that tourists come to cherish.

TRANSPORTATION. Trains run from the station (☎284 32 50 56) 1km outside of town to: **Évora** (1½hr., 5 per day 7:45am-8:40pm, €6.50); **Faro** (3½hr.; 9:30am, 9:13pm; €8.50) via **Funcheira; Lisbon** (2½-3hr., 4 per day 5am-7:20pm, €8.50). The **bus station** (☎284 31 36 20) is on R. Cidade de São Paulo, near the corner of Av. Brasil. Buses go to: **Évora** (1hr., 5 per day 7:10am-7:15pm, €7.20); **Faro** (3½hr., 3 per day 10:10am-7:20pm, €9); **Porto** (8½-10hr., 4 per day 9am-2:30pm, €17) via **Lisbon; Lisbon** (3¼hr., 6 per day 7:10am-3pm, €9.40); **Picalho,** a border town with connections to destinations in Spain (2hr., 5 per day 10:50am-9:15pm, €6).

PRACTICAL INFORMATION. The **tourist office,** R. Capitão J. F. de Sousa, 25, provides luggage storage. To get to the tourist office from the bus station, take a left out of the station onto Av. Brasil. Make your next right onto R. Albuquerique. After a block turn left onto R. Camoes and after the *biblioteca* take a right onto R. Biscainha, which ends in R. de Sousa. (☎/fax 284 31 19 13. Open May-Sept. M-F 9am-8pm, Sa 10am-1pm, 2-6pm; Oct.-Apr. M-Sa 10am-1pm and 2-6pm.) **Banks** are open M-F 8am-3pm. **ATMs** are plentiful around the train station and on R. de Sousa near the tourist office. Exchanging traveler's checks can be difficult in Beja, so be sure to have an alternate source of cash. **Luggage storage** is also available at the bus station on weekdays (€1.75 per day). Services include: **emergency** ☎112; the **police** on R. D. Nuno Álvares Pereira (☎284 32 20 22), one block downhill from the tourist office. To get to the **post office,** on Lgo. do Correio, take a left out of the tourist office, then a right on R. Infantaria 17. **Poste Restante** and **fax service** (€2.20 per page) are available. (☎284 31 12 70. Open M-F 9am-6pm.) **Postal code:** 7800.

ACCOMMODATIONS. Beja is a very pleasant place to stay for the night, and there are several truly excellent options for accommodations. Most are located within a few blocks of the tourist office. **Pousada de Juventude de Beja (HI) ❶,** R. Professor Janeiro Acabado. From the front of the bus station, walk away from the center (and the Pr. Tavares traffic circle) on R. Cidade de São Paulo, then take a right on R. Professor Janeiro Acbado; the hostel is on the left. This hostel offers a living room with TV and games, laundry room, and a kitchen. (☎284 32 54 58; fax 284 32 54 68. June 16-Sept. 15 dorms €10; doubles €21, with bath €23; Sept. 16-June 15 €8/€18/€19. Open 8am-noon and 6pm-midnight.) **Residencial Rosa do Campo ❸,** R. Liberdade, 12. Take a right out of the tourist office and walk three blocks down as R. de Sousa becomes R. Liberdade; the house will be on the right after the park on the left. The extremely kind owners offer spacious, air-conditioned rooms in their newly-renovated private home. All rooms come with TV and private bath. (☎284 32 35 78. Singles €27.50; doubles €35-40; room with 4 beds €15 per person.) A secluded **annex ❷** just around the block has one huge (70 sq. m) room with five beds, a bath, and a refrigerator, and rivals youth hostel prices. Stay there alone and you practically have a studio apartment for the night. For one person €15, 2 for €25, 3-5 people for €10 per person. **Residencial Bejense ❸,** R. Capitão J. F. de Sousa, 57. Take a left out of the tourist office and walk just a little

UNREQUITED LOVE The city is known for a tale of passion: when the French troops came to Portugal during the war of Restoration in 1666, the young nun Mariana Alcoforado fell hopelessly in love with the knight Chimilly, whom she saw passing by from her now-famous window overlooking the Porta de Mértola. The nun wrote five passionate letters to her love, and these were soon published in Paris under the title *Five Love Letters of a Portuguese Nun*. Mariana died at the age of 83, but her letters remained to tell her story of unrealized passion and to inspire future artists and lovers. Whether the nun ever spoke to her object of her desire is unknown.

bit down the street. This three-star lodging house, with *azulejo*-lined hallways, has large rooms with tiled floors, TVs, phones, and A/C. (☎284 31 15 70; fax 284 31 15 79. Singles €28; doubles €40, with 3rd bed €50. AmEx/MC/V.)

FOOD AND NIGHTLIFE. Beja is one of the best places to taste authentic (and affordable) Alentejo cuisine. The municipal **market** sets up in a building on Lgo. de Mercado, one block up and one block to the right from the bus station (open M-Sa 6am-1:30pm). **Restaurante Casa de Risto o Saiote,** R. Biscainha, 6, off R. Capitão J. F. de Sousa, to the right before the intersection of R. Portas de Mertola, gets loud and busy at lunchtime. Although the fluorescent-lit interior provides less romance than other restaurants in the center, the reasonable prices and large servings keep patrons happy. (☎284 32 02 59. *Calhamares* €4.25. Open M-Sa noon-3:30pm, 7-10:30pm.) At night, locals head to **Ritual,** R. Moeda, 9, down the street from Pr. República. A classier bar, it's popular for pre-clubbing and peaks at 1am. (☎968 02 33 68. Beer €1.50, mixed drinks €2.50. Open M-Sa 10pm-4am.)

SIGHTS. Beja's sites are scattered, but the outstanding **Museu Rainha Dona Leonor** makes an excellent starting point. Take a right from the tourist office and walk into the Pr. Diogo Fernandes de Beja. Go right on R. Dr. Brito Camacho, and through Lgo. de São João to Lgo. da Conceiçao; the museum is on the right. Built on the site where Sister Mariana Alcoforado fell in love with the French officer, the museum features a replica of the cell window through which the nun watched the object of her passion. Inside, the church's 18th-century *azulejo* panels depict the lives of Mary and St. John the Baptist. Nearby are panels of *talha dourada* (gilded carvings) and *intaglio* marble altars. (Lgo. de Conceição. ☎284 32 33 51. Open Tu-Su 9:30am-12:30pm and 2-5:15pm. €0.50, Su free. Ticket also good for the **Museu Visigótico** behind the castle, which displays artifacts. Same hours.)

One block downhill from the Museu Rainha Dona Leonor is the 13th-century **Igreja de Santa María da Feira,** transformed into a mosque during the Moorish invasion and back into a church when the city reverted to Portuguese control; the result is a notable mix of architectural styles. A miniature bull on its corner column symbolizes the city's spirit. (Largo de Santa María. Church open daily 10am-1pm and 3-7pm. Free. Mass daily 6-6:30pm, also Su noon.) From here, R. Aresta Branco leads past handsome old houses to the **Castelo de Beja,** built around 1300 on the remnants of a Roman fortress. (Open May-Sept. Tu-Su 10am-1pm and 2-6pm; Oct.-Apr. 9-11:30am and 1-3:30pm. Free.) The castle still has an enormous marble keep, vaulted chambers, stones covered with cryptic symbols, and walls covered with ivy. The castle's **Torre de Menagem** provides an impressive view of the vast Alentejan plains (€0.50 to go up the tower). Between the police station and the center of town lies the **Convento de São Francisco**, R. Dr. Nuno Alvares Pereira (☎284 32 84 41). The convent has been turned into a state-run luxury pousada; however, you can still go in and see the lobby and cloister of the convent.

RIBATEJO AND ESTREMADURA

Serrated cliffs and whitewashed fishing villages line Estremadura's Costa de Prata (Silver Coast), whose beaches rival even those of the Algarve. Throngs of tourists and summer residents populate seafront Nazaré and Peniche. Smaller, less touristed towns with sparkling beaches line the coast, and the rugged, beautiful Ilhas Berlingas lie just offshore. Nearby, the fertile region of the Ribatejo ("banks of the Tejo")

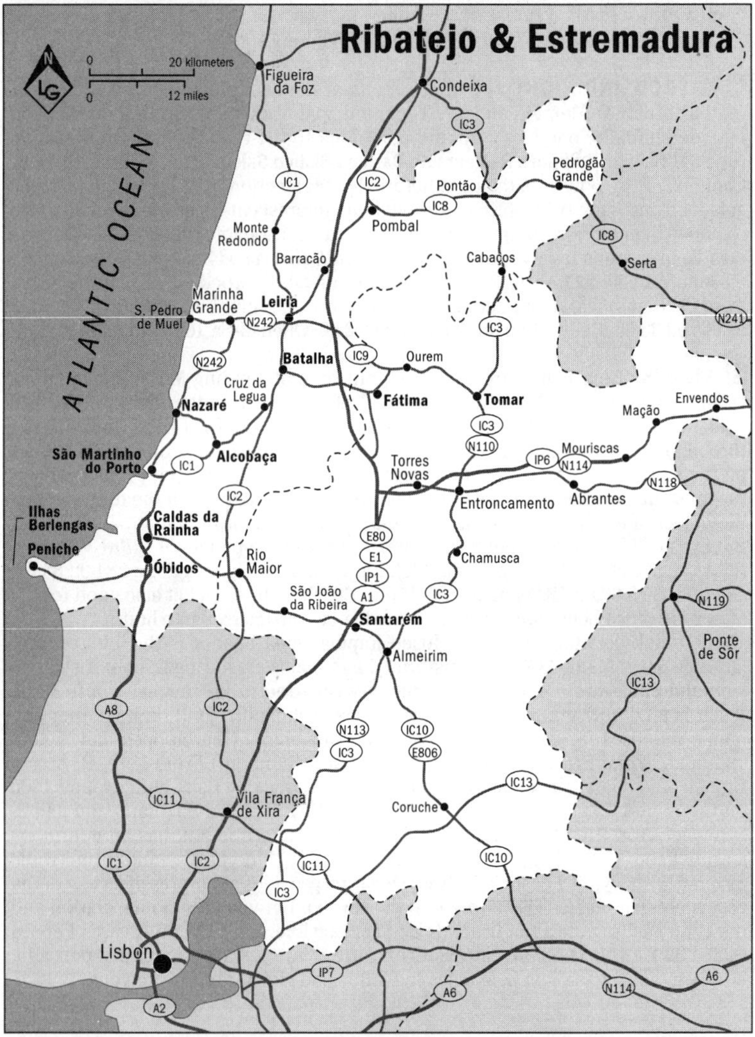

is perhaps the gentlest and greenest in the entire country. Known as the "Heart of Portugal," the Ribatejo is famous for pastures bordering the arid Alentejan plain and Estremaduran wetlands. Home to the ornate monasteries in Alcobaça and Batalha and the mysterious medieval town of Óbidos, the Ribatejo boasts some of the country's finest sights.

SANTARÉM ☎243

Perhaps the most charming of Ribatejo's cities, Santarém (pop. 50,000) presides atop a rocky mound over the calm Rio Tejo. Once a ruling city in the ancient Roman province of Lusitania and later a flourishing medieval center, Santarém has a long history of prosperity. It was also the capital of Portuguese Gothic style, and its many appealing churches display a mind-boggling range of architectural trends.

TRANSPORTATION

Trains: Station, Estrada da Estação (☎243 32 11 99), 2km outside town. **Bus** service to and from the station (10min., every 30min.-1hr. 7:30am-7pm, €1.10). To: **Coimbra** (2hr., 11 per day 6:25am-1:10am, €5.25-7); **Faro** via Lisbon (4hr., 6 per day, €8.50); **Lisbon** (1hr., 37 per day 4:40am-3:55am, €3.30-5.25); **Portalegre** (3hr., 4 per day 8:50am-9pm, €5.60); **Porto** (4hr., 4 per day 9:55am-8:55pm, €8.50-12); **Tomar** (1hr., every hr. 6:20am-1:25am, €2.60).

Buses: Rodoviária do Tejo, Av. Brasil (☎243 33 32 00), not far from the main *praça*. To: **Braga** (5hr.; 10:45am, 6:45pm; €11); **Caldas da Rainha** (1½hr., 3-5 per day 7:20am-6:20pm, €3.90); **Coimbra** (2hr.; 10:45am, 6:45pm; €7.25); **Faro** (7hr., 4 per day 10:30am-4:30pm, €13); **Leiria** (1½hr., 5 per day 8:15am-6:45pm, €4.60-7.75); **Lisbon** (1¼hr., 10 per day 7am-7:15pm, €5.50); **Nazaré** (1¼hr.; 8:15am, 5:30pm; €4.50); **Porto** (4hr.; 10:45am, 6:45pm; €11).

Taxis: Scaltaxis (☎243 33 29 19) has a stand across the park from the bus station.

ORIENTATION AND PRACTICAL INFORMATION

The densely packed streets between **Praça Sá da Bandeira** (the main square) and the park **Portas do Sol** (above the Tejo) form the core of Santarém. **Rua Capelo Ivêns,** which begins at the *praça*, is home to the tourist office and many hostels.

Tourist Office: R. Capelo Ivêns, 63 (☎243 30 44 37). Maps and info on festivals, accommodations, and transportation. Friendly and helpful English-speaking staff. Open Tu-F 9am-7pm; Sa-Su 10am-12:30pm, 2:30-5:30pm; M 9am-12:30pm, 2-5:30pm.

Currency Exchange: Banco Nacional Ultramarino (☎243 33 30 07), at R. Dr. Texeira Guedes and R. Capelo Ivêns. €5 commission. Open M-F 8:30am-3pm.

Luggage Storage: Bus station. €0.50 per bag. Open M-F 9am-1pm, 2-7pm.

Emergency: ☎112. **Police:** Av. Brasil (☎243 32 20 22), near the bus station.

Hospital: Av. Bernardo Santareno (☎243 30 02 00). From Pr. Sá da Bandeira, walk up R. Cidade da Covilhã as it becomes R. Alexandre Herculano and then Av. Bernardo Santareno. English spoken.

Internet Access: Free at the **Instituto Português da Juventude,** downstairs from the youth hostel, M-F 9am-8pm (30min. limit). **E-planet,** Av. Madre Andaluz, 16B (☎914 95 47 80). From the youth hostel, turn left and walk 5min. down the road; it's on the right. €1.50 per 30min. Open daily 2pm-2am.

Post Office (☎243 30 97 00), on the corner of Lgo. Cândido and R. Dr. Texeira Guedes. Open M-F 8:30am-6:30pm, Sa 9am-12:30pm. **Postal Code:** 2000.

ACCOMMODATIONS

Prices are fairly high year-round, increasing during the Ribatejo Fair (10 days starting in early June). The tourist office can help find a room in a private house.

Residencial Muralha, R. Pedro Canavarro, 12 (☎243 32 23 99; fax 243 32 94 77), across the park from the bus station and next to the medieval wall. Comfortable rooms, all with TV, most with large private bath. Reserve a week ahead in summer. Singles €15, with bath €25-33; doubles €22-25, with bath €35. ❷

Residencial Abidis, R. Guilherme de Azevedo, 4 (☎243 32 20 17 or 243 32 20 18), around the corner from the tourist office. Centrally located, with hotel-style lodging, adequate rooms, and a living room on each floor. Breakfast included. Singles €18-20, with bath €28; doubles €22-25, with bath €35. ❷

Pensão José Rodrigues, Tr. do Froes, 14 (☎243 32 30 88). Cheap rooms in a central location. Popular during the summer, so call ahead. Singles €12.50; doubles €25. ❶

Pousada da Juventude de Santarém (HI), Av. Grp. Forcados Amadores de Santarém, 1 (☎/fax 243 39 19 14), near the bullring. From the bus station, turn right onto Av. Brasil, walk 4 blocks, then turn right onto Lgo. Cândido dos Reis, following it as it becomes Av. Dom Afonso Henriques and then curves past the bullring; the hostel is on the left, upstairs from the Instituto Português da Juventude. Rooms are clean and comfortable.

Breakfast included (8:30-10am). Reception 8am-noon and 6pm-midnight. Check-in after 6pm and check-out before 11am. Lockout 11am-6pm. June 16-Sept. 15 dorms €9.50; doubles with bath €23. Sept. 16-June 15 €7.50/€19. ❶

FOOD

Eateries cluster around the parallel R. Capelo Ivêns and R. Serpa Pinto. The **municipal market,** in the pagoda on Lgo. Infante Santo near the Jardim da República, sells fresh produce. (Open M-Sa 8am-2pm.) **Supermercado Minipreço,** R. Pedro Canavarro, 31, is along the street leading from the bus station to R. Capelo Ivêns. (Open M-Sa 9am-8pm.) If you're in the mood for home-style cooking, **Casa d'Avó ❶,** R. Serpa Pinto, 62, serves Portuguese dishes (€4.75-6) as well as sandwiches (€1-1.75) and sweets (€0.55-1.75) on petite tables surrounded by cast-iron garden chairs. (☎243 32 69 16. Open M-F 9am-7pm, Sa 9am-2pm. Closed Aug.) **Pastelería Eureka ❶,** R. Capelo Ivêns, 12, has 70 years of experience making its own pastries (€0.60) and bread. (☎243 42 90 23. Open M-Sa 8am-7pm.)

SIGHTS

GARDENS. **Portas do Sol,** a paradise of flowers and fountains surrounded by Moorish walls, is best visited on a clear day, when the walls offer a lovely view of the plains and the Tejo. *(Take R. Serpa Pinto from Pr. Sá da Bandeira to Pr. Visconde de Serra Pilar, then continue on R. Cons. Figueiredo Leal, and bear left on Av. 5 de Outubro after the art-deco theater. The Portas do Sol is at the end of the street. Open daily 8am-11pm. Free.)*

PRAÇA VISCONDE DE SERRA PILAR. Centuries ago, Christians, Moors, and Jews gathered for social and business affairs in this *praça*. *(Take R. Serpa Pinto from Pr. Sá da Bandeira.)* The 12th-century **Igreja de Marvila,** off the *praça*, has a 17th-century *azulejo* interior and a Manuelian style exterior. *(Open Tu-Su 9:30am-12:30pm and 2-5:30pm. Free.)* The early Gothic purity of nearby **Igreja da Graça** contrasts sharply with Marvila's overflowing exuberance. Within Graça's chapel lies Pedro Alvares Cabral, the explorer who "discovered" Brazil and one of the few to live long enough to return to his homeland. *(Open Tu-Su 9:30am-12:30pm and 2-5:30pm. Free.)*

IGREJA DO SEMINÁRIO DOS JESUÍTAS. The austere facade of the Igreja do Seminário dos Jesuítas dominates Pr. Sá da Bandeira, Santarém's main square. Stone friezes carved as ropes separate the three stories, and Latin biblical mottos embellish every doorway. *(Open Tu-Su 9:30am-12:30pm and 2-5:30pm. Free. If it is closed, enter through the door to the right of the entrance and ask the sacracristan to unlock it.)*

TORRE DAS CABAÇAS. The medieval Torre das Cabaças (Tower of the Gourds) was named after the eight earthen bowls installed in the 16th century to amplify the bell's ring. Inside the tower is the Museu de Tempo (Time Museum), with clocks, clocks, and more clocks. *(Take R. São Martinho from Pr. Visconde de Serra Pilar. Open Tu-Su 9:30am-12:30pm and 2-5:30pm. €1 for each, €1.75 for both.)*

ENTERTAINMENT

Around the corner and two blocks down from the bus station is **Cervejão,** Av. António Maria Baptista, 10. The name means "big beer," and lots of it can be found here. (☎243 26 43 33. Beer €1-2. Cocktails €2.50. Open M-Sa 4pm-midnight.) For unrestrained daytime partying, try the **Feira Nacional de Agricultura** (also known as the Feira do Ribatejo). Thousands of people come for a 6- to 10-day bullfighting and horse-racing orgy in early June.

"G" RATED The story of Santarém's founding could have been a Disney movie. All the elements are there: beautiful girl, frustrated love, bitter jealousy, a little bit of magic, and no sex whatsoever. The daughter of two 7th-century nobles, Iria was sent to a convent at an early age to live a life of purity and devotion. Soon Iria fell in love with a noble named Britaldo. The two contented themselves with innocent hand-holding and tried to live happily ever after. Enter Remígio, a former teacher of Iria's, now madly in love with her as well. Cue the jealous rage. Remígio decided if he can't have Iria, no one can, and slips a potion into her soup that makes her look pregnant. Needless to say, sex is a convent no-no, so the townspeople cast Iria into the river. Her nun friends form a search party and eventually find her body washed up on the shore. Before anyone can give her a proper burial, the river rises, giving the girl a watery grave. Santarém was founded on this tragic site, "Santarém" being derived from "Santa Iria." A statue of her by the river marks the spot where Iria is said to lie still.

ÓBIDOS

Óbidos has a medieval heart: the 12th-century village defended by formidable walls remains the center of any visit. The red-tiled roofs of the hilltop town are barely visible above the complete castle wall's collective reach. Though Óbidos is quite small, its beauty is deserving of a stop-over for travelers in the area. The **castelo** on the coast, a Moorish fortress rebuilt in the 12th century, gradually lost its strategic importance as the ocean receded. Although the castle itself, now a luxury *pousada* is opened only to guests, everyone is free to walk the 1.5km of its **walls.** The 17th-century *azulejo*-filled **Igreja de Santa Maria,** to the right of the post office in the central *praça*, displays Josefa de Óbidos's vivid canvases off the main altar. It was also the site of the 1441 wedding of 10-year-old King Afonso V to his 8-year-old cousin, Isabel. (Open daily Apr.-Sept. 9:30am-12:30pm and 2:30-7pm; Oct.-Mar. 9:30am-12:30pm and 2:30-5pm. Free.)

The **tourist office** is a small, green cottage just up the steps from the bus stop, across from Porta da Vila. (☎262 95 92 31; fax 262 95 50 14. Open May-Sept. M-F 9:30am-7pm, Sa-Su 10am-7pm; Oct.-Apr. M-F 9:30am-6pm, Sa-Su 10am-6pm.) There are many private rooms for rent in Óbidos, as advertised by the signs on and around R. Direita, but it may be difficult to find a good price. **ÓbidoSol ❷,** R. Direita, 40, is a charming 17th-century home that has three rooms with window seats, an *azulejo*-covered common bath, and a large living room. Reservations recommended, especially during the summer. (☎262 95 91 88. June-Sept. double bed €25; doubles €30. Oct.-May €20/€25. Ask for a €5 discount if you are traveling alone.) "Typical" **restaurants** (most with typical tourist prices) and several **markets** cluster on and around R. Direita. Eat light and save your euros for Óbidos's signature *ginja* (wild cherry liqueur); stores on R. Direita sell bottles for €1.75.

Buses, which stop just outside the town gate, are more convenient than trains to Óbidos. Connections to: **Caldas da Rainha** (20min., 24 per day 7:35am-8:35pm, €0.85); **Lisbon** (1¼hr., M-F 4 per day 7:05am-4:10pm, €5.50); **Peniche** (40min.; M-F 10 per day 8:10am-7:40pm, Sa 7 per day 8:10am-7:40pm, Su 5 per day 9:40am-7:40pm; €2). On weekends you must stop in Caldas da Rainha to go to Lisbon (1½hr., 5-7 per day 7am-9pm, €5). Buses stop a few stairs down from the main gate. No bus schedules are posted here, so ask at the tourist office.

PENICHE ☎262

Many travelers overlook Peniche, a seaport town 22km west of Óbidos, en route to the Ilhas Berlengas, missing this lively city close to popular beaches. Home to Portugal's second largest fishing fleet, Peniche used to dedicate an entire festival just to the sardine; it now celebrates fishing and seafood in general.

TRANSPORTATION

Buses: R. Dr. Ernesto Moureira (☎262 78 21 33), on an isthmus outside the town walls. To: **Alcobaça,** via Caldas da Rainha (1¾hr., 3 per day 10:45am-5:10pm, €5.75); **Caldas da Rainha** (1hr., 8 per day 8am-7:30pm, €2.50-4); **Leiria,** via Caldas da Rainha (2hr., 3 per day 10:45am-5:10pm, €7); **Lisbon** (2hr., 12 per day 6am-8:45pm, €5.50); **Nazaré** (1½hr., 4 per day 10:45am-6pm, €3.70-5.50); **Porto** (6½hr., 3 per day 7am-6pm, €11); **Santarém,** via Caldas da Rainha (1½hr., 3 per day 7am-5:10pm, €4.75). Peniche is accessible only by bus.

Taxis: (☎262 78 44 24 or 262 78 29 10) in Pr. Jacob Pereira and Lgo. Bispo Mariana.

ORIENTATION AND PRACTICAL INFORMATION

Most of Peniche's points of interest are situated in or around the grid of streets between **Largo Bispo Mariana** and the **fortaleza** on the coast. **Praça Jacob Rodrigues Pereira** marks the center of town, near the tourist office and the start of **Avenida do Mar,** which runs along the river to the docks and fishing port.

Tourist Office: R. Alexandre Herculano (☎/fax 262 78 95 71). From the bus station, take a left and cross the river over Ponte Velha to the right. Turning left on R. Alexandre Herculano, walk alongside the public garden, and follow signs to the office. English spoken. Open July-Sept. daily 9am-8pm; Oct.-May 10am-1pm and 2-5pm; June 9am-7pm.

Bank: Caixa Geral de Depósitos, on R. Alexandre Herculano, down the street from the tourist office. Open M-F 8:30am-3pm.

Emergency: ☎112. **Police:** R. Herois Ultramar (☎262 78 95 55).

Hospital: R. Gen. Humberto Delgado (☎262 78 17 00). From the tourist office, turn right onto R. Alexandre Herculano and take the 1st left onto R. Arquitecto Paulino Montez; walk all the way up the street, passing the post office, then take a right onto R. Gen. Humberto Delgado, and the hospital is down the road on the left.

Internet Access: On Line Cyber Café, R. António Cervantes, 5 (☎966 85 77 49), near the *fortaleza,* has 4 fast computers. €0.60 per 15min., €0.50 per 15min. after the first hr. Coffee €0.40-0.60. Beer €0.75. Mixed drinks €2.50. Open daily 11:30am-2am.

Post Office: R. Arquitecto Paulino Montez (☎262 78 00 60). From the tourist office, turn right on R. Alexandre Herculano, left on R. Arquitecto Paulino Montez, and walk 3 blocks. **Posta Restante** and **fax.** Open M-F 9am-6pm. **Postal Code:** 2520.

ACCOMMODATIONS AND CAMPING

Peniche's budget accommodations are located above restaurants of the same name; look for signs to find a *residencial* on or behind Av. do Mar. Hostels do fill quickly, especially from June to August; try to arrive early in the day. Persistent elderly matrons renting rooms in their private houses gather in Pr. Jacob Rodrigues Pereira. Rooms in private houses may be good budget options, but insist on seeing them first and inquire about hot water and amenities.

Residencial Marítimo, R. António Cervantes, 14 (☎262 08 34 07), off the *praça* in front of the fortress. Newly decorated rooms, all with TV and private bath. Breakfast included. Reserve ahead. Singles €15-22; doubles €30-45. ❷

Residencial Mira Mar, Av. Mar, 40-44 (☎262 78 16 66), near the docks and above the seafood restaurant of the same name. Large rooms with terraces, TV, and bath. Reserve 2 weeks ahead in summer. July-Sept. singles €20; doubles €35. Oct.-June €15/€30. AmEx/MC/V. ❷

Municipal Campground (☎262 78 95 29; fax 262 78 96 96), 2km outside of town, at least a 30min. walk from downtown. From the bus station, turn left onto Av. Porto de Pesca to reach EN 114, following it through the traffic circle and past the waterpark; the campsite is on the left. Or take a taxi (about €2.50 from downtown). Open year-round. €2 per person, €1.10 per child age 6-12, under 6 free. €1.50-4 per tent. €1.50 per car. Free hot showers. ❶

FOOD

The restaurants lining **Av. do Mar** serve excellent fresh grilled seafood. Despite the multilingual menus, the prices are reasonable and there are plenty of locals mixed in among tourists. Peniche's *sardinhas* (sardines) are exceptional, as are the seafood *espetadas* (skewers). The outdoor cafes on **Pr. Jacob Rodrigues Pereira** are lively, particularly on Sundays, when the rest of town is quiet. The **market,** on R. António da Conceição Bento, stocks fresh produce (open Tu-Su 7am-1pm).

Restaurante Mira Mar, Av. do Mar, 42 (☎262 78 16 66). One of the best of the string of restaurants along Av. do Mar. The place gets loud and happily busy at dinner time, especially 9-10pm. Entrees €4.50-7. Excellent *crème de marisco* (shellfish chowder; €2). Open 10am-11:30pm; meals noon-3pm and 8-10:30pm. AmEx/MC/V. ❶

Ristorante Il Boccone, Av. do Mar, 4 (☎262 78 24 12), at the beginning of row of restaurants along Av. do Mar. A reprieve from seafood. Pizza (€5-8) and pasta dishes (€4.50-14.50). Open Tu-Su 10am-2am; meals noon-4pm, 8pm-midnight. ❷

Café Oceano, Pr. Jacob Pereira, 12-13 (☎262 78 23 15). Popular cafe with outdoor seating. Sandwiches €1-3.50. Coffee €0.40-0.85. Gourmet ice cream €0.80-4. Specialty *pasteis de Peniche* (almond pastries; €0.70). Open daily 8am-midnight. ❶

SIGHTS

FORTALEZA. António Salazar, Portugal's longtime dictator, chose Peniche's formidable 16th-century fortress for one of his four high-security political prisons. Its high walls and bastions later became a camp for Angolan refugees. It now houses the **Museu de Peniche,** highlighted by a chilling walk through the cells of Salazar's prison. In an annex outside of the museum, a small anti-Fascist exhibition traces the dictatorship and underground resistance from the seizure of power in 1926 to the coup that toppled the regime on April 25, 1974. *(Campo da República, near the dock where boats leave for the Ilhas Berlengas. Fortaleza open Tu-Su 10:30am-noon and 2-6pm. Free. Museum ☎262 78 01 16. Open Tu-Su 10:30am-noon and 2-6pm. €1, under 16 free.)*

BEACHES. For sun and surf, head to any of the town's three beaches. The beautiful but windy **Praia de Peniche de Cima,** along the north crescent, has the warmest water. It merges with another beach at **Baleal,** a small fishing village popular with tourists. The southern **Praia do Molho Leste,** known to many as "super-tubos" because of its big surf, is a bit cooler. Beyond it is the crowded **Praia da Consolação.** The strange humidity at this beach supposedly cures bone diseases. Unfortunately, on windless days, it also traps the less than tantalizing aroma of nearby sewers. *(Buses 7am-7pm, €0.90. Check with the tourist office for changes.)*

FESTIVALS AND NIGHTLIFE

Although Peniche may seem sleepy during the day, the town's nightlife heats up from the after-dinner hours until late, especially during the summer. The town caters to every kind of taste. Peniche's biggest festival takes place on the first Sunday of

August, when boats bedecked in wreaths of flags and flowers process into the harbor to launch the two-day **Festa de Nossa Senhora da Boa Viagem,** celebrating the protector of sailors and fishermen. The town lets loose with carnival rides, live entertainment, wine, and seafood. Mid-September brings the **Sabores do Mar** festival, focused on fishing, *fado*, and folklore.

Café Cartaxo, Tv. dos Proletários, 3 (☎96 436 66 80), behind the Igreja São Pedro. An unpretentious 100-year-old Celtic bar. Chess boards are available on the shelf near the entrance. Port wine €1.50-4.50. Open M-Sa 1:30pm-2am.

Bar No. 1, R. Afonso Albuquerque, 14 (☎262 78 45 41), close to the intersection with R. José Estevão. Popular with both tourists and locals; its friendly owner works the DJ booth during the late-night hours. The bar hosts 10 small art exhibits per year. Beer and shots €0.75-1.50. Mixed drinks €3. Open daily noon-2am.

Karas, Estrada Marginal Norte (EN-114), complex #1 (☎262 78 55 79), a 10-15min. walk from Pr. Jacob Pereira along the coast. The most popular disco within walking distance gets moving at 3-5am. Minimum consumption €5. Beer €2. Mixed drinks €3.50. In Aug., open Tu-Su midnight-6am; during the rest of year, open only Sa, same hours.

HIKING

To truly enjoy the ocean air, hike around the peninsula (8km). Start at Papôa, just north of Peniche. From Pr. Jacob Pereira, take R. Alexandre Herculano and then Av. 25 de Abril and follow the signs along the coast. Stroll out to the tip, where orange cliffs rise from a swirling blue sea. Nearby lie the sparse ruins of an old fortress, Forte da Luz. The endpoint of the peninsula, Cabo Carvoeiro, is the most popular and dramatic of Peniche's natural sights. The fortress's *farol* (lighthouse) punctuates the extreme west end of the peninsula. The Nau dos Corvos (Crow's Ship), an odd rock formation, delivers a seagull's-eye perspective.

DAYTRIPS FROM PENICHE

ILHAS BERLENGAS (1HR.)

Several companies operate boats from Peniche's public dock. Largest is Viamar ferry (☎262 78 56 46; fax 262 78 38 47. Ticket booth open 8:30am-5:30pm), which offers 3 crossings per day. (40min.; July-Aug. 3 per day 9:30, 11:30am, 5:30pm; return trips at 10:30am, 4:30, 6:30pm. To stay overnight, buy a €10 1-way ticket each way. May 15-June and Sept. 1-15 10am, returns 4:30pm. Same-day round-trip ticket €15, children age 5-12 €10, under 5 free.) Reserve 3-4 days in advance. Arrive 1 hr. in advance, 2½ hr. in Aug. The crossing from Peniche to the island is rough. (To get through the ordeal, try inhaling as the boat goes up and exhaling as it goes down.) Trips by Berlenga Turpesca (☎262 78 99 60) include visits to the Berlenga caves. Berlenga Praia (☎917 60 11 14) also offers crossing.

The rugged Ilhas Berlengas (Berlenga Islands) rise out of the Atlantic Ocean, 12km northwest of Peniche. The main island of Berlenga and archipelago of several smaller islands (the Farilhões, Estelas, and Forcados), are inhabited by thousands of screeching seagulls. The **Reserva Natural da Berlenga** is home to wild black rabbits, lizards, and a very small fishing community. Deep gorges, natural tunnels, and rocky caves carve through the main island. The only beach accessible by foot lies in a small cove by the landing dock. For beach-goers willing to brave the cold, dips in the calm water bring instant respite from the heat. Hikers can trek to the island's highest point for a gorgeous view of the 17th-century **Forte de São João Batista,** now a hostel run by the Associação Amigos da Berlenga (AAB).

NAZARÉ ☎262

It's hard to tell where authenticity stops and tourism starts in Nazaré. Fishermen clad in traditional garb stroll barefoot and women typically don seven petticoats, thick shawls, and gold earrings. The day's catch dries in the hot sun and streetside entrepreneurs sell everything from fishing nets to seashell necklaces. "Traditional" lifestyle has become the basis of Nazaré's most thriving business: tourism. But if Nazaré is part theater, at least it puts on a good show.

TRANSPORTATION

Buses: Av. Vieira Guimarães (☎262 55 11 72), perpendicular to Av. República. More convenient than taking the train (6km away). To: **Alcobaça** (30min., 14 per day 7:10am-8pm, €1.15); **Batalha** (50min., 5 per day 7:10am-6:45pm, €2.50); **Caldas da Rainha** (1¼hr., 11 per day 6:30am-7:15pm, €2.30); **Coimbra** (2hr., 5 per day 6:25am-7:25pm, €7); **Fátima** (1½hr., 3 per day 7:10am-5pm, €3); **Leiria** (1¼hr., 10 per day 6:45am-7:10pm, €2.50-3); **Lisbon** (2hr., 8 per day 6:50am-8pm, €6.50); **Peniche** (1½hr., 6 per day 8:35am-6pm, €3.80); **Porto** (3½hr., 5 per day 6:25am-7:25pm, €11); **São Martinho do Porto** (20min., 11 per day 6:50am-8pm, €1.25); **Tomar** (1½hr., 3 per day 7:10am-5pm, €4.30).

Taxis: ☎262 55 31 25.

ORIENTATION AND PRACTICAL INFORMATION

All of the action in Nazaré—beaches, nightlife, and most restaurants—takes place in the **new town** along the beach. Its two main squares, **Praça Sousa Oliveira** and **Praça Dr. Manuel de Arriaga,** are near the cliffside away from the fishing port. Either the cliffside funicular or a winding road leads up to the **Sítio,** the old town, which preserves a sense of calm and tradition less prevalent in the crowded resort below. To get to the tourist office from the bus station, take a right toward the beach and then a right onto Av. República; the office is a 5min. walk along the shore, between the two major *praças*.

Tourist Office (☎262 56 11 94), beachside on Av. República. English-speaking staff provides maps as well as information on entertainment and transportation. Open daily Apr.-June 15 10am-1pm and 3-7pm; June 15-30 10am-1pm and 3-8pm; July-Aug. 10am-10pm; Sept. 10am-8pm; Oct.-March 9:30am-1pm and 2:30-6pm.

Banks: Several major banks on and around Av. República. Open M-F 8:30am-3pm.

Emergency: ☎112. **Police** (☎262 55 12 68), 1 block from the bus station at Av. Vieira Guimarães and R. Sub-Vila.

Hospital: Hospital da Confraria da Nossa Senhora de Nazaré (☎262 56 11 16), in the Sítio district on the cliffs above the town center. **Centro de Saúde** (☎262 55 11 82), in the new part of town.

Internet Access: Cultural Center, Av. Manuel Remigio (the continuation of Av. República in the direction of the fishing port), there are kiosks with computers for public use. Open M-Sa 9:30am-1pm and 2-7pm, Su 4-7pm.

Post Office: Av. Independência Nacional, 2 (☎262 56 16 04). From Pr. Souza Oliveira, walk up R. Mouzinho de Albuquerque. 1 block past Pensão Central. **Fax** and **Posta Restante**. Open M-F 9:30am-12:30pm and 2:30-6pm. **Postal Code:** 2450.

ACCOMMODATIONS AND CAMPING

Nazaré is home to the most aggressive room-renters in Portugal; insistent old ladies swarm arriving buses at the station and line Av. República, waving colored signs and relentlessly proffering rooms in their houses. Be sure to check that the owners are authorized by the tourist office (in the form of an authorization card from the city or the tourist bureau) and insist on seeing the room (and feeling the hot water) before settling the deal. Bargaining is fair practice. For lodging, look above the restaurants on Pr. Dr. Manuel de Arriaga and Pr. Sousa Oliveira.

Vila Turística Conde Fidalgo, Av. da Independência Nacional, 21-A (☎/fax 262 55 23 61), 3 blocks uphill from Pr. Sousa Oliveira. Prices skyrocket in July-Aug., but for rooms with private baths, some in an apartment-like setting, and a big patio in front, it's a great deal the rest of the year. Reception 9am-1am. Reservations recommended in the summer and require 50% pre-payment if far in advance. Sept.-June singles €15-20; doubles €25-30, with kitchen €25. July €30/€35/€60. August €40/€45/€60. ❷

Hospedaria Ideal, R. Adrião Batalha, 98 (☎262 55 13 79), between the 2 main *praças*. Reception 10am-10pm in the restaurant downstairs. 5 rooms with high ceilings and comfortable beds share a clean bath. Check if they are offering the "Pensão Completa" package, which includes a double room and all 3 meals for 2 people for only €70. Sept. 16-June singles €15-20; doubles €25-30. July-Sept. 15 €30/€40-45. ❸

Camping: Vale Paraíso, Estrada Nacional 242 (☎262 56 18 00; fax 262 56 19 00), 2½km out of town. Take the bus to Alcobaça or Leiria (15min., 8 per day 7am-7pm). Also rents bungalows and apartments. Swimming pools, a restaurant-bar, a supermarket, occasional Internet access, and laundry. Pool open June-Sept. €1.75; Apr.-May and Oct. free; Nov.-Mar. closed. June-Sept. €3.25 per person, €2.70-3.90 per tent, €2.70 per car. Apr.-May and Oct. €2.70/€2.30-3.25/€2.50. Nov.-Mar. €2/€1.90-2.50/€1.75. Free showers. AmEx/MC/V. ❶

FOOD

For groceries, check out the **market** across from the bus station. (Open daily July-Sept. 8am-1pm; Oct.-June Tu-Su 8am-1pm.) **Supermarkets** line R. Sub-Vila, parallel to Av. República. (Open daily June-Aug. 9am-10pm; Sept.-May 9am-8pm.)

A Tasquinha, R. Adrião Batalha, 54 (☎262 55 19 45), 1 block left of Pr. Dr. Manuel de Arriaga. Perhaps the only restaurant in Nazaré with a Portuguese-only menu; locals and tourists pack this popular restaurant between 1-2pm and 8-9pm. Carlos, the friendly English-speaking owner, is happy to help with ordering. Most entrees €4-6.50. Open Tu-Su noon-3pm and 7-11pm. AmEx/MC/V. ❶

THE LOCAL STORY

RUNNING FROM FAME

On July 2, 2002 at Ta Bar Es in Nazaré, Ábilio Ferro told Let's Go *about his experience as a musician in Portugal. Look for Ábilio's debut CD, scheduled for release in December 2002.*

Q: What kind of music do you play? What are your influences?

A: All types of music—jazz, bossa nova, *fado*, blues, rock-n-roll. I've had many influences: Led Zeppelin, the Who, and Floyd. I'm 46 and I'll be 47 in July, and I am still trying to discover myself. I have all kinds of influences and I am not sure which I'm going to follow. I love rock-n-roll, the blues, and reggae.

Q: Where did you pick up these musical influence—here in Portugal?

A: Both here in Portugal, and when I turned 16 and I sailed all over the world. I've been to 70 countries. When I went to Canada and the United States, I met a lot of good musicians. I've already played with Nick McGrain from Iron Maiden and with Nellie Furtado. I know all the star music artists here in Portugal. I've learned a lot, but my base is here. My friends like to hear me play. I've just been running away from fame.

Q: Where do you play?

A: Here in the bars and I've done a few tours through Europe, to the Azores, to Canada. Finally, I came back [to Portugal] four years ago and I've played all over the country. But now I want to get some rest. I need to rest my voice.

Q: How do you fit into the music scene here in Nazaré?

A: I see what the audience wants. If they want more *fado* or more reggae, then I'll play more *fado* or more reggae. It's easy; I like all kinds of music.

O Borges, R. Mouzinho de Albuquerque, 4 (☎262 57 91 03), near Pr. Sousa Oliveira. Bright and roomy, this upscale restaurant serves both fish and other meats. *Platos do día* are tasty and affordable (€5-7). The specialty is *arroz com mariscos* (€19 for 2 people). Open daily noon-10pm. AmEx/MC/V. ❷

Pastelaria Batel, R. Mouzinho de Albuquerque, 2 (☎262 55 11 47), at the corner of Pr. Sousa Oliveira. The best known pastry shop in Nazaré, with a 33-year history. The place to try sweet local specialties. All pastries €0.70. Try the *tamáres* (little boats with egg filling capped with chocolate), *sardinhas* (flaky pastry, not fish), and *Nazarenos* (almond pastry). Open June-Aug. daily 8am-2am; Sept.-May Th-Tu 8am-2am. ❶

SIGHTS AND ENTERTAINMENT

Nazaré's main attraction is the expansive **beach** running along the main road. After catching the sun's rays, you can take the **funicular** (3min.; every 15min. 7:15am-9:30pm, every 30min. 9:30pm-midnight; €0.60 1-way, €1.40 for 6 trips) which runs from R. Elevador off Av. República to the **Sítio,** a clifftop area of Nazaré. With its uneven cobbled streets, weathered buildings, and staggering views of the town and ocean, Sítio makes for a perfect picnic. Around 6pm, fishing boats return to the **port** beyond the far left end of the beach; eavesdrop as local restaurateurs spiritedly bid for the most promising catches at the **fish auction** (M-F 6-10pm).

Cafes in Pr. Sousa Oliveira teem with people past midnight. The intimate bar **Ta Bar Es,** R. de Rio Maior, 20-22, off R. Mouzinho Albuquerque near Pr. Dr. Manuel de Arriaga, is a mellow haven from the sun by day but livens up at night with live Brazilian and Portuguese music most summer evenings after 11pm. (☎262 08 21 73. Coffee €0.50. Before 7pm, beer €0.75-2, mixed drinks €2.50. After 7pm, beer €1-2.50, mixed drinks €3.50. Open daily 2pm-4am. Closed 1st 2 weeks of Nov.)

On Saturday afternoons in May and June, locals dress in traditional outfits and haul the fishing nets out of the water, enacting the old-fashioned technique in an event known as **Arte Xávega.** During the summer, look out for late-night **folk music** gatherings on the beach. **Bullfights** are also popular; Nazaré is on the schedule that brings *corridas* to a different city in the province each summer weekend (usually Sa 10pm; tickets start at €24.50).

DAYTRIPS FROM NAZARÉ

ALCOBAÇA

Buses are the best way to reach Alcobaça. The bus station on Av. Manuel da Silva Carolino (☎262 58 22 21) offers service to: Batalha (30min., 8 per day 7:30am-7:10 pm, €2); Coimbra (2hr.; 7:30am, 4:25pm; €6.75); Leiria (1hr., 7 per day 7:30am-7:10pm, €2.50); Lisbon (2hr.; M-F 5 per day, Sa-Su 3 per day 6:30am-6pm; €6.50); Nazaré (25min., 12-15 per day 7:30am-8:20pm, €1.25); Porto (3½hr., 4:25pm, €10).

A sleepy town in the hills not too far from the coast, Alcobaça welcomes thousands of visitors each year for one reason: its dominating **Mosteiro de Santa Maria de Alcobaça,** the oldest church in Portugal. The town was founded in 1153, following King Afonso Henriques's expulsion of the Moors, as a grant from the king to Cistercian monks. Afonso was attempting to secure Christianity in the region, so the monks began construction of their new monastery in 1178. Additions continued over the course of several centuries. Today it is the largest building of the Cistercian order in all of Europe and was recently granted UN World Heritage status. In the smaller naves adjacent to the towering central one, the **tombs** of King Pedro I and his wife Inês de Castro display sophisticated carvings, immortalizing one of Portugal's great love stories (see **Eat your heart out, Don Juan,** p. 686). Surrounding the monastery's cloisters are numerous Gothic rooms, most notably the immense

kitchen and **refectory** (the monks could roast more than 6 oxen at a time), and the **Sala dos Monges** (Monk's Hall). (☎262 50 51 20. Monastery open daily Apr.-Sept. 9am-7pm; Oct.-Mar. 9am-5pm. Cloisters open daily Apr.-Sept. 9am-6:30pm; Oct.-Mar. 9am-4:30pm. €3, students 14-25 €1.50, under 14 free. Su before 2pm free.)

The **Museu da Vinha e do Vinho** (Museum of Wine and Winemaking), 5min. from the bus station on R. Leiria (which branches off R. dos Combatentes on the way out of town), houses a comprehensive exhibit about the history and methods of Portugal's wine industry. (☎262 58 22 22. Open May-Sept. Tu-F 9am-12:30pm and 2-5:30pm, Sa-Su 10am-12:30pm and 2-6pm; Oct.-Apr. M-F 9am-12:30pm and 2-5:30pm. €1.50, students €0.75.)

The **tourist office** sits on the corner of Pr. 25 de Abril. To get there, take a right out of the bus station, then take the first right onto Av. dos Combates, and follow the road towards the monastery. The English-speaking staff hands out accommodation lists and town maps that fold into wallet-size cards. (☎262 58 23 77. Open daily May-Sept. 10am-1pm and 3-7pm; Oct.-Apr. 10am-1pm and 2-6pm.) Although Alcobaça can be easily appreciated as a daytrip, should you spend the night, **Pensão Corações Unidos ❶,** R. Frei António Brandão, 39, off Pr. 25 de Abril, has 20 rooms. (☎/fax 262 58 21 42. Reception 8am-midnight. July-Sept. singles €15, with bath €17.50; doubles €30, with bath €35. Oct.-June €12.50/€15/€25/€30.)

SÃO MARTINHO DO PORTO

Trains run from the station (☎262 98 94 85) to Leiria (1½hr., 5 per day 9:50am-8:10pm, €2) and other points north and south. Buses, faster and more convenient, run to Nazaré (20min., 7 per day 9:30am-7:30pm, €1.25) and other towns. Both train and bus schedules are posted in the tourist office. The bus stops on the main road leading into town.

Countless ages of crashing surf hollowed out surrounding coastal cliffs to create the bay of São Martinho do Porto. Nearly enclosed on all sides, the town lies at the base of the inlet, while its windless, swimmer-friendly **beach** sweeps 3km along and around the bay, forming an almost perfect circle. With its red-roofed houses crowding down a palm-studded hillside to a small and colorful fishing harbor, São Martinho do Porto has an almost Mediterranean charm; it's an ideal escape from crowded Peniche and Nazaré. Vacationers crash the peace in July and August.

The **tourist office,** on Lgo. Frederico Ulrich at the end of Av. 25 de Abril, provides a list of private rooms. (☎262 98 91 10. Open June-Sept. Tu-Su 10am-1pm and 3-7pm; Oct.-May Tu-Su 10am-1pm and 2-6pm.) A congenial place to stay is **Casa Luz ❷,** R. José Bento da Silva, 3, at the top of R. D. Pedro V; it's the white house to the left of the stairs. (☎262 98 91 39. Open May-Sept. only. Reserve at least a month ahead for August. May-July and Sept. singles €20; doubles €25. Aug. €25/€30.)

LEIRIA ☎244

Transport hub Leiria fans out from a fertile valley, 22km from the coast. An impressive ancient castle peers over the city, gazing down upon countless shops, a shady park, and a slow, algae-covered river. Chosen to host the Euro Cup 2004 soccer finals, Leiria is busy preparing itself for the crowds that will soon flood the city. Leiria makes a practical base for exploring the nearby region, with frequent buses to Alcobaça, Batalha, and Fátima, and the beaches of the Costa da Prata.

TRANSPORTATION

Trains: Leiria train station is 3km outside town (☎244 88 20 27). Buses run between the station and the tourist office (15min., every hr. 7:05am-7:20pm, €0.75). To: **Coimbra** (1½hr., 10 per day 2am-10:15pm, €5.75); **Figueira da Foz** (1hr., 3 per day 10:30am-5:45pm, €5.75); **Lisbon** (1¾hr., 9 per day 3am-11pm, €7).

Buses (☎244 81 15 07), just off Pr. Paulo VI, next to the main park and near the tourist office, in an exhaust-filled building; the ticket office is down the steps in back. Buses are the most convenient transport out of Leiria. Express buses are twice the price of regional buses. To: **Alcobaça** (50min., 6 per day 7:15am-7:10pm, €2.40-4.80); **Batalha** (20min., 9 per day 7:15am-7:10pm, €1.20); **Coimbra** (1hr., 11 per day 7:15am-2am, €5.80); **Fátima** (1hr., 6 per day 7:15am-7:05pm, €1.90-4); **Figueira da Foz** (1½hr., M-F 8 per day 7:55am-6:35pm, €5.90); **Lisbon** (2hr., 11 per day 7:15am-11pm, €7); **Nazaré** (1hr., 6-9 per day 7:50am-7:10pm, €2.50-5.50); **Porto** (3½hr., 10 per day 7:15am-2am, €9); **Santarém** (2hr., 5 per day 7:15am-7:05pm, €4.50-8); **Tomar** (1½hr.; M-F 7:15am, 5:45pm; Sa 6:15pm; €3-6).

Taxis: ☎244 81 59 00 or 244 88 15 50. Taxis gather at the Jardim Luís de Camões.

ORIENTATION AND PRACTICAL INFORMATION

The **Jardim Luís de Camões** lies at the center of Leiria. The castle up on the hill is a 20min. climb from the town below.

Tourist Office (☎244 82 37 73; fax 244 83 35 33), in the Jardim Luís de Camões, across the park from the bus station. English-speaking staff has maps, accommodations lists, and a precise model of Batalha's monastery—made entirely of sugar. Obtaining hard information, however, may prove a struggle. Free short-term **luggage storage.** Open daily May-Sept. 10am-1pm and 3-7pm; Oct.-Apr. 10am-1pm and 2-6pm.

Emergencies: ☎112. **Police:** Lgo. Artilharia, 4 (☎244 81 37 99).

Hospital (☎244 81 70 00), on R. Olhalvas, along the road to Fátima.

Internet Access: The **library,** Lgo. Cândido dos Reis, 6 (☎244 82 08 50), a few doors down from the HI hostel, offers free Internet access (1hr., twice a week); sign up in advance. Open M 1-5:45pm, Tu-F 10am-12:30pm and 1-5:45pm; Oct.-May also Sa 3-6:30pm. Both post offices charge €6 per hr.

Post Office: Downtown office (☎244 82 04 60), in Lgo. Santana on Av. Combatentes da Grande Guerra, between the tourist office and the youth hostel. Label **Posta Restante** mail "Estação Santana." Open M-F 8:30am-6pm. **Main office,** Av. Herois de Angola, 99 (☎244 84 94 10), a bit farther away, past the bus station toward the mall. Open M-F 8:30am-6:30pm, Sa 9am-12:30pm. **Postal Code:** 2400.

ACCOMMODATIONS

Pousada da Juventude de Leiria (HI), Lgo. Cândido dos Reis, 9 (☎/fax 244 83 18 68). From the bus station, walk to the cathedral and exit Lgo. da Sé (next to Lgo. Cónego Maia) onto R. Barão de Viamonte. Lgo. Cândido dos Reis is 6 blocks ahead. Kitchen, TV room, and game room with pool table (€2 per hr.). Breakfast included 8:30-10am. Reception daily June 16-Sept. 15 8am-midnight; Sept. 16-June 15 8am-noon and 6pm-midnight. Lockout noon-6pm (bag drop-off still available). June 16-Sept. 15 dorms €10.50; doubles €27. Sept. 16-June 15 €8.50/€21. AmEx/MC/V. ❶

Residencial Dom Dinis, Tr. Tomar, 2 (☎244 81 53 42; fax 244 82 35 52). Turn left after exiting the tourist office, cross the bridge over Rio Lis, walk 2 blocks. Turn left again; the hostel is on the right. 24 comfortable rooms with bath, telephone, and cable TV. Breakfast 8-10:30am. Singles €22; doubles €32.50; triples €40-42. AmEx/MC/V. ❷

Pensão Alcôa, R. Rodrigues Cordeiro, 24 (☎244 83 26 90), off Pr. Rodrigues Lobo, and next to the restaurant of the same name. All 16 rooms come with bath and cable TV. Breakfast included 8:30-10:30am. June 16-Sept. singles €22; doubles €32; triples €38. Oct.-June 15 €20/€30/€35. ❷

FOOD

The **market,** on Av. Cidade de Maringá, sells fresh produce (open M-F 8am-4pm, Sa 8am-1pm). Groceries and fresh baked bread are at **Supermercado Ulmar,** Av. Heróis de Angola, 56, just past the bus station. (☎244 83 30 42. Open M-Sa 8am-9pm, Su 10am-1pm and 3-8pm.) Budget eateries line the side streets between the park and the castle; other quality finds are near Pr. Lobo and the youth hostel.

Os Novos, Av. Combatentes da Grande Guerra, 77 (☎244 82 58 90), near the youth hostel. Inexpensive cafe/restaurant offers combination plates (€3.80-4). Daily specials €4.50-5. Open 10am-11pm; meals served noon-3pm and 7-11pm. ❶

Restaurante O Rocha, R. Dr. Correria Mateus, 54 (☎244 40 93 73). One in a series of popular, moderately priced restaurants on the pedestrian mall. Entrees €4-7. Large half portions €3.50-5. Open M-Sa noon-3pm and 7:30-10:30pm. ❷

SIGHTS AND BEACHES

From the main square, follow the signs past the austere **sé** (cathedral) to the city's most significant monument, the **Castelo de Leiria.** Built by Dom Afonso Henriques after he snatched the town from the Moors, this granite fort presides atop the crest of a volcanic hill on the north edge of town. Left to crumble for hundreds of years, the castle retains only the **torre de menagem** (homage tower), the **sala dos namorados** (lovers' hall), and a restored wall. The terrace opens onto a panoramic view of the town and river. *(☎244 81 39 82. Castle open Apr.-Sept. M-F 9am-6:30pm, Sa-Su 10am-6:30pm; Oct.-Mar. M-F 9am-5:30pm, Sa-Su 10am-5:30pm. €1; students €0.50.)* Several nearby beaches are easily accessible via bus. Buses run from the station July-Sept. 14 to: **Praia de Viera** (45min., 9 per day 7am-6:35pm, €0.80; last return 7:25pm); **Praia Pedrógão** (1hr., 6 per day 8:25am-6:35pm, €0.90; last return 6:15pm); **São Pedro de Muel** (45min.; M-F 8 per day 7:55am-6:30pm, Sa 7 per day 6:55am-5:30pm, Su 7 per day 7:55am-5:30pm; €0.80; last return 7:15pm).

BATALHA ☎244

The only reason to visit Batalha (pop. 7500) is the gigantic **Mosteiro de Santa Maria da Vitória,** rivaling Belém's Mosteiro dos Jerónimos in its monastic splendor.

TRANSPORTATION. Buses stop in Lgo. 14 de Agosto de 1385 across the street from the monastery. Inquire at the tourist office for info or call the bus station in Leiria (☎244 81 15 07). Buses from Batalha to: **Leiria** (20min., 10 per day 7:50am-8:25pm, €1.10); **Lisbon** (2hr., 6 per day 7:25am-6:55pm, €6); **Nazaré** (1hr., 13 per day 7:35am-6:50pm, €2.60) via **Alcobaça** (45min., €2); **Tomar** (1½hr.; 8:05am, noon, 6pm; €2.60) via **Fátima** (40min., €1.45).

ORIENTATION AND PRACTICAL INFORMATION. The **tourist office** is on Pr. Mouzinho de Albuquerque along R. Nossa Senhora do Caminho, just across from the monastery. Its friendly English-speaking staff offers maps and bus information, as well as accommodation lists and **luggage storage**. (☎244 76 51 80. Open daily May-Sept. 10am-1pm and 3-7pm; Oct.-Apr. 10am-1pm and 2-6pm.) In case of **emergency** call ☎112 or the **police** at ☎244 76 51 34, on R. Mouzinho de Albuquerque, across the street from the bus stop. The **health center** is on Estrada da Freiria, next to a school (☎244 76 52 46). **Internet** access is available for free at the Instituto Português da Juventude, the Edificio dos Antigos Paços do Concelho; it's across Pr. Mouzinho de Albuquerque from the tourist office, with the entrance in back. (☎244 76 63 21. 1 computer; flexible 15min.

time limit. Open M-F 1:30-5:30pm.) The **post office,** in Lgo. Papa Paulo VI, near the freeway entrance, has **fax** (€2.20 per page) and **Posta Restante.** (☎244 76 51 11; fax 244 76 91 06. Open M-F 9:30am-1pm and 2:30-6:30pm.) **Postal code:** 2440.

ACCOMMODATIONS AND FOOD. **Pensão Residencial Gladius ❷,** Pr. Mouzinho de Albuquerque, 7, has seven comfortable rooms, all with TV, nifty globe lamps, and bath. Two rooms have a view of the plaza. (☎244 76 57 60. Reception 9am-11:30pm. June-Sept. singles €25; 1 double €30; triples €40. Oct.-May €5 less.) **Pensão Vitória ❷,** on Lgo. da Misericórdia next to the bus stop, has three rooms, each with one double bed; solo travelers can ask for a discount. (☎244 76 56 78. Reception 9am-midnight. Rooms €18.) The **restaurant** below offers daily specials for €4.50-7 and *frango assado na brasa* (half-chicken, €4.50). Meals are served daily noon-3pm and 7-11pm. Several inexpensive *churrasqueiras* (barbecue houses) line the squares flanking the monastery.

SIGHTS. Batalha's **monastery complex** has been granted UN World Heritage status. Its flamboyant facade soars upward in Gothic and Manueline style, opulently decorated and topped by dozens of spires. The **Capela do Fundador,** immediately to the right of the church, shelters the elaborate sarcophagi of Dom João I, his English-born queen Philippa of Lancaster, and their son Prince Henry the Navigator. The rest of the complex is accessible via a door in the nave of the church; enter through the broad Gothic arches of the **Claustro de Dom João I,** the delicate columns of which initiated the Manueline style. Adjacent to the cloister lies the **Tomb of the Unknown Soldier,** always guarded by two motionless men in uniform. Through the **Claustro de Dom Afonso V,** out the door and to the right are the unique **Capelas Imperfeitas** (Unfinished Chapels), with massive buttresses designed to support a large dome that was never actually constructed; the project was abandoned when Manuel I ordered his workers to build the monastery in Belém instead. (Open daily Apr.-Sept. 9am-6pm; Oct.-Mar. 9am-5pm. €3, under 25 and seniors €1.50, under 14 and Su before 2pm free. Church free.)

Twenty minutes out of town lies a series of spectacular underground *grutas* (caves) in Estremadura's natural park between Batalha and Fátima. The **Grutas de Mira de Aire** are the deepest; though **Grutas de Santo António** and **Alvados** are equally impressive. From Batalha, take a bus to **Torre Novas** (20min., 6 per day 7:35am-7:40pm, €1.75; last bus back to Batalha 6:30pm). Ask the driver to stop at the *grutas.* (Caves open daily July-Aug. 9:30am-8:30pm; June and Sept. 9:30am-7pm; Oct.-Mar. 9:30am-5:30pm; Apr.-May 9:30am-6pm. €3.50, students and seniors €2.50.)

FÁTIMA ☎249

Until 1917, when the Virgin Mary appeared to three peasant children, Fátima was a sheep pasture. Now the once-quiet village has become a religious center, defined by its total immersion in holy fervor. A sign at the entrance of the town's holy Santuário complex states, "Fátima is a place for adoration; enter as a pilgrim." Only Lourdes rivals this site in popularity with Catholic pilgrims, as the miracles believed to have occurred here attract an endless international procession of religious groups. The plaza in front of the church, larger than St. Peter's Square in the Vatican, floods with pilgrims on the 12th and 13th of each month.

TRANSPORTATION

Trains: The **Caxarias** station (☎249 57 43 50), 10km out of town, is closer than the Fátima station (☎249 56 61 22), 22km away. From Caxarias to: **Coimbra** (1hr., 14 per day 5:25am-1:55am, €3.50); **Lisbon** (2½hr., 9 per day 6:50am-11:30pm, €5.20);

Porto (4hr., 12 per day 5:25am-1:55am, €6.80); **Santarém** (1½hr., 10 per day 6:50am-9:35pm, €3.20). **Buses** run between the Caxarias train station and the bus station (30min., 7 per day 7:50am-7:50pm, €1.80) as well as between the Fátima train and bus stations (45min., 5 per day 6:10am-6:35pm, €2.20).

Buses: Av. Dr. José Alves Correia da Silva (☎249 53 16 11). To: **Batalha** (30min., 3 per day 9am-6:35pm, €1.45); **Coimbra** (1½hr., 9-13 per day 7:45am-7:40pm, €7.50); **Leiria** (1hr., 13 per day 7:45am-8pm, €2.50-4); **Lisbon** (1½-2½hr., 11-17 per day 7am-5pm, €7); **Nazaré** (1½hr.; 9am, 1:55, 6:25pm; €3); **Porto** (3-3½hr.; 11 per day 7:45am-9:30pm, Sa last bus 5:30pm; €9.50); **Santarém** (1hr., 7 per day 7:30am-5:45pm, €5.90); **Tomar** (1¼hr.; 8:30am, 12:30, 6:35pm; €2.40).

Taxis: Call ☎249 53 21 92, or catch one next to the bus station.

ORIENTATION AND PRACTICAL INFORMATION

Activity in Fátima centers around the basilica complex. The **Santuário de Fátima** is the huge, open *praça* that fills with visitors on special occasions and the 12th and 13th of each month. The bus station and tourist office are on **Avenida D. José Alves Correia da Silva,** which runs just south of the Santuário. The **tourist office** is in a lovely stone building with a wooden roof. From the bus station, take a right and walk 10min.; the office is a short way past the Santuário. (☎249 53 11 39. Open daily June-Sept. 10am-1pm and 3-7pm; Oct.-May 10am-1pm and 2-6pm.) Pl. Santuário has its own information office, on the left side when facing the basilica. English-speaking staff. (☎249 53 96 23. Open M-Sa 9am-6pm, Su 9am-5pm.) Several major **banks** have branches along the commercial center of R. Jacinta Marto (open 8:30am-3pm). Services include: **emergency:** ☎112; **police:** Av. D. José Alves Correia da Silva (☎249 53 97 30), **Centro de Saúde,** on R. Jacinta Marto (☎249 53 18 36); **Internet access** at **X-Medi@,** R. S. João de Deus, 13 (☎249 53 22 60), in the Edificio Varandas de Fátima, a few blocks behind and to the right of the basilica. The **post office** is on R. Cónego Formigão. (☎249 53 18 10. Open M-F 8:30am-6pm.) **Postal Code:** 2495.

ACCOMMODATIONS AND FOOD

Scores of hostels surround the basilica complex; prices vary little. During the grand pilgrimages of the 12th and 13th of every month, the population and prices rise. It's always best to reserve one week ahead,

THE LOCAL STORY

A HOPE AND A PRAYER

Corina Diaz is a Latin American Pilgrim to Fátima. An estimated five to six million religious pilgrims visit the site every year.

Q: Why was it important for you to come to Fátima?

A: I come from a rural town that is very religious, very Catholic. I remember learning the story of the three little shepherd children and how the Virgin appeared to them, and so I always wanted to come and visit since I was a girl.

Q: What special significance does an apparition have in this modern era?

A: Well, it is very important because it was looked at scientifically. Since this miracle happened in modern times and the Vatican was able to study it and confirm that there was no natural explanation for it, this apparition is more believable than earlier ones because some could just say, "Oh, those were hallucinations or optical illusions." But with Fátima, we were able to look at it through modern, skeptical eyes and prove that the miracle occurred, so it is very important that it happened when it did.

Q: When you see all the pilgrims in Fátima from so many different countries and cultures, what do you think?

A: I was so happy to see all the different people, because it means that hope is still alive and that people still have a love of God. One of the central messages of Fátima was to bring peace to the world, and so to see all the people here, you know that the hope is still there.

and at least a month prior on summer weekends and holidays. The plain but comfortable rooms of **Residencial São Francisco ❶**, R. Francisco Marto, 100, just off the Santuário, all come with TV, phone, and private baths, and some have private balconies. (☎249 53 30 17; fax 249 53 20 28. Reception 7:30am-midnight. Breakfast included. Singles €15; doubles €25; triples €35.) **Residência São Jorge ❷**, R. Santa Cruz, 4, off R. Jacinta Marto near the Wax Museum, has hotel-like rooms with TV, private bath, and flower-lined balconies. During the day, enter through the souvenir shop next door on the left. (☎/fax 249 53 14 64. Reception 8am-midnight. Lockout midnight. Singles €20; doubles €30; triples €45. AmEx/MC/V.) **Restaurants** and snack bars cluster in commercial centers along R. Francisco Marto, R. Santa Isabela, and R. Jacinta Marto.

SIGHTS

SANTUÁRIO DE FATIMA. The modern holy sanctuary is a visually overwhelming site. Many of the devout travel the length of the plaza on their knees, all the way from the cross to the *capelinha*, praying for divine assistance or giving thanks to the Virgin Mary. After decades of fervent speculation, the Vatican disclosed the closely guarded "third secret" of Fàtima in 2000, ending fears that it revealed the apocalypse. The Virgin is said to have prophesied the 1981 assassination attempt on Pope John Paul II in St. Peter's Square. The Pope now credits the Virgin with saving his life and had the bullet placed in the Madonna's crown here.

At the end of the plaza rises the **Basílica do Rosário** (erected in 1928), featuring a crystal cruciform beacon atop the tower's seven-ton bronze crown. Inside are the tombs of two of the children who witnessed the apparitions; Francisco lies in the right nave, while Jacinta is in the left. *(Open daily 7:30am-10:30pm. Mass daily at 7:30, 9, 11am, 3, 4:30, and 6:30pm.)* To the left, in front of the Basílica do Rosário, is the **Capelinha das Aparições,** where the miracles allegedly took place. Sheltered beneath a metal and glass canopy, the Little Chapel of the Apparitions was built in 1919 at the site of the apparitions. Religious groups from all over the world make pilgrimages to the site and perform Mass at the chapel; an international Mass in many languages is held there every Thursday at 9am. A candlelight procession is held every evening at 9:30pm from April to October.

MUSEUMS. The **Museu de Arte Sacra e Etnologia** exhibits Catholic icons from various centuries. *(R. Francisco Marto, 5. 3 blocks from the basilica. ☎249 53 94 70. Open Apr.-Oct. Tu-Su 10am-7pm; Nov.-Mar. noon-5pm. €2, seniors and students €1.)* The **Museu Fátima 1917 Aparições** uses light, sound, and special effects to re-create the apparition. *(R. Jacinta Marto. To the left of the basilica, through the park, in the complex beneath the Hotel Fátima. ☎249 53 28 58. Open daily Apr.-Oct. 9am-7pm; Nov.-Mar. 9am-6pm. €2, children under 12 €1).*

TOMAR ☎249

The arcane Knights Templar—part monks, part warriors—plotted crusades from Tomar (pop. 22,000) for centuries. A celebrated convent-fortress sitting high above the old town served as the knights' powerful and mysterious headquarters. Known as the Convento de Cristo, the complex ingeniously combines architectural styles from the 12th to 17th centuries. Today, Tomar rests peacefully in the shade of the eucalyptus and sycamore trees lining the banks of the Rio Nabão.

TRANSPORTATION

Trains: Av. Combatentes da Grande Guerra (☎249 31 28 15), at the southern edge of town. As Tomar is the northern end of a minor line, most destinations require a transfer at Entroncamento; be sure to check your ticket. **Ticket office** open M-F 5am-8:30pm and 9:30-10:30pm; Sa 5:30-8:30am, 9:30am-6:30pm, and 7:30-10:30pm; Su 6:30am-10:30pm. To: **Coimbra** (2½hr., 6 per day 6:05am-6:05pm, €4.80-6); **Lisbon** (2hr., 18 per day 5:05am-10:05pm, €5-10); **Porto** (4½hr., 7 per day 8:05am-8:05pm, €7.70-11); **Santarém** (1hr., 12 per day 5:05am-10:05pm, €2.60-4.20).

Buses: Rodoviária Tejo, Av. Combatentes da Grande Guerra (☎249 31 27 38), next to the train station. Express buses are twice the price of regular buses. To: **Coimbra** (2½hr., 7am, €8.25); **Fátima** (30min., 3 per day 7:50am-5:20pm, €2.40-5); **Figueira da Foz** (4½hr., 7am, €8.25); **Lagos** (9hr.; M-Sa 9:15am via Santarém and Évora, 10:15am via Lisbon, Su 10:15am via Lisbon; €16); **Leiria** (1hr.; M-F 7:15am, 5:45pm; Sa 7am; €3-6); **Lisbon** (2hr., 4 per day 9:15am-6pm, €6); **Nazaré** (1½hr., 3 per day 7:50am-5:20pm, €4.40-9); **Porto** (4hr., 7am); **Santarém** (1hr.; 9:15am, 6pm; €6).

Taxis: ☎249 31 37 16 or 31 23 73. Cabs cluster near the bus and train stations, as well as on R. Santa Iria, across the river.

ORIENTATION AND PRACTICAL INFORMATION

The **Rio Nabão** divides Tomar. Almost everything travelers need—the train and bus stations, accommodations, and sights—lies on the west bank. The lush **Parque Mouchão** straddles the two banks, while the ancient **Ponte Velha** (old bridge) connects the two. From the **Ponte Nova** (new bridge), **Av. Dr. Cândido Madureira** leads to **Pr. Infante Dom Henrique,** behind which lie the trails of the **Parque da Mata Nacional dos Sete Montes.** (Park open daily 10am-6pm. Free.) The **bus** and **train stations** sit next to each other on **Av. Combatentes da Grande Guerra,** near the outskirts of town. The pedestrian-only **R. Serpa Pinto** cuts across the town from the river to the castle and connects the Ponte Velha to **Praça da República,** the main square.

Tourist Office: Casa Vieira Guimarães, R. Serpa Pinto (☎/fax 249 32 24 27 or 249 32 98 14), on the corner of Av. do Marquês de Tomar, across the street from the regional tourist office and the Ponte Velha. From the bus or train station, take a right onto Av. Combatentes da Grande Guerra, then take a left onto Av. Torres Pinheiro, and continue straight past the traffic circle on R. Everaro; the office is on the left, just past the bridge. Short-term **luggage storage.** Open daily July-Sept. 10am-8pm, Oct.-June 10am-6pm.

Emergency: ☎112. **Police:** R. Dr. Sousa (☎249 31 34 44).

Hospital: Av. Cândido Madureira (☎249 32 11 00), down from the tourist office.

Internet Access: INCA, R. João do Santos Simões, 60 (☎249 32 16 06), over the bridge, off R. Marqués Pombal. €2 per 30min. Open M-F 9:30am-1pm and 3-7pm, Sa 10am-1pm. Available free at nightspot **Casablanca,** R. São João, 83 (☎249 31 47 57), between the tourist office and Pr. República. Open M-Sa 10pm-4am.

Post Office: Av. Marquês de Tomar (☎249 31 04 00; fax 249 31 04 06), across from Parque Mouchão. **Fax** and **Posta Restante** available. Open M-F 8:30am-6pm, Sa 9am-12:30pm. **Postal Code:** 2300.

ACCOMMODATIONS AND CAMPING

Finding accommodations is only a problem during the **Festival dos Tabuleiros,** which takes place once every four years (next in 2003). **R. Serpa Pinto** is lined with quality lodging, while cheaper options lie closer to the bus and train stations.

Residencial União, R. Serpa Pinto, 94 (☎249 32 31 61; 32 12 99), halfway between Pr. República and the bridge. The nicest budget accommodation in Tomar, in a central location. 28 rooms all have TV, phone, and private bath. Well-stocked bar. Breakfast included. Reception 8am-midnight. Reservations recommended for July and Aug. Apr.-Sept. singles €25; doubles €35; 3rd person €5 more. Oct.-Mar. €20/€33/€2.50. ❷

Residencial Luz, R. Serpa Pinto, 144 (☎/fax 249 31 23 17; www.residencialluz.com), close to Residencial União. 14 clean and comfy rooms, most with private bath, TV, and phone. May 16-Sept. singles €20, with bath €22; doubles €30, with bath €35; 1 quad with bath €45-60. Oct.-May 15 €15-18/€18-20/€23-25/€25-30/€35-45. ❷

Casa de Dormidas, R. de D. Aurora de Macedo, 46 (☎249 31 19 03 or 249 32 28 78). Go to the Casa Costa shop on Av. Dr. Cândido Madureira, 18, near the traffic circle, and speak with owner José Fernandes Costa. Singles €15; doubles €25. For the absolute rock bottom deal in town, ask about his rooms without bath at **Casa de Dormidas Convento,** Av. Combatentes da Grande Guerra, 7. Singles €10; doubles €15. ❶

Camping: Parque Municipal de Campismo (☎249 32 98 24; fax 249 32 26 08), on the river, across Pte. Velha and to the left. Thickly forested campground with pool. Free showers. Reception daily 8am-1pm and 3-5pm. June-Sept. €2.30 per person, €2 per tent, €2.20 per car, €1.50 for electricity; Oct.-May 50% less. ❶

FOOD

The lush **Parque Mouchão,** across from Av. Marquês Tomar, is the perfect spot for a picnic. The **market,** across the river on the corner of Av. Norton de Matos and R. Santa Iria, provides all but the red-checkered blanket. (Open Tu, Th-F 8am-2pm. The larger F market has a flea market portion as well.) Several inexpensive **mini-markets** line the side streets between the tourist office and Pr. República.

Ristorante/Pizzeria Bella Italia, R. Everard, 91 (☎249 32 29 96), near the river, between the 2 main bridges. Family serves delicious pastas (€4-7) and pizzas (€4-9). Specialties include *pasta mista* (€12; serves 2). The *tiramisú* (€2.50) is the most popular dessert. Open daily noon-3pm and 7-11pm. ❶

Salsinha Verde, Pr. da República, 19 (☎249 32 32 29), at the corner of the main plaza, to the left when facing the town hall. Local students pop *petingas* (small fish; €0.15) at the bar. Entrees served in the dining room €3.50-7. Cheaper *pratos do dia* (daily specials, €3). Open M-Sa 8am-midnight. ❶

SIGHTS AND ENTERTAINMENT

From the tourist office, take the second right and bear left at the fork to reach the mysterious grounds of the **Convento de Cristo,** which display an intriguing range of architecture and landscaping. (Pedestrians can take the steeper dirt path a bit after the fork on the left or follow the cars up the paved road. From Pr. República, walk behind the *praça* and pick up the path.) The first structure was built by the Knights Templar in 1160, but successive centuries have added an eclectic collection of various cloisters, convents, and buildings. An ornate octagonal canopy protects the high altar of the **Templo dos Templares,** modeled after the Holy Sepulchre in Jerusalem. Below stands the **Janela do Capítulo** (chapter window), an exuberant tribute to the Age of Discovery. One of Europe's masterpieces of Renaissance architecture, the **Claustro dos Felipes** honors King Felipe II of Castile, who was crowned here as Felipe I of Portugal during Iberia's unification (1580-1640). Stairs spiral upward to the sweeping views of the **Terraço da Cera.** Tucked behind the Palladian main cloister and the nave is the **Claustro da Santa Bárbara,** where grotesque gargoyle rain-spouts writhe in pain as they cough up a fountain.

On the northeast side of the church is the Gothic **Claustro do Cemitério.** (☎249 31 34 81. Open daily June-Sept. 9am-6pm; Oct.-May 9am-5pm. €3, under 14 free.) The **Museu Luso-Hebraico Abraáo Zacuto** is Portugal's most significant reminder of its once-vibrant Jewish community. This synagogue, built between 1430 and 1460, now houses a small museum of international Jewish history, with a collection of tombstones, inscriptions, and pieces from around the world. (R. Dr. Joaquim Jaquinto, 73. Open daily 10am-1pm and 2-6pm. Free.) For a week near the end of June, handicrafts, folklore, *fado*, and theater storm the city during the **Feira Nacional de Artesanato,** but the biggest party in Tomar is the **Festa dos Tabuleiros,** which takes place only once every four years (the next will occur in 2003). Tomar also hosts four summer **bullfights;** look for large, brightly colored posters advertising the *corridas*.

THE THREE BEIRAS

The Three Beiras region offers a sampling of the best of Portugal: the pristine beaches of the coast, the rich greenery of the interior, and the ragged peaks of the Serra de Estrela. The Beira Litoral (Coastal Region) encompasses the unspoiled Costa da Prata (Silver Coast) beginning at the resort town of Figueira da Foz and passing through up-and-coming Aveiro on the way to Porto. The soil in this region yields some of Portugal's best farmland, and the countryside is dotted with red-roofed farmhouses surrounded by endless expanses of corn, sunflower, and wheat fields. A vibrant university city, Coimbra overlooks the region from its perch above the Rio Mondego. The mountainous extremes of the region, Beira Alta and lowland Beira Baixa, have retained their wealth in tradition.

COIMBRA ☎239

The country's only university city from the mid-16th to the early 20th century, Coimbra is still a mecca for youth and backpackers alike. A slew of cheap cafes and bars, coupled with an energetic student body, keep Coimbra swinging from September through May.

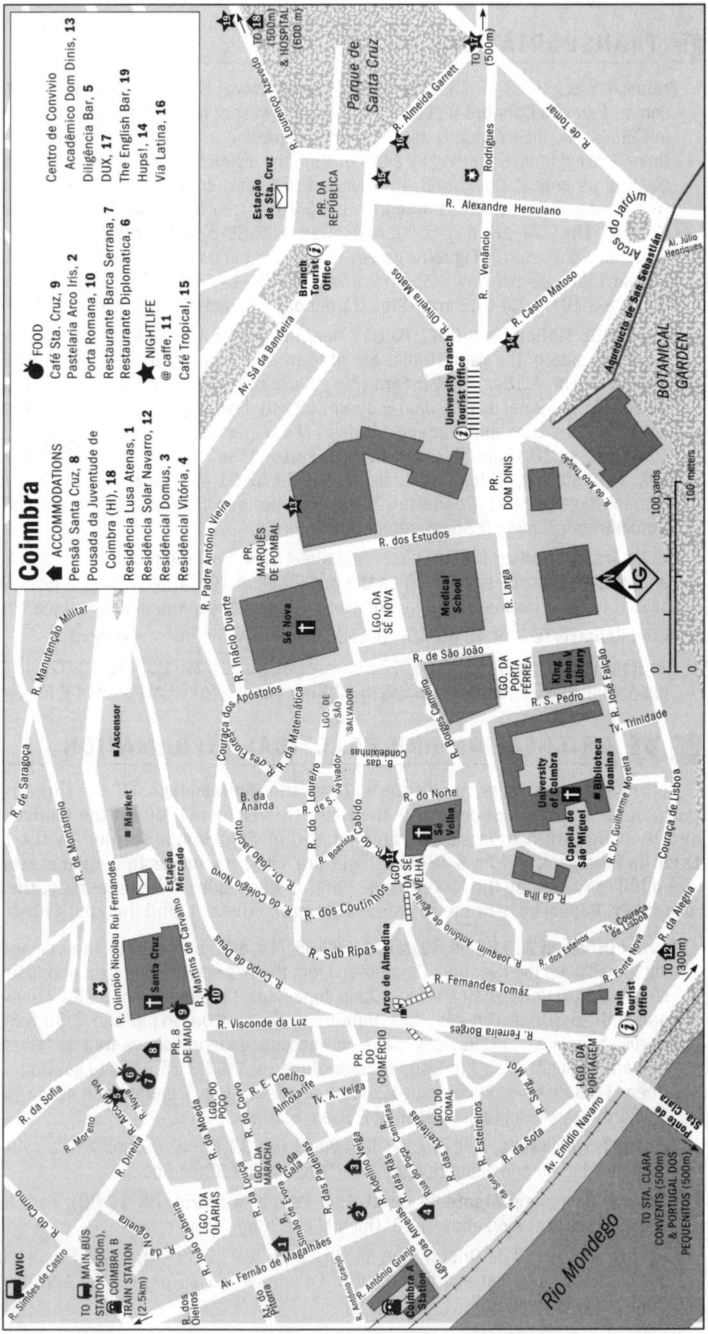

THREE BEIRAS

TRANSPORTATION

Trains: Info ☎239 83 49 98. **Estação Coimbra-A (Nova)** is 2 blocks from the lower town center. **Estação Coimbra-B (Velha)** is 3km northwest of town. Regional trains stop first in Coimbra-B, then continue to Coimbra-A, departing in reverse order. Long-distance trains arriving from/departing for cities outside the region stop in Coimbra-B only. If your train stops only at Coimbra-B, it is easiest to take a connecting train to Coimbra-A (4min., immediately after trains arrive, €0.70 or free if transfer). Trains to: **Aveiro** (30min.-1hr., 22 per day 5:10am-3:10am, €2.80-6.50); **Braga** (3hr.; 9:55am, 7:55pm; €6.10-8.20); **Figueira da Foz** (1¼hr., 24 per day 5:20am-12:20am, €1.45); **Lisbon** (3hr., 23 per day 5:35am-2:20am, €7.70-13.50); **Ovar** (1½hr., 21 per day 5:10am-3:10am, €4-6); **Porto** (2hr., 21 per day 5:10am-3:10am, €5.20-9.50).

Buses: RBL station (☎239 82 70 81), near the end of Av. Fernão Magalhães, on the university side of the river 10min. out of town, and past Coimbra-A. Buses to: **Évora** (4hr.; 9:30am, 4:15pm; €12); **Faro** (8hr., 3 per day 9:25am-2:10am, €15); **Figueira da Foz** (1½hr., 9 per day 7:20am-6:35pm, €2.80); **Lisbon** (2½hr., 17 per day 7:30am-2:15am, €9); **Luso** and **Buçaco** (45min.; M-F 7 per day 7:35am-7:20pm; Sa 9am, 12:45pm; Su 10:15am, 5:30pm; €2.50); **Porto** (1½hr., 10 per day 8:30am-9:30pm, €7). **AVIC station,** R. João de Ruão, 18 (☎239 82 01 41), between R. Sofia and Av. Fernão Magalhães. To **Condeixa** (25min., 14 per day 7:35am-7:35pm, €1.25) and **Conímbriga** (30min.; 9:35am, return bus 6pm; €1.40).

Public Transportation: SMTUC buses and street cars. Round-trip ticket €0.80 at kiosks and vending machines or €1.20 on the bus. Book of 10 €4; 3-day tourist pass €6.20 sold at vending machines at Lgo. Portagem, Pr. República, and throughout the city.

Taxis: Politaxis (☎239 48 40 45). Outside Coimbra-A and the bus station.

Car Rental: Avis (☎/fax 239 83 47 86; reservations toll-free 800 20 10 02), in Coimbra-A. Min. age 21. Open M-F 8:30am-12:30pm and 3-7pm. Cars start at €75 per day.

ORIENTATION AND PRACTICAL INFORMATION

Coimbra's steep streets rise in tiers above the **Rio Mondego.** Of the three major parts of town, the most central is the **Baixa** (lower town), site of the **tourist office** and the Coimbra-A **train station,** and set within the triangle formed by the river, **Largo da Portagem,** and **Pr. 8 de Maio.** Coimbra's historic **university district** is atop the steep hill overlooking the lower town. On the other side of the university, the area around **Pr. República** is home to cafes, a shopping district, and the youth hostel.

Tourist Office (☎239 85 59 30; fax 239 82 55 76), off Lgo. Portagem, in a yellow building 2 blocks up the river from Coimbra-A. From the bus station, turn right and follow the street to Lgo. Portagem (15min.). Open June-Sept. M-F 9am-7pm, Sa-Su 10am-1pm and 2:30-5:30pm; Oct.-May M-F 9am-6pm, Sa-Su 10am-1pm and 2:30-5:30pm. English-speaking staff provides maps and accommodation lists as well as transportation and regional info. **University branch office** (☎239 83 25 91), in Lgo. Dom Dinis. Open M-F 9am-6pm, Sa-Su 9am-12:30pm and 2-5:30pm. Other **branch office** (☎239 83 32 02) in Pr. República. Open M-F 10am-6:30pm.

Budget Travel: Tagus, R. Padre António Vieira (☎239 83 49 99; fax 239 83 49 16). Handles student and youth budget travel. Open M-F 9:30am-6pm.

Currency Exchange: Montepio Geral, Lgo. Portagem (☎239 85 17 00), near tourist office. €5 commission above €50. Open M-F 8:30am-3pm.

Luggage Storage: Café Cristal, Lgo. Anreias, 5 (☎239 82 39 44), off Av. Fernão Magalhães, across the street and to the left of Coimbra-A. €1.25 per bag for 4hr. drop off. Open daily 5:30am-10pm.

Laundromat: Lavandaria Lucira, Av. Sá da Bandeira, 86 (☎239 82 57 01). Self-service wash and dry €5.50 per load. Open M-F 9am-1pm and 3-7pm, Sa 9am-1pm.

Emergency: ☎112. **Police:** ☎239 82 95 65. Special division for foreigners *(Serviço de Estrangeiros),* R. Venâncio Rodrigues, 25 (☎239 82 37 67).

Hospital: Hospital da Universidade de Coimbra (☎239 40 04 00 or 239 40 05 00), Lgo. Professor Mota Pinto and Av. Dr. Bissaya Barreto. Take bus #7 or 29.

Internet Access: Central Modem, Escada de Quebra Costas, down the stairs from Lgo. da Sé Velha. €0.55 per 15min. Open M-F 10am-10pm. **Post Net,** R. Antero de Quental, 73 (☎239 84 10 25), between Pr. República and the youth hostel. €0.75 per 15min.; €2.50 per hr. Open M-F 10am-midnight, Sa 2pm-midnight, Su 7pm-midnight. **@ caffé,** Lgo. da Sé Velha, 4-8 (☎239 83 81 64), across from the old cathedral. €1.50 per hr.

Post Office: Central office (☎239 85 07 70; toll-free 800 20 68 68), in the pink building on Av. Fernão Magalhães. Open M-F 8:30am-6:30pm. **Telephones** and **fax** service available. **Branch office** (☎239 85 18 20; fax 239 85 18 26), Pr. República, between the youth hostel and the university. Label **Posta Restante** "Estação Santa Cruz." Open M-F 9am-6pm. **Postal Code:** 3000 for central Coimbra.

THREE BEIRAS

ACCOMMODATIONS

Pensão Santa Cruz, Pr. 8 de Maio, 21, 3rd fl. (☎/fax 239 82 61 97; www.pensaosantacruz.com), directly across from the Igreja da Santa Cruz. From Lgo. Portagem, follow R. Ferreira Borges as it becomes R. Visconde da Luz and leads to the plaza. A family pension with comfortable rooms, most with cable TV and some with bath. 2 rooms share a balcony overlooking the plaza, ideal for viewing free summer concerts. July-Sept. singles or doubles €20, with bath €30; triples €25, with bath €35. Oct.-June €5 less. Discounts for extended stays. ❷

Pousada da Juventude de Coimbra (HI), R. Henrique Seco, 14 (☎239 82 29 55; fax 239 82 17 30). From the tourist office, walk up R. Ferreira Borges to Pr. 8 de Maio. Walk 20min. uphill along R. Olímpio Nicolau Rui Fernandes to Pr. República, then up R. Lourenço Azevedo (to the left of the park); take the 2nd right. Kitchen, TV room, and heavenly showers. Laundry €5 per load. Reception 8am-noon and 6pm-midnight. Lockout noon-6pm. Bag drop-off available (except M-F 1-2pm and Sa-Su noon-6pm). June 16-Sept. 15 dorms €10.50; doubles with bath €29. Sept. 16-June €8.50/€24. ❶

Residencial Vitória, R. da Sota, 11-19 (☎239 82 40 49; fax 84 28 97), across from Coimbra-A. Rooms with prices to suit any budget. Newly renovated rooms with bath, phone, TV, and A/C. 24hr. reception. New rooms: singles €25; doubles €35; triples €45. Older rooms: singles €15, with shower €18; doubles €20-€25. MC/V. ❷/❶

Residência Solar Navarro, Av. Emídio Navarro, 60-A, 2nd floor (☎239 82 79 99), past the tourist office and across from the park; look for the green Delta sign. All rooms with bath and TV, some with balconies and views of the park. 24hr. reception. Singles €15; 1 double €30; 1 triple €38; 1 enormous room with 5 beds €62. ❶

Residencial Domus, R. Adelino Veiga, 62 (☎239 82 85 84; fax 239 83 88 18), between Coimbra-A and Pr. do Comércio. A 3-star *residencial* with a more economical annex across the street in the Residencial Moderna building. Central location, kind staff, and large rooms. Main rooms all have bath, phone, and cable TV; annex rooms are without bath. 24hr. reception. July-Sept. main rooms: singles €30; doubles €40; 1 triple €45. Annex: singles €23; doubles €30. Oct.-June main rooms: €23/€35/€38; Annex: €20/€23. Discounts for extended stays. ❸

Residência Lusa Atenas, Av. Fernão Magalhães, 68, upstairs (☎239 82 64 12; fax 239 82 01 33), between Coimbra-A and the bus station, next to Pensão Avis. Rooms with bath, phone, A/C, and cable TV in a classic building. TV room with cushy brown couches. Reception 8am-midnight. July-Aug. singles €20-25; doubles €30-35; triples €45; quads €50. May-June €20/€30/€38/€40. Sept.-Apr. €18/€25/€30/€40. ❷

FOOD

For eats, check out the areas around R. Direita off Pr. 8 de Maio, the side streets between the river and Lgo. Portagem, and university-side Pr. República. Restaurants offer steamy portions of *arroz de lampreia* (rice with lamprey meat). The cheapest meals around are found at **UC Cantina,** the university's student cafeteria, on the right side of R. Oliveiro Matos. An international student ID is (theoretically) mandatory. Get your fruit at the enormous green warehouse **mercado,** on the right just past the post office and uphill on R. Olímpio Nicolau Rui Fernandes (open M-Sa 8am-1pm). **Supermercado Minipreço,** R. António Granjo 6C, is in the lower town center. (☎239 82 77 57. Open M-Sa 8:30am-8pm, Su 9am-1pm and 3-7pm.)

Porta Romana, R. Martins de Carvalho, 10 (☎239 82 84 58), just up from the Igreja da Santa Cruz in Pr. 8 de Maio. Amiable staff serves surprisingly affordable Italian dishes. Pizzas €4-7, pastas €4.70-7.50, salads €3.50-4. Open July-Aug. M-Sa 7am-midnight, Su 6pm-midnight; Sept.-June M-F 7am-midnight. ❷

Pastelaria Arco Iris, Av. Fernão Magalhães, 22 (☎239 83 33 04), across from the Coimbra-A station. A colorful variety of pastries (€0.50-0.80) are displayed in the glass cases. Coffee €0.45-0.90. A large selection of sandwiches is also available (€1-2.50). Open M-Sa 7:15am-8:30pm, Su 8am-8:30pm. ❶

Restaurante Barca Serrana, R. Direita, 46 (☎239 82 06 16), down R. Direita from Pr. 8 de Maio. A popular and inexpensive lunch spot. Enjoy an entree (€3.80-7) in the dining room in back or at the wide counter. 2 specials per day (€3.50). Open M-F 9am-11pm, Sa 9am-4pm; meals served M-F 11:30am-3pm and 8-11pm, Sa 8-11pm. ❷

Café Santa Cruz, Pr. 8 de Maio, 5 (☎239 83 36 17), right next to the church. Formerly part of the cathedral, this is the city's most famous cafe–a popular place for coffee (€0.50-1) and people-watching. Features a vaulted ceiling and stained-glass windows. Best on summer nights during the free concerts in the square. Sandwiches €1.25-2.50. Open May-Sept. M-Sa 7am-2am, Oct.-Apr. M-Sa 7am-midnight. ❶

Restaurante Diplomática, R. Nova, 15 (☎239 82 37 84). From Pr. 8 de Maio, walk up R. Sofia; look for the sign on the right. A popular spot for traditional fare in a laid-back setting. Entrees €5-10. Open M-Sa noon-3:30pm and 7-10pm. ❷

SIGHTS

OLD TOWN. Take in Coimbra's old town sights by making the arduous climb from the river up to the university. Begin the ascent at the ancient **Arco de Almedina,** a remnant of the Moorish town wall, one block uphill from Lgo. Portagem, next to the Banco Pinto e Sotto Mayor. The gate leads to a street aptly named R. Quebra-Costas (Back-Breaker Street). Up a narrow stone stairway looms the 12th-century Romanesque **Sé Velha** (Old Cathedral). Don't miss the peaceful cloister upstairs from the main nave. *(Open M-Th 10am-noon and 2-7:30pm, F-Su 10am-1pm. Cathedral free. Cloisters €1, students €0.75.)* Follow the signs to the nearby 16th-century **Sé Nova** (New Cathedral), whose exterior was completed by architects for the resident Jesuit community. *(Open Tu-Sa 9am-noon and 2-6:30pm. Free.)*

THE UNIVERSITY. Though many buildings have since been built from 1950s reinforced concrete, the original law school still retains its spot on the architectural Dean's List. Enter the center of the old university through the **Porta Férrea** (Iron Gate), off R. São Pedro. *(Uphill from the new cathedral. Open daily May-Sept. 9am-7:30pm; Oct.-Apr. 9:30am-12:30pm and 2-5:30pm.)* The staircase at right leads up to the **Sala dos Capelos** (Graduates' Hall), where portraits of Portugal's kings (6 of whom were born in Coimbra) hang below a 17th-century ceiling. *(Open daily 9:30am-12:30pm and 2-5pm. €2.50.)* The **university chapel** and mind-boggling, gilded 18th-century **Biblioteca Joanina** lie past the Baroque clock tower. *(☎239 85 98 41. Open daily May-Sept. 9am-7:30pm, Oct.-Apr. 9:30am-noon and 2-5:30pm. A limited number of people allowed at a time, so there is generally up to 1hr. wait. €2.50, teachers and students free. A booklet of tickets for all university sights can be purchased for €4 from the office in the main quad.)*

ACROSS THE RIVER. Cross the bridge in front of Lgo. Portagem to discover the 14th-century **Convento de Santa Clara-a-Velha.** Today, more than half of its structure is submerged in the morass. Abandoned in 1687, the convent was recently renovated to reveal an ancient church founded in 1330 by Queen Isabel, wife of Dom Dinis. The Queen's Gothic tomb was relocated uphill to the ornate **Convento de Santa Clara-a-Nova.** *(☎239 44 16 74. Interior closed until summer 2003 for massive renovation. Church open M-Sa 9am-noon and 2-6pm. Cloisters and sacristy €1.)*

NIGHTLIFE

After dinner, outdoor cafes surrounding Pr. República buzz with animated conversation from midnight to 2am, after which crowds move on to the bars and clubs further afield. Nights are best September through May, when the students are in town. Bars and clubs are listed in chronological order by peak hour. Figueira da Foz (see p. 681) offers more nightlife options and makes a popular "night-trip."

Café Tropical, Pr. República, 35 (☎239 82 48 57). Fills with students after midnight. Beer €0.70-1.25. Mixed drinks €3.50. Open M-Sa 9am-2am.

Diligência Bar, R. Nova, 30 (☎239 82 76 67), off R. Sofia. Shamelessly touristy during the summer, yet still intimate and pleasant. Excellent *fado* performed nightly after 10pm. Sangría €9.20 per liter. Open M-Sa 6pm-2am, Su 7pm-2am.

The English Bar, R. Lourenço de Almeida Azevedo, 24 (☎919 50 94 39). Bottom floor restaurant serves traditional English pub grub, while a top floor DJ spins 70s and 80s music to an age 20-40 bar-side crowd. Huge backyard patio. Beer €1.50-2. Mixed drinks €3-4. Best F-Sa at midnight. Open M-Sa 10pm-4am.

Centro de Convívio Acadêmico Dom Dinis, Lgo. D. Dinis (☎239 83 85 38), near Sé Nova. A study hall by day, the university-owned Centro wakes with a DJ M-Th and live music by student groups F-Sa 1-3am. ISIC or college ID required. Beer €0.80. €0.50 minimum. Best Sept.-May after 1am, especially Th. Open Sept.-July M-Sa 10pm-3am.

@ caffé, Lgo. da Sé Velha, 4-8 (☎239 83 81 64). Much more than an Internet spot, this is one of Coimbra's newest dance clubs. Stone, wood, and metal walls reverberate with house, Brazilian, African, and pop. Beer €1.25. Mixed drinks €2.50. Minimum €2.50 after 11pm. Open June-Sept. 15 M-Sa 11am-4am; Sept. 16-May M-Sa 9pm-4am.

Hups!, R. Castro Matoso, 11 (☎932 22 21 02). One of the few spots open Sunday night, this club attracts a mostly 25-40 crowd. African music on W. Beer €1.50. Mixed drinks €4-5. Minimum €5 for men, €2.50 for women. Open Tu-Su 10pm-5am.

Via Latina, R. Almeida Garrett, 1 (☎239 82 02 93). Large dance club popular with students M-Th and older Coimbra residents F-Sa. Latin music Sa-Th, F house. 2 1100-liter tanks of bar-side Super Bock fuel the whole operation. Tu ladies' night (3 drinks with entrance). Beer €1.50. Mixed drinks €3.50-4. Minimum M-Th €2.50 for men and €1.50 for women, F-Sa €5/€3.50. Open M-Sa 11pm-7am.

DUX, Av. Afonso Henriques, 43 (☎239 40 40 47), near the youth hostel. Partly owned by well-known Portuguese magician Luís de Matos, this modernist maze is a playground for the elite crowd. Stern "greeters" guard its bright white entrance. Best 3-4am. Beer €2. Mixed drinks €4. Minimum €6 for men, €3 for women. Open F-Sa 11pm-6am.

FESTIVALS

Students run wild during Coimbra's infamous week-long festival, the **Queima das Fitas** (Burning of the Ribbons), in the first or second week of May. The festivities begin when graduating seniors set fire to their narrow freshman ribbons and receive wide, ornamental replacements. Live choral music echoes in the streets during the **Festas da Rainha Santa,** held the first week of July. During even-numbered years, two processions of the statue of Rainha Santa (one at the beginning, one at the end) more visibly reflect the festival's religious roots, from whence all of this rollicking came. The firework-punctuated **Feira Popular** in the second week of July offers carnival rides and games across the river.

DAYTRIPS FROM COIMBRA

CONÍMBRIGA

*AVIC **buses** (☎239 82 37 69) run each morning from Coimbra (30min.; M-F 9:05, 9:35am; Sa-Su 9:35am only; €1.50) and return in the afternoon (M-Sa 1, 6pm; Su 6pm only). Buses run more frequently to Condeixa, 2km away from Conímbriga (25min.; 6-30 per day M-F 6:35am-10pm, Sa-Su 7:05am-6:05pm; €1.40). If you're ready to head back to Coimbra early, walk the 30min. or take a taxi (☎239 94 12 43) to Condeixa.*

Sixteen kilometers south of Coimbra, Conímbriga is home to the **Ruínas de Conímbriga,** Portugal's largest preserved Roman site. Highlights include a 3rd-century town wall, an ancient, luxurious villa, and baths complete with sauna and furnace room. Stunningly well-preserved mosaics are visible under the shelter of a glass canopy. (Open Mar. 16-Sept. 15 daily 9am-8pm; Sept. 16-Mar. 15 9am-6pm. Ticket office closes 30min. before the ruins. €3, under 25 and seniors €1.50, under 14 free.) The ticket price for the ruins includes nearby **Museu Monográfico de Conímbriga** and its displays of regional artifacts. (☎239 94 11 77. Same hours as the ruins, but closed M.) The **tourist office** is inside the museum. (☎239 94 47 64; fax 239 94 14 74. Open daily 9am-12:30pm and 2-5:30pm.)

BUÇACO FOREST AND LUSO

***Buses** run from Coimbra to Buçaco (45min.; M-F 7 per day 7:35am-7:20pm; Sa 9am, 12:45pm; Su 10:15am, 7:20pm; €2.50), before continuing on to Viseu. Buses back to Coimbra depart a few blocks from the Luso tourist office, across from the natural springs (35min.; M-F 5 per day 7:35am-6:35pm; Sa 10:35am, 6:35pm; Su 4:35pm; €2.50).*

Home to Portugal's most revered forest, Buçaco (also spelled Bussaco) is a favorite weekend retreat for many residents of Coimbra. The forest has drawn wanderers in their escape from the city for centuries. Benedictine monks settled the Buçaco area in the 6th century, established a monastery, and remained in control until the 1834 disestablishment of all religious orders. The forest owes its fame, however, to the Carmelites, who arrived here nearly 400 years ago. Selecting the forest for their *desertos* (isolated dwellings for penitence), the Carmelites planted over 700 types of trees and plants brought from around the world by missionaries. In the center of the forest, adjoining the old Carmelite convent, is Dom Carlos's exuberant **Palácio de Buçaco.** Now a luxury hotel, the building is a flamboyant display of neo-Manueline architecture. The *azulejos* on the outer walls depict scenes from *Os Lusíadas*, the great Portuguese epic about the Age of Discovery (see **Literature,** p. 585). In the forest itself, landmarks include the lovely **Fonte Fria** (Cold Fountain), the **Vale dos Fetos** (Fern Valley), and the **Porta de Rainha** (Queen's Gate). A 1hr. hike along the Via Sacra leads past 17th-century chapels to a sweeping panorama of the countryside from the **Cruz Alta** viewpoint.

A 3km walk downhill from Buçaco leads to the quiet town of **Luso,** Portugal's greatest source of bottled water. The town has a spa, fountains, baths, swimming pools, and a **bottling plant** (guided tours Tu, Th 3pm; reserve in advance at the casino near the tourist office). Locals visit the crisp, cold spring **Fonte de São João** at all hours to refill their water bottles. The **tourist office,** R. Emídio Navarro, 136, in the center of town, has a friendly English-speaking staff that provides maps and short-term **luggage storage.** (Open July-Sept. M-F 9:30am-1pm and 2-7pm, Sa-Su 10am-1pm and 3-5pm; Oct.-June M-F 9:30am-12:30pm and 2:30-6pm, Sa 10am-1pm; occasional longer hours.)

FIGUEIRA DA FOZ

Figueira da Foz may work best as a night-trip—if you're up to it. The ambitious arrive in the evening, and return to Coimbra on a morning train, bleary-eyed but content after a night of wild partying. Figueira peaks during July and August. The town's daytime highlight is a grand 3 sq. km beach of Sahara-like sand with tons of free recreational opportunities and a long boardwalk. At night, rowdy youths crowd the bars and discos, trying their luck at Figueira's infamous casino.

TRANSPORTATION. Trains are the best transport from Coimbra to Figueira da Foz (1½hr.; M-Sa 20-24 per day 5:20am-12:20am, Su 17 per day 6:19am-12:20am; €1.45). From Figueira station, it's an easy stroll to the tourist office and the beach (25min.). With the river on your left, follow Av. Saraiva de Carvalho as it becomes R. 5 de Outubro at the fountain and then curves into Av. 25 de Abril.

ORIENTATION AND PRACTICAL INFORMATION. Packed with hotels, beachfront **Avenida 25 de Abril** runs the length of Figueira, turning into **Avenida Foz do Mondego** after the fortress, before becoming **Avenida de Saraiva de Carvalho,** as it leads toward the train station. Four blocks inland and parallel to Av. 25 de Abril, **Rua Bernardo Lopes** is lined with semi-affordable hostels and restaurants, as well as the casino-cinema-disco heart of the city's nightlife. The **tourist office,** Av. 25 de Abril, 24, is next to the Hotel Mecure, facing the beach. (☎233 40 28 27; fax 233 40 28 28. Open June-Aug. daily 9am-midnight; Sept. 9am-11pm; Oct.-May M-F 9am-5:30pm, Sa-Su 10am-12:30pm and 2:30-6:30pm.) The **police** are on R. Joaquim Carvalho (☎233 42 88 81), by the bus station. Take the "Gala" or "Hospital" bus (from in front of the market on R. 5 de Outubro; €0.60) or catch a cab (about €5) to the **hospital** (☎233 40 20 00), across the river in the Gala district. Above the Bompreço supermarket is the **Crackport Ciber Café,** R. Rancho das Cantarinhas, 68. (☎233 41 32 48. €0.60 for 15min. Open daily 2:30pm-1am.)

ACCOMMODATIONS AND FOOD. A smattering of hostels line R. Bernardo Lopes and R. Miguel Bombarda. Two blocks from the tourist office and above an Indian restaurant of the same name, the rooms of **Pensão Residencial Bela Figueira ❷,** R. Miguel Bombarda, 13, are clean and close to the beach. (☎233 42 27 28; fax 233 42 99 60. Singles €15-25, with bath €20-35; doubles €20-35, with bath €25-45; triples €25-40, with bath €30-50. AmEx/MC/V.) To reach the **Parque Municipal de Campismo da Figueira da Foz Municipal ❶** on Estrada Buarcos, walk up Av. 25 de Abril with the beach on your left, turn right at the roundabout on R. Alexandre Herculano, then left at Parque Santa Caterina. A taxi from the bus or train station runs €3. Swank grounds have an Olympic-size pool (€1.75 per day), tennis courts, market, and currency exchange. (☎233 40 28 10. 2-person min. per party. Reception daily June-Sept. 8am-8pm; Oct.-May 8am-7pm. Quiet hours midnight-7am. Showers €0.60 for 7min. Sites €2 per person, €1.50-2 per tent, €1.50 per car.)

Several restaurants and snack bars are scattered along **R. Bernardo Lopes** and the beach. A local **market** where fruit, bread, and beach gear are offered sets up beside the municipal garden between Av. Foz do Mondego and R. Dr. Francisco A. Dinis (open daily June-Sept. 15 7am-7pm; Sept. 16-May M-Sa 7am-4pm). Fill your beach basket at **Supermercado Ovo,** on the corner of R. Francisco António Dinis and R. Bernardo Lopes. (☎233 42 00 52. Open M-Sa 8am-8pm, Su 9am-2pm.) At **Restaurante Andaluz ❷,** R. Maestro David de Sousa, 91, the dark wood interior creates a striking contrast to the sunny beach outside, but excellent and generous meals are served at some of the most reasonable prices in this resort town. *Pratos de dia* €5-10. (☎233 41 23 90. Open daily noon-3:30pm and 7:30-10:30pm. AmEx/V/MC.)

SIGHTS AND ENTERTAINMENT. Just up from the public gardens on R. 5 de Outubro, the **Museu Municipal Dr. Santos Rocha,** in Parque Abadias, displays ancient coins and the fashions of Portuguese nobility. (R. Calouste Gulbenkian. ☎233 40 28 40. Open Tu-Su 9:30am-5:15pm. Free.) On R. Joaquim Sotto Mayor, the continuation of R. da Liberdade running parallel to the beach, the modest exterior of **Palácio Sotto Mayor** conceals the shameless extravagance within; lavish green marble columns line the main hallway, and gold leafing covers the ceiling. (☎233 42 20 41. Open Sept.-May Sa-Su 2-6pm, June-Aug. Tu-Su 2-6pm. €1.) Figueira's partying lifestyle shifts from high gear to warp speed during the month-long **Festa de São João,** usually starting in mid-June and continuing through the first week of July. On the night of June 23, the eve of the **Dia de São João,** crowds of partygoers dance in the streets and on the beach, gleefully bonking each other on the head with plastic noisemakers. After a spectacular fireworks display at 1am, crowds continue the in-town party or congregate around bonfires along the beach until the 5am *banho santo* (holy bath), when the brave take a dip in the ocean. The popular **casino complex,** on R. Dr. Calado, at the corner of R. Bernardo Lopes, houses a nightclub, cinema, and arcade. (☎233 40 84 00. Entrance 18+ with ID. Casino open daily 3pm-3am. Slot machines and bingo free. Game room open July-Aug. 4pm-3am; Sept.-June M-F 5pm-3am, Sa-Su 4pm-3am. Day pass €3.50. Cinema Tu-Su €3.30, M €2.50. No shorts or sneakers.)

NIGHTLIFE. The summer nightlife in Figueira da Foz limbers between 10pm and 2am and runs on until dawn. Many bars and clubs with nightly summer hours are only open F-Sa during the rest of the year. On winter weekdays, nightlife remains back in Coimbra. Crowds fill several nearby bars before hitting the club scene. Grab a Bacardi (€3) at Cuban bar **Havana,** R. Cândido dos Reis, 86. It's best around 11pm. (☎233 43 48 99. Beer €0.75. Open Tu-Su 8pm-4am.) The versatile new **Art Café,** Esplanada Silva Guimarães, 3, on the terrace above the tourist office, features a downstairs dance floor and a chill bar and art gallery upstairs. Enter through the door to the left of the downstairs bar. (☎233 42 08 82. Beer €1. Mixed drinks €3.50. Minimum downstairs €2.50. Downstairs open June 15-Sept. 15 daily noon-4am, Sept. 16-June 14 M-W noon-midnight, Th-Sa noon-4am. Upstairs year-round M-Sa 8pm-4am.) **Rolls Bar** is an Irish bar on R. Poeta Acácio Antunes, 1E. (Beer €1.50-2.50. Mixed drinks €3-4. 1 drink minimum. Open July-Aug. daily; Sept.-June M-Sa 5pm-6am.) Club **Katigo** spins pop music until 4am, then house music until dawn. The action peaks at 3am. (Beer €1.75. Mixed drinks €3.50. Minimum €5. Open July-Aug. daily; Sept.-June Th-Sa midnight-6am.) End the night and bring on the morning at the **Discoteca Bergantim,** R. Dr. Lopes Guimarães, a block up from the beach. Crowds groove to pop and rock 5-7am; don't bother coming before 4am. (☎233 42 71 29. Beer €1.50. Mixed drinks €4. Minimum €4 for women, €5 for men. Open July-Aug. daily Sept.-June F-Sa 2-8am.)

AVEIRO ☎234

A network of canals winds through the old center of Aveiro, along which traditional *moliceiros* (colorful fishing boats reminiscent of Venice's gondolas) drift out to sea. The canonized princess Santa Joana once lived in the convent here (see p. 685), but Aveiro is perhaps best known for its numerous beaches.

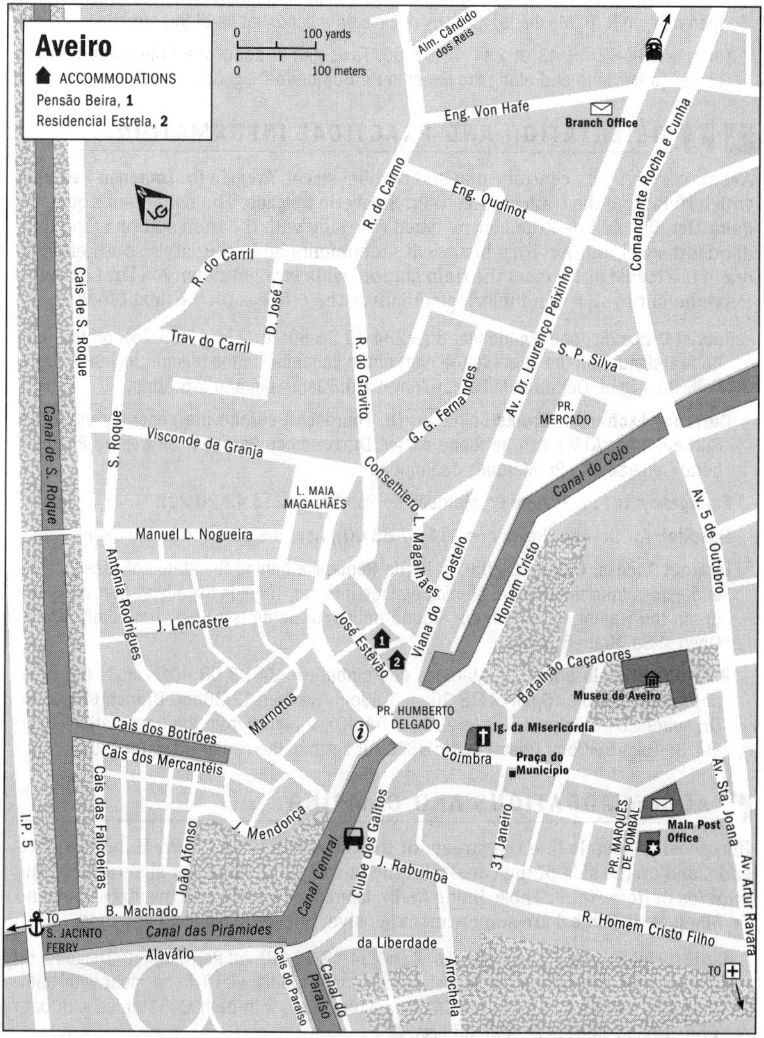

TRANSPORTATION

Trains: Lgo. Estação (☎234 38 16 32), at the end of Av. Dr. Lourenço Peixinho. Trains to: **Braga** (2hr.; 10:35am, 8:35pm; €4.90); **Coimbra** (1hr., every hr. 6:10am-1:10am, €2.75-6.50); **Lisbon** (5hr., 14 per day 6:45am-8:50pm, €9-16.20); **Ovar** (20min., 21 per day 4:35am-1:10am, €1.40); **Porto** (1¼hr., 21 per day 4:35am-1:10am, €1.70).

Ferries: TransRia (☎234 33 10 95) ferries depart for the beach at **São Jacinto** from the Vera Cruz docks, the site of the old fish auction (M-F 9 per day 7:05am-12:45am, Sa-Su 8 per day 8:20am-12:45am, last return ferry at midnight; €1.30). From the tourist office follow R. João Mendonça as it winds around the park, turn left on R. João Afonso, and then right on R. B. Machado; the ferry dock is on a continuation of this street.

Taxis: ☎234 42 29 43 or 234 42 37 66. Taxis gather about the train station on Av. Lourenço Peixinho and along the canal in Pr. Humberto Delgado.

ORIENTATION AND PRACTICAL INFORMATION

Aveiro is split by its central canal and parallel street, **Avenida Dr. Lourenço Peixinho,** which runs from the train station to **Pr. Humberto Delgado.** The fishermen's quarter, **Beira Mar,** lies north of the central canal (the side with the train station). The residential district and Aveiro's historical monuments lie in the city's south end. To reach the **tourist office** from the train station, walk straight down Av. Dr. Lourenço Peixinho until you reach the bridge (15min.); the office is on the next block.

Tourist Office: R. João Mendonça, 8 (☎234 42 36 80; fax 234 42 83 26), off Pr. Humberto Delgado, on the street to the right of the canal facing the lagoon. July-Sept. open daily 9am-8pm; Oct.-June M-F 9am-7pm, Sa 9:30am-1pm and 2-5:30pm.

Currency Exchange: Banks lining Av. Dr. Lourenço Peixinho are generally open M-F 8:30am-3pm. **ATMs** can be found on Av. Dr. Lourenço Peixinho, as well as Pr. Humberto Delgado and Pr. Marquês de Pombal.

Emergency: ☎112. **Police:** Pr. Marquês de Pombal (☎234 42 20 22).

Hospital: Av. Dr. Artur Ravara (☎234 37 83 00), near the park across the canal.

Internet Access: Cidade Digital, in Pr. da República behind the statue of José Estevão and across from the *Câmara Municipal.* Free Internet. There is usually a short wait; sign up on the waiting list and hang around until your name is called. Time limit 30min. Open M-Sa 10am-8:30pm.

Post Office: Main office, Pr. Marquês de Pombal (☎234 38 08 40), across the canal and up R. Coimbra. Open M-F 8:30am-6:30pm, Sa 9am-12:30pm. **Branch office,** Av. Dr. Lourenço Peixinho, 169B (☎234 38 04 90), 2 blocks from the train station. Open M-F 8:30am-6:30pm. **Postal Code:** 3800 for north of the canal, 3810 for south.

ACCOMMODATIONS AND CAMPING

Inexpensive hostels line the streets of the old town, north of Pr. Humberto Delgado, and on the side of the canal with the tourist office; look for signs advertising *quartos* or *dormidas*. Those lining **Av. Dr. Lourenço Peixinho** and the streets around **Pr. Marquês de Pombal** are somewhat expensive, but serve as good backups.

Residencial Estrela, R. José Estêvão, 4 (☎234 42 38 18), off Pr. Humberto Delgado, on the right 1 block before the tourist office. Bright rooms with TV and most with bath. June-Aug. singles €25, with bath €30; doubles €35, with bath €45; triples with bath €55; 1 quad €60. Sept.-May €5 less. ❸

Pensão Beira, R. José Estêvão, 18 (☎234 42 42 97), off Pr. Humberto Delgado beyond Residencial Estrela. Large rooms, all with TV and most with private bath. Apr.-Sept. singles €20, with bath €30-40; doubles €30, with bath €45-50. Slightly less Oct.-Mar. ❷

Residencial Palmeira, R. de Palmeira, 7-11 (☎234 42 25 21 or 234 81 56 58). Take a left out of the tourist office, turn left on the 1st street, and then take a left on the street before the post office. On a quiet side street, but in a great location close to many bars and restaurants. Fancier rooms with TV and bath. 24hr. reception. Reserve 2 weeks ahead in summer. June-Sept. singles €25; doubles €35; 1 triple €40. Oct.-May €20/€30/€35. 1 single without bath €2.50 less. ❷

Hospedagem Rossio, R. Dr. Barbosa de Magalhães, 24 (☎234 42 98 57), past the tourist office, and across from the park. These are the cheapest beds in town. Adequate but worn rooms. Payment required in advance. Singles €15, with bath €20; doubles €20, with bath €25; 1 triple €25. ❶

Camping Municipal de Aveiro (☎/fax 234 33 12 20), in São Jacinto. Reception 8am-7pm. €1.80 per person, €1 per tent, €0.60-1.80 per car. Open Jan.-Nov. ❶

FOOD

Seafood restaurants cluster around the fish market off Pr. do Peixe ("fish square"), in the old town, a few blocks behind the tourist office. Aveiro's specialty-pastry, called *ovos moles* (sweetened egg yolks), can be sampled at most of the *pastelarias* (pastry shops) along Av. Dr. Loureço Peixinho and R. J. Mendonça. **Supermercado Pingo Doce,** R. Batalhão Caçadores, 10, is across the canal from the tourist office. (☎234 38 60 42. Open daily 9am-10pm.)

Restaurante Zico, R. José Estêvão, 52 (☎234 42 96 49), off Pr. Humberto Delgado. Filled with locals looking for a quick, quality meal. Entrees €4-20; half-portions €3.50-5. Open M-Sa 8am-2am; serving noon-4pm and 7-11:30pm. ❸

Casa Necas, R. Tenente Resende, 51-53 (☎234 42 37 81), just off Pr. do Peixe. A small but solid Portuguese menu. Friendly staff and friendly prices. Entrees €3.50-4 for large half-portions and €6-7 for full portions. *Menú* €8. House specialty is *vitela assada* (veal, €4 half-portion). Open M-Sa noon-2:30pm and 7-9:30pm. ❷

SIGHTS

The old town's main attraction is the **Museu de Aveiro,** R. Sta. Joana Princesa. It was here that King Afonso and his daughter Infanta Joana, who wished to become a nun despite her father's objections, fought it out in 1472. Luckily for the poor and sick of Aveiro, she won. Beneath *azulejo* panels depicting the story of her life is one of the most famous works of art in Portugal, Santa Joana's Renaissance tomb supported by the heads of four angels. (☎234 42 32 97. Open Tu-Su 10am-5:30pm. €2.50, students and seniors €0.75, under 14 and Su before 2pm free.) Simple but strikingly blue *azulejos* cover the walls of the **Igreja da Misericórdia,** in Pr. República, across the canal and a block uphill from the tourist office. (☎234 42 67 32. Open M-F 10am-12:30pm and 2:30-5pm.) In the same square, the regal **Câmara Municipal** (city hall) displays its French design and bell tower.

BEACHES AND ENTERTAINMENT

Some of the beach towns near Aveiro boast beautiful sand dunes well worth a daytrip from Aveiro. Like the natural reserve at the **Dunas de São Jacinto** (10km away), most of them are easily accessible by ferry (see **Ferries,** p. 684). Closer to Aveiro,

EAT YOUR HEART OUT, DON JUAN There's love, and then there's *love.* Dom Pedro I was in the latter. While a prince, he fell head-over-heels for Inês de Castro, the daughter of a Spanish nobleman and lady-in-waiting to his first wife. Pedro's father, Afonso IV, objected to the romance, fearing that such an alliance would open the Portuguese throne to Spanish domination. Despite his father's opposition to the marriage, Pedro fled with Inês to Bragança, where the couple secretly wed. Soon thereafter, the disgruntled Afonso had Inês killed. Upon rising to the throne two years later, Pedro personally ripped out the hearts of the men who had slit his young wife's throat and proceeded to eat them. Henceforth, the hardy king became known as Pedro the Cruel. In a macabre ceremony, he had Inês's body exhumed, dressed her meticulously in royal robes, set her on the throne, and officially deemed her his queen; he even, according to legend, made his court kiss her rotting hand. She was eventually reinterred in an exquisitely carved tomb in the king's favorite monastery, the Mosteiro de Santa Maria de Alcobaça. The king later joined her. The inscription on their tombs reads, *"Até ao fim do mundo"* (until the end of the world).

the beaches **Barra** and **Costa Nova** can be reached by bus from the *canal central* or train station stops (15min.; July-Aug. 17 per day 7:10am-8:45pm; Sept.-June M-F 14 per day 7:10am-8:10pm, Sa-Su 11-12 per day 8:20am-8:10pm; €1.75).

At night, the bars around **Pr. do Peixe** fill up quickly. Other popular places line R. Canal de São Roque. Check out **Salpoente,** on Cais de São Roque, or neighboring **Estrondo Bar** and **Urgência,** on R. São Roque.

DOURO AND MINHO

Although their landscapes and Celtic history invite comparison with northwestern Spain, the Douro and Minho regions of northern Portugal are more populated, developed, and wealthy than Spanish Galicia. Thanks to the area's rich mineral deposits, these regions have had a prosperous history. The evidence is everywhere from the abundance of luxurious villas to the traditional female dress, which customarily feature layers of gold charm-encrusted necklaces. Wealth and history take a backseat to the region's spectacular greenery—Douro and Minho are a haven for nature lovers. Hundreds of trellised vineyards burgeoning with grapes for *porto* and *vinho verde* wines beckon connoisseurs, and houses tiled in brilliant *azulejos* draw visitors to peaceful streets. The region's mild coastal climate is too cool to attract the beach crowd until July, and only a few ambitious travelers ever make it past Porto and the Douro Valley to the greens and blues of the Alto Minho, which hugs the Spanish border. The cities of Braga, Viana do Castelo, and Guimarães will reward the intrepid traveler with their unspoiled charm.

PORTO (OPORTO) ☎22

Porto is one of Portugal's most sophisticated and modern cities. The source of its greatest fame is its sugary-sweet port wine. Founded by English merchants in the early 18th century, the port industry is at the root of the city's successful economy and is reason enough to visit, but there's more to Porto than port. Magnificently situated on a gorge cut by the Douro River, just 6km from the sea, Portugal's second-largest city is characterized by an elegance reminiscent of Paris or Prague and often seems more vibrant than Lisbon. Porto was named a Cultural Capital of Europe in 2001 and a place on the UNESCO World Heritage list.

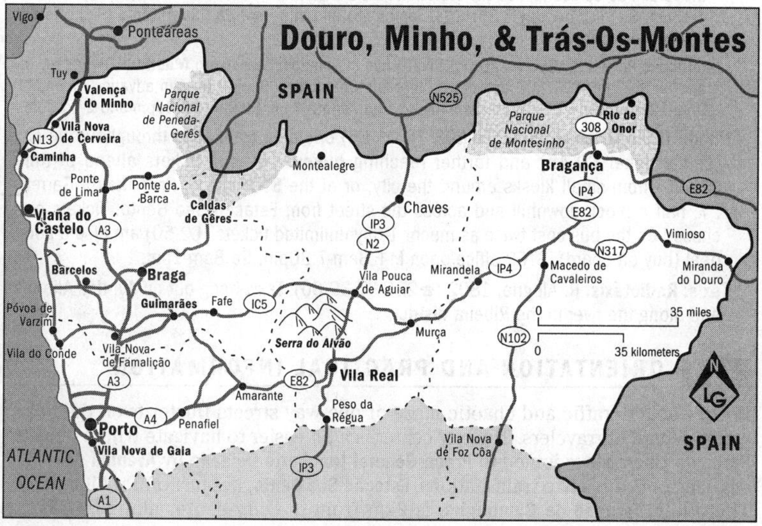

TRANSPORTATION

Flights: Aeroporto Francisco de Sá Carneiro (☎229 41 32 60), 20km from downtown. City bus (#56) goes to the airport from R. Carmo (in front of Hospital São António) but can be very slow due to multiple stops. The **aerobus,** which leaves from Av. dos Aliados near Pr. Liberdade, is more efficient (40min., every 30min. 7am-6:30pm, €2.50). Buy tickets on board. **Taxis** are even quicker (20-30min., about €15-18). **TAP Air Portugal,** Pr. Mouzinho de Albuquerque, 105 (☎226 08 02 31), flies to major European cities.

Trains: Estação Campanhã (☎225 36 41 41), on R. da Estação east of the center. Most trains pass through this main station. Trains run to: **Aveiro** (1¼hr., 30 per day 5:05am-11:15pm, €1.65); **Braga** (1½-1¾hr., 21 per day 5:20am-11:20pm, €2.50); **Coimbra** (2hr., 17 per day 5:05am-12:05am, €5.30); **Faro** (9hr.; Tu, Th, Su 10:10pm; €14.50); **Lisbon** (3½-4½hr., 14 per day 6am-8:05pm, €11-19); **Madrid** (13-14hr., 6:10pm, €48), with transfer at Entroncamento; **Viana do Castelo** (1½-2hr., 12 per day 5:35am-12:35am, €2); **Vigo, Spain** (2½hr.; 7:40am, 6:55pm; €11.50). **Estação São Bento** (☎222 00 27 22), Pr. Almeida Garrett, centrally located 1 block off Pr. Liberdade, serves trains with mostly local and regional routes. Frequent connections to **Estação São Bento** (5-10min., every 20-30min. 5:55am-11:10pm, €0.75). Buses #34 and 35 also connect Campanhã to downtown (every 30min., €0.90).

Buses: There is no central bus station; over 20 different companies operate out of garages all over the downtown area.

Rede Expresso, R. Alexandre Herculano, 366 (☎222 05 24 59), in the Garagem Atlântico, has buses to: **Braga** (1¼hr., 8 per day 9:25am-12:15am, €4.40); **Bragança** (5hr., 7 per day 7:15am-8:15pm, €7.50); **Coimbra** (1½hr., 11 per day 7:15am-12:45am, €7); **Lisbon** (4hr., 12 per day 7:15am-12:45am, €12); **Viana do Castelo** (1¾hr.; 10:55am, 6:40pm; €7.50). **REDM,** R. Dr. Alfredo Magalhães, 94 (☎222 00 31 52), 2 blocks from Pr. República, has buses to **Braga** (1hr.; M-F 26 per day 6:45am-8pm, Sa-Su 9-12 per day 7:15am-8pm; €3.30).

Rodonorte, R. Ateneu Comercial do Porto (☎222 00 43 98), 1 block from R. Sá da Bandeira, goes to **Vila Real** (1¾hr.; M-F 16 per day 6:50am-10:30pm, Sa 7 per day 6:50am-9:20pm, Su 7 per day 6:50am-10:30pm; €5.50) via **Amarante** (1hr., €4.25). A little secret: ask for a free bottle of water on Rodonorte buses. **Renex,** Campo dos Martires da Patria (☎222 00 33 95), in front of the Jardim de Cordoaria, has express service via Lisbon to **Lagos** (8½hr.; M-F 6 per day 5:30am-1:15am, Sa-Su 5 per day 7:30am-1:15am; €18) and **Vila Real de São António** (9½hr., 5 per day 9am-1:15am, €18).

Internorte, Pr. Galiza, 96 (☎226 05 24 20) has international service to **Madrid** (10½hr.; Tu, Th, and Sa-Su 9am; €27.50), as well as other European cities. Book 3 days in advance. Open M-F 9am-12:30pm and 2-6:30pm, Sa 9am-12:30pm and 2-4pm, Su 9am-12:30pm and 2-5:30pm.

Public Transportation: STCP (☎808 20 01 66) operates **tram** lines throughout the city (single ticket €0.45) and farther reaching **buses.** Buy bus tickets ahead of time (€0.40) from small kiosks around the city, or at the **STCP** office, Pr. Almeida Garrett, 27, half a block downhill and across the street from Estação São Bento. Tickets purchased on the bus cost twice as much. 1-day unlimited tickets (€2.50) are also a good deal (buy on-board). STCP office open M-F 8am-7:30pm, Sa 8am-1pm.

Taxis: Radiotáxis, R. Alegria, 1802 (☎225 07 39 00). Taxis hang out on Av. dos Aliados and along the river in the Ribeira district.

ORIENTATION AND PRACTICAL INFORMATION

Porto's heavy traffic and chaotic maze of one-way streets fluster even the most well-oriented of travelers. The city center is a bit easier to navigate where hillside **Praça da Liberdade** is joined to **Praça General Humberto Delgado** by **Avenida dos Aliados.** One of Porto's two train stations, **Estação São Bento,** lies just off Pr. Liberdade. The other, **Estação de Campanhã,** is 2km from the city center along the river.

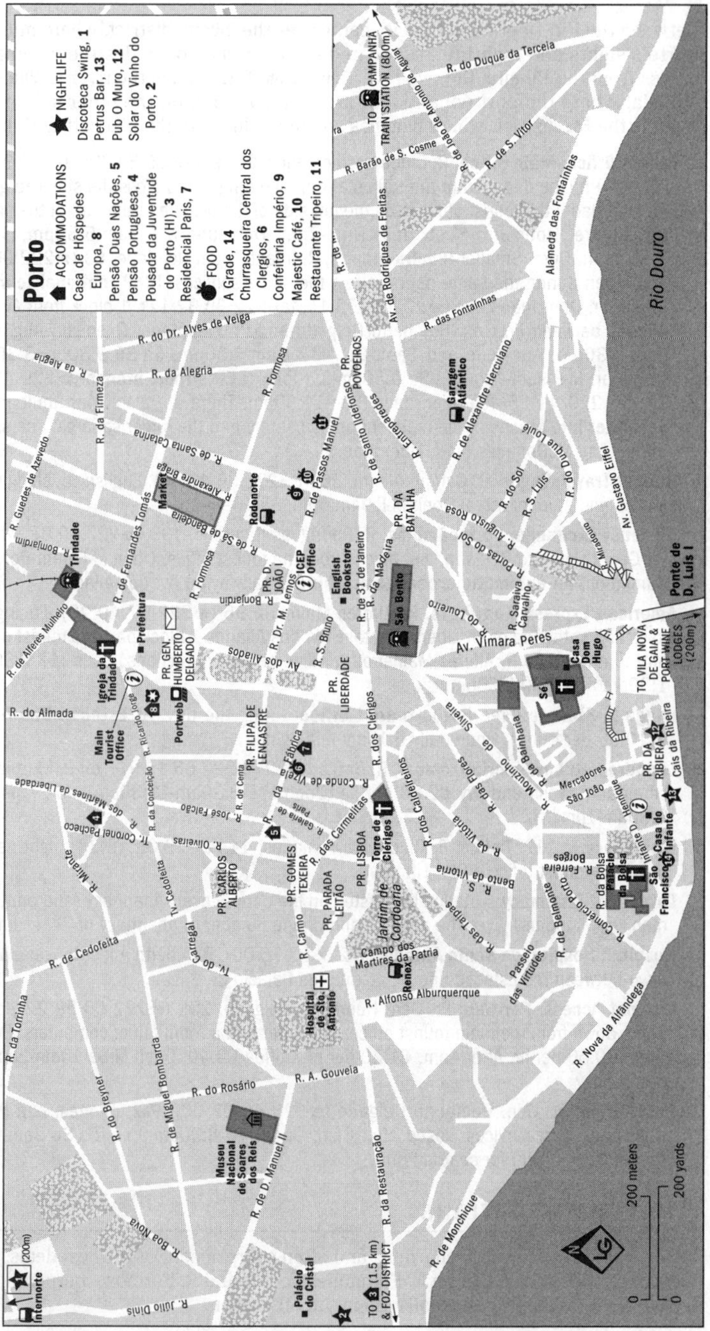

DOURO AND MINHO

Between the Rio Douro and the city center lies the **Ribeira** district, where much of Porto's sights and nightlife are located on steep, narrow sidestreets. Directly across from the Ribeira, the two-level **Ponte Dom Luís I** spans the river to **Vila Nova de Gaia,** where the port wine-lodges are located. Back on the other side of the river, is the **Foz** district, where beaches and nightclubs are the main attraction.

Tourist Office: Main office, R. Clube dos Fenianos, 25 (☎223 39 34 72; fax 223 32 33 03), off Pr. Liberdade. From the train station, take a right and cross the street to get to Pr. Liberdade; the tourist office is on the left side of the avenue farther up, at the end of the square. Open July-Sept. daily 9am-7pm; Oct.-June M-F 9am-5:30pm, Sa-Su 9:30am-4:30pm. Smaller **Ribeira branch,** R. Infante Dom Henrique, 63 (☎222 00 97 70), open during the same hours, offers the same services. **ICEP (national tourism) office,** Pr. Dom João I, 43 (☎222 05 75 14; fax 222 05 32 12), 1 block from Av. dos Aliados between Pr. Gen. Humberto Delgado and Pr. Liberdade. Open July-Aug. daily 9am-7:30pm; Apr.-June and Sept.-Oct. M-F 9am-7:30pm, Sa-Su 9:30am-3:30pm; Nov.-Mar. M-F 9am-7pm, Sa-Su 9:30am-3:30pm. **ICEP airport branch** (☎229 41 25 34; fax 229 41 25 43) open daily 8am-11:30pm. There are also 24hr. multilingual **computer info stands** in the main shopping centers and the larger squares; one sits in front of the McDonald's in Pr. Liberdade.

Budget Travel: Tagus, R. Campo Alegre, 261 (☎226 09 41 46). English-speaking staff; advice and student rates. Open M-F 9am-6pm, Sa 10am-1pm.

Currency Exchange: Portocâmbios, R. Rodrigues Sampaio, 193 (☎222 00 02 38), off Pr. Gen. Humberto Delgado, just across from the tourist office. Open M-F 9am-6pm, Sa 9am-noon. An **automatic exchange machine** is halfway up Av. dos Aliados.

American Express: Top Tours, R. Alferes Malheiro, 96 (☎222 07 40 20). Facing the town hall at the top of Pr. Liberdade, take Av. dos Aliados 1 block past the tourist office, and turn left onto R. Alferes Malheiro. Handles all AmEx functions. Open M-F 9:30am-1:30pm and 2:30-6:30pm.

Luggage Storage: Free in the **tourist office** during the day. At **Estação São Bento** (€10.50 per 48hr.). Open daily 5:15am-midnight.

Laundromat: Lavanderia Tropical, R. Bragas, 329 (☎222 05 13 97), off R. Mártires da Liberdade. Wash and dry €2.50 per kg. Open M-F 8:30am-12:30pm and 2-7pm, Sa 9:30am-1pm.

Emergency: ☎112. **Police:** R. Clube dos Fenianos, 11 (☎222 08 18 33), right next to the main tourist office off Pr. Liberdade.

Late-Night Pharmacy: Rotation list posted on the door of every pharmacy (and printed in many newspapers) gives the address and phone number of pharmacy of 24hr. duty.

Hospital: Hospital de Santo António (☎222 07 75 00), R. Alberto Aires Gouveia, downtown between the Estação São Bento and the Palácio de Cristal.

Internet Access: Portweb, Pr. Gen. Humberto Delgado, 291 (☎222 00 59 22), a few doors down from the main tourist office, has a bar and a room full of computers. Before 4pm, €0.50 per hr. After 4pm, €1.20 per hr. Coffee €0.40. Open M-Sa 10am-2am, Su 3pm-2am.

Post Office: Pr. Gen. Humberto Delgado (☎223 40 02 00). **Fax,** phones, and **Posta Restante.** Most services closed after 6pm. Open M-F 8:30am-9pm, Sa-Su 9am-6pm. **Postal Code**: 4000 for central Porto.

ACCOMMODATIONS

Hostels in Porto are rarely charming and often overpriced. For the best deals, look west of Av. dos Aliados, or on R. Fernandes Tomás and R. Formosa, perpendicular to Av. dos Aliados. Prices usually dip in the off-season.

Pensão Duas Nações, Pr. Guilherme Gomes Fernandes, 59 (☎222 08 96 21 or fax 222 08 16 16). From the train station, cross the street and turn right into Pr. Liberdade and then left onto R. Dr. Artur de Magalhães Basto, which turns into R. Fábrica and then R. Sta. Teresa; it's across the square at the top. Popular with young travelers from around the world. Rooms have large windows with small terraces and TV. Laundry €7 per load. Internet €0.50 per 15min. Reserve ahead. Singles €15, with bath €20; doubles €20, with bath €25-30; triples €30, with bath €35; quads €40, with bath €45; 1 room with 6 beds and bath €11 per person. ❷

Residencial Paris, R. da Fábrica, 27-29 (☎222 07 31 40). From the train station, cross Pr. da Liberdade and take a left on R. da Fábrica; it's 1 block up on the left. In a charming old building with marble staircases; all rooms come with private bath, TV, and A/C. Apr.-Oct. singles €35; doubles €45. Nov.-Mar. €5 less. ❹

Pousada da Juventude do Porto (HI), R. Paulo da Gama, 551 (☎226 17 72 57; fax 226 17 72 47), 3km from town center in the Foz district. Bus #35 from Estação Campanha and Pr. Liberdade or #36 from Boavista stop in front of the hostel. In a somewhat dodgy neighborhood; women should be cautious walking about at night. Reception daily 8am-midnight. Checkout 11am. June-Sept. dorms €15; doubles with bath €42. Oct.-May dorms €12.50; doubles with bath €35. MC/V. ❷

Pensão Portuguesa, Tr. Coronel Pacheco, 11 (☎222 00 41 74), off R. Mártires da Liberdade, up the street from Pr. Carlos Alberto. Cheap and adequate rooms on a quiet street a few blocks from the bustle of the city center. July-Aug. singles €12.50, with bath €15; doubles €15, with bath €20; Sept.-June €10/€13/€13/€18. ❶

Casa de Hóspedes Europa, R. do Almada, 398 (☎222 00 69 71), near the corner of R. Dr. Ricardo Jorge, up the street from the main tourist office. Above a restaurant of the same name. Friendly owners. May 16-Sept. 15 singles €13, with bath €18; doubles €20, with bath €25. Sept. 16-May 15 €10/€15/€18/€20. AmEx/MC/V. ❶

Camping: Prelada (☎228 31 26 16), on R. Monte dos Burgos, in Quinta da Prelada, 3km from the town center and 5km from the beach. Take bus #6, 50, 54, or 87 from Pr. Liberdade (only #50 and 54 run at night). Reception 8am-1am. €3.30 per person, €2.50-3 per tent, €2.60 per car. **Salgueiros,** R. do Campismo (☎227 81 05 00; fax 227 81 01 36), near Praia Salgueiros in Vila Nova de Gaia, is less accessible and less equipped campsite, but it is also less expensive and closer to the beach. To get there, catch the green Espírito Santo bus from Pr. da Batalha in front of the Teatro Nacional de São João (€1.10). €1.50 per person, €1.50-2 per tent, €0.75 per car. ❶

FOOD

The city center is full of mediocre snack bars, but there are also plenty of good deals for lunch and afternoon munchies at restaurants and cafes. Budget meals can be found near Pr. Batalha on R. Cimo de Vila and R. Cativo. Places selling *bifanas* (small pork sandwiches) line R. Bomjardim. At dinnertime, the Ribeira district along the river is the place to look for quality and affordable restaurants, particularly on C. Ribeira, R. Reboleira, and R. Cima do Muro. Adventurous eaters can try the city's specialty, *tripas à moda do Porto* (tripe and beans). The **Mercado de Bolhão,** on the corner of R. Formosa and R. Sá de Bandeira, has fresh bread, cheese, meats, and excellent olives, as well as fresh produce on its upper level (open M-F 8:30am-5pm, Sa 8:30am-1pm). If you are in the mood to spend, the more expensive (touristy) restaurants border the river in the Ribeira district, particularly on C. Ribeira, R. Reboleira, and R. Cima do Muro.

Majestic Café, R. de Santa Catarina, 112 (☎222 00 38 87). Capturing the decadence of old Porto with a classical decor of chandeliers and *patina*-covered mirrors, this is the city's oldest and most famous cafe. Sandwiches €2-8.75. Elaborate pastries €1-3.25. A selection of fine cigars €6-23. Open M-Sa 9:30am-midnight. AmEx/MC/V. ❷

Churrasquería Central dos Clerigos, R. da Fábrica, 69 (☎222 57 49 21). A lively and cheerful restaurant lined with *azulejos*, this *churrasquería* offers assorted grilled fish and meat dishes accompanied by generous portions of salad and other extras. Entrees €2.50-7. Open M-Sa noon-3:30pm and 7:30-10:30pm. ❶

A Grade, R. de S. Nicolau, 9 (☎223 32 11 30), in the Ribeira. Up from Lgo. de Terreiro, just past Adega S. Nicolau. A welcoming restaurant furnished with old-fashioned wooden tables and benches. Tasty lunch *menú* (€5). Entrees are €5-10, while specialties like *polvo assado no forno* (octopus) and *cabrito assado no forno* (goat) run about €8.85. Open daily M-F 8am-midnight; meals served noon-3:30pm and 7:30-11pm. ❷

Confeitaria Império, R. de Santa Catarina, 149-151 (☎222 00 55 95), across from the Majestic Café. Founded in 1941, this *pastelaría* has excellent pastries and inexpensive lunch specials (€3) served in the back dining room. Try the *especialidade Império* pastry (€0.60). Open M-Sa 7:30am-8:30pm. A new branch at R. Fernandes Tomás, 755, is the largest self-service cafe in the city, selling a variety of meals and snacks. ❶

Restaurante Tripeiro, R. de Passos Manuel, 195 (☎222 00 58 86), half a block up from R. Santa Catarina. Well-prepared dishes, including regional specialties. Entrees €8-15. Open M-Sa noon-3:30pm and 11pm. ❸

SIGHTS

Your first brush with Porto's rich stock of fine artwork may be, of all places, at the **São Bento train station,** home to a celebrated collection of *azulejos*. Outside the station and at the top of adjacent **Pr. da Liberdade,** the formidable **Prefeitura** (City Hall) is a monument to Porto's late 19th-century greatness.

CATHEDRAL. Fortified on the hilltop slightly south of the train station is Porto's imposing Romanesque *Sé*. Built in the 12th and 13th centuries, the Gothic, *azulejo*-covered cloister was added later in the 14th century. The **Capela do Santíssimo Sacramento,** to the left of the high altar, shines with solid silver and plated gold. During the Napoleonic invasion, crafty townspeople whitewashed the altar to protect it from vandalism. Climb the staircase to the **Renaissance chapter house** for a splendid view of the old quarter. *(Terreiro da Sé. ☎222 05 90 28. From Pr. Liberdade, walk past Estação São Bento and uphill on Av. Afonso Henriques; the cathedral is on the right. Open M-Sa 9am-12:30pm and 2:30-6pm, Su 2:30-6pm. Cloister €1.25.)*

PALÁCIO DA BOLSA. The elegant Palácio da Bolsa (Stock Exchange) was built from 1842 to 1910 over the ruins of the Convento de São Francisco, after the convent was destroyed by fire in 1832. At the entrance is the **Pátio das Nações** (Hall of Nations), which served as the trading floor of the stock exchange. The domed ceiling is decorated with the coats of arms of 20 countries friendly with Portugal. Leading up to the top floor is the **Escadaria Nobre** (Noble Staircase), decorated with carved granite, and topped with two giant bronze chandeliers. Among the exquisitely decorated rooms is the **Sala dos Retratos** (Portrait Room), which features a wooden table that took three painstaking years to carve. The most striking room of the Palácio is the opulent **Sala Árabe** (Arabic Hall). The green crests on the ceiling proclaim "Allah above all," and its gold and silver walls are covered with the oddly juxtaposed inscriptions "Glory to Allah" and "Glory to Queen Maria II." Note that the door to the hall is set slightly off-center—an intentional alteration to symbolize that only Allah is perfect. The various rooms of the Palácio are now used for occasional ceremonies and official receptions. *(R. Ferreira Borges. ☎223 39 90 00. From the town center, walk past Estação São Bento and downhill on R. Mouzinho da Silveira to the square; signs lead the way. Open daily 9am-7pm. Multilingual tours every 30min. €4.)*

MUSEU DE ARTE CONTEMPORÂNEA. This museum rotates temporary exhibits of contemporary Portuguese art and architectural design. The building crowns an impressive 44 acres of sculpted gardens, fountains, and old farmland tumbling down toward the Douro River. *(R. D. João de Castro, 210. ☎226 15 65 00. Several km out of town, on the way to the beach. Bus #78 leaves from Av. dos Aliados; ask the driver to stop at the museum (30min., return buses run until midnight). Museum open Tu-Th 10am-10pm, Sa-Su 10am-8pm. Park closes at sundown. €4. Free Su before 2pm.)*

IGREJA E TORRE DOS CLÉRIGOS. The 18th century **Igreja dos Clérigos** is decorated with Baroque and Rococo carvings. Its **Torre dos Clérigos** is the city's tallest landmark, reaching a height of 75.6m. Atop the 200 steps await spectacular views of Porto and the Rio Douro Valley. *(R. dos Clérigos. ☎222 00 17 29. Church open M-Th 10am-noon and 2-5pm, Sa 10am-noon and 2-8pm, Su 10am-1pm. Tower open daily June-July 10am-7pm, Aug. 10am-10pm, Sept.-May 10am-noon and 2-5pm. Church free; tower €1.)*

MUSEU NACIONAL DE SOARES DOS REIS. A former royal residence, this 18th-century museum houses an exhaustive collection of 19th-century Portuguese painting and sculpture, much of it by Soares dos Reis, often called Portugal's Michelangelo. *(R. Dom Manuel II, 44. ☎223 39 37 70. From the town center, walk down R. Clérigos and R. Restauração, then take R. Dom Manuel II past the churches and forested park (10min.). Open Tu 2-6pm, W-Su 10am-6pm. €3, seniors and students €1.50.)*

IGREJA DE SÃO FRANCISCO. The Gothic and Baroque Igreja de São Francisco glitters with one of the most elaborately gilded wooden interiors in Portugal. Under the floor, thousands of human bones are stored in preparation for Judgment Day. *(R. Infante Dom Henrique. ☎222 06 21 00. From Pr. Liberade, follow the directions to Palácio da Bolsa. Open daily 9am-6pm. €2.50, students €1.25.)*

JARDINS DO PALÁCIO DE CRISTAL. These beautiful gardens lie outside the Palácio de Cristal (Glass Palace), near the hospital, with geese, swans, ducks, peacocks, and fountains. *(R. D. Manuel II. ☎226 05 70 80. Exit Pr. Liberdade on R. Clérigos and follow the road around the hospital (right on R. Alberto Gouveia) before taking a left on R. Dom Manuel II. The park and palace are on the left, after the Museu Nacional de Soares dos Reis (10-15min.). Park open daily until dark.)*

BEACH AND ESPLANADE. Porto's rocky beach, in the ritzy **Foz** district in the west end of the city, is a popular destination despite the pollution. Beyond the Foz district, on the city's western coastline, are the beaches of **Matosinhos.** *(Bus #1 from the São Bento train station heads to both Foz and Matosinhos.)* Between Foz and downtown, at the bottom of the hill on R. Alfândega, past a marvelous dock filled with shops and restaurants, runs the esplanade in **Ribeira.** *(Bus #1 from the São Bento train station or tram #1 from the Igreja de São Francisco.)*

PORT LODGES

Now for the reason you came to Porto. All of the port wine lodges are located across the river in the nearby suburb, **Vila Nova da Gaia.** To get there, walk down to the Ribeira district and cross the lower level of the large **Ponte Dom Luís I.** Most of the lodges offer free tasting tours, on which you can note the differences between British and Portuguese lodges. Be measured in your tasting; it's easy to get carried away with all the free port. You still need to cross the bridge to get back to the city.

Taylor's, R. do Choupelo, 250 (☎223 71 99 99), up the hill over the other Port lodges. From Av. Diogo Leite (the main street), take a left on R. de França, which turns into R. do Choupelo. Follow it uphill as it curves; Taylor's is on the right. In this quiet and elegant lodge, have your wine in comfortable chairs that overlook a colorful garden or on the terrace, with an amazing view of the Rio Douro. Free tours (every 20-30min.) and tasting. Open Aug. M-Sa 10am-6pm, Sept.-July M-F 10am-6pm; last visit starts 5pm.

Sandeman, Lgo. Miguel Bombarda, 3 (☎223 74 05 33), just off Av. Diogo Leite. The bigshot of Vila Nova da Gaia, with costumed guides and a souvenir shop. Tours (every 15min.) last about 30min. €2.50 entrance, under 16 free. Tickets are good for a €2.50 discount at the gift shop. Open Apr.-Sept. daily 10am-12:30pm and 2-6pm; Oct.-Mar. M-F 9:30am-12:30pm and 2-5pm. AmEx/MC/V.

Ferreira, R. Carvalhosa, 19 (☎223 74 61 00), 1 block up from the end of Av. Ramos Pinto. Sip your port in the tasting room among heavy wooden tables and untapped casks filled with more burgundy *liquor.* Tours €2.50, credited toward purchase of a bottle of port. Open Apr.-Oct. every 20min. M-F 10:15am-12:30pm and 2-5:45pm, Sa 10:30am-12:30pm; Nov.-Mar. every hr. M-F 9am-noon and 2-5pm. AmEx/MC/V.

NIGHTLIFE

The place to party on weekend nights is the **Ribeira,** where bars vibrate with the rhythms of Brazilian and Latin tunes. Pr. Ribeira, M. Bacalhoeiros, and R. Alfândega harbor most of the bars and pubs. Be cautious, as Pr. Ribeira and Cais do Ribeira can be unsafe at night. Most clubs are located along the river in the **Foz** district and in the new industrial zones; nightlife in Porto is hard to follow without a car. Bus #1 runs all night from Pr. Liberdade to the beach at Matosinhos, passing Foz along the way. A taxi to Foz from downtown costs about €3.50.

Solar do Vinho do Porto, R. Entre Quintas, 220 (☎226 09 47 49), off R. Dom Manuel II, by the Palácio de Cristal. Take the 1st left after the palace park, continue downhill to the fork, turn left at the park, then right at the fountain and down some stairs. Sister of the *Solar* in Lisbon, this is a good choice if you're still not tired of tasting port. Once a manor house, its upscale lounge has a terrace with a gorgeous river view. Port starts at €1.50 and climbs to over €15. Open M-Sa 2pm-midnight. MC/V.

Petrus Bar/Wine Caffé, R. Fonte Taurina, 97 (☎919 86 77 80), with 1 entrance through the patio on Cais do Ribeira and another on the narrow street leading from Lgo. de Terreiro. The patio is a perfect spot to enjoy the view of the wine lodges across the river. During the day, Petrus is a cool escape from the sun. At night, lounge music cools to jazz, soul, and blues. Live music on the patio Sa 3-7pm, inside W 10am-2pm. Beer €1.50-2.50. Mixed drinks €3.50. Open daily 10:30am-5am.

Pub O Muro, Muro dos Bacalhoeiros, 87-88 (☎222 08 34 26), on a pedestrian street in the Ribeira district. A restaurant at dinnertime, but also a good place to start the night with a few drinks overlooking the river. Beer €1. Open Tu-Su noon-2am.

Discoteca Swing, Praceta Engenheiro Amaro Costa, 766 (☎226 09 00 19), near R. Júlio Dinis. Swinging action for a mixed gay-straight crowd grooving to alt-rock, new wave, and pop. Cover €5. Open daily 11pm-4am, but the fun starts around 1am.

ENTERTAINMENT AND FESTIVALS

Porto hosts the **Fantasporto Film Festival** (2 weeks in Feb.), screening international fantasy, sci-fi, and horror flicks for crowds of film enthusiasts. Early June brings the **Festival Internacional de Teatro de Expressão Ibérica,** which has free performances of Portuguese and Spanish theater, including pieces from the nations' former colonies. Porto's biggest party, however, is the **Festa de São João** (June 23-24), when locals storm the streets for free concerts, folklore, *fado*, and (of course) wine. The tourist office doles out info detailing Porto's upcoming events to celebrate its status as a Cultural Capital of Europe.

BRAGA ☎253

Braga (pop. 160,000) is distinct among Portuguese cities for its extensive historic district packed with colorful gardens, sprawling plazas, and large fountains. The town's attractive, historic character has earned it the nickname "Portuguese Rome." Originally the capital of a district founded by Celtic tribes in 300 BC, in 27 BC it became "Bracara Augusta," a Roman administrative center. Today, the city is widely considered to be the most politically conservative in all of Portugal. Not surprisingly, the 1926 coup that paved Salazar's path to power was launched from here. During Holy Week, religious processions cross flower-carpeted streets and somber devotion explodes at night into fireworks and dancing. Those who come to Braga expecting just to pass through often end up staying for several days, as the city makes a convenient base for several worthwhile daytrips.

TRANSPORTATION

Trains: Lgo. Estação (☎253 26 21 66), 2 blocks downhill from the Porta Nova. Trains to: **Coimbra** (4hr.; 7:50am, 6:50pm; €5.75); **Lisbon** via (7:50am, 6:50pm; €14), **Porto** (1½hr., 11 per day 5:20am-10:05pm, €1.15). To get to **Valença, Viana do Castelo,** and **Vila Nova de Cerveira,** make a connection at **Nine** (20min., 14 per day 5:20am-10:05pm, €0.90).

Buses: Central de Camionagem (☎253 61 60 80 or 253 68 31 33), a few blocks north of the city center. **Rodoviária** to: **Coimbra** (3hr., 6-9 per day 6am-11:30pm, €8); **Faro** (12-15hr., 9 per day 6am-11:30pm, €17); **Guimarães** (1hr., every 30min. 7am-8pm, €1.90); **Lisbon** (5¼hr., 8-9 per day 9:30am-11:30pm, €12); **Porto** (1¾hr., every 45min. 6:45am-8pm, €3.80). **Hoteleira do Gerês** to: **Caldas de Gerês** (1½hr., 17-18 per day 6am-11:30pm, €7.50).

Taxis: ☎253 61 40 19.

ORIENTATION AND PRACTICAL INFORMATION

Braga's focal point is the **Praça da República,** the large central square full of fountains and cafes. **Av. Liberdade** stems out from the square. Pedestrian thoroughfare **R. do Souto** begins at the tourist office corner of Pr. República, eventually becoming R. Dom Diogo de Sousa and then R. Andrade de Corvo, before leading straight to the **train station.** To get to Pr. República from the **bus station,** take a left with your back to the entrance, and turn right up the commercial street. Continue straight under the modern building's overpass onto Pr. Alexandre Herculano, then take R. dos Cháos straight ahead into the square.

Tourist Office: Av. Central, 1 (☎253 26 25 50), on the corner of Av. Liberdade in Pr. República. Short-term **luggage storage.** Open July-Sept. M-F 9am-7pm, Sa-Su 9am-12:30pm and 2-5:30pm; Oct.-June M-F 9am-7pm, Sa 9am-12:30pm and 2-5:30pm.

Budget Travel: Tagus, Pr. Município, 7 (☎253 21 51 44). Student flights and other services. Open June-Sept. M-F 9am-6pm, Sa 9am-12:30pm; Oct.-May M-F 9am-12:30pm and 2:30-6pm. AmEx/MC/V.

Currency Exchange: Caixa Geral de Depósitos, Pr. República (☎253 60 01 00), across from the tourist office. Open M-F 8:30am-3pm.

English Bookstore: Livraria Central, Av. Liberdade, 728 (☎253 26 23 83), next to Residência Avenida. A small selection of books and travel guides in English. Open M-F 9am-12:30pm and 2:30-7pm, Sa 9am-1pm. AmEx/MC/V.

Emergency: ☎112. **Police:** R. dos Falcões, 12 (☎253 20 04 20).

Hospital: Hospital de São Marcos, Lgo. Carlos Amarante (☎253 61 38 00).

Internet Access: Instituto Português da Juventude, R. de Santa Margarida, 6 (☎253 20 42 50), in the same building as the youth hostel. 1hr. free. Open M-F 9am-6pm. **Videoteca Municipal,** R. do Raio, 2 (☎253 26 77 93), has 10 computers. Free, 1hr. limit. Open M-Sa 10am-12:30pm and 2-6:30pm.

Post Office: Av. Liberdade (☎253 20 03 64), 2 blocks downhill from the tourist office, in the grand building on the right side of the street. For **Posta Restante,** indicate "Estação Avenida" in the address. Telephones, **fax,** and other services. Open M-F 8:30am-6pm. **Postal Code:** 4700.

ACCOMMODATIONS AND CAMPING

Pensão Grande Residência Avenida, Av. Liberdade, 738, 2nd fl. (☎253 60 90 20; fax 60 90 28), steps from Pr. da República. Rooms with phones and cable TV overlook the lively avenue. Breakfast included. June-Sept. singles €20, with bath €22.50; doubles €25, with bath €30; triples €33. Oct.-May €15/€20/€23/€28/€30. MC/V. ❷

Pousada da Juventude de Braga (HI), R. Santa Margarida, 6 (☎/fax 253 61 61 63). From the tourist office entrance, take a right and follow Av. Combatentes before turning left at the intersection with R. Santa Margarida; the hostel is up the hill on the left. A taxi from the train station costs €4. Crowded dorm rooms, with 8-10 beds each, are offset by a friendly atmosphere and a convenient location. Fills with school groups Apr.-May and tourists June-Aug. Reception 8am-midnight. June 16-Sept. 15 dorms €9.50; double with bath €26.50. Sept. 15-June 15 dorms €7.50/€21. MC/V. ❶

Pensão Residencial Francfort, Av. Central, 7 (☎253 26 26 48). A large red tiled building in a premium location. Some of the slightly worn rooms overlook the fountain in Pr. República. Reception 8am-midnight. Midnight curfew. May-Sept. singles €15, with bath €25; doubles €20, with bath €30. Oct.-Apr. €13/€20/€18/€25. ❷

Residencial Dona Sofia, Lgo. S. João do Souto, 131 (☎253 263 160). From Pr. República, head downhill on R. S. Marco, take the 1st left, and it's on the far side of the square. Offers an excellent break from budget hostels. The rooms are huge and newly-decorated, and all have cable TV, bath, and large windows. Singles €45; doubles €55. ❹

Camping: Parque da Ponte (☎253 27 33 55), 2km down Av. Liberdade from the center, next to the stadium and the municipal pool. Buses every 20min. 6:30am-11pm. Laundry facilities. €1.80 per person, €1.40 per tent, €1.50 per car.

FOOD

Braga has many cafes and several superb restaurants, but little in between. A **market** sets up in Pr. Comércio, two blocks from the bus station (open M-Sa 7am-3pm). For fast meals around a food court and a movie theater, head to the **BragaShopping** mall, facing the plaza (☎253 20 80 10).

Churrasqueira da Sé, R. D. Paio Mendes, 25 (☎253 26 33 87), on the street running from the front entrance of the cathedral. An efficient and popular restaurant, serving generous half-portions to lunchtime crowds. The *prato do dia* (€3.50-5.50) is always a good deal. Open Th-Tu 9:30am-3pm and 6:30-9:30pm. ❶

Café Vianna, Pr. República, 87 (☎253 26 23 36). Marble and velvet-filled cafe is packed at midnight in summer. *Prato do dia* €4.25. Sandwiches €3.50-5. Open May-Sept. daily 8am-2am. Oct.-Apr. closed Su. AmEx/MC/V. ❶

Abade de Priscos, Pr. Mouzinho de Albuquerque, 7, 2nd fl. (☎253 27 66 50). Named after a priest widely considered to be Portugal's best chef, this restaurant serves traditional Portuguese cuisine. Small menu of entrees prepared with care (€6-10). Open Tu-Sa noon-3:30pm and 7:30-9:30pm, M 7:30-9:30pm. Closed last 3 weeks of July. ❷

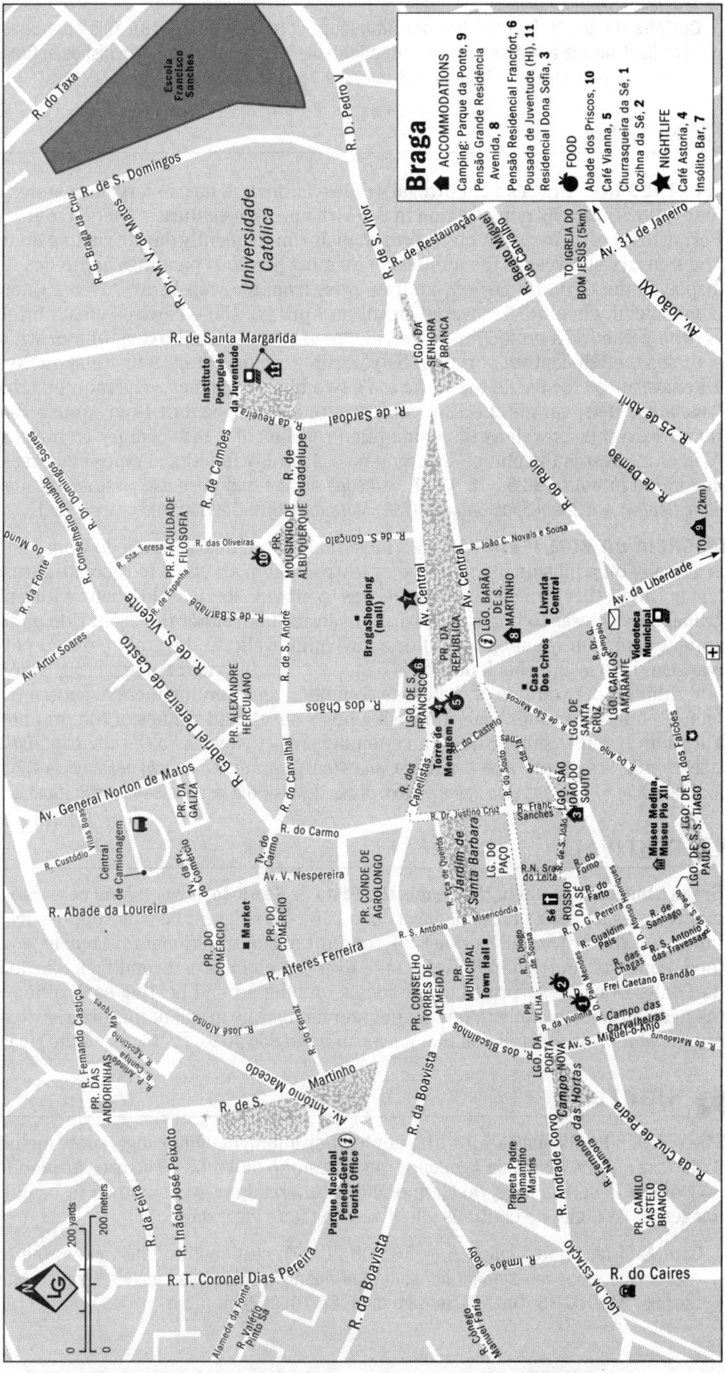
Braga
ACCOMMODATIONS
Camping: Parque da Ponte, 9
Pensão Grande Residência Avenida, 8
Pensão Residencial Francfort, 6
Pousada de Juventude (HI), 11
Residencial Dona Sofia, 3
FOOD
Abade dos Priscos, 10
Café Vianna, 5
Churrasqueira da Sé, 1
Cozihna da Sé, 2
NIGHTLIFE
Café Astoria, 4
Insólito Bar, 7
Escola Francisco Sanches
Universidade Católica
Instituto Português da Juventude
BragaShopping (mall)
Torre de Menagem
Casa Dos Crivos
Livraria Central
Videoteca Municipal
Museu Medina, Museu Pio XII
Central de Camionagem
Market
Town Hall
Sé
Jardim de Santa Barbara
Parque Nacional Peneda-Gerês Tourist Office
TO IGREJA DO BOM JESÚS (5km)
TO 9 (2km)
Av. Central
Av. da Liberdade
Av. 31 de Janeiro
Av. João XXI
R. de Santa Margarida
R. de S. Domingos
R. do Taxa
R. D. Pedro V
R. de S. Vitor
R. de Restauração
R. Beato Miguel de Carvalho
R. 25 de Abril
R. de Damão
R. do Raio
R. João C. Novais e Sousa
R. de Sardoal
R. da Reveira
R. de Camões
R. das Oliveiras
R. de S. Gonçalo
R. de S. Barnabé
R. de S. André
R. dos Chãos
R. do Carvalhal
R. de S. Vicente
R. Gabriel Pereira de Castro
Av. General Norton de Matos
R. do Carmo
Av. V. Nespereira
R. Abade da Loureira
R. Alferes Ferreira
R. José Alfonso
Av. António Macedo
R. de S. Martinho
R. da Boavista
R. T. Coronel Dias Pereira
R. Inácio José Peixoto
R. da Feira
R. Andrade Corvo
R. da Cruz de Pedra
R. do Caires
LGO. DA ESTAÇÃO
Av. S. Miguel-o-Anjo
Campo das Carvalheiras
Frei Caetano Brandão
R. dos Biscainhos
R. do Matadouro
R. dos Capelistas
R. do Castelo
R. de São Marcos
R. do Anjo
R. dos Falcões
LGO. DE S. FRANCISCO
LGO. BARÃO DE S. MARTINHO
LGO. DA SENHORA A BRANCA
LGO. DE SANTA CRUZ
LGO. CARLOS AMARANTE
LGO. SÃO JOÃO DO SOUTO
LGO. DE S. TIAGO
LGO. DE S. PAULO
LGO. DO PAÇO
LGO. DA PORTA NOVA
ROSSIO DA SÉ
PR. DA REPÚBLICA
PR. MOUSINHO DE ALBUQUERQUE
PR. ALEXANDRE HERCULANO
PR. FACULDADE FILOSOFIA
PR. DA GALIZA
PR. CONDE DE AGROLONGO
PR. DO COMÉRCIO
PR. MUNICIPAL
PR. CONSELHO TORRES DE ALMEIDA
PR. DAS ANDORINHAS
PR. CAMILO CASTELO BRANCO
Praceta Padre Diamantino Martins
Campo Novo
Campo das Hortas
200 yards
200 meters

Cozinha da Sé, R. D. Frei Caetano Brandão, 95 (☎253 27 73 43). This spot boasts excellent service and some of the most affordable and well-prepared fish dishes in Braga. Entrees €5-10. Open Tu-Su noon-3:30pm and 7:30-10:30pm. ❷

SIGHTS

CATHEDRAL. Braga's **Sé,** Portugal's oldest cathedral, has undergone a series of renovations since its construction in the 11th and 12th centuries. Guided tours (in Portuguese) of its treasury, choir, and chapels run frequently during visiting hours. The treasury showcases the archdiocese's most precious paintings and relics. On display is the *Cruz do Brasil*, an iron cross from the ship Pedro Álvares Cabral commanded when he discovered Brazil on April 22, 1500. Perhaps most curious are the cathedral's collection of *cofres cranianos* (brain boxes), one of which contains the 6th-century cortex of São Martinho Dume, Braga's first bishop. Near a Renaissance cloister lie the cathedral's two historic chapels. The more notable, **Capela dos Reis,** guards the 12th-century stone sarcophagi of Dom Afonso Henriques's parents as well as the mummified remains of a 14th-century archbishop. Also of interest is the choir—its organ has 2424 fully functional pipes elaborately decorated in gold. *(☎253 26 33 17. Cathedral and treasury open daily June-Aug. 8:30am-6pm; Sept.-May 8:30am-5pm. Cathedral free. Mass daily 5pm. Treasury and chapels €2.)*

IGREJA DO BOM JESUS. Braga's most famous landmark, Igreja do Bom Jesus, is actually on a hillside 5km outside of town. Built in an effort to recreate Jerusalem in Braga, this 18th-century church was to provide Iberian Christians with a pilgrimage site closer to home. To visit Bom Jesus, take either the 285m ride on the antique funicular (8am-8pm, €1) or a 25-30min. walk up the granite-paved pathway. On the way up, check out the 365-step zig-zagging **staircase** depicting, among other things, the stations of the cross, fountains representing the five senses (the "smell" fountain spouts water through a boy's nose), and statues of the prophets. The church, a few small cafes, and stunning sunset views await at the top. *(Buses labeled "#02 Bom Jesus" depart at 10min. and 40min. past the hr. in front of Farmácia Cristal, Av. Liberdade, 571. Buses stop at the bottom of the stairway; the last bus is around 8:30pm. €1.)*

FESTIVALS

Braga's biggest festival of the year is the **Festa de São João,** a week-long celebration that reaches its peak on the night of June 23rd. The biggest bash is supposedly in Porto, but the *bracarenses* don't fall too far behind; traditional folk music, good food, concerts, and general revelry take over Av. da Liberdade and Lgo. São João da Ponte. Don't be surprised to see locals running around beating each other on the head with toy hammers; few seem to remember the origin of this bizarre ritual, but the older folk will tell you that it's a tribute to Sao João, Protector of the Head.

NIGHTLIFE

The cafes in **Pr. República** fill with people after midnight. Other nightspots include **R. do Taxa** and **Pr. Conde de Agrolongo** (a.k.a. Campo da Vinha). The area around Pr. do Comércio between Tr. do Carmo and R. Alferes Ferreira is known to be quite dangerous at night; be cautious when walking here after dark.

Café Astória, Pr. República, 5 (☎966 08 36 97), next door to Café Vianna. The bar upstairs is a popular student hangout after midnight. Wide-eyed angels hang from the ceiling. Beer €0.75. Open M-Sa 8am-4am, Su 10am-2am.

Insólito Bar, Av. Central, 47 (☎968 01 62 40), between Pr. República and the youth hostel. Owned by the city academic association. Live music in the large yard out back attracts a university crowd of students and professors. Beer €1. Mixed drinks €2.50. Minimum consumption M-Th €1, F-Sa €2.50. Open M-Sa 10pm-4am. Closed Aug.

DAYTRIPS FROM BRAGA

MOSTEIRO DE TIBÃES

A city bus labeled "Sarrido" heads 6km from Braga to the monastery. Buses leave from Pr. Conde de Agrolongo, 1 block up R. Capelistas from Pr. República. (25min., every 2hr. at 5 and 35min. past the hr., 8:05am-7:35pm, €1.10).

Surrounded by unspoiled forest, this peaceful 11th-century Benedictine monastery has suffered from centuries of neglect. Stones rattle underfoot in the weathered cloister. (The monastery is undergoing much-needed restoration; check with the tourist office in Braga or the monastery office to find out what areas are open for visits.) Adjoining the cloister is an exceptionally well-preserved church. (☎253 62 26 70. Open Tu-Su 10am-noon and 1-6:30pm. €4, age 14-25 €2, under 14 free.)

GUIMARÃES

REDM buses (☎253 51 62 29) run from Braga to Guimarães (40min.; M-F 19 per day 7:15am-8:35pm, Sa-Su 13-15 per day 8am-8:35pm; €2), and return (40min.; M-F 19 per day 6:30am-8:30pm, Sa-Su 13-15 per day 6:55am-8:30pm; €2).

Ask any Portugal native about the city of Guimarães (pop. 60,000), and they will tell you that it was the birthplace of the nation. As the hometown of the first king of Portugal, Alfonso Henrique, Guimarães represented the starting point for *la Reconquista* from the Moors and the site of his initial court in the 12th century. One of Portugal's most gorgeous palatial estates, the **Paço dos Duques de Bragança** (Ducal Palace), is modeled after the manor houses of northern Europe. A museum inside includes furniture, silverware, tapestries, and weapons once used at the palace. Don't miss the elaborate Pastrana tapestries in the **Sala dos Pasos Perdidos** (Hall of Lost Footsteps) or the interesting display of archaic weaponry in the **Sala das Armas** (Arms Room). Up a few steep steps from the courtyard is the **Capela.** (Chapel open daily 9:30am-12:30pm and 2-5:30pm. €3, seniors and students €1.50. Su mornings free.) Overlooking the city is the **Monte da Pena,** home to an excellent campsite as well as picnic areas, mini-golf, and cafes. To get there, take the **teleférico** (skyride) which runs in summer from Lgo. das Hortas to the mountaintop. (☎253 51 50 85. June-July and Sept. M-F 11am-7pm, Sa-Su 10am-8pm; Aug. daily 10am-8pm. €1.50, €2.50 round-trip.)

The main **tourist office** is on Alameda de São Dámaso, 83, facing Pr. Toural. From the bus station, take Av. Conde Margaride to the right, walk uphill, and turn right at the fork onto R. Paio Galvão; the tourist office is on the far corner of Pr. Toural. The English-speaking staff distributes maps and brochures, and offers short-term **luggage storage.** (☎253 41 24 50. Open June-Sept. M-Sa 9:30am-7pm; Oct.-May M-Sa 9:30am-6pm.) The **train station** is a 10min. walk down Av. Afonso Henriques from the tourist office. The **bus station** (☎253 51 65 29) is in the **GuimarãeShopping** complex, on Alameda Mariano Felgueiras. To get there, follow Av. Conde Margaride downhill. Services include: **emergency** ☎112; **police** on Alameda Alfredo Pimenta (☎253 51 33 34); **hospital** on R. dos Cutileiros (☎253 51 26 12). Follow the crowds for lunch at **Restaurante O Pinguim ❷,** Tr. do Picoto, off R. Picoto. From Lgo. Navarros de Andrade, go up Av. Humberto Delgado (across the square from the post office) and take a left onto R. Picoto up the hill, then another left off the street as it curves to the right. Their specialty is *bacalhau à pinguimu,* a salted cod dish (€12.25, serves 2). Other entrees run €4.75-9. (☎253 41 81 82. Open Tu-Su 8am-10:30pm; serves meals 11:30am-3:30pm and 7-10:30pm. AmEx.)

ROOSTER JUSTICE A few days in Portugal and you'll start to notice something of a national obsession with roosters. A very special rooster, that is—*o galo de Barcelos* (the famous rooster of Barcelos). This particular animal, with flowers and hearts on its wings and tail, may seem like a psychedelic symbol of sorts, but it actually serves an altogether nobler cause. Once upon a time in the sleepy town of Barcelos, an innocent man was condemned to die for a crime he didn't commit. As his last wish he asked to have dinner with the judge so that he could try one last time to prove his innocence. The judge, who was having roast chicken for dinner that night, obliged. When the man saw the chicken at dinner, he announced that the rooster would crow to prove his innocence. And sure enough the *galo* did—or so the story goes—forever securing itself a special place in Portuguese folklore as a symbol of truth, justice, and faith.

BARCELOS

Getting from Braga to Barcelos and back is easy. REDM buses (☎253 80 83 00) leave from Av. Sidónio Pais, 245, across from Campo da República, and run frequently to Braga (40-50min.; M-Sa 6:30am-7:20pm, Su 7:30am-7:20pm; €1.60).

Though Barcelos is known throughout Portugal for its famous rooster, the town also hosts one of the largest weekly markets in Europe—vendors from the entire region come on Thursdays to sell everything from produce to local ceramics. This market, the **Feira de Barcelos,** was inaugurated in 1412 by Dom João I. Vendors begin arriving at the huge **Campo da República** late Wednesday night to set up, and by 8am on Thursday, the market is going at full force. Old ladies carry live roosters by the feet, artisans display inexpensive traditional ceramics, and aggressive pastry sellers work from trucks on the square's edge along Av. da Liberdade. Even if you miss market day, it's still worth the trip to visit Barcelos. The **Templo do Bom Jesus,** in main Lgo. da Porta Nova, built in 1704, is an octagonal Baroque church with a golden altar. In Lgo. do Município is the 17th-century **Igreja Matriz,** a Gothic church built by Count Alfonso. Behind the church is the 14th century **Paço Condal,** site of the famous monument to the Barcelos cock. The Paço has also hosted the **Museu Arqueológico** since 1920. (All sights open daily 9am-noon and 1-5pm. Free.)

The **tourist office** is in the Torre da Porta Nova, part of the town's original 15th-century wall and the only remaining of three towers that once formed the entrance to the ancient city. The office provides short-term **luggage storage.** (☎253 81 18 82. Open Mar.-Oct. M-F 10am-6pm, Sa 10am-12:30pm and 2:30-5:30pm, Su 2:30-5:30pm; Nov.-Feb. M-F 9:30am-5:30pm, Sa 10am-12:30pm and 2:30-5pm.) Services include: **emergency** (☎112) and the **police** on Av. Dr. Sidónio Pais (☎253 80 25 70).

PARQUE NACIONAL DE PENEDA-GERÊS

A crescent-shaped natural reserve along the Spanish border, the Parque Nacional de Peneda-Gerês became Portugal's first protected area in 1971. This park consists of the northern Serra da Peneda and the southern Serra do Gerês. The main base is Caldas de Gerês, a spa town in the south. The park is one of the most popular destinations for Portuguese vacationers in July and August, but those who venture farther away from Caldas de Gerês can find areas to relax any time of year.

TRANSPORTATION AND PRACTICAL INFORMATION. Empresa Hoteleira do Gerês (☎253 61 58 96) runs **buses** between **Gerês** and **Braga** (1½hr.; M-Sa 10-17 per day 6:30am-6:30pm, Su 7 per day 6:30am-9pm; €3). To get to the **tourist office** from the bus stop, walk uphill along Av. Manuel Francisco da Costa; the office is surrounded by a semicircle of shops. The English-speaking staff provides info on the national park and short-term **luggage storage.** (☎253 39 11 33. Open M-Sa 9am-12:30pm and

2:30-6pm.) The **police** (☎253 39 11 37) are just off Av. Manuel Francisco da Costa. The **post office** is located off the rotary that leads uphill into the center. (☎253 39 00 10; fax 253 39 00 16. Open M-F 9am-12:30pm and 2-5:30pm.)

ACCOMMODATIONS AND FOOD. There are plenty of *pensões* in Gerês. One option is **Casa de Ponte ❷,** on Av. D. João V. From the bus stop, head downhill until you see the hostel on the left corner where the road splits, next to the Escola Primaria. The rooms have baths and TV, most have porches overlooking the garden. English-speaking owner. (☎253 39 11 25. Midnight curfew. Aug.-Oct. singles €25; doubles €40; triples €45. May-July €20/€30/€35. Nov.-Apr. €15/€20/€35.) For camping, try **Camping Vidoeiro ❶,** by the river and 1km out of town. Facing the tourist office, take the uphill road to the left. (☎253 39 12 89. Open May 15-Oct. 15. Reception 8am-7pm. €2 per person, €1.75-2.25 per tent, €2.25 per car.) Meals are available at the *pensões* throughout town. **Restaurants** and **cafes** lie along Av. Manuel Francisco da Costa, around the corner from the bus stop.

HIKING. The main park information office is located in **Braga,** on Av. António Macedo. (☎253 20 34 80; fax 253 61 31 69. Open M-F 9am-12:30pm and 2:30-5:30pm.) The **Gerês branch office** (☎253 39 01 10), on Av. Manuel Francisco da Costa uphill from the municipal tourist office, has an English-speaking staff that can assist with hike-planning. More casual hikers tend to stay south where the few roads provide scenic and manageable journeys, while more dedicated visitors head to the trails of the north. In both areas, numerous hamlets and villages offer accommodations, campsites, and food. Serious hikers can attempt the 10-12hr. trek along an ancient Roman road beginning in Braga; the route runs along the **Vilarinho das Furnas** reservoir, an optimal place for swimming and camping. In the height of summer, one might be able to catch a view of the village that was submerged when the river was dammed. Another possible hike follows the road toward **Portela do Homem,** a small town on the Portuguese-Spanish border with a river pool at the bottom of the **Minas dos Carris** valley. Southeast of Gerês is Miradouro do Gerês, a popular site overlooking the **Caniçada** reservoir—beware the en masse migration of weekend picnickers. The village of **Rio Caldo,** at the base of the Caniçada reservoir just 8km south of Gerês, offers windsurfing and waterskiing. The main attraction in Gerês proper is the **Spa Caldas de Gerês,** open May to October. The spa complex includes a pool, tennis, horseback riding, hiking services, canoeing, and nautical sports, along with its famed waters. Next door, **Parque das Termas** has flourine mineral waters. (☎253 39 11 13. €0.85, under 12 €0.40. Pool open Apr.-July and Sept. 10am-6pm, Aug. 10am-8pm. €3.50; under 7 €2.)

VIANA DO CASTELO ☎258

Visited mainly as a beach resort, Viana do Castelo (pop. 20,000) has a lively historic district, centered around the Praça da República. The surrounding hilltops offer excellent views of the fertile landscape and the sea. Those intending to pass through en route to Galicia soon discover the town's charm, excellent food and beaches, and intriguing architecture including a bridge designed by Gustave Eiffel.

TRANSPORTATION

Trains: (☎258 82 13 15) The station is at the top of Av. Combatentes da Grande Guerra, under the Santa Luzia hill. Trains to: **Porto** (2hr., 13-14 per day 5am-9:27pm, €4); **Vigo, Spain** (2½hr.; 9:18am, 8:30pm; €7.80); **Vila Nova de Cerveira** via **Caminha** (1hr., 8 per day 7:44am-8:30pm, €1.60).

Buses: Rodoviária (☎258 82 50 47) departs from **Central de Camionagem,** on the eastern edge of town and a 20min. walk from the center, to **Braga** (1½hr.; M-Sa 6-8 per day 7am-6:35pm, Su 4 per day 8:15am-6:35pm; €3.50). **AVIC** (☎258 82 97 05) and **Auto-Viação do Minho** (☎258 80 03 41) go to **Porto** (2hr.; M-F 9 per day 6:45am-6:30pm, Sa-Su 4-6 per day 8:20am-6:30pm; €3.50-5.25) and **Lisbon** (5½hr.; Su-F 3 per day 8am-11:45pm, Sa 7am and 2:30pm; €18).

Taxi: Táxis Vianenses (☎258 82 66 41 or 82 23 22). Taxis can be found along Av. Combatentes da Grande Guerra.

ORIENTATION AND PRACTICAL INFORMATION

Wide, main **Av. dos Combatentes da Grande Guerra** runs from the **train station** to the port. Most accommodations and restaurants are located on or just off the Avenida. The **historic center** stretches east of the Avenida around **Praça da República,** while the fortress and sea lie to the west.

Tourist Office (☎258 82 26 20; fax 258 82 78 73), R. do Hospital Velho, corner of Pr. Erva. From the train station, take the 4th left at the sharp corner onto R. da Picota, then a quick right onto Pr. Erva. Open May-July and Sept. M-Sa 9am-1pm and 2:30-6pm, Su 9:30am-1pm; Aug. daily 9am-7pm; Oct.-Apr. M-Sa 9am-12:30pm and 2:30-5:30pm.

Currency Exchange: Montepio Geral, Av. Combatentes da Grande Guerra, 332 (☎258 82 88 97), near the train station. Open M-F 8:30am-3pm. On-site 24hr. **ATM.**

Emergency: ☎112. **Police:** R. de Aveiro (☎258 82 20 22).

Hospital: Hospital de Santa Luzia, Estrada de Sta. Luzia (☎258 82 90 81), off Av. 25 de Abril.

Internet Access: Free at the **Biblioteca Municipal** (public library) on R. Cândido dos Reis (☎258 80 93 02), up from Pr. República. 5 computers. ID required. Strict 30min. limit; often a 1hr. wait. Open M-F 9:30am-12:30pm and 2-7pm, Sa 9:30am-12:30pm.

Post Office: Av. Combatentes da Grande Guerra (☎258 80 00 80), across from the train station. **Posta Restante** and **fax.** Open M-F 8:30am-6pm. **Postal Code:** 4900.

ACCOMMODATIONS AND CAMPING

Accommodations in Viana do Castelo are easy to find, although they are not particularly cheap. *Quartos particulares* (private rooms) are the best option in the center of town. Check the tourist office's list of accommodations or look on side streets off Av. Combatentes da Grande Guerra.

Pousada de Juventude de Viana do Castelo (HI), R. da Argaçosa (☎258 80 02 60; fax 258 82 08 70), right on the marina, off Pr. de Galiza. Rooms with balconies and great views of the marina. Lounge with a pool table (€3 per hr.) and free ping-pong. Bar, common kitchen, and dining hall (lunch 12:30-1:30pm, dinner 7:30-8:30pm; €4.75). Laundry €5 per load. Internet access €1.50 per 30min., €2.50 per hr. Reception 8am-midnight. Checkout 10am. Reservations recommended. June 16-Sept. 15 dorms €12.50; doubles with bath €30. Sept. 16-June 15 €10/€25. ❶

Pensão Guerreiro, R. Grande, 14 (☎258 82 20 99; fax 258 82 04 02), at Av. Combatentes da Grande Guerra. June-Sept. 15, Dec. 16-31, Apr. singles €18; doubles €28; triples €30; quads €33. Rest of year €8 discount. ❷

Pensão Dolce Vita, R. Poço, 44 (☎258 82 48 60), across from the tourist office. Rooms with baths surround a common TV lounge. July 15-Sept. singles €20; doubles €30; Oct.-July 15 €10/€20. MC/V. ❶

Pensão Vianense, Av. Conde da Carreira, 79 (☎258 82 31 18), across from the train station on a side street off the top of Av. Combatentes da Grande Guerra. 9 rooms without bath. June-Sept. singles €15; doubles €30. Oct.-May €12.50/€25. MC/V. ❶

Residencial Viana Mar, Av. Combatentes da Grande Guerra, 215 (☎/fax 258 82 89 62). Large, hotel-like *residencial* with TV and A/C. Singles €22.50, with shower €25, with bath €30; doubles €32.50, with shower €35, with bath €45. AmEx/MC/V. ❷

Camping: Orbitur (☎258 32 21 67; fax 258 32 19 46), at Praia do Cabedelo. Catch a TransCunha "Cabedelo" bus (6 per day 7:35am-6:45pm, €0.75) from the bus station or from Lgo. 5 de Outubro. A well-equipped campsite with free showers. Apr.-Sept. €3-3.50 per person, €2.50-5 per tent, €2.50-3 per car. Oct.-Nov. and Jan.-Mar. €2/€1.50-2.75/€1.75. Open Jan. 16-Nov. 30. ❶

FOOD

People eat well in Viana do Castelo. The local specialties are *arroz de sarabulho* (rice cooked with blood and served alongside sausages and potatoes) and *bacalhau à Gil Eanes* (cod cooked with milk, potato, onion, garlic, and oil). Most budget restaurants lie on the small streets off Av. Combatentes da Grande Guerra. The **municipal market** is on Av. Rocha Paris, in front of Pr. Dona Maria II. (☎258 82 26 57. Open M-Sa 8am-3pm.) A **weekly market,** attracting many of the same vendors as the market in Barcelos, is held on Fridays in Campo do Castelo, in front of the castle. For groceries, go to the **Pingo Doce** on R. de Aveiro (open daily 9am-10pm).

Restaurante Dolce Vita, R. Poço, 44 (☎258 82 48 60), at the corner of Pr. Erva, across the square from the tourist office. Brick-oven pizzas with generous, fresh toppings (€4.50-5.25) are served to a bustling crowd. Portuguese dishes and pastas €4.50-10. Open daily noon-3pm and 7:30-10:30pm. MC/V. ❶

Confeitaria Natário, R. Manuel Espregueira, 37 (☎258 82 23 76), just off Av. Combatentes da Grande Guerra. People line up at 10:30am to catch the meat and fish pastries hot out of the oven (€0.60-1). Their delicious specialty is *bolas de berlim* (€0.75), a sweet pastry made with fresh egg cream. Open W-M 9am-10pm. ❶

Arcada, R. Grande, 34-36 (☎258 82 36 43). Take a right out of the tourist office and then the 2nd right; it's on the left. This traditional *casa de pasto* is the oldest in the historic center (founded in 1950). Entrees €5-8.50. Freshest fish Tu-Th. Open May-Sept. daily noon-3pm and 7-11pm; Oct.-Apr. M-F noon-3pm and 7-11pm. V. ❷

Ruela Bar, Av. Campo do Castelo, 11 (☎258 81 10 72), on the street below the castle, across from the square. Popular with students for its *prato do dia* (€3.50), as well as its burgers and sandwiches (€1-2.50). Open M-Sa 11:30am-3pm and 6pm-midnight. ❶

A Matriz, R. do Tourinho, 82 (258 33 12 16), on the corner with R. Sacadura Cabral. A quiet restaurant with excellent fish and meat dishes. Entrees €6-12. Open Tu-Su noon-3:30pm and 7:30-10:30pm. ❷

SIGHTS

Even in a country famed for its impressive squares, Viana do Castelo's **Pr. da República** is remarkable. Its centerpiece is a 16th-century fountain encrusted with sculptures and crowned with a sphere bearing a cross of the Order of Christ. The small **Paço do Conselho** (1502), formerly the town hall, seals off the square to the east. Diagonally across the plaza, granite columns support the playful and flowery facade of the **Igreja da Misericórdia** (1598, rebuilt in 1714). Known for its *azulejo* interior, the **Monte de Santa Luzia,** overlooking the city, is crowned by magnificent Celtic ruins and the **Templo de Santa Luzia,** an early 20th-century neo-Byzantine church. Though the funicular no longer runs, you can always reach the hilltop

DOURO AND MINHO

by walking up the long stairway beginning behind the train station. The view of Viana from the hill is fantastic, especially from the top of the church; take the elevator (€0.65) up the tower, or climb the narrow stairway that leads to the **Zimbório** at the very top. For more great views of the harbor and ocean, visit the **Castelo de São Tiago da Barra,** built in 1589 (around a 14th-century tower) by Felipe I of Spain. To reach the castle from the train station, take the second right off Av. Combatentes da Grande Guerra onto R. General Luís do Rego and walk five blocks.

BEACHES

Viana do Castelo and the surrounding coast feature excellent beaches that satisfy everyone from sunbathers to windsurfers. **Praia Norte,** at the end of Av. do Atlántico at the west end of town, is easy to reach and has swimming pools. **Praia da Argaçosa,** a small beach on Rio Lima next to the youth hostel and marina, fills with sunbathers in summer. Getting to the beaches on the other side of the river requires taking the TransCunha bus from Lgo. 5 de Outubro across the bridge (6 per day, 7:35am-6:45pm, €0.75) to the **Praia do Cabedelo,** a great beach for windsurfing. A short train ride north of Viana leads to the **Praia do Bico** in Afife, frequented by surfers (10min.), and the large **Praia de Âncora** (15min.). Farther north are the beaches of **Moledo** and **Caminha.**

ENTERTAINMENT AND NIGHTLIFE

The cafes and bars around Pr. República fill up in the evening. The most popular place in Viana is **Bar Glamour,** R. da Bandeira, 183, down the street from the plaza and away from the main avenue. The interior dance floor and garden feature live music on Thursdays and karaoke on Tuesdays. (☎258 82 29 63. Minimum consumption Su-Th 1 drink. Cover F-Sa €2.50. Open daily 10pm-4am.) Viana's biggest festival of the year is the **Festa de Nossa Senhora da Agonia,** in August.

TRÁS-OS-MONTES

The country's roughest and most isolated region, Trás-Os-Montes ("behind the mountains") is a land of extremes. *Trasmontanos* to describe their seasons as "nine months of winter and three months of hell." The region's isolation, beauty, and tranquility are its biggest draws. Rocky hilltops give way to fields of grapes and corn, which in turn are followed by arid stretches, good only for growing olives. The *trasmontanos* themselves, though known for their toughness, are quite possibly the friendliest people in Portugal.

Trás-Os-Montes has long been home to Portugal's political and religious exiles. Dom Sancho I practically had to beg people to settle here after he incorporated it into Portugal in the 12th century, and it was here that the Jews chose to hide during the Inquisition. Today, it is one of the last outposts of traditional Portugal. The gastronomic specialties, served in generous portions, hint at the region's rustic character: *cozido à portuguesa* is made from sausages, pig parts, carrots, and turnips, and it takes some serious hikes to burn off the hearty *feijoada à trasmontana* (bean stew). The most prized dish is probably *posta a mirandesa*, locally bred beef that locals claim is the most tender in the world.

BRAGANÇA ☎273

Wedged in a narrow valley between two steep slopes, Bragança (pop. 40,000) is a steadfast wilderness outpost. While most visitors come for clean air, blue skies, and olive-covered hillsides—or perhaps the massive 12th-century castle—the people of Bragança make it unique; its substantial distance from the rest of Portugal seems to have preserved an almost archaic sense of hospitality and festivity. Bragança is also the perfect base for exploring the Parque Natural de Montesinho, which extends north into Spain. The town has launched an extensive revitalization project that includes new commercial centers and an updated bus station.

TRANSPORTATION

Trains: No train service. Nearest station is **Mirandela,** 1hr. away and accessible by bus.

Buses: The temporary bus station is 2km from the center of town, on Av. Dom Sancho I. The new bus station, scheduled to open in the spring of 2003, will be at the top of Av. João da Cruz. **Rodonorte** (☎273 30 01 83) buses go to: **Lisbon** (8hr., 3 per day 6-11am, €14) and **Porto** (5hr., 4-6 per day 6am-5pm, €7.80) via **Mirandela** and **Vila Real. Rede Expressos** (☎273 33 18 26) buses go to: **Coimbra** (6hr.; M-F 6 per day, Sa 5 per day 6am-9:30pm; €9); **Lisbon** (8hr.; M-F 8 per day, Sa-Su 6 per day 6am-9:30pm; €14); **Porto** (5hr.; M-F 8 per day, Sa-Su 6 per day 6am-11pm; €8); **Vila Real** (2hr.; M-F 6 per day, Sa-Su 3 per day 2-7pm; €6.75). **Internorte** runs to **Braga** (5hr.; 4:15pm, 1:15am; €8.50) and **Zamora, Spain** (2½hr.; M-Sa 2pm, Su 5:45pm; €11).

Taxis (☎273 32 21 38). Cabs congregate near the post office and temporary bus station (fare to town €2.80-4).

ORIENTATION AND PRACTICAL INFORMATION

The new bus station will be at the top of **Avenida João da Cruz;** from the bottom of this avenue, downward-sloping R. Almirante Reis leads to budget *pensões* and the **Praça da Sé** at the heart of the old town. **Avenida Sá Carneiro,** wide and commercial, leads to the local Instituto Politécnico. To reach the **fortress,** situated on a hill west of Pr. Sé, take **Rua Combatentes da Grande Guerra** from Pr. Sé, walk uphill, and enter through the opening in the stone walls.

Tourist Office: Av. Cidade de Zamora (☎273 38 12 73; fax 30 42 98). From Pr. da Sé, take R. Abilio Beca and then the 2nd left onto R. Marqués. Turn right onto Av. Cidade de Zamora; the office is on the left, across the grass. Short-term **luggage storage.** Open May-Sept. M-F 10am-6pm, Sa 10am-12:30pm and 2-5pm, Su 10am-1pm; Oct.-Apr. M-F 10am-12:30pm and 2-5pm, Sa 10am-12:30pm.

Currency Exchange: Banco Nacional Ultramarino, Av. João da Cruz, 2-6 (☎273 33 12 65), next to the post office, has **ATMs.** Open M-F 8:30am-3pm. **San Vitur** (☎273 33 18 26), run by Rede Expressos with an office at the bus station and on Av. Joã da Cruz, also does exchange.

English Bookstore: Livraría Mário Péricles, R. Combatentes da Grande Guerra, 180 (☎273 32 25 49). Open M-F 9:30am-noon and 2-7pm, Sa 9:30am-1pm. AmEx/MC/V.

Emergency: ☎112. **Police:** R. Dr. Manuel Bento (☎273 30 34 00), by the town hall.

Hospital: Hospital Distrital de Bragança, Av. Abade de Baçal (☎273 31 08 00), before the stadium on the road to Vinhais.

Post Office: (☎273 31 00 71), at the corner of R. Almirante Reis and R. 5 de Outubro, at the end of Av. João da Cruz. Open M-F 9am-5pm. **Postal Code:** 5300.

TRÁS-OS-MONTES

ACCOMMODATIONS AND CAMPING

Plenty of cheap *pensões* and *residenciales* line Pr. da Sé and R. Almirante Reis; the youth hostel is near the temporary bus station and the modern area of town.

Pousada de Juventude—Bragança (HI), Forte de São João de Deus (☎273 30 46 00; fax 273 32 61 36), off Av. 22 de Maio. A 20min. walk from Av. João da Cruz, but very close to the temporary bus station. From the station, turn right and take the 1st left onto Av. 22 de Maio. The hostel is the large, white building on the left. 24 dorms with 4 beds each. Kitchen, playroom, sitting room, and beautiful terrace seating. Laundry facilities. Check-in after 6pm. June 16-Sept. 15 dorms €12.50; doubles with bath €35. Sept. 16-June 15 €10/€28. MC/V. ❶

Pensão Poças, R. Combatentes da Grande Guerra, 200 (☎273 33 14 28 or 273 33 12 16). From Pr. da Sé, walk toward the castle and bear right; it's just ahead on the left. Clean common baths with showers. Includes breakfast (8:30-11am). Reception in restaurant. Singles with or without bath €10; doubles €20; triples €30. AmEx/MC/V. ❶

Camping: Parque de Campismo Municipal do Sabor (☎273 33 15 35), 6km from town on the edge of the Parque Natural de Montesinho, on the road to Portelo (N103-7) park. The #7 STUB bus (yellow and blue) toward Meixedo goes by the campground, leaving from the Caixa Geral de Depósitos on Av. João da Cruz (10min.; M-F 12:44, 6pm, also Sept.-June 2:10pm; Sa 1:35pm; €0.75). If you choose to hike, be careful—roads are narrow and curvy. Reception 8am-midnight. Open May-Oct. €1.50 per person and per car, €1.50-2.25 per tent. Electricity €1. ❶

FOOD

The region is celebrated for its *presunto* (cured ham) and *salsichão* (sausages), as well as the local delicacy, *alheiradas*, sausages made with bread and various meats (see **That Can't be Kosher,** p. 710). You can find these and fresh produce at the stores that surround the *mercado municipal*, two blocks down from the Pr. da Sé. Restaurants in Bragança tend to serve generous quantities of food; half-portions are almost always enough for one person. Be prepared for lots of meat.

Restaurante Poças, R. Combatentes da Grande Guerra, 200 (☎273 33 14 28), off Pr. da Sé. One of the best places to try local specialties. Entrees €5-9. Open 8am-midnight; serves meals noon-3pm and 7-10:30pm. AmEx/MC/V. ❷

Restaurante Dom Fernando, R. Rainha D. Maria II, 197 (☎273 32 62 73), in the Cidadela (inside the castle walls), upstairs above the bar. Given its location, this restaurant should be more touristy, more expensive, and less good. Fortunately, it's not. Entrees €4.50-7.50. *Menú* €6. Open June-Sept. daily, Oct.-May F-W, 9am-10pm. ❷

Solar Bragançano, Pr. de Sé (☎273 32 38 75). A Victorian setting with chandeliers dripping crystal and a beautiful garden on the back patio of this renovated mansion. Entrees (€6.50-15) include traditional dishes as well as wild game options. Excellent vegetarian soups (€2) and vegetarian omelettes available. Open daily noon-3:30pm, 7:30-10pm. ❸

SIGHTS

Uphill from Praça da Sé is the old town and its 12th-century **castelo;** the castle's tower is from the 15th century. The castle is encircled by massive restored walls that provide phenomenal views of Bragança and Spain. Inside the walls, the castle's **Museu Militar** has a wide range of military paraphernalia that traces Portugal's war history, from the medieval treaties with Spain to the Portuguese efforts in WWI and the African campaigns. (Open F-W 9-11:45am and 2-4:45pm. €1.25. Free Su mornings.) The venerable **pelourinho** (pillory) in the square behind the castle bears a coat of arms. At the base of the whipping post is a granite pig, a vestige of pagan ideology and the place where sinners and criminals were bound during the Middle Ages. The **Domus Municipalis,** behind the church across the square from the castle, once served as the city's municipal meeting house. Today, it is the only existing example of Roman civil architecture on the Iberian Peninsula.

FESTIVALS AND NIGHTLIFE

The most important festival in Bragança is the **Festa de Nossa Senhora das Graças,** celebrated annually in mid-August. The biggest day is August 22nd; the holiday is marked with fireworks on the night of the 21st. During the **Festa do Estudante,** the town's *tunas* (student music groups) gather to play for the entire town. Students from the polytechnic institute ensure good nightlife in the city. A popular student hangout, especially after 1am on weekends, is **Zona+,** Av. Sá Carneiro, 2A, downstairs, below Confeitaria Veneza with the door to the right. (☎933 37 63 95. Open M-Sa 10pm-3am.) A classier place is **Central Pub,** R. do Poço, 18, above Pr. da Sé, on a cross street between R. Almirante Reis and R. 5 de Outubro. An elegant upstairs pub plays 60s music and rotates art exhibitions every three weeks; there's a disco/bar downstairs. (☎273 33 13 09. Open daily 1-3pm.)

DAYTRIP FROM BRAGANÇA

PARQUE NATURAL DE MONTESINHO

Inquire at the information office in Bragança, R. Cónego Albano Falcão, 5 (in Bairro Salvador Nunes Teixeira). Walk downhill from the tourist office on Av. Cidade de Zamora, take the 1st left on a paved street and the 1st left again; it's at the end of the street on the right. Park trails are unmarked, but the office has maps and can help plan hikes. (☎273 38 14 44; fax 273 38 11 79. Open M-F 9am-12:30pm and 2-5:30pm.) The info office (☎273 38 12 34 or 38 14 44) rents Casas Abrigos (traditional houses, also called Casas de Naturaeza). Doubles €25-38; quads €50. Getting to the park can be complicated. Buses to the border village of Rio de Onor leave from Bragança on Av. João da Cruz, in front of Banco Nacional Ultramarino near Pr. da Sé (Sept.-June daily, and the 3rd, 12th, and 21st of summer months, 2:09pm; return bus runs year-round Su-F 6:50pm).

ON THE PROWL The **Festa dos Rapazes,** an ancient ritual enacted in the villages of the Parque Natural de Montesinho, is certainly not lacking for erotic innuendo. The festival, which coincides with the winter solstice, has regional variations but the general idea is the same everywhere. On December 26th or January 6th, the single young men of the villages dress up as *caretos,* wearing shaggy colored suits and diabolic painted masks, and prowl around in groups in search of lone females. Upon finding a *rapariga,* they surround her and one of the *caretos* grabs and shakes her, knocking the bells attached to his belt against her hips (the verb is *chocalhar*). The *festa* continues today, as shy young men use the event to meet and flirt with local girls.

One of the largest protected areas in Portugal, the **Parque Natural de Montesinho** covers 290 square miles between Bragança and the Spanish border. The park consists of 88 traditional *aldeias* (villages). Rich with tradition, these villages preserve age-old communal customs and enact ancient rituals, from the carving of pigs to lively festivals such as the **Festa dos Rapazes** (see **On the Prowl,** p. 708). Some of the villages can be reached in a day's hike or bike ride, but visitors with more time often design multi-day hikes between villages.

Old mountain paths lead through rolling woodlands of oak, chestnut, pine, and cherry trees. *Pombais pombales* (pigeon lofts) dot the landscape, and the land is home to many rare and endangered species including the Iberian wolf, royal eagle, and black stork, among others. Trout fishing, hiking, and horseback riding are popular. The riverbanks are ideal for picnics. If you have only one day to visit the park, the most worthwhile trip is to **Rio de Onor,** a village near the northeast corner, on the border with Spain. Here the Portuguese and Spanish have lived together for centuries, intermarrying and even speaking their own hybrid dialect, *rionorés.* A subtle stone post, with a "P" for "Portugal" carved into one side and an "E" for "España" on the other, marks the border. Villagers cross into Spain for groceries and back into Portugal for coffee at **Cervejaria Preto,** a bar that's not hard to find, as it's the only one in town. You can eat on the stone tables overlooking the river.

VILA REAL ☎259

Vila Real (pop. 25,000) presides over the edge of the gorges of the Corgo and Cabril Rivers in the foothills of the Serra do Marão. The small, historic town center is surrounded by new neighborhoods reaching into the hills, a lively main street, and a few cafes. As the principal commercial center for the southern farms and villages of Trás-Os-Montes, Vila Real is a good point of departure for excursions into the fields and slopes of the Serra do Alvão and Serra do Marão.

TRANSPORTATION. **Trains** run from Av. 5 de Outubro (☎259 32 21 93) to **Porto** (4½hr., 5 per day 7:20am-7:45pm, €5). To get to Vila Real's center, walk up Av. 5 de Outubro over the iron bridge onto R. Miguel Bombarda and turn left on R. Roque da Silveira. Continue to bear left until Av. 1 de Maio. Trains take longer than buses and require transfers at Régua. **Rodonorte buses,** R. D. Pedro de Castro (☎259 34 07 10), are on the square directly uphill from the tourist office. To: **Bragança** (2hr.; 5-9 per day 8:45am-11pm; €7.50); **Guimarães** (1½hr.; M-W 4 per day 6:25am-5:20pm, Th-F 5 per day 6:25am-7pm, Sa 10am, Su 3 per day 4:30-7pm; €5.50); **Lisbon** (6½hr.; M-F 8am, 1:10, 5:20pm; Sa 9:30am, 1:10, 5:20pm; Su 5 per day 9:30am-10:40pm; €13); **Porto** (1¾hr.; 8-13 per day M-F 6:25am-8:20pm, Sa 8am-7pm, Su 8am-10:30pm; €5.50). **Ruicar,** R. Gonçalo Cristóvão, 16 (☎259 32 47 61), up the street across from Rodonorte, sells tickets for Rede Expressos, which stop in front of Rodonorte. It has less service and extremely complicated schedules. It's most useful for late-night weekend buses. Cabs cluster along Av. Carvalho Araújo; try calling **Radiotáxis** (☎259 37 31 38).

ORIENTATION AND PRACTICAL INFORMATION. Vila Real's old neighborhood is centered around **Avenida Carvalho Araújo,** a broad tree-lined avenue that runs downhill from the bus station to the Câmara Municipal. Most of the town's cafes, shops, and hostels are here. The bus stops at Rodonorte Station on **Rua Don Pedro de Castro;** go right upon exiting to get to the main avenue. The **Tourist Office,** Av. Carvalho Araújo, 94 (☎259 32 28 19; fax 259 32 17 12), is to the right and downhill from the bus station, across the street. It's English-speaking staff offers short-term **luggage storage.** (Open June-Sept. M-F 9:30am-7pm, Sa-Su 9:30am-12:30pm and 2-6pm; Oct.-Mar. M-F 9:30am-12:30pm and 2-5pm, Sa 10am-12:30pm and 2-4:30pm; Apr.-May M-F 9:30am-12:30pm and 2-7pm, Sa 10am-12:30pm and 2-5pm.) **Currency exchange** is at **Realvitur,** Lgo. Pioledo, 2 (☎259 34 08 00), 4 blocks uphill from the tourist office and to the right. (Open M-F 9am-7pm, Sa 9am-1pm.) The **post office,** Av. Carvalho Araújo (☎259 33 03 00), is across the street from and to the right of the tourist office. (Open M-F 8:30am-6pm, Sa 9am-12:30pm.)

ACCOMMODATIONS AND CAMPING. Rooms in Vila Real are cheap and plentiful, making the town a convenient place to stay either as a stopover or as a base for exploring the region. Several cafes along Av. Carvalho Araújo advertise rooms. **Residencial São Domingos ❶,** Tr. de São Domingos, 33 (☎259 32 20 39), is the last of 3 hostels on a side street off Av. Carvalho Araújo, to the right of the cathedral. Its rooms are old, but all but 1 have private bath, TV, and phone. (Singles €12.50; doubles €25; triples €30.) **Residencial Mondego ❶,** Tr. de São Domingos, 11 (☎259 32 30 97), just up the street, has the same owners and prices and uses the reception desk at São Domingos. Camp at **Parque de Campismo Municipal de Vila Real ❶,** R. Dr. Manuel Cardona (☎259 32 47 24), beside the river and past the youth hostel, at the end of the street on the right. The site offers free showers. (Reception daily June-Aug. 8am-11pm; Sept.-May 8:30am-5pm. Open Jan. 16-Dec. 15. €2.75 per person, €1.75 per tent and per car.)

TRÁS-OS-MONTES

FOOD

Eating well in Vila Real is easy and inexpensive. There are plenty of options, with lots of good restaurants and cafes located along the central streets. The main avenue (Av. Carvalho Araújo) and the parallel R. Antonio de Azevedo are good places to look; restaurants on R. Teixeira de Sousa tend to be more touristy, but there are some cheaper ones there as well. The cafes along Av. Carvalho Araújo and in the square at the bottom of the avenue fill with people at night. The **Mercado da Praça,** R. D. Maria das Chaves, 75, hosts a large regional market twice a week (Tu and F 8am-noon) and a regular market more frequently (M-Sa 8am-7pm). **Churrasqueira Real ❶,** R. Teixeira Sousa, 14, midway up the street, is very popular, and has a large selection of grilled meats. (☎259 32 20 78. Entrees €2.50-8.50. Open Tu-Su 9am-11pm; meals noon-2pm and 7-9:30pm. Another branch at R. D. Pedro Castro, 15.) **Restaurante Museu dos Presuntos ❶,** Av. Cidade de Orense, 43, at R. D. Afonso III and R. Morgado de Mateus, is a bit of a hike from the town center, but it's worth it for the *presunto* combinations. From the tourist office, cross Av. Carvalho Araújo, take a right, and continue up R. D. Pedro de Castro. After passing the Rodonorte station, bear right onto R. D. Pedro de Menezes, then take a right onto R. D. Afonso III, and it will be at the end of the street across the intersection. (☎259 32 60 17. Open W-Th and Sa-M 12:30-2:30pm and 7-9:30pm, F 7-9:30pm only.)

THAT CAN'T BE KOSHER The *alheira* sausage, a specialty of the Trás-Os-Montes region, was invented by escaping Jews as part of an ingenious plan to save themselves from the Spanish Inquisition. At the time, all Portuguese households had pork sausages hanging from the kitchen ceiling. To blend in without using pork, Jews began to make look-alike sausages filled with chicken, turkey, duck, and pigeon. Officers of the Spanish Inquisition who saw the sausages concluded that the residents could not possibly be Jews and continued on their way. Today, *alheiras* have been adopted by Christians and are made with pork, among other ingredients.

SIGHTS AND EXCURSIONS

Vila Real makes a good base for seeing the nearby natural parks, but the churches in town are worth visiting before you go. The 15th-century **Sé** (cathedral), with its simple interior divided by thick, arched columns, looms at the lower end of Av. Carvalho Araújo. (Open only for Mass M-F 7:30am and 6:30pm, Sa-Su 9am, noon, and 6pm.) Two blocks east of the cathedral, at the end of R. Central, the **Capela Nova** (New Chapel) blushes behind a floral facade. (Open daily 8:30am-6pm. Free.) One block up R. 31 de Janeiro, in Lgo. São Pedro, the **Igreja de São Pedro** is resplendent with 17th-century *azulejos*. (Open daily 9am-5pm. Free.) At the corner of R. Teixeira de Sousa and Av. 1 de Maio is the 16th-century **Igreja da Misericordia,** now open after years of renovations. (Open daily 9am-5pm. Free.) The **Parque Natural do Alvão** is a protected area reaching to the edge of the mountainous Serra country 15km north of Vila Real. For maps and hiking info, visit the **park information office,** Lgo. dos Freitas, at the bottom of Av. Carvalho Araújo behind the Câmara Municipal. (☎259 30 28 30; fax 259 30 28 31. Open M-F 9am-12:30pm and 2-5:30pm.)

MOROCCO المغرب

DIRHAM (DH)		
	US $1 = 10.70DH	1DH = US $0.09
	CDN $1 = 6.91DH	1DH = CDN $0.15
	EUR €1 = 10.52DH	1DH = EUR €0.09
	UK £1 = 16.40DH	1DH = UK £0.06
	AUS $1 = 5.82DH	1DH = AUS $0.17
	NZ $1 = 4.97DH	1DH = NZ $0.20
	SAR 1 = 0.98DH	1DH = ZAR 1.02

Country Code: 212. **International dialing prefix:** 00.

LIFE AND TIMES

On a clear day, you can stand on a hill in southernmost Andalucía and see across the Strait of Gibraltar, where the faint ridges of the Atlas Mountains swell along the horizon. From this perspective, Morocco easily fulfills its fabled role as the gateway to the Orient. On the ground, things are a little different—Morocco has much more to offer than grizzled expatriates trading tales of hash smoking with Jimi Hendrix. The North African influence permeating Andalucía often piques the curiosity of intrepid budget travelers, who take advantage of the close proximity of the two continents to hop down. This path is well trod, serving for centuries as a trading route for language, religion, Arab archwork, and the occasional imperial dynasty. Fortunately for the modern traveler, the trek has only become easier.

Morocco's identity was carved by a host of influences: African, European, and Middle Eastern. Arab culture and religion, African history and landscape, and European dominance and rule, all met here. Now, the country teeters between the past and present, as both a civilization descended from nomads and a modern nation that has struggled against imperial powers for its sovereignty.

Coverage of Morocco is included here to provide a guide for a brief visit during more extensive travel in Spain and Portugal, featuring the accessible highlights of Morocco rather than an exhaustive survey. So, as the draw of Morocco pulls you south through Andalucía, skim across the Strait and give in to Morocco.

OFFICIAL NAME: Kingdom of Morocco.

GOVERNMENT: Constitutional monarchy.

CAPITAL: Rabat.

POPULATION: 30,645,305.

LAND AREA: 446,550 sq. km.

GEOGRAPHY: Mountainous in interior and north; rich coastal plains.

CLIMATE: Mediterranean, more extreme in interior.

MAJOR CITIES: Agadir, Casablanca, Fez, Marrakech, Rabat, Tangier.

LANGUAGES: Arabic, French, Berber dialects.

RELIGIONS: Islam (98.7%).

AVERAGE INCOME PER CAPITA: US$3,500.

MAJOR EXPORTS: Phosphates and fertilizers, food and beverages, minerals.

HISTORY

PRE-ISLAMIC. Archaeological evidence along Morocco's Atlantic coast suggests that regions of the country have been settled for anywhere from 100,000 to 1,000,000 years. The **Berber** people arrived between 4000 and 2000 BC; evidence of the use of early Berber tools can still be found in rock carvings scattered throughout the High Atlas Mountains. Though the **Phoenicians** began to explore the area in the 12th century BC and developed colonies along the coast, they exerted little control or influence over the area. The **Romans** sacked Carthage, near modern Tunis in Tunisia, eventually becoming dependent on North Africa's agricultural supply and creating the province of Mauritania Tingitana in what is now Morocco. When the *Pax Romana* deteriorated in the 4th century AD, the Romans abandoned Morocco. By 420 the country was ruled by the Vandals, followed by a period of brief **Byzantine** rule. Each of these civilizations faced similar problems—it was impossible to exert any control over the land without a reliable overland route. As a result, the majority of the country remained unexplored for centuries.

THE RISE AND FALL OF ISLAM (669-1554 AD). Morocco achieved stability in the late 7th and early 8th century when Muslim armies invaded North Africa. In AD 669, **Uqba bin Nafi al-Fihri** spread the religion of the prophet Mohammed to Morocco. The Berbers could not hold off the Muslim troops, so they made peace with the leader Musa ibn Nusayr, and many converted to Islam. This set the stage for the Arab invasion of Spain less than 50 years later. This Arab rule was short-lived in Morocco, ending in AD 740. Although Arabs remained in the Maghreb, they would not regain power until the 20th century. Instead, a series of local Muslim dynasties rose up to take control of the area, claiming descent from Mohammed to legitimize their rule. **Idris ibn Abdullah,** after fleeing Arabia, founded the first truly Moroccan state in 789. Idris was poisoned in 791, and his kingdom did not last. Over the next few hundred years, Morocco was conquered by one minor dynasty after another, the most important of which was the **Almoravid Dynasty** that founded Marrakesh in 1062, and the **Almohad Dynasty** that conquered it in 1160.

MOROCCO

A golden age during the reign of the **Marinid** (a Berber dynasty that ruled from the 13th to 15th centuries) and then **Wattasid** rule (1244-1554) promoted a cultural and intellectual boom and tied Morocco to Spain. As Muslim influence in Christian Iberia waned, however, the Spanish became aggressive. During the Spanish Inquisition in 1492, a wave of Jewish immigrants from Spain fled to Morocco when forced to choose between conversion or death. By the early 1500s, the Iberians had established control over Moroccan ports and a number of inland territories.

THE EUROPEAN CONTENDERS (1415-1912). The **Saadis** reunited Morocco. Under **Ahmed al-Mansur,** known as Ahmed the Gilded, Morocco expanded its trade in Timbuktu and parts of the Sudan. When the **Alawite dynasty** overthrew the Saadis in 1659, they took over Marrakesh and Fez. The Alawite dynasty rules to this day.

Morocco was one of the first African countries to be colonized by Europe. In 1415, Portugal seized Ceuta (Sebta) and began erecting forts along the coast. Spain took possession of Melilla in 1497; it is still a Spanish enclave. The Saadis were able to push the Iberians back for several centuries, ruling the rest of the country from Marrakesh and remaining in power until the 17th century. England took possession of Tangier in 1662, and Spain controlled the northern coast. France invaded after winning the battle of Isly in 1844, but their major stroke of luck did not come until the death of Sultan Hassan in 1893 and the ascension of his 13-year-old son Abd al-Aziz to the throne. Under the **Treaty of Fez,** March 30th, 1912, Morocco became a protectorate of France. The northernmost part of the country fell to the Spanish, while Tangier was governed by a European council.

STRUGGLE FOR INDEPENDENCE (1921-1977). In 1921, **Abd al-Krim,** now considered the founder of modern Morocco, organized a rebel army that fought Spain over control of the Rif Country. Rifian tribes managed to get as far as Fez before a combined French and Spanish army drove them out in 1927.

Morocco's nationalist movement began in 1944 with the founding of the Independence Party, **Istiqlal;** by 1947 it had gained the support of the Moroccan Sultan, **Moulay Muhammad V.** The French deported nationalist leaders and exiled Muhammad in 1953. The ensuing popular unrest, combined with revolt in Algeria, forced the French to concede. Muhammad was returned to the throne on November 18, 1955 and signed a treaty of independence for French Morocco on March 2, 1956. The independence of most of Spanish Morocco followed one month later.

Muhammad V's successor, **King Hassan II,** ascended the throne in 1961 and introduced a constitution favoring monarchists. This was heavily protested by the opposition party UNFP: in 1963, ten of UNFP's leaders, including **Ben Barka,** were implicated in a plot to overthrow the monarchy and sentenced to death. In 1965, King Hassan declared a national **state of emergency,** snagging direct control of executive and legislative powers. Hassan's 1970 constitution ended the emergency and restored limited parliamentary government, but two military coups and governmental divisions delayed democratic parliamentary elections until 1977.

Perhaps the most significant of Hassan's political triumphs was the **Green March** in 1975. The Spanish, who had long since controlled the Spanish Sahara, were confronted with a Saharan rebel group—the **Polisario Front**—precisely as General Franco (see p. 67) lay dying. Hassan capitalized on Spanish weakness, marching his troops into the Sahara. Because the Polisario Front was disorganized and the Spanish were preoccupied, Hassan was successful. Unfortunately, peace did not come easily or immediately. The Polisario Front gained support from the Algerians, but they were at war in the Sahara until the UN declared a cease-fire in 1989.

MODERN MOROCCO (1977-2003). Today Morocco is nominally a **constitutional monarchy:** though assisted by a parliament and Chamber of Representatives, the king and his advisers make the more important decisions. Under Hassan, censorship ruled out opposition from such groups as trade union activists and university radicals. A drought further sapped support of the monarchy, but after sluggish industrial growth, riots, and the drain of war in the Western Sahara, Morocco began to recover in the 90s. Islamist movements throughout North Africa have kept Morocco cautious, though King Hassan's regime was stable in comparison to those in neighboring countries. Morocco's relations with neighbors are strained, particularly with Algeria, where illegal arms shuttling resulted in the closing of the Morocco-Algeria border in 1994. Southern Europe, also aligned against Islamist infiltration, has been taking a greater interest in Morocco, and has advocated tighter border controls in light of a flow of illegal immigration.

King Mohammed VI's three-year reign has generally brought progress and reform to Morocco, most notably when he released thousands of political prisoners. Commentators anticipated that the 2002 parliamentary election would be "the freest that Morocco has ever had." In March 2002, King Mohammed made waves with his semi-public marriage to a computer engineer. Traditionally, royal marriages were strictly kept secrets; the public release of the name and photograph of the king's bride were presented as heralding an era of openness and modernity.

Despite the country's advances, Morocco remains a nation where a significant percentage of the population lives below the poverty line, sometimes on less than a dollar a day. Morocco's social problems—unemployment, illiteracy, high infant mortality rate—generally outpace those of similar countries.

IN RECENT NEWS

DIRE STRAITS

Electrical fences now enclose the Spanish enclaves of Ceuta and Melilla, which are on the African continent surrounded by Morocco. The 9m strait between the two countries once facilitated exchange of people and ideas, but today the coast guard arrests would-be migrants in dinghies and the more desperate souls who dare swim the strait. In a trend of border-closing sweeping Europe, Spain is enforcing new immigration policies to keep Moroccans and sub-Saharan Africans from crossing the borders.

For the Africans flooding the shores, a land of economic opportunity awaits across the sea—the chance to escape lands rife with poverty and joblessness, the chance to work and send money home. Spain argues that it cannot assimilate the heavy flow of immigrants, but is nonetheless aware that Moroccans fill the jobs that fewer and fewer Spaniards are willing to take. To further complicate matters, the issue is no longer solely an economic one. After September 11th, patrolling borders became crucial to international security.

Morocco has accused Europe of demanding the passage of goods while denying the passage of labor, and says it is doing as much as it can to police borders. They have appealed to the EU, presenting investment as the only long-term solution for countering the lure of Europe.

Meanwhile, an average of five people a day drown in the Strait of Gibraltar. Children are escorted from Spain to the Moroccan border and left to fend for themselves, and the detention centers in Spain are overflowing.

CURRENT EVENTS

In the wake of the terrorist attacks of September 11, 2001, tourism in Morocco suffered a blow as already weak consumer spending abroad was aggravated by a reluctance to fly and hesitation to visit Arab countries. In April 2002, a delegation from Fez was sent to New York to assure Americans that Morocco still welcomed their tourism. September 11 continued to affect Morocco even more directly, as local authorities cracked down on the **al-Qaeda** presence in their country, arresting suspected agents of Osama Bin Laden's terrorist ring. In June 2002, the government arrested three Saudis on Moroccan soil, announcing that it had foiled an al-Qaeda plot to attack American and British ships in the Strait of Gibraltar.

Controversy continues to broil in the dispute over control of the **Western Sahara.** In June, officials in Rabat accused Polisario, the Saharawi independence movement, of holding 1,362 Moroccans for over 20 years. The Foreign Ministry said it had released all Polisario and Algerian prisoners to honor the 1991 peace agreement engineered by the United Nations. In 2002, the European Union moved to send $13.3 million in aid to refugees from the Western Sahara, now displaced to southwestern Algeria.

Military sparring over the tiny island of **Perejil** further strained relations between Morocco and Spain, which have clashed over immigration, fishing rights, oil exploration in disputed waters, and the Western Sahara. The island, called Leila (Night) by Morocco, was occupied by Moroccan soldiers in late July 2002 before being reoccupied in a peaceful operation by an elite team of Spanish commandoes. Morocco, which claims sovereignty over the island, justified sending troops there by saying it was maintaining an observation post to tackle illegal immigration and drug smuggling across the Strait of Gibraltar.

LANGUAGE

Morocco is a paradise for polyglots. Although Classical Arabic *(al-Fusha)* is the official language of Morocco, it is rarely spoken and has become an almost exclusively written language. Most Moroccans speak the modern dialect called *Darija,* a compacted **Arabic** peppered with **Spanish** and **French,** as well as French proper. Whether Arabic, French, or Spanish, each language absorbed into Morocco has been sprinkled and spiced. In this book, **city names** appear first in English, then in Arabic. (Fez written neither as Fès, the French spelling, nor Faas, the Arabic spelling.) A massive naming shift from European to Arabic is underway on **street signs**, so some of the streets mentioned in this book may go by a different title (here they are listed in both French and Arabic when necessary). *Rues* and *avenues* may become *zanqats*, *derbs*, or *sharias*.

RELIGION

The religion of Islam was founded by the Arab prophet Mohammed in AD 622. Informed of his prophetic calling by the angel Gabriel, Mohammed is believed by Muslims to be the end of a long chain of visionaries that includes Abraham, Moses, Elijah, and Jesus. Mohammed led his followers until his death in 632, during which time his words and deeds were recorded in *hadith* (sayings) that comprise the *Sunna*, or examples of Mohammed. Following his death, the issue of who would rule divided Muslims into two branches, the Sunni and the Shi'a. The Sunni wanted Mohammed's successor chosen from a community of men; they believe strongly in God's will and predestination, while the Shi'ites believe in free will and insist on his successor being a blood relative of their prophet. More than 99% of Moroccans are Sunni Muslim, though Morocco also has a small Jewish minority and an even smaller Christian one. Islam is the official state religion.

At the heart of the Islamic faith is the Arabic word *islam*, meaning submission. The believer, or *Muslim*, accepts complete submission to the will of God *(Allah)* as embodied in the Qur'an (book of recitation). This Arabic text is considered by Muslims to be a miracle—perfect, immutable, and untranslatable; it replaces all earlier revealed books and is the final definitive form of God's word. Unlike the Christian conception of Jesus, the Islamic view considers Mohammed a human messenger of God. All practicing Muslims must adhere to the five pillars of Islam: the formal profession of faith, prayer toward Mecca five times daily, alms-giving, fasting during the month of Ramadan, and, if possible, a pilgrimage to Mecca.

Moroccan Islam is somewhat unique. While there is the inevitable difference between popular and orthodox Islam in Morocco, there is less of a gap between the religious intellectuals and the general public than in other Arab countries. Sufism is a mystical twist to Islam that is based on the belief that Muslims will find the truth of God's love and knowledge through a personal experience with God. Sufis were once quite politically influential; they are still a large presence, but their influence in politics has faded. Morocco has had its share of Islamic fundamentalist movements, but they have been substantially weaker than those in other North African countries, due to the popular belief that the king is a religious as well as political leader.

RAMADAN 101 It is believed that Mohammed received the Qur'an during the month of **Ramadan.** Fasting during this holy month is the fourth pillar of Islam. Between dawn and sunset, Muslims are not permitted to smoke, have sexual intercourse, or let any food or water pass their lips; exceptions are made for pregnant or menstruating women, the sick, and travelers (though all must make up the fast at a later date). Fasting is meant to teach Muslims to resist temptation and thereby control all their unchaste urges. Ideally, Muslims read the Qur'an during the daylight hours. By experiencing hunger they are meant to better understand the plight of the poor and to be more thankful for the food which God has provided them. It is insensitive to eat in public during Ramadan. Ramadan inspires a sense of community. As soon as the sun sets, the fast is broken and a night of feasting and visiting of friends and relatives begins. The revelry lasts until dawn, when the fast begins again.

CULTURE

FOOD AND DRINK

Moroccan chefs lavish aromatic and colorful spices on their dishes—pepper, ginger, cumin, saffron, honey, and sugar are culinary staples. The distinctive Moroccan flavor comes from a unique blend of spices, known as *ras al-hanut*. However, no matter how delicious everything may seem, be prepared to get sick at least once, as Morocco is full of things to which tourists are not immune. Taking extra precautions may help. Bottled mineral water is the way to go, as is peeling all fruits and vegetables. The truly cautious may avoid salads as well, or ensure that their vegetables are washed in purified water. Most food sold on the street, especially meat, can be quite risky and should be regarded as such.

TYPICAL FARE

Moroccan cuisine consists mainly of couscous, *tajine*, and soups. **Tajine** is a stew steamed in a cone-shaped clay dish. It consists of meat (chicken, lamb, or pigeon) along with an assortment of vegetables, olives, and prunes. Vegetarian forms of *tajine* are common as well. **Couscous** is a semolina-grain pasta about the size of sesame seeds, and is served with meat or vegetables. The most popular of the Moroccan soups is **harira,** a salty chick-pea soup, sometimes containing meat (it is served every day during Ramadan). **Baguettes** and **honey-soaked pastries** are everywhere, as are delicious Moroccan breads.

Other common dishes include **poulet** (chicken), which can be prepared either *rôti* (roasted on a spit with olives) or *limon* (with lemon). Pricier and harder-to-find specialties include **mechoui,** whole lamb spitted over an open fire, and **pastilla,** a combination of pigeon or chicken, onions, almonds, eggs, butter, cinnamon, and sugar under a pastry shell. For a lighter treat, slurp sweet natural yogurt with mounds of peaches, nectarines, or strawberries, or try an oily Moroccan salad with finely chopped tomatoes, cucumbers, and onions. Snackers munch briny olives (1dh per scoop), roasted almonds, dried chick-peas, and cactus buds (1dh per bud). Oranges abound as the cheapest, sweetest, safest fruit in the country.

EATING OUT

The restaurant scene in Morocco depends on whether you're in a big city or small town. As eating out isn't common practice for locals, eateries in large, modern cities cater mainly to foreign tourists, featuring comprehensive menus of typical French or Moroccan cuisine. Seeking out **authentic** regional cuisine in larger cities often requires an adventurous expedition into the maze of the medina. Tiny restaurants hide the most tantalizing dishes. A complete meal includes a choice of entree (*tajine*, couscous, or perhaps a third option), salad or *harira*, a side of vegetables, and yogurt or an orange for **dessert.** Less expensive *tajine* is made with *kefta* (a ground beef cooked in an array of herbs and spices) and often served on a baguette, as is *merguez* (a spicy beef or lamb sausage). Almost every Moroccan main course includes meat; *cous aux légumes* (couscous with vegetables) will usually be the closest **vegetarian** option. The best bet for strict vegetarians is to cook with produce from the market, or to request an omelette at restaurants. Lunchtime runs from noon to 2pm, dinner 7 to 9pm. If a service charge isn't automatically included, a 10% **tip** will suffice.

DRINKING

Although tap water is drinkable in most parts of the country, bottled and purified water is a safer bet. If you get a bottle that isn't completely sealed, return it—

CULT FICTION Paul Bowles has become a cult figure in Morocco and is considered one of America's best expat writers. He initially gained fame through his involvement in radical politics, but Bowles turned to travel after marrying Jane Auer in 1938, and he ultimately settled in Morocco on the advice of Gertrude Stein. It was there that he began to use Moroccan drugs to enhance his creativity and started writing fiction. His first and most famous novel, *The Sheltering Sky* (1949), details the lives of an American couple and their struggle with Moroccan culture. Many reviewers likened the novel to the works of Poe (who was Bowles's childhood idol) and Hemingway. From that point on, most of Bowles's fiction was set in Morocco, though his only other piece to gain much fame was *The Spider's House* (1955). When Jane died in 1973, Bowles's work showed signs of a loss of hope. His career, however, received a boost in the early 1990s when Bernardo Berotolucci made a movie of *The Sheltering Sky* starring Debra Winger and John Malkovich. He died in Tangier in November 1999.

chances are the bottle has been filled with tap water. Orange juice and other fruit drinks are popular, but make sure that they are diluted with purified water.

Despite the Islamic prohibition against alcohol, Morocco is a wine-lover's paradise. While the two best wines are the Cabernet Medallion and Beauvillion (about 80dh), the less expensive Vabernet du President, Amazir, and Guerraine Rouge are also quite good (all 35dh). Moroccan, French, and Spanish **wines** are available in supermarkets and restaurants (but not in the medina). Watery local **beer,** usually Stork or Flag Speciale, isn't particularly good. Moroccan **bars** are entirely male and focus on heavy drinking; otherwise, they are pricey, tourist-oriented, and tend to attract less-than-savory types. More pleasant are the many coffee houses where you can get inexpensive Moroccan **coffee** and **tea.** Espresso is widespread, as is regular coffee, usually sweetened with sugar and milk. Green tea, a staple of the Moroccan diet, is sipped with fresh mint leaves and lots of sugar.

CUSTOMS AND ETIQUETTE

TABOOS. Avoid clothing that exposes too much flesh: modest clothing for both men and women is recommended, particularly in more rural areas. Even properly dressed non-Muslims are barred from entering many of Morocco's active mosques. Taboo topics to avoid in conversation with Moroccans include sex, Israel and Palestine, the Royal Family, and the Western Sahara.

PUBLIC BEHAVIOR. Tourists in larger areas are susceptible to the advances of Moroccans offering to guide them. If you refuse, be polite but insistent. Western women will find that their presence attracts attention from Moroccan men. In general, the best way to react is not at all; toning down public visibility is always smart.

TABLE MANNERS. A traditional Moroccan meal begins with handwashing. Dinner may be served from a communal dish at a low, round table. Avoid directly using your left hand when eating, as this hand is considered reserved for personal hygiene. In more personal settings, such as dining in the home of a Moroccan, vocally praising the food is important; belching may also be appropriate.

THE ARTS

In Morocco, art is lived daily in the form of architecture and crafts such as carpets, pottery, jewelry, and embroidery. Morocco has entranced Western painters for centuries; Orientalism, in the works of painters like Eugene Delacroix, began here.

> **!** Non-Muslims are usually prohibited from entering Moroccan mosques, though visitors may glimpse the splendor of interior courtyards from doorways. Out of respect, non-Muslim guests should keep a distance during services (five times daily; Fridays at midday).

ARCHITECTURE

Diverse architectural forms define Moroccan landscapes and cityscapes. An intense climate, combined with Berber austerity and Islamic privacy, give **Berber architecture** an enclosed and stark nature. *Kasbahs*, the monumental houses of the Berbers, feature central courtyards, narrow passageways, animal shelters, simple high towers, thick walls, and plain facades. *Qsour* (plural of *qsar*, or fortified Berber villages) house densely packed "apartments." Built of *pisé* (packed earth), many are gradually turning to ruins, unable to withstand wind and sand storms.

In the 10th century, Fez residents built the first Moroccan **mosques** (sometimes called *djemmas* or *masajid*), al-Andalus and the Qairaouine. The *qibla* (wall) contains the *mihrab* (prayer niche), which faces Mecca. There are two basic designs for mosques: Arab-style, based on Muhammad's house with a pillared cloister around a courtyard, and Persian-style with a vaulted arch on each side. Attached to most mosques, Qur'anic schools *(madrasas)* have classrooms, libraries, and a prayer hall around a central courtyard and fountain.

In order to avoid idolatry, Muslim artists are forbidden from portraying figures of people, animals, or even plants. The result is a style of incredibly ingenious geometric and calligraphic decorations. Colorful patterns swirl across tiles, woodwork, stone, and ceramic. In less doctrinaire times, Almoravid artists slipped in designs that vaguely resemble leaves and flowers. **Calligraphy,** particularly elegant renderings and illuminations of the Qur'an, became another outlet for creativity as well as religious devotion. Sultans reserved their most dazzling designs for **imperial palaces,** with long, symmetrical reception and dwelling rooms studded with decorative gates, hidden gardens, and tiny pools and fountains.

MOROCCO

CRAFTS

Carpet connoisseurs differentiate between rugs and *kilims*. While rugs are knotted and bordered by a shag ruffle, *kilims* are woven and ruffleless. The most valuable carpets will be older, with detailed embroidery, and colored with vegetable pigments. A sniff test will differentiate currant crimson from Red #5. Higher-quality rugs will also be woven of wool or linen. Berber patterned carpets from the Rif or Middle and High Atlas mountains are filled with colorful markings. Those from Rabat and other coastal cities are modeled on the famed Turkish carpets.

Fez has been the center of a renowned **leather** industry since the 15th century. High-quality Moroccan leather can be purchased where it's made for a fraction of its international price. Fez is also the center for Moroccan **pottery** and is famous for its classic blue-and-white designs. Saharan and Berber **terra-cotta** ware are also common, and the South is known for its distinctive **silver jewelry,** often inlaid with colorful stones or glass. Moroccan woodwork is amazing; craftsmen seem to effortlessly transform blocks of cedar into delicate and intricate pieces.

All of the above are to be found in Moroccan **souqs** (markets). Those in more touristed areas target foreign travelers for the sale of craftwork; the wise will make for local *souqs* to do their real purchasing. Bargaining in Morocco is serious business, as much a cultural art form as an everyday engagement. Approach with vigor: a reasonable final price should be about 50% of your seller's original quote. To avoid unnecessary hassle, declare that you've finished your shopping already or claim penniless student status. If your heart is set on a certain pair of slippers and their price refuses to drop, try walking out the door and down the block: the

> **! HENNA TATTOOS.** A synthetic dye (PPD) found in some forms of henna tattooing can cause severe blisters and permanent scarring. Ask the henna artist to tell you everything that is in their paste before proceeding. Even natural oils and herbs–clove oil, eucalyptus oil, or walnut powder–that other artists use in natural henna paste can be irritating to the skin. If you have sensitive skin, patch test the henna first, or ask the artist for a simple mix of henna powder and lemon juice.

owner is quite likely to chase after you with a better offer. Even if he doesn't, you'll find the same item two stores down. (See also **Bargaining for Dummies,** p. 750.)

MUSIC

In the North, a hybrid genre known as **Andaloussi** is played on instruments like the *bendir* (tambourine), *oud* (lute), and *darbuqa* (percussion), putting classical poetry to complex musical structures. Originally developed in Granada in the 9th century, Arab-Andalucian music thrived in Morocco after the Muslim expulsion from Spain in the late 15th century, and is still performed today. **Berber** music dates back to before the arrival of the Arabs; often emphasizing a storytelling aspect to music, it may be accompanied by *ahidous*, a ritual group dance. **Gnawa** music, a style of religious music derived from sub-Saharan Africa, is performed in a ceremony to deter evil spirits, characterized by a trance-like rhythm. Moroccan popular music is heavily influenced by **Rai,** a rebellious, polyglot pop born in urban Algeria. Artists such as **Cheb Mimoun** and **Cheb Mara** joined the Maghreb canon that includes such international superstars as **Cheb Mami, Rachid Taha,** and **Cheb Khaled.**

SPORTS AND RECREATION

Moroccans are deeply passionate about soccer, and there are intense rivalries between competing clubs. Basketball runs a distant second but is still popular. Team sports remain limited to men, although other participatory sports abound. Skiing is common in the High Atlas Mountains (late December to early March) and is possible in the Middle Atlas Mountains as well. Hiking is available everywhere, water sports are popular on the Atlantic coast, and biking takes place nationwide.

RECOMMENDED READING

LITERATURE ABOUT MOROCCO. Most literature about Morocco focuses on the countries intoxicating culture and landscape. *In Morocco*, by Edith Wharton, gives episodic descriptions of Rabat, Salé, Fez, and Meknes. Walter Harris's *Morocco That Was*, is a turn-of-the-century journalist's diary, featuring a wry account of a Brit's kidnapping by the international bandit Raissouli. *The Voices of Marrakech*, by Bulgarian Nobel Prize recipient Elias Canetti, eloquently records a European Jew's encounter with Moroccan Jews. For insight into the country's social history, pick up *The House of Si Abd Allah*, edited by noted scholar Henry Munson, which recounts an oral history of a Moroccan family. No Moroccan reading list would be complete without *The Sheltering Sky*, *The Spider's House*, and *Days: Tangier Journal*, all by Paul Bowles. These books give a numbingly gorgeous introduction to Morocco and to Bowles (see Cult Fiction, p. 717).

MOROCCAN LITERATURE IN ENGLISH. For a more authentic taste of contemporary Moroccan life, read *Love With a Few Hairs*, *The Lemon*, and *M'hashis*, by Muhammad Mrabet and translated by Paul Bowles. *The Battle of Three Kings*, by Youssef Necrouf, gives an entertaining account of medieval violence and intrigue under the Saadian dynasty. In *Dreams of Trespass (Tales of a Moroccan Girlhood)*, Fatima Mernissa tells her story of growing up in a Fez harem in the 1950s.

ESSENTIALS

The information in this section is designed to help travelers get their bearings once they are in Morocco. For info about general **travel preparations** (including passports and permits, money, health, packing, international transportation, and more), consult the **Essentials** section at the beginning of this guide. Essentials also contains important information about alternatives to tourism and offers tips for travelers with specific concerns: **women travelers** (p. 50); **older travelers** (p. 51); **bisexual, gay, and lesbian travelers** (p. 52); **travelers with disabilities** (p. 52); **minority travelers** (p. 53); **travelers with children** (p. 53); and travelers with **dietary concerns** (p. 54).

ENTRANCE REQUIREMENTS

Passport. Required for all citizens of United Kingdom, Canada, Australia, New Zealand, South Africa, Ireland, and the United States.

Visa: Required in addition to passport for citizens of South Africa.

Driving Permit (p. 722). Required for all those planning to drive in Morocco.

EMBASSIES AND CONSULATES

In Morocco, most embassies and consulates are open Monday through Friday from around 8am to noon; some reopen after lunch until 6pm.

British Embassy: 17 bd. de la Tour Hassan, B.P. 45, **Rabat** (☎037 72 96 96; fax 70 45 31; www.britain.org.ma). **Consulates:** 43 bd. d'Anfa, B.P. 13, #762, **Casablanca** (022 22 16 53); bd. Mohammed V, B.P. 2122, **Tangier** (☎039 94 15 57; fax 94 22 84).

Canadian Embassy: 13 Bis, Jaafar As-Saddik, B.P.709, Agdal, **Rabat** (☎037 68 74 00).

Irish Embassy: Refer to the Irish Embassy in Lisbon (p. 588). In case of emergency, contact any Commonwealth embassy.

Australian Embassy: Refer to the Canadian Embassy in Rabat (above). In case of emergency, contact any Commonwealth embassy.

New Zealand Embassy: Refer to the New Zealand Embassy in Spain (p. 79). In case of emergency, contact any Commonwealth embassy.

South African Embassy: 34 rue de Saadiens, **Rabat** (☎037 70 67 60; fax 70 67 56), opposite the mausoleum.

US Embassy: 2 av. de Mohammed El Fassi, Rabat (☎037 76 22 65, after-hours line 76 96 39; fax 76 56 61). Consulate: 8 bd. Moulay Youssef, Casablanca (☎022 26 45 50; fax 20 41 27).

TRANSPORTATION

BY PLANE

Royal Air Maroc (in Casablanca ☎022 31 41 41 or airport 022 33 90 00; in US 800-344-6726; in UK 7 439 43 61), Morocco's national airline, flies to and from most major cities in Europe, including Madrid and Lisbon. Domestically, a network of flights radiates from the Mohammed V Airport outside Casablanca. Planes fly daily to Marrakesh, Agadir, Tangier, and Fez and, occasionally, to Ouarzazate.

If you hope to see a lot of Morocco in a short time, flying can be a convenient and affordable option; you don't have to commit to a flight until the day before, and the price of the ticket always remains the same, whenever you buy it. Royal Air Maroc (RAM) and its competitor, **Regional Airlines,** fly to all major domestic cities. Regional Airlines (in Casablanca ☎022 54 34 17; www.regionalmaroc.com) flies from Barcelona, Las Palmas, Lisbon, Madrid, and Málaga, and offers many domestic routes, including Agadir, Casablanca, Laayoune, Tangier, and Oujda.

BY FERRY AND HYDROFOIL

For travel from Spain to Morocco, the most budget-minded mode is by sea. Spanish-based **Trasmediterránea** (☎902 45 46 45, within Spain; www.trasmediterranea.es/homei.htm) runs ferries on a shuttle schedule from **Algeciras** (☎956 65 62 44; Recinto del Puerto, s/n) to **Ceuta,** known within Morocco as Sebta (☎956 50 94 11; Muelle Cañonero Dato, 6), and **Tangier.** Trasmediterránea is represented in Tangier by **Limadet** (☎039 93 50 76; 3, rue IBN Rochd., Tangier). "Fast" Ferries run from Algeciras to Ceuta. **Comarit** (☎956 66 84 62; www.comarit.com; Av. Virgen del Carmen, 3-1°Cial) runs from Algeciras to Tangier and offers **vehicle transport.** Check online for Comarit's unpredictable weekly schedule.

BY TRAIN

Trains in Morocco are faster than buses, more comfortable, fairly reliable, and prompt. Second-class train tickets are slightly more expensive than corresponding CTM bus fares; first-class tickets cost around 20% more than those second-class.

The main line runs from Tangier via Rabat and Casablanca to Marrakesh. A spur connects Fez, Meknes, and points east. There is one *couchette* train between Fez and Marrakesh. Tickets bought on board cost at least 10% more and may cause trouble with the conductor. No student fares are available. Be wary of old schedules that show times for the Atlantic coast, south of Casablanca—this route has been out of service for a few years now. InterRail (see p. 43) is valid in Morocco, but Eurail is not. Fares are so low, however, that InterRail is not worth it.

BY BUS

In Morocco, bus travel is less frequent and less reliable than in Spain or Portugal. Plan well ahead if you plan to use buses as your method of transport. They're not all that fast or comfortable, but they are extremely cheap and travel to nearly every corner of the country. **Compagnie de Transports du Maroc (CTM),** the state-owned line, has the fastest, most luxurious, most reliable, and generally most expensive buses (though "expensive" here means just a few more dirham). In many cities, CTM has a station separate from other lines; reservations are usually not necessary. *Let's Go* lists CTM stations in each city. Several dozen private companies operate as well. Though they may offer more frequent departures, the comfort level is so low, you'll probably wish you had waited for the next CTM. Other private companies, called **cars publiques** (a.k.a. *souq* buses), have more departures and are slower, less comfortable, and cheaper. In bus stations, each company has its own info window; window-hop for information on destinations and schedules.

The **baggage check** at CTM bus depots is usually safe. Your bags, however, may not be accepted for storage if you don't have padlocks on the zippers. Private bus companies also have baggage checkrooms; they're generally very trustworthy.

BY TAXI

Two separate hordes of taxis prowl Moroccan streets: intra-urban *petit taxis* and inter-urban *grand taxis*, both dirt cheap by European standards. *Petit taxis*, small Renaults or Fiats that can each hold a strict maximum of three passengers, are all painted in one color depending on the municipality (red in Fez, blue in Meknes, etc.) and can't leave the city or take you to the airport. Make sure the driver turns the meter on; they are required to do so by law. If the driver won't turn it on, agree on the price before you go (around 50% of what the driver asks is fair). There is a 50% surcharge after 8pm. Don't be surprised if the driver stops for other passengers or picks you up with other passengers in the car, but if you are picked up after the meter has been started, note the initial price.

Grand taxis, typically beige or dark-blue Mercedes sedans, are the most expensive way to travel, but do go just about everywhere. Unlike their *petit* cousins, they don't usually cruise for passengers, congregating instead at a central area in town. They hold up to six passengers (four in the back, two in the front), but if you plan on taking a long ride, you might buy two spaces to allow for extra room. A taxi won't go until it is filled with passengers going in the same direction. Ask other passengers what they are paying to avoid being ripped off.

BY CAR AND BY THUMB

There are two reasons to rent a car in Morocco: large group travel, or travel to areas not reached by Morocco's public transportation system. Otherwise, rental is unnecessary. Roads can be very dangerous; reckless passing maneuvers, excessive speed, shoddy maintenance, and poorly equipped vehicles are all common.

Hertz, Avis, and **Europcar** all rent cars; expect to pay about 400dh per day for an economy car, including taxes and insurance. Large local firms such as **Afric Car, Moroloc,** and **Locoto** offer cars for considerably less money but are also less reliable. Both international and local firms are easy to find in all major cities. Before you leave the lot, make sure that you have a full spare and a complete toolkit.

Once in your car, you face a myriad of complications, the most serious being **security checks.** Virtually any trip you take will bring you to at least one checkpoint. Expect to be pulled over and asked to produce your passport and proof of rental. One tactic if pulled over is to immediately ask for directions, either in French or Arabic. You also may be stopped for **traffic violations,** real or not. The fine is payable on the spot in dirhams and may be negotiable; asking for a receipt could be construed as provocative. Whatever you do, **do not travel with drugs in your car.**

Routes goudronées (principal roads), marked "P," are paved and connect cities. **Pistes** (secondary roads), designated "S," are very rough. If traveling in the **desert,** be sure to bring at least 10L of bottled water for each person and for the radiator. Move rapidly over sand; if you start to bog down, put the car in low gear and step on the gas. If you come to a stop in soft sand, push. **Gas** costs about 10dh per liter.

Driving in Morocco without the **Michelin map** of Morocco all but ensures that you will get lost. Even with the map, you still should inquire about road conditions. One place to make such inquiries is the automobile association, **Touring Club du Maroc,** 3 av. F.A.R., Casablanca (☎022 20 30 64).

Almost no one in Morocco **hitches,** although flagging down buses and trains can feel like hitchhiking. Transportation is dirt cheap by European and North American standards. If Moroccans do pick up a foreigner, they will most likely expect payment for the ride. Hitching is more frequent in the south and in the mountains, where transportation is irregular. *Let's Go* does not recommend hitchhiking.

MONEY

In Morocco, **banking hours** are Monday through Friday 8:30 to 11:30am and 2:30 to 4:30pm, during Ramadan from 9:30am to 2pm. In the summer, certain banks close at 1pm and do not re-open in the afternoon. Do not try the **black market** for currency exchange—you'll be swindled. As in Europe, **ATMs** are the best way to change money. Also know that it is very difficult to change back upon departure.

Taxes are generally included in prices, though in malls and *grandes surfaces* (larger superstores) you will find a 7% Value-Added Tax on food and a 22% tax on luxury goods. **Tipping** a small amount after restaurant meals, while not necessary, is a nice gesture given the extreme degree of poverty of many Moroccan citizens.

Bargaining is a legitimate part of the Moroccan shopping experience—it is most commonly accepted in outdoor markets. There are guidelines to consider when bargaining. Tailor your bargaining to the situation—offering 40% of the asking price may be too much or too little, depending on where the seller started. Decide what the item is actually worth to you, and use that as a benchmark. Do not appear overly eager, instead point out imperfections in the item, or mention that you saw the item elsewhere at a lower price. Walk away when the seller has quoted a "minimum" price. Do not try to bargain in supermarkets or established stores.

SAFETY AND SECURITY

EMERGENCY ☎ **Police:** ☎ 19. **Highway services:** ☎ 177.

Morocco has received a bad rap among travelers. While the **crime rate** is higher than in Spain or Portugal, there is more to Morocco than just hustlers and drugs. Nevertheless, visitors should be suspicious of offers for free food or drinks, as they have been known to be drugged. Large cities like Tangier and Fez are filled with fake guides offering tours of the city for a small price; they should be avoided.

Debates between the Moroccan government and the Algerian-based Polisario Front over possession of the Western Sahara resulted in a guerrilla war until the late 1980s. The UN called a cease-fire in 1991, but there are still unexploded **landmines** in the area. Travel to Western Sahara is difficult and not recommended; those interested can obtain clearance information from the Moroccan embassy.

Women travelers will probably have extra difficulties traveling through Morocco without a male companion. At the very least, they should never travel alone. Visitors will feel safer and more comfortable (and will avoid offending local sensibilities) by not wearing short skirts, sleeveless tops, and shorts; moreover, females should always wear bras. Regardless, non-Moroccan women may be gawked at, commented upon, approached by hustlers, followed in a crowd, or even groped on the street. Moroccan woman may "hiss" at indecently clad female travelers. The best response to male harassers may be silence, but yelling "*shuma*" (meaning shame) may well embarrass them, especially in the presence of onlookers. If an uncomfortable situation persists, look out for a policeman.

HEALTH

All travelers in Morocco face a different set of health issues than in Spain and Portugal; food and waterborne diseases in particular are a common cause of illness. The CDC recommends that travelers drink only bottled or boiled water, avoiding tap water, fountain drinks, and ice cubes. It is also advisable to only eat fruit and vegetables that are cooked and that you have peeled yourself. Stay away from food sold by street vendors, and check to make sure that dairy products have been pasteurized. There is only a slight malaria risk in Morocco, but it would still be wise to take extra precaution against insect bites. Consider getting a vaccine before leaving. For further information, see **Health** on p. 23.

While there is a public health system in Morocco, travelers should seek out private clinics, which offer the most dependent and affordable care. There are few English-speaking doctors, though French is widespread; learn a few basic words of medical vocabulary in French in case of an emergency. Private clinics are found in large cities and university towns with medical schools, such as Casablanca and Rabat. Travelers with significant medical problems that might need sudden and immediate attention are advised to stay in larger cities for accessibility reasons.

ACCOMMODATIONS

YOUTH HOSTELS

The **Federation Royale des Auberges de Jeunesse (FRMAJ)** is the Moroccan Hosteling International (HI) affiliate. Beds cost 30-40dh per night, and there is a surcharge for non-members everywhere but in Casablanca. Some hostels sell HI memberships on the spot. Call ahead for reservations as beds can be popular. To reserve beds in high season, get an International Booking Voucher from FRMAJ (or your nearby HI affiliate) and send it to the hostel four to eight weeks in advance. You'll probably need to bring your own sleepsack and towel, and there are usually curfew and lock-out times. For hostel addresses, write to FRMAJ, Parc de la Ligue Arabe, B.P. 15998, Casa Principale, Casablanca 21000 (☎022 47 09 52; fax 22 76 77). For more info on national youth hostel associations, see **Accommodations,** p. 25.

HOTELS

Although there is an official star system for rating hotels in Morocco, the number of stars reflects little more than price. Hotels that are not part of the system are not necessarily worse—their standards vary greatly—but are usually cheaper. Rooms can vary widely even within a particular hotel, so ask to see another room if you don't like the first, or find another hotel, often next door. Cheap hotels in Morocco are really cheap—as little as 50dh per night. Listings are generally divided between medina and *ville nouvelle* establishments. Medina hotels are usually cheaper than their *ville nouvelle* counterparts, but less comfortable and with fewer amenities. Hot showers, when available, may cost extra (usually less than 10dh). Cold showers are usually free. Many hotels offer laundry service.

CAMPING

Camping is popular and cheap (about 15dh per person), especially in the desert, mountains, and beaches. Like hotels, conditions vary widely. You can usually expect to find restrooms, but electricity is not as readily available. Use caution if camping unofficially, especially on the beaches, as theft is a problem.

KEEPING IN TOUCH

Most useful communication information (including international access codes, calling card numbers, country codes, operator and directory assistance, and emergency numbers) is listed on the inside back cover of this book.

TELEPHONES. Morocco has recently invested hundreds of millions of dollars into modernizing its telephone system, markedly improving services. Pay phones accept only phone cards. Available at post offices, cards are usually in denominations too large to be practical. Entrepreneurial Moroccans hang around phone banks and let you use their phone cards. You pay for the units used—typically 2dh per unit. To use the card, insert and dial 00. Once the dial tone turns into a tune, dial the number.

Phone offices *(téléboutiques)* are located in most cities. If you can't find one, head to the post office—they always have at least one phone for international calls. To make a collect call, ask the desk attendant at the local telephone office to place a call *en P.C.V.* ("ahn PAY-SAY-VAY"). Write down your name and the country, state, city, and telephone number you want to call. Collect calls can also be made from payphones; simply dial 12 and ask to call *en P.C.V.* Remember that the initial zero (0) in **city codes** is dialed only when calling from another area within Morocco;

from outside of Morocco the number is omitted. Local calls do not require dialing any portion of the city code.

The best way to make international calls is with a **calling card** (see **By Telephone,** p. 32). To **call home with a calling card,** contact the operator for your service provider in Morocco by dialing the appropriate toll-free access number (see page 32).

MAIL. Sending something **Air mail** *(par avion)* can take a week to a month to reach the US or Canada (about 10dh for a slim letter, postcards 4-7dh). Less reliable **surface mail** *(par terre)* takes up to two months. **Express mail** *(recommandé* or *exprès postaux)*, is faster than regular air mail and more reliable. Post offices and *tabacs* sell **stamps.** For fast service (2 days to the US), your best bet is DHL (www.dhl.com), which has drop-off locations in major cities, or FedEx, (www.fedex.com).

EMAIL. Yes, email has reached Morocco. Cybercafes are common in major cities and more touristed towns. *Let's Go* lists Internet access where applicable.

NATIONAL HOLIDAYS

Moroccans celebrate several secular and Islamic holidays. The dates of all Muslim holidays, which begin at sundown before the day listed, are based on the lunar calendar and are valid for 2003 only. Be aware that many establishments are closed during most holidays, particularly the religious ones (and if the holidays fall near a weekend, places are likely to remain closed for an extended period.)

DATE	FESTIVAL
January 1	New Year's Day
January 11	Independence Manifesto
February 12	'Eid al-Adha
March 5	Islamic New Year
May 1	Labor Day
August 14	Reunification Day
August 20	Anniversary of the King's and People's Revolution
August 21	Young People's Day
November 6	Anniversary of the Green March
November 18	Independence Day
October 26-November 23	Ramadan
November 24-27	'Eid al-Fitr

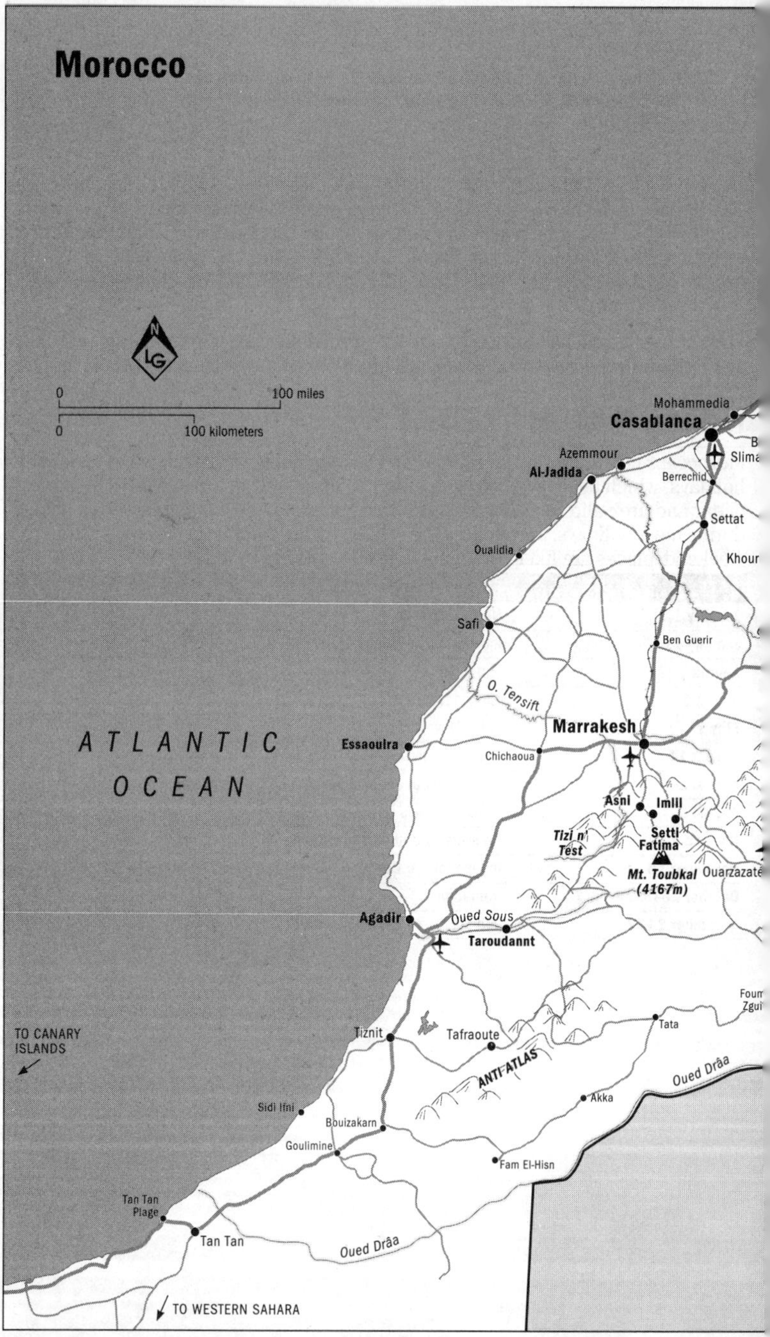
Morocco
100 miles
100 kilometers
0
0
ATLANTIC
OCEAN
Mohammedia
Casablanca
Azemmour
Al-Jadida
Berrechid
Settat
Khour
Oualidia
Safi
Ben Guerir
O. Tensift
Marrakesh
Essaouira
Chichaoua
Asni
Imlil
Tizi n' Test
Setti Fatima
Mt. Toubkal (4167m)
Ouarzazate
Agadir
Oued Sous
Taroudannt
Tiznit
Tafraoute
Tata
ANTI-ATLAS
Oued Drâa
Akka
Sidi Ifni
Bouizakarn
Goulimine
Fam El-Hisn
Tan Tan Plage
Tan Tan
Oued Drâa
TO CANARY ISLANDS
TO WESTERN SAHARA

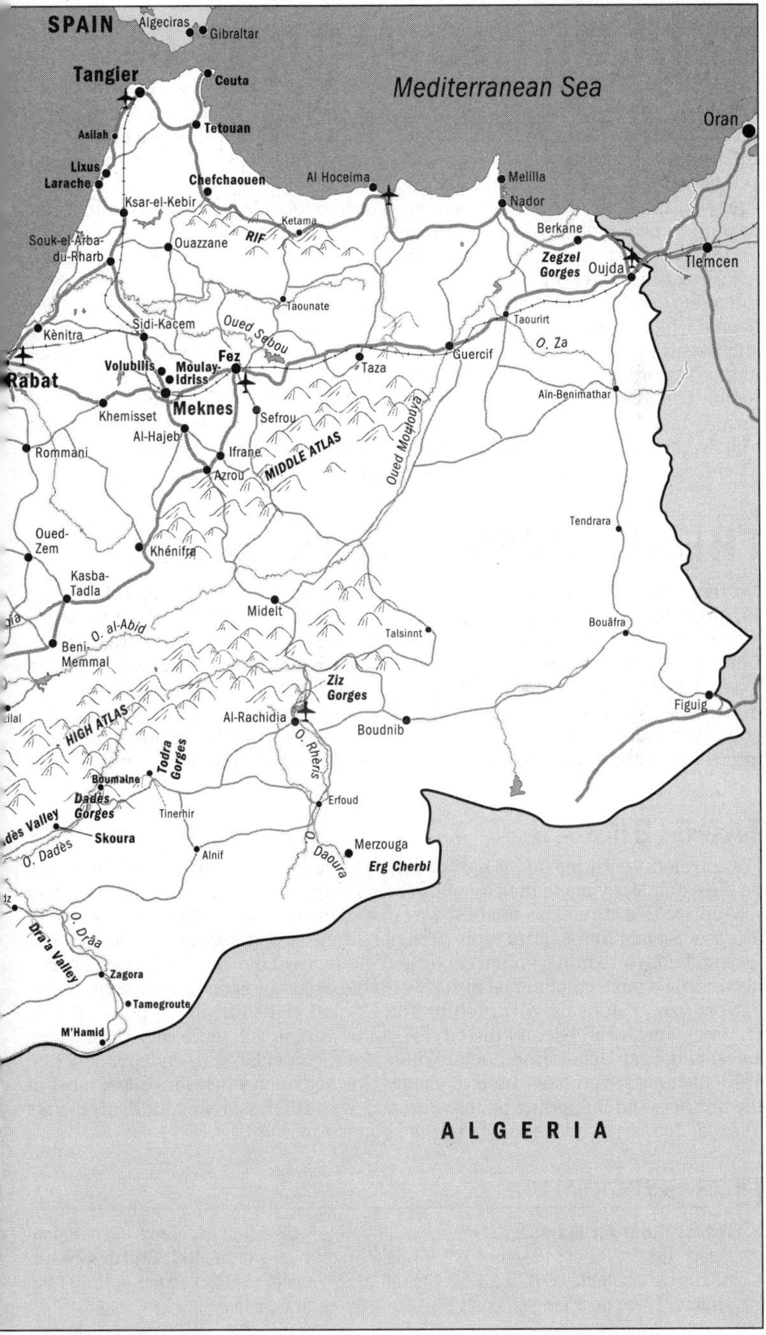
SPAIN
Algeciras
Gibraltar
Tangier
Ceuta
Mediterranean Sea
Oran
Tetouan
Asilah
Lixus
Larache
Chefchaouen
Al Hoceima
Melilla
Nador
Ksar-el-Kebir
Ketama
RIF
Berkane
Souk-el-Arba-du-Rharb
Ouazzane
Zegzel Gorges
Oujda
Tlemcen
Taounate
Sidi-Kacem
Oued Sebou
Taourirt
Kènitra
O. Za
Fez
Taza
Guercif
Volubilis
Moulay-Idriss
Rabat
Aïn-Benimathar
Meknes
Khemisset
Sefrou
Al-Hajeb
Rommani
Ifrane
MIDDLE ATLAS
Oued Moulouya
Azrou
Tendrara
Oued-Zem
Khénifra
Kasba-Tadla
Midelt
Talsinnt
Bouâfra
O. al-Abid
Beni-Memmal
Ziz Gorges
Figuig
HIGH ATLAS
Al-Rachidia
Boudnib
O. Rhèris
Todra Gorges
Boumalne
Dadès Gorges
Tinerhir
Erfoud
Dadès Valley
Skoura
O. Dadès
Alnif
Merzouga
O. Daoura
Erg Cherbi
O. Drâa
Dra'a Valley
Zagora
Tamegroute
M'Hamid
ALGERIA

EXPLORING MOROCCO

For many travelers weary of visiting Spanish cathedrals, a short excursion across the Strait of Gibraltar into Morocco becomes an unexpected highlight of their trip. In Morocco, passersby don't pass you by; everyone wants to know your name. Fruits and vegetables are sold right off the street—next to stinking fish. Old men squat on the side of the road, wrapped in hooded garments. Excitement and adventure need not be planned or paid for lavishly; just step outside your hotel door and wander down an ancient medina street. While Morocco offers a manageable, if at times stressful, introduction to both the Islamic and African worlds, it's the proud and hospitable nation's own unique blend of languages, landscapes, and people which defy any preconceptions and exceed all expectations. The country, still largely inhabited by an ancient race of people known as Berbers, has a fascinating history as the crossroads between two rich continents. Physically, the nation contains unparalleled raw beauty in the form of lush valleys, enormous desert dunes, ancient imperial cities, and North Africa's highest mountains. Finally, there is Morocco in its modern mutation, a nation that struggles to balance a youthful and striving face with its traditional ways.

THE MEDITERRANEAN COAST

Northern Morocco is comprised of Mediterranean ports, beaches, and the jagged Rif Mountains. The most accessible region from Spain, the Mediterranean coast is a common point of entry into the country; precisely because of its proximity to Europe and the prevalence of European influence throughout its history, this area where French, Spanish, and Arabic architecture, lifestyles, and language overlap is rarely considered "real Morocco." The Mediterranean cities provide a taste of the country, but they may not leave visitors with the most favorable impression. Those interested in observing true Moroccan culture should keep pushing south.

MOROCCO

TANGIER طنجة ☎039

For travelers venturing out of Europe for the first time, Tangier (pop. 500,000) can be stressful. Many make the city out to be a living nightmare, but despite the very real difficulties, it remains the best way to enter from Spain. While it is not one of Morocco's main tourist attractions, Tangier interests visitors with its complex history and edgy urban pace. For centuries, the region bounced from one imperial power to the next, culminating in 1923 with the declaration of Tangier as an "international zone" loosely governed by the US and eight European powers. Law enforcement dwindled, and the city began to attract rich heiresses, drug users, spies, and Beat Generation poets. When Morocco declared its independence in 1956, the new government tried to change Tangier's image, closing down most of the brothels and increasing police presence. Nevertheless, rising tourism (thanks to expanded ferry service) has propelled Tangier forward.

TRANSPORTATION

Flights: Royal Air Maroc, pl. France (☎039 37 95 08). Domestic and international flights. **Iberia,** 35 bd. Pasteur (039 93 61 78), flies daily to **Madrid. British Airways,** 83 rue de la Liberté (☎039 93 52 11), off of pl. France, flies to **London.** A taxi to the **airport,** 16km from Tangier, costs 80-100dh for up to 6 people.

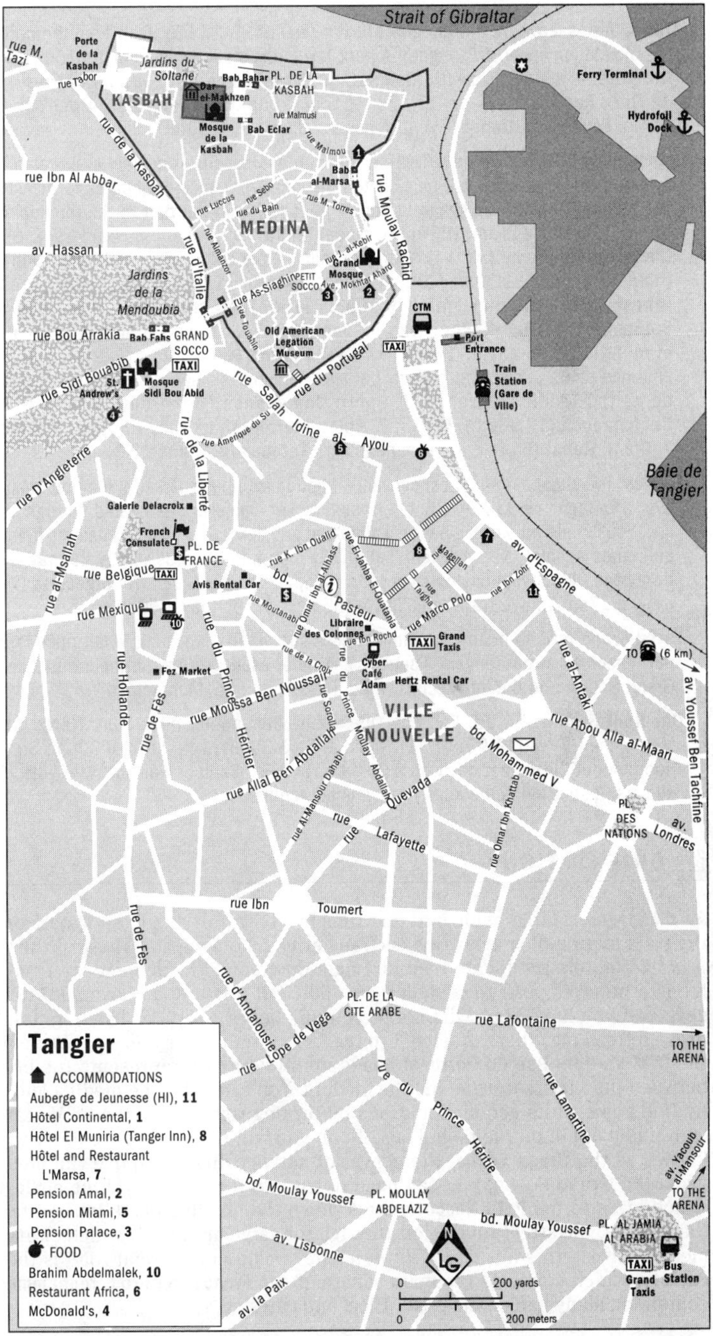
Strait of Gibraltar
Porte de la Kasbah
rue M. Tazi
rue Tabor
Jardins du Soltane
KASBAH
Dar el-Makhzen
Bab Bahar
PL. DE LA KASBAH
Mosque de la Kasbah
Bab Eclar
rue Malmusi
rue Malmou
Bab al-Marsa
rue de la Kasbah
rue Ibn Al Abbar
rue Luccus
rue Sebo
rue du Bain
rue M. Torres
MEDINA
rue Moulay Rachid
av. Hassan I
rue d'Italie
rue Almanzor
rue J. al-Kebir
Grand Mosque
Ave. Mokhtar Ahard
PETIT SOCCO
rue As-Siaghin
Jardins de la Mendoubia
rue Touahin
CTM
Port Entrance
Old American Legation Museum
rue Bou Arrakia
Bab Fahs
GRAND SOCCO
TAXI
Train Station (Gare de Ville)
rue Sidi Bouabib
St. Andrew's
Mosque Sidi Bou Abid
rue du Portugal
rue Salah Idine al-Ayou
rue Amerique du Su
rue de la Liberté
Ferry Terminal
Hydrofoil Dock
Baie de Tangier
rue D'Angleterre
Galerie Delacroix
French Consulate
PL. DE FRANCE
rue K. Ibn Oualid
rue El-Jahba El-Ouatania
Magellan
av. d'Espagne
rue al-Msallah
rue Belgique
Avis Rental Car
bd. Pasteur
rue Omar ibn al-Alhass
rue Targha
rue Ibn Zohr
rue Mexique
rue Moutanabi
Libraire des Colonnes
rue Ibn Rochd
rue Marco Polo
Grand Taxis
TO (6 km)
rue de la Croix
Cyber Café Adam
Hertz Rental Car
rue al-Antaki
Fez Market
rue Hollande
rue du Prince Héritier
rue Moussa Ben Noussair
rue Sorolla
rue du Prince Moulay Abdallah
VILLE NOUVELLE
av. Youssef Ben Tachfine
rue Abou Alla al-Maari
rue de Fès
bd. Mohammed V
rue Allal Ben Abdallah
rue Al-Mansour Dahabi
rue Quevada
rue Omar Ibn Khattab
PL. DES NATIONS
av. Londres
rue Lafayette
rue Ibn Toumert
rue de Fès
rue d'Andalousie
PL. DE LA CITE ARABE
rue Lope de Vega
rue Lafontaine
TO THE ARENA
rue du Prince Héritie
rue Lamartine
av. Yacoub al-Mansour
TO THE ARENA
bd. Moulay Youssef
PL. MOULAY ABDELAZIZ
bd. Moulay Youssef
PL. AL JAMIA AL ARABIA
Bus Station
Grand Taxis
av. Lisbonne
av. la Paix
N
LG
0 200 yards
0 200 meters
Tangier
ACCOMMODATIONS
Auberge de Jeunesse (HI), 11
Hôtel Continental, 1
Hôtel El Muniria (Tanger Inn), 8
Hôtel and Restaurant L'Marsa, 7
Pension Amal, 2
Pension Miami, 5
Pension Palace, 3
FOOD
Brahim Abdelmalek, 10
Restaurant Africa, 6
McDonald's, 4

Trains: Trains leave from **Mghagha Station** (☎039 95 25 55), 6km from the port (not the old station on av. d'Espagne). A *petit taxi* to the station costs around 15dh. To: **Asilah** (1hr., 4 per day 7am-10:30pm, 13dh); **Casablanca** (6hr., 4 per day 8am-11pm, 117dh); **Fez** (5½hr., 4 per day 8am-11pm, 96dh); **Meknes** (5hr., 4 per day 8am-11pm, 80dh); and **Rabat** (5½hr., 4 per day 8am-11pm, 91dh).

Buses: Non-CTM buses leave from av. Yacoub al-Mansour at pl. Jamia al-Arabia, 2km from the port entrance. Ask blue-coated personnel or check the boards for ticket info. The standard price for luggage is 5dh. A *petit taxi* from the port to the terminal costs 8dh. To: **Asilah** (11am, 4:30pm); **Casablanca** (6hr., every hr. 5am-1am, 69dh); **Chefchaouen** (7am, 2:45pm); **Ceuta** (40min., 7 per day 6:15am-5:45pm, 10dh); **Fez** (6hr., 11 per day 11:30am-9:30pm, 63dh); **Larache** (11 per day 5:30am-6pm); **Marrakesh** (10hr.; 6:45am, 4:20, 8:30pm; 115dh); **Meknes** (5hr., 8 per day 6am-5:45pm, 57dh); **Rabat** (5hr., every hr. 5am-1am, 57dh); and **Tetouan** (1hr., at least 2 every hr. 5:30am-10pm, 14dh). The **CTM Station** (☎039 93 11 72) near the port entrance offers pricier and posher, but less frequent bus service to the same destinations. To: **Agadir** (11am, 4:30, 9pm); **Casablanca** (6 per day 11am-midnight); **Chefchaouen** (12:30pm); **Fez** (3, 7, 9pm); **Marrakesh** (11am, 4:30pm); **Meknes** (3, 7, 9pm); **Rabat** (6 per day 11am-midnight); **Tetouan** (7:45am, 12:30pm).

Ferries: The cheapest and most convenient option is to buy a ticket at the port agent, 46 ave. d'Espagne (☎039 94 26 12), though ticket agencies are located throughout the city. You'll need a boarding pass (available at any ticket desk) and a customs form (ask uniformed agents). Near the terminal, pushy men with ID cards will try to arrange your ticket and fill out your customs card for 10dh; just do it yourself. To: **Algeciras** (2½hr., every hr. 7am-9pm, 210dh) and **Tarifa** (35min., 3-5 per day, 200dh).

Taxis: *Grand taxis* to nearby locations. Prices subject to bargaining; a fair price is 20dh per person for 6 passengers. Found everywhere, especially by the main bus stop, the Grand Socco, and the intersection of bd. Pasteur and bd. Mohammed V.

Car Rental: Avis, 54 bd. Pasteur. Open daily 8am-noon and 2-7pm. **Hertz,** 36 av. Mohammed V (☎039 93 30 31). Open M-Sa 8:30am-noon and 2-6:30pm, Su 9am-noon. About 250dh per day with a 20% tax for a Fiat Palio or Fiat Uno. Min. age 25 for all cars. A special international license is not required.

ORIENTATION

Av. d'Espagne, a large boulevard that runs from the port along the waterfront to the train station 6km away, makes Tangier easy to navigate. Many of the *ville nouvelle* hotels are located about 1.5km down av. d'Espagne away from the ferry terminal (a *petit taxi* should cost 5dh, but if you don't have a lot of baggage and you have your wits about you, it's better to walk). Hustlers tend to prey on fresh meat here. Adjacent to the ferry terminal area on av. d'Espagne is the **CTM station. Rue du Portugal** heads uphill here and represents the border between the *ville nouvelle* and the medina. You can enter the medina and easily find some of its accommodations by turning right above the CTM station, continuing uphill on rue de la Plage. Soon you will reach the large, busy rotary known as the **Grand Socco,** the center of activity directly above the medina. From the Grand Socco, you can head down into the medina via **rue al-Siaghin,** which leads to the **Petit Socco** or walk down the bustling **rue d'Italie** (if facing the medina, the street on the left through the large archway), which skirts the medina's western wall. The *ville nouvelle's* main commercial road is the **bd. Pasteur,** which connects the main square, **pl. de France,** with **bd. Mohammed V,** containing many banks, the post office, and cafes.

PRACTICAL INFORMATION

Tourist Office: 29 bd. Pasteur (☎039 94 80 50). Some English, French, and Spanish spoken. Glossy brochures and basic map of the city, but nothing to get excited about. List of accommodations available. Open M-F 8:30am-7:30pm.

Currency Exchange: There is a branch of **BMCE** on most ferries and one in the port complex, although these only change cash. BMCE's **main office** in Tangier is located at 21 bd. Pasteur (☎039 93 11 25). No commission here, but other Moroccan banks charge fees for exchanging traveler's checks. Open M-F 8:15am-2:15pm. Major banks line bd. Pasteur and bd. Mohammed V, several of which have **ATMs.** Travel agencies near the port are required to change money at official rates. There are **Western Union** locations at pl. de France and the main post office.

Luggage Storage: At the **train station** (5dh per bag). Open 24hr. Also at the **bus station** (4dh per bag). Open daily 5:30am-12:30am.

English Bookstore: Librairie des Colonnes, 54 bd. Pasteur (☎039 93 69 55), near pl. France. English classics, French and Spanish fiction, and literature on Moroccan culture. Open M-F 9:30am-12:30pm and 4-7pm, Sa 9:30am-1pm.

Police: ☎19, at the port and main train station.

Medical Services: Red Cross, 6 rue al-Monoui Dahbi (☎039 94 25 17), runs a 24hr. English-speaking medical service. **Ambulance:** ☎039 31 27 27.

Internet Access: Several cafes in the *ville nouvelle,* including **Cyber Café Adam,** 2 rue Ibn Roched, off bd. Pasteur and bd. Mohammed V. 10dh per hr. Open daily 8:30am-2am. **Espace Net** and **Euronet** are on ave. de Mexique, 1 block from pl. de Paris.

Post Office: 33 bd. Mohammed V (☎039 93 25 18), on the downhill continuation of bd. Pasteur. **Poste Restante.** Open M-Th 8:30am-6:30pm, Sa 8:30am-12:15pm. Parcels are received around the corner from main entrance, on the back side of the building.

ACCOMMODATIONS

Whether you stay in the *ville nouvelle* or the medina, you are bound to meet some hustlers "welcoming" you to Morocco. Accommodations in the *ville nouvelle* are often more comfortable. Reserve ahead, be cautious, and have a sense of where you're going when you hit town. Expect to pay around 50-60dh for a single and 80-100dh for a double. Rates may decrease in winter.

MEDINA

The most convenient hostels are near **rue Mokhtar Ahardan** (formerly rue des Postes), off the Petit Socco. From the Grand Socco, take the first right down rue al-Siaghin to the Petit Socco, which is really a small intersection. Rue Mokhtar Ahardan begins at the end of the Petit Socco closest to the port. At night, the smaller streets off the medina can be unsafe.

Pension Amal, 5 rue Mokhtar Ahardan (☎039 93 36 00), at the bottom of the Petit Socco on the right. Rooms are clean and plain, if a bit dingy. Free cold showers. Singles 50dh; doubles 100dh. ❶

Pension Palace, 2 rue Mokhtar Ahardan (☎039 93 61 28). Downhill, on the alley exiting the Petit Socco to the right. Stark rooms inhabited by students. The courtyard starred in Bertolucci's adaptation of *The Sheltering Sky.* Singles 40dh; doubles 80dh, with bath 120dh; triples 120dh/150dh; quads 120dh/200dh. ❷

Hôtel Continental, 36 Dar Baroud (☎039 93 10 24; fax 039 93 11 43), overlooking the port. From the ferry terminal, bear right around the CTM station, and follow the many signs. A grand hotel furnished with a mix of Moroccan ornament and Art Deco. Home to newbie visitors and aging hippies. Breakfast included. Showers hot only in the mornings. Reservations recommended. Singles 284dh; doubles 365dh; triples 435dh. ❺

THE LOCAL STORY

THE ROYAL TREATMENT

Ahmed Soussi Tamli is the proprietor of Brahim Abdelmalek, credited with introducing sandwiches to Morocco.

"The idea of making sandwiches came only accidentally to my father. In 1960, the Casino players, mostly European, would come in hungry late at night, asking my father for a piece of bread with tuna. They loved it. They started calling my father the King of the Sandwiches.

"King Hassan II visited Tangier around 1964, walking the streets at night to see how the people lived. He came to the shop at about 3am, asking for a sandwich. My father didn't recognize him because he was wearing dark sunglasses. He took a piece of bread to make him a sandwich. But the King didn't didn't eat anything but salami and olives; he just wanted to talk. My father started thinking, Who is this person who doesn't want to eat?

"They were talking about life in Tangier when a Jew came in asking for a sandwich. When he'd left, the King said, 'Why do you speak to the other man very gently, and not to me? My father said, 'I don't know you. That is my customer, I see him everyday.' The King gave my father a 20dh bill, and said to keep the change. That was a lot of money back then. My father said, 'Take your change and come tomorrow.' They laughed, and the King gave him 10dh instead. Then he saw the King's limousine with the star and the flag. The King took off the glasses and laughed.

"This is the story of the sandwich."

VILLE NOUVELLE

Hotels line av. d'Espagne as it heads away from the port. The best values lie a few blocks uphill toward bd. Pasteur and bd. Mohammed V.

Hôtel El Muniria (Tanger Inn), rue Magellan (☎039 93 53 37). From the port, walk south along the tree-lined pedestrian walkway; take 1st right after Hôtel Biarritz on av. d'Espagne walking away from the medina, and follow as it winds uphill. William Burroughs wrote *Naked Lunch* in room #9 (now the owner's room). Ask for room #4, where Jack Kerouac and Allen Ginsberg stayed. A great deal for Tangier, with spacious rooms, hot showers, and towels. Singles 100dh; doubles 130dh. ❸

Auberge de Jeunesse (HI), 8 rue al-Antaki (☎039 94 61 27), down av. d'Espagne away from the port and half a block up the steep road to the right, after Hôtel Marco Polo. A backpacker hotspot. New, firm dormitory beds. Common area with TV. Hot showers 5dh. Office open M-Sa 8-10am, noon-3pm, and 6-11pm, Su 8-10am and 6pm-midnight. Closes around 10:30pm in winter. HI members 27dh; non-members 29.50dh. ❶

Pension Miami, 126 rue Salah Eddine al-Ayoubi (☎039 93 29 00), off av. d'Espagne. 45 rooms, carved high ceilings, and a balcony on each floor. Basic communal bathroom. Hot showers 10dh. Singles 50dh; doubles 80dh; triples 120dh; quads 160dh. ❶

Hôtel L'Marsa, 92 av. d'Espagne (☎039 93 23 39), away from the port on the main drag. Clean rooms with closets, some with terrace. Hot showers outside 7dh. Laundry 5dh per piece. Singles 50dh; doubles 100dh; quads 200dh. MC/V. ❶

FOOD

MEDINA

Begin at the **Grand Socco,** where you can stall-hop for delights of all types, and then head toward the Petit Socco for a slew of inexpensive local eateries. On the corner near the pl. France sprawls a huge **market.** The best pastries in town are at **Café Patisserie Charaf,** 28 rue Smarine, just below the Grand Socco in the medina.

Restaurant Hammadi, 2 rue de la Kasbah (☎039 93 45 14), the continuation of rue d'Italie just outside the medina walls. Specialties are *tajine* (40dh) and couscous (45dh). Beer and wine served. Entrees 40-60dh. A 10% tax is added to each meal. Open daily 11am-3pm and 7pm-midnight. MC/V. ❷

Restaurant Dar Tagine, 29 rue de Commerce, Petit Socco (☎068 425 500). When coming down the hill from the Grand Socco, take the 1st left; restaurant is on the left. Some of the best Moroccan cuisine in the city. Elegant and immaculate Moroccan-style decor. Set price for 5-course meal is 110dh. Open daily. MC/V. ❹

VILLE NOUVELLE

The restaurants along av. d'Espagne tout unspectacular and overpriced *menus touristiques* for 50dh and up. Beachfront restaurants run by the high-end hotels are just what you'd expect—expensive and boring. You're better off scouting around **pl. France.** For a snack, hot sandwiches can be found all along bd. Pasteur. The restaurant with the best view in the city may also afford a guilty break from Morocco cuisine: the **McDonald's** in Le Dawliz complex, above the Grand Socco.

L'Marsa, 92 av. d'Espagne (☎039 93 19 28). This popular restaurant/cafe has outdoor dining and a mixed Italian and Moroccan menu. Praiseworthy pizzas (23-35dh), pasta, and Italian ice cream (12-25dh). Women traveling alone should avoid the rooftop terrace, a choice pick-up spot for Moroccan men. Entrees 25-70dh. Open daily June-Aug. 5am-3am; Sept.-May 5am-midnight. MC/V. ❷

Restaurant Africa, 83 rue Salah Eddine al-Ayoubi (☎039 93 54 36), just off av. d'Espagne near Pension Miami, opposite old train station. A quiet, dimly lit place by Moroccan standards. Omelettes (15dh) and *tajine* (30dh). Beer served. Big 4-course *menu du jour* 50dh. Entrees 25-80dh. Open daily 9am-12:30am. ❷

Brahim Abdelmalek, 14 rue de Mexique (☎039 93 17 96), under an off-white awning. King Hassan II lunched here. You can too, for less than 15dh. Owner claims to have invented Moroccan sandwich craze in 1960. (See **The Local Story,** left.) Open daily 10:30am-3am. ❶

SIGHTS

IN AND NEAR THE MEDINA

OLD AMERICAN LEGATION. The Old American Legation is an austere and refined escape. In 1821, this became the first foreign property acquired by the United States. The museum contains correspondence between George Washington and his "great and magnanimous friend" Sultan Moulay ben Abdallah, among other exhibits. (Morocco was the first nation to recognize America's independence, thus forever solidifying friendly relations between the countries.) Visit the room dedicated to famous expat writer Paul Bowles, featuring photographs from Tangier's storied "interzone" days. The friendly curators will give excellent tours on request, but calling first is recommended. *(8 rue d'America. Enter the medina via the large white steps on rue du Portugal and look for the yellow archway emblazoned with the US seal. ☎039 93 53 17. Open M-F 10am-1pm and 3-5pm. Donation suggested.)*

DAR AL-MAKHZEN. An opulent palace, currently under renovation, with hand-woven tapestries, inlaid ceilings, and foliated archways, the Dar al-Makhzen was once home to the ruling pasha of Tangier and is now the Museum of Moroccan Art. The collection includes intriguing exhibits of ceramics, carpets, silver jewelry, weapons, and musical instruments, with plaques in French and English. *(Currently undergoing renovations; call to see if it has reopened. The easiest way to reach the museum and the pl. de la Kasbah grounds is to enter the medina from the porte de la Kasbah gate and stick to the rampart wall until you reach the wide open space of pl. de la Kasbah. The museum is to the right. ☎039 93 20 97. Open W-M 9am-12:30pm and 3-5:30pm. 10dh.)*

MARKETS. The medina's commercial center is the **Grand Socco.** This busy square and traffic circle is cluttered with fruit vendors, parsley stands, and *kebab* and fish stalls. Off of rue de Fez is the small, colorful **Fez Market,** where local merchants cater to Tangier's Europeans. *(Uphill on rue de la Liberté, across pl. France, and 2 blocks down rue de Fez on the right.)* Rif Berbers come to the **Dradeb district** every Thursday and Sunday bearing pottery, olives, mint, and fresh fruit, but unless Tangier is your only stop, buy crafts elsewhere. *(West of the Grand Socco along rue Bou Arrakia and rue de la Montagne.)*

OTHER SIGHTS. Rue Riad Sultan runs alongside the **Jardins du Soltane,** where artisans weave carpets, and continues to **pl. de la Kasbah,** a sunny courtyard with a promontory offering spectacular views of Spain and the Atlantic Ocean. With your back to the water, walk toward the far right corner of the plaza; just around the corner to the right the **Mosque de la Kasbah** rears its octagonal minaret. Outside of the medina, 17th- and 18th-century bronze cannons hide in the **Jardins de la Mendoubia,** a welcome escape from the excitement of the Soccos. *(Opposite rue de la Liberté, where rue Bou Arrakia joins the Grand Socco, through the white gate marked #50.)*

ENTERTAINMENT

The most popular evening activity in Tangier is sipping mint tea in front of a cafe on pl. de France or bd. Pasteur. The **Café de Paris,** 1 pl. de France, hosted countless meetings between spies during WWII. Coming from the Grand Socco, look to the left. (☎039 93 84 44. Tea and coffee 5-6dh. Open daily 7am-11:30pm.) Inside the medina, **Café Central** was a favorite of William S. Burroughs (off the Petit Socco; same hours and prices). **Cafe Hafa,** near the *Kasbah,* has a great view of Spain on a clear day. Cafes tend to attract a male crowd, but female tourists should not be afraid to grab a table and an orange juice—it's perfectly acceptable. **Kandinsky Plaza,** 30 route Malabata, a chic cafe and gourmet ice cream shop, is a popular with men and women, foreign and Moroccan. For a no-hassle beer, head to the **Tanger Inn,** rue Magellan (open 9pm-late); for a quiet drink, try **Negresco,** 20 rue Mexique, off the pl. France. The city's longest-running bar is full of expats and backpackers. (☎039 93 80 97. Beer 15-18dh. Mixed drinks 30-35dh. Open daily 10am-midnight.) I

CEUTA (SEBTA) سبتة ☎039

Travelers hoping to avoid Tangier altogether may opt to ferry to the Spanish enclave Ceuta (pop. 70,000; called *Sebta* within Morocco) and from there cross the Moroccan border, only 5km away. Most visitors don't stay in Ceuta, moving on immediately to Tetouan (35min. away) or Chefchaouen (allow 4hr.). If you're trapped in Ceuta, try the helpful **tourist booth** (☎956 50 62 75) in the ferry terminal, which has a map. If you need to spend the night, accommodation options do exist.

TETOUAN تطوان ☎039

For a small city, Tetouan (pronounced *tet-ta-wan)* maintains a remarkable pace. The city contains its share of hustlers and the down-and-out, both of whom tourists will inevitably encounter. If at all possible, the bus station, where most of them congregate, should be avoided by solo travelers. The two pleasant plazas, pl. Moulay al-Mehdi and pl. Hassan II, connected by C. Mohammed V, offer some respite. To reach **pl. Moulay al-Mehdi,** the heart of the *ville nouvelle,* from the **bus station,** follow av. Mohammed V four blocks uphill. The medina, the palace, and the spacious pl. Hassan II are halfway between the station and the plaza, while the plaza itself is home to Pension Iberia, the **BCME bank,** the **post office** (open M-F 8:30am-12:15pm and 2:30-6:30pm, Sa 8:30-11:30am) and **telephones. Internet** (10dh per hr.) can be found just down the street to the left of the

> **BORDER CROSSING.** To reach the Moroccan border from Ceuta, grab a taxi from the town center (€4.80) or take **bus #7** (€0.47); to reach the bus stand from the ferry (5min. away), exit the terminal and take a left onto the main street. At the end of the street, near a roundabout with a fountain in the middle (and near the water), take a right up the hill, and then another right to the stand. Taxis and buses stop short of the border; you must cross on foot and have your passport stamped. Expect to be accosted by guides wanting to escort you to their cousin's rug emporium. Just head straight to the parking lot, where **grand taxis** await (see p. 720). **Cash** exchange is also available at the border; do it here rather than in Ceuta. From the border, full *grand taxis* to Tetouan are 15-20dh per person. From there you can connect to the more mellow Chefchaouen, by catching a bus or taxi. If you are heading to Algeciras (see p. 259) from Ceuta, there are sixteen **fast-ferry** departures (35min., 7:30am-10:30pm, €21). Don't forget about the 2hr. time difference between Spain and Morocco.

BMCE. **CTM buses** (☎039 31 20 61) provide a receipt for luggage (5dh). Buses to **Casablanca** (7hr., 120dh); **Chefchaouen** (1½hr., 25dh); **Fez** (5hr., 60dh); **Rabat** (6hr., 100dh); and **Tangier** (1½hr., 15dh) are relatively frequent as several companies run out of Tetouan. **Grand taxis** (15-20dh) to Ceuta also leave from near the bus station. Taxis to Chefchaouen (25dh when full) run from a stand 10min. away; walk from pl. Moulay al-Mehdi away from the bus station along rue Achra Mai and bear left onto rue al-Jazair. The **tourist office** is a half block down av. Mohammed V toward the medina, and has a map and info on guides. (Open M-F 8:30am-noon and 2:30-6:30pm.) Reach **police** at ☎19.

For accommodations, by far the best option is **Pension Iberia ❶,** pl. Moulay al-Mehdi, on the third floor above BMCE. Clean, breezy rooms make up for a long walk upstairs. (☎039 96 36 79. Hot showers 5dh. Singles 40dh; doubles 70dh; triples 105dh.) **Hotel Príncipe ❶,** 20 rue Youssef, has archaically furnished rooms with bath and toilet. (☎039 96 27 95. Singles 70dh; doubles 100dh.) The pocket-sized *pastillas* (lamb-filled pastries; 6dh) at **Café-Patisserie Smir ❶,** 17 Calle Mohammed V, make a perfect lunch-on-the-go, though there's also a balcony on which to enjoy the pastries (1-5dh). Popular with Moroccan families, it's also comfortable for women. (Open daily 6am-9pm.)

CHEFCHAOUEN (CHAOUEN) شفشوانخ ☎039

High in the Rif Mountains lies the mellow, whitewashed Chefchaouen (pop. 30,000). Chefchaouen's relaxed atmosphere and cool mountain air refresh even the weariest of travelers, who are attracted by its manageable, Mediterranean medina and the proximity to *kif* (hashish) farms. There are also some breathtaking natural wonders within hiking distance.

TRANSPORTATION The **bus station** (☎039 98 95 73) is far downhill from town. **Buses** heading south fill up, so get tickets early. **CTM** and other **buses** go to: **Fez** (5hr.; 1:15, 3pm; 45-55dh); **Ouazzene,** the best bet for connections (1hr.; 7am, 1:15, and 3:30pm; 18dh); **Tangier** (via Tetouan, 28-33dh); and **Tetouan** (1½hr., 7 per day 6:45am-6pm, 16-18dh). To get to **Ceuta,** you must go through Tetouan. Private companies also have daily buses to Fez and Meknes. There is a **second bus station** only four blocks down the hill from Plaza Mohammed V, on rue Mohammed Abduh, that has buses to several locations at better prices than CTM. **Grand taxis** are the easiest way to get to **Tetouan** (24dh) and **Ceuta,** although they often take a while to fill. **Taxis** leave a block downhill from pl. Mohammed V.

MOROCCO

PRACTICAL INFORMATION. From both **bus stations,** head up the steep hill and turn right after several blocks onto the large road, which leads to the tree-filled, circular pl. Mohammed V; it's about a 20min. walk to the center of town (or a few dirhams for a cab). Cross the plaza and continue east on **av. Hassan II,** the *ville nouvelle's* main road. Here you'll find currency exchange at the **BMCE** (open M-F 8:15am-2:15pm), the **post office** with **telephones** (open M-F 8:30am-12:15pm and 2:30-6:30pm), and **Internet** at **IRIC,** 10 av. Hassan II. (☎039 98 97 15; 10dh per hr. Open daily 9am-midnight.) Chefchaouen has no tourist office. Av. Hassan II ends at the Bab al-Ain, the main gate into the **medina.** From Bab al-Ain, the main street twists uphill to **place Uta al-Hammam,** the plaza at the heart of the medina. **Hospital Mohammed V** is a block west from pl. Mohammed V, and **police** are at ☎19.

ACCOMMODATIONS AND FOOD. Chefchaouen has a slew of colorful budget hotels. Inside the medina, head uphill from Bab al-Ain; hotels are clustered along this street and around pl. Uta al-Hammam. The best of the lot is **Hotel Andalus ❶,** 1 rue Sidi Salem, directly behind Credit Agricola on pl. Uta al-Hammam, in the medina. Friendly owner Ahmed takes great pride in this clean, comfortable, and relaxing pension. With cheap rates, a gorgeous terrace, and a large common room, it's one of Morocco's best deals. (☎039 98 60 34. Singles 30dh; doubles 60dh; triples 90dh; quads 120dh; lovely terrace 20dh. Prices include hot shower.) Tucked in the corner of whitewashed walls and next to a *hammam*, **Pension la Castellana ❶,** 4 Sidi Ahmad Bouhali, caters almost exclusively to backpackers and encourages long stays. Walk to the end of pl. Uta al-Hammam to get there. (☎039 98 62 95. Communal kitchen and common room with stereo. Free hot showers. Singles 30dh; doubles 60dh; triples 90dh; quads 120dh.) **Pension Znika ❶,** 4 rue Znika, in the medina, has well-kept rooms. (☎039 98 66 24. Singles 30dh, doubles 60dh, triples 90dh.) **Hotel Rif ❶,** rue Hassan II, is just outside the medina walls. Follow rue Hassan II to the right around the medina; it's on the left after a few blocks. Rif has clean rooms, great views, a TV lounge, and terraces decorated in an odd combination 16th-century Moroccan and 1970s Americana motifs; they also can help with **mountain hikes**—just ask for affable owner Younes. (☎/fax 039 98 69 82. Singles 50dh, with shower 90dh; doubles 80dh/120dh; triples 120dh/160dh. MC/V.) For a quick bite, **Chez Aziz ❶,** just outside Bab al-Ain, the medina's gate, has cheap, tasty snacks. (Open daily noon-midnight.) Inside the medina, outdoor seating is available in pl. Uta al-Hammam at various restaurants; **Al Kasaba ❶** is one of the best. (Open daily 8am-11pm.) More upscale choices are along av. Hassan II.

MOROCCO

SIGHTS. Chefchaouen's steep **medina** is one of Morocco's best. It's uncrowded and more relaxed than those of larger cities. Enter through Bab al-Ain and walk uphill toward pl. Uta al-Hammam, the center of the medina. In the *place* are several outdoor cafes, the 16th-century **Grand Mosque** with its red-and-gold minaret, and a 17th-century *kasbah* built by Moulay Ismail, Morocco's famous rogue. Inside the *kasbah* stands the 15th-century **Tower of Homage.** *(Open daily 9am-1pm and 3-6:30pm. 10dh.)* Chefchaouen's **souq** operates Mondays and Thursdays outside the medina and below both av. Hassan II and av. Allal ben Abdalallah.

HIKING. For trailhead or map info, see Ahmed at Hotel Andalus or Younes at Hotel Rif. To obtain a friendly guide, contact Mouden Abdeslam (mobile ☎062 11 39 17). Follow the **Ras al-Ma River** (still known as Hippie River from the days Chefchaouen attracted many) upstream into the hills for just a few kilometers for spectacular results. For a view of the city, hike to the Hotel Asmaq (follow signs for the *ville nouvelle*). Behind the hotel, there's a path that winds up the peak to the left, and then runs down into the valley. Try reaching the "Spanish mosque" about halfway up the peak to the right of the medina, or the spectacular rocky arch known as the **Pont de Dieu** (God's Bridge). Most of the hikes are 1hr. round-trip, though it takes a full day to reach the Pont de Dieu. Consider taking a taxi to the base of God's Bridge. Finally, with much planning or a guide, an **overnight hike** to villages in the mountains where Berbers will host you, can be unforgettable.

THE MIDDLE ATLAS الاطلس المتوسط

The Middle Atlas is Morocco's heartland, where traditional culture and political dynasties were formed. Home to the Roman ruins of Volubilis and the imperial cities of Meknes and Fez, the region is full of historical points of interest. Modernization creates stunning contrasts; thousands of satellite dishes face skyward from Fez's medieval medina homes.

MEKNES مكناس ☎055

After uniting Morocco under his brutal rule, the rogue Sultan Moulay Ismail chose Meknes as his seat of power in 1672 and tried to turn this relative backwater into a capital to rival Versailles. Though less arresting than Morocco's other imperial cities, Meknes remains a pleasant and manageable city where visitors can take leisurely enjoyment of a few impressive monuments left by Moulay Ismail as well as the nearby world-renowned ruins of Volubilis. Named for the Berber tribe Meknassa, this provincial capital has the largest Berber population in Morocco.

TRANSPORTATION

Trains: Meknes has 2 stations with nearly identical service. Use the **Meknes al-Amir Abdelkader Station,** rue d'Alger (☎055 51 61 35), 2 blocks from av. Mohammed V. The **Meknes Main Station** is farther from the center of town. To: **Casablanca** (3¾hr., 7 per day 8am-3:30am, 81-119dh); **Fez** (50min., 9 per day 9:55am-2am, 16.50dh); **Marrakesh** (8hr., 7 per day 8am-3:30am, 153-228dh); **Rabat** (2½hr., 6 per day 10:35am-3:30am, 56-80dh); **Tangier** (4hr., 4 per day 7:50am-2:15am, 75-117dh).

Buses: CTM, av. des F.A.R. (☎055 51 47 59), a shiny, new station about 5 blocks from av. Mohammed V (take a left when exiting the station; av. Mohammed V will be to the right). To: **al-Rachidia** (6hr., 10pm, 80dh) via Fez; **Casablanca** (4hr., 8 per day 8:30am-3am, 63dh); **Fez** (1hr., 9 per day 4am-11pm, 18dh); **Marrakesh** (8hr., 7pm, 132dh); **Rabat** (3hr., 8 per day 8:30am-3am, 38dh); **Tangier** (5hr., 3 per day 2-7pm, 70dh). **Private companies** depart from a station on av. Mellah just outside Bab al-Khemis, on the far side of the medina away from the *ville nouvelle.* A *petit taxi* is necessary. To: **al-Rachidia** (4 per day 9am-2pm); **Casablanca** (12 per day 5:30am-4pm); **Erfoud** (9pm); **Fez** (10am, 5:30pm); **Larache** (3:15 and 10pm); **Marrakesh** (4 per day 5:30am-6:30pm); **Rabat** (3 per day 6:30am-12:45pm); **Tangier** (6 per day 4:45am-3pm); **Tetouan** (7 per day 5am-10pm).

Taxis: *Grand Taxis* cluster, among other places, on av. des F.A.R., across from Hotel Continental, next to the private bus station, and outside the al-Amir Abdelkader train station. To: **Fez** (17dh), **Moulay Idriss** (8dh), **Rabat** (40dh).

ORIENTATION AND PRACTICAL INFORMATION

The river **Oued Boufrekane** divides Meknes into three "boroughs": the **medina,** the neighboring **imperial city,** and the modern **ville nouvelle.** The train and CTM buses deposit passengers in the *ville nouvelle.* Tree-lined **avenue Mohammed V,** the new city's main drag, intersects with av. Hassan II at a large roundabout surrounded by cafes and shops. From the intersection, follow av. Hassan II, which turns into av. Moulay Ismail, to approach the medina via Bab Bou-Amir. To reach **Bab al-Mansour** (the entrance to the imperial complex) and **Plaza al-Khedim** (the medina's main square), head uphill from Bab Bou-Amir, take a right on rue Roumazine and then a left on rue Dar Smen. Local buses #5, 7, and 9 (1.50-2.30dh) shuttle between the CTM bus station and Bab al-Mansour (a 20min. walk); a *petit taxi* should cost 8dh. The private bus station deposits passengers at Bab al-Khemis.

Tourist Office: 27 pl. Administrative (☎055 52 44 26; fax 055 51 60 46). From the Abdelkader train station, go straight 2 blocks, turn left on av. Mohammed V, and make an immediate right. Cross rue Allal ben Abdallah, continue toward the Hôtel de Ville, and veer right. The tourist office is on the right just after the post office. Some English spoken. Brochure with basic map of city. Guides are only necessary if you want more historical information about the sites, as Meknes is quite easy to navigate. Tours half day 120dh, full day 150dh. Open July-Sept. M-F 8am-6:30pm; Oct.-June M-F 8:30am-noon and 2:30-6:30pm. **Syndicat d'Initiative** (☎055 52 01 91), on Esplanade de la Foire, off av. Moulay Ismail, inside the yellow gate. Open M-F 8:30am-noon and 3-6pm.

Currency Exchange: BMCE, 98 av. des F.A.R. (☎055 52 03 52), has **ATMs.** Exchange window open daily 10am-2pm and 4-8pm. **Hôtel Rif,** on Zenkat Accra, cashes traveler's checks for a fee. **Banks** line both Mohammed V and Hassan II.

Late-Night Pharmacy: Red Crescent Emergency Pharmacy (☎055 52 33 75), in pl. Administrative, across from the Petrol station. Open daily 8:30am-8:30pm.

Hospitals: Hôpital Moulay Ismail (☎055 52 28 05 or 055 52 28 06), on av. des F.A.R.

Internet Access: Many choices in the *ville nouvelle,* including **Cyber Paris,** rue de Accra, which claims to have the fastest connection in the city. 6dh per hr. Open daily 9am-late. In the medina, try **Meetnet,** 38 rue Roumazine. 6dh per hr. Open Sa-Th 10:30am-11:45pm, F 10:30am-12:20pm and 3-11:45pm.

Post Office: pl. Administrative. **Poste Restante** at the side entrance. Open M-Sa 8am-3:30pm. **Branch office** on rue Dar Smen, near the medina.

MOROCCO

ACCOMMODATIONS

MEDINA

Rue Roumazine and rue Dar Smen house most of the medina's budget hotels, although even backpackers opt for plusher accommodations in the *ville nouvelle.*

Maroc Hôtel, 7 rue Roumazine (☎055 53 00 75). Clean, small rooms. Cold showers and squat toilets. Breakfast 20dh. Hot showers 10dh. 60dh per person. ❷

Hôtel de Paris, 58 rue Roumazine. Look for the sign that says "Hôtel." Basic and clean. Shower and *hammam* next door, both 6dh. Singles 35-40dh; doubles 70dh; triples 90dh; nice terrace for 20dh, but beds are rough. ❶

Municipal Camping Agdal (☎055 55 53 96), on the ramparts of the medina behind Agdal Basin. Follow signs from Bab Mansour (15min. walk) or Bab Bou-Amir. Cheap rates and proximity to Meknes's tourist sights outdo many hotel options. Set in a beautiful, wooded park. Hot showers (7dh), kitchen and restaurant. Reception daily 8am-1pm and 4-8pm. 17dh per adult, 12dh per child, 10dh per tent, 17dh per car. ❶

VILLE NOUVELLE

The *ville nouvelle* offers greater comfort and easier access to banks, CTM buses, and trains, but prices are higher than in the medina. Most of the cheapest hotels lie around av. Mohammed V and rue Allal ben Abdallah.

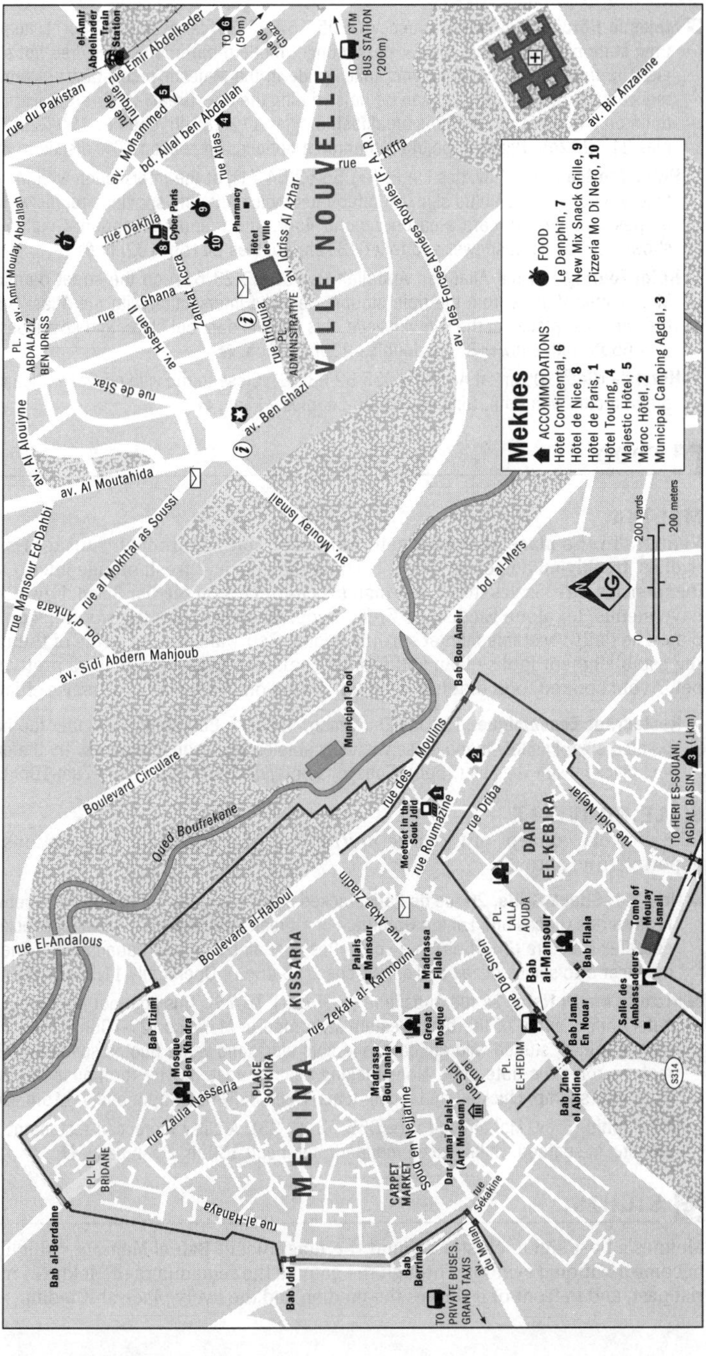
Meknes
ACCOMMODATIONS
Hôtel Continental, 6
Hôtel de Nice, 8
Hôtel de Paris, 1
Hôtel Touring, 4
Majestic Hôtel, 5
Maroc Hôtel, 2
Municipal Camping Agdal, 3
FOOD
Le Danphin, 7
New Mix Snack Grille, 9
Pizzeria Mo Di Nero, 10
VILLE NOUVELLE
MEDINA
KISSARIA
DAR EL-KEBIRA
el-Amir Abdelhader Train Station
TO 6 (50m)
TO CTM BUS STATION (200m)
TO HERI ES-SOUANI, AGDAL BASIN, 3 (1km)
TO PRIVATE BUSES, GRAND TAXIS
rue du Pakistan
rue Emir Abdelkader
rue de Turquie
av. Mohammed V
bd. Allal ben Abdallah
rue Atlas
rue de Ghaza
rue Dakhla
Cyber Paris
Pharmacy
Hôtel de Ville
av. Idriss Al Azhar
rue Kiffa
av. des Forces Armées Royales (F. A. R.)
av. Bir Anzarane
PL. Amir Moulay Abdallah
PL. ABDALAZIZ BEN IDRISS
rue Ghana
Zankat Accra
av. Hassan II
rue Ifriquia
PL. ADMINISTRATIVE
rue de Sfax
av. Al Alouiyne
av. Ben Ghazi
av. Al Moutahida
rue Mansour Ed-Dahbi
rue al Mokhtar as Soussi
av. Moulay Ismail
bd. d'Ankara
av. Sidi Abdern Mahjoub
bd. al-Mers
Bab Bou Ameir
Municipal Pool
Boulevard Circulare
Oued Boufrekane
rue des Moulins
rue El-Andalous
Boulevard al-Haboul
Meetnet in the Souk Jdid
rue Roumazine
rue Driba
rue Sidi Nejjar
PL. LALLA AOUDA
rue Akba Ziadin
Palais Mansour
Madrassa Filale
rue Zekak al-Karmouni
Great Mosque
Bab al-Mansour
Bab Filala
Tomb of Moulay Ismail
Salle des Ambassadeurs
Bab Jama En Nouar
Bab Zine el Abidine
PL. EL-HEDIM
rue Dar Smen
Bab Tizimi
Mosque Ben Khadra
PLACE SOUKIRA
rue Zauia Nasseria
Madrassa Bou Inania
rue Sidi Amar
Souq en Nejjarine
CARPET MARKET
Dar Jamai Palais (Art Museum)
rue Sekakine
PL. EL BRIDANE
rue al-Hanaya
Bab al-Berdaine
Bab Jdid
Bab Berrima
av. du Mellah
S314
0 200 yards
0 200 meters

MOROCCO

Majestic Hôtel, 19 av. Mohammed V (☎055 52 20 35; fax 055 52 74 27), near the train station. Comfortable rooms, cozy lounge, modern bathrooms, and free hot showers. The friendly and helpful owner takes pride in the Majestic's constant upkeep, but renovations and construction can be noisy during the day. Breakfast 24dh. Backpacker dorm on terrace 60dh, includes breakfast. Singles 112-189dh; doubles 150-225dh; triples 217-292dh. Prices depend on bathroom options. Off-season 10% discount. ❸

Hôtel Continental, 92 av. des F.A.R. (☎055 52 54 71), at the intersection with Mohammed V. Look for neon blue sign. An adequate choice, offering spacious rooms with red drapes, lounge and cafe area on second floor, and friendly reception. Singles with shower 109dh, with shower and toilet 137dh; doubles 141dh/162dh. ❸

Hôtel Touring, 34 rue Allal ben Abdallah (☎055 52 23 51), on the street parallel to Mohammed V away from the train station, near the intersection with rue Atlas. One of the cheapest places in the *ville nouvelle,* this hotel is dark but clean and spacious. Singles 65dh, with shower 85dh; doubles 90dh/110dh. ❷

Hotel de Nice, 10 Zankat Accra (☎055 52 03 18). Close to the *ville nouvelle.* Clean and bright rooms with bath. Singles 185dh; doubles 217dh. ❹

FOOD

MEDINA

Vendors in the **place al-Khedim** sell *merguez* (spicy Moroccan sausage) sandwiches, freshly-made potato chips, corn on the cob, and fresh orange juice. Other inexpensive fare sizzles in the one-man *brochetteries* on **rue Dar Smen.** Few places have menus, let alone English or French copies—most have their options on display. The daily **vegetable market** sprouts beside Bab Mansour. As a rule of thumb, if the establishment looks clean and food is cooked in front of you, it's a pretty safe bet. Avoid cooked food that has been left sitting out, especially rotisserie chicken.

Restaurant Economique, 123 rue Dar Smen, opposite Bab Mansour, under the hand-painted sign. Friendly manager serves tasty staples at reasonable prices. Try the excellent chicken with veggies (25dh). Couscous or *tajine* 25dh. Open daily 7am-10pm. ❶

VILLE NOUVELLE

Like the very concept of the *ville nouvelle* itself, most of the best options are imported from abroad.

New Mex Snack Grille, 20 rue de Paris, tucked away in an alley off rue de Paris between Festival des Glaces and Lahlon Optique. For a break from Moroccan cuisine, shockingly good Tex-Mex fare (34-45dh) in a very refreshing, air-conditioned atmosphere. Friendly manager also serves pizzas and sandwiches (30-45dh). Open daily 11:30am-11pm. ❷

Pizzeria Mo Di Nero, 14 rue Antisirabe (☎055 51 76 76). This gourmet pizza shop and eatery offers some of the best Western-style food in Morocco (27-70dh). Brick walls, marble tables, stuffed wild animals, and chic black and white photos somehow mix to make a romantic date spot. Non-smoking section upstairs. Try the house specialty, pizza with shrimp, chicken, and mushrooms. Open daily noon-3pm and 7-11pm. ❷

Le Dauphin, 5 av. Mohammed V (☎055 52 34 23). A glitzy Moroccan restaurant specializing in seafood. Highly recommended. Set *menù* 130dh. Open daily. ❺

SIGHTS

Meknes's best sights cluster around the magnificent **Bab al-Mansour,** which has become a national symbol. Through the gate lie the remainders of Meknes's imperial past, and in front of it thrives the medina and the lively place al-Khedim.

IMPERIAL MEKNES

Weakened by war, weather, and the Great Earthquake of 1755, the ramparts of the **Dar al-Kebira** (Imperial City) testify to Meknes's former glory. Sultan Moulay Ismail, who, along with Hassan II, is perhaps Morocco's most revered visionary, personally supervised the building of over 25km of protective **walls** for his city within a city. Strolling about the site with a pick-ax and whip in hand, the sultan criticized and occasionally decapitated workers who displeased him. Gathering materials from sights all over Morocco, including Roman marble from the ruins at Volubilis, Moulay Ismail created a radiant city. Ismail razed part of the medina to create **place al-Khedim** (Plaza of Destruction), an approach to **Bab al-Mansour,** Morocco's finest gate. Today, only the walls and several large monuments remain.

TOMB OF MOULAY ISMAIL. The tomb, along with its accompanying **mosque,** is one of only two Muslim buildings in all of Morocco open to non-Muslims and is well worth a visit. After several bright yellow antechambers lies a larger courtyard. At the far left end is an ornately designed room from which you can view the tomb itself. The tomb is flanked by two functioning grandfather clocks, a consolation prize from Louis XIV after he refused Moulay Ismail's proposal to his daughter (don't feel sad for ol' Moulay; he already had over 300 lovers). Photographs are allowed. *(Through the two blue arches, and then immediately to the left. Open Sa-Th 9am-noon and 3-6pm, F 3-6pm. Free, but donations requested in the room of the tomb.)*

SALLE DES AMBASSADEURS. Standing by itself in an open court is the green-tiled roof of the recently restored Salle des Ambassadeurs, where Ismail conducted affairs of state. Ask the guard to unlock the doors to the so-called **"Christian Dungeon,"** a 6 sq. km. underground storehouse and granary for the Sultan, his entourage, and their horses. This storehouse is said to have once housed some 50,000-100,000 Christian prisoners. Since the "dungeon" remains a cool 15°C even in summer, it is the perfect place to avoid the midday sun. *(From pl. al-Khedim, go through Bab al-Mansour or one of the nearby smaller gates, walk straight, and follow the wall on the right around the bend. Open daily 9am-noon and 3-6pm. 10dh.)*

OTHER IMPERIAL CITY SIGHTS. A short trek from Moulay Ismail's tomb is the **Heri al-Souani** (storehouse), a cool granary with immense cisterns designed to withstand prolonged sieges. Trees and birds have invaded, giving it a jungle-like feel. Do not, under any circumstances, pay for guided tours; they're overpriced and unnecessary. *(Open daily 9am-noon and 3-6pm. 10dh.)* Below lies the **Agdal Basin,** once Moulay Ismail's private country club and his reservoir in case of siege. His wives (more than 300 of them) and their 800 kids were said to swim here to escape the stifling summer heat. Today, it is a nice place for an evening stroll. *(To get to the Heri al-Souani and Agdal Basin from Bab al-Mansour, take a petit taxi for 7dh. Free.)*

MEDINA

Meknes's medina is more pleasant, tranquil, and compact than those of the other imperial cities. Facing the Dar Jamaï Museum of Moroccan Art, take the alley to the left of the entrance. Push straight ahead to **Souq al-Nejjarine,** a major street. Heading left here brings you first to the **textile souq,** the **carpenters' souq,** and the **carpet market.** The rest of the medina is best explored like any other: wander until you get lost, then try to find your way out.

GREAT MOSQUE AND MADRASA BOU. While everything except the green-glazed minaret of the Great Mosque *(al-masjid al-kebira)* is off-limits to non-Muslims, the breathtaking 14th-century Madrasa Bou Inania, across from it, is not. A college of theology and Muslim law, this *madrasa* typifies traditional Merenid architecture—the courtyard combines cedar, stucco, and mosaics with characteristic flair. Upstairs are a number of cells, each of which snugly hosted at least two students.

The roof, which you may have to unlock yourself, offers a splendid view of the minaret of the Great Mosque and the rooftops of Meknes. *(Face Dar Jamaï in pl. al-Khedim, turn right onto rue Sidi Amar, and enter the medina. Follow the alley as it turns left, then fork right. Madrasa open daily 9am-noon and 3-6pm. 10dh.)*

DAYTRIP FROM MEKNES

VOLUBILIS تجوليبيليس

There are no direct buses to Volubilis: a ***taxi*** *is the most reliable and convenient method of transport. While you can hire a grand taxi near the private bus station in Meknes, you need a 6-person party to get the cheapest fare, and taxis rarely fill up; alone it will cost 100dh. The surest way is to take a* grand taxi *to Moulay Idriss (45 min., 8dh per place). Even taxis to Moulay Idris can take a long time to fill up. From Moulay Idriss, either walk if it's not too hot (4km, 40min., straight from junction with Moulay Idriss and then left at the sign for Oualili), or save your energy and take another taxi from Moulay Idriss (10dh total). Alternatively, you can also try grabbing a* ***bus*** *from Meknes to Ouezzane (every hr. 7am-7pm, 10dh) and asking the driver to drop you off near the ruins. To get back to Meknes, hop on a tour bus or wait by the parking lot for a taxi; they are infrequent but not rare. Don't try to return too late though; rides become scarcer the later it gets. In general, leave yourself at least 1.5 hr. to enjoy the ruins.*

Thirty-three kilometers from Meknes lie the dramatic ruins of Volubilis, the best-preserved Roman site in Morocco and perhaps all of North Africa. Surrounded by beautiful country-side and containing an extensive collection of **Roman mosaics,** Volubilis has deservedly earned must-see status. Once a major center for the olive oil trade, the city flourished under Roman rule, reaching its zenith in the 2nd and 3rd centuries AD when it became the capital of the kingdom of Mauritania. The Romans, who viewed their North African possessions as a bread basket for their European citizens, ordered the deforestation of the area to make room for grain crops; from that point on local resources dwindled and the city began to decline. When Moulay Idriss took control of the city in the 18th century, he siphoned off much of the residential population to Fez and Meknes and claimed many of the city's pillars and stones for his own palace. The Lisbon Earthquake of 1755, which wreaked devastation all along the Atlantic seaboard, finally sealed the city's fate.

When US General George C. Patton visited the ruins, he declined an offer of a guided tour—he believed he had been stationed here as a Roman centurion in his previous life and thus knew his way around. If you've been equally lucky, stop reading here. Otherwise, head past the ticket office and over a bridge, take a left and climb the steps to the top, where among the ruins of a housing and industrial area are several **olive presses.** In this area you'll also find the **House of Orpheus,** which includes a few well-preserved mosaics, one of which depicts the Orpheus myth. Nearby is a small building containing a restored olive press and then further on are the towering columns of the **capitol** (dating from 218 AD) and arches of the **basilica.** The basilica, despite its name, served as the courthouse during Roman times. Follow the path to the **House of the Athlete** on the left, named for its mosaic depicting the victor of a *desultor* race (which involved mounting a moving horse). In the middle of town looms the **Triumphal Arch,** built in AD 217 to celebrate Emperor Caracalla and his scheming mother Julia Domna. Julia assured her son's power by helping him murder his rival Gota in AD 212. The gate marks the beginning of the town's main street, **Decumanus Maximus.** The houses along the street, including the **House of the Ephebus** and the **House of the Knight,** have impressive mosaics of Dionysus, Hercules, Orpheus, and other mythical figures. From the top of the hill is an amazing panoramic view of Volubilis. The **Tangier Gate,** with the **Gordien Palace** just before it, is atop the hill. Walk down the hill and head toward the only tree in front. Under it is the **Cortege of Venus,** which holds several mosaics including *Chariot Race*, *Bacchus Surrounded by the Four Seasons*, *Diana Bathing*, and the *Abduction of Hylas by Nymphs*, all dating as far back as the late 2nd or early 3rd century AD. Cross the stream back to the ticket gate to see the ruins of a **Temple** dedicated to Jupiter, Juno, and Minerva.

The ruins are open daily sunrise to sunset (admission 20dh; bring exact change). They are more peaceful and scenic in the early morning or late afternoon. Be sure to bring a hat, sunscreen, water, and sunglasses (if possible) if you are visiting in

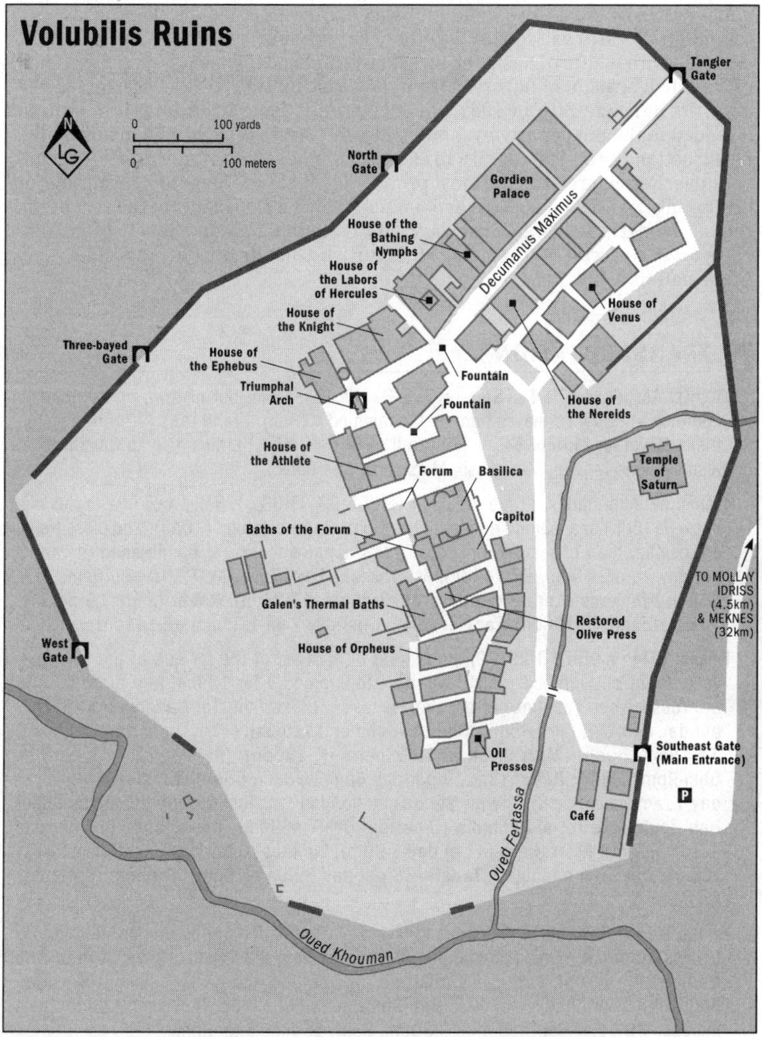

MOROCCO

the afternoon, as the sun can be ferocious. You may be nearly alone at the ruins; the isolation makes you feel like you've stumbled on the ruins yourself. Bring a picnic; there is only one small, overpriced cafe. Volubilis is one place where you might seriously consider hiring a guide (through the ticket office for roughly 20-30dh per person)—placards labeling sights are very brief.

FEZ فاس ☎055

Fez's bustling, colorful medina epitomizes Morocco—no visit to the country is complete without seeing it. Artisans bang out sheets of brass, donkeys strain under crates of Coca-Cola, children balance trays of dough on their heads, and tourist groups struggle to stay together. The scent of *brochettes* on open grills combine with whiffs of hash, the sweet aroma of cedar shavings, and the stench of fresh fish brought at daybreak from the coast. Since UNESCO designated Fez a World Heritage Site in 1981, the city's walls have been largely restored. Founded in the 8th century by Moulay Idriss I, Fez rose to prominence with the construction in the 9th century of the Qairaouine, one of the world's first universities. Fez emerged as the most prominent city in the Maghreb, nurturing (or destroying) political dynasties and handing down legal rulings to the rest of the region. Modern Fez is an expansive city containing a conspicuously middle-class *ville nouvelle*, but remains at the artistic, intellectual and spiritual helm of the nation.

TRANSPORTATION

Flights: Aérodrome de Fès-Saïs (☎055 62 47 12), 12km out of town on the road to Immouzzèr. Bus #16 leaves from pl. Mohammed V (3dh). *Grand taxis* (120dh) also run there. **Royal Air Maroc,** 54 av. Hassan II (☎055 62 55 16), flies daily to **Casablanca.** Also services Tangier, Marrakesh, Marseilles, and Paris.

Trains: av. Almohades, at rue Chenguit (☎055 93 03 33), a 5min. taxi ride to the *ville nouvelle* (5dh) or a 10min. ride to the medina's Bab Boujeloud (10dh). 2nd-class trains are comfier than buses and only cost a few dirhams more. To: **Casablanca** (4½hr., 8 per day 7am-2:45am, 97-144dh); **Marrakesh** (9hr., 7per day 7:15am-2:40am, 171-255dh); **Meknes** (1hr., 8 per day 7am-2:45am, 17-24dh); **Rabat** (3½hr., 8 per day 7am-2:45am, 72-106dh); **Tangier** (5hr., 4 per day 7am-1:35am, 96-141dh).

Buses: CTM (☎055 73 29 92) stops near pl. d'Atlas, at the far end of the *ville nouvelle.* From pl. Florence, walk down bd. Mohammed V for 15min. and turn left onto av. Youssef ben Tachfine. At pl. d'Atlas, take the 1st right. To: **Casablanca** (5hr., 9 per day 6am-2:30am, 85dh); **Chefchaouen** and **Tetouan** (4hr., 2 per day 11am and 11:45pm, 50dh); **Marrakesh** (8hr., 2 per day, 130dh); **Meknes** (1hr., 7 per day 6am-9pm, 18dh); **Rabat** (3hr., 9 per day 6am-2:30am, 55dh); **Tangier** (6hr., 3 per day 11am-1am, 85dh). The private bus station in Fez is just outside the medina near Bab Boujeloud. To: **al-Rachidia** (5 per day 7:30am-9pm); **Casablanca** (25 per day 4:30am-1pm); **Marrakesh** (4 per day 3-9pm); **Meknes** (6 per day 6am-8pm); **Rabat** (16 per day 5am-midnight); **Tangier** (8 per day 6:30am-10pm); **Tetouan** (3 per day 6am-8pm).

Public Transportation: Pl. Mohammed V and pl. Résistance are the major hubs for city buses. Important routes include: bus #9 and 11 from the Syndicat d'Initiative to **Bab Boujeloud** and **Dar Batha;** #3 from the train station and pl. Mohammed V to **Bab Ftouh;** #4 from pl. Résistance to **Bab Smarine** in Fez al-Jdid. They cost 2.20dh; fares increase 20% July-Sept. 15 after 8:30pm, Sept. 16-June after 8pm.

Car Rental: Avis, 50 bd. Chefchaouni (☎055 62 67 46). **Hertz,** 1 Kissauiat de la Foire (☎055 62 28 12). Open M-Sa 8:30am-noon and 2-6:30pm, Su 9am-noon. Both agencies charge 250-500dh per day with a 20% tax, not including mileage. Min. age 25 for all cars except the smallest ones (Fiat Palio or Uno), for which the minimum age is 23, though many offices don't ask for proof of age. An international license is not required.

Taxis: Some prices are fixed, such as *grand taxis* to: Meknes (400dh); Rabat (800dh); Volubilis/Moulay Idriss (800 round-trip). A loop of Fez and around the medina costs 200dh. See the tourist office if you have questions. Stands at the post office, Syndicat d'Initiative, Bab Boujeloud, and Bab Guissa. *Petit taxis* should always use a meter. Fares increase 50% July-Sept. 15 after 8:30pm, Sept. 16-June after 8pm.

ORIENTATION AND PRACTICAL INFORMATION

Fez is large and spread out but still manageable. It is essentially three cities in one: the fashionable, French-built **ville nouvelle,** 1.5km from the medina; the Arab **Fez al-Jdid** ("New Fez"), containing the Jewish cemetery and the palace of Hassan II, next to the medina; and the enormous medina of **Fez al-Bali** ("Old Fez") housing nearly 500,000 residents. The *ville nouvelle* is most convenient for services and has the quietest accommodations; its two central streets are **av. Hassan II** and **bd. Mohammed V,** which intersect at **pl. Florence,** the center of activity. Walking down av. Moulay Youssef from the *ville nouvelle* brings you to pl. Alaouites in Fez al-Jdid, directly in front of the king's palace, **Dar al-Makhzen.** After passing through Bab Smarine on the left, rue Fez al-Jdid takes you the length of the palace. At the end, a right through Bab Dakakeen leads to Fez al-Bali and its main gate **Bab Boujeloud.** The two main streets of Fez al-Bali are **Tala'a Kebira** and **Tala'a Seghira,** although they are barely wide enough for its shops, a donkey, and your backpack.

Tourist Office: Syndicat d'Initiative, pl. Mohammed V (☎055 62 34 60). Helpful *Fassi* (citizens of Fez) answer almost any question. Limited English spoken. Same meager maps from the Moroccan National Tourism Office. Hire official local guides here for 120dh for half-day or 150dh for full-day; national guides for 150dh for half-day, 250dh for full day. Open M-F 8:30am-noon and 2:30-6:30pm, Sa 8:30am-noon.

Currency Exchange: BMCE, pl. Mohammed V, opposite the Syndicat d'Initiative and to the right of the main bank entrance. Handles MC/V and traveler's checks transactions and has **ATMs.** Open M-F 8:15am-2:15pm. **Sheraton Fez Hôtel,** at the end of av. Hassan II, 4 blocks from the post office, has after-hours exchange.

Luggage Storage: At the train station. 2.50dh per bag per day. Open 24hr. Also at the CTM station. 5dh per bag per day. Open 24hr.

Police: ☎19.

Late-Night Pharmacy: Municipalité de Fès, av. Moulay Youssef (☎055 62 33 80), off Pl. Résistance, 5min. uphill from the royal palace. Open daily 8pm-8am.

Hospital: Ghastani (☎055 62 27 76), at the end of av. Hassan II.

Internet Access: There are several Internet cafes in the *ville nouvelle;* just look for the "Cyber" sign. One of them is **Soprocon,** off pl. Florence, upstairs from a teleboutique. 10dh per hr. Open daily 9am-11pm.

Post Office: At the corner of av. Hassan II and bd. Mohammed V in the *ville nouvelle.* **Branch offices** at pl. d'Atlas and in the medina at pl. Batha. All open July-Sept. 15 M-F 8:30am-2:30pm; Sept. 16-June M-F 8:30am-12:15pm and 2:30-6:30pm.

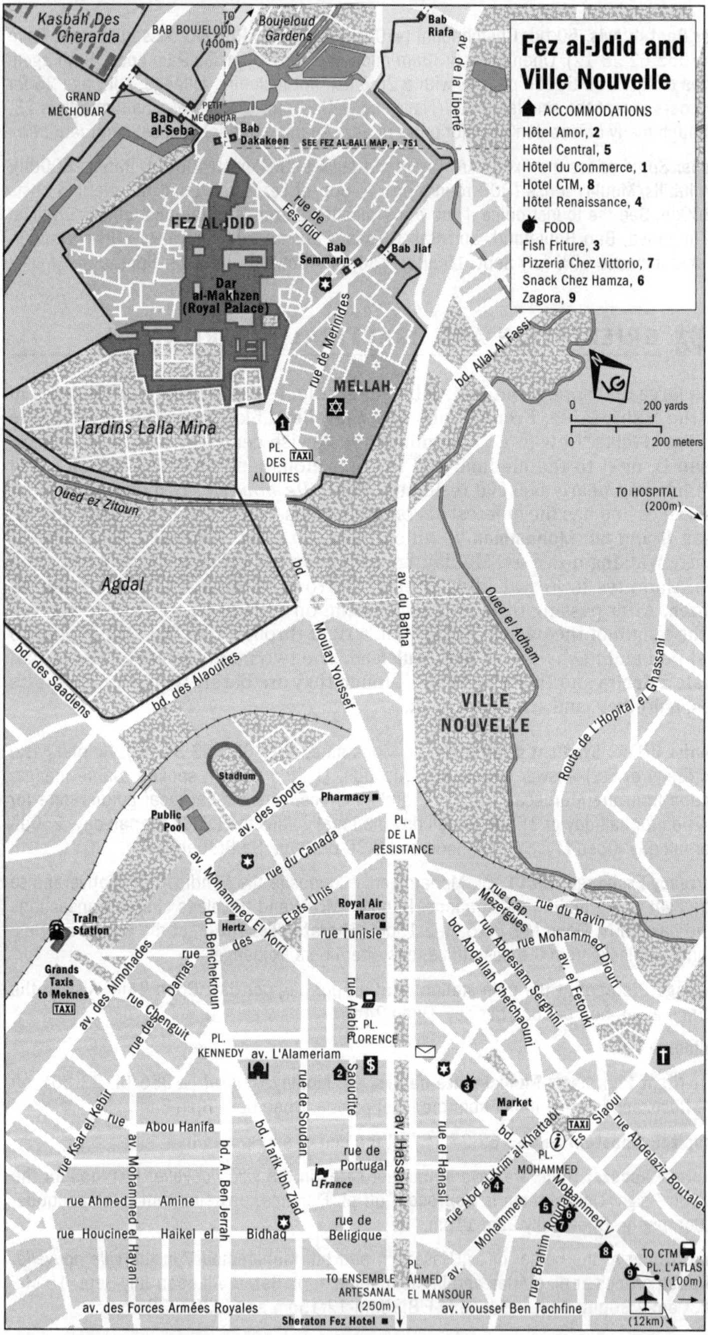
Fez al-Jdid and Ville Nouvelle
ACCOMMODATIONS
Hôtel Amor, 2
Hôtel Central, 5
Hôtel du Commerce, 1
Hotel CTM, 8
Hôtel Renaissance, 4
FOOD
Fish Friture, 3
Pizzeria Chez Vittorio, 7
Snack Chez Hamza, 6
Zagora, 9
0 200 yards
0 200 meters
Kasbah Des Cherarda
TO BAB BOUJELOUD (400m)
Boujeloud Gardens
Bab Riafa
GRAND MÉCHOUAR
PETIT MÉCHOUAR
Bab al-Seba
Bab Dakakeen
SEE FEZ AL-BALI MAP, p. 751
av. de la Liberté
FEZ AL-JDID
rue de Fes Jdid
Bab Semmarin
Bab Jiaf
Dar al-Makhzen (Royal Palace)
rue de Merinides
MELLAH
bd. Allal Al Fassi
Jardins Lalla Mina
PL. DES ALOUITES
TAXI
Oued ez Zitoun
TO HOSPITAL (200m)
Agdal
bd. Moulay Youssef
av. du Batha
Oued el Adham
bd. des Saadiens
bd. des Alaouites
VILLE NOUVELLE
Route de L'Hopital el Ghassani
Stadium
Public Pool
av. des Sports
Pharmacy
PL. DE LA RESISTANCE
rue du Canada
av. Mohammed El Korri
des Etats Unis
Royal Air Maroc
rue Tunisie
Hertz
rue du Ravin
rue Cap. Mezergues
rue Abdeslam Serghini
rue Mohammed Diouri
av. el Fetouki
bd. Abdallah Chefchaouni
bd. Benchekroun
Train Station
Grands Taxis to Meknes
av. des Almohades
rue Damas
rue des Chenguit
rue Arabie
PL. FLORENCE
PL. KENNEDY
av. L'Alameriam
Saoudite
rue de Soudan
av. Hassan II
rue el Hanasli
Market
bd. Abd al-Krim al-Khattabi
Es Slaoui
rue Abdelaziz Boutaleb
PL. MOHAMMED
Mohammed V
rue Ksar el Kebir
rue Abou Hanifa
av. Mohammed el Hayani
bd. A. Ben Jerrah
bd. Tarik ibn Ziad
rue de Portugal
France
rue Ahmed Amine
rue Houcine Haikel el Bidhaq
rue de Beligique
av. Mohammed
rue Brahim Roudani
TO CTM
PL. L'ATLAS (100m)
(12km)
TO ENSEMBLE ARTESANAL (250m)
PL. AHMED EL MANSOUR
av. des Forces Armées Royales
av. Youssef Ben Tachfine
Sheraton Fez Hotel

MOROCCO

ACCOMMODATIONS

VILLE NOUVELLE

Rooms here are convenient to local services and more comfortable than those in the medina. The cheapest lodgings are just off bd. Mohammed V, between av. Mohammed al-Slaoui near the bus station and av. Hassan II near the post office.

Hôtel Central, 50 rue Brahim Roudani (☎055 62 23 33), off pl. Mohammed V. Clean rooms with better-than-average furnishings. Singles 59dh, with shower 89dh; doubles 89dh/119dh; triples 150dh/180dh. ❷

Hôtel Amor, 31 rue Arabie Saoudite (☎055 62 27 24), off pl. Florence. A good choice for those with a little more to spend. All rooms are clean, nicely furnished, and have private bath. Singles 164dh; doubles 198dh. ❹

Hotel CTM (☎055 62 28 11), off bd. Mohammed V, between pl. Mohammed V and the CTM bus station. Look for the huge sign on the pinkish wall. Clean and cheap rooms with rock-hard beds. Singles 60dh, with shower 80dh; doubles 80dh/100dh. ❷

Hôtel Renaissance, 29 rue Abd al-Krim al-Khattabi (☎055 62 21 93), just before pl. Mohammed V coming from pl. Florence down at the end of the pedestrian walkway. All rooms have a window or a view of the terrace. Squat toilets. Hot showers 6dh. Singles 50dh; doubles 90dh; triples 120dh; quads 140dh. ❶

FEZ AL-JDID

Fez al-Jdid has only one hotel of note, but the location is perfect—close to the medina without the annoyance of hustlers.

Hôtel du Commerce, pl. Alaouites (☎055 62 22 31), by the Royal Palace. Friendly owners, comfortable rooms, and affordable prices. Offers views of palace grounds. Cold showers. Singles 50dh; doubles 90dh. ❶

FEZ AL-BALI

Head to the area around the Bab Boujeloud for budget rooms. Although accommodations are less pleasant than those in the *ville nouvelle*, and hustlers may seem to have tourist radar, they're still perfect for that 24hr. medina experience.

Hôtel Cascade, 26 Serrajine Boujeloud (☎055 63 84 42), just inside Bab Boujeloud and to the right. Friendly staff, free hot showers, free luggage storage, a modern toilet, a tap for hand-washing clothes, and a laundry service (30dh for 15-20 pieces). Popular with backpackers and families. Rooms are clean and basic. The terrace provides a bird's-eye view of Bab Boujeloud and the medina. 50dh per person; terrace 20dh. ❶

Hôtel Lamrani, Tala'a Seghira (☎055 63 44 11). Enter Bab Boujeloud; take the 1st right, then left and through the arch. Unusually clean, with in-room sinks. Head here when the Cascade is full. Nearby *hammam* 6dh. Singles 40-60dh; doubles 80-120dh; triples 150-180dh. ❶

Hôtel Erraha (☎055 63 32 26). Follow the alley on the right of the cafe just before Bab Boujeloud. Basic rooms. Singles 50dh; doubles 80dh; triples 120dh. ❶

Hôtel Mauritania, 20 Serrajine Boujeloud (☎055 63 35 18), to the right after the Bab Boujeloud. Small rooms. Hot showers 10dh. Singles 60dh; doubles 120dh. ❷

FOOD

VILLE NOUVELLE

Cheap sandwich dives, cafes, and juice shops line both sides of bd. Mohammed V. The *ville nouvelle* is stricken with more than its fair share of western-style fast food joints that offer a time-out for those overwhelmed by real Moroccan fare.

IN RECENT NEWS

BEASTS OF BURDEN

For many first-time visitors to Fez, the overwhelming presence of donkeys is as novel a sight as the ancient, labyrinthine streets of the medina. The animals carry everything from fruit and fish to crates of Coca-Cola and old televisions. But more than medieval relics of a time before technological advancement, the abundance of overworked and under-fed animals, with their open sores and bruises, is a testament to the present-day levels of poverty in Morocco.

As the cheapest form of animal power, the donkey is within the reach of even the poorest of the poor, often constituting a substantial part of family wealth. In a country where 47% of the population works in agriculture, and nearly as many work in the markets, the unhealthy conditions of the donkeys pose an omnipresent threat to the livelihood of working families, as well as an immediate risk to the animals' lives.

The Society for the Protection of Animals in North Africa (SPANA) is working to combat these problems. Founded in 1923, SPANA targets the biggest problems–insufficient funds to care for the animals, general ignorance, and neglect–with education and veterinary care. They have produced a teachers' handbook in Arabic that is now used in over 4500 primary schools, and have trained teachers from different regions to give lessons in environmental education. Working from base clinics, veterinary technicians visit markets or villages every day, where they will see up to 1000 donkeys, horses, and mules daily.

For those in search of local eats, poke through stalls of fresh food at the **central market** on bd. Mohammed V, two blocks up from pl. Mohammed V. (Open daily 7am-1pm.)

Restaurant Fish Friture, 138 bd. Mohammed V (☎055 94 06 99), tucked away off bd. Mohammed V, near pl. de Florence. A small and relaxing maritime-themed restaurant with friendly service. Good for lunch or dinner with excellent fish brochettes (60dh) and other Moroccan standards (entrees 35-50dh; set *menús* up to 130dh). Open daily 10am-3pm and 6pm-midnight. MC/V. ❷

Zagora, 5 bd. Mohammed V (☎055 94 06 86), in a shopping center behind Au Derby Shoe store. Look for the red neon sign. Elegant, air-conditioned restaurant with Moroccan fare. Set *menú* includes soup or puff pastry, couscous, brochettes or chicken pastilla, and dessert (140dh). Open 9:30am-11:30pm. MC/V. ❺

Pizzeria Chez Vittorio, 21 rue Brahim Roudania (☎055 62 47 30), just down from Hotel Central. This dark, cool restaurant with charming Italian countryside decor serves beer, wine, and spirits. Pizzas, ravioli, and spaghetti 45-50dh. Meat entrees 90-100dh. ❸

Snack Chez Hamza, 25 rue Brahim Roudani (☎055 93 02 14), across the street from Hotel Central. Pleasant, clean stop for fresh sandwiches or brochettes. ❶

FEZ AL-BALI

Food stalls line Tala'a Kebira and Tala'a Seghira, near the Bab Boujeloud entrance to Fez al-Bali and a couple minutes further down. A feast of *harira* (spicy lentil soup), roasted peppers and eggplant, potato fritters, and bread will only set you back 10dh at the stalls inside, while a good *kefta* (ground meat) sandwich goes for 15dh. Directly across from Hotel Cascade and Restaurant des Jeunes by Bab Boujeloud, **La Kasbah** ❷ has a pleasant rooftop terrace perfect for a quiet meal (*tajine* and couscous 40dh; 60dh for the house specialty *pastilla*). For some of the cheapest eateries in Morocco, go left from Tala'a Kebira at Madrasa al-Atarrine (see p. 751), and head into the medina toward pl. Achabine. Also, consider splurging on one of the Moroccan specialty restaurants listed below.

Restaurant des Jeunes, 16 rue Serrajine (☎055 63 49 75), next to Hotel Cascade. A tourist favorite. Regional favorites. Set *menú* 35dh. Open daily 6am-midnight. ❶

Restaurant Asmae, 4 Derb Jeniara (☎055 741 210), located near the Qairouine Mosque. Choose from 10 4-course meals (120-250dh). Open daily noon-midnight. ❺

Restaurant Dar Jamai, 14 Foundouk Lihoudi (☎055 63 56 85), 100m from the Palais Jamai. Traditional feasting and royal treatment at affordable prices in this pillow-filled hideaway. 4-course *menú* 100dh. Open daily noon-11pm. ❹

SIGHTS

FEZ AL-BALI

Fez's medina is the handicraft capital of the country. With over 9000 streets and nearly 500,000 residents, the crowded medina is possibly the most difficult to navigate in all Morocco. But it is also the most rewarding, containing fabulous mosques, *madrassas*, *souqs*, and unparalleled frenzy. Craftsmen work at trades completely untouched by modern industry and machinery. The medina is quieter and less crowded between noon and 3pm. If you definitely want to make a purchase at the medina, it's best to wait until after 5pm, when shop owners will be more flexible with prices for some quick money before closing.

WITH A GUIDE. This approach is simple and recommended in spite of the cost: hire an official guide. **Official guides** are available at the Syndicat d'Initiative. They'll save you time, discourage hustlers, and provide detailed explanations. (Don't assume that they'll help you bargain for goods, though.) You can choose between a local or national guide for either a half-day (3hr.) or full-day (5+hr.) tour. Both types are adequate, though national guides have earned a higher qualification and therefore can provide tours of the whole country. Local guides cost 120-150dh and national guides 150-200dh. Based in Fez, national guide Hassan Elkhader is highly recommended (☎067 33 44 11). He offers friendly and informative tours of Fez in English or French. Though much cheaper, **unofficial guides** are illegal, often lack historical knowledge, and usually take travelers only to shops from which they will get a 25% commission. Whichever type of guide you hire, nail down an itinerary and price beforehand and establish your aversion to shopping.

WITHOUT A GUIDE. To keep hustlers and merchants at bay, ignore calls or hisses and simply say "non, merci" or "la shukran" to those who approach you directly. Remember: walking downhill will take you farther into the medina, while trekking uphill will lead you out to Bab Boujeloud. Without a guide, there are two classic approaches to exploring the medina. The first is to head to the main gateway Bab Boujeloud and wander down **Tala'a Kebira** from there. Virtually all of the sights in Fez's medina lie along the Tala'a Kebira (or the Grand Tala'a), old Fez's main street and an essential reference point for anyone attempting to navigate the medina. The Tala'a Kebira heads downhill from Bab Boujeloud to the Qairaouine Mosque area. The **Bab Boujeloud** is the main entrance to the medina; faux guides tend to gather here. Once you pass the gate, however, they will tend to leave you alone. Built in 1912 by the Frenchman Maréchal Lauyote to gain the confidence of the locals, the *bab* is tiled in blue on one side (the color of Fez) and green on the other (the favorite color of Mohammed and consequently the color most identified with Islam). The square just inside the *bab* is where the Moroccan revolution against the French occupation began. Down to the right is the **Tala'a Seghira,** Fez's other main street, lined mostly by shops catering to locals (i.e., the famed underwear *souq*). The second classic approach is to taxi inside the medina to the more centrally located **Place Rsif** nearby the Qaraouine Mosque. This choice puts you right near the center of the sights described below. The final option, though you'll be vulnerable to hustlers, is simply to get lost in the magnificent atmosphere that is Fez's medina. When you're done, ask merchants or women how to get to Tala'a Kebira and follow it back uphill to Bab Boujeloud.

BARGAINING FOR DUMMIES You'll have to do it for everything from carpets to camel treks, so you might as well do it right. Know that you never have to buy anything just because you look in the shop; feel free to say nothing interests you, and move on. Once you've found something you want, let the shopkeeper be the first to offer a price. You'll be expected to make a counter-offer; don't be intimidated by the shopkeeper's enthusiasm or claim that he's "making you a good price." Decide what you want to ultimately pay (anywhere from one-tenth to half of the initial price) then offer one-third to half of *that*. The shopkeeper may respond by laughing or calling you a Berber (the true skinflints), at which point you may choose to politely but firmly walk out. (Generally, you should leave at least once when haggling over a big purchase.) Invariably, you will be dragged back in. You can gauge the seller's willingness to negotiate by how quickly (and by how much) he drops his price. If you're with a friend, it can be useful to play good-cop/bad-cop with the storekeeper, one of you always saying the item is too expensive or that you need to move on. If you're at an impasse, you can try any of the following: 1) You've seen the same thing elsewhere for X (lower) price. 2) You like it but it's flawed; point out blemishes. 3) You're a student/budget traveler (sellers scale their prices to what you look like you can pay). 4) Tell them you've made your final offer.

In larger *souqs*, the same goods are often available at several stores, so don't be afraid to try a couple of negotiations until you find a price you like. By the fourth haggle of your day, you will be much more comfortable. Be wary of shopkeepers trying to sell you something that is somehow "unique"–there are no special years, months, or weeks on the calendar of Berber carpet makers, so don't pay as if there were.

BOU INANIA MADRASA. At the head of the main thoroughfare Tala'a Kebira is the spectacular Bou Inania Madrasa and mosque, a school built in 1326 for teaching the Qur'an and Islamic sciences. The intricacy of the cedar and stucco work make this arguably the best *madrasa* in Morocco and perhaps even the world. Classes were held in the courtyard and the adjacent salons, and students lived three or four to a 2x2m cell on the upper floor. When the Merenid Sultan Abou Inan was presented with the totals for the construction, he threw them into the canal, claiming that no price tag could be placed on beauty. *(Closed for renovations in 2002; reopening date uncertain. Open daily 9am-5:30pm. 10dh.)*

MOROCCO

FUNDUQS. Plunging ahead down Tala'a Kebira, you'll notice a series of *funduqs* (old inns now used as factories) on the left side. First is the drum *funduq*, where skins are stretched over hoops to produce the right tone. Next is the *funduq* for honey, olive oil, and butter, which was formerly a mental hospital. Last, you'll sniff the products of the **sheepskin funduq,** just after the parking lot on the left.

NEJJARINE MUSEUM OF ART. The easiest way to get to the **place Nejjarine,** with its tiled fountain, is to go all the way down Tala'a Seghira until it turns into Tala'a Kebira. Turn around, facing the direction you just came from, and go down the steps that are about 10m in front of you. At the bottom of the steps, follow the path to the small square; the museum is just off this small courtyard. The displays are of tools, instruments, decorated doors, etc. Today, its rooftop **salon de thé** (tea room) offers a tranquil escape from the rushing traffic of peddlers and tourists, as do its bathrooms, Morocco's finest. *(Open daily 10am-5pm. 10dh.)*

SPICE SOUQ AND OTHER MARKETS. Back on the Tala'a Kebira, the **Attarine (Spice) Souq,** perhaps the most exotic market, awaits. Off to the right at the beginning of the spice *souq* is the **Henna Souq,** which sells the plant used to temporarily tattoo women at weddings. At the far end is the **Maristan Sidi Frej,** which was built in 1286, where the depressed were treated with music, sexual stimulation, and herbs and spices. It was the model for the first Western psychiatric hospitals in southern Spain. Toward the end of the Attarine Souq are passageways leading into a **cloth market,** selling slippers and *djellabas* (robes), and a **dried fruit market.**

MADRASA AL-ATTARINE. The Tala'a Kebira ends at Madrasa al-Attarine, which dates from 1324. Though often overlooked by visitors, this could be the most peaceful place in the old city. Built by Abou Siad, a Merenid, it is one of the smallest *madrasas* in Morocco, but is notable for its details and mosaics. The intricacies of the carvings are spectacular—they rival the Bou Inania's both in beauty and in style. *(Open daily June-Aug. 9am-6pm; Sept.-May 9am-5pm. 10dh.)*

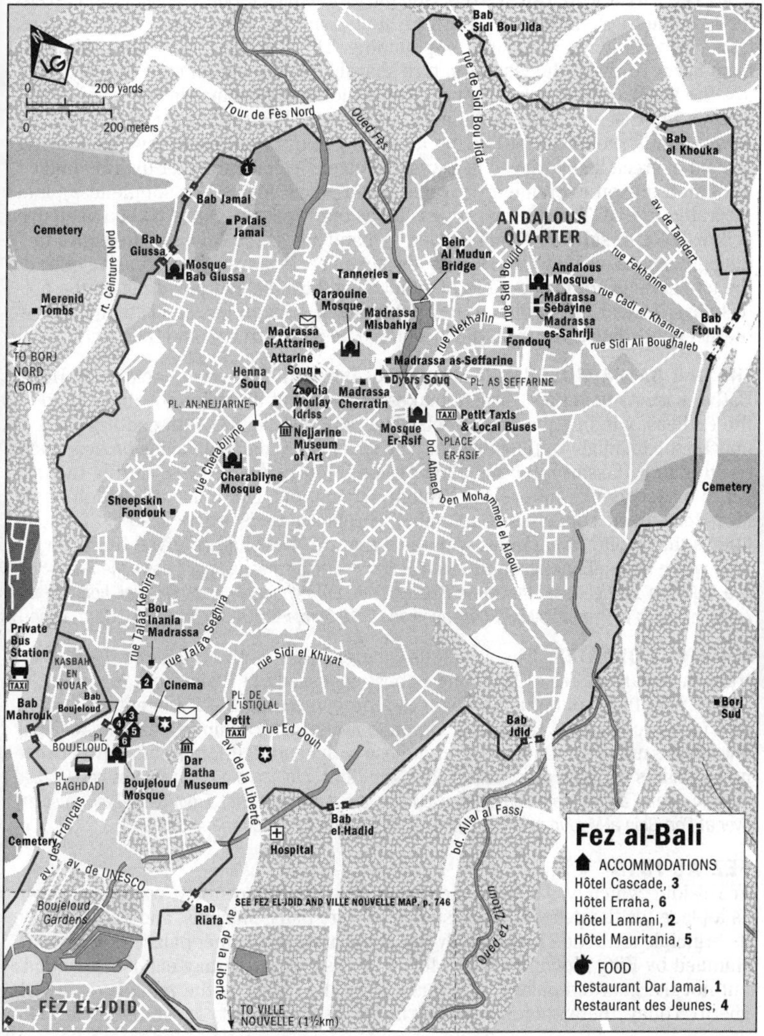

MOROCCO

QAIRAOUINE MOSQUE. Exiting the *madrasa*, turn left, and then left again; a few meters down is a little opening into the Qairaouine mosque. It contains 14 gates, six fountains (3 for men and 3 for women), and can hold up to 20,000 worshippers (second only to Hassan II in Casablanca). Founded in 857 by Fatima al-Fihri, a woman, the mosque is also one of the oldest universities in the world. It trained students in logic, math, rhetoric, and the Qur'an, while Europe stumbled through the Dark Ages. You can thank (or curse) the mosque for educating Pope Sylvester II, who introduced algebra and the modern number system. Non-Muslims can take pictures through the portals but may not enter. Its library, off-limits to tourists, holds what some think is the oldest manuscript of the Qur'an in North Africa.

METAL SOUQ AND TANNERIES. Keeping the mosque on the right, you'll eventually come to pl. Seffarine, known for its fascinating **metal souq,** which deafens travelers with incessant cauldron-pounding. There are several potential routes from here. To reach the **tanneries**, turn sharply left and continue to bear left (follow the worn, 6-sided cobblestones). Once the smell becomes intense, head right down a microscopic alley (a tannery *"guardien"* has probably grabbed you by now; 10dh is the basic fee). From a balcony above, you may view skins being soaked in green liquid, rinsed in a washing machine/cement-mixer hybrid, dunked in diluted pigeon excrement or waterlogged wheat husks (for suppleness), and saturated in dye. The dyeing process takes one week (except for the expensive yellow color of saffron, which is dyed by hand and takes 2 days). The entire tanning process takes up to two weeks for one piece. Beware—the pervasive odor of the tanneries is not for the faint of stomach and can be overpowering on the hottest days. To exit the medina or reach **Bab al-Rcif,** a major bus and cab hub, follow the street heading away from the mosque to its end, turn left, and then right.

THE DAR BATHA MUSEUM. The beautiful Dar Batha Museum, located by Hotel Batha, with its well-kept garden, makes an excellent diversion for those tired of the endless, winding medina streets. The building itself, a 19th-century palace, may be the highlight of the museum. The spacious Andalucian mansion headquartered Sultan Hassan I and his playboy son, Moulay Abd al-Aziz, during the last years of decadence before the French occupation. The museum, which hosts Moroccan music concerts in September, chronicles Fez's artistic history. The keynote is the display of ceramics with the signature "Fez blue" (derived from cobalt) on a white enamel background. *(Start at Bab Boujeloud, head straight down the Tala'a Seghira, take the 1st right past the movie theater, then turn right again at pl. l'Istiqlal, home to the museum. Open W-Th and Sa-M 8:30am-noon and 2:30-6pm, F 8:30-11:30am and 3-6pm. 10dh.)*

ANDALOUS QUARTER. The Andalous Quarter is across the Oued Fez (Fez River) from the heart of Fez al-Bali, and is best accessed via Place Rcif. Many of the Moors who fled from Muslim Spain to Morocco during the 15th-century *Reconquista* settled around the grand Almohad house of worship in Fez, the **Andalous Mosque.** Its main attraction is the grandiose 13th-century doorway, mainly because non-Muslims can't go any further than the door. *(To find the mosque, cross pl. Rcif, go through a small arched gate, turn right, and follow the wall on the right. From Fez al-Bali, cross the river at Port Bein al-Mudun near the tanneries and head straight down rue Seffrah.)*

FEZ AL-JDID

Fez al-Jdid, which was built by the Merenids in the 13th century, was once known as a place for the peaceful coexistence of Christians, Muslims, and Jews. Today, its principle attraction is the gaudy **Dar al-Makhzen,** the former palace of Hassan II, shunned by King Mohammed VI's for its excess. Tourists may enter the grounds but not the guarded palace, of course. Near the palace is the *mellah* or Jewish ghetto. Today, there are few Jews left in Fez, as the majority left for Israel in 1948.

The placement of the ghetto near to the palace is not arbitrary as here the Jews could be easily protected and, more importantly, easily taxed. Diagonally off the plaza, grande rue des Merinides runs up to Bab Smarine and its seven bronze gates installed by King Hassan II in 1968. Just before the beginning of the main street is a peaceful, 17th-century **Jewish cemetery,** the resting place for over 12,000 people. *(Cemetery open daily dawn-dusk; free, though a donation may be requested.)* Off this boulevard, the meter-wide streets open into miniature underground tailors' shops, and half-timbered houses. The **jewelers' souq** glitters at the top of grande rue des Merinides. Cackling chickens, salty fish, and dried okra abound in the **covered market,** inside Bab Smarine at the entrance to Fez al-Jdid proper.

Bear left at the end of rue des Fez al-Jdid into the **Petit Méchouar;** on the left is **Bab Dakakeen,** the back entrance to the Dar al-Makhzen. **Bab al-Seba,** an imperial gate, opens onto the **Grand Méchouar,** a roomy plaza lined with street lamps. From here it's an easy walk to Bab Boujeloud—turn through the opening to the right of Bab al-Seba, continue straight for 250m, veer to the right, and pass through a large arch at the end of the road. The entrance to the refreshing **Boujeloud Gardens,** a refuge from the midday sun, is on the right. *(Open Tu-Su. Free.)* The gardens were a gift from Hassan I to the people of the medina. Inside is the delightful **Café Restaurant Noria,** known as Lovers' Café, a pleasant place for female travelers (as well as male) to relax under the grape-leaf arbor. Coffee 5dh. Couscous 35dh. **Bab Boujeloud** lies another 300m down the street.

OUTSIDE THE MEDINA

For fantastic views of Fez, head to the hills on either side of the city. The ramparts of Borj Nord (Arms Museum), the Merenid Tombs, and the Palais des Merenides provide good vantage points. All three are located on the same hill overlooking Fez. Be careful after dark, as aggressive hustlers are known to frequent the area.

BORJ NORD AND THE MERENID TOMBS. To reach Borj Nord and the nearby tombs (they can be spotted from the ground), grab a *petit taxi* from the medina (5dh) or exit the medina through a small gate to the right on pl. Baghdadi when walking from Bab Boujeloud toward Fez al-Jdid. Turn right on the main road, walk past the bus station 200m, then take a small path that winds its way up the hillside; the tombs are to the right and Borj Nord is to the left. The **Palais des Merenides,** a five-star hotel, overlooks the tombs from one of the most picturesque hillsides in the Maghreb. From here, the medina reveals itself with the delicate beauty that inspired Paul Bowles and countless other Orientalist writers. The panorama is particularly impressive in the half-light of dawn or dusk; during calls to prayer, when over a hundred *muezzin* summon the faithful, the experience is almost mystical.

SHOPPING AND CRAFTS

The medina of Fez is world-famous, particularly for its twice-baked blue pottery and tannery. In general, try to get an idea of prices before heading into a shop and don't be afraid to walk away once inside. Quality of products—from *djellabas* (the hooded garment) to rugs—can vary widely. Don't pay top dollar for something that's a dirham a dozen (for more bargaining strategy, see **Bargaining 101,** p. 750). The following quality shops are located in the medina, with the exception of the pottery shop. They are as interesting for their managers and buildings as they are for their products. If you're looking to buy, discreetly return without your guide to avoid commission charges.

Société Fakhkhari, 16 Quartier des Potiers, Route Sidi Harazem (☎055 64 93 22), outside the medina in the hills by Borj Sud. Take a tour (ask for Ahmed) of fascinating work areas and buy a fresh piece of pottery from the 450° oven. A *petit taxi* here 7-10dh.

MOROCCO

Berber House, 51 Derb Sidi Moussa (☎055 74 12 68). From Zaouia Moulay Idriss II, turn left after the wooden bar and go straight for 50m. Specializes in Berber tribe blankets and *kilims* and sells cheaper blankets made on location. Open daily 9am-9pm.

El Haj Ali Baba, 10 Hay Lablida (☎055 63 66 25). This shop offers wonderful views of the enormous tannery and dye wells below and sells a vast array of goods.

Dar Zaouia, 4 Derb Jeniara Blida (☎055 63 55 12). A 15th-century house now filled with modern rugs and Berber *kilims* instead of harems. Open daily 8:30am-7:30pm.

Herboriste Ibn Sina, 6 Fondouk Lihoudi Zaouia (☎055 63 74 17). Herbal medicine recipes kept in the family and dispensed in little bottles. Open daily 8am-9pm.

L'Art Islamique, 36 Derb Touil (☎055 74 12 04). Berber jewelry, Judaica, and antiques. Open daily 8am-7:30pm.

THE ATLANTIC COAST

The towns along Morocco's Atlantic coast are undoubtedly more laid-back than their conservative cousins in the interior. Men and women alike sunbathe, swim, surf, and windsurf. The west coast contains Morocco's industrial boom towns—Casablanca, the country's commercial center, and Rabat, its most westernized city—which, while very much part of the modern country, are avoided by those with limited time in their itinerary. If you're headed to the coast, your best bets are the peaceful and tranquil smaller cities like Essaouira and Asilah.

ASILAH أصيلة ☎039

Just a short trip from Tangier, Asilah offers sandy shores, a laid-back atmosphere, and a brilliant, clean medina. Over the last 1000 years, every European power from the Vikings to the French have sent flotillas, armies, and even a crusade to wrench tiny Asilah from Moroccan hands, but rarely did Europeans last more than a generation or two before being sent packing. Except for the international art festival (the first 2 weeks in Aug.), Asilah is a peaceful spot for Atlantic sun-soaking.

TRANSPORTATION. The **train station** (☎039 41 73 27) is a 25min. walk from town on the Tangier highway, past a strip of campgrounds. To get to town from the station, simply follow the road by the beach, keeping the sea to the right. A taxi to town costs about 10dh. **Trains** run to: **Casablanca** (6hr., 3 per day 8:35am-11:35pm, 101-150dh); **Fez** (5-6hr., 4 per day 7:45am-11pm, 81-119dh); **Marrakesh** (9hr., 3 per day 8:35am-11:35pm, 174-259dh); **Meknes** (4-5hr., 4 per day 8:35am-11:35pm, 65-94dh); **Rabat** (5hr., 4 per day 8:35am-11:35pm, 77dh); and **Tangier** (40min., 4 per day 5:30am-9:25pm, 14-20dh). **CTM Buses** run to: **Casablanca** via **Rabat** (4½-5½hr., 11:45am and 5:15pm, 60dh); **Marrakesh** continuing on to **Agadir** (9hr., another 4hr. to Agadir; 5:15pm; 130dh); **Meknes** via **Fez** (3½hr.-4½hr., 3:45 and 7:45pm, 55dh); and **Tangier** (1hr., 12:15 and 4:15pm; 10dh). **Private buses** go to the same destinations and more with greater frequency. To: **Fez** (5 per day 10:45am-11pm); **Larache** (5 per day 11:45am-5:15pm); **Meknes** (5 per day 10am-11pm); **Rabat** via **Casablanca** (8 per day 5:45am-10pm); and **Tangier** (6 per day 7:45am-5:15pm). Many buses arrive full, so get to the station early. **Grand taxis** cluster in pl. Mohammed V, by the bus station, and head to Tangier (12dh) and Larache (12dh).

ORIENTATION AND PRACTICAL INFORMATION. The main street heading into town is bd. Mohammed V, which ends at the town's center, **pl. Mohammed V** (a traffic circle). Here you'll find a **BMCE bank** and a **Banque Populaire,** both with **ATMs.** The main strip of restaurants, accommodations, and cafes are located on rue Zallakah, which radiates from pl. Mohammed V and the adjoining av. Hassan II which borders the medina. There is a small **liquor shop** on rue Zallakah, marked with a *Speciale Flag* sign, two doors down from Hotel Marhaba (closes at 9pm). The town **market** takes place on av. Hassan II and continues along the medina. **Internet** can be found across from the medina on av. Hassan II. (8dh per hr. Open daily 9am-late.) To get to the **post office** from pl. Mohammed V, take bd. Mohammed V and turn right onto pl. Nations Unies. The post office is 20m up on the left. (☎039 41 72 00. Open M-F 8am-noon and 2:30-6:30pm.)

ACCOMMODATIONS AND FOOD. Most hotels cluster around pl. Mohammed V and off av. Hassan II. In July and August, they brim with French and Spanish beachgoers; call at least a day in advance to reserve a room. If you want to splurge on a slightly nicer bed, **Hotel Patio de la Luna ❹,** 12 Plaza Zelaka, is a good place to do it. The airy rooms, all with shower and toilet, are spotlessly clean. (☎039 41 60 74. Singles 200dh; doubles 320dh.) Back to normal budget fare, **Hôtel Sahara ❷,** 9 rue Tarfaya, a block inland from av. Mohammed V and two blocks before pl. Mohammed V, has immaculate rooms maintained by a Spanish-speaking staff, a 10min. walk from the action in and around the medina. (☎039 41 71 85. Hot showers 5dh. Singles 98dh; doubles 126dh; triples 186dh; quads 252dh.) A sign on av. Hassan II points you to **Hôtel Belle Vue ❷,** where rooms with dressers, couches, and murals of sunbathers on the walls await. (☎/fax 039 41 77 47. June-Aug. singles 100dh; doubles 200dh; triples 300dh; quads 400dh. Sept.-May 50dh/120dh/180dh/250dh.) To be by the beach, try **Camping As-Saada ❶,** 700m toward town from the train station, tidier and cheaper than neighboring Echrigui. (☎039 41 73 17. Showers 10dh. 12dh per person, 10dh per tent and per car. Bungalows 100dh.)

The restaurants and cafes along Hassan II all have similar prices and fare. Those facing the ramparts just before heading up av. Hassan II specialize in seafood and serve good meals for 40dh and up. **Al Kasaba ❸,** rue Zallakah, toward the ocean and past Hôtel Marhaba, is the best restaurant in town. (☎039 41 70 12. Entrees 30-100dh. Open daily 9am-4pm and 7pm-midnight. Closes earlier in winter. MC/V.)

SIGHTS AND BEACHES. Asilah's stunning **medina** is bounded by heavily fortified 15th-century Portuguese walls. The Bab Kasaba, the gate off rue Zallakah, leads past the **Grand Mosque.** Right across from the mosque is the modern and spacious **Centre Hassan II des Rencontres Internationales,** which houses an excellent collection of art created during the great **International Festival,** held the first 2 weeks of Aug. (☎039 41 70 65. Open 9am-12:30pm and 3:30-7:30pm. Free.) The city glows with artistic flair year-round; walls are covered with murals, music fills the air, and locals seem to be constantly dancing on the beaches. There are two popular beaches. The closest is toward the train station along the Tangier-Asilah highway (15min. from the medina). The nicest, in the opposite direction, is the enclosed **Paradise Beach,** an hour's walk from the medina. Horse-drawn wagons from the intersection of av. Mohammed V are around 150-200dh round-trip; or, try to persuade a taxi to make the bumpy trip. Some men might jeer at the sight of foreign women swimming; if you feel uncomfortable, walk to a less-crowded area.

LARACHE العرايش ☎039

Without a touristy veneer, the city makes an appealing stop for those with an extra day to spend on the Atlantic Coast. While there isn't too much to do in Larache itself, this former Spanish colony (with the Spanish-style architecture to prove it) does provide a perfect base for a trip to the nearby Roman ruins at Lixus.

TRANSPORTATION. CTM buses go to and from: **Asilah** (50min., 4 per day 11:15am-10:45pm, 13dh); **Casablanca** (4hr., 3 per day 8:15am-6:30pm, 82dh); **Fez** (5hr., 3 per day 4:30-10:15pm, 61dh); **Rabat** (3hr., 3 per day 8:15am-6pm, 56dh);

MOROCCO

Marrakesh (9hr., 6pm, 143dh); **Meknes** (4hr., 3 per day 6:30am-10:15pm, 46dh); and **Tangier** (1½hr., 4 per day 11:15am-10:30pm, 29dh). **Private buses** leave from the same station and send packed buses to the same locations at cheaper prices. **Taxis** park outside the bus station. **Local buses** (2.50dh) depart Kasbah de la Cigogne off av. Mohammed V, traveling to **Lixus** (buses #4 and 5) and the **beaches** (bus #4).

ORIENTATION AND PRACTICAL INFORMATION. Buses to Larache drop off passengers five blocks from the spacious **place de la Libération,** the center of activity. From the station, exit from where the buses enter, turn right, and head down **av. Mohammed ben Abdallah,** which runs into pl. Libération (about 8min.). Branching off pl. Libération to the right is the main artery, **bd. Mohammed V.** Also off pl. Libération, **Bab al-Khemis** (also called Bab Medina) leads to the **medina** and the **Zoco de la Alcaicería** (or Zoco Chico). Larache's **beach,** beyond the medina and across the Loukkos estuary, is accessible by bus (2.50dh) or boat (2dh over, 4dh back). There is no tourist office in Larache. **Banks,** across from the post office on bd. Mohammed V heading away from pl. Libération, exchange money and have **ATMs.** Contact the **police** at ☎19. **Pharmacie Centrale** is located just off pl. Liberation at 1 av. Mohammed ben Abdallah. (Open daily 9am-1pm and 4-8pm.) **Internet** at **M@rnet,** 4 rue Mouatamid ben Abbad, boasts a fast connection. Look for the sign on Ahmed ben Abdallah across from the pharmacy. (☎039 91 68 84. 10dh per hr. Open Sa-Th 10am-midnight, F 10am-3:30pm.) **Telephones** are located in the **post office.** (Open M-F 8:30am-noon and 2:30-6:30pm. Phones inside available M-Sa 8:30am-noon and 2:30-6:30pm.)

ACCOMMODATIONS AND FOOD. While there are extremely basic hotels in the medina, many nicer budget options can be found on av. Mohammed ben Abdallah and off pl. Libération. The best bargain is the **Pensión Amal ❶,** 10 av. Abdallah ben Yassine. From the bus station entrance, turn right and head straight for five blocks until you see the sign. (☎039 91 27 88. Hot showers 6dh; cold showers 2dh. Singles 50dh; doubles 70-80dh; triples 90dh; quads 115dh.) **Hôtel España ❸,** 2 Hassan II, off pl. Libération, is part of the family of once-grand hotels that are worth the extra cash; the large rooms have TVs, and bathrooms are modern. (☎039 91 31 95. Singles 120dh, with bath 204dh; doubles 162dh/243dh; triples 200dh/313dh; quads with bath 350dh). Cheap and redundant **restaurants** line pl. Libération and the Zoko. **Restaurant Eskala ❷** (☎039 91 41 80), immediately to the left after passing through the main medina gate off pl. Liberation. This hole-in-the-wall restaurant serves outstanding couscous for 40dh.

MOROCCO

DAYTRIP FROM LARACHE

LIXUS

Lixus is located 5km north on the highway to Tangier. Let's Go does not recommend hitchhiking, but some report that it is the best way to get to and from Lixus (give the driver a few dh). Alternatively, take bus #4 or 5 from the stop near Kasbah de la Cigogne in Larache (2.50dh) and tell the driver you want to go to Lixus (pronounced "lix-OOS"), or take a petit taxi for 25-30dh. You can't take a bus back, as they don't stop at Lixus. Instead, walk along the highway (45min.), flag down one of the rare taxis, or hitchhike.

Though not as impressive as Volubilis (see p. 742), the Roman ruin of Lixus is one of the Atlantic Coast's most interesting sights. It figured prominently in Greco-Roman mythology as the place where Hercules completed his 11th labor: collecting the golden apples from Mount Atlas. In real life, it was settled by an ancient sun-worshipping cult and became a highly successful **Phoenician settlement** around 1000 BC. The area fell to the Romans around 140 BC, and within a few years it had become a rich trading city occupying an important place in the Roman Empire. Unfortunately, the city lost prominence with the Empire's fall, and by the 5th century, it was totally deserted.

Today, the ruins remain largely abandoned and unmarked, besides a sign at their base on the highway. To explore Lixus on your own, begin along the highway where you'll find the silo and **factory** where *garum*, Lixus's famous fish-intestine paste, was made and stored for shipment. Walking past the factory, along the highway away from Larache, take a path to the left up the hill toward the ruins of a Greco-Roman **theater** featuring what was once one of the ancient world's largest orchestra pits; it was later converted to an **amphitheater** and, during Spanish occupation, a bullring. Located near the theater are the famous **Mosaic of the Sea God** and the **Roman baths.** Follow the fork uphill and head left to temples, villas, churches, and views of the entire site.

RABAT الرباط ☎037

Sedate political capital Rabat has a florid past. Once home to merciless pirate plunderers, today it is overrun by uniformed public servants and a swelling upper-middle class.

TRANSPORTATION

Flights: Rabat is served by its own minor airport, as well as the larger Mohammed V in Casablanca. **Royal Air Maroc,** av. Mohammed V (☎037 70 97 66), across from the train station. Open M-Sa 8:30am-12:15pm and 2:30-7pm. **Air France,** 281 av. Mohammed V (☎037 70 77 28). Open M-F 8:30am-12:15pm and 2:30-7pm, Sa 9am-noon.

Trains: By far the most convenient method of arrival and departure is via the **Rabat Ville Station,** av. Mohammed V (☎037 73 60 60), at av. Moulay Youssef. To: **Casablanca Port** (1hr., 29 per day 6:30am-8:30pm, 29dh); **Casablanca Voyageurs** (1hr., 28 per day 3:30am-11:15pm, 29dh); **Fez** (4hr., 8 per day 7:15am-1:20am, 72dh); **Marrakesh** (5hr., 8 per day 3:30am-11:30pm, 101dh); **Meknes** (3hr., 8 per day 7:15am-1:20am, 55.50dh); **Tangier** (5½hr., 4 per day 7:15am-1:20am, 89dh).

Buses: All buses leave from a huge station at pl. Mohammed Zerktouni (☎037 28 02 62), on the road to Casablanca, several kilometers from the town center. Take a *petit taxi* (12dh) or bus #30 from av. Hassan, near av. Mohammed V (2.50dh). **CTM** at window #15; other windows are private companies. CTM to: **Casablanca** (1hr., 10 per day 3:20am-10:30pm, 30dh); **Fez** (3½hr., 10 per day 8:30am-10:30pm, 58dh); **Meknes** (2½hr., 8 per day 7am-11pm, 49dh); **Marrakesh** (3 per day 1-9:30pm, 100dh) **Tangier** (5hr., 4 per day 7:30am-1am, 90dh); **Tetouan** (6hr.; 6pm, midnight; 92dh).

Taxis: There are stands at the train station, in front of the bus station, and at the entrance to the medina by the corner of av. Hassan II and av. Mohammed V. Expect to pay about 18dh from the bus station to the center of town.

Car Rental: Budget (☎062 38 80 38), in the train station. Fiat Uno starting at 474dh per day, plus 2.50dh per km. Open M-F 8am-noon and 2:30-7pm, Sa 9am-noon and 3-6pm, Su 9am-noon. Min. age 21 for most cars. **Hertz,** 467 av. Mohammed V (☎/fax 037 70 92 27), across from the train station. Starting at 250dh per day for a Fiat Palio or Fiat Uno, plus 2.50dh per km. Min. age 25 for all cars except the smallest ones, for which the min. age is 23. No special international license required.

ORIENTATION AND PRACTICAL INFORMATION

Rabat is easy to navigate. Rabat's main street, **av. Mohammed V,** runs uphill from the **medina** past the post office and train station, to the **Great Mosque (al-Sounna).**

MOROCCO

Exiting the train station (the Rabat Ville stop), turn left up av. Mohammed V to reach most budget hotels and **bd. Hassan II,** which runs perpendicular to av. Mohammed V along the medina's walls. The waterfront area along the Bou Regreg River contains many of Rabat's important sights: the **Kasbah, Hassan Tower,** and **Mausoleum of Mohammed V,** plus sister city **Salé** across the river.

Tourist Office: The **main office** (☎037 68 15 31) is in the posh suburb of Agdal on av. Al Abtal (take a taxi to al-Abtal; the office is on the left side of the street). All info in French. Open M-Th 8:30am-noon and 2-6:30pm, F 8:30am-11:30pm and 3-6:30pm.

Currency Exchange: Banks and **ATMs** line av. Mohammed V and av. Allal ben Abdallah. **BMCE** is at 260 av. Mohammed V (24hr. ATM outside) and at the train station. Open M-F 8:15am-2:15pm.

Luggage Storage: At the train station (15dh per bag per day, locks for sale (7dh) in station). Open daily 7am-10:30pm. At the bus station (3dh per day).

English Bookstores: **English Bookshop,** 7 rue Alyamama (☎037 70 65 93), behind the train station. From the medina, take av. Moulay Youssef off av. Mohammed V past the station and bear right onto rue Alyamama. Used selection has everything from philosophy to feminist criticism to popular fiction. Open M-F 9am-12:30pm and 3:30-7pm.

Emergency: ☎19. **Police:** rue Soekarno, off av. Mohammed V.

Late-Night Pharmacy: Pharmacie de Préfecture, av. Moulay Rachid (☎037 70 70 72). From post office, cross av. Mohammed V and veer right onto rue al-Qahira. On your right a few blocks down and across from Theatre Mohammed V. Open nightly 8:30pm-8am.

Hospital: Hôpital Avicenne, av. Ibn Sina (☎037 67 28 71), at the end of bd. d'Argonne away from the medina. US citizens can also go to the **US Embassy** (see p. 720) for medical assistance.

Internet Access: Cyber-Espace Menara, av. Mohammed V, in the Maroc Telecom building across from the post office. Fast connections. 12dh per hr. Open daily 9am-9pm.

Post Office: av. Mohammed V at rue Soekarno (☎037 72 36 46), to the left when leaving the train station. Open M-Sa 8:30am-6:30pm and Su 8:30-11:30am.

ACCOMMODATIONS

The medina has several good options for bargain-hunters. The cushier hotels are off **av. Mohammed V** and **av. Allal ben Abdallah.** From the train station, turn left onto av. Mohammed V and walk toward the medina; av. Allal ben Abdallah runs parallel, one block to the right. None of the hotels are far from the *ville nouvelle.*

VILLE NOUVELLE

Auberge de Jeunesse (HI), 43 rue Marassa (☎/fax 037 72 57 69), 2 blocks along the medina walls on the road perpendicular to av. Hassan II. Clean dorms and a lush interior garden with comfy couches. Modern toilets; hot showers in the winter. Breakfast 14dh. Reception open June-Aug. 9am-midnight. Dorms 35dh, HI members 30dh. ❶

Hôtel de la Paix, 2 rue Ghazza (☎037 73 20 31 or 037 72 29 26), on the corner of av. Allal ben Abdallah and rue Ghazza, about 10min. from the train station and 2 blocks before the medina. Large, simple rooms with full baths, some with phones. Ask for a balcony. Singles 160dh; doubles 200dh; more spartan rooms 70-90dh. ❸

Hotel Majestic, 121 bd Hassan II (☎037 72 29 97), across from the medina walls. Recently renovated hotel has large, well-furnished rooms with baths. The front rooms have medina views but can be noisy. Singles 189dh; doubles 223dh; triples 286dh. ❹

Hôtel Central, 2 rue al-Basra (☎037 70 73 56; fax 037 72 83 10). From the train station, cross av. Mohammed V, walk 2 blocks toward the medina, and turn right; it's on the corner of rue al-Basra and rue Dimach. Big rooms with high ceilings, sinks, and firm beds. Hot showers 10dh. Singles 80dh, with shower 100dh; doubles 110dh/150dh; triples 150dh/200dh; quads 200dh/250dh. ❷

MEDINA

Hotel D'Alger, 34 rue Souq Semmarine (☎037 72 48 28). Come here for a bargain and a modern bathroom. Clean rooms at very reasonable rates. No reservations. Singles 35dh, with shower and toilet 70dh; doubles 70dh, with shower and toilet 100dh. ❶

Hôtel Dohrmi, 313 av. Mohammed V (☎037 72 38 98), 1½ blocks inside the medina, on the right. Surprisingly modern for a medina hotel, with bright rooms, newly-tiled floors, and toilets. Hot showers 7dh. Singles 100dh; doubles 120dh; triples 180dh. ❹

Hôtel Maghrib El-Jadid, 2 rue Sebbahi (☎037 73 22 07), at av. Mohammed V, a few blocks past Hôtel Dohrmi on the right. Bare-bones and clean. Squat toilets and small beds. Cold showers 4dh; hot showers 7.50dh. Singles 50dh; doubles 90dh; triples 135dh; quads 160dh. Add 10dh during the summer. Additional bed 45dh. ❶

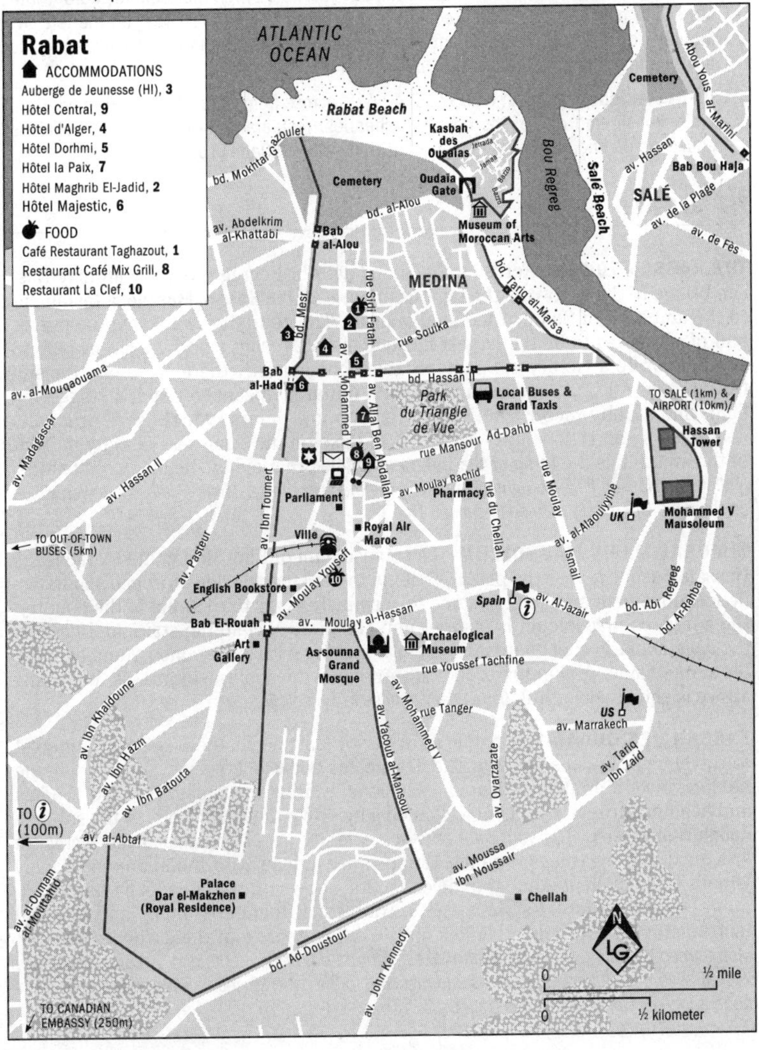

MOROCCO

FOOD

Along with scores of traditional restaurants, Rabat is filled with mediocre international food options. A **food market** sits at the entrance to the **medina** at av. Mohammed V, and there are *brochetteries* and sandwich shops within the medina walls.

Restaurant Café Mix Grill, av. Mohammed V (☎037 20 83 27), 1 block from the post office toward the train station. Westerners will feel right at home at this restaurant, waited on by attentive staff. Crepes (12dh), excellent shawarma (25dh), and pizza (26-50dh) served at a modern and clean spot. Open daily 7:30am-midnight. ❶

Restaurant La Clef, av. Moulay Youssef (☎037 70 19 72). Comfortable restaurant with Moroccan cuisine from 50dh. Facing the train station, take the street on the left, av. Moulay Youseff, and veer left onto the small pedestrian walkway. The restaurant is upstairs from the cafe on the left. Open daily noon-3pm and 7-10:30pm. MC/V. ❷

Café Restaurant Taghazout (☎037 72 40 61), across from Hotel Maghrib El-Jadid. Generally considered one of the best and cheapest restaurants in the medina. Delicious couscous on Fridays. Entrees 23-40dh. Open daily 7:30am-11pm. ❶

SIGHTS

THE HASSAN TOWER. Across town, along av. Abi Regreg (near the Moulay Hassan bridge to Salé), towers the famous minaret of the **Hassan Mosque,** a testament to the ambition of Sultan Yacoub al-Mansur. The courtyard was once the prayer hall of what was to be the largest mosque in the Muslim world, begun in 1195 to commemorate a victory in Spain but abandoned shortly thereafter upon the sultan's death. All that remains are the 44m minaret (meant to reach a staggering 60m) and stubby reconstructions of the support pillars (which were originally destroyed by an 18th-century earthquake). Also on the same site, directly in front of the minaret, is the **Tomb of the Unknown Soldier,** marked by the blank tombstone. *(Follow bd. Hassan II to the right when facing the medina; after a 15min. walk, the tower will be on the right. Open daily sunrise to sunset. Free.)*

MOHAMMED V MAUSOLEUM. The Mausoleum of King Mohammed V faces the Hassan Mosque across the plaza. A tribute to the king who led Morocco's independence movement and lent his name to seemingly every third street in the country, the gorgeous mausoleum is open to non-Muslims. Ascend the stairs and pass by the spectacularly clad guards who keep company with Mohammed V and his marble sarcophagus. Make sure to look up—not just down at the tomb—as the ceiling above is equally beautiful. *(Open daily sunrise to sunset. Free.)*

KASBAH DES OUDAIAS. Compared to Fez or Marrakesh, there is little of interest to travelers in Rabat's medina. The **Kasbah des Oudaias,** however, just outside the medina, once a pirate stronghold, is striking. Exiting the *kasbah* via Bab Oudaia and heading through the keyhole-shaped gate down the stairs leads to the sublime **Andalucian gardens**. *(On your right after you enter the gate.)* The **Museum of Moroccan Arts,** next to the gardens, was the 17th-century hideaway of the infamous Moulay Ismail. The excellent ethnographic collection shows off the sultan's private apartment, signature Rabat-style carpets, traditional local costumes, and musical instruments. A charming **cafe** lies on the opposite side of the garden. *(Follow av. Mohammed V through the medina and take a right on bd. al-Alou to its end, a 15min. walk. The kasbah is to the left and the gardens and museum to the right. Museum and gardens open 8am-noon and 2-7:30pm. Museum entrance 10dh.)*

THE CHELLAH. Beyond the city walls at the end of av. Yacoub al-Mansour loom the deteriorating but nonetheless remarkable ruins of the Chellah, a former Roman city. In the 14th century, the ruling Merenids encircled the city with walls and converted it into a royal necropolis. Because of its tranquil aura and spectacular views, the Chellah is often called one of the most romantic sites in Morocco. Storks have completely taken over the site, building their enormous nests throughout the ruins and lush gardens. Still, the Chellah makes for pleasant wandering. From the gate, descend through the overgrown gardens to reach the necropolis and its ruined mosque. Step inside for the 13th-century tombs of Sultan Abu Yacoub Youssef and the adjacent stork-filled minaret. *(Follow av. Mohammed V to the al-Sounna Mosque (see below) and continue, keeping palace wall on the right. At the end of the road (25min.). The Chellah is across the square to the left. Open daily, sunrise to sunset. 10dh.)*

ARCHAEOLOGICAL MUSEUM. Near the al-Sounna Mosque, the Archaeological Museum houses some of Morocco's oldest artifacts. The small museum traces prehistoric and pre-Islamic history and contains wonderful collections from the ruins of Volubilis and Lixus, including an assortment of Hellenistic bronze works, all cast before 25 BC. For those travelers with Volubilis or Lixus on their itineraries, this is a very rewarding stop, though information plaques are only in French and Arabic. *(Walk down av. Mohammed V away from the medina and bear left at the Grand Mosque onto Abd al-Aziz; the museum is on the next street off Abd al-Aziz to the left, near the Hôtel Chellah. ☎037 70 19 19. Open daily 9am-5:30pm. 10dh.)*

ENTERTAINMENT AND NIGHTLIFE

The centrally-located **Henry's Bar,** across from the train station, is a decent place to get a drink, where you'll find the usual clientele of older Moroccan men. **Hotel Balima** (☎037 70 77 55), on Mohammed V across from the post office, has a bar and nightclub that cater to a younger and more integrated crowd. One of the medina's best nightclubs is **Amnesia,** 18 rue Monastir, near the Royal Movie Theater. (☎037 70 18 60. Dress code. Open W-Sa midnight-4am.) The **Royal Movie Theater,** on av. Allal ben Abdallah, a few blocks off the medina, shows popular films dubbed in French. (1 screen, 4 shows per day; 20dh.)

CASABLANCA الدار البيضاء ☎022

Though sprawling Casablanca (known as "Casa") is famous in the West, there is little to see here other than the grandiose Hassan II Mosque. Unfortunately, there is no Rick's Café Américain in the *kasbah*, and no one looking at you, kid, except the hustlers who prowl the port and medina. Casa is little more than a transportation hub. In the country's economic capital and Africa's largest port, Western dress predominates, and women participate actively in city life. With its early 19th-century French boulevards, parks, and decaying Art Deco buildings, Casablanca can feel more like a European city whose sun has set until one visits the spectacular modern wonder, the Hassan II Mosque, the third largest mosque in the world.

TRANSPORTATION

The **Casa Port train station** is near the youth hostel and the city center; the **Casa Voyageurs train station** is a 50min. walk from Casa Port or a 30dh *petit taxi* ride. The **private bus station** is even farther away. To get from Casa Port to the convenient downtown **CTM bus station,** cross the street, follow bd. Houphëit-Boigny to the head of pl. Nations Unies. At the rotary, take a sharp left onto the wide av. Armée Royale, and watch for Hôtel Safir on the right; the station is behind and to the right of the hotel. Expect to be offered "help" when disembarking in Casablanca, and be wary of *petit taxi* drivers offering highly inflated rates; demand that drivers turn on the meter. Alternatively, walk a few blocks from the station for a taxi. Accommodations are almost all within walking distance, but be careful at night.

Flights: Aéroport Mohammed V (☎022 53 90 40) handles all flights. Trains run between the airport terminal and the Casa Port train station (45min., 9 per day 5:15am-8:45pm, 30dh), stopping at Casa Voyageurs en route. Make sure to get on a train that runs to Casa Port. **Royal Air Maroc** (☎022 31 41 41), at the airport and 44 av. des F.A.R. Open M-F 8:30am-12:15pm and 2:30-7pm, Sa 8:30am-noon and 3-5pm.

Trains: There are 2 main train stations: **Casa Port** (☎022 27 18 37), on the waterfront close to the heart of the city, and **Casa Voyageurs** (☎022 24 38 18), 4km outside the city center on bd. Ba Hammed. Casa Port has northbound service to **Rabat** (1hr., every 30min. 6:30am-8:30pm, 27dh). Casa Voyageurs has southbound service to: **Fez** (5¼hr., 8 per day 7:15am-11:15pm, 97dh) via **Meknes** (4½hr., 81dh); **Marrakesh** (3½hr., 8 per day 4:55am-1:30am, 75dh); **Tangier** (6hr., 4 per day 6:15am-12:15am, 116dh; possible transfer at Sidi Kacem).

Buses: Arriving by **CTM** rather than with a private company is worth the extra money and effort in Casablanca; the private bus station is a long taxi ride away from the city center. **CTM,** 23 rue Léon L'Africain (☎022 45 80 00), off rue Chaouia. To: **Agadir** (10hr., 8 per day 6:30am-11pm, 145dh); **al-Jadida** (1½hr., 5 per day 6:30am-3pm, 25dh); **Essaouira** (5½hr., 2 per day 5:30am and 7pm, 110dh); **Fez** (6hr., 11 per day 7am-10pm, 80dh); **Marrakesh** (4hr., 10 per day 7:30am-11pm, 70dh); **Meknes** (5hr., 10 per day 7am-2am, 68dh); **Rabat** (1½hr., 18 per day 6am-11:30pm, 30dh); **Tangier** (6½hr., 4 per day 6am-11:30pm, 120dh).

Car Rental: Though travelers don't need a car in Casa, the city has dozens of rental companies. **Avis,** 19 av. des F.A.R. (☎022 31 24 24). Open M-F 8am-7pm, Sa 8am-noon and 2-5pm, Su 8am-noon. **Hertz,** 25 rue de Foucauld (☎022 84 09 39), same hours. Min. age 25, 23 for small cars. **Budget,** 15 av. des F.A.R. (☎022 31 31 24). Min. age 21. Open M-F 8:30am-noon and 2:30-7pm, Sa 9am-noon and 3-6pm, Su 9am-noon.

> In Casablanca, **petit taxi** drivers are particularly flagrant in failing to turn on the meter and taking scenic routes. Be sure to double-check the meter and have a sense of the route. The daytime meter should start at 1.40dh, the nighttime meter at 2.10dh. Taxi drivers are required by Moroccan law to use their meter.

MOROCCO

ORIENTATION AND PRACTICAL INFORMATION

The city has two main squares, **pl. Nations Unies,** below the landmark clock tower and a 5min. walk from Casa Port, and **pl. Mohammed V.** Pl. Nations Unies spreads out in front of the Hyatt Regency at the intersection of bd. Mohammed V, av. Hassan II, and av. Forces Armées Royales (F.A.R.). Pl. Mohammed V lies six blocks away from the port along av. Hassan II. Budget accommodations lie around rue Allal ben Abdallah, parallel and in between bd. Mohammed V and av. des F.A.R.

Tourist Office: Syndicat d'Initiative et de Tourisme, 98 bd. Mohammed V (☎/fax 022 22 15 24), at rue Chaouia, about 4 blocks down from pl. Nations Unies. English spoken. Offers an overpriced guided tour of Casablanca for 450dh, including taxi. Open M-F 8:30am-noon and 2:30-6:30pm, Sa 9am-1pm, Su 8:30am-noon and 3-5:30pm. The **Office de Tourisme,** 55 rue Omar Slaoui (☎022 27 95 33 or 022 27 11 77; fax 022 20 59 29), has similar services. From pl. Mohammed V, take av. Hassan II, turn left on rue Reitzer, and then right. Open M-F 8:30am-noon and 2:30-6:30pm.

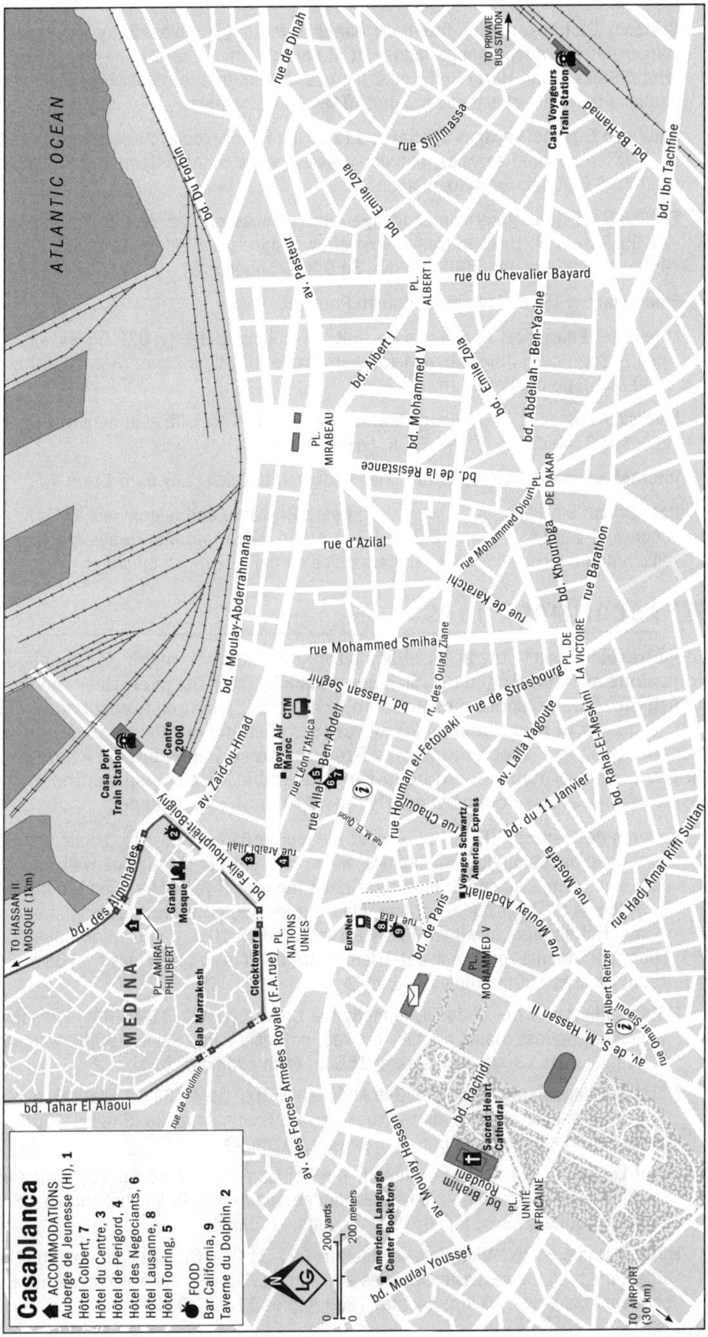
Casablanca
ACCOMMODATIONS
Auberge de Jeunesse (HI), 1
Hôtel Colbert, 7
Hôtel du Centre, 3
Hôtel de Perigord, 4
Hôtel des Negociants, 6
Hôtel Lausanne, 8
Hôtel Touring, 5
FOOD
Bar California, 9
Taverne du Dolphin, 2
0 200 yards
0 200 meters
ATLANTIC OCEAN
TO HASSAN II MOSQUE (1km)
TO PRIVATE BUS STATION
TO AIRPORT (30 km)
MEDINA
Casa Port Train Station
Casa Voyageurs Train Station
Centre 2000
Grand Mosque
Clocktower
Bab Marrakesh
PL. AMIRAL PHILIBERT
PL. NATIONS UNIES
PL. MIRABEAU
PL. ALBERT I
PL. DE DAKAR
PL. DE LA VICTOIRE
PL. MOHAMMED V
PL. UNITE AFRICAINE
Royal Air Maroc
CTM
EuroNet
Voyages Schwartz/ American Express
Sacred Heart Cathedral
American Language Center Bookstore
bd. des Almohades
bd. Tahar El Alaoui
rue de Goulmin
bd. Felix Houphet-Boigny
av. Zaïd-ou-Hmad
rue Araibi Jilali
av. des Forces Armées Royale (F.A.rue)
bd. Moulay-Abderrahmana
bd. Du Forbin
av. Pasteur
rue de Dinah
bd. Emile Zola
rue Sijilmassa
bd. Ba-Hamad
bd. Ibn Tachfine
rue du Chevalier Bayard
bd. Albert I
bd. Mohammed V
bd. Abdellah - Ben-Yacine
bd. de la Résistance
rue d'Azilal
rue Mohammed Diouri
rue de Karatchi
bd. Khouribga
rue Barathon
rue Mohammed Smiha
bd. Hassan Seghir
r. des Oulad Ziane
rue de Strasbourg
rue Houman el-Fetouaki
av. Lalla Yacoute
rue Léon l'Africa
Ben-Abdell
rue Allal
rue M. El Quori
rue Chaouia
bd. du 11 Janvier
bd. Rahal-El-Meskini
rue Mostafa
rue Hadj Amar Riffi Sultan
rue Moulay Abdallah
rue Tata
bd. de Paris
av. de S. M. Hassan II
bd. Albert Reitzer
rue Omar Slaoui
bd. Rachidi
bd. Brahim Roudani
av. Moulay Hassan I
bd. Moulay Youssef

MOROCCO

Currency Exchange: When the many **banks** in the city are closed, try the airport and larger hotels, which change money at Morocco's official rates. The **Hyatt Regency, Hôtel Suisse,** and **Hôtel Safir,** near the bus station, and the other big hotels near pl. Nations Unies are all safe bets. 24hr. **ATMs** are everywhere.

American Express: Voyages Schwartz, 112 av. du Prince Moulay Abdallah (☎022 22 29 47). Offer standard services, but won't receive wired money. Open M-F 8:30am-noon and 2:30-6:30pm, Sa 8:30am-noon.

English Bookstore: American Language Center Bookstore, bd. Moulay Youssef (☎022 27 95 59), at pl. Unité Africaine. Vast array of novels and reference books. Open M-F 9:30am-12:30pm and 3:30-6:30pm, Sa 9:30am-noon.

Emergency: ☎19. **Police** on bd. Brahim Roudani.

Late-Night Pharmacy: Pharmacie de Nuit, pl. Nations Unies (☎022 26 94 91). Open nightly 8pm-8am. Other pharmacies with normal day-time hours (8am-12:30pm and 2:30-8pm) are on almost any city block.

Medical Assistance: Croix-Rouge Marocaine, 19 bd. al-Massira al-Khadra (☎022 25 25 21). **S.O.S. Medicins,** 81 av. F.A.R. (☎022 44 44 44).

Internet Access: EuroNet, 51 rue Tata. 10dh per hr. Open daily 8am-11pm.

Post Office: bd. Paris, at av. Hassan II. **Poste Restante** and telephones. M-Th 8:30am-noon and 2:30-6:30pm, F 8:30-11:30am and 3-6:30pm. As always, packages are shipped and received from a separate office on the side of the building.

ACCOMMODATIONS

Most travelers don't stay in Casablanca for more than one night. For budget deals, look along **rue Chaouia** and **rue Allah Ben Abdallah;** avoid the overpriced medina. It's worth the effort to scout out the room first or visit a couple hotels before choosing, as quality of rooms and beds can vary significantly even within hotels. Casa is very noisy, so try to get a room away from the street. Depending on where you are in Casa, a street name could be in French, Arabic with transliteration, or both; some listings below note particularly recent or confusing changes.

Auberge de Jeunesse (HI), 6 pl. Ahmed Bidaoui (☎022 22 05 51), 10min. from Casa Port. Head right along bd. Almohades, which runs outside the medina wall, and go left up a small ramp-like street; blue signs point the way. If you don't mind the lack of privacy, this is the best budget option. Pleasant lounge, clean dorms, and modern bathrooms. Hot showers in winter. Breakfast included (8-10am). Reception open daily 8-10am and noon-11pm. Lock-out 10am-noon; be sure to check out by 10am. Dorms 45dh; doubles 120dh; triples 180dh. ❶

Hôtel Colbert, 38 rue Chaouia, formerly rue Colbert (☎022 31 42 41). Friendly staff maintains spotless rooms. Usually booked, so arrive early. Singles 90dh, with shower 125dh; doubles 130dh, with shower 165dh; each additional person 36dh. ❷

Hôtel des Negociants, 116 Allah Ben Abdallah (☎022 31 40 23). A relatively new addition to the block, and it shows—rooms and bathrooms sparkle. Singles 105dh, with shower 168dh; doubles 165dh, with shower 207dh. ❸

Hôtel Lausanne, 24 rue Tata, formerly rue Poincaré (☎022 26 86 90). Catch up on Egyptian soap operas and Arab news in modern rooms with TV and hot showers. Singles 229dh; doubles 273dh; triples 350dh; quads 427dh. ❺

Hôtel Touring, 87 av. Allah Ben Abdallah (☎022 31 02 16). A budget hotel that offers little more than the necessities; tables and electrical outlets are welcome bonuses. Hot showers 2dh. Singles 62dh; doubles 78dh; triples 114dh. ❷

Hôtel Perigord, 56 rue Arabi Jilali, formerly rue Foucauld (☎022 22 10 85). From bd. Felix Houpheit-Boigny, left onto av. des F.A.R., then the 1st right. Basic budget option with clean rooms. Shared hot shower. Singles 62dh; doubles 82dh; triples 127dh. ❷

Hôtel du Centre, (☎022 44 61 80) at av. de F.A.R. and Sidi Balyout. Walking from pl. Nations Unie, it's the 1st intersection on the left. Upscale option. Large rooms, modern bathrooms, and shower. Singles 173dh; doubles 214dh; triples 286dh. ❹

FOOD

Cosmopolitan Casa offers everything from French *haute cuisine* to McDonald's, but most restaurants are geared toward the city's wealthy business clientele. The casual and inexpensive rotisserie chicken restaurants, which line the bottom of **rue Chaouia** in the *ville nouvelle* around the corner from rue Allah Ben Abdallah, are safe bets. Restaurants near pl. Nations Unies and in the medina are also good values, though prices are a bit higher. For fresh meats and produce, try haggling at the **central market,** 7 rue Chaouia (open daily 8am-1pm). Two blocks away from the center is **L'Oliveri,** at 132 Hassan II, the best ice cream shop around.

O'Dissea, 19 av. Hassan II (☎022 22 49 21). A trendy Moroccan restaurant painted in bright colors with mahogany highlights. Delicious *menú* (try the catch of the day) for 48dh. Also has a *patisserie* and ice cream shop. ❷

Restaurant Snack Bar California, 19 rue Tata (☎022 29 49 44), midway down the street. A welcoming atmosphere for women. Its spectacular vegetarian couscous (40dh) is a rarity in Casa. A darling of the travel guidebooks; locals probably wouldn't be caught dead here. Entrees 20-50dh. Open daily 10am-1am. ❷

Taverne au Dauphin, 115 bd. Felix Houphëit-Boigny (☎022 22 12 00), up the road from the port. Entrance on the right side of building. House specialties include *crevettes grillées* (grilled shrimp; 55dh) and *filet de lotte* (fish filet; 70dh). Limited selection of non-seafood options. Beer 15dh. Open M-Sa noon-3pm and 7-11pm. V. ❸

Point Central, 89 rue Allah ben Abdallah, next door to Hotel Touring. Tajine and couscous dishes 18-28dh. Open M-F noon-2pm and 8-9:30pm, Sa 8-9:30pm. ❶

SIGHTS

HASSAN II MOSQUE. The glorious Hassan II Mosque is the third largest mosque in the world. If you're within striking distance of Casa, it warrants a special trip or detour. Built on the orders of former Moroccan king Hassan II, it's very easy to find; from anywhere in Casa, look toward the sea and spot the minaret (200m high, the tallest in the world). Begun in 1980 and inaugurated in 1994, this massive structure cost over US$800 million (much of it collected from the Moroccan people through "universal voluntary conscription"). Designed by a Frenchman, the mosque was constructed by 3300 master Moroccan craftsmen who worked day and night to complete the project. The prayer hall, much larger than St. Peter's in Rome, combines glass, marble, and precious wood and holds over 25,000 under the glow of 56 chandeliers. The plaza accommodates another 80,000. At one end of the prayer hall, silver electric gates weighing over 34 tons open only once a year—during the birthday celebration for the prophets—for a grand entrance by his living descendant, the King himself. The hall also boasts a retractable roof, a heated floor, and a 20 mi. long laser beam that shoots from the minaret toward Mecca. Hassan II graciously wanted his mosque to be accessible to non-Muslims (unlike every other mosque in the country); take advantage of the tour which offers access to otherwise restricted areas in order to truly appreciate the Moroccan craftsmanship and awe-inspiring beauty of this national and religious monument. *(Walk past the medina along the coastal road for about 15min., or take a* petit taxi *(no more than 10-15dh though drivers will often ask for an unmetered 20dh). Tours take 1hr. and are given Sa-Th 9, 10, 11am, and 2pm. Tours in English, French, and Arabic. 100dh, students 50dh. Elevator up the side of the minaret 10dh.)*

OTHER SIGHTS AND ENTERTAINMENT. There's a reason Hassan II chose Casa as the site for his mosque—there just isn't much else here. Casa is too preoccupied with commerce to maintain a romantic veneer. A small and decaying **medina** disappoints veterans of Fez and Marrakesh, and the portside **Centre 2000,** meant to be a tourist draw, is just a collection of unexciting western cafes and restaurants. Two blocks farther south along av. Hassan II sprawls the **Parc de la Ligue Arabe,** the grandest of Casa's parks. In the northwest corner you can enjoy a nice **picnic** in the shadows of the old **Sacred Heart Cathedral,** built in 1930.

AL-JADIDA الجديدة ☎023

Al-Jadida (pop. 150,000) is one of Morocco's largest Atlantic beach towns. With its quiet Cité Portugaise, palmy boulevards, and some of the country's most pleasant beaches, al-Jadida serves as a prime destination for foreign and domestic tourists.

TRANSPORTATION

Trains: The train station is 5km outside the city center, in a remote area. When arriving in al-Jadida, move as quickly as possible to the taxi stand outside, as taxis seldom come out unless there's a train arriving. A *petit taxi* should cost you about 12dh. There are 2 outgoing trains to **Casablanca** (5:30am, 3:40pm; 25dh), with connecting service to **Marrakesh, Rabat, Tangier, Fez,** and **Meknes.**

Buses: CTM, on bd. Mohammed V., sends **buses** to **Casablanca** (2hr., 4 per day 8:30am-4:30pm, 24dh) and **Essaouira** (3hr., 8:15am, 54dh). The CTM bus to Essaouira begins in Casablanca and often has few seats left by the time it arrives in al-Jadida; buy a ticket in advance. Slightly cheaper and less reliable **non-CTM buses** run from the same station to: **Agadir** (7 per day 5:30am-midnight); **Casablanca** (almost every hr. 4:15am-7:30pm, 21dh); **Essaouira** (5 per day 7:30am-5pm); **Marrakesh** (every hr. 4am-4pm, 35dh); **Rabat** (10 per day 4:15am-5:30pm).

Taxis: Many **petit taxis** in al-Jadida don't have meters, so agree on a price beforehand.

ORIENTATION AND PRACTICAL INFORMATION

From the **bus station,** exit left on bd. Mohammed V and continue up to the city center (10min.). First you'll reach **pl. Mohammed V,** the center of town, which joins bd. Mohammed V at the post office. Most services, including the tourist office and post office, are nearby. Straight ahead from pl. Mohammed V is **pl. al-Hansali** (a pedestrian square), which is packed at night, and finally **pl. Mohammed ben Abdallah,** which connects bd. Suez to the conspicuous, walled **Portuguese city.**

Tourist Office: Syndicat, in pl. Mohammed V, next to Bata Shoes. Extremely friendly service. Some English spoken. Open Th-Tu 9am-12:30pm and 3-7pm.

Currency Exchange: There are many banks in and around pl. Mohammed V. **Wafabank,** on pl. Mohammed V, has a 24hr. **ATM.** Bank open M-F 8:15am-2:15pm.

Police: ☎19. Stations at the bus station, by the city beach, and on av. al-Jamia al-Arabi.

Late-Night Pharmacy: Pharmacie de Nuit (☎023 35 52 52). From pl. Mohammed V, face the post office; take av. Jamai al-Arabia to the left of the post office; walk about 100m and take the 2nd left into the small arcade area. Open nightly 9pm-8am.

Medical Assistance: Hospital, rue Roux (☎023 34 20 04 or 023 34 20 05), near rue Boucharette in the south of town. **Ambulance:** ☎023 34 37 30. **Clinique Ennakil,** on av. Jamai Ababia, is preferable to the hospital.

Internet Access: Cyber Abir, off rue Zerktouni, past Hotel el-Jadida. 8dh per hr.

Post Office: Pl. Mohammed V. **Poste Restante** at the 1st window to the right. Open M-F 8:30am-noon and 2:30-6:30pm.

ACCOMMODATIONS AND CAMPING

Al-Jadida has a decent number of budget hotels. As usual, ask to see a room before you commit; rooms vary in quality even within a hotel. Reserve in July and August.

Hôtel Bourdeaux, 47 rue Moulay Ahmed Tahiri (☎023 37 39 21). A few narrow streets away from pl. al-Hansali; follow signs at the end of the pl. al-Hansali toward the medina (about 100m). Don't be fooled by the less-than-clean streets; step inside to find the best of the budget hotels, with bright, clean, and modern rooms. Rooftop lounge. Hot shower 5dh. Singles 41dh; doubles 57dh; triples 78dh. ❶

Hôtel de Provence, 42 rue Fquih Mohammed Errafil (☎023 34 23 47; fax 023 35 21 15). From the bus station, turn left off av. Mohammed V (away from the beach) at the post office. Just outside the busiest part of the medina, this quiet, upmarket hotel is popular with older travelers. Spotless rooms include shower, toilet, towels, and nice sheets. Hotel has restaurant, bar, currency exchange, and parking. Continental breakfast (33dh). Singles 186dh; doubles 229dh; triples 384dh. MC/V. ❹

Camping Caravaning International, 1 av. des Nations Unies (☎023 34 27 55). From pl. Mohammed V, take av. Jamia al-Arabi to left of post office; take 6th right. Clean and well-kept campground with electricity, showers, and bungalows (231dh for 2). 14dh per adult, 20dh per tent, 8.5dh per car plus 6dh *emplacement* and 10% tax. ❶

FOOD

Cheap eateries serve *brochettes* on **pl. Mohammed V.** Restaurants cluster in and around **pl. al-Hansali,** and many cafes dot the waterfront. On Sundays, a **souq** selling everything from fruit to cow lungs is by the lighthouse near rue Zerktouni.

Snack Ramses, around the corner from Hotel Magreb and Hotel France, toward the waterfront. A heaping plate of fresh fried fish, calamari, and shrimp will fill you up for 24dh. Open daily noon-4am. ❶

La Broche, 8 pl. al-Hansali (☎023 37 26 49), next to Paris Cinema. Moroccan standards, veggie options, and *paella* (20-60dh). Open M-Sa noon-3pm and 7-11pm. ❶

Snack Le Dauphin, 18 av. Fquih Mohammed Errafil, by pl. Mohammed V. A cheery spot with tasty Lebanese-style schwarma (23dh). Open daily 11am-2:30am. ❶

SIGHTS AND BEACHES

CITÉ PORTUGAISE. The heart of al-Jadida is its lovely ramparted **Cité Portugaise,** completed in 1502 by Portuguese traders. In 1769, Moroccan forces, in a siege led by Sultan Sidi Mohammed ben Abdallah finally sent them packing, but not before the retreating Portuguese blasted the old town walls to bits. After Sultan Moulay Abd ar-Rahman renovated the ramparts in the 19th century, the city was rebuilt as a Jewish settlement (*mellah*) mostly populated by merchants. The city is much smaller and quieter than Morocco's other ancient cities, with only a few shops on the main thoroughfare. Don't be afraid to venture into the quaint neighborhoods. Enter through the first fortified gate off pl. Mohammed ben Abdallah at the top of bd. Suez. Up rue

Mohammed Hachemi Bahbai on the left, a yellow plaque marks the entrance to the famed **Portuguese Cistern,** a Gothic structure lucky enough to have survived the Portuguese bombardment. It was designed in 1514 as an arsenal and later converted into a cistern. The water, illuminated by a shaft of light from the roof, reflects the cistern's columns and arches. The riot scene in Orson Welles's *Othello* was filmed here. *(Open Oct.-Apr. 9am-1pm and 3-6pm; May-Sept. 9am-1pm and 3-7:30pm. Guided tour available but unnecessary.)*

BEACHES. The town beach is excellent but crowded with football-playing and sun-bathing locals. It stretches south and is ideal for long walks. Buy your refreshments in town or be prepared to pay inflated prices. For less populated beaches, head south of town beyond the Cité Portugaise. The favorite **Sidi Bouzid,** 5km to the south, is sprawling and chic with wide beaches and good swimming. Take a *grand taxi* (5dh per person) or the #2 bus (2.50dh) from near the Cité Portugaise. The bus, which stops 10min. short of the beach just outside the walls of the Cite Portugaise, makes frequent return trips. A taxi may be preferable, as the bus makes many stops and can be crowded. The splendid **Oualidia,** about 78km south of al-Jadida (20dh per person in a *grand taxi,* or get one of the buses headed to Safi or Essaouira to drop you off), may be Morocco's best beach.

ESSAOUIRA الصويرة ☎044

Essaouira is one of Morocco's most enchanting communities. Piracy boosted this port in the 18th century, when Sultan Muhammad ben Abdallah leveled the Portuguese city of Mogador. In the late 1960s, Jimi Hendrix and Cat Stevens triggered a mass hippie migration. Essaouira achieved international fame as an expat enclave and music center. Though most of the hash smoke has cleared, Essaouira remains one of Morocco's most laid-back cities. The miles of beautiful beaches are often too windy for sunbathing (the wind is calmest in the early morning), but the fortified medina and splendid scenery provide ample diversion. In mid-June, acclaimed musicians descend on the town for the annual Festival of Essaouira, a celebration of the local, African influenced *Gnaoua* music and international jazz.

TRANSPORTATION

Buses: CTM runs from the station outside the medina, a 15min. walk from pl. Moulay Hassan. To: **Agadir** (2½hr., 1:30pm, 46dh); **Al-Jadida** (3½hr., 11:15am, 76dh); **Casablanca** (6½hr.; 11:15am, midnight; 88dh/105dh). **Supratours** buses leave from the Bab Marrakesh, across the square from Agence Supratours (☎044 47 53 17), to **Marrakesh** (2½hr.; 6:10am, 4pm; 55dh). Buy tickets at the office. Private companies make daily runs to the cities listed above, plus **Casablanca, Meknes, Rabat,** and **Taroudannt.**

ORIENTATION AND PRACTICAL INFORMATION

Buses arrive at the **bus station,** about 1km from the medina along bd. Industrie. Exit the rear of the station (where the buses park) and walk to the right, passing two *souqs* (or deserted wastelands, depending on the hour), to reach the medina gate, **Bab Doukkala** (10min.). The gate opens onto **av. Mohammed Zerktouni,** one of two main arteries; the other is the parallel **rue Mohammed ben Abdallah.** To reach the city center from Bab Doukkala, continue on av. Mohammed Zerktouni as it becomes av. l'Istiqlal (at an intersection surrounded by *souqs*). Walk until you see a clock tower and gate on the right. Go through the gate, pass through the square, and follow the road as it winds to **pl. Moulay Hassan,** the heart of Essaouira.

Tourist Office: Syndicat d'Initiative du Tourism, rue de Caire (☎044 47 50 80). From the top of pl. Hassan (away from the port), take a right and follow the road as it zig-zags 1 block beyond a gate. Some English spoken. Open M-F 9am-noon and 2:30-6:30pm.

Currency Exchange: Banks cluster around pl. Moulay Hassan. **Bank Credit du Maroc,** pl. Moulay Hassan (☎044 47 58 19), cashes traveler's checks and has an **ATM.** Open M-F 8:30am-2:15pm. **BMCE** (same hours as above) with ATM is at the end of pl. Moulay Hassan, near Ben Abdallah.

Luggage Storage: Available 24hr. at the bus station (5dh per bag).

Police: ☎19, in the *ville nouvelle* near the tourist office.

Hospital: av. al-Moquamah (☎044 47 27 16), next to the post office.

Bookstore: Galerie Aida, 2 rue de la Skala (☎044 47 62 90), off pl. Moulay Hassan. An interesting collection of crafts, used books, and art. Open daily 10am-8pm.

Internet Access: Several teleboutiques offer Internet access, but the cheapest is **Mogador Informatique,** av. Oqba ben Nafil, 3rd fl. (☎044 47 50 65), 2 blocks away from the post, on the left. Wait for Computer #4; the others are painfully slow. 10dh per hr. Vague hours, usually daily 9am-midnight. The more expensive but centrally located **Cyber Espace** is at the top of pl. Moulay Hassan (15dh per hr.).

Post Office: av. al-Moqamah at Lalla Aicha, the 1st left after Hôtel les Isles walking away from the medina by the shore. **Poste Restante.** Open 8:30am-noon and 2:30-6:30pm.

ACCOMMODATIONS

Once Morocco's best kept secret, Essaouira has lost its anonymity. There are a number of nice, cheap hotels, but reservations may be necessary in summer.

Hotel Cap Sim, 11 Ibu Rochd (☎044 78 58 34). Standing in pl. Moulay Hassam facing Credit du Maroc, make a left on rue Skala, the street along the ramparts right next to Banque Populaire. Make a right just before the archway and follow the street around to the hotel. A beautiful new hotel decorated with local art. Rooms are bright and clean with huge modern baths. Singles or doubles 158dh, with shower 258dh. MC/V. ❸

Hôtel Smara, 26 rue Skala (☎044 47 56 55). Standing in pl. Moulay Hassan, facing Credit du Maroc, make a left on rue Skala, right next to Banque Populaire (3min.). Rooms are a little damp, what with ocean waves crashing only 100m away. Arrive early—this is the most popular hotel among backpackers. Breakfast 10dh. Laundry 2dh per piece. Some English spoken. Breakfast served on terrace with a view of the sea. Singles 62dh; doubles 94dh, with ocean view 124dh; triples 156dh; quads 196dh. ❷

Hôtel Souiri, 37 rue Attarine (☎044 47 53 39), off rue Sidi Mohammed Ben Abdallah. The comfort is worth the extra dirham. Modern and well-decorated. Singles 95dh, with shower 220dh; doubles 150dh/310dh; triples 225dh/375dh. MC/V. ❸

Hôtel Tafraout, 7 rue Marrakesh (☎044 47 62 76). In pl. Moulay Hassan, walk past the restaurants and cafes and take a left onto the busy rue Sidi Mohammed ben Abdallah. Look for the sign a few blocks up. Newly renovated rooms. Hot showers 7dh. Singles 100dh, with shower 150dh; doubles 150dh/250dh. Extra bed 50dh. ❸

Hôtel Majestic, 40 rue Derb Laalouj (☎044 47 49 09). From pl. Moulay Hassan, head away from the port down the street to the right; take a quick left and then another. A good value. Free hot showers. Singles 70dh; doubles 130; triples 160dh. ❷

FOOD

Informal dining, mostly geared to tourists, is near the port and **pl. Moulay Hassan. Fish grilles,** fried sardines (with fish, bread, and tomatoes; 20dh) and grilled shrimp (25dh) are sure bets. The **Berber cafes,** near Porte Portugaise and off av. l'Istiqlal, have low tables, straw mats, and fresh fish *tajine* (20dh). Establish prices before eating.

Restaurant Laayoune (☎044 47 46 43). From the top of pl. Moulay Hassan (away from the port), take a right and continue past rue Sidi ben Mohammed Abdallah. Follow the road as it turns right; the restaurant is ahead on the left. Outstanding Moroccan food at reasonable prices, served in a beautiful, well-decorated setting. Fills up at night; be prepared to wait. 4 set *menús* 45-72dh. Open daily noon-4pm and 7-11pm. ❷

Chez Sam (☎044 47 65 13), past the food stalls, at the very end of the port. Pricey and touristy. Ocean view and one of the town's few liquor licenses. Almost identical **La Coquillage** is next door. Steaming heap of mussels 50dh. Fish dishes 80-100dh. *Menús* 85-200dh. Open daily noon-3pm and 7:30-10:30pm. AmEx/MC/V. ❹

Dar Baba Restaurant, 2 rue Marrakesh (☎044 47 68 09), near the Hôtel Tafraout. Home to the city's best Italian cuisine. Entrees 35-45dh. Open Tu-Su 6:30-9:30pm. ❶

SIGHTS

While many flock to Essaouira to simply sit back, relax, and do nothing at all, the ramparts, shops, museums, and the beaches can distract one for hours on end.

RAMPARTS AND PORT. Essaouira has two *skalas* (forts) that sit high atop fortifications. Buttressed by formidable ramparts, dramatic, sea-sprayed **Skala de la Kasbah,** up the street from Hôtel Smara away from the main square, is the nicer of the two (it's also free). Visitors can go up the large turret and artillery-lined wall to where the cannons, gifts to the sultan from European merchants, face the sea and the medina. The other fort, **Skala de Port,** has a view of the port and medina. *(10dh.)*

MEDINA SHOPS AND MUSEUMS. Follow the sound of pounding hammers and the scent of *thuya* wood to the **carpenters' district,** comprised of cell-like niches set in the **Skala Stata de la Ville.** The craftsmen here inlay cedar and *thuya* with lemonwood and ebony to create some of the best woodwork in Morocco. On sale are unique masks and statues, as well as the more typical boxes, drums, chess sets, dice, and desk tools. For a quality overview of Essaouira's goods and prices, go to the cooperative **Afalkai Art,** 9 pl. Moulay Hassan (open daily 9am-8pm) and browse the many shops lining **rue Abd al-Aziz al-Fechtaly** (off rue Sidi ben Abdallah). For silver jewelry, head to the *souq*, located just outside the medina walls on Av. Oqba ben Nafil. Look for the sign that says "*bijoux*" above the entrance on the right, about a block from rue de Caire on the right. **Museum Mohammed ben Abdallah,** near the Hôtel Majestic on rue Derb Laalouj, is in the former residence of a *pasha*. It features antique woodwork and important manuscripts, including a 13th-century Qur'an. *(☎044 47 53 00. Open W-M 9am-noon and 3-6:30pm. 10dh.)* Galleries dot the medina—the best one, **Galerie of Frederic Damgaard,** near the clock tower, displays modern art crafted by local artists. *(Open daily 9am-1pm and 3-7pm. Free.)*

BEACHES. Though infamous for its winds, the wide beach of Essaouira is still one of Morocco's finest. Join locals at the free courts for basketball and volleyball along its pedestrian walkway. To get to the sand, head to the port and veer left; you can't miss it. Windsurfing clubs cluster on the beach and rent boards. Try **Fanatic Fun Center** for good rental deals. *(☎044 34 70 13. Windsurfing boards with harness and wet-suit 100dh per hr., 300dh for a half day; bodyboards 20dh per hr., 150dh per day; jet-skis 60dh per 15min; windsurfing lessons 180-230dh per hr. depending on skill level.)*

PURPLE ISLES. Just off-shore from Essaouira are the famed Purple Isles, where rare birds still hang out and get high. Dominated by the **Isle of Mogador,** the Isles are now a nature reserve for the rare Eleanora's falcons. A Berber king from Mauritania, Juba II, set up dye factories here around 100 BC, producing the purple dye used to color Julius Caesar's cape, among other things, and giving the Isles their name. In 1506, the Portuguese, under King Manuel, built a fortress, and Moulay Hassan added a prison. Visiting the Isles is possible, but requires permission from the municipal office, which can take a few days. A tip may expedite the process.

PURPLE ISLES HAZE While certain stimulants are still available (especially for foreigners), Essaouira's heyday of "good times" was in the early 1970s when Jimi Hendrix and fellow hippies took over the isles. The fort on the beach, **Borj al-Berad,** and the inland ruins supposedly inspired Hendrix's song *Castles Made of Sand.* When he tried to buy the Berber village-turned-hippie-colony of **Diabat,** the Moroccan government decided that it had had enough of Hendrix and his long-haired expat friends and expelled most non-Moroccans. Today, the village residents have almost forgotten their raucous past; the Purple (Isles) Haze has burned away.

THE HIGH ATLAS الاطلس الاعلى

Hollywood has deemed southern Morocco one of the most beautiful regions in the world, as evidenced by the numerous movies filmed here over the last fifty years—*Lawrence of Arabia*, *Kundun*, *The Mummy*, *Spy Game*, and *Black Hawk Down*, to name a few. The terrain in the mountains and their foothills is the most varied in the country. At the feet of the High Atlas lies Marrakesh, a city overflowing with unique architecture, exotic bazaars, and magical energy. Falling southeast from the Atlas ranges and stretching through Ouarzazate to the sand-dune seas of the Sahara is Morocco's desert. Mountainous and desolate, its deep reds and oranges are softened only by the rare, green veins of oases that creep through the valley floors. Set into this landscape are fantastic Berber towns and *kasbahs*, where *pizid* (mud and straw) castles tower over the road. Excursions are possible by local transportation, but a rental car is best for exploring this region.

MARRAKESH مراكش ☎044

The imperial city of Marrakesh has always exerted an unshakable grip on the traveler. Djema'a al-Fna, the medina's main square, is home to lively crowds of snake charmers, musicians, boxers, acrobats, mystics, dentists, scribes, and storytellers practicing their crafts. Marrakesh's *souqs* and craftwork are some of Morocco's best and, in general, the bustling city is more tourist-friendly (and tourist-ridden) than the rest of Morocco. The Almoravid dynasty founded the city in 1062, elevating an infamous highwayman's outpost to the status of cultural capital and infusing it with Andalucian influences from their Spanish empire.

TRANSPORTATION

Flights: Aéroport de Marrakesh Menara (☎044 44 79 10 or 044 44 78 65), 5km south of town. Taxi from town 10dh per person. Bus #11 from the Koutoubia Mosque to the airport (about 7am-10pm, 3dh). Domestic and international flights on **Royal Air Maroc,** 197 av. Mohammed V (☎044 42 55 00). Open M-F 8:30am-12:15pm and 2:30-7pm.

Trains: Av. Hassan II (☎044 44 65 69). Going away from the medina on av. Mohammed V, turn left on av. Hassan II (40min.). A taxi to or from pl. Djema'a al-Fna costs 10dh.

! In Marrakesh, **petit taxi** drivers are particularly notorious about taking scenic routes or failing to turn on the meter. Be sure to double check the meter to make sure it's on—don't be afraid to insist—and have a clear sense of the route. If the driver doesn't oblige, get out and find another who will.

THE INSIDER'S CITY

MARRAKESH MEANDERING

Guéliz is the 20th century industrial area of Marrakesh, catering to the city's expatriate community and populated by shops, hotels, pavement cafes, bars and restaurants. Though mainly geared towards the city's lucrative tourist trade, Guéliz provides a much-needed break from the traditional and time-honored medina.

1. For fresh produce and home-cookin' ingredients, head to **Star Foods** for the expat grocery shopping experience.
2. Stock up on goods and gifts at the **French Market,** complete with a bakery. Here you'll discover hard-to-find items like alcohol and pork.
3. Indulge your sweet tooth at the **Jeff de Bruges Chocolatier;** everything is better with chocolate.
4. Hungry? Get your grub on at **Charly's Cabana Pub.**
5. If sightseeing and shopping have got you worn down, catch a flick at Guéliz's **movie theater.**
6. Sip on a cocktail and catch a beautiful Moroccan sunset from the rooftop bar of **Hôtel Tachfine.**

To: **Casablanca** (4hr., 8 per day 5:15am-9pm, 111dh); **Fez** (8hr., 6 per day 5:15am-5pm, 225dh); **Meknes** (7hr., 6 per day 5:15am-5pm, 228dh); **Rabat** (5hr., 8 per day 5:15am-9pm, 154dh); **Tangier** (8hr., 3 per day 9am-9pm, 188dh). There is an **overnight train** for Tangier that leaves at 9pm with stops in Casablanca and Rabat. For a *couchette* (200dh including train fare) book 1 day in advance. 1st class is often a good option; 2nd class is often overbooked, leaving many people standing.

Buses: (☎044 43 39 33), outside the medina walls by Bab Doukkala. To get there, walk out of the medina on av. Mohammed V, pass through Bab Larissa, and then turn right, continuing along the walls to Bab Doukkala. The station is to the left. Arrive 30min.-1hr. early, as seats fill quickly. **CTM** is window #10. To: **Agadir** (4hr.; 8am, 4pm; 75dh); **Casablanca** (4hr.; 12:30, 3:30pm; 70dh); **Fez** (10hr., 1 per day, 135dh); **Meknes** (8-9hr., 11pm, 145dh); **Ouarzazate** (4½hr., 5pm, 70dh); **Rabat** (5hr., 10 per day 5am-9pm, 55dh); **Zagora** (4-5hr., 10:30pm, 79dh). **Private companies** run frequently to destinations throughout Morocco, including **Agadir** (14 per day 4:45am-5pm), **al-Jadida** (9 per day 6am-4pm), **Asni** (every 30min. 8am-5pm, 10dh), **Casablanca** (every hr. 4am-8pm), **Essaouira** (8 per day 4am-5pm); **M'hamid** and **ar-Rachidia** (4am, 5pm); **Rabat** (12 per day 5am-9pm); and **Zagora** (4 per day 10am-10pm).

Grand Taxis: It's best to start from Bab al-Rob, where you can share a taxi to Asni or Setti Fatma. 15dh per person for 6 passengers; slightly more for smaller groups. As always, you have to wait for the taxi to fill up. If you already have a group assembled, there's no need to head to Bab al-Rob; take one of the grand taxis waiting at Djema'a al-Fna.

Car Rental: Hertz, 154 bd. Mohammed V (☎044 43 99 84). **Avis,** 137 bd. Mohammed V (☎044 43 37 27). Both agencies charge 250dh per day for a Fiat Palio or Fiat Uno, plus 2.50dh per km. Min. age 25 for all cars except the smallest ones, for which the min. age is 23, though many offices don't require proof of age. No special international license required. Open M-F 8am-noon and 3-6:30pm, Sa 9am-noon and 3-6pm, Su 9am-noon. Many hotels (like Hôtel Ali) also arrange rentals. Don't hesitate to bargain.

ORIENTATION AND PRACTICAL INFORMATION

Marrakesh and its medina are more spacious than Morocco's other imperial cities but just as crowded and noisy. Most of the excitement, as well as bud-

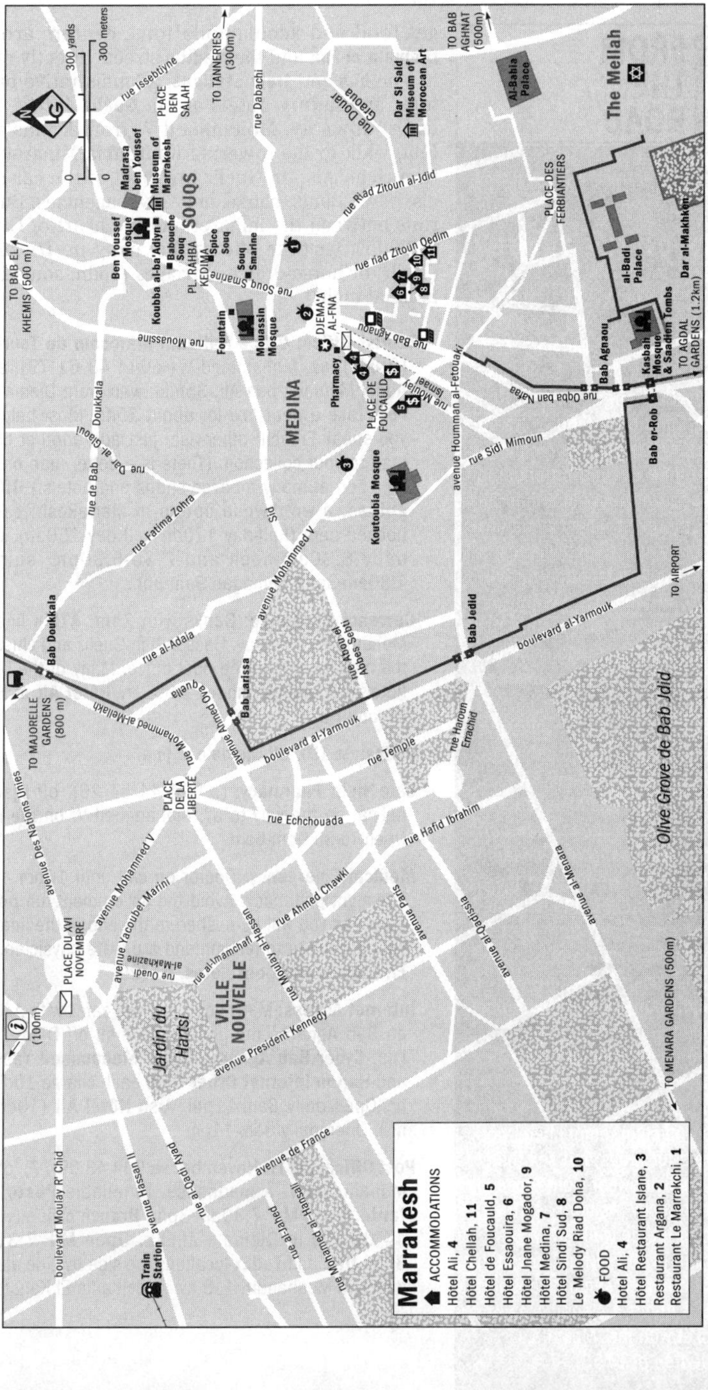

Marrakesh
ACCOMMODATIONS
Hôtel Ali, 4
Hôtel Chellah, 11
Hôtel de Foucauld, 5
Hôtel Essaouira, 6
Hôtel Jnane Mogador, 9
Hôtel Medina, 7
Hôtel Sindi Sud, 8
Le Melody Riad Doha, 10
FOOD
Hotel Ali, 4
Hôtel Restaurant Islane, 3
Restaurant Argana, 2
Restaurant Le Marrakchi, 1
MEDINA
VILLE NOUVELLE
SOUQS
The Mellah
Jardin du Hartsi
Olive Grove de Bab Jdid
DJEMA'A AL-FNA
PLACE DE FOUCAULD
PLACE DE LA LIBERTÉ
PLACE DU XVI NOVEMBRE
PLACE DES FERBIANTIERS
PLACE BEN SALAH
PL. RAHBA KEDIMA
Koutoubia Mosque
Mouassin Mosque
Fountain
Ben Youssef Mosque
Madrasa ben Youssef
Museum of Marrakesh
Koubba al-ba'Adiyn
Babouche Souq
Spice Souq
Souq Smarine
Pharmacy
Dar Si Saïd Museum of Moroccan Art
Al-Bahia Palace
al-Badi Palace
Dar al-Makhzen
Kasbah Mosque & Saadien Tombs
Bab Doukkala
Bab Larissa
Bab Jdid
Bab Agnaou
Bab er-Rob
Train Station
TO BAB EL KHEMIS (500 m)
TO TANNERIES (300m)
TO BAB AGHMAT (500m)
TO AGDAL GARDENS (1.2km)
TO AIRPORT
TO MENARA GARDENS (500m)
TO MAJORELLE GARDENS (800 m)
(100m)
300 yards
300 meters
rue Issebtiyne
rue Dabachi
rue Douar Graoua
rue Riad Zitoun al-Jdid
rue riad Zitoun Qedim
rue Souq Smarine
rue Mouassine
rue Bab Agnaou
rue Moulay Ismael
rue Qbba ban Nâtaa
rue Sidi Mimoun
avenue Houmman al-Fetouaki
rue de Bab Doukkala
rue Dar al-Glaoui
rue Fatima Zohra
avenue Mohammed V
rue al-Adaia
rue Abou el Abbes Sebti
boulevard al-Yarmouk
avenue Ahmed Ouaquella
rue Mohammed al-Mellakh
rue Temple
rue Haroun Errachid
rue Echchouada
rue Hafid Ibrahim
avenue Des Nations Unies
avenue Yacoubel Marini
rue Ahmed Chawki
rue Moulay al-Hassan
rue Ouadi al-Makhazine
rue al-Imamchafi
avenue Paris
avenue al-Qadissia
avenue al-Menara
avenue President Kennedy
avenue de France
avenue Hassan II
rue al-Qadi Ayad
boulevard Moulay R' Chid
rue al-Jahed
rue Mohamed al-Hansali

MOROCCO

get food and accommodations, centers around **Djema'a al-Fna** and the **medina** streets directly off of it. The **bus** and **train stations,** administrative buildings, and luxury hotels are in **Guéliz** *(ville nouvelle)* down av. Mohammed V; from Djema'a al-Fna, walk to the towering Koutoubia Minaret and turn right. Also in Guéliz are most of the car rentals, newsstands, banks, and travel agencies. Bus #1 runs between the minaret and the heart of Guéliz (1.50dh). Or take one of the many *petits taxis* (10dh) or horse-drawn carriages (15dh, sometimes more at night).

Tourist Office: Office National Marocain du Tourisme (ONMT), av. Mohammed V (☎044 43 61 79), at pl. Abdel Moumen ben Ali; 35min. walk from Djema'a al-Fna. Take a *petit taxi* for about 15dh. Most helpful if you speak French; otherwise, just add another cheap map to your collection. (There is a better map on sale for 15dh at many tobacco shops and hotels.) **Official guides,** a worthwhile option in Marrakesh, can be booked here (half-day 120dh, full day 150dh). Open daily 8:30am-noon and 2:30-6:30pm; summer 7:30am-3pm; Ramadan 9am-3pm.

Currency Exchange: Banks with 24hr. **ATMs** line av. Mohammed V and av. Hassan II in Guéliz and cluster in the medina around the post office. Many of the busier hotels will change money 24hr. Try **Hôtel Ali** or **Hôtel Essaouira.**

Police: (☎19), off Djema'a al-Fna.

Late-Night Pharmacy: (☎044 44 54 26), off Djema'a al-Fna, on the way to av. Mohammed V, on the right. Open Tu-Su 9pm-6am.

Medical Emergency: Doctor on call until 10pm at the late-night pharmacy. Avoid the government-run *polyclinique,* as you will be pushed to the end of the line; ask your consulate to recommend a private physician. See **Embassies and Consulates,** p. 720.

Internet Access: Many good Internet cafes with A/C are on Bab Agnaou, the pedestrian mall off Djema'a al-Fna. **Cyber Bab Agnaou, Cyber Mohammed Yassine,** and **Hanan Internet Cyber Cafe** each charge 10dh per hr. Open daily 8am-11pm. Also **Hôtel Ali** (10dh per hr.). Open daily 8am-11pm.

Post Office: Pl. 16 Novembre (☎044 43 09 77), off av. Mohammed V. A madhouse. Unreliable **Poste Restante.** Open M-F 7:30am-3pm. **Branch office** (☎044 44 09 77) in Djema'a al-Fna. Open M-F 7:30am-3pm. **DHL** and **FedEx** locations are side by side at Residence Al Mouhandiz, 113 av. AbdelKarim El Kahattabi.

FROM THE ROAD

TRICKS OF THE TRADE

I'm starting to believe that there is an annual Moroccan hustlers' convention, definitely held in Tangier, most likely at My First Cousin's Craft, Carpet, Money Exchange, and Tourist Welcoming Emporium (you've heard of it?). The keynote address on finessing the fine line between friendship and extortion is given in more than 23 languages, the most recent additions being Sanskrit and Choctaw. I can't think of a better explanation for why every hustler in Morocco has put me through the same routine, using the same tactics to try to swindle me out of my dirham; they must get together and talk about it.

I first fell victim to their shady ways when I was in Tangier; I had only been in Morocco for about a week. A man approached me and initiated the nationality guessing game: *bonjour,* hello, hi, *buenos dias, ça va, salaamu aleikum,* hi, sssss! He showed me a business card and offered to help me. He took me everywhere but where I wanted to go—hardware stores, Internet cafes, a Jewish bookstore—and I followed right along, an idiot hoping for a miracle.

In the summer heat, fatigue eventually chiseled away at his "Nice Guy" facade and his true character blazed through—an off-color remark here, persistent offers for drugs and sex there, strings of English swear words pieced together incorrectly. As hard as I tried, he refused to let me walk away.

Later on in my trip, I had arrived in Asni late, hoping to secure transport on to Imlil, without a sleeping bag or even a jacket with me. Mustafa,

continued on p. 775

ACCOMMODATIONS

Marrakesh's inexpensive accommodations are in abundant supply near Djema'a al-Fna. It's always worthwhile to see your room before taking it. Many places allow you to sleep on the rooftop terrace for about 20dh, a good option in the summer when rooms get hot, and a nice way to meet other travelers.

Hôtel Ali, rue Moulay Ismail (☎044 44 49 79; fax 044 44 05 22), past the post office off Djema'a al-Fna. A self-contained tourist compound. Suites with soap, towels, usually A/C, and toilet paper. English spoken. Also has a restaurant, Internet cafe, and currency exchange, and arranges expeditions in the High Atlas (350dh per day). If it's full, don't agree to go to Hôtel Farouk; it's too far away. Ali gets quite hectic in summer; head to Essaouira or Sindi Sud (see below) for a more laid-back atmosphere. Breakfast included. Dorms or terrace 40dh. Singles with fan and shower 100dh; doubles with A/C and shower 150dh; triples with A/C 200dh. ❸

Hôtel Essaouira, 3 Derb Sidi Bouloukat (☎044 44 38 05). From Djema'a al-Fna, facing the post office, head down the road in the left corner, just beyond Café de France, through an archway. Take the 1st right after the Hôtel de France and look for the signs. A colorful and stylish hotel with a cafe and laundry basins. One of the best sleeping terraces in town. Hot showers 5dh. Luggage storage 5dh per day. 40dh per person, but there are few singles; doubles 80dh; terrace 25dh. ❶

Hôtel Sindi Sud, 109 Riad Zitoun al-Qedim (☎044 44 33 37), just off the intersection with Derb Sidi Bouloukat, across from Hôtel Essaouira. This 2-year-old hotel is a great value for your money. Popular with American Peace Corps workers, it has clean, well-furnished rooms, a nice indoor courtyard, laundry basins, and friendly staff. Hot shower and breakfast included. 40dh per person; terrace 25dh. ❶

Hôtel Medina, 1 Derb Sidi Bouloukat (☎044 44 29 97), beside Hôtel Essaouira. Laid-back atmosphere, spotless beds, and a colorful courtyard adorned with traditional mosaic patterns. Laundry basins, drying lines, and a terrace cafe. Breakfast 14dh. Hot showers 5dh. 40dh per person, students 35dh; terrace 20dh. ❶

Le Melody Riad Doha, 10 Riad Zitoun Lakdim Derb Lakhdar (☎044 42 65 94). Treat yourself to this intimate and luxurious Moroccan townhouse run by an attentive staff. Beautifully-decorated, traditional Moroccan interior illuminated by sunlight. A world away from the hustle of Djema'a al-Fna. Breakfast included. Doubles 400dh; solo travelers should negotiate the price. ❺

sporting a boyish base-baseball cap, shooed away the two drunkards harassing me and spoke to me in English. "That's all you have? You're gonna freeze up there!" He insisted that I was mistaken in my belief that the refuge accommodations would suffice.

He took me back to his Berber village and gave me one of his very own blankets. What a kind man! He stayed with me as I waited for transportation up the mountain, and when it never arrived, he let me spend the night. That evening he asked to "borrow" some money to buy propane for his family. I was hesitant, but I still gave him quite a bit of cash.

He never came back–didn't even sleep at his own home, as I learned when his wife and mother asked me where he went. I tracked him down the next day and got my money back, but I have to admit that Mustafa was damn good.

Still, you can outsmart even the best of them. If someone approaches you, he wants something–period. He may say, implicitly or explicitly, "I am not a hustler. I am not like those *other* people." Whoever says this is a hustler. You may consider running away as fast as you can, but don't. When he says, "I have a cousin (or brother, or friend) from your country," try saying with a straight face, "Oh really, New York City? I've never heard of that." He will be utterly confused and may walk away. The most important thing is to maintain your sense of humor.

–Mosi Secret

Jnane Mogador Hotel, 116 Riad Zitoun al-Qedim (☎044 42 63 23), off Derb Sidi Bouloukat by Hotel Medina; look for the big, wooden door. A nice step up from budget accommodations. Rooms have fancy, modern bath, stained glass windows, and large, comfortable beds. English spoken. Terrace cafe. Singles 250-300dh; doubles 300dh; triples 380dh; quads 460dh. ❺

Hôtel de Foucauld, off pl. de Foucauld (☎044 44 54 99), about 200m from Djema'a al-Fna. If you're desperate for A/C, Foucauld is the best bet. Also a great spot for a drink. English spoken. Breakfast included. Singles 189dh; doubles 248dh. ❹

Hôtel Chellah, 14 Riad Zitoun al-Qedim (☎044 44 29 77). From Djema'a al-Fna, walk down the same street as to Hôtel Essaouira, but take the next right. Clean and pleasant. Hot showers 15dh, cold showers 2.50dh. Breakfast 15dh. Rooms 50dh per person. ❶

FOOD

For delicious dinner bargains, take a chance and head for the **food stalls** in Djema'a al-Fna. Dozens of stalls deal from early evening until after midnight. Follow the crowds to the best *harira* (spicy bean soup; 2dh), *kebab* (skewered meat; 2dh each), and fresh-squeezed orange juice (2.50dh). On the other end of the price spectrum, Marrakesh also boasts many **"palace restaurants"** where music, outrageous portions, and liquor combine for a memorable, if expensive, evening (usually 300-600dh per person). **Restaurant Yacout** ❺ is pricey (500-600dh per person) but superb. (☎044 38 29 00. Reservations required.) For lunch, the restaurants off Bab Agnaou are popular with tourists. For pastries, try the **Patisserie des Princes** on Bab Agnaou or the understated **Mik Mak,** next to Hôtel Ali. Two **markets** peddle fresh produce along the walls surrounding the city, far from Djema'a al-Fna.

Hôtel Ali (see **Accommodations,** above). A tasty all-you-can-eat Moroccan buffet dinner situated 4 floors above the bustle of Djema'a al-Fna on the rooftop of Hôtel Ali. Try to arrive early before the food gets too cold, though lines may be long. A hearty breakfast is served on the 1st fl. as well. A good place for women traveling alone. 50dh for Ali guests, 60dh for all others. Served daily 6:30-10pm. ❷

Restaurant Le Marrakchi, 52 rue des Banques (☎044 44 33 77), off Djema'a al-Fna. If you have a few extra dirham to spend, this excellent restaurant has authentic Moroccan decor and great views of Djema'a al-Fna and the Koutoubia Mosque. Ask to sit near the front windows. Live music and belly dancing. Moroccan menus from 250-450dh. ❺

Hôtel Restaurant Islane, av. Mohammed V (☎044 44 00 81), on the roof of Hôtel Islane across from the Koutoubia Mosque. Brick-oven pizza and pasta (60-80dh) and a nice view of the mosque. Slightly overpriced, but a refreshing break from typical Moroccan fare. Good for women traveling alone. Open daily noon-3pm and 7-11pm. MC/V. ❸

Restaurant Argana, off Djema'a al-Fna. It's more about the views than the food here, though pastas and Moroccan fare (60-85dh) are fine. Open daily 5am-11:30pm. ❸

SIGHTS

DJEMA'A AL-FNA. Welcome to Djema'a al-Fna (Assembly of the Dead), one of the world's most frantically exotic squares, where sultans once beheaded criminals and displayed the remains. Crowds of thousands participate in the bizarre bazaar that picks up in the late afternoon and peters out after midnight. Individuals consult with potion dealers and fortune tellers; crowds encircle preachers, storytellers, and musicians; women have their children blessed by mystics; and promoters encourage bets on boxing matches between young boys (and girls).

SEEING RED One may see the hands, feet, and hair of Moroccan women decorated with the original temporary tattoo, *henna.* Stemming from the Arabic words meaning "tenderness" and "good luck," henna is made from the leaf of the *tafilat* plant, ground into a powder and mixed with warm water or tea to make a paste. The dye comes in different colors, including red, black, and green, and it has three main uses: as a medicine; for pregnant women in their seventh month; and for marriage ceremonies and the "Festival of the Girls" on the 27th day of Ramadan. The application of the design to the skin, which can take hours, is both an art and a ceremony unto itself. The intricate motifs are painted on freehand or using a pattern and are left to sit anywhere from a couple of hours to an entire day before being rubbed off. The resulting decorations may last on the skin for weeks. Tourists can get a henna hand tattoo in Marrakesh for 10-15dh. For an important warning, see **Henna Tattoos,** p. 719.

MEDINA AND SOUQS. Second only to Fez in size, Marrakesh's medina contains a fantastic array of crafts and artisans. The best place in Morocco to buy spices, the medina is also where you'll find the most colorful iron and sheepskin lampshades. A worthwhile survey of the medina (primetime, which you'll want to avoid if you don't like packed crowds, is 5-8pm) begins at the *souqs.* If you get lost, ask a merchant for directions, or a child will lead you out for a few dirhams. From Djema'a al-Fna, enter the medina directly across from the Café-Restaurant-Hôtel de France. This path runs to the medina's main thoroughfare; turn toward the enormous **souq smarine** (textiles) by taking a quick left after the **pottery souq;** look for the sign on the arched gate. Berber blankets and yarn pile up in the alleyways of the **fabric souq.** Head through the first major orange gateway and make a quick right to the Rahba Kedina, a small plaza containing the **spice souq,** complete with massive sacks of saffron, cumin, ginger, and orange flower, as well as the apothecaries' more unusual wares—goat hoof for hair treatment, ground-up ferrets for depression, and live chameleons for sexual frustration. Nearby is **La Criée Berbère** (the Berber Auction), once a slave-trading center. Nowadays it hosts aggressive carpet merchants. Farther on are the bubbling vats of the **dye souq.** Fragrant whiffs of cedar signal the nearby **carpentry souq,** where workers carve chess pieces with astounding speed. Go left through these stalls to see the 16th-century **Mouassin Fountain** bathe its colorful, but grime-covered, carvings. On the road going right where the **souq attarine** (perfume) forks, an endless selection of colorful leather footwear glows at the **babouche souq** (untinted yellow is traditional for men; women wear the fancier models). The right fork at the end of the street leads to the **cherratine souq,** which connects the *babouche souq* to the **souq al-kebir,** the leather *souq.* Those with strong stomachs can visit the **tanneries;** continue through the *souqs* and take a right after the Madrasa ben Youssef; head straight for 10min. through a run-down stretch of the medina; the tanneries are on your right.

Among the shops that stand out from the rest in terms of quality of products and information is **Chateau des Souks** which sells Berber rugs and carpets. *(44 Souq Smarine. ☎044 42 64 10.)* At **Herboristerie Avenzoar** you can hear fascinating explications of the healing qualities of herbs and spices in fluent English. *(78 Derb N'Khel, off the Rahba Kedina. ☎044 042 69 10.)* **Caverne de Tissage** sells traditional Moroccan pieces in untraditional fabrics like silk, cashmere, and velvet. *(rue Rahba Lakdima, off the Rahba Kedina. ☎044 42 67 90.)*

AL-BAHIA PALACE. The ruthless late-19th-century vizier Si Ahmad Ibn Musa, also known as Ba Ahmed, constructed this palace, naming it al-Bahia (The Brilliance). Serving as the de facto seat of government for the man who ruled in the sultan's stead, al-Bahia was built in an effort to assert Morocco's historical and cultural significance and thus stave off European domination. Today, its impressive ceilings are beautifully preserved, although little artwork or furniture adorn its halls. Occasionally it serves as a gallery for modern art. *(From Djema'a al-Fna, walk down rue Riad Zitoun al-Qedim to its end at pl. Ferbiantiers, then turn left and follow the road as it curves to a red archway, which opens onto a long, tree-lined avenue leading to the palace door. Open Sa-Th 8:30-11:45am and 2:30-5:45pm, F 8:30-11:30am and 3-5:45pm. 10dh. Summer travelers may find that the palace is closed for restorations in late June.)*

MADRASA BEN YOUSSEF. In 1565, Sultan Moulay Abdallah al-Ghalib raised the Madrasa ben Youssef in the medina center, the largest Qur'anic school in the Maghreb until its closing in 1960. One of the most beautiful buildings open to non-Muslims, the Madrasa was designed in the Andalucian architectural style, including the calligraphy, courtyard, and intricate floral designs. Visitors can roam the students' cells and appreciate the size of their hostel rooms. *(Walk down the main souq street, rue Souq Smarine, and bear right onto rue Souq al-Kebir; follow it to its end. Open June-Aug. Tu-Su 9am-1pm and 2:30-6pm; Sept.-May Tu-Su 9am-6:30pm. 20dh, children 10dh.)*

DAR SI SAID. This 19th-century palace was built by Si Said, brother of Grand Vizier Ba Ahmed and chamberlain of Sultan Moulay al-Hassan. It houses the **Museum of Moroccan Art,** with Berber carpets, pottery, jewelry, Essaouiran ebony, and Saadian woodcarving. One of the best classical Moroccan art museums in the country, it's well worth a visit. *(Go toward al-Bahia, and continue on rue Zitoun al-Jadid, taking the 2nd right heading toward Djema'a al-Fna and the 1st left onto the alley where the museum resides. Open W-Th and Sa-M 9-11:45am and 2:30-5:45pm, F 9-11:30am and 3-5:45pm. 10dh. Summer travelers may find the museum closed for renovations in late June.)*

MUSEUM OF MARRAKESH. Featuring both thematic exhibits on Moroccan culture and private collections, this is one of Morocco's best museums. The building itself, a 19th-century palace, is lavishly decorated and contains a traditional *hammam* for visitors to explore. There is also a pleasant cafe and shop on site. *(Off the open plaza at the end of rue Souq Smarine in the back of the medina, around the corner from the Madrasa and Koubba al-Ba'Adiyn. ☎ 044 39 09 11. Open daily 9am-6pm. 30dh, students 10dh.)*

MOROCCO

KOUTOUBIA MOSQUE. Almost every tour of Marrakesh begins at the 12th-century Koutoubia Mosque, whose magnificent **minaret** stands 70m over the Djema'a al-Fna. Crowned by a lantern of three golden spheres, the minaret is the oldest (and best) surviving example of the art of the Almohads who made Marrakesh their capital from 1130 to 1213. At their peak, their rule stretched from Spain to Tunisia, and one of the minaret's two siblings is the Giralda in Sevilla (see p. 221). The name Koutoubia comes from the Arabic *koutoubiyyin* (of the books), because the design of the minaret was inspired by one of the first four authorized editions of the Qur'an. After 5pm, visit the beautiful Koutoubia rose garden; when in full bloom, it's perfect for an evening stroll. *(Entrance is forbidden to non-Muslims.)*

KOUBBA AL-BA'ADIYN MONUMENT. Beside the Madrasa ben Youssef protrudes the unpainted cupola of 12th-century Koubba al-Ba'adiyn, the oldest monument in town, the only relic of the Almoravid dynasty and the original from which all other Moroccan buildings have borrowed their unique style. Though excavated around the middle of the 20th century, much remains hidden either underground or by other structures. Ask the guard to open an ancient wooden door to the subterranean cisterns. *(Walk down the main souq street, rue Souq Smarine, bear right onto rue Souq al-Kebir, and turn left at the madrasa. Open daily 9am-5:30pm. Bang on the door if it's closed. 10dh, plus 5-10dh tip for the custodian-guide.)*

SAADIAN TOMBS. Modeled after the interior of the Alhambra in Granada, the Saadian Tombs served as the royal Saadian necropolis during the 16th and 17th centuries, until Moulay Ismail walled them off to efface the memory of his predecessors. In 1912, the burial complex was rediscovered during a French aerial survey. The first room after the entrance is home to the mother of Sultan Ahmed al-Mansur (the Victorious). Next door is his own tomb, the most impressive **Hall of the Twelve Columns** where the trapezoidal tombs of the Sultan and his sons rise from a pool of polished marble. The walls of the **mausoleum,** dating from the late 16th century, brim with illuminated mosaic tilework. The sultan's four wives, 23 concubines, and the most favored of his hundreds of children are buried in the third room; the unmarked tombs belong to the women. The minaret of the Mosque of the Kasbah, al-Mansour's personal mosque, towers above the complex. *(From Djema'a al-Fna, walk away from the souqs to the walkway left of Banque de Maghreb and walk 5min. to Bab al-Rob; take a left through Bab Agnaou and follow the signs. English tours. Open daily 8:30-11:30am and 2:30-5:45pm. 10dh.)*

GARDENS. Since the 12th century, rulers have dealt with the sun by constructing massive irrigated gardens. Only the most extravagant and least Moroccan of these gardens, the **Majorelle Gardens,** allows for a true escape from the heat. Designed by French painter Jacques Majorelle in the 1920s, the gardens are owned and maintained today by fashion designer Yves Saint-Laurent. On the same site is the small **Museum of Islamic Art.** *(From Djema'a al-Fna, walk toward Koutoubia Mosque and take a right on av. Mohammed V. After exiting the medina, take a right and follow the walls to the bus station. Bear left onto bd. Safi and turn right onto av. Yacoub al-Mansour; the gardens are on the left. Better yet, take a petit taxi for 10dh. Open June-Aug. daily 8am-noon and 3-7pm; Sept.-May 8am-noon and 2-5pm. Gardens 20dh; museum 10dh.)* The luxurious **gardens at Hotel La Mamounia,** Marrakesh's most extravagant hotel (once frequented by Winston Churchill) can be visited in the morning though you must act and dress smartly. *(The hotel is 5min. from Djema'a al-Fna on av. Houman el Fetouaki just before exiting through Bab Jedid. Open to the public until 2pm, although the doormen will often turn you away even earlier.)*

NIGHTLIFE

Most travelers hang around Djema'a al-Fna or in one of the terrace cafes that overlooks it for most of the night. Alternatively, try the **bars** at the **Tazi** (☎044 44 27 87) and **Foucauld** (☎044 44 54 99) hotels, where locals and tourists mix with the help of 15dh *Spéciale Flag.* (Both bars open at 9pm. Cover 50dh.) To find the Tazi, head away from Djema'a al-Fna 200m down the street to the left of the Banque du Maroc. For Foucauld, turn right by the Tazi onto the road that becomes av. Mohammed V and walk two blocks. International karaoke bar **Safran et Cannelle** is at av. Hassan II (☎044 43 59 69). Marrakesh has the closest thing in Morocco to a club scene. Try **Diamant Noir,** in Hotel Marrakesh on Mohammed V in Guéliz, or the city's best and largest club, **Paradise,** at the far end of Guéliz. Both are a taxi ride away from Djema'a al-Fna.

DAYTRIPS FROM MARRAKESH

Travelers should make every effort to push farther south for excursions into the High Atlas Mountains (see p. 781) or east toward the Cascades D'Ouzoud. Morocco's most dramatic landscape lies beyond the High Atlas in the *kasbah*-filled oases of the southern deserts (see p. 784). **Hôtel Ali** (see **Accommodations,** p. 775) organizes trips (1-4 days) to the Cascades, into the mountains, and through the gorges and deserts of the south. Prices depend on group size, averaging around 300-400dh per person per day (usually includes transport, room, and meals).

CASCADES D'OUZOUD

Travel options to the Cascades are rental car, grand taxi, or bus. A car is the easiest, fastest way (3hr., 167km northeast on S508). Buses for Azilal (window #18) run from the main station in Marrakesh (3½hr., 2 per day 8:30am-2pm, 40dh). Ask to be dropped off at the turn-off for the Cascades and then join a grand taxi (10dh) for the rest of the way or, to be safe (as you could wait quite a while for a taxi to fill up), continue to Azilal and grab a place in one of the taxis headed to the falls (40min., 15dh). The return trip may be difficult. If you miss one of the two evening buses running from Azilal to Marrakesh (2:30 and 7:30pm), organize a group to share a grand taxi back to Marrakesh from either Azilal or, if you're lucky, the falls themselves (400dh). Alternatively, arrange a round-trip grand taxi from Djema'a al-Fna for about 550dh, or try round-trip transportation from Hôtel Ali.

The Cascades d'Ouzoud (Ouzoud Waterfalls) adorn posters in hotel rooms across Morocco for good reason: they are the stuff lazy vacations are made of. At the Cascades, you can swim in refreshing pools, search for Barbary apes in the surrounding valley trees, or kiss behind a waterfall. Once you get beyond the unnecessary guides at the top of the waterfall, you can find relative tranquility by the river below where the falls crash into a large pool. You can also jump from the rock precipices high above the pools, or swim directly underneath the falls, but exercise appropriate caution. From the top of the falls, take the path to the left and descend the stairs. You are better off crossing the river (water taxi is 2dh) and hiking down to the many more secluded pools below. Spending the night at the Cascades can be highly enjoyable, as there are plenty of excellent campgrounds (10-20dh per person; 5dh per tent) where you can fall asleep to the sound of rushing water and be completely free to explore the surrounding valley (no tent is necessary as thin mattresses and blankets are provided). If you must have a roof above your head, **Hotel Challal d'Ouzoud** ❷ is the best option with clean, well-furnished rooms. (☎023 45 96 60. Singles 65dh; doubles 120dh; triples 180dh; terrace 25dh.)

SETTI FATMA

To get to Setti Fatma, take a minibus from Marrakesh's Bab al-Rob station, which is not the main bus station (1½hr., 6am-noon, 10dh); buses run back to Marrakesh at 4 or 5pm and 7:30am. Grand taxis also make frequent runs (15dh). If you have a car, go 57km south on S513; ignore the first "P" (for parking) sign in Asgaour, even if men try to tell you you can't drive farther. You can in fact drive right to Setti Fatma, where you can find a limited number of free parking spaces.

MOROCCO

The **Ourika Valley,** just south of Marrakesh, is a popular vacation destination for city residents, with its grassy farmlands, lush greenery, and hillside roses. The area is a renowned skiing spot. In the summer, the town's collection of seven small waterfalls and cool pools are a favorite. Getting to the first of the falls from the town requires a fair amount of hiking, but can be done without a guide. Start by crossing the river at one of the several makeshift bridges near the farthest cluster of hotels and cafes, and look for the arrows painted in black on several large boulders. Clamber up to the first, most popular and accessible cascade (45min.). To enjoy the best of what Setti Fatima has to offer, you'll need a guide. Ask for the highly-respected Ahmed Ait Kaid at the helpful **tourist office** or the main parking lot, both in the town center. All the waterfalls can be explored in just a few hours. During the **moussem** (festival) in early August, hundreds of Moroccans descend upon the tiny town. For some traditional Berber villages, continue past the line of cafes and hotels to the end of the road and then head along the river or the village mule paths into the valley. When you walk by, you'll certainly be the object of attention. The village is not accessible without a guide. Finally, Setti Fatma marks the end of the Imlil-Setti Fatma hike through the High Atlas Mountains (see below). If you're spending the night in the area, first try the clean and adequate **Café-Restaurant Asgaour ❶** near the bridge (singles 50dh; doubles 70dh; triples 100dh) or the hodgepodge of rooms at **Auberge Tafoukt ❷,** a bit farther from the center of town (heading back toward Marrakesh), high above the river (singles or doubles 100dh).

HIGH ATLAS MOUNTAINS الاطلس الاعلى

With manageable hikes and access to isolated Berber villages, the High Atlas mountains are one of the highlights on any Moroccan itinerary. The range's trails have yet to be fitted for tourists, and the valleys below remain green, unspoiled, and very accessible. Even travelers with limited funds, time, and skills can huff to the summit of **Djebel Toubkal,** North Africa's highest peak (4167m), in only two days—little more than a sleeping bag, food, water, and sturdy shoes is necessary. Treks of up to two weeks are also possible, but unless one is skilled and equipped with a full outfit of backpacking equipment (i.e. stove, tent, water purification system, compass, maps, etc.), the services of a guide and/or mule and muleteer are rather essential for long trips, as there are numerous unmarked trails. **Official guides** (ask to see their papers) or **mules** can be hired in **Imlil** for 250dh per day and 75dh per day respectively (not including tip). Alternatively, treks can be organized in Marrakesh at **Hôtel Ali** (see p. 775) for about 300dh per day per person, with everything from food-and-shelter deals to guide-and-mule setups. **Altitude sickness** is a potential risk, as the altitude change from Marrakesh is drastic (about 3700m). *The Atlas Mountains, Morocco* by Robin G. Collomb is a great hiker's resource.

ASNI ☎044

Grand taxis and buses from Marrakesh will go no farther than Asni, making a stop here on your way to Imlil inevitable. There's no reason to hang around for long, although Asni is a good place to stock up on provisions; you can get everything from sardines to a can-opener here. Most people move on to Imlil for their first night or to arrange for guides and/or mules. If you get stuck, there is a surprisingly good, bare-bones **youth hostel ❶** at the far end of town (if walking along the paved road, turn left before the abandoned Hôtel du Toubkal), which has free cold showers and cooking facilities (30dh per bed; camping 30dh). Avoid hustlers and offers to stay in the nearby village; too many in Asni are out to take advantage of your belief in Berber hospitality. To get to Asni from Marrakesh, take one of the frequent **buses** (dawn to dusk, 10dh) or a *grand taxi* (about 15dh per person) from the Bab al-Rob station (1½hr.). It's best to make the trip early in the day, as rides from Asni to Imlil dry up quickly.

IMLIL ☎044

The tiny village of Imlil is the ideal base for trips into the High Atlas. There are plenty of places to stay, eat, and stock up on supplies, and the crisp mountain air and constant sound of running water soothe tired climbers and invigorate future ones. Martin Scorsese used this village as the setting for his film *Kundun,* which told the story of the Dalai Lama, substituting the Atlas Mountains for the Himalayas and the village mosque for a Buddhist temple. In the center of town, next to the Club Alpine Français refuge, is the **official bureau of guides** (☎/fax 044 48 56 26). Ask questions and pick a personal guide (250dh per day) from the photos on the wall, although if you're only aiming to top Toubkal, no guide is necessary (see **The Toubkal Trek,** below). To get to Imlil from Asni, hop on the first truck up (20dh). The ride is an experience in itself; stand in the back, and don't let anyone try to charge you more or take you to any shops. If you have a car, park in front of the Bureau for 10dh.

There are many high-quality hotels that will provide meals (with a few hours' notice) and store luggage as you trek. **Hôtel El'Aine ❶,** at the start of town on the right, boasts a lovely courtyard, garden, terrace, and even a library of old French mountain books. The owners are extremely helpful with any trekking info you might need, though little English is spoken. (☎044 48 56 25. Hot showers included. 50dh per person.) **Hôtel Café Soleil ❶** has hot showers and clean rooms with futons on the floor. (☎/fax 044 48 56 22. 40dh per person.) It also serves quality food (entrees 25-35dh) and rents hiking gear. **Café Aksoual ❶** (☎044 48 56 12) has rooms with hot shower for 30dh a person. You can also sleep on its nice terrace (15dh) and store luggage (10dh). The **Shopping Center** right next door rents boots (30dh per day) and skis (150dh per day) and also sells groceries.

THE TOUBKAL TREK

The ascent of **Djebel Toubkal** is the most popular hike in the High Atlas and requires no special preparation. The entire hike can be completed from Imlil in two days with an overnight stay at the Toubkal Refuge (3-4hr. from the summit).

Beginning from Imlil, the first challenge of the hike is finding the trailhead, which is about an hour's walk on foot. Walk uphill on the village's only road, taking a sharp right when you see three large boulders on your right. After about 50m, veer onto a smaller path to the left (look for the Toubkal Kasbah sign on a building). Follow this path up past the *kasbah* for about 15min. until it joins a dirt road, weaving to the left; there are blue arrows showing the way. After 5-10min. you'll see the pleasant village of **Aroumd** on the opposite bank of the river. You'll reach a small fork in the road. You can go either way; the narrow path on the left is a little steeper and has less secure footing, but is quicker than the longer and flatter path on the right. Past Aroumd, you descend into a broad valley. The trailhead is through a small village on the opposite side; look for the very small yellow sign. This path is clear the entire way up the mountain. At about the 2-2½hr. mark you'll reach the tiny outpost of **Sidi Chamarouch,** home to a fiercely guarded marabout shrine and expensive beverages. A room here costs 50dh and *tajine* is 100dh (talk about a cornered market). The village marks the spring snow line, so be prepared for icy conditions through late April.

Another 3hr. gets you to the **Toubkal** (or Neltner) **Refuge,** where hikers from all over the world trade stories at night (32dh with CAF card, 48dh with other club cards, 64dh without; breakfast 30dh and lunch 50dh; gas burner 7dh). The refuge provides bunk beds, camping mattresses, blankets, kitchen and washing facilities, and luggage storage. If you don't stay at the refuge, any use of its facilities is strictly prohibited. It gets mighty cold during all parts of the year at this altitude, so most hikers choose to spend the night here and ascend to the summit (3-4hr.) early the next morning. This strategy also allows for the best view, as clouds tend to move in during the afternoon. To ascend the summit, choose between the south or north routes. The south is a bit easier though both are characterized by fields of loose rock (scree) which can make both the ascent and descent rather difficult. After reaching the summit, most people descend back to Imlil on the same day.

IMLIL TO SETTI FATMA TREK

This moderate three-day/two-night trek passes through ancient Berber villages and over stunning mountain passes. No guide or special equipment is necessary, and provisions such as water and accommodations are available on the route. Regardless, some hikers choose to hire a guide or a mule in **Imlil** for convenience.

DAY 1: IMLIL TO OUNESCRA. In Imlil, hike up the main road for a few minutes and then veer left past a large boulder and over a bridge spanning the river; pick up the dirt road on the other side. Most of the first day's trek is along this road as it winds through the valley. After 1½hr., a trail leaves the road for the steep ascent to the top of the mountain pass (although one can stick to the road to reach the same point). Views from the pass are tremendous. From the top, the rest of the day is a steady and enjoyable downhill hike. After 1hr., at the road's end, veer left across the river to Ounescra; you'll backtrack a bit past the orange schoolhouse to the wonderful **Gite de Soleil** (30dh per person; water and meals available) for your first night's stay. *Gites* are Berber houses sanctioned and regulated by the government to provide accommodation for travelers. (Approx. 4hr. for the entire day.)

DAY 2: OUNESKRA TO LAUSENNE OR TIMICHI. The hardest day of the hike, this stage often takes a full 8hr. From Ouneskra, follow the mule path as it clings to the left bank of the river and climbs steadily toward the mountain pass (which will always be in sight). After 1hr., the ascent becomes gradually steeper and more difficult until it transforms into long, but relatively mellow, switch-backs for the 45min. climb over the pass. From the windy pass, the rest of the day consists of a steady downhill on rocky switchbacks that can be tough on the legs. The descent passes juniper trees and becomes more relaxed as it approaches **Lausenne,** where the excellent and tranquil **Gite de labasen** offers beds for 30dh. Otherwise, continue another 20min. to **Timichi** where there's another *gite* at the bottom of the hill across the river from the mosque. (Approx. 7-8hr. for the entire day.)

DAY 3: TO SETTI FATMA. The last day has a few climbs but is mostly a steady downhill run. From Timichi, stick to the path for 1hr. as it follows the river through the valley until it forks. Take the left route which climbs rather steeply for 20min. before becoming a well-beaten mule path. This path winds through the valley towards **Setti Fatma** for nearly 2hr. It ends at the riverbed where a small stand sells soda. To reach Setti Fatma proper and its stand of *grand taxis* heading for **Marrakesh,** walk along the river for 20min. until you reach a paved road, then continue past the cafes and hotels. For details on Setti Fatma, a pleasant place to spend an afternoon, see p. 780. (Approx. 4hr. for the entire day.)

TIZI-N-TEST

The direct route between Marrakesh and Taroudannt, the **Tizi-n-Test** is one of the most entertaining and most dangerous drives in the country. Built by the French in the 1920s and 30s, the road is still deemed so laborious and time-consuming that almost all buses take a longer, roundabout path via Agadir. While a car offers much better access to the region, drivers should be forewarned of the danger of the drive—at the top of the pass where switchbacks are tight, heavy cloud and mist often cut visibility to near zero. Road accidents are an everyday occurrence; fatalities are frighteningly frequent. If you are brave (or crazy) enough to make the drive, **Ijoukak** can be a good base along the way for trekking, although it's not as established as other parts of the High Atlas. The **Tin Mal Mosque,** an excellently preserved specimen of 12th-century Almohad architecture, offers a rare chance for non-Muslims to see what is usually kept secret from visitors.

TIZI-N-TICHKA

The route from Marrakesh to Ouarzazate, known as the Tizi-n-Tichka, is not as breathtaking as its western cousin Tizi-n-Test, but the diverse landscape is eye-catching. As you wind south from Marrakesh, the land becomes more and more arid, with numerous terraced plateaus. **Buses** run quite often (see the Marrakesh and Ouarzazate sections), as do **grand taxis** (500dh total). Renting a car from Marrakesh with a Ouarzazate drop-off might be worth the expense. **Hertz, Avis, National, and Europcar** all allow you to do so.

MEN AT WORK Ever wonder how wilderness guides get away with being the most expensive things you'll ever have to pay for in Morocco? Well, there are only 44 of them (licensed, that is). Every year, the Club Alpine Français sends delegates to Casablanca to administer a three-day test. For the first two days, would-be guides are given a practical exam in Arabic and French on topics ranging from Berber history to wilderness survival. On the third day, applicants are sent to the backcountry to hike 40km in under 6hr. Those who make the cut are each required to take the Club Alpine representatives on a guided hike. Delegates can ask any question they can think of, from the height of the summit to the length of the hike to what to do with toilet paper in the woods. Correct answers mean applicants are made certified guide, legally required to collect 250dh per day (as opposed to the unlicensed 100dh).

About 2hr. south of Marrakesh by car is the town of **Telouet,** 21km from the main road (P31) and home to a remarkable **Glaoui Kasbah.** Inhabited by the powerful Glaoui family until the middle of this century, the walls of this extravagant palace are slowly crumbling. Ask the caretaker to let you in (tip about 10dh) and he'll explain how the one preserved part of the *kasbah* was used for feasts. The skylights and mosaics in the main quarters are particularly noteworthy. Transport to Telouet is difficult and expensive, so it's better done as a short excursion en route from Marrakesh or as a daytrip from Ouarzazate.

THE SOUTHERN DESERTS

From *kasbah*-hopping to camel caravans, the Southern Deserts fulfill romantic visions of Morocco. Though public transportation can be complicated (a rental car is often a good choice), the Dadés and Dra'a valleys, with their grand, palm-filled oases, charming villages, and staggering landscapes, are endlessly rewarding.

MOROCCO

OUARZAZATE ☎044

Ourzazate found its niche as one of Morocco's most convenient little staging towns. You can arrange everything here for your journey south, from picking up a rental car to buying some *bon bons* or *stylos* for the kids you meet along the way.

TRANSPORTATION. The **CTM station** (☎044 88 24 27) is located in the center of town, one block from the main street. **Buses** go to: **Marrakesh** (4hr.; 8am, 9pm; 70dh); **M'Hamid** (6½hr., 4:30pm, 68dh); and **Zagora** (4:30pm, 46dh). For destinations in the **Dadés Valley** (Skoura, Boumalne du Dadés, and Tinerhir), it's necessary to take a **private bus.** To reach the private bus company, go all the way down Mohammad V, past all the buildings, to a large roundabout; the bus station will be on your right. **Grand taxis** line up by the bus station and run fairly often to destinations such as **Marrakesh** (4hr., 70dh), **Skoura** (1hr., 13dh), and **Zagora** (3hr., 45dh). If the taxis are not full (fewer than 6 people crammed in), be prepared to pay for the empty spaces. There are a dozen **rental car** agencies in Ouarzazate, including Hertz, Avis, and Europcar, all on av. Mohammed V. Larger companies charge about 500dh per day for a Fiat Uno (unlimited mileage); local companies offer fewer services but charge half that. Try **LocaSud,** 33 av. Mohammed V, for rates as low as 350dh per day with unlimited mileage. (Min. age 21. Open M-F 8:30am-noon and 2:30-8pm, Sa-Su 8:30am-noon and 2-8pm.) Check out any car—especially the spare tire and repair kit—before making any payments, and don't hesitate to bargain. Hôtel Royal rents **mopeds** (150dh per half-day, 250dh per day; haggling acceptable).

ORIENTATION AND PRACTICAL INFORMATION. The main street in Ouarzazate is **av. Mohammed V,** home to most administrative buildings, budget hotels, and restaurants. The helpful **tourist office,** on av. Mohammed V where the road forks to follow the Oued Dra'a and the Oued Dadès, offers bus info and a directory of hotels in the Dra'a and Dadès Valleys. (☎044 88 24 85. Open M-Th 8:30am-noon and 2:30-6:30pm, F 8:30-11:30am and 3-6:30pm.) **Currency exchange** and **ATMs** at the banks on av. Mohammed V; four- and five-star hotels will only exchange cash. **Librairie Chaab,** 12 av. Mohammed V, sells 30dh basic **maps.** (Open daily 8am-noon and 2-10pm.) **Internet** access is at **Info-Ouar,** around the corner from Café-Restaurant Essalam on rue de Marché. (☎044 88 45 60. 10dh per hr. Open daily 9am-midnight.) The **post office,** with **telephones,** is on av. Mohammed V by the tourist office. (Open M-F 8:30am-3:30pm.)

ACCOMMODATIONS AND FOOD. For inexpensive lodging, look on av. Mohammed V or the parallel streets. **Hôtel Royal ❶,** 24 av. Mohammed V next to Chez Dimitri and across from Hotel Essalam, has welcoming if simple rooms and can help with rental cars and expeditions. (☎044 88 22 58. Cold showers free. Warm showers 10dh. Singles 36dh, with shower 81dh; doubles 72dh/92dh; triples 73dh/93dh; quads with bath 134dh.) The **Hôtel Bab Es Sahara ❶,** in the plaza across from the Shell station just off of Mohammed V, has big, cheap rooms, a restaurant, currency exchange, and accepts credit cards. (☎044 88 47 22; fax 044 88 44 65. Singles 50dh, with bath 80dh; doubles 80dh, with bath 130dh; triples with shower 160dh.) The **supermarket** on av. Mohammed V, across the street from Hôtel Royal, has an unrivaled selection of cured meats, canned goods, chocolate, wine, cold beer, and European goods. The best restaurant value in town is the **Café-Restaurant Essalam ❷,** av. Prince Héritier Sidi Mohammed, just off av. Mohammed V. The *tajine* or couscous *menú* is 50dh; big parties can order a pigeon *pastilla* for a negotiable 200dh. (☎044 88 23 76. Open daily 7am-11pm.)

SIGHTS. The nearest example of desert architecture is the **Taourirt Kasbah,** once a Glaoui stronghold. The *kasbah*, 1½km east of town, was built in the mid-18th century and occupied until 1956. Recently restored, its interior is an entertaining maze of winding streets, stairways, and balconies. To get there, walk down av. Mohammed V, bear left at the tourist office, and head toward Club Med; it's right before the blue awning of **Café de la Kasbah.** (Open daily 8:30-6:30pm. 10dh.)

NEAR OUARZAZATE

The area to the north of Ouarzazate is a hot and dusty palette of desert browns and greens, periodically interrupted by small Berber **kasbahs.** The plateaus of the pre-Sahara here are spectacular in their vastness; the scale of towns is difficult to determine against such a background. Perhaps the most well-known of the *kasbahs* is in the village **Aït Benhaddou,** 21km on the road toward Marrakesh. Built in the 17th century, the *kasbah* has been designated a UNESCO World Heritage site but is still home to a few Berber families. A member of the family will show you around for a 10dh tip. Some rooms still have intricate stone carvings and vegetable-dyed cedar wood ceilings. The terrace has a great view of the surrounding mountains. Movie buffs may recognize the forest of tapered turrets and backdrop—they're the region's film stars, featured in *Lawrence of Arabia* and *Jesus of Nazareth.* The best way to get here is to take a *grand taxi* from Ouarzazate (about 250dh min. round-trip; the driver will wait, but don't pay him until the journey is complete). It's also a beautiful ride on a rented moped with a full gas tank. From Marrakesh, take the second signed road (the paved one) to Aït Benhaddou and drive until restaurants appear on the right (10km). Park in front, and walk (5min.) toward the *kasbah* in the distance. Cross a riverbed to get to the entrance.

THE DRA'A VALLEY وادي درعة

South of Ouarzazate, passing through Agdz and Zagora and ending in M'Hamid, is the narrow Dra'a Valley, along which stretches a nearly continuous grove of palm trees strewn with *kasbahs* and *qsours* (fortified strongholds). This scenic route is best covered by rental car, although people also hop from village to village by bus, or taxi. At the end of the road lies M'Hamid, perhaps the best place in Morocco to stage treks into the desert. Avoid the touristy desert excursions that stop at every shop along the way, and find a more authentic experience of Berber life in the desert. Allow at least two days to reach M'Hamid. Expeditions by camel or 4x4 vehicles are best taken from M'Hamid, but those pressed for time or money may choose to wait until Erg Chebbi for their desert excursion.

OUARZAZATE TO ZAGORA

The route south from Ouarzazate (P31) is unexciting for the first 15km, although a lunar landscape extends in all directions. Volcanic rock soon gives way to an oasis of sorts; a small road to the left leads to the **al-Mansour al-Dahbi reservoir,** formed by heavy rains in 1989. **Aït Saoun** is the first *qsour* along the way and marks the beginning of a steep ascent over the **Tizi-n-Tinifift,** which ultimately reaches an altitude of 1660m. On the way back down, the road passes by several kilometers of stratified rock until the start of the Dra'a's main oases. The first city to take advantage of the waters is **Agdz,** 67km south of Ouarzazate. Set below **Djebel Kissane,** an imposing peak of the Djebel Sharo to the east, the town mainly functions as a resting point before continuing south; buses stop for 30min. to allow passengers to grab a drink. If you have time and your own vehicle, there is a **palmery** to the left when approaching from Ouarzazate, with a few small *kasbahs* within.

Just a few kilometers south of Agdz, the real *qsours* begin. The road intersects the Dra'a River, at which point there is a remarkable series of villages: each community is divided into several clusters surrounding an oasis, with smaller homes adjoining central, fortified *kasbahs*. **Tamnougalt,** 6km south of Agdz, was once the area's capital. The next *qsour*, **Timiderte,** boasts another Glaoui Kasbah worth investigating only if you have not yet seen one. Next is **Tangihlit** and its explosion of palm trees; its neighbor **Tamezmoute** has another large *kasbah*. Just 37km north of Zagora, the larger **Tinezouline** has a *kasbah* and a lively Monday *souq*. At the **Azlag Pass** just before Zagora, the valley opens again to a vast ocean of palms.

HUSTLERS AND HITCHERS. Many hustlers pose as hitchhikers or victims of auto breakdowns along the Ouarzazate to Zagora road. Don't stop; just smile and wave as you go by.

ZAGORA تجكورة ☎044

Stiflingly hot, Zagora is the traditional jumping-off point for treks and excursions into the valley or desert. It is perhaps most famous for the half-serious sign at the lower end of town: "To Tombouktou 52 *jours*—by camel." Zagora itself is not a very appealing place, and for those who wish to take a camel trek, M'Hamid offers a more authentic experience. The only time worth spending in Zagora is during the Mouloud, when the city celebrates the **Moussem of Moulay Abdelkader Jilali.**

Numerous **trek agencies** line av. Mohammed V, with the best deals at the hotels or campgrounds (**Hôtel des Amis** and **Camping Sindibad** are good bets). Expect to pay around 200-250dh per person per day for trips around Zagora and 300dh per person per day to trek near M'Hamid (transportation included). The more people trekking, the cheaper the price per person. If you plan to take a long trip out into the desert, it's best to push on to M'Hamid, where you'll find better deals.

The best-priced accommodation is the **Hôtel des Amis ❶,** in the middle of av. Mohammed V, with slightly dingy but decent rooms. (☎044 84 79 24. Singles with shower 35dh; doubles 50dh, with shower 60dh; triples with shower 75dh; 20dh to sleep on the roof. MC/V.) Signs indicate the way to **Camping Sindibad ❶,** av. Hassan II, just off av. Mohammed V. Spots are shaded by rare trees and covered with grass; there is also a pool at no extra charge. (☎044 84 75 53. Hot showers 5dh. 10dh per person, 5dh per car, 10dh per caravan.) Both accommodations have restaurants. All **buses** stop on av. Mohammed V, the road that the highway turns into, although **CTM** (☎044 84 73 27) stops on the far side of town while other private companies stop on the near side, along with **grand taxis.** CTM buses run to: **Casablanca** (12hr., 6pm, 170dh); **Marrakesh** (6hr., 6pm, 82-110dh); and **Ouarzazate** (2hr., 6pm, 36-45dh). The best way to get to M'Hamid is by *grand taxi* (25dh). Every sort of tourist and financial service is along av. Mohammed V, including **banks,** the **post office,** an **Internet cafe,** and most hotels and restaurants.

SOUTHERN DRA'A

To cross the Dra'a at the southern edge of Zagora, travel out of town (away from Ouarzazate) for 3km and watch for a dirt road on the left (at the sign for Camping de la Montagne de Zagora). This rough track trundles its way to **Djebel Zagora,** a lone volcanic outcrop overlooking the fertile Dra'a. The best time to visit the mountain is at sunset, when the peaks shimmer in the dying light.

TAMEGROUTE. Just off the main highway is the town of Tamegroute, an oasis of date palms and *qsours*. Morocco's best historical resource is here, in what seems to be the middle of nowhere. Tamegroute's **library** contains 4000 Moroccan manuscripts dating from the 11th to the 18th centuries. The collection includes a history of Fez, a copy of Bukhari's *Hadish*, poetry of al-Andalusi, countless astronomical algebraic charts, Mohammed's family tree, and a history of Egypt. The library's most treasured document is a history of Islam written on gazelle skin in 1063 by the great legal authority Iman Malik. To get to the library, ignore the painted *bibliothèque* signs (a scam) and turn left (coming from Zagora) down the only paved road. Just after the pavement ends, walk straight for a block and look for a large gate on the right; this leads to the library courtyard. (Open daily 9am-noon and 3-6pm. Free, but tip the multilingual caretaker around 5dh.)

TINFOU. Just south of Tamegroute along the main road, the **Dunes of Tinfou** rise from the valley floor in smooth golden mounds. They are rare in that they can be easily reached by foot or any kind of car from the main road. Just watch for a well-marked dirt turn-off on the left as you come from Zagora. **Hotel Repos du Sables ❸** is located on the road to M'Hamid (27 km from Zagora and 7km from Tamegroute) with the dunes of Tinfou as a dramatic backdrop. It is one of the best places to spend the night in all of Morocco, worth the effort. The owner offers a short 1hr. excursion to the dunes, but it's better to venture out on your own. (☎044 84 85 66. Singles 100dh; doubles 150dh.)

M'HAMID ☎044

M'Hamid is literally the end of the road. Forty-five kilometers from the Algerian border and 97km from Zagora, M'Hamid stands as the outpost at the edge of the great deserts. M'Hamid lacks all but the most basic facilities; electricity made its debut a few years back. If you're in town on a Monday, check out the weekly market where nomads come from the desert to sell their goods. M'Hamid is the best place for guided **camel treks** into the Sahara (300-350dh per person per day with meals included). **Four-by-four trips,** and even trips with your own car, can be arranged as well. The best place to arrange excursions is at

ROCK THE KASBAH Most of the ruined structures you'll pass while traveling in Morocco are **kasbahs,** four-towered fortified structures built for one family and its livestock. **Qsours,** while not necessarily larger, are fortified villages with any number of towers, designed for any number of families. Either of these (or a section of a city) may be referred to as a **mellah,** which means it was once inhabited by Jews. The structures were almost all built with **pizid,** a mixture of straw and mud that needs to be reapplied every year; that is why there are so many ruined *kasbahs* that date back only 40 or 50 years. The first floor of each is generally used for animals, the second for dining and the kitchen, and the third for living and sleeping. The prefixes **Ben** and **Aït** modify the family name: Ben means "son of," while Aït refers to the entire family.

Sahara Services, the only agency in M'Hamid, in the town's center. They charge 300-350dh per person per day with meals and tent accommodations included. (☎061 77 67 66; fax 044 84 80 26.) **L'Hôtel Iriqui** (☎044 84 80 23; www.iriqui.com; booking in Ourzazate ☎044 88 57 99. MC/V) has slightly more expensive tours. If you start in M'Hamid instead of in Zagora, you can reach endless seas of sand dunes and isolated oases within five or six days and very impressive landscapes in only one or two days. The **Chagaga Dunes,** arguably bigger and better than the dunes in Merzouga, are about 60km from M'Hamid. Locals claim they reach 300m high and are 40km wide. The way to the dunes leads you past impressive landscapes and isolated oases. It's a five-day trip by camel or an overnight trip by 4x4. If you don't have time to make the trip to the Chagaga Dunes, there are smaller and less impressive dunes only 15km away. The best times to go are in November or December, when temperatures are least extreme. Spend the night at the newly expanded **Hôtel-Restaurant Sahara ❶,** which offers rooms with free hot showers. (Singles 40dh; doubles 75dh; triples 105dh; sleeping in a Berber tent 10dh.) The hotel also serves food, including camel meat (entrees 15-50dh). To reach M'Hamid by bus, you'll have to come from Casablanca or Marrakesh. A **CTM bus** leaves Casablanca (13hr., 8:30pm, 180dh), and private buses leave from Marrakesh (10hr.; 8:30am, 7pm; 110dh). To make the return trip, one **CTM bus** leaves each day for **Marrakesh** via Ouarzazate and Zagora (11hr., 5am, 100dh), as well as one privately-owned bus (11hr.; 7am, 2pm; 90dh). **Taxis** and trucks to Zagora are more frequent. There are no banks and only a tiny **post office.**

THE DADÈS VALLEY وادى دادس

Broader and drier than the Dra'a Valley, the Dadès Valley stretches eastward from Ouarzazate. The valley's main attractions are the **Dadès** and **Todra Gorges,** extending north into the dry escarpment of the High Atlas. The *kasbahs* of the **Skoura** oasis make for an interesting stop on the way to the gorges. A four-wheel drive vehicle is required to get from Dadés to the Todra across the **Djebel Sharo** range.

SKOURA ☎044

Forty-two kilometers east of Ouarzazate is the *kasbah*-filled oasis of Skoura, surrounded by fields of grain and roses. From Ouarzazate, turn left off the highway to reach the first *kasbah*, **Ben Moro.** Recently restored and converted into a hotel, it was previously owned by five generations of Moros; the first Moro built it in the 17th century. The hill and horse decorations above the doorways indicate that the Moro family was once a nomadic Berber tribe. Walking about 200m down any of the paths directly behind Ben Moro leads to the **Amridil Ksar,** located just across the river. An old Glaoui home, it gained fame with its appearance on the 50dh bill.

Still inhabited by the Nassar family, it is usually open to visitors; just knock on the front door. You can spend the night for 100dh or just tour the grounds with the caretaker. Nearby is the **mellah** Kasbah Aït Sidi Maocti, with its intricate exterior carvings. The owner of the Ben Moro Kasbah, Mohammed Sibir, is happy to show anyone around (tip 10-20dh). The town of Skoura itself has little to offer, so plan to move on once you've seen the *kasbahs*. **Buses** may stop on the Ouarzazate to al-Rachidia route, but a *grand taxi* from Ouarzazate should cost no more than 20dh.

BOUMALNE DU DADÈS ☎044

At a key junction between the Dadès Gorge and the Djebel Sharo, Boumalne du Dadès has succeeded where its neighbors have failed: not a single faux guide bothers visitors to this tourist-friendly, attractive town. Its vantage point from a steep cliff over the Dadès River has made sunset-watching a popular local pastime. If you can't make it up to the Dadès Gorge itself by nightfall (a much nicer place to spend the night), the best place to stay in Boumalne is in the clean, plain rooms of the recently expanded **Hôtel Al Manadar ❸,** five minutes up the hill from the main square. (☎044 83 01 72. Singles 100dh; doubles 130-160dh; triples 180dh.) Its **restaurant ❷** serves good food with a minimal wait (*menú* 60dh; entrees 35dh). The highway turns into the main road (P32) and goes through town and up the cliff to reach the plateau above. Private **buses** arrive on the lower part of this street. Buses go to **al-Rachidia** (5 per day 5am-4:30pm, 50dh); **Casablanca** and **Rabat** (3 per day 9:30am-6:15pm, 120-130dh); **Erfoud** (9am, 2:30pm; 60dh); **Fez** (4:30pm, 120dh); **Marrakesh** (5 per day 6am-6:15pm, 75dh); **Ourzazate** (6:15pm); and **Zagora** (2pm, 60dh). **Grand taxis** leave from near the bus station for Ouarzazate and Tinerhir, while minibuses and pickup trucks will carry you up the Dadès Gorge for around 15-20dh. The **post office,** with several **téléboutiques,** is on top of the hill (a left at the Shell gas station; a 20min. walk). There are two **Internet cafes, Dades Net** and **Cyber Cafe,** in the center of town behind a brown mosque and its large gravel parking lot (10dh/hr.).

Sixteen kilometers on the drive from Boulmane du Dadès to the Dadès Gorge awaits the geographical wonder **Fingers of the Monkey.** Look for a large gravel shoulder about 50m wide on the right side of the road and pull over. The owner of **Camping-Restaurant Le Dades,** on the other side of the road, can show you where the path begins. The scenery is heavenly, with a small creek flowing through lush gardens filled with bright flowers and tiny frogs, set against the fantastic rock structure known by the locals as "Monkey Fingers." Cross the river at a shallow point, and one of the locals can show you where you can enter the rock structure. Walk through the rocks until you reach the top for breathtaking results.

MOROCCO

DADÈS GORGE ☎044

Bizarre limestone rock formations, *kasbahs*, and sweeping changes in color mark the winding road through the Dadès Gorge, more tranquil and beautiful than its neighbor, the Todra Gorge. A single paved road runs up into the gorge from Boumalne, past small villages and lush palmeries for over 50km. If driving, the route is best taken slowly and with frequent stops to enjoy the landscape changes, or for hikes down into the valley. For those without transport, lorries run quite frequently to and from the gorge, or taxis can be hired in Boumalne. Base yourself at one of the hotels listed below; an hour's walk from either reveals great scenery.

There are many places to stay and eat along the road, the best being the **Restaurant Hôtel La Gazelle du Dadès ❷,** at 27km from Boumalne, which has a friendly atmosphere and a breathtaking location. (☎044 83 17 53. Singles 70dh; doubles 80-100dh; triples 100dh; *salon* or terrace 25dh with mattress and shower; **camping** 10dh per person with shower.) Through the hotel, hire a **guide** (300dh per person for 24hr. with meals), arrange **rafting expeditions** when the water is high (Jan.-Apr.;

200dh per person per day), and rent **bikes** (60dh per day). Its **restaurant** also serves filling meals (3-course *menú* 60dh). Another solid option in the gorge is the **Auberge des Gorges du Dadès ❸,** at 25km from Boumalne. The hostel arranges **treks,** and has a restaurant. (☎044 83 17 10. Singles 100dh; doubles 140dh.)

TINERHIR (TINGHIR) ☎044

While it's preferable to stay the night in Todra Gorge itself, Tinerhir provides the nearest conveniences. The eastern part of town (on the right when coming from Ouarzazate) contains an old medina and *mellah* worthy of exploration.

The highway turns into av. Mohammed V as it reaches the town. **Buses** arrive just off it, in pl. Principale. Parallel to av. Mohammed V is av. Hassan II, where most of the cheaper hotels and restaurants are located. A **CTM bus** goes to **Casablanca** via **Meknes** and **Rabat** (7pm). **Private buses** go to **Agadir** (8, 9:30pm); **al-Rachidia** (2pm); **Erfoud** (3pm); **Fez** (9:30am, 5:30 pm); **Meknes** (3 per day 8am-7pm); and **Tangier** (2pm). **Grand taxis** running east and west and **lorries** going up the gorge (15-20dh) leave on the other side of the garden between the two main roads. **Banks** line av. Mohammed V. The **post office** is near the taxi stand on av. Hassan II.

For accommodations, try **Hôtel Tomboktou ❸,** Av. Bir Anzarane. From Ourzazate, turn right onto the paved road before the center of town. Enjoy Tomboktou's traditionally-decorated rooms in a restored *kasbah*. (☎044 83 51 81; fax 011 83 35 05. Singles 89dh, with bath 250dh; doubles 156dh/350dh.) For a cheaper stay, budget hotels line av. Hassan II opposite the park. Next to the CTM office is the student-oriented **Résidence El Fath ❶,** 56 av. Hassan II. The owner will arrange **bike rentals** for exploring the gorge, and its **restaurant** serves good rotisserie chicken. (☎044 83 48 06. Bikes 100dh per day. Singles 40dh; doubles 80dh; triples 90dh.) Just outside of town toward Ouarzazate is **Camping Ourti ❶,** av. Mohammed V, with bungalow-type rooms (35dh per person) and a swimming pool which is 10dh but free for guests. (☎044 83 32 05. Camping 12dh per person, 10dh per tent, 8dh per car.) Camping Ourti will also arrange outings up the gorge and to palmeries.

TODRA GORGE ☎044

MOROCCO

The road out of Tinerhir snakes up the **Todra River Valley** for 14km before reaching the mouth of the **gorge.** From here, hike up between the towering walls. Todra is more developed than the Dadès; while more extensive facilities are available, privacy and the sense of wilderness are lost. Still, the hike is spectacular. Almost 1000 ft. high, the sienna walls frame a blue strip of sky above and fall to a rocky riverbed below. A half-day hike is enough to appreciate the magnificence of the gorge, but a few days, or even a week, will allow you to climb well into the High Atlas. Rock climbing is popular, but there are no agencies with equipment or guides. Along the way to the gorge are a trio of beautiful campgrounds. **Auberge de l'Atlas ❶** is slightly better than the other two facilities. Rooms are big and bright with pine furniture, and the campsites are well shaded. (☎/fax 044 89 50 46. Camping 10dh per person, 15dh per tent, 15dh per car. Doubles 100dh; triples 140dh; Berber tent 15dh; terrace 20dh.) Its **restaurant ❷** serves standard fare (*menú* 50-60dh). **Café-Restaurant Auberge Étoile des Gorges ❶** has eight worn rooms and a restaurant; better yet, sleep on the roof below the gorge walls. (☎044 89 50 55. Singles 50dh; doubles 100dh; salon 20dh; roof 10dh.). You can also arrange rock climbing and guided trips here. At the end of the road is the comfortable **Hôtel Les Roches ❹,** which is frequented by tour groups and has a rooftop terrace. (☎044 83 48 14; fax 044 83 36 11. Singles 150dh; doubles 200dh; triples 275dh; terrace 50dh. AmEx/MC/V.) The **restaurant ❷** serves average food (entrees 50dh for hotel guests, 70dh otherwise). A small **tourist office** is on av. Le Prince Moulay Abdullah, just off the main road.

THE ZIZ VALLEY

AL-RACHIDIA الرشيدية ☎044

Al-Rachidia's university and successful businesses have brought the town an air of prosperity and friendliness; it offers little to do or see, but makes a pleasant stop for travelers heading into the southern deserts and gorges. **Buses** arrive in town at the main bus station (☎044 57 20 24) at pl. Principale, just off the town's main street, av. Moulay Ali Cherif. Buses go to **Casablanca** via **Rabat** (16hr.; CTM 9:15pm, private companies 5 per day 5:30-10pm; 110-130dh); **Erfoud** and **Rissani** (1hr.; private companies 5 per day 7:30am-7:30pm; 15-20dh); **Fez** (8hr.; CTM 10pm, private companies 10 per day 7am-11:15pm); **Meknes** (7 hr.; CTM 10pm, private companies 4 per day 6am-10pm; 80dh). **Grand taxis** go to: **Erfoud** (16dh); **Rissani** (20dh); **Tinerhir** (about 50dh). There are several **banks** in town; the BCME in the town square has an **ATM.** Services include **police** ☎19, at the bus station, and a dingy **Red Crescent,** av. Moulay Ali Cherif next to Restaurant Imilchil.

Most budget hotels are near the bus station. **Hotel El Ansar ❶,** 34 rue Ibn Batouta, behind the bus station and to the left, has the best value, with sparkling rooms and free hot showers. You can arrange to take the owner's 4x4 directly to Merzouga. (☎044 57 39 19. Singles 40dh; doubles 60dh; triples 80dh.) Also good is **Hotel Renaissance ❷,** just behind Restaurant Echajara. (☎055 57 26 33. Doubles with hot shower 70dh.) For fresh produce, try the **supermarket,** across from Hotel M'Daghra. (Open Sa-Th 8am-1pm and 4-9:30pm.) **Café-Restaurant Echajara ❶,** 38 av. Moulay Ali Cherif (☎067 36 62 18), serves a complete *menú* for 35dh. Try the house specialty *qualia* (a mix of beef, fried egg, and desert spices), which the owner claims is served nowhere else in Morocco. Larbi Lamhamdi (☎070 13 75 75), arranges sunrise/sunset **tours** to **Merzouga dunes** (200dh with your own car).

ERFOUD ارفود ☎044

Although famous for its marble fossils and its annual date festival (Oct.), Erfoud itself has little to entertain visitors. If you're heading for the dunes of Merzouga, you're better off avoiding Erfoud and its hustlers by staying the dunes themselves.

One CTM **bus** departs from av. Mohammed V, Erfoud's main street, and goes to **Meknes** (8hr., 8:30pm, 95dh). More frequent private buses leave from pl. des F.A.R., at the far end of av. Mohammed V and go to **Casablanca** (8:30pm, 130dh); **Fez** (3 per day 6:30am-11pm, 97dh); **Marrakesh** (7am, 6:15pm, 130dh); **Meknes** (8am, 95dh); **Ourzazate** (3pm, 160dh); **Rabat** (5:30pm, 120dh); and **Zagora** (8:30, 9:30am; 75-110dh). **Grand taxis** go to **al-Rachidia** (16dh) and **Rissani** (6dh), departing from the intersection of av. Mohammed V and av. Moulay Ismail. **Banks** (1 with an **ATM**) the **hospital,** and the **post office** are there as well. Most of Erfoud's hotels are expensive. A good budget option, **Hôtel Merzouga ❷,** 114 av. Mohammed V, outshines the rest, offering spotless and cheery rooms with showers. (☎044 57 65 32. Singles 60dh; doubles 80dh; triples 120dh; terrace 25dh.) The hotel's **restaurant** serves traditional Moroccan cuisine (3-course *menú* 40dh).

NEAR ERFOUD: THE DUNES OF MERZOUGA

About 50km south of Erfoud is one of Morocco's most enduring images: the fantastic **al-Chebbi** dunes of Merzouga. The largest in the world—some claim they are up to 125m tall—they are most enchanting at sunrise and sunset. It is said that submersion in the sweltering sand cures heart disease and rheumatism. Arrange excursions from Erfoud—hire a 4x4 *grand taxi* (5-6hr., 400-500dh per taxi) in pl. des F.A.R. or join the air-conditioned package tour (600dh per car) leaving from Hôtel Merzouga. You can also take a *grand taxi* from Erfoud to one of the dune

MOROCCO

accommodations and arrange your excursion there. Those with cars should consider enlisting a guide to navigate through the sand-blown *piste.* One highly recommended guide is Rachid from **Merzouga Car;** save money by booking directly through him (☎067 76 63 44; rachid212@yahoo.com). Arrange to stop in the oasis and the flamingo pond. In Merzouga town, Berber families rent camels for dune treks (50dh per hr.). Ask any driver or hotel owner to point you to them.

Dune "hotels" are mud and straw buildings; most arrange dune tours where you can sleep on the sand under the stars. **Auberge-Restaurant-Camping La Caravane ❶** has a free campground-type enclosure, as well as small rooms with Berber blankets. (☎044 35 16 54; fax 044 57 52 19. Singles 50dh; doubles 100dh; triples 120dh.) Austere **Hotel Er-Chebbi ❷** has a telephone. (☎044 35 16 26. 60dh for 1 or 2 people.)

APPENDIX

CLIMATE

In the following charts, the first two columns for each month list the average daily minimum and maximum temperatures in degrees Celsius and Fahreinheit. The rain column lists the average number of days of rain that month.

SPAIN	JANUARY			APRIL			JULY			OCTOBER		
	°C	°F	Rain	°C	°F	Rain	°C	°F	Rain	°C	°F	Rain
Barcelona	4-13	40-55	5	8-17	47-62	9	19-27	66-81	4	12-21	54-70	9
Madrid	0-11	32-51	8	6-17	42-63	9	16-32	61-90	2	8-20	47-68	8
Málaga	7-16	45-61	7	11-20	51-68	6	20-29	68-84	0	14-23	58-74	6
Santiago de Compostela	5-10	41-50	21	8-18	46-64	7	13-24	55-75	1	11-21	52-70	10
Sevilla	6-16	42-61	8	10-22	50-71	7	19-35	66-95	0	13-26	56-78	6

PORTUGAL	JANUARY			APRIL			JULY			OCTOBER		
	°C	°F	Rain	°C	°F	Rain	°C	°F	Rain	°C	°F	Rain
Faro	7-16	45-61	9	10-19	50-67	9	18-28	64-83	0	14-23	61-72	6
Lisbon	8-14	46-58	15	8-17	46-63	15	15-24	63-81	2	14-22	58-72	9
Porto	5-13	41-56	18	9-18	48-64	18	15-25	59-76	5	11-21	52-69	15

MOROCCO	JANUARY			APRIL			JULY			OCTOBER		
	°C	°F	Rain	°C	°F	Rain	°C	°F	Rain	°C	°F	Rain
Fez	4-16	39-61	8	9-23	49-73	9	18-36	64-97	1	13-26	55-79	7
Marrakesh	4-18	39-64	7	11-26	52-79	6	19-38	66-100	1	14-28	57-82	4
Rabat	8-17	46-62	9	11-22	52-72	7	17-28	63-73	0	14-25	57-77	6
Tangier	8-16	46-61	10	11-18	52-64	8	18-27	64-81	0	15-22	59-72	8

TIME DIFFERENCES

Spain is 1 hour ahead of Greenwhich Mean Time (GMT) and 6 hours ahead of US EST. **Portugal** and **Morocco** are on GMT and 5 hours ahead of EST. Thus, when it is noon in New York, it is 5pm in Portugal and Morocco and 6pm in Spain. Spain and Portugal, together with the rest of Europe, switch to Daylight Savings Time about one week before the US does; they switch back at the same time. Morocco does not switch, and thus is 4 hours ahead of US EST and 2 hours behind Spain in the summer.

ADDRESSES

Spain and Portugal: "Av.," "C.,""R.," and "Tr." are abbreviations for street, "Po." and "Pg." for promenade, "Pl." and "Pr" for plaza, and "Ctra." for highway. A building's number follows the street name; "s/n" stands for *sin numero* (without number). **Morocco:** "av.," "bd.," "rue," and "calle" mean street; "pl." is a plaza. The building number comes before the street name, when there is one. When hunting for an address, note that many streets are being renamed in Arabic; "rue" and "calle" may be replaced by "zankat," "derb," or "sharia."

SPANISH PHRASEBOOK

Spanish pronunciation is fairly intuitive. Most consonants are the same as English. Important exceptions are: *j* ("h" in *hello*), *ll* ("y" in *yes*), *ñ* ("ny" in *canyon*), and *rr* (trilled "r"). The consonant *h* is always silent; *x* retains its English sound.

ENGLISH	SPANISH	ENGLISH	SPANISH
		The Bare Minimum	
Yes/No	Sí/No	**Do you speak English?**	¿Habla (usted) inglés?
Hello	Hola (Sí on the phone)	**I don't understand**	No entiendo
Good morning	Buenos días	**I don't speak Spanish**	No hablo español
Good afternoon	Buenas tardes	**What/When**	¿Qué?/¿Cuándo?
Good evening/night	Buenas noches	**Where/How**	¿Dónde?/¿Cómo?
Goodbye	Adiós/Hasta luego	**Who/Why**	¿Quién?/¿Por qué?
Please/Thank you	Por favor/Gracias	**How are you?**	¿Cómo está (usted)?
Excuse me	Perdón/Perdóname	**Good/Bad/So-so**	Bién/Mal/Así así
Help	¡Socorro!	**What time is it?**	¿Qué hora es?
No smoking/Got a lighter (cigarette)?	No fumar/¿Tiene fuego (un cigarillo)?	**How much does it cost?**	¿Cuánto cuesta?
Here/There/Left/ Right/Straight	Aquí/Allí/Izquierda/ Derecha/Recto	**Can you drop me off here?**	¿Usted me puede dejar aqui?
Open/Closed	Abierto/Cerrado	**My name is...**	Me llamo...
Hot/Cold	Caliente/Frío	**What is your name?**	¿Cómo se llama?
Where is a late-night pharmacy?	¿Dónde está una farmacia de guardia?	**Is there a telephone that I could use?**	¿Hay un teléfono que podría usar?
Where is the toilet?	¿Dónde está el lavabo?	**I'm sick.**	Estoy enfermo/a.
		Accommodation and Transportation	
I want/I would like	Quiero/Quisiera	**How do I reach...?**	¿Cómo llego a...?
I would like a room	Quisiera un cuarto	**One ticket to...**	Un billete para...
Do you have any rooms?	¿Tiene cuartos libres?	**Bus (Train) station/ Airport**	Estación de Autobús (Tren)/Aeropuerto
I would like to reserve a room, please.	Quisiera reservar una habitación, por favor.	**How much is the fare to...?**	¿Cuánto vale el billete a...?
bath/shower/water	baño/ducha/agua	**train/plane/bus**	tren/avión/autobús
key/sheets	llave/sábanas	**round-trip**	ida y vuelta
Air conditioning	aire acondicionado	**How long is the trip?**	¿Cuánto dura el viaje?
Hotel/Hostel/Campgrounds/Inn	Hotel/Hostal or Albergue/Camping/Posada	**At what time does it leave/arrive?**	¿A qué hora sale/llega?
		Food and Dining (also see Glossary)	
breakfast	desayuno	**the check, please**	la cuenta, por favor
lunch	almuerzo	**drink**	bebida
dinner	cena	**dessert**	postre
Can I get this without the meat?	¿Me puede preparar este plato sin carne?	**Can you please bring me...?**	¿Me puede traer...por favor?
		Days	
Sunday	domingo	**today**	hoy
Monday	lunes	**tomorrow**	mañana
Tuesday	martes	**day after tomorrow**	pasado mañana
Wednesday	miércoles	**yesterday**	ayer
Thursday	jueves	**day before yesterday**	antes de ayer/anteayer
Friday	viernes	**week**	semana
Saturday	sábado	**weekend**	fin de semana

PORTUGUESE PHRASEBOOK

Portuguese words are often spelled like their Spanish equivalents, although Portuguese pronunciation can be baffling to Spanish speakers. In additional to regular vowels, Portuguese has nasal vowels as in French; vowels with a *til* (*ã*, *õ*, etc.) or before an *m* or *n* are pronounced with a nasal twang. At the end of a word, *o* is pronounced *oo* as in *room*, and *e* is sometimes silent (usually after a *t* or *d*). The consonant *s* is pronounced *sh* or *zh* when it occurs before another consonant. The consonants *ch* and *x* are pronounced *sh*, although the latter is sometimes pronounced as in English; *j* and *g* (before an *e* or *i*) are pronounced *zh*. The combinations *nh* and *lh* are pronounced "ny" as in *canyon* and "ly" as in *billion*.

ENGLISH	PORTUGUESE	PRONUNCIATION
Yes/No	Sim/Não	seeng/now
Hello	Olá	oh-LAH
Good day, afternoon/night	Bom dia, Boa tarde/noite	bom DEE-ah, BO-ah tard/noyt
Goodbye	Adeus	ah-DAY-oosh
Please	Por favor	pur fah-VOR
Thank you	Obrigado (male)/Obrigada (female)	oh-bree-GAH-doo/dah
Sorry	Desculpe	dish-KOOLP
Excuse me, please	Desculpe	dish-KOOLP
Do you speak English?	Fala inglês?	FAH-lah een-GLAYSH?
I don't understand	Não entendo	now ayn-TAYN-doo
Where is...?	Onde é que é ...?	OHN-deh eh keh eh...?
How much does this cost?	Quanto custa?	KWAHN-too KOOSH-tah?
Do you have a single/double room?	Tem um quarto individual/duple?	tem om KWAR-toe een-dee-vee-du-AHL/DOO-play?
Help!	Socorro!	so-KO-ro!

MOROCCAN PHRASEBOOK

Moroccan Arabic, though it is historically related to Classical Arabic, is difficult to understand even for those who have studied the Classical language. Particularly daunting is the language's seeming lack of vowels; the alien language in Frank Herbert's *Dune* is allegedly based on the Moroccan dialect. The consonants *'ayin* (written ') and *hha'* (written *hh*) are pronounced deep in the throat; *'alif* (written ') is a glottal stop. Some consonants, the so-called "emphatics," are pronounced with the throat constricted and the tongue tensed; often this constriction spreads over entire syllables or words. *Let's Go* recommends that you stick with French.

ENGLISH	MOROCCAN ARABIC	FRENCH
Hello (polite)	assa-LAA-mu-'a-LEY-kum / 'a-LEY-kum as-sa-LAAM (response)	Bonjour (day) / Bonsoir (night)
Hello/How are you?	la-BAS?	Ça va?
Fine, thanks	la-BAS, al-HAM-du-lil-lah	Tres bien, merci
Yes/No	EE-yeh/LA	Oui/Non
Please	min FAD-lak (m), min FAD-lik (f)/'AF-fak (m), 'AF-fik (f)/al-LAH-yikhaleek	S'il vous plaît
Thank you	shukran/mercee	Merci
I want (I would like)...	bgheet...	Je voudrais...
I need/I don't need	khuss-NEE/ma-khuss-NEESH	J'ai besoin de/Je n'ai pas besoin de
Where is...?	feen...?	Où est...? / Où se trouve...?
When is...?	fo-QASH...?	A quelle heure est...?
Bus/Taxi/Train	u-tu-BEES/TAK-see/MA-shina	Bus/Taxi/Train

APPENDIX

ENGLISH	MOROCCAN ARABIC	FRENCH
Hotel/Bathroom	u-TEEL/twa-LET or ham-MAM	Hôtel/Toilette
Is there a room?	wesh kayn beet?	Est-ce qu'il y a une chambre libre?
I don't speak Arabic (French)	ma-kan-tkal-LAMSH al-'arabi (al-fransawee)	Je ne parle pas arabe (français)
Do you speak English?	wesh-kat-TKAL-lim in-GLEE-zee?	Parlez-vous anglais?
How much does it cost?	sh-HAL ta-MAN?	Combien ça coute?
Let's work on a better price.	DIR-l-na shee taman mezyan / wa-TSOW-wab m'ana (very colloquial)	Faites-moi un bon prix.
A lot/A little bit	bez-ZAF/sh-WEEY-ya	Beaucoup/Un peu
Cheap/Expensive	ri-KHEES/GHEH-lee	Pas cher/cher
I'm not interested	ma bagh-EESH	Je ne suis pas interessé
Excuse me	SMEH-li	Pardon
Help!	an-NAJ-da! an-qee-DOO-nee!	Au secours!

ARABIC NUMERALS										
0	1	2	3	4	5	6	7	8	9	10
٠	١	٢	٣	٤	٥	٦	٧	٨	٩	١٠
sifir	waahid	itnayn	talaata	arba'a	khamsa	sitta	sab'a	tamaniya	tis'a	'ashara

GLOSSARY

In the following glossary we have tried to include the most useful shortlist of common terms possible, particularly words we use in the text and those that you will encounter frequently in food menus. Non-Castilian words are specified as **C** (Catalan), **B** (Basque), or **G** (Galician), respectively. In the Morocco glossary section, **A** stands for Moroccan Arabic and **F** refers to French.

SPAIN: TRAVELING

abadía: abbey
abierto: open
ajuntament (C): city hall
albergue: youth hostel
alcazaba: Muslim citadel
alcázar: Muslim palace
autobús: bus
avenida: avenue
avinguda (C): avenue
ayuntamiento: city hall
bahía: bay
bakalao: Spanish techno
baños: baths
barcelonés: of Barcelona
barrio viejo: old quarter
biblioteca: library
bodega: wine cellar
buceo: scuba diving
cajero automático: ATM
calle: street
cambio: currency exchange
capilla: chapel
carrer (C): street
casa particular: lodging in a private home
caseta: party tent for Sevilla's *Feria de Abril*
castell (C): castle
castillo: castle
catedral: cathedral
cerrado: closed
calabacín: zucchini
caldo gallego: white bean and potato soup
carretera: highway
churrigueresco: ornate Baroque architecture style
ciudad vieja: old city
ciutat vella (C): old city
colegio: school
consigna: luggage storage
Correos: post office
corrida: bullfight
cripta: crypt
croquetas: fried croquettes
encierro: running of the bulls
entrada: entrance
ermida (C): hermitage
ermita: hermitage
església (C): church
estación: station
estanco: tobacco shop
estanque: pond
estany (C): lake
extremeño: of Extremadura
fachada: façade
feria: outdoor market or fair
ferrocarriles: trains
fuente: fountain
gallego: of Galicia
gitano: gypsy
glorieta: rotary
iglesia: church
igrexa (G): church
IVA: value-added tax
jardín público: public garden
judería: Jewish quarter
kiosco: newsstand
librería: bookstore
lista de correos: poste restante
litera: sleeping car (in trains)
llegada: arrival
madrileño: Madrid resident
madrugada: early morning
manchego: from La Mancha
menú: full meal with bread, drink and side dish
mercado: market
mercat (C): market
mezquita: mosque
mirador: lookout point
monestir (C): monastery
monte: mountain
mosteiro (G): monastery

APPENDIX

Mozárabe: Christian art style
Mudéjar: Muslim architectural style
muelle: wharf, pier
muralla: wall
museo: museum
museu (C): museum
palau (C): palace
parador nacional: state-owned luxury hotel
paseo, Po.: promenade
passeig, Pg. (C): promenade
plaça, Pl. (C): square
plateresque: architectural style noted for its facades
platja (C): beach
plaza, Pl.: square
praza, Pr. (G): square
puente: bridge
rastro: flea market
real: royal
REAJ: the Spanish HI youth hostel network
Reconquista: the Christian reconquest of the Iberian peninsula from the Muslims
refugio: shelter, refuge
reina/rey: queen/king
retablo: altarpiece
ría (G): estuary
río: river
riu (C): river
rua (G): street
sacristía: part of the church where sacred objects are kept
sala: room or hall
salida: exit, departure
Semana Santa: Holy Week, leading up to Easter Sunday; **Setmana Santa** in Catalan
serra (C): mountain range
seu (C): cathedral
sevillanas: type of flamenco
SIDA: AIDS
sierra: mountain ranges
sillería: choir stalls
tienda: shop or tent
tesoro: treasury
torre: tower
universidad: university
v.o.: *versión original,* a foreign-language film subtitled in Spanish
valle: valley
zarzuela: Spanish light opera

SPAIN: FOOD & DRINK

a la plancha: grilled
aceite: oil
aceituna: olive
adabo: battered
aguacate: avocado
ahumado/a: smoked
ajo: garlic
al horno: baked
albóndigas: meatballs
alioli: Catalan garlic sauce
almejas: clams
almuerzo: midday meal
alubias: kidney beans
anchoas: anchovies
anguila: eel
arroz: rice
arroz con leche: rice pudding
asado: roasted
atún: tuna
bacalao: salted cod
bistec: steak
bocadillo: sandwich
bollo: bread roll
boquerones: anchovies
brasa: chargrilled
cacahuete: peanut
café con leche: coffee w/ milk
café solo: black coffee
calamares: calamari, squid
caldereta: stew
calimocho: red wine and coke
callos: tripe
camarones: shrimp
caña: small beer in a glass
canelones: cannelloni
cangrejo: crab
carne: meat
cava (C): champagne
cebolla: onion
cena: dinner
cerdo: pig, pork
cereza: cherry
cervecería: beer bar
cerveza: beer
champiñones: mushrooms
choco: cuttlefish
chorizo: spicy red sausage
chuleta: chop, cutlet
chupito: shot
churros: fried dough sticks
cocido: cooked; meat and peas stew
conejo: rabbit
coñac: brandy
copas: drinks
cortado: coffee with little milk
crudo: raw
cuchara: spoon
cuchillo: knife
cuenta: the bill
desayuno: breakfast
dorada: sea bass
empanada: meat/pastry pie
ensaladilla rusa: vegetable salad with mayonnaise
entremeses: hors d'oeuvres
escabeche: pickled fish
espagueti: spaghetti
espárragos: asparagus
espinacas: spinach
fabada asturiana: bean soup with sausage and ham
flan: crème caramel
frambuesa: raspberry
fresa: strawberry
frito/a: fried
galleta: cookie
gambas: prawns
gazpacho: cold soup with garlic and tomato
guindilla: hot chili pepper
guisantes: peas
helado: ice cream
horchata: sweet almond drink
horneado: baked
huevo: egg
jamón dulce: cooked ham
jamón serrano: cured ham
jatetxea (B): restaurant
jerez: sherry
langosta: lobster
langostino: large prawn
lechuga: lettuce
lomo: pork loin
manzana: apple
manzanilla: dry, light sherry
mejillones: mussels
melocotón: peach
menestra de verduras: vegetable mix/pottage
merienda: tea/snack
merluze: hake
migas: fried breadcrumb dish
morcilla: blood sausage (black pudding)
muy hecho: well-done (steak)
natillas: creamy milk dessert
paella: rice and seafood dish
pastas: small sweet cakes
patatas bravas: potatos in spicy tomato sauce
patatas fritas: French fries
pavo: turkey
pechuga: chicken breast
pepino: cucumber
pescaíto frito: tiny fried fish
picante: spicy
pimienta: pepper
piña: pineapple
pintxo (B): Basque for tapa
plancha: grilled
plátano: banana
plato del día: daily special
plato combinado: entree and side order
poco hecho: rare (steak)
pollo: chicken
pulpo: octopus
queso: cheese
rabo de toro: bull's tail
ración: small dish
rebozado: battered and fried
refrescos: soft drinks
relleno/a: stuffed
salchicha: pork sausage
sangría: red wine punch
seco: dried
sesos: brains
setas: wild mushrooms
sidra: cider
solomillo: sirloin
sopa: soup
taberna: tapas bar
tapa: bite-sized snack
tenedor: fork
ternera: beef, veal
terraza: patio seating

tinto: red (wine)
tortilla española: potato omelette
tostada: toast
trucha: trout
tubo: tall glass of beer
uva: grape
vaca, carne de: beef
verduras: green vegetables
vino: wine
vino blanco: white wine
vino tinto: red wine
xampanyería (C): champagne bar
yema: candied egg yolk
zanahoria: carrot
zarzuela de marisco: shellfish stew
zumo: fruit juice

PORTUGAL: TRAVELING

alto/a: upper
autocarro: bus
bairro: town district
baixo/a: lower
berrões: stone pigs found in Trás-Os-Montes
biciclete tudo terrano: mountain bike
bilhete: ticket
bilheteria: ticket office
câmara municipal: town hall
camioneta: coach
capela: chapel
casa de abrigo: shelter-house, usually in parks
castelo: castle
centro de saúde: state-run medical center
chegadas: arrivals
cidade: city
claustro: cloister
conta: bill
coro alto: choir stalls
Correios: post office
cruzeiro: cross
Dom, Dona: courtesy titles, usually for kings and queens
domingo: Sunday
entrada: entrance
esquerda: left (abbr. E, Esqa)
estação rodoviária: bus station
estrada: road
feriada: holiday
floresta: forest
fortaleza: fort
grutas: caves
horario: timetable
igreja: church
ilha: island
intercidade: inter-city train
lago: lake
largo: small square
ligação: connecting bus/train
livraria: bookstore
miradouro: lookout
mosteiro: monastery
mouraria: Moorish quarter
mudança: switch/change
obras: construction
paco: palace
paragem: stop
partidas: departures
pelourinho: stone pillory
pensão (s.), pensões (pl.): pension(s)/guesthouse(s)
ponta: bridge
porta: gate
pousada da juventude: youth hostel
pousada: state-run hotel
praça: square
praça de touros: bullring
praia: beach
PSP: Polícia de Seguranca Pública, the local police force
quarta-feira: Wednesday
quarto de casal: room with double bed
quinta-feira: Thursday
quiosque: kiosk; newsstand
res do chão: ground floor, abbr. R/C
residencial: guesthouse, more expensive than *pensões*
retablo: altarpiece
ribeiro: stream
rio: river
romaria: pilgrimage-festival
rossio: rotary
rua: street
sábado: Saturday
saída: exit
sé: cathedral
segunda-fiera: Monday
selos: stamps
sexta-feira: Friday
terça-feira: Tuesday
termas: spa
tesouro: treasury
tourada: bullfight
turismo: tourist office
vila: town

PORTUGAL: FOOD AND DRINK

açorda: thick soup with bread
adega: wine cellar, bar
aguardente: firewater
alface: lettuce
alho: garlic
almoço: lunch
ameijoas: clams
Antigua: aged grape brandy
arrufada de Coimbra: raised dough cake with cinnamon
assado (no forno): baked
azeitonas: olives
bacalhau: cod
bacalhau à Gomes de Sá: cod with olives and eggs
bacalhau à transmontana: cod braised with cured pork
balcão: counter in bar or café
batata: potato
batido: milkshake
bem passado: well done
bica: espresso
bifinhos de vitela: veal filet with wine sauce
bitoque de porco: pork chops
bitoque de vaca: steak
bolachas: cookies
café com leite: coffee with milk, in a mug
café da manhã: breakfast
caldeirada: shellfish stew
caldo: broth/soup
caldo verde: cabbage soup
camarões: shrimp
caneca: pint-size beer mug
caracóis: snails
carioca: cafe mixed with hot water; like American coffee
carne: meat
carne de vaca: beef
cebola: onion
cerveja: beer
chourico: sausage
churrasqueira: BBQ house
cogumelos: mushrooms
conta: bill
couvert: cover charge added to bill for bread
cozido: boiled
ementa: menu
ervilhas: green peas
esacalfado: poached
espadarte: swordfish
espetadas: skewered meat served with melted butter
esturjão: sturgeon
fatia: slice
feijao: bean
frango: chicken
frito: fried
galão: coffee with hot milk
gasosa: lemonade
gelado: ice cream
grao: chick peas
grelhado: grilled
guisado: stewed
hamburger no prato: hamburger patty with fried egg
imperial: tall thin beer glass
jantar: dinner
lagosta: lobster
laranja: orange
linguiça: very thin sausage
maca: apple
manteiga: butter
mariscos: shellfish
massapão: marzipan
mexilhões: mussels
no churrasco: barbequed
no forno: baked
padaria: bakery
panado: breaded
pao: bread
pastelaria: pastry shop
peru: turkey
pimentos: peppers
polvo: octupus
porço: pork
posta: slice of fish or meat

APPENDIX

prato do dia: dish of the day
presunto: ham
quiejo: cheese
recheado: stuffed
salmão: salmon
sande: sandwich
sobremesa: dessert
sopa juliana: soup with shredded vegetables
sumo: juice
tasca: bistro/cafe
tigelada: sweet egg dessert
tomatada: rich tomato sauce
tosta: grilled cheese
tosta mista: grilled ham and cheese sandwich
toucinho do ceu: "Bacon of Heaven," an egg dessert
verdures: vegetables
vinho branco: white wine
vinho de casa: house wine
vinho verde: young wine
vitela: veal

MOROCCO

adhan (A): call to prayer
agneau (F): lamb
aguelmane (A): lake
aourir (A): small mountain
aujourd'hui (F): today
azrour (A): rock
auberge de jeunesse (F): youth hostel
azib (A): shepherd's hut
bastilla (A): pigeon pie
bab (A): gate
beurre (F): butter
bière (F): beer
billet (F): ticket
birra (A): beer
blanc (F): white
boeuf (F): beef
borj (A): tower
boulettes de viande (F): meatballs
brochettes (F): shish-kebab, usually lamb
bus (F): bus
chambre (F): room
chameau (F): camel
chaud (F): hot
compris (F): included
consigne (F): left luggage
couscous (F): semolina grain
couscous bidaoui (A): couscous with 7 vegetables
cornes de gazelles (F): pastry horns with marzipan
coûter (F): to cost
crevettes (F): shrimp
demain (F): tomorrow
djebel (A): mountain peak
douche (F): shower
droite (F): right
ejben (A): cheese
erg (A): sand dune
fassi (A): resident of Fes
fermé (F): closed
forsheta (A): fork
frites (F): French fries
froid (F): cold
fromage (F): cheese
gare (F): train station
gare routière (F): bus station
gauche (F): left
glace (F): ice cream
hadj (A): Mecca pilgrimage
hammam (A): public bath
harira (F): Moroccan lamb-based soup
hier (F): yesterday
huile (F): oil
djellaba (A): traditional Moroccan garment
djoutia (A): flea market
kasbah (A): family fortress
kefta (F): Moroccan burger
l-habra (A): steak
l'houli (A): mutton
légume (F): vegetable
lehmama (A): pigeon
litham (A): veil
louer (F): to rent
louz (A): almonds
madrassa (A): school
makhzen (A): government
malka (A): spoon
mechoui (A): roast lamb
medina (A): old Arabic city
mellah (A): Jewish quarter
mihrab (A): prayer niche
msalla (A): prayer area
moos (A): knife
mosquée (F): mosque
moussem (A): festival
musée (F): museum
nouveau/nouvelle (F): new
oignons (F): onions
ouvert (F): open
pain (F): bread
palais (F): palace
pastilla (F): chicken, almond paste, and spices in a pastry
piscine (F): pool
poisson (F): fish
poste (F): post office
poulet (F): chicken
qahwa: coffee
qniya (A): rabbit
qsar, qsour (pl.) (A): fortified village with curved, white-washed houses
rouge (F): red
rue (F): street
salle de bain (F): bathroom
shrab (A): wine
souq (A): market
tajine (F): Moroccan stew
timbre (F): stamp
tmer (A): dates
toilette (F): toilet
train (F): train
viande (F): meat
vieux/vielle (F): old
ville (F): city
vin (F): wine
voiture (F): car
zelidj (A): decorative tiles

AVERAGE TRAVEL TIMES IN SPAIN AND PORTUGAL

	Algeciras	Badajoz	Barcelona	Bilbao	Córdoba	Granada	León	Málaga	Madrid	Pamplona	Salamanca	San Sebastián	Santiago	Sevilla	Toledo	Valencia	Zaragoza
Algeciras																	
Badajoz	10hr.																
Barcelona	19½hr.	13½hr.															
Bilbao	11-13hr.	10-11½hr.	8-11hr.														
Córdoba	5-6hr.	6hr.	11hr.	9-11hr.													
Granada	5-7hr.	7½-9½hr.	12-13hr.	10-12hr.	3hr.												
León	11hr.	8½hr.	11½hr.	7hr.	7-9hr.	10hr.											
Málaga	5½hr.	7-8hr.	13hr.	11-13hr.	2½-3hr.	2hr.	9-11½hr.										
Madrid	6hr.	4½hr.	7hr.	5-7hr.	2-6hr.	5hr.	4½-5½hr.	4-6hr.									
Pamplona	11hr.	9½hr.	6-8hr.	2hr.	9hr.	10hr.	4hr.	9-11hr.	5hr.								
Salamanca	9hr.	5½hr	11½hr.	5½-6½hr.	6-8hr.	8hr.	3hr.	7-9hr.	3hr.	6-7hr.							
San Sebastián	12-14hr.	10-12hr.	7-10hr.	11hr.	10-12hr.	11-13hr.	5¼hr.	12-14hr.	6-8hr.	1-2hr.	5½-6½hr.						
Santiago de Compostela	14hr.	12-13hr.	15hr.	11hr.	11-13hr.	13hr.	5½hr.	12-14hr.	7½-8hr.	12hr.	7-8hr.	12hr.					
Sevilla	4-5hr.	4½hr.	13-16hr.	8-11hr.	1½hr.	3-5hr.	7-9hr.	2½-3hr.	2½-3½hr.	8hr.	8hr.	9-11hr.	11hr.				
Toledo	6hr.	5hr.	7hr.	6-8hr.	3-5hr.	14hr.	6hr.	5-6hr.	1½hr.	9hr.	4hr.	7-9hr.	12hr.	3hr.			
Valencia	13-15hr.	10hr.	4-6hr.	12hr.	7hr.	8hr.	10-13hr.	11hr.	5-7½hr.	10hr.	8-10½hr.	10hr.	11hr.	9hr.	5-7½hr.		
Zaragoza	9hr.	8hr.	4hr.	4hr.	6-8hr.	8hr.	5½-6hr.	7-9hr.	3hr.	2hr.	7hr.	4hr.	11-12hr.	8½hr.	4hr.	6hr.	

Braga	Coimbra	Évora	Faro	Fátima	Lisbon	Porto	
	4hr.	9-10hr.	12-15hr.	5½hr.	8½hr.	2hr.	Braga
		6hr.	12hr.	1½hr.	3hr.	3hr.	Coimbra
			6hr.	5½hr.	3hr.	7hr.	Évora
				7½hr.	5hr.	8½hr.	Faro
					2½hr.	3½hr.	Fátima
						6hr.	Lisbon
							Porto

LSA Language Studies Abroad, Inc.

Enforex

Total Immersion in Spain and Portugal

Study in:

Spain:
Alcalá
Alicante
Almuñecar
Avila
Barcelona
Benalmadena
El Puerto
Granada
Madrid
Málaga
Marbella
Nerja
Salamanca
San Sebastian
Sevilla
Tenerife
Valencia
Valladolid

Portugal:
Faro
Lisbon
Porto

Your Window to Success!

We offer:
- *Youth, Adult and Senior Programs*
- *Language and Culture*
- *University Programs*
- *Business Courses*
- *Internships*
- *Flexible Start Dates*
- *Studies from 1 week to 1 year*
- *No Credit or Credit for Universities or High Schools*
- *Very Reasonably Priced*
- *Excursions and Activities*
- *Small Classes for all Ages*
- *Flexible Course Duration*
- *Homestay Total Immersion*
- *Variety of Optional Courses*

Language Studies Abroad, Inc.
Web.............www.languagestudiesabroad.com
Email...........info@languagestudiesabroad.com

Tel...800-424-5522

INDEX

A

B

Stay in Touch While Traveling!
With the LET'S GO Phonecard
Powered by ekit
The Global Phonecard with More!
• Save up to 85% on calls & receive messages wherever you go.
• Friends and Family can leave voice messages for FREE!
• Access to FREE internet services designed especially for travelers!
Activate your Let's Go Phonecard today!
Go to www.letsgo.ekit.com or call 1-800-706-1333 in the US. Receive 15 minutes FREE* when you charge $20 by quoting reference code LGMAG01.
*based on call UK to US using economy access numbers. All amounts in US$.
LG
LET'S GO

AMERICA'S FAVORITE
LUCKY BRAND
REG. DUNGAREES T.M.
LUCKY BRAND
AMERICA'S FINEST
BLUE JEANS
HANDMADE WITH THE FINEST DENIM FABRICS
BUY A PAIR
DO IT TODAY
RTM
RN:80318
WWW.LUCKYBRANDJEANS.COM
L. B. Mfg. Co.
AMERICAN DENIM STANDARD LA Ca.
LB

Book your air, hotel, and transportation all in one place.
Hotel or hostel? Cruise or canoe? Car? Plane? Camel? Wherever you're going, visit Yahoo! Travel and get total control over your arrangements. Even choose your seat assignment. So. One hump or two? travel.yahoo.com
powered by hp
YAHOO!
Travel
Do You Yahoo!?

MAP INDEX

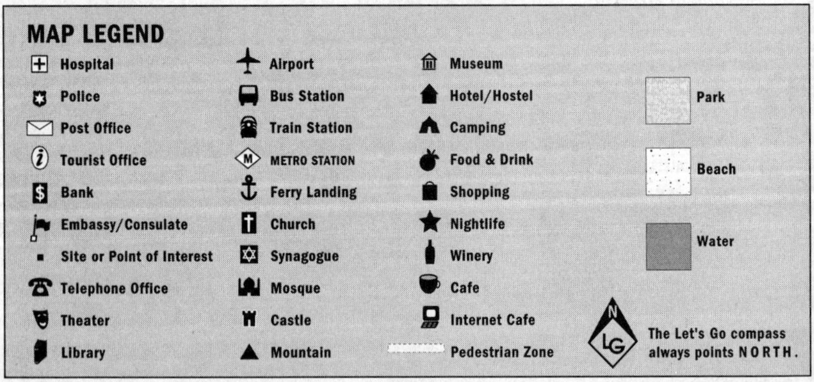

MAP LEGEND
Hospital
Police
Post Office
Tourist Office
Bank
Embassy/Consulate
Site or Point of Interest
Telephone Office
Theater
Library
Airport
Bus Station
Train Station
METRO STATION
Ferry Landing
Church
Synagogue
Mosque
Castle
Mountain
Museum
Hotel/Hostel
Camping
Food & Drink
Shopping
Nightlife
Winery
Cafe
Internet Cafe
Pedestrian Zone
Park
Beach
Water
N
LG
The Let's Go compass always points NORTH.